June 10–13, 2014
Munich, Germany

**Association for
Computing Machinery**

Advancing Computing as a Science & Profession

ICS'14
Proceedings of the 28th ACM
International Conference
on Supercomputing

Sponsored by:
ACM SIGARCH

Technical Supporters:
Intel, IBM, MegWare, SGI, & T-Platforms

Editors:
Arndt Bode, Michael Gerndt, Erwin Laure, & Per Stenström

Association for Computing Machinery

Advancing Computing as a Science & Profession

The Association for Computing Machinery
2 Penn Plaza, Suite 701
New York, New York 10121-0701

ISBN: 978-1-4503-2642-1

Additional copies may be ordered prepaid from:

ACM Order Department
PO Box 30777
New York, NY 10087-0777, USA

Phone: 1-800-342-6626 (USA and Canada)
+1-212-626-0500 (Global)
Fax: +1-212-944-1318
E-mail: acmhelp@acm.org
Hours of Operation: 8:30 am – 4:30 pm ET

Printed in the USA

General Chairs' Welcome

Welcome to the 28th ACM International Conference on Supercomputing (ICS), the oldest and longest running conference on high-performance computing. ICS is a premier forum for researchers to present and discuss latest results and perspectives on the state-of-the-art in supercomputing with their colleagues. ICS 2014 continues the strong focus on excellent technical presentations, motivating keynote addresses, and a small collection of carefully selected workshops and tutorials. The conference follows a cycle of four years visiting twice the United States, once Europe and Asia. This year ICS is taking place in Munich, the center of Bavaria in Germany. The venue is the Bavarian Academy of Sciences with a long tradition going back to 1759. The Academy is running the Leibniz Supercomputer Centre with its 3 Petaflops SuperMUC system.

The success of ICS 2014 is the result of an outstanding team of people. We want to thank the organizing committee at Technische Universität München and the Leibniz Supercomputer Centre for their dedication in setting up and running the conference. The excellent technical program was brought together by the PC chair Per Stenström and the area co-chairs Barton P. Miller, Lawrence Rauchwerger and Martin Schulz. Thanks to the huge reviewing effort of the program committee and the extended review committee, 34 excellent papers were selected from over 160 submissions. We would also like to thank the workshops chair Bernd Mohr, the tutorials chair Michael Bader and the poster chair Erwin Laure for broadening the scope of ICS 2014 with additional activities. The publicity chair Beniamino Di Martino put a lot of effort into attracting submissions and participants to the conference. Shajulin Benedict cooperated with ACM-Sheridan Proceedings Service in the publication of the proceedings. Josef Weidendorfer, Herbert Huber and Carsten Trinitis worked closely together in the local organization team taking care of the local logistics, the sponsoring and the financial accounting. Finally, we thank the steering committee and especially its chair Alex Veidenbaum for giving us the opportunity to run this prestigious conference in Munich.

The continued sponsorship of ACM SIGARCH for ICS is the basis for 28 events of this conference series and for even more to come. We also want to thank the industrial sponsors of this year's conference enabling us to have enjoyable and fruitful days in Munich.

Finally, our thanks go to all the authors of papers submitted to the conference for taking the effort in presenting their latest research results. Without their contributions, this conference would not be such a stimulating meeting.

Arndt Bode and Michael Gerndt

Table of Contents

Keynote Address II
Session Chair: Per Stenström *(Chalmers University of Technology)*

Session: MPI
Session Chair: Martin Schulz *(Lawrence Livermore National Laboratory)*

Poster Session
Session Chair: Erwin Laure *(KTH)*

Session: I/O and NVRAM

Session Chair: Michael Gerndt *(Technische Universität München)*

Session: Modeling and Optimization

Session Chair: Philip Roth *(Oak Ridge National Laboratory)*

Keynote Address III

Session Chair: Lawrence Rauchwerger *(Texas A&M University)*

Session: Accelerators

Session Chair: Cosmin Oancea *(Copenhagen University)*

Session: Interconnect and Microarchitecture

Session Chair: Ronald Brightwell *(Sandia National Laboratory)*

Session: Multi- and Many-core Systems

Session Chair: Todd Gamblin *(Lawrence Livermore National Laboratory)*

Author Index

ICS 2014 Organization

General Co-Chairs: Arndt Bode, *Technische Universität München and Leibniz Rechenzentrum, Germany*

Michael Gerndt, *Technische Universität München, Germany*

Program Chairs: Per Stenström, *Chalmers University of Technology, Sweden*

Lawrence Rauchwerger, *Texas A&M University, USA*

Barton Miller, *University of Wisconsin, USA*

Martin Schulz, *Lawrence Livermore National Laboratory, USA*

Workshops Chair: Bernd Mohr, *Jülich Supercomputer Center, Germany*

Tutorials Chair: Michael Bader, *Technische Universität München, Germany*

Poster Chair: Erwin Laure, *KTH, Sweden*

Local Chair: Josef Weidendorfer, *Technische Universität München, Germany*

Finance Chair: Carsten Trinitis, *TUM, Germany, and University of Bedfordshire (UK)*

Sponsoring Chair: Herbert Huber, *Leibniz Rechenzentrum, Germany*

Publicity Chair: Beniamino Di Martino, *Seconda Università di Napoli, Italy*

Proceedings Chair: Shajulin Benedict, *SXCCE, Anna University, India*

Program Committee: Boris Grot, *University of Edinburgh, UK*

Elisa Heymann, *Autonomous University Barcelona, Spain*

Torsten Hoefler, *ETH Zurich, Switzerland*

Adolfy Hoisie, *Pacific Northwest National Lab, USA*

Yutaka Ishikawa, *University of Tokyo, Japan*

Daniel Jimenez, *Texas A&M, USA*

Wolfgang Karl, *Karlsruhe Institute of Technology, Germany*

Jaejin Lee, *Seoul National University, Korea*

Mikko Lipasti, *University of Wisconsin, Madison, USA*

Andrew Lumsdaine, *Indiana University, USA*

Jason Mars, *University of Michigan, USA*

Patrick McCormick, *Los Alamos National Laboratory, USA*

Bilha Mendleson, *Consultant, Israel*

ICS'14 Sponsors & Supporters

Conference Sponsors

acm Association for Computing Machinery   SIGARCH

Conference Supporters

intel   IBM   MEGWARE

sgi   PLATFORMS

HPC for the Human Brain Project

Thomas Lippert
Forschungszentrum Jülich
Jülich Supercomputing Centre
52425 Jülich
Germany
th.lippert@fz-juelich.de

Abstract

The Human Brain Project, one of two European flagship projects, is a collaborative effort to reconstruct the brain, piece by piece, in multi-scale models and their supercomputer-based simulation, integrating and federating giant amounts of existing information and creating new information and knowledge about the human brain. A fundamental impact on our understanding of the human brain and its diseases as well as on novel brain-inspired computing technologies is expected.

The HPC Platform will be one of the central elements of the project. Including major European supercomputing centres and several universities, its mission is to build, integrate and operate the hardware, network and software components of the supercomputing and big data infrastructures from the cell to full-scale interactive brain simulations, with data management, processing and visualization.

In my contribution, I will discuss the requirements of the HBP on HPC hardware and software technology. These requirements follow the multi-scale approach of the HBP to decode the brain and recreate it virtually. On the cellular level, hardware-software architectures for quantum mechanical ab-initio molecular dynamics methods and for classical molecular dynamics methods will be included in the platform. On the level of the full-scale brain simulation, on the one hand, a development system to "build" the brain by integration of all accessible data distributed worldwide as well as for tests and evaluation of the brain software is foreseen, and, on the other hand, a system that acts as the central brain simulation facility, eventually allowing for interactive simulation and visualization of the entire human brain. Additionally, the brain needs to be equipped with the proper sensory environment, a body, provided by virtual robotics codes developed on a suitable hardware system. It is expected that the human brain project can trigger innovative solutions for future exascale architectures permitting hierarchical memory structures and interactive operation.

Categories and Subject Descriptors

B.0 [Hardware]: General; D.0 [Software]: General

Keywords

Decoding the human Brain; exascale architecture; interactive simulation and visualization; molecular dynamics methods

Short Bio

Prof. Dr. Dr. Thomas Lippert received his diploma in Theoretical Physics in 1987 from the University of Würzburg. He completed Ph.D. theses in theoretical physics at Wuppertal University in the field of computer science. Since 2004 he is director of the Jülich Supercomputing Centre at Forschungzentrum Jülich. Thomas Lippert is the executing director of the John von Neumann Institute for Computing of the Helmholtz Association (NIC) and the director of the Jülich Aachen Research Alliance section HPC (JARA-HPC). Moreover he heads the division "High Performance Computing" within the HBP. He is the coordinator of the implementation project 1IP, 2IP and 3IP of the Partnership for Advanced Cpmputing in Europe (PRACE) and also acts as coordinator in the EU Exascale Project DEEP and DEEP-ER. His research interests include the simulation of field theories, numerical and parallel algorithms as well as computer architectures and system software. Thomas Lippert has published about 200 scientific articles.

ICS'14, June 10–13, 2014, Munich, Germany.
ACM 978-1-4503-2642-1/14/06.
http://dx.doi.org/10.1145/2597652.2616584

LAWS: Locality-Aware Work-Stealing for Multi-socket Multi-core Architectures

Quan Chen
Shanghai Key Laboratory of
Scalable Computing and
Systems,
Department of Computer
Science and Engineering,
Shanghai Jiao Tong University
chen-quan@sjtu.edu.cn

Minyi Guo[*]
Shanghai Key Laboratory of
Scalable Computing and
Systems,
Department of Computer
Science and Engineering,
Shanghai Jiao Tong University
guo-my@cs.sjtu.edu.cn

Haibing Guan
Shanghai Key Laboratory of
Scalable Computing and
Systems,
Department of Computer
Science and Engineering,
Shanghai Jiao Tong University
hbguan@sjtu.edu.cn

ABSTRACT

Modern mainstream powerful computers adopt Multi-Socket Multi-Core (MSMC) CPU architecture and NUMA-based memory architecture. While traditional work-stealing schedulers are designed for single-socket architectures, they incur severe shared cache misses and remote memory accesses in these computers, which can degrade the performance of memory-bound applications seriously. To solve the problem, we propose a Locality-Aware Work-Stealing (LAWS) scheduler, which better utilizes both the shared cache and the NUMA memory system. In LAWS, a load-balanced task allocator is used to evenly split and store the data set of a program to all the memory nodes and allocate a task to the socket where the local memory node stores its data. Then, an adaptive DAG packer adopts an auto-tuning approach to optimally pack an execution DAG into many cache-friendly subtrees. Meanwhile, a triple-level work-stealing scheduler is applied to schedule the subtrees and the tasks in each subtree. Experimental results show that LAWS can improve the performance of memory-bound programs up to 54.2% compared with traditional work-stealing schedulers.

Categories and Subject Descriptors

D.3.4 [**Processors**]: Run-tume environments

Keywords

Shared cache; NUMA; Auto-tuning; DAG packing

1. INTRODUCTION

Although hardware manufacturers keep increasing cores in CPU chips, the number of cores cannot be increased unlimitedly due to physical limitations. To meet the urgent need for

---

[*]Minyi Guo is the correspondence author of this paper.

ICS'14, June 10–13, 2014, Munich, Germany.
Copyright 2014 ACM 978-1-4503-2642-1/14/06 ...$15.00.
http://dx.doi.org/10.1145/2597652.2597665.

powerful computers, multiple CPU chips are integrated into a Multi-Socket Multi-Core (MSMC) architecture, in which each CPU chip has multiple cores with a shared last-level cache and is plugged into a socket.

To efficiently utilize the cores, programming environments with dynamic load-balancing policies are proposed. *Work-sharing* [3] and *work-stealing* [4] are two best-known dynamic load balancing policies. For instance, TBB [25], XKaapi [14], Cilk++ [22] and X10 [21] use work-stealing, OpenMP [3] uses work-sharing. With dynamic load balancing polices, the execution of a parallel program is divided into a large amount of fine-grained tasks and is expressed by a task graph (aka. Directed Acyclic Graph or DAG [16]). Each node in a DAG represents a task (i.e., a set of instructions) that must be executed sequentially without preemption.

While all the workers (threads, cores) share a central task pool in work-sharing, work-stealing provides an individual task pool for each worker. In work-stealing, most often each worker pushes tasks to and pops tasks from its task pool without locking. When a worker's task pool is empty, it tries to steal tasks from other workers, and that is the only time it needs locking. Since there are multiple task pools for stealing, the lock contention is low even at task steals. Therefore, work-stealing performs better than work-sharing due to its lower lock contention.

However, modern shared-memory MSMC computers and extreme-scale supercomputing systems often employ NUMA-based (*Non-Uniform Memory Access*) memory system, in which the whole main memory is divided into multiple memory nodes and each node is attached to the socket of a chip. The memory node attached to a socket is called its local memory node and those that are attached to other sockets are called remote memory nodes. The cores of a socket access its local memory node much faster than the remote memory nodes. Traditional work-stealing is very inefficient in this architecture.

In work-stealing, since a free worker *randomly* selects victim workers to steal new tasks when its own task pool is empty, the tasks are distributed to all the workers nearly randomly. This randomness can cause more accesses to remote memory in NUMA as well as more shared cache misses inside a CPU chip, which often degrades the performance of memory-bound applications in MSMC architectures (the problem will be discussed in detail in Section 2).

To reduce both remote memory accesses and shared cache

misses, this paper proposes a Locality-Aware Work-Stealing (LAWS) scheduler that automatically schedules tasks to the sockets where the local memory nodes store their data and executes the tasks inside each socket in a cache friendly manner. LAWS targets iterative divide-and-conquer applications that have tree-shaped execution DAG. While existing work-stealing schedulers incur bad data locality, to the best of our knowledge, LAWS is the first locality-aware work-stealing scheduler that improves the performance of memory-bound programs leveraging both NUMA optimization and shared cache optimization.

The main contributions of this paper are as follows.

- We propose a load-balanced task allocator that automatically allocates a task to the particular socket where the local memory node stores its data and that can balance the workload among sockets.

- We propose an adaptive DAG packer that can further pack an execution DAG into *Cache Friendly Subtrees* (CF subtrees) for optimizing shared cache usage based on online-collected information and auto-tuning.

- We propose a triple-level work-stealing scheduler to schedule tasks accordingly so that a task can access its data from either the shared cache or the local memory node other than the remote memory nodes.

The rest of this paper is organized as follows. Section 2 explains the motivation of LAWS. Section 3 presents locality-aware work-stealing, including balanced data allocator, adaptive DAG packer and triple level work-stealing scheduler. Section 4 gives the implementation of LAWS. Section 5 evaluates LAWS and shows the experimental results. Section 6 discusses the related work. Section 7 draws conclusions.

2. MOTIVATION

Similar to many popular work-stealing schedulers (e.g., Cilk [5] and CATS [10]), this paper targets iterative *Divide-and-Conquer* (D&C) programs that have tree-shaped execution DAG. Most stencil programs [26] and algorithms based on jacobi iteration (e.g., *Heat distribution* and *Successive Over Relaxation*) are examples of iterative D&C programs.

Fig. 1 gives a general execution DAG for iterative D&C programs. In a D&C program, its data set is recursively divided into several parts until each of the leaf tasks only processes a small part of the whole data set.

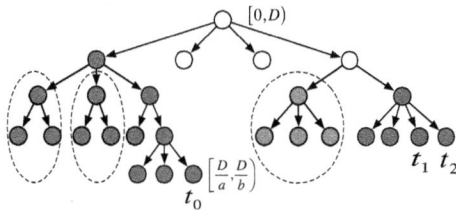

Figure 1: A general execution DAG for iterative D&C programs.

Suppose the execution DAG in Fig. 1 runs on an MSMC architecture with a NUMA memory system as shown in Fig. 2. In the MSMC architecture, a memory node N_i is attached to the socket ρ_i. In Linux memory management for NUMA, if a chunk of data is first accessed by a task that is running on a core of the socket ρ, a physical page from the local memory node of ρ is automatically allocated to the data. This data allocation strategy employed in Linux kernel and Solaris is called *first touch strategy*. In this work, we take advantage of this strategy of memory allocation.

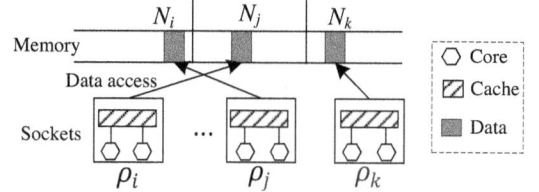

Figure 2: The data access pattern in traditional work-stealing.

For a parallel program, its data set is often first accessed by tasks in the first iteration or in an indepedent initialization phase. By scheduling these tasks to different sockets, the whole data set of the program that has the execution DAG in Fig. 1 is split and stored in different memory nodes as shown in Fig. 2 due to the first touch strategy.

However, traditional work-stealing suffers from two main problems when scheduling the execution DAG in Fig. 1 in MSMC architectures. First, most tasks have to access their data from remote memory nodes in all the iterations. Second, the shared caches are not utilized efficiently.

As for the first problem, suppose the whole data set of the program in Fig. 1 is $[0, D)$, and the task t_0 is the first task that accesses the part of the data $[\frac{D}{a}, \frac{D}{b})$ ($a > b \geq 1$). If task t_0 is scheduled to socket ρ_i, the part of the data $[\frac{D}{a}, \frac{D}{b})$ is automatically allocated to the memory node, N_i, of socket ρ_i, due to the first touch strategy. Suppose task t_r in a later iteration processes the data $[\frac{D}{a}, \frac{D}{b})$. Due to the randomness of work-stealing, it is very likely that t_r is not scheduled to socket ρ_i. In this situation, t_r cannot access its data from its fast local memory node, instead it has to access a remote memory node for its data.

As for the second problem, neighbor tasks (e.g., task t_1 and task t_2 in Fig. 1) are likely to be scheduled to different sockets due to the randomness of stealing in traditional work-stealing schedulers. This causes more shared cache misses as neighbor tasks in DAG often share some data. For example, in Fig. 1, both t_1 and t_2 need to read all their data from the main memory if they are scheduled to different sockets. However, if we could schedule t_1 and t_2 to the same socket, their shared data is only read into the shared cache once by one task, while the other task can read the data directly from the shared cache.

To solve the two problems, we propose the *Locality-Aware Work-Stealing* (LAWS) scheduler that consists of a load-balanced task allocator, an adaptive DAG packer and a triple-level work-stealing scheduler. The load-balanced task allocator can evenly distribute the data set of a program to all the memory nodes and allocate a task to the socket where the local memory node stores its data. The adaptive DAG packer can pack the execution DAG of a program into *Cache-Friendly Subtrees* (CF subtrees) so that the shared cache of each socket can be used effectively. The triple-level work-stealing scheduler schedules tasks accordingly to balance the workload and reduce shared cache misses.

4

LAWS ensures that the workload is balanced and most tasks can access data from either the shared cache or the local memory node. The performance of memory-bound programs can be improved due to balanced workload and shorter data access latency.

3. LOCALITY-AWARE WORK-STEALING

In this section, we first give a general overview of the design of LAWS. Then, we present the load-balanced task allocator, the adaptive DAG packer and the triple-level work-stealing scheduler in LAWS, respectively. Lastly, we verify the effectiveness of LAWS through theoretical analysis.

3.1 Design of LAWS

Fig. 3 illustrates the processing flow of an iterative program in LAWS.

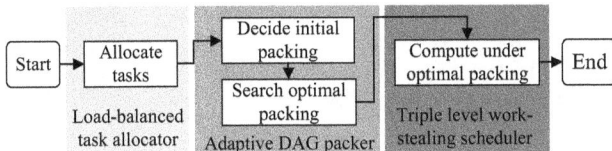

Figure 3: The processing flow of an iterative D&C program in LAWS.

In every iteration, the task allocator carefully allocates tasks to different sockets to evenly distribute the data set of the program to all the memory nodes and allocate each task to the socket where the local memory node stores its data. In this situation, the workload of different sockets is balanced in general since the time for processing the same amount of data is similar among tasks in D&C programs. There may be some slight load-unbalance which will be resolved by the triple-level work-stealing scheduler.

For each socket, LAWS further packs the tasks allocated to it into a number of CF subtrees based on runtime information collected in the first iteration, so that shared cache can be better utilized. For example, in Fig. 1, the subtree in each ellipse is a CF subtree. In the first several iterations, the packer automatically adjusts the packing of tasks to search for the optimal one that results in the minimum makespan. Because the execution DAGs of different iterations are the same and the tasks in the same position of the execution DAGs work on the same part of the data set in D&C programs, the optimal packing for the completed iterations is also optimal for future iterations. Once the optimal packing is found, LAWS packs the tasks in all the following iterations in a way suggested by the optimal packing.

LAWS adopts a triple-level work-stealing scheduler to schedule tasks in each iteration. The tasks in the same CF subtrees are scheduled within the same socket. If a socket completes all its CF subtrees, it steals a CF subtree from a randomly-chosen victim socket in order to resolve the possible slight load-unbalance from the task allocator.

Because tasks in the same CF subtree often share some data, the shared data is only read into the shared cache once but can be accessed by all the tasks of the same CF subtree. In this way, the shared cache can be better utilized and cache misses can be reduced.

It is worth noting that LAWS does not need users to provide any information. All the information needed is obtained automatically at runtime by LAWS.

3.2 Load-balanced task allocator

The load-balanced task allocator is proposed based on an assumption that a task divides its data set into several parts evenly according to its branching degree. This assumption is true in most of the current D&C programs.

The load-balanced task allocator should satisfy two main constraints when allocating tasks to sockets. First, to balance workload, the size of data processed by tasks allocated to each socket should be same in every iteration. Second, to reduce shared cache misses, the adjacent data should be stored in the same memory node since adjacent data is processed by neighbor tasks that should be schedule to the same socket. Traditional work-stealing schedulers do not satisfy the two constraints due to the randomness of stealing.

Suppose a program runs on an M-socket architecture. If its data set is D, to balance workload, the tasks allocated to each socket need to process $\frac{1}{M}$ of the whole data set. Without loss of generality, LAWS makes sure that the tasks allocated to the i-th ($1 \leq i \leq M$) socket should process the part of the whole data set ranging from $(i-1) \times \frac{D}{M}$ to $i \times \frac{D}{M}$ (denoted by $[(i-1) \times \frac{D}{M}, i \times \frac{D}{M})$).

To achieve the above objective, we need to find out each task processes which part of the whole data set. For a task α_2 in Fig. 4, to find out it will process which part of the data set, LAWS analyzes the structure of the dynamically generated execution DAG when α_2 is spawned. Suppose task α_2 is task α_1's i-th sub-task and the branching degree of α_1 is b. If α_1 processes the part of data $[D_s, D_e)$, Eq. 1 gives the part of data that α_2 will process.

$$[(i-1) \times \frac{D_e - D_s}{b} + D_s, i \times \frac{D_e - D_s}{b} + D_s) \quad (1)$$

Fig. 4 gives an example of allocating the tasks to the two sockets of a dual-socket architecture. The range of data beside each task is calculated according to Eq. 1.

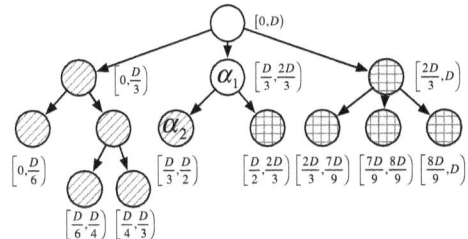

Figure 4: Allocate the tasks to the two sockets of a dual-socket architecture.

In the dual-socket architecture, the tasks that process the data set $[0, \frac{D}{2})$ and $[\frac{D}{2}, D)$ should be allocated to the first socket and the second socket respectively. For instance, in Fig. 4, because α_2 is responsible for processing data range $[\frac{D}{3}, \frac{D}{2})$ that is within $[0, \frac{D}{2})$, it should be allocated to the first socket. Due to the same reason, the slash-shaded tasks should be allocated to the first socket and the mesh-shaded tasks should be allocated to the second socket.

Note that, if a task is allocated to a socket, all its child tasks are allocated to the same socket. For example, all the tasks rooted with α_2 will be allocated to the first socket.

Because the load-balanced task allocator allocates a task according to the range of its data set, in the following iterations, the tasks processing the same part of the whole data set will be allocated to the same socket. In this way, the tasks in all the iterations can find their data in the local memory node. Therefore, the first problem discussed in Section 2 in traditional work-stealing will be solved.

3.3 Adaptive DAG packer

After the tasks are allocated to appropriate sockets, each socket will still have to execute a large number of tasks. The data involved in these tasks are often too large to fit into the shared cache of a socket. To utilize the shared cache efficiently, LAWS further packs the tasks allocated to each socket into CF subtrees that will be executed sequentially.

3.3.1 Decide initial packing

LAWS makes sure that the data accessed by all the socket-local tasks in each CF subtree can be fully stored into the shared cache of a socket. Note the tasks in the same CF subtree (called *Socket-local tasks*) are scheduled in the same socket and the root task of a CF subtree is called a *CF root task*. In this way, the data shared by tasks in the same CF subtree is read into the shared cache once but can be shared and accessed by all the tasks.

To achieve the above objective, we need to know the size of shared cache used by each task, which cannot be collected directly. To circumvent this problem, in the first iteration, for any task α, LAWS collects the number of last level private cache (e.g. L2) misses caused by it. The size of shared cache used by α can be estimated as the number of the above cache misses times the cache line size (e.g., 64 bytes).

The approximation is reasonable due to two reasons. First, the core c that executes α does not execute other tasks concurrently. All the last level private cache misses of c during the execution are caused by α. Second, once a last level private cache miss happens, c accesses the shared cache or memory and will use a cache line in the shared cache.

For task α, we further calculate its *SOSC*, which represents the *Size Of Shared Cache used by all the tasks in the subtree rooted with α*. SOSC of α is calculated in the bottom-up manner. Suppose α has m direct child tasks $\alpha_1, ..., \alpha_m$ and their SOSCs are $S_1, ..., S_m$ respectively. SOSC of α (denoted by S_α) can be calculated in Eq. 2, where M_α equals to the number of last level cache misses caused by α itself times the cache line size.

$$S_\alpha - M_\alpha + \sum_{i=1}^{m} S_i \qquad (2)$$

Once all the tasks in the first iteration are completed, SOSCs of all the tasks are calculated. Based on SOSCs of all the tasks, the DAG packer can group the tasks into CF subtrees by identifying all the CF root tasks as follows.

Let S_c represent the shared cache size of a socket. Suppose α's parent task is β, and their SOSCs are S_α and S_β respectively. Then, if $S_\alpha \leq S_c$ and $S_\beta > S_c$, α is a CF root task, which means all the data involved in the descendent tasks of α just fit into the shared cache. If $S_\beta < S_c$, α is a socket-local task.

Once all the CF root tasks are identified, the initial packing of tasks into CF subtrees is determined.

3.3.2 Search optimal packing

If S_α in Eq. 2 precisely equals to the real size of shared cache used by the subtree rooted with α, the data involved in any CF subtree would not exceed the capacity of a socket's shared cache.

However, S_α is only a close approximation due to the following reasons. Suppose tasks α_1 and α_2 in the subtree rooted with α share some data. Although they are allocated to the same socket by the load-balanced task allocator, they can be executed by different cores. In this case, both α_1 and α_2 need to read the shared data to the last level private cache and thus the size of the shared data is accumulated twice in Eq. 2. On the other hand, if some data stored in the shared cache has already been pre-fetched into the private cache before, it does not incur last level private cache misses and the size of the pre-fetched data is missed in Eq. 2. The multiple accumulation of shared data and the pre-fetching make S_α of Eq. 2 slightly larger or smaller than the actual size of shared cache used by the subtree rooted with α.

Therefore, the initial packing of tasks into CF subtrees is only a near optimal packing. LAWS further uses an auto-tuning approach to search the optimal packing. In the approach, LAWS packs tasks into CF subtrees differently in different iterations, records the execution time of each iteration, and chooses the packing that results the shortest makespan as the optimal packing.

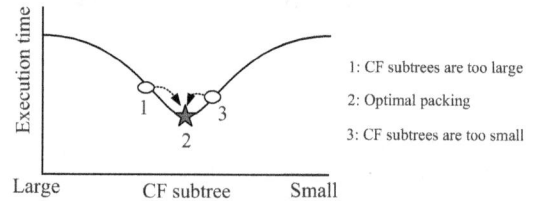

Figure 5: Execution time of an iteration when the execution DAG is packed differently.

Fig. 5 shows the execution time of an iteration when tasks are packed differently. If CF subtrees are too large (contain too many socket-local tasks, point 1 in Fig. 5), the data accessed by tasks in each CF subtree cannot be fully stored in the shared cache of a socket. On the other hand, if CF subtrees are too small (contain too few socket-local tasks, point 3 in Fig. 5), the data accessed by tasks in each CF subtree is too small to fully utilize the shared cache.

Starting from the packing of the execution DAG into CF subtrees in Section 3.3.1, LAWS first evaluates smaller CF subtrees. If smaller CF subtrees result in shorter execution time, CF subtrees in the initial packing are too large. In this case, LAWS evaluates smaller and smaller CF subtrees until the packing that results in the shortest execution time (point 2 in Fig. 5) is found. If smaller CF subtrees result in longer execution time, CF subtrees in the initial packing are too small. In this case, LAWS evaluates larger and larger CF subtrees instead until the optimal packing is found.

Algorithm 1 gives the auto-tuning algorithm for searching the optimal way to pack the tasks allocated to a socket into CF subtrees. To generate larger or smaller CF subtrees, we select the parent tasks or child tasks of the current CF root tasks as the new CF root tasks.

Since the initial packing is already near-optimal, LAWS can find the optimal packing in a few iterations. Theoretically, it has a small possibility that some CF subtrees are too large while some other CF subtrees are too small. However, since there are a great many CF subtrees in an execution DAG, it is too complex to tune the size of every CF subtrees independently in a small number of iterations at run-

---

Algorithm 1: Algorithm for searching the optimal way to pack the execution DAG into CF subtrees

---

Input: $\alpha_1, ..., \alpha_m$ (CF root tasks in the initial packing)
Input: T (Execution time under the initial packing)
Output: Optimal CF root tasks

```
1  int Tn = 0, Tc = T ;          // New & current makespan
2  int EvalLarger = 1 ;          // Eval. larger subtrees?
3  while CF root tasks have child tasks do
4  │   Set child tasks of the current CF root tasks as the
   │   new CF root tasks ;
5  │   Execute an iteration under the new packing ;
6  │   Record the execution time Tn ;
7  │   if Tn < Tc then // Point 1 in Fig. 5
8  │   │   Tc = Tn ;
9  │   │   Save new CF root tasks ;
10 │   │   EvalLarger = 0 ;
11 │   else break ;
12 if EvalLarger == 1 then // Point 3 in Fig. 5
13 │   Restore CF root tasks to {α1, ..., αm} ;
14 │   Tc = T ;
15 │   while CF root tasks have parent tasks do
16 │   │   Set parent tasks of the current CF root tasks as
   │   │   the new CF root tasks ;
17 │   │   Execute an iteration under the new packing ;
18 │   │   Record the execution time Tn ;
19 │   │   if Tn > Tc then break ;
20 │   │   else Tc = Tn ; Save new CF root tasks ;
```

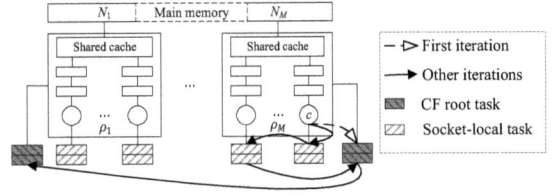

Figure 6: Architecture of LAWS on an M-socket multi-core architecture.

time. To simplify the problem, we increase or decrease the size of all the CF subtrees at the same time in Algorithm 1 of this paper. Actually, according to the experiment in Section 5.2, our current auto-tuning strategy in Algorithm 1 works efficiently.

The approach of packing DAG into CF subtrees in LAWS partially origins from CATS [9], which also packs the execution DAGs of parallel programs into subtrees for optimizing shared cache usage. However, once an execution DAG is packed in CATS, the packing cannot be adjusted even if the packing is not optimal. Experiment in Section 5.2 shows that the performance of applications can be further improved with the auto-tuning algorithm described in Algorithm 1 for searching the optimal packing. Worse, CATS did not consider the NUMA memory system at all and suffered from a large amount of remote memory accesses. We will further compare the performance of CATS and LAWS in detail in Section 5.

3.4 Triple-level work-stealing scheduler

Fig. 6 gives the architecture of LAWS on an M-socket multi-core architecture, and illustrates the triple-level work-stealing policies in LAWS. In Fig. 6, the main memory is divided into M memory nodes and node N_i is the local memory node of socket ρ_i. In each socket, core "0" is selected as the head core of the socket.

For each socket, LAWS creates a *CF task pool* to store CF root tasks allocated to the socket and the tasks above the CF root tasks in the execution DAG. For each core, LAWS creates a *socket-local task pool* to store socket-local tasks.

Suppose a core c in socket ρ is free, in different phases, it obtains new tasks in different ways as follows.

In the first iteration of an iterative program (and the inde-

pendent initialization phase if the program has the phase), there is no socket-local task and all the tasks are pushed into CF task pools since the tasks have not been packed into CF subtrees. In the period, c can only obtain a new task from CF task pool of ρ. Core c is not allowed to steal a task from other sockets because the data set of a task will be stored into the wrong memory node if it is stolen in the first iteration due to the first touch strategy.

Starting from the second iteration, the tasks in each iteration have been packed into CF subtrees. Adopting triple level work-stealing, free core c can steal a new task from three levels: socket-local task pool of other cores in its socket ρ, CF task pool of ρ, and CF task pools of other sockets.

More precisely, when c is free, it first tries to obtain a task from its own socket-local task pool. If its own task pool is empty, c tries to steal a task from the socket-local task pools of other cores in ρ. If the task pools of all the cores in ρ are empty and c is the head core of ρ, c tries to obtain a new CF root task from ρ's CF task pool.

LAWS allows a socket to help other sockets execute their CF subtrees. For instance, after all the tasks in the CF task pool of ρ are completed, the head core of ρ tries to steal a task from CF task pools of other sockets. Although ρ needs longer time to process the CF subtrees that are allocated to other sockets, the workload is balanced and the performance of memory-bound programs can be improved.

In LAWS, cores in the same socket are not allowed to execute tasks in multiple CF subtrees concurrently. This policy can avoid the situation that tasks in different CF subtrees pollute the shared caches with different data sets. Also, a socket is only allowed to steal entire CF subtrees from other sockets for optimizing shared cache usage.

3.5 Theoretical Validation

A memory-bound D&C program has three features. First, only leaf tasks physically access the data while other tasks divide the data set recursively into smaller pieces. Second, each leaf task only processes a small part of the whole data set of the program. Third, the execution time of a leaf task is decided by its data access time. Based on the three features, we prove that LAWS can improve the performance of memory-bound D&C programs theoretically.

Consider a memory-bound program that runs on an M-socket architecture. Suppose a leaf task α in its execution DAG is responsible for processing data of S bytes and α still accesses B bytes of boundary data besides its own part of data. Let V_l and V_r represent the speeds (bytes/cycle) of a core to access data from local memory node and remote memory nodes respectively. Needless to say, $V_l > V_r$.

If we adopt a traditional work-stealing scheduler to schedule the program, the probability that α can access all the data from local memory node is $\frac{1}{M}$. Therefore, the cycles expected for α to access all the needed data in traditional work-stealing (denoted by T_R) can be calculated in Eq. 3.

$$T_R = \frac{S+B}{V_l} \times \frac{1}{M} + \frac{S+B}{V_r} \times \frac{M-1}{M} \quad (3)$$

If we adopt LAWS to schedule the program, benefit from the task allocator, α can access its own part of data from local memory node. As a consequence, the cycles needed by α to access all the needed data in LAWS (denoted by T_L) can be calculated in Eq. 4, because α also has a high chance to access its boundary data from local memory node.

$$T_L \le \frac{S}{V_l} + \frac{B}{V_r} \quad (4)$$

Deduced from Eq. 3 and Eq. 4, we can get Eq. 5.

$$T_R - T_L \ge (\frac{1}{MV_r} - \frac{1}{MV_l}) \times [(M-1)S - B] \quad (5)$$

In Eq. 5, because $V_r < V_l$, we know $\frac{1}{MV_r} - \frac{1}{MV_l} > 0$. Therefore, $T_R - T_L > 0$ if $(M-1)S - B > 0$ that is always true in almost all the D&C programs empirically since a task's own data set (S) is always far larger than its boundary data (B). In summary, we prove that α needs shorter time to access all the needed data in LAWS.

Because leaf tasks need shorter time to access their data in LAWS than in traditional work-stealing schedulers, LAWS can always improve the performance of memory-bound D&C programs even when the optimization on reducing shared cache misses in LAWS is not taken into account.

4. IMPLEMENTATION

We implement LAWS by modifying MIT Cilk, which is one of the earliest parallel programming environments that implement work-stealing [13].

Existing work-stealing schedulers adopt either parent-first policy or child-first policy when generating new tasks. In parent-first policy (called *help-first policy* in [17]), a core continually executes the parent task after spawning a new task. In child-first policy (called *work-first policy* in [5]), a core continually executes the spawned new task once the child is spawned. Parent-first policy works better when the steals are frequent, while child-first policy works better when the steals are infrequent [17].

During the first iteration, LAWS adopts the parent-first policy to generate new tasks, because it is difficult to collect the numbers of last level private cache misses caused by each task with the child-first policy. If a core is executing a task α, with the child-first policy, it is very likely the core will also execute some of α's child tasks before α is completed. In this case, the number of last level cache misses caused by α itself, which is used to calculate SOSCs of tasks, may not be collected correctly as it could include the number of last level private cache misses of α's child tasks.

Starting from the second iteration, LAWS generates tasks above CF root tasks with the parent-first policy since the steals are frequent in the beginning of each iteration. LAWS generates socket-local tasks with the child-first policy since the steals are infrequent in each CF subtree.

We have modified the compiler of MIT Cilk to support both the parent-first and child-first task-generating policy while the original Cilk only support the child-first policy. If a task α is spawned in the first iteration, the task is spawned with the parent-first policy and is pushed to the appropriate CF task pool based on the method in Section 3.2. If α is spawned in the later iterations and it is a socket-local task, LAWS spawns α with the child-first policy and pushes α into the socket-local task pool of the current core. Otherwise, if α is a CF root task or a task above CF root tasks, and it is allocated to socket ρ, it is spawned with the parent-first policy and pushed into ρ's CF task pool.

We use the "libpfm" library in Linux kernel to program Hardware Performance Units for collecting last level private cache misses of each task. We have also modified the work-stealing scheduler of MIT Cilk to implement the triple-level work-stealing algorithm in Section 3.4.

5. EVALUATION

We use a server that has four AMD Quad-core Opteron 8380 processors to evaluate the performance of LAWS. Each socket has a 512K private L2 cache for each core and a 6M L3 cache shared by all four cores. The server has 16GB RAM and runs Linux 3.2.0-14. Therefore, each socket has a 4GB memory node.

We compare the performance of LAWS with the performance of Cilk [5] and CATS [9]. Cilk uses the pure child-first policy to spawn and schedule tasks. Similar to LAWS, CATS also packs the execution DAG of a parallel program into subtrees to reduce shared cache misses in MSMC architectures. Once an execution DAG is packed in CATS, the packing cannot be adjusted at runtime even the packing is not optimal. In addition, CATS did not consider the underlying NUMA memory system.

For fairness in comparison, we also implement CATS by modifying Cilk and we have improved CATS so that it also allocates the data evenly to all the memory nodes in the first iteration as LAWS does. The Cilk programs run with CATS and LAWS without any modification.

Table 1: Benchmarks used in the experiments

Name	Description
Heat/Heat-ir	2D heat distribution (regular/irreg.)
SOR/SOR-ir	Successive Over-Relaxation (regular/irreg.)
GE/GE-ir	Gaussian elimination alg. (regular/irreg.)
9p/9p-ir	2D 9-point stencil comp. (regular/irreg.)
6p/6p-lr	3D 6-point stencil comp. (regular/irreg.)
25p/25p-ir	3D 25-point stencil comp. (regular/irreg.)

In order to evaluate the performance of LAWS in different scenarios, we use benchmarks listed in Table 1 that have both regular execution DAG and irregular execution DAG in the experiment. Most of the benchmarks are examples in the MIT Cilk package. We port the other benchmarks in the same way the examples of MIT Cilk are developed. *Heat-ir, GE-ir, SOR-ir, 9p-ir, 6p-ir* and *25p-ir* implement the same algorithm as their counterparts respectively, except their execution DAGs are irregular. We create the programs with irregular execution DAGs in the same way as suggested in [9]. If all the nodes (except the leaf tasks) in the execution DAG have the same branching degrees, the execution DAG is regular. All benchmarks are compiled with "-O2".

5.1 Performance of LAWS

Fig. 7 shows the performance of all the benchmarks in Cilk, CATS and LAWS.

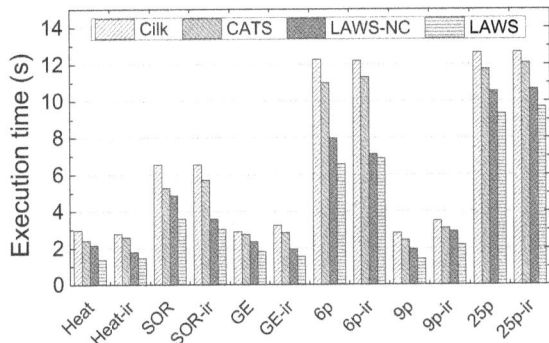

Figure 7: The performance of all the benchmarks in Cilk, CATS and LAWS.

In this experiment, for *Heat*, *Heat-ir*, *SOR* and *SOR-ir*, the input data used is a 8096 × 1024 matrix. For *GE* and *GE-ir*, the input data used is a 2048 × 2048 matrix due to algorithm constraint. For *6p*, *6p-ir*, *25p* and *25p-ir*, the input data is a 8096 × 64 × 64 3D matrix.

As we can see from Fig. 7, LAWS can significantly improve the performance of benchmarks compared with Cilk while the performance improvement ranges from 23.5% to 54.2%. CATS can also improve the performance of benchmarks up to 19.6% compared with Cilk.

In MSMC architectures, the performance of a memory-bound application is decided by the *straggler socket* that seldom access data from its local memory node because the tasks in the straggler socket need the longest time to access their data. Note that, during the execution of a memory-bound application, any socket can be the straggler socket.

To explain why LAWS outperforms both Cilk and CATS for memory-bound applications, we collect the shared cache misses (Event 4E1H) and the local memory accesses (Event 1E0H) of the straggler socket. The information about the events of hardware performance units can be found in [2]. For each benchmark, Table 2 lists its shared cache misses and the local memory accesses of the straggler socket in Cilk, CATS and LAWS.

Observed from Table 2, we can find that the shared cache (L3) misses are reduced and the local memory accesses of the straggler socket are prominently increased in LAWS compared with Cilk and CATS. Since LAWS schedules tasks to the sockets where the local memory nodes store their data, the tasks can access their data from local memory node and thus the local memory accesses have been significantly increased. Furthermore, since LAWS packs tasks allocated to each socket into CF subtrees to preserve shared data in shared cache, the shared cache misses are also reduced.

Only for *GE* and *GE-ir*, the local memory accesses of the straggler socket are not increased in LAWS. This is because their input data is small enough to be put into the shared cache directly. In this situation, most tasks can access the data from the shared cache directly and do not need to access the main memory any more. Because the L3 cache misses are prominently reduced, LAWS can still significantly improve the performance of *GE* and *GE-ir*.

The performance improvement of the benchmarks in CATS is due to the reduced shared cache misses. However, since CATS cannot divide an execution DAG optimally like LAWS, it still has more shared cache misses than LAWS as shown in Table 2.

Surprisingly, CATS can also slightly increase the local memory accesses of the straggler socket. As mentioned before, we have improved CATS so that the adjacent data is stored in the same memory node. Although tasks have the same possibility ($\frac{1}{M}$ on an M-socket architecture) to find its data in the local memory node in Cilk and CATS, if a task can find its own data in the local memory node in CATS, it has higher possibility to also find its boundary data in the local memory node. The local memory accesses of the straggler socket in CATS are increased in consequence.

Careful readers may find that CATS performs much worse here than in the original paper [9]. While CATS can only improve the performance of benchmarks up to 19.6% here, it can improve their performance up to 74.4% in [9]. The reduction of performance improvement of CATS comes from the much larger input data set used in this paper. This result matches with the findings in [9]. That is, with the increasing of the size of the input data set, the percentage of shared data among tasks decreases and the effectiveness of CATS degrades in consequence.

5.2 Effectiveness of the adaptive DAG packer

To evaluate the effectiveness of the adaptive DAG packer in LAWS, we compare the performance of LAWS with LAWS-NC, a scheduler that only schedules each task to the socket where the memory node stores its part of data but does not further pack the tasks into CF subtrees.

From Fig. 7 we find that LAWS-NC performs better than both Cilk and CATS. This is because most tasks in LAWS-NC can access their data from local memory nodes. However, since tasks are not packed into CF subtrees for optimizing shared cache in LAWS-NC, LAWS-NC incurs more shared cache misses and performs worse than LAWS.

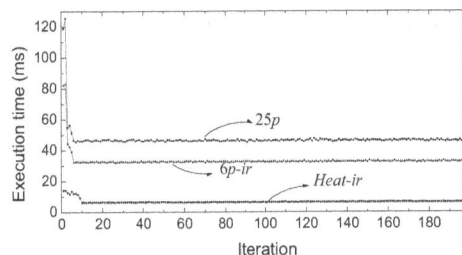

Figure 8: Execution time of each iteration in 25p, 6p-ir and Heat-ir.

To evaluate the auto-tuning approach (Algorithm 1) proposed to optimally pack tasks into CF subtrees, Fig. 8 gives the execution time of 200 iterations of *Heat-ir*, *25p* and *6p-ir* in LAWS. From the figure we find that the execution time of an iteration in all the benchmarks is significantly reduced after the optimal packing is found in several iterations.

In summary, the adaptive DAG packer in LAWS is effective and the auto-tuning algorithm for searching the optimal packing of tasks in Algorithm 1 works also fine.

5.3 Scalability of LAWS

To evaluate scalability of LAWS, we compare the performance of benchmarks with different input data sizes in Cilk, CATS and LAWS.

During the execution of all the benchmarks, every task divides its data set into several parts by rows to generate

Table 2: Shared cache misses and local memory accesses of the straggler socket (*1E6)

		Heat	Heat-ir	SOR	SOR-ir	GE	GE-ir	6p	6p-ir	9p	9p-ir	25p	25p-ir
L3	Cilk	572	574	1151	1013	220.3	230.1	2518	2543	573.2	577	2484	2477
Cache	CATS	531	541.8	1070	886	147.4	113.3	2420	2361	539.1	469.2	2383	2372
Misses	LAWS	462	504.5	1005	876	29.1	28.7	2375	2345	504.5	446.03	2340	2354
Local	Cilk	16.1	17.2	32.8	29	6.1	5.64	81.5	74.4	17.2	15.3	83.2	81.5
Memory	CATS	21.3	18.6	41.4	30.4	4.5	3.58	100.5	97.3	21.9	19.3	90.6	85.8
Accesses	LAWS	25.8	27.5	57.1	39.3	0.65	0.47	151.9	134.7	27.2	24.8	125	117.7

child tasks unless the task meets the cutoff point (i.e., the rows of a leaf task, and 8 rows is used in the experiment). Since the data set size of the leaf tasks affects the measurement of scalability, we ensure that the data set size of the leaf tasks is constant by using a constant cutoff point for the leaf tasks. If the input data is an $x \times y$ 2D matrix, we set $y = 1024$ for all the input 2D matrix. If the input data is an $x \times y \times z$ 3D matrix, we set $y = 64$ and $z = 64$ for all the input 3D matrix. We only adjust the x of the input matrices in the experiment. In this way, we can measure the scalability of LAWS without the impact of the granularity of the leaf tasks. In all the following figures, the x-axis represents the x of the input matrixes.

We use *Heat-ir* and *6p* as benchmarks to evaluate the scalability of CATS in scenario that applications with a regular execution DAG and an irregular execution DAG. All the other benchmarks have similar results.

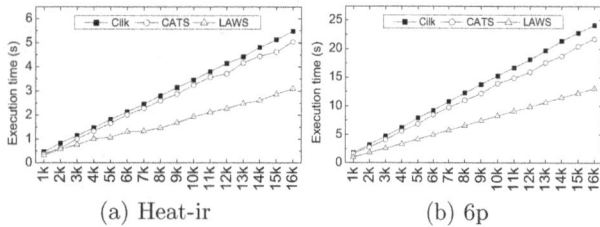

(a) Heat-ir   (b) 6p

Figure 9: Performance of Heat-ir and 6p with different input data sizes.

Fig. 9 shows the performance of *Heat-ir* and *6p* with different input data sizes in Cilk, CATS and LAWS. We can find that *Heat-ir* and *6p* achieve the best performance in LAWS for all input data sizes. When the input data size is small (i.e., $x = 1k$), LAWS reduces 30.4% execution time of *Heat-ir* and reduces 36.6% execution time of *6p* compared with Cilk. When the input data size is large (i.e., $x = 16k$), LAWS reduces 43.6% execution time of *Heat-ir* and reduces 45.8% execution time of *6p* compared with Cilk.

In Fig. 9, the execution time of benchmarks in Cilk, CATS and LAWS increases linearly with the increasing of their input data sizes. Since their execution time increases much slower in LAWS than in Cilk and CATS, for all the input data sizes, LAWS can always reduce the execution time of memory-bound applications. In summary, LAWS is scalable in scheduling both regular execution DAGs and irregular execution DAGs.

Corresponding to Fig. 9, Fig. 10 and Fig. 11 show the L3 cache misses and the local memory accesses of the straggler socket in executing *Heat-ir* and *6p* with different input data sizes. Observed from the figure, we can find that the shared cache misses are reduced, while the local memory accesses of

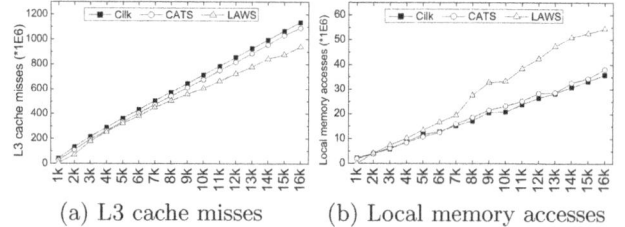

(a) L3 cache misses   (b) Local memory accesses

Figure 10: L3 cache misses and local memory accesses of the straggler socket in Heat-ir.

the straggler socket are increased in LAWS. When the input data size is small (i.e., $x = 1k$), LAWS can reduce 82% L3 cache misses and increase 132.1% local memory accesses compared with Cilk. When the input data size is large (i.e., $x = 16k$), LAWS can reduce 17.3% L3 cache misses and increase 70.6% local memory accesses compared with Cilk.

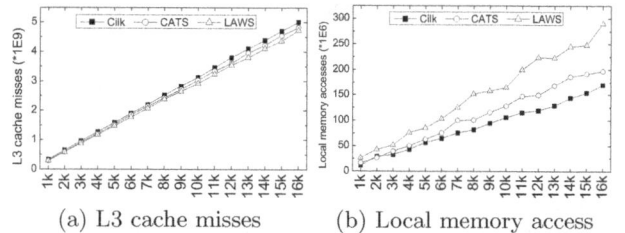

(a) L3 cache misses   (b) Local memory access

Figure 11: L3 cache misses and local memory accesses of the straggler socket in 6p.

Fig. 10 and Fig. 11 further explain why LAWS performs much better than CATS. Since LAWS can optimally pack tasks into CF subtrees through auto-tuning, it can reduce more L3 cache misses of memory-bound benchmarks than CATS. In addition, since LAWS can schedule a task to the socket where the local memory node stores its data, it significantly increases local memory accesses. The two key advantages of LAWS result in the better performance of LAWS.

As we all know, if the input data of a memory-bound program is small, the shared cache is big enough to store the input data. In this case, if the shared cache misses are greatly reduced, the performance of memory-bound programs can be improved. If the input data is large, the performance bottleneck of the program is the time of reading data from main memory. Therefore, CATS performs efficient when the input data size is small but performs poor when the input data size is large. On the contrary, because LAWS can increase more local memory accesses when input data size gets larger, it performs even better when the input data is large as shown in Fig. 10 and Fig. 11. This feature of LAWS is promising as the data size of a problem is becoming larger and larger.

5.4 Overhead of LAWS

Because LAWS aims to reduce remote memory accesses and shared cache misses, LAWS is neutral for CPU-bound programs. Based on the runtime information, if LAWS finds that a program is CPU-bound, LAWS schedules tasks of the program in traditional work-stealing. Another option is to use techniques in WATS [7, 8] scheduler to improve the performance of CPU-bound programs by balancing workloads among cores.

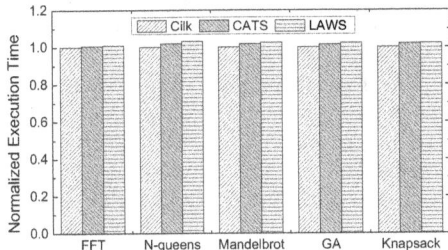

Figure 12: Performance of CPU-bound benchmarks in Cilk, CATS and LAWS.

Fig. 12 shows the performance of several CPU-bound applications in Cilk, CATS and LAWS. The applications in this experiment are examples in Cilk package. By comparing the performance of CPU-bound applications in Cilk, CATS and LAWS, we can find the extra overhead of LAWS.

Observed from Fig. 12, we see the extra overhead of LAWS is negligible compared with Cilk and CATS. The extra overhead of LAWS mainly comes from the overhead of distributing data to all the memory node evenly and the profiling overhead in the first iteration of a parallel program, when LAWS can determine if the program is CPU-bound or memory-bound based on the profiling information.

5.5 Discussion

LAWS assumes that the execution DAGs of different iterations in an iterative program are the same. The assumption is true for most programs. Even if a program does not satisfy this assumption, LAWS can still ensure that every task can access its data from local memory node since the load-balanced task allocator allocates tasks to sockets in each iteration independently according to their data set in the current iteration. However, in this situation, the optimization on shared cache utilization is not applicable since the optimal packing for the past iterations may not be optimal for future iterations due to the change of the execution DAG. In summary, even the above assumption is not satisfied, LAWS can improve the performance of memory-bound programs due to the increased local memory accesses.

6. RELATED WORK

Work-stealing is increasing popular due to its automatic load balancing feature and high performance. There are many works have been done to improve its performance [18, 9] and energy efficiency [27] on various hardwares. However, most existing work-stealing schedulers are designed for single-socket architectures and degrade the performance of memory-bound programs in MSMC architectures with

NUMA memory system. There are two main approaches for improving the performance of memory-bound programs in MSMC architectures: *increasing local memory accesses* and *reducing shared cache misses.*

Many studies have been done to improve the performance of a particular application [26, 6] or general applications [28, 23] by increasing local memory accesses in NUMA memory system (i.e., the first approach).

In [26], nuCATS and nuCORALS improved the performance of iterative stencil computations for NUMA memory system by optimizing temporal blocking and tiling. While nuCATS and nuCORALS focused on the tiling scheme for stencil programs, through online scheduling, LAWS can improve the performance of iterative stencil programs without changing the tiling scheme. In [28], a dynamic work-stealing strategy is proposed for on-chip NUMA multi-core processors based on the topology of underlying hardware. Based on Charm++ [19], NUMALB [23] is proposed to improved the performance of parallel programs. NUMALB balances the workload while avoiding unnecessary migrations and reducing across-core communication. While the above schedulers only increase local memory accesses, LAWS can further reduce the shared cache misses and thus performs better for memory-bound programs.

Using the second approach, there are also several work-stealing schedulers [1, 18, 24, 15] are proposed to tackle the cache-unfriendly problem in various parallel architectures (e.g., multi-CPU and multi-GPU architectures [15]). In [12], the authors analyzed the cache misses of algorithms using traditional task-stealing, focusing on the effects of false sharing. In SLAW [18], workers are grouped into *places* and a worker is only allowed to steal tasks from other workers in the same place. The scheduling policy is similar to the triple-level work-stealing policy in LAWS. However, SLAW did not consider the NUMA memory systems and did not pack tasks for optimizing shared cache usage as LAWS does.

Similar to LAWS, HWS [24] and CAB [11] used a rigid boundary level to divide tasks into global tasks and local tasks (similar to socket-local tasks in LAWS). By scheduling local tasks within the same socket, the shared cache misses can be reduced. However, users have to give the level manually in HWS or provide a number of command line arguments for the scheduler to calculate the boundary level in CAB. To relieve the above burden, CATS [9] was proposed to divide an execution DAG based on the information collected online, without extra user-provided information. While the adaptive DAG packer in LAWS can find the optimal packing of tasks into CF subtrees through auto-tuning, all the above schedulers cannot optimally partition an execution DAG. In addition, they did not consider the NUMA memory system at all. Our experiment results also show that LAWS significantly outperforms CATS.

In [29], an offline graph-based locality analysis framework based on METIS [20] is proposed to analyze the inherent locality patterns of workloads. Leveraging the analysis results, tasks are grouped and mapped according to cache hierarchy through recursive scheduling. Because the framework relied on offline analysis, a program has to be executed at least one time before it can achieve good performance in the framework. On the contrary, LAWS can improve the performance of programs online without any prerequisite offline analysis, because it can optimally pack tasks into CF subtrees based on online collected information and auto-tuning.

7. CONCLUSIONS

Traditional work-stealing schedulers pollute shared cache and increase remote memory accesses in MSMC architectures with NUMA-based memory system. To solve the two problems, we have proposed the LAWS scheduler, which consists of a load-balanced task allocator, an adaptive DAG packer and a triple-level work-stealing scheduler. The task allocator evenly distributes the data set of a program to all the memory nodes and allocates a task to the socket where the local memory node stores its data. Based on auto-tuning, for each socket, the adaptive DAG packer can optimally pack the allocated tasks into CF subtrees. The triple-level work-stealing scheduler schedules tasks in the same CF subtree among cores in the same socket and makes sure that each socket executes its CF subtrees sequentially. In this way, the shared cache misses are greatly reduced and the local memory accesses are prominently increased. Experimental results demonstrate that LAWS can achieve up to 54.2% performance gain for memory-bound applications compared with traditional work-stealing schedulers.

8. ACKNOWLEDGMENTS

This work was supported by Program for Changjiang Scholars and Innovative Research Team in University (IRT1158, PCSIRT) China, NSFC (Grant No. 61272099) and Scientific Innovation Act of STCSM (No.13511504200). This work was also partially supported by NRF Singapore under its Campus for CREATE Program.

9. REFERENCES

[1] U. Acar, G. Blelloch, and R. Blumofe. The data locality of work stealing. *Theory of Computing Systems*, 35(3):321–347, 2002.

[2] AMD. *BIOS and Kernel Developer Guide (BKDG) For AMD Family 10h Processors*. AMD, 2010.

[3] E. Ayguadé, N. Copty, A. Duran, J. Hoeflinger, Y. Lin, F. Massaioli, X. Teruel, P. Unnikrishnan, and G. Zhang. The design of OpenMP tasks. *IEEE TPDS*, 20(3):404–418, 2009.

[4] R. D. Blumofe. *Executing Multithreaded Programs Efficiently*. PhD thesis, MIT, Sept. 1995.

[5] R. D. Blumofe, C. F. Joerg, B. C. Kuszmaul, C. E. Leiserson, K. H. Randall, and Y. Zhou. Cilk: An efficient multithreaded runtime system. *Journal of Parallel and Distributed Computing*, 37(1):55–69, 1996.

[6] M. Castro, L. G. Fernandes, C. Pousa, J.-F. Méhaut, and M. S. de Aguiar. NUMA-ICTM: A parallel version of ICTM exploiting memory placement strategies for NUMA machines. In *IPDPS*, pages 1–8, 2009.

[7] Q. Chen, Y. Chen, Z. Huang, and M. Guo. WATS: Workload-aware task scheduling in asymmetric multi-core architectures. In *IPDPS*, pages 249–260, 2012.

[8] Q. Chen and M. Guo. Adaptive workload aware task scheduling for single-ISA multi-core architectures. *ACM Transactions on Architecture and Code Optimization*, 11(1), 2014.

[9] Q. Chen, M. Guo, and Z. Huang. CATS: Cache aware task-stealing based on online profiling in multi-socket multi-core architectures. In *ICS*, pages 163–172, 2012.

[10] Q. Chen, M. Guo, and Z. Huang. Adaptive cache aware bi-tier work-stealing in multi-socket multi-core architectures. *IEEE Transactions on Parallel and Distributed Systems*, 24(12):2334–2343, 2013.

[11] Q. Chen, Z. Huang, M. Guo, and J. Zhou. CAB: Cache-aware bi-tier task-stealing in multi-socket multi-core architecture. In *ICPP*, pages 722–732, 2011.

[12] R. Cole and V. Ramachandran. Analysis of randomized work stealing with false sharing. In *IPDPS*, pages 985–989, 2013.

[13] M. Frigo, C. E. Leiserson, and K. H. Randall. The implementation of the Cilk-5 multithreaded language. In *PLDI*, pages 212–223, 1998.

[14] T. Gautier, J. V. Lima, N. Maillard, and B. Raffin. XKaapi: A runtime system for data-flow task programming on heterogeneous architectures. In *IPDPS*, pages 1299–1308, 2013.

[15] T. Gautier, J. V. F. Lima, N. Maillard, B. Raffin, et al. Locality-aware work stealing on Multi-CPU and Multi-GPU architectures. In *MULTIPROG*, 2013.

[16] A. Gerasoulis and T. Yang. A comparison of clustering heuristics for scheduling directed acyclic graphs on multiprocessors. *Journal of Parallel and Distributed Computing*, 16(4):276–291, 1992.

[17] Y. Guo, R. Barik, R. Raman, and V. Sarkar. Work-first and help-first scheduling policies for async-finish task parallelism. In *IPDPS*, pages 1–12, 2009.

[18] Y. Guo, J. Zhao, V. Cave, and V. Sarkar. SLAW: a scalable locality-aware adaptive work–stealing scheduler. In *IPDPS*, pages 1–12, 2010.

[19] L. V. Kale and S. Krishnan. *CHARM++: a portable concurrent object oriented system based on C++*. ACM, 1993.

[20] G. Karypis and V. Kumar. A fast and high quality multilevel scheme for partitioning irregular graphs. *SIAM Journal on Scientific Computing*, 20(1):359–392, 1998.

[21] J. Lee and J. Palsberg. Featherweight X10: a core calculus for async-finish parallelism. In *PPoPP*, pages 25–36, 2010.

[22] C. Leiserson. The Cilk++ concurrency platform. In *DAC*, pages 522–527, 2009.

[23] L. L. Pilla, C. P. Ribeiro, D. Cordeiro, A. Bhatele, P. O. Navaux, J.-F. Méhaut, L. V. Kalé, et al. Improving parallel system performance with a NUMA-aware load balancer. *TR-JLPC-11-02*, 2011.

[24] J.-N. Quintin and F. Wagner. Hierarchical work-stealing. In *EuroPar*, pages 217–229, 2010.

[25] J. Reinders. *Intel threading building blocks*. Intel, 2007.

[26] M. Shaheen and R. Strzodka. NUMA aware iterative stencil computations on many-core systems. In *IPDPS*, pages 461–473, 2012.

[27] S. Sridharan, G. Gupta, and G. S. Sohi. Holistic run-time parallelism management for time and energy efficiency. In *ICS*, pages 337–348, 2013.

[28] B. Vikranth, R. Wankar, and C. R. Rao. Topology aware task stealing for on-chip NUMA multi-core processors. *Procedia Computer Science*, 18:379–388, 2013.

[29] R. M. Yoo, C. J. Hughes, C. Kim, Y.-K. Chen, and C. Kozyrakis. Locality-aware task management for unstructured parallelism: a quantitative limit study. In *SPAA*, pages 315–325, 2013.

Effective Automatic Computation Placement and Data Allocation for Parallelization of Regular Programs

Chandan Reddy
Indian Institute of Science
Bangalore 560012 India
chandan.g@csa.iisc.ernet.in

Uday Bondhugula
Indian Institute of Science
Bangalore 560012 India
uday@csa.iisc.ernet.in

ABSTRACT

This paper proposes techniques for data allocation and computation mapping when compiling affine loop nest sequences for distributed-memory clusters. Techniques for transformation and detection of parallelism, and generation of communication sets relying on the polyhedral framework already exist. However, these recent approaches used a simple strategy to map computation to nodes – typically block or block-cyclic. These mappings may lead to excess communication volume for multiple loop nests. In addition, the data allocation strategy used did not permit efficient weak scaling. We address these complementary problems by proposing automatic techniques to determine computation placements for identified parallelism and allocation of data. Our approach for data allocation is driven by tiling of data spaces along with a scheme to allocate and deallocate tiles on demand and reuse them. We show that our approach for computation mapping yields more effective mappings than those that can be developed using vendor-supplied libraries. Experimental results on some sequences of BLAS calls demonstrate a mean speedup of $1.82\times$ over versions written with ScaLAPACK. Besides enabling weak scaling for distributed memory, data tiling also improves locality for shared-memory parallelization. Experimental results on a 32-core shared-memory SMP system shows a mean speedup of $2.67\times$ over code that is not data tiled.

Categories and Subject Descriptors

D.3.4 [**Programming Languages**]: Processors—*Compilers, Optimization, Code generation*

General Terms

Algorithms, Design, Experimentation, Performance

Keywords

automatic parallelization; distributed memory; polyhedral model; data distribution; computation placement

1. INTRODUCTION AND MOTIVATION

A significant amount of work has been done in the past two decades on parallelizing for distributed-memory. A majority of this work was done in developing compiler technology for high performance Fortran. However, even in domains where it was suitable, namely programs with regular accesses, there was limited success. Several steps involved in achieving good performance remained manual. The quality of communication code as well as the ability to automatically apply complex transformations was a big limitation. Hence, even for programs that involve regular accesses such as sequences of linear algebra kernels, the approach currently used to obtain the best performance is to rely on highly tuned libraries. In addition, none of the previous approaches on automatic distributed-memory parallelization and code generation have been directly employed so far even in domain-specific language compilation. MPI still happens to be the dominant and de facto programming model due to the lack of any compiler support. The objective of our paper is to further improve automatic compiler and runtime support for distributed-memory clusters of multicores with emphasis of exploiting locality.

Some of the limitations in parallelization and code generation for regular programs, in particular, affine loop nests, have been addressed in recent years [2, 4, 3, 7]. These works provide techniques for transformation and detection of parallelism, and generation of communication sets relying on the polyhedral framework. However, these works use a simple strategy to map identified parallelism – typically block or block-cyclic. Previous automatic data distribution works [11, 5, 10, 12] also employed only block or block-cyclic mappings for loop nests with the possibility to re-distribute in between. In spite of a good choice of loop transformations and structure, these strategies to map identified parallelism significantly impact communication volume and load balance. Some specialized mappings such as multipartitioning [14, 6] were known and implemented in dHPF, but these works did not provide any automatic way to determine such mappings. In addition to this, there has been significant room for improvement in the way data allocation was handled – to better exploit locality in conjunction with compute transformations. This paper provides an effective solution to these missing steps.

Our approach for data allocation works by tiling of data spaces. A *data tile* is the granularity at which data is allocated and it is itself contiguous in main memory. Data local to a node as well as that which is received from remote nodes is accessed by first addressing a data tile and then indexing into it. A compiler-based approach with light-weight runtime helper functions handles on-demand allocation and deallocation of tiles, and their reuse. The approach can work in conjunction with either static or dynamic scheduling of compute tiles. Besides enabling weak scaling for distributed memory, data tiling improves locality for shared-memory parallelization – by reducing cache conflict misses, data TLB misses, and false sharing, and allowing better prefetching.

Although manual distributed-memory parallelization as seen by a programmer often starts with the step of data decomposition followed by computation decomposition, we show that this seemingly natural approach is not the efficient one when designing flexible and automatic compiler support. We argue that emphasis should first be placed on determining the right computation transformation and a placement. If good computation distributions are found, the initial data distribution only impacts "first-read" and "last write" communication. Determining a data distribution and then a compute distribution as done by some previous approaches may even prevent certain computation distributions where the owner of data has to change in order to exploit locality. Our approach neither has the notion of an owner for data, nor that of fixed distribution, nor re-distribution. Instead data that is accessed for a piece of computation is allocated on demand (if not already allocated), with communication data flowing from one node to another as dictated by computation mappings. In summary, the contributions of our work are that of:

- developing a technique to map identified parallelism after transformation encompassing block, block-cyclic and other specialized and arbitrary mappings,

- devising a data allocation technique based on data tiling to provide improved locality and enable weak scaling for distributed memory parallelization,

- and demonstration through experiments that our approach is significantly better than previous approaches and the code generated outperforms that which can be written even using vendor supplied BLAS libraries.

More specifically, for some sequences of BLAS calls, the code we automatically generate beats code manually written using Intel ScaLAPACK library by a mean factor of $1.82\times$ while running on a 32-node InfiniBand cluster of multicores. Shared-memory parallelization results obtained on a 32-core shared-memory NUMA SMP system show a mean speedup of $2.67\times$ over code that is not data tiled.

The rest of this paper is organized as follows. Section 2 describes our approach to find computation placements. Section 3 describes how data tilings are found. We describe in Section 4 how allocation is performed based on a tiled view of data spaces. Experimental results are presented in Section 5. Related work and conclusions are presented in Section 6 and 7 respectively.

2. FINDING COMPUTATION PLACEMENT

In this section, we describe how we find a suitable way of mapping available parallelism to a set of nodes. In particular, the presented strategy subsumes commonly used distributions like block, block-cyclic as well as more complex mapping schemes. The mappings are obtained for all parallel loop nests together. In the rest of this paper, the term *node* is used to refer to a set of processors that have shared memory, typically, an SMP system of general-purpose multicores. Multiple nodes are connected over an network interconnect.

To be self-contained, we briefly describe certain distribution patterns – although some of them are very well-known. A *block* distribution distributes a set of iterations into equal or nearly equal contiguous chunks where the number of chunks is equal to the number of processors. A *cyclic* distribution distributes a set of iterations

across processors in a round-robin manner at the granularity of a single iteration. When this granularity is changed to a contiguous chunk of some fixed size, the resulting mapping is a *block-cyclic* mapping. We define another specialized mapping that we call a *sudoku* mapping due to its similarity with the popular number placement puzzle of the same name. A *sudoku* mapping assigns tiles from an n-dimensional view to processors in a way such that all tiles along any of the ($n-1$ dimensional) canonical hyperplanes are mapped on to distinct processors. We will see that such a mapping (Figure 5a) has interesting properties in minimizing communication if two pieces of computation require an array to be distributed in conflicting ways. Multipartitioning [14] implemented in dHPF is one possible perfect sudoku mapping and such a mapping was used in the manually parallelized versions of NAS BT and SP.

The computation mapping of a statement S_i, denoted by π_{S_i}, maps computation tiles to nodes. The chosen computation mappings have a significant impact on the execution time of a program. Two key factors to be considered while deciding computation mappings are communication volume and load balance. We call a computation mapping for a given program optimal if it leads to the lowest communication volume and perfect load balance. Consider the sample tiled ADI code shown in Figure 2. The optimal computation mapping π_{S1} for the forward x sweep loop is the block distribution along ii loop iterations. This distribution leads to no communication and all nodes gets equal number of iterations. Similarly, the optimal mapping π_{S2} for the y sweep is the block distribution of jj. However, these mappings are not optimal for the entire program as they demand a transpose of array X between the nests of $S1$ and $S2$, and thus a large amount of communication. Significantly better mappings exist and in this section, we will describe a technique to find such computation mappings automatically.

```
//forward x sweep
for (i=0; i<N; i++)
 for (j=1; j<N; j++)
  X[i][j] = X[i][j] - X[i][j-1] * A[i][j] / B[i][j-1]; //S1

//upward y sweep
for (j=0; j<N; j++)
 for (i=1; i<N; i++)
  X[i][j] = X[i][j] - X[i-1][j] * A[i][j] / B[i-1][j]; //S2
```

Figure 1: Sample ADI program with only forward x and y sweeps.

We model the problem of finding optimal computation mappings as a graph partitioning problem on the inter-tile communication graph (TCG). Each vertex in the TCG represents a computation tile of the program. An edge e is added between two vertices if and only if there is communication between the corresponding two tiles when they are executed on different nodes. The weight of the edge e_w will be equal to the communication volume between the two tiles. Finding the optimal computation mappings is equivalent to partitioning the TCG into p (number of nodes) equal size partitions with the objective to minimize the sum of those edge weights that straddle partitions. This objective function represents the total communication volume for the entire program execution. The resulting computation mappings will thus have lower communication volume.

Figure 3a illustrates the tiled iteration domain along with RAW dependences for the ADI example. A vertex is added to TCG for each of the tiles. Previous work [7] describes techniques (FOIFI) to determine the communication sets and receiving tiles for a given tile. Dependence edges that cross tile boundaries are used to determine the necessary communication sets and receiving tiles. We use these techniques to build the TCG. For a given tile, an edge is added to each of its receiving tiles. The size of the communication set between sender and receiver tiles is set as the weight of edge

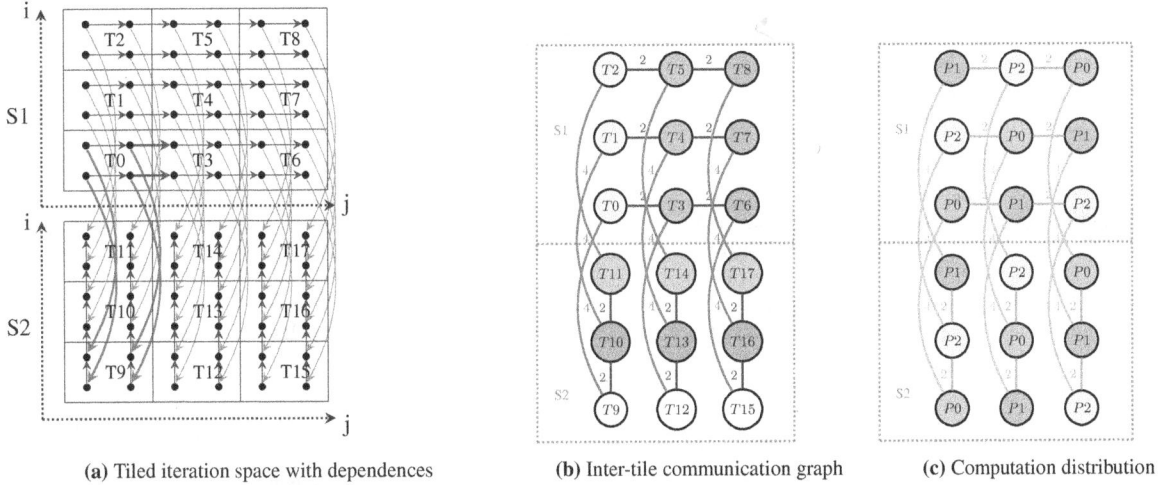

(a) Tiled iteration space with dependences   **(b)** Inter-tile communication graph   **(c)** Computation distribution

Figure 3: ADI

```
//forward x sweep
for (jj=0; jj<floord(N, 128); jj++) //serial loop
 for (ii=0; ii<floord(N, 128); ii++) //parallel loop
  for (i=max(1, ii*128); i<min(ii*128+127, N); i++)
   for (j=max(1,jj*128); j<min(jj*128+127, N); j++)
    X[i][j] = X[i][j] - X[i][j-1] * A[i][j] / B[i][j-1]; //S1

//upward y sweep
for (ii=0; ii<floord(N, 128); ii++) //serial loop
 for (jj=0; jj<floord(N, 128); jj++) //parallel loop
  for (j=max(1, jj*128); j<min(jj*128+127, N); j++)
   for (i=max(1, ii*128); i<min(ii*128+127, N); i++)
    X[i][j] = X[i][j] - X[i-1][j] * A[i][j] / B[i-1][j]; //S2
```

Figure 2: Tiled ADI program, tile size = 128

between them. In the Figure 3b, edges are added from $T0$ to its receivers $T3$ and $T9$, with the edge weights 2 and 4 respectively.

2.1 Load balancing constraints

A parallel phase is a contiguous band of parallel loops/dimensions that have been identified for potential extraction of parallelism. Programs often consist of multiple parallel phases. To achieve good load balance, it is essential that an equal or a nearly equal number of tiles are allocated to all nodes in each parallel phase. We identify the tiles that belong to a parallel phase and add constraints that will minimize load imbalance within each parallel phase. Vertex weights are used to distinguish between tiles that belong to different parallel phases. The vertex weight is a vector of size equal to the total number of parallel phases. All tiles which belong to the ith parallel phase will have a vertex weight with the ith component set and rest zero. Let S_i be the sum of the ith vertex weight component of all vertices belonging to a single partition. For each vertex weight component, we add load balancing constraints that minimizes the difference between S_is of any two partitions. These constraints make sure that the resulting compute tile mappings will assign an equal or a nearly equal number of tiles to each node in each parallel phase.

When performing static scheduling, all tiles belonging to a band of tiled parallel loops, for a given value of surrounding sequential loops, are said to belong to a single parallel phase. Figure 2 shows the tiled code for the ADI example. For the first loop, ii is the innermost tiled parallel loop. All the iterations of ii, for a particular value of outer sequential loop jj, belong to the same parallel phase. In case of dynamic scheduling, we do a topological sort of the TCG to identify tiles that belong to the same parallel phase – all tiles at

the same level belong to a single phase. For the ADI example in Figure 3b there are six parallel phases. All tiles belonging to the same parallel phase are marked with the same color. Tiles $T0$, $T1$ and $T2$ belong to same parallel phase and each will have vertex weights as $\langle 1, 0, 0, 0, 0, 0 \rangle$. Similarly $T9$, $T12$ and $T15$ belong to same parallel phase and will have vertex weight as $\langle 0, 0, 0, 1, 0, 0 \rangle$. The load balancing constraints ensures that Tiles $T0$, $T1$ and $T2$ are equally divided among all nodes.

The above formulation finds partitions that have an equal number of tiles in each partition. If number of iterations in the tiles are not equal, assigning equal number of tiles to each partition could lead to load imbalance. To overcome this issue, we set number of iteration in the tile as the vertex weight component. Load balancing constraints on vertex weights ensures that each partition will have an equal number of iterations, in each parallel phase.

Figure 3c shows one of the optimal solutions for graph partitioning of the ADI example. In each parallel phase, equal number of tiles are assigned to all the nodes, which ensures perfect load balance. Computation mapping is identical for both $S1$ and $S2$. Computation tile $\langle ii, jj \rangle$ of $S1$ and $\langle ii, jj \rangle$ of $S2$ are mapped to the same node, thus eliminating communication between $S1$ and $S2$. We call this type of computation mapping a 'sudoku' mapping, since all nodes are assigned equal numbers of tiles along each row and column. Multi-partitioning mappings [14] are similar to sudoku mappings. Sudoku mappings may not have modulo shift mappings of nodes as defined in multi-partitioning mappings. Figure 4a shows the computation mappings for stencil programs with near-neighbor communication, which is exactly the block distribution. Figure 4b shows the obtained computation mappings for tapered iteration spaces. This mapping is slightly different from block-cyclic mapping. In this mappings, first and last columns are mapped to node $P0$, where as in block-cyclic mappings first and fourth columns will be mapped to node $P0$. The obtained mappings has slightly better load balance than block-cyclic distribution, as equal number of tiles are allocated to all the nodes.

The graph partitioning solution of the TCG also determines the optimal dimensionality of the computation mapping. Note that a higher dimensional mapping is not necessarily optimal for an entire sequence of loop nests being optimized. Consider a program with the first loop nest (forward x sweep) of ADI. The TCG of this program contains only the upper half of Figure 3b with just nodes of $S1$. The optimal computation mapping for this graph is a 1-d block distribution of ii loop. Similarly, for the lower half with the second loop nest (upward y sweep), the optimal computation mapping is a 1-d block distribution of the jj loop. Our graph partitioning approach is able to find these solutions.

2.2 Scalability of graph partitioning

Graph partitioning with load balancing constraints is an NP-hard problem. Solutions to these problems are generally derived using heuristics and approximation algorithms. Open-source software packages such as METIS [15] and SCOTCH [17] can be used to solve graph partitioning problems. As the problem sizes in our input program increase, the number of vertices and edges in the TCG also increase. The number of load balancing constraints also increases as we add load balancing constraints to each parallel phase, and this depends on the problem size. Even state-of-the-art graph partitioning software such as these do not scale as the problem size increases. For example, to partition a TCG of ADI with 64 vertices into 4 partitions, METIS takes around 240s. If the problem size is increased further, both the time taken and the memory required for partitioning increases drastically. Another major problem is that the quality of the obtained solution degrades as the problem size increases. For the ADI example, we observe that perfect "sudoku" mappings are not obtained for more than 32 vertices.

In order to make our approach scalable for larger problem sizes, we use an approximation to partition the TCG. Note that the dependence patterns typically do not change as the problem size is increased beyond a certain point. Hence, the optimal mappings for a larger problem size can often be obtained by scaling the optimal mappings for a smaller one. The computation mappings for larger problem sizes and the actual number of processors are derived from the computation mappings for a smaller problem size and number of processors. At compile time, we build the TCG for a smaller problem size. Problem sizes are chosen such that the number of vertices in each parallel phase is a particular number that is sufficient to distinguish the nature of the obtained mapping. The number of processors is fixed at four which we found to be sufficient in practice, and the problem size is set so that we have at least two times the number of processor tiles along each parallel dimension. This allows us to distinguish between block and block-cyclic mappings. The edges weights and vertex weights are computed for this smaller graph, and this is partitioned using METIS. Partitioning the initial small graph into four partitions takes less than 0.6s in all cases (avg: 0.2s, min: 0.01s). At runtime, when the problem size is known, the partitioning solution for the input problem size is obtained from the solution of the smaller representative graph. The mapping obtained is first classified as either being block, block-cyclic, sudoku or an arbitrary one. If a mapping is identified as block, sudoku, or arbitrary, then we perform a "block" scaling of the mapping for the right problem size and the number of processors. This is illustrated in Figure 5 which shows the computation mapping obtained for larger problems sizes for the ADI example. We then generate a function that returns the correct mapping for any given number of nodes.

For block and sudoku mappings, block scaling ensures that the respective property continues to hold. For arbitrary mappings, we find the block scaling to be a reasonable approach though we have not seen cases where we found arbitrary mappings. When the solution obtained through graph partitioning corresponds to a cyclic or a block-cyclic mapping, we perform a cyclic scaling analogous to the block scaling described above. Overall, this approximate approach of using a representative graph and then scaling the solution analytically based on an identified template mapping does not take more than a second on any of the examples considered for evaluation.

Actual communication costs finally depend on network topology – finding computation mappings that are optimal for a given network topology is beyond the scope of this work and is left for future.

3. DATA TILING

As introduced earlier, the idea is to tile the data space similar to tiling an iteration space, compute data required by a compute tile at the granularity of data tiles, and allocate only the required data tiles on-demand at a node. A node itself could comprise multiple cores that share memory.

3.1 Finding data tiling hyperplanes

In this section, we describe techniques to find the shape of the computation and data tiles. We determine the shape of computation and data tiles such that the data accessed by a computation tile is packed into as few data tiles as possible.

Let $S_1, S_2, \ldots, S_n$ be the statements of a program. Let D_{S_j} be the domain of S_j. Let E be the set of dependences edges with each edge $e \in E$ characterized by a dependence polyhedron P_e. P_e is a set of linear constraints that relate source iterators and target iterators that are in dependence. A one-dimensional affine transformation for S_j, denoted by ϕ_{S_j}, is defined as

$$\phi_{S_j}(\vec{i}) = \vec{h}^{S_j} \cdot \vec{i} + h_0^{S_j}. \tag{1}$$

ϕ_{S_j} can be viewed as a function mapping iterations of S_j to numbers that represent virtual processor ids. For example, $\phi_{S_j}(\vec{i}) = (1, 0)^T \cdot \vec{i} + 0$ maps all iterations (i, j) to virtual processor i. ϕ_{S_j} partitions the iteration space of S_j, and $\vec{h} = (1, 0)$ represents the orientation of the hyperplane that partitions it. When ϕ_{S_j} satisfies certain properties, we call it a tiling hyperplane.

Similarly, for arrays we define an array mapping function ψ_{A_k} that maps array elements to virtual processors represented by

$$\psi_{A_k}(\vec{a}) = \vec{d}^{A_k} \cdot \vec{a} + d_0^{A_k}, \tag{2}$$

where $\vec{d}$ represents the orientation of the hyperplane that partitions the array space, d_0 is the constant offset, and $\vec{a}$ is a data element in A_k. We call these mappings data tiling hyperplanes if they are found to satisfy certain properties that we will describe later in this section.

Consider the first loop nest of the ADI example shown in Figure 1. Assume that the computation mapping for S1 is $\phi_{S_1}(\vec{i}) = (1, 0)^T \cdot \vec{i}$. Different iterations of the i loop will be mapped to different virtual processors. For the array access $X[i][j]$, different iterations of i loop access different rows of array X. Hence, the first dimension of X has to be partitioned. This corresponds to the array mapping $\psi_X(\vec{a}) = (1, 0)^T \cdot \vec{a}$, which in turn corresponds to a row distribution of X. If the array access had been $X[j][i]$, then for $\phi_{S_1}(\vec{i}) = (1, 0)^T \cdot \vec{i}$, the corresponding data mapping would be $\psi_X(\vec{a}) = (0, 1)^T \cdot \vec{a}$, i.e., a column-wise distribution of X. Hence, the choice of data partitioning hyperplanes, for a given computation mapping, is driven by the array accesses.

Let F_{s_j, A_k}^i be the ith access function of array A_k in statement S_j. In our model, F is an affine function of loop iterators and program parameters. $\phi_{s_j}(\vec{i})$ is the virtual processor to which iteration $\vec{i}$ will be mapped. $F_{s_j, A_k}^i(\vec{i})$ represents data accessed by $\vec{i}$. $\psi_{A_k}(F_{s_j, A_k}^i(\vec{i}))$ is the virtual processor to which the data accessed by $\vec{i}$ will be mapped. Now, we require that the data accessed by $\vec{i}$ be mapped to the same virtual processor as the one $\vec{i}$ is mapped to, i.e.,

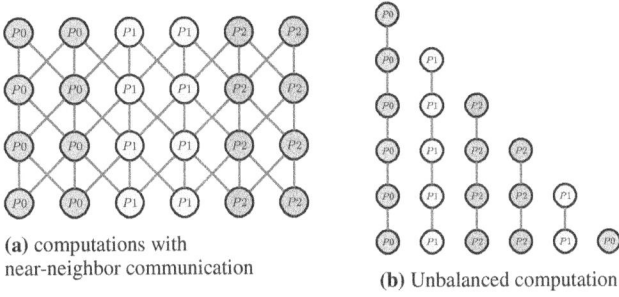

(a) computations with near-neighbor communication

(b) Unbalanced computation

Figure 4: Computation distributions

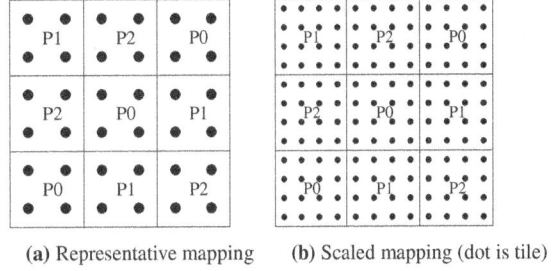

(a) Representative mapping   **(b)** Scaled mapping (dot is tile)

Figure 5: Scaling a computation mapping for ADI

$$\phi_{s_j}(\vec{i}) = \psi_{A_k}(F^i_{s_j,A_k}(\vec{i})). \tag{3}$$

The above condition is conceptually the same as that used by Anderson and Lam [1], but it was in a form that worked only for perfect loop nests and uniform dependences, and hence the subsequent approach relying on it was also different. It is not obviously always possible to ensure condition (3) since multiple iterations can access the same data. Hence, what we try to capture is the difference between the LHS and RHS of (3) as follows and try to minimize it:

$$\gamma^i_{s_j,A_k}(\vec{i}) = |\phi_{s_j}(\vec{i}) - \psi_{A_k}(F^i_{s_j,A_k}(\vec{i}))| \ \ \vec{i} \in D_{s_j}. \tag{4}$$

The above definition is thus used to connect compute and data tiling hyperplanes. We now first describe the existing technique to characterize and choose from valid compute tiling hyperplanes, and then show how data tiling constraints and objectives are integrated into it to minimize γs. Previous work [4] provided an automatic approach to find compute tiling hyperplanes that exposed maximal course-grained parallelism and locality based on an Integer Linear Programming formulation. To enforce validity for tiling for an edge e with dependence polyhedron P_e, the following constraint ensures non-negative dependence components that is sufficient for tiling:

$$\phi_{s_j}(\vec{t}) - \phi_{s_i}(\vec{s}) \geq 0, \ \ \langle \vec{s}, \vec{t} \rangle \in P_e. \tag{5}$$

Then, the following cost function has been used to select the best hyperplane among the set of valid tiling hyperplanes.

$$\delta_e(\vec{t}, \vec{s}) = \phi_{s_j}(\vec{t}) - \phi_{s_i}(\vec{s}), \ \ \langle \vec{s}, \vec{t} \rangle \in P_e \tag{6}$$

This cost function is a measure of communication volume or reuse distance – and the ILP is solved to minimize it.

We now add data tiling hyperplane coefficients to the ILP described above and use (4) to relate compute and data tiling hyperplane coefficients. (4) cannot be directly added as it leads to non-linear constraints between hyperplane coefficients and loop iterators. The bounding function technique [9] can again be used here obtain constraints in a linear form. When the iteration spaces are bounded, one can obtain an upper bound on $\gamma^i_{s_j,A_k}(\vec{i})$. The maximum mismatch quantified by γ occurs when the iterations and the entire data accessed by them are mapped onto different virtual processors. This mismatch can be bounded by an affine function of program parameters $\vec{p}$, i.e., there exists $v_{A_k}(\vec{p}) = u_{A_k} \cdot \vec{p} + w$ such that

$$v_{A_k}(\vec{p}) - \gamma^i_{s_j,A_k}(\vec{i}) \geq 0, \ \ \vec{i} \in D_{s_j} \tag{7}$$

By minimizing the bounding function coefficients $\vec{u}_{A_k}$, we indirectly minimize (4). Now the affine form of the Farkas lemma can be applied to (7).

$$v_{A_k}(\vec{p}) - \gamma^i_{s_j,A_k}(\vec{i}) \equiv \lambda_{s_j,A^i_{k0}} + \Sigma_t \lambda_{s_j,A^i_{kt}}(a_t\vec{i} + b_t), \tag{8}$$

where $\lambda_{s_j,A^i_{kt}} \geq 0$ are the Farkas multipliers and $a_t\vec{i} + b_t \geq 0$ are the faces of D_{s_j}. The coefficients of $\vec{i}$ and $\vec{p}$ in the resulting equations are eliminated using Fourier-Motzkin elimination to obtain constraints in a linear form.

The resulting ILP system with tile validity conditions (5), cost function constraints (6) and data hyperplane constraints (7) is solved using PIP [8] to get both compute and data tiling hyperplanes. PIP computes the lexicographical minimal solution for the ILP. Hence, the order of variables is important. We add separate bounding function coefficients for each of the arrays to ensure that non-zero bounding coefficients of one array do not affect the choice of data hyperplanes for the other arrays. Let u_s, w_s be the bounding function coefficients from the (6), u_{A_k}, w_{A_k} be the bounding function coefficients for array A_j resulting from (7), and h_{s_j} be the vector of compute hyperplane coefficients, and d_{A_k} that of the data tiling hyperplane coefficients. (9) shows the order of variables used for the lexicographic minimal solution:

$$min_\prec(u_s, u_{A_1}, \ldots, w_s, w_{A_1}, \ldots, h_{s_1}, \ldots, d_{A_1}, \ldots). \tag{9}$$

Consider the example shown in Figure 6. For compute tiling hyperplane (1,0), there is no need to tile array $v1$ and $v2$, as all iterations of i loop access entire $v1$ and $v2$ arrays. Once we solve the ILP, we obtain a compute tiling hyperplane for each of the statements, ϕ_{S_j}, and a data tiling hyperplane for each of the arrays, ψ_{A_k}. A data tiling hyperplane ψ_{A_k} is considered to be invalid for all $F^i_{S_j,A_k}$ if the ϕ_{S_j} lies in the union of the null spaces of all array access functions, $F^i_{S_j,A_k}$. If this condition is satisfied, then all iterations of S_j access the entire array A_k. Hence, it is not necessary to tile the array space even if the iteration space of S_j is tiled with ϕ_{S_j}. It is necessary to tile the data space only when different partitions of the iteration space, due to ϕ_{S_j}, access different parts of array A_k.

```
for (i=0; i<N; i++)
  for (j=1; j<N; j++)
    B[i][j] = A[i][j] + u1[i]*v1[j] + u2[i]*v2[j];
```

Figure 6: First loop nest of gemver

3.2 Iteratively finding all hyperplanes

A statement can have as many compute tiling hyperplanes as the dimensionality of its iteration space. Similarly, an array can have as many data tiling hyperplanes as its dimensionality. Solving the ILP formulation described in the previous section gives us a single compute tiling hyperplane for all statements and a single data tiling hyperplanes for all arrays. We add new constraints to the ILP to ensure that subsequent compute tiling hyperplanes are linearly independent of ones already found. However, for data tiling

17

hyperplanes, linear independence constraints are only added with respect those that were found to be valid. Algorithm 1 describes the complete procedure to find all compute and data tiling hyperplanes. For the ADI example 1, the first compute hyperplane for $S1$ and $S2$ is (1,0), corresponding data tiling hyperplane for arrays X, A and B is (1,0). The second compute hyperplane for $S1$ and $S2$ is (0,1), corresponding data tiling hyperplane for arrays X, A and B is (0,1). Since, each of the data tiling hyperplanes are linearly independent of each other, they form a full rank matrix.

Algorithm 1: Finding compute and data hyperplanes

Input: Data dependences (E), array access functions (**F**)
Output: $\phi_{S_j} \ \forall S_j, \psi_{A_k} \ \forall A_k$

1 $C \leftarrow \emptyset$;
   valid_hyperplanes_$S_j \leftarrow \emptyset \ \forall S_j$;
   valid_hyperplanes_$A_k \leftarrow \emptyset \ \forall A_k$;
   num_valid_hyperplanes_$S_j \leftarrow 0 \ \forall S_j$;
   num_valid_hyperplanes_$A_k \leftarrow 0 \ \forall A_k$;
   max_num_hyperplanes $\leftarrow \max(dim(S_j)) \ \forall S_j$;
   for each $e \in E$ *within fused loops* **do**
2 $\quad$ Add validity constraints resulting from $\phi_{s_j}(\vec{t}) - \phi_{s_i}(\vec{s}) \geq 0$ to C
3 **for each** $e \in E$ **do**
4 $\quad$ Add the bounding function constraints resulting from
   $\quad |v(\vec{p}) - \delta_e(\vec{t}, \vec{s})| \geq 0$ to C;
5 **for each** $F^i_{s_j, A_k} \in \mathbf{F}$ **do**
6 $\quad$ Obtain constraints resulting from $\phi_{s_j}(\vec{i}) - \psi_{A_k}(F^i_{s_j, A_k}(\vec{i})) \geq 0$
   $\quad$ and $\psi_{A_k}(F^i_{s_j, A_k}(\vec{i})) - \phi_{s_j}(\vec{i}) \geq 0$ to C;
7 **while** *max_num_hyperplanes ≥ 0* **do**
8 $\quad$ Solve the ILP with constraints in C;
   $\quad$ max_num_hyperplanes $\leftarrow$ max_num_hyperplanes - 1;
   $\quad$ **for each** ϕ_{S_j} *found* **do**
9 $\quad\quad$ **if** *num_valid_hyperplanes_$S_j < dim(S_j)$* **then**
10 $\quad\quad\quad$ Add ϕ_{S_j} to valid_hyperplanes_S_j;
   $\quad\quad\quad$ num_valid_hyperplanes_S_j++;
   $\quad\quad\quad$ Add constraints to exclude hyperplanes linearly
   $\quad\quad\quad$ dependent on ϕ_{S_j};
11 $\quad$ **for each** ψ_{A_k} *found* **do**
12 $\quad\quad$ **if** ψ_{A_k} *is a valid data tiling hyperplane* **then**
13 $\quad\quad\quad$ **if** *num_valid_hyperplanes_$A_k < dim(A_k)$* **then**
14 $\quad\quad\quad\quad$ Add ψ_{A_k} to valid_hyperplanes_A_k;
   $\quad\quad\quad\quad$ num_valid_hyperplanes_A_k ++;
   $\quad\quad\quad\quad$ Add constraints to exclude hyperplanes linearly
   $\quad\quad\quad\quad$ dependent on ψ_{A_k};

---

4. DATA ALLOCATION

In this section, we describe how data is indexed and managed once data tiling hyperplanes for each array have been determined. The data accessed for array A_k through access function F in S_j can be computed by taking the image of the D_{S_j} under F. However, we are interested in computing data accessed by a particular compute tile. This enables us to allocate only the data required for the tile on the node it executes on. To accomplish this, the image of the access function is computed while treating dimensions outer to the tile, that we call inter-tile iterators, as parameters. The resulting image will be a set, parametric in the inter tile iterators. By plugging in a particular value for these inter tile iterators, precise data accessed by that particular compute tile can be obtained. The shaded rectangle in Figure 7 shows the parametric data region of compute tile (1,0) due to the array access $A[i][j-1]$.

When the data tiling hyperplanes are used, the parametric data regions obtained above end up getting tiled as well in the same way iteration spaces are tiled. Same tile sizes are used when tiling the

iteration space using compute tiling hyperplanes and the parametric data region using the corresponding data tiling hyperplane. After tiling, the dimensions of the parametric data region include the newly added inter data tile iterators, intra data tile iterators and the inter compute tile iterators. For a particular value of compute tile iterators, inter data tile iterators enumerate all data tiles accessed, and intra data tile iterators scan data points inside a data tile.

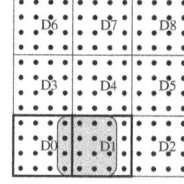

Figure 7: Accessed data for compute tile (0,1) for $A[i][j-1]$ in ADI

On-Demand data tile memory allocation: Projecting out the inter data tile iterators, we get parametric polyhedron that can be used to enumerate all the data tiles that a compute tile accesses. We use this polyhedron to generate a function that will allocate memory for the data tiles required by a given compute tile. This function will be called just before the execution of a compute tile. This will ensure that data required by a compute tile is allocated only on that node which will execute the compute tile. For the ADI example generated function returns data tiles $D0$ and $D1$ for the compute tile (0,1), and only $D0$ for the compute tile (0,0).

Algorithm 2: Determine accessed data tiles for array A_k

Input: Parametric data region D_{A_k} of array A_k, data tiling
$\quad\quad$ hyperplanes ψ_{A_k}, tile sizes τ_k
Output: Parametric data tiles accessed

1 **for each** *data tiling hyperplane* $\psi_{A_k}(\vec{a}) = \vec{d_k} \cdot \vec{a} + d_{k0}$, *tile size* τ_k
   do
2 $\quad$ add a inter data tile dimension $\vec{a_T}$, corresponding to $\vec{a}$
   $\quad$ add the following two constraints to D_{A_k}
   $\quad \tau_k * (\vec{d_k} \cdot \vec{a_T}) \leq \vec{d_k} \cdot \vec{a} + d_{k0} \leq \tau_k * (\vec{d_k} \cdot \vec{a_T}) + \tau_k - 1$
3 Project out the intra-tile data dimensions $\vec{a}$ in D_{A_k}
   return D_{A_k}

Allocation of first-read data: Input data of the program being compiled has to be initialized and distributed before start of program execution. We thus also need to allocate that part of the input data that is "live in" to the compute tiles to be executed on that node. We call this the first-read data. First-read data of an array A is set of all array elements whose values are first read by a compute tile before a write is performed if at all. This set is identified by computing the data accessed all read accesses, and then subtracting out data accessed by target iterations of RAR and RAW dependences entering the tile.

Data tile buffer reuse: Programs access different parts of the array during the entire execution of the program. Often, we can reuse the data tile buffers, rather than allocating new buffers for every new data tile. A data tile buffer can be safely reused when all the compute tiles that require this data tile have finished their execution. We can precisely count the number of compute tiles that require a given data tile. Per data tile ref-count is used to capture number of compute tiles that need this data tile. We generate a function that will enumerate all the compute tiles executed by the given processor and use Algorithm 2 to get all the data tiles accessed by tile, and increment their ref-count. This function is invoked at the start of the program. Once the compute tile has finished its execution and data required by other tiles is packed, we decrement the ref-count of all the data tiles accessed by this compute tile. If the ref-count becomes zero we add the data tile buffer pointer to free-buffers queue. When we want to allocate a new buffer for data tile, the free-buffer queue is checked fist, if it is non empty, one of its buffers is returned. A new allocation is done only when free-buffer queue is empty. Per data tile ref-count is used to track the liveness information of data tiles. Since, we use dynamic scheduling, actual schedule will be decided at runtime. Above techniques provide an efficient, dynamic and schedule independent mechanism for data tile buffer reuse.

Algorithm 3: initialize_ ref_counts ()

Input: Set of all compute tiles
Output: data tile ref-counts

1 **for each** *data tile* $\vec{d}$ **do**
2   ref_count_$\vec{d}$ ← 0;
3 **for each** *compute tile* $\vec{t}$ **do**
4   **if** $\pi(\vec{t}) = node\_id$ **then**
5   required_data_tiles ← determine required data tiles ($\vec{t}$);
     for each *data tile* $\vec{d}$ ∈ *required_data_tiles* **do**
6   ref_count_$\vec{d}$ ++;

Data tiling with dynamic scheduling: We have integrated data tiling with a dynamic scheduling framework which schedules at the granularity of compute tiles. First, we determine the computation mappings π_S for a given problem size and the number of nodes. The dynamic scheduling runtime distributes compute tiles according to π_S. The read-in data is allocated and data tile reference counts are initialized as per π_S mappings. All compute tiles that are mapped to a single node are dynamically scheduled. Before start of tile execution, we call the on-demand allocate function (Algorithm 2), which will allocate all required data tiles if they had not been already allocated. After the tile has finished execution, we call the pack function which packs data required by other nodes from the current node. Packed data is sent to its receive nodes using asynchronous MPI primitives. Once the pack function is finished, we decrement the ref-counts of data tiles used. Besides being called at schedule time, the on-demand allocate function is also called before data received from other nodes is unpacked. A concurrent queue is used to maintain a list of free data tile buffers. Atomic increment and decrement are used to modify data tile ref-counts, and a compare-and-swap to update data tile buffer pointers. Thus, the whole implementation is thread-safe and lock-free.

4.1 Re-indexing data spaces

After we perform data tiling transformation, the memory layout of the arrays is changed. Array elements within the data tile are now packed in contiguous memory locations. So we need to modify the original array access functions such that they access correct elements in the new memory layout. The dimensionality of array A is double because of the new tile dimensions that are added. There should be an one-to-one mapping between original array dimensions and new tiled dimensions to ensure correctness. We use following equation to obtain new array accesses from original array accesses.

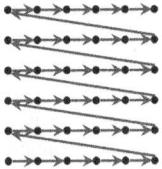

Figure 8: Original memory layout

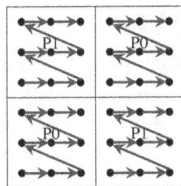

Figure 9: Tiled memory layout

$$\vec{T} = (\psi_{A_k} \cdot \vec{a})/\tau_k$$
$$\vec{t} = (\psi_{A_k} \cdot \vec{a})\%\tau_k \qquad (10)$$

where $\vec{T}$ is the access vector corresponding to inter-tile dimensions, $\vec{t}$ to intra-tile dimensions, ψ_A is the data tiling hyperplane, and τ is the tile size. Since the array tiling hyperplanes form a full-ranked matrix, a one-to-one mapping exists between original and new array accesses. $\vec{T}$ represents inter data tile dimensions which enumerates data tiles and $\vec{t}$ scans points inside a data tile. If the data tiling hyperplanes used are (1,0) and (0,1) and tile sizes τ_1, τ_2, the new array access will be $A[i/\tau_1][j/\tau_2][i\%\tau_1][j\%\tau_2]$. The size of the data tile that is to be allocated is $\tau_1 * \tau_2$.

To selectively allocate only the required data tiles, we split the transformed array access $A_t[ii_t][jj_t][i_t][j_t]$ into two parts, (i) $ptr = A_t[ii_t][jj_t]$ which returns the pointer to data tile (ii_t, jj_t), and (ii) $ptr[i_t][j_t]$ which indexes the array element within a data tile. A_t is used as an array of pointers to data tiles. Only when a particular data tile (ii_t, jj_t) is required by a node, a new data tile buffer is allocated and stored in $A_t[ii_i][jj_t]$.

Simplification of access expressions: Modified access functions obtained after transformation have the additional cost of a divide, a mod, and an additional memory access (to obtain the data tile pointer) for each array access. This could lead to significant overhead and may prohibit other optimizations such as vectorization. We hoist the divide, mod and array dereference operations out of the innermost loop by splitting it. Consider the data tiled code shown in Figure 10. The transformed code is shown in Figure 11. After simplification of access expressions, Intel's compiler was able to vectorize the innermost loop which led to a large performance improvement of about 4x.

```
//forward x sweep
for (jj=0; jj<floord(N, 128); jj++)
 for (ii=0; ii<floord(N, 128); ii++)
  for (i=max(1,ii*128); i<min(ii*128+127, N); i++)
   for (j=max(1,jj*128); j<min(jj*128+127, N); j++)
    X[i/128][j/128][i%128][j%128] =
     X[i/128][j/128][i%128][j%128] -
     X[i/128][(j-1)/128][i%128][(j-1)%128] *
     A[i/128][j/128][i%128][j%128] /
     B[i/128][(j-1)/128][i%128][(j-1)%128]; //S1
```

Figure 10: Data tiled ADI example

```
//forward x sweep
for (jj=0; jj<floord(N, 128); jj++)
 for (ii=0; ii<floord(N, 128); ii++)
  for (i=max(1, ii*128); i<min(ii*128+127, N); i++){
   j = max(1, jj*128);
   //peeled iteration
   X[i/128][j/128][i%128][j%128] =
       X[i/128][j/128][i%128][j%128] -
       X[i/128][(j-1)/128][i%128][(j-1)%128] *
       A[i/128][j/128][i%128][j%128] /
       B[i/128][(j-1)/128][i%128][(j-1)%128]; //S1
   j++;
   X_ptr = X[i/128][j/128];
   A_ptr = A[i/128][j/128];
   B_ptr = B[i/128][j/128];
   i_mod = i%128;
   lb = max(1, jj*128+1);
   for (j=max(1,jj*128+1); j<min(jj*128+127, N); j++)
    X_ptr[i_mod][j-lb] = X_ptr[i_mod][j-lb] -
        X_ptr[i_mod][j-lb-1] * A_ptr[i_mod][j-lb] /
        X_ptr[i_mod][j-lb-1]; //S1
}
```

Figure 11: Optimized data tiled ADI example

5. EXPERIMENTAL EVALUATION

This section presents experiments demonstrating improvement over existing techniques. Our framework is implemented as a part of a publicly available source to source polyhedral tool chain. The input for our framework is sequential C code which can be arbitrarily nested affine loop nests. Compilable code to find computation placements and to distribute data is automatically generated. Cloog-isl [2] is used to generate code from the polyhedral representation. METIS [15] is used to partition the initial graph (Section 2), and to determine computation distributions.

Benchmarks: We present results for Floyd-Warshall (floyd), LU Decomposition (lu), Cholesky Factorization (cholesky), Alternating Direction Implicit solver (adi), 2mm (2mm), and 3mm (3mm) benchmarks. All these benchmarks are chosen from the publicly available Polybench/C 3.2 suite [16]. For comparing against ScaLAPACK programs, we use atax, BiCG Sub Kernel (bicg), gemver, gesummv, and matrix vector product and transpose (mvt) benchmarks, also from the Polybench/C 3.2 suite [16]. All benchmarks use double-precision floating-point operations. The compiler used for all experiments is ICC 13.0.1 with options -O3 -ansi-alias -fp-model precise. *pluto-data-tile-gp* refers to our code. Where applicable, we compare or comment on solutions that would have been found by previous approaches [12, 14, 3], and we also mention the specific mapping found by the graph partitioning approach. Problem sizes used are listed in Table 1 and 2.

Benchmark	Problem size
floyd	4096 x 4096
cholesky	4096 x 4096
lu	8192 x 8192
2mm	2048 x 2048
3mm	2048 x 2048

Table 1: Problem sizes for shared memory evaluation

Benchmark	Problem size per processor
gemver	20000 x 20000
bicg	40000 x 40000
gesummv	30000 x 30000
mvt	30000 x 30000
atax	30000 x 30000
floyd	2048 x 2048
lu	4096 x 4096
adi	128 x 4096 x 4096

Table 2: Problem size (per proc) for distributed-memory evaluation

5.1 Distributed memory

The experiments were run on a 32-node InfiniBand cluster of dual-SMP Xeon servers. Each node on the cluster consists of two quad-core Intel Xeon E5430 2.66 GHz processors with 12 MB L2 cache and 16 GB RAM. The InfiniBand host adapter is a Mellanox MT25204 (InfiniHost III Lx HCA). All nodes run 64-bit Linux kernel version 2.6.18. The cluster uses MVAPICH2-1.8.1 as the MPI implementation. We measured a point-to-point latency of 3.36 μs, unidirectional and bidirectional bandwidths of 1.5 GB/s and 2.56 GB/s respectively. We developed ScaLAPACK versions of the benchmarks using multi-threaded ScaLAPACK routines of Intel MKL (version 11.0.1) library. All experiments are run with 8 threads per node.

Figure 12 shows the weak scaling performance for both ScaLA-PACK code and our framework. ScaLAPACK internally uses 2-d block cyclic distributions for all routines. Our framework computes the optimal computation placements for each of the benchmarks. For gemver, our framework finds the *sudoku* distribution that significantly outperforms 2-d block cyclic distribution. As we are able to fuse the first two loop nests in gemver and perform data tiling, our single thread performance is improved by about 3x. For mvt, bicg and gesummv benchmarks, transformations applied result in an outer parallel loop. The output of our framework is a 1-d block distribution with no communication, and this results in near ideal scaling. For atax benchmark ScaLAPACK code performs slightly better than our code because there was no benefit with loop fusion and the obtained computation placement led to same communication volume as that of two separate ScaLAPACK library calls. Figure 13c shows the weak scaling performance for adi. Previous schemes [3, 12] would have chosen 1-d block distribution for adi, that leads to $O(n^2)$ communication (nxn being the data size), and does not scale. On the other hand, our framework finds the sudoku-like placement that has only $O(n)$ communication. Figure 13a shows the weak scaling performance for floyd. The performance of *pluto-data-tile-gp* is very close to manually written 2-d blocked floyd. 2-d block distribution performs better than a 1-d block one due to a higher ratio of computation to communication – in this case, it leads to a 3× reduction in communication volume. Our framework also implicitly finds the optimal dimensionality of the distribution leading to the minimum communication volume. Note that a higher dimensional mapping may not be necessarily optimal for an entire sequence of loop nests being optimized.

5.2 Shared memory

The experiments were run on a four socket machine with AMD Opteron 6136 CPUs (2.4 GHz, 128 KB L1, 512 KB L2, and 6 MB L3 cache). The shared memory has a NUMA architecture and numactl to bind threads and pages appropriately for all our experiments. When not performing data tiling (for comparison), we did a simple interleaving of pages across all NUMA nodes.

Figure 14 shows that data tiling leads to a significant improvement in single thread performance, and hence benefits shared-memory parallelization as well. Data tiling enhances the spatial locality of space tiled loops. After data tiling, data accessed by a compute tile is contiguous in memory. There will only be cold caches for all accesses to a data tile, i.e., conflict misses are eliminated. It also reduces TLB misses and false sharing. Due to simplification of the modified access functions, we completely eliminated associated overhead from the innermost loop. This results in a geometric mean speedup of 2.67× over code with no data tiling. For cholesky we see a very high speedup of 5.42×. This is also due to data tiling enabling vectorization. cholesky kernel had spatially conflicting accesses in a single statement. This kernel is not readily vectorizable by icc as the memory accesses are not contiguous. If j is the innermost loop, then consecutive access of $A[j][i]$ are array size apart. However, after data tiling, accesses due to $A[j][i]$ are tile size apart, and icc can vectorize the code. So, in addition to enhancing locality, data tiling may also enable vectorization.

6. RELATED WORK

Our approach is built on top of and coupled with communication set generation and distributed-memory code generation works of Bondhugula [3] and Dathathri et al [7]. The communication set construction scheme of [7] is used and the volume of communication for a given transformation does not increase due to data tiling.

The works of Kennedy and Kremer [12], Chapman et al [5], Garcia et al [10], Gupta and Banerjee [11] have addressed the problem

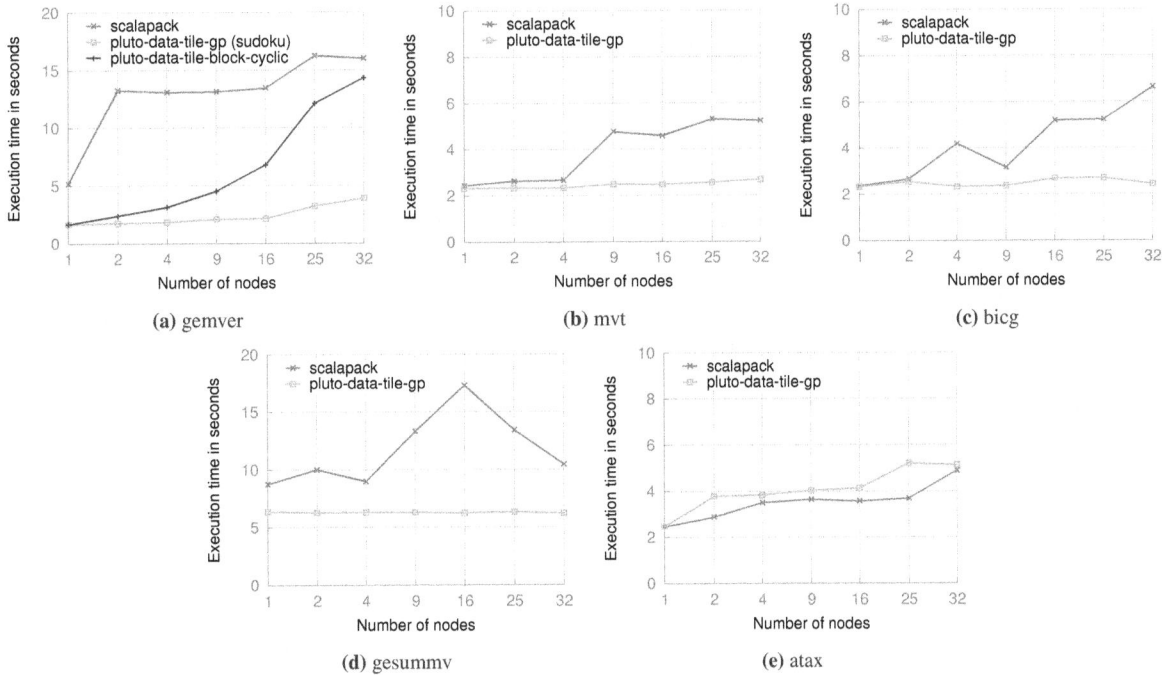

(a) gemver   **(b)** mvt   **(c)** bicg

(d) gesummv   **(e)** atax

Figure 12: Weak scaling performance of scalapack and pluto-data-tile-gp on up to 32 nodes (256 cores)

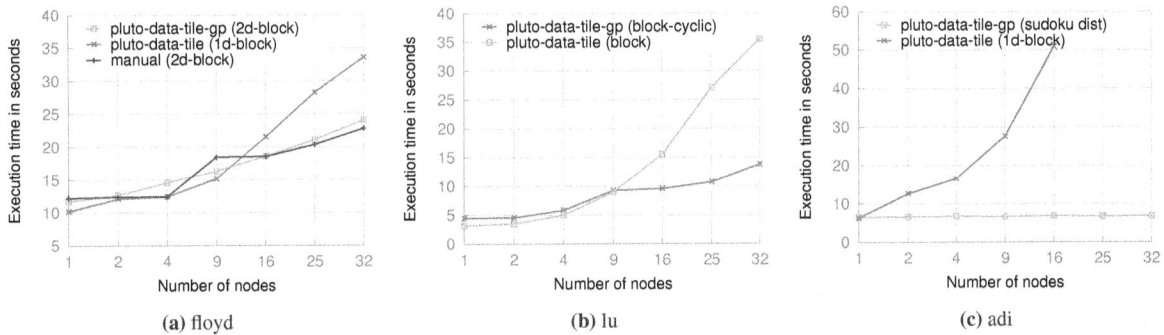

(a) floyd   **(b)** lu   **(c)** adi

Figure 13: Weak scaling performance of pluto-data-tile-gp on up to 32 nodes (256 cores)

of finding automatic data distributions for distributed memory architectures in the context of regular programs. These approaches first decompose the input program into regions (also called phases) at the granularity of loop nests. An array has a single distribution throughout a phase and data is remapped between phases (dynamic distributions). Within each phase, data distributions and array alignments are found that lead to the least communication volume. The solution space of these works only includes data distributions typically supported by HPF (High Performance Fortran), i.e., block or block-cyclic. On the other hand, our technique first determines computation placements and the data distributions are then derived from it. It thus automatically captures array alignments, static and dynamic distributions, and array replications modeled in the previous approaches. To provide this flexibility, our approach included an elaborate data allocation scheme. To summarize, our approach has the following advantages over all previous works: (i) our solution space includes arbitrary mappings including multipartitioning-style, not just block and block cyclic, (ii) it has the flexibility to apply locality-enhancing transformations such as time tiling since we do not adhere to the "owner computes" rule,

and (iii) it minimizes both communication volume and load imbalance.

The work of Anderson and Lam [1] deals with finding computation and data distributions in a unified manner. It only deals with sequences of perfectly nested loops, and finds affine computation and data mappings to virtual processors. Heuristics are then used to map virtual processors to actual physical processors, which again only support block or block-cyclic mappings.

Multipartitioning [14] and generalized multipartitioning [6] were specialized computation mapping schemes implemented in dHPF that provided excellent scaling for SP and BT from NAS parallel benchmarks. They are also suitable for the smaller *gemver* and *adi* codes we used for evaluation. However, a general mapping strategy that automatically deduced multipartitioning as a suitable mapping while also incorporating block, block-cyclic, and other arbitrary mappings for affine loop nests did not exist prior to this work.

Many recent works [13] and [19] addressed the problem of optimizing data layouts for shared-memory architectures. Lu et al [13] proposed a data layout framework to enhance locality on NUCA-based chip multiprocessors. They find a single "localizable" data

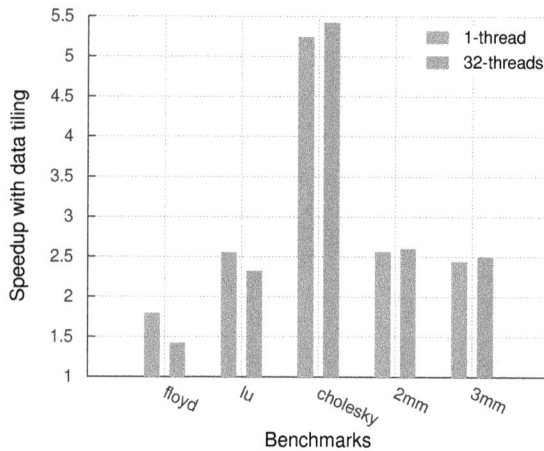

Figure 14: Speedup with data tiling over no data tiling on shared-memory setup. Sequential execution times for floyd, lu, cholesky, 2mm, 3mm are 225s, 494s, 297s, 93s, and 109s respectively.

and computation partitioning, and the data is tiled along only one dimension. On the other hand, we find a full-ranked computation and data mapping in a unified manner, and data is thus tiled along multiple dimensions. This approach is required due to our problem context being very different from that of [13]. Zhang et al [19] proposed techniques to determine data tiling hyperplanes and computation-to-core mappings. They too formulate a graph partitioning problem to find the computation-to-core-mapping to minimize communication volume. However, they do not consider load balance and use simple heuristics to partition the graph. Both the approaches do not address on-demand allocation and buffer reuse and their techniques do not provide the flexibility to support any arbitrary computation mapping.

Siek et al [18] propose techniques to optimize sequences of BLAS kernels calls for shared-memory architectures. They develop a domain-specific language to express linear algebra operations and their BTO (Build to Order) compiler performs optimizations such as loop fusion and tiling across sequences of BLAS calls. Our approach fits well in such domain-specific compilers as well to allow targeting distributed memory.

7. CONCLUSIONS

We proposed techniques for data allocation and computation mapping when compiling affine loop nest sequences for distributed-memory clusters. These techniques allowed us to complete missing steps in allowing effective end-to-end distributed-memory parallelization of affine loop nests. Our approach for data allocation relies on a tiled view of data spaces. The scheme allocates and deallocates tiles on-demand and exploits their reuse. We showed how our approach for computation mapping is able to come up with more effective mappings than those that can be used with vendor-supplied BLAS libraries. These mappings that were automatically determined also subsume mappings with similar properties that were implemented and used manually in previous works. Experimental results on some sequences of BLAS calls demonstrated a mean speedup of $1.82\times$ (and a maximum speedup of $4\times$) over versions written with ScaLAPACK while running on a 32-node cluster. Besides enabling weak scaling for distributed memory, data tiling also improves locality for shared-memory parallelization. Experimental results on a 32-core shared-memory NUMA SMP system show a mean speedup of $2.67\times$ over code that is not data tiled.

Acknowledgments

This work was supported in part by a research gift from AMD. We would also like to acknowledge the Department of Science and Technology, India for a grant under the FIST program. We would like to thank all our reviewers from ICS 2014 for their detailed and useful reviews.

8. REFERENCES

[1] J. M. Anderson and M. S. Lam. Global optimizations for parallelism and locality on scalable parallel machines. In *PLDI*, pages 112–125, 1993.

[2] C. Bastoul. Code generation in the polyhedral model is easier than you think. In *PACT*, pages 7–16, 2004.

[3] U. Bondhugula. Compiling affine loop nests for distributed-memory parallel architectures. In *Supercomputing (SC)*, page 33. ACM, 2013.

[4] U. Bondhugula, M. Baskaran, S. Krishnamoorthy, J. Ramanujam, A. Rountev, and P. Sadayappan. Automatic transformations for communication-minimized parallelization and locality optimization in the polyhedral model. In *ETAPS CC*, 2008.

[5] B. M. Chapman, T. Fahringer, and H. P. Zima. Automatic support for data distribution on distributed memory multiprocessor systems. In *LCPC*, pages 184–199, 1993.

[6] A. Darte, J. Mellor-Crummey, R. Fowler, and D. Chavarría-Miranda. Generalized multipartitioning of multi-dimensional arrays for parallelizing line-sweep computations. *JPDC*, 63:887–911, Sep 2003.

[7] R. Dathathri, C. Reddy, T. Ramashekar, and U. Bondhugula. Generating efficient data movement code for heterogeneous architectures with distributed-memory. In *PACT*, 2013.

[8] P. Feautrier. Parametric integer programming. *RAIRO Recherche Opérationnelle*, 22(3):243–268, 1988.

[9] P. Feautrier. Some efficient solutions to the affine scheduling problem: Part I, one-dimensional time. *International Journal of Parallel Programming*, 21(5):313–348, 1992.

[10] J. Garcia, E. Ayguade, and J. Labarta. A novel approach towards automatic data distribution. In *Supercomputing*, pages 78–78. IEEE, 1995.

[11] M. Gupta and P. Banerjee. Paradigm: A compiler for automatic data distribution on multicomputers. In *ICS*, pages 87–96. ACM, 1993.

[12] K. Kennedy and U. Kremer. Automatic data layout for distributed-memory machines. *ACM TOPLAS*, 20(4):869–916, 1998.

[13] Q. Lu, C. Alias, U. Bondhugula, et al. Data layout transformation for enhancing data locality on nuca chip multiprocessors. In *PACT*, pages 348–357, 2009.

[14] J. Mellor-Crummey, V. Adve, B. Broom, D. Chavarria-Miranda, R. Fowler, G. Jin, K. Kennedy, and Q. Yi. Advanced optimization strategies in the rice dHPF compiler. *Concurrency: Practice and Experience*, pages 741–767, 2002.

[15] METIS -Family of Graph and Hypergraph Partitioning Softwares. http://glaros.dtc.umn.edu/gkhome/views/metis.

[16] Polybench. http://polybench.sourceforge.net.

[17] Scotch - Sequential and parallel graph partitioning software. http://www.labri.fr/perso/pelegrin/scotch.

[18] J. G. Siek, I. Karlin, and E. R. Jessup. Build to order linear algebra kernels. In *IPDPS 2008*, pages 1–8, 2008.

[19] Y. Zhang, W. Ding, M. Kandemir, J. Liu, and O. Jang. A data layout optimization framework for nuca-based multicores. In *IEEE/ACM MICRO*, pages 489–500, 2011.

On the Conditions for Efficient Interoperability with Threads: An Experience with PGAS Languages Using Cray Communication Domains

Khaled Z. Ibrahim, Katherine Yelick
Lawrence Berkeley National Laboratory
One Cyclotron Road, Berkeley, CA 94720, USA
{KZIbrahim, Kayelick}@lbl.gov

ABSTRACT

Today's high performance systems are typically built from shared memory nodes connected by a high speed network. That architecture, combined with the trend towards less memory per core, encourages programmers to use a mixture of message passing and multithreaded programming. Unfortunately, the advantages of using threads for in-node programming are hindered by their inability to efficiently communicate between nodes.

In this work, we identify some of the performance problems that arise in such hybrid programming environments and characterize conditions needed to achieve high communication performance for multiple threads: addressability of targets, separability of communication paths, and full direct reachability to targets. Using the GASNet communication layer [6] on the Cray XC30 as our experimental platform, we show how to satisfy these conditions. We also discuss how satisfying these conditions is influenced by the communication abstraction, implementation constraints, and the interconnect messaging capabilities.

To evaluate these ideas, we compare the communication performance of a thread-based node runtime to a process-based runtime. Without our GASNet extensions, thread communication is significantly slower than processes–up to $21\times$ slower. Once the implementation is modified to address each of our conditions, the two runtimes have comparable communication performance. This allows programmers to more easily mix models like OpenMP, CILK, or pthreads with a GASNet-based model like UPC, with the associated performance, convenience and interoperability advantages that come from using threads within a node.

Categories and Subject Descriptors

C.2.4 [**Computer Communication Networks**]: Distributed Systems—Network operating systems; D.1.3 [**Programming Techniques**]: Concurrent Programming—Parallel and Distributed programming

ACM acknowledges that this contribution was authored or co-authored by an employee, contractor or affiliate of the national government of United States. As such, the Government retains a nonexclusive, royalty-free right to publish or reproduce this article, or to allow others to do so, for Government purposes only..
ICS'14, June 10–13 2014, Munich, Germany.
Copyright is held by the owner/author(s). Publication rights licensed to ACM.
ACM 978-1-4503-2642-1/14/06 ...$15.00.
http://dx.doi.org/10.1145/2597652.2597657.

Keywords

Interoperability, Communication Paradigms, Programming Languages, Processes, Threads

1. INTRODUCTION

As hardware designers continue to take advantage of transistor density increases while addressing power issues, computing systems are growing increasingly complex, with tens of cores per chip and and multiple chips organized into shared or distributed memory systems. HPC platforms have witnessed multiple transitions, with vector machines using mostly shared memory, massively parallel processors using distributed memory, and multicore processors again using shared memory. The multicore era in HPC has brought back shared memory programming within the node, because it is both convenient for programmers and efficient in terms of memory usage and intra-node communication.

Extreme-scale systems currently use hierarchal shared and distributed resources, which leads to multiple programming models. Software abstractions to efficiently deal with resource sharing are typically different from those requiring privatization and protection. Processes provide the natural abstraction for protection, while threads provide the lowest overhead abstraction for sharing. For instance, the Message Passing Interface, MPI uses processes as the default mechanism for parallel execution, while OpenMP is built on top of threads.

In a threaded model, access to shared resources such as network buffers involves mutual exclusion to coordinate access to the resource. Processes simplify access to these resources through privatization and protection, allowing concurrent accesses without worrying about serialization at the user level. On the other hand, processes have disadvantages for parallelism within a node, leading to memory overhead due to replication of data and time overhead due to expensive sharing mechanisms, *i.e.*, mmap files for data sharing or RPC for code sharing. While most node programming models use threads to provide low-overhead shared-memory programming, these threads cannot initiate communication efficiently to other nodes in scalable systems. We measure up to $41\times$ slowdown for transferring small messages by threads compared with processes. These constraints also influence the application tuning efforts and strategies while using hybrid programming.

Many research efforts discussed techniques for reducing the overhead associated with using threads while injecting messages to the interconnect [2, 4, 16, 3, 15]. The main theme of these efforts is to parallelize message injection by reducing the size of critical regions that protect shared resources, including the use of multiple communication endpoints when allowed by the underlying messaging system. This only partly solves the problem because it never fully eradicates serialization. As such, the performance gap between threads and processes continues to increase with the number of cores per node, on all systems we explored.

In this work, we identify the necessary conditions to make threads communicate efficiently enough that they are comparable to process performance. These conditions are targeting *addressability*, *separability*, and *reachability*. The addressability condition requires precisely specifying the target of a transfer before initiating it. The separability condition assures a fully parallel transfer management for independent messages. The reachability condition requires having a direct path to each possible target. We show the details of how to satisfy these conditions to improve a pthread-based implementation of GASNet [6]. Our implementation currently works on Cray Gemini and Aries interconnects, used by multiple machines of the top ten supercomputers in the world [18]. Our technique is conceptually simple but effective. It combines the creation of multiple communication domains with redundant registration for memory segments with interconnect driver to create fully parallel communication paths for threads. Through the performance of microbenchmarks and applications, we show that GASNet can deliver the same performance regardless of the composition of threads and processes chosen by the runtime.

The contributions of this work include: a detailed description and analysis of our work to improve the support for threading in GASNet, and our definition of the necessary conditions to allow threads to communicate efficiently. To the best of our knowledge, our released software is the only publicly available solution on latest Cray supercomputers, where the inter-node communication performance of processes and threads matches. The presented work can easily be implemented on other platforms as well. It also enables efficient integration of PGAS programming languages, such as UPC, with programming models that rely on threading models, for instance, HabaneroC and OpenMP.

The rest of this paper is organized as follows: After describing experimental setup in Section 2, we briefly describe, in Section 3, the motivation of supporting programming models based on processes and threads in modern runtimes and the challenges in achieving efficient interoperability. We present GASNet and our work to achieve efficient interoperability between processes and threads in Section 4. We also layout the necessary conditions to achieve optimal interoperability in general. Performance analysis of our scheme is presented in Section 5. We discuss related work in Section 6, and conclude in Section 7.

2. EXPERIMENTAL SETUP

We used NBP benchmarks written in UPC, which are distributed with Berkeley UPC. We also use a UPC implementation of the UTS benchmark [12]. For micro-benchmarking, we used a modified version of an OSU microbenchark [14] to measure the bidirectional latency of data transfers with concurrent communication.

Most of the presented experiments in this study are carried out on Cray XC30 supercomputer (Edison) [1], installed at NERSC. Edison peak performance is 2.39 petaflops/sec.

Each node has two socket Ivy-Bridge processors at 2.4GHz and 64 GB memory. The Edison interconnect (named Aries) has a Dragonfly topology [5]. Aries uses tiled router architecture, where 4 nodes are connected to each router. Traffics from different nodes are multiplxed by the router on a packet-by-packet basis thus allowing nodes to exceed their fair share of the bandwidth. The messaging unit can be programmed using the Generic Network Interface (GNI), and the Distributed Shared Memory Application (DMAPP) APIs. GASNet library, similar to Cray MPI implementation, is developed on top of GNI. The same APIs are used on earlier generation Cray XE06 (Hopper), with the Gemini interconnect. We also conducted microbenchmarking of other runtimes on the IBM BlueGene/Q BGQ (Mira) at Argonne National Laboratory, and the Trestles infiniband cluster at San Diego Supercomputing Center.

3. SCALABLE RUNTIME DESIGNS

Most scalable runtimes, such as MPI [9] and UPC [19], rely on processes in designing their runtimes because they provide a protection mechanism in accessing resources. The operating system provides replicated software data structures to manage shared hardware resources such as the network interface (NIC). This relieves the messaging runtime from using mutual exclusion to access the interconnect. Threads can be used within a compute node to utilize shared memory programming models such as OpenMP, but they suffer long latencies to communicate across nodes due to serialization, as detailed in this section.

3.1 Process-based Runtimes

The namespace (address space) replication mechanism with processes matches well distributed hardware resources, which are dominant in scalable machines. Figure 1 shows the communication domain abstraction used in Cray XE06 and XC30 supercomputers. The job spawner creates and distributes application processes on computational nodes based on the user request. These processes collectively create a communication domain using the information provided by the spawner runtime. Each process creates endpoints, and completion queues through which it can inject transfers, track their completions, or get notifications for incoming messages. Applications typically register part of their memory to allow faster communication. With memory registration, the OS guarantees not to change the mapping between the virtual and physical memory. Depending on the programming model, the registration information can be exchanged at the beginning of the application by the runtime, or on demand. GNI provides two communication mechanisms, a messaging mechanism with mailbox like semantics, and a Remote Direct Memory Access (RDMA) mechanism for one-sided communication. The messaging mechanism allows efficient two-sided small transfers, while the RDMA mechanism delivers higher performance for large transfers.

A single communication domain is typically created by the runtime for an application, except when multiple runtimes are used by the same application, for instance, mixing UPC and MPI or using GNI messaging and DMAPP collectives.

3.2 Thread-based Runtimes

The advent of multicore to node designs makes memory sharing within a node and thus hierarchal designs more common in HPC systems. Threading is an attractive abstrac-

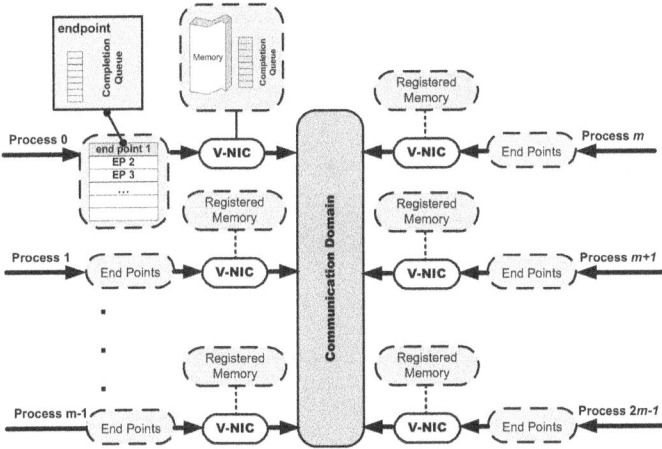

Figure 1: Cray GNI Communication Domain abstraction: each process is assigned a unique access point that can be used without mutual exclusion.

tion for sharing architectural resources because they expose sharing to the application and the runtime using a single namespace (virtual address space). The resource sharing makes the development of runtimes for shared-memory programming models, such as OpenMP, much simpler. It also makes the development of tasking runtimes, such as HebaneroC, more efficient. In these models, the workload is distributed between working threads to achieve load balancing. At the OS level, threads share the page tables, file resources, etc. This means that no protection is provided between executing threads, but a smaller memory footprint is used by the application.

The only limitation for threads is that a correct access to mutable shared resources could require mutual exclusion. Applications and runtimes can use locks, atomics or transactions to enforce serialization. For HPC workloads, one of the most critical shared resources for performance is the network interface. Enforcing serialization for accessing the network leads to a significant performance penalty. For instance, accessing the network massaging endpoint is not thread-safe in Cray GNI, leading to the serialized multiplexing depicted in Figure 2. Other massaging system, such as IBM PAMI, provides a thread-safe access to endpoints [8] when multiple threads do not share the context of an endpoint.

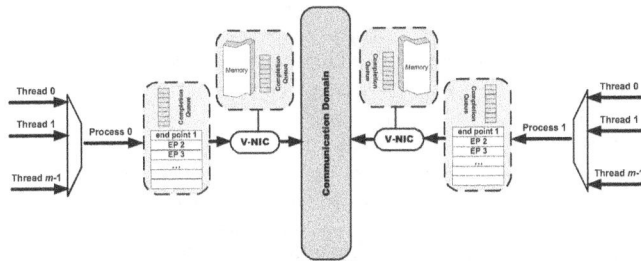

Figure 2: Default support of multithreading through multiplexing threads, with runtime mutual exclusion, into the same interconnect access point.

3.3 Internode Communication Performance of Processes vs. Threads

To quantify the performance of using threads to send messages (or memory transfers) to remote nodes, we show two

scalable programming models, MPI for two-sided communication and UPC (based on GASNet) for one-sided communication. Although MPI also provides one-sided communication support, it is not well tuned on all the implementations we explored, including Cray MPI implementation, OpenMPI and MPICH.

The bidirectional latency microbenchmark is based on OSU benchmarks [14]. We measure the latency by issuing a single non-blocking send and posting a non-blocking receive to the target rank, then waits for the completion of both messages. Ranks are placed such that each pair resides in different nodes. The communication between a pair is bi-directional. We report the average latency over thousands of messages after warming.

When threads are used with MPI, we used different tags to resolve pairing ambiguity. We also use different communicators between threads because some runtimes use a hash of the rank and the communicator to parallelize the injection to the network [8]. Communicators have per rank membership, thus allowing different threads to use different communicator leads to subscription of each rank with all communicators. For threading with MPI, we experimented with three modes: `MPI_THREAD_MULTIPLE`, which allows all threads to inject messages to the interconnect, `MPI_THREAD_FUNNELED` where the main thread injects the messages of all threads, in addition to the default mode of one thread per process. For funneling, we do not account for the extra synchronization to notify the main thread with the readiness for messages of other threads.

We created a UPC version of the same benchmark using one-sided `get` transfers with similar to MPI benchmark pairing of threads. We report for Berkeley UPC, based on GASNet, which supports processes and threads models; whereas Cray UPC supports only processes. Because the shared address space of each UPC thread is semantically similar, whether the runtime (GASNet) uses processes or pthreads, we did not need any additional handling at the application level. GASNet supports three threading modes analogous to MPI [6].

As shown in Figure 3, for 8B messages, processes deliver the lowest latency for data transfers, independent of the concurrency level. This observation is valid for both programming languages, UPC and MPI, and different implementations of MPI. The network can sustain more traffic, thus runtime overhead and serialization dictate the performance. The use of threads increases the latency of transferring messages because most runtimes serialize the access to their data structure using locks, atomics, or transactions. For 8B messages at concurrency level of 24, Figure 3.a&b, the latency increase for MPI threads over processes by $41\times$, while for UPC the increase is $21\times$. The gap increases with the level of concurrency, which is an alarming trend because future systems are expected to have more cores. The difference decreases as the message size increases because the performance becomes bounded by the available bandwidth. For 2KB messages using UPC, the latency ratio for threads to processes gets reduced to $12\times$ and approaches $1\times$ for 2MB messages. Using funneling to the main thread can lead to better performance than parallel injection by all threads.

We found similar performance trends, to those shown in Figure 3, on other runtimes including OpenMPI [13], MPICH [10], MVAPICH [11] on different interconnects including Cray Gemini and Infiniband clusters. In some runtimes, such as

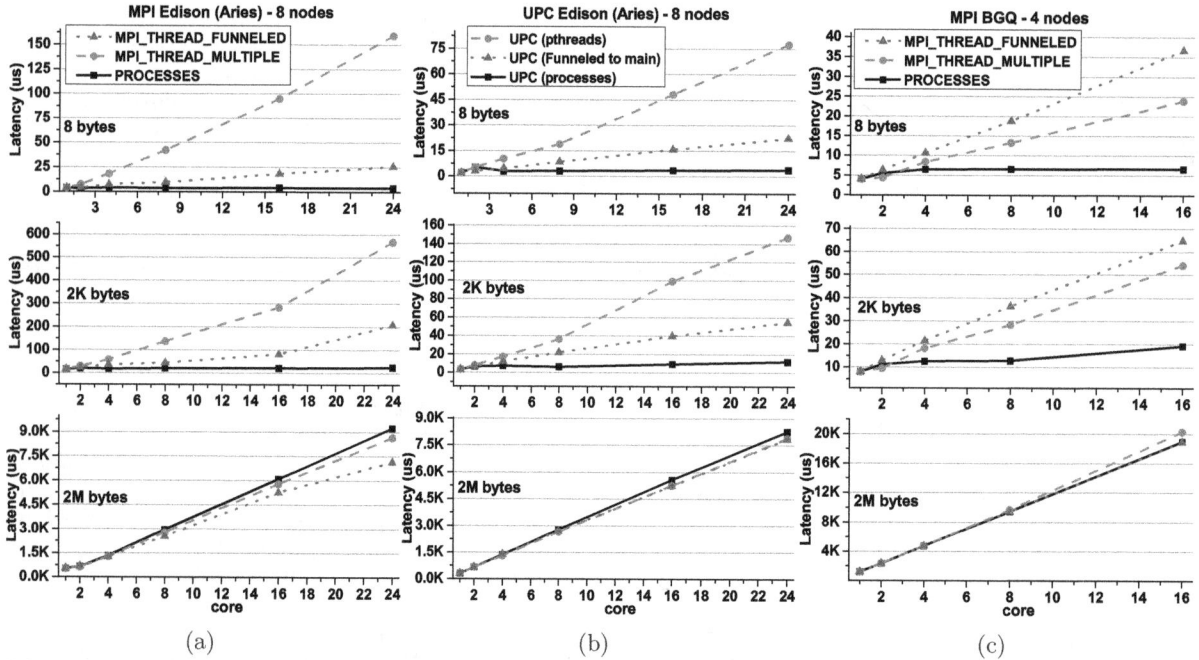

Figure 3: bidirectional Latency microbenchmark of UPC and MPI programming models for processes vs. two threading models (THREAD_MULTIPLE for full threaded injection to the interconnect, and THREAD_FUNNELED for relaying communication to the main thread).

OpenMPI, the high performance byte transport layer is disabled when threading is enabled. This leads to a larger performance gap between threads and processes. As such, many scalable runtimes disable threading support by default. We measured up to 366× latency increase for threads compared with processes for MPICH implementation on Infiniband cluster (Trestles) at a concurrency level of 32. MVAPICH has up to 96× latency increase on the same cluster.

In the systems we explored, the best runtime in handling this problem is IBM MPI implementation on BGQ systems, shown in Figure 3.c. The latency difference between processes and threads is at most 4× for 16-way concurrency. BGQ systems support L2 atomic locks that lower the serialization overhead. These efficient locks are suitable for single socket nodes, which is a distinct path for architecting nodes that is not prevalent. IBM MPI implementation uses PAMI endpoints and context abstractions, which could allow fully concurrent injection of messages to the interconnect. Processing incoming messages with threads cannot be fully parallelized [8], though.

4. IMPROVING GASNET THREADING SUPPORT USING MULTIPLE COMMUNICATION DOMAINS

We argue for a runtime to support full concurrent communication by an execution abstraction, such as threads, it needs to satisfy three conditions: unambiguous *addressability* of remote targets, *separability* of communication paths, and full direct *reachability* between all communication parties. In this section, we discuss the challenges associated with these conditions and the way we handled them in GASNet [6], Global Address Space Networking, to improve one-sided communication primitives.

4.1 GASNet Runtime and Base Threading Support

GASNet is a scalable communication library that provides, at the core of its functionality, APIs supporting active messages (AMs). Memory segments are typically registered for communication between ranks of an application. Likewise, AM handler functions are registered with the library. An AM carries both a payload and a handler *id* of the task to be executed at the remote side. AMs give unique ids only to processes (calling them nodes).

GASNet provides another set of communication primitives for one-sided memory transfers and collectives, called extended APIs, which does not require any remote side processing of the data. These primitives typically exploit network accelerated remote memory access (RMA) mechanisms.

GASNet library is used by multiple parallel partitioned global address space (PGAS) programming languages such as UPC, Titanium, and Co-Array Fortran. Each of these languages uses a different subset of GASNet functionality. The library supports pthreads in three modes resembling MPI's support, where the language runtime should declare if one or more threads need to concurrently call GASNet. If threading support is requested, GASNet enforces serialization of accesses to shared runtime resources through mutual exclusion (using locks or atomics). GASNet provides different builds depending on the level of threading support. This allows removing unnecessary handling for thread safety if only one thread per process is used.

4.2 One-sided Primitives and Threading

One-sided communication typically involves transfer between a local memory and a remote memory, using either **put** or **get** primitives. The remote memory can either reside locally (within a node) or at a remote node. Most interconnect HPC systems provide a hardware acceleration mechanism for one-sided primitives. Although these APIs are not the core APIs for GASNet, they are the most critical to performance for many high-level programming languages, such as UPC. In this section, we focus on how to improve the support of threaded one-sided communication in GASNet.

4.2.1 Addressability of the Remote Destination

One-sided communication in GASNet uses a tuple of a registered address and process *id* for the remote part of the transfer. The process *id* is used solely to resolve the affinity of the memory address to a particular compute node. The affinity is enough for GASNet runtime to manage the transfer, and the participation of the remote process is typically not needed. PGAS languages, such as UPC, use these tuples to create a global unique name for each shared memory address. One-sided communication in GASNet does not care about which entity is going to operate on the data at the remote location. Thus, the use of threads within a process does not pose any address ambiguity challenge.

4.2.2 Separability of Communication Paths

Separability of communication paths is the condition where independent transfers do not get serialized unnecessarily by the runtime. Full separability requires special handling during data transfer injection, progress and advancement, and reception. Separability of communication paths necessitates carful communication resource allocation and management.

Communication resources include the runtime data structures used in holding the communication state. Communication management involves mechanisms and state machines used in initiating communication, advancing the progress, and checking for completions. We argue that to support threads efficiently we need full separability of resources and management by each thread.

To achieve separability of resources at the GASNet runtime level, we use exclusive per thread resource pools. This alleviates the need for locks or atomics in the case of having shared resources. Examples of these resources are communication handles and descriptors, and internal bounce buffers. Likewise, we ensured that all used libraries do not use any shared resources. For instance, most memory allocation libraries use the shared heap to allocate memory, thus causing serialization. We made sure that the memory allocator uses a distinct heap per thread.

The challenge we faced is that the interface of the Cray GNI library is not thread-safe. Assigning a distinct endpoint to a thread is not enough to achieve concurrent injection to the interconnect. In this work, we solve this problem by creating a separate communication domain for each thread (or group of threads). When each thread is assigned a separate domain, as shown in Figure 4, all threads can concurrently inject to the GNI layer without any serialization.

4.2.3 Full Direct Reachability to All Remote Targets

The challenge with the creation of multiple communication domains is that it makes it potentially difficult to have full reachability to all memory addresses. Using multiple domains, each thread subscribes to a different communication domain. Registering the memory of affinity to a particular thread leads to unreachable destination memory segments because each thread can only see the memory of threads subscribing to its domain. The shared memory is typically split between executing units. A shared memory segment always has affinity to one execution unit, which is responsible for registering this segment of the shared memory with the messaging runtime. It is also responsible for exchanging information about these segments. In the base implementation, only the main thread does the registration of the whole memory assigned to the process. Multiple processes sharing a node register their segments independently and then exchange information. Thus, each memory segment is registered once with the interconnect.

To solve this problem, we register the whole memory of affinity to the process that this thread belongs to. This leads to redundant registrations of the same memory depending on the number of communication domains created by the runtime. These redundant registrations (aliasing), shown in Figure 4, allow full direct reachability for each thread to the whole shared address space. In fact, this allows multipath reachability to each memory location. Fortunately, this does not affect the consistency model provided by GASNet because GASNet always guarantees remote completion of put operations. The implication of redundant registration on the registration resources is discussed in Section 5.2.

4.3 Active Messages and Threading

GASNet active message APIs allow sending a request to execute a handler procedure at a remote destination. The request carries the data, the destination and the handler *id*. It supports a strict request reply mechanism, thus the destination can send at most one reply to the sender. The target *id* in a reply is implicit (the sender of the request). GASNet AMs can be used in many management tasks by high-level programming languages, for instance, to implement synchronization primitives and collectives.

4.3.1 Addressability of the Remote Destination

The destination of an active message, similar to MPI, is only a process, and the handler can be executed by any thread belonging to the process. Unlike one-sided primitives, the destination process strictly specify the partner responsible for processing the message, not just the affinity of the destination memory. The specification of processes as the only valid target arose when most HPC node architectures were a single core, or processes were thought as the main scalable runtime abstraction. GASNet AMs do not recognize threads as addressable entities. Allowing the active message handler to be executed by any thread belonging to the target process can be looked at as a flexibility because it allows low-loaded threads to execute the handler. If multiple communication domains are used, this causes complexity in runtime design to maintain correct execution as discussed in the next sections.

4.3.2 Separability of Communication Paths

Active message (AM) requests and replies require explicit resource allocation at the sender side. The receive side resources is transparently managed by the runtime. This makes concurrent injection of AMs by different threads an easy task using multiple communication domains. The receiver of an AM does not post any explicit receive, thus resource management at the receive side is completely controlled by the runtime. Separability of resources management is complicated because processing an incoming AM should not be done by multiple threads. Thus, the reception cannot be fully parallelized and a centralized decision with a mutual exclusion mechanism needs to be used.

4.3.3 Full Direct Reachability to All Remote Targets

The reliance of active messages (AM) on addressing processes makes direct reachability achievable with one communication domain even with multithreading. The reachability of AMs is dependent on not only the arrival of the data to the destination but also on the execution of the handler by the target. The data reachability for large messages is achieved using multiple domains, using the one-sided RDMA. The handler information are sent using small messages, where most vendors provide a mechanism for efficient mailbox short messages on pre-allocated buffers. The messaging mechanism is solely used for the data and the AM descriptor when the payload in small.

The GASNet AM specification of the handler execution imposes the following runtime behavior: any thread trying to make progress should check for arrival of AMs because of the possibility that this thread is the only one doing so. If multiple paths of arrival are possible, all paths should be checked for incoming messages. On the other hand, if multiple threads are ready to execute a handler only one should do so. Thus, the use of multiple domains for AMs creates the possibility for all threads advancing all domains. Each advancement requires a mutually exclusive access of the communication domain. Therefore, having multiple reachability paths can lead to a significant serialization problem.

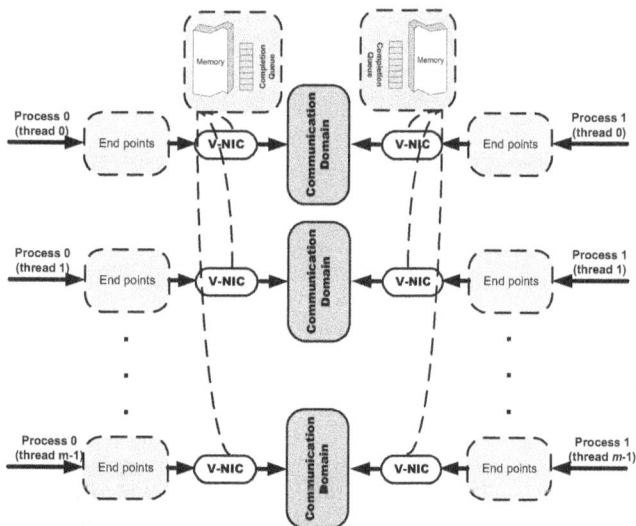

Figure 4: Multipath through the use of multiple communication domains. Each thread can subscribe to a distinct domain. The same address space is redundantly registered in multiple domains.

If all threads are addressable, then we will need for direct reachability communication domain count equals the square of thread concurrency. The resources needed for a communication domain make the number allocatable of domains limited, as detailed in Section 5.2.

In our implementation, we made the choice of restricting AM handler processing to the first domain to minimize the potential serialization. The data transfer part can go through any domain, especially for large transfers. The first domain is by default accessible to the first thread of a process. Given that some languages using GASNet may use other than the first thread for receiving and processing AMs, we make all threads infrequently advance the progress of the

first domain AMs. Only the first thread within a process has a low latency in processing the AM reception. We use an environment variable to control how frequently each thread should check and advance the AM domain.

5. ANALYSIS OF THE USE OF MULTIPLE COMMUNICATION DOMAINS

In this section, we show that the use of multiple communication domains improves the performance of threaded one-sided communication dramatically. We also show the impact on the performance of active messages. We finally discuss the resource issues associated with the use of multiple communication domains.

5.1 Improvement of the performance of one-sided primitives

In Figure 5, we show that the performance of a one-sided get, with different levels of thread concurrency and domain count. We show the latency for small to medium message sizes on Cray XC30 (Edison). We plot performance of threads relative to using pure processes for communication, for the microbenchmark presented in Section 3.3. The first observation is that using domain count matching the number of threads yields performance equivalent to process-based implementation (at most 8% difference for small messages) due to infrequent handling active messages. Without active messages, the performance perfectly matches, and even yields a slightly better performance for threads.

The improvement is larger for high thread concurrency and small messages. The improvement for threads performance is up to $31.5\times$ for 8B messages with 24-thread concurrency. The improvement decreases with the increase of the message size because the bottleneck shifts to bandwidth availability. For 2KB messages the improvement is up to $14.6\times$. The largest message we observed improvement for is 128KB. In earlier generation Cray Machines, XE 06 (Hopper), the largest message to see benefit is 32KB, smaller than that for XC30 (Edison).

The second observation is that using a domain count less than the thread count significantly reduces the latency of injection. The latency is reduced monotonically with the number of domains. Thus depending on the resource constraints of allocating domains, increasing the domain count can bring the internode communication of the threads closer to processes.

5.2 Resources Allocation

Multiple resource constraints affect the approach presented in this work: the maximum domain count allowed by the messaging library, and the available memory registration resource, and memory allocation per process. In this section, we discuss the implication of these resource limits.

Most interconnect runtimes impose a restriction on the number of domains that can be allocated. On Cray XE06 (Hopper), we can allocate at most 30 domains. On Cray XC 30 (Edison), the number of domains is at most 120. On other architectures such as IBM BGQ, PAMI allows 48-64 communication contexts. The impact of this restriction is that we cannot have communication domains equal to the square of the thread concurrency, up to 64 in most recent supercomputers. This makes direct reachability using separate domains not feasible for active messages. One-sided

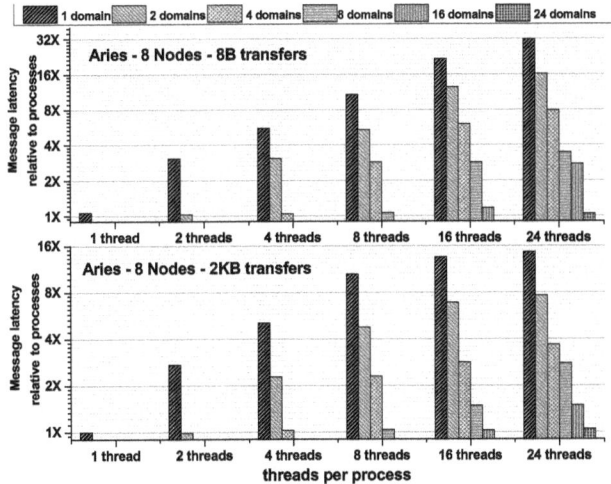

Figure 5: Improvement of message latency with the number of domains for small to medium message sizes on Cray Edison (Aries interconnect).

communication requires domain count at most equal to the number of cores.

A more challenging restriction is the limited registration resources of the memory with the NIC. Some interconnects, such as Gemini (Cray XE06), have limited hardware resources for storing the registration information. This limits the number of memory pages registered per domain. Having redundant registration stress the limited centralized resource. Accelerated RDMA mechanisms rely heavily on memory registration. Fortunately, the registration resources depend mostly on the page count, not the page size. As such, the use of huge pages allows allocating larger registerable memory per thread. In Table 1, we show that the registration resources decline with the number of domains, especially with small pages (4KB), to reach only 64MB per thread when 24 communication domains are used. Using huge pages significantly alleviates this restriction and push the limit to 4GB. Fortunately, for the newer generation Cray XC30, this restriction is no longer an issue, and the registration resources are designed such that it can hold the maximum allocatable memory per process for any number of communication domains.

We also observed a restriction that the maximum allocatable memory, by libc, for a process is 8GB, which is smaller than the available physical memory. It is possible to allocate larger memory using posix allocators. The consequence of the last two restrictions is that we may need to use multiple processes to achieve optimal resource allocation. For instance, we allocate one process per NUMA node and use threads to exploit all cores within that node.

Table 1: Cray Hopper max. registration per thread

Domain Count	small pages	huge pages (8MB)
1	512MB	8GB
2	512MB	8GB
4	256MB	8GB
8	128MB	4GB
24	64MB	4GB

Another comment is that even though the requested network resources are increased with the creation of multiple

communication domains, the use of threads usually reduces the physical memory used by the application compared with processes. The saving for threads comes from sharing code segments, and using a single page table per process (shared by all threads). Applications developers also do not use data replication in thread-based programming model, which is typical with processes in distributed programming languages. The runtimes developed over threads are also known to have a smaller memory footprint.

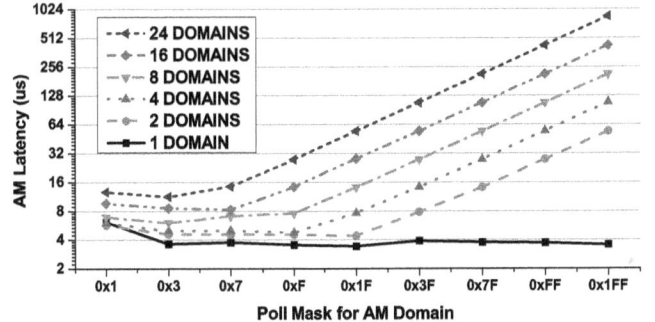

Figure 6: Impact of the choice of polling masks on the latency of GASNet Active Messages.

5.3 Impact on Active Message Performance

As discussed earlier, to avoid frequent locking of communication domains by all threads, we make active message (AM) descriptors go through the first communication domain. To guarantee forward progress, we allow all threads to infrequently advance the AM engine using a mask value[1]. The larger the mask, the less frequent advancement to the AM domain. This leads to the trends shown in Figure 6 by TestAM benchmark[2]. The latency can increase by up to $76\times$, when the polling mask changes from 1 to 511. Obviously the difference gets smaller as we reduce the number of domains. These latency values are the max for all threads. Note, the performance of the first thread is typically not impacted by the use of multiple domains or the polling mask.

Figure 7 shows the impact on one-sided transfer latencies when the mask is changed. We notice that the mask value of one increases the latency of messages by at most $2.73\times$ for the smallest messages. The difference decreases with the increase in message size until it becomes neutral for messages above 128K. The other observation is that with the smallest mask (highest frequency of polling), the latency is much smaller than using a single domain, shown in Figure 3, by up to $7.3\times$.

The trends shown in Figures 6 & 7 may suggest that to balance the performance of one-sided primitives with AMs we need to choose a mask value of 0x7. We do not follow that because we know that most languages using GASNet rely more on the one-sided primitives performance. Consequently, we made the default value 0x1FF. To alleviate the impact on AMs, we modify the use pattern of upper layer runtimes to GASNet. For instance, unified parallel C (UPC) runtime is modified such that synchronizations that use GASNet always elect the first thread to receive AMs. The default behavior is such that threads within a process

---

[1]The mask value is set using the environment variable `GASNET_AM_DOMAIN_POLL_MASK`.
[2]TestAM is a benchmark distributed with GASNet.

elect a thread (normally the last arrival) to perform AMs in behalf of the process. We will show that this strategy proves suitable for applications written in UPC in the following section.

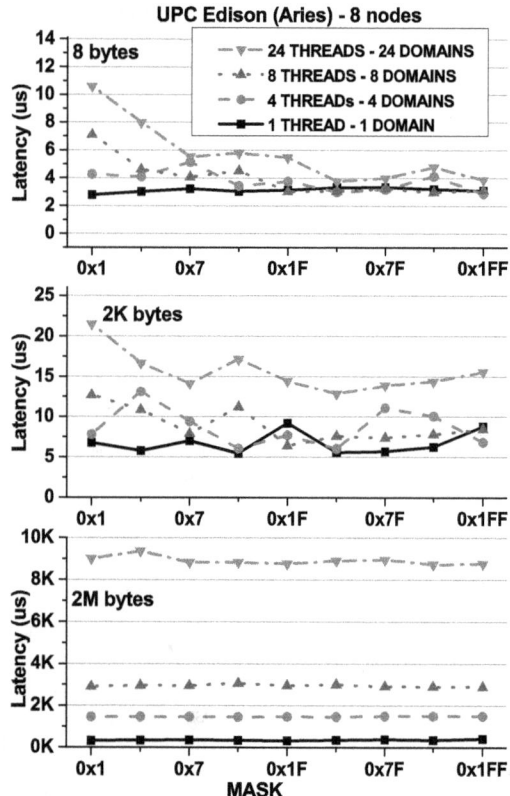

Figure 7: Impact of choice of polling masks on the latency of get operations.

5.4 UPC Application Performance with Communication Domains

To test the efficiency of the presented scheme, we use multiple UPC applications from NBP benchmark. Our objective is to measure the impact of using programming models relying on processes with those relying on threads. Fortunately, Berkeley UPC can run with single threaded processes, or with multi-threading. A UPC thread is mapped either to a process or a thread. Berkeley UPC uses GASNet communication library to achieve portability. All UPC threads (processes or pthreads) initiate communication (no funneling). The presented applications mostly rely one-sided primitives for communication. They also use synchronization primitives and collectives that use AMs. We use 16 UPC threads per node and 16 nodes to make it easier to create power of two, or square processes needed to run these benchmarks. We varied the mapping of UPC threads within a node from using two processes per node and 8 threads per process to mapping all UPC threads to processes. We did not extend our run to one process (16 pthreads) per node because Cray XC30 has two NUMA domains per node. All the studied applications do not have explicit NUMA locality control and system utilities on Cray machines allow controlling NUMA allocation only at the process level. All the runs are relative to process-based implementation, which use xpmem shared memory, between processes for intra-node communication.

The base performance is that associated with one communication domain. As shown in Figure 8, the performance degrades as we use more threads with a single communication domain. For CG, the slowdown can reach up to 5.5× for the use of 8 threads per process. For other applications, the slowdown is at most 61%. The amount of slowdown depends on the message sizes used by the application. The smaller the message sizes the higher the performance slowdown. As shown Figure 8, as we increase the number of communication domains the performance improves monotonically for all applications. The difference between processes and threads implementations becomes bounded to less than 10%. The processing of active messages is a contributing factor to the small mismatch between processes and threads implementations. Our choice of the mask for frequency of polling AMs proves efficient for overall performance of the studied applications. Although, we modified the UPC runtime to make AM calls done by the first thread, we still need for compliance with GASNet specifications do infrequent advancement from all threads to the active message domain. As per GASNet specifications, in a threaded mode any thread should be able to advance the progress of the runtime. This infrequent polls cause a small serialization overhead. We should note that allowing highly concurrent access could reduce the performance because of congestion.

5.5 Remarks on Efficient Interoperability Conditions

Satisfying the presented conditions for concurrent wait-free communication are influenced by multiple factors: the specifications by the programming model, the runtime design constraints and implementation strategy, and the capabilities of the messaging systems of the interconnect.

The specifications can influence the addressability of the target with different execution abstractions. We showed that communication primitives in one-sided models do not suffer any addressability issue whether we use processes or threads, while AMs in GASNet suffer an addressability problem for reasons embedded in their specifications. Addressability can be tackled by either having a convention of using communication resources or by amending the specifications. We argue that long-term solution should consider modifying the specification, for the convention might be difficult to follow or to enforce.

Separability of paths and full reachability are typically opposing forces. One can have separable resources and management on current programming models that lead to limited reachability. Berkeley UPC provides teams, conceptually similar to MPI communicators, which allow independent progress within each team. Participation in a single team can lead to a reachability problem to some targets, and dynamic change of teams can lead to a separability problem. Separability is also influenced by the language specifications. If a language imposes certain ordering semantic for thread execution, then this limits the separability while processing transfers.

What eased the integration of this work to GASNet is that it was done transparently with respect to its legacy interfaces and specifications. For instance, although multiple domains and reachability paths are introduced, the completion semantic and ordering guarantees are not modified. Part of this ease came from the fact that addressability in

PGAS languages does not rely on the execution abstraction (processes or threads).

This work shows encouraging results for the integration projects of UPC with other programming models that rely on threading. These results guarantee threads to be able to communicate without serialization by the runtime.

This will not only simplify runtime integration, but will also simplify application development activities. Application developers, being aware of inefficiency of initiating communication from threads, add additional code for preprocessing and postprocessing messages. A main thread typically collects partial results from all compute threads and distributes incoming messages, which involves unnecessary synchronization. Efficient communication by threads can make such practice obsolete.

The importance of this work is likely to increase in future systems because the number of cores per node is increasing. The trends for memory size growth does not show them coping up. Most applications are also likely to run in strong-scaling regime, forcing them to rely on the performance of small messages at high concurrency.

6. RELATED WORK

Interoperability of scalable runtimes, such as MPI and UPC, with shared memory programming has become critically important with the advent of multi and manycore designs to node architectures. The support of thread-based programming models, in scalable communication runtimes, is the subject of many research proposals and prototypes [2, 4, 16, 3, 15]. Most of these proposals target two-sided MPI programming model. MPI, up to 3.0 specifications, deals with threads as non-addressable entities [9, 7], and requires the ability to reason a serial order of concurrent pthreads execution.

The first issue these proposals tried to address is making threads addressable. They propose assigning threads rank *ids* [17], or using an endpoint per thread [8, 16, 3]. While mapping ranks to threads conflicts with the MPI specification, most endpoint proposals try to use some convention to resolve the mapping between threads and the communication resources. For instance, they associate each thread with a unique endpoint that can be mapped to a communication context within the communication rank.

These proposals assume thread-safety of accessing endpoints, which is true on IBM PAMI [8, 16] if each context is associated with a unique endpoint. Allowing low-overhead injection of messages does not guarantee the creation of fully separable communication paths. Separability of managing the communication resources is typically challenging at the receive side. Contexts are typically collectively advanced, which can be done by a communication thread. The cost of advancing all contexts is typically small in IBM BGQ because locking relies on a low-overhead L2 atomic, which is suitable only for single-socket node designs. Kumar et al [8] details why it is tricky to parallelize MPI_IRecv and MPI_WaitAll with threads, even with the use of PAMI endpoints because of the specification constraints of MPI.

The other approach to address thread support is to reduce the runtime overhead of implementing mutual exclusion. Proposals of fine-grained locking or lock-free atomics show promising results in reducing the impact of serialization [2]. Their objective is to make serialization event very brief. Fine-grained per object locking requires a special care

to preserve single ordering in locking or deadlocks become a possibility. In large scale runtimes, this simple requirement can be a challenge. This approach looks at the serialization within the interconnect driver as an orthogonal issue. We note that the base GASNet [6] implementation uses lock-free data structures (manipulated with atomics) and still suffer a large penalty as we scale the number of cores especially for small messages. The overhead in serialized access to a non thread-safe messaging APIs (such as Cray GNI) was their main performance bottleneck.

This work introduces a comprehensive analysis for this problem and provides a solution suitable for PGAS languages, which rely one-sided primitives. Our work is publicly released thus allowing other runtime designers to experiment with it, especially those targeting one-sided abstractions.

7. CONCLUSIONS

Hybrid shared and distributed memory are becoming the standard for massively parallel machines. While threads have both a lower memory footprint and some performance advantages for intra-node programming, we have shown that they often exhibit significant performance problems in interconnect communication. This penalty was as high as $21\times$ for UPC and $41\times$ for MPI in our measurements. We present the necessary conditions for efficient interoperability of process-based scalable programming languages with thread-based node models. We implemented this in the context of an extension to GASNet communication library. The first condition, addressability, is found orthogonal to the execution abstraction, processes or threads, for one-sided communication. The second condition, separability, requires restructuring the runtime to avoid having shared resources between threads and also the creation of multiple communication domains on top of the messaging library. The third condition, reachability, is addressed by using redundant registration (aliasing) of the shared memory segments.

GASNet active messages are shown bounded by their limitation of restricting the addressability to processes leading to a difficulty in achieving full parallelization of their transfers with threads. Overall, our approach significantly improves performance of inter-node thread-based communication, allowing it to match the performance of processes in microbenchmarks. We also compared these in an application setting and measured up to $5\times$ performance improvement for NBP benchmarks build with a hybrid implementation using processes and threads. Aside from improving the performance of GASNet-based programming languages, our analysis also identifies the key features that lower level network APIs and hardware need to support for good hybrid performance. We believe these design principles will be increasingly important as the number of cores per node continues to grow.

Acknowledgments

This research used resources of the National Energy Research Scientific Computing Center, which is supported by the Office of Science of the U.S. Department of Energy under Contract No. DE-AC02-05CH11231, and resources of the Argonne Leadership Computing Facility at Argonne National Laboratory, which is supported under contract DE-AC0206CH11357.

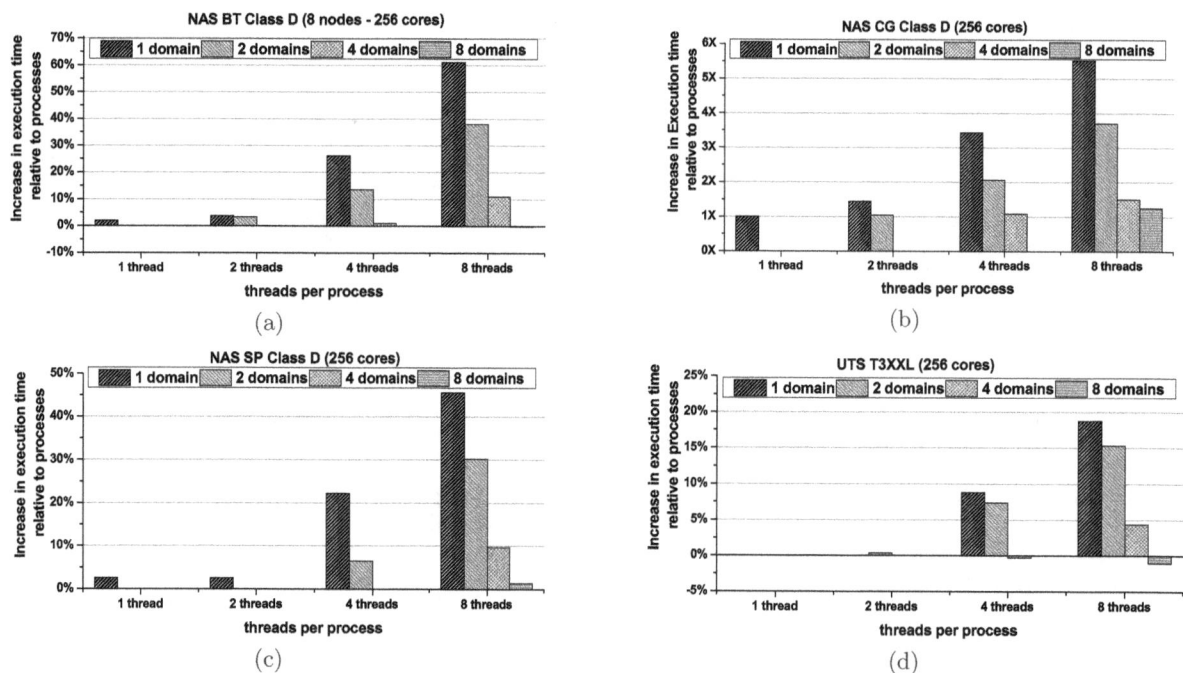

Figure 8: Performance of UTS and NPB applications using different thread concurrency levels and communication domains. All runs use 16 UPC threads per node and 16 Cray XC30 (Edison) nodes.

8. REFERENCES

[1] National Energy Research Scientific Computing Center, Edison Supercomputer. http://www.nersc.gov/users/computational-systems/-edison/configuration.

[2] P. Balaji, D. Buntinas, D. Goodell, W. Gropp, and R. Thakur. Fine-grained multithreading support for hybrid threaded mpi programming. *IJHPCA*, 24(1):49–57, 2010.

[3] J. Dinan, P. Balaji, D. Goodell, D. Miller, M. Snir, and R. Thakur. Enabling MPI Interoperability Through Flexible Communication Endpoints. *EuroMPI*, pages 13–18, 2013.

[4] G. Dozsa, S. Kumar, P. Balaji, D. Buntinas, D. Goodell, W. Gropp, J. Ratterman, and R. Thakur. Enabling concurrent multithreaded mpi communication on multicore petascale systems. *Recent Advances in the Message Passing Interface, Lecture Notes in Computer Science*, 6305:11–20, 2010.

[5] G. Faanes, A. Bataineh, D. Roweth, T. Court, E. Froese, B. Alverson, T. Johnson, J. Kopnick, M. Higgins, and J. Reinhard. Cray cascade: a scalable HPC system based on a Dragonfly network. *The International Conference on High Performance Computing, Networking, Storage and Analysis*, pages 103:1–103:9, 2012.

[6] Global-Address Space Networking (GASNet). Specification v1.8. http://gasnet.lbl.gov.

[7] W. Gropp and R. Thakur. Thread-safety in an MPI implementation: Requirements and analysis. *Parallel Computing*, 33(9):595 – 604, 2007.

[8] S. Kumar, A. Mamidala, D. Faraj, B. Smith, M. Blocksome, B. Cernohous, D. Miller, J. Parker, J. Ratterman, P. Heidelberger, D. Chen, and B. Steinmacher-Burrow. PAMI: A Parallel Active Message Interface for the Blue Gene/Q Supercomputer. *The 26th IEEE International Parallel Distributed Processing Symposium (IPDPS)*, pages 763–773, 2012.

[9] Message Passing Interface Forum. MPI: A Message-Passing Interface Standard Version 3.0. www.mpi-forum.org/docs/mpi-3.0/mpi30-report.pdf, Sept 2012.

[10] MPICH2 v 3.0.4. http://www.mcs.anl.gov/research/projects/mpich2/ .

[11] MVAPICH2 v 2.0b. http://mvapich.cse.ohio-state.-edu/overview/mvapich2/.

[12] S. Olivier, J. Huan, J. Liu, J. Prins, J. Dinan, P. Sadayappan, and C.-W. Tseng. UTS: An Unbalanced Tree Search Benchmark. *The 19th Intl. Workshop on Languages and Compilers for Parallel Computing (LCPC 2006)*, Nov. 2006.

[13] OpenMPI v 1.7.3. http://www.open-mpi.org.

[14] OSU benchmarks. OMB 4.2. Network-Based Computing Laboratory, Ohio State University, http://mvapich.cse.ohio-state.edu/benchmarks/.

[15] G. Saxena. Thread safety for hybrid programming in thread-as-rank model. Master's thesis, The University of Edinburgh, Aug. 2013.

[16] G. Tanase, G. Almasi, H. Xue, and C. Archer. Network endpoints for clusters of smps. *The 24th IEEE International Symposium onComputer Architecture and High Performance Computing (SBAC-PAD)*, pages 27–34, 2012.

[17] H. Tang and T. Yang. Optimizing threaded mpi execution on smp clusters. *The 15th International Conference on Supercomputing*, pages 381–392, 2001.

[18] Top 500 Supercomputers. http://www.top500.org.

[19] UPC Consortium. http://upc.lbl.gov/docs/user/upc_spec_1.2.pdf.

HOMR: A Hybrid Approach to Exploit Maximum Overlapping in MapReduce over High Performance Interconnects *

Md. Wasi-ur-Rahman, Xiaoyi Lu, Nusrat S. Islam, Dhabaleswar K. (DK) Panda
Department of Computer Science and Engineering
The Ohio State University
{rahmanmd,luxi,islamn,panda}@cse.ohio-state.edu

ABSTRACT

Hadoop MapReduce is the most popular open-source parallel programming model extensively used in Big Data analytics. Although fault tolerance and platform independence make Hadoop MapReduce the most popular choice for many users, it still has huge performance improvement potentials. Recently, RDMA-based design of Hadoop MapReduce has alleviated major performance bottlenecks with the implementation of many novel design features such as in-memory merge, prefetching and caching of map outputs, and overlapping of merge and reduce phases. Although these features reduce the overall execution time for MapReduce jobs compared to the default framework, further improvement is possible if shuffle and merge phases can also be overlapped with the map phase during job execution. In this paper, we propose HOMR (a Hybrid approach to exploit maximum Overlapping in MapReduce), that incorporates not only the features implemented in RDMA-based design, but also exploits maximum possible overlapping among all different phases compared to current best approaches. Our solution introduces two key concepts: Greedy Shuffle Algorithm and On-demand Shuffle Adjustment, both of which are essential to achieve significant performance benefits over the default MapReduce framework. Architecture of HOMR is generalized enough to provide performance efficiency both over different Sockets interface as well as previous RDMA-based designs over InfiniBand. Performance evaluations show that HOMR with RDMA over InfiniBand can achieve performance benefits of 54% and 56% compared to default Hadoop over IPoIB (IP over InfiniBand) and 10 GigE, respectively. Compared to the previous best RDMA-based designs, this benefit is 29%. HOMR over Sockets also achieves a maximum of 38-40% benefit compared to default Hadoop over Sockets interface. We also evaluate our design with real-world workloads like SWIM and PUMA, and observe benefits of up to 16% and 18%, respectively, over the previous best-case RDMA-based design. To the best of our knowledge, this is the first approach to achieve maximum possible overlapping for MapReduce framework.

* This research is supported in part by National Science Foundation grants #OCI-1148371, #CCF-1213084 and #CNS-1347189. It used the Extreme Science and Engineering Discovery Environment (XSEDE), which is supported by National Science Foundation grant number OCI-1053575.

Categories and Subject Descriptors

C.4 [**Performance of Systems**]: Design Studies

Keywords

MapReduce; Shuffle Algorithm; High Performance Interconnects; Overlapping Execution

1. INTRODUCTION

In the past several years, there has been an immense surge of interest for Big Data. Big Data provides ground breaking opportunities for enterprise information management and decision making. The 2011 International Data Corporation (IDC) study [1] on Digital Universe indicated the beginning of 'Information Age', where the foundation of economic value is largely derived from information vs. physical things. The rate of information growth appears to be exceeding Moore's Law and it is expected that 35 zettabytes of data will be generated and consumed by the end of this decade. According to the Market Strategy and BI Research group [2], data volumes are doubling every year. Moreover, 42.6 percent of respondents are saving more than three years of data for analytical purposes. Therefore, Big Data applications are in demand of highly efficient solutions for both computational and storage purposes in order to keep up with the need to ingest, process and store the vast amount of data.

MapReduce [5] has emerged as one of the most popular parallel computing models for processing data of the petabyte scale. With the growing popularity and volume of web-based contents, MapReduce is being widely used by many reputed organizations such as Yahoo!, Google, Amazon, Facebook, etc. The key advantages of MapReduce, like easy programming, transparent parallelization, high scalability, and fault tolerance, make it the de facto standard for large scale data analysis. As the most successful open-source implementation of MapReduce, Hadoop [24] has become synonymous with MapReduce. Hadoop Distributed File System (HDFS) [20] is the underlying file system of Hadoop MapReduce and Hadoop Database HBase [4].

However, recent studies [11, 17, 25] have illustrated the inability of the current Hadoop framework in taking advantage of high-performance interconnects in modern clusters. InfiniBand [9], on the other hand, is used by many HPC systems due to its low latency and high bandwidth properties. According to the latest Nov. 2013 TOP 500 list, 41% of supercomputing systems use InfiniBand as the primary communication network. In scientific computing domains, with the Message Passing Interface (MPI) as the underlying basis, most applications have made extensive use of InfiniBand. Recently, cloud computing systems are also being widely deployed on HPC clusters [3]. A popular example is the 'Greenplum Analytics Workbench' [6], which is a 1000+ nodes HPC cluster with In-

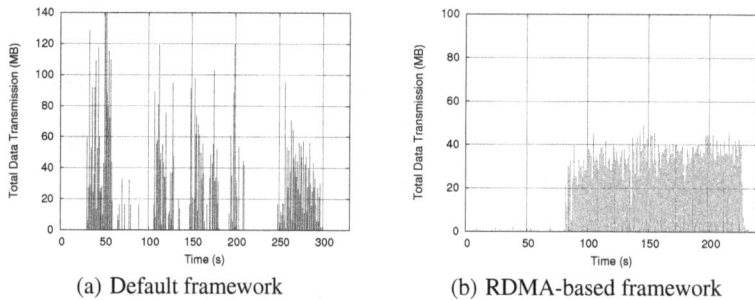

(a) Default framework   (b) RDMA-based framework

Figure 1: Profiling of data transmission in shuffle phase

finiBand, running regular integration testing on the Apache Hadoop trunk.

Research works [11, 13, 17, 25] have shown huge performance improvement potentials for different Big Data analysis middleware using InfiniBand networks. The researchers in [17, 25] have provided RDMA-based designs for data shuffle in Hadoop MapReduce on InfiniBand network. The design presented in [17] shows significantly better performance compared to the default architecture [24] over high performance interconnects. Such RDMA-based designs of Hadoop MapReduce have alleviated major performance bottlenecks with the implementation of many novel features such as in-memory merge, prefetching, caching of map outputs, and overlapping of merge and reduce phases. Although these designs introduce new features compared to the default framework, they do not guarantee maximum possible overlapping among all the phases of the framework to achieve maximum utilization of all resources. This leads to an important question: *Can we devise a new scheme that can leverage features from both RDMA-based design and default framework to get maximum possible overlapping among all different phases of a MapReduce job and obtain substantial performance benefits compared to the previous best case?*

2. MOTIVATION AND CONTRIBUTIONS

2.1 Motivation

The existing RDMA-based designs of Hadoop MapReduce [17, 25] have significant architectural changes (described in Section 3.2) compared to the default framework. Four key design features in this new framework are as follows.
(1) RDMA-based shuffle engine
(2) In-memory merge
(3) Overlapping between merge and reduce phases
(4) Pre-fetching and caching of map phase outputs
This enhanced MapReduce framework can gain significant performance benefits compared to the default architecture running over high performance interconnects or protocols such as 10 GigE and IPoIB. In addition to the in-memory merge operations, overlapping between merge and reduce phases minimizes the number of disk operations in the ReduceTask. However, unlike the default architecture, this new framework does not take into account the overlapping among map, shuffle, and merge phases. This clearly introduces some differences in the utilization of the network resources between these two architectures. Figure 1 illustrates one of these scenarios. In this figure, profiling of the total amount of data transmission in shuffle phase is presented during a small MapReduce job execution (20 GB TeraSort in a cluster size of 4). Here, X-axis represents the progress of time from the beginning of job execution to the end and Y-axis represents the average amount of data shuffled across all nodes at each point during the entire execution of the job.

As shown in Figure 1(a), in the default MapReduce architecture, data transmission in shuffle starts at the very beginning of the job execution process. Thus, it starts to utilize the underlying network from the beginning of the job execution and continues to do so till the end. However, due to a large number of disk operations, many stalls exist in the overall shuffle phase, which is clearly visible in Figure 1(a). This proves the fact that in default MapReduce architecture, pipeline efficiency among different phases is very low.

On the other hand, RDMA-based designs [17, 25] eliminate most of the disk operations by introducing in-memory merge mechanism with overlapping of reduce phase. To fit data from all maps in memory, this design shuffles only a small portion of data initially from each map location, which can also be validated from Figure 1(b). This phenomena clearly states that in the early stage of job execution, current RDMA-based designs are not utilizing full network capacity. As soon as all maps finish execution, this design starts fetching more data and utilizes the network with almost no stalls. This proves that pipeline efficiency for this design is high during the latter part of the job execution process compared to the default framework.

Figure 1 also presents another key difference between these two frameworks which is the peak amount of data shuffled at a single point of time. The default framework can obtain higher peak as it transmits all the packets back to back on a single request. Whereas, in the RDMA-based design, only one packet is transferred per request to keep all packets from all map locations reside in-memory for merge operation.

These observations motivate us to the following research challenges.

1. Can a hybrid approach between these two designs be taken which can utilize the network more efficiently compared to current best approaches?

2. Can this hybrid approach guarantee maximum possible overlapping among all the phases in the MapReduce framework?

3. In this hybrid approach, how efficiently can one design switch to another without affecting the overall job execution time?

4. Can this hybrid approach be efficiently implemented on different high performance interconnects by both Sockets and RDMA?

5. With this new scheme, what will be the performance improvement for MapReduce applications compared to the previous best-case design and default MapReduce over high performance interconnects?

We address these challenges in detail in Section 4 and Section 5.

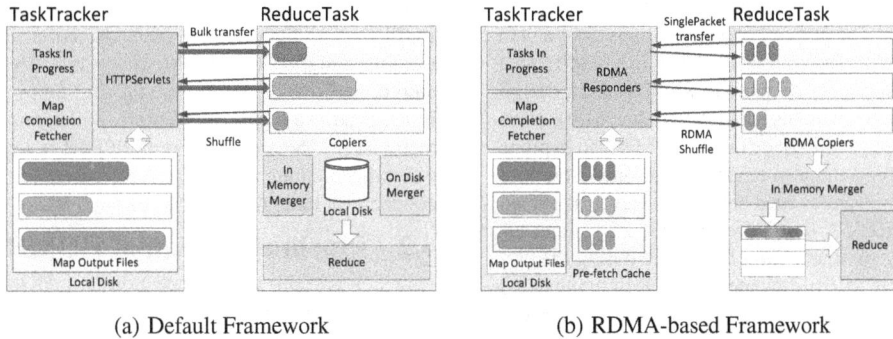

(a) Default Framework   (b) RDMA-based Framework

Figure 2: Comparison between default framework and RDMA-based design

2.2 Contributions

In this paper, we propose a new hybrid scheme, HOMR, which can exploit maximum possible overlapping among all phases of MapReduce jobs. Through HOMR, we propose a new Greedy Shuffle Algorithm which utilizes the network for shuffle in a more optimized manner compared to current approaches. For skewed data distribution, we propose On-demand Shuffle Adjustment, that helps MapReduce jobs to progress faster. We keep our architecture simple but generalized enough to work over different high performance interconnects including Sockets and RDMA over InfiniBand. We also perform extensive evaluations with HOMR and compare the performance with the previous best-case design [17] as well as the default MapReduce framework over different interconnects. Performance evaluations show that, for regular benchmarks such as Sort and TeraSort, our new design can achieve up to 29% benefit in terms of job execution time compared to previous best-case design [17] over RDMA. HOMR over Sockets can achieve 38% benefit compared to default Hadoop over Sockets. Performance benefits of HOMR over RDMA compared to default Hadoop over IPoIB can go up to 54% for the same workloads.

3. EXISTING ARCHITECTURES

In this section, we first discuss the default architecture of Hadoop MapReduce. Then, we discuss the RDMA-enhanced MapReduce architecture.

3.1 Default MapReduce Architecture

Hadoop [24] is a popular open source implementation of the MapReduce [7] programming model. The Hadoop Distributed File System (HDFS) [20, 24] is the primary storage for Hadoop cluster. A Hadoop cluster consists of two types of nodes: NameNode and DataNode. The NameNode manages the file system namespace and the DataNodes store the actual data. The NameNode has a JobTracker process and all the DataNodes can run TaskTracker processes. These processes, together, act as a master-slave architecture for a MapReduce job. A MapReduce job usually consists of three basic stages: map, shuffle/merge/sort and reduce. JobTracker is the service within Hadoop that distributes tasks to specific nodes in the cluster. A single JobTracker and a number of TaskTrackers are responsible for successful completion of a MapReduce job.

Each TaskTracker can launch several MapTasks, one per split of data. The map function converts the original records into intermediate results and stores them on the local file system as map output files. Each of these files are sorted into many data partitions, one per ReduceTask. The JobTracker then launches the ReduceTasks as soon as the map outputs are available from the MapTasks. As shown in Figure 2(a), each ReduceTask starts fetching the map outputs from the map output locations that are already completed. TaskTracker tracks the finished map tasks through TasksInProgress

and MapCompletionFetcher units. Data from various map output locations are sent and received via HTTP requests and responses. While receiving these data from various locations, a merge algorithm is run to merge sort these data in the local disk to be used as an input for the reduce operation. Then each ReduceTask loads and processes the merged outputs using the user defined reduce function. The final result is then stored into HDFS.

3.2 RDMA-based MapReduce Architecture

As mentioned in Section 2.1, RDMA-based design of MapReduce has four key features introduced in the framework. These features not only improve the overall job execution time for MapReduce framework, but also enhance the pipeline efficiency by introducing overlapping between merge and reduce phases.

RDMA-based shuffle engine: As shown in Figure 2(a), ReduceTasks send HTTP requests to the TaskTracker for the retrieval of map output data. TaskTracker receives these HTTP requests over Java Sockets and then uses Servlets to respond.

In RDMA-based design, this shuffling of data is implemented over RDMA. RDMA Copiers send requests to TaskTrackers for recently completed map output data. RDMA Responders in TaskTrackers receive those requests and responds back to ReduceTasks fetching the data from cache. As shown in Figure 2(b), each response consists of only one packet of data to facilitate in-memory merge operation.

In-memory merge: In the RDMA-based design, entire merge operation can take place in-memory, which reduces significant number of disk operations in the ReduceTask. As in RDMA, data can be retrieved much faster, it creates the opportunity to transfer one map output file in multiple communication steps instead of one. By doing this, the merge phase can start as soon as some key-value pairs from all map output files reach at the reducer side.

Overlapping of merge and reduce: For default MapReduce, merge starts immediately with shuffle. But reduce cannot start until all data has been merged and kept in disk.

However, RDMA-based design can start reduce operation as soon as first merge process completes its sorting. The beauty of this design is that it can overlap merge and reduce functionality through efficient pipelining between these two phases.

Prefetching and caching of map output: RDMA-based design of MapReduce implements an efficient caching technique for the intermediate data residing in map output files in local disk. Figure 2(b) shows the Pre-fetch Cache in the TaskTracker side.

4. DESIGN OF HOMR

4.1 Architectural Overview of HOMR

For efficient utilization of all resources in MapReduce framework, we propose HOMR (Hybrid approach to exploit maximum

Overlap in MapReduce). Figure 3 presents the high-level architectural overview of HOMR. The primary objective of this design is to combine all possible overlapping among all phases in a MapReduce job. Since the huge performance benefits in RDMA-based design compared to default framework relies heavily on reduced disk overheads in both TaskTrackers and ReduceTasks, HOMR also exploits this observation by keeping the in-memory merge operation with overlapping between merge and reduce phases. However, as shown in Section 2.1, current RDMA-based designs [17, 25] cannot efficiently utilize network communication for shuffle during the earlier stage of the job execution. To alleviate this, HOMR emphasizes maximum overlapping among all phases of MapReduce framework by carefully utilizing the available resources in the most efficient manner possible.

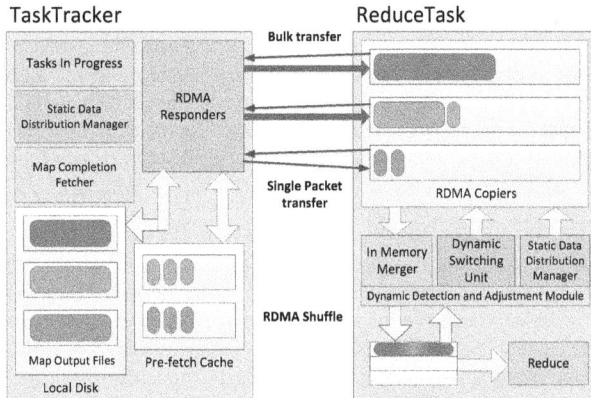

Figure 3: Architecture of HOMR

The high-level architecture for HOMR is shown in Figure 3. Compared to the previous RDMA-based architecture, HOMR introduces the following units.

Static Data Distribution Manager (SDDM): Both TaskTrackers and ReduceTasks contain SDDMs to assign static weights on how much data to shuffle. Initially, ReduceTasks do not have the knowledge of how much data from each map output file are assigned to it. After one round of communication, ReduceTasks gather this knowledge. SDDM assigns a static weight to each completed map location which signifies the amount of data that would be shuffled in the initial stage. In the TaskTracker side, it defines how much data needs to be cached in the Pre-fetch cache based on the weight distribution. Depending on the shuffle scheme, discussed in Section 4.3, SDDM decides on efficient weight distribution.

Dynamic Switching Unit (DSU): Added in the ReduceTask, DSU detects the switching point of one design framework to another dynamically. Operationally, HOMR executes similarly as in default MapReduce framework when the map phase starts, thus bringing statically assigned map output data in response to a single request. This can ensure the high peak rate of data transmission during the early stage of job execution. HOMR then switches its mode of operation to the RDMA-based design [17] with the help of DSU, depending on the shuffle scheme used for SDDM. The main objective of DSU is to decide and switch the operations from one framework to another in a correct and efficient manner.

Dynamic Detection and Adjustment Module (DDAM): After the completion of switching, HOMR continues to operate in RDMA-based mode. However, depending on the intermediate data distribution to the ReduceTasks, some map output may be required more than others for faster progression of merge and reduce phases. DDAM works in the ReduceTask side to facilitate this. The objective of this module is to monitor the merge and reduce progress

inside ReduceTasks. It detects those map outputs that need to be shuffled more than others. After detection, it quickly adjusts the weights assigned by SDDM to dynamically control the shuffle, merge, and reduce phases so that maximum possible overlapping is achieved. To adjust the weights, it maintains a queue of priority map tasks. The architecture of HOMR is kept simple as well as generalized enough to work over different high performance interconnects including GigE networks and RDMA over InfiniBand.

4.2 Pipelined Design of HOMR

In this section, we elaborate on how HOMR exploits overlapping among all different phases in MapReduce framework using the new architectural features mentioned in the previous section. However, map and reduce phase can not overlap with each other for the semantics of the MapReduce programming model. To exploit maximum overlapping in different phases of MapReduce job execution, HOMR maintains these steps.

Step One: Overlapping map and shuffle at the beginning: During job startup, map phase starts execution by running several map tasks in different nodes in the cluster. After each map completion event, HOMR interrupts SDDM to collect all map output information for that particular map. This information is needed to compute static weights for both TaskTracker and ReduceTask. TaskTracker uses this weight to determine how much data it needs to cache for a particular map, whereas ReduceTask uses this value as the fraction of data that it can expect to receive on a single request. Based on the shuffle algorithms described in Section 4.3, SDDM uses different weight assignment.

Step Two: Overlapping map, shuffle, and merge: Unlike previous RDMA-based designs, HOMR brings more data during early shuffle. Because of this reason, merge also starts with shuffle and keeps building up the priority queue as well as merges newly shuffled data to the queue. In this way, as soon as maps complete their execution, merge phase almost has entire shuffled data merged and ready for reduce. This helps to start reduce immediately after the last map's first data packet is merged to the priority queue.

Step Three: Map completes, switching starts: As soon as the last map completes, ReduceTask interrupts DSU. Depending on data distribution assigned by SDDM, DSU detects the switching point and dynamically switches shuffle and merge phases to run in RDMA-based mode as in [17, 25]. Reduce phase also starts after this switching point.

Step Four: Overlapping shuffle, merge, and reduce: As soon as DSU switches the mode, shuffle, merge, and reduce phases continue to run as in RDMA-based designs [17, 25]. So, each shuffle request brings single packet of data for each map, reducing the amount of memory to be merged at any time. DDAM monitors the overall progress of merge and reduce phases at all times and dynamically adjusts weights of map outputs to be shuffled.

A comparison of overlapping among different phases of different MapReduce frameworks is shown in Figure 4. We differentiate the bulk transfer mode in default architecture (Figure 4(a)) and single packet transfer in RDMA-based architecture (Figure 4(b)) here. HOMR utilizes the network by incorporating both of these architectures (Figure 4(c)). Similar hybrid approach is taken for merge phase. From this figure, we can see that HOMR has maximum overlapping possible among all phases for MapReduce framework.

4.3 Efficient Shuffle Algorithms

We first describe a simple algorithm for shuffle, All-Average.

4.3.1 All-Average Algorithm

The simplest way to assign weights on shuffle data would be assigning equal weights to all map locations. In this algorithm,

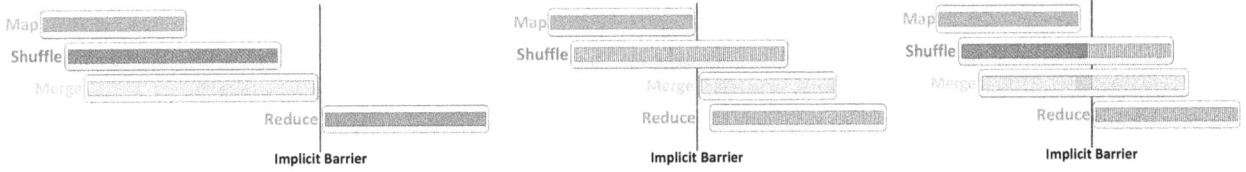

Figure 4: Overlapping of different phases in MapReduce job: (a) Default architecture, (b) RDMA-based architecture [17, 25], (c) HOMR architecture

SDDM follows this approach based on the available memory in each ReduceTask. For this algorithm, DSU can start switching to the RDMA-based mode as soon as last map's output is merged into memory. So each map output will share equal memory space in ReduceTask before DSU starts switching. In HOMR, ReduceTask sends this weight along with the request message to TaskTracker. We name this weight as f_{HOMR}. This weight signifies the amount of data from each map output that can fit in ReduceTask's memory to perform in-memory merge operation.

In All-Average, SDDM calculates f_{HOMR} using the following equation.

$$f_{HOMR} = \frac{availableMemory}{mapLocations * expectedOutputSize} \quad (1)$$

$expectedOutputSize$ is equal to the average map output size that this reducer expects from one map location. Each MapTask stores partition size of its output. We estimate $totalOutputSize$ by combining partition sizes from the completed maps and then extrapolating it for all. $totalOutputSize$ is then divided by total maps to get $expectedOutputSize$. TaskTracker sends this information to each Reducer during the first round of shuffle. If $availableMemory > (mapLocations * expectedOutputSize)$, then f_{HOMR} would be greater than 1, which signifies that the total memory in the ReduceTask is enough for all map output data. In that case, ReduceTask can get all map outputs during map phase and thus assigns a weight of 1 to all map locations. However, for most of the cases, f_{HOMR} would be less than 1. On subsequent requests to the TaskTracker, ReduceTask sends this fraction value. When TaskTracker gets this fraction value, it sends map output data packets back to back until it reaches that fraction of the total data size. This communication pattern would sustain until any of the maps are still running.

Although this approach is very simple, it can have several issues causing performance degradation.

High volume of request messages: All-Average does not assign a fraction of 1.0 to any map location unless the available memory is already enough to hold all map output data. This means that for each of the map output location, at least two requests must be needed to get all the data to ReduceTask's memory. This increases the number of request-response messages during shuffle.

Increased cache miss: For All-Average, after map phase, all the map locations still need to be cached in TaskTracker side for faster response. This happens due to the same reason mentioned above. This introduces more cache misses.

Switching may become costly: In All-Average, all the map locations have same f_{HOMR} value, which takes more time for merge to extract all the sorted key-value pairs from the Priority Queue.

Based on the above observations, we propose another approach, Greedy Shuffle Algorithm.

4.3.2 *Greedy Shuffle Algorithm*

In this algorithm, SDDM assigns different f_{HOMR} to different map locations. This algorithm starts assigning the fraction f_{HOMR} to 1.0 starting from the beginning of the completed maps list. Before assigning this value, it checks whether the whole map output data from this location combining with other map locations that

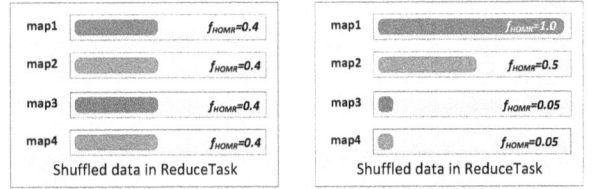

(a) All-Average Algorithm   (b) Greedy Shuffle Algorithm

Figure 5: Sample weight assignment for both algorithms

are already assigned a 1.0 value, can fit in the available memory. If it can, then SDDM assigns a value of 1.0 to this map's f_{HOMR}. Otherwise, this algorithm assigns f_{HOMR} as follows.

$$f_{HOMR} = f_{singlePacket} = \frac{packetLength}{expectedOutputSize} \quad (2)$$

After this first round of assignment, each map location is assigned a value as per following.

$$f_{HOMR}(m_i) = \begin{cases} 1.0 & \text{if } \sum_0^i rawLength + \\ & \sum_{i+1}^n packetLength \leq \\ & availableMemory \\ f_{singlePacket} & \text{otherwise} \end{cases}$$

Here, n represents total map locations and $packetLength$ is a configurable parameter of shuffle packet size. After this assignment, this algorithm applies another round of assigning larger fraction values starting from those map locations which have been assigned $f_{singlePacket}$ in the first round. In the second round, it tries to assign a value of 0.5 instead of 1.0. In this way, the algorithm approaches, each time assigning the fraction from the previous round but dividing it by two, similar to the well-known exponential back-off algorithm.[1] This continues until the fraction becomes less than $f_{singlePacket}$. Similar to All-Average, Greedy Shuffle Algorithm also sends the assigned f_{HOMR} to the TaskTracker and then expects to receive that much data. As the most recently completed map locations have significantly lower f_{HOMR}, DSU can switch very efficiently and the number of request messages from each ReduceTask also keeps to a low value.

A sample comparison of shuffled data from different map locations for Greedy and All-Average is shown in Figure 5. Performance comparisons between these two approaches is presented in Section 5.2.1.

4.4 On-demand Shuffle Adjustment

After SDDM applies weights on how much data to shuffle using one of the algorithms mentioned in Section 4.3, and DSU switches the framework to operate as in RDMA-based designs [17, 25], all the map locations start to shuffle single packet of data for correctly executing in-memory merge. Shuffling only single packet of data

---

[1]Exponential back-off refers to algorithm commonly used in network congestion, where a rate of repeated transmission of some data is decreased multiplicatively based on some feedback.

helps merge and reduce phases to execute in an overlapping manner without swamping the available memory. This may be an ideal scenario for most of the applications that are running MapReduce jobs over randomly distributed data. However, for a skewed data distribution, this situation may not help since some of the map outputs are needed more than the others. SDDM, assigning weights at the very beginning with the help of Greedy Algorithm, would have no idea of how skewed the data distribution is.

To overcome this, DDAM applies on-demand shuffle adjustment as soon as it finds out some map outputs are needed to be shuffled more than others. DDAM achieves this in two steps.

Monitor and Detection: DDAM has a light-weight monitoring unit that monitors the overall progress of merge and reduce phase with a counter for each map location data. It uses a detection algorithm to find out whether some map outputs are merged and reduced faster than other map outputs. This signifies that the data distribution is skewed and the corresponding reducer needs this map output more than the others to progress faster on merge and reduce phases. After detection, it puts this map location on a queue which signifies the data structure for holding priority map locations.

Dynamic Adjustment: DDAM waits on the queue for priority map locations for any entry made by the detection logic. As soon as it finds one map location in the queue, it quickly adjusts its weight of shuffled data. The next time when the shuffle begins for this map location, instead of shuffling only one packet for this location, TaskTracker sends back-to-back packets for this map location until it reaches the adjusted weight assigned by ReduceTask. Performance improvement for applying on-demand shuffle is discussed in Section 5.2.2.

4.5 Implementation

We implement different functional units of HOMR in Hadoop MapReduce. We choose the stable versions from different repositories (hadoop-0.x.y and hadoop-1.x.y) for this implementation. First, we implement SDDM in both TaskTrackers and ReduceTasks, which starts as a daemon thread and assigns fractions to all completed map locations obtained from Map Completion Fetcher. The Greedy Shuffle and All-Average Algorithms are implemented as generalized routines that can assign these fraction values to the input set of map locations. After initial assignments are done, SDDM goes to sleep until it is interrupted by DDAM. DSU and DDAM are implemented only inside ReduceTasks. Unlike SDDM, DSU initially goes to sleep. After all map completion events, DSU is notified by one of the copiers to start switching to RDMA-enhanced mode of operation. During this process, DSU maintains different data structures and controls values for copiers and mergers so that they can commence after the switching is complete. DDAM has different functional units implemented inside ReduceTask. It has a monitoring thread that continuously monitors the currently shuffled data from all map locations and yet to be merged. Through some simple detection logic using user-defined parameters, it notifies SDDM to dynamically adjust fractions for different map locations. The monitoring unit inside DDAM runs as a daemon thread, starting from the beginning of ReduceTask execution till task completion. For RDMA communication, both TaskTrackers and ReduceTasks have JNI adaptive interface which enables the Java code to make use of RDMA functionalities, implemented in native C. We keep the implementation specifics of RDMA communication similar to the previous RDMA-based design [17].

5. PERFORMANCE EVALUATION

In this section, we present detailed performance evaluations of HOMR and comparisons with other architectures over different high performance interconnects. Our performance evaluation can

be divided into three broad categories:
(1) Performance analysis of HOMR
(2) Evaluation of Micro-benchmarks
(3) Evaluation of Macro-benchmarks

5.1 Experimental Setup

We have used three different cluster configurations.

(1) Intel Westmere Cluster with larger memory (Cluster A): This cluster has 9 nodes and each node in this cluster has Xeon Dual quad-core processor operating at 2.67 GHz. Each node is equipped with 24 GB RAM and two 1TB HDDs. These nodes also have NetEffect NE020 10Gb Accelerated Ethernet Adapter (iWARP RNIC) that are connected using a 24 port Fulcrum Focalpoint switch. Each node is also equipped with MT26428 QDR ConnectX HCAs (32 Gbps data rate) with PCI-Ex Gen2 interfaces and are interconnected with a Mellanox QDR switch. Each node runs Red Hat Enterprise Linux Server release 6.1 (Santiago) at kernel version 2.6.32-131 with OpenFabrics version 1.5.3.

(2) Intel Westmere Cluster (Cluster B): This is a larger cluster with 65 nodes that has the same processors with 12GB RAM and a single 160GB HDD. It also has similar QDR HCAs as in Cluster A.

(3) TACC Stampede [21] (Cluster C): Each node in this cluster is dual socket containing Intel Sandy Bridge (E5-2680) dual octa-core processors, running at 2.70GHz. It has 32GB of memory, a SE10P (B0-KNC) co-processor and a Mellanox IB FDR MT4099 HCA. The host processors are running CentOS release 6.3 (Final). Each node is equipped with a single 80 GB HDD. We use 65 nodes from this cluster.

In all our experiments, we have used hadoop-1.2.1 and JDK 1.7.0. We have also tested on hadoop-0.20.2 and observed similar results. The HDFS block-size used is 256 MB for all experiments. Throughout this section, HadoopA-IB, MRoIB (MapReduce over InfiniBand), and MRoIB-HOMR legends in the graphs refer to the RDMA based design of HadoopA [25], RDMA based design of MapReduce over InfiniBand [17], and HOMR with RDMA over InfiniBand, respectively. For HadoopA-IB, we used the patch provided by Mellanox [15] for hadoop-1.x.y. For MRoIB [17], we use the RDMA for Apache Hadoop [18] release package.

5.2 Performance Analysis of HOMR

In this section, we first evaluate two shuffle algorithms presented in Section 4.3 and compare their performances. After that, we show the benefits of applying on-demand shuffle adjustment for skewed data distribution. Lastly, we provide some profiling analysis for the HOMR architecture.

5.2.1 Shuffle Algorithms: All Average vs Greedy

To compare the performance of these two algorithms, we evaluate each with increasing number of map locations. In MapReduce, map locations represent the local data directories where the output from each map are stored. In this experiment, each map location possess five blocks of data where block size is 256 MB. Each reducer needs to shuffle the data assigned to it from each map location. We launch a total of 32 reducers in 4 nodes in Cluster A and measure the average shuffle time across all the reducers to determine which algorithm can respond to the shuffle request fastest.

Table 1: Comparison of average shuffle times

No. of map locations	All Average	Greedy Shuffle
160	116.31 sec	82.9 sec
240	259 sec	205.18 sec
320	367.65 sec	300.4 sec

Table 1 shows the average shuffle times for both algorithms. We can see that Greedy Algorithm performs 18-28% faster compared to All Average. As mentioned in Section 4.3.1, the total number of request response messages is much higher in All Average compared to the Greedy Algorithm. In our experiment, we find that All Average has 32% more request response messages in shuffle compared to the Greedy algorithm. Pre-fetch cache misses also rise by 24% for All Average compared to the Greedy approach because of the reasons mentioned in Section 4.3.1.

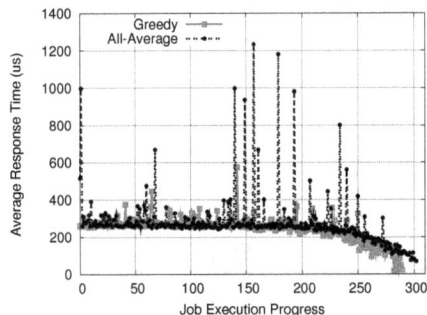

Figure 6: Average response time for shuffle algorithms

We measure the total time taken for handling each request message. Figure 6 presents one such snapshot. Here X-axis represents the job execution progress after all maps have completed writing the outputs to local disks and Y-axis represents average response times for each request message sent from ReduceTasks. As expected, All Average has larger response times compared to the Greedy approach during the job execution process due to the increase in cache miss events and total number of request messages.

5.2.2 Benefits from On-demand Shuffle Adjustment

In this experiment, we show performance benefits that can be achieved through on-demand shuffle adjustment mentioned in Section 4.4.

Table 2: Benefits of on-demand shuffling with HOMR

	Non-skewed data	Skewed data
Without on-demand shuffle	247 sec	301 sec
With on-demand shuffle	239 sec	247 sec

Table 2 shows the performance comparison of a 20 GB Sort on 4 nodes with on-demand shuffle adjustment applied on both a randomly distributed data as well as a skewed data distribution. For the skewed data distribution across reducers, we use an input data set where most of the data is shuffled to 50% of the reducers. The rest of the reducers process a small fraction of data. Job execution times are taken on the HOMR architecture with and without enabling the on-demand shuffle. We can see that, for non-skewed data, on-demand shuffle adjustment cannot guarantee significant performance benefit. However, for a skewed data distribution, on-demand shuffle adjustment achieves a performance benefit of 18% compared to HOMR without on-demand shuffle.

Reasons for the performance benefit with on-demand shuffle adjustment can be verified from Figure 7. Here, in X-axis, we show job progress in seconds after the maps are completed and in Y-axis, we show number of segments that resides in ReduceTasks' memory and not yet reduced. The reason behind taking the job execution times after map completion in X-axis is that the reduce phase starts after all the maps are completed. From this figure, we see that as the data distribution is skewed, shuffle without on-demand adjustment makes the merge and reduce progress much slower and thus the number of in-memory segments keeps increasing. With on-demand shuffle adjustment, DDAM can detect the slowness in

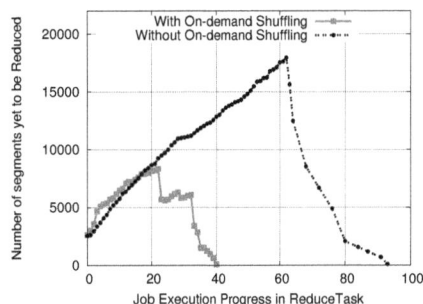

Figure 7: Merge-reduce progress for skewed data distribution

merge and reduce progress and thus adjusts the fractions so that it gets more desired data from all map locations.

5.2.3 HOMR Profiling

In this experiment, we show how the map and reduce phases progress with respect to time and observe the trend for both MRoIB and MRoIB-HOMR. We conduct 20 GB TeraSort experiment in 4 nodes of Cluster A to observe this behavior.

Figure 8(a) shows the trend for maps and compares between MRoIB and MRoIB-HOMR. Here X-axis represents time in seconds, Y-axis represents job execution progress in percentage. Figure 8(a) shows that map phases in both the designs progress similarly and finish their execution almost at the same time.

Whereas, for the progress in reduce, as shown in Figure 8(b), MRoIB-HOMR starts earlier because of its overlapping features and achieves a benefit of 27.7% over MRoIB at the end of the execution. This shows clearly that the early overlap among different phases in the ReduceTask and efficient network utilization can enhance the performance by a significant margin.

Figure 8(c) contrasts both Figure 1(a) and Figure 1(b) and shows that how MRoIB-HOMR can utilize the network bandwidth more efficiently in the shuffle phase compared to MRoIB [17] and default architecture.

5.3 Evaluation of Micro-benchmarks

In this section, we evaluate and compare micro-benchmark performance for different architectures over different interconnects. We use the sort benchmarks, Sort and TeraSort, for this evaluation.

5.3.1 Comparison with Hadoop over Sockets

In this section, we evaluate HOMR with underlying networks of 10 GigE and IPoIB and compare with default Hadoop over these interconnects.

Figure 9 shows these experiments with TeraSort as the benchmark. We conduct these experiments first in Cluster A. For larger cluster experiments, we use Clusters B and C. Figure 9(a) shows Cluster A experiments where we use 8 nodes and vary data size from 60 GB to 100 GB. Here we can see that, for 100 GB TeraSort, HOMR running over IPoIB (shown as IPoIB-HOMR) has 40% benefit compared to default Hadoop over IPoIB. For the same data size, HOMR over 10 GigE has 38% benefit compared to default Hadoop over 10 GigE. However, MRoIB-HOMR gets 14% further improved performance compared to IPoIB-HOMR (54% compared to IPoIB) and 18% improved performance compared to 10GigE-HOMR (56% compared to 10 GigE). In Cluster B (Figure 9(b)), we vary the cluster size from 16 to 64, while increasing the data size from 100 GB to 400 GB. Here, we see that HOMR over IPoIB gets a reduced performance benefit of 13% compared to default Hadoop over IPoIB for a data size of 400 GB in 64 nodes. However, MRoIB-HOMR has 31% benefit compared to default Hadoop over IPoIB for the same data size in 64 nodes. Similar results are shown

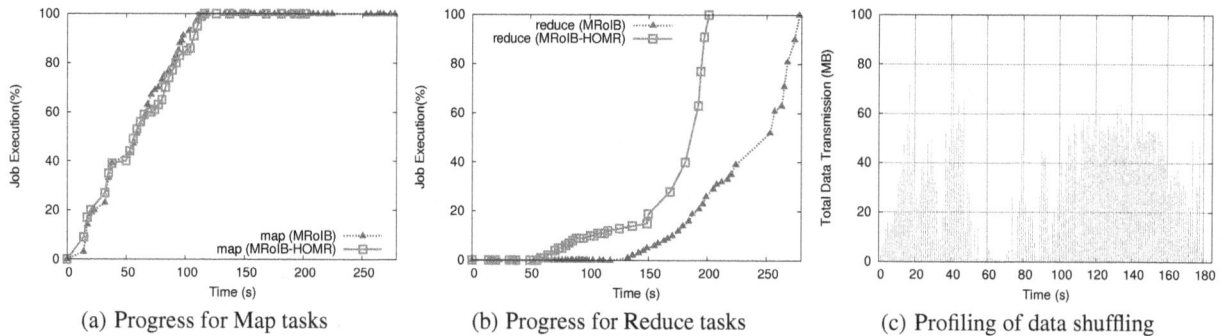

| (a) Progress for Map tasks | (b) Progress for Reduce tasks | (c) Profiling of data shuffling |

Figure 8: Profiling of HOMR

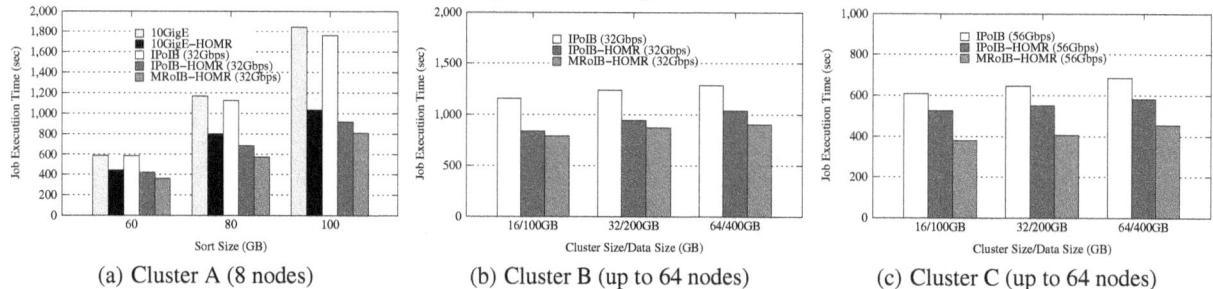

| (a) Cluster A (8 nodes) | (b) Cluster B (up to 64 nodes) | (c) Cluster C (up to 64 nodes) |

Figure 9: Comparison of TeraSort between default architecture and HOMR

for Cluster C in Figure 9(c). Here also, with 400 GB data size in 64 nodes, we see MRoIB-HOMR outperforms default Hadoop over IPoIB by 34%.

We also evaluate Sort benchmark which differs from the TeraSort as it generates key-value pairs of random length.

As shown in Figure 10(a), for 40 GB Sort experiment in Cluster A, HOMR over IPoIB outperforms default Hadoop over IPoIB by 33%, whereas HOMR over 10GigE has a benefit of 22% compared to default Hadoop over 10 GigE. MRoIB-HOMR still has 10% further benefit compared to IPoIB-HOMR. In Cluster B, we vary the data size from 60 GB to 240 GB which increasing the cluster size from 16 to 64. With 64 nodes and a data size of 240 GB, IPoIB-HOMR has a benefit of 19% compared to default Hadoop over IPoIB. MRoIB-HOMR has further 25% benefits for the same experiment. For Cluster C, we vary the data size from 80 GB to 320 GB and MRoIB-HOMR achieves 35% benefit compared to default Hadoop over IPoIB for 320 GB data in 64 nodes.

From these experiments, it is evident that HOMR architecture over any network has significant benefit compared to the default architecture over the same network. HOMR with RDMA over IB has the largest benefit compared to all other architectures.

5.3.2 Comparison with Hadoop over RDMA

In this section, we evaluate HOMR with RDMA over IB and compare the results with previous best-case RDMA-based Hadoop architectures. Figure 11(a) shows such performance comparisons in a cluster size of 8. We vary the data size from 60 GB to 100 GB. It shows that MRoIB-HOMR can obtain significant performance benefits compared to the previous best-case, MRoIB [17]. For example, in 100 GB TeraSort, MRoIB-HOMR outperforms MRoIB by 24%. For the same data size, it achieves an improvement of 49% compared to HadoopA-IB.

In Figure 11(b), we show performance comparison for the same benchmark in larger cluster sizes of Cluster B. Here, we vary the cluster size from 16 to 64 while the data size varies from 100 GB to 400 GB. In this experiment, MRoIB-HOMR outperforms MRoIB by 15% for the cluster size of 64. For Cluster C (Figure 11(c)), with

the same scale, MRoIB-HOMR achieves a performance benefit of 16% and 20% compared to MRoIB and HadoopA-IB, respectively.

For Sort experiments in Cluster A, as shown in Figure 12(a), we vary the data size from 25 GB to 40 GB. Here we observe 29% benefit for MRoIB-HOMR compared to the previous best-case MRoIB. Compared to HadoopA-IB, the performance gain goes up to 46% for the same sort size.

For large sort size, we conduct experiments in Cluster B (Figure 12(b)) with the data size varying from 60 GB to 240 GB while the cluster size is varied from 16 to 64. With 240 GB sort running in 64 nodes, MRoIB-HOMR achieves a performance benefit of 16% and 38% compared to MRoIB and HadoopA-IB, respectively. For experiments in Cluster C, with similar scale in Cluster B, we vary the data size from 80 GB to 320 GB and observe a benefit of 10% compared to MRoIB.

From the micro-benchmark evaluation, we can summarize the performance as shown in Table 3. In this table, we normalize the execution time of 100 GB TeraSort with respect to the MRoIB-HOMR and calculate the normalized execution times for all other architectures over interconnects. These normalized execution times can be generated from any benchmark evaluation and for each case, the values may slightly differ. However, based on all our micro-benchmark evaluation, we can safely propose this as the expected behavior from different MapReduce architectures. We choose the three different architectures based on overlapping among different phases in MapReduce as shown in Figure 4.

Table 3: Normalized execution times for 100GB TeraSort

Arch. over Network	10 GigE	IPoIB	IB
Default	2.13	2.04	N/A
Previous RDMA designs [17, 25]	1.79	1.67	1.32
HOMR	1.47	1.35	1

From Table 3, we can see that for default architecture, IPoIB delivers better performance compared to 10 GigE. For RDMA-based designs, IB provides the best performance compared to other interconnects [17, 25, 26]. For HOMR also, IB performs better than any other interconnects. In this perspective, for macro-benchmark eval-

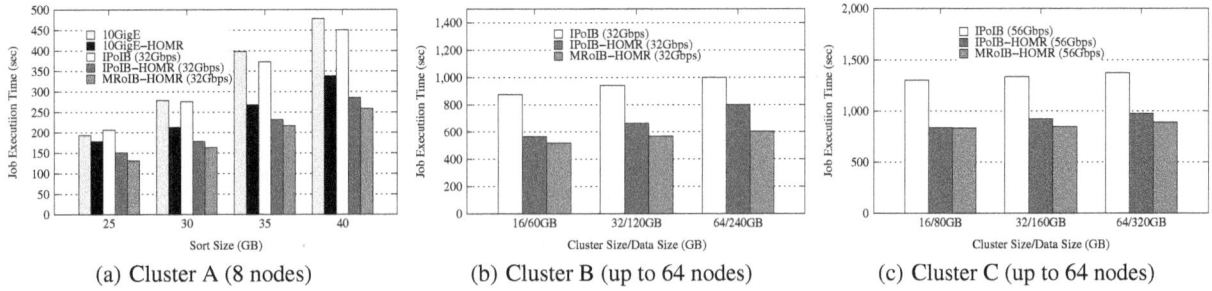

(a) Cluster A (8 nodes)   (b) Cluster B (up to 64 nodes)   (c) Cluster C (up to 64 nodes)

Figure 10: Comparison of Sort between default architecture and HOMR

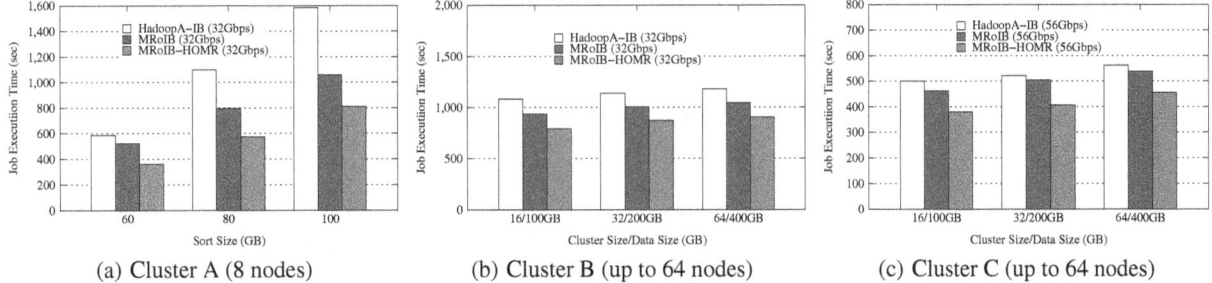

(a) Cluster A (8 nodes)   (b) Cluster B (up to 64 nodes)   (c) Cluster C (up to 64 nodes)

Figure 11: Comparison of TeraSort across RDMA-based designs

uation in Section 5.4, we evaluate three best scenarios from three different architectures.

5.4 Evaluation of Macro-benchmarks

In this section, we evaluate macro-benchmarks that closely resembles real application behavior.

5.4.1 Evaluation using SWIM

In this section, we evaluate the performance of our design by using realistic workloads from production system, such as SWIM [22]. SWIM contains suites of workloads consisting of thousands of jobs, with complex data, arrival, and computation patterns. It also contains workload synthesis tools to generate representative test workloads by sampling historical MapReduce cluster traces.

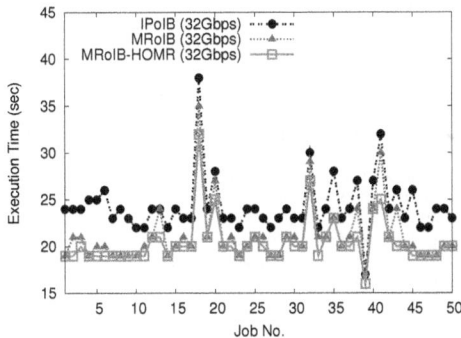

Figure 13: Facebook SWIM workload evaluation

Most of the workloads in SWIM are generated from historical Hadoop traces on large clusters at Facebook. In this experiment, we generate one such workload from existing Facebook's workload. We evaluate this experiment on Cluster B with four nodes. Figure 13 presents these results.

The representative workload that is used here consists of 50 short duration MapReduce jobs. Here, MRoIB-HOMR achieves a maximum gain of 27% over IPoIB and 16% over MRoIB in case of individual jobs. Also, from Figure 13, we observe that MRoIB-HOMR is always better or equal to MRoIB in terms of job execution time. Table 4 summarizes the results for SWIM.

Table 4: Summary of benefits for SWIM

	IPoIB	MRoIB [17]
Maximum Benefit	27%	16.67%
Average Benefit	15.72%	4.09%

5.4.2 Evaluation using PUMA

In this section, we evaluate our design with PUMA [16]. Here, we conduct our experiments on Cluster A with eight nodes and measure the job execution times over IPoIB, MRoIB, and MRoIB-HOMR. The benchmarks that we use here are Adjacency List, Self Join, Word Count, Sequence Count and Inverted Index.

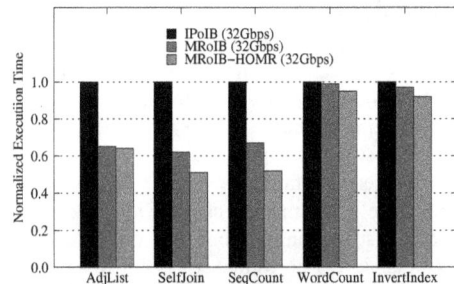

Figure 14: Evaluating PUMA workloads

Figure 14 shows the performance of the PUMA workloads for different MapReduce designs. As each workload varies significantly in terms of job duration, we present normalized job execution times here to clearly depict the performance improvement for each workload. The highest benefit is obtained for SelfJoin with 80 GB data size. MRoIB-HOMR outperforms MRoIB and IPoIB by 18% and 49%, respectively. For SequenceCount, MRoIB-HOMR achieves a benefit of 23% and 48% over MRoIB and IPoIB, respectively. From Figure 14, we observe that for WordCount and InvertedIndex, the benefits of MRoIB-HOMR compared to IPoIB are significantly less than that for other benchmarks. The reason is that these workloads are map-intensive and the reduce tasks have very little to contribute in the total job execution time.

6. RELATED WORK

Recent studies have paid more attention to improve the performance of the MapReduce framework. Hadoop-A [25] provides a

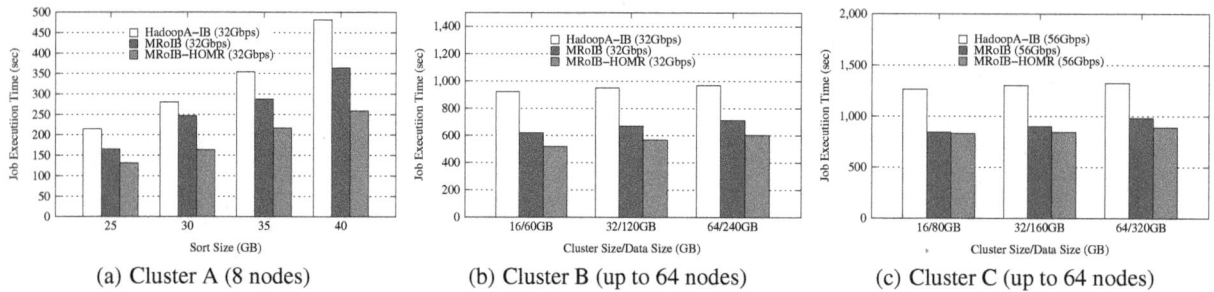

| (a) Cluster A (8 nodes) | (b) Cluster B (up to 64 nodes) | (c) Cluster C (up to 64 nodes) |

Figure 12: Comparison of Sort across RDMA-based designs

new merge method for Hadoop MapReduce by utilizing RDMA over InfiniBand. Different from Hadoop-A, our previous RDMA-based design [17] has some major enhancements with respect to pre-fetching, caching, overlapping, etc. Authors in [26] have presented another approach to obtain efficient shuffle through bypassing JVM. But, this work still follows same overlapping of phases as in previous RDMA designs. Authors in [12] have presented a comprehensive performance evaluation of MapReduce and have shown that the performance of MapReduce jobs can be improved by tuning. In [19], the authors have proposed techniques of pre-fetching and pre-shuffling into MapReduce. From their results, these techniques can improve the job execution performance in Hadoop MapReduce. The research in [14] has demonstrated that there is an impressive space for performance improvement inside Hadoop MapReduce compared to traditional HPC technologies, such as MPI. Some research works have been dedicated to improve different Hadoop components on high-performance interconnects (such as 10 GigE and InfiniBand). In [23], the authors have revealed the potential performance benefits for HDFS by utilizing high-performance networks. In [8, 10, 11, 13], the authors have designed high-performance RDMA-based designs for HBase, HDFS, and RPC, respectively over InfiniBand.

7. CONCLUSION

In this paper, we present HOMR, a hybrid approach that exploits maximum overlapping among all different phases in MapReduce framework. In this architecture, we introduce Greedy Shuffle Algorithm and On-demand Shuffle Adjustment, both of which are essential to achieve significant performance benefits. HOMR also supports both Sockets interface as well as RDMA over IB. Through On-demand Shuffle Adjustment, it can provide faster performance for skewed data distribution. Performance evaluations show that, our design can achieve a performance benefit of as large as 29% for a variety of MapReduce applications compared to the previous best-case RDMA design. This design can also enhance the performance of MapReduce jobs by up to 49%, 54%, and 56% over HadoopA-IB [25], IPoIB, and 10 GigE, respectively. As a future work, we plan to investigate more on the performance impacts for reduce-intensive MapReduce workloads.

References

[1] 2011 IDC Digital Universe Study. http://www.emc.com/leadership/programs/digital-universe.htm.

[2] 2012 DataNami Study. http://www.datanami.com/datanami/2012-07-16/top_5_challenges_for_hadoop_mapreduce_in_the_enterprise.html.

[3] J. Appavoo, A. Waterland, D. Da Silva, V. Uhlig, B. Rosenburg, E. Van Hensbergen, J. Stoess, R. Wisniewski, and U. Steinberg. Providing A Cloud Network Infrastructure on A Supercomputer. In *Proceedings of the 19th ACM International Symposium on High Performance Distributed Computing*, HPDC, New York, NY, USA, 2010.

[4] F. Chang, J. Dean, S. Ghemawat, W. C. Hsieh, D. A. Wallach, M. Burrows, T. Chandra, A. Fikes, and R. Gruber. Bigtable: A Distributed Storage System for Structured Data. In *Proceedings of the 7th Symposium on Operating System Desgin and Implementation*, OSDI, Seattle, WA, USA, 2006.

[5] J. Dean and S. Ghemawat. MapReduce: Simplified Data Processing on Large Clusters. In *Proceedings of the 6th Symposium on Operating Systems Design and Implementation*, OSDI, San Francisco, CA, USA, 2004.

[6] Greenplum Analytics Workbench. http://www.greenplum.com/news/greenplum-analytics-workbench.

[7] Hadoop Map Reduce. The Apache Hadoop Project. http://hadoop.apache.org/mapreduce/.

[8] J. Huang, X. Ouyang, J. Jose, M. W. Rahman, H. Wang, M. Luo, H. Subramoni, C. Murthy, and D. K. Panda. High-Performance Design of HBase with RDMA over InfiniBand. In *Proceedings of the IEEE International Parallel and Distributed Processing Symposium*, IPDPS, Shanghai, China, 2012.

[9] Infiniband Trade Association. http://www.infinibandta.org.

[10] N. S. Islam, X. Lu, M. W. Rahman, and D. K. Panda. Can Parallel Replication Benefit Hadoop Distributed File System for High Performance Interconnects? In *The Proceedings of IEEE 21st Annual Symposium on High-Performance Interconnects*, HOTI, San Jose, CA, 2013.

[11] N. S. Islam, M. W. Rahman, J. Jose, R. Rajachandrasekar, H. Wang, H. Subramoni, C. Murthy, and D. K. Panda. High Performance RDMA-based Design of HDFS over InfiniBand. In *The Proceedings of International Conference for High Performance Computing, Networking, Storage and Analysis*, SC, Salt Lake City, Utah, USA, 2012.

[12] D. Jiang, B. C. Ooi, L. Shi, and S. Wu. The Performance of MapReduce: an In-depth Study. *Proceedings of VLDB Endowment*, 2010.

[13] X. Lu, N. S. Islam, M. W. Rahman, J. Jose, H. Subramoni, H. Wang, and D. K. Panda. High-Performance Design of Hadoop RPC with RDMA over InfiniBand. In *Proceedings of IEEE 42nd International Conference on Parallel Processing*, ICPP, Lyon, France, 2013.

[14] X. Lu, B. Wang, L. Zha, and Z. Xu. Can MPI Benefit Hadoop and MapReduce Applications? In *Proceedings of IEEE 40th International Conference on Parallel Processing Workshops*, ICPPW, 2011.

[15] Mellanox Technologies. Unstructured Data Accelerator. http://www.mellanox.com/page/products_dyn?product_family=144.

[16] Purdue MapReduce Benchmarks Suite (PUMA). http://web.ics.purdue.edu/.

[17] M. W. Rahman, N. S. Islam, X. Lu, J. Jose, H. Subramoni, H. Wang, and D. K. Panda. High-Performance RDMA-based Design of Hadoop MapReduce over InfiniBand. In *International Workshop on High Performance Data Intensive Computing, in conjunction with IPDPS*, HPDIC, Boston, USA, 2013.

[18] RDMA for Apache Hadoop: High-Performance Design of Hadoop over RDMA-enabled Interconnects. http://hadoop-rdma.cse.ohio-state.edu/.

[19] S. Seo, I. Jang, K. Woo, I. Kim, J.-S. Kim, and S. Maeng. HPMR: Prefetching and Pre-shuffling in Shared MapReduce Computation Environment. In *Proceedings of IEEE International Conference on Cluster Computing and Workshops*, CLUSTER, 2009.

[20] K. Shvachko, H. Kuang, S. Radia, and R. Chansler. The Hadoop Distributed File System. In *Proceedings of the IEEE 26th Symposium on Mass Storage Systems and Technologies*, MSST, 2010.

[21] Stampede at Texas Advanced Computing Center. http://www.tacc.utexas.edu/resources/hpc/stampede.

[22] Statistical Workload Injector for MapReduce. https://github.com/SWIMProjectUCB/SWIM/wiki.

[23] S. Sur, H. Wang, J. Huang, X. Ouyang, and D. K. Panda. Can High Performance Interconnects Benefit Hadoop Distributed File System? In *Workshop on Micro Architectural Support for Virtualization, Data Center Computing, and Clouds, in Conjunction with MICRO*, Atlanta, GA, 2010.

[24] The Apache Software Foundation. The Apache Hadoop Project. http://hadoop.apache.org/.

[25] Y. Wang, X. Que, W. Yu, D. Goldenberg, and D. Sehgal. Hadoop Acceleration through Network Levitated Merge. In *Proceedings of International Conference for High Performance Computing, Networking, Storage and Analysis*, SC, Seattle, WA, USA, 2011.

[26] Y. Wang, C. Xu, X. Li, and W. Yu. JVM-Bypass for Efficient Hadoop Shuffling. In *Proceedings of the IEEE 27th International Symposium on Parallel and Distributed Processing*, IPDPS, Boston, MA, USA, 2013.

DTail: A Flexible Approach to DRAM Refresh Management

Zehan Cui[†‡], Sally A. McKee[§], Zhongbin Zha[†‡], Yungang Bao[†], Mingyu Chen[†]
[†]State Key Laboratory of Computer Architecture, Institute of Computing Technology, CAS
[‡]University of Chinese Academy of Sciences
[§]Chalmers University of Technology
{cuizehan,zhazhongbin,baoyg,cmy}@ict.ac.cn   mckee@chalmers.se

ABSTRACT

DRAM cells must be refreshed (or rewritten) periodically to maintain data integrity, and as DRAM density grows, so does the refresh time and energy. Not all data need to be refreshed with the same frequency, though, and thus some refresh operations can safely be delayed. Tracking such information allows the memory controller to reduce refresh costs by judiciously choosing when to refresh different rows.

Solutions that store imprecise information miss opportunities to avoid unnecessary refresh operations, but the storage for tracking complete information scales with memory capacity. We therefore propose a flexible approach to refresh management that tracks complete refresh information within the DRAM itself, where it incurs negligible storage costs (0.006% of total capacity) and can be managed easily in hardware or software. Completely tracking multiple types of refresh information (e.g., row retention time and data validity) maximizes refresh reduction and lets us choose the most effective refresh schemes. Our evaluations show that our approach saves 25-82% of the total DRAM energy over prior refresh-reduction mechanisms.

1. INTRODUCTION

Main memory systems are commonly composed of cheap, dense Dynamic Random Access Memory (DRAM) devices. DRAM devices store data as charges on cell capacitors, and these charges leak over time. Data thus must be periodically refreshed — read and rewritten — to maintain integrity.

The storage cells are arranged in banks of rectangular arrays indexed by row (wordline) and column (bitline). DRAM accesses *open* a row by loading its entire contents into a bank of sense amplifiers (or a *row buffer*) from which data may be read or written. When data in a different row are needed, the memory controller *closes* the row by writing the contents back to the storage array and precharging the row buffer. Refresh simply opens and closes rows without servicing intervening accesses. We find that, on average, refresh operations on current 4Gb DRAMs impose performance and energy overheads of 7.2% and 18.9%, respectively.

ICS'14, June 10–13 2014, Munich, Germany.
Copyright 2014 ACM 978-1-4503-2642-1/14/06 ...$15.00.
http://dx.doi.org/10.1145/2597652.2597663.

Since the length of the DRAM wordlines is constrained by the energy required to drive the bitlines and to open and close the row, memory designers increase density by adding more rows to each bank [13, 14]. This, in turn, requires that more rows be refreshed before data values degrade, causing the refresh time and energy to increase, as well.

DRAM memory systems already account for up to 40% of total system power, which represents up to 60% of the power for each processor-node (CPUs and DRAMs) [18, 3]. For exascale systems, DRAM is predicted to consume about 75% of processor-node power budgets [4]. Within four generations, almost half the memory's contribution to system power will come from refresh instead of useful accesses [20]. This means that even small refresh reductions will be more significant as memory power grows to dominate system power.

A smart memory controller can avoid unnecessary refreshes based on certain information: rows that maintain data integrity longer can be refreshed less often, and rows without meaningful data need not to be refreshed. Since completely tracking such information — termed *refresh data* (RD) — incurs significant costs, previous smarter-refresh approaches compromise by storing imprecise refresh data [20, 2], which reduces their opportunities to optimize refresh. In addition, the ways in which these prior approaches track refresh data make it difficult to leverage multiple types of RD information. For instance, Bloom filters [20] work well for tracking the long tail distribution of retention time variation, but they are impractical for tracking data validity.

We aim to build a smart-refresh memory system that:

1. stores refresh data with negligible cost,
2. tracks multiple types of refresh data,
3. coordinates the memory controller and all levels of software stack, and
4. performs necessary refreshes efficiently.

To this end, we propose *DTail*[1], a flexible, low-overhead DRAM refresh management scheme. The key idea of DTail is to store refresh data in the DRAM itself. Doing so greatly reduces the storage cost because DRAM capacity is much larger and cheaper than either SRAM or registers. Since DRAM data can be accessed with normal memory instructions, the memory controller can collaborate with all levels of the software stack to track and leverage the RD. The row-by-row behavior of refresh makes simple prefetching and caching mechanisms effective for masking access latencies. We further leverage the RD to dynamically select either automatic refresh or explicitly controlled refresh, whichever is likely to perform better. Our contributions are:

---

[1] We choose this mnemonic because we try to "dovetail" different types of refresh data to create a strong, stable, smart refresh mechanism.

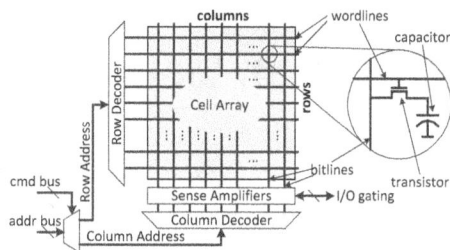

Figure 1: Bank Structure

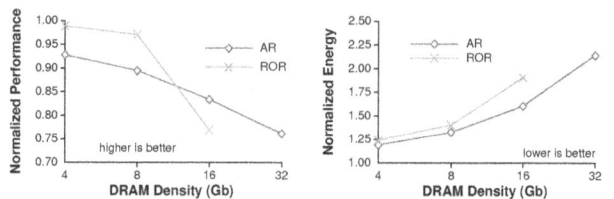

(a) Performance   (b) Energy

Figure 2: Performance and energy overheads for using auto refresh (AR) and RAS-only refresh (ROR) for various DRAM densities. Results are normalized to an ideal system that omits refresh entirely.

- We propose DTail, which can completely track multiple types of refresh data and coordinate with all levels of the software stack. DTail introduces negligible storage cost for refresh data — 0.006% of memory capacity — and maximizes refresh reduction;
- We propose to dynamically select among different refresh implementations by predicting the most effective way to perform necessary refreshes;
- We find that by tracking complete refresh data, DTail respectively saves 23.3% and 9.05-41.7% (depending on memory utilization) DRAM energy over two prior mechanisms; and
- We find that by tracking and combining multiple types of refresh data, DTail respectively saves between 25.9-40.0% and 24.6-81.9% (depending on memory utilization) of the DRAM energy over two prior mechanisms.

2. BACKGROUND AND MOTIVATION

We briefly outline DRAM organization and operation. Figure 1 shows the typical organization of a DRAM bank. Each bank comprises a two-dimensional array of cells, sense amplifiers, row and column decoders, and peripheral circuits. To access a bit in the array, the memory controller (MC) sends a row address strobe (RAS)[2] that loads the row into the row buffer (sense amplifiers). The memory controller then sends one or more column address strobes (CASs) to access specific bits. When the memory controller finishes accessing a row, it sends a precharge (PRE) command to write the values back to the storage array and prepare the row buffer for the next access. Multiple banks, which can be accessed in parallel, are organized into ranks, and channels connect one or more ranks to the MC.

2.1 Refresh Operation

To simplify hardware design, refresh operations are traditionally performed for all rows within a period short enough to guarantee data integrity for the most leaky cells[3]. Instead of refreshing all rows sequentially in a burst, refresh operations are usually staggered across the period to avoid blocking normal memory accesses. Each operation may affect one or more rows, depending on the implementation.

JEDEC makes *auto refresh* (AR) a standard for DDRx SDRAMs. The DRAM chip internally maintains a row address counter (RAC) pointing to the next row to refresh. The MC issues a refresh command every $tREFI$ cycles, at which point all DRAM banks simultaneously refresh a number of rows — making the rank unavailable for $tRFC$ cycles

— and increase their RAC accordingly. The number of rows to refresh at a time depends on density.

In *RAS-only refresh* (ROR) [24], the MC issues a row address strobe to load the specified row into the row buffer. The row is eventually written back to the DRAM array by a subsequent precharge command. In this case the MC maintains its own RAC. The controller periodically increments the RAC and issues a row address strobe. Refresh proceeds one row at a time, but the MC chooses which refreshes to schedule when. Note that the granularity of auto refresh is much larger than that of RAS-only refresh.

2.2 Performance and Energy Overheads

Table 1 shows refresh timing parameters (auto refresh) for x8/x16 width devices in the JEDEC DDR4 specification [14] at extended temperature ranges. (Devices of x4 width have twice the number of rows.) The interval between two consecutive auto refresh commands, $tREFI$, remains constant. Thus, the number of rows per refresh command doubles each generation. However, the increase in the refresh delay, $tRFC$, is only 1.3× because modern DRAM banks comprise multiple subarrays [17] that can refresh multiple rows in parallel. The portion of time that a rank is unavailable is 8.97% for 8Gb chips and 16.4% for 32Gb chips.

If refresh blocks too many normal memory accesses, the MSHRs (miss status holding registers) or load/store queue slots fill, preventing the issue of other memory access instructions. Delaying critical loads needed by instructions in flight quickly stalls the pipeline. Figure 2 shows performance and energy overheads for a system using auto refresh or RAS-only refresh compared to a system that omits refresh entirely: these overheads grow as density increases, e.g., auto refresh incurs 23.8% performance overhead and 114% energy overhead versus a 32Gb refresh-less system.

Figure 2 omits data for RAS-only refresh at 32Gb because at this density it fails to refresh all rows in our evaluated DRAM organizations. Table 1 shows that 512 rows need to be refreshed every $3.9\mu s$ for 32Gb DRAMs, which requires a

Table 1: JEDEC DDR4 Refresh Timing Parameters of x8/x16 Devices at Extended Temperature Range

Density	#rows per refresh command	$tREFI$	$tRFC$	$tRFC/tREFI$
2Gb	16×2[a]	$3.9\mu s$	160ns	4.10%
4Gb	16×4	$3.9\mu s$	260ns	6.67%
8Gb	16×8	$3.9\mu s$	350ns	8.97%
16Gb	16×16	$3.9\mu s$	480ns[b]	12.3%
32Gb	16×32	$3.9\mu s$	640ns[b]	16.4%

[a] DDR4 has 16 banks, with multiple rows per bank refreshed each time.
[b] We use the projection from Mukundan et al. [27] for 16Gb and 32Gb.

---

[2]The name RAS is now commonly replaced by ACT for *activate*, but we choose RAS for historical consistency.

[3]For DDRx SDRAM, the period is respectively 64ms and 32ms at normal (0-85 °C) and extended (85-95 °C) temperature ranges.

RAS command to be issued every six cycles ($3.9\mu s/1.25ns/512$). A subsequent precharge command is required to write the row back to the DRAM array, which means the address bus would need to transmit two commands every six cycles for each device. This is not possible in our DRAM organization with four ranks sharing one bus.

2.3 Limitations of RAS-only Refresh

RAS-only refresh allows fine-grained control of selective refreshes, and it outperforms auto refresh for lower density devices (4Gb/8Gb) due to DRAM bank-level parallelism. However, it must adhere to the DRAM timing constraints. Specifically, the MC must observe $tRRD$ (the activate-to-activate command delay) and $tFAW$ (four activate window). The former defines the minimum interval between two consecutive RAS commands to the same DRAM device, and the latter specifies a sliding window during which no more than four RAS commands can be issued to the same DRAM device.

As DRAM density increases, the number of rows that need to be refreshed doubles with each generation (Table 1), which means more RAS-only refreshes must be issued. Constrained by $tRRD$ and $tFAW$, RAS-only refresh hurts performance and energy efficiency at higher DRAM densities. Since auto refresh can operate on multiple rows simultaneously, it becomes relatively more efficient at higher densities. Figure 2 shows that auto refresh exhibits higher performance and energy efficiency at a 16Gb density. This suggests that it may be better to dynamically choose between auto refresh and RAS-only refresh, depending on the number and location of rows needing to be refreshed.

3. RELATED WORK

Memory systems incorporating intelligent refresh must decide: 1) when to schedule refresh operations with respect to other memory commands, and 2) which rows to refresh. We briefly survey approaches to making the former decision before treating solutions to the latter in more detail.

3.1 Deciding When to Schedule Refreshes

Refresh schedulers can be classified according to how they schedule refresh operations [35] and whether they schedule regular accesses around [27] or within them (for multi-row refresh granularities) [28]. Stuecheli et al. propose *Elastic Refresh* [35] to dynamically fit the refresh period to the currently executing workload. To prevent the MC queue from stalling useful accesses when filled with commands to a bank being refreshed, Mukundan et al. [27] propose Dynamic Command Expansion (DCE) and Preemptive Command Drain (PCD). The former delays commands to banks under refresh, and the latter proactively schedules commands to banks about to undergo refresh. Nair et al. [28] call for pausable refresh operations that allow regular accesses to proceed with less delay.

3.2 Deciding What Not to Refresh

Intelligent refresh schemes can also be classified according to the kinds of refresh data on which they base their scheduling decisions: cell retention time ($\mathbf{R}$), error tolerance of the data ($\mathbf{T}$), access recency ($\mathbf{A}$), and row validity ($\mathbf{V}$), i.e., whether the OS has allocated the physical pages containing those cells. We use this **RTAV** RD taxonomy

to survey the rich prior work in DRAM refresh reduction, a summary of which is shown in Table 2.

Retention. Retention time refers to the period during which cells hold valid values as charge gradually leaks. Process variation [10][16] causes the retention time of DRAM cells to vary across the chip. Note that approaches that exploit $\mathbf{R}$ information are insensitive to system workloads and global memory usage, which makes them attractive components for a refresh-optimized memory subsystem.

In hardware, $\mathbf{R}$-based approaches can employ multi-period schemes to refresh cells with long retention times less frequently, as in the Variable Refresh Architecture (VRA) of Ohsawa et al. [29] and the Retention-Aware Intelligent DRAM Refresh (RAIDR) of Liu et al. [20]. VRA stores each row's expected refresh period in registers inside the DRAM. RAIDR exploits the fact that very few rows need a high refresh rate, and it tracks these inside the MC.

In software, the OS can increase the refresh period of the device by only allocating addresses that map to cells with sufficent retention. The Retention-Aware Placement in DRAM (RAPID) of Venkatesan et al. [36] and Refresh Incessantly but Occasionally (RIO) of Baek et al. [2] are two such $\mathbf{R}$-based solutions that lower the device refresh rate by isolating physical page frames that require frequent refresh.

Tolerance. Applications like games, media processing, machine learning, and unstructured information analysis tolerate errors in portions of their data and still produce acceptably accurate results. Approximate computation [31, 8] exploits this approximate data to realize tradeoffs among performance, energy, and accuracy. Cells containing such error-tolerant $\mathbf{T}$ data need not be refreshed as often as those containing critical data. How many cells fall into this category depends on application characteristics.

Liu et al. [22] partition DRAM banks into critical and noncritical regions and extend the self-refresh time to refresh non-critical regions less frequently. Their solution, Flikker, targets smartphones, which keep DRAM in self-refresh mode when (frequently) idle, but a similar technique could be applied to auto refresh in operating mode. If workload characteristics change such that more data become critical, the DRAM must be repartitioned. This partitioning is coarse-grained (e.g., it requires regions to be 1/4, 1/2, or 3/4 the capacity), which simplifies hardware and reduces area overhead but misses opportunities for finer optimization.

Access Recency. DRAM accesses imply refresh operations, and so a subsequent refresh to the same row can be postponed. The number of rows affected depends on how many different rows are accessed within the maximum refresh period, which may be few for many workloads. Ghosh et al. [9] propose Smart Refresh, which divides the refresh period into phases and maintains a per-row timeout counter in the MC. The MC decrements the counters each phase and issues a RAS-only refresh when a counter hits zero.

Emma et al. [7] create smarter refresh policies for embedded DRAM caches: ECC provides error-tolerance and time stamps guide scheduling selective refreshes. Agrawal et al. [1] similarly target eDRAM caches with Refrint, employing eager writeback for seldom used lines in addition to tracking access recency. Since the number of rows in eDRAM is limited, overheads for tracking $\mathbf{A}$ information are much more tolerable than they are for main memory.

Validity. If the OS has not allocated the page frame, its data are meaningless, and refreshes to it are wasteful. Sev-

Table 2: Summary of Intelligent Refresh Approaches

Information	Technique	Information Tracked		Implementation
		acquisition	storage	
R (retention time)	T. Ohsawa et al. [29] (VRA)	profiling	DRAM	DRAM skips refresh
	J. Liu et al. [20] (RAIDR)		MC	MC skips refresh
	R. Venkatesan et al. [36] (RAPID)		OS	OS deletes pages
	S. Baek [2] (RIO)			
T (tolerance to data errors)	S. Liu et al. [22] (Flikker)	programer annotations	page number	DRAM is split into two refresh regions
A (access recency)	M. Ghosh and H. Lee [9] (smart)	MC tracking	MC	MC skips refresh
	P. Emma et al. [7]	cache controller tracking	cache controller	cache controller skips refresh
	A. Agrawal et al. [1] (refrint)			
V (validity of row data)	T. Ohsawa et al. [29] (SRA)	OS tracking	DRAM	DRAM skips refresh
	C. Isen and L. John [12] (ESKIMO)			
	S. Baek et al. [2] (PARIS)		MC	MC skips refresh

eral software approaches thus attempt to trigger refreshes only for rows with valid data. The effectiveness of schemes using such **V** refresh information is sensitive to the total memory usage of the system.

In addition to VRA, Ohsawa et al. [29] propose a Selective Refresh Architecture (SRA) that uses an **A** bit per row to decide whether to refresh it. This scheme modifies the ISA so that the compiler, OS, or MC can prevent refreshes to dead data. In their combined hardware/software ESKIMO approach, Isen and John [12] adapt SRA to track data significance (e.g., the values of uninitialized data in a newly allocated memory region are insignificant). The OS maintains information on allocation and deallocation of virtual addresses. Baek et al. [2] extract physical memory usage information from the OS instead of monitoring virtual addresses. Their Placement-Aware Refresh In Situ (PARIS) improves SRA by maintaining RD bits in the memory controller. Storage overheads can be reduced by tracking **V** bits for larger row granularities, but this imprecision increases unnecessary refreshes.

3.3 Implementation Issues

Not only do intelligent refresh schemes differ with respect to what refresh information they track — they differ in how they acquire that data, where they store them, and how they use them to decide when to skip refreshes (see Table 2).

The main drawback of most of these methods is that RD storage costs are proportional to memory capacity, potentially adding megabytes of SRAM to the cache controller or memory controller [9, 2] (as shown in Figure 3) or adding up to 20% area overhead to DRAM dies [29]. The economics of manufacturing commodity DRAMs may hinder adoption of such solutions.

In general, **R**-based approaches have the potential to perform well regardless of system load or application behavior, but their implementation poses challenges. **R**-based software solutions fragment memory, which can hurt performance and limit adoptability, since modern operating systems use physical superpages for the kernel, framebuffer, device drivers, and some application data regions. RIO [2] thus restricts deleted pages to be fewer than 0.1% of all page frames, which in turn limits its impact. Current **R**-based hardware solutions (ours included) statically measure retention distributions, but basing refresh-period lengths on off-line information may hurt reliability because retention time fluctuates with time and temperature [37, 30, 19]. Obvious solutions are to somehow monitor retention times dynamically or to adopt overly conservative refresh periods (reducing the benefit of these optimizations). **T**, **A**, and **V** approaches are more reliable, but less broadly effective, depending on application behavior. **A** approaches grow less ef-

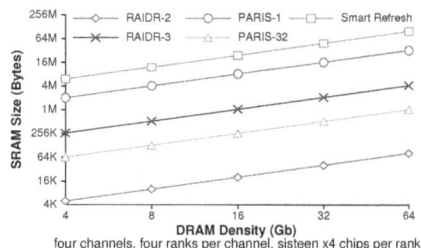

Figure 3: Comparative Storage Costs (instances of approaches from Table 2). RAIDR-n maintains n bloom filters; PARIS-m represents m rows per bit.

fective as DRAM density increases, since relatively few rows are likely to be accessed during any refresh period. Our study therefore does not address the use of **A** information.

4. DTAIL OVERVIEW

Here we describe DTail, a framework that supports multiple refresh reduction techniques. We can mitigate the storage costs of refresh data by acting on two observations:

- only a small part of the RD collection is useful at any refresh decision point, and those points occur infrequently compared to normal memory accesses; and
- RD accesses exhibit high spatial locality, since most refresh schemes rely on a row address counter (RAC) to sequentially cycle through rows of a DRAM bank.

Based on the first observation, we choose not to store RD information within specialized registers or buffers within the memory controller because paying such high overheads for infrequently used data wastes area and power. We instead store the data within the DRAM itself, where, based on the second observation, we employ prefetching to hide the latency of accessing slower storage.

Figure 4 depicts the logical building blocks of DTail: the software and hardware negotiate a contiguous physical memory space in which to store RD entries for all rows. The refresh data must be acquired through software or hardware and then written to the RD space in main memory. As always, the memory controller periodically generates refresh commands, but here it uses the RAC of a potential refresh operation to access the RD entry for that row (already prefetched into the memory controller) to compute whether the potential refresh can be squashed. DTail can make use of any of the **RTV** information types discussed above, either alone or in combination.

Placing refresh information in DRAM avoids the need for a separate device or new interface, and it facilitates hardware/software coordination by allowing the memory con-

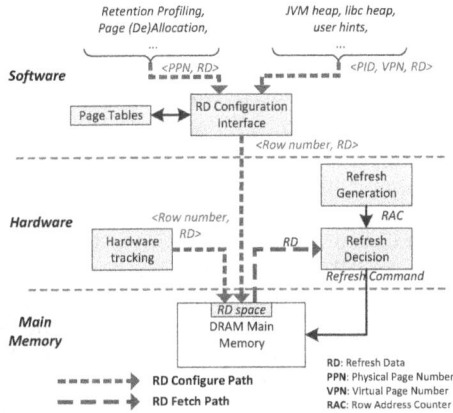

Figure 4: Building Blocks of DTail

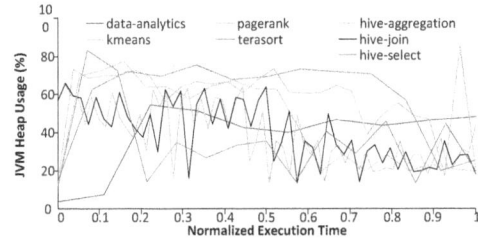

Figure 5: JVM Heap Usage

troller, OS, compiler, and even the user to participate in refresh management.

The refresh decision logic in Figure 4 can take advantage of prefetched RD to predict the gain of different refresh methods and make the most efficient choice[4].

5. DESIGN DETAILS

In this section, we discuss the design of DTail, including changes to the OS, MC, and DRAM devices.

5.1 Maintaining Refresh Data

5.1.1 Refresh Data Acquisition

Prior work discusses how to acquire the **RTV** refresh data. For example, gathering retention time information requires profiling to determine which DRAM cells hold their data at several discrete refresh rates [2, 19]. The programmer must identify error-tolerant data to guide OS page allocation [22]. Given this requirement, we do not consider data error-tolerance in the current study.

Note that the refresh data may exist in any layer of the software stack. For example, an application (e.g., memcached or JVM) may allocate large chunks of memory at startup and then self-manage it (possibly with garbage collection). The OS may consider a page valid even if it is not currently assigned to an object. Figure 5 shows JVM heap usage for several Java applications (profiled every five seconds). Total execution times range from 50 seconds to 300 seconds, and each application's time is normalized to its total execution time. On average, the "true" valid data only account for 34.6-58.3% of the heap size.

5.1.2 Configuration Interface

DTail provides an easy RD configuration interface to store aquired refresh data of different types from various layers. Refresh data acquired by the OS (e.g., from page allocation/deallocation) can be tagged by the physical page number (PPN). This makes it straightforward to configure the RD space in memory, given the address mapping between rows and pages. If refresh data are acquired from upper layers (e.g., the JVM GC or user hints), a system call passes the process ID (PID) and virtual page number (VPN) to the OS. The OS indexes the page table to translate the tuple <PID,

VPN> into the PPN. In case the virtual-to-physical translation is not yet established[5], we add a few bits to the page table entry (PTE) to temporarily store the RD while the OS maps the page.

5.1.3 Refresh Data Storage

The RD entries for all rows can be stored in simple tables. Retention and validity information can be represented by the *expected refresh period* and a *valid bit*, respectively. Representing data error-tolerance as the expected refresh period simplifies the refresh decision logic; critical data require the normal period, but non-critical data are assigned relaxed refresh periods according to their error-tolerance levels.

Since both the expected refresh period and validity are seldom updated (at system boot time and upon events such as page allocation and garbage collection), we merge them, as in Table 3. These RD tables should be stored in contiguous physical memory that the OS allocates at boot time and for which it configures the MC (with physical addresses and lengths). This simplifies MC circuitry: simple state machines can control accesses to these dense structures.

Table 3: Refresh Data (RD) Format

RD (four bits)				expected refresh period
0	X	X	X	no refresh
1	0	0	0	64ms
1	0	0	1	2×64ms
1	0	1	0	4×64ms
...	...			...
1	1	1	1	128×64ms

5.2 Deciding When to Refresh

The DTail hardware uses information in the RD tables to support different refresh reduction techniques: retention-aware multi-period refresh, validity-aware selective refresh, and tolerance-aware multi-period refresh. The MC generates both auto refresh and RAS-only refresh synchronously, and DTail dynamically selects which refresh method to use based on gain prediction. Figure 6 shows the decision process.

5.2.1 Per-Row Refresh Decisions

Since each RD entry is four bits, each RD access (typically 64 bytes) fetches multiple entries and buffers them in a FIFO within the MC. Simple next-line prefetching helps mask lookup latency.

When a RAS-only refresh command is generated, the refresh decision logic decides whether it will be issued based on the RD entry. If the refresh is not squashed, the expected refresh period (assumed here to be $N \times 64ms$) indicates how often a row must be refreshed. The decision logic in Figure 6 ensures that a refresh occurs once every N periods. The hash function avoids "refresh bursts" by distributing refresh oper-

---

[4]We do not address global scheduling of memory operations here, but DTail supports intelligent scheduling schemes.

[5]Linux uses demand paging, which allocates a physical page only when the virtual page is accessed.

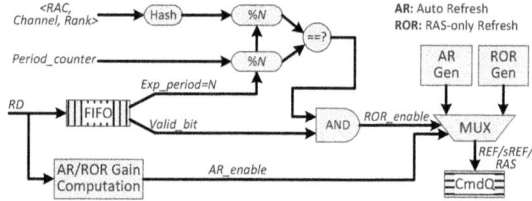

Figure 6: DTail Decision Process

ations for different rows over N periods and by distributing refreshes across the channels, ranks, and banks.

5.2.2 Refresh Choice

DTail can choose between RAS-only refresh and auto refresh. Table 1 shows that multiple rows across all banks — termed a *super-row* to simplify further dicussion — are refreshed on each auto refresh command. DTail predicts the most efficient way to refresh a super-row, issuing either one auto refresh command (refreshing all rows) or multiple RAS-only refresh commands (refreshing rows selectively). As per Section 2.3, auto refresh is more efficient when many rows need to be refreshed in high density DRAMs.

Whenever an RD entry is fetched into the MC, the DTail logic uses it to predict which type of refresh will generate the least overhead. Upon reaching the boundary of a super-row, the gain computation block in Figure 6 computes whether auto refresh should be enabled to refresh the current super-row, and it clears its internal state to compute the choice for the next super-row. If RAS-only refresh is indicated, the per-row RD entries are used to further decide which rows need refreshing. The FIFO depth is equal to the size of a super-row, so FIFO entries will not be consumed until the choice of refresh mode has been made.

This gain computation function can be arbitrarily complex. Our initial implementation checks whether the number of RAS-only refreshes exceeds a given threshold, and if so, it switches to auto refresh. Deriving a smarter algorithm that considers workload characteristics like memory intensiveness and bank-level parallelism is part of ongoing work.

5.2.3 Refresh Issue

If the gain computation indicates that auto refresh is better, a REF command is issued. Otherwise, RAS-only refreshes are used. Each DRAM maintains its own row address counter (RAC), so simply omitting the REF command leaves the RAC in DRAM pointing to the current row.

Here we propose a new refresh command — silent refresh, or $sREF$ — to be added to the DDRx protocol. Upon receiving an $sREF$, the DRAMs increase their RACs, but do not perform the refresh. This synchronizes the RAC values between the MC and the DRAMs. For RAS-only refresh, an unnecessary refresh can be eliminated by omitting the issue of the RAS command.

5.3 Overhead Analysis

DTail incurs storage overheads for the tracked refresh data and fetch-latency and traffic overheads for accessing the data.

Storage Overheads. DTail stores refresh data within the DRAM, which is much cheaper than SRAM or special-purpose registers. For RAS-only refresh, we keep one entry per row in the RD table. In our investigations, we assume four bits suffice to record **RTV** refresh data information for

each 8KB DRAM row (1KB per chip and eight chips per rank). The capacity overhead is thus 4bits/8KB = 0.006%.

Fetch Overheads. The small size and high locality of RD table entries trigger minimal fetch traffic. For example, each memory read typically accesses 64 bytes containing 128 RD table entries. For a four-rank system using 4Gb devices at extended temperature ranges, 256 RD table entries are required (for all rows in a super-row per rank) every $tREFI$, which results in two memory reads every $3.9\mu s$. These RD reads account for 0.77% of the total memory accesses, on average. As density increases, the traffic overhead may grow to 5.61% at 32Gb density. (Average traffic overhead is 3.51% for all but our least memory-intensive workloads.) Nonetheless, evaluation results show that DTail still performs better and saves more energy than prior mechanisms that access RD in SRAMs inside the MC. Sending more reads for each prefetch further reduces the fetch overhead by exploiting row buffer locality to save RAS operations.

Other Runtime Overheads. RD acquisition incurs a few other runtime overheads. For instance, the overhead of paging amounts to checking the status of several (OS) pages in the DRAM row and updating the row's RD, which involves several (but not a great many) memory accesses. For upper-layer RD collection mechanisms, the overheads are a system call to do virtual-to-physical mapping and then several memory accesses to update the RD in DRAM. (We have the kernel do the RD update for security.) The execution overhead depends on how frequently such events happen, and here we assume them to be infrequent. Nonetheless, runtime overheads must be managed properly. For instance, JVM divides the heap into young, old, and permanent generations. Tracking RD for the young generation would require frequent (kernel) address translations: an obvious optimization is to track RD only for the other generations. Addressing the young generation is ongoing work.

6. EVALUATION METHODOLOGY

We briefly describe our tools and workloads.

6.1 Simulation Setup

We evaluate our design space by running traces on the USIMM cycle-accurate memory simulator [5]. The original processor model considers only the reorder buffer and issue/retire widths. To generate reasonable access rates, we augment USIMM to model the load/store queue, multiple load/store ports, a three-level cache hierarchy (including MSHRs), and dependences between memory instructions.

We use Pin [23] to generate memory instruction traces with data dependence hints. We capture the read-after-write (RAW) relationships between non-memory instructions and pass the dependences through the CPU registers to generate memory instruction dependences (similarly to Zsim [32]). We omit write-after-read, write-after-write, and control dependences, and instead assume that ideal register renaming and branch prediction can fully resolve them. The original USIMM memory model uses DDR3 SDRAM. We minimally modify it to model the new features of the JEDEC DDR4 specification (such as bank groups).

Table 4 details the system configuration in our evaluations. We choose a 4:1 core-to-channel ratio, a likely configuration in contemporary high-end and future systems. Table 5 shows timing parameters from the JEDEC DDR4 specification, and Table 1 shows refresh-related parameters.

Table 4: System Configuration

Parameter	Detail
Number of cores	4
Core frequency	3.2GHz
ROB size	128
Issue/retire width	4/2
Pipeline depth	10
Load/store queue size	48/32
Load/store ports	2/1
L1 private Dcache	64KB per core, 4-cycle
L2 private cache	256KB per core, 10-cycle
L3 shared cache	4MB, 40-cycle
MSHR	8 entries per core
Read/write queue size	32/24
Scheduling policy	FC-FRFS, open page
Address mapping	row:rank:bank:column:offset
DRAM frequency	800MHz (DDR4-1600)
DRAM device width	x8
DRAM device density	4Gb/8Gb/16Gb/32Gb
Channels	1
DIMMs per channel	2
Ranks per DIMM	2
Banks per rank	16
Rows per bank	32768/65536/131072/262144
Columns per bank	8192

Table 5: DDR4 Timing Parameters

Timing parameter	Value[a]	Timing parameter	Value
$tRCD$	11	$tWTR\_S$	2
tRP	11	$tWTR\_L$	6
$tCAS$	11	$tRTP$	6
tRC	39	$tCCD\_S$	4
$tRAS$	28	$tCCD\_L$	5
$tRRD\_S$	4	$tCWD$	5
$tRRD\_L$	5	$tRTRS$	2
$tFAW$	20	tXP	5
tWR	12	$tBURST$	4

[a] All timing parameters are in DRAM cycles.

Table 6: DDR4 Power Parameters of 4Gb Devices

Power parameter	IDD	IPP
Supply voltage (VDD/VPP)	1.2V	2.5V
One bank active-precharge current (IDD0/IPP0)	40mA	3mA
Precharge standby current (IDD2N/IPP2N)	30mA	1.8mA
Precharge power-down current (IDD2P/IPP2P)	17mA	1.8mA
Active standby current (IDD3N/IPP3N)	37mA	1.8mA
Active power-down current (IDD3P/IPP3P)	25mA	1.8mA
Burst read current (IDD4R/IPP4R)	125mA	1.8mA
Burst write current (IDD4W/IPP4W)	120mA	1.8mA
Burst refresh current (IDD5B/IPP5B)	110mA	15mA

Table 7: Retention Time Distribution of Evaluated DRAM System

Retention time	Probability of cells	Number of rows @ 4Gb
64-128ms	2.93E-10	40
128-256ms	7.78E-09	1069
256-512ms	1.53E-06	200078
512-1024ms	1.91E-05	1353119
1024-2048ms	3.42E-04	542846
>2048ms	~1.00	0

We enhance the Micron power model [25] to derive energy numbers. The model reflects the activating power supply (VPP) and Pseudo-Open Drain (POD) termination [33] of JEDEC DDR4. Table 6 shows the IDD/IPP currents of a 4Gb DDR4 DRAM device according to the Micron document [26]. We project the IDD/IPP currents of higher density devices: all IDD/IPP currents except IDD5B/IPP5B (burst refresh current) remain the same, assuming that technology scaling compensates for the costs of increasing device density and that the current consumed by auto-refresh increases $1.3\times$ as device density doubles. ($tRFC$ grows much less than $2\times$, which means more rows are refreshed in the same amount of time, which increases current.)

Each simulation models a 1024ms execution (about 3.28 billion cycles at 3.2GHz). We adopt a constant-threshold-based low-power mode management method [6] that incurs less than 2% performance overhead and reduces background power by 35%. We report results at extended temperature ranges since the DRAM operating temperature is usually greater than 85 °C in servers and data centers [21].

6.2 Workloads

To create multiprogrammed workloads from the SPEC CPU2006 benchmark suite [11], we first classify the 29 applications according to memory intensity. We consider an application memory-intensive if the last-level cache misses per kilo instructions (MPKI) is over five. We randomly generate twelve four-program workloads for five intensity categories (based on the number of memory-intensive benchmarks in the mix), creating 60 workloads in total.

To evaluate retention-aware refresh, we extract the retention distribution for a 50nm technology node from Kim and Lee [16] and randomize the physical position of weak cells [2]. Table 7 shows the retention distribution for our evaluated DRAM system using 4Gb devices.

To evaluate validity-aware refresh, we allocate dummy pages in the simulator to model five memory capacity utilization levels. By allocating the desired memory on a real server with 32GB DRAM and scanning the Linux kernel's *mem_map* structure, we obtain the distribution of allocated pages for a 32GB capacity, and on this we base our derivations of distributions for other capacities.

6.3 Metrics

We use *Weighted Speedup* (WS) [34] to measure the system performance of multi-programmed workloads. We normalize each benchmark IPC to that of the solo execution IPC and calculate weighted speedup as the sum of all normalized benchmark IPCs. Since we run each simulation a fixed number of cycles, higher performing mechanisms execute more memory instructions and thus expend more energy. For a fair comparison, we use *Energy Per Access* (EPA) to report DRAM system power.

7. RESULTS

We compare the following mechanisms:

- RL: refresh-less, in which no refresh is performed.
- AR: the auto refresh method.
- ROR: the RAS-only refresh method.
- RAIDR: the Retention-Aware Intelligent DRAM Refresh method proposed by Liu et al. [20]. We track retention information in two Bloom filters (at reasonable storage costs — see Figure 3).
- PARIS: the Placement-Aware Refresh in Situ method proposed by Baek et al. [2], which skips refreshes for rows with invalid data. We use one bit per 32 rows (64 pages), which results in acceptable storage costs and an average performance overhead of 7.95%.[6]
- DTail-R: DTail with retention information.
- DTail-V: DTail with validity information.
- DTail-RV: DTail with combined retention and validity information.

---

[6] Defined as missed opportunities for refresh reduction. Representing more rows per bit reduces storage costs but increases the performance overhead to 14.8% for 64 rows and 28.2% for 128 rows, on average.

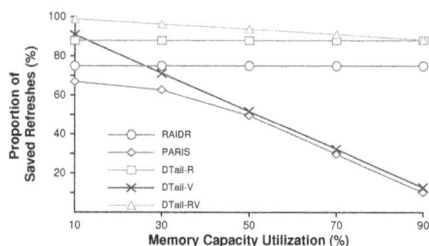

Figure 7: Refresh Reduction of Various Methods

All performance (*weighted speedup*) and power (*energy per access*) results in this section are normalized to those of a refresh-less (RL) system. Recall that Figure 2 shows results for AR and ROR.

7.1 Overview of Refresh Reductions

Figure 7 gives an overview of the number of refreshes saved (compared to a system that always refreshes all rows) by various methods for 4Gb DRAMs under different memory utilization rates. Both RAIDR and DTail-R are based on the process variation of the DRAMs themselves, and thus their behaviors are independent of the utilization rate. RAIDR eliminates 75.0% of total refreshes, and DTail-R eliminates 87.9%. The additional 12.9% comes from DTail-R's storing complete per-row refresh data.

The number of refreshes saved by both PARIS and DTail-V decreases when more memory rows store valid data. DTail-V avoids more refreshes than PARIS, again because it stores complete per-row refresh data. The advantage of DTail-V is more significant at low memory utilization, e.g., an additional 24.0% and 8.45% of refreshes are saved at 10% and 30% memory utilization, respectively. Note that the default Linux buddy page allocator preserves a certain amount of continuity among allocated physical pages, and thus using one bit to represent a small number of pages (rows) results in modest overhead at high memory utilization. However, some advanced page allocation mechanisms [15] may break the continuity, increasing the overhead of PARIS.

By taking advantage of both retention and validity information, DTail-RV saves the most refreshes, from 88.2% at high memory utilization to 98.9% at low memory utilization.

7.2 Retention-Aware Methods

We compare DTail-R with RAIDR [20] to evaluate the retention-aware methods. Figure 8 and Figure 9 show the normalized weighted speedups and energy per access of both methods at 4Gb together with projections for higher densities. Results in the projected figures are averaged across all five categories of memory-intensiveness.

Figure 8(a) shows that RAIDR and DTail-R perform similarly to the ideal refresh-less configuration at 4Gb. RAIDR has already cut down 75% of the refreshes, and the performance impact of the remaining refreshes is negligible, especially when RAS-only refresh can utilize the DRAM bank-level parallelism. DTail-R saves an additional 12.9% of the refreshes, which makes its performance advantage grow as DRAM density increases (Figure 8(b)).

Although the "small" number of refreshes saved by DTail-R compared to RAIDR has little performance impact, the benefit in energy savings is apparent. Figure 9(a) shows that DTail-R consistently saves more energy: compared to

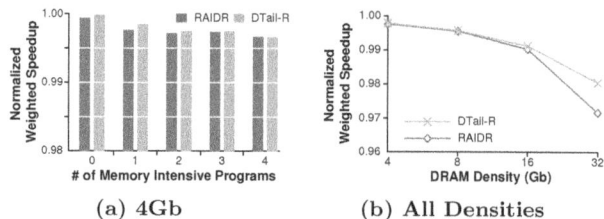

(a) 4Gb (b) All Densities

Figure 8: Performance Comparison between RAIDR and DTail-R (higher is better)

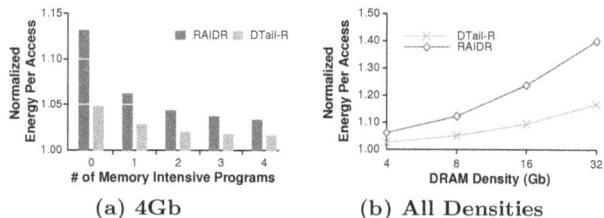

(a) 4Gb (b) All Densities

Figure 9: Power Comparison between RAIDR and DTail-R (lower is better)

RAIDR, DTail-R reduces the energy overhead by an average of 3.54% (up to 8.53%) at 4Gb. Figure 9(b) shows that the benefit grows with DRAM density: from 3.54% energy savings at 4Gb to 23.3% at 32Gb. DTail-R saves about half the refreshes that RAIDR does, but the energy reduction is a bit more than half. For example, at 32Gb the energy overheads of RAIDR and DTail-R compared to a refresh-less system are 40.0% and 16.7%, respectively. This additional energy savings comes from two factors: first, more refreshes force the DRAMs to exit the low power state for low-intensity workloads, increasing background power; second, refresh may unnecessarily precharge open rows that will be reused in the near future, increasing the number of RAS operations and the corresponding energy consumption.

7.3 Validity-Aware Methods

To evaluate the validity-aware methods, we compare DTail-V with PARIS [2]. Figure 10 and Figure 11 show the normalized weighted speedup and energy per access of the two methods at different memory utilizations for various densities. Results are again averaged across all five memory-intensity categories (60 workloads). PARIS fails to work at 32Gb because there is insufficient time to issue all the commands for RAS-only refresh.

Performance decreases and energy consumption increases as the portion of valid DRAM rows grows. For example, Figure 10(c) and Figure 11(c) show that at the 16Gb density the normalized weighted speedup decreases by 14.2% and energy per access increases by 65.2% for PARIS when we go from 10% to 90% memory utilization.

Figure 7 shows that DTail-V saves more refreshes when memory utilization is low (10-30%) because it stores complete refresh data. This contributes to higher performance (Figure 10) and lower energy consumption (Figure 11) at low memory utilization. However, Figure 10(c) and Figure 11(c) show that DTail-V also performs better at high memory utilizations for higher density DRAMs. For example, with 90% memory utilization at 16Gb, DTail-V improves performance by 4.44% and saves energy by 41.7% compared to PARIS. This is because DTail-V dynamically detects the system page placement behavior and chooses between auto

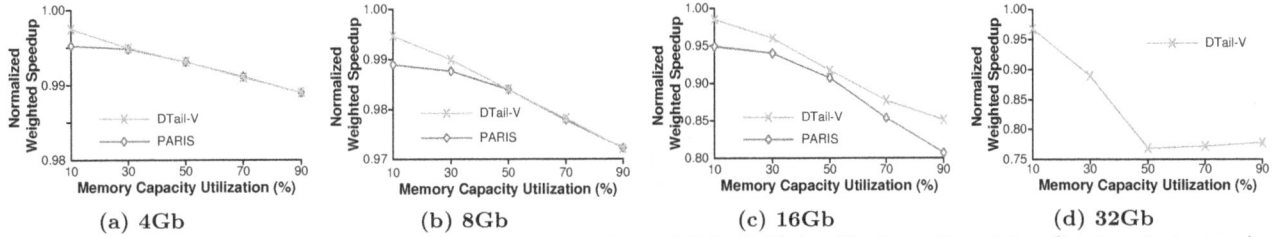

Figure 10: Performance Comparison between PARIS and DTail-V for Various Densities (higher is better)

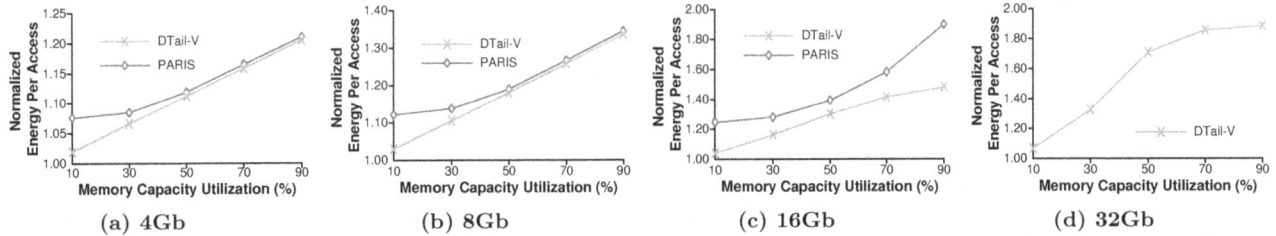

Figure 11: Power Comparison between PARIS and DTail-V for Various Densities (lower is better)

refresh and RAS-only refresh. DTail-V's lack of performance improvement at 50%, 70%, and 90% utilization for 32Gb density is due to our heuristic switching mechanism.

7.4 Combining R and V Information

DTail is easy to reconfigure to adopt both retention and validity information. We call this implementation DTail-RV. Figure 12 and Figure 13 show the performance and energy benefits of DTail-RV at different memory utilizations for various densities. We compare to RAIDR [20] for retention-awareness and to PARIS [2] for validity-awareness. Results are averaged across all five memory-intensivity categories (60 workloads). Recall that PARIS fails to work for 32Gb.

Figure 12 shows that RAIDR and DTail-RV perform close to an ideal refresh-less system. DTail-RV is slightly better than RAIDR, especially at higher densities.

Figure 13 shows that DTail-RV can save significantly more energy than RAIDR and PARIS. Compared to RAIDR and PARIS, DTail-RV reduces energy by 15.8-23.8% and 24.6-81.9% (depending on memory utilization), respectively, for 16Gb DRAMs. For 32Gb DRAMs, the energy savings of DTail-RV relative to RAIDR ranges from 40.0% at 10% memory utilization to 25.9% at 90% memory utilization.

8. CONCLUSION

We have introduced DTail, a low-overhead DRAM refresh-management scheme that stores refresh information within the DRAM itself. This small, intuitive innovation delivers high payoff. The capacity overhead is negligible compared to growing DRAM capacities, and the latency of relatively infrequent accesses is easily masked by prefetching.

Technology trends make frameworks like DTail that store refresh data at negligible cost increasingly attractive. Consider emerging high-density 3D-Stacked DRAM technologies whose (many) more rows greatly increase the amount of refresh data to track. Furthermore, 3D-stacked technologies face thermal challenges that increase leakage, which in turn increases the required refresh frequency (e.g., an 8ms refresh period at 95-115 °C). This raises the performance and energy overheads of performing refresh.

Finally, storing the data in regular memory makes it accessible to all levels of the software stack: making it easier

for hardware and software to collaborate to minimize refresh performance and energy overheads opens up an interesting design space of hybrid refresh approaches.

9. ACKNOWLEDGMENTS

We thank the anonymous reviewers for their valuable feedback. This work is supported by the National Natural Science Foundation of China (NSFC) under grant number 61221062, 61272132, and 61331008, the National Basic Research Program of China (973 Program) under grant number 2011CB302502, the Strategic Priority Research Program of the Chinese Academy of Sciences under grant number XDA06010401, and Huawei Research Program under grant number YBCB2011030. Yungang Bao is partially supported by a CCF-Intel Young Faculty Research Program (YFRP) grant.

10. REFERENCES

[1] A. Agrawal, P. Jain, A. Ansari, and J. Torrellas. Refrint: Intelligent refresh to minimize power in on-chip multiprocessor cache hierarchies. In *High-Performance Computer Architecture*, pages 400–411, Feb 2013.

[2] S. Baek, S. Cho, and R. Melhem. Refresh now and then. *IEEE Transactions on Computers*, 2013.

[3] L. Barroso and U. Hölzle. The datacenter as a computer: An introduction to the design of warehouse-scale machines. *Synthesis Lectures on Computer Architecture*, 4(1):1–108, 2009.

[4] S. Borkar. The exascale challenge. In *Keynote of Parallel Architectures and Compilation Techniques*, Sep 2011.

[5] N. Chatterjee, R. Balasubramonian, M. Shevgoor, S. Pugsley, A. Udipi, A. Shafiee, K. Sudan, M. Awasthi, and Z. Chishti. USIMM: the utah simulated memory module. *University of Utah, Techincal Report UUCS-12-002*, 2012.

[6] V. Delaluz, M. Kandemir, N. Vijaykrishnan, A. Sivasubramaniam, and M. Irwin. DRAM energy management using software and hardware directed power mode control. In *High-Performance Computer Architecture*, pages 159–169, Jan 2001.

[7] P. Emma, W. Reohr, and M. Meterelliyoz. Rethinking refresh: Increasing availability and reducing power in DRAM for cache applications. *IEEE Micro*, 28(6):47–56, 2008.

[8] H. Esmaeilzadeh, A. Sampson, L. Ceze, and D. Burger. Architecture support for disciplined approximate programming. In *Architectural Support for Programming Languages and Operating Systems*, pages 301–312, Mar 2012.

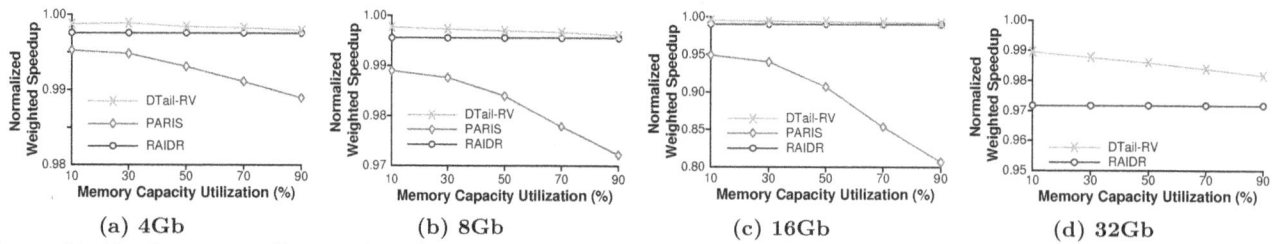

Figure 12: Performance Comparison between RAIDR, PARIS and DTail-RV for Various Densities (higher is better)

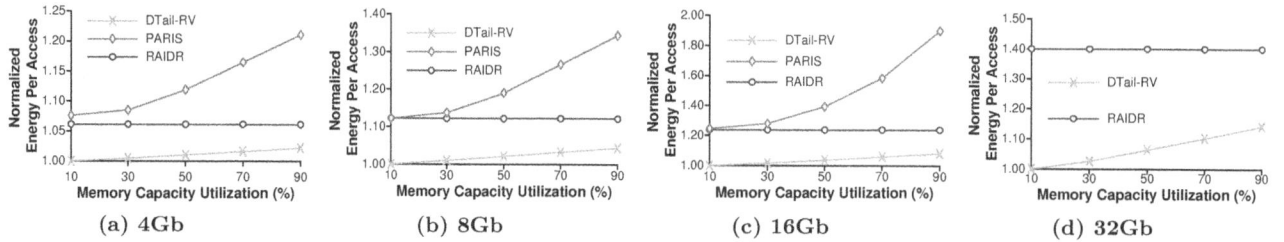

Figure 13: Power Comparison between RAIDR, PARIS and DTail-RV for Various Densities (lower is better)

[9] M. Ghosh and H. Lee. Smart refresh: An enhanced memory controller design for reducing energy in conventional and 3D die-stacked drams. In *MICRO*, pages 134–145, Dec 2007.

[10] T. Hamamoto, S. Sugiura, and S. Sawada. On the retention time distribution of dynamic random access memory (DRAM). *IEEE Transactions on Electron Devices*, 45(6):1300–1309, 1998.

[11] J. Henning. SPEC CPU2006 benchmark descriptions. *ACM SIGARCH Computer Architecture News*, 34(4):1–17, 2006.

[12] C. Isen and L. John. ESKIMO: Energy savings using semantic knowledge of inconsequential memory occupancy for DRAM subsystem. In *MICRO*, pages 337–346, Dec 2009.

[13] JEDEC. JESD79-3E: DDR3 SDRAM specification, 2010.

[14] JEDEC. JESD79-4: DDR4 SDRAM specification, 2012.

[15] R. Kessler and M. Hill. Page placement algorithms for large real-indexed caches. *ACM Transactions on Computer Systems*, 10(4):338–359, 1992.

[16] K. Kim and J. Lee. A new investigation of data retention time in truly nanoscaled DRAMs. *IEEE Electron Device Letters*, 30(8):846–848, 2009.

[17] Y. Kim, V. Seshadri, D. Lee, J. Liu, and O. Mutlu. A case for exploiting subarray-level parallelism SALP in DRAM. In *International Symposium on Computer Architecture*, pages 368–379, Jun 2012.

[18] C. Lefurgy, K. Rajamani, F. Rawson, M. Kistler, and T. Keller. Energy management for commercial servers. *IEEE Computer*, 36(12):39–48, 2003.

[19] J. Liu, B. Jaiyen, Y. Kim, C. Wilkerson, and O. Mutlu. An experimental study of data retention behavior in modern DRAM devices: Implications for retention time profiling mechanisms. In *International Symposium on Computer Architecture*, pages 60–71, Jun 2013.

[20] J. Liu, B. Jaiyen, R. Veras, and O. Mutlu. RAIDR: Retention-aware intelligent DRAM refresh. In *International Symposium on Computer Architecture*, pages 1–12, Jun 2012.

[21] S. Liu, B. Leung, A. Neckar, S. Memik, G. Memik, and N. Hardavellas. Hardware/software techniques for DRAM thermal management. In *High-Performance Computer Architecture*, pages 515–525, Feb 2011.

[22] S. Liu, K. Pattabiraman, T. Moscibroda, and B. Zorn. Flikker: Saving DRAM refresh-power through critical data partitioning. In *Architectural Support for Programming Languages and Operating Systems*, pages 213–224, Mar 2011.

[23] C.-K. Luk, R. Cohn, R. Muth, H. Patil, A. Klauser, G. Lowney, S. Wallace, V. J. Reddi, and K. Hazelwood. Pin: building customized program analysis tools with dynamic instrumentation. In *Programming Language Design and Implementation*, pages 190–200, Jun 2005.

[24] Micron. TN-04-30: Various methods of DRAM refresh, 1999.

[25] Micron. TN-41-01: Calculating memory system power for DDR3, 2007.

[26] Micron. DRAM memory in high-speed digital designs. http://www.home.agilent.com/upload/cmc_upload/All/5Micron.pdf, 2013.

[27] J. Mukundan, H. Hunter, K.-h. Kim, J. Stuecheli, and J. Martínez. Understanding and mitigating refresh overheads in high-density DDR4 DRAM systems. In *International Symposium on Computer Architecture*, pages 48–59, Jun 2013.

[28] P. Nair, C. Chou, and M. Qureshi. A case for refresh pausing in DRAM memory systems. In *High-Performance Computer Architecture*, pages 627–638, Feb 2013.

[29] T. Ohsawa, K. Kai, and K. Murakami. Optimizing the DRAM refresh count for merged DRAM/logic LSIs. In *International Symposium on Low Power Electronics and Design*, pages 82–87, Aug 1998.

[30] P. Restle, J. Park, and B. Lloyd. DRAM variable retention time. In *International Electron Devices Meeting*, pages 807–810, Dec 1992.

[31] A. Sampson, W. Dietl, E. Fortuna, D. Gnanapragasam, L. Ceze, and D. Grossman. EnerJ: approximate data types for safe and general low-power computation. In *Programming Language Design and Implementation*, pages 164–174, Jun 2011.

[32] D. Sanchez and C. Kozyrakis. Zsim: fast and accurate microarchitectural simulation of thousand-core systems. In *International Symposium on Computer Architecture*, pages 475–486, Jun 2013.

[33] J.-H. Shin, S.-I. Kim, Y.-M. Ahn, Y.-K. Han, and S.-J. Seo. Methodology on power estimation of memory modules with pseudo-open drain and center-tab termination type termination schemes. In *Open Server Summit*, Nov 2011.

[34] A. Snavely and D. Tullsen. Symbiotic jobscheduling for a simultaneous mutlithreading processor. *ACM SIGPLAN Notices*, 35(11):234–244, 2000.

[35] J. Stuecheli and D. Kaseridis. Elastic refresh: Techniques to mitigate refresh penalties in high density memory. In *MICRO*, pages 375–384, Dec 2010.

[36] R. Venkatesan, S. Herr, and E. Rotenberg. Retention-aware placement in DRAM (RAPID): software methods for quasi-non-volatile DRAM. In *High-Performance Computer Architecture*, pages 155–165, Feb 2006.

[37] D. Yaney, C. Lu, R. Kohler, M. Kelly, and J. Nelson. A meta-stable leakage phenomenon in DRAM charge storage—variable hold time. In *International Electron Devices Meeting*, pages 336–339, Dec 1987.

Last-level Cache Deduplication

Yingying Tian‡   Samira M. Khan†‡   Daniel A. Jiménez‡   Gabriel H. Loh§

‡Texas A&M University   †Carnegie Mellon University   ‡Intel Labs   §AMD Research

‡{tian,djimenez}@cse.tamu.edu   †samirakhan@cmu.edu   §gabriel.loh@amd.com

ABSTRACT

Caches are essential to the performance of modern microprocessors. Much recent work on last-level caches has focused on exploiting reference locality to improve efficiency. However, value redundancy is another source of potential improvement. We find that many blocks in the working set of typical benchmark programs have the same values. We propose cache deduplication that effectively increases last-level cache capacity. Rather than exploit specific value redundancy with compression, as in previous work, our scheme detects duplicate data blocks and stores only one copy of the data in a way that can be accessed through multiple physical addresses. We find that typical benchmarks exhibit significant value redundancy, far beyond the zero-content blocks one would expect in any program. Our deduplicated cache effectively increases capacity by an average of 112% compared to an 8MB last-level cache while reducing the physical area by 12.2%, yielding an average performance improvement of 15.2%.

1. INTRODUCTION

Caches play an essential role in modern microprocessors to bridge the gap between fast processor speed and high access latency of main memory. A simple solution to improve cache performance is to increase the cache size. However, increased cache size leads to increased power and area consumption. In a chip-multi processor (CMP), often more than half of the chip area is occupied by caches that contribute to significant power consumption [37, 18, 31]. In a conventional cache, each block is associated with a requested memory block address and a copy of the data. Different cache blocks with different addresses can contain copies of identical data. These duplicated blocks waste cache capacity because they store redundant information. As an example, Figure 1 shows the average percentage of duplicated blocks stored in a 2MB last-level cache (LLC) in 18 randomly selected SPEC CPU2006 benchmarks [11]. Thirteen of 18 benchmarks have more than 20% duplicated cache blocks. For benchmarks *zeusmp* and *GemsFDTD*, more than 90% of cache blocks are duplicated. On average, 35% of cache blocks store duplicated data in the LLC.

Cache compression has been proposed to improve effective cache capacity [1, 2, 4, 19, 20, 40, 38, 10, 28]. Storing compressed cache blocks potentially reduces cache misses by increasing effective capacity. However, the processes of com-

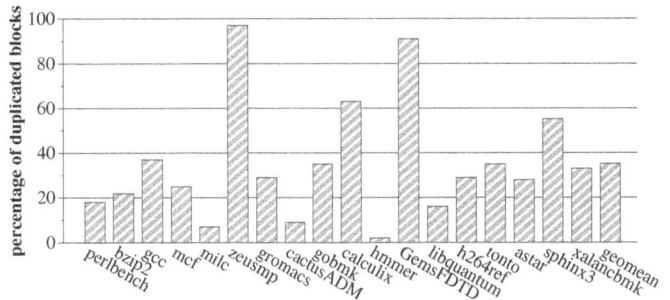

Figure 1: Average percentage of duplicated blocks in LLC.

pression and decompression significantly increase cache access latency, thus degrading performance. The zero-content augmented cache [8] was proposed to reduce the storage of cache blocks that contain null data. Storing only physical addresses and valid bits of null blocks in an augmented cache saves cache area and improves overall performance. However, the percentage of zero-content blocks is relatively small on average, the performance improvement is also small.

We propose cache deduplication to improve performance significantly by exploiting value redundancy to increase effective cache capacity. Cache deduplication eliminates duplicated data stored in the cache. Instead of storing different copies of identical data, duplicated blocks are stored as references to distinct data. The saved capacity can be used to store more blocks to increase the overall effectiveness of the cache, reducing the frequency of costly off-chip memory accesses.

This paper makes the following contributions:

- We find that widespread duplication exists in caches and quantify the cache duplication effect in 18 SPEC CPU2006 benchmarks.

- We propose a unified cache-deduplication technique to improve cache performance with increased effective cache capacity. By exploiting block-level value redundancy, cache deduplication significantly increases cache effectiveness with limited area and power consumption.

- We propose a novel LLC design with cache deduplication. Compared to a conventional LLC, the deduplicated LLC uses similar chip area and power consumption while performing comparably to a double-sized conventional LLC.

Based on our experiments, cache deduplication improves performance by 15.2% compared to a baseline 8MB LLC, which is comparable to a conventional 16MB LLC and superior to 12MB and 14MB caches, while using 12.2% less physical area than a conventional 8MB LLC.

In this paper, Section 2 motivates the proposed technique. Section 2.2 describes cache deduplication in detail, followed by a novel design of deduplicated LLCs in Section 3. Section 4 discusses the experimental methodology we use, followed by the experimental results in Section 5. A detailed analysis is presented in Section 6. Related work is discussed in Section 7, and we conclude in Section 8.

2. MOTIVATION AND CHALLENGES

2.1 Motivation

Conventional cache design wastes capacity because it stores duplicated data. When a memory request is issued, the data fetched from the main memory also is brought into caches for future requests. This data is associated with a tag derived from its physical memory address. However, cache blocks with different block addresses may contain identical data. The same chunk of data is duplicated in the cache because the tags differ.

We measure the percentage of distinct blocks stored in a 2MB 16-way LLC during the execution of 18 SPEC CPU2006 benchmarks, each running for an interval of one billion instructions. We count the number of distinct blocks every 10 million instructions. The ratio of distinct blocks varies with the workload, but there always are duplicated blocks stored in the cache for all the benchmarks. Among the benchmarks, *hmmer* has the smallest percentage of duplicated blocks (2.7% on average) and *zeusmp* has the largest percentage of duplicated blocks (97.8%). On average, 35.1% of cache blocks are duplicated for all the benchmarks.

```
if (serEng.needToStoreObject(objToStore)) {
    int vectorLength = objToStore->size();
    serEng<<vectorLength;
    for ( int i = 0; i < vectorLength; i++) {
        XercesStep* data = objToStore->
            elementAt(i);
        serEng<<data;
    }
}
```
Listing 1: storeObject() in XTemplateSerializer.cpp

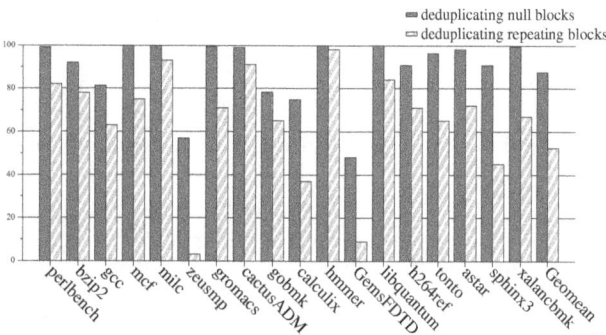

Figure 2: Percentage of distinct blocks for null-block deduplication and all repeating-block deduplication.

This phenomenon happens mainly because of program behaviors and input characteristics. Program behavior such as copying and assignment generate duplicate data stored at different memory locations. Listing 1 shows a code snippet of assignment in the SPEC CPU2006 benchmark *xalancbmk*. Elements in the vector *objToStore* are stored in the buffer

serEng. After running this code, there are two copies of the same data stored in the cache. A similar phenomenon happens with memory operations like $memcpy()$ [1].

Another source of duplication is program input. For example, the input of the SPEC CPU2006 benchmark *zeusmp* is "a spherical blastwave with radius r=0.2 and located at the origin" [11], which contains perfect symmetry, leading to a significant amount of data similarity (97.8% of cache blocks are duplicated in our experiment). Similar input characteristics exist in benchmark *GemsFDTD*, in which more than 90% of cache blocks are duplicated. Symmetric data is common especially in scientific workloads, causing copious duplication of non-zero values.

Previous cache-compression techniques proposed to compress specific values that cause data duplication [1, 8, 28] such as zero. Based on our experiments, eliminating zero-content (null) blocks can save only 13% of the cache capacity, while eliminating all possible duplication leads to 47.5% of cache blocks removed/invalidated, as shown in Figure 2. In other words, almost half of the cache capacity can be saved with data deduplication.

The majority of duplication contains non-zero data values resulting from input and/or computation with a random distribution of the number of copies depending on program behavior. As an example, we take a random execution point of *xalancbmk* to show the nature of duplication degree and duplicated data. At a random execution point, in a 2MB cache, there are 14,931 distinct blocks out of 29,278 of cache blocks (i.e., 51% of blocks are distinct). There are 2,414 chunks of data associated with two tags each, so 16% of blocks are duplicated once. There are 1,157 zero-content blocks. If only zero-content blocks are compressed, only 4% of total capacity is saved. If all the duplication can be eliminated from the cache, more than 38% of the capacity of the 2MB cache can be saved, which is about three times larger than a modern processor's typical 256KB L2 cache.

2.2 Challenges of Cache Deduplication

Data deduplication is a specific compression technique to eliminate duplicated copies of repeating data. It has been used widely in disk-based storage systems [6, 39, 12]. With data deduplication, only a single instance of identical data is stored physically. The redundant data is stored as references to the corresponding data in a deduplicated data storage to improve storage utilization. Although commonly used in disk storage and main-memory compression, data deduplication is a challenge in caches with limited overhead due to the following concerns:

How to detect duplication: The first challenge is the way to compare data to detect possible duplication. Duplication can be detected by comparing the analyzed data either with all the stored data or to a specific part of a tree-based data array. Because caches contain a large number of blocks, direct comparison with all blocks is prohibitively expensive. A tree-based structure requires more metadata to maintain the tree while the time complexity is still too high for a large number of nodes. Indexing using a hash function is a fast solution to find the data with which to compare. However, simply using a hash function to index the data array is inefficient because of underutilization of

---

[1] Some compilers and ISAs generate specialized code so that certain copies bypass the cache. For instance, Intel's C compiler and libraries will use a non-temporal store for $memcpy()$ if the size of the data moved is larger than 256KB [9]. However, shorter instances of copying continue to lead to significant cache data duplication.

the data array. A practical duplication-detection technique must be fast as well as storage-efficient.

When to detect duplication: The second challenge is the point at which to process duplication detection. Caches play an important role in bridging the performance gap between processors and the main memory, in which access latency is critical to the overall system performance. The process of duplication detection should not affect the cache latency.

Deduplication granularity: Previous work [40, 38, 2, 1, 8, 28] used sub-block level granularity to compress all possible compressible data. Granularity at the sub-block-level may lead to a higher rate of deduplication, but it also causes increased access latency, additional power overhead, and more complex hardware design. Although the effective capacity can be increased more with sub-block-level deduplication, the system performance may be degraded because of the increased access latency. The trade-offs among compression degree and increased cache latency and overhead makes compression granularity another challenge for cache deduplication.

Write hit and replacement of duplicated blocks: The last challenge in cache deduplication design is dealing with write hits and replacement of duplicated blocks. When a store instruction writes duplicate data, the updated block must be allocated a new entry to differentiate from the previous value. When duplicate data is invalidated or evicted from a deduplicated cache, all tags that are associated with this data also should be invalidated. Previous work proposed storing all possible tags in each data entry [23], which is impractical in a cache design due to the limited capacity. An intelligent and low-overhead data management is required in a practical cache deduplication design.

3. DEDUPLICATED LAST-LEVEL CACHE

We propose a practical LLC design eliminating duplicated cache blocks that we call a deduplicated LLC. To address the challenges cited in the previous section, deduplicated LLC uses augmented hashing to detect duplication, which is fast and makes the most of the utilization of the cache capacity. It uses post-process detection [17] to hide possibly increased cache latency. It uses block-level-deduplication granularity to compare the analyzed block with the data already stored in the cache, regardless of its content, to exploit data duplication fully with limited overhead. For the replacement policy of the duplicated blocks, we propose the distinct-first random replacement (DFRR) policy for efficiency.

3.1 Structure

Figure 3 shows the structure of a deduplicated LLC. It consists of three decoupled structures: a tag array, a data array, and a hash table. With cache deduplication, the mapping from the data store to the tag store is no longer one-to-one. The structure of the data store is decoupled from that of the tag store. The data array is used only to place distinct data, while the tag array keeps the semantics of cache blocks by storing blocks with tags, pointers to the data array, and other metadata. More than one tag can share a data block. Cache-management techniques (e.g., intelligent replacement policy, increased number of blocks, and so on) are related only to the tag array. With the decoupled structures, changes in the tag array need not affect the design of the data array.

3.1.1 Tag Array

The tag array is a set-associative structure that keeps the semantics of cache blocks. Each entry in the tag array contains the following fields: required metadata of a cache block as in a conventional cache (e.g., tag bits, LRU bits, valid bit, and dirty bit), a reference that indexes the data array, and two references that point to other tag entries that maintain a doubly-linked list of tags all pointing to the same data block. The reference to a data entry, referred to as a *tag-to-data pointer (Tptr)*, identifies a distinct entry in the data array. When there is a tag match, *Tptr* directly indexes the data associated with this cache block. When a tag is inserted in the tag array, it also is inserted into the doubly-linked list of tags of duplicated blocks (if there are any) associated with the corresponding data.

When a tag is replaced from the tag array, it also is deleted from the linked list. With these pointers, all tags stored in the tag array that share identical data are linked. The linked list of tags of duplicated blocks is referred to as the tag-list and the two pointers in each tag entry are referred to as tag-list pointers. When there is a replacement in the data array, all associated tags can be tracked along with the tag-list of the data block and invalidated. The replacement of the data array will be discussed in Section 3.2.3; in practice, this process has very low latency. The tag array can be treated as a conventional cache storing only metadata. It uses requested memory addresses to search specific sets for matching tags. When cache misses occur, the tag array uses the regular cache replacement policy (i.e., least-recently used (LRU) to choose replacement candidates rather than replacement in the data array, which uses the DFRR policy).

In our experiments, we use the traditional least-recently-used (LRU) replacement policy in the tag array for fair evaluation. The left-most structure shown in Figure 3 gives an example of the tag array in a deduplicated LLC. This tag array is a 4-way set-associative structure, with three sets. As shown at the bottom of the structure, the second (from left to right) tag entry in *set[2]* contains the tag *t9*, the *Tptr* that indexes the corresponding data *d1 - 0x1*. One tag-list pointer to the previous block in the tag-list - *t6* and the other tag-list pointer is set as NULL because there is no next block of *t9*. As drawn in bold in Figure 3, Blocks t3, t2, t1, t5, t4, and t8 are in the tag-list of duplicated data *d0*, and t6 and t9 are in their own list. Blocks t7 and t10 are distinct blocks, because there is only one tag in the tag-list of each data block.

3.1.2 Data Array

Each entry in the data array contains a data frame, a counter, a pointer, and a one-bit deduplication flag. The counter (referred to as *Ctr*) indicates the number of tags stored in the tag array that share this data. When a tag is inserted into the tag array, the corresponding *Ctr* in the data array is incremented by 1. When a tag is replaced or invalidated from the tag array, the corresponding *Ctr* is decremented by 1. When a *Ctr* becomes zero, the data block can be reused. The pointer (referred to as a data-to-tag pointer (Dptr)) identifies the head of the tag-list. *Dptr*s of invalid entries are used to keep a free list of available data entries. The one-bit deduplication flag indicates whether the current data block has been analyzed for deduplication (discussed in Section 3.3). The data array can be treated as a direct-mapped cache, accessed only by *Tptr*s from the corresponding tag entries. The structure shown in the middle of Figure 3 gives an example of a data array. There are six entries in the data array; four of them are valid. Data *d0*, located in *0x0*, is shared by six blocks (*Ctr* equals 6), heading with tag *t3* in the tag-list. Data blocks *d2* and *d3* are distinct blocks, linking to only one tag each, *t7* and

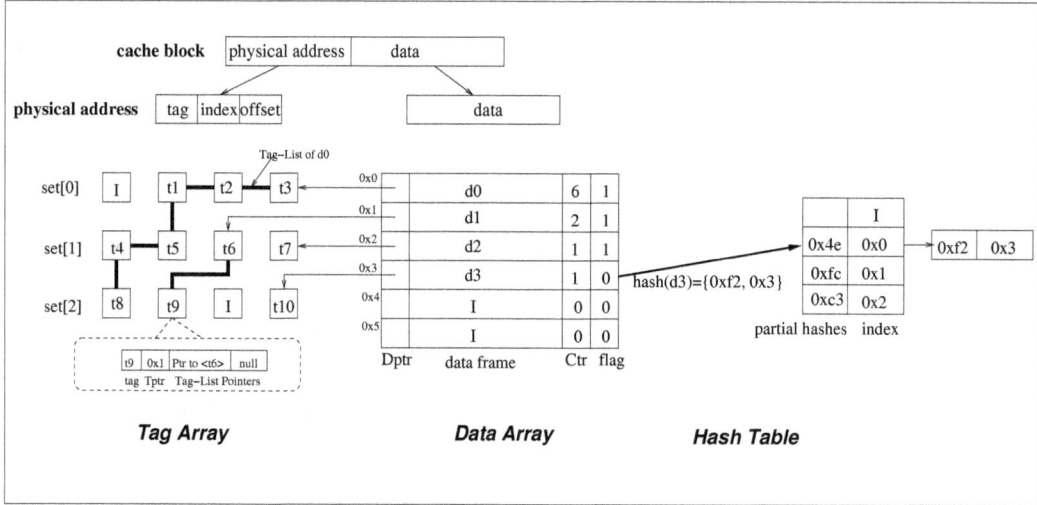

Figure 3: Structure of a deduplicated LLC. Blocks t1, t2, t3, t4, t5 and t8 are duplicated blocks, sharing identical data d0; t6 and t9 share data d1; t7 is a distinct block with data d2; and, t10 is inserted as a distinct block and has not been analyzed for deduplication yet.

t10, respectively. However, *d3* has not been analyzed for duplication detection yet (i.e., the flag is unset).

3.1.3 Hash Table

The third structure in deduplicated LLC is an augmented hash table. We use an augmented hash table to implement a two-level look-up to make the most of the cache capacity. The first level of look-up occurs in the hash table indexed by the hashed data, and the second level occurs in the data array redirected by the indices stored in the hash node. To reduce the number of hash collisions, the hash table is implemented as a sequence of small associative arrays representing buckets. Each node in a bucket contains a 16-bit pointer indexing the data array, a 1-bit valid bit, and a 15-bit partial-hash value.

On each duplication detection, the new data are hashed to a hash table entry containing a bucket of nodes as shown in the right-most structure in Figure 3. To reduce access to the data array, each node stores a partial hash value as well as the index into the data array. The new data is compared with indexed data only if the partial hash values match. For the hash function, we use five-level exclusive-OR gates using the same technology used for hashing long branch history for high-performance branch predictors [35]. Each level of the exclusive-OR gate halves the number of bits by taking the exclusive-OR of the upper half of the input bits with the lower half of the input bits. Hashing is completed within one cycle assuming a clock period of at least 10 FO4 delays.

Based on our experiments, a small hash table is sufficient to keep the percentage of hash collisions extremely low (less than 1%). However, hash collisions are practically unavoidable when hashing a large set of possible keys (cache data). We describe hash collision resolution in Section 3.4.

3.2 Operations

A deduplicated cache has different operations on cache hits and cache misses. On a cache access, the tag of the requested block is compared in parallel with all tags in a specific set of the tag array. If the look-up fails, a cache miss has occurred; otherwise, a cache hit has occurred.

3.2.1 Cache Miss

On a cache miss, the requested block is brought from the main memory as in a conventional cache. The placement of the cache block then is separated into two parts: placement in the tag array and placement in the data array. The data of the block is placed in an invalid data entry randomly chosen from the free list maintained using the *Dptr*s. The tag of the block is placed in the corresponding set of the tag array indexed using the memory address. The *Tptr* in the tag entry and the *Dptr* in the data entry then are updated to point to each other, and *Ctr* is increased by 1. If there is no invalid entry in the set of the tag array, the regular replacement policy (LRU in our experiments) is used to choose a replacement victim. If there is no invalid entry in the data array, we use DFRR to choose a data replacement victim (detailed in Section 3.2.3).

At this time, the requested cache block is not analyzed for duplication (with the deduplication flag unset). Instead, it is placed in the cache directly with an unset deduplication flag, indicating it has not been processed for deduplication, and without incurring any deduplication latency. The duplication detection to this block will not be launched until next cache miss occurs, as described in Section 3.3. The corresponding hash node of the data replacement victim then is invalidated.

3.2.2 Cache Hit

A cache hit can be either a read hit or a write hit. In a deduplicated cache, write hits modify the data of blocks, incurring re-hash of the updated data for another duplication detection, while read hits are unrelated to deduplication. Thus, the operations on read hits and write hits are different:

- When there is a read hit in the tag array, the *Tptr* in the matching entry directly indexes the data array to retrieve the requested data. Replacement information then is updated in the tag array. The data array is unchanged.

- When there is a write hit in the tag array, the requested data is indexed by the *Tptr*. If it is a distinct block (*Ctr* equals 1), the data can be modified immediately and the deduplication flag is unset to indicate an unanalyzed block. If it is a duplicated block, instead of modifying the data array directly, an invalid data entry is allocated to place the updated data. In this case, the write hit to a duplicated data is processed similar to a cache miss. Then the dirty bit in the tag entry is updated as well as the replacement information.

3.2.3 Distinct-first Random Replacement

We use a DFRR policy in data array replacement. To find a replacement candidate, the DFRR policy goes to a random position of the data array and checks if the data is distinct. If it is distinct, the entry is chosen as replacement victim; if not, another random entry is checked. To limit the amount of checking, up to four locations can be checked on each replacement. If there is no distinct block among the checked blocks, the block with the fewest duplicates out of the four entries is replaced. Corresponding tag entries are back-invalidated in the tag array to maintain integrity.

Based on our experiments, on each data replacement, on average 1.004 blocks are checked randomly to find the replacement victim. The intuition behind DFRR is that no invalid data entry means there are too many distinct blocks, so one or two random checks will be enough to find a distinct block to replace. The latency of finding a new data entry can be hidden completely.

3.3 An Example of Hash-based Post-Process Deduplication

We propose to use hash-based post-process duplication detection to process deduplication fast with limited overhead. Hash-based post-process duplication detection is launched on LLC misses to avoid possible increased latency. The cache block that is under deduplication detection is blocked. Delaying the detection process until the cache is less busy and the processed block has less chance to be accessed (due to locality) helps avoid dynamically increased cache latency. Figure 4 gives an example of how it works. In this example, the tag array is a 4-way associative structure with two sets, the data array has three entries, and the hash table has four buckets. Each bucket contains a chain of two nodes. Each valid tag entry contains a *Tptr* pointing to the corresponding data entry. For simple illustration, we do not show the replacement states in the tag array, nor do we show *Dptrs*, *Ctrs*, and deduplication flags in the data array.

On a cache miss to Block A, the requested block is fetched from the main memory. The tag is inserted in the tag array and the data $d1$ is inserted in an invalid data entry, as in Step 1. On the next cache miss to Block B, during the memory access time, the previously placed data $d1$ of Block A is detected for duplication. The hash value of $d1$ indexes a bucket in the hash table (Step 2). Because the bucket is empty, the location of $d1$ and its hash value $hd1$ are placed in this bucket. After Block B is fetched from the memory, it is filled in the cache (Step 3).

On a cache miss to Block C, the previously placed data $d2$ of Block B needs duplication detection. The bucket of $d2$ is also empty, so the position of $d2$, $0x1$, and its hash value $hd2$ are inserted in the bucket (Step 4). Block C later is filled in the cache by placing the tag in the tag array and inserting the data in an empty data entry at $0x2$ (Step 5).

On a cache miss to Block D, the data of Block C (located at $0x2$) hashes to a bucket containing a hash value $hd1$ and index $0x0$. Because the hash of the data of Block C equals $hd1$, the data is compared with the data located at $0x0$, resulting in a match (Step 6). Thus, the *Tptr* of Block C is updated to $0x0$, and the data entry in $0x2$ is invalidated (Step 7). The *Dptr* of $d1$ is updated to point to Block C.

After requested Block D is fetched, it is filled in the cache by placing its data in the empty entry at $0x2$ (Step 8).

On a cache miss to Block E, the previously placed data $d4$ of Block D is analyzed for deduplication. The hash value of $d4$ does not equal the one stored in the hash node, so there is no further data comparison. A hash collision incurs. The location of $d4$ and its hash value are inserted in the chain of the hashed bucket (Step 9).

3.4 Hash Collision Resolution

Hash collisions are unavoidable with a practical hash function. In a deduplicated cache, a hash collision occurs when the hash bucket is full. Thus, a strategy is required for hash collision resolution:

- If there is a distinct block indexed in the current bucket, this block is back-invalidated from the data array and the tag array, respectively. The bucket node then is updated to the location of the colliding data. This procedure can be treated as a replacement in a hash bucket.

- Because of the extremely low probability (lower than 0.1% in our experiments), if data indexed in the current bucket are all duplicated, no replacement occurs in this bucket. The current deduplication procedure just exits and a new detection is launched if there is any unanalyzed data. In this case, we may lose a chance to eliminate a possibly duplicated block. However, it will not cause any extra cache misses to degrade the cache performance because the mapping from the tag to the data is kept one to one.

Based on our experiments, a hash bucket with 16 nodes is sufficient to keep the rate of hash collision as low as 1%. We give detailed analysis concerning hashing in Section 6.4.

4. METHODOLOGY

This section outlines the experimental methodology used in this work.

4.1 Simulation Environment

We use the MARSSx86 cycle-accurate simulator [26], a full-system simulation of the x86-64 architecture that runs both single-core and multi-core workloads to evaluate the proposed deduplicated LLC. It models an out-of-order 4-wide x86 processor with a 128-entry re-order buffer and coherent caches with MESI protocol as well as on-chip interconnections.

The micro-architectural parameters are consistent with Intel Core i7 processors [21], including a three-level cache hierarchy: L1 I-caches and L1 D-caches, L2 caches, and a shared LLC. The L1 and L2 caches are private to each core. The L1 I-cache and D-cache are 4-way 32KB each and the L2 cache is unified 8-way 256KB. The shared LLC is a unified 16-way 2MB-per-core cache. The default replacement policy for each cache is LRU. Access latencies to the L1 cache, L2 cache, LLC, and main memory are 4, 10, 40, and 250 cycles respectively, in keeping with the methodology of recent cache research work [13, 15, 14, 7]; we show in Section 6.6 that our results are not changed significantly with alternate latencies. For the deduplicated LLC, both the number of sets and the associativity of the tag array can be increased to accommodate more blocks. We evaluate both ideas by doubling the number of sets and associativity of the tag array, respectively. The reason to double the size of the tag array is to compare the duplicated LLC with a double-sized conventional LLC. The actual size of the tag array can

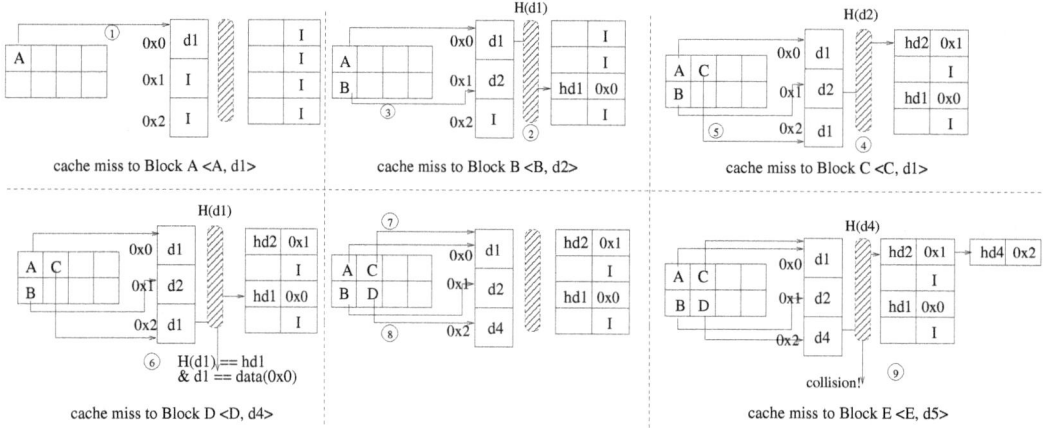

Figure 4: An example of hash-based post-process last-level cache deduplication.

be increased arbitrarily to achieve better performance with commensurate power and area consumption. Based on the experiments, the evaluated deduplicated LLC with a double-sized tag array fits in the area of the LLC of the baseline. We show a detailed cost analysis in Section 6.

The replacement policy in the tag array is LRU, while the replacement policy in the data array is the proposed DFRR.

We also compare our work with two cache-compression techniques: adaptive cache compression [1] and ZCA cache [8]. With adaptive cache compression, the L1 and L2 caches have the same configuration as in a conventional cache hierarchy. Data stored in L1 and L2 caches are uncompressed and only the LLC supports compression. The compressed LLC is a unified 16-way (up to 32-way dynamically) 2MB-per-core set-associative cache with decoupled tag and data stores. Instead of storing a 64-byte data block, the data store is broken into 8-byte segments. An uncompressed 64-byte block is stored as eight 8-byte segments, while a compressed block is compressed into one to seven segments. Data segments are stored continuously in each set with tag order. We conservatively ignore the very high cost of replacement in the contiguous storage variant of the compressed cache.

In our experiments, the access latency of a compressed LLC is constant at 24 cycles. We ignore the decompression latency of 5 cycles to evaluate the cache-deduplication technique better. We also assume that the compression process, occurring on each LLC replacement, can be hidden by the memory-access latency. Thus, the extra compression latency is ignored in our experiments.

With the ZCA cache technique, the L1 and L2 caches have the same configuration as the baseline. The L3 cache is a 2MB-per-core set-associative main cache along with an 8,192-entry, 8-way ZCA cache consuming 156KB of storage overhead. Because accesses to the ZCA cache are in parallel with accesses to the main cache, the access latency is unchanged.

4.2 Benchmarks

The benchmarks used in the experiments are selected randomly from the SPEC CPU2006 benchmark suite. We use SimPoint [29] to identify a single one-billion-instruction characteristic interval (i.e., SimPoint) of each benchmark. Each benchmark is compiled for the x86-64 instruction set and run with the first *ref* input provided by the *runspec* command. Benchmarks are categorized into three groups based on the average percentage of duplicated blocks:

- *Deduplication-sensitive benchmarks*: average percentage of duplicated blocks is greater than 50%;

- *Deduplication-friendly benchmarks*: average percentage of duplicated blocks is between 20% and 50%; and,

- *Deduplication-insensitive benchmarks*: average percentage of duplicated blocks is lower than 20%.

Table 1 shows the group and the percentage of duplicated blocks of each benchmark as well as the LLC misses per 1,000 instructions (MPKI), instructions per cycle (IPC), and the number of instructions fast-forwarded (FFWD) to reach the interval given by SimPoint in a baseline system. Memory-intensive benchmarks are shown in boldface.

Group	Benchmark	% Duplicated Blocks	MPKI (LRU)	IPC (LRU)	FFWD
Dedup-sensitive (S)	zeusmp	97.1%	9.05	0.580	405B
	GemsFDTD	90.6%	16.46	0.466	1060B
	calculix	63%	0.04	1.130	4433B
	sphinx3	54.6%	9.00	0.530	3195B
Dedup-friendly (F)	gcc	37.3%	1.38	1.292	64B
	gobmk	34.9%	0.35	1.072	133B
	tonto	34.9%	0.04	1.259	44B
	xalancbmk	33.4%	35.95	0.144	178B
	h264ref	30%	0.09	1.700	8B
	gromacs	28.8%	0.59	1.244	1B
	astar	27.9%	9.7	0.366	185B
	mcf	24.7%	83.54	0.126	370B
	bzip2	22.1%	0.886	1.127	368B
Dedup-insensitive (I)	perlbench	18.2%	1.67	0.882	541B
	libquantum	16.1%	24.82	0.162	2666B
	cactusADM	9%	24.7	0.22	81B
	milc	7%	1.01	1.299	272B
	hmmer	2.7%	2.75	0.844	942B

Table 1: The 18 SPEC CPU2006 benchmarks with LLC cache misses per 1,000 instructions for LRU, instructions per cycle for LRU in a 2MB cache, and number of instructions fast-forwarded to reach the simpoint (B = billions). Memory-intensive benchmarks in **boldface**.

For multi-core workloads, we randomly generate 12 mixes of quad-core workloads from the 18 benchmarks, listed in Table 2 with their characteristics of duplication. Each benchmark in a workload runs simultaneously with the others, restarting after one billion instructions, until all of the benchmarks have executed at least two billion instructions.

5. EXPERIMENTAL RESULTS

In this section we analyze the performance and overhead of cache deduplication.

Mixes	Benchmarks
mix1 (FFSF)	gcc, gobmk, zeusmp, xalancbmk
mix2 (ISSF)	milc, sphinx3, zeusmp, gobmk
mix3 (SSSF)	GemsFDTD, zeusmp, calculix, xalancbmk
mix4 (FFSS)	astar, gobmk, calculix, GemsFDTD
mix5 (FISF)	sphinx3, milc, zeusmp, xalancbmk
mix6 (IFSS)	hmmer, gcc, sphinx3, calculix
mix7 (IFFF)	hmmer, gcc, xalancbmk, gromacs
mix8 (FSSF)	gcc, calculix, GemsFDTD, h264ref
mix9 (FFII)	gobmk, gromacs, hmmer, perlbench
mix10 (FIIF)	h264ref, hmmer, libquantum, xalancbmk
mix11 (IISF)	libquantum, hmmer, GemsFDTD, tonto
mix12 (ISFF)	perlbench, zeusmp, mcf, gcc

Table 2: 12 mixes of quad-core workload ('F' stands for deduplication-friendly, 'S' for deduplication-sensitive and 'I' for deduplication-insensitive).

5.1 Performance Improvement

In a deduplicated cache, both the number of sets and the associativity of the tag array can be increased to place more cache blocks. In a compressed cache, the number of sets cannot be increased and the associativity is increased dynamically up to twice as large as an uncompressed cache. In a ZCA cache, up to 64MB null blocks can be mapped.

We compare the performance of each technique with a double-sized conventional cache as an upper bound (doubled-sets). In our experiments, we show the performance improvement (normalized to an 8MB conventional LLC) of an 8MB compressed LLC, an 8MB deduplicated LLC with doubled number of sets (16,384 sets, 16-way), an 8MB deduplicated LLC with doubled associativity (8,192 sets, 32-way), an 8MB conventional LLC with a 8,192-entry ZCA cache, and a 16MB conventional LLC (16,384 sets, 16-way).

Figure 5 shows the LLC cache misses normalized to an 8MB conventional LLC of each technique for quad-core workloads. On average, ZCA cache reduces the LLC misses by 5.5%. Cache compression reduces the LLC misses by 12%. Cache deduplication in a doubled-set LLC reduces average misses by 18.5%. Cache deduplication in a doubled-associativity LLC reduces average misses by 19%. The doubled-size conventional LLC reduces the cache misses by 18.4%.

Reducing cache misses translates into improved performance. Figure 6 shows the performance improvement of each technique normalized to an 8MB conventional LLC. The ZCA cache improves performance by 6.9%. The compressed cache yields an average speed-up of 10.8% compared to the baseline. Cache deduplication in a doubled-set LLC gives an improvement of 15%, and cache deduplication in a doubled-associativity LLC yields a speed-up of 15.2%. The upper-bound 16MB conventional cache delivers an average speed-up of 15.1% compared to the 8MB baseline. A 12MB conventional LLC delivers an 8.7% speed-up, and a 14MB LLC delivers an 8.9% speed-up.

Overall, the deduplicated LLC performs comparably to a double-sized conventional LLC.

6. DETAILED ANALYSIS

In this section, we give detailed analysis of cache deduplication with respect to capacity, storage, and power overhead, hashing effectiveness, and the cache sensitivity to different sizes of hash table.

6.1 Effective Cache Capacity

Figure 7 shows the average amount of duplication in each quad-core workload. On average, each block of data stored in the data array is shared by 2.23 tags. In other words,

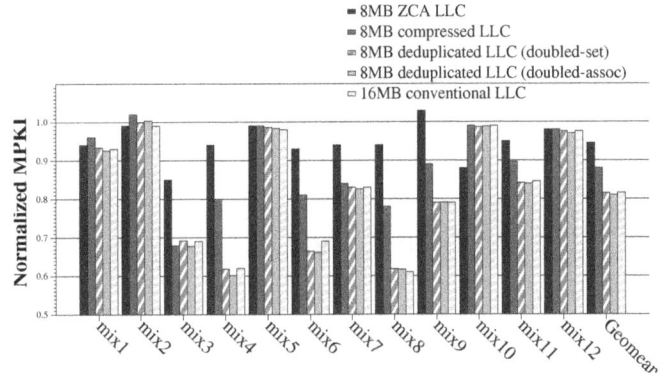

Figure 5: Reduction in LLC misses normalized to 8MB conventional LLC.

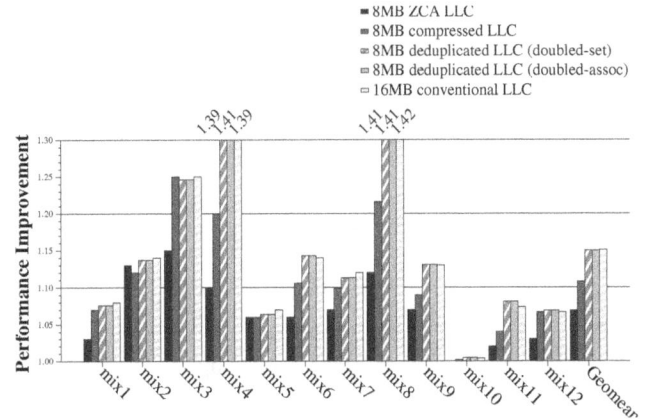

Figure 6: Performance Improvement normalized to 8MB conventional LLC.

effective cache capacity is increased by 112% with cache deduplication. For workloads mix6, mix7, mix9, mix10, and mix11, which all contain the most deduplication-insensitive benchmark *hmmer*, cache deduplication still works by eliminating duplication by about 38%.

6.2 Storage

Although the effective capacity is increased, the physical area is reduced. Table 3 shows the detailed storage requirements of both the baseline and the deduplicated LLC in a quad-core CMP. The 8MB deduplicated LLC occupies 87.8% of the physical area of a conventional 8MB LLC (i.e., it reduces physical area by 12.2% compared to the conventional LLC). The area savings lead to reduced leakage power cost, as shown in Section 6.3.

6.3 Power and Energy

Table 4 shows the results of CACTI 6.5 simulations [24] to determine the leakage and dynamic power of the deduplicated LLC compared to the conventional LLC. The tag array is modeled as the tag store of a conventional 16MB set-associative cache. The data array is modeled as a 4MB direct-mapped cache with 37 bits of tags. The hash table is modeled as the data store of a 512KB direct-mapped cache with block size of 4 bytes.

Due to the nature of deduplicated caches, accesses to the LLC are increased while accesses to the main memory are decreased. Based on the experiments, compared to an 8MB

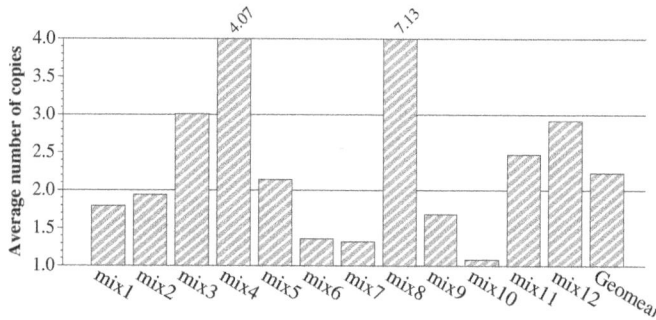

Figure 7: Average amount of duplication.

	Conventional LLC	Deduplicated LLC
Each tag store entry contains:		
Tag	29 bits	28 bits
Status (valid+dirty+LRU)	6 bits	6 bits
Tptr	-	17 bits
Rptrs	-	36 bits
Number of tag entries	131,072	262,144
Total size of tag store	560KB	2784KB
Each data store entry contains:		
Data	512 bits	512 bits
Dptr	-	18 bits
Ctr	-	18 bits
Dedup flag	-	1 bit
Number of data entries	131,072	65,536
Total size of data store	8192KB	4392KB
Additional structure(s):		
Size of hash table	-	8,192
Length of chain	-	16
Size of node	-	32 bits
Total size of hash table	-	512KB
TOTAL SIZE	8,752KB	7,688KB

Table 3: Storage cost analysis.

conventional cache, the number of accesses to the tag array of the 8MB deduplicated cache is increased by 38% and the number of accesses to the data array is increased by 33%. The number of accesses to the off-chip main memory is decreased by 26% with the deduplicated cache.

Compared to the energy cost of accessing caches, the energy cost of accessing the off-chip memory is significantly higher. According to the results of previous work [33], the energy consumed to activate and precharge a page and to read a block is $5nJ$ with a row buffer size of 8KB. Thus, as shown in Table 5, the average dynamic energy consumption of the deduplicated LLC accesses is 3.3% higher than that of the conventional LLC, while the dynamic energy cost of the memory accesses is reduced by 34.5% with the deduplicated LLC.

	Structures	Dynamic Energy per Read Port (nJ)	Dynamic Power per Read Port at max freq (W)	Leakage Power per Bank (W)
Conventional	Tag store	0.0389	0.0605	0.5205
	Data store	1.3148	2.0482	3.0297
	Total	1.3537	2.1087	3.5502
Deduplicated	Tag array	0.1225	0.2564	0.9207
	Data array	0.8793	2.3149	1.8441
	Hash table	0.0234	0.0746	0.0445
	Total	1.0543	2.6534	2.9278

Table 4: Dynamic and leakage power of each LLC design.

6.4 Hashing

Number of Look-ups.

Figure 8 shows the average number of look-ups in each deduplication process. On each duplication detection, the analyzed data is compared with all the data indexed in the hash bucket until a match occurs or it mismatches with all the data. On average, there are 4.9 look-ups in each

	Structures	Dynamic Energy (J)
Conventional	Tag store	0.0005
	Data store	0.0175
	Memory	0.0222
Deduplicated	Tag array	0.0021
	Data array	0.0156
	Hash table	0.0009
	Memory	0.0165

Table 5: Dynamic energy cost of each LLC and main memory.

duplication detection. The number of look-ups is related to the deduplication latency, described in Section 6.5. For workloads such as mix6, mix10, and mix11, the number of look-ups is higher because of the nature of deduplication-insensitive benchmarks: most analyzed data is distinct, causing more look-ups in each duplication detection.

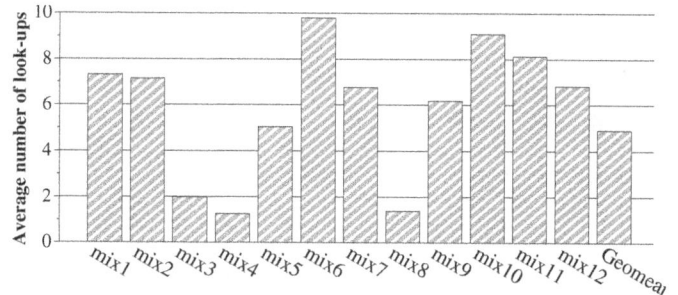

Figure 8: Average number of look-ups for data comparison.

Hash Collisions.

With a practical hash algorithm, hash collisions are unavoidable. Figure 9 shows the average percentage of hash collisions for each quad-core workload. On average, the percentage of hash collisions is as low as 1%.

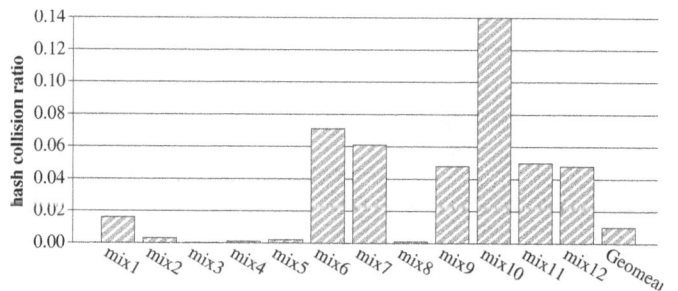

Figure 9: Hash collision.

6.5 Process Latency

The deduplication latency is hidden by the memory access. On each LLC miss, the duplication detection is launched to analyze a previously stored cache block. The analyzed data is hashed to a bucket and compared with all the data indexed in that bucket until a match occurs or mismatches with all the indexed data. Data comparison is completed well within one cycle using a simple circuit, assuming 12 FO4 delays [2]. Thus, the duplication detection takes *(number of look-ups × (1 + data comparison))* cycles on average, which is less than 10 cycles and thus totally hidden by the memory-access latency of 250 cycles.

In adaptive cache compression, as claimed in [1, 2], compression latency is 3 cycles and decompression latency is 5 cycles. The extra access latency is on the critical path to degrade performance. Even if the compression latency of 3 cycles can be hidden by the memory-access latency, the decompression latency is unavoidable.

6.6 Hash Table Sensitivity

The size of the hash table in our experiments is 8,192 buckets with 16 nodes per bucket, leading to a 512KB storage overhead. Reducing the size of the hash table to 4,096 buckets leads to an increased number of look-ups of 5.7 on average, and the percentage of hash collision is increased to 1.3%. The performance improvement is barely changed; the difference is 0.1%. We performed experiments to measure the behavior of our technique in the presence of context switching. Space constraints prevent a full discussion, but our results indicate that our technique yields at least the same improvement compared to the baseline configuration in the presence of OS context-switching among multiple applications.

7. RELATED WORK

Data deduplication is used in disk-based storage systems to reduce storage consumption [6, 39, 12]. Address correlation [32] analyzed the phenomenon of data duplication in the L1 cache without giving a feasible implementation. Non-redundant data cache [22] proposed a sub-block-level cache-deduplication technique, requiring value-based data storage and an extra value search on the critical path. Content-based block caching [23] was an inline deduplication technique designed to improve disk-based storage systems requiring significant storage overhead, which is impractical in caches. The mergeable cache architecture [3] proposed to merge blocks from different processes with the same address and similar data. Villa *et al.* [36] proposed compressing zero-content data in the cache for energy reduction. Dusser *et al.* [8] proposed an augmented cache to store null blocks to increase effective cache capacity. The HICAMP architecture [5] applies deduplication to main memories. It uses an associative hash table, suffers from underutilization, practical design issues, and lack of consideration for collisions in the hash table. CATCH [16] proposed using cache-content-deduplication only in instruction caches without data modification.

Data compression is another technology to eliminate redundant data. Yang *et al.* [38] proposed frequent value compression in first-level caches. Zhang *et al.* [40] proposed the frequent value cache (FVC) based on the observation of frequent value locality to hold only frequently accessed values in a compressed form. Alameldeen *et al.* [2] proposed frequent pattern compression (FPC), a pattern-based compression scheme for L2 caches. By storing common word patterns in a compressed form with certain prefixes, FPC provides a compression ratio comparable to more complex schemes. To reduce useless decompression overhead, Alameldeen *et al.* [1] proposed an adaptive policy to trade dynamically between the benefit of compression with the cost overhead. Hallnor *et al.* [10] proposed a unified compression scheme to compress and decompress data in the LLC, main memory, and memory channels. Although the unified compression scheme eliminates the additional compression and decompression expense required in transferring data between the LLC and the main memory, it cannot avoid compression/decompression overhead incurred with data transferring between different cache levels. Base-delta-immediate compression [28] is another data-compression algorithm representing data using a base value and an array

of differences. For value- or pattern-based compression, besides the complex compression and decompression logic and unavoidable decompress latency, another drawback is that most cache-management policies cannot be used efficiently in a compressed cache because of the variation of block sizes. Linearly compressed pages [27] is another recently proposed technique for main memory compression.

The V-way cache [30] was proposed to vary the associativity of a cache on a per-set basis to increase the effective cache capacity. Line distillation was proposed to retain only used words and evict unused words in a cache block to increase effective cache capacity. Motivated by skew-associative caches [34] and cuckoo hashing [25], Zcache [31] was proposed to provide higher associativity than the number of physical ways by increasing the number of replacement candidates.

8. CONCLUSION

We propose a practical deduplicated last-level cache with limited overhead to improve performance by increasing effective cache capacity. By exploiting block-level data duplication, cache deduplication significantly increases the effectiveness of the cache with limited area and power consumption. Compared to a conventional LLC, a deduplicated LLC uses similar chip area and power consumption while performing comparably to a double-sized conventional LLC.

This paper evaluates cache deduplication in LLCs. In future work, we will extend cache deduplication to core caches and exploit redundant information-elimination techniques in other storage units. The sequentially allocated nature of the data array in the deduplicated cache offers opportunities for power gating.

9. REFERENCES

[1] A.R. Alameldeen and D.A. Wood. Adaptive cache compression for high-performance processors. In *Proceedings of the 31st Annual International Symposium on Computer Architecture*, pages 212–223. IEEE, 2004.

[2] A.R. Alameldeen and D.A. Wood. Frequent pattern compression: A significance-based compression scheme for l2 caches. *Dept. of Computer Sciences, University of Wisconsin-Madison, Tech. Rep*, 2004.

[3] S. Biswas, D. Franklin, A. Savage, R. Dixon, T. Sherwood, and F.T. Chong. Multi-execution: multicore caching for data-similar executions. In *ACM SIGARCH Computer Architecture News*, volume 37, pages 164–173. ACM, 2009.

[4] D. Chen, E. Peserico, and L. Rudolph. A dynamically partitionable compressed cache. In *Proceedings of the Singapore-MIT Alliance Symposium*, January 2003.

[5] D. Cheriton, A. Firoozshahian, A. Solomatnikov, J.P. Stevenson, and O. Azizi. Hicamp: architectural support for efficient concurrency-safe shared structured data access. In *Proceedings of the seventeenth international conference on Architectural Support for Programming Languages and Operating Systems*, pages 287–300. ACM, 2012.

[6] T.E. Denehy and W.W. Hsu. Duplicate management for reference data. *Research Report RJ10305, IBM*, 2003.

[7] L. Domnitser, A. Jaleel, J. Loew, N. Abu-Ghazaleh, and D. Ponomarev. Non-monopolizable caches: Low-complexity mitigation of cache side channel attacks. *ACM Transactions on Architecture and Code Optimization (TACO)*, 8(4):35, 2012.

[8] J. Dusser, T. Piquet, and A. Seznec. Zero-content augmented caches. In *Proceedings of the 23rd international conference on Supercomputing*, pages 46–55. ACM, 2009.

[9] R. W. Green. Memory movement and initialization: Optimization and control. http://software.intel.com/, April 4th, 2013.

[10] E.G. Hallnor and S.K. Reinhardt. A unified compressed memory hierarchy. In *High-Performance Computer Architecture, 2005. HPCA-11. 11th International Symposium on*, pages 201–212. IEEE, 2005.

[11] J.L. Henning. Spec cpu2006 benchmark descriptions. *ACM SIGARCH Computer Architecture News*, 34(4):1–17, 2006.

[12] B. Hong, D. Plantenberg, D.D.E. Long, and M. Sivan-Zimet. Duplicate data elimination in a san file system. In *Proceedings of the 21st Symposium on Mass Storage Systems (MSSâĂŹ04), Goddard, MD*, 2004.

[13] A. Jaleel, E. Borch, M. Bhandaru, SC Steely, and J. Emer. Achieving non-inclusive cache performance with inclusive caches: Temporal locality aware (tla) cache management policies. In *Microarchitecture (MICRO), 2010 43rd Annual IEEE/ACM International Symposium on*, pages 151–162. IEEE, 2010.

[14] A. Jaleel, H.H. Najaf-Abadi, S. Subramaniam, S.C. Steely, and J. Emer. Cruise: cache replacement and utility-aware scheduling. In *ACM SIGARCH Computer Architecture News*, volume 40, pages 249–260. ACM, 2012.

[15] S.M. Khan, Y. Tian, and D.A. Jimenez. Sampling dead block prediction for last-level caches. In *Microarchitecture (MICRO), 2010 43rd Annual IEEE/ACM International Symposium on*, pages 175–186. IEEE, 2010.

[16] M. Kleanthous and Y. Sazeides. Catch: A mechanism for dynamically detecting cache-content-duplication and its application to instruction caches. In *Proceedings of the conference on Design, automation and test in Europe*, pages 1426–1431. ACM, 2008.

[17] P. Koutoupis. Data deduplication with linux. *Linux Journal*, 2011(207):7, 2011.

[18] N.A. Kurd, S. Bhamidipati, C. Mozak, J.L. Miller, T.M. Wilson, M. Nemani, and M. Chowdhury. Westmere: A family of 32nm ia processors. In *Solid-State Circuits Conference Digest of Technical Papers (ISSCC), 2010 IEEE International*, pages 96–97. IEEE, 2010.

[19] J.S. Lee, W.K. Hong, and S.D. Kim. Design and evaluation of a selective compressed memory system. In *Computer Design, 1999.(ICCD'99) International Conference on*, pages 184–191. IEEE, 1999.

[20] J.S. Lee, W.K. Hong, and S.D. Kim. Adaptive methods to minimize decompression overhead for compressed on-chip caches. *International journal of computers & applications*, 25(2):98–105, 2003.

[21] D. Levinthal. Performance analysis guide for intel core i7 processor and intel xeon 5500 processors. *Intel Performance Analysis Guide*, 2009.

[22] C. Molina, C. Aliagas, M. García, A. Gonzàlez, and J. Tubella. Non redundant data cache. In *Proceedings of the 2003 international symposium on Low power electronics and design*, ISLPED '03, pages 274–277, New York, N.Y., USA, 2003. ACM.

[23] C.B. Morrey III and D. Grunwald. Content-based block caching. In *Proceedings of 23rd IEEE Conference on Mass Storage Systems and Technologies*, College Park, Maryland, May 2006.

[24] N. Muralimanohar, R. Balasubramonian, and N.P. Jouppi. Cacti 6.0: A tool to model large caches. *Research report hpl-2009-85, HP Laboratories*, 2009.

[25] R. Pagh and F.F. Rodler. Cuckoo hashing. *Journal of Algorithms*, 51(2):122–144, 2004.

[26] A. Patel, F. Afram, and K. Ghose. Marss-x86: A qemu-based micro-architectural and systems simulator for x86 multicore processors. In *1st International Qemu Users' Forum*, pages 29–30, 2011.

[27] G. Pekhimenko, V. Seshadri, Y. Kim, H. Xin, O. Mutlu, P. B. Gibbons, M. A. Kozuch, and T. C. Mowry. Linearly compressed pages: a low-complexity, low-latency main memory compression framework. In *Proceedings of the 46th Annual IEEE/ACM International Symposium on Microarchitecture*, pages 172–184. ACM, 2013.

[28] G. Pekhimenko, V. Seshadri, O. Mutlu, T. C. Mowry, P. B. Gibbons, and M. A. Kozuch. Base-delta-immediate compression: A practical data compression mechanism for on-chip caches. In *Proceedings of the 21st ACM International Conference on Parallel Architectures and Compilation Techniques (PACT)*, 2012.

[29] E. Perelman, G. Hamerly, M. Van Biesbrouck, T. Sherwood, and B. Calder. Using simpoint for accurate and efficient simulation. In *Proceedings of the 2003 ACM SIGMETRICS international conference on Measurement and modeling of computer systems*, SIGMETRICS '03, pages 318–319, New York, N.Y., USA, 2003. ACM.

[30] M.K. Qureshi, D. Thompson, and Y.N. Patt. The v-way cache: Demand-based associativity via global replacement. In *Computer Architecture, 2005. ISCA'05. Proceedings. 32nd International Symposium on*, pages 544–555. IEEE, 2005.

[31] D. Sanchez and C. Kozyrakis. The zcache: Decoupling ways and associativity. In *Microarchitecture (MICRO), 2010 43rd Annual IEEE/ACM International Symposium on*, pages 187–198. IEEE, 2010.

[32] R. Sendag and P.F. Chuang. Address correlation: Exceeding the limits of locality. *IEEE Comput. Architecture Letters*, 1(1):13–16, January 2002.

[33] O. Seongil, S. Choo, and J.H. Ahn. Exploring energy-efficient dram array organizations. In *Circuits and Systems (MWSCAS), 2011 IEEE 54th International Midwest Symposium on*, pages 1–4. IEEE, 2011.

[34] A. Seznec. A case for two-way skewed-associative caches. In *ACM SIGARCH Computer Architecture News*, volume 21, pages 169–178. ACM, 1993.

[35] A. Seznec. Analysis of the o-geometric history length branch predictor. In *Computer Architecture, 2005. ISCA'05. Proceedings. 32nd International Symposium on*, pages 394–405. IEEE, 2005.

[36] L. Villa, M. Zhang, and K. Asanovic. Dynamic zero compression for cache energy reduction. In *Microarchitecture, 2000. MICRO-33. Proceedings. 33rd Annual IEEE/ACM International Symposium on*, pages 214–220, 2000.

[37] D.F. Wendel, R. Kalla, J. Warnock, R. Cargnoni, S.G. Chu, J.G. Clabes, D. Dreps, D. Hrusecky, J. Friedrich, S. Islam, et al. Power7, a highly parallel, scalable multi-core high end server processor. *Solid-State Circuits, IEEE Journal of*, 46(1):145–161, 2011.

[38] J. Yang, Y. Zhang, and R. Gupta. Frequent value compression in data caches. In *Proceedings of the 33rd annual ACM/IEEE international symposium on Microarchitecture*, pages 258–265. ACM, 2000.

[39] T. Yang, H. Jiang, D. Feng, Z. Niu, K. Zhou, and Y. Wan. Debar: A scalable high-performance de-duplication storage system for backup and archiving. In *Parallel & Distributed Processing (IPDPS), 2010 IEEE International Symposium on*, pages 1–12. IEEE, 2010.

[40] Y. Zhang, J. Yang, and R. Gupta. Frequent value locality and value-centric data cache design. In *ACM SIGOPS Operating Systems Review*, volume 34, pages 150–159. ACM, 2000.

Block Value based Insertion Policy for High Performance Last-level Caches

Lingda Li, Junlin Lu, and Xu Cheng
Microprocessor Research and Development Center, Peking University, Beijing, China
{lilingda, lujunlin, chengxu}@mprc.pku.edu.cn

ABSTRACT

Last-level cache performance has been proved to be crucial to the system performance. Essentially, any cache management policy improves performance by retaining blocks that it believes to have higher *values* preferentially. Most cache management policies use the access time or reuse distance of a block as its value to minimize total miss count. However, cache miss penalty is variable in modern systems due to i) variable memory access latency and ii) the disparity in latency toleration ability across different misses. Some recently proposed policies thus take into account the miss penalty as the block value. However, only considering miss penalty is not enough.

In fact, the value of a block includes not only the penalty on its misses, but also the reduction of processor stall cycles on its hits, i.e., *hit benefit*. Therefore, we propose a method to compute both miss penalty and hit benefit. Then, the value of a block is calculated by accumulating all the miss penalty and hit benefits of its requests. Using our notion of block value, we propose *Value based Insertion Policy (VIP)* which aims to reserve more blocks with higher values in the cache. VIP keeps track of a small number of incoming and victim block pairs to learn the relationship between the value of the incoming block and that of the victim. On a miss, if the value of the incoming block is learned to be lower than that of the victim block in the past, VIP will predict that the incoming block is valueless and insert it with a high eviction priority. The evaluation shows that VIP can improve cache performance significantly in both single-core and multi-core environment while requiring a low storage overhead.

Categories and Subject Descriptors

B.3.2 [**Memory Structures**]: Design Styles—*cache memories*

General Terms

Design, Performance

ICS'14, June 10–13 2014, Munich, Germany.
Copyright 2014 ACM 978-1-4503-2642-1/14/06 ...$15.00.
http://dx.doi.org/10.1145/2597652.2597653.

Keywords

Value; Miss penalty; Hit benefit; Insertion; Last-level cache

1. INTRODUCTION

Cache performance, especially last-level cache performance, is crucial to the system performance due to the increasing memory access latency. In order to reduce the processor stall cycles on cache misses, a large amount of cache management policies have recently been proposed. Essentially, any cache management policy improves cache performance by retaining blocks which it believes to have higher *values*[1] longer, and replacing valueless blocks preferentially. Most of recent proposals treat the access time or reuse distance of a cache block as its *value* to reduce the absolute cache miss count [14, 25, 27, 29, 38, 40, 46, 48]. These proposals implicitly assume that all cache requests result in equal performance degradation when they miss in the cache. However, this assumption is inaccurate in modern systems for two reasons.

The first reason is that memory access latency is not uniform in modern systems. First, in modern DRAM systems, memory requests need additional serving time when request queue and bank conflicts occur, and memory requests that access the same row as previous requests are served faster. Second, the interconnect network introduces variable access latency in a non-uniform memory access system. Moreover, in future systems, multiple memory techniques can be used simultaneously (e.g., eDRAM, PCRAM, STT-RAM [47]). Such systems also tend to use hybrid memory hierarchies such as 3D-stacked DRAM caches [32]. Therefore, the disparity in memory latency will become even larger.

The other reason for the disparity in miss penalty is that modern processors make use of various techniques such as non-blocking caches [28] and prefetching [45] to serve multiple cache misses in parallel. Using these techniques makes the processor stall cycles on a cache miss depend not only on its memory access latency, but also on other concurrent misses. The memory access latency of cache misses which can be served in parallel can be partly hidden by that of other concurrent misses, and these misses thus have small performance impact. On the other hand, cache misses that occur in isolation can incur greater performance loss.

The variation of miss penalty suggests that the cache management policy should use the miss penalty as a part of block value. Some recently proposed cache management policies take into account the miss penalty on replacement [16, 19,

---

[1]In this paper, the value of a block refers to its worth or merit, not its data value.

22, 39, 43]. These proposals compute and record the miss penalty when a block is inserted into the cache, and preferentially replace blocks with small miss penalty.

However, only considering miss penalty is not enough. Let us assume that there are two blocks A and B: A has a miss penalty of 200 cycles on its insertion and receives no hit; B has a smaller miss penalty of 100 cycles, nevertheless, it receives 3 hits, and each hit prevents the processor from stalling for another 100 cycles. In such a scenario, reserving B will potentially save an aggregate penalty of 400 cycles, while it is 200 cycles for A. Thus, the cache should reserve B instead of A. However, if we only consider the penalty on cache misses, A will incorrectly be preferred.

Therefore, the *value* of a cache block depends on all its requests. It includes not only the increment of processor stall cycles on its misses (i.e., *miss penalty*), but also the reduction of processor stall cycles on its hits (i.e., *hit benefit*). To evaluate cache block values, we propose a simple hardware mechanism to compute both miss penalty and hit benefit for superscalar processors. Then, the value of a block can be calculated by accumulating all the miss penalty and hit benefits of its requests during a period of time.

Based on our notion of value, we propose *Value based Insertion Policy (VIP)* to improve cache performance by reserving more blocks with higher values. VIP learns and predicts the relationship between the value of the incoming block and that of the victim block selected by the baseline replacement policy on cache misses. On the insertion of an incoming block, if its value is predicted to be lower than that of the victim block, VIP will insert the incoming block with a high eviction priority, and thus that block will be replaced preferentially on following misses.

VIP can be applied to the current cache design with negligible modification, and it can cooperate with any baseline replacement policy. Moreover, VIP is both thread-aware and prefetch-aware.

We evaluate the performance of VIP with NRU, LRU, and SRRIP [14]. Our evaluation shows that VIP can improve cache performance significantly while requiring a low storage overhead. On average, VIP outperforms LRU by 8.2% and 5.9% for single-core and 4-core workloads respectively in the absence of prefetching, and it can also achieve significant performance improvement in the presence of prefetching. VIP also outperforms other state-of-the-art techniques, including SBAR [39], DIP [38], DRRIP [14], PIPP [48], UCP [40], and SHiP-PC [46].

The rest of this paper is organized as follows. Section 2 discusses some related work. Section 3 introduces the computation method for miss penalty and hit benefit and the notion of block value. Section 4 describes the design and implementation of VIP. Section 5 shows the experimental methodology, and then Section 6 analyzes the results. Finally, Section 7 concludes this paper.

2. RELATED WORK

Extensive research on cache management has been done to improve cache performance. Based on the goal, they can be classified into two categories: miss count based policies which aim to reduce the miss count, and miss penalty based policies which aim to reduce the miss penalty. We will introduce the primary work of these two types of policies respectively in this section.

2.1 Miss Count based Cache Management

A lot of studies propose to improve cache performance by reducing the miss count. DIP [38] dynamically inserts most incoming blocks into the LRU position to avoid thrashing when the working set is larger than the cache size. Pseudo-LIFO [3] uses a fill stack and prioritizes to replace blocks on the top of fill stack. Keramidas *et al.* proposed to explicitly predict the reuse distance to guide replacement [24]. RRIP [14] distinguishes reused blocks from no reused ones, and evicts no reused blocks preferentially. SHiP [46] can further improve the performance of RRIP with a signature-based re-reference interval predictor, and their signatures include memory region, PC, and instruction sequence. PDP [5] protects cache blocks within a predicted reuse distance. Jiménez proposed a low cost replacement policy based on tree-based Pseudo LRU [20].

Dead block prediction techniques try to identify and preferentially evict blocks that will not be accessed again (i.e., *dead blocks*). Dead block prediction can be classified into three categories based on how to identify dead blocks: trace based [29], time based [10], and counter based [27]. Cache burst predictor [31] improves dead block prediction accuracy by making prediction for continuous access sequences. SDBP [25] samples a part of sets to reduce conflicts in the predictor for low overhead and high prediction accuracy.

Bypass techniques improve cache performance by bypassing blocks with poor locality. Based on how to predict the locality, these techniques can be classified into address based [15, 21, 41] and PC based [4, 8, 44]. DSB [6] adjusts the bypass probability based on the reuse order of the incoming block and the victim block. Gaur *et al.* proposed a bypass and insertion algorithm for exclusive last-level caches [7]. OBM [30] learns and predicts the behavior of the optimal bypass to make bypass decisions.

To improve shared cache performance, some recent work proposed to partition shared caches to minimize the aggregate miss count of multi-core processors. UCP [40] collects the cache utility information for each core to allocate cache space for minimizing the total miss count. TADIP [13] extends DIP to select the best insertion policy for each core. PIPP [48] adjusts the insertion and promotion policy of different cores to partition shared caches implicitly. NUcache [33] improves shared cache performance by retaining blocks accessed by selected PCs longer. Vantage [42] partitions shared caches at cache block granularity to make it applicable in many-core systems. PriSM [34] adjusts the eviction probabilities of different cores to partition shared caches.

Miss count based cache management policies implicitly assume that all cache misses are equal. However, the penalty of different misses can change dramatically in modern systems. Thus, only reducing the miss count is not enough, and it is important for cache management policies to take into account the variation of miss penalty.

2.2 Miss Penalty based Cache Management

Jeong and Dubois first proposed to take into account the miss cost in cache management [16, 17, 18]. They extend LRU to distinguish the miss cost of local memory from that of remote memory in CC-NUMA multiprocessors. In uniprocessor environment, Jeong *et al.* proposed to distinguish the miss penalty between load and store misses [19].

Critical cache [22] and LACS [26, 43] both estimate the miss penalty using the number of issued instructions during

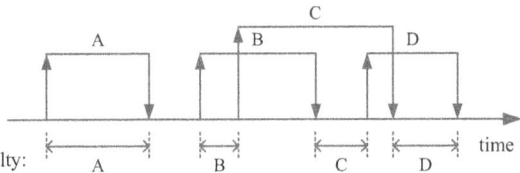

Figure 1: Example for miss penalty computation of demand misses.

the cache miss. Critical cache dedicates a part of cache to preserve critical loads, and LACS replaces blocks with small miss penalty preferentially.

Qureshi *et al.* proposed to take into account the variation of miss penalty since modern processors can serve multiple misses in parallel, which is called the Memory Level Parallelism (MLP) cost [39]. They use the reciprocal of the in-flight miss number to represent the MLP cost. On replacement, the MLP-aware policy selects the block with the minimum weighted sum of MLP cost and LRU stack position as the victim. In case that the MLP-aware policy can hurt performance sometimes, SBAR is introduced to adaptively select the policy that has better performance between the MLP-aware policy and LRU. MLP-DCP [36] and MCFQ [23] both partition shared caches based on the MLP cost.

These previous miss penalty based policies only take into account the miss penalty on the insertion of cache blocks, and they do not consider the received benefits on the hits. On the other hand, our policy takes into account both miss penalty and hit benefit to represent cache block values.

3. BLOCK VALUE

In order to reduce the total processor stall cycles on cache misses, caches should retain blocks that can hurt the performance most when they are not resident in the cache. Therefore, we use the aggregate increasing processor stall cycles if a block is not reserved by the cache as its *value*, which depends on all requests of that block. The value of a cache block includes both the processor stall cycles on its misses (i.e., *miss penalty*) and the reduction of processor stall cycles due to its hits (i.e., *hit benefit*). We need to compute and accumulate all miss penalty and hit benefits of a block to get its value. Therefore, at first, we will introduce how to compute miss penalty and hit benefit respectively for superscalar processors.

3.1 Miss Penalty Computation

Miss penalty reflects the increment of processor stall cycles due to the cache miss. We describe how to compute miss penalty based on the request type.

Demand misses. After a long-latency demand miss, the processor will run out of resources and stall soon. Therefore, the number of processor stall cycles on a miss can be approximated by the number of cycles that the cache spends on waiting for the memory.

Figure 1 presents an example for miss penalty computation, where A, B, C, and D denote different miss requests. For an isolated miss such as A, the processor has to wait until the memory returns its data. Therefore, the miss penalty of isolated misses is their memory access latency. For parallel misses such as B and C, their miss penalty is the non-overlapping fraction of their memory access latency, as shown in Figure 1. The reason behind it is that if a parallel

miss is removed, only its non-overlapping fraction of memory access latency is reduced from the total cache serving cycles.

To compute miss penalty, we extend MSHR (Miss Status Holding Register) [28]. MSHR is used to record in-flight cache misses. Each cache miss is allocated with an MSHR entry before it is sent to memory, and the MSHR entry is released when the memory completes the request. We append each MSHR entry with a counter T_p for its miss penalty computation. When an MSHR entry is allocated, its T_p is initialized to 0. Each cycle, if there is only one demand miss, the T_p of the isolated miss is increased by 1 to indicate that this miss should be responsible for this cache serving cycle. Otherwise, it indicates that there are either multiple or no demand misses, and no miss needs to take responsibility in either case. C_{demand_miss} is used to count the number of in-flight demand misses. Algorithm 1 shows the algorithm for computing demand miss penalty.

Writeback and prefetch misses. Writeback requests are generated by inner caches on replacement, and they do not affect the processor performance directly. Prefetch misses do not stall the processor, too. Thus, the miss penalty of writeback and prefetch requests is 0.

For demand misses, prefetch misses can affect their miss penalty in two ways. One is that for a prefetch request which is not timely, although the following demand request to the prefetched block cannot get the data immediately, its miss penalty becomes smaller. In such scenarios, we only need to reset the corresponding T_p and restart the miss penalty counting when the address of an in-flight prefetch request recorded in an MSHR entry is found to be identical to that of the current demand request. The other way is that prefetch requests contend with demand requests for memory bandwidth, which will eventually affect the memory access latency of demand requests. However, our method for miss penalty computation takes into account variable memory latency. Consequently, our miss penalty computation method is applicable in the presence of prefetching.

3.2 Comparison with Other Miss Penalty Computation Methods

Jeong and Dubois proposed the optimal offline miss cost based policy, and it uses two static costs to distinguish the miss penalty of local memory from that of remote memory in CC-NUMA multiprocessors [16]. When the latency toleration ability of modern processors is taken into account, using two static costs is inaccurate since miss costs can change dynamically and have many different values.

Critical cache [22] and LACS [26, 43] use the number of issued instructions during a cache miss to represent its penalty. The more the issued instructions, the lower the miss penalty. However, when memory access latency is long enough, the number of issued instructions will show no d-

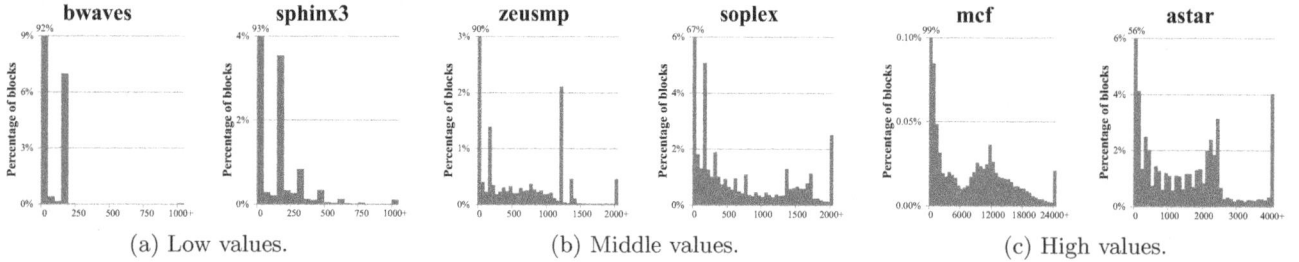

(a) Low values.   (b) Middle values.   (c) High values.

Figure 2: Value distribution for SPEC CPU2006 representative programs. The x-axis represents block values in cycles.

ifference, and thus using it to estimate miss penalty is not accurate. Besides, such information is difficult to obtain by last-level caches.

The MLP cost computation method proposed by Qureshi *et al.* [39] takes into account both variable memory latency and latency toleration ability. When multiple misses are served in parallel, unlike our method, their method divides the serving cycles equally for all in-flight misses, which indicates that all concurrent misses share the responsibility for these cycles. Since the MLP cost computation needs division operations, their method is more complex. While our method only needs plus-one operations, and at most one adder is used in one cycle. We evaluate the performance of our proposed policy using the MLP cost computation method instead of ours in Section 6, and its performance is similar to that of our original policy.

3.3 Hit Benefit Computation

Demand hits. Hit benefit represents the reduction of processor stall cycles on a cache hit. To compute it, we pretend the hit request to be a miss and then use the miss penalty computation method introduced above.

Unlike miss requests, cache hit requests do not need to access the memory and allocate MSHR entries. Thus, we propose a structure called *Hit Benefit Calculator (HBC)* to record cache hit requests for hit benefit computation. HBC is similar to MSHR. Each HBC entry includes a valid bit, the address of request, a latency counter to count the remaining hypothetic memory access latency, and T_b for hit benefit computation. On a demand hit, an HBC entry is allocated with its latency counter initialized to its hypothetic memory access latency and T_b initialized to 0. Since we model a desktop-like system in our experiments, where the variation of memory latency is not large, we use a static estimated memory access latency (150 cycles) for all hit requests in our experiments. For more complex systems where memory latency can change dramatically, a small address indexed latency predictor can be potentially employed, since cache block address usually determines its location in the memory system, and thus roughly determines its access latency. Each cycle, the latency counter is decreased by 1, and the T_b is increased by 1 if C_{demand_miss} is equal to 0, since in such scenarios, the hypothetic miss converted from the hit request will be an isolated miss. When the latency counter of an HBC entry is reduced to 0, its T_b represents the hit benefit.

Computing hit benefits for all hit requests will require a large HBC. Fortunately, we only need to compute hit benefits for a small fraction of cache hits as we will introduce later, and thus a small HBC is enough.

Writeback and prefetch hits. Their hit benefits are always 0 since there is no influence on the processor execution time when they are converted into misses.

3.4 Analysis of Block Value

Using the methods described above, the value of a cache block can be calculated by accumulating both miss penalty and hit benefits of its requests within a certain period of time. We analyze the values of cache blocks for SPEC CPU2006 benchmarks in an LRU-managed 2MB L2 cache without prefetching. To calculate the block value in a longer time, we double the associativity of the L2 cache tag array, so we can accumulate all miss penalty and hit benefits of a block as its value from the time when it is placed in the 2MB cache to the time when it is evicted from the virtual 4MB cache. Figure 2 presents the block value distribution for some representative programs.

First, we observe that a large amount of blocks have 0 values. The reason is that since L1 caches filter out most of the locality, L2 cache requests generally show poor locality and many blocks receive no cache hits. For mcf, although 99% of blocks have 0 values, the remaining blocks have extremely large values (> 10000 cycles). Therefore, it is important to make sure that 99% of valueless blocks do not interfere 1% of valuable blocks for mcf.

Our second and more important observation is that the disparity in block values is large. The cache requests of some programs always occur in isolation, such as sphinx3, and thus most of their block values are multiples of memory access latency ($\approx$ 150X cycles). While for other programs such as zeusmp and soplex, there are more parallel requests.

Moreover, in multi-core system where the cache is shared, the variation of values exists not only between different blocks of the same core, but also between blocks of different cores. For instance, when bwaves and astar are executing in parallel, the cache management policy should allocate more cache space for astar since its blocks have larger values.

The disparity in block values motivates the need for a block value based cache management policy, which can be aware of the variation of cache block values and retain blocks with higher values preferentially.

3.5 Predictability of Block Value

To enable block value based cache management, block values must be predictable. A simple scheme to predict the value of a block is to use the last value when it is retained by the cache. Note that we only use this simple value prediction scheme to study the predictability of block value, and we do not use it in our proposed policy. We evaluate the feasibility of this scheme by measuring the difference between the values of a block during its two successive cache residence time. The *absolute difference* is calculated by subtracting the smaller value from the larger one, and the *relative difference* is calculated by dividing the absolute difference by the larger value. If either relative difference < 10% or absolute difference < 15 cycles (10% of memory access latency) for two successive values of the same block, the value prediction is considered to be accurate.

Among the 16 SPEC CPU2006 benchmarks used in our experiments, for most programs, more than 80% of their value prediction is accurate. Only the block values of bzip2, zeusmp, and gobmk show poor predictability. Therefore, we conclude that the block value is predictable, and it can be used to guide the cache management policy.

4. VALUE BASED INSERTION POLICY

Our goal is to design a cache management policy that focuses on increasing the aggregate values of blocks reserved by the cache to improve performance. In order to increase the aggregate values of cache blocks, on a cache miss, if the value of the incoming block is lower than that of the victim block, the incoming block should be inserted with a high eviction priority, so that it can be evicted from the cache quickly.

To that end, we propose *Value based Insertion Policy (VIP)*. VIP makes insertion decisions by learning and predicting the relationship between the value of the incoming block and that of the victim.

4.1 Overview

Figure 3 shows the structure of VIP, where grey modules are added for VIP. VIP uses *Replacement History Table (RHT)* to compare the value of the incoming block with that of the victim block selected by the baseline replacement policy. On a cache miss, an RHT entry is allocated to keep track of the current incoming block and the corresponding victim. Each RHT entry contains a *value comparer (VC)* to record the difference between the value of the incoming block and that of the victim, and the VC is initialized to 0 on the allocation of an RHT entry. On the following access to the incoming block of an RHT entry, the miss penalty computed by the MSHR or the hit benefit computed by the HBC is added to its VC. While on the following access to the victim of an RHT entry, the miss penalty or hit benefit is subtracted from its VC. If VC exceeds a positive threshold, it indicates that the incoming block has a higher value. Otherwise, if VC exceeds a negative threshold, it indicates that the value of victim block is higher.

Then, a PC indexed saturating counter table called *Relative Value Prediction Table (RVPT)* is employed to record value comparison results. The numerical value of a counter in the RVPT indicates whether the value of the incoming block generated by the corresponding PC is larger than that of the victim block recently. All counters of RVPT are initialized to 0. When a value comparison completes, the PC of the incoming block is used to index the RVPT to update its corresponding counter: If the incoming block is learned to have a higher value, the counter is increased by 1; if the victim block has a higher value, it is decreased by 1.

On the insertion of an incoming block, VIP consults the RVPT to predict whether the incoming block has a smaller value. If the counter indexed by its PC is less than 0, it indicates that the values of previous incoming blocks accessed

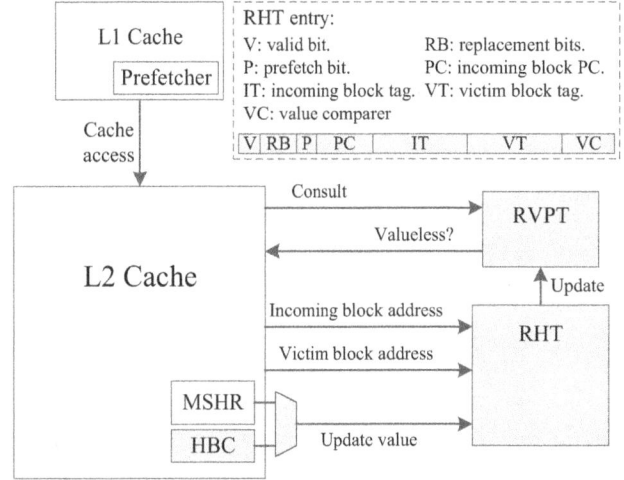

Figure 3: The structure of VIP.

by the same PC are smaller than those of the victim blocks. In such scenarios, VIP predicts that the current incoming block also has a smaller value. Otherwise, it indicates that the values of previous incoming blocks accessed by the same PC are larger than those of the victims, and thus VIP predicts the current incoming block is valuable and should be retained longer in the cache.

VIP associates each cache block with an *eviction bit (EB)* to indicate its eviction priority. If an incoming block is predicted to have a smaller value compared to the victim, its EB is set to 1 to indicate its high eviction priority. Otherwise, its EB is set to 0.

Upon replacement, blocks whose EBs are 1 are selected as the victim preferentially. If there are no such blocks, the baseline replacement policy is used to select the victim. In doing so, VIP prevents incoming blocks with smaller values from evicting blocks with higher values in the cache, and thus increases the aggregate values of cache blocks.

Algorithm 2 shows the detailed algorithm of VIP. The threshold of VC is chosen as the estimated memory access latency (150 cycles). The reason is that assuming the value of block A minus that of block B is larger than the memory latency, even though B shows a higher value in a long term, B can be brought into the cache on its next miss. Since the miss penalty on the next miss of B must be smaller than or equal to the memory latency, it is also smaller than the value difference between A and B, and thus the total values of cache blocks increase by reserving A first and then B next.

VIP can cooperate with any baseline replacement policy. In our experiments, we evaluate the performance of VIP with various replacement policies, including Not Recently Used (NRU) policy, LRU, and SRRIP [14].

4.2 Implementation Details

The RHT can be organized as fully associative, set associative, or direct mapped. Our experiments show that a 128-entry 8-way set-associative RHT is enough. Since the set number of RHT (16) is smaller than that of the cache (2048 for the 2MB cache in our experiments), the set index field of RHT (9th to 6th bits of address) is a subset of the cache set index field (16th to 6th bits of address for the 2MB cache). Hence, the incoming and victim blocks from the same cache set are also in the same RHT set. Each RHT

Algorithm 2 The algorithm of VIP
```
1:  On an access to block X:
2:  if X is a demand miss then
3:      benefit = ComputeMissPenalty();
4:  else if X is a demand hit then
5:      benefit = ComputeHitBenefit();
6:  else
7:      benefit = 0;
8:  end if
9:  for each valid entry A in the corresponding RHT set do
10:     if X.tag == A.IT then
11:         A.VC += benefit;
12:         if A.VC >= VALUE_THRESHOLD then
13:             RVPT[A.PC]++;
14:             Invalidate A;
15:         end if
16:     else if X.tag == A.VT then
17:         A.VC -= benefit;
18:         if A.VC <= -VALUE_THRESHOLD then
19:             RVPT[A.PC]--;
20:             Invalidate A;
21:         end if
22:     end if
23: end for
24: if X is a miss then
25:     Y = Cache.SelectVictimEB1(X);
26:     Z = Cache.SelectVictimBaseline(X);
27:     if Y != NULL then
28:         Replace Y with X;
29:     else
30:         Replace Z with X;
31:     end if
32:     if RVPT[X.PC] >= 0 then
33:         X.EB = 0;
34:     else
35:         X.EB = 1;
36:     end if
37:     if RHT.Record(X) == true then
38:         B = RHT.SelectVictim(X);
39:         B.PC = X.PC;
40:         B.IT = X.tag;
41:         B.VT = Z.tag;
42:         B.VC = 0;
43:     end if
44: end if
```

entry contains 7 fields: A valid bit indicates whether the entry is valid, and an entry is invalidated when its VC exceeds the threshold; replacement bits are used to select an RHT entry to record the current incoming block and victim block when there is no invalid entry, and the replacement policy of RHT is similar to LRU; a prefetch bit indicates whether the request is a prefetch request, and we will introduce how to use it later; PC bits keep the PC of incoming block; VC stores the value difference; IT and VT store the tags of incoming and victim blocks respectively, and we use partial tags to reduce the storage overhead, so that IT and VT only store the lower 18 bits of tags instead of the whole tags.

It is not necessary to record the incoming and victim block pairs of all misses in the RHT. We record the miss in the RHT only if there are invalid entries in the corresponding set of RHT or a small probability is satisfied. Our experiments show that for the 128-entry RHT and 2MB L2 cache, VIP performs well enough when the probability is $1/256$. A small RHT can also reduce the number of HBC entries. We only need to compute hit benefits for hit requests that hit in the RHT. Our experiments show that a 4-entry HBC is enough. When there is no available HBC entry, the extra request for hit benefit computation is simply dropped.

Besides PC, other signatures of cache requests can also be used to index the RVPT, such as block address. Previous studies have shown that using PC to classify cache requests is more effective compared to other methods [46], and thus we use the instruction PC which causes the miss to classify incoming blocks in this paper. Our experiments show that a 256-entry RVPT with 3-bit counters can achieve enough performance gain. Therefore, the RHT entry only needs to keep the 9th to 2nd bits of PC, since the benchmarks are compiled to Alpha binaries, and the lower 2 bits of PC in Alpha instructions are always 0. The shortened 8-bit PC is delivered along with the cache request in the cache hierarchy like all prior cache policies using PC [25, 29, 30, 46].

4.3 Thread-awareness

In multi-core environment where the last-level cache is shared, the values of blocks from different cores can show significant disparity. Therefore, it is necessary for VIP to make insertion decisions for each individual core. Due to the PC based design of VIP, it can distinguish cache blocks from different cores. The only extension that VIP needs for multi-core environment is to assign a $C_{\text{demand\_miss}}$ for each core to enable its miss penalty and hit benefit computation.

4.4 Prefetch-awareness

Prefetching is widely used in modern processors to enhance cache performance. However, incorrect prefetch requests cannot provide any performance improvement, and they can hurt performance by prematurely evicting valuable blocks from the cache. Therefore, it is necessary for VIP to make insertion decisions for demand and prefetch requests separately. To be prefetch-aware, each RHT entry needs a prefetch bit to indicate whether it is a perfetch request, and the PC bits are used to store the core number instead of PC when recording a prefetch request in the RHT entry. We also assign an additional saturating counter in the RVPT for each core which is dedicated to prefetch requests. Its value indicates whether the EB of the block prefetched by a specific core should be set to 1.

4.5 Design Issues for Inclusive Caches

In this paper, we evaluate the performance of VIP in an inclusive L2 cache. In an inclusive cache hierarchy, when a cache block is evicted from the L2 cache, the same block must be evicted by L1 caches to satisfy the inclusion property, and these evicted L1 cache blocks as a result of inclusion are called *inclusion victims*. Inclusion victims may show good locality in L1 caches, and thus evicting them early can hurt the performance [12].

To eliminate inclusion victims, the cache management policy should avoid replacing blocks resident in L1 caches. To that end, the L1 cache sends an *explicit eviction notification* to the L2 cache on the replacement of a clean block, so that the L2 cache can have the accurate information about which cores are caching the block [35]. Upon replacement, the L2 cache preferentially selects the victim among blocks which are not resident in L1 caches. If there are no such blocks, the replacement policy will select the victim block from all blocks in the cache set. This method is similar to a recently proposed inclusive cache management policy [1]. To make a fair comparison, we evaluate the performance of all techniques using this extension in our experiments. Our experiments show that the performance of all techniques can improve slightly with this extension, and the increasing traffic due to explicit eviction notifications is very small.

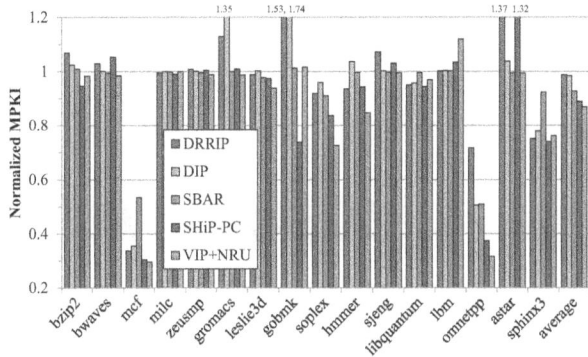

Figure 4: Normalized MPKI for various techniques.

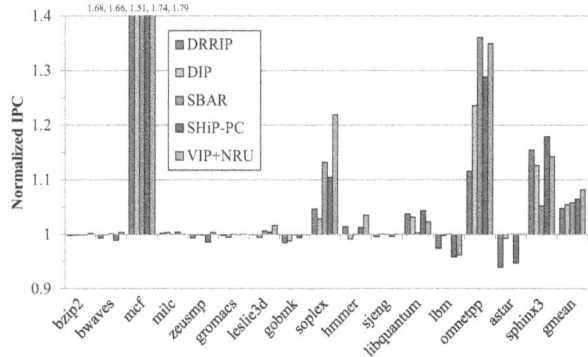

Figure 5: Normalized speedup for various techniques.

4.6 Bypass Instead of Insertion in Non-inclusive and Exclusive Caches

In non-inclusive and exclusive cache hierarchies, last-level caches do not have to keep the same blocks in L1 caches. In such scenarios, valueless blocks can be bypassed directly. Therefore, VIP converts to *Value based Bypass Policy (VBP)*. VBP does not need to append each block with an eviction bit, and thus it consumes less storage overhead. This paper focuses on the study of VIP, and we leave the study of VBP as part of our future work.

5. EXPERIMENTAL METHODOLOGY

The simulator we used is gem5 [2]. The microarchitecture parameters of the simulator are shown in Table 1, and the configuration of the processor is similar to that of the Intel Nehalem [11]. The simulator models a two-level inclusive cache hierarchy using the MESI coherence protocol. The L1 caches are private to each core, while the L2 cache is shared by all cores. In single-core configuration, the L2 cache is 16-way 2MB. In multi-core configuration, the L2 cache is 4MB for 4 cores and 8MB for 8 cores. The simulator also models a hardware stream prefetcher for each core, and prefetched blocks are inserted into both the L1 and L2 caches.

Table 1: Parameters of the simulator.

Parameter	Configuration
Processor	4-wide, 128-entry ROB, 48-entry Load Queue, 32-entry Store Queue
L1 ICache	32KB, 64B block size, 4-way, 3-cycle hit latency, PLRU
L1 DCache	32KB, 64B block size, 4-way, 3-cycle hit latency, PLRU, 32-entry MSHR
L2 Cache	2MB/4MB/8MB, 64B block size, 16-way, 16-cycle hit latency, 64-entry MSHR
Memory	1 channel, 2 dimms, 2 ranks per dimm, 8 banks per rank, bank conflicts modeled, 150-cycle minimal access latency

We use SPEC CPU2006 benchmarks [9] with the first reference inputs to do evaluation. SimPoint [37] is used to obtain a single representative 200 million instructions for each benchmark. Among the benchmarks that can be addressed by our simulation infrastructure, `gamess`, `namd`, `povray`, `calculix`, `h264ref`, and `wrf` are not evaluated because their working sets are very small and their misses per thousand instructions (MPKI) are less than 0.1 in a 2MB L2 cache under LRU. The rest of 16 benchmarks are used in our experiments.

For the performance evaluation in multi-core environment, we choose several benchmarks out of 16 selected SPEC CPU2006 benchmarks at random to combine into a multi-core workload. Totally, we create 20 4-core workloads and 8 8-core workloads. We quantify the performance in multi-core environment with the following three widely used metrics: weighted speedup $= \sum_{i=1}^{n} \frac{IPC_i}{SingleIPC_i}$, throughput $= \sum_{i=1}^{n} IPC_i$, and fair speedup $= n / \sum_{i=1}^{n} \frac{SingleIPC_i}{IPC_i}$, where n is the number of cores, and $SingleIPC_i$ is got when program i runs alone.

6. RESULTS AND ANALYSIS

6.1 Performance on Single-core Workloads

At first, we evaluate the performance of VIP when NRU is used as the baseline replacement policy and prefetching is disabled. Besides VIP with NRU (VIP+NRU), we also investigate the performance of other state-of-the-art techniques, including miss count based DIP [38], DRRIP [14], and SHiP-PC [46], and miss penalty based SBAR [39].

Figure 4 and Figure 5 show MPKI and IPC both normalized to LRU for various techniques respectively. Compared to LRU, VIP+NRU reduces MPKI by 13.0% on average and achieves a geometric mean speedup of 8.2%, while the geometric mean speedup is 4.8% for DRRIP, 5.5% for DIP, 5.8% for SBAR, and 6.5% for SHiP-PC.

DIP, DRRIP, and SHiP-PC only consider the recency information of a block as its value, and thus VIP+NRU outperforms them since they are not aware of the variation of miss penalty. For instance, we observe that the MPKI of SHiP-PC for `bzip2` is lower than that of VIP+NRU, but since these reduced misses are at the expense of more costly ones, the IPC of VIP+NRU is slightly higher than that of SHiP-PC for `bzip2`. For `libquantum` and `sphinx3`, SHiP-PC reduces more misses and outperforms VIP+NRU because it uses a larger predictor. SBAR takes into account both miss penalty and recency information, but as we stated, it is also important to take into account hit benefit. VIP+NRU thus outperforms SBAR consistently except `omnetpp`, for which SBAR has slightly better performance since it uses a more complex miss penalty computation method as stated in Section 3.2. When VIP+NRU uses the same computation method as SBAR, they have similar performance for `omnetpp`. For `lbm`, a small number of blocks occasionally show huge values, and their behaviors are very difficult to

69

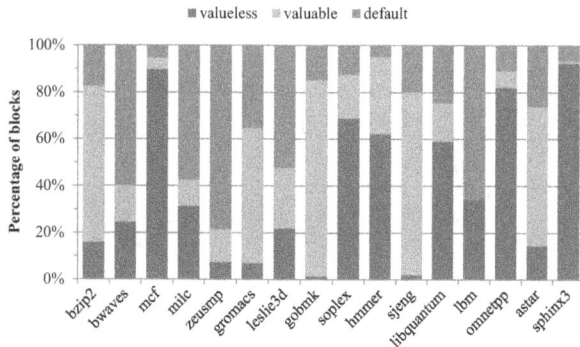

Figure 6: Prediction results of VIP+NRU.

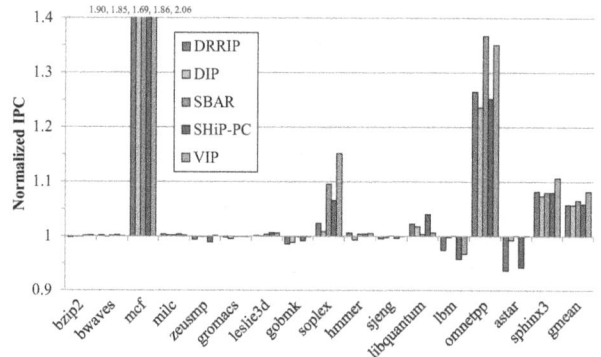

Figure 7: Normalized speedup in the presence of prefetching.

predict. Thus, only LRU and techniques that can dynamically switch to LRU (DIP and SBAR) perform well for `lbm`.

Figure 6 shows the prediction results of VIP+NRU. For programs such as `bwaves` and `lbm`, neither the incoming block nor the victim block is valuable in most cases. In such scenarios, VIP+NRU cannot learn their value relationship (the RVPT counter is 0) and does not set the eviction bit by default. For programs where majority of blocks have low values such as `mcf` and `sphinx3` in Figure 2, most of incoming blocks are predicted to be valueless and VIP+NRU performs well. While for programs which have higher block values such as `astar`, VIP+NRU correctly predicts most blocks to be valuable and thus does not hurt their performance.

To illustrate how VIP improves performance, Figure 8 compares the miss penalty distribution under LRU, SHiP-PC, and VIP+NRU for `soplex`. The miss numbers of SHiP-PC and VIP+NRU are both normalized to the total miss number of LRU. Compared to LRU, both SHiP-PC and VIP+NRU can reduce the aggregate miss count. While the miss counts with small penalty of SHiP-PC and VIP+NRU are almost the same, VIP+NRU reduces more misses with higher penalty ($\geq$ 150 cycles) by retaining more valuable blocks compared to SHiP-PC.

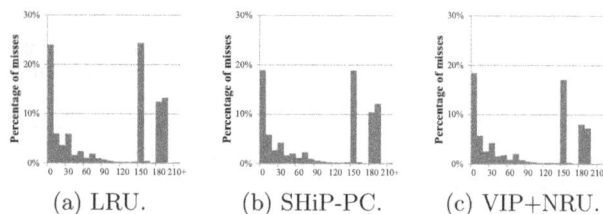

(a) LRU.   (b) SHiP-PC.   (c) VIP+NRU.

Figure 8: Miss penalty distribution for soplex.

Our evaluation also shows that considering hit benefits as parts of block values is essential. When only miss penalty is considered, the average performance improvement of VIP+NRU is merely 0.1% compared to LRU. Besides, the performance gain of VIP+NRU decreases to 7.3% when the hit benefit is fixed to a static number (150 cycles), which demonstrates that an accurate hit benefit computation method is necessary.

We also study the performance of VIP when the MLP cost computation method proposed by Qureshi et al. [39] is used to compute miss penalty and hit benefit. VIP+NRU using the MLP cost computation achieves a geometric mean speedup of 8.4%, which is similar to that of our original

method. Since the MLP cost computation method requires complex calculation, our method is easier to implement.

Besides NRU, we also investigate the performance of VIP when LRU or SRRIP [14] is used as the baseline replacement policy. VIP+LRU and VIP+SRRIP outperform LRU by 8.3% and 8.2% on geometric mean respectively. Compared to SRRIP, VIP+SRRIP outperforms it by 5.8%. These results show that VIP can cooperate with various replacement policies. Since NRU needs the lowest storage overhead and is the simplest among these policies, and the performance of VIP+NRU is similar to that of VIP+LRU and VIP+SRRIP, we focus on the study of VIP+NRU. In the rest of this paper, VIP+NRU is referred to as VIP.

Next, we study the performance of VIP in the presence of prefetching. Figure 7 shows the speedup of various techniques when prefetching is enabled. The speedup is normalized to that of LRU in the presence of prefetching. VIP reduces average MPKI by 11.5% and achieves a performance gain of 8.2%, and it also outperforms other techniques. Compared to LRU without prefetching, VIP outperforms it by 23.9%, while LRU with prefetching outperforms it by 14.5%. These experiments show that VIP can also improve cache performance in the presence of prefetching.

6.2 Performance on Multi-core Workloads

For multi-core workloads, we compare the performance of VIP with other state-of-the-art shared cache management policies including TADIP [13], TADRRIP, UCP [40], PIPP [48], and SHiP-PC. TADIP and TADRRIP are the thread-aware versions of DIP and DRRIP respectively, and SHiP-PC itself is already thread-aware.

Figure 9 presents the s-curve of the weighted speedup normalized to LRU for 20 4-core workloads in the absence of prefetching. The s-curve is plotted by sorting the data from the lowest to the highest. Compared to LRU, VIP achieves a geometric mean weighted speedup improvement of 5.9%, while it is 2.0% for PIPP, 3.1% for UCP, 4.0% for TADIP, 4.3% for TADRRIP, and 4.2% for SHiP-PC. While other techniques incur performance loss for some workloads, VIP does not degrade the performance for any workload. Due to the variation of block values across different cores, the performance benefits of VIP for multi-core workloads are more significant than those for single-core workloads, especially for multi-core workloads where programs with high values and those with low values execute in parallel. On average, VIP predicts that 69.7% of incoming blocks are valueless for 20 4-core workloads.

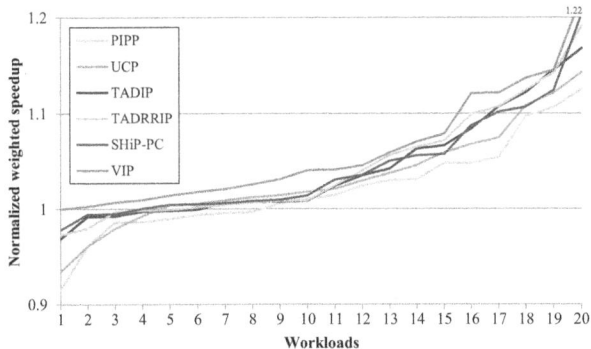

Figure 9: S-curve for normalized weighted speedup on 4-core workloads in the absence of prefetching.

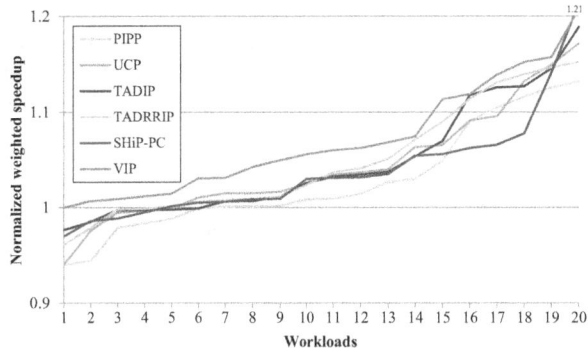

Figure 10: S-curve for normalized weighted speedup on 4-core workloads in the presence of prefetching.

We also study the results on throughput and fair speedup respectively. The throughput improvement of VIP is 5.7% on geometric mean, and the fair speedup improvement of VIP is 8.3%. VIP also outperforms other state-of-the-art techniques on the metrics of throughput and fair speedup. The performance improvement of VIP on fair speedup is the most, since VIP rarely causes performance degradation for any program in a multi-core workload.

Figure 10 shows the s-curve of the normalized weighted speedup on 4-core workloads when prefetching is enabled. Compared to LRU with prefetching, the weighted speedup improvement is 6.9% for VIP, while it is 4.7% for TADRRIP which performs best among the rest of techniques.

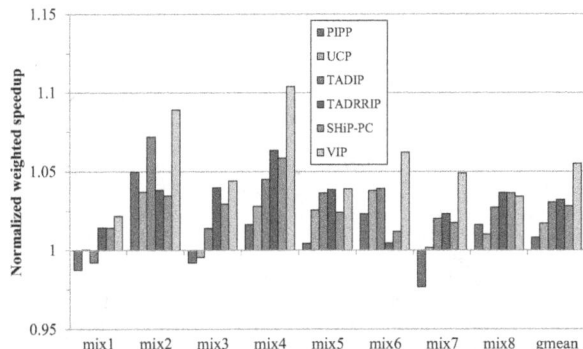

Figure 11: Normalized weighted speedup for 8-core workloads in the absence of prefetching.

To study the scalability of VIP with the number of cores, we evaluate the performance of VIP on 8-core workloads. Figure 11 presents the normalized weighted speedup for 8-core workloads in the absence of prefetching. Compared to LRU, the weighted speedup improvement of VIP is 5.5%, which is significantly better than the improvement of other techniques in which TADRRIP performs best and outperforms LRU by 3.2%.

6.3 Storage Overhead

Table 2 compares the storage overhead of various techniques for the 4MB L2 cache used in 4-core configuration. The storage overhead of VIP+NRU comes from per-block eviction bit and NRU bit, RHT, RVPT, and the structures for miss penalty and hit benefit computation. Each cache block needs 1 eviction bit and 1 NRU bit. For a 128-entry

8-way RHT, each RHT entry consists of 1 valid bit, 3 replacement bits, 1 prefetch bit, 8-bit PC, 18-bit IT, 18-bit VT, and 9-bit VC. Each RVPT counter needs 3 bits. For miss penalty and hit benefit computation, each core requires a 7-bit $C_{\text{demand\_miss}}$, and each MSHR entry requires an 8-bit T_p. Each HBC entry requires a valid bit, an 8-bit T_b, an 8-bit latency counter, and a 36-bit address. It totally consumes 17.09KB of extra storage to implement VIP, which is roughly 0.4% of the total storage of a 4MB L2 cache. Compared to other recent proposals, the storage overhead of VIP+NRU is close to that of TADRRIP and lower compared to that of others. The storage overhead of VIP+NRU in single-core configuration is also very low.

Table 2: Storage overhead of various techniques.

	Storage per block	Extra storage	Total
LRU	4 bits	0	32KB
PIPP	4 bits	5KB	37KB
UCP	6 bits	5KB	53KB
TADIP	4 bits	40 bits	32KB
TADRRIP	2 bits	40 bits	16KB
SHiP-PC	2 bits	24.5KB	40.5KB
VIP+NRU	2 bits	1.09KB	17.09KB

7. CONCLUSION

Every cache management policy tries to improve cache performance by retaining blocks with higher *values* longer. Traditionally, the access time or reuse distance of a cache block is treated as its value. However, cache miss latency is variable in modern systems. As a result, the cache management policy should also be able to take into account the performance impact of each cache request when it results in miss. This paper achieves this goal by making the following contributions:

1. We illustrate that the *value* of a cache block depends on all its requests. It includes not only the performance loss on its misses (i.e., *miss penalty*), but also the performance gain due to its hits (i.e., *hit benefit*).

2. We propose a hardware mechanism to compute miss penalty and hit benefit, which only requires negligible modification to the current cache design. Then the value of a block can be calculated by accumulating all its miss penalty and hit benefits.

3. We propose *Value based Insertion Policy (VIP)*. VIP learns and predicts the relationship between the value

of the incoming block and that of the victim block on a cache miss. If the value of the incoming block is predicted to be lower, it is assigned with a high eviction priority so that it can be evicted from the cache quickly.

Our evaluation shows that VIP can improve cache performance for both single-core and multi-core workloads. In future systems with heterogeneous multiprocessors and hybrid memory hierarchies, the values of different cache blocks can even change more dramatically. To apply VIP in such systems is part of our future work.

8. ACKNOWLEDGMENTS

This work is supported by the National Science and Technology Major Project of the Ministry of Science and Technology of China under grant 2009ZX01029-001-002-2. We would like to acknowledge Dong Tong, Zichao Xie, and the anonymous reviewers for their helpful comments.

9. REFERENCES

[1] J. Albericio, P. Ibáñez, V. Viñals, and J. M. Llabería. Exploiting reuse locality on inclusive shared last-level caches. *ACM Trans. Archit. Code Optim.*, 9(4):38:1–38:19, 2013.

[2] N. Binkert, B. Beckmann, G. Black, S. K. Reinhardt, A. Saidi, A. Basu, J. Hestness, D. R. Hower, T. Krishna, S. Sardashti, R. Sen, K. Sewell, M. Shoaib, N. Vaish, M. D. Hill, and D. A. Wood. The gem5 simulator. *SIGARCH Comput. Archit. News*, 39(2):1–7, 2011.

[3] M. Chaudhuri. Pseudo-LIFO: The foundation of a new family of replacement policies for last-level caches. In *MICRO-42*, 2009.

[4] C.-H. Chi and H. Dietz. Improving cache performance by selective cache bypass. In *HICSS-22*, 1989.

[5] N. Duong, D. Zhao, T. Kim, R. Cammarota, M. Valero, and A. V. Veidenbaum. Improving cache management policies using dynamic reuse distances. In *MICRO-45*, 2012.

[6] H. Gao and C. Wilkerson. A dueling segmented LRU replacement algorithm with adaptive bypassing. In *JWAC-1*, 2010.

[7] J. Gaur, M. Chaudhuri, and S. Subramoney. Bypass and insertion algorithms for exclusive last-level caches. In *ISCA-38*, 2011.

[8] A. González, C. Aliagas, and M. Valero. A data cache with multiple caching strategies tuned to different types of locality. In *ICS-9*, 1995.

[9] J. L. Henning. SPEC CPU2006 benchmark descriptions. *SIGARCH Comput. Archit. News*, 34:1–17, 2006.

[10] Z. Hu, S. Kaxiras, and M. Martonosi. Timekeeping in the memory system: Predicting and optimizing memory behavior. In *ISCA-29*, 2002.

[11] Intel. Intel Core i7 processor. http://www.intel.com/products/processor/corei7/.

[12] A. Jaleel, E. Borch, M. Bhandaru, S. Steely, and J. Emer. Achieving non-inclusive cache performance with inclusive caches: Temporal locality aware (TLA) cache management policies. In *MICRO-43*, 2010.

[13] A. Jaleel, W. Hasenplaugh, M. Qureshi, J. Sebot, S. Steely, Jr., and J. Emer. Adaptive insertion policies for managing shared caches. In *PACT-17*, 2008.

[14] A. Jaleel, K. B. Theobald, S. C. Steely, Jr., and J. Emer. High performance cache replacement using re-reference interval prediction (RRIP). In *ISCA-37*, 2010.

[15] J. Jalminger and P. Stenstrom. A novel approach to cache block reuse predictions. In *ICPP '03*, 2003.

[16] J. Jeong and M. Dubois. Optimal replacements in caches with two miss costs. In *SPAA-11*, 1999.

[17] J. Jeong and M. Dubois. Cost-sensitive cache replacement algorithms. In *HPCA-9*, 2003.

[18] J. Jeong and M. Dubois. Cache replacement algorithms with nonuniform miss costs. *Computers, IEEE Transactions on*, 55(4):353–365, 2006.

[19] J. Jeong, P. Stenström, and M. Dubois. Simple penalty-sensitive replacement policies for caches. In *CF-3*, 2006.

[20] D. A. Jiménez. Insertion and promotion for tree-based PseudoLRU last-level caches. In *MICRO-46*, 2013.

[21] T. Johnson, D. Connors, M. Merten, and W.-M. Hwu. Run-time cache bypassing. *Computers, IEEE Transactions on*, 48(12):1338 –1354, 1999.

[22] R. D.-c. Ju, A. R. Lebeck, and C. Wilkerson. Locality vs. criticality. In *ISCA-28*, 2001.

[23] D. Kaseridis, M. Iqbal, and L. John. Cache friendliness-aware management of shared last-level caches for high performance multi-core systems. *Computers, IEEE Transactions on*, 2013.

[24] G. Keramidas, P. Petoumenos, and S. Kaxiras. Cache replacement based on reuse-distance prediction. In *ICCD-25*, 2007.

[25] S. M. Khan, Y. Tian, and D. A. Jimenez. Sampling dead block prediction for last-level caches. In *MICRO-43*, 2010.

[26] M. Kharbutli and R. Sheikh. LACS: A locality-aware cost-sensitive cache replacement algorithm. *Computers, IEEE Transactions on*, 2013.

[27] M. Kharbutli and Y. Solihin. Counter-based cache replacement and bypassing algorithms. *Computers, IEEE Transactions on*, 57(4):433 –447, 2008.

[28] D. Kroft. Lockup-free instruction fetch/prefetch cache organization. In *ISCA-8*, 1981.

[29] A.-C. Lai, C. Fide, and B. Falsafi. Dead-block prediction & dead-block correlating prefetchers. In *ISCA-28*, 2001.

[30] L. Li, D. Tong, Z. Xie, J. Lu, and X. Cheng. Optimal bypass monitor for high performance last-level caches. In *PACT-21*, 2012.

[31] H. Liu, M. Ferdman, J. Huh, and D. Burger. Cache bursts: A new approach for eliminating dead blocks and increasing cache efficiency. In *MICRO-41*, 2008.

[32] G. H. Loh and M. D. Hill. Efficiently enabling conventional block sizes for very large die-stacked dram caches. In *MICRO-44*, 2011.

[33] R. Manikantan, K. Rajan, and R. Govindarajan. NUcache: An efficient multicore cache organization based on next-use distance. In *HPCA-17*, 2011.

[34] R. Manikantan, K. Rajan, and R. Govindarajan. Probabilistic shared cache management (PriSM). In *ISCA-39*, 2012.

[35] M. M. K. Martin, M. D. Hill, and D. J. Sorin. Why on-chip cache coherence is here to stay. *Commun. ACM*, 55(7):78–89, 2012.

[36] M. Moreto, F. Cazorla, A. Ramirez, and M. Valero. MLP-aware dynamic cache partitioning. In *HiPEAC '08*. 2008.

[37] E. Perelman, G. Hamerly, M. Van Biesbrouck, T. Sherwood, and B. Calder. Using simpoint for accurate and efficient simulation. *SIGMETRICS Perform. Eval. Rev.*, 31:318–319, 2003.

[38] M. K. Qureshi, A. Jaleel, Y. N. Patt, S. C. Steely, and J. Emer. Adaptive insertion policies for high performance caching. In *ISCA-34*, 2007.

[39] M. K. Qureshi, D. N. Lynch, O. Mutlu, and Y. N. Patt. A case for MLP-aware cache replacement. In *ISCA-33*, 2006.

[40] M. K. Qureshi and Y. N. Patt. Utility-based cache partitioning: A low-overhead, high-performance, runtime mechanism to partition shared caches. In *MICRO-39*, 2006.

[41] J. A. Rivers, E. S. Tam, G. S. Tyson, E. S. Davidson, and M. Farrens. Utilizing reuse information in data cache management. In *ICS-12*, 1998.

[42] D. Sanchez and C. Kozyrakis. Vantage: Scalable and efficient fine-grain cache partitioning. In *ISCA-38*, 2011.

[43] R. Sheikh and M. Kharbutli. Improving cache performance by combining cost-sensitivity and locality principles in cache replacement algorithms. In *ICCD-28*, 2010.

[44] G. Tyson, M. Farrens, J. Matthews, and A. R. Pleszkun. A modified approach to data cache management. In *MICRO-28*, 1995.

[45] S. P. Vanderwiel and D. J. Lilja. Data prefetch mechanisms. *ACM Comput. Surv.*, 32(2):174–199, 2000.

[46] C. Wu, A. Jaleel, W. Hasenplaugh, M. Martonosi, S. Steely Jr, and J. Emer. SHiP: Signature-based hit predictor for high performance caching. In *MICRO-44*, 2011.

[47] Y. Xie. Modeling, architecture, and applications for emerging memory technologies. *Design Test of Computers, IEEE*, 28(1):44–51, 2011.

[48] Y. Xie and G. H. Loh. PIPP: Promotion/insertion pseudo-partitioning of multi-core shared caches. In *ISCA-36*, 2009.

Multi-Stage Coordinated Prefetching for Present-day Processors

Sanyam Mehta
Department of Computer
Science and Engineering
University of Minnesota
Minneapolis, MN USA
sanyam@cs.umn.edu

Zhenman Fang
School of Computer Science
Fudan University
Shanghai, China
fangzhenman@gmail.com

Antonia Zhai
Department of Computer
Science and Engineering
University of Minnesota
Minneapolis, MN USA
zhai@cs.umn.edu

Pen-Chung Yew
Department of Computer
Science and Engineering
University of Minnesota
Minneapolis, MN USA
yew@cs.umn.edu

ABSTRACT

Latest microarchitectures provide support for both hardware and software prefetching. However, the architectural features supporting either are different. In addition, these features can vary from one architecture to another. As a result, the choice of the right prefetching strategy is non-trivial for both the programmers and compiler-writers.

In this paper, we study prefetching techniques in the context of different architectural features that support prefetching on existing hardware platforms. These features include, the size of the line fill buffer or the Miss Status Handling Registers servicing prefetch requests at each level of cache, the effectiveness of the hardware prefetchers and their interaction with software prefetching, the nature of the instruction pipeline (in-order/out-of-order execution), etc. Our experiments with two widely different processors, a latest multi-core (SandyBridge) and a many-core (Xeon Phi), show that these architectural features have a significant bearing on the prefetching choice in a given source program, so much so that the best prefetching technique on SandyBridge performs worst on Xeon Phi and vice-versa. Based on our study of the interaction between the host architecture and prefetching, we find that coordinated multi-stage prefetching that brings data closer to the core in stages, yields best performance. On SandyBridge, the mid-level cache hardware prefetcher and L1 software prefetching *coordinate* to achieve this end, whereas on Xeon Phi, pure software prefetching proves adequate.

Categories and Subject Descriptors

D.3.4 [**Processors**]: Compilers, Optimization

Keywords

Coordinated prefetching; SandyBridge; XeonPhi

1. INTRODUCTION

Data prefetching proves very effective for hiding the large memory latency. It is for this reason that latest processors are equipped with improved hardware prefetching logic, and their instruction sets provide support for software prefetch instructions that can selectively prefetch data to different levels of cache. However, while such an extensive support exists in the form of hardware, software, or coordinated hardware-software prefetching, the choice of the right prefetching strategy among the various options continues to remain a mystery for programmers and compiler writers.

The choice of the right prefetching strategy is a function of the various features supporting prefetching in the host architecture. One such feature is the nature of hardware prefetcher - its effectiveness, aggressiveness and behavior in the presence of software prefetch instructions. For example, on SandyBridge, the Mid-level cache (MLC) streamer hardware prefetcher is very effective and prefetches data to the L2 cache. Unlike software prefetching, it is not limited by the small size of the Line Fill Buffer at the L2 cache that allows very few outstanding prefetch requests, but can effectively prefetch data for 32 streams. Further, it can be trained by the software prefetch requests to the L2 cache for prefetching data to the L1 cache. This makes for an ideal scenario for *coordination* between the MLC streamer prefetcher and the L1 software prefetches that together fetch the data all the way to the L1 cache and make up for the not-so-effective L1 hardware prefetcher. The L1 software prefetching also provides other advantages: (1) Using a larger prefetch distance helps to increase the limit of look-ahead prefetch distance of the hardware prefetcher as the existing limit of 20 cache lines proves insufficient for small loops (as in matrix multiplication). (2) The hardware prefetcher stops at page boundaries. However, using a large prefetch distance in the software prefetch instructions helps to re-trigger the hardware prefetcher in time to prevent incurring any stalls at page boundaries. (3) The hardware prefetcher can track a maximum of 32 streams. Thus, for programs with more than 32 streams, software prefetch instructions prove particularly helpful to improve the prefetch coverage by prefetching data for the remaining streams directly to the L1 cache.

On the other hand, on Xeon Phi, there is similarly an effective L2 streamer prefetcher but it does not prefetch data in the presence of L1 software prefetch instructions. Thus, the advantages of coordinated hardware-software prefetching cannot be realized on

Xeon Phi. However, unlike SandyBridge that supports very few outstanding software prefetch requests at the L2 cache, each core on Xeon Phi supports a much larger number of outstanding software prefetch requests at the L2 cache. Thus, like SandyBridge, the data can be brought all the way to the L1 cache through coordinated multi-stage prefetching. But, unlike SandyBridge, the *coordination* is between software prefetch instructions at different levels of cache, i.e. data is first prefetched using a larger prefetch distance at the larger last level cache, while a smaller prefetch distance is used at the L1 cache to prefetch data from the next level cache. A smaller prefetch distance at the L1 cache allows for fewer outstanding prefetches, thus minimizing contention in the 8-entry MSHR file at the L1 cache. It is interesting to note that Xeon Phi with in-order cores and blocking caches, is more sensitive to the choice of prefetching technique than SandyBridge because pipeline stalls due to inadequate prefetching cannot be tolerated through out-of-order execution capability as in SandyBridge.

In recent past, hardware-based coordinated multi-stage prefetching has been implemented in IBM's Power6 microarchitecture [11] where the L1 hardware prefetcher coordinates with the L2 hardware prefetcher to bring the data to the L1 cache in stages. However, as noted above, software prefetches can be used in a similar manner to achieve this coordination and overcome the limitations of the existing hardware prefetchers. Also, there has been some work [6, 15, 18] that has considered employing software to aid hardware prefetching, but in such cases, the hardware was built around achieving such coordination. This, however, is not true for existing processors, and thus achieving such coordination while considering other hardware features is non-trivial. Recently, Lee et al. [12] have studied the interaction between software and hardware prefetching but have not proposed any particular prefetching strategy.

In this paper, we make the following contributions:

1. We study the influence of various hardware features on data prefetching and their impact on the choice of prefetching technique for different hardware platforms.

2. Based on our study, we propose a coordinated multi-stage prefetching algorithm for 2 different state-of-the-art processors (SandyBridge and Xeon Phi). The means of achieving the coordination, is however, different on each platform depending on the hardware supporting prefetching.

3. We evaluate the performance of the different prefetching techniques possible on both platforms and identify the reasons for their respective behaviors in different programs. Our experiments with prefetching in multithreaded environment further provides useful insights about the interaction between hardware and prefetching, and leads us to an interesting compiler optimization to tackle pronounced contention for resources in Xeon Phi. The coordinated multi-stage prefetching proposed in this work is a static compiler technique with no hardware overhead and can thus be incorporated in existing production-quality compilers, or serve as an effective tool in the hands of a programmer.

Our multi-stage prefetching algorithm works in three phases, (1) identifying *what* to prefetch, (2) identifying *where* to insert the prefetch instructions, and (3) identifying *when* to prefetch, or what prefetch distance to use at each level. The choice of prefetch instructions and the prefetch distance at each level is carefully chosen to achieve the desired coordination. We have implemented our prefetching algorithm in the ROSE source-to-source compiler framework that transforms the original source code to include the prefetch instructions. The generated transformed code is then compiled using the Intel compiler as the back-end vendor compiler. We tested our algorithm using various memory-intensive benchmarks

from the SPEC CPU2006 and OMP2012 suites on Intel Sandy-Bridge and Xeon Phi processors. Experimental results show that our multi-stage prefetching achieves a speedup of 1.55X over the Xeon Phi hardware prefetcher, and that of 1.3X over the state-of-the-art Intel compiler for Xeon Phi. On SandyBridge that employs an effective hardware prefetcher, an improvement of 1.08X is obtained.

The rest of the paper is organized as follows. Section 2 provides the background for this work and reinforces our motivation through an example. We describe our multi-stage prefetching algorithm with its three phases in Section 3. The interaction of our prefetching algorithm with the multithreading technique is also discussed in this section. Section 4 describes our compiler framework for implementing the prefetching algorithm. We present experimental results and discuss the results obtained using different prefetching strategies on individual benchmarks in Section 5. Related work is presented in Section 6 and we conclude in Section 7.

2. BACKGROUND AND MOTIVATION

In the literature, there have been many schemes proposed, both for hardware-based and software-directed prefetching. In hardware-based prefetching, some special hardware monitors data access patterns to a particular cache and identifies data suitable for prefetching based on obtained information. Current processors employ multiple hardware prefetchers for streaming as well as strided accesses. Software-directed prefetching, on the other hand, involves the insertion of prefetch instructions into the original code by the programmer or the compiler that request data needed a few iterations later. This distance in the number of loop iterations is called the prefetch distance. Like hardware prefetchers that sit on multiple levels of cache and can prefetch data to those levels, the latest instruction sets provide prefetch intrinsics for prefetching data at different levels of cache. In software-directed prefetching, it is the responsibility of the programmer to ensure timeliness and prevent redundant prefetches by deciding the data to prefetch and the prefetch distance. The hardware prefetchers usually ensure timeliness through aggressive prefetching, i.e. maintaining a prefetch degree of more than one. For example, the streamer hardware prefetchers on SandyBridge and Xeon Phi have prefetch degrees of 2 and 4, respectively, and can maintain a prefetch distance of a maximum of 20 cache lines. Depending on implementation, software prefetch instructions can also be used to train and thus control the prefetch distance at which the hardware prefetcher operates. Comparing software-directed and hardware-based prefetching, software-directed prefetching has the advantage of being used in a controlled manner, but is associated with an additional instruction overhead which may compete with the gains.

While the above-mentioned facts about prefetching are better known, the impact of other hardware features influencing prefetching are less well understood. The hardware tracks the outstanding prefetch requests through a buffer or a queue. This hardware structure is called the line fill buffer (LFB) in SandyBridge and MSHR (Miss Status Handling Registers) file in Xeon Phi, and is responsible for rendering the data prefetch requests *non-blocking*. The size of the LFB or the MSHR file, among other factors, has a significant bearing on the most appropriate choice of prefetching strategy on a particular architecture. This is because, on Xeon Phi, if the MSHR file is full, the pipeline stalls. On SandyBridge, if the LFB is full, subsequent prefetches/loads enter the load buffer, which when full, stalls the pipeline.

On all hardware platforms, the size of the LFB or MSHR file at the L1 cache is usually small. This is because any arriving data requests initiates a fully associative search across the structure to eliminate redundant requests, which is costly in terms of power usage and time delay, restricting its size. Chip area concerns also limit their size since these are located close to the core. It is for these reasons that both SandyBridge and Xeon Phi allow for only 8 outstanding prefetch requests at the L1 cache. However, clearly, such a small number of requests are insufficient to hide the large memory latencies on modern processors as pipeline stalls will result once the MSHR file or the load buffers are full. As a result, a multi-stage prefetching algorithm that brings the data from the memory in stages being cognizant of the resource availability at each level, is necessitated. This is more clearly illustrated through the following example of a well known memory-intensive weather prediction benchmark from SPEC OMP2012 suite, *swim*. The Xeon Phi processor is considered below, and similar arguments hold for a multicore processor as well.

```
for (i=0; i<M; i++) {
  for (j=0; j<N; j++) {
    S1: UNEW[i+1][j] = UOLD[i+1][j]+C1*(Z[i+1][j+1]+Z[i+1][j])
        *(CV[i+1][j+1]+CV[i][j+1]+CV[i][j]+CV[i+1][j])-C2*(H[i+1][j]-H[i][j]);
    S2: VNEW[i][j+1] = VOLD[i][j+1]-C1*(Z[i+1][j+1]+Z[i][j+1])
        *(CU[i+1][j+1]+CU[i][j+1]+CU[i][j]+CU[i+1][j])-C3*(H[i][j+1]-H[i][j]);
    S3: PNEW[i][j] = POLD[i][j]-C2*(CU[i+1][j]-CU[i][j])
        -C3*(CV[i][j+1]-CV[i][j]);
  }
}
```

Figure 1: An example loop nest in the *swim* benchmark.

Figure 1 shows one of the three computationally (and memory) intensive loop nests in *swim*. The loop nest shown has 14 array references that access different cache lines, or in other words 14 data streams that need to be prefetched. When testing on Intel Xeon Phi that has a maximum memory latency of 1000 cycles, we observe that a minimum prefetch distance of 6 cache lines is needed to hide the memory latency. That is, there can be a maximum of 14*6 (= 84) outstanding prefetches per thread for *swim*. Thus, for the data to be prefetched directly to the L1 cache, the L1 cache should provide 84 MSHRs per thread (in the ideal scenario when there is enough off-chip memory bandwidth available), or at least much more than the currently available 8 MSHRs per thread. Such a large MSHR file at L1 cache is not feasible. To make things worse, the 8 MSHRs at L1 cache are shared by the 4 SMT threads on each core on Xeon Phi.

Thus we implement a coordinated multi-stage data prefetching strategy, where data is first brought to the lower-level cache, e.g., L2 cache (that on Xeon Phi, has more MSHRs to allow holding more requests for hiding larger memory latencies) using a large prefetch distance (6 cache lines in case of *swim*). Subsequently, data is brought from the lower-level cache (e.g., L2 cache) to the higher-level cache (e.g., L1 cache) using a smaller prefetch distance (1 cache line in case of *swim*) since the data is already in the next-level cache. As a result, a small MSHR file at the L1 cache proves sufficient to hide the small L2-to-L1 latency, and prevent stalls due to contention. On SandyBridge, the same coordinated multi-stage prefetching strategy is implemented, but the coordination is between the L1 software prefetches and the L2 hardware prefetcher, which is more effective than its software counterpart due to its ability to hold many more outstanding prefetch requests.

3. COORDINATED MULTI-STAGE DATA PREFETCHING

As stated in Section 1, our coordinated multi-stage data prefetching algorithm works in three phases, namely, *what* to prefetch, *where* to insert prefetch instructions, and *when* to prefetch. For each of these phases, we discuss our specific choices for the two hardware platforms considered and reasons behind those specific choices.

3.1 What to Prefetch

This is the first of the three phases in which the references that should be prefetched are identified. Such references include (1) those whose future memory accesses can be determined, and (2) those when prefetched will benefit application performance.

A recent work [12] classified memory references into 5 types - (1) direct-indexed *streaming* array references, (2) direct-indexed *strided* array references, (3) *indirect*-indexed array references, (4) recursive data structures (RDS), and (5) hashing data structures. In our compiler framework, we only handle memory references of types (1) through (3), as references of types (4) and (5) need to be handled differently.

Further, even among references whose future access patterns can be statically determined, prefetching all of them is not always beneficial. For example, references that have temporal locality in the inner loops such as references A and C in *matmul* (shown in Figure 2) have small reuse distances and thus, the data referenced by them stays in the cache with a high probability. Such references occur often in SPEC benchmarks and lead to redundant prefetches that reduce performance gains, especially when the amount of computation in loop-nests is small (as in *matmul*). Although Mowry et al. in [13] proposed prefetch predicates in the form of IF statements (or its equivalent) to eliminate redundant prefetches, we empirically observe that the instruction overhead of such predicates usually offset the performance gain from data prefetching. These predicates also hinder automatic vectorization by the compiler. It is for these reasons that we do not consider such references as profitable candidates for prefetching. In addition, for references that have group reuse, such as $CV\ i\ j$ and $CV\ i\ j$ in statement S1 in *swim* (shown in Figure 1), we prefetch only for the *leading* reference $CV\ i\ j$ as it is the one that accesses new data first and caches it for later use.

```
for(i = 0; i < N; i++)
  for(k = 0; k< N; k++)
    for(j = 0; j < N; j++)
      C[i][j] += A[i][k] * B[k][j];
```

Figure 2: The *matmul* kernel.

For all references that are thus marked for prefetching, our prefetching algorithm inserts prefetch instructions for just the L1 cache in case of SandyBridge since it relies on the hardware prefetcher for prefetching data to other levels. In case of Xeon Phi, however, the algorithm inserts prefetch instructions for all levels of cache to implement pure software-directed coordinated multi-stage prefetching.

3.2 Where to Insert Prefetch Instructions

Having identified the array references to be prefetched, the next phase is to determine *where* prefetch instructions for the identified references should be inserted. For all identified references, we insert prefetch requests in the innermost loop. This simplifies the insertion of prefetch instructions and prefetch distance calculation by the compiler. However, even in the innermost loop, the placement of prefetch instructions is important. For example, in the loop nest from the *swim* benchmark shown in Figure 1, if prefetch requests for all 14 array references are placed contiguously in the source code without any intermittent computation, then it might lead to pipeline-stalls because prefetches will be blocked waiting for the availability of MSHRs. This is particularly true for L1 prefetch instructions given the small size of the L1 LFB or MSHR file. Such stalls are particularly visible on Xeon Phi where the pipeline is stalled immediately upon unavailability of MSHRs, whereas incoming requests could be buffered in the load buffer in case of dynamically scheduled SandyBridge processor. Thus, our compiler framework inserts prefetch requests *between* individual statements requesting data needed by the array references in that statement - this introduces computation between a batch of prefetch requests providing adequate time for them to finish and free MSHRs. Further, prefetch requests for different levels of cache are intermingled, creating additional cycles for an L1 prefetch request to prefetch data from a lower-level cache.

3.3 When to Prefetch

This is the last phase of our prefetching algorithm that determines *when* to prefetch data for a memory reference. In particular, this phase determines for each array reference, the prefetch distance to be used when prefetching data to a particular level of cache. Prefetch distance calculation involves calculation of the loop iteration time, which is hard to precisely determine for processors with out-of-order execution capability. Thus, in this section, we treat the prefetch distance calculation for the in-order many-core Xeon Phi and the out-of-order multi-core SandyBridge separately.

3.3.1 Calculating Prefetch Distance in Xeon Phi

Mowry et al. in one of the earliest works on software prefetching [13] defined prefetch distance as $\lceil \frac{Lat}{LIT} \rceil$, where Lat and LIT are the prefetch **Lat**ency and the **L**oop **I**teration **T**ime, respectively. Of the two parameters, Lat is a machine specific parameter and can be known from vendor's data sheets or measurements. LIT, on the other hand, must be estimated by the compiler. In our framework, we estimate LIT using Equation 1 below. This estimated value of LIT is then used to calculate the prefetch distances for prefetches to any level of cache, using measures of the corresponding prefetch latencies.

$$ LIT \quad nrefs * Lat_{L1} \quad nrefs * C_p * i \quad \sum_{comp=1}^{n} C_{comp} \quad (1) $$

where $nrefs$ is the number of distinct array references in the loop nest, Lat_{L1} is the latency of accessing a data item in the L1 cache, C_p is the number of cycles spent in executing a prefetch instruction, and C_{comp} is the cost of one of n computations in the loop nest measured in the number of cycles.

The above formula for calculating the loop iteration time (LIT) assumes that all array references in the loop nest are accessed from the L1 cache (i.e. L1 cache hits). This is because we accomplish a multi-stage data prefetching where the data is prefetched all the way up to the L1 cache. This assumption holds for all but the initial few iterations of the loop nest, which can be considered as the warm-up phase. Also, since our framework inserts one prefetch instruction for each level of the cache memory per array reference, the instruction overhead in each loop iteration is calculated as $nrefs * C_p * i$, where i is the number of levels in the cache memory hierarchy. To facilitate further discussion in this section, we assume a 2-level cache memory hierarchy as in the Xeon Phi processor.

Once LIT is determined, the prefetch distance at each of the two levels is calculated as,

$$ PD_{L1} \quad \left(\left\lceil \frac{Lat_{L2}}{LIT} \right\rceil \right) * \alpha * \beta \quad (2) $$

and

$$ PD_{L2} \quad \left(\left\lceil \frac{Lat_{memory}}{LIT} \right\rceil \right) * \alpha * \beta \quad (3) $$

where α and β are program dependent constants as explained below

When calculating the prefetch distance, it is important to consider whether or not the innermost loop is vectorized. This is because, the prefetch distance computed using the formula, $\lceil \frac{Lat}{LIT} \rceil$, gives the prefetch distance in the number of loop iterations. How-

ever, if the innermost loop is vectorized, the same formula (using appropriate computation costs for vector operations) gives the prefetch distance in the number of vector iterations. We accommodate this in our algorithm by the parameter α, where α is size of the vector (in the number of data elements) when the innermost loop is vectorized and 1, otherwise. The prefetch distance is further multiplied by the constant stride, β, for an array reference that exhibits strided access pattern. The prefetch distance is also rounded to the next higher multiple of the cache line size in cases when the innermost loop is not vectorized.

From Equations 2 and 3, we observe PD_{L2} is much larger than PD_{L1} (as $Lat_{memory} >> Lat_{L2}$). As a result, data is prefetched first to the larger L2 cache using a larger prefetch distance, and this data is then prefetched to the L1 cache a fewer iterations ahead. Thus, the 2 stages of data prefetching coordinate to timely fetch the data to the L1 cache. As discussed earlier, using a smaller L1 prefetch distance facilitated by this strategy minimizes contention (and also prevents a possible cache pollution due to early prefetches).

3.3.2 Calculating Prefetch Distance in SandyBridge

Unlike the many-core Xeon Phi that has single-wide in-order issue and in-order execution, the multi-cores are usually superscalar processors with dynamic scheduling capability. As a result, it is non-trivial to statically determine the iteration time of loops on a multi-core processor. It is for this reason that Lee et al. [12] use the IPC values from benchmark profiling in their prefetch distance calculation. Their calculation gives a lower bound on the prefetch distance. The prefetch distance can, however, be increased without any negative effects until the newly prefetched data begins to replace the previously prefetched but unused data. A larger prefetch distance for L1 prefetches is, infact, required as this helps to increase the prefetch distance for the hardware prefetcher. This, as explained earlier, helps to prevent stalls at page boundaries and in particular, helps small loops that need large prefetch distances. In our algorithm we prevent the replacement of useful data from the L1 cache by ensuring that the amount of unused prefetched data does not exceed a fourth of the L1 cache size. We restrict ourselves to a fourth of the L1 cache size as misses due to cache interference can set in much before the cache capacity is reached. The prefetch distance is thus calculated as

$$ PD_{L1} \quad \left\lceil \frac{Size_{L1}}{* \ nrefs * Size_{elem}} \right\rceil \quad (4) $$

where $Size_{L1}$ is the L1 cache size, and $Size_{elem}$ is the size of each data element. The L1 software prefetch instructions use this prefetch distance and in turn trigger the L2 hardware prefetcher which in time runs sufficiently ahead of the L1 prefetches to timely bring the data to the L2 cache. Thus, like Xeon Phi, coordinated multi-stage prefetching that prefetches the data all the way to the L1 cache with minimal contention in L1 LFB, is accomplished on SandyBridge.

3.3.3 Prefetch Distance for Tiled Code

While the formula for calculating the prefetch distances as derived above proves applicable to most programs, it nevertheless assumes long contiguous streaming/strided access patterns, i.e. array references where the entire array is referenced in all loop nests within an application. Such access patterns are not observed, however, in tiled codes and certain other scientific codes where the computational domain is split into parts, as in *gemsfdtd* and *mgrid* benchmarks from the SPEC suite.

We use a simple example of tiled *matmul* to illustrate such a case and the prefetching strategy applied therein. Figure 3(b) shows

```
for (iT=0; iT< N/I; iT++)              for (iT=0; iT< N/I; iT++)              for (iT=0; iT< N/I; iT++)
  for (kT=0; kT< N/K; kT++)              for (kT=0; kT< N/K; kT++)              for (kT=0; kT< N/K; kT++)
    for (jT=0; jT< N/J; jT++)              for (jT=0; jT< N/J; jT++)              for (jT=0; jT< N/J; jT++)
      for (i = I*iT ; i < I*iT + I-1 ; i++)    for (i = I*iT ; i < I*iT + I-1 ; i++)    for (i = I*iT ; i < I*iT + I-1 ; i++)
        for (k = K*kT ; k < K*kT + K-1 ; k++)    for (k = K*kT ; k < K*kT + K-1 ; k++)    for (k = K*kT ; k < K*kT + K-1 ; k++)
          for (j = J*jT ; j < J*jT + J-1 ; j++)    for (j = J*jT ; j < J*jT + J-1 ; j++) {    for (j = J*jT ; j < J*jT + J-1 ; j++) {
          {                                          prefetch (&B[k][j+PD_L1], _L1_);          prefetch (&B[k+1][j], _L1_);
            C[i][j] += A[i][k] * B[k][j];           prefetch (&B[k][j+PD_L2], _L2_);          prefetch (&B[k+2][j], _L2_);
          }                                          C[i][j] += A[i][k] * B[k][j]; }           C[i][j] += A[i][k] * B[k][j]; }

              (a)                                         (b)                                       (c)
```

Figure 3: (a) Tiled *matmul*; (b) Tiled *matmul* with prefetching as in the *general* case; (c) Tiled *matmul* with prefetching as in the *special* case.

the tiled *matmul* code with prefetch instructions inserted assuming contiguous streaming access patterns - B k j is identified as suitable for prefetching and prefetch instructions are inserted in the innermost loop as shown. However, as a result of tiling, the access pattern is no longer contiguous - only J elements of array B are accessed contiguously, followed by another J elements from the next row of B. Thus, if a prefetch distance, PD_{L2} (that is likely to be greater than J), as calculated using Equation 3 is used, *useless* prefetches could result. Since the data does not arrive at L2 cache in time for L1 prefetches, 2-stage prefetching becomes ineffective.

Our framework identifies such cases of accesses to non-contiguous data chunks (where the size of the innermost loop is a fraction of the array size) as in tiled *matmul*, and inserts prefetches as shown in Figure 3(c). It prefetches one of the next array rows instead of prefetching elements that are a few cache lines (= prefetch distance) away. Thus, useless prefetches are reduced to only those that are prefetched while processing the last few rows of a tile of array B. Since correct data does arrive in time in L2 cache, 2-stage prefetching again becomes very effective. In such cases, the prefetch distance is calculated in the number of *array rows*, instead of elements as in the *general* case above discussed. It is given as follows.

$$PD_{L1}^s \quad max\left(\ , \frac{PD_{L1}^g}{lc}\right) \quad (5)$$

and

$$PD_{L2}^s \quad max\left(\ , \frac{PD_{L2}^g}{lc}\right) \quad (6)$$

where PD^s is the prefetch distance in this *special* case, PD^g is the prefetch distance in the *general* case (calculated in the number of elements) and lc is the loop count of the innermost loop, or tile size in case of tiled codes. In the formula, the lower bounds of 1 and 2 for L1 and L2 prefetch distance is to ensure sufficient time for the data to arrive in both L1 and L2 cache. In SandyBridge, our framework inserts prefetch requests for just the L1 cache using the above formula, and relies on the hardware to prefetch the data to L2 cache.

3.4 Multi-stage Prefetching in multi-threaded environment

Chip multiprocessing (CMP) and simultaneous multithreading (SMT) can both be used to extract the inherent instruction-level parallelism in programs run in a multithreaded environment. Both these techniques interact closely with prefetching. In CMP, threads on each core simultaneously place demands for data from the memory, and pronounced bandwidth contention results. The net effect of this is an increase in the effective memory latency. As a result, pipeline-stalls due to unavailability of slots in the load/store buffer (in multi-cores) tend to be more prominent in such cases. Data prefetch requests that are additional requests to the regular loads, also occupy slots in the load buffer and thus end up contributing to these stalls. It is for this reason that we observe that for certain

memory-intensive benchmarks such as *swim*, *bwaves* and others, the performance advantage due to software-directed prefetching to L1 over the hardware prefetcher, is lost. For other benchmarks that are less memory-intensive such as *bt*, *cactus* and *matmul*, the performance advantage persists. In a many-core processor such as Xeon Phi that has blocking loads, there is no load buffer and thus data prefetch requests and regular loads do not share common resources. As a result, prefetching does not cause a side-effect to parallel performance as in multi-cores as long as useful data is timely prefetched.

In SMT, multiple SMT threads on a core share the LFB or the MSHR file. As a result, the increased data access rate puts pressure on the shared MSHR file, resulting in potential stalls due to contention. Precisely, a contention results when the maximum number of outstanding prefetches are less than the available MSHRs.

Since MSHRs are already scarce for a single thread, we observe that prefetching generally adversely affects performance of programs run in an SMT environment. In case of Xeon Phi, however, prospects of an interesting compiler optimization to reduce contention for MSHRs emerge for several reasons. Xeon Phi employs GDDR5 memory that has significantly higher latency and the latency increases when there are multiple active data streams or the number of distinct array references in a loop. It is for this reason that our framework detects contention for MSHRs and performs loop distribution prior to the insertion of prefetch instructions. This reduces the number of active streams in a loop by distributing statements in the original nest to multiple nests and thus benefits from reduced contention for MSHRs due to reduced memory latency. It is important to note that in cases where there is reuse among array references in original nest, loop distribution hurts temporal locality and thus reuse. However, since we distribute at the innermost loop, only L1 cache locality is hurt, which is more than compensated by effective data prefetching rendered possible by reduced contention. In multi-cores that employ a DDR3 memory, the latency does not increase significantly with the number of active streams, and thus loop distribution is not beneficial.

4. THE COMPILER FRAMEWORK

Figure 4 gives an overview of our compiler framework for co-ordinated multi-stage data prefetching. Our prefetching strategy is implemented in the open-source ROSE [14] compiler, which performs source-to-source transformations and provides many APIs for program analysis and transformations based on its Abstract Syntax Tree (AST). As shown in Figure 4, there are mainly five steps to insert multi-stage prefetches to the input source code after it is parsed to the AST. Steps 1 through 3 determine *what* to prefetch - all array references in the innermost loops are recognized and those with either temporal or group locality are discarded for prefetching. Step 4 is the key step to determine the prefetch distances or, *when* to prefetch, for multi-stage prefetching. As stated in Section 3, prefetch distance for each cache level is calculated using Equations (2)-(6). This requires information such as the total number of array references as well as the number and type of computations involved in the loop nest, which are obtained by querying the AST. The last step is to insert those prefetches with the calculated prefetch distance into the AST. After our multi-stage prefetching transformation, ROSE unparses the AST to the transformed source code with prefetch instructions. Finally, a back-end vendor compiler is used to compile the transformed source code to the final executable.

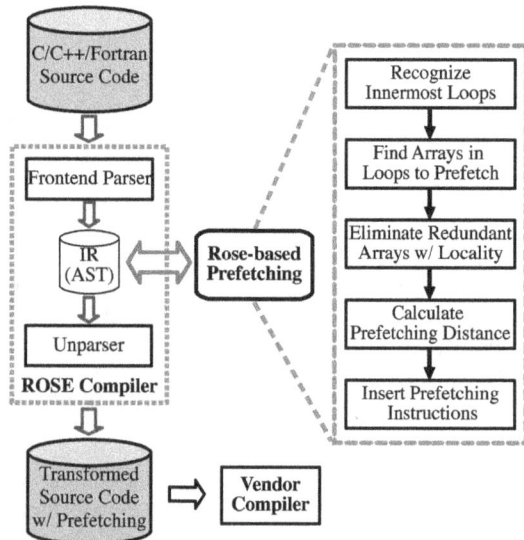

Figure 4: Compiler framework for coordinated multi-stage prefetching.

5. EXPERIMENTAL RESULTS AND DISCUSSION

In this section, we present the results of our coordinated multi-stage data prefetching and compare it with other prefetching strategies in both SandyBridge and Xeon Phi processors. Results comparing multi-stage prefetching and other strategies in a multithreaded environment are also presented.

5.1 Experimental Environment

Benchmark	Benchmark Suite	Category	Problem Size
cactus	SPEC CPU2006	General Relativity	Ref Input
hmmer	SPEC CPU2006	Search Gene Sequence	Ref Input
libquantum	SPEC CPU2006	Quantum Computing	Ref Input
gemsfdtd	SPEC CPU2006	Computational Electromagnetics	Ref Input
bwaves	SPEC OMP2012	Fluid Dynamics	Ref Input
swim	SPEC OMP2012	Weather Prediction	Ref Input
mgrid	SPEC OMP2012	Fluid Dynamics	Ref Input
bt	SPEC OMP2012	Fluid Dynamics	Ref Input
matmul	BLAS	Matrix-Matrix Multiplication	N=4000
spmv	General-purpose	Sparse Matrix-Vector Multiplication	N=10000

Table 1: Summary of benchmarks with problem sizes.

We first present our experimental setup. We chose a diverse set of memory-intensive benchmarks from the SPEC CPU2006 and OMP2012 benchmark suites that have high cache miss rates. We also chose two frequently used kernels, *dense matrix-matrix multiplication* (that can be tiled) and *sparse matrix-vector multiplication* (that involves indirect array indexing). Table 1 lists all the benchmarks used with their problem sizes.

We ran our experiments on the two different hardware platforms discussed in the paper - the multi-core Intel SandyBridge and the recently released many-core Intel Xeon Phi. The micro-architectural details of the two processors are compared in Table 2. Also, Xeon Phi contains instructions for prefetching data as 'exclusive' into either of the two caches, whereas SandyBridge does not provide this functionality. On Xeon Phi, we use the 'exclusive' prefetches to prefetch writes. Since Xeon Phi has 2-level cache hierarchy and SandyBridge (with 3-level cache hierarchy) also allows to prefetch only to the L1 and L2 caches, the coordinated prefetching strategy is implemented in **2** stages on both platforms. After generating the transformed source code that contains the prefetch instructions, we use the Intel compiler (v13) [1] as the back-end compiler to generate the executable.

Microarchitecture	Cache	No. of Cores	SMT	Hardware prefetcher
SandyBridge	Non-blocking	8	2-way	Streaming, Strided (L1+L2)
Xeon Phi	Blocking	60	4-way	Streaming (L2 only)

Table 2: Details of the microarchitectures

5.2 Results for Multi-stage Prefetching in Single-threaded environment

Strategy	Description
Hardware prefetching	The prefetching strategy used by Intel processors
L1 SW pref.	Data is prefetched only to L1 cache
L2 SW pref.	Data is prefetched only to L2 cache
2-stage SW pref.	Data is prefetched to both L1 and L2 cache using carefully chosen prefetch distances
2-stage HW-SW pref.	Data is prefetched to L1 cache assuming that hardware prefetcher brings the data to the L2 cache
icc SW pref.	The prefetching strategy used by the Intel compiler
Baseline pref.	The baseline configuration with all prefetching disabled

Table 3: Summary of different prefetching strategies.

Figure 5 compares the performance results obtained on Sandy-Bridge and Xeon Phi, respectively, for the different prefetching strategies summarized in Table 3. In addition to the inherent hardware-based prefetching on Intel processors and the icc-directed prefetching, we implemented four other prefetching strategies for the purpose of comparison. As discussed in the paper, we propose a 2-stage coordinated software prefetching for Xeon Phi and 2-stage coordinated hardware-software prefetching for SandyBridge. Of the seven different strategies listed in Table 3, we could not implement the baseline prefetching on Xeon Phi because the BIOS did not provide the facility to turn off the hardware prefetcher as in SandyBridge. Thus, the hardware-based prefetching serves as the baseline in case of Xeon Phi. On the other hand, the Intel compiler for multi-cores is largely passive in the matter of prefetching and relies primarily on the hardware prefetcher. Thus, in our results for SandyBridge, we do not show the performance results for icc-directed prefetching which performs similar to the hardware-based prefetching for all benchmarks. In our analysis, we explain the behavior of the prefetching strategy adopted by the Intel compiler by studying the assembly code generated for different benchmarks.

According to the data access pattern, we divide the benchmarks into four categories: 1) programs with streaming or strided accesses, 2) programs with indirect array indexes, 3) programs with array of structures (and pointers), and 4) programs with loop sizes that are fractions of the problem size.

1. Programs with streaming or strided accesses. Among the benchmarks used for our experiments, *cactus*, *hmmer*, *bwaves*, *swim*, and *matmul* involve streaming array accesses whereas *bt* involves streaming as well as strided accesses. Results show that on

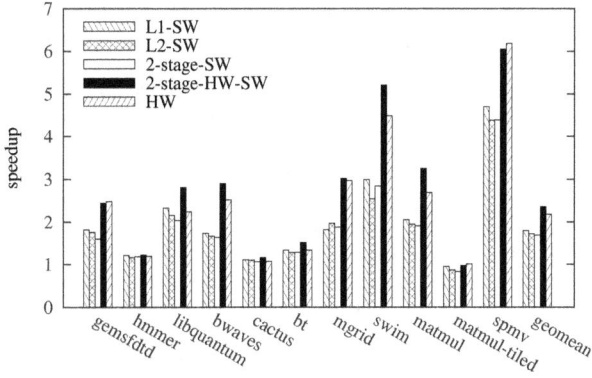

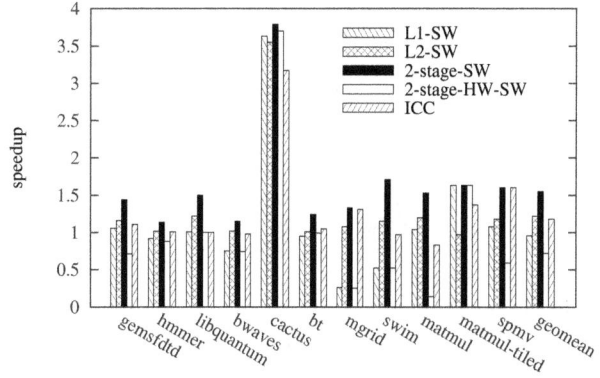

Figure 5: Performance speedup of different prefetching strategies on single thread in (a) SandyBridge (results normalized wrt baseline pref.) (b) Xeon Phi (results normalized wrt hardware pref.)

both hardware platforms, 2-stage coordinated prefetching as proposed for the respective platform, either outperforms or performs close to the best performing prefetching strategy for all benchmarks. It is interesting to note that 2-stage coordinated hw-sw prefetching which is the best performing strategy on SandyBridge, is the worst performing on Xeon Phi owing to the difference in interaction between hardware and software prefetching on the two platforms. On Xeon Phi, the software prefetches cannot train the hardware prefetcher and both cannot co-exist. On SandyBridge, on the other hand, we employ software-based prefetching to train the hardware prefetcher (because such an opportunity is provided by hardware) to overcome its limitations, and thus outperform other strategies. It is similarly interesting that the 2-stage sw prefetching which is the best performing strategy on Xeon Phi performs poorly on SandyBridge. This is because of a very small LFB at the L2 cache in SandyBridge. The L2 sw prefetching performs poorly on SandyBridge for the same reason. The L1 sw prefetching performs worse than the L2 sw prefetching on Xeon Phi due to fewer MSHRs at L1 cache (and thus more contention), whereas it performs slightly better than the L2 sw prefetching on SandyBridge due to prefetching the data to the L1 cache (that has same-sized LFB as L2 cache). The performance results for each benchmark are discussed in more detail below.

swim, bwaves and matmul. These benchmarks involve streaming access patterns with long loops. Although *matmul* has temporal locality, it behaves like other streaming benchmarks when it is not tiled since the data set size is much larger than L2 cache size. Here, multi-stage prefetching performs considerably better than the other prefetching strategies. It wins over the hardware and L2 sw prefetching for hiding the L2-to-L1 latency by prefetching the data to the L1 cache. The improvement is significant since the L1 misses are significant given the streaming nature and large working sets in these benchmarks. On SandyBridge, the 2-stage coordinated hw-sw prefetching improves considerably over the hardware-based prefetching in case of *matmul* even though the L1 hardware prefetcher proves sufficient for the small number of streams in *matmul*. This is because L1 software prefetches with large prefetch distances help in increasing the prefetch distance of the hardware prefetcher that is essential for the small loops in *matmul*. The L1 hardware prefetcher on SandyBridge prefetches only the next cache line, and thus cannot sufficiently increase the prefetch distance of the L2 hardware prefetcher. It is for this reason that we observe (using the Vtune performance monitoring tool [2]) that a significantly more number of loads that miss the L1 cache hit the LFB, in case of *matmul* that uses the hardware prefetcher against

the one which uses our 2-stage coordinated software prefetching. The higher number for the former suggests pending prefetch requests at the L2 cache because of insufficient prefetch distance. On Xeon Phi, the Intel compiler performs worse than even the hardware prefetcher in *matmul*, because of inserting redundant prefetch instructions for the array reference (reference $C_{i\ j}$ in Figure 2) that has temporal locality in an inner loop. In *swim*, the Intel compiler performs poorly as it does not prefetch data for all references. In addition, the data is prefetched only to the L2 cache and not to the L1 cache. In *bwaves*, the Intel compiler performs worse than coordinated prefetching because of issuing redundant prefetches for references that have temporal locality in the innermost loop, while leaving out references that have spatial locality in the innermost loop. We believe that it makes a wrong decision because of performing loop interchange optimization. It also does not prefetch data to the L1 cache in this case.

cactus. In *cactus*, bulk of the computation and memory references happen in a very large loop nest. Each iteration of the loop nest provides sufficient cycles to hide the memory latency. Since the loop nest involves significant computation, even requests to prefetch the data directly to the L1 cache are finished without much stalls. As a result, all software prefetching strategies perform similarly. The multi-stage prefetching achieves slightly better performance as compared to the L1 or L2 prefetching because of achieving better performance in other smaller loop nests that also involve streaming accesses. On Xeon Phi, the Intel compiler performs slightly worse because of inserting all prefetch instructions at the end of the loop instead of interleaving them with the computation. This leads to stalls due to contention at L1 cache that hurts performance. An important observation here is that the baseline hardware prefetcher on Xeon Phi performs significantly worse than the other strategies. This is because, the large loop nest contains streams (81 data streams) that are much larger than that can be handled by the hardware prefetcher (16, in case of Intel Xeon Phi). The performance difference is much less on SandyBridge for 2 reasons, (1) the hardware prefetcher can prefetch data for 32 streams instead of 16, and (2) the out-of-order execution tolerates most of the stalls since there is significant computation interspersing memory requests in the large loop nest in cactus.

hmmer. In *hmmer*, a subroutine called *P7Viterbi* is most computationally intensive and contains small loops. All the data referenced in the subroutine fits the L2 cache. Thus, although 2-stage prefetching that brings the data to the L1 cache wins over other strategies, the performance difference is small. On Xeon Phi, the Intel compiler also prefetches to both the L1 and L2 cache, but uses a much larger prefetch distance which proves costly, given the small loops.

bt. In *bt*, four subroutines, *compute_rhs*, *x_solve*, *y_solve* and *z_solve* contribute almost entirely to the execution time. These subroutines contain both streaming as well as strided accesses, and the working set is large. Thus, although a likely candidate for significant performance gains from 2-stage prefetching as in *swim*, the performance gains are small. This is because, the loop nests in *bt*, particularly some of the time-consuming nests in *x_solve*, *y_solve* and *z_solve*, are dominated by computation than by memory references. The performance improvement achieved by coordinated prefetching on SandyBridge is smaller than that achieved on Xeon Phi because higher computation in loop nests allows for tolerance of stalls due to out-of-order execution. Most of the performance improvement achieved by 2-stage prefetching stems from prefetching for strided accesses. These strided accesses are missed by even the strided hardware prefetcher in SandyBridge (that can detect strides upto 2K bytes) since the strides are long, given loops with large trip count. On Xeon Phi, the Intel compiler does not yield much improvement over the baseline because of not adequately prefetching for strided accesses.

```
void quantum_cnot( quantum_reg *reg, ... )
    ...
    for (i = 0; i < reg->size; i++)
        prefetch(&reg->node[i+PDL1], _L1_E ); // exclusive
        prefetch(&reg->node[i+PDL2], _L2_E );
        if (reg->node[i].state & ... )
            reg->node[i].state ^= ...
    ...
```

Figure 6: An example loop nest with prefetching instructions to L1 and L2 cache in the *libquantum* benchmark.

2. Programs with array of structures (and pointers). In *libquantum*, the computationally intensive loop-nests contain an array of structures, that is responsible for bulk of the memory accesses. One such loop-nest is shown in Figure 6, and the memory reference *reg* → *node* is an array of structures, that has *state* as one of its fields. In such cases, our multi-stage prefetching algorithm determines the size of the structure and prefetches the entire structure on the assumption that majority of the fields of the structure will be referenced - this may lead to prefetching more than a single cache line. However, in *libquantum*, the structure has only 2 fields and a size of 16 bytes, so we prefetch just one cache line. Our multi-stage prefetching wins over the hardware based prefetching, as the hardware prefetcher cannot run sufficiently ahead of the program counter for timely prefetching, given the small computation in the loop-nests and larger size of the data structure. It is for this reason that on SandyBridge, coordinated hw-sw prefetching where L1 software prefetches train and thus help in increasing the prefetch distance of the hardware prefetcher outperforms all other strategies. The performance improvement of coordinated sw prefetching over the baseline hardware prefetcher on Xeon Phi is more significant since there is no hardware prefetcher at L1 in Xeon Phi to prefetch to the L1 cache. On Xeon Phi, the Intel compiler does not prefetch array of structures and thus performs as well as the hardware prefetcher.

3. Programs with indirect array indexes. An example program with indirect array indexes is *sparse matrix-vector multiplication* as shown in Figure 7, where the array reference *B colIdx j* is indirectly indexed. In such cases, we prefetch data for the directly indexed reference, *colIdx*, that is used to reference the indirectly indexed reference *B*. We also prefetch the array reference *values*, but not reference *C* that has temporal locality in the innermost loop *j*. On Xeon Phi, we get considerable perfor-

mance improvement over the baseline hardware prefetcher due to prefetching to L1 cache. On SandyBridge, however, the hardware prefetcher performs slightly better than the 2-stage coordinated hw-sw prefetching as even the hardware prefetcher at L1 cache is successful in bringing the data to the L1 cache given few memory references in the loop nest. The slight better performance of the hardware prefetcher is due to no instruction overhead of prefetching. It is important to note that the loop iteration time in *spmv* is not as small as in *matmul* due to an indirectly indexed array reference that hurts efficient vectorization, and thus the benefit from increasing the prefetch distance of the hardware prefetcher through software prefetches is not significant. On Xeon Phi, the Intel compiler performs similar to the coordinated sw prefetching since it also prefetches to both the L1 and L2 cache using different distances. Although it uses a much larger distance that needed for the L1 prefetches, the performance is not hurt due to very long data streams.

```
for (i=0; i<M; i++)
    int start = row_start[i], stop = row_start[i+1];
    for (j=start; j<stop; j++)
        prefetch (&values[j+PDL1], _L1_ );
        prefetch (&values[j+PDL2], _L2_ );
        prefetch (&colIdx[j+PDL1], _L1_ );
        prefetch (&colIdx[j+PDL2], _L2_ );
        C[i] += values[j] + B[colIdx[j]];
```

Figure 7: *Sparse matrix-vector multiplication* with prefetching instructions to L1 and L2 cache.

4. Programs with loop sizes that are fractions of the problem size. This category of programs include both the tiled codes and various scientific codes that compute in parts such as the *gemsfdtd* and *mgrid* benchmarks from SPEC suite. In such codes, our multi-stage prefetching algorithm prefetches data in the following array rows instead of prefetching a few cache lines ahead as shown earlier in Figure 3(c). This helps to not only avoid prefetching useless data but also allows to timely prefetch useful data. On Xeon Phi, coordinated software prefetching wins over the hardware prefetcher and other software prefetching strategies primarily due to prefetching the data to L1 cache and also eliminating redundant prefetches. On SandyBridge, hardware-based prefetching and coordinated hw-sw prefetching win over others due to employing an efficient hardware prefetcher (with no resource contention) to prefetch data to the L2 cache. Other details regarding performance results for the 3 benchmarks in this category are discussed as follows.

gemsfdtd. On SandyBridge, the coordinated hardware-software prefetching performs slightly worse than the hardware prefetcher because although this benchmark computes in 2 parts, most of the execution belongs to one of those 2 parts. As a result, aggressive prefetching by hardware enables timely prefetching for the 2 parts although at the cost of some useless prefetches. The overhead due to both the useless prefetches and not prefetching the data to the L1 cache are tolerated by the out-of-order execution since the loops nests are not highly memory-intensive and involve considerable computation. On Xeon Phi, the Intel compiler does not achieve improvement over the hardware prefetcher due to insertion of useless prefetches by prefetching using large prefetch distances.

mgrid. On SandyBridge, the improvement achieved by coordinated hw-sw prefetching over the hardware prefetcher is small because this benchmark is highly memory intensive, and thus we observe significant pipeline stalls due to filled up load buffer, when prefetch requests are inserted. Using Vtune, we observe that the stalls due to filled up load buffer in a code with L1 software prefetch instructions increase by a factor of 3 over a code that contains no prefetch instructions. On Xeon Phi, however, there are no addi-

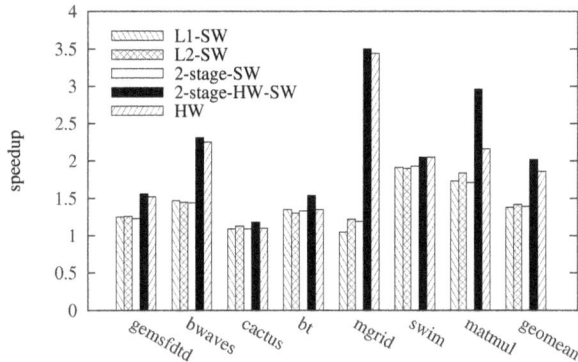

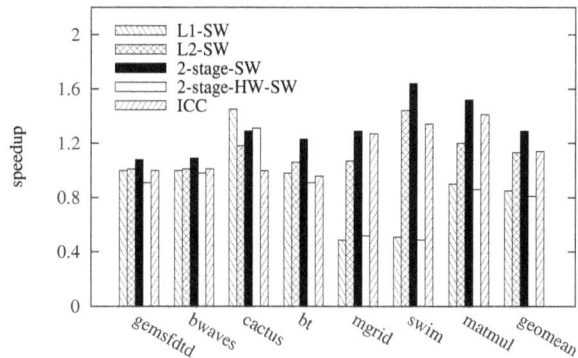

Figure 8: Performance speedup of different prefetching strategies using CMP technique in (a) SandyBridge (results normalized wrt baseline pref.) (b) Xeon Phi (results normalized wrt hardware pref.)

tional stalls due to prefetching and thus significant improvement is obtained over the hardware prefetcher. The Intel compiler in this case inserts prefetches for both the L1 and L2 caches using different distances. The L1 prefetch distance is again larger than needed but does not hurt performance since this benchmark is less sensitive to prefetch distance.

matmul-tiled. We tile *matmul* using the same tile size as chosen by *icc*, i.e. 128. As a result of using a tile size of 128, the working is reduced such that it exceeds the L1 cache size, but is well within the L2 cache size. Thus, a single tile always fits the L2 cache, and once fetched, the data needs to only be prefetched from the L2 cache in subsequent executions of the tile. This gives interesting performance results on Xeon Phi - all prefetching strategies that prefetch the data to the L1 cache perform as well as the coordinated sw prefetching. However, *icc* performs slightly worse because of inserting redundant prefetches for references with locality in the inner loops as in *matmul*. On SandyBridge, the L1 hardware prefetcher effectively prefetches data to the L1 cache, given few references involved, and thus performs slightly better than coordinated hw-sw prefetching. The other strategies only perform slightly worse since the working set occupies the L2 cache, and part of the L2-L1 latency can be tolerated through out-of-order execution.

5.3 Results for Multi-stage Prefetching in multithreaded environment

Figure 8 shows the performance results of our coordinated prefetching strategies for SandyBridge and Xeon Phi on 8 and 32 cores, respectively, in CMP environment. On SandyBridge, as discussed in Section 3.4, the performance improvements achieved by coordinated hw-sw prefetching using single thread diminish for benchmarks that are highly memory-intensive due to increased stalls from resource contention. The benchmarks in this list are *swim*, *gemsfdtd*, *bwaves* and *mgrid*. Other less memory intensive benchmarks such as *bt* and *cactus* continue to show improvement. *Matmul*, although memory intensive, shows significant improvement owing to the increase in hardware prefetch distance achieved through software prefetching. On Xeon Phi, the benchmarks behave similar in both the CMP and single thread environment since prefetching does not cause additional stalls in the CMP environment as in SandyBridge.

As discussed in Section 3.4, memory intensive benchmarks with many references in the loop nest benefit from loop distribution optimization on Xeon Phi on account of reduced contention. Figure 9 shows the performance gains of loop distribution (followed by multi-stage prefetching) in 3 memory-intensive parallel benchmarks, *swim*, *gemsfdtd* and *cactus*. Using the recommended 2-way

SMT on Xeon Phi, loop distribution achieves another 13% average speedup over multi-stage prefetching on the 3 benchmarks.

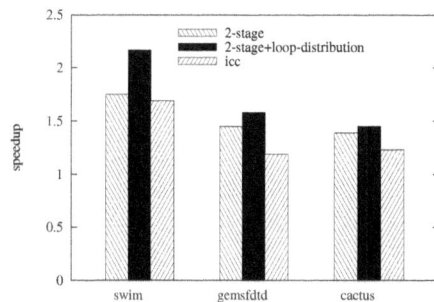

Figure 9: Performance speedup with loop distribution in Xeon Phi (results normalized wrt hardware pref.)

6. RELATED WORK

In the past, there has been significant research on tuning the prefetch distance and reducing overhead due to software prefetching [3, 4, 9, 13]. Mowry et al. [13] defined prefetch distance in terms of the prefetch latency and loop iteration time. Mowry et al. also proposed prefetch predicates to eliminate redundant prefetches. Badawy et al. in [3] proposed to insert prefetch instructions in the epilogue and prologue. Recently, Lee et al. [12] have proposed to calculate the loop iteration time using the average IPC of the application obtained through program profiling. Such an adjustment to prefetch distance is necessary for modern multicores that execute out-of-order. In our work, however, since we only use software to prefetch to the L1 cache in multi-cores, we show that using a large prefetch distance such that it does not cause evictions in the L1 cache is a better choice for several reasons. This has the advantage of being loop-based and not program-based, and is calculated statically.

In recent past, coordinated prefetching was proposed and implemented in IBM's Power6 microarchitecture [11]. On Power6 (and its follow-ons), the L2 hardware prefetcher that can hold 32 outstanding prefetch requests, prefetches data from memory using a larger distance (at most 24 lines) and the L1 hardware prefetcher that can hold 8 prefetch requests, prefetches data from L1 using a smaller distance (at most 2 lines). In this work, we use a similar idea to achieve coordination, but through software prefetching. On SandyBridge, software prefetching at L1 coordinates with the

L2 hardware prefetcher that allows us to significantly increase the prefetch distance (without polluting the cache - Section 3.3.2) and overcome the limitations of the hardware prefetcher as mentioned in Section 1. On Xeon Phi, the coordination is achieved entirely through software prefetching. Lee et al. [12] have considered coordination between hardware and software prefetching on existing multi-cores. They manually insert software prefetch instructions and identify benchmarks for their positive, neutral or negative interaction with the existing hardware prefetchers (primarily through simulation). Their work is thus focused on studying the interaction between hardware and software prefetching, but does not propose any particular prefetching strategy. In their tests, they use cooperative hardware-software prefetching where both software and hardware prefetching co-exist; ours is a coordinated hardware-software prefetching technique, where the software prefetches actively train the hardware prefetcher to achieve coordination.

In the past, Santhanam et al. [16] and Caragea et al. [5] have also proposed reduction of prefetch distance due to limited resources in the form of number of outstanding prefetch requests that can be handled by the hardware. However, these works consider HP PA-8000 and a many-core research machine, XMT, respectively, both of which employ single-level cache. Thus, unlike our work, they do not employ the facility to prefetch to multiple levels of cache as in existing architectures, to tackle the problem of resource contention. A recent work from Intel [10] talks about prefetching the data to both the L1 and L2 cache - a technique implemented in the existing version of the Intel compiler for Xeon Phi. However, they do not describe any strategy to prefetch the data to the L1 and L2 cache such that a coordination is achieved. We observe in our results that the Intel compiler for Xeon Phi does not always insert prefetch requests for L1 and L2 cache, and generally uses a larger prefetch distance at L1 than needed. As a result, it cannot match the performance of our coordinated prefetching on Xeon Phi.

Among other works in software-based prefetching are those that employ helper threads to predict future load addresses [7, 8, 17]. The authors in [7, 8] use an idle thread as the helper thread to prefetch data for another compute thread, whereas Son et al. [17] extend the helper-thread prefetching to work with multiple cores by assigning a customized helper thread to a group of compute threads. These works, however, have not evaluated the impact of resource contention due to aggressive prefetching by the helper-thread. In our experiments, we find the impact of resource contention to be important, particularly on many-cores that have blocking caches, and thus implement a simple and low-overhead software prefetching strategy that is different from helper-thread based prefetching.

7. CONCLUSION

In this work, we study software prefetching in light of various architectural features that support prefetching in existing processors. Based on our study of those features, we implement a coordinated multi-stage prefetching strategy for two widely different state-of-the-art processors, the multi-core SandyBridge and the many-core Xeon Phi. However, the means of achieving this coordination is different on either - in SandyBridge, it is achieved through the MLC hardware prefetcher prefetching data to the L2 cache and L1 software prefetches further bringing it to L1 cache; in Xeon Phi, the coordination is achieved through carefully tuned software prefetching at different levels of cache. Results establish the efficacy of these strategies on respective platforms and also the importance of an awareness of the influence of different architectural features on prefetching as studied in this work. The performance results achieved using the 7 different prefetching strategies are discussed for each benchmark considered. Further, the performance of these strategies in multithreaded environment is also presented and discussed. Since our multi-stage coordinated prefetching is a simple, static prefetching technique, and does not require any special hardware, it can be readily incorporated in production-quality compilers for existing architectures.

8. ACKNOWLEDGEMENTS

We would like to acknowledge NSF grants CNS-0834599 and CCF-0708822 for supporting this work.

9. REFERENCES

[1] Intel compiler. Available at http://software.intel.com/en-us/intel-parallel-studio-xe.

[2] Intel's VTune. Available at www.intel.com/Software/Products.

[3] A.-H. Badawy, A. Aggarwal, D. Yeung, and C.-W. Tseng. The efficacy of software prefetching and locality optimizations on future memory systems. *JILP'2004*, 6(7).

[4] D. Callahan, K. Kennedy, and A. Porterfield. Software prefetching. pages 40–52.

[5] G. C. Caragea, A. Tzannes, F. Keceli, R. Barua, and U. Vishkin. Resource-aware compiler prefetching for many-cores. In *ISPDC'2010*, pages 133–140.

[6] T.-F. Chen and J.-L. Baer. A performance study of software and hardware data prefetching schemes. In *ISCA'94*, pages 223–232.

[7] M. Kamruzzaman, S. Swanson, and D. M. Tullsen. Inter-core prefetching for multicore processors using migrating helper threads. In *ASPLOS'11*, pages 393–404.

[8] D. Kim and D. Yeung. Design and evaluation of compiler algorithms for pre-execution. In *ASPLOS'02*, pages 159–170.

[9] A. C. Klaiber and H. M. Levy. An architecture for software controlled data prefetching. In *ISCA'91*, pages 43–53.

[10] R. Krishnaiyer, E. Kultursay, P. Chawla, S. Preis, A. Zvezdin, and H. Saito. Compiler-based data prefetching and streaming non-temporal store generation for intel xeon phi coprocessor. In *Workshop on Multithreaded Architectures and Applications*, 2013.

[11] H. Q. Le, W. J. Starke, J. S. Fields, F. P. O'Connell, D. Q. Nguyen, B. J. Ronchetti, W. M. Sauer, E. M. Schwarz, and M. T. Vaden. Ibm power6 microarchitecture. *IBM Journal of Research and Development*, 51(6):639–662, 2007.

[12] J. Lee, H. Kim, and R. Vuduc. When prefetching works, when it does not, and why. *TACO'2012*, 9(1):29.

[13] T. C. Mowry, M. S. Lam, and A. Gupta. Design and evaluation of a compiler algorithm for prefetching. In *ASPLOS'92*, pages 62–73.

[14] D. J. Quinlan, M. Schordan, B. Philip, and M. Kowarschik. The specification of source-to-source transformations for the compile-time optimization of parallel object-oriented scientific applications. In *LCPC'01*, pages 383–394.

[15] R. H. Saavedra and D. Park. Improving the effectiveness of software prefetching with adaptive executions. In *PACT'96*, pages 68–78.

[16] V. Santhanam, E. H. Gornish, and W.-C. Hsu. Data prefetching on the hp pa-8000. In *ISCA'97*, pages 264–273.

[17] S. W. Son, M. Kandemir, M. Karakoy, and D. Chakrabarti. A compiler-directed data prefetching scheme for chip multiprocessors. In *PPOPP'09*, pages 209–218.

[18] Z. Wang, D. Burger, K. S. McKinley, S. K. Reinhardt, and C. C. Weems. Guided region prefetching: A cooperative hardware/software approach. In *ISCA'03*, pages 388–398.

Evaluation of Methods to Integrate Analysis into a Large-Scale Shock Physics Code

Ron A. Oldfield
Sandia National Laboratories
P.O. Box 5800
Albuquerque, NM 87185-1327
raoldfi@sandia.gov

Kenneth Moreland
Sandia National Laboratories
P.O. Box 5800
Albuquerque, NM 87185-1326
kmorel@sandia.gov

Nathan Fabian
Sandia National Laboratories
P.O. Box 5800
Albuquerque, NM 87185-1326
ndfabia@sandia.gov

David Rogers
Los Alamos National
Laboratory
P.O. Box 1663
Los Alamos, NM 87545
dhr@lanl.gov

ABSTRACT

Exascale supercomputing will embody many revolutionary changes in the hardware and software of high-performance computing. For example, projected limitations in power and I/O-system performance will fundamentally change visualization and analysis workflows. A traditional post-processing workflow involves storing simulation results to disk and later retrieving them for visualization and data analysis; however, at Exascale, post-processing approaches will not be able to capture the volume or granularity of data necessary for analysis of these extreme-scale simulations. As an alternative, researchers are exploring ways to integrate analysis and simulation without using the storage system. In situ and in transit are two options, but there has not been an adequate evaluation of these approaches to identify strengths, weaknesses, and trade-offs at large scale. This paper provides a detailed performance and scaling analysis of a large-scale shock physics code using traditional post-processsing, in situ, and in transit analysis to detect material fragments from a simulated explosion.

Categories and Subject Descriptors

I.6.6 [**Simulation Output Analysis**]; H.3.4 [**Systems and Software**]: Performance evaluation (efficiency and effectiveness)

Keywords

Case study, fragment detection, in situ analysis, in transit analysis, shock physics

ICS'14, June 10–13 2014, Munich, Germany.
ACM 978-1-4503-2642-1/14/06.
http://dx.doi.org/10.1145/2597652.2597668..

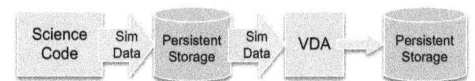

(a) Traditional post-processing VDA.

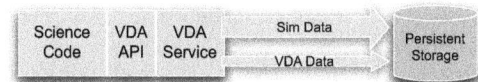

(b) Embedded in situ analysis VDA.

(c) Service-oriented in transit VDA.

Figure 1: Traditional and emerging workflow diagrams showing the flow of information from simulation to persistent storage.

1. INTRODUCTION

High-performance computing (HPC) applications produce complex datasets that are increasingly difficult to explore and understand using traditional post-processing workflows. The primary reason is the increasing gap between computation and communication performance and the performance of parallel file systems. This gap has been a known problem for several decades [13,15] and has motivated numerous innovations to improve parallelism [16,31], caching [32], processing [33], and scheduling [7] in I/O systems. Despite these innovations, the gap widens at an alarming rate. At Exascale, with a projected storage system rate of 60 TB/s [3], I/O system throughput will be less than 1% of the generating capacity of an HPC simulation. These trends are driving an evolution away from application workflows consisting of sequences of independent simulation and analysis steps to integrated approaches that perform these steps concurrently.

This paper provides a comprehensive evaluation of three approaches (see Figure 1) to integrate visualization and data analysis (VDA) with scientific simulations on one of the Department of Energy's largest HPC platforms, the Cray XE6 (Cielo) system at Los Alamos National Laboratories. The three approaches studied are traditional post-processing analysis, in situ analysis, and in transit analysis.

Post-processing **analysis** performs analysis and simulation in two distinct steps. The simulation outputs important "raw" data to global file system, then a separate application reads the data and performs the analysis. This approach is the simplest to implement because it provides a clean separation between simulation and analysis steps. However, as the I/O gap continues to widen, the cost of writing the "raw" data to the file system could be prohibitive. In addition, management of intermediate data products and scheduling of analysis tasks can be cumbersome on the user.

In situ **analysis** embeds analysis into the simulation code, either through code-specific operations, or by incorporating a separate library. Analysis executes on the same compute resources as the simulation, making it easy to deploy. Depending on the complexity of the analysis, however, in situ approaches may have substantial memory, computation, and communication costs that create stability, scalability, and resilience issues for highly-tuned production codes.

In transit **analysis** offloads analysis to a separate partition of compute resources, using the high-speed network rather than the file system for communication. This approach requires a thin client library to aggregate and communicate important data structures to the VDA service, effectively creating a parallel pipeline that allows overlap of simulation and analysis. Although this approach is less intrusive than in situ approaches, it requires additional compute resources and is more complicated to coordinate the allocation and execution of an application and a service.

This paper describes background and related work (Section 2); an application use case that detects material fragments from a simulated explosion (Section 3); our implementation of fragment detection using in situ, in transit, and post-processing workflows (Section 4); and finally results and conclusions (Sections 5 and 6).

2. BACKGROUND AND RELATED WORK

Although there is a recent upsurge of interest in running data analysis in tandem with the simulation, it has been studied for many years. The basic concept of in situ visualization is described in the 1987 National Science Foundation Visualization in Scientific Computing workshop report [20], which is often credited with launching the field of scientific visualization.

Several solutions for library-level (i.e., in situ) coupling of visualization and data analysis with simulation have been implemented. Most of these are small, specialized codes written for and part of a particular simulation. Some general purpose libraries that are still active include SciRUN [30], pV3 [14], and RVSLIB [9]. There also exist libraries built on top of existing scientific visualization applications to provide the dual benefit of in situ processing and offline post-processing. The Catalyst library built on top of ParaView [11] and the Libsim library built on top of VisIt are popular libraries for this purpose.

In transit approaches have also been around for some time. One of the first demonstrations of the benefits of pipelining simulation and analysis in an HPC code came from a seismic imaging code that used a separate partition of nodes to

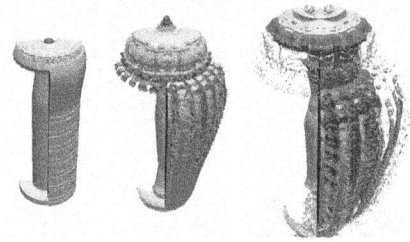

Figure 2: Simulation of an exploding pipe, which presents many prototypical fragment analysis challenges.

perform data transformations [29]. More recent work has looked at general-purpose frameworks for developing "data services". Nessie [19, 28], DataStager [1], GLEAN [36], and I/O delegation [24] are examples of these frameworks. Although the initial motivation for these frameworks was to "stage" data to avoid bursty I/O patterns [26], it has also shown value as a tool for offloading analysis from a running simulation. Such capabilities exist for fusion modeling [37], Magneto Hydro Dynamics [37], combustion modeling [6], and shock physics [23].

Although a number of publications discuss the merits of in situ and in transit analysis, this paper provides details on how to apply these techniques on a real scientific problem at large scale, and represents the most comprehensive performance-based evaluation of the two approaches to date. Our results are the culmination of several years of development of the in situ and in transit analysis codes, 6 months of performance evaluations, and over ten million processor-hours of machine time on one of the Department of Energy's (DOE) premier capability-class systems. Our experiments evaluate a number of different algorithms, and include detailed analysis of runtime, resource usage, and variance. Such a complete evaluation contributes real data to the previously conjectured merits of the two approaches.

3. APPLICATION DRIVER

For this work, we explore the problem of characterizing fragments in an explosion simulation. Simulation is a vital part in understanding shock physics. Although experimentation will always be a necessary tool for scientific inquiry and corroboration, the amount of data we can retrieve with experimentation is limited. Experiments in shock physics usually involve high energy, high velocities, and high variability, all of which hinder detailed, accurate, and repeatable observations. When measurements cannot be taken during the experiment, they must be taken after the experiment by observing the remaining material. Much can be learned in this manner, but the transient states during the experiment are lost.

Another limiting factor of experimentation is its high cost and slow turnaround. To create shock physics experiments, physical devices must be fabricated. These devices are then usually destroyed during the experiment. Safety and political issues also often plague shock physics experiments. In some cases, experimentation is simply not feasible. Thus, simulation plays a major role in shock physics analysis.

In our experiments, we use an example simulation of an exploding pipe shown in Figure 2. This example provides an accurate representation of the types of problems studied

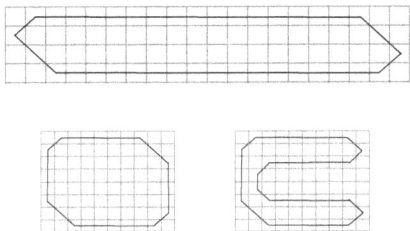

Figure 3: Examples of potential fragments that we would like to characterize.

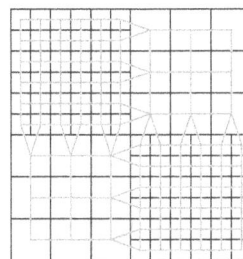

Figure 4: A 2D AMR example with 2 different refinement levels (blue lines) and the conforming dual grid we build with it (yellow lines).

at SNL and also provides results at many different levels of refinement, allowing us to scale the problem from hundreds to tens-of-thousands of cores. In addition, this problem has features like discrete compute, communication, and I/O phases common in a large number of HPC codes, not just shock physics, making this a great example to study the general applicability of analysis techniques.

One of the most important features in shock-physics analysis is material fragments. The physical properties of the fragments, including mass, volume, and shape, as well as their trajectories, can all be important. In particular, shape can be an important characteristic. Consider the example fragments given in Figure 3. The top fragment is long and sharp, making it more likely to penetrate objects. In comparison, the bottom left fragment is rounded and could have less damage potential. However, the U-shaped fragment in the bottom right may be harmful depending on the scenario, but could be difficult to distinguish from the round fragment in many shape metrics.

We used the CTH [17] simulation code for our experiments. CTH is an Eulerian shock physics code that uses an adaptive mesh refinement (AMR) data model. These adaptive finite volumes can take up different amounts of space depending on where they are in the model and how closely the simulation is refining the space.

In order to correctly find fragments, we must first determine what is and is not a fragment. The simulation operates on a finite volume and comprises a set of simulated materials, which each take up a certain fraction of finite cells within that volume. We treat any connected region of cells with material volume fraction above a given threshold as a fragment of that material. Generally speaking, when a simulation begins, each material comprises usually one connected region, which we refer to as the main mass. As the simulation progresses, this region breaks apart and gaps occur between pieces of material, filled either by another material or by the surrounding air. Once there is a gap as wide as at least one cell, we determine that a fragment as formed. The challenge when finding these fragments on a large scale parallel system is that regions that make up the fragments straddle process boundaries, requiring communication between the processes to determine the full shape of a fragment.

Because the number of fragments a shock physics simulation can generate are so numerous, it is seldom realistic for a person to examine every one. It is therefore more beneficial to first perform computational analytics that provide useful summary statistics and identify particularly interesting fragments. This analysis has the added benefit of reducing the amount of memory required to represent it. Therefore, fragment analysis is a good candidate for in situ processing.

Here we characterize an algorithm for determining just the shape of the fragment, or fragment boundary. This in itself is a non-trivial problem that is a useful starting point for performance characterization–the purpose of this paper.

Determining shape is done in the following steps:

1. *Find block neighbors.* This includes determining block neighbors located on different process.
2. *Build a conforming mesh over the AMR boundaries.* AMR has inconsistent interpolation at interfaces between blocks of different refinements. The conforming mesh resolves the interpolation.
3. *Identify the boundaries of fragments.* We estimate the boundary as the contour at a threshold between high and low volume fraction.

The creation of fragment boundaries is nontrivial because the surface needs to be "watertight" in that the representative mesh surface is conforming and closed. Making a surface from an AMR mesh watertight is challenging because the AMR mesh is nonconforming at boundaries between adjacent regions at different levels of refinement.

To generate this watertight fragment surface, we first build a dual mesh of the original AMR mesh. The dual mesh contains a vertex at the center of each cell in the original mesh and allows us to run a standard contouring algorithm (i.e., Marching Cubes) over the cell-centereed vertices in the dual. If the original mesh were a regular grid, it would be straightforward to build a conforming mesh as the contour edges would always align correctly at the original cell faces.

Instead, we have different levels of refinement at AMR boundaries, as shown in Figure 4. We then merge the disconnected contour edges by creating degenerate shapes at the boundary between two AMR neighborhoods, otherwise T-joint gaps form in the fragment. In a distributed parallel job, neighborhood information must be shared between regions that might be located on different processes. Resolving this neighborhood information requires a significant amount of communication, limiting the scalability of the algorithm.

Efficient communication of boundary elements first requires that each process knows the location of the neighbors for each region it holds. If data is loaded with no knowledge of its decomposition, which is typical in the postprocessing of data, then this neighborhood information can be retrieved only through global communication. Our initial *baseline* algorithm starts with this global communication, which severely limits the scalability of the algorithm.

When running the surface creation algorithm as an embedded in situ component of CTH, this global communication of finding neighbors is wasteful because CTH already has this information. To take advantage of this neighborhood information, we make a small change to CTH to pass this data decomposition information through its I/O layer to Catalyst. With this data, our *refined* algorithm skips the global communication leaving only the more scalable boundary-data passing. Our analysis shows that the refined algorithm is much more scalable than the baseline algorithm [10]. Unfortunately, we cannot apply the refined algorithm in the in transit workflow because this workflow redistributes the data and invalidates this neighborhood information from CTH.

4. IMPLEMENTATION APPROACH

To implement the various workflows, we developed components to support in situ and in transit fragment-detection using the Catalyst in situ library and Nessie framework for data services. In this section, we provide descriptions of each of these software components, along with modifications made to support the fragment-detection use case.

4.1 Catalyst

The Catalyst library and the algorithms we use within CTH are an accumulation of several years work, starting with the development of fragment analysis algorithms with our post-processing tools [22], described in more detail in Section 3. Subsequent work lead to the development of Catalyst [11] and the scaling of algorithms used in conjunction with CTH [10].

Catalyst is a general purpose, full-featured library that leverages existing implementations of analysis and visualization capabilities. The intent in doing this is threefold. First, by leveraging existing visualization and data analysis libraries we can benefit from the accumulation of over two decades of visualization research and development. Second, by making the library general purpose we can quickly apply our in situ visualization and data analysis capabilities to many simulations as opposed to a single simulation. Third, by using our existing code we can integrate the in situ tools with our traditional post-processing tools, providing familiar capabilities that are seamlessly integrated across the entire analysis tool chain.

Catalyst is a C++ library with an API available in C, FORTRAN, and Python. It is built atop the Visualization Toolkit (VTK) [35] and ParaView [4]. This means that Catalyst takes advantage of a large number of algorithms including writers for I/O, rendering algorithms, and processing algorithms such as isosurface extraction, slicing, and flow particle tracking. Catalyst uses ParaView to implement and manage the visualization and data analysis, which is defined using a visualization pipeline [21]. Although it is possible to construct pipelines entirely in C++, a more flexible approach is defining pipelines with Python scripts. We used Python scripts for the experiments presented in this paper.

We do not expect most scientific codes to use the Catalyst API directly. Instead, we rely on adapters — which are small pieces of code written for each new linked simulation — to translate data structures between the simulation's code (for our use case the CTH shock physics code) and Catalyst's VTK-based architecture, as shown in Figure 5a. The adapter provides a mechanism that allows the simulation to define a visualization pipeline and periodically invoke the

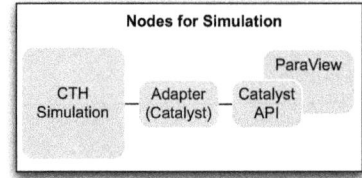

(a) In situ coupling.

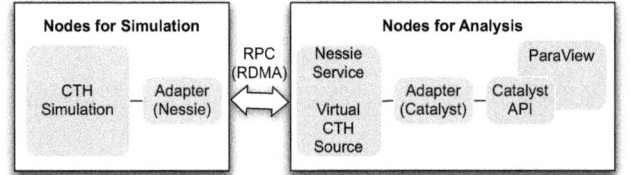

(b) In transit coupling.

Figure 5: Coupling a simulation with Catalyst.

data analysis while running the simulation. In our case, the CTH input deck identifies the frequency and type of analysis performed throughout the simulation.

To conserve memory, our adapter directly interfaces the visualization and data analysis code to the data structures defined by CTH. This interface is challenging because although the blocks of data are represented sequentially in both CTH and VTK, the multidimensional order is different. To address this, our adapter contains an interface wrapper above the standard VTK array. The wrapper re-implements the array's accessor functions to handle the order difference between the two systems. Although there is a minor overhead in additional pointer arithmetic and virtual method calls, it saves us from a deep-memory copy.

4.2 Nessie

The NEtwork Scalable Service Interface, or Nessie, is a framework for developing parallel client-server data services for large-scale HPC systems [28]. Nessie includes a number of features that address scalability, efficient data movement, and support for heterogeneous architectures. Features of particular note include 1) asynchronous methods for most of the interface to prevent client blocking while the service processes a request; 2) server-directed bulk-data transport to efficiently manage network bandwidth between the client and servers; 3) separate channels for control and data traffic; and 4) XDR encoding for the control messages (i.e., requests and results) to support heterogeneous systems of compute and service nodes.

A Nessie service consists of one or more processes that execute as a serial or parallel job on the compute nodes or service nodes of an HPC system. The client and service communicate through a remote procedure call (RPC) interface layered on top of the Nessie Network Transport Interface (NNTI) [27], an RDMA abstraction layer that provides near hardware rates for supported HPC interconnects. NNTI currently has support for most major HPC vendor interconnects, including Cray XT (Seastar), Cray XE (Gemini), InfiniBand, and the IBM BlueGene/P (DCMF).

For the in transit coupling of CTH and Catalyst, illustrated in Figure 5b, we developed a client-side *Nessie* adapter that is a drop in replacement for the in situ Catalyst adapter.

For efficiency reasons, our implementation of the in transit adapter does not simply forward all the functions to the service. In many cases, we aggregate metadata to reduce the number of small messages sent to the service. For example, the adapter API includes "setup" functions to initialize data structures, assign cell and material field names, and set cell and material fields pointers. Most of these operations do not require immediate interaction with the data service. Instead, we synchronize metadata and the data between client and the server at the beginning of the *pvspy_viz* operation that initiates ParaView coProcessing on the remote service.

The in situ implementation for the Catalyst adapter has the notion of a "CTH source" that allows Catalyst to work directly on the memory of the CTH application without making copies. Since the in transit service does not have access to the physical memory of the CTH application, we created a virtual CTH source on the service that emulates the data structures on the CTH application. That allows our service to use the same library the client uses for in situ analysis.

With the exception of the operations to transfer metadata and data to the analysis service, all remote operations are asynchronous, allowing the data analysis on the service to execute in parallel with computation on the CTH application. If one remote visualization operation is not complete by the time CTH is ready to do another visualization operation, CTH has to wait.

5. RESULTS

This section documents the results of experiments designed to characterize the performance of our data-analysis workflows. In particular, we are interested in determining the additional overhead our data analysis places on the simulation and the efficiency with which it can be done. These data summarize evaluations run over the course of 10.58 million processor-hours of execution. The results come from measurements taken from instrumented code as well as the HPCToolkit profiling tool [2].

5.1 Experimental Setup

We performed all experiments on the Cielo [8] supercomputer housed at Los Alamos National Laboratory. Cielo is an 8,944-node Cray XE6 resource for the Advanced Simulation and Computing (ASC) program and is jointly managed by Sandia National Laboratories and Los Alamos National Laboratory under the New Mexico Alliance for Computing at Extreme Scale (ACES) project. Each node contains two AMD Opteron 6136 (Magny-Cours) 8-way processor chips for a total of 16 cores per node. Each core has a peak computational speed of 2.4 GHz, leading to a total theoretical peak of 1.37 Petaflops for the machine. The compute nodes each have 32 GB of memory. The interconnect consists of a proprietary Cray Gemini Network with a 3D Torus topology and has a peak throughput rate of 6 GB/s/link.

We investigate the following application workflows:

In situ baseline: Analysis on the compute nodes where the simulation treats the analysis library as a "black box". The analysis code performs a communication-intensive step to find AMR block neighbors for each visualization operation.

In situ refined: Analysis on the compute nodes using an approach where CTH shares block-neighbor information with the analysis code, resulting in a more efficient analysis algorithm.

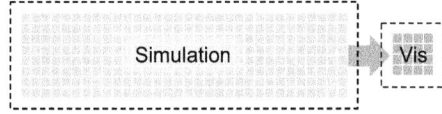

(a) In transit extra.

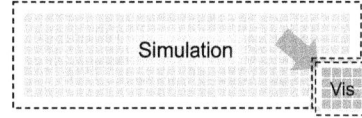

(b) In transit internal.

Figure 6: We used two allocation schemes for the in transit experiments: one that allocates extra nodes for the service, and one that "carves" out a set of nodes for the service.

Table 1: Scaling Overview

Data Set	CTH Cores (16/node)		Server Cores (8/node)
	standard	internal	
33k blocks	128	96	16
	256	224	16
	512	480	16
	1024	992	16
218k blocks	1024	768	128
	2048	1,792	128
	4096	3,840	128
	8192	7,936	128
1.5m blocks	4096	2,496	800
	8192	6,592	800
	16384	14,784	800
	32768	31,168	800

In transit extra: Analysis on service nodes using an extra allocation of nodes for the service (Figure 6a). This represents the case where there might be "special" nodes available for staging and analysis, such as the proposed "burst-buffer" architecture for Exascale systems [18].

In transit internal: Analysis on service nodes that are subtracted from the nodes normally allocated to the CTH job (Figure 6b). In this workflow, the total number of resources used is identical to an in situ workflow.

Post-processing: A CTH job that writes files instead of doing data analysis. Later a data analysis job, the same size as the in transit extra service, is run on the saved data to detect fragments.

Note that all the in transit workflows use the baseline algorithm for analysis on the service. In the post-processing workflow, there is no neighbor information to transfer from the CTH code because CTH is no longer executing. For the in-transit workflows, relaying neighbor information to the services is complicated, but possible. We did not have time to implement such improvements for this paper, but are planning this for future work.

All applications complete 500 cycles (i.e., timestep calculations) of the CTH code, performing exactly 51 analysis (or I/O) operations, approximately once every 10 cycles. For the post-processing workflow, we summed the time to run the simulation, read and write files, and perform the post-processing analysis to get a run time comparable to the in situ and in transit workflows.

For each application, we ran strong scaling experiments for three different datasets. Each data set comes from the

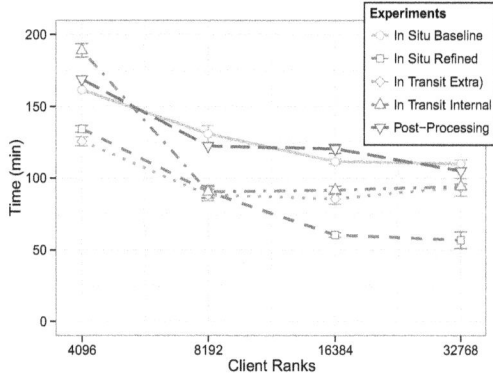

Figure 7: Total runtime for 1.5M block dataset.

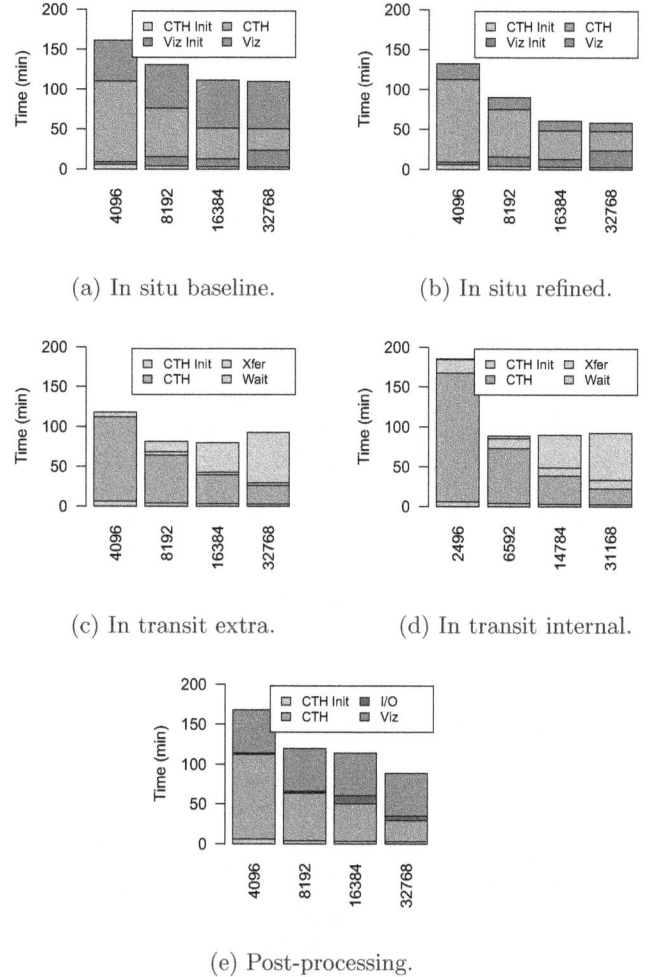

(a) In situ baseline.

(b) In situ refined.

(c) In transit extra.

(d) In transit internal.

(e) Post-processing.

Figure 8: Illustration showing the contributions of selected operations to the total execution times for each application.

same initial conditions but with a different maximum level of refinement. Thus, measurements of different job sizes with different data set sizes provides a weak scaling overview. Table 1 shows the range of core sizes used for the various experiments. For every application we used the maximum 16 cores-per-node for the CTH client, since CTH is primarily bound by computation and scales very well. The second number in the CTH cores column shows the reduced number of cores used for CTH in the in transit internal workflow due to the node allocation scheme we used for that case.

The number of service nodes used for the experiments was purely based on the memory requirements of the various experiments. Based on preliminary trials, we found that a server could manage around 16k blocks of CTH data without running out of memory. We designed our experiments to fit within that constraint. A second issue for the servers is computational requirements. Ideally, the server would have just enough compute capability to complete one analysis step before CTH requests another. A perfect balance of simulation and analysis would identify the optimal number of required service node resources given a particular size problem and algorithm for analysis. In our experiments, we did not attempt to use an "optimal" number of resources. Instead, we focused on memory constraints first, then experimented with different numbers of server cores to find an appropriate balance. Based on preliminary results that showed an 8-core/node allocation to be preferable, we chose to use 8 cores for each service node. We discuss this decision in more detail in Section 5.4.

5.2 Total Execution Time

In the interest of saving space, we focus most of our discussion on the large-scale results for the 1.5m block dataset. Although the smaller sets are interesting, results from the large data set clearly show where the two approaches differ. In addition, the large-scale results are more interesting from a supercomputing perspective because they demonstrate capability not possible on smaller clusters. For a complete look at all the results, see our ASC milestone final report [34].

Figure 7 shows the total runtime of each workflow for the large data set. The points represent the mean over at least five independent runs on different node allocations, with error bars indicating the standard deviation from the mean. The results clearly show a "sweet spot" at 8K cores where the in transit approach, even though it is using a less scalable algorithm, performs the same as the the refined version

of in situ. At 16K and 32K, none of the codes show significant improvement, the baseline in situ and the in transit approaches actually take longer. We believe the biggest reason is that there is not enough work for the compute nodes. At 32K cores, each core processes around 46 blocks/node. The same size problem using 4K nodes process 366 blocks/node. The key to making the in transit approach successful is being able to overlap computation and data analysis. If the data analysis portion does not scale particularly well, the compute nodes need sufficient work to hide the analysis cost.

To better understand exactly where the time is being spent, we collected detailed timings of each application using a combination of instrumented timers and profiling tools (HPCToolkit). Figure 8 shows the total runtime performance of the five workflows as stacked bar plots illustrating the portion of runtime associated with select functions. For the in situ workflows, we measure the initialization and computational time of CTH and the analysis/visualization. For in transit workflows, we measure the initialization cost of CTH, the cost of transferring data to the service, and the time the client waits for analysis of the previous set of data to complete. Since remote analysis is an asynchronous operation, CTH computation and Catalyst analysis execute concurrently. Wait time should be non-zero only if the time to perform analysis is larger than the CTH computation time.

Results from Figure 8a show that there is a clear scaling problem with the data analysis portion (labeled "Viz") of the baseline in situ workflow. It almost appears as if the execution time is more dependent on the problem size than the number of cores performing the data analysis. The refined version dramatically improves the performance. This corroborates our previous work [10].

Another important issue these timings reveal is the initialization cost of the visualization and data analysis. Although the CTH initialization cost appears to decrease as the core count increases, the initialization cost for data analysis, "Viz Init," increases, accounting for more than 1/3 of the total time for a 500-cycle run. For long runs, the initialization cost will get amortized, but is still large enough to warrant further study.

The in transit results in Figure 8c show that in transit extra successfully hides most of the cost of data-analysis at 4K and 8K nodes, but the wait time at larger core counts eliminates any benefit of using in transit analysis at these scales. Observe that the total time for the 16K and 32K runs of in transit extra are roughly the same as the sum of the *Viz* and *Viz Init* costs of the in situ baseline experiments in Figure 8a. We expect that if the in transit service were using the refined algorithm for analysis, the cost of analysis would be the sum of the initialization and analysis costs shown in Figure 8b, small enough that the client would not have to wait even for the large-scale runs. This experiment is left for future work.

The in transit workflow, shown in Figure 8d, which carves out a subset of 100 nodes for data analysis, has interesting results as well. Observe that the number of cores used for CTH is much smaller, leading to an increase in the time spent doing CTH computation. Even with this increase in computational cost, there is still benefit. At 4K and 8K, all of the data analysis cost is hidden. At 8K, the total runtime is slightly less than the refined version of in situ, even though both experiments use the exact same number of resouces and the in transit workflow uses a much less scalable algorithm for analysis. Although CTH takes longer for the in transit approach because it has fewer compute nodes, the analysis portion is completely hidden, compensating for the difference in CTH time. This particular configuration represents a near perfect balance of the resources required for computation and analysis.

One particularly surprising result is the performance of the post-processing workflow. For the data sets we studied, this application performed quite well, showing that the Lustre file system on Cielo is quite strong. The plots include the time spent writing the spyplot files during the experiment and the measured time to perform the data analysis as a post-processing step. One anomaly we notice in Figure 8e is that for the largest data set the I/O time jumps from around 2 minutes with 8192 cores to 10 minutes on 16,384 cores. Looking closer at our log files, we see that we have two experiments contributing to this value. One experiment required about 4.5 minutes to write whereas the other required about 15.5 minutes. We speculate that this second measurement comes from an anomalous condition on Cielo, but we do not have enough data to diagnose further.

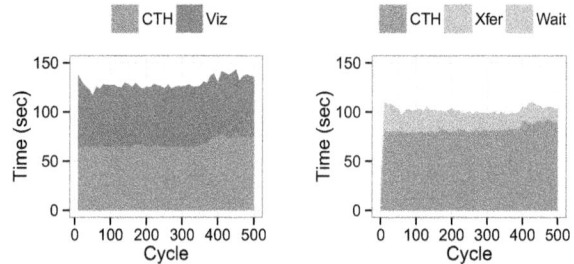

(a) In situ baseline. (b) In transit internal.

Figure 9: Time-series analysis of the in situ baseline and in transit internal workflows at 8K cores of the 1.5m block dataset.

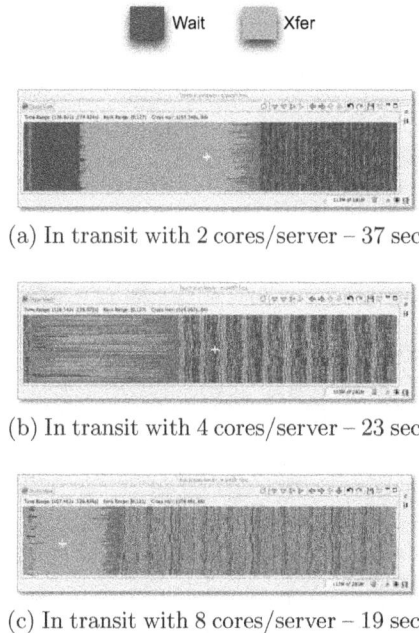

(a) In transit with 2 cores/server – 37 sec.

(b) In transit with 4 cores/server – 23 sec.

(c) In transit with 8 cores/server – 19 sec.

Figure 10: HPCToolkit-generated traces showing a 10-cycle window of execution for a 128-core job using 2, 4, and 8 cores for the analysis server.

5.3 Time-Series Analysis

A time-series analysis of the in situ baseline and in transit internal workflows at the "sweet spot" (illustrated in Figure 9) shows that time spent for computation and analysis is roughly equal for the baseline algorithm. Notice in the in transit workflow that as the CTH compute time gradually rises, the wait time goes to zero, illustrating to point where the application transitions from analysis bound to compute bound. This demonstrates a near perfect balance in the ratio of compute to service nodes for this particular data point. The goal of future research is to achieve this balance for arbitrary problems.

5.4 Server Scaling

For a scaling analysis of in transit, we evaluate performance of the in transit workflows when using different numbers of cores/node. Figure 10 shows HPCToolkit time traces of a small experiment we performed early in the project to

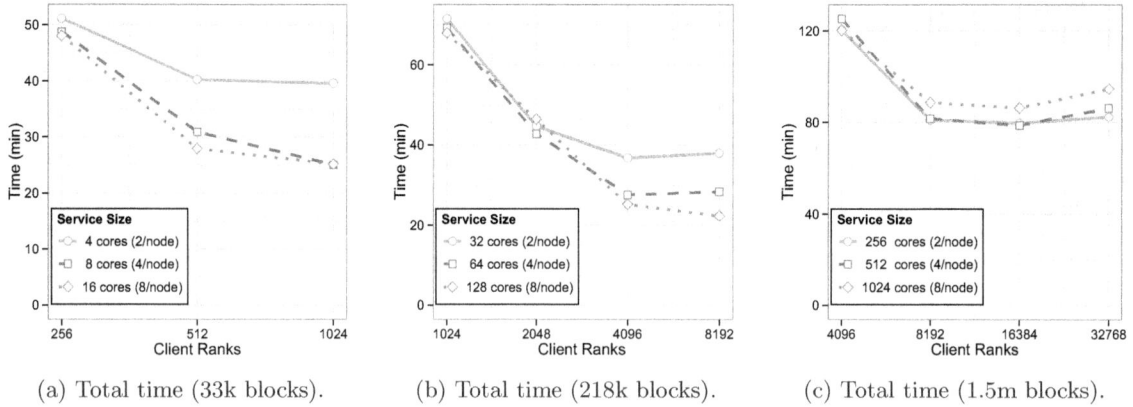

(a) Total time (33k blocks).   (b) Total time (218k blocks).   (c) Total time (1.5m blocks).

Figure 11: In transit performance for 2, 4, and 8 cores per server node.

decide on the core count for our complete set of experiments. The traces show a 10-cycle window of execution for a 128-core job using 1 server node. For this small experiment, we used a dataset of only 5k blocks.

The tracing results show a dramatic difference in network performance and wait time between all three of the experiments. We believe the relatively poor network performance in the 2-core experiment is caused by contention. Because only 2 cores can process the bulk-data requests at a time, the clients are either waiting for network transfers to complete, or they are waiting for the server to finish copying the data to a server buffer, causing the request to sit in the server's pending queue. The larger wait time on the 2-core experiment tells us that for this size problem, there is a computational benefit to increasing the number of cores performing the data analysis.

At larger scales, however, these results change. The plots in Figure 11 show differences in the total times for the 2, 4, and 8 cores/node runs of the in transit (extra) application for the three different data sets. While the smaller datasets show clear benefit of using more cores/node for analysis, the inverse seems to be true for the large datasets. Perhaps for the large runs, we have reached a scaling limit where increasing the number of cores no longer results in a performance improvement for the analysis code. Unfortunately, these conclusions are just speculation. We did not run enough experiments of this type to make definitive claims.

5.5 Variance

Page limitations prevent a full coverage of the variance studies, but we highlight two interesting results from our experiments in Figure 12. In Figure 12a, we overlay timings of six different runs of the 8K-core, 1.5M block dataset. The plots show two interesting anomalies that only occur in one run. This variance could come from any number of sources, perhaps the most likely cause is OS noise [12] or network congestion caused by a sudden burst in activity.

The plot in Figure 12b shows significant variance in network transfers for in transit workflows. The transfer of data from simulation to visualization is bandwidth constrained, and this bandwidth can vary considerably across different nodes in the network topology. The high variance we observe indicates the job scheduler might be doing a bad job optimizing the connection between the simulation and visualization [25].

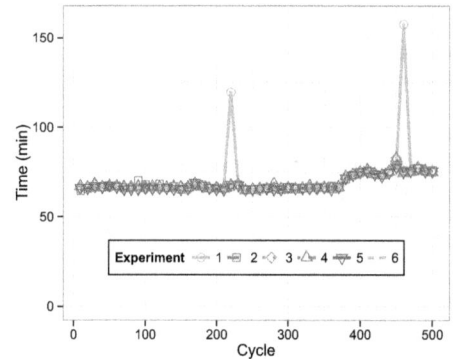

(a) CTH variance.

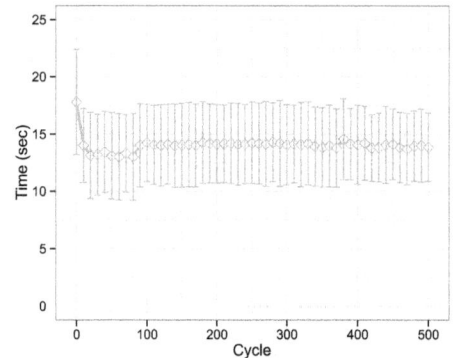

(b) In situ data-transfer variance.

Figure 12: Variance results for selected operations. (a) shows an overlay of CTH performance for 6 runs of CTH for the 8K-core, 1.5M block dataset. (b) shows the mean in transit data-transfer performance of the same set of runs with error bars showing standard deviation from the mean.

5.6 Memory Overheads

A preliminary memory analysis of the two approaches showed that the in situ experiments required 30% to 50% more memory than CTH. The in transit workflows needed 10% to 50% more memory than CTH. At large scales, memory overhead of the in transit workflows was less than half the overhead of in situ, but the amount of memory added for in transit seems to be nearly constant, independent of the number of cores on a particular node. Since in transit only allocates transfer buffers and metadata structures, further evaluation is needed to find the source of this overhead.

6. SUMMARY AND CONCLUSIONS

This document summarizes the results of a significant scaling study to evaluate performance of visualization and data analysis for a shock-physics application. Most of these workflows benefit from running in tandem with the simulation to analyze its transient data before it is written to storage. Based on this analysis, we make the following conclusions.

In situ is great for lightweight analysis. For analysis codes that do not severely hinder the scalability of the simulation, an in situ approach is extremely effective, and will likely be the simplest and best choice because the cost of analysis would be less than the cost of allocating extra nodes and transferring the data.

In transit is ideal for complex analysis. Offloading complex analysis algorithms to a separate set of nodes with perhaps large quantities of addressable memory is a practical way to integrate complex analysis and simulation with little impact on the scalability of the simulation code.

In transit analysis requires balance. Effective use of in transit analysis requires a good balance between the time spent in simulation and analysis. Such a balance requires a detailed understanding of the overheads imposed by both simulation and the analysis code.

Initialization time matters. Most efforts focus on scalability of algorithms invoked during the run of a simulation, but disregard the initialization cost. Based on our results, the cost of initialization can become quite significant at high process counts and should be evaluated and tuned with the same level of rigor as the rest of the code.

Disk-based I/O is not dead... yet. Our post-processing workflow shows that although I/O incurs a large cost, it is still a practical approach for this particular example. Thus, we expect the vast majority of users to continue to use the offline post-processing visualization and data analysis approach in the near term.

Current job scheduling support is inadequate. One of the existing technical challenges in transit workflows is scheduling the simulation and analysis to execute in tandem. Capabilities of HPC schedulers are inadequate for our needs. We cannot start, stop, or connect independent jobs dynamically. These issues will also need to be addressed in order to take advantage of burst buffers in future architectures. This particular issue helped drive a new effort, sponsored by the DOE/ASCR program, to explore operating system and runtime support for composition of application workflows [5].

We need all three types of analysis. This study was not meant to choose a "winner". Instead, it demonstrates that in situ, in transit, and even post-processing analysis approaches are required. As we evolve toward a more integrated model for analysis, we expect complex integrated workflows to leverage both in situ and in transit approaches. For example, future work will explore in situ for identification of fragments and in transit for analysis of fragments, with the expectation that the fragment analysis presents memory and scaling requirements that hinder the scalability of the simulation. Finally, in situ and in transit analysis does not displace the need for post-processing visualization, they provide complimentary tools that accelerate the rate at which a scientist can gain insight from simulated results.

7. ACKNOWLEDGEMENTS

We thank the National Nuclear Security Administration (NNSA) Office of Advanced Scientific Computing (ASC) for funding as well as access to the Cielo parallel supercomputer at Los Alamos National Laboratory. A special thanks to Joel Stevenson, John Noe, and Bob Ballance for resolving technical issues and reviewing performance results. Finally, the ASC milestone review committee consisting of Becky Springmeyer (LLNL), Berk Geveci (Kitware, Inc), Ron Brightwell (SNL), Mike Glass (SNL), Kim Mish (SNL), Dino Pavlakos (SNL), Kendall Pierson (SNL), and Jason Wilke (SNL) provided guidance and appropriate critiques of this work.

Sandia National Laboratories is a multi-program laboratory managed and operated by Sandia Corporation, a wholly owned subsidiary of Lockheed Martin Corporation, for the U.S. Department of Energy's National Nuclear Security Administration under contract DE-AC04-94AL85000.

8. REFERENCES

[1] H. Abbasi, M. Wolf, et al. Datastager: scalable data staging services for petascale applications. In *Proceedings of the 18th IEEE International Symposium on High Performance Distributed Computing*, pages 39–48, Garching, Germany, 2009.

[2] L. Adhianto, S. Banerjee, et al. Hpctoolkit: tools for performance analysis of optimized parallel programs. *Concurrency and Computation: Practice and Experience*, 22(6):685–701, 2010.

[3] S. Ahern, A. Shoshani, K.-L. Ma, et al. Scientific discovery at the exascale. Report from the DOE ASCR 2011 Workshop on Exascale Data Management, Analysis, and Visualization, February 2011.

[4] U. Ayachit et al. *The ParaView Guide: A Parallel Visualization Application*. Kitware, Inc., 4th edition, 2012.

[5] R. B. Brightwell, R. A. Oldfield, A. B. Maccabe, and D. E. Bernholdt. Hobbes: Composition and virtualization as the foundations of an extreme-scale OS/R. In *Proceedings of the International Workshop on Runtime and Operating Systems for Supercomputers*, ROSS '13, pages 2:1–2:8, Eugene, OR, June 2013.

[6] J. H. Chen et al. Terascale direct numerical simulations of turbulent combustion using S3D. *Computational Science & Discovery*, 2(1):31pp, 2009.

[7] A. Choudhary, I. Foster, et al. Languages, compilers, and runtime systems support for parallel input-output. Technical Report CCSF-39, Scalable I/O Initiative, Caltech Concurrent Supercomputing Facilities, Caltech, 1994.

[8] D. Doerfler, M. Vigil, S. Dosanjh, and J. Morrison. The Cielo petascale capability supercomputer. In *Cray User Group Meeting*, Fairbanks, Alaska, May 2011.

[9] S. Doi, T. Takei, and H. Matsumoto. Experiences in large-scale volume data visualization with RVSLIB. *Computer Graphics*, 35(2), May 2001.

[10] N. Fabian. In situ fragment detection at scale. In *Proceedings of the 2012 IEEE Symposium on Large Data Analysis and Visualization (LDAV)*, pages 105–108, October, 2012.

[11] N. Fabian, K. Moreland, D. Thompson, et al. The paraview coprocessing library: A scalable, general

purpose in situ visualization library. In *IEEE Symposium on Large Data Analysis and Visualization (LDAV)*, pages 89–96, October 2011.

[12] K. B. Ferreira, P. G. Bridges, and R. Brightwell. Characterizing application sensitivity to OS interference using kernel-level noise injection. In *Proceedings ofSC2008: High Performance Networking and Computing*, pages 1–12, Austin, Texas, 2008.

[13] G. A. Gibson, J. S. Vitter, and J. Wilkes. Strategic directions in storage I/O issues in large-scale computing. *ACM Computing Surveys*, 28(4):779–793, December 1996.

[14] R. Haimes and D. E. Edwards. Visualization in a parallel processing environment. In *Proceedings of the 35th AIAA Aerospace Sciences Meeting*, number AIAA, January 1997.

[15] J. L. Hennessy and D. A. Patterson. *Computer architecture (2nd ed.): a quantitative approach.* Morgan Kaufmann Publishers Inc., 1996.

[16] R. Jain, J. Werth, and J. C. Browne, editors. *Input/Output in Parallel and Distributed Computer Systems*, volume 362 of *The Kluwer International Series in Engineering and Computer Science*. Kluwer Academic Publishers, 1996.

[17] E. S. H. Jr. et al. CTH: A software family for multi-dimensional shock physics analysis. In R. Brun and L. Dumitrescu, editors, *Proceedings of the 19'th International Symposium on Shock Waves*, volume 1, pages 377–382, Marseille, France, July 1993.

[18] N. Liu, J. Cope, et al. On the role of burst buffers in leadership-class storage systems. In *IEEE Conference on Mass Storage Systems and Technologies*, pages 1–11, April 2012.

[19] J. Lofstead, R. A. Oldfield, and T. H. Kordenbrock. Experiences applying data staging technology in unconventional ways. In *13th IEEE/ACM International Symposium on Cluster, Cloud and Grid Computing (CCGrid)*, Delft, The Netherlands, May 2013.

[20] B. H. McCormick et al., editors. *Visualization in Scientific Computing (special issue of Computer Graphics)*, volume 21. ACM Press, 1987.

[21] K. Moreland. A survey of visualization pipelines. *IEEE Transactions on Visualization and Computer Graphics*, 19(3):367–378, March 2013.

[22] K. Moreland, C. C. Law, L. Ice, and D. Karelitz. Analysis of fragmentation in shock physics simulation. In *Proceedings of the 2008 Workshop on Ultrascale Visualization*, pages 40–46, November 2008.

[23] K. Moreland, R. Oldfield, et al. Examples of in transit visualization. In *Proceedings of the 2nd International Workshop on Petascale Data Analytics: Challenges and Opportunities*, PDAC '11, pages 1–6, Seattle, WA, November 2011.

[24] A. Nisar, W. Liao, and A. Choudhary. Scaling parallel I/O performance through I/O delegate and caching system. In *Proceedings of the 2008 ACM/IEEE conference on Supercomputing*, SC '08, pages 9:1–9:12, Piscataway, NJ, USA, 2008.

[25] R. A. Oldfield. Lightweight storage and overlay networks for fault tolerance. Technical Report SAND2010-0040, Sandia National Laboratories, Albuquerque, NM, January 2010. LDRD Final Report.

[26] R. A. Oldfield, S. Arunagiri, et al. Modeling the impact of checkpoints on next-generation systems. In *Proceedings of the 24th IEEE Conference on Mass Storage Systems and Technologies*, San Diego, CA, September 2007.

[27] R. A. Oldfield, T. Kordenbrock, and P. Widener. Data-movement approaches for HPC storage systems. In A. Gavrilovska, editor, *Attaining High Performance Communication: A Vertical Approach*, chapter 17, pages 329–351. CRC Press, 2009.

[28] R. A. Oldfield, G. D. Sjaardema, et al. Trilinos I/O Support (Trios). *Scientific Programming*, 20(2):181–196, August 2012.

[29] R. A. Oldfield, D. E. Womble, and C. C. Ober. Efficient parallel I/O in seismic imaging. *The International Journal of High Performance Computing Applications*, 12(3):333–344, Fall 1998.

[30] S. Parker and C. Johnson. SCIRun: A scientific programming environment for computational steering. In *Proceedings of the IEEE/ACM SC95 Conference*, November 1995.

[31] D. Patterson, G. Gibson, and R. Katz. A case for redundant arrays of inexpensive disks (RAID). In H. Jin, T. Cortes, and R. Buyya, editors, *High Performance Mass Storage and Parallel I/O: Technologies and Applications*, chapter 1, pages 3–14. IEEE Computer Society Press and Wiley, New York, NY, 2001.

[32] R. H. Patterson, G. A. Gibson, et al. Informed prefetching and caching. Technical Report CMU-CS-95-134, School of Computer Science, Carnegie Mellon University, 1995.

[33] E. Riedel, C. Faloutsos, G. A. Gibson, and D. Nagle. Active disks for large-scale data processing. *IEEE Computer*, 34(6):68–74, June 2001.

[34] D. Rogers, K. Moreland, R. Oldfield, and N. Fabian. Data co-processing for extreme scale analysis. Technical Report SAND2013-1122, Sandia National Laboratories, March 2013. L2 ASC Milestone 4745.

[35] W. Schroeder, K. Martin, and B. Lorensen. *The Visualization Toolkit An Object-Oriented Approach To 3D Graphics*. Kitware, Inc., 4th edition, December 2006.

[36] V. Vishwanath, M. Hereld, et al. Topology-aware data movement and staging for I/O acceleration on Blue Gene/P supercomputing systems. In *Proceedings of 2011 International Conference for High Performance Computing, Networking, Storage and Analysis*, SC '11, pages 19:1–19:11, New York, NY, USA, 2011.

[37] F. Zheng, H. Abbasi, et al. PreDatA - preparatory data analytics on Peta-Scale machines. In *Proceedings of the International Parallel and Distributed Processing Symposium*, pages 1–12, Atlanta, GA, April 2010.

Input-adaptive Parallel Sparse Fast Fourier Transform for Stream Processing

Shuo Chen
Department of ECE
University of Delaware
Newark, DE, USA
schen@udel.edu

Xiaoming Li
Department of ECE
University of Delaware
Newark, DE, USA
xli@udel.edu

ABSTRACT

Fast Fourier Transform (FFT) is frequently invoked in stream processing, e.g., calculating the spectral representation of audio/video frames, and in many cases the inputs are sparse, i.e., most of the inputs' Fourier coefficients being zero. Many sparse FFT algorithms have been proposed to improve FFT's efficiency when inputs are known to be sparse. However, like their "dense" counterparts, existing sparse FFT implementations are input oblivious in the sense that how the algorithms work is not affected by the value of input. The sparse FFT computation on one frame is exactly the same as the computation on the next frame. This paper improves upon existing sparse FFT algorithms by simultaneously exploiting the input sparsity and the similarity between adjacent inputs in stream processing. Our algorithm detects and takes advantage of the similarity between input samples to automatically design and customize sparse filters that lead to better parallelism and performance. More specifically, we develop an efficient heuristic to detect the similarity between the current input to its predecessor in stream processing, and when it is found to be similar, we novelly use the spectral representation of the predecessor to accelerate the sparse FFT computation on the current input. Given a sparse signal that has only k non-zero Fourier coefficients, our algorithm utilizes sparse approximation by tuning several adaptive filters to efficiently package the non-zero Fourier coefficients into a small number of bins which can then be estimated accurately. Therefore, our algorithm has runtime sub-linear to the input size and gets rid of recursive coefficient estimation, both of which improve parallelism and performance. Furthermore, the new heuristic can detect the discontinuities inside the streams and resumes the input adaptation very quickly. We evaluate our input-adaptive sparse FFT implementation on Intel i7 CPU and three NVIDIA GPUs, i.e., NVIDIA GeForce GTX480, Tesla C2070 and Tesla C2075. Our algorithm is faster than previous FFT implementations both in theory and implementation. For inputs with size $N = 2^{24}$, our parallel implementation outperforms FFTW

for k up to 2^{18}, which is an order of magnitude higher than prior sparse algorithms. Furthermore, our input adaptive sparse FFT on Tesla C2075 GPU achieves up to 77.2× and 29.3× speedups over 1-thread and 4-thread FFTW, 10.7×, 6.4×, 5.2× speedups against sFFT 1.0, sFFT 2.0, CUFFT, and 6.9× speedup over our sequential CPU performance, respectively.

Categories and Subject Descriptors

G.1.0 [**General**]: Parallel Algorithms

Keywords

Sparse FFT; Input Adaptive; Stream Processing; Parallel Algorithm

1. INTRODUCTION

The Fast Fourier Transform (FFT) calculates the spectrum representation of time-domain input signals. If the input size is N, the FFT operates in $O(NlogN)$ steps. The performance of FFT algorithms is known to be determined only by input size, and not affected by the value of input. Therefore, prior FFT optimization efforts, for example the widely used library FFTW, have been largely focused on improve the efficiency of FFT for various computer architectural features such as cache hierarchy, but have generally put aside the role of input characteristics in FFT performance.

So far the only feature of input value having been leveraged to improve FFT performance is input sparsity. In real world applications, input signals are frequently sparse, i.e., most of the Fourier coefficients of a signal are very small or equal to zero. If we *know* that an input is sparse, the computational complexity of FFT can be reduced. Sub-linear sparse Fourier algorithm was first proposed in [14], and since then, has been extensively studied in the literatures when applied to various fields [13, 6, 2, 7, 12, 1]. However, their runtimes have large exponents in the polynomials of k and $logN$, and their complex algorithmic structures restrict fast and parallel implementations.

A recent highly-influential work [9] presented an improved algorithm in the runtime of $O(k\sqrt{NlogN}logN)$ that makes it faster than FFT for the sparsity parameter k up to $O(\sqrt{N/logN})$. The follow-up work [10] proposed an algorithm with runtime $O(klogNlog(N/k))$ or even the optimal $O(klogN)$. Just like the "dense" FFT algorithms and the earlier sparse FFT algorithms, the latest sparse FFT algorithms are oblivious to input characteristics, because input sparsity is assumed but not measured. Furthermore, the sparse FFT algorithms' design is fixed for all inputs of the same size. No part in the algorithms is adapted to other input characteristics.

Here we make an interesting observation. We know that in many real-world FFT applications not only inputs are sparse, but at the same time adjacent inputs are similar. For example, in video compression, two consecutive video frames usually have almost identical sparse distribution in their spectrums, and differ only in the magnitudes of some spectrum coefficients. If the FFT on the prior input has been computed, i.e., its spectrum representation is known, and the current input has a similar sparse distribution to the prior input, can the similarity help computing the sparse FFT on the current input? To answer the question, we need to tell whether an input is similar to its predecessor, and how the knowledge about the predecessor's spectral representation can help. This paper answers the two questions and propose a new sublinear and parallel algorithm for sparse FFT. The main contributions of this paper are: 1) a heuristic to detect the sparsity homogeneity, so that we can know when the FFT computation can be simplified with prior knowledge; and 2) an efficient input adaption process to use the sparsity homogeneity as a template to design the customized filters for subsequent similar inputs, so that the filters lead to less waste of calculation on those zero coefficient bins and can better express parallelism in sparse FFT.

Particularly interesting is that the input sparsity and the input simularity make it easier to parallelize FFT calculation. From a very high point of view, our sparse FFT algorithm applies the custom-designed sparse filters to disperse the sparse Fourier coefficients of inputs into separate bins directly in the spectrum domain. During the dispersion, the calculation on those bins are independent. Therefore it leads our sparse FFT to produce a deterministically correct output, and to be non-iterative with high arithmetic intensity as well. Substantial data parallelism is able to be exploited from our algorithm.

Next we briefly introduce existing sparse FFT algorithms and overview our approach. Then we present how we customize filters based on the sparse template, and how we use the designed filters to reduce the overhead and the number of iterations in the sparse FFT algorithm presented in [9], which our work is based on. Moreover, we show how our input adaption process efficiently and effectively classifies homogeneous and discontinuous signals and automatically recovers from input discontinuity. Finally, we evaluate the performance and accuracy of our input-adaptive sparse FFT with FFTW, CUFFT and the latest sparse FFT implementation on synthetic and real video inputs.

2. BACKGROUND AND OVERVIEW

In this section we overview FFT algorithms, including prior works on sparse Fourier transform, and then introduce our contribution in that context.

2.1 Prior Work on Sparse FFT

A naive discrete Fourier transform of a N-dimensional input series $x(n)$, $n = 0, 1, ..., N - 1$ is presented as $Y(d) = \sum_{n=0}^{N-1} x(n) W_N^{nd}$, where $d = 0, 1, ..., N - 1$ and N-th primitive root of unity $W_N = e^{-j2\pi/N}$. Fast Fourier transform algorithms recursively decompose a N-dimensional DFT into

several smaller DFTs [4], and reduce DFT's operational complexity from $O(N^2)$ into $O(NlogN)$. There are many FFT algorithms, or in other words, different ways to decompose DFT problems. Prime-Factor (Good-Thomas) [8] decomposes a DFT of size $N = N_1 N_2$, where N_1 and N_2 are coprime numbers. Twiddle factor calculation is not included in this algorithm. Additionally, Rader's algorithm [15] and Bluestein's algorithm [3] can factorize a prime-size DFT as convolution.

So far, the runtimes of all FFT algorithms have been proved to be at least proportional to the size of input signal. However, if the output of a FFT is k-sparse, i.e., most of the Fourier coefficients of a signal are very small or equal to zero and only k coefficients are large, sparse Fourier transform is able to reduce the runtime to be only sublinear to the signal size N. Sublinear sparse Fourier algorithm was first proposed in [14], and since then, has been extensively studied in many application fields [13, 6, 2, 7, 12, 1]. All these sparse algorithms have runtimes faster than original FFT for sparse signals. However, their runtimes still have large exponents (larger than 3) in the polynomials of k and $logN$, and their complex algorithmic structures are hard to parallelize.

A highly influential work [9] presented an improved algorithm with the complexity of $O(k\sqrt{NlogN}logN)$ to make it faster than FFT for k up to $O(\sqrt{N/logN})$. The work in [10] followed up with an improved algorithm with runtime $O(klogNlog(N/k))$ or even the optimal $O(klogN)$. Basically, the algorithms permute input with random parameters in time domain to approximate expected permutation in spectral domain for binning the large coefficients. The probability has to be bounded to prevent large coefficients being binned into the same bucket. In addition, these algorithms iterate over passes for estimating coefficients, updating the signal and recursing on the reminder. Because dependency exists between consecutive iterations, the algorithms cannot be fully parallelized. Moreover, the selections of the permutation probability and the filter, which are crucial to the algorithms' performance, are predetermined and are oblivious to input characteristics.

2.2 Our Approach

In this paper, we address these limitations by proposing a new sublinear as well as parallel algorithm for sparse Fourier transform. Our algorithm has a quite simple structure and leads to a low big-Oh constant in runtime. Our sparse FFT algorithm works efficiently in the context that the sparse FFT is invoked on a stream of input signals, and neighboring inputs have very similar spectrum distribution including the sparsity parameter k. The assumption is true for many real-world applications, for example, for many video/audio applications, where neighboring frames have almost identical spectral representations in the locations of large Fourier coefficients, and only differing in the coefficient magnitudes. Our algorithm adapts to the homogeneity in signal spectrums by utilizing the output of the previous FFT, i.e., the spectral representation of the previous input, as a template to most efficiently compute the Fourier transform for the current input signal. When the homogeneity is found to be broken, our algorithm re-calculates the template and restarts the input-adaptation. An effective heuristic is proposed in this paper to detect such discontinuity in frame spectrums.

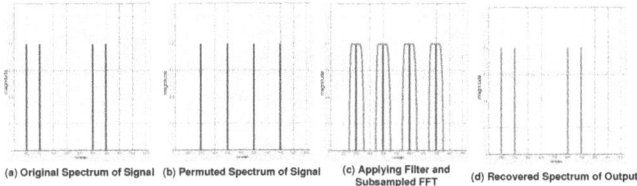

Figure 1: Binning of non-zero Fourier coefficients.

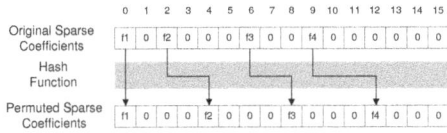

Figure 2: Hash table based permutation.

To help understand the role of spectral template, Figure. 1 illustrates the binning process in our algorithm. Large Fourier coefficients are binned into a small number of buckets and each bucket is designed to have only one large coefficient whose location and magnitude can be then determined. The bucket is represented by an n-dimensional filter D, that is concentrated both in time and frequency [9, 10], to ensure the runtime to be sublinear to N. What binning does is essentially to convolute a permuted input signal with a well-selected filter in spectral domain. During the binning, each bucket receives only the frequencies in a narrow range corresponding to the length of filter D's pass region, and pass regions of different buckets are disjoint. The prerequisite of a pass region having only one large coefficient is to make it possible to evenly space all adjacent coefficients in spectrum later. The information of likely coefficient locations used in the filter tuning is derived from the sparsity template. Particularly, to achieve the expected equal distanced permutation, we make use of a hash table structure to directly permute coefficients in the spectral domain. Fig. 2 shows the example of our hash table based permutation in spectral domain, where f_i denotes non-zero Fourier coefficients and the numbers shown above represent locations of the coefficients.

Note that we do not permute input in time domain to approximate the equal distanced permutation with a certain probability bound, but rather directly permute in spectral domain. In addition, each bucket certainly bins only one large coefficient. Therefore our sparse FFT algorithm is always capable of producing a determinative as well as correct output. Once each bucket bins only one large coefficient, we also need to identify its magnitudes and locations. Instead of recovering the isolated coefficients using linear phase estimation [10], we can easily look up the hash table reversely to identify binned coefficients. As a result, our algorithm has the runtime at most $O(k^2 log N)$.

Furthermore, if the distances of all adjacent frequencies are larger than the minimum length of filter's pass region, we can reduce the number of permutations and therefore further improve the runtime to $O(k log N log(k log N))$.

Another desirable trait of our algorithm, compared with prior sparse FFT algorithms, is its capability to be fully parallelized. Since our algorithm is non-iterative with high arithmetic intensity, substantial data parallelism can be exploited from the algorithm. The graphical processing units (GPUs) are utilized for the well-suited data parallel computations. In this work we parallelize three main steps in

our algorithm on GPU: input permutation, subsampled FFT and coefficient estimation.

3. INPUT ADAPTIVE SPARSE FFT

In this section, we go over several algorithm versions to explain the evolution from a general sparse FFT algorithm to the proposed input-adaptive parallel sparse FFT algorithm. We first describe a general input adaptive sparse FFT algorithm which comprises of input permutation, filtering non-zero coefficients, subsampling FFT and recovery of locations and magnitudes. Subsequently, we discuss how to save the number of permutations and propose an alternatively optimized version for our sparse FFT algorithm to gain runtime improvement. Moreover, the general and the optimized versions are hybridized so that we're able to choose a specific version according to input characteristics. Additionally, we show how the performance of our implementation can be parallelized for GPU and multi-core CPU. Finally, an example of real world application is described to illustrate our input adaptive approach.

3.1 General Input-Adaptive Sparse FFT

3.1.1 Notations and Assumptions

For a time-domain input signal x with size N (assuming N is an integer power of 2), its DFT is $\hat{x}$. The sparsity parameter of input, k, is defined as the number of non-zero Fourier coefficients in $\hat{x}$. In addition, $[q]$ refers to the set of indices $\{0, ..., q-1\}$. $supp(x)$ refers to the support of vector x, i.e. the set of non-zero coordinates, and $|supp(x)|$ denotes the number of non-zero coordinates of x. Finally, this initial version of algorithm assumes input homogeneity, that is, the locations loc_j of non-zero Fourier coefficients can be estimated from similar prior inputs, where $j \in [k]$. The location template is computed only once for a sequence of signal frames that are similar to each other. The computing of the template by our input-adaptive mechanism is described in section 3.5.

When we find that homogeneity is broken, our algorithm re-calculates the template and restarts the input-adaptation.

3.1.2 Hashing Permutation of Spectrum

The general sparse FFT algorithm starts with binning large Fourier coefficients into a small number of buckets by convoluting a permuted input signal with a well-selected filter in spectral domain. To guarantee that each bucket receives only one large coefficient so that its location and magnitude can be accurately estimated, we need to permute large adjacent coefficients of input spectrum to be equidistant. Knowing the possible Fourier locations loc_j and their order $j \in [k]$ from the template, we can customize a hash table to map spectral coefficients into equally distanced positions.

DEFINITION 1. *Define a hash function H: $idx = H(j) = j \times N/k$, where idx is index of permuted Fourier coefficients and $j \in [k]$.*

Next we want to determine the shifting distance s between each original location loc and its permuted position idx to be $s_j = idx_j - loc_j, j \in [k]$. Since shifting one time moves all non-zero Fourier coefficients with a constant factor, so in the worst case, only one Fourier coefficient will be permuted into the right equidistant location. In addition, since we need to permute in total k non-zero coefficients, at most k-time shiftings have to be performed to permute all the coefficients into their equal distanced positions.

Moreover, the shifting factors obtained in spectral space should be translated into correspondent operations in time domain so that they are able to take effect with input signal $x_i, i \in [N]$. In effect, shifted spectrum $\hat{x}_{loc-s}$ is equivalently represented as $x_i \omega^{si}$ in time domain, where $\omega = e^{b2\pi/N}$ is a primitive n-th root of unity and $b = \sqrt{-1}$.

DEFINITION 2. *Define the permutation $P_{s(j)}$ as $(P_{s(j)}x)_i = x_i \omega^{is(j)}$ therefore $\hat{P_{s(j)}x_i} = \hat{x}(loc_j - s(j))$, where $s(j)$ is the factor of j-th shifting.*

Therefore, each time when we change the factor $s(j)$, the permutation allows us to correctly bin the large coefficient at location loc_j into the bucket. The length of bucket is determined by the flat window function designed in the next section.

3.1.3 Flat Window Functions

In this paper, the method of constructing a flat window function is same as that used in [9]. The concept of flat window function is derived from standard window function in digital signal processing. Since window functions work as filters to bin non-zero Fourier coefficients into a small number of buckets, the pass region of filter is expected to be as flat as possible. Therefore, our filter is constructed by having a standard window function convoluted with a box-car filter [9]. Moreover, we want the filter to have a good performance by making it to have fast attenuation in stopband.

DEFINITION 3. *Define $D(k, \delta, \alpha)$, where $k >= 1$, $\delta > 0$, $\alpha > 0$, to be a flat window function that satisfies:*
1. *$|supp(D)| = O(\frac{k}{\alpha} log(\frac{1}{\delta}))$;*
2. *$\hat{D}_i \in [0, 1]$ for all i;*
3. *$\hat{D}_i \in [1-\delta, 1+\delta]$ for all $|i| \leq \frac{(1-\alpha)N}{2k}$;*
4. *$\hat{D}_i < \delta$ for all $|i| \geq \frac{N}{2k}$;*

In particular, a flat window function acts as a filter to extract a certain set of elements of input x. Even if the filter consists of N elements, most of the elements in the filter are negligible and there are only $O(\frac{k}{\alpha} log(\frac{1}{\delta}))$ significant elements when multiplying with x in time domain. In addition, the flat window functions are precomputed in our implementation to save execution time, since their constructions are not dependent on input x but only dependent on N and k. We can lookup each value of the window function in constant time.

Fig.3 shows an example of Gaussian, Kaiser and Dolph-Chebyshev flat window functions. Note that the spectrum of our filters D is nearly flat along the pass region and has an exponential tail outside it. It means that leakage from frequencies in other buckets can be negligible. By comparing the properties of the three window functions, Dolph-Chebyshev window is the optimal one for us due to its flat pass region as well as its quick and deep attenuation in stopband.

3.1.4 Subsampled FFT

The coefficients binning process convolutes input spectrum with flat window function. In our algorithm, this

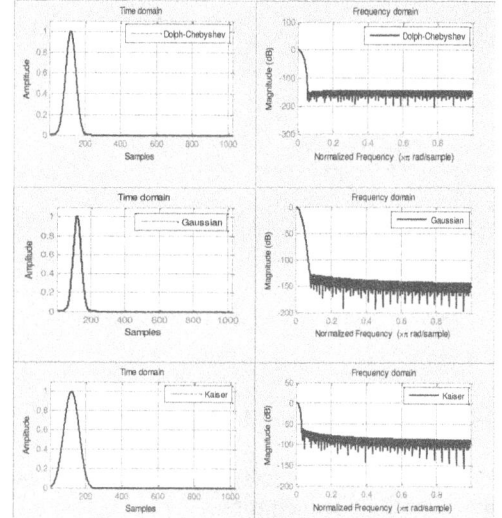

Figure 3: Dolph-Chebyshev, Gaussian and Kaiser flat window functions for $N = 1024$.

convolution is actually performed in time domain by first multiplying input with filter and then computing its subsampled FFT. Suppose we have one N-dimensional complex input series x with sparsity parameter k for its Fourier coefficients, we define a subsampled FFT as $\hat{y}_i = \hat{x}_{iN/k}$ where $i \in [k]$ and N can be divisible by k. The FFT subsampling expects the locations of Fourier coefficients in spectrum domain have been equally spaced. The proof of k-dimensional subsampled FFT has been shown in [9] and the time cost is in $O(|supp(x)| + klogk)$.

3.1.5 Reverse Hash Function for Location Recovery

After subsampling and FFT to the permuted signal, the binned coefficients have to be reconstructed. This is done by computing the reverse hash function H_r.

DEFINITION 4. *Define a reverse hash function H_r: $rec = H_r(idx) = \frac{idx}{(N/k)}$, where idx is index of permuted Fourier coefficients and rec is the order of recovered coefficients.*

Therefore, the recovery of Fourier locations can be estimated as loc_{rec} by using the reconstructed order of frequencies.

3.1.6 Basic Algorithm

Combining the aforementioned steps, we can piece together a baseline sparse FFT algorithm. Note that up to this point, we have not introduced input adaptability, yet. Assuming we have a Fourier location template with k known Fourier locations loc and a precomputed filter D,

1. For $j = 0, 1, 2, ..., k-1$, where $j \in [k]$, compute hash indices $idx_j = H(j)$ of permuted coefficients, and determine shifting factor $s_j = idx_j - loc_j$.
2. Compute $y = D \cdot P_s(x)$, therefore $|supp(y)| = |s| \times |supp(D)| = O(|s|\frac{k}{\alpha} log(\frac{1}{\delta}))$. We set $\delta = \frac{1}{4N^2V}$, where V is the upperbound value of Fourier coefficients and $V \leq N$.
3. Compute $u_i = \sum_{l=0}^{\frac{|supp(y)|}{k}-1} y_{i|y|+lk}$ where $i \in [k]$.
4. Compute k-dimensional subsampled FFT $\hat{u}_i$ and make $\hat{z}_{idx} = \hat{u}_i$, where $i \in [k]$.
5. Location recovery for $\hat{z}_{idx}$ by computing reverse hash function to produce $rec = H_r(idx)$ and finally output $\hat{z}_{loc(rec)}$.

The computational complexity The computational complexity of our general sparse FFT algorithm can be derived from the complexity of each step: Step 1 costs $O(k)$; step 2 and 3 cost $O(|s|\frac{k}{\alpha}log(\frac{1}{\delta}))$; step 4 costs $O(klogk)$ for a k-points FFT; step 5 costs $O(k)$. Therefore the total running time is $O(|s|\frac{k}{\alpha}log(\frac{1}{\delta}))$. It is very rarely that initial Fourier coefficients have equidistant locations, therefore $|s|$ equals to $|k|$ in general and the runtime becomes $O(\frac{k^2}{\alpha}log(\frac{1}{\delta}))$ which is asymptotic to $O(k^2logN)$.

3.2 Optimized Input-Adaptive Sparse FFT

In this section we introduce several transformations of our algorithm that may improve performance and facilitate parallelization. The complexity of the general adaptive sparse Fourier algorithm is asymptotic to $O(|s|\frac{k}{\alpha}log(\frac{1}{\delta}))$ if initially no adjacent Fourier coefficients are equally distanced. However, if the number of permutations can be reduced, then $|s|$ will be decreased. In fact, it is unnecessary to permute all the Fourier locations to make them equidistant between each other. Since binning the sparse Fourier coefficients is a process of convoluting permuted input spectrum with a customized filter, it is guaranteed that if length of filter's pass region ϵ is less than or equal to half of the shortest distance $dist_{min}$ among all the adjacent locations of non-zero coefficients, i.e. $\epsilon <= dist_{min}/2$, then we don't need to permute all coefficients before we do a FFT. Moreover, in this way, we can get rid of aliasing distortions during the binning and each pass region essentially receives only one large coefficient. If we do not do this, aliasing error occurs and we have to permute all spectral samples.

Next we continue to apply the flat window function D to compute filtered vector $y = Dx$ and then a FFT is computed for y to produce the final output $\hat{y}$. The form of FFT we use here is not a k-dimensional subsampled FFT described previously, since the subsampled FFT requires that locations of non-zero Fourier coefficients are permuted to be equidistant. Instead, we apply a general FFT subroutine into calculation of $\hat{y}$. The size of the FFT is dependent on the length of non-zero elements in y, which is $O(\frac{k}{\alpha}log(\frac{1}{\delta}))$ determined by non-zero region of window function D. We treat the size of this FFT as a region with length $O(\frac{k}{\alpha}log(\frac{1}{\delta}))$ (i.e. $O(klogN)$) truncated from size N. Total number of such truncated regions is $\frac{N}{klogN}$. In addition, since k sparse Fourier coefficients are distributed in a region consisting of N elements, we have to identify whether the output of $O(\frac{k}{\alpha}log(\frac{1}{\delta}))$-dimensional FFT contains all non-zero Fourier coefficients. If not, we would like to shift the unevaluated non-zero coefficient into the truncated region. Our algorithms determines whether to do the shifting before computing FFT. Since the locations of non-zero coefficients and the length of truncated region are known from template, we compare the locations with boundary of truncated region to determine the shifting factor sf.

3.2.1 Input-Adaptive Shifting

There are two ways to shift non-zero coefficients. 1) If $k <= \frac{N}{klogN}$, we shift the first unevaluated non-zero coefficient into the truncated region each time; or 2) If $\frac{N}{klogN} < k$, we shift the unevaluated non-zero coefficient by a constant factor $klogN$ each time;

In the worst case, the first method performs shifting at most $O(k)$ times, while the second version uses at most $O(\frac{N}{klogN})$. However, if all large coefficients reside in only one truncated region, we need no shifting and hence we obtain the best case. Meanwhile, the shifting sf_i to spectral

coefficients, i.e. $\hat{y}_{i+sf_i}$ is equivalent to a time domain operation by multiplying input signal y_n with a twiddle factor, i.e. $y_n e^{-b2\pi sf_i n/N}$ where $b = \sqrt{-1}$. Therefore, the cost of shifting for one time is the length of filtered vector y, i.e. $O(klogN)$.

3.2.2 Optimized Algorithm

Adding the optimization heuristics and the input-adaptive shifting, the improved sparse FFT algorithm works as following:

1. Apply filter to input signal x:
Utilize a flat window function D to compute the filtered vector $y = Dx$. Time cost RT_1 is $O(\frac{k}{\alpha}log(\frac{1}{\delta}))$, i.e. $O(klogN)$.

2. Spectrum shifting: Compare k and $\frac{N}{klogN}$ to select one of the two shifting methods and then do the shifting to filtered vector y. The step-2's runtime RT_2 is $O(klogN) \leq RT_2 < O(min\{k, \frac{N}{klogN}\}\frac{k}{\alpha}log(\frac{1}{\delta}))$, i.e. $O(klogN) \leq RT_2 < O(min\{k, \frac{N}{klogN}\}klogN)$.

3. For $e \in \{1, 2, ..., min\{k, \frac{N}{klogN}\}\}$, each shifting event I_e is to compute $O(\frac{k}{\alpha}log(\frac{1}{\delta}))$-dimensional (i.e. $O(klogN)$-dimensional) FFT $\hat{z}_e$ as $\hat{z}_{e,i} = \hat{y}_i$ in current truncated region, for $i \in [O(\frac{k}{\alpha}log(\frac{1}{\delta})) = O(klogN)]$. Final output is $\hat{z}$. The step-3's runtime RT_3 is $O(klogNlog(klogN)) \leq RT_3 < O(min\{k, \frac{N}{klogN}\}klogNlog(klogN))$.

Therefore, total runtime RT of the improved sparse FFT algorithm is
$$O(klogNlog(klogN)) \leq RT < O(min\{k, \frac{N}{klogN}\}klogNlog(klogN)).$$

3.3 Hybrid Input-Adaptive Sparse FFT

It is clear from the complexity analysis of our general and optimized sparse FFT algorithms that the two algorithm versions are best suited for different input characteristics. That is, the "optimized" version does not perform better than the general version on all cases. We hybridize the two approaches by at runtime selecting the most appropriate version based on input characteristics.

In our optimized version of sparse FFT algorithm, it is worth mentioning that if the required length of pass region is too short, such a filter becomes hard to construct in practice. Therefore, we define a threshold $dist_{TD}$ of minimum distance $dist_{min}$. If $dist_{min} >= dist_{TD}$, then the filter can be constructed to have expected pass region. If $dist_{min} < dist_{TD}$, then our general sparse FFT has to be applied and all the Fourier locations have to be permuted to be equidistant. The threshold can be obtained by offline empirical search.

Therefore, the two algorithm versions are selected based on the following heuristic:

1. Determine the shortest distance $dist_{min}$ among all adjacent locations of k large coefficients: Initialize minimum distance $dist_{min} = 0$; For $j \in 1, 2, ..., k-1$, compute distances $dist_j = loc_j - loc_{j-1}$ between all k adjacent sparse Fourier locations loc_{j-1} and loc_j; Then if $dist_j <= dist_{min}$, update $dist_{min} = dist_j$. The runtime is $O(k)$.

2. If $dist_{min} >= dist_{TD}$, we choose the optimized approach to avoid large number of permutations; If $dist_{min} < dist_{TD}$, then our general sparse FFT has to be applied and all the Fourier locations have to be permuted to be equidistant. The threshold can be obtained by empirical search in our filter design process.

The cost for the selecting process is only $O(k)$, which can be neglected compared with the runtime of either the general version or the optimized version.

3.4 Parallel Input-Adaptive Sparse FFT

Compared with the "dense" FFT algorithms or the existing sparse FFT algorithms, our input-adaptive sparse FFT algorithm can be better parallelized. Specifically, our algorithm is non-iterative with high arithmetic intensity in most portions. The non-iterative nature exposes good coarse-grain parallelism. Moreover, the data parallelism in each substep can also be exploited. In this paper, we use the Graphic Processing Units (GPUs) for the data parallel computations. Several architectural-oriented transformations are applied to fine-tune the algorithm for the GPU architecture.

We use the general sparse FFT implementation to demonstrate how we parallelize our input-adaptive sparse FFT algorithms. The parallelization of the optimized version is similar. Data parallelism exists in the hashed index computation, input filtering and permuting, subsampling FFT, and location recovery. Therefore, we implement a GPU computational *kernel* for each step. First of all, the kernel $HashFunc()$ is responsible to compute hashed indices of permuted coefficients and to determine shift factors. The loop of size k is decomposed into k threads and each thread concurrently works at each index j in the algorithm. In addition, the kernel $Perm()$ with $k^2 logN$ threads is used to apply filter and permutation to input. Each thread multiplies the filter and the shifting factor with input for one element. We parallelize the subsampling of input in kernel $Subsample()$ with total k threads before launching the FFT kernel $TunedFFT()$. Finally we obtain output from location estimation kernel $Recover()$ with k threads parallelizing the loop of algorithm.

3.4.1 Tuned GPU based FFT Library

Our GPU kernel decomposes a 1D FFT of size $N = N_1 \times N_2$ into multi-dimensions N_1 and N_2. Therefore it enables the exploitation of more parallelism for parallel FFT implementation on GPU architectures. All N_1 dimensional 1D FFTs are first calculated in parallel across N_2 dimension. If the size of N_1 is still large after decomposition, we would further decompose each $N_1 = N_{11} \times N_{12}$ sized 1D FFT into two dimensional FFTs with smaller sizes N_{11} and N_{12}, respectively. On GPU, the device memory has much higher latency and lower bandwidth than the on-chip memory. Therefore, shared memory is utilized to increase device memory bandwidth. $N_1W \times N_{11} \times N_{12}$ sized shared memory needs to be allocated, where N_1W is chosen to be 16 for half-warp of threads to enable coalesced access to device memory. The number of threads in each block, for both N_{11} and N_{12}-step FFTs, is therefore $N_1W \times max(N_{11}, N_{12})$ to realize maximum data parallelism on GPU. To calculate each N_1-step 1D FFT, a size N_{11} FFT is executed to load data from global memory into shared memory for each block. Next, all threads in each block are synchronized before data in shared memory is reused by the N_{12}-step FFT and subsequently written back to global memory. Experiment tests show that such shared memory technique effectively hides global memory latency and increases data reuse, both contributing to the performance on GPU. Fig.4 shows the working flow of our GPU based parallelization.

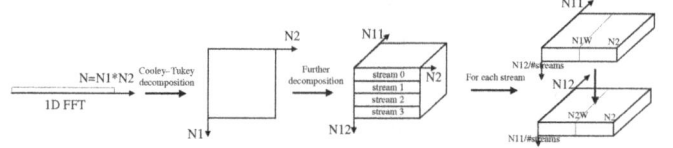

Figure 4: Working flow of GPU parallelization.

3.5 Input Adaption Heuristics and Process

In this section, we describe our overall input adaption process. We first detail when and how Fourier location templates are generated. Then, we elaborate how our sparse FFT adapts to inputs with homogeneous and discontinuous characteristics.

3.5.1 Scenario Establishment

Assume we use a fix video camera to record the movement of a 2D object for a duration of time. Each frame of the object can be represented as a 2D matrix $img(g, h)$ whose values stand for color digits, where # of rows is ro, # of columns is col, and $g \in [ro]$, $h \in [col]$. In this paper, we flatten the 2D matrix into a row-major 1D signal $x_i = x(i = g * col + h) = img(g, h)$. If the interval between the same object in two time-adjacent video frames is m in X dimension and v in Y dimension, it is clear that the shifting factor (m, v) to $img(g, h)$ is the same as x_i since $img(g-v, h-m) = x(g*col - v*col + h - m) = x_{i-v*col-m}$. Therefore, the process of video recording is modeled as a time shifting process to x_i, and we want to compute its Fourier transform $\hat{x}_j$.

3.5.2 Input Adaption for Homogeneous Signals

If the scene doesn't switch to another scene, i.e., the shifted object signals are homogeneous, the signals will have same amplitudes but differ in the X dimensional displacement. As a result, in the spectral domain, the neighboring frames have identical Fourier locations but differ in the coefficients.

In the beginning, the input signal $x_{i,T0}$ is captured in a video frame at the initial time slot T_0. We generate the Fourier template Tmp once by calculating $x_{i,T0}$'s Fourier transform $\hat{x}_{j,T0}$ using a dense FFT if $\hat{x}$ is not sparse or using a sparse FFT if $\hat{x}$ is sparse. The Fourier template Tmp containing all the locations of non-zero Fourier coefficients and their order for $\hat{x}_i$ at T_0. The cost includes runtime of a full FFT, i.e. $O(FFT)$, plus the time to identify sparse Fourier locations, i.e. $O(N)$. Next, we need to compute Fourier transform for x_{i-m_1} at time T_1. Since the time-shifted x_{i-m_1} corresponds to $\hat{x}_j e^{-b2\pi m_1 j/N}$ in spectral domain, where $b = \sqrt{-1}$, hence the locations of non-zero Fourier coefficients in $\hat{x}_{j,T1}$ is same as those in $\hat{x}_{j,T0}$, but only the coefficients differ. As a consequence, the Fourier template Tmp is used to compute sparse FFT for $x_{i-m_1,T1}$ at T_1 and for $x_{i-m_t,Tt}$ in the following time slots T_t. Therefore, we only compute dense FFT once on each segment of homogeneous inputs. Except for the first input in the segment, our adaptive sparse FFT is used.

3.5.3 Input Adaption for Discontinuous Signals

When the homogeneity is broken, the input-adaptation restarts by re-calculating the spectral template. There are two types of discontinuity: *Case 1*, the signal size is invariable, but its amplitudes vary; *Case 2*, both signal size and amplitudes vary.

Table 1: Sub-steps parameters of input adaption

Parameters	Functionality
#frames	Total # of video frames per segment.
#segment	Total # of stream segments.
Full_FFT	Time of the full dense or sparse FFT to generate Fourier location template.
Partial_FFT	Time of the partial-size FFT to detect discontinuity.
T_loc	Time to find sparse Fourier locations.
IA_sFFT	Time of our input-adaptive sparse FFT.

We develop an effective heuristic to detect such discontinuity in frame spectrums. Conceptually, if the standard FFT is computed for each input and the output is compared with the output of our sparse FFT, the deviations between the two will be small in the case of homogeneity, but will become large at the discontinuity point. However, we cannot run a $O(NlogN)$-time standard FFT to detect the discontinuity, which will void all performance advantage of the sparse FFT. Instead, we use sampling. A partial size FFT is calcuated as the standard, and its runtime is limited to $klogN$ so that the complexity of our library plus partial standard FFT is still kept to be strictly sublinear to N and to be smaller than the runtime of other sparse FFTs as well. We tried two sampling methods: *First-Partial Method*, simply chooses the first $klogN$ portion from the output; and *Partial Sampling Method*, samples the output by a rate of $\frac{N}{klogN}$.

Subsequently, we need to quantitively define discontinuity. We use the first-level deviation dev_i by comparing the outputs of our sparse FFT with that of sampled FFT. We further conduct a second-level deviation metric $dev\_2nd(dev_i, dev_{i-1})$ to determine the relative degree of difference between dev_i for current signal x_i and dev_{i-1} for signal x_{i-1} in the prior frame $i-1$. From the evaluation in section 4.2, if discontinuity occurs at frame i, $dev\_2nd(dev_i, dev_{i-1})$ at the discontinuous point will be much larger than $dev\_2nd(dev_{i-m}, dev_{i-m-1})$, $1 \leq m < \#frames$, of the previously homogeneous cases, and can be accurately separated. Since we only need compute the second-level metric once, the cost for the entire detection is $O(our\_sparse\_fft) + klogN + O(1)$ and is asymptotic to only $O(our\_sparse\_fft)$. Finally, after the discontinuity has been detected, our algorithm re-calculates the template and resumes the input-adaptation.

The overall performance of our input-adaptive sparse FFT algorithm can be decomposed into the time components listed in Table 1. Suppose there are $\#segment$ segments of inputs in a stream. In each segment, the first $\#frames - 1$ frames are homogeneous and discontinuity occurs at the last frame. The execution time of our algorithm over the whole stream can be summarized as $Time = Full\_FFT + T\_loc + (IA\_sFFT + Partial\_FFT) \times (\#frames - 1) \times \#segments + (Full\_FFT + T\_loc + IA\_sFFT) \times \#segments$.

4. EXPERIMENTAL EVALUATION

In this section we evaluate our input-adaptive sparse FFT implementation and its performance in a real-world-like application. All inputs are double-precision. The evaluation is conducted on three heterogeneous computer configurations. The sequential version is implemented on the Intel i7 920 CPU and the parallel implementation is tuned for three different NVIDIA GPUs, i.e. GeForce GTX480, Tesla

C2070 and Tesla C2075. For both sequential and parallel versions, we evaluate our general and optimized sparse FFT approaches, and compare them against four highly-influential FFT libraries: 1) FFTW 3.3.3 [5], the latest FFTW which is one of the most efficient implementations of dense FFT. In FFTW, Streaming Single Instruction Multiple Data Extensions (SSE) on Intel CPU is enabled for better performance. Furthermore, we use two levels of optimizations in FFTW, i.e. ESTIMATE (a basic optimization level marked as 'FFTW' in the plots) and MEASURE (a more aggressively optimized version marked as 'FFTW OPT'). The 4-thread enabled FFTW is used in evaluation of the parallel version. 2) sFFT 1.0 and 2.0 [9], which is one of the fastest sublinear algorithms of sparse FFT. 3) AAFFT 0.9 [11], which is another recent sublinear algorithm with fast empirical runtime. 4) CUFFT 3.2, the NVIDIA CUDA FFT library for GPU-based dense FFT implementation. The GPU performance reported in this paper includes the time for both computation and data transferring between host and device. The configurations of GPUs and CPU are summarized in Table 1.

Table 2: Configurations of GPUs and CPU

GPU	Memory	NVCC	PCI
GeForce GTX480	1.5GB	3.2	PCIe2.0 x16
Tesla C2070	6GB	3.2	PCIe2.0 x16
Tesla C2075	6GB	3.2	PCIe2.0 x16
CPU	Frequency/Cores	Memory	Cache
Intel i7 920	2.66GHz/4 cores	24GB	8192KB

4.1 Input-Adaptive Sparse FFT

We evaluate both the sequential and the parallel versions of our general sparse FFT in two cases: First, we fix the sparsity parameter $k = 64$ and plot the execution time of our library and the other libraries for 18 different signal sizes from $N = 2^{10}$ to 2^{27}. Second, we fix the signal size to $N = 2^{24}$ and evaluate the running time under different numbers of non-zero frequencies, i.e. k.

4.1.1 *Sequential Input-Adaptive Sparse FFT*

Fig. 5 and Fig. 6 show our sequential sparse FFT on an Intel i7 CPU. The basic version of our library is labeled as flag 'General', and the average and the best case of our optimized version is marked as 'OPT-AVG' and 'OPT-BEST', respectively. Specifically, our optimized version performs best when all large coefficients reside in only one truncated region of length $O(klogN)$ so that no shifting is needed. The 'OPT-AVG' case instead runs on a random input for 10 times and then takes an average.

In Fig. 5, we fix $k = 64$ but vary N. The running time of FFTW is linear in the signal size N and sFFT 1.0/2.0 shows approximately linear in N when $N > 2^{20}$. However, our sparse FFT's performance appears almost constant as the signal size increases, which reflects the sub-linear complexity of our algorithm. In addition, AAFFT 0.9 is stable over different N but its performance is lower than ours and sFFT. Overall, our approach outperforms over sFFT, FFTW and AAFFT. Our general version, the average case and the optimal case of our optimized library become faster than FFTW with $N \geq 2^{18}$, $N \geq 2^{17}$, and $N \geq 2^{14}$, respectively, while sFFT and AAFFT achieve this goal with much larger input sizes, i.e., $N \geq 2^{19}$ and $N \geq 2^{24}$, respectively.

In Fig. 6, we fix $N = 2^{24}$ but change k. FFTW shows invariance in performance since its complexity is $O(NlogN)$ which is independent to k. Our general sparse FFT main-

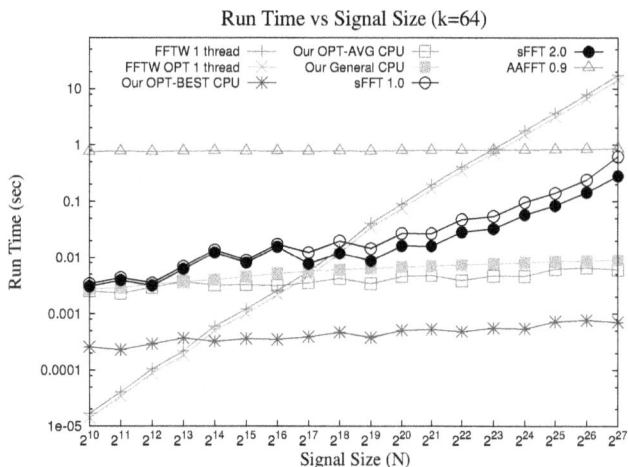

Figure 5: Sequential performance vs. signal size.

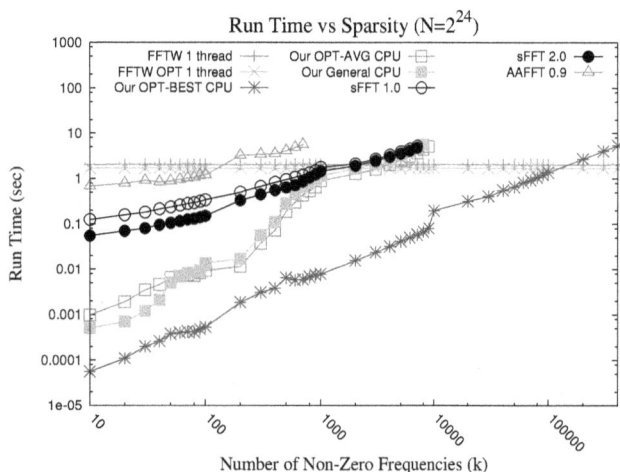

Figure 6: Sequential performance vs. sparsity.

tains its performance superiority over FFTW for k up to 3000 and 2000, respectively. Our optimal version shows a faster performance than FFTW before k reaches 100000. However, sFFT 1.0, sFFT 2.0 and AAFFT 0.9 are faster than basic FFTW only when k is less than 900, 1000 and 100. Therefore, our approach extends the range of input sparsity parameter k in which a sparse FFT outperforms a dense FFT, the range being an indicative and widely used efficiency metric when evaluating a sparse FFT algorithm. Furthermore, our library performs better than all other compared FFT libraries on average.

4.1.2 *Parallel Input-Adaptive Sparse FFT*

Fig. 7 shows the parallel versions of our sparse FFT on three GPUs. Since there is no parallel version of either sFFT or AAFFT, we only compare to the 4-thread FFTW and CUFFT. In Fig. 7, we fix $k = 64$ and vary N. Both 4-thread FFTW and CUFFT are linear in the signal size N, however, our parallel performance appears constant as N increases. Our general version implementations on the three GPUs are faster than the 1-thread FFTW, the 4-thread FFTW and CUFFT when $N \geq 2^{14}$, $N \geq 2^{16}$ and $N \geq 2^{17}$. Furthermore, the optimal performance of our parallel case is faster

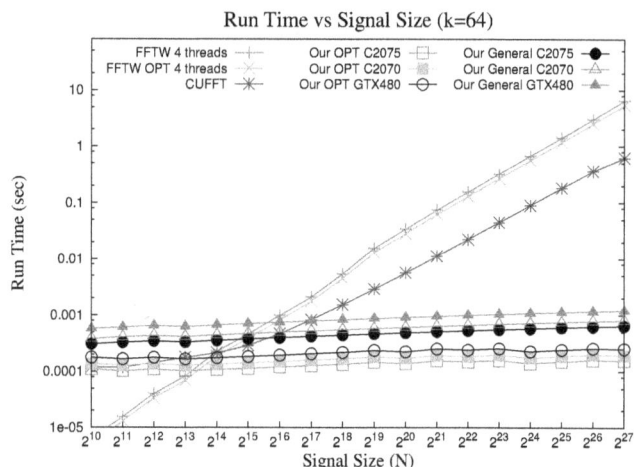

Figure 7: Parallel performance vs. signal size.

than 1-thread FFTW, 4-thread FFTW and CUFFT when $N \geq 2^{12}$, $N \geq 2^{14}$ and $N \geq 2^{14}$.

In Fig. 8, we fix $N = 2^{24}$ and change k. Specifically, our parallel performance of basic version on GTX480, Tesla C2070 and C2075 has a runtime faster than 1-thread FFTW for k up to 30000, 40000, 50000, faster than 4-thread FFTW before k reaches to 20000, 30000, 30000, and faster than CUFFT for k less than 6000, 8000, 9000, respectively. Additionally, the optimal performance of our parallel case is better than 1-thread FFTW, 4-thread FFTW, CUFFT for k up to 500000, 100000, 40000, respectively.

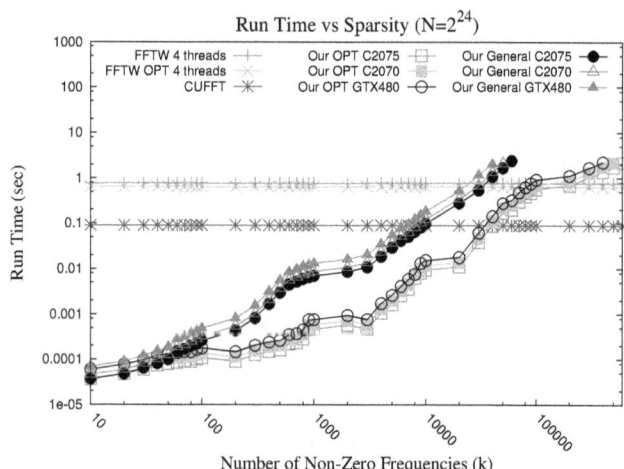

Figure 8: Parallel performance vs. sparsity.

4.2 Detection for Signal Discontinuity

In section 4.1, the performance of our pure sparse-FFT library is evaluated based on homogeneous input signals. When the homogeneity is broken, the heuristic introduced in the section 3.5 is used to detect when the discontinuity happens. Next, we evaluate how well our heuristic works and how much overhead it incurs.

We use test cases similar to the image streaming processing scenario described in section 3.5.3. In total 3 segments of image frames are used. In each segment, the frames are homogeneous except for the last frame at which discontinuity occurs. For the case-1 discontinuity, we keep to use the

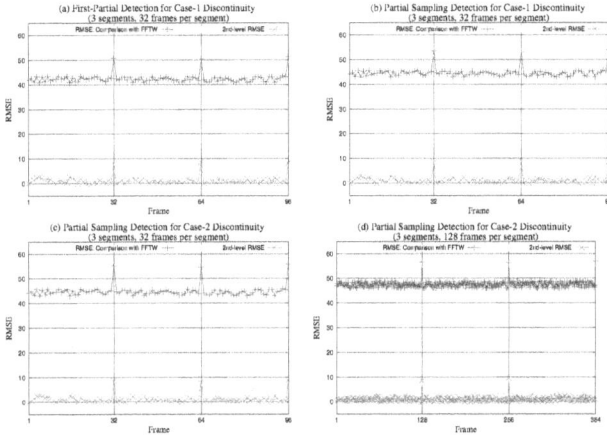

Figure 9: Detection for signal discontinuity.

same signal size N, but re-generate signal with randomly picked amplitudes differing from the homogeneous signals. For the case-2 discontinuity, the signal size is cut down to $N/2$ and its amplitudes are randomly re-generated. The size of each image signal is $N = 2^{22}$ and the sparsity parameter $k = 64$.

Fig. 9(a) and Fig. 9(b) show the first-partial method and the partial sampling detection method for the case-1 discontinuity. There are 3 segments and 32 frames per segment. For each homogeneous frame, it shifts by a displacement of 2^{17} points. We use the Root-Mean-Square-Error (RMSE) between the sampled FFT and our sparse FFT as the deviation metric (Sec. 3.5.3). The RMSE is defined as $\sqrt{\frac{\sum_{i=0}^{N-1}[(F_x-f_x)^2+(F_y-f_y)^2]}{2N}}$.

As shown in Fig. 9(b), our library and the sampled FFT produce almost the same results for homogeneous frames with the 1st-level RMSEs in the small range of $(4.43 \times 10^1, 4.52 \times 10^1)$. However, the outputs are significantly different at the three discontinuity points with the 1st-level RMSEs being 5.35×10^1, 5.31×10^1 and 5.41×10^1, respectively. The spectrally similar signals will produce much closer RMSEs than the discontinuous cases. We can further calculate the 2nd-level RMSE as the RMSE of the 1st-level RMSEs of adjacent frames. The line in the figure represents the 2nd-level RMSE clearly shows values smaller than 2.7 for the homogeneous cases and larger than 8.5 for the discontinuous points. The two boundaries are separated by a large margin. Therefore, the discontinuity is accurately detected at frame 32, 64 and 96 by both sampling methods . Fig. 9(c) shows the partial sampling detection method for case-2 discontinuity with 3 segments and 32 frames per segment. Each homogeneous frame shifts by 2^{17} points. Similarly, discontinuities are detected at frame 32, 64 and 96, and the RMSE of case-2 discontinuity is larger that of the case-1. Fig. 9(d) shows the partial sampling detection for case-2 discontinuity with 3 segments and 128 frames per segment. For each homogeneous frame, it shifts by a factor of 2^{15}. The discontinuities at the frames 128, 256 and 384 are also successfully detected.

4.3 Performance of Input Adaption Process

When discontinuity is detected by the heuristic, the Fourier templates will be re-generated. This section evaluates the impact of this input adaption process to the overall performance.

In this section, the input size is $N = 2^{22}$ and the sparsity parameter $k = 64$. The overall performance is measured including the overhead of the detection heuristic, the recalculation of spectrum templates when discontinuity is found, and the adaptive sparse FFT. Clearly, the more frequently the spectrum templates are calculated, the higher the overhead is, and the lower the performance advantage of our adaptive sparse FFT over the existing input oblivious algorithms. Therefore, we try to determine the break-even point by varying the number of homogeneous frames in a video segment, i.e., in each segment all frames are homogeneous except for the last frame where discontinuity occurs.

Fig. 10 and Fig. 11 illustrates the performance of our input adaption process with 3 segments of frames on CPU and GPUs, respectively. In Fig 10, when the $\#frames \geq 8$, our sequential library on Intel i7 920 CPU is faster than both 1-thread and 4-thread FFTW, while when $\#frames \geq 32$, our library is faster than sFFT 1.0 and 2.0. Moreover, when $\#frames = 128$, on average our algorithm gains $30.2\times$, $11.5\times$ speedup over the 1-thread and the 4-thread FFTW, and $4.2\times$, $2.6\times$ speedup over sFFT 1.0 and 2.0, respectively. In Fig. 11, when the $\#frames \geq 8$, our parallel library on the three GPUs is faster than both 1-thread and 4-thread FFTW, while when $\#frames > 16$, our library is faster than sFFT 1.0, 2.0 and CUFFT. Furthermore, when $\#frames = 128$, our implementation on Tesla C2075 GPU achieves $77.2\times$, $29.3\times$ speedup over 1-thread and 4-thread FFTW, and $10.7\times$, $6.4\times$, $5.2\times$ speedup over sFFT 1.0, sFFT 2.0 and CUFFT, respectively. Meanwhile, when $\#frames = 128$, our optimal performance on Tesla C2075 obtains $6.9\times$ speedup against that of our own sequential CPU version.

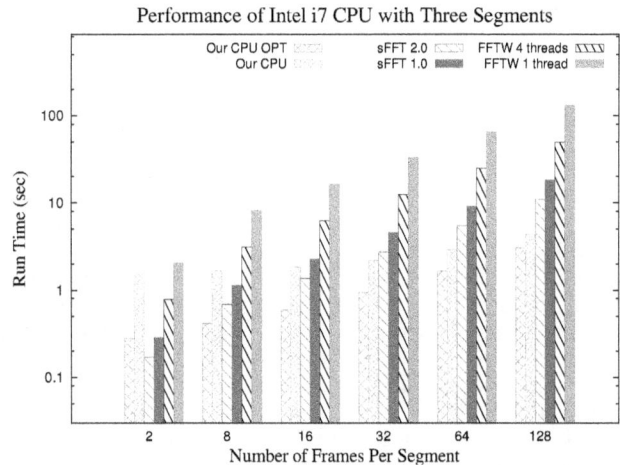

Figure 10: CPU performance with 3 video segments.

4.4 Precision of Our Sparse FFT

The accuracy of our sparse FFT implementation is verified by comparing its complex Fourier transform (F_x, F_y) with the output (f_x, f_y) of FFTW, which is a widely used standard FFT library, for the same double-precision input. The difference in output is quantified as RMSE which has been defined in section 4.2. Lower RMSE value means the two computation routines produce more similar result.

The RMSEs of different signal sizes N and sparsity parameters k are shown in Fig. 12. The RMSE is extremely

Performance of Three GPUs with Three Segments

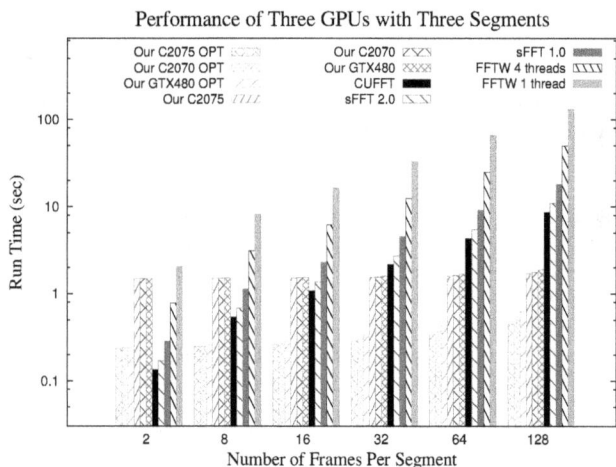

Figure 11: GPU performance with 3 video segments.

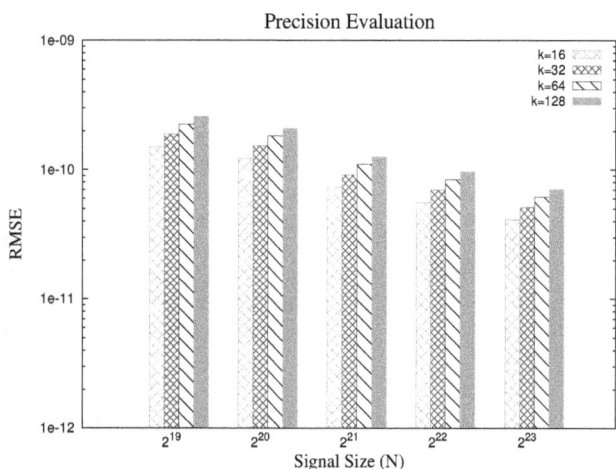

Figure 12: Precision of our algorithm.

small and is in the range of $(4.1 \times 10^{-11}, 1.5 \times 10^{-10})$. Additionally, the RMSE of k-sparse coefficients between our output and FFTW has been measured and is in the range of $(1.61 \times 10^{-8}, 3.12 \times 10^{-8})$. In other words, our sparse FFT produces the same accurate results as FFTW. Interestingly, with the decrease of k for each N, the RMSE decreases. Meanwhile, under the same k, when N increases, the RMSE shows a slight decrease.

5. CONCLUSION

The main contribution of this paper is the exploitation of the similarity between sparse input samples in stream processing to improve the efficiency of sparse FFT. Specifically, our work develops an effective heuristic to detect input similarity, and dynamically customizes the algorithm design to achieve better performance. In particular, we integrate and tune several adaptive filters to package non-zero Fourier coefficients into sparse bins which can be estimated accurately. Moreover, our algorithm is non-iterative with high computation intensity such that parallelism can be exploited for multi-CPUs and GPU to improve performance. Overall, our algorithm is faster than other FFTs both in theory and implementation, and the range of sparsity parameter k that our approach can outperform dense FFT is larger than that of other sparse Fourier algorithms.

Acknowledgement: This work is partly supported by NSF Grant 1115771, AFOSR Grant FA9550-13-1-0213, and gifts from NVIDIA.

6. REFERENCES

[1] A. Akavia. Deterministic sparse fourier approximation via fooling arithmetic progressions. In *The 23rd Conference on Learning Theory*, pages 381–393, 2010.

[2] A. Akavia, Goldwasser, and S. S., Safra. Proving hard-core predicates using list decoding. In *The 44th Symposium on Foundations of Computer Science*, pages 146–157. IEEE, 2003.

[3] L. Bluestein. A linear filtering approach to the computation of discrete Fourier transform. *Audio and Electroacoustics, IEEE Transactions on*, 18(4):451–455, 1970.

[4] P. Duhamel and M. Vetterli. Fast fourier transforms: a tutorial review and a state of the art. *Signal Process.*, 4(19):259–299, Apr. 1990.

[5] M. Frigo and S. G. Johnson. The design and implementation of fftw3. *Proceeding of the IEEE*, 93(2):216–231, 2005.

[6] A. Gilbert, S. Guha, P. Indyk, M. Muthukrishnan, and M. Strauss. Near-optimal sparse fourier representations via sampling. In *Proceedings on 34th Annual ACM Symposium on Theory of Computing*, pages 152–161. ACM, 2002.

[7] A. Gilbert, M. Muthukrishnan, and M. Strauss. Improved time bounds for near-optimal space fourier representations. In *Proceedings of SPIE Wavelets XI*, 2005.

[8] I. Good. The interaction algorithm and practical Fourier analysis. *Journal of the Royal Statistical Society, Series B (Methodological)*, 20(2):361–372, 1958.

[9] H. H., I. P., D. Katabi, and P. E. Simple and practical algorithm for sparse fourier transform. In *Proceedings of the 23th Annual ACM-SIAM Symposium on Discrete Algorithms*, pages 1183–1194. ACM, 2012.

[10] H. Hassanieh, P. Indyk, D. Katabi, and P. E. Nearly optimal sparse fourier transform. In *Proceedings of the 44th symposium on Theory of Computing*, pages 563–578. ACM, 2012.

[11] M. Iwen. AAFFT (Ann Arbor Fast Fourier Transform) http://sourceforge.net/projects/aafftannarborfa/, 2008.

[12] M. Iwen. Combinatorial sublinear-time fourier algorithms. *Foundations of Computational Mathematics*, 10(3):303–338, 2010.

[13] Y. Mansour. Randomized interpolation and approximation of sparse polynomials. In *The 19th International Colloquium on Automata, Languages and Programming*, pages 261–272. Springer, 1992.

[14] A. Nukada and S. Matsuoka. Learning decision trees using the fourier spectrum. In *Proceedings of the Conference on High Performance Computing Networking, Storage and Analysis*, pages 455–464. ACM, 1991.

[15] C. Rader. Discrete Fourier transforms when the number of data samples is prime. *Proceedings of the IEEE*, 56(6):1107–1108, 1968.

Thread-cooperative, Bit-parallel Computation of Levenshtein Distance on GPU

Alejandro Chacón
Universitat Autònoma de
Barcelona (UAB)
Bellaterra 08193, Spain
alejandro.chacon@uab.es

Santiago Marco-Sola
Centro Nacional de Análisis
Genómico (CNAG)
Barcelona 08028, Spain
santiagomsola@gmail.com

Antonio Espinosa
Universitat Autònoma de
Barcelona (UAB)
Bellaterra 08193, Spain
antoniomiguel.espinosa@uab.es

Paolo Ribeca
Centro Nacional de Análisis
Genómico (CNAG)
Barcelona 08028, Spain
paolo.ribeca@gmail.com

Juan Carlos Moure
Universitat Autònoma de
Barcelona (UAB)
Bellaterra 08193, Spain
juancarlos.moure@uab.es

ABSTRACT

Approximate string matching is a very important problem in computational biology; it requires the fast computation of string distance as one of its essential components. Myers' bit-parallel algorithm improves the classical dynamic programming approach to Levenshtein distance computation, and offers competitive performance on CPUs. The main challenge when designing an efficient GPU implementation is to expose enough SIMD parallelism while at the same time keeping a relatively small working set for each thread.

In this work we implement and optimise a CUDA version of Myers' algorithm suitable to be used as a building block for DNA sequence alignment. We achieve high efficiency by means of a cooperative parallelisation strategy for (1) very-long integer addition and shift operations, and (2) several simultaneous pattern matching tasks. In addition, we explore the performance impact obtained when using features specific to the Kepler architecture.

Our results show an overall performance of the order of tera cells updates per second using a single high-end Nvidia GPU, and factor speedups in excess of $20\times$ with respect to a sixteen-core, non-vectorised CPU implementation.

Categories and Subject Descriptors

D.1.3 [**Programming Techniques**]: Concurrent Programming; C.1.2 [**Processor Architectures**]: Multiple Data Stream Architectures (Multiprocessors); Single-instruction-stream, multiple-data-stream processors (SIMD)

Keywords

SIMD; GPU; CUDA; Myers' algorithm

1. INTRODUCTION

Current DNA sequencing technologies produce billions of sequence reads, with hundreds of bases per read, in a single instrument run. Downstream data analysis for resequencing projects requires alignment (or *mapping*) of all these reads to a reference genome. Sequencing errors, sequence divergence from the reference and the growing length of reads require efficient approximate pattern matching algorithms.

Recent sequence alignment software tools, like BWA [10] or GEM [16], use a two-step alignment strategy. The first step (based on a seeded search in the case of BWA, or on filtration in the case of GEM) extracts substrings from the query (or *read*); such substrings are searched in the reference genome (which has been previously turned into an indexed form allowing fast pattern matching, for instance an FM-index [3]) generating candidate match positions. The second step uses online approximate string matching [18] to verify the similarity between the query and the region adjacent to every candidate position; it returns as valid matches the regions that differ from the query, in terms of some string distance, by less than a value specified by the user.

In the context of biological sequence alignment one often employs *Levenshtein distance*, i.e. the minimum number of *edit operations* needed to transform the query into the match. Each operation can be either a substitution, or an insertion, or a deletion of a single character. Levenshtein distance is typically evaluated in terms of *dynamic programming* (DP, [22]), which casts the problem into the computation of (a subset of) a suitable integer-valued matrix. Improving upon a vast previous literature, Myers [17] devises an algorithm to compute the DP matrix using bit-wise operations; each multi-bit operation can handle several matrix cells simultaneously, thus reducing both the total computational work and memory storage requirements.

CUDA-enabled Graphic Processing Units (GPUs) are high-performance, cost-effective and power-efficient many-core architectures appropriate for accelerating the execution of a wide range of algorithms [11]. They provide overall peak computation throughput and memory bandwidth about an order of magnitude higher than general-purpose latency-oriented processors. GPUs need Single Instruction Multiple Data (SIMD) or vector parallelism and Multiple Instruction

Multiple Data (MIMD) parallelism to feed their computational cores. They also strongly rely on H/W multithreading (excess of Thread-Level Parallelism, or TLP) to hide the latency of memory accesses and pipeline dependencies. In general an algorithm must exhibit massive and regular data-level parallelism, converted into both SIMD/vector parallelism and TLP, to achieve high GPU execution efficiency.

The larger computation capability of GPUs comes at the expense of having an order of magnitude less on-chip memory capacity (registers and cache memories) than that of CPUs. As a result, GPUs put more pressure on reducing the overall working set of running threads to make it fit into fast on-chip memory; applications with moderate ratio between computation and memory operations will need to reuse data stored in fast on-chip memory not to become memory-bound.

A typical read-mapping job turns billions of query sequences into tens of billions of candidate regions. This provides plenty of task-level parallelism in the form of multiple DP matrix calculations. While *inter-task parallelism* is a simple way of benefiting from the MIMD and H/W multithreading capabilities of GPUs, however, it is not adequate to efficiently exploit their SIMD/vector potential. In addition, running a pattern matching task per thread would not scale with the query size, due to the impossibility of fitting the working sets of the threads into available on-chip GPU memory even for relatively short queries.

Within the low-memory DP framework of Myers', we propose and analyse a scheme to make several threads cooperate on one or multiple pattern matching tasks (through *intra-task parallelism*). This approach allows us to tune the amount of data per thread, which enables the efficient usage of GPU registers and shared memory. We test different cooperative mechanisms, among them the new Kepler *shuffle* instruction.

Finally, we present a performance analysis methodology to identify the most relevant bottlenecks of our GPU algorithm. From it, we derive a new solution that uses register memory effectively by means of thread cooperation, and we are able to (1) overcome the memory-bandwidth bottleneck and (2) achieve a more efficient use of computational resources.

Our main contributions can be summarised as follows:

- We develop an algorithmic approach to solve the problem of computing Levenshtein distance in a thread-cooperative way, suited to a SIMD-based computational model. It relies upon a fast method to communicate carries by means of collective very-long integer add and shift operations

- We provide a CUDA-specific implementation of our algorithm, describing our optimisation strategies on the GPU

- We present an in-depth performance analysis showing that our CUDA code is computation-bound and scalable, and more efficient than simpler task-parallel CPU and GPU implementations. Performance is on the order of TCUPS (Tera Cells Updated Per Second).

In section 2 we review some terminology and prerequisites about Levenshtein distance, Myers' algorithm and GPU architectures. Section 3 contains our parallelisation proposal (first, by using a task-parallel approach, and next by introducing a thread-cooperative approach). In section 4, we present the experimental results we obtain when benchmarking our proposal on several GPU systems. Section 5 discusses related work and, finally, section 6 summarises our results, describing future work.

2. BACKGROUND

2.1 Computing Levenshtein distance

Let Σ be an alphabet of size σ, and the *pattern* $P_{[1..m]}$ and the *text* $T_{[1..n]}$ two strings over Σ. DNA strings generated by sequencing machines can usually be represented with the alphabet {A,C,G,T,N}, where A,C,G and Ts encode bases adenine, cytosine, guanine and thymine, respectively, and N indicates a base which is unknown due to some technical problem occurred during sequencing.

Levenshtein distance can be computed with DP techniques by using the following recurrence [22] to fill a score matrix C, with $0 \leq i \leq m$ and $0 \leq j \leq n$:

$$\begin{cases} C_{i,0} = i, \ C_{0,j} = 0 \\ C_{i,j} = min\{C_{i-1,j-1} + \delta(i,j); C_{i-1,j} + 1; C_{i,j-1} + 1\} \end{cases}$$
(1)

where δ(i,j) is 0 if $P_{[i]} = T_{[j]}$, and 1 otherwise. A score value $C_{m,j} = k$ identifies an occurrence of P with Levenshtein distance k, ending at text character $T_{[j]}$. An example of score matrix is given in Table 1.a. The time complexity of the classical DP algorithm is $O(nm)$, i.e. proportional to the number of cells in matrix C.

We define the *maximum allowed error rate* as $\epsilon = k/m$.

2.2 Myers' bit-parallel algorithm

Ukkonen [25] noticed that adjacent values in matrix C can differ at most by ± 1. A matrix of differences equivalent to C can be represented using two bits per cell. Table 1.b shows a matrix of vertical differences, Δv, where $\Delta v_{i,j} = C_{i+1,j} - C_{i,j}$. Myers [17] used these adjacency properties to exploit bit parallelism and compute difference cells using bitwise logical, shift, and addition operations. Time complexity becomes $O(n)$ if an m-cell column of Δv fits into a computer word of size w (typically w=32 or 64). Otherwise, a block

Table 1: Dynamic Programming tables for sequences P=TAGAC and T=ATCGAG

	A	T	C	G	A	G
	0	0	0	0	0	0	0
T	1	1	0	1	1	1	1
A	2	1	1	1	2	1	2
G	3	2	2	2	1	2	1
A	4	3	3	3	2	1	2
C	5	4	4	3	3	2	2

(a) C: Score Matrix

+1	+1	0	+1	+1	+1	+1
+1	0	+1	0	+1	0	+1
+1	+1	+1	+1	-1	+1	-1
+1	+1	+1	+1	+1	-1	+1
+1	+1	+1	0	+1	+1	0

(b) Δv: vertical-differences

	A	C	G	T
T	1	1	1	0
A	0	1	1	1
G	1	1	0	1
A	0	1	1	1
C	1	0	1	1

(c) Query profile $\equiv \delta()$

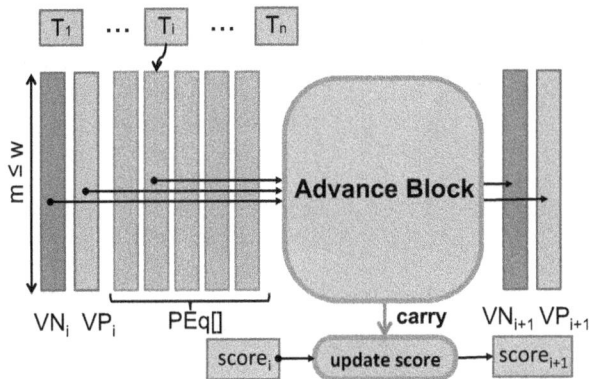

Figure 1: Core operation of Myers' basic algorithm

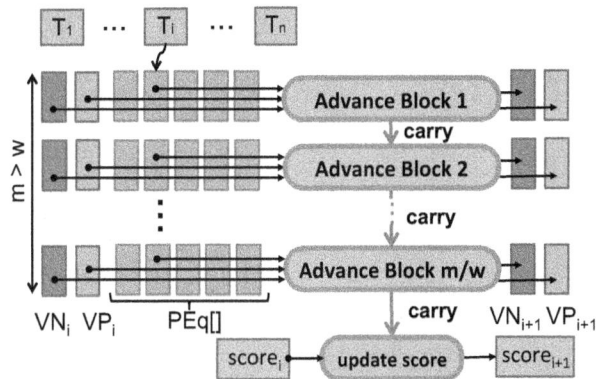

Figure 2: Myers' blocked-based algorithm

strategy achieves complexity $O(n\lceil m/w \rceil)$. Hyyrö et al. [7] improved Myers algorithm by reducing the number of bit-wise operations.

Function $\delta()$ can be implemented using a *query profile* (see Table 1.c). Each of the σ different columns is a bit-vector codifying the occurrences of each letter into the query. Also, if matrix C is constructed column-wise only one column needs to be kept in memory at a time, resulting in total memory space requirements of $O(\sigma \times m)$ (measured in bits).

Algorithm 1 shows pseudo-code for Myers' proposal. The main program and variables are at the top, while the time-consuming code, invoked once for each of the n columns, is at the bottom. PV and NV are w-bit vectors encoding positive and negative differences in a given column. Text T is scanned symbol by symbol, and each symbol $T_{[i]}$ determines the appropriate query profile in PEq[]. Function *advance_block()* executes 17 logical/arithmetic operations to transform the input (i.e. the previous column encoded as PV and NV) into the next column, i.e. to compute m new vertical cells. It also provides a carry (the last cell in the column), which is the penalty to be added to the alignment score.

The basic algorithm assumes $m \leq w$ and is depicted in Fig.1. Patterns larger than w can be partitioned into w-bit blocks [17]. The block-based strategy needs to generate and send special carries between consecutive blocks, as shown in Fig.2. This is achieved by means of a slightly modified version of function *advance_block()*.

2.3 GPU Architectures

GPUs are composed of tens of processing components, called streaming multiprocessors (SMs) by Nvidia [11]. SMs share a L2 cache of hundreds of KBytes, and an external global memory of several GBytes. Each SM contains hundreds of SIMD cores that perform in-order execution of instructions. Each SM contains tens of KBytes of local storage that is partitioned into explicitly-managed registers and shared memory banks, and several implicitly-managed cache memories.

Tens of thousands of threads must be launched simultaneously to achieve high performance. The CUDA programming model is based on a hierarchy of threads executing the same program on different sets of data. A *thread-block* is a group of threads that may cooperate using the registers and shared memory available in a given SM. Thread-blocks

in a *grid* (or *kernel*) are scheduled non-deterministically for independent MIMD execution into SMs. A thread-block is divided into batches of 32 threads, called *warps*, which are the smallest scheduled unit. Between 32 and 64 warps from one or multiple thread-blocks are dynamically scheduled for execution in the same SM. This mechanism, often known as H/W multithreading, is the main latency-hiding strategy on GPUs.

A warp is executed in a SIMD/vector fashion: threads in a warp are executed in a lock-step manner operating on 32 values in parallel. If threads in the same warp need to follow different control flows, all paths must be executed one after another, with some threads active and the remaining threads stalled. An instruction executed by a subset of the warp threads is said to be divergent. Divergence is an inherent performance limitation of SIMD architectures, and must be addressed when designing the algorithm.

Another critical performance issue is the memory access pattern of the algorithm. When executing a SIMD/vector load or store instruction, the memory addresses provided by all the threads in the same warp are combined, or *coalesced*, to generate one or multiple memory block access requests (memory blocks of 32 to 128 Bytes). High memory performance is achieved only when all the data requested from global memory is really needed by the program. In practice, that means requested data is coalesced into one or a few memory blocks. Warp-level, cooperative instructions may help reducing the need for global and shared memory accesses.

3. PARALLELISATION ANALYSIS

This section describes and discusses two CUDA implementation strategies for Myers' bit-parallel algorithm: (1) task-parallel and (2) thread-cooperative. The work presented addresses the computation of Levenshtein distance for DNA strings, but can easily be extended to different alphabets.

3.1 Task Parallel Approach

We assume there is a large number of input sequence reads, and each query must be compared to multiple regions in a large genome text. Having lots of independent query-text comparisons provides a straightforward source of task parallelism. This approach has been used on GPUs very recently in [9] [24]. We have developed our own implementa-

---

Algorithm 1: Myers' algorithm for $m \leq w$

---

input : $P=pattern$, $T=text$, $m=|P|$, $n=|T|$, $\sigma=|\Sigma|$
output: $(minScore, position)$ with lower # differences

begin
   $bitvector{<}w{>}$ PV, NV, HMASK, EQ, PEq[σ]
   (PV, MV) $\longleftarrow$ ($\sim$0, 0)
   HMASK $\longleftarrow$ $1 \ll (m-1)$
   PEq[σ] $\longleftarrow$ $preprocess($ P, σ)
   for $i=1$ **to** n **do**
      EQ $\longleftarrow$ PEq[$T_{[i]}$]
      (c, PV, NV) $\longleftarrow$ $advance\_block$(EQ, PV, NV)
      score $\longleftarrow$ score + c
      if ($score < minScore$) **then**
         (minScore, position) $\longleftarrow$ (score, i)
      end
   end
   return (minScore, position)
end

Function $advance\_block$ ($bitvector{<}w{>}$ EQ, PV, NV)
begin
   $bitvector{<}w{>}$ XV, XH, PH, NH
   XV $\longleftarrow$ EQ | NV
   XH $\longleftarrow$ (((EQ & PV) + PV) $\wedge$ PV) | EQ
   PH $\longleftarrow$ NV | $\sim$ (XV | PV)
   NH $\longleftarrow$ PV & XH
   carry $\longleftarrow$ (PH & HMASK) $-$ (NH & HMASK)
   PH $\longleftarrow$ PH $\ll$ 1
   NH $\longleftarrow$ NH $\ll$ 1
   PV $\longleftarrow$ NH | (XV | PH)
   NV $\longleftarrow$ PH & XV
   return (carry, PV, NV)
end

Algorithm 2: Thread-Cooperative m-bit Addition and Shift functions executed by each thread

---

Function $thread\_cooperative\_add$ ($bitvector{<}w{>}$ a, b)
begin
   $bitvector{<}w{>}$ result
   (result, c_add) $\leftarrow$ a + b
   while ($check\_any\_thread$ (c_add $!=$ 0)) **do**
      next_c $\leftarrow$ $send\_to$ (**threadID**+1, c_add)
      (result, c_add) $\leftarrow$ result + next_c
   end
   return (result)
end

Function $thread\_cooperative\_shift$ ($bitvector{<}w{>}$ a)
begin
   $bitvector{<}w{>}$ result
   c_shft $\leftarrow$ a $\gg$ (w - 1)
   next_c $\leftarrow$ $send\_to$ (**threadID**+1, c_shft)
   result $\leftarrow$ (a $\ll$ 1) | next_c
   return (result)
end

---

tion, putting our best effort on optimising the code. Apart from some implementation details described at the end of this section, the most performance-critical issue is handling the local storage for each task.

Bit-vectors PV, NV and PEq[] are accessed n times during the algorithm execution. For the sake of performance, it is important to reuse this intermediate data, keeping them in on-chip memory and avoiding costly main memory transfers. The problem is that the aggregated size of this intermediate data grows both with the query size and with the number of running threads. For moderate and large query sizes either (1) memory performance suffers because intermediate data exceed the available on-chip GPU memory, or (2) GPU occupancy is sacrificed to make intermediate data fit into on-chip memory. Section 4 evaluates performance when storing intermediate data either in local memory or shared memory.

3.2 Thread Cooperative Approach

One way to deal with the previous problem is making threads cooperate on the same task (intra-task parallelism) so that the amount of intermediate data per thread is reduced. Another advantage of thread cooperation is to enable the allocation of GPU registers for all intermediate variables. Registers provide more storage capacity and throughput than any other kind of on-chip memory.

3.2.1 Intra-task SIMD vectorisation: 1 warp per task

Finding enough intra-task parallelism to be efficiently exploited by even a single warp (SIMD operation) is challenging. Dynamic programming approaches present a well-known dependence pattern: any cell of the score matrix can be computed only after the values of the left and above cells are known.

There is potential parallelism when computing cells on the same anti-diagonal, but it is difficult to exploit, since it grows and diminishes as the anti-diagonal enlarges and shrinks while traversing the score matrix. Having said that, Myers' method for computing Levenshtein distance is interesting, as it allows processing all cells in a column simultaneously.

We revisit Myers' idea to exploit bit parallelism not only at the word level, but also at the SIMD level. Each thread (or SIMD lane) holds a word-size slice of the column information stored in bit-vectors PEq[], PV and NV. This scheme reduces and fixes the total local memory required per thread, which is now independent of m, the query size. Then, the CUDA compiler can easily allocate registers for the local data of each thread.

Most of the bit-wise operations on Algorithm 1 are inherently parallel (and, or, xor, not ...) and are trivially converted to SIMD/warp instructions. The exceptions are the add and shift operations inside $advance\_block()$ function. Algorithm 2 depicts the pseudo-code of our proposed thread-cooperative m-bit addition and shift operations. Each thread executes the code, receives a portion of each bit-vector input and generates a portion of the output. The cooperative shift requires one extra carry propagation step between neighbour threads. The cooperative addition uses a simple ripple-carry scheme. First, all threads perform a bit-wise addition of their corresponding portion of the input. Then, a cooperative loop of communication and carry addition steps iterates until no carries need to be propagated. Most times, it takes just one or two loop iterations to complete.

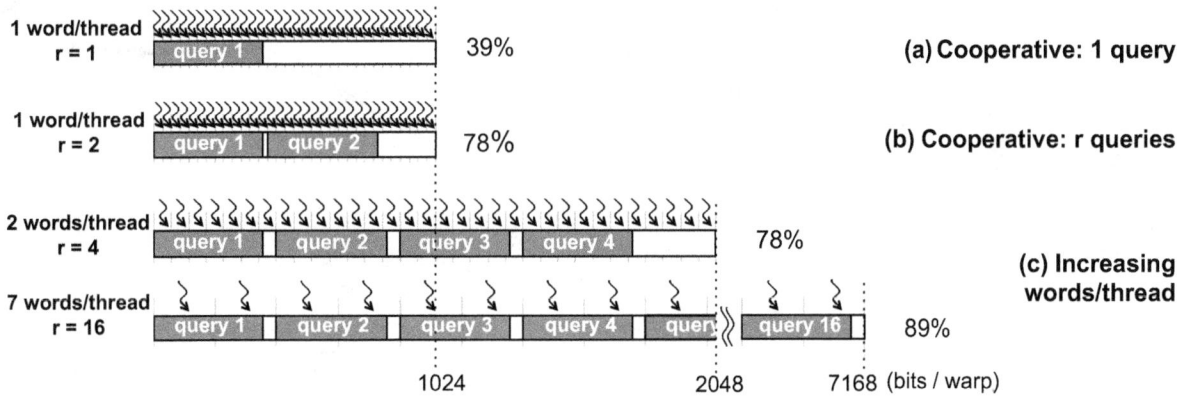

Figure 3: Thread Cooperation: r queries (m=400) and varying #words processed per thread

It is not surprising to find that most of the complexity falls in the addition operation. Indeed the "magic" of Myers's method resides in converting cell dependencies into the carry dependencies within the addition operation. This strategy ultimately benefits from the very efficient hardware implementation of the addition operation, which solves the carry chain dependence very quickly.

The 1-*warp-per-task* strategy works reasonably well for certain query sizes, but fails with others. Fig. 3.a shows how a query of size m=400 is partitioned into 13 words, and exactly 13 threads cooperate on the matching task while the remaining 19 threads are idle. This case involves a disappointing thread utilisation of 39%. The next step to achieve high GPU performance requires the threads in a warp to cooperate on processing several queries.

3.2.2 Intra- and Inter-task SIMD: 1 warp per r tasks

Combining intra- and inter-task parallelism enables two types of performance improvements. First, several small queries may be used to "fill" a 1024-bit SIMD vector and provide useful work for as many threads in a warp as possible. Fig. 3.b shows how r=2 queries of size m=400 occupy 2×13=26 words (and threads), with an utilisation that raises to 78% (800 bits used from 1024).

Second, we can use a larger number of queries per warp in order to increase the total work per thread. In this case, more words are handled by each thread, as measured by the quantity *words/thread*. Increasing work per thread helps reducing query fragmentation and increase SIMD efficiency. Fig. 3.c shows examples for *words/thread*=2 and 7 (r=4 and 16 queries), with thread utilisation rising to 89%.

But the most important advantage of increasing the amount of work per thread is the reduction of the total number of overhead instructions: those not included in the 17 bit-wise original operations in Myers' algorithm. The extra instructions needed for inter-thread carry propagation represent an important portion of this overhead. The drawback of increasing *words/thread* is that the amount of local memory required per thread also increases; this may compromise the efficient usage of GPU registers and GPU occupancy. As we will show in the next section, the best *words/thread* configuration depends on the query size but also on the GPU architecture.

An extreme thread-cooperative configuration with r=32 is in fact purely task parallel, as there is no actual need of thread cooperation. This option, however, only makes sense for small queries. An advantage with respect to previous proposals is that the static declaration of variables allows using GPU registers instead of local memory.

The mechanism to let several threads cooperate on several queries requires identifying those threads responsible of the last slice of each query. They must be inhibited on carry propagation phases, but are responsible for generating the final result for each query.

3.3 Optimisation details

We simplify the inner code loop as much as possible to reduce the amount of divergence and instruction overhead. We help the compiler to generate non-divergent code by replacing conditional control flow structures by computation.

Since the input text can be very large, it is stored in binary form, with several symbols packed into a single w-bit data word. Divergence appears when threads access multiple text regions simultaneously and extract symbols from different positions of a data word. We apply a loop peeling optimisation [14] to move the extra control instructions and the associated divergence out of the main loop.

Additionally, divergence and instruction overhead outside the main loop is further reduced by extending text regions to start and finish in aligned locations.

Query pre-processing is moved out of the main code, so that each query is preprocessed just once, and not once for each candidate text region. All query profiles are created and stored into global memory before running the comparison code. For small alphabet sizes, like DNA, query profiles are just slightly larger than the original query strings.

Special GPU assembly instructions (*adc* and *add.cc*) implement carry propagation for local extended additions. Also, the Kepler-specific *funnelshift* instruction is used to propagate the carry in extended shift operations.

Thread-cooperative operations are implemented using thread communication at the warp level. We take advantage of the warp's lock-step execution to avoid synchronisation primitives. Several intra-warp communication techniques for carry propagation (shared memory, ballot and shuffle instructions) are implemented and evaluated. The Kepler-specific *shuffle* instruction is the most efficient alternative, with an improvement close to 20%.

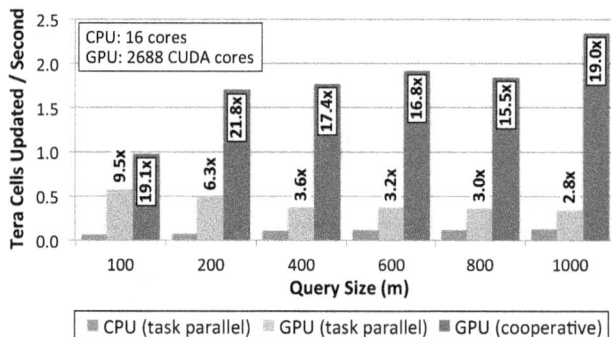

Figure 4: Performance overview

4. EXPERIMENTAL RESULTS

We ran several implementations of Myers algorithm on different multi-core and GPU platforms. We first assess overall performance and then present a detailed analysis in order to identify the main architectural bottlenecks.

4.1 Experimental setup and methodology

The experimentation platform is a heterogeneous CPU-GPU node. The CPU is a dual-socket Intel Xeon E5-2650, with eight 2-way hyperthreaded cores per socket running at 2.0Ghz. Most of the GPU measurements were done on an Nvidia GTX Titan with 14 Kepler SMs (993Mhz). We also used a Tesla 2090 with 16 Fermi SMs (1.3 Ghz) and a Tesla K20c with 13 Kepler SMs (705Mhz).

Commonly-used simulation tools [5] [20] are a standard way of providing the query input sets. Each input set contains a million reads. We have used a modified version of GEM [16] to generate all the candidate matching positions in the human genome (GRCh37) for such inputs. The accepted error rate is ϵ=0.2. At most 20 million query-candidate pairs (i.e., at most 20 candidates per query) are processed. The genome text and query profiles reside in CPU and GPU memory before starting execution measurements. Results are obtained by averaging over the 3 best executions, and expressed in terms of cell update operations per time unit. The variability of the measures is very low (on the level of the 1%).

The multi-core CPU implementation is task-parallel, with 16×2 threads (OpenMP) to exploit hyperthreading, and is not vectorized. GPU implementations set the thread-block size to 128 for Kepler and 256 for Fermi, since they provide the highest performance.

4.2 Overall Performance Results

Fig. 4 shows performance on CPU (task-parallel approach) and GPU (both using task parallelism and thread cooperation) for increasing query sizes (m from 100 to 1000). The presented results correspond to the best-performing configuration for each query size and implementation version.

The thread-cooperative GPU algorithm provides the best performance, surpassing the Tera-CUP barrier (from 1.0 up to 2.3). These results are between 15× and 22× better than those obtained by the multi-core CPU. Additionally, on the GPU the cooperative approach outperforms the task-parallel scheme by 2×-7×.

In general, longer queries provide better relative performance. This is expected since the relative weight of the ini-

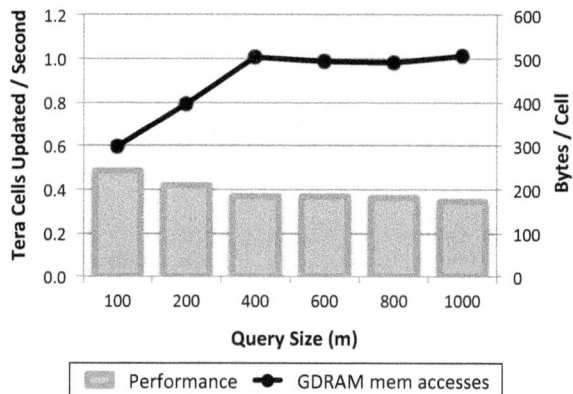

Figure 5: GPU Task Parallel: local memory

tialisation phase and parallelisation overheads are reduced. However, the performance of the GPU task-parallel version reduces by a factor of up to 0.6× as the query length increases. This unexpected result is studied in detail in the next subsection. The analysis done helps understanding the reasons behind the thread-cooperative solution results.

4.3 Task Parallel: Performance limiters

The task parallel scheme uses one thread for each query-candidate pair. This is a coarse-grained approach that performs well on a CPU but not on GPUs. In the next sections, we analyse the performance bottlenecks of the GPU implementation, either using local or shared memory to describe the reasons for these results.

4.3.1 Using Local Memory: high miss rate

Square bars on Fig.5 quantify how performance degrades up to 1.41× when increasing query size and using local memory. The solid line indicates an increase of 1.7× in the number of GDRAM memory accesses, from 297 to 506 Bytes/cell. There is a clear correlation between increasing the amount of GDRAM accesses and performance reduction.

The amount of local memory needed by the application grows linearly with the number of simultaneous queries and the query size. The number of queries is determined by the total number of threads launched for execution. Increasing query size decreases temporal locality and the L1 and L2 GPU caches become less effective to filter GDRAM accesses. For example, with a query size of m=1000, 94% of L1 and 79.5% of L2 accesses are misses.

Once GDRAM memory is identified as the main performance bottleneck, we need to see if the problem is latency- or bandwidth-bound. We measured empirical GDDR5 bandwidth to be between 185 GB/s and 210 GB/s, which range between 85% and 95% of the maximum bound provided by the Nvidia bandwidth test. Therefore, we conclude that the task-parallel GPU implementation using local memory is bound by GDRAM bandwidth. In contrast, owing to larger on-chip caches the CPU implementation is not memory- but computation-bounded.

4.3.2 Using Shared Memory: low GPU occupancy

The classical solution to overcome GDRAM bandwidth memory problems is to foster data reuse by explicitly using shared memory. The best performance is achieved when we

108

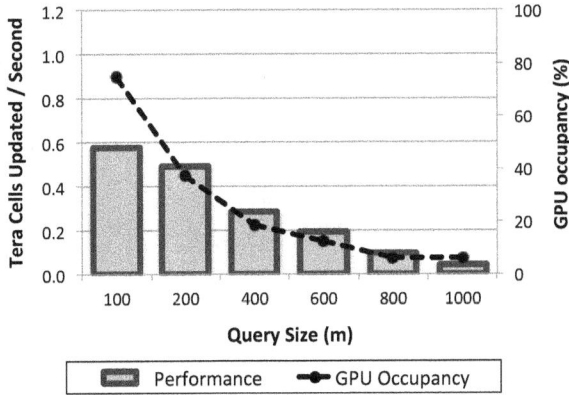

Figure 6: GPU Task Parallel: shared memory

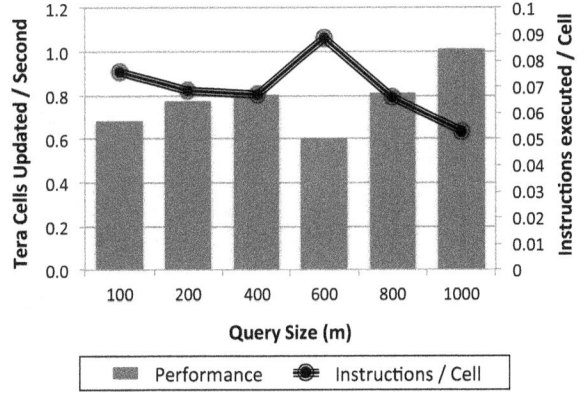

Figure 7: GPU Thread Cooperative: 1 *word/thread*

store columns PV and NV in shared memory, but maintain query profiles, PEq[], in local memory. Measured GDRAM bandwidth values for query sizes m=100, 200, 400, 600, 800, 1000 are now 41.2, 8.30, 1.56, 0.98, 0.72, 0.57 GB/s. Therefore, using shared memory actually prevents GDRAM bandwidth from becoming a bottleneck.

Table 2 compares effective GDRAM memory accesses with an estimation of best local data reuse. The estimation assumes that all data requests imply no additional GDRAM accesses if elements are already placed in on-chip memory.

A task parallel approach with local memory exhibits very limited data reuse. The use of shared memory increases the latter, but there is a significant amount of requests that are still fetched from GDRAM and not from on-chip memory.

Fig. 6 shows the performance of the shared memory implementation. Bars indicate a performance degradation from 1.18× to 13.66× as query size increases. Again, this is due to the higher amount of local data, but now the effect is revealed by a reduction of GPU occupancy (i.e. the percentage of active versus potential running threads, depicted by the dashed line in Fig. 6). Shared memory is a scarce resource that must be assigned equally to each thread. The GPU cannot allocate the same amount of active threads if each thread requires more memory; as a result, GPU occupancy is reduced to levels that strongly reduce overall performance.

Comparing Fig. 5 and Fig. 6 we conclude that using shared memory only benefits small query size cases, $m \leq 200$, when GPU occupancy is high enough to hide memory latencies.

4.4 Thread Cooperative: Performance limiters

We analyse performance and limiting factors of the cooperative approach. We first address the case of assigning a slice of the column to each thread, using one word per thread. Subsequently, we explore the performance advantage of using several words per thread. Finally, we analyse the execution in detail to find out performance bottlenecks.

4.4.1 Cooperation: one word/thread

Fig. 7 presents results for the best combination of m (query size) and r (tasks or queries assigned to each warp). Performance varies between 0.6 and 1.0 TCUPS, always higher than the results obtained with the task parallel approach.

Table 2 shows that the cooperative approach drastically reduces the amount of GDRAM memory accesses, almost reaching the theoretical minimum. In fact, effective measured GDRAM bandwidth is lower than 7 GB/s for all query sizes. Also, all the executions achieve 100% GPU occupancy. Therefore, neither memory nor GPU occupancy are performance bottlenecks here.

We measured the total instruction count (in warp instructions) and computed the cell-normalised rate, that we denote by *instructions/cell*. This metric is depicted by the solid line in Fig.7 and exhibits a strong correlation with performance, which is inversely proportional to *instructions/cell*. This result suggests that GPU execution is now computation-bound.

In fact, the reason for the performance variations discovered in Fig. 7 has to be found elsewhere. Warp instructions can simultaneously operate with 32 bits × 32 threads = 1024 cells. For each query size m, we must adjust the number of simultaneous queries r to use a total number of bits as close to 1024 as possible. Fig. 3 was showing the problem of low thread utilisation. For the cases of Fig. 7, thread utilisation is 78%, 78%, 78%, 59%, 78% and 97%, respectively. Considering that overhead instructions are relatively less frequent for larger query sizes, thread utilisation correlates almost perfectly with *instructions/cell*.

4.4.2 Cooperation: several words/thread

Fig. 8 depicts the performance impact of increasing the amount of work per thread (measured in *words/thread*) by processing more queries per warp. For fixed values of m and *words/thread* the optimal value of r is derived empirically.

Table 2: Ratio of effective GDRAM accesses versus estimated GDRAM accesses

Query size (m)	100	200	400	600	800	1000
Task parallel (Local Mem.)	54071×	145270×	368912×	546418×	724375×	931655×
Task parallel (Shared Mem.)	7515×	3042×	1149×	1082×	1059×	1058×
Cooperative (1 word/thread)	1.60×	1.28×	1.14×	1.11×	1.07×	1.05×

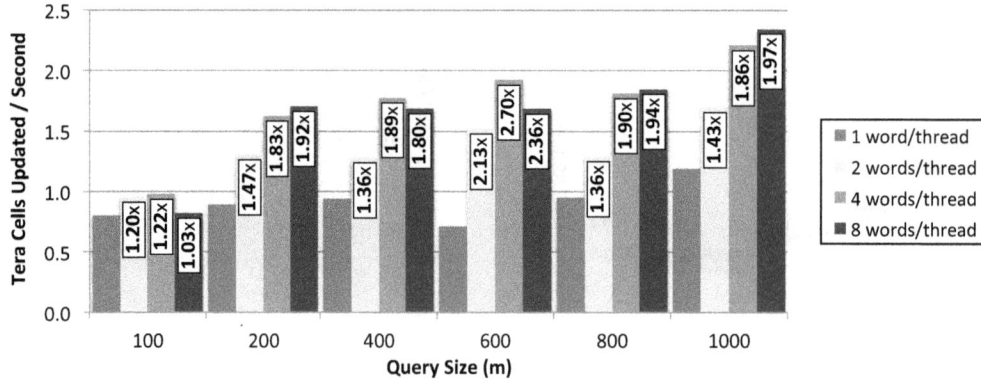

Figure 8: Performance for varying *words/thread*

Results show performance speedups from 1.22× to 2.70× when increasing the amount of work per thread.

Also for this scenario we carried out an in-depth performance analysis, which can help generating new optimisation ideas. Fig. 9 shows the performance trade-off involved when increasing the amount of work assigned to each thread.

On one hand, *instructions/cell* is reduced between 1.39× and 2.33× when increasing *words/thread*. This is due to the reduction of the instructions devoted to communication and synchronisation among the cooperating threads, and explains why the overall performance increases.

On the other hand, GPU occupancy falls sharply. As local data increases, more registers per thread are required and, hence, GPU occupancy decreases. In the examples shown in the Figure, the numbers of allocated registers are 28, 38, 56, and 92, respectively. The sharp plunge of GPU occupancy explains why overall performance flattens and even worsens.

In summary, for each query size m one can find a configuration of r (number of queries) and *words/thread* that maximises performance.

4.4.3 Detailed Performance Analysis

We also measured the performance impact of using Kepler-specific instructions such as *shuffle* and *funnelshift*. Execution time is improved up to 28% and an average of 18%, meaning that Kepler GPUs have an important performance advantage with respect to previous-generation Fermi GPUs.

Table 3 provides data from relevant experiments with selected maximum performance values of m and *words/thread* to help understand the final performance limits of our GPU implementation. The first row of the table shows the empirical number of bitmap operations needed to compute a column, which varies between ~24 and ~33. The theoretical minimum is 17 bitmap operations [17] but this value does not consider the operations for score calculation, management of conditional structures, synchronisation and memory access. We conclude from those results that the parallelization overhead is limited and acceptable.

The second row of Table 3 shows the ratio between effective and estimated GDRAM accesses. This is a measure of data reuse, which is between 1.02 and 5.39. Effective GDRAM bandwidth is listed in the third row of the Table, and complements previous information. Measured bandwidth is found to be between 1.3 GB/s and 29 GB/s, very far from GPU memory system limits. From those results we conclude that memory reuse is very effective.

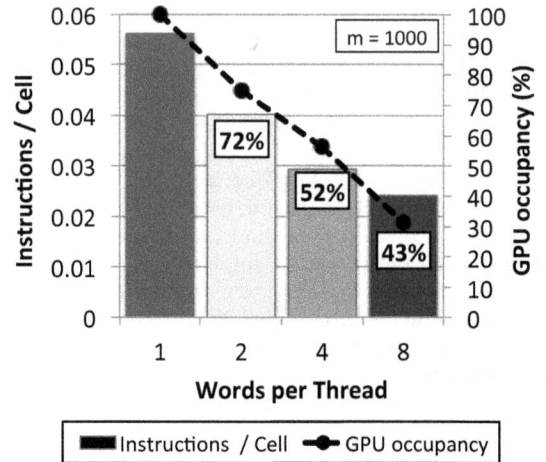

Figure 9: Impact of varying *words/thread* on *instructions/cell* and GPU occupancy

Finally, Table 3 shows an IPC (Instructions Per Cycle) value between 2.59 and 4.73. We consider these figures as quite close to the limit: the theoretical architecture maximum is 7, and many sources from Nvidia state that values above 4.5 are rarely obtained in real applications.

As a conclusion, the cooperative solution is computation-bound and exploits all GPU resources very efficiently.

4.4.4 Performance on different GPUs

We have repeated our performance analysis on different GPU architectures, namely Fermi and Kepler. Speedups with respect to the 16-core CPU are also included as a reference in Fig.10. The normalised performance obtained for all the GPUs is between 0.5 and 0.86 GCUPS per core and GHz. For a fixed query size, normalised performance (obtained by factoring out the architectural advantage of the Kepler instructions) is very similar in all three GPUs. This means that performance scales fairly well with the number of cores and clock frequency, even when using GPUs with different CUDA capabilities (Fermi and Kepler). Such results back the expectation that our proposal will show a good performance scaling even on future, more powerful GPUs.

Table 3: Detailed performance metrics for best performing cases

(m, words/thread)	(100, 4)	(200, 8)	(400, 4)	(600, 4)	(800, 8)	(1000, 8)
Bitmap operations/Column	29.23	26.95	33.35	29.49	30.17	24.09
Effective/Estimated GDRAM accesses	5.39	1.57	1.12	1.07	1.03	1.02
Bandwidth (GB/s)	29.19	7.25	2.69	1.85	1.29	1.29
IPC	2.59	3.66	4.73	4.52	4.00	4.06

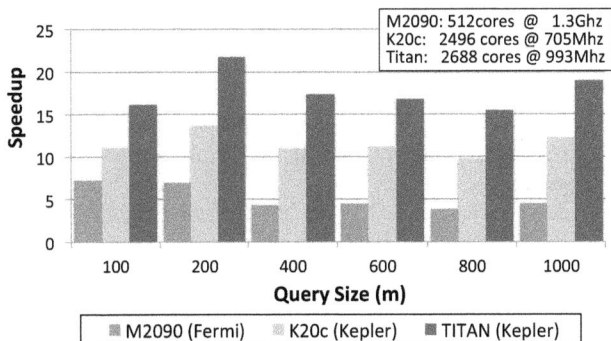

Figure 10: Speedup of several GPUs vs CPU

5. RELATED WORK

Two recent works implement a task-parallel scheme of Myers' algorithm on the GPU. On one hand Langner et al. [9] analyse GPU implementations of Levenshtein and Damerau distances. They aim to integrate the GPU code into SeqAn [1], a library of bioinformatics algorithms and data structures. They propose a task-parallel design, and evaluate the use of shared memory. On the other hand Tristam et al. [24] use a task-parallel design to evaluate the difficulty of the required GPU optimisations. Their setup includes an interleaved layout for the input strings, the usage of 16-Byte loads, and a tuned kernel scheduling. Due to the many differences it's difficult to directly compare such results with ours, but their performance hardly reaches 100 GCUPS.

Both works address the optimal usage of the different GPU memories. They recognise memory bandwidth as the main bottleneck, and the need for cooperative strategies; however, they apparently do not take into account register memory. In fact, with the present paper we demonstrate for the first time that an efficient use of register memory by means of thread cooperation is key to overcome the memory-bandwidth bottleneck. Of note, both works also propose the usage of banded and cutoff techniques [6] to reduce the number of cells to be computed; we too plan to include these techniques into our implementation in the future.

First works on GPU were focused on the Smith-Waterman algorithm [23] for general score functions, using a substitution matrix and affine gap penalties. Manavski and Valle [15] exploited task parallelism by allocating one pairwise sequence alignment task to each single thread. Liu et al. [12] [13] have implemented several versions of CUDASW++. The first version of CUDASW++ [12] adopted a task-parallel approach for small sequences (≤ 3072) and thread cooperation for large sequences, exploiting anti-diagonal (wavefront) parallelism. Hains et al. [4] improve the cooperative version using tiling and more efficient register usage. They achieve performance in the range of 10s of GCUPS. Liu et al.

[13] employ GPU SIMD parallelisation using PTX instructions to gain additional data parallelism. They also address concurrent CPU and multi-GPU processing and present a performance of about 120 GCUPS on a single Kepler GPU (GTX 680). However, the usage of general distances prevents the use of simple bit-parallel strategies, making the parallelisation more complex. Farivar et al. [2] apply tiling strategies similar to [4], but using a global alignment algorithm [19].

Bit-level parallelism can also be exploited for the Longest Common Subsequence (LCS) problem, which is similar to, but simpler than, the problem of computing Levenshtein distance. Kawanami and Fujimoto [8] implement the first GPU solution, which exploits task parallelism. Ozsoy et al. [21] propose an improved GPU design that reaches 1 TCUPS using 3 Fermi GPUs. The cooperative scheme proposed in this paper should be useful to obtain a better solution for the LCS problem as well.

6. CONCLUSIONS AND FUTURE WORK

Upcoming sequencing technologies will produce longer reads at reduced cost. This will put additional stress on current sequence alignment algorithms, that will quickly become the bottleneck of the pervasive analysis pipelines used to process resequencing data.

In this work we improve on the GPU Myers' algorithm, which computes the Levenshtein distance between two strings and constitutes a basic block of several popular aligners. Experimental results show that our best implementation obtains on a single GPU performance speedups of $20\times$ with respect to a sixteen-core, non-vectorised CPU version, providing a peak performance of 2.3 TCUPS.

The solution presented here is ready to be efficiently executed on any current GPU. To tune it to the target architecture it is sufficient to adjust the work-per-thread ratio; if more local memory is available on the GPU, an appropriate reconfiguration will improve performance.

From a methodological standpoint, this paper provides an example of how task-parallel CPU approaches can be redesigned into cooperative multi-thread algorithms adapted to many-core architectures like the GPU; the main principle guiding our implementation has been to get the most from local memory system and reduce the number of instructions. We have also demonstrated how specific Kepler architecture instructions can be used to further improve algorithmic performance.

From the standpoint of the analysis of sequencing data, we have shown that GPUs are computational platforms suitable to efficiently implement string-comparison algorithms. Our results indicate that GPUs can become an additional source of computational power in order to perform high-quality alignment of longer sequence reads in acceptable times.

As future work, we will implement on the Intel MIC architecture a version of the cooperative-parallel algorithm that uses explicit SIMD instructions; its performance will provide us with a comparison of the benefits offered by the two architectures. Also, we plan to integrate our GPU algorithm into the GEM mapper [16], thus demonstrating the practical relevance of our results.

7. ACKNOWLEDGMENTS

This research has been supported by MICINN-Spain under contract TIN2011-28689-C02-01. The authors would like to thank Nvidia for supporting our research with the donation of a K20c Kepler GPU card.

8. REFERENCES

[1] A. Döring, D. Weese, T. Rausch, and K. Reinert. SeqAn an efficient, generic C++ library for sequence analysis. In *BMC bioinformatics*, 9(1):11, 2008.

[2] R. Farivar, H. Kharbanda, S. Venkataraman, and R. H. Campbell. An algorithm for fast edit distance computation on GPUs. In *Innovative Parallel Computing (InPar 2012)*, pages 1–9. IEEE Computer Society, 2012.

[3] P. Ferragina and G. Manzini. Opportunistic data structures with applications. In *Proceedings of the 41st Symposium on Foundations of Computer Science (FOCS 2000)*, pages 390–398. IEEE Computer Society, 2000.

[4] D. Hains, Z. Cashero, M. Ottenberg, W. Bohm, and S. Rajopadhye. Improving CUDASW++, a parallelization of Smith-Waterman for CUDA enabled devices. In *IEEE International Symposium on Parallel and Distributed Processing Workshops and Phd Forum (IPDPSW 2011)*, 2011:490–501, 2011.

[5] M. Holtgrewe. Mason - A read simulator for second generation sequencing data. *Technical Report FU Berlin*, 2010.

[6] H. Hyyrö. A Bit-Vector algorithm for computing Levenshtein and Damerau edit distances. In *Nordic Journal of Computing*, 10(1):29–39, 2003.

[7] H. Hyyrö and G. Navarro. Faster bit-parallel approximate string matching. In *Proceedings of the 13th Annual Symposium on Combinatorial Pattern Matching (CPM 2002)*, pages 203–224, 2002.

[8] K. Kawanami and N. Fujimoto. GPU accelerated computation of the longest common subsequence. In *Facing the Multicore-Challenge II*, volume 7174 of *LNCS*, pages 84–95. Springer Berlin Heidelberg, 2012.

[9] L. Langner, K. Reinert, and D. Weese. Myers Bit-Vector Algorithm on GPU for SeqAn. Master's thesis, Freie Universität Berlin, 2011.

[10] H. Li and R. Durbin. Fast and accurate short read alignment with Burrows-Wheeler transform. In *Bioinformatics*, 25(14):1754–1760, 2009.

[11] E. Lindholm, J. Nickolls, S. Oberman, and J. Montrym. NVIDIA Tesla: a unified graphics and computing architecture. In *IEEE Micro*, 28(2):39–55, 2008.

[12] Y. Liu, B. Schmidt, and D. Maskel. CUDASW++2.0: enhanced Smith-Waterman protein database search on CUDA-enabled GPUs based on SIMT and virtualized SIMD abstractions. In *BMC Research Notes*, 3:93, 2010.

[13] Y. Liu, A. Wirawan, and B. Schmidt. CUDASW++ 3.0: accelerating Smith-Waterman protein database search by coupling CPU and GPU SIMD instructions. In *BMC Bioinformatics*, 14(1):117, 2013.

[14] S. A. Mahlke, D. C. Lin, W. Y. Chen, R. E. Hank, and R. A. Bringmann. Effective compiler support for predicated execution using the hyperblock. In *Proceedings of the 25th annual international symposium on Microarchitecture (MICRO 1992)*, volume 23, pages 45–54. IEEE Computer Society, 1992.

[15] S. Manavski and G. Valle. CUDA compatible GPU cards as efficient hardware accelerators for Smith-Waterman sequence alignment. In *BMC Bioinformatics*, 9(Suppl 2):S10, 2008.

[16] S. Marco-Sola, M. Sammeth, R. Guigo, and P. Ribeca. The GEM mapper: fast, accurate and versatile alignment by filtration. In *Nature Methods*, 9(12):1185–1188, 2012.

[17] G. Myers. A fast Bit-Vector algorithm for approximate string matching based on dynamic programming. In *Journal of the ACM*, 46(3):395–415, May 1999.

[18] G. Navarro. A guided tour to approximate string matching. In *ACM Computing Surveys*, 33(1):31–88, 2001.

[19] S. Needleman and C. Wunsch. A general method applicable to the search for similarities in the amino acid sequence of two proteins. In *Journal of Molecular Biology*, 48:443–453, 1970.

[20] Y. Ono, K. Asai, and M. Hamada. PBSIM: PacBio reads simulator-toward accurate genome assembly. In *Bioinformatics*, 29(1):119–121, 2013.

[21] A. Ozsoy, A. Chauhan, and D. M. Swany. Achieving teraCUPS on longest common subsequence problem using GPGPUs. In *The 19th IEEE International Conference on Parallel and Distributed Systems (ICPADS 2013)*. IEEE Computer Society, 2013.

[22] P. H. Sollers. The theory and computation of evolutionary distances: Pattern recognition. In *Journal of Algorithms*, 1(4):359 – 373, 1980.

[23] T. Smith and M. Waterman. Identification of common molecular subsequences. In *Journal of Molecular Biology*, 147:195–197, 1981.

[24] D. Tristram and K. Bradshaw. Evaluating the acceleration of typical scientific problems on the GPU. In *Proceedings of the South African Institute for Computer Scientists and Information Technologists Conference (SAICSIT 2013)* pages 17–26, ACM, 2013.

[25] E. Ukkonen. Finding approximate patterns in strings. In *Journal of algorithms*, 6(1):132–137, 1985.

Load Balancing N-Body Simulations with Highly Non-Uniform Density

Olga Pearce*†, Todd Gamblin†, Bronis R. de Supinski†,
Tom Arsenlis†, Nancy M. Amato*

*Department of Computer Science and Engineering, Texas A&M University, College Station, TX, USA
{olga,amato}@cse.tamu.edu
†Center for Applied Scientific Computing, Lawrence Livermore National Laboratory, Livermore, CA, USA
{olga,tgamblin,bronis,arsenlis1}@llnl.gov

ABSTRACT

N-body methods simulate the evolution of systems of particles (or bodies). They are critical for scientific research in fields as diverse as molecular dynamics, astrophysics, and material science. Most load balancing techniques for N-body methods use particle count to approximate computational work. This approximation is inaccurate, especially for systems with high density variation, because work in an N-body simulation is proportional to the particle *density*, not the particle count. In this paper, we demonstrate that existing techniques do not perform well at scale when particle density is highly non-uniform, and we propose a load balance technique that efficiently assigns load in terms of interactions instead of particles. We use adaptive sampling to create an even work distribution more amenable to partitioning, and to reduce partitioning overhead. We implement and evaluate our approach on a Barnes-Hut algorithm and a large-scale dislocation dynamics application, ParaDiS. Our method achieves up to 26% improvement in overall performance of Barnes-Hut and 18% in ParaDiS.

Categories and Subject Descriptors

D.1.3 [**Programming Techniques**]: Concurrent Programming— *Parallel programming*; G.2.2 [**Discrete Mathematics**]: Graph Theory—*Hypergraphs*; I.6.8 [**Simulation and Modeling**]: Types of Simulation—*Parallel*

Keywords

load balance; parallel algorithm; performance; simulation

1. INTRODUCTION

N-body methods simulate the dynamic evolution of a system of particles (*bodies*) under the influence of physical forces. These algorithms are critical to many scientific fields, including astrophysics, computational biology, chemistry, and material science [17, 27, 28, 34]. In an N-body simulation, each particle may exert a force on any other. The simulation progresses by repeatedly computing force *interactions* between pairs of particles, then updating the particles to reflect the force's effect. These forces typically comprise the bulk of the simulation's execution time. If all forces are considered, a naïve N-body algorithm runs in $O(n^2)$ time with respect to the number of particles. Modern algorithms such as Barnes-Hut [5] and the fast multipole method [31] use more sophisticated algorithms to reduce the number of interactions that need to be computed, resulting in $O(n \log n)$ or $O(n)$ runtime, but even with these algorithms, the interaction computation dominates the runtime. Large N-body simulations may involve billions of particles, and they need to be run on parallel computers.

Load balance is a major performance problem for N-body methods at scale. For the best parallel performance, computational work must be evenly decomposed over all processing elements of the machine. Currently, many N-body simulations use a geometric domain decomposition to assign groups of *particles* to processes, and each process computes the interactions involving the particles it is assigned. However, the work in N-body simulations is proportional to the number of *interactions* each process computes, i.e., the local density of particles in the simulated domain. Particle decompositions can therefore distribute work unevenly when there is high particle density variation. This type of load imbalance is particularly expensive at scale, because hundreds of thousands of idle processors may wait on a single overloaded processor.

We show that particle-based decompositions are prohibitively imprecise at scale, particularly when interaction density is highly non-uniform, and we present a load balancing method that explicitly balances the real work: interactions. Current approaches do not balance interactions explicitly because of memory and performance concerns: interactions greatly outnumber particles. Our approach makes balancing interactions affordable by using adaptive sampling to select uniformly sized groups of interactions, which we call *work units*. We then apply a hypergraph partitioner to the work units and to assign them to processes. The overhead of this approach is low because the coarse granularity of the work units and their uniform size make the hypergraph partitioner run efficiently.

We apply our load balancing technique to a Barnes-Hut benchmark and a large scale dislocation dynamics application, ParaDiS. This paper makes the following contributions:

1. An algorithm for load balancing interactions in N-body simulations, using work unit selection and hypergraph partitioning to assign interactions to processes explicitly;
2. An adaptive sampling approach to select work units with uniform sizes for good load balance, and coarse granularity for good partitioning performance;

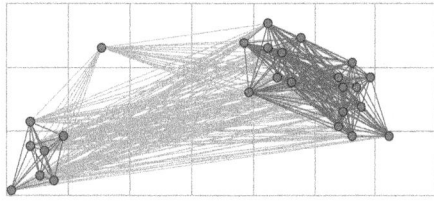

Figure 1: Particles Shown as Circles (n); Short-Range and Long-Range Interactions Shown as Black and Blue Edges

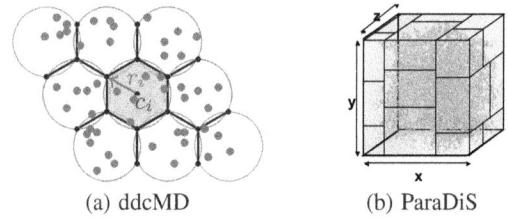

(a) ddcMD   (b) ParaDiS

Figure 2: Geometric Domain Decomposition

3. Demonstration of significantly improved load balance, low overhead, and overall performance improvements of up to 26% on Barnes-Hut and 18% on ParaDiS.

To our knowledge, we present the first approach to load balancing interactions explicitly with low overhead. Section 2 summarizes traditional load balance methods for N-body applications. Section 3 describes our algorithm for load balancing interactions, which uses an adaptive sampling approach for selecting work units and hypergraph partitioning for assignment to processes, as detailed in Sections 3.1 and 3.2. Section 4 outlines our implementation and its application to Barnes-Hut and ParaDiS. We evaluate the performance of our approach in Section 5.

2. LIMITATIONS OF EXISTING N-BODY LOAD BALANCING TECHNIQUES

N-Body methods simulate the evolution of systems of particles (*bodies*) by computing force *interactions* on groups of particles. For forces like gravity and electromagnetism, interactions involve pairs of particles, but in other systems they may involve larger groups. Once the force is evaluated, particle positions are updated and the cycle repeats. Figure 1 shows a system of particles (circles) and the interactions between them (edges). In nearly all N-body simulations, force computation is the bulk of the work. Modern algorithms such as Barnes-Hut [5] and fast multipole [31] compute weak long-range forces (blue edges) less frequently than stronger near-range forces (black edges). These algorithms use a *cutoff radius* to determine whether an interaction is near- or long-range; the cutoff radius is determined based on the particular physics simulated. This optimization reduces the number of interactions computed. Still, the force computation dominates the running time.

The largest N-body simulations comprise billions of particles and require a parallel computer in order to run. Implementing an efficient parallel N-body algorithm is difficult because the algorithm must evenly distribute work to all processes; this task of dividing work is called *domain decomposition*. Since N-body systems are dynamic, the interactions that each process evaluates change over time, and we must load balance frequently. Finally, in addition to evenly dividing work, parallel N-body load balancers must effectively manage *locality*. To compute a force interaction, the simulation needs information on all particles involved. If the particles are owned by different processes, then each process must gather information on remote particles. Local copies of remote particles are called *ghosts*. Ghost communication is expensive, so load balancers must allocate particles to minimize such communication.

Plimpton [23] classifies N-Body load balancing algorithms into three categories: particle decomposition, force decomposition, and spatial decomposition. The remainder of this section discusses these methods and their limitations in terms of the above criteria.

Particle Decomposition. In a system of N particles running on P processes, *particle decomposition* (also called row-wise decomposition) assigns N/P particles to each process. Each particle and its associated interactions comprise a single *row* in the force matrix. Each interaction is computed by the process that owns the particles involved. If particles in an interaction are owned by different processes, a tiebreaker determines which process should compute the interaction. Unless extra care is taken to preserve particle locality, particle decomposition does not minimize ghost communication. Work is balanced by moving the *particles* from process to process. However, with a cutoff radius, the number of interactions per particle varies with the local density of the system. Interactions are the bulk of computation, so particle decompositions become increasingly imbalanced the more density varies.

Force Decomposition. Rather than assigning *rows* of the force matrix as in particle decomposition, force decomposition assigns *blocks* of the force matrix. Because particle ordering in the matrix has no geometric correspondence, force decomposition methods do not minimize ghost communication. This method works well for a naive N-body algorithm that does not use a cutoff radius, because the force matrix is densely populated. However, it does not work well when there is a cutoff radius because each matrix block may contain very different numbers of interactions. To balance work efficiently, blocks of the force matrix must be uniformly dense.

Spatial Decomposition. Most modern N-body simulations use spatial decomposition, in which the simulated physical domain is divided geometrically into subdomains, which are then assigned to processes. Examples include orthogonal recursive bisection [7, 34], octrees [26, 35], fractiling [4], and space-filling curves [10]. Orthogonal recursive bisection divides space recursively into cuboids until each contains approximately N/P particles. Octree methods similarly divide three-dimensional subspaces into octants until octants contain a similar number of particles. Other spatial decomposition methods include Voronoi cell decomposition [28], where each process is assigned a centroid and owns the particles nearest its centroid (Figure 2(a)), and prismatic schemes [8], a variation on recursive bisection allowing subspaces to be divided more than twice (Figure 2(b)). Spatial decomposition methods preserve locality of particles and therefore reduce ghost communication.

In all of these methods, each process owns the computation associated with the particles in its subdomains and the work is balanced by adjusting the subdomain boundaries. Particles are moved among subdomains as part of balancing. Some methods use the number of particles per subdomain as an approximation of the workload, while others [36] weight each particle by the number of interactions in which it participates. Our method can split the work on one particle between multiple processes. Many of these methods (e.g., octrees and recursive bisection) impose limits on *how* the space can be subdivided. Together, these approximations lead to less accurate load balancing, which limits application speedup.

Limitations. No existing method balances N-body interactions directly with high precision. Particle and spatial decomposition attempt to assign similar numbers of interactions to processes by assigning *particles*, introducing a high degree of approximation. The force decomposition *does* balance forces directly, but it assumes a dense force matrix, but many simulation force matrices are sparse. Spatial and particle decompositions reduce bookkeeping costs; tracking spatial boundaries or even individual particles is still no worse than $O(n)$ in the number of particles; tracking individual interactions would quickly become intractable. Even the force decomposition assigns *blocks* rather than individual interactions, thus reducing bookkeeping overhead. Our new method that allows fine-grained *interaction* balancing also avoids the memory and performance overheads of tracking individual interactions.

3. AN INTERACTION-BASED BALANCER

The load balancer must be precise to achieve the evenly balanced load required for performance at scal. In particular, to address the limitations discussed in Section 2, the load balancer must:

1. Balance interactions directly with fine granularity;
2. Preserve locality to reduce ghost communication;
3. Run fast and not incur excessive bookkeeping overhead.

In this section, we present a load balancing algorithm that satisfies all three criteria. It consists of the following steps:

1. **Select work units with sampling.** Sample interactions; use samples to divide interactions into subsets, or *work units*.
2. **Construct model.** Use work units, proximity information.
3. **Partition model.** Assign work units to p processes by partitioning the work units into p groups.

Optimal partitioning is NP-hard [18] with many heuristic partitioning algorithms. However, while existing partitioning algorithms are sufficient for off-line use, our challenge is to use them in a dynamic, on-line load balancer. Even with an efficient heuristic algorithm, the number of interactions on each process is $O((\frac{N}{P})^2)$. Repeatedly partitioning a system this large at runtime is too slow.

The crux of our approach is to reduce the number of work units under consideration by several orders of magnitude using *sampling*. Further, we exploit two key aspects of any partitioner, namely that the partitioner has a higher likelihood of finding an optimal solution [18] and will therefore run faster if: 1) work unit sizes are small compared to process load, and 2) the sizes are relatively uniform in size. We have developed adaptive techniques to split large sample groups and to narrow distribution of work unit sizes. We have also experimented with different sample granularities to find a sufficiently fine granularity without excessive overhead.

To our knowledge, our load balancing algorithm is the first online algorithm that directly partitions interactions instead of particles. Our technique is also the first algorithm to sample *interactions* in a large-scale N-body problem. We discuss our adaptive sampling techniques in detail in Section 3.1, and we present our techniques for model construction and partitioning in Section 3.2.

3.1 Selecting Work Units

As discussed, using a hypergraph partitioner on the full set of interactions in an N-body simulation is infeasible. Thus, we have developed an *adaptive sampling strategy* that works in two ways. First, sampling *coarsens* the data set by several orders of magnitude, which allows us to solve a much smaller partitioning problem. Second, our sampling strategy is adaptive: it samples denser regions of the problem space more finely so that work units are relatively uniform in size, avoiding many of the pitfalls of the decompositions discussed in Section 2. Our strategy ensures that the partitioning is both fast and accurate.

Algorithm 1 outlines the steps of our approach. Our algorithm takes as input the set of particles P, a set of interactions I, and an *adaptive sampling threshold s*. Our algorithm's output is a set of *work units*. A work unit is a sampled interaction and an associated

---

Algorithm 1 Adaptive Interaction Sampling

Input. $P \leftarrow$ particles, $I \leftarrow$ interactions, $s \leftarrow$ adaptive sampling threshold
1: $count_{avg} = |I|/|P|$
2: **for all** $p_j \in$ P **do**
3:    i_{p_j} = set of interactions of p_j
4:    nSubsets$_j$ = max$(1, s \times |i_{p_j}|/count_{avg})$
5:    take nSubsets$_j$ samples from i_{p_j}
6:    **if** $nSubsets_j > 1$ **then**
7:       build k-d tree from samples taken
8:       **for all** interactions of p_j **do**
9:          select the subset w_{jk} to which interaction belongs
10:          $|w_{jk}|$++
11:       **end for**
12:       $w_{j_{avg}} = |i_{p_j}|/$nSubsets$_j$
13:       **for all** subset$_{jk} \in$ subsets$_j$ **do**
14:          **if** $w_{jk} > s \times w_{j_{avg}}$ **then**
15:             adaptively sample within subset$_{jk}$, calculate weights
16:          **end if**
17:       **end for**
18:    **end if**
19: **end for**
Output. $W \leftarrow$ work units with desired size and $\sim$uniform size distribution

---

neighborhood. Each work unit represents all samples in a particular neighborhood, and it consists of the sampled interaction, an associated *centroid*, and a number of non-sampled interactions.

On line 2, Algorithm 1 starts by iterating over all particles. For each particle, on lines 4 and 5, the algorithm samples at least one interaction. If a particle is involved in more than the average number of interactions, then we take more samples. The adaptive sampling threshold, s, determines the number of additional samples to take, and the caller can use s to adjust the aggressiveness of sampling in dense regions of the domain. The number of interactions sampled from particle p_j is stored in $nSubsets_j$.

Once we have a sampled interaction, we assign it a coordinate in space based on the *centroid* of the particles that it involves. For a pairwise force, like gravity, the centroid is the midpoint between two particles. For more complex forces, it is the center of mass of the polygon defined by the member particles (Figure 3(a)). To define neighborhoods for work units, each sampled interaction's centroid is used as the center of a *Voronoi cell* that defines the neighborhood. A centroid's Voronoi cell is the set of points closest to that centroid. Figure 3(b) shows a set of points and their enclosing Voronoi cells. Any interactions in a sampled interaction's Voronoi cell are considered part of its work unit.

Our adaptive sampling technique ensures that each Voronoi cell contains approximately the same number of interactions. If a cell contains too many interactions, e.g., the cell in Figure 3(c), then we increase the number of samples in its neighborhood, effectively splitting it into subcells. Thus, our work units have nearly uniform granularity and are easy to partition. However, the splitting is potentially expensive. With one sample per particle, we can easily track which interactions belong to a particular work unit by associating the interactions with their owning particle. With multiple samples for a particle, we need another ownership mechanism. For particles with multiple samples, we use a k-d tree [14] to determine which interactions are closest to each sample.

Right-Tailed Distribution. Using a k-d tree ensures that each work unit has high locality and the accuracy of our sampling scheme. However, constructing it is expensive. We must therefore be careful to set the adaptive sampling threshold to a value that balances granularity with range query cost.

Fortunately, an obvious way to set s exists for nearly all N-body systems, In the natural sciences, the density of samples of objects

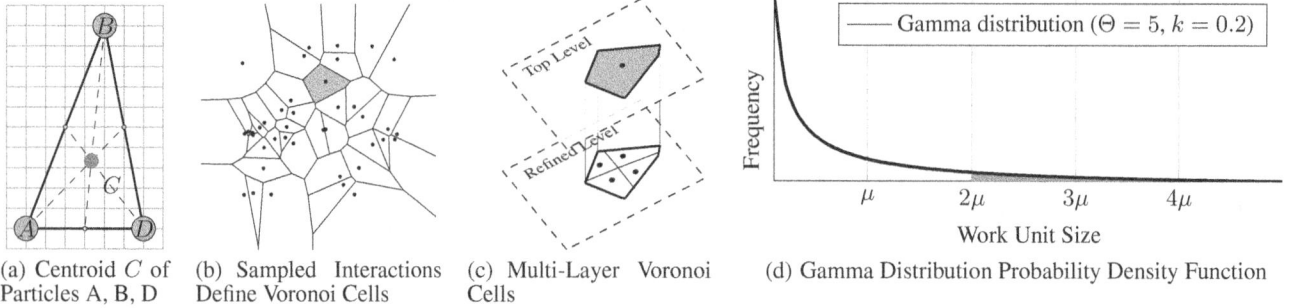

(a) Centroid C of Particles A, B, D (b) Sampled Interactions Define Voronoi Cells (c) Multi-Layer Voronoi Cells (d) Gamma Distribution Probability Density Function

Figure 3: Defining Interaction Subsets

Algorithm 2 Hypergraph Construction

Input. P (set of particles), SI (set of sampled interactions)
Output. $H = (V, E^H)$ (graph of particles and interactions)
1: **for** $p_j \in$ P **do**
2:     H.insert(e_i) to represent the particle
3:     **for** $i \in$ subsets$_j$ **do**
4:         H.insert(v_{ij})
5:         add edges from v_{ij} to all e_i, hyperedges needed to compute v_{ij}
6:     **end for**
7: **end for**

---

in physical and natural processes (such as particles in a dynamical system) obey a power law distribution [13]. This phenomenon is known as *Taylor's Law* in ecology and the *fluctuation scaling law* in physics. For our purposes, it implies that random sampling leads to work units with sizes that can be fit to a gamma distribution:

$$\mathbb{P}(x) = \frac{1}{\Theta^k} \frac{1}{\Gamma(k)} x^{k-1} e^{-\frac{x}{\Theta}} \qquad (1)$$

where k is a *shape* parameter, Θ is a *scale* parameter, and $\Gamma(k)$ is the *gamma function* evaluated at k. While the parameters vary, all examples that we have considered exhibit a long right tail as shown in Figure 3(d), which implies that relatively few samples have a larger than average number of interactions. Thus, we can achieve an even distribution of work unit weights by splitting relatively few work units into smaller pieces. The (red) shaded area under the tail of the gamma distribution in Figure 3(d) depicts the number of work units that are larger than 2μ, or $2\times$ the mean. Thus a domain scientist can easily pick a good value for s for a particular problem: s should generally be chosen to "chop off" all or part of the tail off the gamma distribution. In Section 5, we show empirically that our method produces work units with relatively uniform sizes, and we demonstrate the positive impact on the resulting load balance.

3.2 Assigning Work Units to Processes

Section 3.1 described how we select uniformly sized work units for load balancing; next, we construct a model from these work units to represent both parallel computation and communication. A hypergraph is a well suited model for this problem because hypergraphs have been used extensively to represent the behavior of parallel applications [16]. Further, we can use well established hypergraph partitioning algorithms to guide load balancing.

Hypergraphs are a generalization of graphs. Where a graph contains vertices, and pairs of vertices are connected by edges, in a hypergraph, each *hyperedge* may connect *one or more* of vertices. Thus, if we represent interactions with vertices, particles are a natural fit for hyperedges, because a particle may be involved in many interactions. Hyperedges also accurately represent ghost communication in N-body simulations, because if two interactions in the

---

Algorithm 3 Sampling-based Interaction Load Balancer

$n \leftarrow$ number of particles, $p \leftarrow$ number of processes,
$m \leftarrow$ number of interactions, $s \leftarrow$ adaptive sampling threshold

Step		Cost
1:	Build list of interactions per particle	*incurred*
2:	Adaptively sample interactions (Alg. 1)	$O(s\frac{n}{p} + \frac{m}{p}\log(s))$
3:	Construct hypergraph (Alg. 2)	$O(s\frac{n}{p})$
4:	Partition hypergraph	$O(s\frac{n}{p}\log(s\frac{n}{p}))$
5:	Redistribute particles, samples, setup ghosts	*incurred*
6:	Build list of interactions per particle	*incurred*
7:	Interaction $\rightarrow$ particle $\rightarrow$ subset $\rightarrow$ process	$O(\frac{m}{p}\log(s))$

---

same partition share a hyperedge that represents a remote particle, a single ghost node will need to be fetched. Partitioning a hypergraph tries to minimize the number of hyperedges cut by partition boundaries, and thus minimizes interprocess communication.

Formally, given a weighted *hypergraph* $H = (V, E^H)$ where V is a set of vertices and E^H is a set of hyperedges, hypergraph partitioning divides V into k sets based on the following two objectives:

1. **Equal partitions:** Vertices are assigned to processes so that the total vertex weight on each process is approximately equal.
2. **Minimized hyperedge cut:** Minimize the number of shared particles cut by the partitions.

In our hypergraph, the *vertices* are the work units selected in Section 3.1 (to represent interactions), and *hyperedges* represent particles (storage units). Algorithm 2 shows our procedure. We first add all particles as hyperedges to the sampled interaction hypergraph H to ensure the graph is connected (line 2). We add the work units from Section 3.1 as vertices (line 4) that will be partitioned into equal partitions. We add edges between the vertices (work units) and the needed hyperedges (particles) to preserve the *spatial proximity* information in the graph (line 5). We use a hypergraph partitioner to partition the resulting hypergraph.

3.3 Interaction-Based Load Balancer Using Sampling and Hypergraph Partitioning

Algorithm 3 shows all steps of our approach together with phases of a host N-body application. To quantify the asymptotic overhead of our algorithm, we list the computational complexity of each phase. Again, since we have chosen to use a hypergraph as our model, the complexities reflect those of hypergraph partitioning. For all complexities, p is the number of processes, n is the number of particles, m is the number of interactions, and s is our sampling threshold. The complexities of some phases are listed as *incurred*. These are phases that an N-body application would perform regardless of whether it uses our load balancing approach, so we do not count the runtime of these phases as overhead.

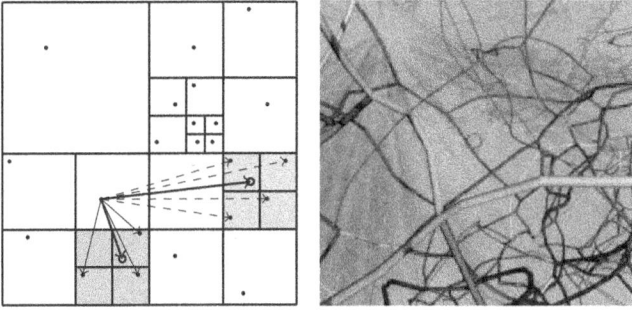

Figure 4: Octree in Barnes-Hut Benchmark

Figure 5: Dislocation Nodes and Arms in ParaDiS

Figure 6: Imbalance over Time in ParaDiS with Built-in Recursive Bisection Load Balancer

Our load balancer starts by building interaction lists for each particle. The application would need this step (or at least a loop, if not a list) to compute interactions, so the cost is not part of overhead. The list of interactions is then passed to Algorithm 1, which samples interactions and constructs work units. We then construct a model, in this case a hypergraph, from the work units in Algorithm 2. We pass this model to partitioning. Assuming a power law distribution as mentioned in Section 3.1, the number of work units added to the hypergraph is $O(n)$. The work units in the tail of the hypergraph do not increase this upper bound. Because the graph is constructed in a distributed manner across all processes, the cost is $O(s\frac{n}{p})$. This cost can vary based on the load balance of the input graph, but for this analysis, we assume that the input is not highly imbalanced initially, which is true for all but the first invocation, assuming our algorithm is run frequently.

Hypergraph partitioning is $O(|V|log(|V|))$, in the size of the input graph, and for our graph, $|V| = s\frac{n}{p}$, which gives $O(s\frac{n}{p}log(s\frac{n}{p}))$ for phase 4. Thus, the complexity is in terms of n and our algorithm partition n objects instead of $m = p(\frac{n}{p})^2$ interactions.

After partitioning, we rely on the application to distribute work according to the outcome of partitioning. These costs are incurred. Last, during the force computation, we must add logic to check each interaction computation against our computed assignment, which is $O(\frac{m}{p}log(s))$. The extra $log(s)$ factor reflects the range lookup required for the small number of particles with split interactions.

4. APPLICATIONS & IMPLEMENTATION

Our load balancer implementation requires support libraries for partitioning and for geometric range queries. Several hypergraph partitioning libraries are freely available [11, 24]. In this work, we use the hypergraph partitioner from Zoltan [12]. We use the k-d tree implementation from the CGAL [2] Computational Geometry Library for the nearest neighbor computation.

4.1 Barnes-Hut

The first application to which we have applied our framework is an implementation of the classic Barnes-Hut algorithm. We created a distributed version of Barnes-Hut [5] based on a shared memory implementation from the Lonestar suite in Galois [9, 22]. The code is written in C++ and uses MPI for communication. Its force calculation phase uses an octree to compute approximately the force that the n particles in the system exert on each other (e.g., through gravity). The n leaves of the octree are the individual particles, while the internal nodes summarize information about the particles contained in the subtree (i.e., combined mass and center of gravity). This octree effectively partitions the volume hierarchically around the n particles into successively smaller cells. While a pre-

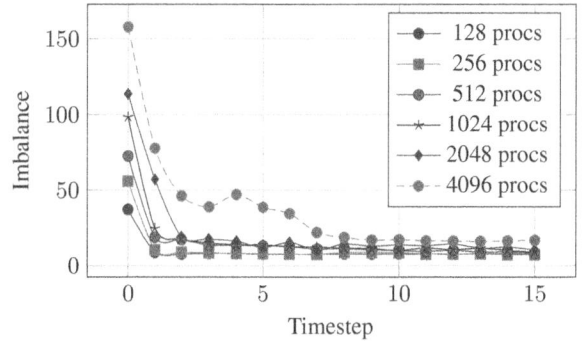

cise computation would have to consider $O(n^2)$ interactions, the Barnes-Hut algorithm uses the summary information contained at each level of the hierarchy to approximate interactions for far away particles. Particles that interact with other particles in nearby cells are computed directly, but for interactions with cells that are sufficiently far away, one force computation with the cell is sufficient.

This algorithm has $O(n\log(n))$ complexity. For example, consider the two-dimensional hierarchical subdivision of space in Figure 4. The algorithm checks the distance to the red cell's center of gravity (red circle). Because the distance is not large (red arrow), interactions with all bodies in the red cell are computed (black arrows). Because the blue cell's center (blue circle) is far enough away, only the interaction with the center is computed (blue arrow, a single computation), instead of for each body (dashed arrows).

We run our load balance algorithm at the end of each timestep. We generate our hypergraph by extracting the particle interactions from the octree data structure. Once partitioned, we redistribute the particles and assign interactions. As a baseline comparison for our results, we use a decomposition that allows assignment of any particle (along with its interactions) to any process, which is more flexible than many implementations of spatial decomposition. To preserve locality, we ordered the atoms by a space filling curve as done by Winkel, et al. [36], Warren and Salmon [35], and used with modifications by Sundar, et al. [29]. The related work shows speedup for 'homogeneous' and 'non-homogeneous' particle distributions; the drop in scalability for 'non-homogeneous' particle distributions reveals that this load balancing scheme is insufficient for this case, which our work targets. Unfortunately, the prior work does not explicitly quantify the load imbalance.

4.2 ParaDiS

ParaDiS (Figure 5) is the second application that we use in our experiments [3, 8]. This large-scale dislocation dynamics simulation, which is written in C/C++ with MPI for interprocess communication, is used to study the fundamental mechanisms of plasticity. It computes short-range forces directly and uses multipole expansion [15, 31] to compute long-range forces. ParaDiS simulations grow in size as they progress, necessitating periodic rebalancing.

Currently, ParaDiS uses a spatial domain decomposition and has several methods for adjusting the decomposition at runtime. Recursive sectioning or recursive bisection can be used to decompose the domain into spatial prisms, and one prism is assigned to each process. The 3-dimensional recursive sectioning decomposition first segments the domain in the X direction, then in the Y direction within X slabs, and finally in the Z direction within XY slabs, as demonstrated in Figure 2(b). The recursive bisection algorithm bisects the space in the X, Y and/or Z dimensions into octants, quar-

117

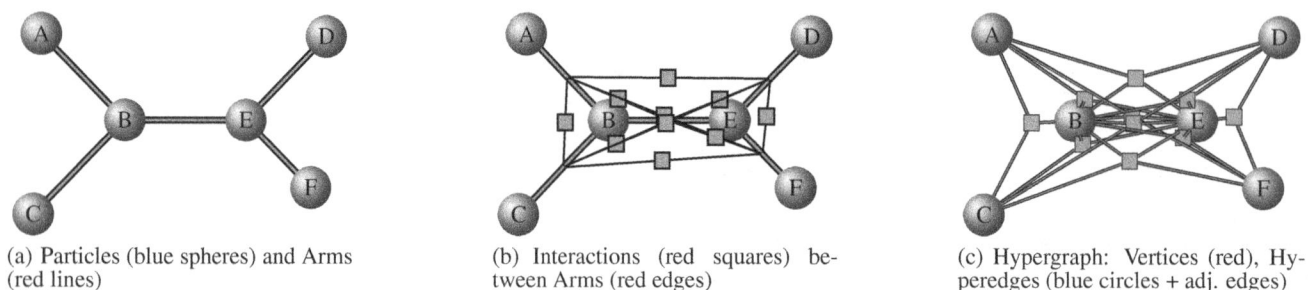

(a) Particles (blue spheres) and Arms (red lines)

(b) Interactions (red squares) between Arms (red edges)

(c) Hypergraph: Vertices (red), Hyperedges (blue circles + adj. edges)

Figure 7: ParaDiS Computation as a Hypergraph

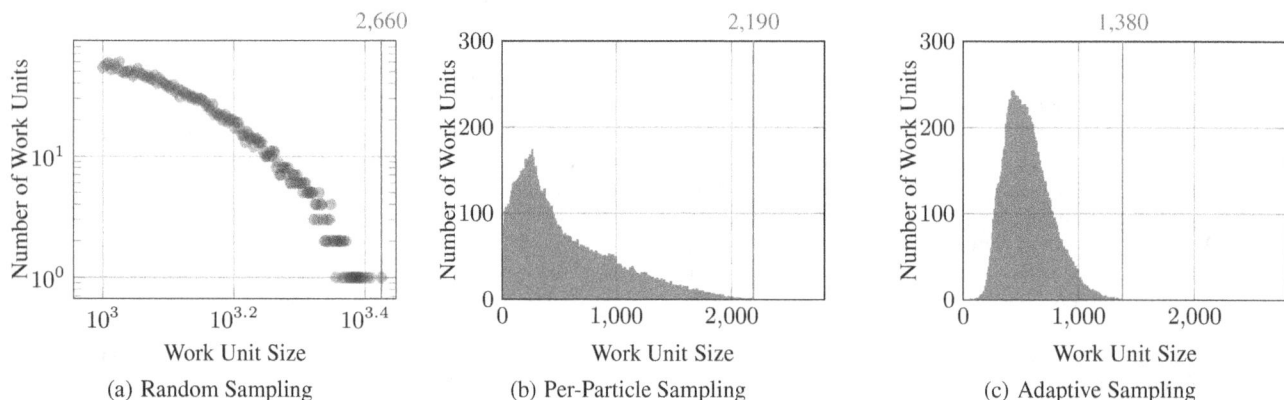

(a) Random Sampling

(b) Per-Particle Sampling

(c) Adaptive Sampling

Figure 8: Effect of Sample Size and Technique on Work Unit Size Variability in Barnes-Hut

ters or halves (depending on the number of domains specified per dimension) such that the computational cost of each sub-partition is roughly the same; the decomposition is then recursively applied to each of the sub-partitions.

ParaDiS uses empirical measurements as an input to its load balancing algorithm. It estimates load by timing the computation that the developers consider most important for load balance. The load balancing algorithm adjusts work per process by shifting the boundaries of the sections. The size of neighboring domains constrains the magnitude of a shift since the algorithm does not move a boundary past the end of a neighboring section.

Figure 6 shows the effectiveness of the recursive bisection load balancer. This fully distributed approach improves load balance over time. However, beyond some point, it cannot improve load balance further due to its approximate assignment of interactions. We use the lowest load imbalance values achievable by the built-in balancer as the baseline for our comparisons in Section 5.3.

Figure 7 demonstrates how we describe the ParaDiS computation as a hypergraph of dislocation nodes (particles) and interactions, where a *dislocation node* is a degree of freedom in the problem. Dislocation nodes are the units of data stored in application data structures, and *arms* or *segments* are the connecting edges, as shown in Figure 7(a). ParaDiS imposes a regular grid of cells to discretize the space, which is used to determine proximity and divide the interactions into short and long range. A segment interacts with all other segments in its own cell and the cells surrounding it, 27 cells in total (assuming periodic boundaries). A *segment interaction* is a unit of work in ParaDiS, as illustrated by red squares in Figure 7(b). Each interaction involves three or four dislocation nodes (particles), unlike many n-body applications which define interactions between pairs of particles. Figure 7(c) demonstrates

the hypergraph that we use for ParaDiS. The *dislocation nodes* and *segment interactions* are the same as in Figure 7(b) (shown as blue spheres and red squares). The *dislocation nodes* become the hyperedges, connected to all interactions that they support.

5. PERFORMANCE EVALUATION

For our experiments, we use a Linux cluster with nodes consisting of two Hex-core Intel Xeon EP X5660 processors running at 2.8 GHz, with twelve cores per node and 22,272 cores total. All nodes are connected by QDR Infiniband. We use GCC 4.4.7 and MVAPICH v0.99 on top of CHAOS [1], an HPC variant of RedHat Enterprise Linux (RHEL), running at Linux kernel version 2.6.32.

5.1 Distribution of Work Unit Sizes and Impact on Performance

This section examines the distribution of work unit sizes under the sampling strategies described in Section 3.1, and how more uniform distribution leads to more evenly distributed load. These experiments use a Barnes-Hut problem with 32K particles, which we strong scale from 8 to 2,048 processes. We chose this problem since it is the largest problem that can fit into memory for 8 processes. We chose strong scaling since reproducing density variations for weak scaling is difficult. Strong scaling allows us to use the same problem at all scales so data points are comparable.

Figure 8 shows the effect of sample size and sampling strategy on the variability of work unit size in Barnes-Hut. As discussed in Section 3.1, sampling a simulated domain with high density variability results in a power law distribution of work units, as Figure 8(a) shows (note that the horizontal axis is log-scale). The maximum work unit size (2,660) is indicated at the top of the figure. We can partially mitigate the density properties by proportionally sampling

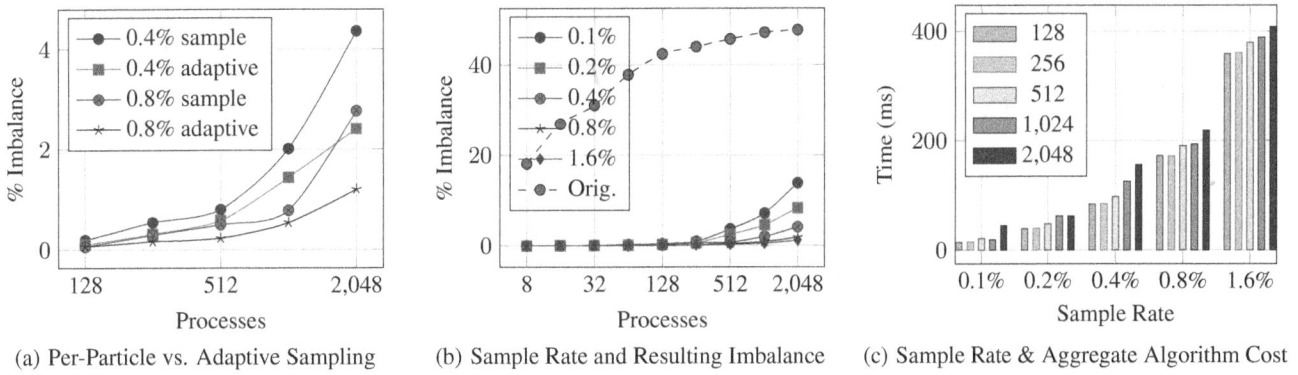

(a) Per-Particle vs. Adaptive Sampling   (b) Sample Rate and Resulting Imbalance   (c) Sample Rate & Aggregate Algorithm Cost

Figure 9: Impact of Sampling Strategy on Resulting Imbalance and Cost of Load Balancing Algorithm

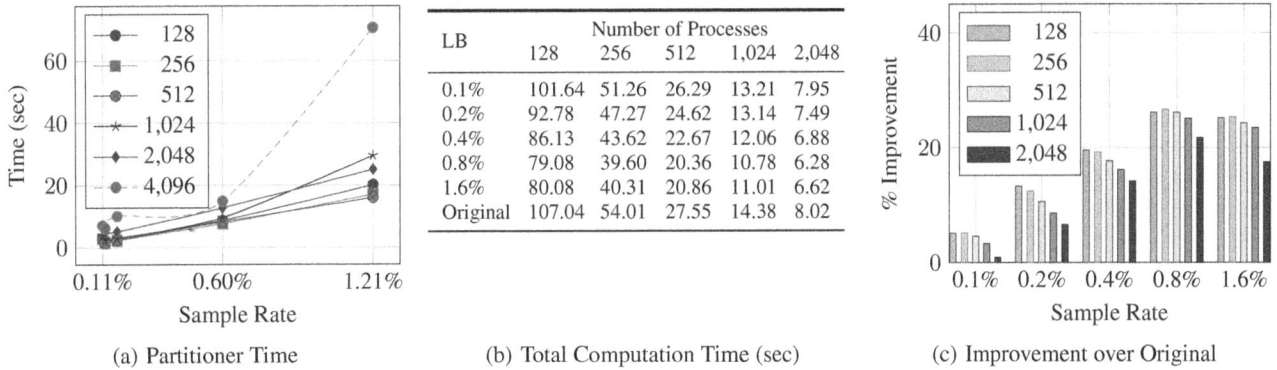

LB	Number of Processes				
	128	256	512	1,024	2,048
0.1%	101.64	51.26	26.29	13.21	7.95
0.2%	92.78	47.27	24.62	13.14	7.49
0.4%	86.13	43.62	22.67	12.06	6.88
0.8%	79.08	39.60	20.36	10.78	6.28
1.6%	80.08	40.31	20.86	11.01	6.62
Original	107.04	54.01	27.55	14.38	8.02

(a) Partitioner Time   (b) Total Computation Time (sec)   (c) Improvement over Original

Figure 10: Impact of Sampling Rate on Performance of Graph Partitioner and Barnes-Hut Application

interactions per-particle (Figure 8(b)). By running Algorithm 1 *without* any adaptation, we achieve a maximum work unit size of 2,190. We achieve a tighter, nearly normal distribution of the interactions that each work unit represents by using the full adaptive sampling approach from Algorithm 1, as Figure 8(c) shows. Here, the maximum work unit size is 1,380.

Figure 9 demonstrates the impact of the sample size and strategy. Figure 9(a) compares how the two approaches to sampling impact the ability of the load balancer to assign equal partitions to processes, where imbalance is:

$$\text{imbalance} = \frac{\text{maximum load - average load}}{\text{average load}}$$

Because adaptive sampling makes the distribution of sample weights more uniform, it results in better partition quality (lower imbalance), as Figure 9(a) shows. Roughly, adaptive sampling can achieve the same partitioning quality as doubling the sample size, and keeps the number of resulting work units roughly the same as its non-adaptive version. Since the number of work units directly impacts the cost of our load balancing method, using a sampling approach that more uniformly distributes work unit sizes is of increasing importance as process count increases.

We also evaluate the quality of the load balance achieved by our load balancing approach, measured by the percent imbalance. We compare the different sampling rates and the traditional particle-based approach. Figure 9(b) shows that, while imbalance of the application using a particle-based method grows quickly as the number of processes increases, our direct interaction assignment scheme is able to achieve much lower levels of imbalance. Because our method is sampling based, quality is, to a large extent, a function

of the number of samples, or the work units assigned to processes. When the number of work units is too small, quality partitioning is difficult to achieve. However, even modest sample sizes of under 1% of all interactions allows for quality partitions. Samples above 1% show diminishing returns on partition quality.

The imbalance increases with the number of processes in this strongly scaled example since we have fewer individual work units to assign to each process. Thus the job of the partitioner is more difficult. One of the strengths of our method is that we can choose the number of work units that we select, which allows us to trade off between cost and accuracy.

Figure 9(c) shows the aggregate overhead of our load balancer. As mentioned earlier, sample count directly impacts the cost of our load balancer because it determines the cost of partitioning, sampling and nearest-neighbor assignment. The figure clearly demonstrates the linear relationship between the sample size and the cost of our balancer. The same size bars within a sample size group would indicate consistent aggregate compute time across all processes, i.e., perfect scaling. While the sampling and nearest-neighbor assignment scale well, the overhead numbers show some degradation in scalability due to the limited scalability of the partitioner. The latter is a well known problem, but can be remedied. Since our method is sampling based and the resulting graph of work units is small, we could gather this graph on a smaller number of processes for partitioning, and then scatter the results. This optimization would allow us to pick the optimal scale for the partitioner independent of the scale at which the application is run, and thus reduce overall runtime. We leave this optimization for future work.

Sampling enables us to use the graph partitioning when partitioning the entire graph would be prohibitively expensive. Figure 10(a)

119

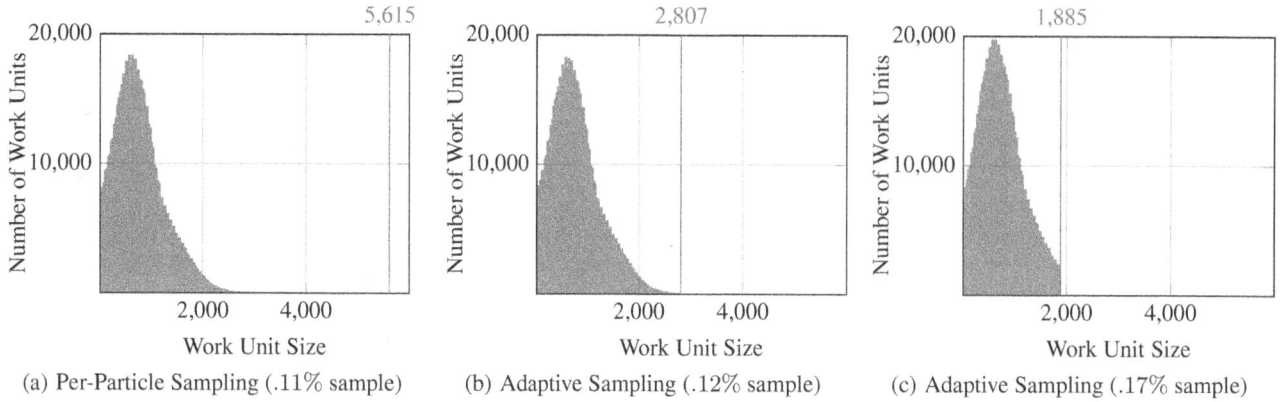

(a) Per-Particle Sampling (.11% sample)   (b) Adaptive Sampling (.12% sample)   (c) Adaptive Sampling (.17% sample)

Figure 11: Effect of Sample Size and Technique on Work Unit Size Variability in ParaDiS

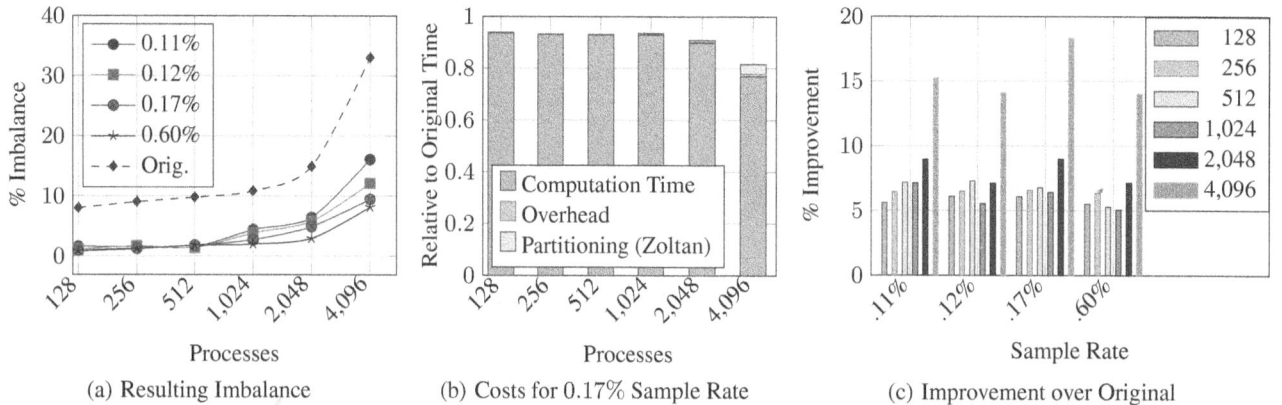

(a) Resulting Imbalance   (b) Costs for 0.17% Sample Rate   (c) Improvement over Original

Figure 12: Effect of Sampling Technique on Load Balance and Application Performance

shows the hypergraph partitioner time (Zoltan) for different sample rates using our ParaDiS data set. The complete graph for this data set has 1M particles and 547M interactions. It takes seconds to partition the graph with just 0.11% of the interactions sampled; partitioning the complete graph would be extremely expensive.

Overall, our sampling approach is an effective way to reduce the size of the graph to be partitioned while preserving the quality of the resulting partitions. The savings in partitioner time make the approach of explicitly load balancing the interactions affordable. As mentioned in Algorithm 3.3, we have effectively reduced the complexity of balancing interactions to that of balancing particles.

5.2   Impact on Barnes-Hut Performance

We show the impact of our load balancer on performance of the Barnes-Hut benchmark in Figure 10. The total times for our 32K particle simulation with different sampling rates are listed in Figure 10(b); Figure 10(c) illustrates these total times relative to the original load balancer. With 0.1% sample, our method shows marginal performance improvement over the original load balancer; poor performance is due to undersampling and the partitioner's inability to form equal partitions from the work units provided. With more sampling, our method outperforms the original method; in this example, the point of diminishing returns is apparent for the sampling ratio of 1.6%. Although our method gains more from its accuracy at scale, two reasons inhibit its performance when the sampling ratio is held constant while increasing the process count. First, the partitioner has fewer work units to divide between a larger

LB	Number of Processes					
	128	256	512	1,024	2,048	4,096
0.11%	6118.71	3061.16	1529.36	774.96	405.14	228.51
0.12%	6086.44	3059.56	1527.47	788.39	408.94	231.51
0.17%	6089.01	3056.97	1536.31	780.96	405.07	220.05
0.60%	6126.13	3064.07	1560.99	792.21	413.34	231.80
Original	6482.01	3271.84	1647.85	834.33	445.09	269.57

Figure 13: Total Computation Time of ParaDiS (sec)

number of partitions, resulting in slight increase in load imbalance. In a more realistic scenario, one would chose the sampling ratio relative to both the problem size and the number of partitions needed, thus not observing this performance degradation. Second, the partitioner scales poorly when partitioning the same small graph on more processes (as discussed previously), necessitating the decoupling of the partitioner scale from the problem scale.

Our interaction-based balancer with sufficient sampling performs well and clearly outperforms the particle-based load balancer. Overall, we observe 23-26% improvement for the optimal sampling rate.

5.3   Impact on ParaDiS Performance

We evaluate the impact of our load balancer on the performance of ParaDiS. We use a highly dynamic crystal simulation input set for ParaDiS, with 1M degrees of freedom at the beginning of the simulation growing to 1.1M degrees of freedom by the end of the run. We strongly scaled this simulation up to 4,096 processes.

Figure 11 shows the effect of the sample size and strategy on work unit size variability. Per-particle sampling results in a distribution with a long right tail, as demonstrated in Figure 11(a). The maximum work unit represents 5,615 interactions, and the sample size is 0.11% of the interactions in the problem. As shown in Figure 11(b), with an only 0.01% increase in sample size (for a total sample rate of 0.12%), we decrease the maximum work unit size to 2,807. With an additional 0.05% increase in sample size (for a total sample rate of 0.17%), we decrease the maximum work unit size to 1,885, as Figure 11(c) shows.

Figure 12 details performance of the load balancer and the application with different sampling strategies. Figure 12(a) demonstrates the impact that the different sampling strategies have on load imbalance, along with the lowest possible load balance achieved by the built-in balancer. With an addition of more work units to partition and more uniform work unit size distribution, the hypergraph partitioner achieves lower levels of load imbalance. As the number of processes grows, the imbalance increases in this strong scaling problem due to the partitioner having to divide the same number of work units into more partitions. The partitioner needs more work units to work with at scale; a higher sampling rate or a bigger problem with the same sampling rate would allow the partitioner to accomplish similar levels of imbalance at scale.

Figure 12(b) shows the cost break down for a sample rate of 0.17% relative to the performance using the existing load balancer. The computation time required with our load balancer is lower, especially at larger process counts when the existing load balancer performs significantly worse. The time spent in the hypergraph partitioner increases as the process count increases because the partitioner does not scale optimally and must partition the same number of work units into more partitions, a more difficult problem to solve. As already discussed, our future work will address this issue.

Figure 12(c) shows the runtime of the problem with different sampling levels, relative to the runtime of the problem with the built-in balancer. For all sampling levels, our method shows greater improvement as the number of processes grows, due to larger improvement in load balance. Further improvement is possible over the per-particle sampling (0.11% sample) because our adaptive sampling improves the distribution of work unit sizes. Because the cost of our algorithm is dependent on the sample size, a sample rate of 0.17% only slightly outperforms one of 0.12%. Performance degrades with the 0.60% sample due to the costs outweighing the benefit of sampling more. Figure 13 lists the total runtimes.

We compare to the *second*, optimized load balance scheme that the ParaDiS developers implemented. Overall, we achieve improvement in performance of 6-18% over this already highly optimized and dynamically load balanced production application.

6. RELATED WORK

Section 2 discussed related work on N-body applications. Related work also includes applications and frameworks that use geometric and graph-based load balancing methods.

In theoretical work on load balancing hierarchical N-body applications, Teng partitions the communication graph [30] and proves certain sub-types of communication graphs can be partitioned. Teng builds a communication graph between the boxes in the hierarchy, and adds edges between the leaf boxes and the actual particles. Noting that edge density makes graph partitioning difficult, Teng then combines some of the edges and shows that the in- and out-degree of the communication graph is bounded by $O(\log n + \mu)$, where n is the number of boxes and μ is a measure of uniformity. Thus,

the graph becomes more dense as the problem or non-uniformity grow. On the contrary, the density of our hypergraph is not tied to the size of the input but rather the sampling rate, or the granularity needed by the partitioner to create quality partitions. Teng's approach assigns weights to particles to meet the load balancing criteria. However, graph partitioners perform poorly with the large variation in weights. By design, our algorithm achieves relatively uniform vertex weights, improving partition quality.

Other types of scientific applications employ geometric load balancers. SAMRAI [37] is a structured AMR application that orders boxes by their spatial location by placing a Morton curve (or Z-curve) [19] through the box centroids to increase the likelihood that the neighboring patches will reside on the same processor after load balancing. PLUM [20, 21] is a load balancing framework for adaptive grid applications. It can use any partitioning algorithm and assists in efficient processor assignment and remapping of the computation. DRAMA [6] is a dynamic load balancing library for finite element methods that includes geometric and graph partitioning algorithms. Its repartitioning modules include iterative pairwise load balancing, recursive coordinate bisection (RCB). Implicit treatment of work units and inherent approximations make these approaches fast but lead to higher imbalance at scale.

An alternative to geometric methods are partitioners that work with mesh, graph, or hypergraph representation of computation, i.e., ParMetis [24, 25], Jostle [32, 33], and Zoltan [11, 12]. Our work determines an appropriate representation for the problem, and leverages these powerful tools by providing them with inputs that enable quality solutions to the problem.

7. CONCLUSIONS

Traditional parallel N-body load balance algorithms use approximate methods to assign computational work, or *interactions* to processes. Those that do balance interactions directly, such as force decomposition, do so with coarse granularity because the interaction graph is large and costly to partition directly. We have developed the first approach for explicitly balancing interactions in N-body applications at runtime. Our approach uses sampling to reduce the size of the interaction hypergraph by several orders of magnitude, and aggressive *adaptive* sampling to even the size of sampled work units. The combination of these two techniques enables extremely efficient partitioning. Using these techniques in conjunction with a hypergraph partitioner to minimize inter-process communication, we have shown for two optimized parallel applications, Barnes-Hut and the ParaDiS dislocation dynamics code, that our method achieves 23-26% and 6-18% improvement in overall performance. To our knowledge, our approach is the first to balance interactions directly with such fine granularity.

8. ACKNOWLEDGMENTS

The research of Amato and Pearce supported in part by NSF awards CNS-0551685, CCF-0833199, CCF-0830753, IIS-0916053, IIS-0917266, EFRI-1240483, RI-1217991, by NIH NCI R25 CA090301-11, by DOE awards DE-AC02-06CH11357, B575363, and by Samsung, Chevron, IBM, Intel, and Oracle/Sun. Pearce supported in part by an NSF Graduate Research Fellowship, a Department of Education Graduate Fellowship (GAANN), and the Lawrence Scholar Program Fellowship. This work was performed under the auspices of the U.S. Department of Energy by Lawrence Livermore National Laboratory under Contract DE-AC52-07NA27344 (LLNL-CONF-648577).

9. REFERENCES

[1] chaos-release: Linux Distribution for High Performance Computing. http://code.google.com/p/chaos-release/wiki/CHAOS_Description.

[2] CGAL, Computational Geometry Algorithms Library. http://www.cgal.org.

[3] A. Arsenlis, W. Cai, M. Tang, M. Rhee, T. Oppelstrup, G. Hommes, T. G. Pierce, and V. V. Bulatov. Enabling Strain Hardening Simulations with Dislocation Dynamics. *Modelling and Simulation in Materials Science and Engineering*, 15(6):553, 2007.

[4] I. Banicescu and S. Flynn Hummel. Balancing Processor Loads and Exploiting Data Locality in N-Body Simulations. In *SC*, 1995.

[5] J. Barnes and P. Hut. A Hierarchical O(N log N) Force-Calculation Algorithm. *Nature*, 324:446–449, 1986.

[6] A. Basermann, J. Clinckemaillie, T. Coupez, J. Fingberg, H. Digonnet, R. Ducloux, J. M. Gratien, U. Hartmann, G. Lonsdale, B. Maerten, D. Roose, and C. Walshaw. Dynamic Load-Balancing of Finite Element Applications with the DRAMA Library. *Applied Mathematical Modelling*, 25(2):83–98, 2000.

[7] M. J. Berger and S. H. Bokhari. A Partitioning Strategy for Nonuniform Problems on Multiprocessors. *IEEE Transactions on Computers*, 1987.

[8] V. Bulatov, W. Cai, J. Fier, M. Hiratani, G. Hommes, T. Pierce, M. Tang, M. Rhee, K. Yates, and T. Arsenlis. Scalable Line Dynamics in ParaDiS. In *SC*, 2004.

[9] M. Burtscher and K. Pingali. An Efficient CUDA Implementation of the Tree-based Barnes-Hut N-Body Algorithm. In *GPU Computing Gems Emerald Edition*, 2011.

[10] A. R. Butz. Convergence with Hilbert's Space Filling Curve. *Journ. of Computer & System Sciences*, 3(2):128–146, 1969.

[11] K. Devine, E. Boman, R. Heaphy, B. Hendrickson, J. Teresco, J. Faik, J. Flaherty, and L. Gervasio. New Challanges in Dynamic Load Balancing. *Applied Numerical Mathematics*, 52(2-3), 2005.

[12] K. Devine, B. Hendrickson, E. Boman, M. St. John, and C. Vaughan. Design of Dynamic Load-Balancing Tools for Parallel Applications. In *Intl. Conf. on Supercomputing (ICS)*, 2000.

[13] Z. Eisler, I. Bartos, and J. Kertesz. Fluctuation Scaling in Complex Systems: Taylor's Law and Beyond. *Advances in Physics*, 57(1):89–142, 2008.

[14] J. H. Friedman, J. L. Bentley, and R. A. Finkel. An Algorithm for Finding Best Matches in Logarithmic Expected Time. *ACM Trans. Math. Softw.*, 3(3):209–226, Sept. 1977.

[15] L. Greengard and V. Rokhlin. A Fast Algorithm for Particle Simulations. *Journal of Computational Physics*, 135:280–292, 1987.

[16] B. Hendrickson and T. G. Kolda. Graph Partitioning Models for Parallel Computing. *Parallel Computing*, 26(12):1519–1534, 2000.

[17] N. Komatsu, T. Kiwata, and S. Kimura. Thermodynamic Properties of an Evaporation Process in Self-Fravitating N-Body systems. *Phys. Rev. E*, 82, Aug 2010.

[18] S. Martello and P. Toth. Knapsack Problems: Algorithms and Computer Implementations. *Chichester: John Wiley and Sons*, 1990.

[19] G. Morton. A Computer Oriented Geodetic Data Base and a New Technique in File Sequencing. *IBM tech report*, 1966.

[20] L. Oliker and R. Biswas. Efficient Load Balancing and Data Remapping for Adaptive Grid Calculations. In *ACM Symposium on Parallel Algorithms and Architectures (SPAA)*, 1997.

[21] L. Oliker and R. Biswas. PLUM: Parallel Load Balancing for Adaptive Unstructured Meshes. *Journal of Parallel and Distr. Computing*, 52(2):150–177, 1998.

[22] K. Pingali, D. Nguyen, M. Kulkarni, M. Burtscher, M. A. Hassaan, R. Kaleem, T.-H. Lee, A. Lenharth, R. Manevich, M. Méndez-Lojo, D. Prountzos, and X. Sui. The Tao of Parallelism in Algorithms. In *Programming Language Design and Implementation (PLDI)*, 2011.

[23] S. Plimpton. Fast Parallel Algorithms for Short-Range Molecular Dynamics. *Journal of Computational Physics*, 117(1):1 – 19, 1995.

[24] K. Schloegel, G. Karypis, and V. Kumar. A Unified Algorithm for Load-Balancing Adaptive Scientific Simulations. In *SC*, 2000.

[25] K. Schloegel, G. Karypis, and V. Kumar. Parallel Multilevel Algorithms for Multi-Constraint Graph Partitioning. In *Intl. Euro-Par Conf. on Parallel Processing*, 2000.

[26] J. P. Singh, C. Holt, J. L. Hennessy, and A. Gupta. A Parallel Adaptive Fast Multipole Method. In *SC*, 1993.

[27] C. D. Snow, E. J. Sorin, Y. M. Rhee, and V. S. Pande. How Well Can Simulation Predict Protein Folding Kinetics and Thermodynamics? *Annual Review of Biophysics and Biomolecular Structure*, 34(1):43–69, 2005.

[28] F. Streitz, J. Glosli, M. Patel, B. Chan, R. Yates, B. de Supinski, J. Sexton, and J. Gunnels. Simulating Solidification in Metals at High Pressure: The Drive to Petascale Computing. *Journal of Physics: Conference Series*, 46:254–267, 2006.

[29] H. Sundar, R. S. Sampath, and G. Biros. Bottom-Up Construction and 2: 1 Balance Refinement of Linear Octrees in Parallel. *SIAM Journal on Scientific Computing*, 30(5):2675–2708, 2008.

[30] S. Teng. Provably Good Partitioning and Load Balancing Algorithms for Parallel Adaptive N-Body Simulation. *SIAM Journal on Scientific Computing*, 19(2):635–656, 1998.

[31] K. S. Thorne. Multipole Expansions of Gravitational Radiation. *Reviews of Modern Physics*, 52:299–340, 1980.

[32] C. Walshaw and M. Cross. Parallel Optimization Algorithms for Multilevel Mesh Partitioning. *Parallel Computing*, 2000.

[33] C. Walshaw, M. Cross, and M. G. Everett. Parallel Dynamic Graph Partitioning for Adaptive Unstructured Meshes. *Journal of Parallel and Distributed Computing*, 47(2), 1997.

[34] M. S. Warren and J. K. Salmon. Astrophysical N-Body Simulations Using Hierarchical Tree Data Structures. In *SC*, 1992.

[35] M. S. Warren and J. K. Salmon. A Parallel Hashed Oct-Tree N-Body Algorithm. In *SC*, 1993.

[36] M. Winkel, R. Speck, H. Hübner, L. Arnold, R. Krause, and P. Gibbon. A Massively Parallel, Multi-Disciplinary Barnes-Hut Tree Code for Extreme-Scale N-Body Simulations. *Computer Physics Communications*, 183(4):880–889, 2012.

[37] A. M. Wissink, D. Hysom, and R. D. Hornung. Enhancing Scalability of Parallel Structured AMR Calculations. In *Intl. Conf. on Supercomputing (ICS)*, 2003.

21st Century Computer Architecture Keynote at 2014 International Conference on Supercomputing (ICS)

Mark D. Hill

Computer Sciences Department
University of Wisconsin-Madison
markhill@cs.wisc.edu

Abstract

This talk has two parts. The first part will discuss possible directions for computer architecture research, including architecture as infrastructure, energy first, impact of new technologies, and cross-layer opportunities. This part is based on a 2012 Computing Community Consortium (CCC) whitepaper effort led by Hill, as well as other recent National Academy and ISAT studies. See: http://cra.org/ccc/docs/init/21stcenturyarchitecturewhitepaper.pdf

The second part of the talk will discuss examples of cross-layer research advocated in the first part. First, our analysis shows that many "big-memory" server workloads, such as databases, in-memory caches, and graph analytics, pay a high cost for page-based virtual memory: up to 50% of execution time wasted. Via small changes to the operating system (Linux) and hardware (x86-64 MMU), this work reduces execution time these workloads waste to less than 0.5%. The key idea is to map part of a process's linear virtual address space with a new incarnation of segmentation, while providing compatibility by mapping the rest of the virtual address space with paging. Second, we will briefly discuss memory consistency models for graphic processing units (GPUs) and other accelerators that support synchronization on a subset of threads called "scopes."

Categories and Subject Descriptors

C. [Computer Systems Organization], D. [Software].

General Terms

Algorithms, Measurement, Performance, Design, Economics, Reliability, Security, Languages, Verification.

Keywords

Computer systems; architecture; programming methods; performance; energy; new technology.

Biography

Mark D. Hill (http://www.cs.wisc.edu/~markhill) is the Gene M. Amdahl Professor of Computer Sciences and Electrical & Computer Engineering at the University of Wisconsin--Madison, where he also co-leads the Wisconsin Multifacet project. His research interests include parallel computer system design, memory system design, computer simulation, and transactional memory. He earned a PhD from University of California, Berkeley. He is an ACM Fellow, a Fellow of the IEEE, co-inventor on 30+ patents, and ACM SIGARCH Distinguished Service Award recipient. His accomplishments include teaching more than 1000 students, having 40 Ph.D. progeny so far, developing the 3C cache miss taxonomy (compulsory, capacity, and conflict), and co-developing "sequential consistency for data-race free" that serves as a foundation of the C++ and Java memory models.

ICS'14, June 10-13, 2014, Muenchen, Germany.
ACM 978-1-4503-2642-1/14/06.
http://dx.doi.org/10.1145/2597652.2597687

MT-MPI: Multithreaded MPI for Many-Core Environments

Min Si
University of Tokyo, Tokyo, Japan
msi@il.is.s.u-tokyo.ac.jp

Antonio J. Peña
Argonne National Laboratory, USA
apenya@mcs.anl.gov

Pavan Balaji
Argonne National Laboratory, USA
balaji@mcs.anl.gov

Masamichi Takagi
NEC Corporation, Kawasaki, Japan
m-takagi@ab.jp.nec.com

Yutaka Ishikawa
University of Tokyo, Tokyo, Japan
ishikawa@is.s.u-tokyo.ac.jp

ABSTRACT

Many-core architectures, such as the Intel Xeon Phi, provide dozens of cores and hundreds of hardware threads. To utilize such architectures, application programmers are increasingly looking at hybrid programming models, where multiple threads interact with the MPI library (frequently called "MPI+X" models). A common mode of operation for such applications uses multiple threads to parallelize the computation, while one of the threads also issues MPI operations (i.e., MPI FUNNELED or SERIALIZED thread-safety mode). In MPI+OpenMP applications, this is achieved, for example, by placing MPI calls in OpenMP critical sections or outside the OpenMP parallel regions. However, such a model often means that the OpenMP threads are active only during the parallel computation phase and idle during the MPI calls, resulting in wasted computational resources. In this paper, we present MT-MPI, an internally multithreaded MPI implementation that transparently coordinates with the threading runtime system to share idle threads with the application. It is designed in the context of OpenMP and requires modifications to both the MPI implementation and the OpenMP runtime in order to share appropriate information between them. We demonstrate the benefit of such internal parallelism for various aspects of MPI processing, including derived datatype communication, shared-memory communication, and network I/O operations.

Categories and Subject Descriptors: D.4 [Communications Management]: Message sending

Keywords: MPI; OpenMP; hybrid MPI + OpenMP; threads; many-core; Xeon Phi;

1. INTRODUCTION

Although multicore processor chips are the norm today, architectures such as the Intel Xeon Phi take such chips to a new level of parallelism, with dozens of cores and hundreds of hardware threads. With the number of processing cores increasing at a faster rate than are other resources in the system (e.g., memory), application programmers are looking at hybrid programming models, comprising a mixture of processes and threads, that allow resources on a node to be shared between the different threads of a process. In such models, one or more threads utilize a distributed-memory programming system, such as MPI, for their data communication. The most prominent of the threading models used in scientific computing today is OpenMP [5]. In OpenMP, the application developer annotates the code with information on which statements need to be parallelized by the compiler and the associated runtime system. The compiler, in turn, translates these annotations into semantic information that the runtime system can use to schedule the computational work units on multiple threads for parallel execution.

A common mode of operation for hybrid MPI+OpenMP applications involves using multiple threads to parallelize the computation, while one of the threads issues MPI operations (i.e., MPI FUNNELED or SERIALIZED thread-safety mode). This is achieved, for example, by placing MPI calls in OpenMP critical sections or outside the OpenMP parallel regions. However, such a model often means that the OpenMP threads are active only in the computation phase and idle during MPI calls, resulting in wasted computational resources. These idle threads translate to underutilized hardware resources on massively parallel architectures.

In this paper, we present MT-MPI, an internally multithreaded MPI implementation that transparently coordinates with the threading runtime system to share idle threads with the application. We designed MT-MPI in the context of OpenMP, which serves as a common threading runtime system for the application and MPI. MT-MPI employs application idle threads to boost MPI communication and data-processing performance and increases resource utilization. While the proposed techniques are generally applicable to most many-core architectures, in this paper we focus on Intel Xeon Phi as the architectural testbed (in "native mode," where applications are executed directly on the coprocessor).

To demonstrate the performance benefits of the proposed approach, we modified the Intel OpenMP runtime (http://www.openmprtl.org) and the MPICH implementation of MPI (http://www.mpich.org). Specifically, we modified the MPI implementation to parallelize its internal processing using a potentially nested OpenMP parallel instantiation (i.e., one OpenMP parallel block inside another). We studied new algorithms for various internal processing steps within MPI that are more "parallelism friendly" for OpenMP to use. In theory, such a model would allow both the application and the MPI implementation to expose their parallelism requirements to the OpenMP runtime, which in turn can schedule

ACM acknowledges that this contribution was authored or co-authored by an employee, contractor or affiliate of the United States government. As such, the Government retains a nonexclusive, royalty-free right to publish or reproduce this article, or to allow others to do so, for Government purposes only.

ICS'14, June 10–13 2014, Munich, Germany.

them on the available computational resources. In practice, however, this has multiple challenges:

1. The modified algorithms for internal MPI processing, while efficient for OpenMP parallelism, are in some cases not as efficient for sequential processing. Consequently, they can improve performance only when sufficient OpenMP parallelism is available. However, the actual number of threads that will be available at runtime is unknown. Depending on the application's usage of threads, this can vary from none to all threads being available to MPI for processing. Thus, if not designed carefully, the algorithms can perform worse than the traditional sequential implementation of MPI.

2. Unfortunately, the current implementation of the Intel OpenMP runtime does not schedule work units from nested OpenMP parallel regions efficiently. It simply creates new pthreads for each nested parallel block and allows the operating system to schedule them on the available cores. This results in creating more threads than the available cores, and degrading performance.

To work around these limitations, we modified the Intel OpenMP runtime to expose information about the idle threads to the MPI implementation. The MPI implementation uses this information to schedule its parallelization only when enough idle resources were available. Furthermore, such information allows the MPI implementation to selectively choose different algorithms that trade off between parallelism and sequential execution in order to achieve the best performance in all cases.

We present our parallelization designs for three different parts within the MPI implementation: (1) packing and unpacking stages involved in derived datatype processing and communication, (2) shared-memory data movement in intranode communication, and (3) network I/O operations on InfiniBand. We also present a thorough experimental evaluation, validation, and analysis using a variety of micro- and macrokernels, including 3D halo exchanges, NAS MG benchmark, and the Graph500 benchmark [11].

2. BACKGROUND

In this section we provide some details about the Intel Xeon Phi architecture and the different threading modes defined by MPI for multithreaded environments.

2.1 Intel Xeon Phi Architecture

The Intel Xeon Phi architecture features a large number of CPU cores inside a single chip. The Xeon Phi cards run their own Linux-based operating system and can launch full operating system processes. In the native mode, system calls that cannot be handled directly on the Xeon Phi card are transparently forwarded to the host processor, which executes them and sends the result back to the issuing process. Although these devices also offer the possibility of running in *offload mode*, following a GPU-like approach, this mode is not considered in our research because it does not allow the coprocessors to run hybrid MPI + OpenMP applications.

When MPI processes are launched on a combination of multiple nodes and adapters, these processes internally communicate with each other using a number of mechanisms. Processes on the same Xeon Phi card communicate with each other using shared memory. Processes on the same node communicate using the PCIe peer-to-peer capabilities.

When communicating outside the node, for some networks such as InfiniBand, communication is performed directly without host intervention through the PCIe root complex.

The first generation of the product released to the public, code-named Knights Corner [4], features a minimum of 60 simple cores each capable of 4 hardware threads, providing a total of 240 hardware threads per coprocessor. The card is equipped with 8 GB of GDDR5 RAM. One difference between this architecture and GPU architectures is the fully private and coherent cache provided to each processing unit: 32 KB instruction + 32 KB data L1, and 512 KB L2 (unified), offering high data bandwidth. Further details on the Intel Xeon Phi architecture can be found in [9, 4].

2.2 Hybrid Programming Models

The MPI standard provides four levels of thread safety.

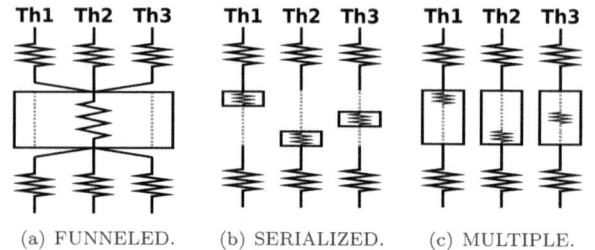

(a) FUNNELED.   (b) SERIALIZED.   (c) MULTIPLE.

Figure 1: Threading modes in MPI. A line represents a thread; the zigzag part represents an active thread in an OpenMP region; the straight part represents a thread outside an OpenMP region; the dotted part represents an idle thread in an OpenMP region; the boxes represent MPI calls.

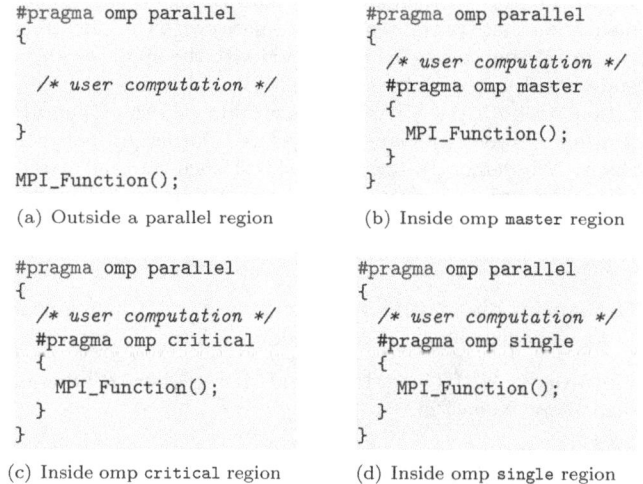

```
#pragma omp parallel
{

    /* user computation */

}

MPI_Function();
```
(a) Outside a parallel region

```
#pragma omp parallel
{
    /* user computation */
    #pragma omp master
    {
        MPI_Function();
    }
}
```
(b) Inside omp master region

```
#pragma omp parallel
{
    /* user computation */
    #pragma omp critical
    {
        MPI_Function();
    }
}
```
(c) Inside omp critical region

```
#pragma omp parallel
{
    /* user computation */
    #pragma omp single
    {
        MPI_Function();
    }
}
```
(d) Inside omp single region

Figure 2: Different use cases in hybrid MPI+OpenMP.

MPI_THREAD_SINGLE. In this mode, a single thread exists in the system. This model is commonly referred to as the MPI-only model, where a bunch of MPI processes communicate with each other and no threads are involved.

MPI_THREAD_FUNNELED. In this mode, multiple threads can exist, but only the master thread (the one that initialized MPI) is allowed to make MPI calls. Different threads can parallelize computational phases, but all MPI communication has to be funneled through the main thread (see Figure 1(a)). In typical OpenMP environments, this involves making MPI calls either outside the OpenMP parallel region (Figure 2(a)) or within OpenMP master regions (Figure 2(b)).

MPI_THREAD_SERIALIZED. In this mode, multiple threads can exist, and any thread can make MPI calls but only one thread at a time. Different threads can parallelize computational phases, but the threads need to synchronize in order to serialize their MPI calls (Figure 1(b)). In typical OpenMP environments, this involves making MPI calls within OpenMP critical regions (Figure 2(c)) or single regions (Figure 2(d)).

MPI_THREAD_MULTIPLE. In this mode, multiple threads can exist, and any thread can make MPI calls at any time (Figure 1(c)). The MPI implementation is responsible for using appropriate synchronization to protect accesses to shared internal data structures.

In this paper we focus on FUNNELED/SERIALIZED modes.

3. DESIGN AND IMPLEMENTATION

In this section we describe the design of MT-MPI, including modifications to the MPICH implementation of MPI (v3.0.4) and the Intel OpenMP runtime (version 20130412).

3.1 OpenMP Runtime

As described in Section 1, for MPI to share OpenMP parallelism with the application, two challenges need to be addressed. The first is the different MPI internal algorithms that trade off between parallelism and faster sequential execution. The second is the behavior of nested parallel regions in current OpenMP implementations, including that of the Intel OpenMP runtime that is used on Xeon Phi architectures. Specifically, the OpenMP runtime creates new pthreads for each nested OpenMP region, thus creating more threads than the available cores and degrading performance.

To handle these issues, we modified the Intel OpenMP runtime to expose the number of idle threads to the MPI implementation. The idea is for the OpenMP runtime system to track how many threads are being used by the application vs. how many threads are idle (e.g., because they are in an OpenMP barrier or outside an OpenMP parallel region). Then, the OpenMP runtime can provide this information through a new runtime function. The expectation in this model is that MPI could query for the number of idle threads and use this information to (1) choose the most efficient internal parallelization algorithms and (2) use only as many threads in the nested OpenMP region as there are idle cores, by explicitly guiding the number of threads in OpenMP (using the `num_threads` clause in OpenMP).

Arguably, the second challenge described above (additional pthreads created in nested OpenMP regions) is an issue only with the current implementation of the Intel OpenMP runtime. An alternative OpenMP runtime that internally uses user-level threads (e.g., [12]) might not face this challenge. However, given that most OpenMP implementations today use pthreads internally and that Intel OpenMP is the only formally supported OpenMP implementation on the Xeon Phi architecture, we consider this to be a real problem that needs to be addressed.

3.1.1 Exposing Idle Threads

To expose the number of idle threads in OpenMP, we need to understand the status of threads in the following cases.

MPI call made outside the OpenMP parallel regions (Figure 2(a)). In this case, all threads except the main thread are idle (often equal to `OMP_NUM_THREADS`). Thus, we

expect MPI to be able to benefit from a large number of idle threads.

MPI call made in an OpenMP single region (Figure 2(d)). OpenMP single regions provide an implicit barrier on exit. Thus, we can ideally expect threads to be available "soon" if the number of idle threads is queried within an OpenMP single region. In practice, however, not all threads might have reached the barrier yet, for example, because there is some skew between the threads or because they are working on a user computation. Thus, the number of idle threads available can vary anywhere between zero and the maximum number of threads. We modified the OpenMP runtime to track each thread in order to return the actual number of idle threads. In this case, the amount of parallelism available to MPI is unknown in the general case. However, for OpenMP parallel regions where the work shared between threads is mostly balanced and threads are reasonably synchronized, the number of idle threads is expected to be close to the maximum number of threads.

MPI call made in an OpenMP master region or single region with a nowait clause (Figure 2(b)). This case is similar to the previous case (single region) with the primary difference that there is no implied barrier at the end of such a region. Hence, there is no natural synchronization point for the threads. Nevertheless, depending on how the application is written, it is possible to have an external synchronization point (such as a user-specified OpenMP barrier) that would cause more idle threads to be available. Consequently, we use a similar solution here as in the previous case, that is, to track the number of idle threads. In practice, however, we do not expect too many idle threads to be available for MPI to use in this case.

MPI call made in an OpenMP critical region (Figure 2(c)). OpenMP critical regions force some synchronization between threads because only one thread can enter a critical region at a time. While this is not quite an implicit barrier, its behavior with respect to the availability of threads can be similar to that of an OpenMP single region. Specifically, when the first thread enters the OpenMP critical region, the remaining threads can be ideally expected to be idle "soon." As discussed earlier, this is not necessarily true if the other threads are busy with the user computation or are skewed, but it can give a reasonable model for us to consider. When the second thread enters the OpenMP critical region, the first thread is no longer expected to be idle because it has already finished executing its critical region. Similarly, when the last thread enters the critical region, none of the remaining threads are expected to be idle because they have all finished executing their critical regions. As in the previous cases, we track the number of idle threads inside the OpenMP runtime, although we expect that the number of idle threads would be high for the first few threads entering the critical section and low for the last few threads.

In some of the cases described above (e.g., single region with nowait), utilizing the idle threads can be risky because their status can change at any time. For example, they might have been idle because they were in an unrelated critical section that has now completed. This would cause those idle threads to become active again, degrading performance. In our implementation, we distinguish how many threads are "guaranteed to be idle" and how many are "temporarily available at the current time." To understand this distinction, we need to look into when a thread can be idle. There are two cases when a thread can be idle: (1) if it is waiting in a barrier waiting for other threads in the team to arrive or (2) if it is outside a critical section waiting to enter it.

A thread that is in a barrier is guaranteed to be idle till all other threads in that team reach the barrier. Thus, when a thread in that team queries for the number of guaranteed idle threads, all the threads that are waiting in the barrier will contribute to the returned value. Waiting to enter a critical section is a bit more tricky in that a thread is guaranteed to wait only till the thread that is already in the critical section does not exit the critical section. Thus, if the thread that is already in the critical section queries for the number of guaranteed idle threads, the threads waiting to enter the critical section will contribute to the returned value. For all other threads, the threads waiting to enter the critical section will not contribute to the guaranteed idle threads but will contribute to the temporarily available threads.

Thus, the following semantics hold true for the number of guaranteed idle threads:

1. It is thread-specific. At a given point of time, depending on which thread is querying for the information, the returned value might be different (it can increase or decrease).

2. It is OpenMP-region specific. If the querying thread enters a new OpenMP region (e.g., critical or single) or exits it, the returned value might be different (it can increase or decrease).

3. It is time-specific. At two different points of time the returned value might be different (e.g., if more threads reached a barrier). However, if the same thread queries for the value and it is in the same OpenMP region, the value can only increase, not decrease.

We modified the OpenMP runtime to keep track of which type of OpenMP region each thread is in, in order to return both the guaranteed number of idle threads and the number of temporarily idle threads. We note that our implementation treats a thread as idle only when it is not engaged in any OpenMP activity, including OpenMP parallel loops and OpenMP tasks. We also note that in our implementation the performance overhead associated with tracking whether a thread is actively being used by the OpenMP runtime is too small to be observed and hence is not demonstrated in this paper.

3.1.2 Thread Scheduling for Nested Parallelism

For well-balanced OpenMP parallel loops with little to no skew, thread synchronizations such as barriers are often short-lived because threads tend to arrive at the barrier at approximately the same time. Thus, when a thread arrives at a barrier, if it is put to sleep while waiting for the other threads to arrive, only to be woken up in a short amount of time, performance is degraded because of the cost of waking up threads from a sleep state. To work around this situation, the Intel OpenMP runtime does not put threads to sleep immediately when they reach a barrier. Instead, they spin waiting for other threads to arrive, for a configurable amount of time: KMP_BLOCKTIME. A large value for this variable would mean that threads do not become truly idle for a long time. While this situation is not a concern for regular OpenMP parallel loops, it can degrade performance for nested OpenMP parallel loops since the Intel OpenMP runtime creates more threads than the number of cores in such

cases. Having the primary threads spin for KMP_BLOCKTIME would cause more threads to be active than the number of available cores for that much time.

When MPI calls are outside the application OpenMP parallel region (such as in Figure 2(d)), this is not a concern since MPI would use the same threads as the application in its parallel region. When MPI calls are inside the application parallel region, however, this would require MPI to use a nested OpenMP parallel region. And since the threads that arrived at the barrier would not yield the available cores immediately, this would either require MPI to utilize lesser parallelism by only using the idle cores or cause thread thrashing on the available cores for KMP_BLOCKTIME amount of time. Neither solution is ideal.

In MT-MPI, to be able to employ these resources as soon as possible, we implemented and exposed a new function in the OpenMP runtime: set_fast_yield. This function plays two roles. First, it forces the threads in the current team to skip the active wait during the barrier operation and immediately yield the core. Second, it continuously yields the core using sched_yield calls instead of simply sleeping. We used this approach primarily because of the overhead associated with sleep vs. that of yield. We found that yielding allows us to manage the cores with a much lower overhead (about 30 μs even with 240 threads) compared with sleeping (more than 100 μs even at 16 threads).

We note that (1) our thread scheduling optimization impacts only those threads that are guaranteed to be idle (e.g., threads waiting in an OpenMP barrier); (2) the fast yield setting is performed internally inside the MPI call and reset once the internal parallelism in MPI is complete, so future OpenMP barriers are not affected by it; and (3) the proposed thread scheduling optimization affects only that case when MPI uses nested OpenMP parallelism (e.g., when an MPI function is called in an OpenMP single region) and does not affect the case when the MPI function is called outside the OpenMP parallel region.

3.2 MPI Internal Parallelism

Using the information about the idle threads exposed by our extended OpenMP runtime, the MPI implementation can schedule its internal parallelism efficiently to obtain performance improvements. In this section, we demonstrate the benefit of such internal parallelism for various aspects of the MPI processing, including derived datatype communication, shared-memory communication, and network I/O operations. In our MPI implementation, we utilize only those idle threads that are guaranteed to be available. Although here we do not utilize temporarily available threads, one could envision cases (e.g., short MPI operations) where they could be. In our implementation, when all threads are idle (e.g., when the MPI call is outside the OpenMP parallel region), we do not specify the number of threads to be utilized by OpenMP; instead, we let it manage such parallelism internally. If fewer than the maximum number of threads is idle, however, we direct the amount of thread parallelism to use through the num_threads OpenMP clause.

3.2.1 Derived Datatype Processing

MPI allows applications to describe noncontiguous regions of memory using user-derived datatypes such as *vector*, *indexed*, and *struct*. These derived datatypes can be used to describe arbitrarily complex data layouts to be processed

```
for (i=0; i<count; i++){          #pragma omp parallel for
   *dest++ = *src;                   for (i=0; i<count; i++){
   src += stride;                       dest[i] = src[i * stride];
}                                    }
   (a) Sequential implementation.     (b) Parallel implementation.
```

Figure 3: Sequential and parallel data packing.

by MPI for packing/unpacking data to/from a contiguous buffer (using `MPI_PACK` and `MPI_UNPACK`) or to send/receive data. When communicating using derived datatypes, MPI implementations typically internally pack data into contiguous buffers, communicate these contiguous buffers, and internally unpack them into the recipient buffer. Halo exchanges [19] are a well-known example of communications that are well suited to employ derived datatypes.

The pack and unpack processing stages consist of a set of local memory copies. A typical implementation traverses the derived datatype tree and copies each noncontiguous chunk of data separately. Some implementations of MPI optimize such processing by representing the entire datatype as a stack structure so that it can be iteratively traversed rather than using a recursive traversal [14]. Given that each noncontiguous data chunk is copied to a different location and there are no dependencies among the different data elements, such copies are a good candidate for OpenMP parallelization. Moreover, thanks to the relatively large private caches per core on the Xeon Phi architecture, concurrent accesses to separate memory regions by the different threads are expected to be highly efficient. Therefore, we modified the MPI implementation to parallelize the datatype data copy using OpenMP. We note that only the lowest level of a nested datatype (e.g., a vector of vectors) is parallelized in MT-MPI.

One issue that we found using MT-MPI was an unintended consequence of the compiler vectorization. The original datatype copy code that is used in MPICH is shown in Figure 3(a). While this code works correctly for sequential data copy, it cannot be easily parallelized by using OpenMP because the compiler cannot understand the constant stride of accesses used through all iterations. We therefore modified the code as shown in Figure 3(b). While this new implementation makes it easier for the compiler to understand the computation and thus parallelize it, the implementation also makes it easier for the compiler to vectorize the code. This situation in itself is not a concern. However, the Intel compiler is inefficient in vectorizing strided loops with large stride values when the amount of data copied in each loop is small. Specifically, the compiler does incorrect prefetching in this case, causing additional cache misses and thus losing performance. Consequently, our modification to the code is not always beneficial and can perform worse than the sequential implementation when very few threads are available. To work around this issue, we could either disable vectorization in the parallel implementation or explicitly choose only the parallel approach when a sufficiently large number of threads are available. We chose the latter approach because vectorization is still beneficial in some cases (e.g., when the stride is small or the copy size is large).

We note that the incorrect cache prefetching and additional cache misses that it causes have been experimentally verified, but the results are not shown in this paper because of space restrictions. The issue has also been reported to Intel and has been confirmed by their compiler team. They are expected to fix it in a future release of the compiler.

3.2.2 Shared-Memory Communication

When multiple MPI processes reside on the same node, since each process has a different virtual address space, most MPI implementations, including MPICH, use a pipelined double-copy strategy through shared memory for intranode communication [3]. As shown in Figure 4(a), a shared-memory ring buffer is allocated between the sender and receiver processes and divided into multiple cells; the sender process then copies part of data into an empty cell while the receiver process copies a full cell out.

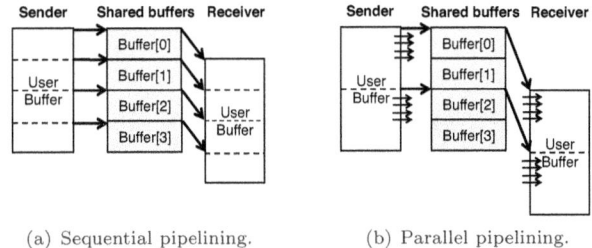

(a) Sequential pipelining.   (b) Parallel pipelining.

Figure 4: Data movement of parallelization and pipelining.

In MT-MPI, we parallelize this copy on both the sender and the receiver side using the available idle threads. We implemented this optimization by extending the pipelined double-copy strategy used within MPICH. As shown in Figure 4(b), in our approach we reserve multiple contiguous available cells and concurrently copy data from the user buffer to these cells on the sender side and from the cells to the user buffer on the receiver side. For messages larger than what can be held in the reserved cells, additional pipelining is used, similar to the sequential case. Compared with the sequential pipelining algorithm, however, the parallel algorithm can degrade performance in the following cases.

Small messages. When the message size is small, there is not enough work in MPI to be parallelized. In such cases, the thread management and synchronization within OpenMP are more expensive than the sequential copy mechanism already used in MPICH. Thus, in this case we do not expect any performance benefit from parallelization.

Large messages but few idle threads. In our parallel implementation, we reserve as many shared-memory cells as possible and parallelize the copy using all of the available idle threads. Thus the receiver process now has to wait until data is filled into all of the reserved cells before it can start its data copy out of shared memory. This approach, in essence, increases the pipeline unit to a much larger size. Thus, while parallelism can improve the performance of each memory copy operation, it can also hurt the data copy pipeline. We note that we cannot simply reduce the size of each shared-memory cell or the maximum number of cells reserved to work around this issue because that would reduce the amount of work done by each thread, thus causing the thread management overhead to dominate. This trend is illustrated in Figure 5. Specifically, compared with sequential pipelining (Figure 5(a)), when the number of threads available to MPI is small, the parallel copy does not improve performance much but delays the receiver process from getting started with its copy (Figure 5(b)). On the other hand, when a large number of threads are available to MPI, the parallel copy is significantly faster, thus balancing the loss of performance due to the reduced pipelining (Figure 5(c)).

(a) Sequential pipelining.

(b) Poor parallelism.

(c) Strong parallelism.

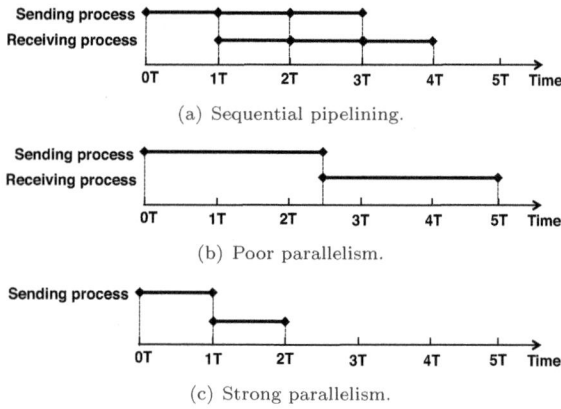

Figure 5: Sequential pipelining vs. parallel data copy.

Few shared-memory cells. The amount of data to be copied is decided not just on the number of available threads but also on the number of available shared-memory cells. Specifically, during the communication process, some cells might be in use for transferring previous messages (or previous parts of the same message). In such cases, there is not enough work to be parallelized, and hence the thread management would add too much overhead to justify the performance improvement through parallelization.

In summary, parallelism would improve performance only when (1) the message size is not too small ($\geq$ 64 Kbytes), (2) the number of threads is not too few ($\geq$ 8), and (3) the total size of free cells is not too small ($\geq$ 64 Kbytes). In our implementation, we utilize the parallel shared-memory communication algorithm only when all three conditions are met; otherwise we fall back to the original sequential algorithm. We note that the above-mentioned thresholds are empirically evaluated on our test platform and must be tuned for different platforms.

3.2.3 Optimizations for the InfiniBand Network

Several MPI implementations are optimized for a variety of networks through a layered software architecture where one of the layers provides network-specific functionality. In MPICH, this layer is called the `netmod layer`. Multiple netmod implementations exist for MPICH over InfiniBand (IB), with more-or-less similar functionality and performance. In this paper we utilize the implementation described in [17].

An MPI implementation utilizing IB needs to create and manage a number of objects, including contexts, protection domains (PDs), queue pairs (QPs), and completion queues (CQs). A process can create one or more IB contexts, each of which maintains a collection of state information associated with the communication. Each context can contain one or more PDs, each of which defines the protection semantics of memory and other objects used by the program, for example to allow different connections access to different sets of memory regions. Within a PD, the program can create one or more QPs, each of which consists of a send queue and a receive queue. A QP is used to communicate between a pair of processes. A PD can also have one or more CQs, each of which is used to check for the completion of communication operations on one or more QPs. IB also provides shared queues for better memory management, but for simplicity we do not describe them here.

The IB software stack [13] is thread-safe. When multiple threads access the same QP or CQ, it internally uses mutexes to maintain state consistency. Such state consistency is expensive, however, and can degrade performance. Therefore, in our approach we try to avoid such usage and instead have different threads manage different QPs in order to maximize performance. Even with this approach some shared data structures still need to be protected. To understand how much performance improvement MPI can gain by parallelizing the posting of network operations, we studied how much potential parallelism there is in the IB stack that can theoretically be exploited. We modified the `ib_write_bw` benchmark from the OpenFabrics Enterprise Distribution (OFED) package [13] to measure the multithreaded point-to-point IB RDMA write bandwidth between two Intel Xeon Phi coprocessors on different nodes. We define three parallelism levels:

IB contexts. Each process has 64 IB contexts, and each context has one QP and one CQ. Each thread handles operations on a different context, CQ and QP.

QPs and CQs. Each process has a single IB context with 64 QPs and 64 CQs. Each CQ is dedicated to a different QP. Each thread handles operations on different QPs and CQs, but they all share the same context.

QPs only. Each process has a single IB context with 64 QPs and one shared CQ. Each thread handles operations on different QPs, but they all share the same context and CQ.

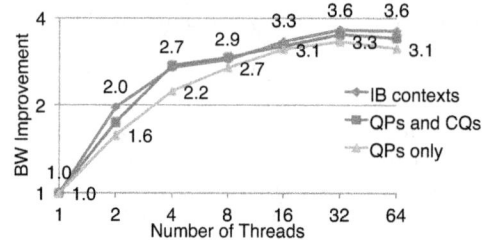

Figure 6: Small (64-byte) IB RDMA write bandwidth.

Figure 6 compares the communication bandwidth of small messages (64 bytes) for the cited parallelism levels. We make two primary observations from the figure. The first is that the performance improvement with increasing threads is higher when the number of shared resources is less. For example, when each thread has a separate context (`IB contexts`), with increasing threads, the parallel performance is 3.6-fold higher than the sequential performance. But when the context and the CQ are shared by all threads (`QPs only`), the parallel performance is only 3.1-fold higher than the sequential performance. This result is expected because more sharing typically means more critical sections and hence more serialization. The second observation is that the maximum parallelism that the IB-stack can provide is 3.6-fold when all resources are dedicated per thread and 3.1-fold when the context and CQ are shared between all the threads. Most MPI implementations are increasingly moving toward more shared resources (i.e., closer to `QPs only`) in order to manage the per-process resource usage. Thus, in current MPI implementations, 3.1-fold improvement is the maximum benefit that we can expect even in the ideal case.

In MT-MPI, each QP is managed by a single thread; multiple QPs might be managed by a single thread, but a single QP is never managed by multiple threads. This strategy minimizes the mutexes that the IB stack needs to do. We also ensure that the number of threads used for parallelism is never more than the number of QPs, in order to minimize thread synchronization overheads.

We note that in the MPICH IB netmod, small-message communication employs temporary buffers that are preregistered with the network. Since the network can communicate only to/from preregistered buffers, user data needs to be copied into these buffers on the sender side and out of these buffers on the receiver side. Each connection uses a separate QP and preregistered buffers, so the data copies on the send and receive side are also part of the parallelism and are executed concurrently by different threads.

Despite the potential for parallelism on many-core architectures, several factors limit the practical parallelism achievable in the MPI implementation. For example, in order to achieve the best parallelism, the MPI implementation can benefit from a large number of operations to be issued to the network, which can be evenly shared between the available threads. However, such ideal conditions are hampered by several practical restrictions in current IB network stacks and applications. For example, the number of operations that can be issued to a QP or to the shared CQ is limited. While the QP or CQ can be configured to allow for a large number of operations, such configuration causes (sometimes large) performance degradation due to the internal bookkeeping associated with these data structures within the IB stack. Consequently, the MPICH IB netmod configures this limit to 1,024 for QPs and 32,768 for CQs, thus forcing the maximum number of network operations each thread can post to 1,024 and the maximum number of network operations posted across all threads to 32,768, before thread synchronization is needed. A similar parallelism-limiting factor is the number of preregistered buffers available at the sender and receiver side.

Still another parallelism constraint comes from the application characteristics. Specifically, since in MT-MPI we exploit parallelism at the granularity of a QP, for ideal parallelism we need the same amount of work per QP—a process should have close to uniform communication with its peer processes. In practice, however, this assumption does not hold; indeed, the amount of communication can vary dramatically between different processes, thus limiting the available parallelism.

4. EVALUATION AND ANALYSIS

In this section, we evaluate the various techniques designed within MT-MPI. All our experiments are executed on the Stampede supercomputer at the Texas Advanced Computing Center (https://www.tacc.utexas.edu/stampede/). Stampede consists of 6400 Dell Zeus C8220z compute nodes, each with two Xeon E5-2680 processors and 32 GB RAM, and an Intel Xeon Phi SE10P coprocessor with 8 GB of onboard RAM connected by an x16 PCIe 2.0 interconnect. The nodes are interconnected by a Mellanox FDR InfiniBand network. All our experiments are executed on the Xeon Phi coprocessor, with every MPI process running on a separate coprocessor.

4.1 Derived Datatype Processing

In this section, we describe three types of experiments that stress derived datatype processing to various degrees: (1) derived datatype packing performance, (2) halo data exchange with derived datatypes, and (3) the NAS multigrid benchmark.

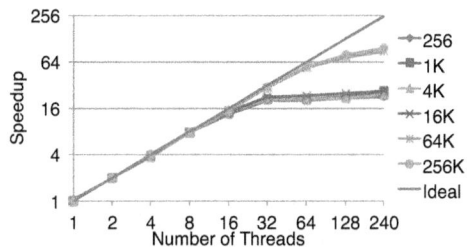

(a) Packing the top surface with varying Z dimension.

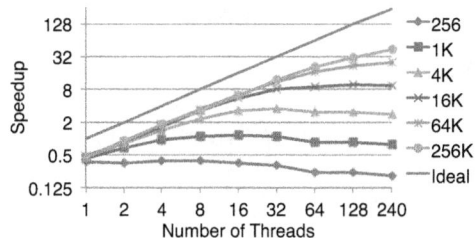

(b) Packing the left surface with varying Y dimension.

Figure 7: Performance of parallel 3D packing.

4.1.1 Derived Datatype Packing

In our experiments with derived datatype packing (using `MPI_PACK`), we utilized a 3D matrix of doubles, with the X dimension as the leading dimension. The matrix volume was fixed at 1 GB, so increasing one dimension would reduce another. Our experiments involved packing different 2D planes of the 3D matrix.

Figure 7(a) shows the performance improvement while packing the top surface (X-Z plane). A vector datatype is utilized in this case, with a block length equal to the length of the X dimension and stride equal to the area of the X-Y plane; the Z dimension indicates the vector count. In our experiment, the Y dimension was fixed to 2 doubles, and the Z dimension varied as indicated on the graph legend (X dimension was varied to maintain the matrix volume). As can be seen in the figure, MT-MPI gets a reasonably good speedup with increasing number of threads, achieving a 96-fold improvement compared with the original sequential version when all 240 threads are used. A larger Z dimension provides better speedup because that leads to a larger iteration count for the contiguous copies and hence more parallelism that can be exploited by MT-MPI.

Figure 7(b) shows the performance improvement while packing the left surface (Y-Z plane). A two-level datatype comprising a vector of vectors is utilized in this experiment. The X dimension was fixed to 2 doubles, and the Y dimension varied as indicated on the graph legend (the Z dimension was varied to maintain the matrix volume). As shown in the figure, MT-MPI still achieves a relatively good speedup compared with the sequential version (42-fold), although less than what it achieved while packing the top surface. This reduction in performance is because the lowest-level vector datatype always has a block length of one double and a count equal to the Y dimension. This restricts the amount of work that is done within each iteration of the contiguous data copy operation and consequently limits the work done by each thread, especially when the number of iterations (i.e., the Y dimension) is small. Furthermore, when the Y dimension is small, the parallel version is worse than the original sequential version (speedup is less than 1) because of the compiler's

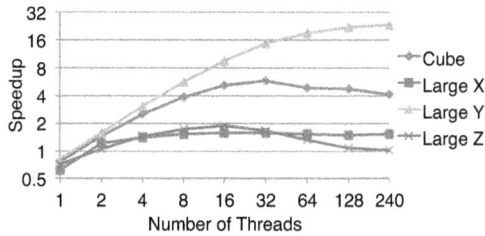

Figure 8: 3D internode halo exchange using 64 MPI processes.

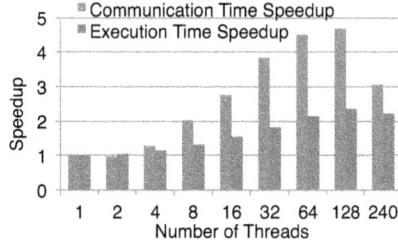

Figure 9: Hybrid MPI+OpenMP NAS MG Class E using 64 MPI processes.

inefficiency in cache prefetching for vectorized code, as described in Section 3.2.1.

4.1.2 Halo Exchange of Data

In our second set of experiments, we measured the performance of 3D halo exchanges of data as used in stencil computations. Both the data and the processes are partitioned into a 3D space. Each process communicates with its neighboring processes with which it shares a plane. For our experiments we define the following four dimension shapes for the local data on each process: (1) Cube, with dimensions $512 \times 512 \times 512$ (doubles); (2) Large X, with dimensions $16K \times 128 \times 64$; (3) Large Y, with dimensions $64 \times 16K \times 128$; and (4) Large Z, with dimensions $64 \times 128 \times 16K$. The MPI processes are evenly distributed in all dimensions.

Figure 8 shows the performance improvement achieved by MT-MPI compared with the sequential version when using 64 MPI processes. Large Y performs much better than the others, delivering a 23-fold speedup with 240 threads. To understand this behavior, we profiled the communication time for the different dimensions. The halo benchmark sends data in all dimensions simultaneously, so it is hard to profile how much time each dimension takes. Therefore, for profiling purposes, we modified it to serialize communication in one dimension at a time, and we observed that communication along the Y-Z dimension takes 85% of the time. While this is obviously not entirely indicative of the true halo benchmark that sends data in all dimensions simultaneously, it does give us some idea of the communication cost.

As demonstrated in Figure 7(b), a large Y dimension helps improve the performance of packing in the Y-Z dimension by providing better parallelism. This results in a large Y impacting the performance of the halo benchmark to the largest extent. With Cube, the Y-dimension is reduced to 512 doubles, thus reducing the speedup to around 5.8-fold as well. With Large X and Large Z, the Y-dimension further reduces to 128 doubles, which in turn reduces the overall speedup to around 1.6-fold and 1.8-fold, respectively.

4.1.3 NAS Multigrid Benchmark

We also evaluated a hybrid MPI+OpenMP version of the NAS Multigrid (MG) kernel [1] . The original MG kernel distributed as a part of the NAS parallel benchmarks does not contain a hybrid MPI+OpenMP version, so we modified the MPI version to (1) parallelize the local computation using OpenMP and (2) employ derived datatype communication instead of manual packing. The MG kernel implements a V-cycle multigrid algorithm to solve a 3D discrete Poisson equation. In every iteration of the V-cycle routine, halo exchanges are performed with various dimension sizes (count of double), from 2 to 514 in class E with 64 MPI processes, and so forth. The communication in all dimensions except the X-Y plane is noncontiguous.

Figure 9 presents the speedup achieved by MT-MPI compared with the original MPICH in class E (X, Y, Z dimension sizes are each 2K) when employing 64 processes. As shown in the figure, MT-MPI helps improve the communication of MG by 4.7-fold, and the overall execution time by 2.2-fold. The speedup in the communication time is still slightly lower than that of the 3D halo exchanges with the Cube shape shown in Figure 8. The reason is that the MG also contains some halo exchanges with very small dimension size whose packing process cannot be parallelized efficiently.

4.2 Shared-Memory Communication

To measure the impact of MT-MPI on intranode shared-memory communication, we evaluated the point-to-point communication benchmarks in the OSU MPI microbenchmark suite version 4.1 (http://mvapich.cse.ohio-state.edu/benchmarks/). In particular, we used the latency, bandwidth, and message rate benchmarks. Both the original MPICH and MT-MPI use an internal shared-memory region of 2 MB, with each cell containing 32 KB.

Figure 10 illustrates the performance of all three benchmarks; the legends in the graph represent different message sizes. We notice that the performance trends of all three benchmarks are similar, with MT-MPI delivering up to a 5-fold performance benefit for message sizes ≥ 1 MB, given enough parallelism. When the number of idle threads is ≤ 4, however, MT-MPI's performance is worse than that of the original MPICH. As discussed in Section 3.2.2, the reason is that MT-MPI loses some of the pipelining capabilities in the original MPICH code in return for thread parallelism. But with a small number of threads, this tradeoff is not beneficial.

Another observation we make in Figure 10 is that the speedup of MT-MPI for message sizes 64 KB and 256 KB is much better than that of other message sizes. This, however, is not because of MT-MPI's superior architecture. Rather, it is because the communication protocol thresholds (i.e., eager vs. rendezvous communication thresholds) in MPICH are tuned for regular Xeon systems, by default, and are too large for the Xeon Phi architecture. We did not change the default configuration of MPICH in order to avoid introducing yet another dimension of variance in the paper. Thus, for 64 KB and 256 KB message sizes, the original MPICH ends up using a suboptimal communication protocol, resulting in MT-MPI's performance falsely appearing to be significantly better as compared to other message sizes.

4.3 InfiniBand Communication Operations

In this section we evaluate the performance benefits achieved by MT-MPI with our modifications to the MPICH IB netmod. We performed two types of experiments: (1) a one-sided communication microbenchmark designed to demon-

(a) Latency. (b) Bandwidth. (c) Message rate.

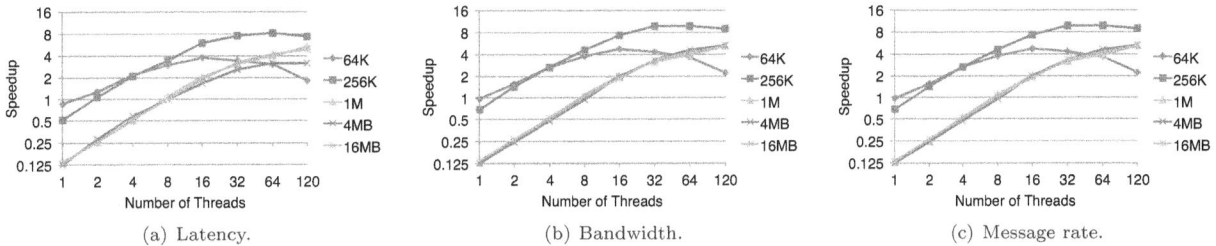

Figure 10: Shared-memory communication performance with varying message size between 2 MPI processes

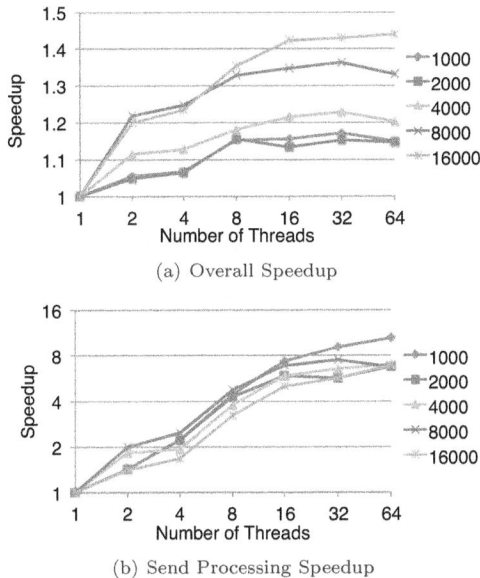

(a) Overall Speedup

(b) Send Processing Speedup

Figure 11: One-sided communication benchmark with IB using 65 MPI processes.

Table 1: Profile of the one-sided communication benchmark.

Nthreads	Execution Time			Speedup	
	Total (s)	SP (s)	SP / Total (%)	Total	SP
1	5.8	2.2	38	1	1
4	4.7	1.3	27	1.2	1.7
16	4.0	0.4	10	1.4	5.0
64	4.0	0.3	8	1.4	6.9

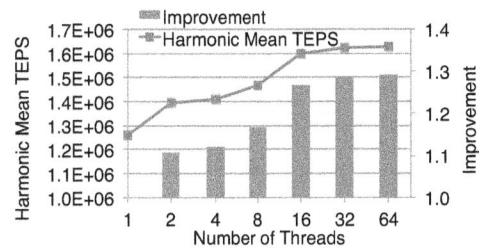

Figure 12: Performance of the Graph500 benchmark using 64 MPI processes.

strate the ideal parallelism that can be obtained within MT-MPI and (2) the one-sided version of Graph500 benchmark [11].

4.3.1 One-Sided Microbenchmark

We designed a microbenchmark in which one MPI process issues many `MPI_PUT` operations to all other processes. Each `MPI_PUT` operation is for 64 bytes. We measured the execution time of the benchmark using 65 MPI processes; thus each process communicates with 64 other processes and internally maintains 64 IB QPs. Figure 11(a) shows the speedup in execution time with MT-MPI compared with the original MPICH. As we increase the number of operations issued from 1,000 to 16,000, MT-MPI delivers an increasing performance benefit, reaching a 1.44-fold speedup when using 64 threads.

This performance benefit, however, is less than the ideal speedup of 3.1-fold that we can get by parallelizing IB communication, as discussed in Section 3.2.3. To understand the reason for this less-than-ideal speedup, we measured the execution time of the netmod send-side communication processing at the root process (SP), which consists only of the copy from the user buffer to a preregistered chunk and the posting of the operations to the IB network. Figure 11(b) shows that the execution time of SP delivers around 8-fold speedup when using 64 threads, which is as expected—we expect around a 3.1-fold speedup due to the parallelization in the posting of network operations, and some additional improvement due to the parallelized memory copy. Table 1

shows the relationship between the time spent in SP and the total execution time when issuing 16,000 operations. Although SP shows the expected performance improvement with MT-MPI, the percentage of time spent in SP is less than 10% when using more than 16 threads. This results in a reduction in the overall performance boost that we achieve.

4.3.2 Graph500 Benchmark

The second benchmark we studied was the Graph500 benchmark [11], which performs a breadth-first vertex-visit operation on large graphs. In particular, we used a scale of 2^{22} and an edge factor of 16 on 64 MPI processes running on different Intel Xeon Phi coprocessors at different nodes. In the one-sided version of the Graph500 benchmark, every process issues many `MPI_Accumulate` operations to the other processes in every breadth-first search iteration.

Figure 12 shows the performance improvement of MT-MPI compared with the original MPICH. MT-MPI delivers a 1.3-fold improvement in the harmonic mean of the traversed edges per second (TEPS) when using 64 threads. As expected, this improvement is on par with the performance improvement we see in the one-sided communication benchmark that we discussed in Section 4.3.1. The slightly smaller speedup compared with the one-sided communication benchmark (which achieves a 1.44-fold speedup) is because the Graph500 benchmark does not uniformly communicate with all peer processes, thus causing some unevenness in MT-MPI's parallelization.

5. RELATED WORK

The hybrid MPI+OpenMP programming model has been extensively used and studied in the past. For instance, Lusk and Chan [10] explored the performance of such a model on a typical Linux cluster, a large-scale system from SiCortex, and an IBM Blue Gene/P system. The authors concluded that some applications performed better with several MPI-only processes on the same node, while others could benefit from the hybridization. While this situation is still true today, an increasing number of applications are moving to hybrid MPI+OpenMP models, not just for performance, but for per-core resource limitations (in particular, memory). Other studies [16] have, on the other hand, reported satisfactory results in porting the finite-difference time-domain algorithm to the hybrid paradigm to adapt it to SMP compute nodes.

Smith and Kent [15] also found that increasing the number of threads decreased the efficiency of the code when implementing the quantum Monte Carlo algorithm on mixed OpenMP/MPI code on an SGI Origin 2000 system. Although this phenomenon was not attributed to the idle-threads issue we address in this paper, it certainly contributes to the reduced efficiency per thread. [18] performed a comprehensive evaluation of multithreaded MPI communications, pointing to the mutually exclusive regions involved in communication as one of the reasons for the suboptimal performance obtained.

Several researchers have also looked at optimizing the MPI implementation in multithreaded environments. For example, the authors of [2, 7, 8] proposed various techniques to minimize locking within the MPI implementation in order to improve the performance of MPI in `MPI_THREAD_MULTIPLE` environments. They presented various techniques to improve performance on traditional Linux clusters as well as the IBM Blue Gene/P systems. The authors in [6] proposed extensions to the MPI standard that would allow the MPI implementation to minimize contention and improve performance in some cases. However, all these optimizations are for `MPI_THREAD_MULTIPLE` applications. A large fraction of today's hybrid MPI applications, however, still use `MPI_THREAD_FUNNELED` and `MPI_THREAD_SERIALIZED` modes, for which these optimizations are not helpful.

6. CONCLUSIONS

In this paper we analyzed the potential benefits of employing idle hardware threads to accelerate MPI processing in hybrid MPI+OpenMP applications on massively parallel many-core architectures. To this end, we modified two widely deployed implementations of these models: the Intel OpenMP runtime and MPICH MPI implementation. We described various optimizations in different parts of MPI implementation, including derived datatype processing, shared-memory communication, and IB network operations. Our experimental evaluation, based on several micro- and macro-kernels, demonstrates considerable performance benefits.

Acknowledgments

This work was financially supported by (1) the CREST project of the Japan Science and Technology Agency (JST) and the National Project of MEXT called Feasibility Study on Advanced and Efficient Latency Core Architecture and (2) the U.S. Department of Energy, Office of Science, Advanced Scientific Computing Research, under Contract DE-AC02-06CH11357. The experimental resources for this paper were provided by the Texas Advanced Supercomputing Center (TACC) on the Stampede supercomputer.

References

[1] D. H. Bailey, E. Barszcz, J. T. Barton, D. S. Browning, R. L. Carter, R. A. Fatoohi, P. O. Frederickson, T. A. Lasinski, H. D. Simon, V. Venkatakrishnan, and S. K. Weeratunga. The NAS Parallel Benchmarks. *The International Journal of Supercomputer Applications*, 1991.

[2] P. Balaji, D. T. Buntinas, D. J. Goodell, W. D. Gropp, and R. S. Thakur. Toward Efficient Support for Multithreaded MPI Communication. In *Euro PVM/MPI*, 2008.

[3] D. Buntinas and G. Mercier. Implementation and Shared-Memory Evaluation of MPICH2 over the Nemesis Communication Subsystem. In *Euro PVM/MPI*, 2006.

[4] G. Chrysos. Intel Xeon Phi Coprocessor - The Architecture. White paper, Intel Corporation, Sept. 2012.

[5] L. Dagum and R. Menon. OpenMP: An Industry Standard API for Shared-Memory Programming. *IEEE Computational Science & Engineering*, 5(1):46–55, 1998.

[6] J. S. Dinan, P. Balaji, D. J. Goodell, D. Miller, M. Snir, and R. S. Thakur. Enabling MPI Interoperability Through Flexible Communication Endpoints. In *Euro MPI*, 2013.

[7] G. Dozsa, S. Kumar, P. Balaji, D. T. Buntinas, D. J. Goodell, W. D. Gropp, J. Ratterman, and R. S. Thakur. Enabling Concurrent Multithreaded MPI Communication on Multicore Petascale Systems. In *Euro MPI*, 2010.

[8] D. J. Goodell, P. Balaji, D. T. Buntinas, G. Dozsa, W. D. Gropp, S. Kumar, B. R. de Supinski, and R. S. Thakur. Minimizing MPI Resource Contention in Multithreaded Multicore Environments. In *IEEE Cluster*, 2010.

[9] Intel Corporation. Many Integrated Core (MIC) Architecture — Advanced. http://www.intel.com/content/www/us/en/architecture-and-technology/many-integrated-core/intel-many-integrated-core-architecture.html, 2013.

[10] E. Lusk and A. Chan. Early Experiments with the OpenMP/MPI Hybrid Programming Model. In *OpenMP in a New Era of Parallelism*, pages 36–47. Springer, 2008.

[11] R. C. Murphy, K. B. Wheeler, B. W. Barrett, and J. A. Ang. Introducing the Graph 500. In *Proceedings of the Cray User's Group Meeting (CUG)*, May 2010.

[12] S. Olivier, A. Porterfield, K. Wheeler, M. Spiegel, and J. Prins. OpenMP Task Scheduling Strategies for Multicore NUMA Systems. *The International Journal of High Performance Computing Applications*, (26(2)):110–124, May 2012.

[13] OpenFabrics Alliance. OpenFabrics Alliance. http://www.openfabrics.org, 2013.

[14] R. Ross and N. Miller. Implementing Fast and Reusable Datatype Processing. In *In EuroPVM/MPI*, pages 404–413, Springer Verlag, 2003.

[15] L. Smith and P. Kent. Development and Performance of a Mixed OpenMP/MPI Quantum Monte Carlo Code. *Concurrency Practice and Experience*, 12(12):1121–1129, 2000.

[16] M. F. Su, I. El-Kady, D. A. Bader, and S.-Y. Lin. A Novel FDTD Application Featuring OpenMP-MPI Hybrid Parallelization. In *International Conference on Parallel Processing (ICPP)*, pages 373–379. IEEE, 2004.

[17] M. Takagi, Y. Nakamura, A. Hori, B. Gerofi, and Y. Ishikawa. Revisiting Rendezvous Protocols in the Context of RDMA-capable Host Channel Adapters and Many-core Processors. In *Euro MPI*, 2013.

[18] R. Thakur and W. Gropp. Test Suite for Evaluating Performance of Multithreaded MPI Communication. *Parallel Computing*, 35(12):608–617, 2009.

[19] A. J. Wallcraft and D. R. Moore. The NRL Layered Ocean Model. *Parallel Computing*, 23(14):2227 – 2242, 1997. Parallel computing in regional weather modeling.

Implementing a Classic:
Zero-copy All-to-all Communication with MPI Datatypes*

| Jesper Larsson Träff | Antoine Rougier | Sascha Hunold |
| traff@par.tuwien.ac.at | rougier@par.tuwien.ac.at | hunold@par.tuwien.ac.at |

Vienna University of Technology (TU Wien)
Faculty of Informatics, Institute of Information Systems
Research Group Parallel Computing
Favoritenstrasse 16/184-5
1040 Vienna, Austria

ABSTRACT

We investigate the use of the derived datatype mechanism of
MPI (the Message-Passing Interface) in the implementation
of the classic all-to-all communication algorithm of Bruck et
al. (1997). Through a series of improvements to the canonical implementation of the algorithm we gradually eliminate
initial and final processor-local data reorganizations, cul-
minating in a *zero-copy* version that contains no explicit,
process-local data movement or copy operations: all necessary data movements are implied by MPI derived datatypes,
and carried out as part of the communication operations.
We furthermore show how the improved algorithm can be
used to solve irregular all-to-all communication problems
(that are not too irregular). The Bruck algorithm serves as a
vehicle to demonstrate descriptive and performance advantages with MPI datatypes in the implementation of complex
algorithms, and discuss shortcomings and inconveniences in
the current MPI datatype mechanism. In particular, we use
and implement three new derived datatypes (bounded vector, circular vector, and bucket) not in MPI that might be
useful in other contexts. We also discuss the role of persistent collectives which are currently not found in MPI for
amortizing type creation (and other) overheads, and implement a persistent variant of the `MPI_Alltoall` collective.

On two small systems we experimentally compare the algorithmic improvements to the Bruck et al. algorithm when
implemented on top of MPI, showing the zero-copy version to perform significantly better than the initial, straightforward implementation. One of our variants has also been
implemented inside `mvapich`, and we show it to perform better than the `mvapich` implementation of the Bruck et al. algorithm for the range of processes and problem sizes where
it is enabled. The persistent version of `MPI_Alltoall` has
no overhead and outperforms all other variants, and in particular improves upon the standard implementation by 50%
to 15% across the full range of problem sizes considered.

Categories and Subject Descriptors

D.1.3 [**Programming techniques**]: Concurrent programming—*Parallel programming*; C.4 [**Performance of Systems**]: Measurement techniques; F.2.2 [**Analysis of algorithms**]: Nonnumerical algorithms and problems—*Routing*

Keywords

All-to-all collective communication; MPI; derived datatypes

1. INTRODUCTION

A now classical algorithm for regular all-to-all collective
communication on fully connected, homogeneous communication networks with a trade-off between number of communication rounds (latency) and communicated data volume (bandwidth) was described in an influential paper on
collective communication by Bruck et al. [1]. This algorithm is well-known in the MPI and collective communication communities, and since long implemented in several
MPI libraries, e.g., `mpich`, OpenMPI, and vendor libraries [7,
9], where it is used for certain ranges of MPI processes and
(smaller) problem sizes.

The communication pattern of the algorithm by Bruck et
al. is inherently non-contiguous. The data elements that
are sent in one communication round have been received
in previous, but non-consecutive rounds, and it is therefore
not possible to organize send and receive operations such
that elements to be sent always form a contiguous sequence.
When the algorithm is implemented, elements will either
have to be communicated directly from/to non-contiguous
segments of memory, or must be reorganized (packed) locally
into contiguous communication buffers.

MPI, the Message-Passing Interface [6], makes it possible to delegate the handling of such non-contiguous data to
the MPI library implementation. MPI's derived datatype
mechanism [6, Chapter 4] facilitates description of arbitrary,
non-contiguous data layouts as derived datatypes to be used
subsequently in communication operations as handles to the

*This work was co-funded by the European Commis-
sion through the EPiGRAM project (grant agreement no.
610598). This work was supported by Austrian FWF
projects "Verifying self-consistent MPI performance guidelines" and "Improving reproducibility of experiments in parallel computing".

data. The algorithm by Bruck et al. (originally implemented with explicit, hand-written packing and unpacking) is an exemplary candidate for the use of MPI derived datatypes. The advantage is a cleaner implementation that separates the algorithmic idea from data reorganization issues that are otherwise handled by customized (manual) packing and unpacking code. Depending on how well the MPI library implements the datatype mechanism and interacts with the communication system, a better performing implementation may be the added benefit (as we shall show).

In this paper we present several such implementations. The small theoretical improvement is the elimination of all process-local reordering steps of the original Bruck et al. algorithm [1], leading to a socalled *zero-copy implementation* in which there are no explicit local copy operations between any communication or intermediate buffers. Data for each communication round are described solely by MPI derived datatypes, and whether data reorganizations (copy-/pack/unpack) are necessary is fully an implementation issue of the MPI library and underlying communication system. The wider significance is the illustration of benefits by using derived datatypes in the implementation of complex algorithms, further in the analysis of shortcomings in the MPI derived datatype specification that lead to descriptive and performance obstacles. We discuss possible extensions that may be of value for a datatype-oriented programming style and thus could be considered in future developments of MPI or other message-passing interfaces. Some have been implemented here, so that their convenience and potential performance impact can be concretely discussed.

In particular, we have implemented the algorithm by Bruck et al. as originally presented [1] using a suitable (new) MPI datatype to implicitly pack and unpack the non-contiguous elements to be sent and received in each communication round (Basic Bruck), an improved algorithm that eliminates the final, post-communication, process local permutation using another (new) derived datatype (Modified Bruck), and finally a version that performs no explicit packing, unpacking or other process local reordering of data (Zero-copy Bruck). The latter variant uses structured, derived datatypes to select the non-consecutive data elements for each communication round from send-, receive- and intermediate buffers, respectively. These variations/improvements to the Bruck et al. algorithm have first been implemented on top of MPI, which allows a fair, differential assessment of the improvements over the original algorithm. The evaluation includes all overheads incurred by creation and destruction of the required MPI derived datatypes. We also measure this overhead in isolation by disabling the actual communication; especially for Zero-copy Bruck overheads are considerable and compromises the implementation for small problems. We also benchmark an implementation in `mvapich` of our modified variant and compare it to the `mvapich` implementation of the standard Bruck et al. algorithm (which uses an MPI indexed datatype). The zero-copy variant has also been implemented as a *persistent collective*, which binds all input parameters in a separate setup operation and thus allows to amortize the type creation and other (algorithm selection) overheads over a number of all-to-all communication operations. Persistent collectives are currently not part of MPI.

It is worth recalling that the Bruck et al. algorithm is designed on the assumption of a homogeneous, fully connected communication network, and that each processor communicates with (only) a logarithmic number of neighbors. Also, since each data element is forwarded a logarithmic number of times, the algorithm is competitive only for smaller problem sizes, which decrease slowly with the number of processes. The Bruck et al. algorithm is therefore only one among many all-to-all algorithms, and its range of concrete applicability depends on many factors. The actual performance benefits by using derived datatypes depends on the quality of the MPI library, and the protocol regimes used (small vs. eager vs. rendezvous; fixed buffers; pipelining). Other improvements (elimination of the post-communication permutation), however, are genuinely MPI independent.

2. THE BASIC ALGORITHM AND A FIRST IMPROVEMENT

We first recapitulate the all-to-all algorithm by Bruck et al. [1] which we for now term *Basic Bruck*. Let p be the number of MPI processes, each bound to a processor or core. The processes are numbered (*ranked*) from 0 to $p-1$. Each process has an individual data *element* to each other process, including an element to itself; elements are the units of communication and can represent larger data. The element from process i, $0 \leq i < p$, to process j, $0 \leq j < p$, is denoted $m_{i \to j}$. We consider first the *regular* all-to-all problem in which all elements have the same size; we denote this element size by n so that every process has to send and receive data of size $(p-1)n$ and possibly copy an element of size n locally.

Basic Bruck has three steps, the second of which involves communication. Each process has a p-element vector R where the elements received so far are stored, and from which the elements to send in the next communication round are also taken. Upon termination, $R[j]$ for process i shall store the element $m_{j \to i}$ from process j to process i. The p processes carry out the same operations with process i, $0 \leq i < p$, doing the following:

1. **Local** shift towards index 0 by i indices: set $R[j] = m_{i \to (i+j) \bmod p}$ for $j = 0, \ldots, p-1$.

2. **Global** communication step with $\lceil \log_2 p \rceil$ rounds. In round $k, 0 \leq k < \lceil \log_2 p \rceil$, all elements $R[j]$ where the kth bit of j is equal to one are sent to process $(i + 2^k) \bmod p$, which receives this element into $R[j]$.

3. **Local** reverse and shift towards index $p-1$ by $i+1$ indices: element $R[j]$ is moved to $R[(p-1-j+(i+1)) \bmod p] = R[(p-j+i) \bmod p]$ for each $j, 0 \leq j < p$.

The second step takes $\lceil \log_2 p \rceil$ communication rounds. In each round, up to $\lfloor p/2 \rfloor$ elements are sent and received, and must be handled as one contiguous message. Over all $\lceil \log_2 p \rceil$ rounds, $\lceil \log_2 p \rceil \lfloor p/2 \rfloor$ elements are sent and received per process. A straightforward all-to-all algorithm that sends each element directly to its destination process sends and receives exactly $p-1$ elements per process, but takes $p-1$ communication rounds to do this. In both cases, the trade-off between number of communication rounds and total volume of data communicated is best possible as shown in [1]. Correctness can be argued as follows. The first step puts the elements into R such that the element to be sent from process i to process $((i+j) \bmod p)$ is in $R[j]$. The

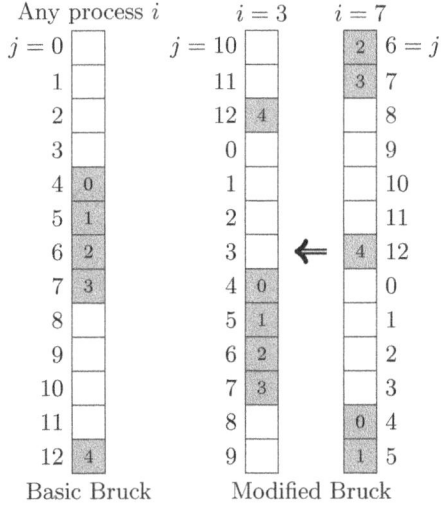

Figure 1: Elements sent in round $k = 2$ with $p = 13$ by Basic Bruck (left), and Modified Bruck for processes $i = 3$ and $i = 7$ (right). Process 7 sends its shaded elements in the indicated order to the shaded positions of process 3.

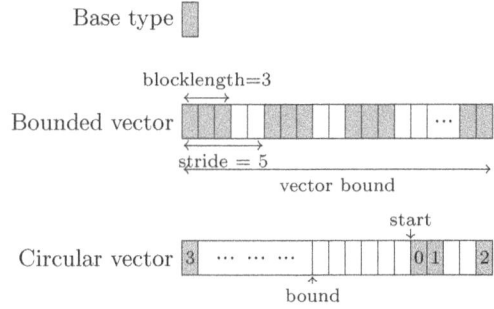

Figure 2: Type maps of bounded and circular vector datatypes for given base type. The bounded vector fits to Basic Bruck, circular vector to Modified Bruck.

second communication step sends element $R[j]$ to its destination process $((i + j) \bmod p)$ by decomposing j into its unique sum of powers of two, $j = 2^{j_0} + 2^{j_1} + 2^{j_2} + \dots$ with $j_0 < j_1 < j_2 < \dots$ corresponding to the one-bits of j, and sending it via processes $(i + 2^{j_0}) \bmod p$, $(i + 2^{j_0} + 2^{j_1}) \bmod p$, $(i + 2^{j_0} + 2^{j_1} + 2^{j_2}) \bmod p, \dots$. Thus, before Step 3, for each process i, $R[j] = m_{(i-j) \bmod p \to i}$. Step 3 accomplishes the permutation resulting in $R[j] = m_{j \to i}$ as desired.

Sending and receiving elements $R[j]$ in Step 2 explicitly or implicitly requires an intermediate buffer in addition to R. The elements for round k can be received into this buffer as a contiguous sequence, and copied into their right, non-contiguous positions in R after the receive operation has completed. When elements are sent out of R, an (implicit) pack operation is needed. Basic Bruck therefore entails a p-element copy operation for Step 1, an unpack and pack operation for each communication round in Step 2, and two full copy operations of $p - 1$ blocks via the intermediate buffer for Step 3. In summary:

THEOREM 1. *Basic Bruck solves the all-to-all problem for p processes and elements of size n in $\lceil \log_2 p \rceil$ communication rounds, with at most $\lceil \log_2 p \rceil \lfloor p/2 \rfloor n$ units of data sent and received per process, and at most $p + 2 \lceil \log_2 p \rceil \lfloor p/2 \rfloor + 2p$ local element copy/unpack/pack operations.*

Assuming a simple, linear cost communication model in which sending and receiving an element of size n takes $\alpha + \beta n$ time units, it follows that Basic Bruck et al. (and the following variants) can be better than a $p - 1$-round, direct all-to-all algorithm when n is $O(\frac{\alpha}{\beta} 2/ \log_2 p)$.

The third, costly process-local reordering step can be eliminated by maintaining the elements in R in a different order. The *Modified Bruck* algorithm has the following two steps in which each process i, $0 \le i < p$, does the following:

1. **Local** reverse and shift towards index i: $R[(i+j) \bmod p] = m_{i \to (i-j) \bmod p}$ for $j = 0, \dots, p-1$.

2. **Global** communication step with $\lceil \log_2 p \rceil$ rounds. In round k, $0 \le k < \lceil \log_2 p \rceil$, all elements $R[(i + j) \bmod p]$ where the kth bit of j is equal to one are sent to process $((i - 2^k) \bmod p)$ which receives these elements into $R[(i - 2^k) \bmod p + j]$.

For both variations of the Bruck et al. algorithm it holds that elements $R[j]$, respectively $R[i + j]$, with the kth bit of j equal to one fall into consecutive sequences of 2^k elements. In Modified Bruck send and receive operations are in the opposite direction of Basic Bruck which ensures that the elements to send in each round are in increasing index order (modulo p). Correctness should be clear: process i initially stores the element $m_{i \to (i-j) \bmod p}$ in $R[(i + j) \bmod p]$, and elements are sent to their destinations following the power-of-two decomposition of j. Note that an element sent from index j by processor i is received at a lower index (modulo p) by the receiving processor; the cyclic shifting of the elements as done explicitly in the first and third step of Basic Bruck is now accomplished as part of the communication. Figure 1 illustrates which elements are communicated in communication round $k = 2$ for the two algorithms.

THEOREM 2. *Modified Bruck solves the all-to-all problem for p processes and elements of size n in $\lceil \log_2 p \rceil$ communication rounds, with at most $\lceil \log_2 p \rceil \lfloor p/2 \rfloor n$ units of data sent and received per process, and at most $p + 2 \lceil \log_2 p \rceil \lfloor p/2 \rfloor$ local element copy/unpack/pack operations.*

3. ELIMINATING EXPLICIT DATA MOVEMENTS WITH DERIVED DATATYPES

We now employ Basic and Modified Bruck to implement the regular, collective all-to-all communication operation of MPI. In an `MPI_Alltoall(sendbuf,sendcount,sendtype,-recvbuf,recvcount,recvtype,comm)` call, each MPI process stores the elements $m_{i \to j}$ to the other processes consecutively in `sendbuf`. Elements can be arbitrarily structured as described by the `sendcount` and `sendtype` arguments. The received elements will be stored in `recvbuf` and can likewise be arbitrarily structured, independently of the structure of the elements to be sent; however, all sent and all received elements have the same structure and size. MPI requires data in `sendbuf` to remain unchanged after the operation, but `recvbuf` can be used for the R vector, as long as the structure of the data to be received is respected.

Listing 1 Communication step of basic Bruck with bounded vector datatype in MPI.

```
1  for (k=1; k<size; k<<=1) {
2    Type_create_vector_bounded((size-k)*recvcount,
3                         k*recvcount,(k<<1)*recvcount,
4                         recvtype,&recvblocktype);
5    MPI_Type_commit(&recvblocktype);
6    MPI_Pack_size(1,recvblocktype,comm,&packsize);
7
8    sendrank = (rank+k)%size;
9    recvrank = (rank-k+size)%size;
10   MPI_Sendrecv((char*)recvbuf+k*recvcount*recvextent,
11            1,recvblocktype,sendrank,BRUCK,
12            interbuf,packsize,MPI_PACKED,recvrank,BRUCK,
13            comm,MPI_STATUS_IGNORE);
14   pos = 0;
15   MPI_Unpack(interbuf,packsize,&pos,
16            (char*)recvbuf+k*recvcount*recvextent,
17            1,recvblocktype,comm);
18
19   MPI_Type_free(&recvblocktype);
20 }
```

Listing 2 Communication step of Modified Bruck with circular vector datatype in MPI.

```
1  for (k=1; k<size; k<<=1) {
2    sendrank = (rank-k+size)%size;
3    recvrank = (rank+k)%size;
4    Type_create_vector_circular(size*recvcount,
5                         recvrank*recvcount,
6                         (size-k)*recvcount,
7                         k*recvcount,
8                         (k<<1)*recvcount,
9                         recvtype,&recvblocktype);
10   MPI_Type_commit(&recvblocktype);
11   MPI_Pack_size(1,recvblocktype,comm,&packsize);
12
13   MPI_Sendrecv(recvbuf,1,recvblocktype,sendrank,BRUCK,
14            interbuf,packsize,MPI_PACKED,recvrank,BRUCK,
15            comm,MPI_STATUS_IGNORE);
16   pos = 0;
17   MPI_Unpack(interbuf,packsize,&pos,
18            recvbuf,1,recvblocktype,comm);
19
20   MPI_Type_free(&recvblocktype);
21 }
```

3.1 Basic Bruck with derived datatypes

In Basic Bruck the sequence of elements sent out of R in each round k is regularly structured: each element $R[j]$, where the kth bit of j is set, is sent. In round k, blocks of 2^k elements with a stride of 2^{k+1} elements, with the last block possibly having fewer than 2^k elements, are sent and received as illustrated in Figure 1 (left). In the original paper [1], hand-coded pack and unpack routines copy the $\lfloor p/2 \rfloor$ elements to be sent into a contiguous buffer, and the received $\lfloor p/2 \rfloor$ elements into their correct positions in R. For an MPI implementation, a natural approach is to use a derived datatype for each communication round to describe the strided pattern of elements to be sent and received. This could be described by an MPI vector datatype, except for the last block that may contain fewer elements. Instead, the layout is described as either a) an indexed type with a possibly smaller last block, as b) an indexed block type where each element is indexed separately, or as c) a structured type consisting of a vector followed by a contiguous type for the last block. The first and second alternative use extra arrays for index and block length information that is mostly redundant, and are thus wasteful both in storage, set-up and processing time. The third alternative is likely to be more efficient. We use it here for the implementation of a derived, derived datatype constructor for *bounded vectors* whose type map is illustrated in Figure 2. The difference from the bounded vector to the MPI vector is that a bound on the total number of (basetype) elements spanned by the datatype is given instead of the count of the number of blocks. Using the bounded vector, the communication step of Basic Bruck can readily be implemented as shown in Listing 1. For the experimental comparison (see Section 4) we consider the following two implementations:

1. Basic Bruck with indexed type (basicBruck-ix)

2. Basic Bruck with bounded vector (basicBruck)

We contend that the bounded vector layout could readily and efficiently be handled by MPI library internal datatype engines, and native support of this datatype would therefore save in both setup and processing overhead compared to

our implementation via existing datatype constructors. We also contend that bounded vector patterns occur in other applications.

In the Basic Bruck outlined in Listing 1, elements are received as a contiguous sequence of `MPI_PACKED` type, and unpacked into the strided blocks of the given `recvbuf` using again the bounded vector datatype. This is a correct MPI solution to the problem of receiving typed data as a contiguous sequence of elements, and necessary since the type signature (see [6, Chapter 4, page 84]) of `recvtype` is not directly known. Note that the `packsize` of an MPI datatype may be larger than the actual size occupied by the elements of that type; also note that sequences of packed elements can only (legally) be accessed through the `MPI_Pack` and `MPI_Unpack` functions. An alternative, more elegant solution would be to provide each MPI (derived) datatype with a datatype corresponding to the signature of the type, that is a contiguous listing of the basic types. Such *signature types* could be used for receiving typed, consecutive sequences and for allocating intermediate buffers without losing type information.

The first and last step of Basic Bruck entail copying elements from `sendbuf` to `recvbuf` and putting the received elements in `recvbuf` into correct order. For Step 3, the MPI pack-unpack functionality suffices if the reordering is done via an intermediate buffer. For Step 1, where elements of `sendtype` have to be copied into a buffer of elements of a possibly different `recvtype`, a *datatyped memory copy* operation is called for. This operation, sometimes called transpacking [5, 8], is not in MPI. In the implementation, we use a process-local `MPI_Sendrecv` to transfer typed data from `sendbuf` to `recvbuf`. Other alternatives are possible, but MPI library support for a datatyped copy operation would be natural and easily more efficient than by-hand solutions.

3.2 Modified Bruck with derived datatypes

Modified Bruck also sends elements from `recvbuf` in a strided pattern, but in round $k, 0 \leq k < \lceil \log_2 p \rceil$, process i sends elements $R[i+j]$ for which the kth bit of j is one. This layout can be described as a strided vector of blocks of 2^k elements starting from offset 2^k, wrapping around at index p to index 0. In order to implement Modified Bruck we introduce another, new datatype constructor for *circular vectors*, the type map of which is also shown in Figure 2. A circular vector is specified by its total extent (in number of basic elements), a bound (as for the bounded vector) on the actual extent to be occupied within the total extent, a start offset, a number of elements per block and a stride between blocks.

With the circular vector, the implementation of Modified Bruck is straightforward, and Listing 2 shows the communication step. The circular vector constructor can be implemented using the existing MPI datatype constructors, but there is a number of tedious, special cases to take care of. A higher type creation overhead is to be expected. As with the bounded vector, we contend that the data accesses specified by this derived datatype could more efficiently be directly embodied in MPI library-internal datatype handling mechanisms. For performance comparison, we give two implementations of Modified Bruck:

1. Modified Bruck with indexed type (modBruck-ix)

2. Modified Bruck with circular vector (modBruck)

3.3 Zero-copy Bruck with derived datatypes

The previous implementations receive elements into an intermediate buffer which is then unpacked into the `recvbuf` before the next communication round. It would be desirable to eliminate this overhead. For instance, a received element which will have to be sent further on in a later communication round could remain in and be sent directly out of the intermediate buffer with no need for unpacking into the `recvbuf`. We now explain in more detail how to completely eliminate any explicit unpacking of the intermediate buffers. We call the resulting implementation *Zero-copy Bruck*; the term was used similarly for other applications in [4].

We use the same communication and storage pattern as in Modified Bruck. When a new element for $R[i+j]$ is received by process i in round k, the kth bit of j is set. In the same round, element $R[i+j]$ is sent. We store the elements to be sent and received alternatingly in the `recvbuf` and an intermediate buffer. If j has no further bits $k' > k$ equal to one, the element is at its destination process and should be received directly into position $i+j$ in `recvbuf`. In general, elements for which the number of set bits $k' > k$ in j is even will be received into `recvbuf`, and elements with an odd number of set bits $k' > k$ will be received into the intermediate buffer. Conversely, elements j with an even number of set bits $k' > k$, will be sent out of the intermediate buffer, elements j with an odd number of set bits after k out of the `recvbuf`. Finally, in each round k, the first element of each segment of 2^k elements is a "new" element, and taken from position $((i-j) \bmod p)$ of `sendbuf` (another way to see this is that such elements have no set bits $k' < k$ in j, and thus have not been received in any previous round); this eliminates the copy operation of Step 1 of Modified Bruck. To implement the alternation between intermediate, send and receive buffer, we need to be able to determine for each index j how many bits are set in j after position k. We do this by computing a table of set bits in $j, 0 \le j < p$, and in round k mask out the bits below k. The number of set bits in all j can easily be (pre)computed in $O(p)$ time steps:

```
1 bits[0] = 0;
2 for (j=1; j<size; j++) bits[j] = bits[j>>1]+(j&0x1);
```

Listing 3 Zero-copy Bruck in MPI using structured send and receive types.

```
1  MPI_Type_get_extent(sendtype,&lb,&sendtotal);
2  MPI_Type_get_extent(recvtype,&lb,&recvtotal);
3  sendtotal *= sendcount; recvtotal *= recvcount;
4  MPI_Type_size(recvtype,&recvsize); recvsize *= recvcount;
5
6  unsigned int mask = 0xFFFFFFFF;
7  for (k=1; k<size; k<<=1) {
8    b = 0; j = k;
9    do { // bit j set
10     sendrank = (rank-j+size)%size;
11     recvrank = (rank+j)%size;
12
13     if ((bits[j&mask]&0x1)==0x1) { // to recvbuf
14       recvblocks[b] = recvcount;
15       recvindex[b] =
16         (MPI_Aint)((char*)recvbuf+recvrank*recvtotal);
17       recvtypes[b] = recvtype;
18
19       if ((j&mask)==j) { // from sendbuf
20         sendblocks[b] = sendcount;
21         sendindex[b] =
22           (MPI_Aint)((char*)sendbuf+sendrank*sendtotal);
23         sendtypes[b] = sendtype;
24       } else { // from intermediate
25         sendblocks[b] = recvsize;
26         sendindex[b] = (MPI_Aint)(interbuf+j*recvsize);
27         sendtypes[b] = MPI_BYTE;
28       }
29     } else { // to intermediate
30       recvblocks[b] = recvsize;
31       recvindex[b] = (MPI_Aint)(interbuf+j*recvsize);
32       recvtypes[b] = MPI_BYTE;
33
34       if ((j&mask)==j) { // from sendbuf
35         sendblocks[b] = sendcount;
36         sendindex[b] =
37           (MPI_Aint)((char*)sendbuf+sendrank*sendtotal);
38         sendtypes[b] = sendtype;
39       } else { // from recv
40         sendblocks[b] = recvcount;
41         sendindex[b] =
42           (MPI_Aint)((char*)recvbuf+recvrank*recvtotal);
43         sendtypes[b] = recvtype;
44       }
45     }
46     b++; // next element
47     j++; if ((j&k)!=k) j += k;
48   } while (j<size);
49
50   MPI_Type_create_struct(b,sendblocks,sendindex,sendtypes,
51                 &sendblocktype);
52   MPI_Type_commit(&sendblocktype);
53   MPI_Type_create_struct(b,recvblocks,recvindex,recvtypes,
54                 &recvblocktype);
55   MPI_Type_commit(&recvblocktype);
56
57   sendrank = (rank-k+size)%size;
58   recvrank = (rank+k)%size;
59   MPI_Sendrecv(MPI_BOTTOM,1,sendblocktype,sendrank,BRUCK,
60            MPI_BOTTOM,1,recvblocktype,recvrank,BRUCK,
61            comm,MPI_STATUS_IGNORE);
62
63   MPI_Type_free(&recvblocktype);
64   MPI_Type_free(&sendblocktype);
65   mask <<= 1;
66 }
```

139

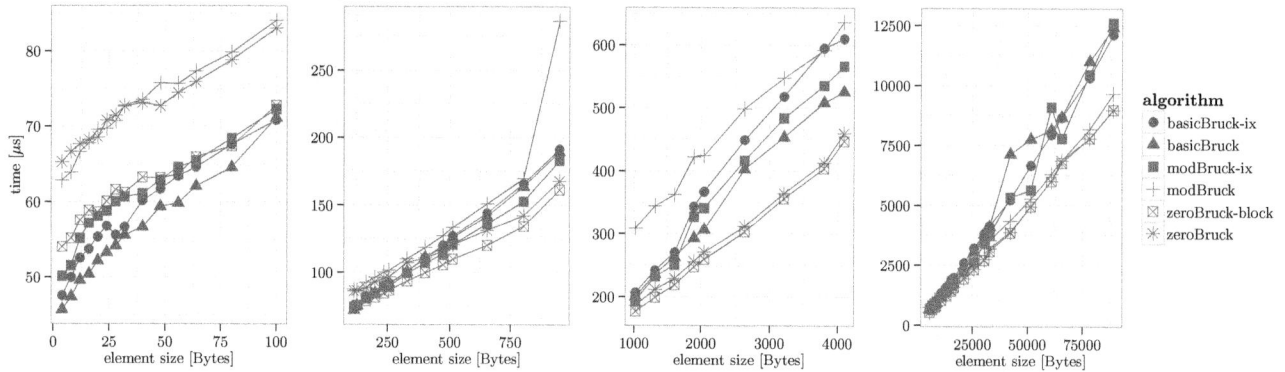

Figure 3: Running times of the six variants on InfiniBand cluster (Jupiter), $p = 36$, element size $n \in [4, 80000]$ Bytes.

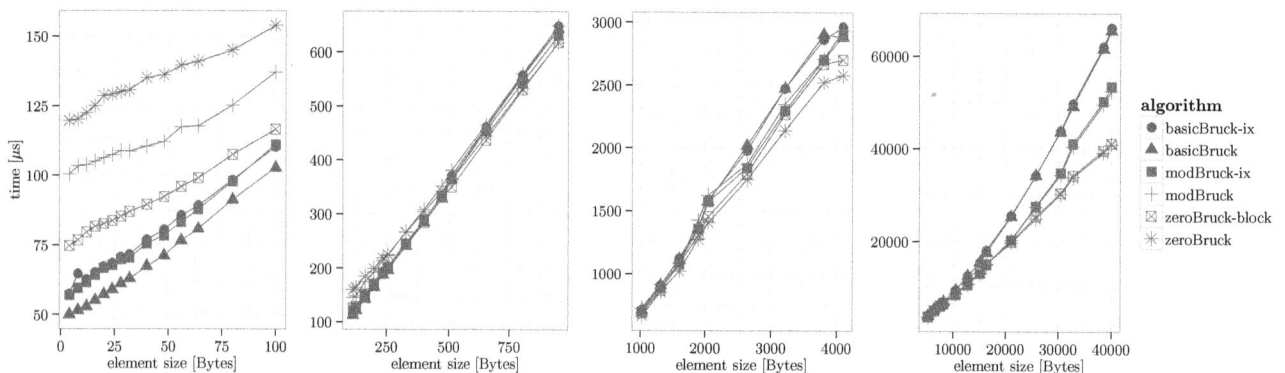

Figure 4: Running times of the six variants on shared-memory system (Mars), $p = 80$, element size $n \in [4, 40000]$ Bytes.

Listing 3 shows the full Zero-copy Bruck. For both the received and the sent blocks separate MPI derived datatypes are computed for each round, and is likely to have a non-negligible overhead. A possible improvement, not shown here, is to collapse consecutive elements into blocks of 2^k and $2^k - 1$ elements. An MPI library with sophisticated datatype preprocessing (*type normalization* [2]) might be able to do such improvements by itself, at the cost of an even higher type creation overhead.

Although structured (determined by the bits in each j), it is much less obvious that these patterns could be of general use, therefore we have not defined a new derived datatype constructor for the zero-copy implementation. Note that the element-wise analysis used to set up the datatypes does not hurt overall complexity, since there are $\lfloor p/2 \rfloor$ elements to be sent anyway.

A final point should be mentioned. Each element in the intermediate buffer is stored as a non-structured, contiguous sequence in order to avoid repeated overheads incurred by possibly structured element `sendtype` and `recvtype`. In the absence of the signature types mentioned in Section 3.1, these contiguous sequences are stored as `MPI_BYTE` sequences; this is not strictly correct since information about basetypes is lost. The `MPI_PACKED` type should have been used as subtype for the elements, but that would have made Listing 3 more confusing.

3.4 Persistent collectives

All three algorithm implementations, Basic Bruck, Modified Bruck and Zero-copy Bruck, create (and free) new, derived datatypes for each communication round. Basic and Modified Bruck use only one derived datatype per round, which is regular enough to be captured using (mostly) MPI vector and contiguous constructors (via the proposed, new type constructors for bounded and cyclic vectors). Hence, the overhead of setting up and using these types might be tolerable. For Zero-copy Bruck separate send and receive datatypes are created, both with a higher overhead by the index analysis and by the use of the MPI struct constructor. In all three cases it would be desirable to be able to amortize the type creation and destruction overheads over a number of `MPI_Alltoall` calls.

The overall structure of the derived datatypes is fully determined by the number of processes p, and could therefore potentially be reused from call to call. Datatypes are static, unchangeable objects in MPI, and since the types are created with `sendtype` and `recvtype` as basetypes and also depend on `sendcount` and `recvcount`, each `MPI_Alltoall` call either has to create (and free) these derived datatypes, or to maintain the created datatypes in a cache. An explicit means for the user to specify caching would be via a persistent version of `MPI_Alltoall`, in analogy with the persistent point-to-point communication operations [6, Section

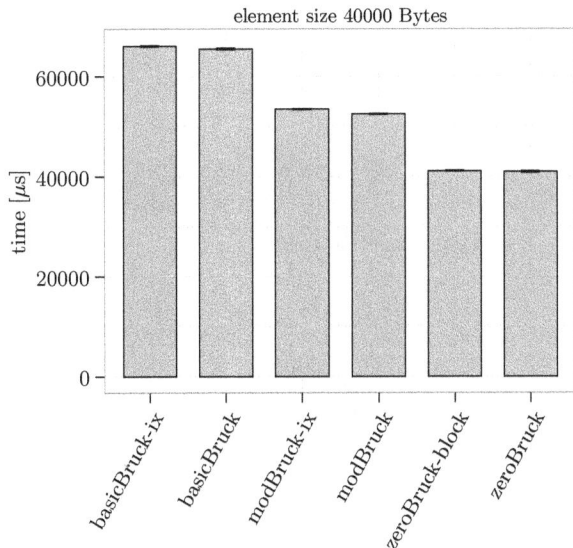

Figure 5: All versions with `mpich` on shared-memory system (Mars), $p = 80$, $n = 40000$ Bytes, 95% confidence intervals.

3.9]. An `MPI_Alltoall` *init* call would take the same arguments as `MPI_Alltoall` and bind these in a special request object also given as parameter to the call; in this object all required datatypes would be precomputed and stored. The corresponding `MPI_Alltoall` *start* operation simply consists of the $\lceil \log_2 p \rceil$-round loop performing the precomputed send and receive operations (that could themselves be persistent).

MPI currently does not specify *persistent collective operations*. To investigate the benefits of factoring out type creation overheads, we have implemented persistent all-to-all operations based on Zero-copy Bruck. As we discuss in the next section, persistence turns out even more beneficial for the irregular counterpart to `MPI_Alltoall`.

3.5 Irregular all-to-all communication

A basic assumption for the analysis of the Bruck algorithm is that elements have the same size. Nevertheless, the Bruck variations could be useful (and efficient) for the implementation of the irregular all-to-all collectives `MPI_Alltoallv` and `Alltoallw` for cases where the element sizes do not differ too much; for very irregular problems, employing an algorithm designed for the regular problem is far from optimal. Employing, for instance, Zero-copy Bruck to implement `MPI_Alltoallv` poses some interesting challenges that we discuss in the following.

A first difficulty is how to determine whether we are in a regular-enough case that Zero-copy Bruck should be used. Perhaps the user has this information, and could assert it to the MPI library; unfortunately, the `MPI_Alltoallv` interface does not provide an easy handle to convey such information. Because of this, the collective would have to do a global analysis to detect whether Zero-copy Bruck should be used. An `MPI_Allreduce` can be used to find the smallest and the largest element size, and based on this, the MPI processes can consistently select the desired algorithm. For regular-enough problems, the processes now allocate inter-

mediate buffers with space enough for $p - 1$ elements of the maximum element size. Such buffers could conveniently be accessed using an MPI derived *bucket datatype* which divides an extent of memory into contiguous buckets of the same maximum size, but with a possibly different actual number of elements in each bucket. This datatype, also not in MPI, is the natural counterpart of the block-indexed datatype: instead of an array of indices and a fixed block size, the bucket type takes as arguments a maximum bucket size and an array of actual element counts for each bucket. Naturally, algorithm selection incurs overhead, which is particular hurtful for the smaller element sizes where the Bruck variations are efficient.

Another difficulty is that the MPI processes do not know in advance the actual sizes of the elements to be received in each of the $\lceil \log_2 p \rceil$ communication rounds. To handle this, each process in each communication round first receives and sends the sizes of the elements it is going to send and receive in that round (using, as in Basic Bruck, a bounded vector of integer counts). This "only" doubles the latency of the communication rounds since count vectors have at most $\lfloor p/2 \rfloor$ entries. With this information, correct, structured datatypes can be constructed, just as shown in Listing 3, using a bucket type for the 2^k-element blocks of differently sized elements. We note here that the trick of using the given `recvbuf` as intermediate buffer will not work, since this buffer may not have space for the possibly larger, intermediate elements. Instead, two intermediate buffers (of size $p - 1$ maximum elements) are allocated; the alternation described for Zero-copy Bruck still works, resulting in a zero-copy algorithm for not too irregular all-to-all communication. On the other hand, using an explicit, intermediate buffer instead of `recvbuf` may have advantages also for the regular problem, namely if `recvtype` is a complicated, structured type: in that case each intermediate element copied into the `recvbuf` is processed by the MPI datatype engine, and could incur an undesired overhead.

Using Zero-copy Bruck to implement `MPI_Alltoallv` incurs a two-element `MPI_Allreduce` overhead and doubles the number of send-receive operations. For small data, such an implementation of `MPI_Alltoallv` would be up to a factor of two slower than the Zero-copy Bruck implementation of `MPI_Alltoall`. However, the extra overhead depends only on p, and on the send-receive types and counts. A persistent version of `MPI_Alltoallv` would make it possible to fully isolate both the algorithm selection and the datatype creation overhead. For comparison, we have implemented such a version, although it has no counterpart in current MPI.

4. EXPERIMENTAL EVALUATION

As can be inferred from Section 3, our hypothesis is that Modified Bruck which saves an $O(pn)$ local reordering step will improve over Basic Bruck, and that Zero-copy Bruck which completely eliminates explicit, local copy operations will improve over Modified Bruck, all on the *assumption that the MPI derived datatype mechanism does not lead to excessive overheads*. To test these expectations, we have implemented the three variations which we term *basicBruck*, *modBruck* and *zeroBruck*, respectively. For additional comparisons *basicBruck-ix* uses an MPI indexed datatype instead of the bounded vector, *modBruck-ix* uses an indexed-block datatype instead of the circular vector, and *zeroBruck-*

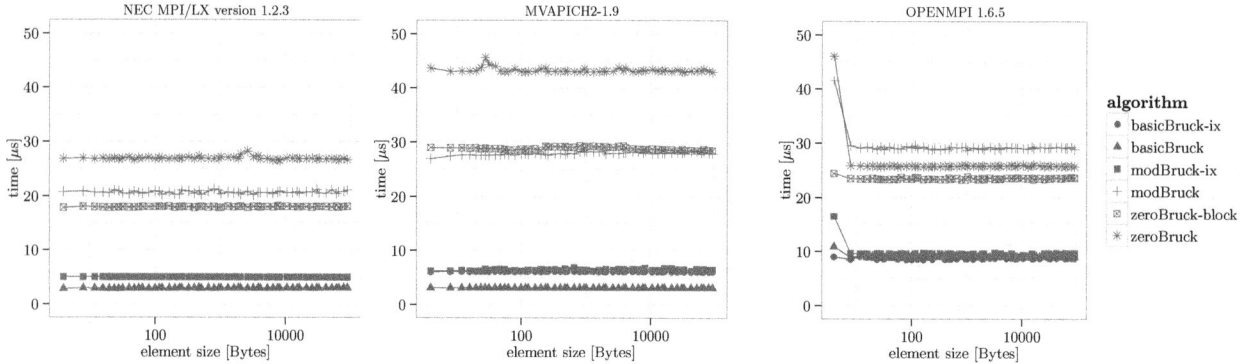

Figure 6: Type creation overheads with vendor MPI, `mvapich` and OpenMPI on InfiniBand cluster (Jupiter).

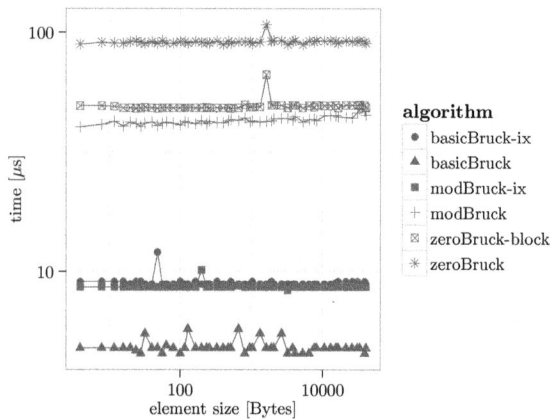

Figure 7: Type creation overheads with `mpich` on shared-memory system (Mars).

blocks creates structured types with fewer, but longer 2^k-element blocks. For each variant, we can disable actual communication in order to measure the derived datatype creation and freeing overheads. Zero-copy Bruck has also been given a persistent implementation, termed *persBruck*; we have also used the zero-copy algorithm to implement `MPI_Alltoallv`, both in non-persistent *zeroBruckV* and persistent *persBruckV* versions. All code is available from the authors upon request. Finally, we also implemented Modified Bruck directly in the `mvapich` library and compared it to the `mvapich` version. Interestingly, `mvapich` (R. Thakur, personal communication) already implements Basic Bruck using an indexed-block datatype; OpenMPI (George Bosilca, personal communication) instead used an indexed type to maintain larger 2^k-element blocks of elements for each round.

For our evaluation we currently have access to two small systems. The first is a 36-node, 576-core InfiniBand cluster (Jupiter) with two 8-core 2.3GHz AMD 6134 Opteron processors/node and a Mellanox MT4036 QDR switch. The second, an 80-core shared-memory system (Mars) based on Intel 10-core 2.0GHz Westmere-EX E7-8850 processors. Although the latter is a shared memory system, we use it as an approximation to a fully connected, homogeneous system. To have as far as possible homogeneous communication be-

tween processes, the measurements on the InfiniBand cluster have been done with one MPI process per node. On the Jupiter InfiniBand cluster we use the vendor MPI library, on the Mars shared-memory system we have used `mpich 3.0.4`.

In our experiments the basic datatype for send and receive buffers is `MPI_INT`, so element sizes are multiples of four bytes. Each single measurement was repeated at least 40 times. To compensate for system noise, sensitive measurements in the microseconds range were repeated 300 times for each element size. We applied Tukey's outlier filter (see, e.g., [3]: for the upper quartile (Q_3) of the sample all measurements larger than $Q3 + 1.5IQR$ are removed, where IQR denotes the interquartile range. We also computed the 95% confidence interval for each element size, but show confidence intervals only in the barcharts. When intervals do not overlap, the results are significantly different at a 95% confidence level.

4.1 Regular all-to-all communication

We first compare the performance of the six implementation variants for regular all-to-all communication on the two systems. Element sizes have been chosen in a larger interval (up to $n = 80000$ Bytes) than that in which the Bruck idea is better than a direct algorithm, in order to amplify the asymptotic differences between the improvements. The results are shown in Figures 3 and 4. We emphasize that the measured implementations are fully self-contained `MPI_Alltoall` algorithms and include all datatype manipulation overheads.

Especially on Mars, Zero-copy Bruck clearly performs asymptotically better than both Modified and Basic Bruck. This is shown in detail in Figure 5, where the improvement is by more than 30% for $n = 40000$ Bytes. For small element sizes the datatype overhead of the zero-copy variants is too large to make these implementations competitive. The best performing variant here is Basic Bruck implemented with the bounded vector type. Modified Bruck with circular vector is surprisingly bad: although a regular layout is described in terms of MPI vector and contiguous types, putting these together with an MPI structured type takes more time than describing the layout by an indexed type.

4.2 Type creation overhead

We explicitly measured the type creation (and destruction) overhead for all six variants by disabling all commu-

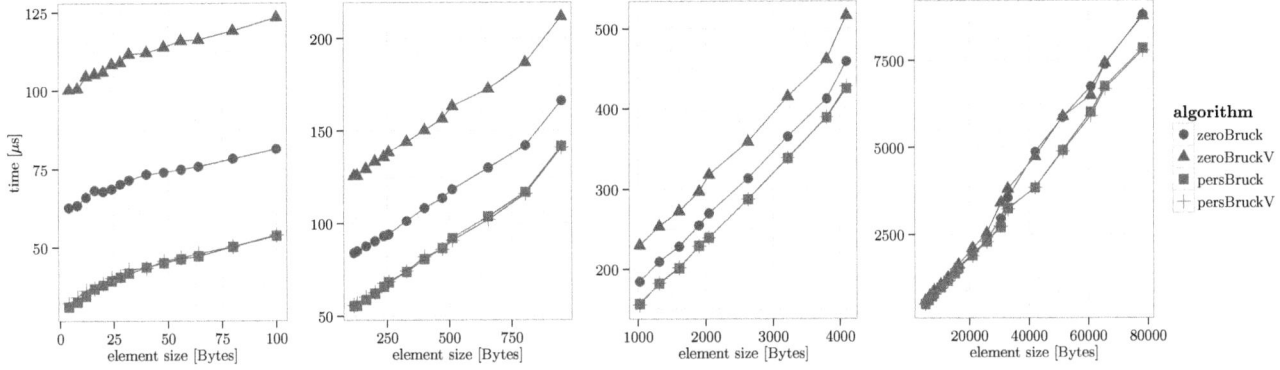

Figure 8: Persistent and irregular Zero-copy Bruck on InfiniBand cluster (Jupiter), $p = 36$, element size $n \in [4, 80000]$ Bytes.

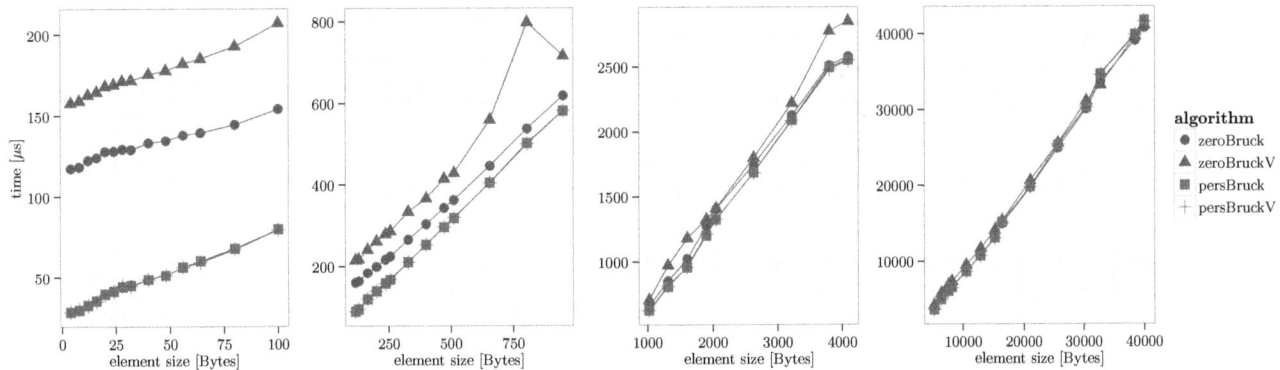

Figure 9: Persistent and irregular Zero-copy Bruck on shared-memory system (Mars), $p = 80$, element size $n \in [4, 40000]$ Bytes.

nication. The results are shown in Figure 6 and 7. The results confirm the speculations: the structured types for Zero-copy Bruck and the circular vector incur significantly higher overheads than the other types. On Jupiter we tried three different MPI libraries, and as Figure 6 shows there are important performance differences, with `mvapich` being particularly slow in the setup/destruction of the structured types for Zero-copy Bruck.

4.3 Persistent and irregular all-to-all communication

We analyze the performance of the persistent versions of Zero-copy Bruck for both `MPI_Alltoall` and `MPI_Alltoallv`. In the experimental setup we use `MPI_Alltoallv` to solve the same regular problem as `MPI_Alltoall`. This gives us an idea of the best-case overhead incurred by using the irregular collective operation. As explained, we expect more than a factor of two difference for small element sizes. This is clearly confirmed by Figures 8 and 9. The persistent versions have no extra overhead. For small element sizes, e.g., 64 Bytes, the persistent versions are more than a factor 2 (for regular all-to-all) and up to a factor 3 (for the irregular version) faster than the non-persistent counterparts. A nice property is that `MPI_Alltoall` and `MPI_Alltoallv` perform equivalently in their persistent variants: all the extra

overhead in the irregular algorithm is taken care of in the `MPI_Alltoallv` *init* operation.

4.4 Incorporating into existing MPI library

Finally, we implemented Modified Bruck (in the version using an indexed type) inside the `mvapich` library; as mentioned `mpich` and `mvapich` have their own implementation of Basic Bruck, which is enabled for a small range of element sizes. The intention is to show that the savings of Modified Bruck indeed give a significantly better (in the statistical sense) implementation than Basic Bruck, also for the range of element sizes where this algorithm is normally employed. The results are shown in Figure 10 for n up to 300 Bytes. Although the difference is only a few percent, it is statistically significant as the barchart shows.

5. SUMMARY AND OUTLOOK

We discussed the use of MPI derived datatypes to implement and improve the all-to-all algorithm of Bruck et al. [1]. Without modifying existing MPI libraries, we showed that the expected improvements can also be achieved in practice, and that the overheads by using datatypes can in many cases be (surprisingly) tolerable with modern MPI libraries.

We made a number of observations for datatype-oriented programming in MPI:

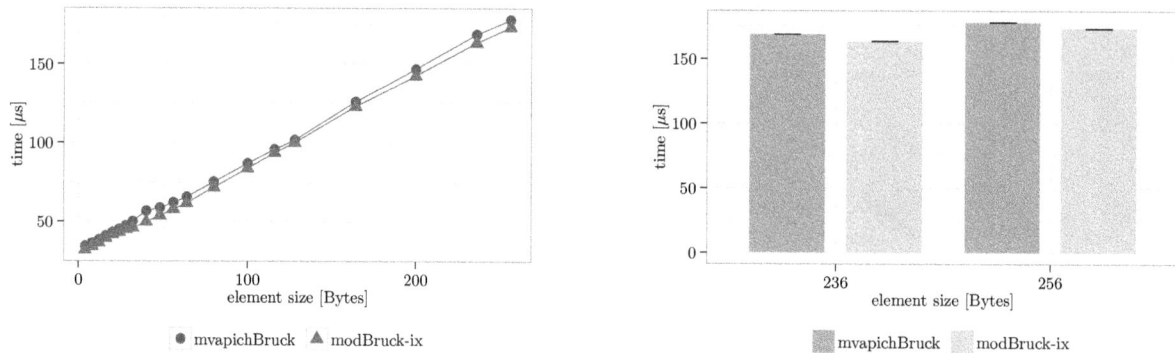

Figure 10: Bruck et al. implementation in mvapich versus Modified Bruck-ix in mvapich on shared-memory system (Mars), $p = 80$, for the interval $n \in [4, 300]$ Bytes.

- For correct handling of intermediate buffers holding elements of a structured type, having access to a *signature type* for (derived) datatypes would be convenient, and would alleviate the need for using MPI_PACKED and the often used, but incorrect resort to MPI_BYTE.

- A *datatyped copy* for process local copying of MPI structured data would likewise be convenient, and can likely be more efficient than work-arounds with process-local MPI_Sendrecv and/or MPI_Pack/MPI_Unpack; in analogy with the MPI_Reduce_local operation introduced in MPI 2.2.

- We proposed new, derived datatype constructors for *bounded* and *circular vectors*; both can more or less easily be implemented with the existing constructors, but a native implementation in the MPI library would likely be more efficient.

- We also discussed a *bucket datatype* constructor which is the natural complement to the MPI block-indexed type.

- Finally we experimentally introduced and evaluated *persistent all-to-all collectives*, and showed that persistence can effectively be used to hide overheads in collective operations.

The discussion in this paper is related to and continues the discussion of (a)symmetries between MPI collective operations and datatypes in [10]. Part of these results were described in the first author's invited talk at EuroMPI 2013.

We mention a small, open problem: Zero-copy Bruck allocates intermediate buffer for p elements, but each round receives at most $\lfloor p/2 \rfloor$ elements. Is it possible to do with only $\lfloor p/2 \rfloor$ element intermediate buffer space and still be zero-copy?

6. REFERENCES

[1] J. Bruck, C.-T. Ho, S. Kipnis, E. Upfal, and D. Weathersby. Efficient algorithms for all-to-all communications in multiport message-passing systems. *IEEE Transactions on Parallel and Distributed Systems*, 8(11):1143–1156, 1997.

[2] W. D. Gropp, T. Hoefler, R. Thakur, and J. L. Träff. Performance expectations and guidelines for MPI derived datatypes: a first analysis. In *Recent Advances in Message Passing Interface. 18th European MPI Users' Group Meeting*, volume 6960 of *Lecture Notes in Computer Science*, pages 150–159. Springer, 2011.

[3] J. Hedderich and L. Sachs. *Angewandte Statistik*. Springer, 14 edition, 2012.

[4] T. Hoefler and S. Gottlieb. Parallel zero-copy algorithms for fast fourier transform and conjugate gradient using MPI datatypes. In *Recent Advances in Message Passing Interface. 17th European MPI Users' Group Meeting*, volume 6305 of *Lecture Notes in Computer Science*, pages 132–141. Springer, 2010.

[5] F. G. Mir and J. L. Träff. Constructing MPI input-output datatypes for efficient transpacking. In *Recent Advances in Parallel Virtual Machine and Message Passing Interface. 15th European PVM/MPI Users' Group Meeting*, volume 5205 of *Lecture Notes in Computer Science*, pages 141–150. Springer, 2008.

[6] MPI Forum. *MPI: A Message-Passing Interface Standard. Version 3.0*, September 21st 2012. www.mpi-forum.org.

[7] H. Ritzdorf and J. L. Träff. Collective operations in NEC's high-performance MPI libraries. In *20th International Parallel and Distributed Processing Symposium (IPDPS)*, page 100, 2006.

[8] R. B. Ross, R. Latham, W. Gropp, E. L. Lusk, and R. Thakur. Processing MPI datatypes outside MPI. In *Recent Advances in Parallel Virtual Machine and Message Passing Interface. 16th European PVM/MPI Users' Group Meeting*, volume 5759 of *Lecture Notes in Computer Science*, pages 42–53. Springer, 2009.

[9] R. Thakur, W. D. Gropp, and R. Rabenseifner. Improving the performance of collective operations in MPICH. *International Journal on High Performance Computing Applications*, 19:49–66, 2005.

[10] J. L. Träff. Alternative, uniformly expressive and more scalable interfaces for collective communication in MPI. *Parallel Computing*, 38(1–2):26–36, 2012.

Value Influence Analysis for Message Passing Applications

Philip C. Roth
Oak Ridge National Laboratory
One Bethel Valley Road
Oak Ridge, TN 37831 USA
rothpc@ornl.gov

Jeremy S. Meredith
Oak Ridge National Laboratory
One Bethel Valley Road
Oak Ridge, TN 37831 USA
jsmeredith@ornl.gov

ABSTRACT

People who develop, debug, and optimize applications are most effective when they understand how those applications function. *Value influence tracking* is an on-line code analysis approach that provides a data-centric perspective on how a value contributes to later computation. Early work on value influence tracking focused on single-process applications. Building upon this early work, we have designed support for performing value influence tracking analyses with applications that use common MPI point-to-point and collective communication operations. In this paper, we describe the design and implementation of an approach for propagating value influence data between the processes of an MPI application that uses these types of operations. To demonstrate and evaluate our approach, we present case studies of using our value influence tracking implementation with the Large-scale Atomic/Molecular Massively Parallel Simulator (LAMMPS) and the Model for Prediction Across Scales (MPAS) ocean climate model running on the Keeneland Initial Delivery System (KIDS) Linux cluster. We also discuss how to extend our approach to support MPI one-sided operations and non-blocking collective communication operations.

Categories and Subject Descriptors

D.2.5 [**Software Engineering**]: Testing and Debugging; D.2.2 [**Software Engineering**]: Design Tools and Techniques

Keywords

Value influence, Message Passing Interface (MPI), dynamic instrumentation

1. INTRODUCTION

People who develop, debug, and optimize applications are most effective when they understand how those applications function. For instance, a user knowing that an application

This manuscript has been authored by UT-Battelle, LLC, under Contract No. DE-AC05-00OR22725 with the U.S. Department of Energy.

ICS'14, June 10–13 2014, Munich, Germany.
Copyright 2014 ACM 978-1-4503-2642-1/14/06 ...$15.00.
http://dx.doi.org/10.1145/2597652.2597666.

applies a particular stencil operation to the elements of a two-dimensional array is better able to determine whether to use a one-dimensional or two-dimensional data decomposition than a person with no knowledge of how the application works. Obtaining this knowledge can be difficult, however. Documentation about an application's implementation is often sparse or non-existent, and most real-world applications are too complex to understand by simply reading the code. Debuggers can be useful for determining how an application works, but they require user interactivity and are best suited for revealing the operation of targeted sections of the code in a single application process. Performance tools can also provide insight into how a program operates, but because they must limit the amount of perturbation to the application under study, they may not expose enough detail about the application's computation or communication.

Value influence tracking [13] is an on-line, direct approach for understanding how a program operates. Value influence tracking allows a user to determine how a *value*—the contents of a variable at a particular point in a program's execution—*influences* later computation. Knowing how a value contributes directly or indirectly to later computation may provide insight into potential program optimizations, program defects, and resilience requirements. For example, if a value influence tracking analysis indicates that a program input parameter was not used to compute a particular program result, but the program's developer expects that it should have been, the developer can use the analysis to determine why the input parameter was not used. In this case, the value influence tracking analysis acts as a debugging aid. As another example, if the value influence tracking analysis shows that a particular value contributed very little to the program's final result, the developer may decide to optimize the program by eliminating the computation and communication required to use the original value in producing the final result.

Initial work on the value influence tracking approach [13] focused on support for single-process programs. The paper describing this work briefly discussed how the approach might support programs that use the Message Passing Interface [3, 4] (MPI) for communication and synchronization between multiple processes, but gave little detail about the approach and did not present evidence of the approach being used with MPI-based applications. Building on the initial value influence tracking work, we have designed value influence tracking support for applications that use MPI two-sided point-to-point and blocking collective communication operations (hereafter called "MPI-1 operations" in this paper). One-sided operations were added in the MPI-2 standard, and non-blocking collective operations were added in the MPI-3 standard. For reasons such as portability, developer inertia, and the newness of the MPI-3 standard, applications that use only the MPI-1 subset of the full MPI interface are common, so limiting our support to MPI-1 operations does not decrease the relevance of our current work.

This paper's contributions include:

- The design of an approach for performing value influence tracking analysis on applications that use MPI-1 operations;
- An implementation of that approach for many of the common MPI-1 operations;
- A discussion of how to extend our current MPI-1 support for MPI-2 one-sided operations and MPI-3 non-blocking collective operations; and
- Case studies describing the use of the value influence tracking approach with two scientific applications.

2. AN OVERVIEW OF VALUE INFLUENCE TRACKING

Value influence tracking [13] is an *on-line, direct* approach. That is, the analysis is performed as the application runs, and is done by observing how values are used in the computation as opposed to reasoning about how they must have been used in the computation. A *value* is the contents of a location L at a specific time during program's execution. The location L can be either a memory location or a register. The *influence* of a value V_i over another value V_j is a measure of how much the value V_i contributed to the computation of the value V_j. An influence I is a real-numbered value in the interval $[0, 1]$. By default, the influence associated with all locations is 0. When a value is initially tagged as being of interest using the value influence tracking tool's application programming interface (API), it is assigned an influence of 1. A value influence analysis maintains a collection of pairs (L, I), updating the influence I associated with a location L whenever location L is assigned a new value. The new influence I is computed using the influences associated with all of the input values used to compute the new value at L. For example, in Figure 1, the values of two variables u and v are summed to produce the value assigned to an output variable *dest*. To compute the influence associated with *dest*, value influence tracking combines the influences associated with u and v. The initial value influence tracking work used the average operator to combine influences; we use the same operator as a combining function in this work. To continue the example, the influences 0.3 and 0.5 associated with u and v, respectively, are averaged to produce an influence 0.4 that is associated with location *dest*.

The value influence tracking approach can be applied using combining operators other than the average operator. For instance, using logical OR as a combining operator provides an analysis that shows which values depend, directly or indirectly, on the initially tagged value, but not how much the initial value contributed to the resulting values. With this combining operator, value influence tracking implements a form of Taint Analysis [6, 2]. More sophisticated combining operators might take into account the operator or even the input values used to compute the output value. For instance, if two values are summed to produce a result, and one is very large compared to the other, it might be benefi-

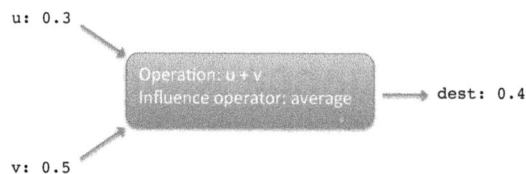

Figure 1: Example of combining value influences as part of an operation.

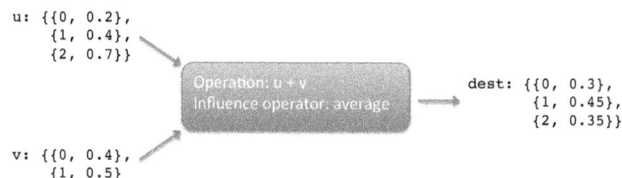

Figure 2: Tracking influences for multiple initial values using unique "colors."

cial to use a combining function that weights the influences associated with the input values based on their magnitude.

The value influence tracking approach described above is sufficient if only a single value's influence is tracked, but it is often useful to be able to track the influences of multiple values simultaneously. To do this, a "color" C is associated with each influence value, and the influence data associated with a location L is a set of $(color, influence)$ pairs. Figure 2 illustrates how a combining operator works when influences for multiple values are being tracked. In the example, the values of variables u and v are being summed to produce a value that is stored in location *dest*. Both u and v have associated influence data; u has three colors of influence (0, 1, and 2), while v has only two colors (0 and 1). The combining operator averages the influence data for each color separately, using an influence value of 0 for any color that is not explicitly represented, and associates the resulting averages by color with the output location *dest*.

Tracking influences for multiple values has a higher overhead in space and time than tracking the influence of a single value. More space is required because of the need to store influences for multiple colors per location, and more time is required because the combining operator must combine the input influence data for each color separately. The actual time and space requirements depend on the number of initial values being tracked (hence the number of colors) and how those values are used in the computation.

For the work described in this paper, we augmented the existing *VIT* value influence tracking tool [13] to add support for applications that use MPI-1 communication operations. *VIT* uses Intel's Pin meta-tool [7] for dynamic instrumentation of the application's machine code. *VIT* examines the application's machine code to determine the instructions that produce an output value, and inserts instrumentation so that whenever such an instruction is executed the tool updates the influence data associated with the output value as described above. *VIT* provides a simple API for tool control, with bindings for both C and Fortran programs. The user instructs *VIT* to start tracking a value's influence by passing its address to `VIT_Track`. The user can use `VIT_Report` to output *VIT*'s influence data, and reset that data using `VIT_Reset`.

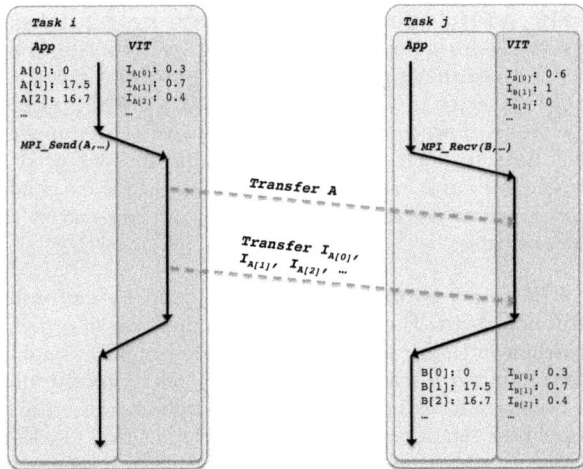

Figure 3: Conceptual picture of propagating value influence for MPI two-sided operations.

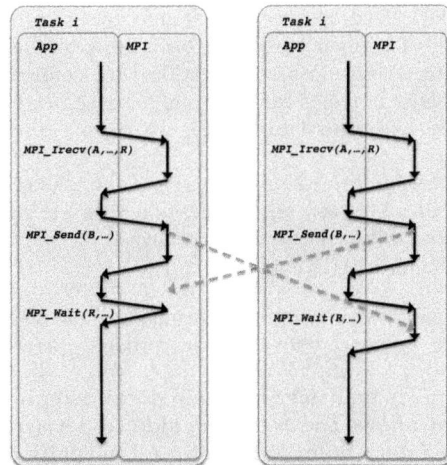

Figure 4: Common implementation of data exchange between two processes using MPI point-to-point operations to overlap computation and communication and avoid deadlock.

3. SUPPORT FOR MPI-1 OPERATIONS

MPI-based applications use MPI communication operations to transfer data between processes. When data in a source process is transmitted to one or more destination processes, any value influence information associated with the data in the source process' address space must also be transmitted to the destination process(es), to be associated with the data after it is received. To do this, *VIT* must be able to detect when a process is involved in a data transfer and must be able to modify the behavior of that transfer. The MPI standard defines a profiling interface, commonly called the *PMPI interface* because its function names are named with the prefix "PMPI," that provides both required capabilities. This interface allows link-time interposition of a function between the caller of an MPI function and the MPI library's implementation of that function. Our version of *VIT* includes a library of interposition functions that transfer value influence data along with the application's data. Others have developed similar "data piggybacking" approaches in tools for MPI-based applications [17, 16, 14, 15], but the existing approaches either lack portability between MPI implementations or are not flexible enough to deal with variable amounts of piggybacked influence data.

We divide the MPI-1 communication operations into two categories: two-sided point-to-point operations and blocking collective operations. Our approach to propagating value influence data between application processes depends on the type of operation used to transfer the application's data.

3.1 Point-to-Point Operations

Propagating value influence data for two-sided MPI point-to-point data transfers is conceptually simple (see Figure 3). Within each application process, *VIT* maintains a set of location-influence pairs for its own address space. When a process (labeled *Task i* in the figure) sends data to another process, it calls an MPI function such as MPI_Send. Because *VIT* interposes a function at the PMPI interface, the sender invokes our version of MPI_Send instead. Our version of this function sends not only the application's array A, but also any influence data associated with array A. To send the application's array, our interposition function uses the PMPI

send operation corresponding to the MPI function called by the application. For instance, if the application called MPI_Isend to initiate transfer of the data, *VIT*'s interposition function would use PMPI_Isend to transmit the data. In the example shown in the figure, the interposition function uses PMPI_Send to transfer the data. When transferring the value influence data, *VIT* uses the same destination specification, communicator, and tag value as was used for the application's data to ensure that the value influence data is delivered to the same receiving process. The receiving process calls an MPI point-to-point receive function such as MPI_Recv, invoking *VIT*'s interposed version of that function. This function receives the application data and then receives the associated influence data and applies it to the data in its receive location (called array B in the receiving process). The application data's location in the destination process address space might not be the same as it was in the source address space. So, the sending *VIT* interposition function converts the location part of the transferred influence data from absolute addresses into offsets into the send-side data buffer. The interposition function in the receiving process converts the offsets back into absolute addresses for locations within the receive-side data buffer. If the source and destination have different architectures (e.g., different byte orders), *VIT*'s interposition functions could adjust the incoming value influence data before applying the $(location, influence)$ data to its receive buffer.

In reality, the transfer of value influence data for point-to-point operations is more complicated than this conceptual picture. This complexity is the result of several inter-related causes:

- The amount of influence data that must be transferred from the sending process to the receiving process is not known *a priori* by the receiving process.

- MPI-1 defines several types of interoperable point-to-point send and receive operations. There are blocking and non-blocking versions, several *communication modes*, and a combined MPI_Sendrecv operation. Many applications pair a `MPI_Send` operation (that may block) with a non-blocking `MPI_Irecv` operation because it may allow the application to overlap computation with communication and because it avoids the potential for deadlock when two processes exchange data (see Figure 4).

- Transparency from the perspective of the application is a *VIT* goal. The way the application uses MPI does not depend on whether it is being analyzed by *VIT* (though the behavior of MPI might).

These causes have several implications for how *VIT* propagates value influence data for point-to-point operations:

1. *VIT* must transfer influence data using a mechanism that allows the receiving side to determine the amount of data being sent before it actually receives the data. Because the receiving process cannot know *a priori* how much data it will receive, the *VIT* receive interposition functions must dynamically determine how much value influence data has been sent and allocate buffers to receive that data. When receiving value influence data (see Figure 5), *VIT*'s interposition function uses `PMPI_Probe` to block until the data arrives, and then uses `PMPI_Get_count` to determine the number of (*location*, *influence*) pairs in the data. It then allocates buffers large enough to hold this data, uses `PMPI_Recv` to receive the data into those buffers, and associates the value influence data with the data in the application's receive buffer. Our initial *VIT* implementation used a separate message to communicate the number of value influence data items from sender to receiver before sending the actual value influence data, but we modified the implementation to use `MPI_Probe` to reduce the number of *VIT* messages required.

2. When the application uses a non-blocking receive, *VIT* must receive the value influence data in the interposition function that *finalizes* the receive. *VIT* cannot receive the value influence data in its `MPI_Irecv` interposition function because it would turn a non-blocking operation into a blocking one, breaking our transparency goal. For instance, consider the data exchange from Figure 4. If *VIT* received its value influence data in the `MPI_Irecv` interposition function, the application would deadlock because both processes will block on the receive and never send their own data. Instead, *VIT* must wait to receive its influence data until the receiving process can block to receive its application data, namely when it calls `MPI_Wait` or one of its variants to finalize the receive (see Figure 5). It is acceptable to use blocking receive operations to receive the value influence data within this interposition function because the process was prepared to block at this point in its execution. There is an additional complication, however. The application provides the information that *VIT* needs to receive and apply the value influence data to the receive buffer when it calls `MPI_Irecv`, but not when it calls `MPI_Wait`. To make this data available to *VIT*'s `MPI_Wait` interposition function, the `MPI_Irecv` interposition function saves the receive buffer length, source, tag, and communicator parameters provided by the application in a map data structure for use later in its `MPI_Wait` interposition function. As a key, it uses the `MPI_Request` provided by the MPI library when *VIT* posted the application's non-blocking receive. The application provides this same `MPI_Request` to

the `MPI_Wait` interposition function, which uses it to retrieve the parameters provided by the application in its `MPI_Irecv` call. Because the application may have provided wildcards for the source or tag parameters, *VIT* uses the `MPI_Status` data provided when it finalized the receive of the application's data to determine the true sender and tag used to transfer the application's data, and uses that same sender and tag to receive the value influence data instead of the wildcard values.

3. *VIT* must transfer application data before value influence data. Handling `MPI_Irecv` imposes an ordering constraint in that it forces *VIT* to transfer application data before influence data so that the non-blocking receive does not become a blocking operation. This ordering must also be adopted for the other point-to-point interposition functions because the MPI point-to-point operations are interoperable. In our *VIT* implementation, we also use this ordering for collective operations. Although this ordering is not required for supporting the MPI-1 blocking collectives, it will be necessary for the MPI-3 non-blocking collective operations and so we adopt the ordering for all functions in the *VIT* interposition library.

4. *VIT* must send influence data using non-blocking sends. In the data exchange scenario of Figure 4, each process posts a receive for the application data it expects to receive. As explained earlier, *VIT* cannot post a non-blocking receive for the value influence data because neither receiver can known *a priori* how much data will be sent. If the *VIT* `MPI_Send` interposition function used a blocking send to transfer the value influence data, the application may deadlock with some MPI implementations because neither process has posted a receive for that data. Because *VIT* cannot use a non-blocking receive to work around this deadlock scenario, it must use non-blocking sends for the value influence data. When the application calls any point-to-point send function, the *VIT* interposition function uses the corresponding PMPI version of the function to initiate the send the application's data, and then uses `PMPI_Isend` to initiate the transfer of the value influence data associated with the application's send buffer. The interposition function saves the `MPI_Request` structures provided by the MPI library in a queue, along with pointers to the dynamically-allocated buffers holding the value influence data. When the process calls another MPI function (including `MPI_Finalize`), the *VIT* interposition function attempts to finalize any outstanding non-blocking sends from that queue and deallocate the memory used to hold the value influence data. In our current *VIT* implementation, we attempt to finalize these influence data sends only in the interposition functions for `MPI_Wait` and `MPI_Finalize`. In the future, we may add these send finalization checks to other interposition functions to control *VIT*'s use of MPI resources and its memory footprint for applications that do not call `MPI_Wait` frequently.

3.2 Collective Operations

Collective communication operations ("collectives") present some additional challenges for propagating value influence data compared to two-sided point-to-point operations. As for point-to-point operations, we use the PMPI interface to interpose our own versions of the collective functions that transfer not only the application data but also our influ-

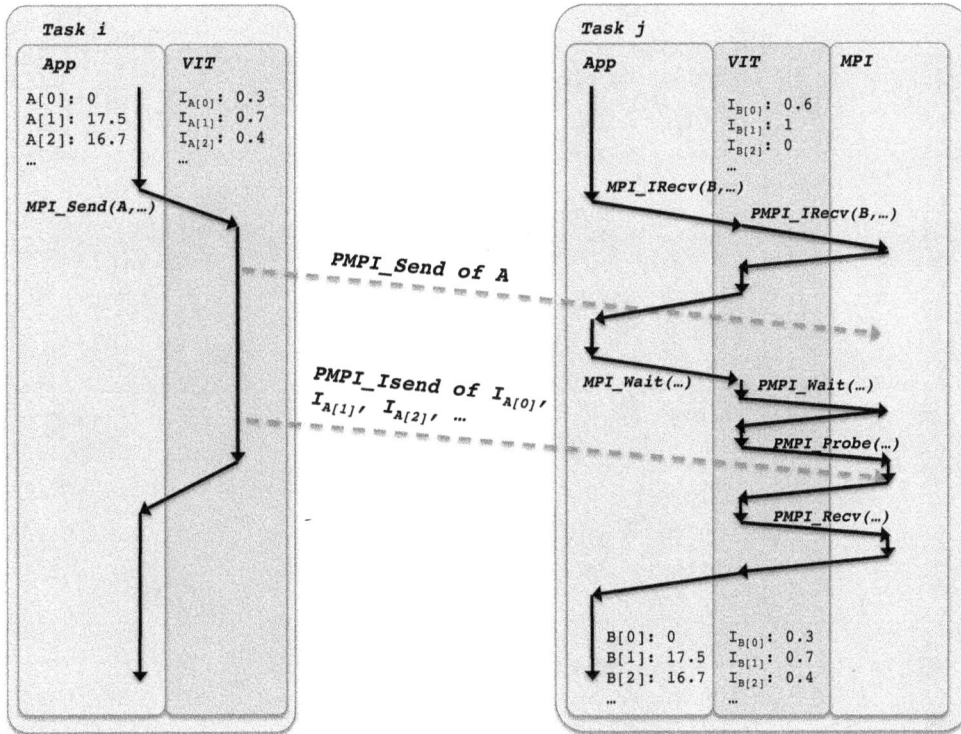

Figure 5: Propagating value influence for a point-to-point transfer using a non-blocking receive.

ence data. Handling collective operations like `MPI_Bcast` and `MPI_Scatter` that transfer data from one root process to one or more destination processes is relatively straightforward. The *VIT* interposition function first calls the PMPI version of the collective operation to transfer the application data. In the root process, the interposition function then determines how many location-influence pairs are associated with the source buffer (or buffers, in the case of functions like `MPI_Scatter`) and uses the PMPI version of the function to distribute this information to the non-root processes. Because there is no analogue to `MPI_Probe` for collective operations, we must use an explicit message for distributing the information about the number of $(location, influence)$ pairs in the influence data. The non-root processes use this number to allocate memory buffers sized appropriately for the influence data being sent. All processes then call the PMPI function to transfer the influence data, and processes apply this influence data to their receive buffers.

Collective operations such as `MPI_Reduce` that apply a combining operation to the input data are even more challenging to support. In addition to applying the operation to the application's input data using the PMPI version of the function, the *VIT* interposition function must also combine any influence data associated with the input buffers using the same MPI operation and an appropriate influence combining operator. For instance, the interposition function for `MPI_Reduce` must call the `PMPI_Reduce` function for the application data, and then apply an appropriate reduction to any influence data associated with the input buffers provided to the `MPI_Reduce` function. Because each process may have influence data associated with a different set of its own locations, this reduction is very complicated to implement if the influence data is left in the sparse form *VIT* normally uses

within its influence data map. To avoid this complexity in our initial *VIT* implementation, processes contributing data to a reducing collective operation first convert their influence data to a dense form, then all processes participate in the collective operation on the influence data, and finally processes that receive data convert the result back to its sparse form and apply it to their receive buffers. Figure 6 illustrates this sequence for a two-process `MPI_Reduce` operation. Both processes provided an array of four integers located at address 0x40000 as input to the operation. Process r is the root process for the collective, and provided a buffer at address 0x50000 to receive the reduction result.

At the outset (Figure 6a, processes r and i both have influence data associated with their input buffers but the data is not associated with the same set of locations within each process' local buffer. *VIT*'s `MPI_Reduce` implementation converts the sparse influence data to a dense form in which zero-valued influence data is explicitly represented (Figure 6b). *VIT* then combines the dense influence data using a reduce operation (Figure 6c). The current *VIT* implementation uses the average operator to combine value influence data (see Section 2), but because the MPI standard does not predefine an `MPI_AVERAGE` reduction operator, we instead use the `MPI_SUM` operator when reducing value influence data and divide the resulting influence values by the number of processes contributing data to the operation (Figure 6d). *VIT* then converts the data back to a sparse form (Figure 6e) and applies the resulting influence data to the root process' receive buffer.

This approach is straightforward but costly in terms of both space (because it explicitly represents all zero influence values associated with the input buffers) and time (because it must convert influence data between sparse and dense

(a) Initial influence data.

(b) After converting to dense form.

(c) After `MPI_SUM` reduction.

(d) After dividing by number of processes.

(e) After converting back to sparse form and applying to receive buffer.

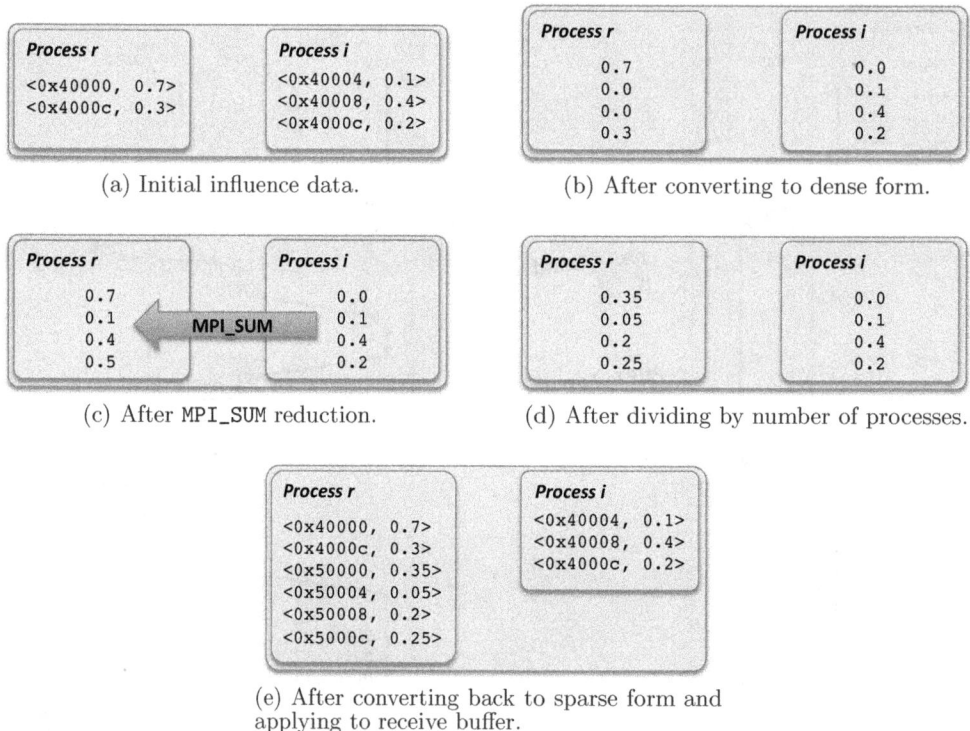

Figure 6: Propagating value influence for collective operations with a reduction, such as `MPI_Reduce`. *In the example, both processes use* `0x40000` *as a send buffer and the root process* r *uses* `0x50000` *as a receive buffer.*

forms). Also, in some scenarios such as that shown in Figure 6, the influence data in sparse form can require more memory than in the dense form. As an optimization, a future *VIT* version may keep its influence data in sparse or dense form on a data-object-specific basis.

In the `MPI_Reduce` example, *VIT* used the `MPI_SUM` built-in operator to combine influence data, and then divided each item in the result using number of processes involved in the collective operation. Determining this number of processes is easier for some collective operations than others. For instance, for an `MPI_Reduce` it is simply the size of the communicator used in the reduction, but for `MPI_Scan` it depends on the rank of the receiving process within that communicator. Supporting more sophisticated value influence combining operators than the average operator is even more challenging. For instance, if the reduction operation is `MPI_SUM`, averaging the influences of the values being reduced may be appropriate. On the other hand, if the reduction operation is `MPI_MAX`, it is more appropriate to simply use the influence associated with the input data having the maximum value. Handling these sophisticated influence combining operators is left for future work.

4. CASE STUDIES

To test, debug, and evaluate our MPI-1 support within *VIT*, we performed case studies of a value influence analysis for two scientific applications running on a Linux cluster.

4.1 Test System

For our case studies, we used the Keeneland Initial Delivery System [18] (KIDS). KIDS is a Georgia Institute of Technology development system deployed at Oak Ridge National Laboratory. The system had 120 HP ProLiant SL390 G7 nodes, each with 24 GB of memory, three NVIDIA M2090 GPUs, and two Intel Xeon X5660 processors running at 2.80 GHz. For our case studies, we did not use the system's GPUs. The nodes were connected using an Infiniband QDR interconnection network. The system used the CentOS 6.3 Linux distribution on its compute nodes, and we used OpenMPI 1.6.1 with the GNU version 4.4.6 C, C++, and Fortran compilers. We used Intel Pin version 2.13-62141 for our *VIT* implementation.

4.2 LAMMPS

The Large-scale Atomic/Molecular Massively Parallel Simulator [9] (LAMMPS) is a framework for molecular dynamics simulations. The application is written in C++ and uses functions from the MPI-1 standard for communication and synchronization. For this case study, we obtained the LAMMPS source code (revision adaba95e dated 2013-12-18) from the project's Git repository. We added a makefile for building LAMMPS on KIDS such that it incorporates the *VIT* PMPI and API libraries into the LAMMPS executable file. We modified the source code slightly to add a call to `VIT_Track` for the x-coordinate of the first atom in the process with MPI rank 0, and added calls to `VIT_Report` at the end of each time step and after the simulation finishes. For this case study, we used the LJ and EAM benchmark problems that are distributed with the LAMMPS source code distribution. We ran these benchmarks in weak scaling mode, varying the number of processes between 12 and 768 processes (i.e., between 1 and 64 nodes with 12 processes per node on KIDS). To control run time, we modified the benchmark problem input files to reduce the number of simulation

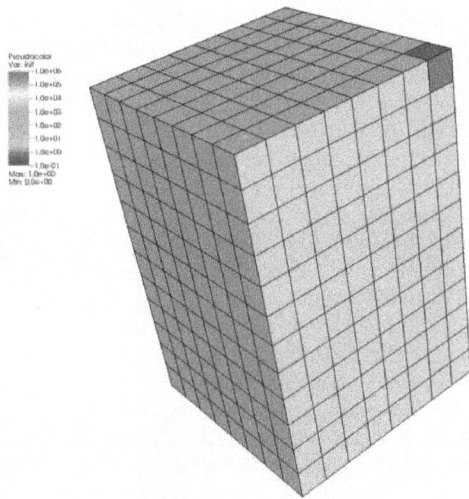

(a) Before time steps.

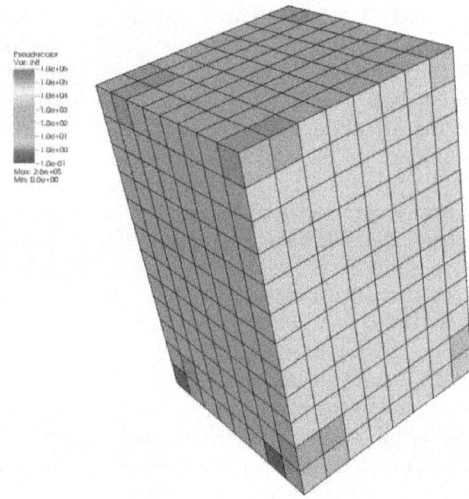

(b) After one time step.

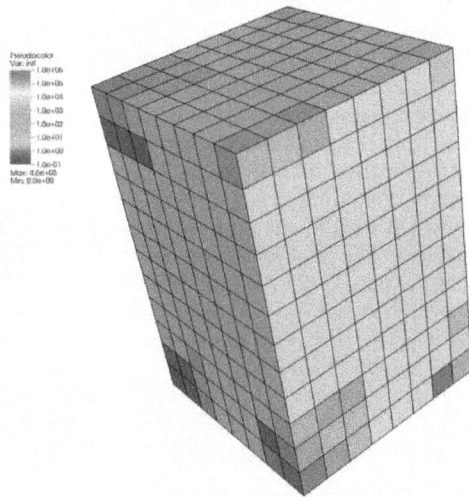

(c) After two time steps.

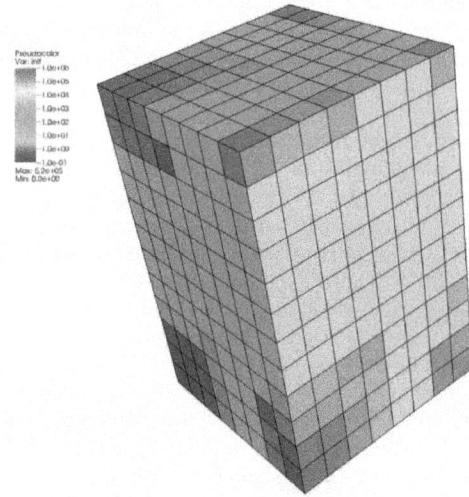

(d) After three time steps.

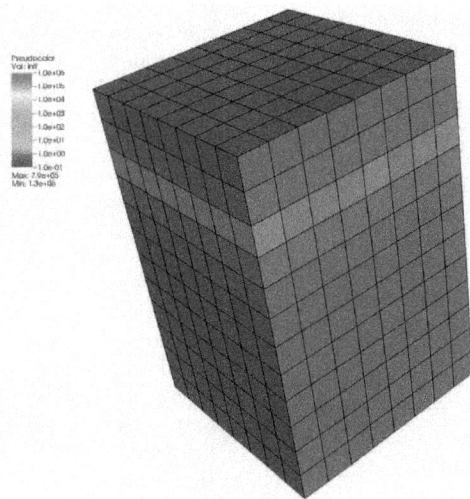

(e) After nine time steps.

Figure 7: Propagation of value influence data from one initial location for a LAMMPS EAM simulation. *Each cell represents a simulation process, and cell color is determined by the number of non-zero influence values in the associated process.*

time steps from 100 to 10 and limited the amount of data per process to approximately 13.15 MB for the LJ problem and 15.30 MB for the EAM problem.

Figure 7 shows how our *VIT* tool propagates value influence data using MPI operations for the LAMMPS EAM benchmark problem. In each plot, a cube represents one MPI process. The color of a cube represents the number of locations within that process' address space that have non-zero value influence data. Before the application has entered its main time stepping loop (Figure 7a), process 0 has one location with non-zero influence, namely the x coordinate of its first atom. During subsequent time steps (Figures 7b through 7d), the value influence data propagates via the application's MPI data transfers to neighboring application processes. By the end of the ninth time step (Figure 7e), the influence of the initial atom's x coordinate value has propagated throughout the problem domain. In this experiment, we tracked the influence of only the x coordinate of one atom, and we see in these images that the influence spreads more quickly in the horizontal direction.

Figure 8a shows the overhead of *VIT* for the LAMMPS benchmark problems. The figure shows the time required to run the application as measured by the GNU time utility. The y axis is logarithmic. The lines labeled "track" show the time required to run the application after having tagged the x coordinate of the first atom in the MPI rank 0 process as having an influence of 1.0. To establish a baseline for the overhead caused by *VIT* instrumentation, we also measured the time required to run the application under *VIT* but without tracking any value influence data. In this scenario, *VIT* instrumentation executes whenever the application encounters an instruction that computes a result, but that instrumentation never had to compute or propagate influence data. These measurements are shown using lines labeled "null" in the figure. Finally, the lines labeled "uninst" show the time required to run the application without *VIT*. As expected for a tool that executes instrumentation for a significant fraction of the application's instructions, the *VIT* overhead is high. To date, we have done very little to optimize *VIT*'s performance to reduce this overhead. Also, the "track" scenario overhead is artificially high in that we saved the value influence data to the file system after every time step so as to produce the visualization of influence propagation shown in Figure 7. Writing a large amount of non-zero influence data after each time step caused high I/O costs, especially for runs with a large number of processes. Although saving influence data with granularity can be useful for some analysis scenarios, in many cases a *VIT* user would save influence data much less frequently. We plan to investigate several potential approaches for reducing overhead such as keeping influence data in a data structure sorted by address for improved performance when querying the set of influence values associated with a location or range of locations (such as a buffer provided to an MPI send function), and better tailoring of *VIT* I/O to the underlying parallel file system when one is available. However, because of the nature of its software-based instruction-level instrumentation, we expect that the overhead for this approach to value influence tracking will remain high.

4.3 MPAS-Ocean

The Model for Prediction Across Scales [8] (MPAS) is a framework for rapid development of dynamical cores for cli-

mate models. MPAS-Ocean [12] is an ocean model built using this framework. The model is written in Fortran and uses functions from the MPI-1 standard for communication and synchronization. We obtained the MPAS 2.0 source code (revision 75fa8ebf7 dated 2013-11-14) from the project's Git repository. We modified the MPAS makefile so that the "gfortran" configuration links against the *VIT* PMPI and API libraries. As with LAMMPS, we modified the source code slightly to add calls to the **VIT_Track** and **VIT_Report** API functions. Unlike LAMMPS, we did not modify the code to write influence data to the file system after every time step, but rather only at the end of the application run. We used the worldOcean_QU_120km benchmark problem. This fixed-size benchmark problem is distributed with partition input files for 64 and 128 processes. We ran the 64 process configuration on 8 KIDS nodes and the 128 process configuration on 16 KIDS nodes. To control run time under *VIT*, we modified the benchmark problem inputs to run for 6 simulation hours (8 time steps) instead of the 360 days specified in the original benchmark problem input file.

Due to space limitations, we provide only *VIT* overhead results for MPAS-Ocean in this paper. Figure 8b shows the overhead of *VIT* for the MPAS-Ocean benchmark problems, with 64 and 128 processes. The bars in this figure are labeled similarly to those in the LAMMPS overhead figure. In the "track" runs, *VIT* exhibited a segmentation fault during program finalization after all time steps had completed, so the actual elapsed time is slightly underreported in the figure. As with LAMMPS, the *VIT* overhead with MPAS-Ocean is high due to the instrumentation's cost and how frequently it is executed. The *VIT* overhead results for MPAS-Ocean shows a larger gap between the "null" and "track" scenarios that for LAMMPS. This indicates that the type of value being tracked, and how it is used in the computation, can have a substantial impact on the tool's overhead.

5. SUPPORT FOR MPI-2 AND MPI-3

Our *VIT* implementation does not support MPI-2's one-sided point-to-point operations nor the non-blocking collectives defined in the MPI-3 standard. However, we believe our approach to supporting MPI-1 operations can be augmented to support both of these types of operations.

For one-sided point-to-point operations, we envision an approach that uses a separate "value influence server thread" running in each application process. When a process calls **MPI_Get** or **MPI_Put**, the *VIT* interposition function would connect to this value influence server thread using an out-of-band channel such as a socket or shadow MPI communicator to either get or put the value influence data associated with the application data being transferred. The *VIT* interposition function for **MPI_Win_fence** associated with the transfer would have to ensure that the value influence data transfer had completed before returning to the caller.

For non-blocking collective operations, our approach would be similar to that we used for non-blocking point-to-point operations. When a process calls a non-blocking collective function like **MPI_Ialltoall**, the *VIT* interposition function would save the parameters provided by the application. When the process later calls a completion function like **MPI_Wait**, the *VIT* interposition function would transfer the value influence data as it does for blocking collective operations (see Section 3.2) and apply it to the process' receive buffers.

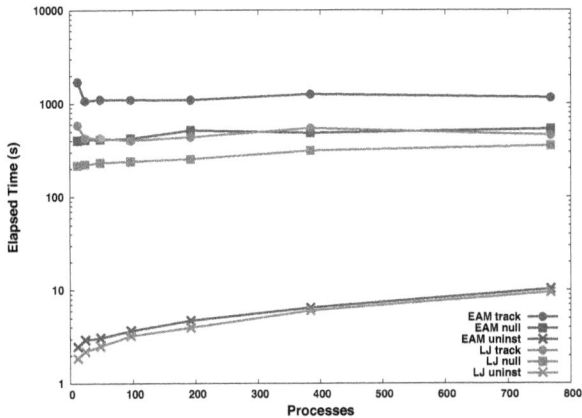

(a) LAMMPS LJ and EAM benchmark problems.

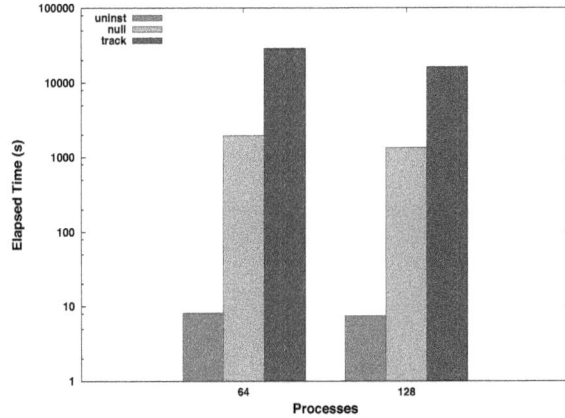

(b) MPAS-Ocean worldOcean_QU_120km problem.

Figure 8: *VIT* **runtime when tracking value influence ("track"), instrumented but not tracking value influence ("null"), and uninstrumented ("uninst").**

6. RELATED WORK

Value influence tracking [13] is a direct, data-centric technique for determining how values are used in a computation. It is related to program slicing [19, 20], chopping [5, 11], Taint Analysis [6, 2], and automatic differentiation [10, 1]. Unlike the code-centric views of forward program slicing and chopping, value influence tracking provides a data-centric view by indicating the values that are computed using a set of initial values, and how much the initial value contributed to those values. Value influence tracking performs a similar analysis to Taint Analysis, but whereas Taint Analysis associates a binary taint metric with all values (i.e., a value is tainted or it is not), value influence tracking associates a real-valued influence with each value. Automatic differentiation could have been used instead of value influence tracking analysis for the case study presented in the initial value influence tracking paper, but value influence tracking can be applied more broadly than automatic differentiation. For instance, a value influence tracking analysis can be applied to the input parameters of a parallel discrete event simulation of traffic congestion, whereas automatic differentiation of this discrete event simulation may be a nonsensical concept.

Our approach to supporting value influence tracking analyses for MPI applications relies heavily on the ability to transparently "piggyback" influence data on an application's normal data transfers. The MPI standard does not define a mechanism for piggybacking data that is transparent to the application, but the functionality is useful for implementing performance tools, MPI communication/synchronization debuggers, and fault tolerant communication protocols, so several approaches to piggybacking data with MPI communication have been used. The first approach uses a modified MPI runtime. For instance, the PHOTON MPI application profiler [17] used a modified MPI runtime to piggyback performance data with the application's message transfers. Although this approach can provide low overhead, it decreases application and tool portability across different MPI implementations. The second approach uses MPI derived types. MPI allows the definition and use of data types derived from its predefined set of types. Shende et al [16] and Schulz [14] use derived types to combine the application's data and their

performance/analysis data into a single data type. In both cases, the piggybacked data was of a known, fixed size (e.g., the size of one timestamp), whereas for value influence tracking we must support variable-length piggybacked data. Furthermore, performance studies of the use of derived data types for piggybacking data [15] suggest that the handling of derived data types by some MPI implementations is very inefficient. The third approach, which we adopt in our value influence tracking approach, uses separate messages for the piggybacked data. This approach can also exhibit high overhead, and requires special handling when receive operations use wildcards for the source task ID and/or message tag. No existing MPI piggybacking approach is ideal, but unless and until the MPI standard defines a piggybacking mechanism, we feel the simplicity of the separate messages approach outweighs its disadvantages compared to the alternatives for use in a value influence tracking tool for MPI applications.

7. SUMMARY

In this paper, we presented an approach for doing a value influence tracking analysis with applications that use MPI two-sided point-to-point operations and blocking collective operations. We described the design and implementation of our approach, and described two case studies of using our value influence tracking analysis tool with the LAMMPS molecular dynamics application and the MPAS-Ocean climate model. We also discussed how our support for MPI-1 applications could be extended to support MPI-2 one-sided operations and MPI-3 non-blocking collective communication operations.

Going forward, we plan to optimize our implementation of value influence tracking for MPI-1 operations to reduce the overhead. We also plan to implement and evaluate our approach for supporting MPI-2 and MPI-3 operations. Finally, we plan to evaluate whether our approach for supporting value influence propagation for MPI applications can be adapted for programs that use accelerators like GPUs.

8. ACKNOWLEDGMENTS

Support for this work was provided through the Scientific Discovery through Advanced Computing (SciDAC) program funded by U.S. Department of Energy, Office of Science, Advanced Scientific Computing Research. The work was performed at the Oak Ridge National Laboratory, which is managed by UT-Battelle, LLC under Contract No. DE-AC05-00OR22725 to the U.S. Government. Accordingly, the U.S. Government retains a non-exclusive, royalty-free license to publish or reproduce the published form of this contribution, or allow others to do so, for U.S. Government purposes.

9. REFERENCES

[1] C. H. Bischof, H. M. Bücker, P. Hovland, U. Naumann, and J. Utke. *Advances in Automatic Differentiation*. Springer Publishing Company, Incorporated, 1st edition, 2008.

[2] M. Ganai, D. Lee, and A. Gupta. DTAM: dynamic taint analysis of multi-threaded programs for relevancy. In *Proceedings of the ACM SIGSOFT 20th International Symposium on the Foundations of Software Engineering*, FSE '12, pages 46:1–46:11, New York, NY, USA, 2012. ACM.

[3] W. Gropp, E. Lusk, and A. Skjellum. *Using MPI: portable parallel programming with the message-passing interface*. Scientific and engineering computation. MIT Press, Cambridge, MA, 2nd edition, 1999.

[4] W. Gropp, R. Thakur, and E. Lusk. *Using MPI-2: Advanced Features of the Message Passing Interface*. MIT Press, Cambridge, MA, USA, 1999.

[5] D. Jackson and E. J. Rollins. Chopping: A generalization of slicing. Technical report, Pittsburgh, PA, USA, 1994.

[6] M. G. Kang, S. McCamant, P. Poosankam, and D. Song. Dta++: Dynamic taint analysis with targeted control-flow propagation. In *NDSS*. The Internet Society, 2011.

[7] C.-K. Luk, R. Cohn, R. Muth, H. Patil, A. Klauser, G. Lowney, S. Wallace, V. J. Reddi, and K. Hazelwood. Pin: building customized program analysis tools with dynamic instrumentation. *SIGPLAN Not.*, 40(6):190–200, June 2005.

[8] MPAS. http://mpas-dev.github.io, 2013.

[9] S. Plimpton. Fast parallel algorithms for short-range molecular dynamics. *Journal of Computational Physics*, 117:1–19, 1995.

[10] L. B. Rall and G. F. Corliss. An introduction to automatic differentiation. In M. Berz, C. H. Bischof, G. F. Corliss, and A. Griewank, editors, *Computational Differentiation: Techniques,*

Applications, and Tools, pages 1–17. SIAM, Philadelphia, PA, 1996.

[11] T. Reps and G. Rosay. Precise interprocedural chopping. *SIGSOFT Softw. Eng. Notes*, 20(4):41–52, Oct. 1995.

[12] T. Ringler, M. Petersen, R. L. Higdon, D. Jacobsen, P. W. Jones, and M. Maltrud. A multi-resolution approach to global ocean modeling. *Ocean Modelling*, 69:211–232, 2013.

[13] P. C. Roth. Tracking a value's influence on later computation. In *Proceedings of the 6th Workshop on Productivity and Performance (PROPER 2013)*, Aug. 2013.

[14] M. Schulz. Extracting critical path graphs from MPI applications. In *Cluster Computing, 2005. IEEE International*, pages 1–10, 2005.

[15] M. Schulz, G. Bronevetsky, and B. R. de Supinski. On the performance of transparent mpi piggyback messages. In A. Lastovetsky, T. Kechadi, and J. Dongarra, editors, *Recent Advances in Parallel Virtual Machine and Message Passing Interface*, volume 5205 of *Lecture Notes in Computer Science*, pages 194–201. Springer Berlin Heidelberg, 2008.

[16] S. Shende, A. D. Malony, A. Morris, and F. Wolf. Performance profiling overhead compensation for MPI programs. In *Proceedings of the 12th European PVM/MPI Users' Group Conference on Recent Advances in Parallel Virtual Machine and Message Passing Interface*, PVM/MPI'05, pages 359–367, Berlin, Heidelberg, 2005. Springer-Verlag.

[17] J. Vetter. Dynamic statistical profiling of communication activity in distributed applications. In *Proceedings of the 2002 ACM SIGMETRICS International Conference on Measurement and Modeling of Computer Systems*, SIGMETRICS '02, pages 240–250, New York, NY, USA, 2002. ACM.

[18] J. Vetter, R. Glassbrook, J. Dongarra, K. Schwan, B. Loftis, S. McNally, J. Meredith, J. Rogers, P. Roth, K. Spafford, and S. Yalamanchili. Keeneland: Bringing heterogeneous GPU computing to the computational science community. *Computing in Science Engineering*, 13(5):90–95, 2011.

[19] M. Weiser. Program slicing. In *Proceedings of the 5th international conference on Software engineering*, ICSE '81, pages 439–449, Piscataway, NJ, USA, 1981. IEEE Press.

[20] M. Weiser. Program slicing. *Software Engineering, IEEE Transactions on*, SE-10(4):352–357, 1984.

Scalable Performance Analysis of ExaScale MPI Programs through Signature-Based Clustering Algorithms *

Amir Bahmani
North Carolina State University
Raleigh, NC
abahman@ncsu.edu

Frank Mueller
North Carolina State University
Raleigh, NC
mueller@ncsu.edu

ABSTRACT

Extreme-scale computing poses a number of challenges to application performance. Developers need to study application behavior by collecting detailed information with the help of tracing toolsets to determine shortcomings. But not only applications are "scalability challenged", current tracing toolsets also fall short of exascale requirements for low background overhead since trace collection for each execution entity is becoming infeasible. One effective solution is to cluster processes with the same behavior into groups. Instead of collecting performance information from each individual node, this information can be collected from just a set of representative nodes. This work contributes a fast, scalable, signature-based clustering algorithm that clusters processes exhibiting similar execution behavior. Instead of prior work based on statistical clustering, our approach produces precise results nearly without loss of events or accuracy. The proposed algorithm combines low overhead at the clustering level with $log(P)$ time complexity, and it splits the merge process to make tracing suitable for extreme-scale computing. Overall, this multi-level precise clustering based on signatures further generalizes to a novel multi-metric clustering technique with unprecedented low overhead.

Categories and Subject Descriptors

I.5.3 [**Clustering**]: Algorithms; D.1.3 [**Programming Techniques**]: Concurrent Programming; D.4.8 [**Performance**]: Measurement

General Terms

Measurement, Performance

Keywords

High-Performance Computing, Message Passing, Tracing, Clustering Algorithms

1. INTRODUCTION

Scientific computing applications continue to push the envelope on ever increasing demand for computational power. This trend is driven by a need to increase model resolution

---

*This research was funded in part by the National Science Foundation, award number 1217748.

by orders of magnitude combined with multi-level simulation combing models at different granularity. High-performance computing (HPC) hardware platforms are struggling to keep peace with these demands as a number of challenges are posed in terms of hardware and software advances for next-generation HPC at exascale Flops (Floating-point operations per second) rates. To effectively utilize such extreme-scale HPC platforms, developers need to observe and tune application behavior to ensure their algorithms still scale to larger number of nodes and cores, a process that is typically repeated for each order-of-magnitude increase in compute capability (Flops). This process is generally aided by collecting detailed information with tracing toolsets to determine algorithmic, software and hardware resource shortcomings. This allows developers to study application behavior of such performance information utilizing performance analysis tools. While applications may be considered "scalability challenged" when exposed to yet another larger platform, current tracing toolsets also fall short of exascale requirements: They can no longer ensure a low background overhead of their tool workload since trace collection for each execution entity is becoming infeasible at extreme scales for hundreds of thousands of cores and beyond. Most tools either obtain lossless trace information at the price of limited scalability, such as Vamipir [3], or preserve only aggregated statistical trace information to conserve the size of trace files, as in mpiP [21].

At extreme scale, tracing tools, linked with applications, could severely affect the efficiency and scalability of the system. The tracing background workload may compete with the application for resources, which can perturb the application's behavior. Moreover, due to the large I/O requirement of tracing data required for applications on top-end HPC platforms, collecting detailed performance information comprehensively may not be feasible from a scalability perspective. Therefore, tool designers need to develop new strategies to address these problems.

One effective solution is to cluster processes with the same behavior into groups; then, instead of collecting performance information from all individual nodes, such information can be collected from just a single node (or a set of representative nodes) per cluster group.

This paper proposes a fast, scalable, signature-based clustering algorithm that clusters processes exhibiting similar execution behavior. We apply our clustering algorithm on trace files created by the public release of ScalaTrace V2 [24], a state-of-the-art MPI message passing tracing toolset. ScalaTrace V2 provides orders of magnitude smaller if not near-constant sized communication traces regardless of the number of nodes while preserving structural information.

ScalaTrace employs a two-stage trace compression technique, namely intra-node and inter-node compression [16,

25]). It utilizes Regular Section Descriptors (RSDs) to capture the loop structures of one or multiple communication events. Power-RSDs (PRSDs) are utilized to recursively specify RSDs in nested loops (see Section 2). After each node has created its own compressed trace file and the program is completing, ScalaTrace performs an inter-node compression over a radix tree rooted in rank 0. During this reduction, internal nodes combine their traces with other task-level traces that they receive from child nodes. While intra-compression is fast and efficient, inter-node compression is a costly operation with $O(n^2 \log P)$ time complexity, where n (typically a constant) is the number of MPI events in PRSD compressed notation and P is the number of processes. Our clustering algorithm addresses the high overhead due to scaling out to 100,000+ processor cores by significantly reducing P to a constant for most cases (or a sub-linear term of P for the remaining ones), thereby effectively eliminating this bottleneck.

The proposed clustering algorithm has two levels, the first of which employs *call-path clustering* based on the stack signature of MPI events. We use the stack signature to distinguish events originating from different call sequences with associated call paths. The call-path signature is the aggregated composition of stack signatures of different events. The first level of clustering distinguishes processes with different execution structures.

Parameter clustering is the second level of clustering. At this level, we use a different signature called the parameter signature. This signature composes parameters of the MPI call event, such as count (number of data elements), type (data type), source, destination, etc., excluding the message content itself. Once the algorithm has clustered processes with different execution structures, with the help of parameter clustering, we distinguish processes with the same execution structure but different parameters.

To evaluate the accuracy and scalability of our algorithm, we also designed a *reference clustering* approach based on a reference signature. The reference signature covers call-path signatures by adding a sequence number to each MPI event as well as parameter clustering by keeping each MPI event's parameters uncompressed. Detailed implementation information about call-path+parameter clustering and reference clustering algorithms are discussed in the following sections.

Contributions: • We provide a novel multi-level clustering algorithm. By separating aspects in a multi-level approach, the algorithmic complexity of clustering is reduced.

• We develop a unique signature-based clustering methodology. Signatures address the shortcoming of past singular metric approaches to clustering. This allows clustering to be extended to multi-dimensional domains of diverse metrics and equally diverse application scenarios. Signatures again reduce computational clustering overheads since signatures are of constant length.

• We design call-path clustering of call sequence signatures suitable for program tracing in general. We further compose domain-specific data via parameter signatures and derive clusters capturing common behavior across different execution instances in a highly parallel environment.

• We evaluate the composition of call-path+parameter clustering for a set of HPC benchmarks showing that their effectiveness is capturing representative application behavior for communication events. The number of clusters is a constant for most benchmarks and scales sub-linearly in the number

of processes for the remaining ones, a significant improvement over linear increases without clustering.

• We demonstrate that application performance is preserved when execution traces composed of a set of just one task per cluster are replayed over the entire original number of processors, where the behavior of other tasks in a cluster is derived from just the singular sampled one.

Overall, a novel technical approach for multi-dimensional clustering is shown to deliver low algorithmic complexity enabling communication tracing at extreme scale in an unprecedented manner.

2. BACKGROUND

Our work builds on ScalaTrace as an MPI tracing toolset. Here, we briefly introduce several of the key ideas and techniques relevant to I/O tracing.

ScalaTrace captures MPI events in the innermost loop as Regular Section Descriptors (RSD), while power-RSDs capture RSDs (PRSDs) of higher-level loop nests represented as a constant sized data structure [15]. Consider the example in the following code snippet:

```
for i = 0 → 1000 do
    for k = 0 → 100 do
        MPI_Send(...);
        MPI_Recv(...);
    end for
    MPI_Barrier(...)
end for
```

Trace compression with PRSDs results in the following tuples: RSD1:<100, MPI_Send1, MPI_Recv1> denotes a loop with 100 iterations of alternating send/receive calls with identical parameters (omitted here), and PRSD1:<1000, RSD1, MPI_Barrier1> denotes 1000 invocations of the former loop (RSD1) followed by a barrier.

ScalaTrace has the following three main properties: (1) ScalaTrace provides location-independent encodings: Communication end-points (task IDs) in SPMD programs often differ from one node to another. However, their position relative to the MPI task ID often remains constant. Therefore, ScalaTrace leverages relative encodings of communication end-points, i.e., an end-point is denoted as $\pm c$ for a constant c relative to the current MPI task ID [16]. Consider Fig. 1 with relative encoding of nodes 5 and 9 in terms of communication end-points -4, -1, $+1$ and $+4$, i.e., these nodes have identical *relative* communication end-points.

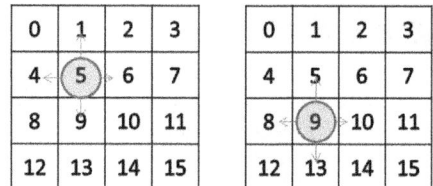

Figure 1: Communication End-point Encoding

(2) ScalaTrace features calling sequence identification: MPI calls, such as a Send, may be scattered over various locations in a program; to distinguish between events from different locations, just recording the MPI event type itself is insufficient. ScalaTrace captures the calling context by recording the calling sequence that leads to the MPI event, which is obtained from the stack backtrace of an MPI event. Each location is represented as a unique signature of the stack trace called the stack signature [16].

156

(3) ScalaTrace provides communication group encoding: ScalaTrace leverages a special data structure called ranklist to represent a communication group. Using EBNF notation, a rank list is represented as ⟨dimension, start_rank, iteration_length, stride, iteration_length, stride⟩, which denotes the dimension of the group, the rank of the starting node, and the iteration and stride of the corresponding dimension, respectively [22]. In Fig. 2(a), the shaded nodes are presented as ranklist ⟨2 5 2 4 2 1⟩, and in Fig. 2(b), they are presented as ranklist ⟨2 0 4 4 4 1⟩. The former reads as a 2D ranklist starting at task 5, two entries in the first dimension with a stride of 4 (implying tasks 5 and 9) and two entries in the second dimension with stride 1 (implying tasks 6 and 10).

0	1	2	3
4	5	6	7
8	9	10	11
12	13	14	15

(a)

0	1	2	3
4	5	6	7
8	9	10	11
12	13	14	15

(b)

Figure 2: Ranklists for Communication Group

3. A NOVEL CLUSTERING ALGORITHM

This section details design and implementation of the call-path+parameter clustering and reference clustering algorithms. Call-path+parameter clustering has two main phases. A first call-path clustering phase discovers processes with different numbers or sequences of events, and a second phase distinguishes processes with the same call-path cluster but different event parameters. As noted previously, the reference signature is the uncompressed version of the call-path+parameter signatures.

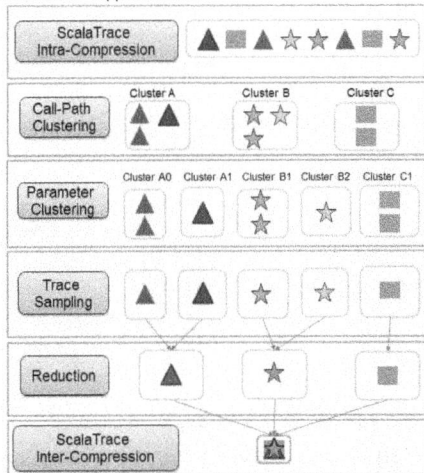

Figure 3: Overview of Proposed Clustering Algorithm

3.1 Call-Path Clustering

Figure 3 illustrates that call-path+parameter clustering has different phases. During the first phase, the algorithm clusters processes with different sequences of MPI calls, which creates so-called "main clusters".

A stack signature consists of a number of backtrace addresses of the program counters (return addresses), one for each stack frame. Our call-path signature is a 64-bit signature. To represent large stack signatures as 64 bits, we computed the exclusive or (XOR) of each part with the current 64-bit signature value.

After creating the 64-bit version of stack signatures, in order to create the call-path signature, we compute the XOR of all 64-bit stack signatures. In most benchmarks, capturing the calling context is sufficient for distinguishing MPI events from each other. However, the Multi-Grid (MG) benchmark from the NAS Parallel Benchmark (NPB) suite features a case where two processes with same number of events and similar calling contexts experience different orders among their events. Therefore, to capture not only the calling context but also the order of events, we multiply the sequence number of each event by the 64-bit stack signature and then use this value in the call-path signature.

Fig. 3 provides a simple illustration of call-path clustering, where processes of different shapes are grouped into different clusters. This operation occurs on a radix tree, i.e., each node receives the call-path signatures of its children. Then, it compares its own call-path signature with those of its children. Finally, it sends different signatures and corresponding ranklists to its parent. At the top of the tree, node 0 receives all of the different signatures and their ranklists.

Node 0 broadcasts the overall clustering result, so all nodes are informed of their respective cluster membership. In our implementation, we considered the start rank of each cluster ranklist the head of the cluster. The computational cost of these two operations is O($\log P$), where P denotes the number of processes.

During the second phase, our algorithm applies parameter clustering. We use a different signature called the parameter signature, which, similar to the call-path signature, is 64 bits long. This signature is composed of the parameters of the MPI event, such as its count, type, source, destination, etc., see Table 1. Note that we did not include the TAG parameter in the parameter signature. While we could easily add the TAG parameter to the signature, we found few differences in the call-path signatures and observed that SRC/DEST parameters could capture the TAG differences in practice for our benchmark set.

3.2 Parameter Clustering

Parameter clustering is the second phase of the proposed algorithm. Similar to the first phase, this phase was implemented over a radix tree. The main difference was that each cluster had similar operations on parameter signatures over a radix tree of its own members. At the end of this phase, the head of the clusters identified in phase one know all of the different parameter signatures in their own "territory" (cluster). Therefore, with the help of parameter clustering, we were able to distinguish processes with the same execution structure but different parameters. Fig. 3 illustrates parameter clustering symbolically, where processes with the same shape but different colors are grouped into different clusters. The computational cost of our clustering algorithm at this phase was also O($\log P$).

By the end of this stage, the algorithm has clustered all processes with disjoint behavior. Then, the algorithm creates the complete trace based on the cluster information.

3.3 Creating a Complete Trace

The next phase consists of selecting a head of each cluster as the representative rank. We choose the start rank from each different sub-cluster. Unlike traditional clustering, which is a top-down process, creating the full trace is a bottom-up process. All similar processes are grouped to-

Table 1: Components of Parameter Signature

Component Descriptions	Bit Positions
Average **COUNT** sent or received for MPI events	0-15
DEST: XOR of the relative address of destinations of MPI events	16-31
SOURCE: XOR of the relative address of sources of MPI events	32-47
MPI Data Types: such as 48:MPI_CHAR, 49:MPI_INTEGER, etc.	48-54
MPI Operation Types: such as 55:MPI_MAX, 56:MPI_MIN, etc.	55-61
MPI Communicator Type: such as 55:MPI_COMM_SELF, etc.	62-63

gether after call-path+parameter clustering, and each representative updates the ranklists accordingly to include the members of its own sub-cluster.

After this process, the representatives are merged within each main cluster. Sub-clusters with different parameters, such as A1 and A2, are merged pairwise linearly at a node within a radix tree (facilitation relative encoding matches [16]) so that the overall reduction over the tree is logarithmic in complexity. For instance, at the reduction phase in Fig. 3, two triangles with different colors are merged into a single triangle. The cost of these two operations is $O(n \log P)$, where n denotes the size of the PRSD-compressed intra-node event trace (typically a constant) and P is the number of processes.

The inter-compression reduction of ScalaTrace [16] at each node in the radix tree is a costly operation with $O(n^2)$ complexity, where n is the size of the PRSD-compressed intra-node event trace. When using ScalaTrace without clustering, all processes participate in this operation over a radix tree. The cost of operation is $O(n^2 \log P)$. With the clustering algorithm, on the other hand, only a set of representatives with different call-path signatures have to participate in this operation. During the last phase of Fig. 3, three different shapes are merged.

As previously mentioned, the cost of the clustering algorithm is $O(\log P)$, the cost of the first level of merging is $O(n \log SC)$, where SC is the maximum number of sub-clusters within a main cluster, and the cost of the second level is $O(n^2 \log MC)$, where MC is the number of different call-path signatures or main clusters.

Due to the nature of parallel programs, as we expected and observed in most of the parallel benchmarks, the number of processes with different execution structures is very small. Since the set of different call-path signatures is so small (mostly just a constant), the clustering algorithm reduces the computation time significantly.

Given the space complexity, the best scenario would be to capture application behavior in only one cluster, meaning there is only one execution sequence / parameter set. In this case, at the root node, there will be one signature and one ranklist containing all the node ranks. The exact size will be eight bytes for the signature and ten bytes, or five integer values, for the ranklist.

In the worst case scenario in which each program has its own unique behavior, processes at different levels of the tree have different complexities. At the bottom of the tree, each leaf node has one ranklist and one signature. On the other hand, the root node has P ranklists and P signatures.

3.4 Reference Signature

As noted previously, to evaluate the accuracy and scalability of our algorithm, we create a reference clustering approach that uses a reference signature. The reference signature is a sequence of events, covers call-path signatures by adding a sequence number to each MPI event, and features parameter clustering by keeping each MPI event's parameters uncompressed. The computational complexity of this clustering is $O(n \times m \times s)$, where n is the number of events after intra-node compression, which is proportional to the number of call-paths leading to MPI calls, m is the number of disjoint events' parameters and s is the number of disjoint reference signatures. The space complexity is a function of the total number of events.

In Section Section 5, we provide the results of the experiments conducted on different benchmarks to compare the results of space complexity for the multi-level call path+parameter clustering approach and the reference signature.

4. EXPERIMENTAL SETUP

We utilized a state-of-the-art cluster at our exposure to conduct experiments. All machines were 2-way SMPs with AMD Opteron 6128 processors with 8 cores per socket. Each node is connected by QDR InfiniBand. This is the largest platform was were able to obtain access to at this time. We tested call-path+parameter clustering, reference clustering and no clustering, which is the default version of Scalatrace for the NAS Parallel Benchmarks (NPB) and Sweep3D. Each experiment was run five times, and the average value and standard deviation were reported. The aggregated wall-clock times across all nodes for the mentioned benchmarks is calculated and reported. We conducted experiments with the NPB suite (version 3.3 for MPI) with class C input size [2] and Sweep3D [10]. Sweep3D is a solver for the 3-D, time-independent, particle transport equation on an orthogonal mesh. It uses a multidimensional wavefront algorithm for "discrete ordinates" in a deterministic particle transport simulation. In our experiments, the problem size is $100 \times 100 \times 1000$.

5. RESULTS AND ANALYSIS

As previously noted, ScalaTrace's inter-compression is a costly operation with $O(n^2 \log P)$ complexity, where n is the size of the PRSD-compressed intra-node event trace and P is the number of processes. To remove this effective bottleneck, we applied our logarithmic algorithm to find processes that exhibit different behavior. Also, we divided the merge process into two steps: (1) merging sub-clusters into main clusters over a local radix tree with $O(n \log SC)$ complexity, where SC is the maximum number of sub-clusters within a main cluster, and (2) merging main clusters over a radix tree with $O(n^2 \log MC)$ complexity, where MC is the number of main clusters. The second level of merging is the most costly operation. Therefore, our first experiment was to determine MC for different benchmarks.

Fig. 4 depicts the topologies of different benchmarks at size 16 (processes). In this figure, main clusters are separated by solid lines, and sub-clusters are separated by dotted lines (e.g., BT has one main cluster and three sub-clusters). Table 2 shows the number of main clusters MC and sub-clusters SC for these benchmarks. According to our experiments, for both weak and strong scaling, the reported number of clusters is constant. Also, the number of clusters is constant for the Sweep3D benchmark with different problem sizes. Notice that the total number of clusters is given by $max(MC, SC)$, which indicates how many different traces ultimately have to be collected for communication characterization.

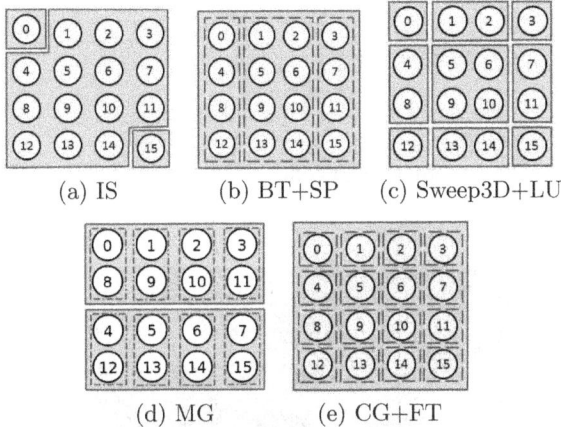

(a) IS   (b) BT+SP   (c) Sweep3D+LU

(d) MG   (e) CG+FT

Figure 4: Topology of Different Benchmarks for 16 Processes Through Call-path+Parameter Clustering

Table 2: Number of Main and Sub Clusters

Benchmarks	Sweep3D	BT	CG	IS	LU	SP	FT	MG
# of Main Clusters MC	9	1	1	3	9	1	1	2
# of Subclusters SC	1	3	4	1	1	3	1	8

Sweep3D: Problem size: $100 \times 100 \times 1000$, # processes: **any** valid one
BT,IS,SP,FT: Class: **any**, # processes: **any** valid one
MG,CG: Class: **any**, # processes: 16

Fig. 4 and Table 2 indicate the following:

(1) Integer Sort (IS) has three main clusters and no sub-clusters. These three groups of processes display very similar execution behavior, except when each process sends its largest key value to the next process. In this phase of the code, process *zero* does not receive any value, and process *comm_size* -1 does not send any value.

(2) The Block Tri-diagonal solver (BT) and the Scalar Penta-diagonal solver (SP) each have only one main cluster, meaning that all processes have the same sequence of MPI events. However, parameter clustering captures three sub-clusters with different communication patterns. Another issue is the COUNT value, which could differ slightly for some events of processes with the same communication pattern (e.g., 9526 and 9500). To compensate for such negligible differences, we implemented a filter that considers two $COUNT$ values to be similar if they differ by only a small percentage (threshold-based filtering), and we record their average. The difference threshold in our experiments is 5%.

(3) The *Sweep3D* neutron-transport kernel and the Lower-Upper Gauss-Seidel solver (LU) have nine main clus-

ters and no sub-clusters, meaning that processes within the same main cluster display the same communication pattern. Sweep3D is a stencil code in which each process must wait for boundary information from neighboring processes to the north and west before computing values within its subdomain [8]. Similar to Sweep3D, LU is also a stencil code [18] that creates nine different main clusters.

(4) The number of main Multi-Grid (MG) clusters is not constant; as shown in Fig. 4, for 16 processes, there are two clusters, and this number increases sublinearly (e.g., (P=32, MC=4), (P=64, MC=8), (P=256, MC=16), etc.) while $SC = 4 \times MC$ for this benchmark. MG is a simplified multigrid kernel that solves 3D Poisson equations. This code requires 2^n processes, where n is an integer number. The partitioning of the grid into processes occurs such that the grid is repeatedly halved along the Z, Y, and X dimensions, respectively [2]. This behavior is due to the following two main reasons [4]: (i) The number of processes assigned to each grid depends on the problem size and the total number of processes P. MG might reduce the number of processors assigned to compute on a coarser grid in order to increase the computation-to-communication ratio. Therefore, some processes may participate in more MPI events; (ii) Two types of communication occur in MG: a boundary exchange and an inter-processor extrapolation/interpolation between two adjacent grid levels. Because MG changes the grid resolution at each iteration of the algorithm, these boundaries change. As the algorithm moves from coarser to finer, more boundaries are created.

(5) Conjugate Gradient (CG) and Fast Fourier Transform (FT) each only have one main cluster, meaning that there is only one execution structure. However, many sub-clusters exist within the main cluster. In CG, each process has its own unique communication pattern. FT has one main cluster and several sub-clusters.

It is beneficial to our approach that these benchmarks only have one main cluster, as this reduces the computational complexity from $O(n^2)$ to $O(n)$. To further reduce the cost of linear compression at the parameter clustering level, one solution is to forcibly "merge" events with different parameters. For example, for CG, the parameter signature indicates that events differ in $SOURCE$ and $DEST$; therefore, all events with $SOURCE$ or $DEST$ may be merged, while other parameters are preserved. This may still result in a large numbers of clusters.

The alternative is for users to supply a plug-in function capturing unique parameters that otherwise would increase the total number of clusters because they can (at best) be merged forcibly. For instance, Fig. 6 shows a CG communication matrix as a heat map for 64 processes, where the x- and y-axes denote mutual communication end-points, and the communication intensity is depicted within a color range (cold/blue=low to hot/red/yellow=high). The orange points (close to the diagonal) in this figure indicate communication occurring with a high frequency. The clustering algorithm can capture the iterative behavior of the orange points easily. However, even though we are using relative addresses for $SOURCE$ and $DEST$, the blue points (further from the diagonal) indicate infrequent communication unique to each process. To capture this secondary communication pattern while simultaneously reducing the number of sub-clusters, we can use the following formula (as a user-provided plug-in function for the CG code):

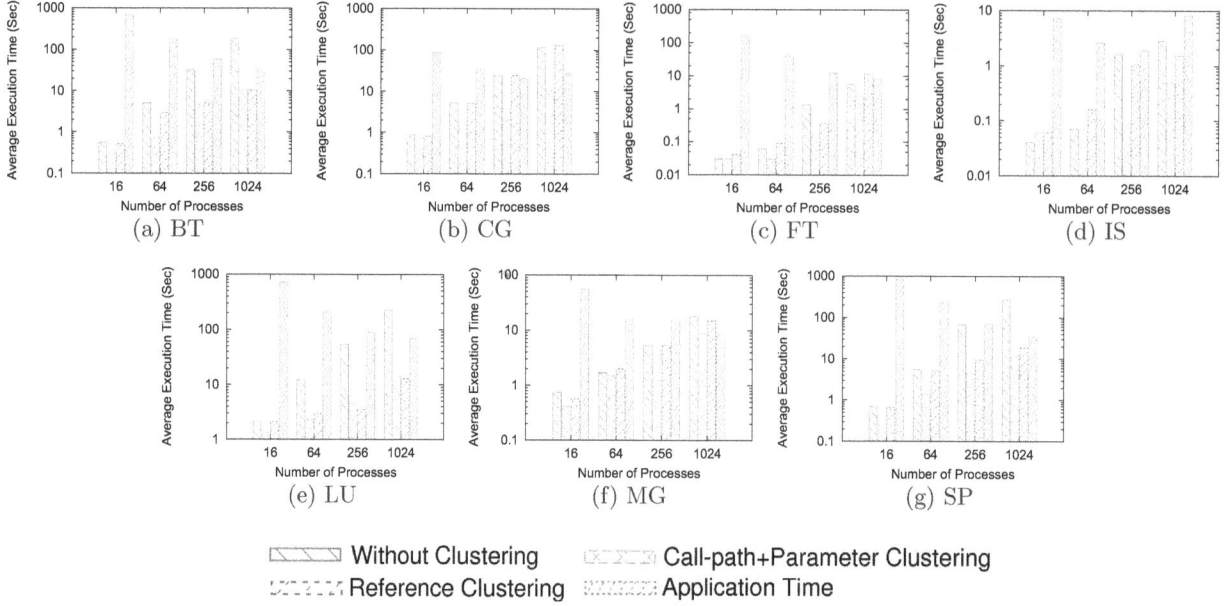

(a) BT   (b) CG   (c) FT   (d) IS

(e) LU   (f) MG   (g) SP

▨ Without Clustering   ▨ Call-path+Parameter Clustering
▨ Reference Clustering   ▨ Application Time

Figure 5: Execution Overhead for NAS benchmarks - Strong Scaling - Nodes/Tasks=1/16

```
if npcols.eq.nprows then
    exch_proc = (me%nprows) × nprows + me/nprows
else
    exch_proc  =  2 × ((me/2%nprows) × nprows +
    me/2/nprows) + (me%2)
end if
```

Here, $npcols$ denotes the number of processes per column, and $nprows$ is the number of processes per row. In CG, the total number of processes equals the number of processes per row times the number of processes per column. If the total number of processes is not a square, then the number of processes per column is twice that of the number of processes per row. $exch\_proc$ is the transpose exchange process, and me is the process rank. The information in Table 3 indicates that once this function is supplied, the number of sub-clusters decreases significantly.

FT solves a three-dimensional partial differential equation (PDE) using fast Fourier transform (FFT). Because all of the processes have the same sequence of events, there is only one main cluster. However, two parameters, $COLOR$ and KEY used in two MPI_Comm_Split events, have different values for different processes. Similar to CG, we can use the following formula (as a user-provided plug-in function for the FT code):

```
if np.eq.1 then
    np2 = 1
else if np.le.nz then
    np2 = np
else
    np2 = np/nz
end if
me1 = me/np2
me2 = (me%np2)
```

Here, me is the process rank, $me1$ and $me2$ are process coordinates, np is the number of processes and nz is the size of the z dimension. Furthermore, $me1$ and $me2$ are assigned to KEY and $COLOR$ in one call and vice versa in another call to MPI_Comm_Split. We also kept track of the global state to assign these values correctly.

The next subsections present results under both strong and weak scaling.

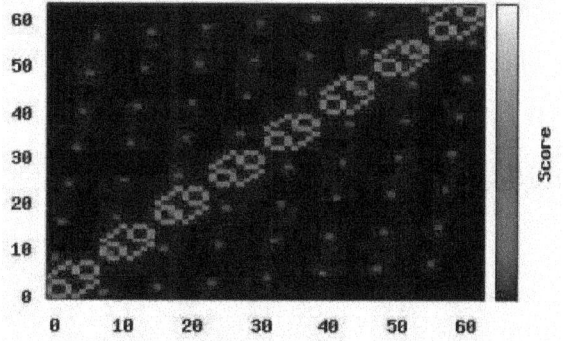

Figure 6: CG Communication Matrix

Table 3: Number of Clusters for CG

Num. of Processes	16	64	256	1024
Number of Main Clusters	1	1	1	1
Number of Subclusters	4	8	16	64

5.1 Strong Scaling

Under strong scaling, the number of processes is increased under the same program input. We tested our clustering algorithm on the NAS benchmarks under strong scaling. Fig. 5 depicts four bars per configuration: (1) the execution overhead for the NAS benchmarks during the inter-compression step for call-path+parameter clustering, (2) reference clustering, (3) without clustering and (4) application execution time with instrumentation. The x-axis of the graph denotes the number of processes participating in inter-node compression. The y-axis is the execution overhead in seconds shown on a logarithmic scale. The execution overhead of without clustering means regular inter-node reduction/compression within ScalaTrace V2.

As the figure shows, call-path+parameter clustering has orders of magnitude smaller overhead than without clustering. For all benchmarks, the overhead of call-path clustering is less than 50% of total program execution time — in contrast to the original inter-node compression without clustering of ScalaTrace, which sometimes exceeds the application runtime for larger number of processes. Notice

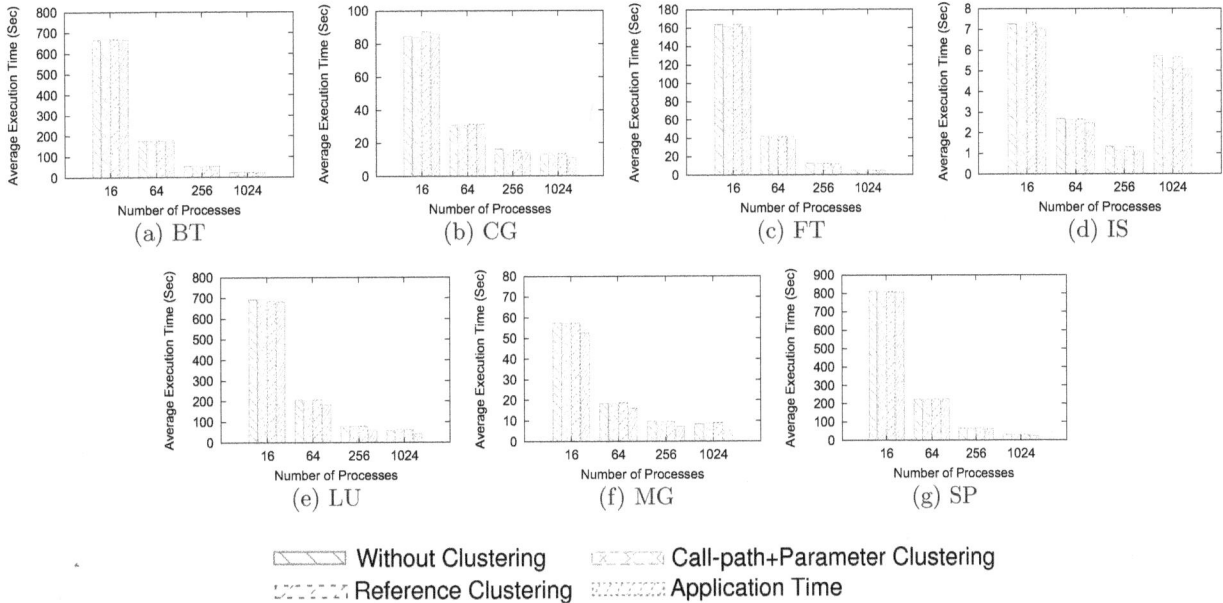

(a) BT   (b) CG   (c) FT   (d) IS

(e) LU   (f) MG   (g) SP

Without Clustering   Call-path+Parameter Clustering
Reference Clustering   Application Time

Figure 7: Replay Time of Traces - Strong Scaling - Nodes/Tasks=1/16

that these benchmark runtimes are relatively short (seconds) while large-scale applications generally run for hours but experience similar inter-node compression overheads as these benchmarks. Call-path+parameter clustering also has orders of magnitude smaller execution overhead than reference clustering for most benchmarks. This is due to the number of processes involved in inter-node compression, as depicted in Table 4 for P=256. For *MG*, call-path+parameter clustering and reference clustering have almost the same number of parameters. Nonetheless, the overhead is smaller than that of reference clustering because most of the clusters in call-path+parameter clustering are sub-clusters. For some *P*s, such as P=256 for BT and LU or P=1024 for SP, the call-path+parameter clustering overhead is very close to the reference signature because, after clustering, the number of processes involved in inter-node compression is in the same order of magnitude. However, at the end of this section, we show that call-path+parameter clustering performs significantly better than reference clustering in terms of space complexity, including but not limited to these configurations. Notice that that application time of IS is lower at P=256 than at P=1024 indicating that there is not enough work per node left at the latter, i.e., it has hit its limit under strong scaling.

Table 4: # Processes Involved in Inter-Node Compression for Clustering Approaches, P=256

Pgm	Call-path+Param Cl.	Ref. Cl.	w/o Clustering
BT	3	41	256
CG	16	256	256
FT	1	256	256
IS	3	21	256
LU	9	16	256
MG	64	72	256
SP	3	53	256

To assess the accuracy of the trace files created by the clustering algorithm, we utilized ScalaReplay, a replay engine operating on the application traces generated by ScalaTrace. It interprets the compressed application traces on-the-fly, issues MPI communication calls accordingly, and simulates

computational overhead as sleeps [23]. We enhanced this replay capability so that the trace of a single node representing a cluster is also replayed by *all other nodes* in the same cluster. These other nodes re-interpret the single node trace and transpose any parameters relative to their task ID automatically because ScalaTrace utilizes relative encodings of end-points, while all other parameters are taken verbatim from the lead node of the cluster. The accuracy of the replay time for traces is defined as

$$ACC = 1 - \frac{|t - t'|}{t}$$

where t is the replay time without clustering and t' is the replay time for clustered traces.

Fig. 7 depicts the overall trace-file replay time, depicted in seconds on a linear y-axis (1) without, (2) with call-path+parameter, (3) with reference clustering and (4) of the non-instrumented original application. The x-axis of these graphs denotes the number of processes participating in the inter-compression phase for the three different methodologies. Replay under call-path+parameter clustering is 88% accurate relative to application runtime over all benchmarks and configurations, which is the same accuracy we observe without clustering, where higher accuracy is observed for longer-running experiments (more representative) than for shorter running ones (an artifact of strong scaling). This equally applies to call-path+parameter clustering with *user-provided functions* (CG+FT) and without (all others) showing that replaying with user-provided specification poses no problems.

5.2 Weak Scaling

Weak scaling typically involves scaling the problem size and the number of processors at the same rate such that the problem size per processor is fixed. (Weak scaling may sometimes also refer to scaling the number of nodes at the same rate as the memory footprint or computational complexity of some algorithm, which we consider as well in the following.) Due to input constraints / lack of weak scaling inputs, we only report these results for the benchmarks for which weak scaling inputs are available natively through the benchmark or when available from other work [22].

As Table 5 indicates, weak scaling and strong scaling produce an equal number of clusters for NAS BT, LU, FT and Sweep3D. The first row of each table indicates the number of processes (MPI tasks); the second one the overall problem size for BT, FT and LU. For Sweep3D, it indicates the per process size; and the last one the number of clusters. We observe the number of clusters for both types of scaling have the same cardinality and identical member sets.

Table 5: Number of Processes Involved in Inter-Node Compression - Weak Scaling

# Processes	16	64	256	1024
BT Prob. Size	60^3	101^3	160^3	255^3
BT # Clusters	3	3	3	3
FT Prob. Size	512×256^2	512^3	$1024^2 \times 512$	2048×1024^2
FT Clusters	1	1	1	1
LU Prob. Size	64^3	128^3	256^3	512^3
LU # Clusters	9	9	9	9
Sweep 3D Problem Size Per Process		$100^2 \times 1000$		
Sw3D # Clus.	9	9	9	9

The execution overheads in seconds on a logarithmic scale on the y-axis of BT, LU, FT and Sweep3D are reported in Fig. 8 for different numbers of processors (x-axis). Just as seen for strong scaling, call-path+parameter clustering has orders of magnitude shorter execution time than without clustering under weak scaling as well. While call-path+parameter and reference result in similar overhead for their cluster formation during tracing, we later show that the former outperforms the latter significantly in terms of space complexity.

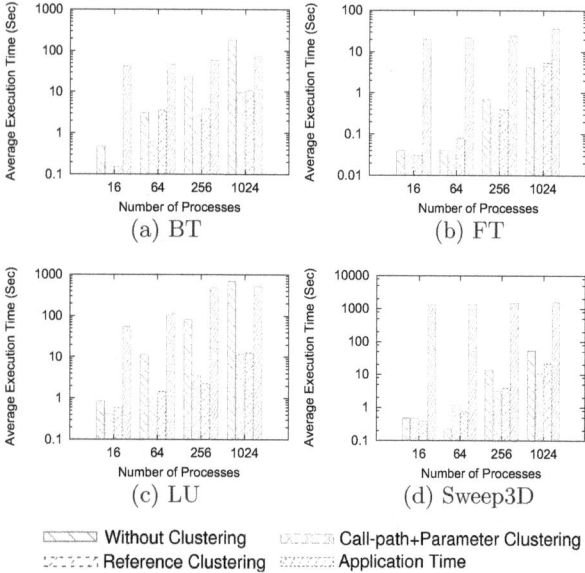

(a) BT   (b) FT

(c) LU   (d) Sweep3D

Without Clustering   Call-path+Parameter Clustering
Reference Clustering   Application Time

Figure 8: Execution Overhead - Nodes/Tasks=1/16

Fig. 9 depicts the replay overhead in seconds on a linear scale (y-axis) for different number of processors (x-axis). In analogy to strong scaling, it illustrates that the overall trace-file replay time under call-path+parameter clustering is 93% relative to application runtime over all benchmarks and configurations, the same as without clustering.

5.3 Space Complexity

The objective of the last experiment is to assess the space complexity. We calculated the number of bytes required for

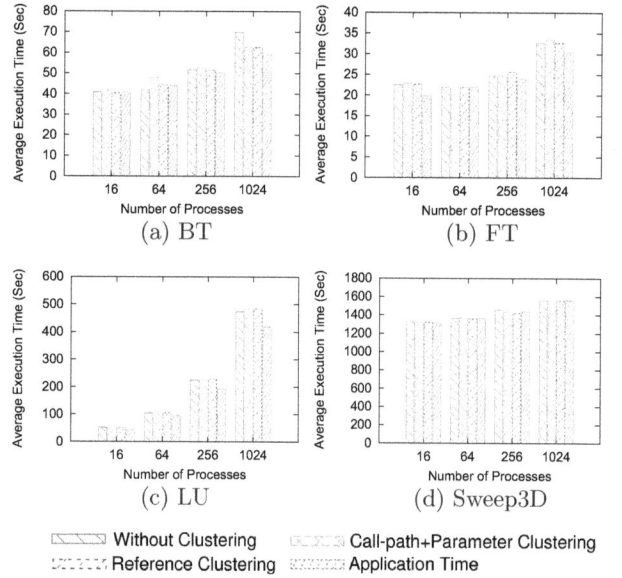

(a) BT   (b) FT

(c) LU   (d) Sweep3D

Without Clustering   Call-path+Parameter Clustering
Reference Clustering   Application Time

Figure 9: Replay Time of Traces - Weak Scaling - Nodes/Tasks=1/16

the different clustering methods. Table 6 shows the space complexity of all benchmarks for P=256.

Average space per process for without clustering is calculated as follows:

$$AvgSpace\,perProcess_{no\,cluster} = \frac{AvgTraceSize \times (P-1)}{P}$$

Here, all processes send their trace files to their parents over a radix tree, except for the root process itself. For reference clustering, the average space is as follows:

$$P1 = AvgTraceSize \times (C-1)$$
$$P2 = P \times AvgSignatureSize$$
$$P3 = AvgSignatureSize \times C \times (P-1)$$
$$AvgSpace\,perProcess_{ref\,cluster} = \frac{P1 + P2 + P3}{P}$$

where C is the number of clusters, $P2$ and $P3$ denote the space of clustering, and $P1$ is the space of inter-node compression. Finally, for Call-path+Parameter clustering, we have

$$P4 = AvgTraceSize \times (MC-1)$$
$$P5 = AvgSignatureSize \times (MC + SC) \times (P-1)$$
$$AvgSpace\,perProcess_{call-path+param} = \frac{P2 + P4 + P5}{P}$$

where MC is the number of main clusters, SC is the number of sub-clusters, $P2$ and $P5$ denote the space of clustering, and $P4$ denotes the space of inter-node compression. Table 6 depicts trace sizes and space metrics for the three clustering types with 256 processes. We observe that reference clustering generally increases the average space per process over no clustering by a factor of 1.4-10 depending on the benchmark — except for Sweep3D, IS and LU, which is due to the small number of clusters involved in inter-node compression for those three benchmarks. Call-path+parameter reduces average space per process by 2-3 orders of magnitudes to 0.1-6% of that without clustering depending on the benchmark. The small size of the signatures and the small number of processes involved in inter-node compression account for this difference. Reference clustering generally sig-

Table 6: Average Space Complexity Per Process - P=256

Pgm	Avg Trace Size	Call-Path+Parameter Clustering			Reference Clustering		Without Clustering	
		MC	SC	Avg Space	# Clusters	Avg Space	# Clusters	Avg Space
BT	72 KB	1	3	0.08 KB	41	108.49 KB	256	71.71 KB
CG	44 KB	1	16	0.36 KB	256	376.32 KB	256	43.82 KB
FT	8 KB	1	1	0.06 KB	256	70.46 KB	256	7.96 KB
IS	8 KB	3	1	0.15 KB	21	3.62 KB	256	7.96 KB
LU	72 KB	9	1	2.43 KB	16	25.05 KB	256	71.71 KB
MG	216 KB	16	64	14.23 KB	72	733.83 KB	256	215.15 KB
SP	68 KB	1	3	0.10 KB	53	133.06 KB	256	67.73 KB
Sweep3D	28 KB	9	1	1.06 KB	9	4.86 KB	256	27.89 KB

nificantly increases the average space per process over call-path+parameter clustering by up to three orders of magnitude, i.e., more specifically a factor of 4.5-1356 depending on the benchmark. The execution overhead for both is comparable because the overhead is a function of the number of clusters, and both clustering methods have a similar number of clusters. However, overheads for call-path+parameter are often lower than reference clustering since $MC + SC$ tends to be lower than C in P3 and P5, respectively, as well as due to more effective multi-level clustering optimizations, including plugins.

Overall, the small footprints of traces and space requirements illustrate the benefits of multi-level clustering, which facilitates analysis without incurring extra cost during tracing or sacrificing accuracy, as results demonstrate.

6. RELATED WORK

A commonly utilized tracing tool for MPI communication is Vampir [3], a commercial post-mortem trace visualization tool. It uses profiling extensions to MPI and facilitates the analysis of message events of parallel execution, helping to identify bottlenecks and inconsistent run-time behavior. While the trace generation supports filtering on trace files, which are stored locally, trace complexity increases with the number of MPI events in a non-scalable fashion. HPC-TOOLKIT [20] uses statistical sampling to measure performance; it provides and visualizes per process traces of sampled call paths. In HPCTOOLKIT, all of the call paths are presented for all samples (in a thread) as a calling context tree (CCT). A CCT is a weighted tree whose root is the program entry point and whose leaves represent sample points. As noted previously, sampling cannot produce accurate data but rather represents a statistical and lossy method. For instance, if the sampling frequency is too low, results may not be representative. Conversely, if it is too high, measurement overhead can significantly perturb the application. In HPCTOOLKIT, finding an appropriate rate of sampling is complicated, and the cost of having a dense CCT is high. In contrast, clustering with ScalaTrace provides a full trace file without resorting to sampling and it does so at very low cost by leveraging a 64-bit stack signature.

Another approach, utilized in [11] and [12], features k-means clustering to select representative data for migration of objects in $CHARM++$. A density-based clustering analysis was proposed in [14], [7] and [6] that can use an arbitrary number of performance metrics to characterize the application (e.g., instructions combined with cache misses to reflect the impact of memory access patterns on performance). The proposed clustering algorithms are expensive in terms of time complexity, especially for extreme-scale sizes. Clus-

tering with ScalaTrace is suitable for exascale computing because it not only utilizes a low overhead clustering algorithm with a $\log P$ complexity, but it also divides clustering and merge processes into two different phases. Separating the clustering algorithm reduces the complexity of the merge process significantly.

Phantom [27], a performance prediction framework, uses deterministic replay techniques to execute any process of a parallel application on a single node of the target system. To reduce the measurement time, Phantom leverages a hierarchical clustering algorithm to cluster processes based on the degree of computational similarity. First, the computational complexity for most hierarchical clustering algorithms is at least quadratic in time, and this high cost limits their application in large-scale data sets [26]. Second, because the paper focuses on performance prediction, it emphasizes computational similarity and does not sufficiently cover communication behavior. Reporting one or two clusters for SP and BT and one cluster for CG shows how their orthogonal objectives result in different clustering decisions.

Another scalable clustering algorithm for tracing toolsets is CAPEK [5], a parallel clustering algorithm based on CLARA [9] that enables in-situ analysis of performance data at run time. Even though the algorithm is logarithmic, the process of clustering and creating the global trace file is based on trace sampling. The merging overhead and the process by which the sample traces are expanded to present the overall behavior of the cluster apply to the duality of "effort and progress" metrics, but this does not generalize to n-dimensional clustering of metrics while our signature-based parameter clustering does.

For instance, a single parameter, such as the count, could produce a significant difference between two processes with the same execution structure. In contrast, our algorithm is not only logarithmic and has low overhead, but it also captures different parameters within the main clusters by means of parameter signatures. It then merges them in a linear manner and captures the different execution structures with by means of call-path signatures.

Since CAPEK is a variant of k-medoids, finding a proper k is a challenge solved via the Bayesian Information Criterion (BIC) [17]. In call-path+parameter clustering, by dividing the merge process, the number of clusters is a function of the number of main clusters. As noted previously, the most costly operation in clustering with ScalaTrace is a function of events, not a function of clusters. Sub-clusters merge in a linear fashion within each main cluster.

TotalView [19] and DDT [1] are debugging tools with demonstrated scalability for large numbers of processes but are prone to extended response time during simple operations (e.g., timeline scroll) due to large amounts of data being processed. The Stack Trace Analysis Tool [13] supports petascale debugging with lightweight tools on an entire parallel application to reduce the problem search space to a manageable subset of tasks. These tools process the entire trace data set of all tasks while we operate on a trace of a small subset of nodes (of just one per cluster).

7. CONCLUSION AND FUTURE WORK

Scalability is one of the main challenges of scientific applications in HPC. This paper contributes a novel multi-level clustering algorithm with $logP$ time complexity and low overhead. The approach relies on signatures to support n-dimensional metrics for cluster selection, much in contrast to a single metric of traditional cluster algorithms. The results of our experiments indicate that our clustering algorithm provides significant reductions in performance overheads making it suitable for extreme-scale computing. Unlike other clustering algorithms designed for large-scale problems, our approach is based on predominantly exact matching rather than on random processes or statistical approaches for sampling with compromised, lower accuracy. Our clustering algorithm is applicable to both strong and weak scaling applications.

We currently apply the clustering algorithm at the end of program execution. However, if we were to group processes with the same execution behavior at interim execution points, e.g., at timestep boundaries of scientific codes, internode compression could be performed online. This would reduce the execution time by overlapping the I/O and computation time. Such online clustering is the focus of our ongoing work beyond the scope of this paper.

8. REFERENCES

[1] Allinea. The distributed debugging tool (DDT), http://www.allinea.com.

[2] D. H. Bailey, E. Barszcz, L. Dagum, and H. D. Simon. Nas parallel benchmark results. *Parallel & Distributed Technology: Systems & Applications, IEEE*, 1(1):43–51, 1993.

[3] H. Brunst, M. Winkler, W. E. Nagel, and H.-C. Hoppe. Performance optimization for large scale computing: The scalable vampir approach. In *Computational Science-ICCS 2001*, pages 751–760. Springer, 2001.

[4] Y. Dotsenko. *Expressiveness, programmability and portable high performance of global address space languages*. ProQuest, 2007.

[5] T. Gamblin, B. R. De Supinski, M. Schulz, R. Fowler, and D. A. Reed. Clustering performance data efficiently at massive scales. In *International Conference on Supercomputing*, pages 243–252. ACM, 2010.

[6] J. Gonzalez, J. Gimenez, and J. Labarta. Automatic detection of parallel applications computation phases. In *International Parallel and Distributed Processing Symposium*, pages 1–11.

[7] J. Gonzalez, K. Huck, J. Gimenez, and J. Labarta. Automatic refinement of parallel applications structure detection. In *Workshop on Large-Scale Parallel Processing*, pages 1680–1687, 2012.

[8] A. Hoisie, O. Lubeck, and H. Wasserman. Performance analysis of wavefront algorithms on very-large scale distributed systems. In *Workshop on wide area networks and high performance computing*, pages 171–187. Springer, 1999.

[9] L. Kaufman and P. J. Rousseeuw. *Finding groups in data: an introduction to cluster analysis*, volume 344. Wiley.com, 2009.

[10] K. R. Koch, R. S. Baker, and R. E. Alcouffe. Solution of the first-order form of the 3-d discrete ordinates equation on a massively parallel processor. *Transactions of the American Nuclear Society*, 65(108):198–199, 1992.

[11] C. W. Lee and L. V. Kalé. Scalable techniques for performance analysis. *Parallel Programming Laboratory, Department of Computer Science, University of Illinois, Urbana-Champaign, Tech. Rep*, pages 07–06, 2007.

[12] C. W. Lee, C. Mendes, and L. V. Kalé. Towards scalable performance analysis and visualization through data reduction. In *International Parallel and Distributed Processing Symposium*, pages 1–8.

[13] G. L. Lee, D. H. Ahn, D. C. Arnold, B. R. De Supinski, M. Legendre, B. P. Miller, M. Schulz, and B. Liblit. Lessons learned at 208k: towards debugging millions of cores. In *High Performance Computing, Networking, Storage and Analysis, 2008. SC 2008. International Conference for*, pages 1–9, 2008.

[14] G. Llort, J. Gonzalez, H. Servat, J. Gimenez, and J. Labarta. On-line detection of large-scale parallel application's structure. In *International Parallel and Distributed Processing Symposium*, pages 1–10, 2010.

[15] J. Marathe, F. Mueller, T. Mohan, B. R. de Supinski, S. A. McKee, and A. Yoo. METRIC: Tracking down inefficiencies in the memory hierarchy via binary rewriting. In *International Symposium on Code Generation and Optimization*, pages 289–300, Mar. 2003.

[16] M. Noeth, P. Ratn, F. Mueller, M. Schulz, and B. R. de Supinski. Scalatrace: Scalable compression and replay of communication traces for high-performance computing. *Journal of Parallel and Distributed Computing*, 69(8):696–710, 2009.

[17] D. Pelleg, A. W. Moore, et al. X-means: Extending k-means with efficient estimation of the number of clusters. In *ICML*, pages 727–734, 2000.

[18] T. Schneider, R. Gerstenberger, and T. Hoefler. Application-oriented ping-pong benchmarking: how to assess the real communication overheads. 2013.

[19] R. Software. Totalview debugger, http://www.roguewave.com/products/totalview.aspx.

[20] N. R. Tallent, J. Mellor-Crummey, M. Franco, R. Landrum, and L. Adhianto. Scalable fine-grained call path tracing. In *International Conference on Supercomputing*, pages 63–74. ACM, 2011.

[21] J. S. Vetter and M. O. McCracken. Statistical scalability analysis of communication operations in distributed applications. In *ACM SIGPLAN Notices*, volume 36, pages 123–132. ACM, 2001.

[22] X. Wu and F. Mueller. Scalaextrap: Trace-based communication extrapolation for spmd programs. In *Proceedings of the 16th ACM symposium on Principles and practice of parallel programming*, pages 113–122. ACM, 2011.

[23] X. Wu and F. Mueller. Scalaextrap: Trace-based communication extrapolation for spmd programs. *ACM Transactions on Programming Languages and Systems (TOPLAS)*, 34(1):5, 2012.

[24] X. Wu and F. Mueller. Elastic and scalable tracing and accurate replay of non-deterministic events. In *International Conference on Supercomputing*, June 2013.

[25] X. Wu, F. Mueller, and S. Pakin. Automatic generation of executable communication specifications from parallel applications. In *Proceedings of the international conference on Supercomputing*, pages 12–21. ACM, 2011.

[26] R. Xu, D. Wunsch, et al. Survey of clustering algorithms. *IEEE Transactions on Neural Networks*, 16(3):645–678, 2005.

[27] J. Zhai, W. Chen, and W. Zheng. Phantom: predicting performance of parallel applications on large-scale parallel machines using a single node. *ACM Sigplan Notices*, pages 305–314, 2010.

An Optimal Distributed Load Balancing Algorithm for Homogeneous Work Units

[Extended Abstract]

Akhil Langer
Department of Computer Science
University of Illinois at Urbana-Champaign, USA
alanger@illinois.edu

ABSTRACT

Many parallel applications, for example, Adaptive Mesh Refinement [1] simulations, need dynamic load balancing during the course of their execution because of dynamic variation in the computational load. We propose a novel tree-based fully distributed algorithm for load balancing homogeneous work units. The proposed algorithm achieves perfect load balance while doing minimum number of migrations of work units.

Categories and Subject Descriptors

G.1.0 [**Mathematics of Computing**]: Parallel algorithms

General Terms

Algorithms, Performance

Keywords

Distributed load balancing; adaptive mesh refinement; complexity analysis; scaling; high performance computing

1. THE DISTRIBUTED LOAD BALANCING ALGORITHM

The proposed algorithm is a spanning-tree based algorithm that is inspired by the distributed algorithm for constructing balanced spanning trees of process subgroups in parallel applications [2]. We form a spanning tree of all the processes, where each vertex of a tree corresponds to a process. The algorithm does two passes over the spanning-tree - the upward pass and the downward pass.

Upward pass: Processes send the count of work units in their subtree (of which the process itself is the root) to the parent process. At the end of the upward pass, each process has the count of work units in each of its child subtrees.

Downward pass: During this pass, migration decisions and work unit migrations take place. The scheme balances the tree while minimizing the number of migrations. The number of work units in the subtree and the size of the subtree

are used to compute the number of work units per process in a perfectly balanced state. The root process and the child subtrees are categorized as either *work supplier* or *work consumer*. Each vertex V of the tree performs a "matchmaking" step, ensuring that each of *work supplier* is assigned one or more of *work consumer* that can absorb the excess work units of the supplier within their subtrees. If V itself needs some work units it requests work units from suppliers for itself. Similarly, if V itself has excess work, it tags itself as a work supplier. A vertex V concludes its role by calling the balancing step on the work suppliers if V was a work receiver or the work receivers if V was a work supplier. This alternation is done in order to ensure that the list of work suppliers and work receivers does not grow long, and in order to minimize the number of messages received by any vertex. Additionally, alternation also helps in early assignment of work units to their final destination processes. This makes it possible to migrate work units concurrently with the downward pass of the algorithm.

Our implementation is based on Charm++ [3], which is an object-based asynchronous message driven parallel programming paradigm.

2. REFERENCES

[1] Akhil Langer, Jonathan Lifflander, Phil Miller, Kuo-Chuan Pan, , Laxmikant V. Kale, and Paul Ricker. Scalable Algorithms for Distributed-Memory Adaptive Mesh Refinement. In *Proceedings of the 24th International Symposium on Computer Architecture and High Performance Computing (SBAC-PAD 2012)*. To Appear, New York, USA, October 2012.

[2] Akhil Langer, Ramprasad Venkataraman, and Laxmikant Kale. Scalable Algorithms for Constructing Balanced Spanning Trees on System-Ranked Process Groups. In Jesper TrÃd'ff, Siegfried Benkner, and Jack Dongarra, editors, *Recent Advances in the Message Passing Interface*, volume 7490 of *Lecture Notes in Computer Science*, pages 224–234. Springer Berlin / Heidelberg, 2012.

[3] Laxmikant Kale, Anshu Arya, Nikhil Jain, Akhil Langer, Jonathan Lifflander, Harshitha Menon, Xiang Ni, Yanhua Sun, Ehsan Totoni, Ramprasad Venkataraman, and Lukasz Wesolowski. Migratable Objects + Active Messages + Adaptive Runtime = Productivity + Performance A Submission to 2012 HPC Class II Challenge. Technical Report 12-47, Parallel Programming Laboratory, November 2012.

ICS'14, June 10–13 2014, Munich, Germany.
ACM 978-1-4503-2642-1/14/06.
http://dx.doi.org/10.1145/2597652.2600108 .

Addressing Bandwidth Contention in SMT Multicores Through Scheduling

Josué Feliu, Julio Sahuquillo, Salvador Petit, and José Duato
Department of Computer Engineering
Universitat Politècnica de València
València, Spain
jofepre@gap.upv.es, {jsahuqui,spetit,jduato}@disca.upv.es

ABSTRACT

To mitigate the impact of bandwidth contention, which in some processes can yield to performance degradations up to 40%, we devise a scheduling algorithm that tackles main memory and L1 bandwidth contention. Experimental evaluation on a real system shows that the proposal achieves an average speedup by 5% with respect to Linux.

Categories and Subject Descriptors

D.4.1 [**Operating Systems**]: Process management—*Scheduling*

Keywords

bandwidth-aware scheduling; bandwidth contention

1. PROPOSED SCHEDULER

Algorithm 1 presents the pseudocode of the devised scheduler. It consists of process selection (lines 2-8) and process allocation (lines 9-12), which deal with main memory and L1 bandwidth contention, respectively, by balancing the memory requests over the workload execution time and the L1 requests among the L1 caches. Previously, the scheduler calculates the average main memory transaction rate of the workload following a similar approach to [2].

In the **process selection**, the proper set of processes is selected to be run during the following quantum. The process not executed for longer is always selected to avoid process starvation. Then, the remaining processes are selected using the fitness function, which quantifies the gap between the TR_{MM} required by a given process and the average bandwidth remaining for each unallocated hardware thread [2].

In the **process allocation**, the selected processes are allocated to the cores. Since the experimental platform implements dual-threaded cores, the L1 bandwidth can be easily balanced by sorting the processes according to its TR_{L1} and then, reiteratively, assigning the processes with highest and lowest bandwidth utilization to the same core [1].

2. EXPERIMENTAL EVALUATION

The experimental evaluation is carried out in an Intel Xeon E5645 processor, with six dual-thread SMT cores, a

ICS'14, June 10–13 2014, Munich, Germany.
ACM 978-1-4503-2642-1/14/06.
http://dx.doi.org/10.1145/2597652.2600109.

Algorithm 1 Bandwidth-Aware Scheduler

Require: Prior calculation of the AVG_WK_TR$_{MM}$
1: **while** there are unfinished processes **do**
2:    Gather TR$_{MM}$ and TR$_{L1}$ of the processes
3:    $BW_{Remain} = AVG\_WK\_TR_{MM}$, $CPU_{Remain} = \#CPUs$
4:    Select the process p at the process queue head and update BW$_{Remain}$ and CPU$_{Remain}$
5:    **while** # selected process < #CPUs **do**
6:      Select the processes p that maximizes:

$$\text{FITNESS(p)} = \frac{1}{\left| \frac{BW_{Remain}}{CPU_{Remain}} - TR^P_{MM} \right|}$$

7:      Update BW$_{Remain}$ and CPU$_{Remain}$
8:    **end while**
9:    Sort the selected processes in ascending TR$_{L1}$
10:   **while** there are unallocated processes **do**
11:     Assign the processes P$_{head}$ and P$_{tail}$ with maximum and minimum bandwidth requirements to the same core
12:   **end while**
13: **end while**

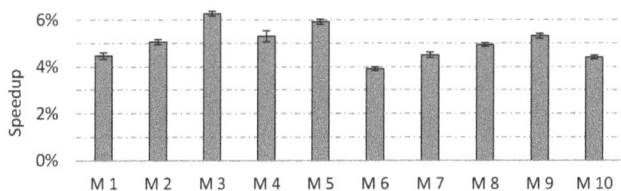

Figure 1: Speedup relative to Linux.

private L1 cache per core and a shared LLC. The algorithm has been implemented in a user-level scheduler. To evaluate the performance of the proposal, a set of ten 24-benchmark mixes was designed.

Figure 1 presents the speedup the devised scheduler achieves compared to the Linux scheduler across all the mixes using the average IPC with 95% confidence intervals. Results show that the scheduler effectively addresses bandwidth contention and improves the Linux performance by 5% on average.

3. ACKNOWLEDGMENTS

This work was supported by the Spanish Ministerio de Economía y Competitividad (MINECO) and Plan E funds, under Grant TIN2012-38341-C04-01, and by the Intel Early Career Faculty Honor Program Award.

4. REFERENCES

[1] J. Feliu, J. Sahuquillo, S. Petit, and J. Duato. L1-Bandwidth Aware Thread Allocation in Multicore SMT Processors. In *PACT*, pages 123–132, 2013.

[2] D. Xu, C. Wu, and P.-C. Yew. On mitigating memory bandwidth contention through bandwidth-aware scheduling. In *PACT*, pages 237–248, 2010.

An Adaptive Cross-Architecture Combination Method for Graph Traversal

Yang You
Tsinghua University, Beijing
you-y12@mails.
tsinghua.edu.cn

Shuaiwen Leon Song
Pacific Northwest National Lab
Richland, WA 99354
Shuaiwen.Song@pnnl.gov

Darren J Kerbyson
Pacific Northwest National Lab
Richland, WA 99354
Darren.Kerbyson@pnnl.gov

ABSTRACT

Breadth-First Search (BFS) is widely used in many real-world applications including computational biology, social networks, and electronic design automation. The combination method, using both top-down and bottom-up techniques, is the most effective BFS approach. However, current combination methods rely on trial-and-error and exhaustive search to locate the optimal switching point, which may cause significant runtime overhead. To solve this problem, we design an adaptive method based on regression analysis to predict an optimal switching point for the combination method at runtime within less than 0.1% of the BFS execution time. Additionally, in order to fully utilize the heterogeneous resources offered by current HPC systems and further improve the performance of the combination method, we propose methodologies to allocate the most suitable computation phases of BFS to the corresponding processing components (i.e. CPUs and accelerators) in the system based on graph information and architecture details. Our adaptive method can predict the switching point with high accuracy (compared with exhaustive search) and achieve up to 695X and 8X speedup over the worst and average case. Our cross-architecture adaptive combination method also improves performance dramatically over the cases conducted on a single architecture.

1. BACKGROUND & CONTRIBUTIONS

Beamer et al. [1] proposed a combination approach that can switch between top-down and bottom-up methods during the BFS execution to achieve better performance, due to their individual performance advantages under different situations: for real world graphs, the number of vertices and edges in the current queue (CQ) is often small at the beginning of the BFS execution, then increases and peaks in the middle, and eventually decreases and becomes small again. The large number of vertices in CQ favors the bottom-up approach because each unvisited vertex will terminate the traversal once it finds its parents. With more vertices in

CQ, the unvisited vertex can find its parents easier. On contrary, the increasing number of vertices in CQ is unfavorable to the top-down approach since the number of edges it needs to travel is increasing. During the different phases of BFS execution, applying one of the two approaches may result in dramatically different performance.

Although the current techniques such as trail-and-error experiments and exhaustive search in theory could help locate a good switching point, it requires manually selecting through a extremely large case space. Moreover, cross-architecture combination (utilizing both CPUs and accelerators) may require more switching points for optimal performance, which is very difficult for the trial-and-error method to be practical.

In order to address the problems above, we propose the following:

- We design an adaptive method based on regression analysis to predict optimal switching point(s) for the combination method at runtime within less than 0.1% of the BFS execution time. Our method achieves high accuracy compared to the theoretical optimal: exhaustive search.

- We propose methodologies to allocate the most suitable computation phases of BFS to the corresponding processing units (i.e. CPUs and accelerators) in the system based on graph information and architecture details, to achieve the optimal performance.

2. RESULTS

Experimental results show that our proposed method obtains both good strong and weak scaling. They also show that our proposed cross-architecture combination method (1 CPU + 1 GPU) outperforms the other combination methods on a single architecture platforms (Intel Xeon Phi Coprocessor, Intel Sandy Bridge CPU, and Nvidia Kepler K20x GPU).

3. REFERENCE

[1] S. Beamer, K. Asanovic, and D. Patterson. Direction-optimizing breadth-first search. In *High Performance Computing, Networking, Storage and Analysis (SC), 2012 International Conference for*, pages 1–10. IEEE, 2012.

ICS'14, June 10–13 2014, Munich, Germany.
ACM 978-1-4503-2642-1/14/06.
http://dx.doi.org/10.1145/2597652.2600110 .

Accelerating Cache Coherence Mechanism with Speculation

Jun Ohno[*]
University of Tokyo
j_ohno@is.s.u-tokyo.ac.jp

Kei Hiraki
University of Tokyo
hiraki@is.s.u-tokyo.ac.jp

ABSTRACT

Directory is one of the common method to maintain cache coherence in multi/many-core systems. However, directory has problems in area, latency and complexity of protocol. Conversely, directoryless coherence mechanism, where each core invalidates its own L1 cache block (tear-off copy) is proposed. The problem of this method is that the cache blocks which are not written by another core are invalidated. We accelerate the coherence mechanism by speculatively executing with the value of these invalidated cache blocks. Our results show 2% acceleration on average over derectory based MOESI protocol in 16 core system.

Categories and Subject Descriptors

B.3.2 [**Hardware**]: MEMORY STRUCTURES—*Design Styles, Cache memories*

Keywords

Multicore; Cache Coherence; Tear-off copy; Speculation

1. BACKGROUND AND MOTIVATION

Performance improvement of processors are shifting from enhancing single-core performance to increasing the multi-core performance. With a common multi-/many-core design, each processor has private L1 cache, which maintains cache coherence. Directory based coherence mechanism is commonly used for solving this problem. Since this method has problems in hardware budgets and access latencies, a coherence mechanism with low latency and additional hardware is now being sought.

Tear-off copy based protocol is known as a simple cache coherence mechanism. Tear-off copy is a cache block which is discarded voluntarily for synchronization. This coherence mechanism has merit in that it requires no invalidation messages and no extra memory as directory. However, this

[*]Master student at May 16, 2014.

ICS'14, June 10–13 2014, Munich, Germany.
ACM 978-1-4503-2642-1/14/06.
http://dx.doi.org/10.1145/2597652.2600111.

method suffers low L1 hit-rate, since each processor invalidates these cache blocks even they are not written by other processors.

In our study we utilize the invalidated cache blocks to gain higher performance, allowing processor to continue execution speculatively on their value. Our method requires little additional hardware, since the speculation circuit is already implemented widely with branch prediction.

2. METHOD AND RESULT

With our simple tear-off copy based coherence protocol, all shared Read / Write (Shared RW) pages classified by the OS are invalidated periodically. On synchronization all shared RW blocks in L1 cache are invalidated voluntarily simultaneously. At the same time the writes to these blocks are globally completed at LLC. Other cache blocks act as normal.

When a processor accesses to an invalidated cache block, the processor initiates request to its home node and speculatively executes the successive instructions. When the LLC returns the correct value, the value used for speculation is compared to it to judge whether the speculation is successful or not.

We have developed a simulator to compare the preformance of our method to directory based MOESI protocol in common CMP environment with x86 consistency model. We used NAS Parallel Benchmarks for evaluation.

We evaluated the performance of our method with increasing the size of the speculation buffer. In many applications the performance saturates at about 24 entries on 4 core, and 48 entries on 16 core. The average speed-up is about 2% with both 4 core and 16 core. Since the size of the speculation buffer is bounded by the number of the physical registers, which is around 128, we concluded that our method outperforms directory based protocol by 2%.

3. CONCLUSIONS

Our study shows that the directory based protocol is not the most suitable coherence mechanism for CMPs. We proposed simple tear-off copy based protocol and accelerated with speculation mechanism widely implemented with branch prediction. Compared to the complicated directory based MOESI protocol, our simple method shows 2% higher performance with realistic size of speculation buffer and consumes less hardware.

Reducing Energy Consumption of NoC by Router Bypassing

Takahiro Naruko
The University of Tokyo
7-3-1, Hongo, Bunkyo-ku
Tokyo, Japan 113-8654
cinccinaru@is.s.u-tokyo.ac.jp

ABSTRACT

As the core-count increases, NoC has more and more impact on performance. It is already known that network latency can be reduced by making packets bypass intermediate routers asynchronously, e.g. SMART. Nevertheless, it is also important to reduce energy consumption of NoC. This work proposes Energy Efficient Router Bypassing (EERB) that employs router bypassing for energy reduction in addition to performance improvement. Simulation results show that EERB reduces dynamic energy consumed in buffers and crossbars by 30% compared to SMART.

Categories and Subject Descriptors

C.2.1 [**Network Architecture and Design**]: Packet-switching networks

Keywords

NoC; Router design; Energy consumption

1. INTRODUCTION

As the core-count increases, network-on-chip (NoC) has more and more impact on performance and energy consumption of the chip. One approach to improve performance is to reduce network latency by a technique which enables flits to traverse multiple hops within a single cycle by bypassing intermediate routers asynchronously. For example, SMART [1] dynamically forms bypassing paths in a cycle-by-cycle basis by sending bypass requests prior to traversals. Meanwhile, reducing energy consumption of NoC has been also an important problem because it occupies large portion of chip power. SMART, however, provides little energy reduction because of two reasons. One is that buffers consume energy when a bypass is stopped halfway at a congested router. The other is that crossbars consume energy even at nonstop routers because bypassing paths are formed via crossbars. In this work, we employ router bypassing for energy reduction in addition to performance improvement.

ICS'14, June 10–13 2014, Munich, Germany.
ACM 978-1-4503-2642-1/14/06.
http://dx.doi.org/10.1145/2597652.2600112.

2. EERB

In order to reduce energy consumption of NoC, we propose Energy Efficient Router Bypassing (EERB), which consists of three techniques: Section Code, Crossbar Bypassing, and Passage Wait. All three techniques are introduced to improve smoothness of router bypassing, which leads to energy reduction in buffers. In addition, Crossbar Bypassing is aimed at reducing crossbar energy. EERB assumes network topology to be 2D-Mesh and restricts bypasses to straight ones, i.e. bypasses at turn routers are not supported.

Section Code is introduced to avoid unnecessary maintenance of order among flits. It is a value calculated by applying a compressor function to source and destination node IDs of a flit and is added into bypass requests.

Crossbar Bypassing is aimed at removing conflicts at input ports of crossbars by doing a selection between a buffer lane and a bypass lane behind a crossbar. Moreover, it cuts down crossbar energy at nonstop routers, where flits no longer have to go through a crossbar.

Passage Wait is introduced to smooth bypasses by making buffered flits in nonstop routers wait for a passing flit when it is predicted that a bypass request will come. Prediction is performed based on a history of bypass requests.

3. RESULTS

Simulation results of PARSEC benchmarks show that although EERB does not reduce an application runtime compared to SMART, it reduces energy consumption in buffers and crossbars by 30%. These results are brought mainly by Crossbar Bypassing, which removes crossbar energy at nonstop routers. Moreover, buffer energy is reduced because of an improvement in smoothness of bypasses.

4. CONCLUSION

This work introduced EERB to reduce energy consumption of NoC and evaluated its performance and energy consumption. The simulation results indicate that EERB reduces energy consumption of buffers and crossbars by 30% compared to SMART.

5. REFERENCES

[1] T. Krishna, C.-H. O. Chen, W. C. Kwon, and L.-S. Peh. Breaking the on-chip latency barrier using SMART. In *Proceedings of the 2013 IEEE 19th International Symposium on High Performance Computer Architecture (HPCA)*, HPCA '13, pages 378–389. IEEE Computer Society, 2013.

Hardware-Assisted Scalable Flow Control of Shared Receive Queue

Teruo Tanimoto   Takatsugu Ono   Kohta Nakashima   Takashi Miyoshi

FUJITSU LABORATORIES LTD.

Kawasaki, Japan

{tanimoto.teruo,ono.takatsugu,nakashima.kouta,miyoshi.takashi}@jp.fujitsu.com

ABSTRACT

The total number of processor cores in supercomputers is increasing while memory size per core is decreasing due to the adoption of processors with multiple cores. Shared Receive Queue is a technique that effectively reduces the memory usage of buffers, but the absence of flow control results in excess buffer pools. We propose a hardware-assisted flow control that reduces flow control latency by 95.1%, thus enabling scalable supercomputers with multi-core processors.

Categories and Subject Descriptors

C.2 [**Computer Systems Organization**]: Computer
-Communication Networks

Keywords

Shared Receive Queue, Flow Control

1. INTRODUCTION

The total number of processor cores in supercomputers is currently increasing by about 1.5 times per year. Co-processors are being considered for use as stand-alone processors in the near future, meaning that the total number of cores will soon be increasing even more. An analysis of the Top500 has shown that, supercomputers which have co-processors have only about 800 MB memory per core. This is because the total DRAM capacity is limited by power and/or cost restrictions. Since scalability is important for super-computers, techniques to lower the latency of inter-node communication have been developed. One way of lowering the latency is having computing processes communicate directly with each other. For this to happen, interconnect needs to be more scalable by reducing memory resources.

Shared Receive Queue (SRQ) is one technique to reduce the number of required buffer resources [1, 2]. However, SRQ cannot avoid buffer underflow because an individual sender cannot discern how many packets an SRQ can receive at a given time. Since InfiniBand implementation does not have flow control capable SRQ, software flow control using interruption has been proposed [2]. However, a rather big buffer is needed to ensure that flow control does not occur, as interruptions can seriously degrade high-performance computing. The current standard per SRQ is now 60 MB [2]. Specifically, if each process is assigned cores that have an SRQ, which occupies 7.5% of available memory, and a system consists of a million cores, the memory resource used for an SRQ buffer is 60 GB.

ICS'14, June 10–13, 2014, Munich, Germany.

ACM 978-1-4503-2642-1/14/06.

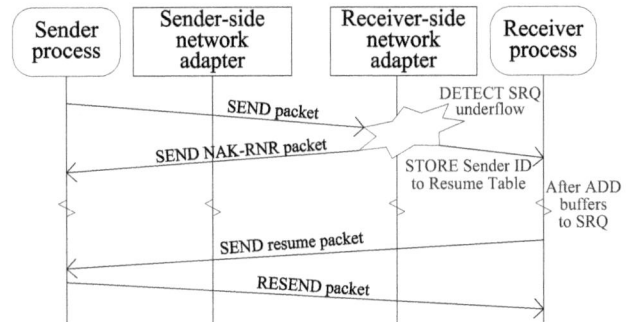

Figure 1: Sequence of proposed flow control.

2. PROPOSED FLOW-CONTROL OF SRQ

We propose a hardware-supported flow control of SRQ that stops a sender if the SRQ of a receiver is not ready. Each SRQ has a resume table in its host memory to record sender processes of sending resume packets. Each sender process takes 1 bit of storage, which in a system with one million cores adds up to 1 MB. The sequence of the proposed flow control is shown in Fig. 1. This flow control does not need interruption because the adapter of any unready receiver stops the sender by NAK. It can be said that resending is inefficient, but this is because the receiver is busy. It is clear that interrupting a busy receiver degrades the overall performance of the application.

We compared the flow control latency of the proposed control with that of a low watermark flow control [2] and found that the proposed was 4.51 us while the low water-mark was 92.8 us. The proposed flow control reduced latency by 95.1%. With the proposed flow control, the buffer size of the SRQ required to prevent queue underflow during the flow control sequence was 56 KB (assuming a 100-Gbps connection, i.e., the bandwidth of InfiniBand EDR 4X). This means the memory size per core can potentially be reduced, which would allow for the incorporation of more processors. We should point out that there was a tradeoff between resource reduction and application performance. Investigating this is our future work.

3. REFERENCES

[1] G. Shipman, T. Woodall, R. Graham, A. Maccabe, and P. Bridges. Infiniband scalability in Open MPI. In *Proc. of the 20th IPDPS*, Apr. 2006.

[2] S. Sur and D. K. Panda. Shared receive queue based scalable MPI design for InfiniBand clusters. In *Proc. of the 20th IPDPS*, Apr. 2006.

Automating and Optimizing Data Transfers for Many-core Coprocessors

Bin Ren[*], Nishkam Ravi[†], Yi Yang[†], Min Feng[†], Gagan Agrawal[*], Srimat Chakradhar[†]

[*]Dept. of Computer Science and Engineering, The Ohio State University

[†]NEC Laboratories America

{ren, agrawal}@cse.ohio-state.edu, {nravi, yyang, mfeng, chak}@nec-labs.com

ABSTRACT

Orchestrating data transfers between CPUs and a coprocessor manually is cumbersome, particularly for multi-dimensional arrays and other data structures with multi-level pointers, which are common in scientific computations. This work describes a system that includes both compile-time and runtime solutions for this problem, with the overarching goal of improving programmer productivity while maintaining performance.

We implemented our best compile-time solution, *partial linearization* with *pointer reset*, as a source-to-source transformation, and evaluated our work by multiple C benchmarks. Our experiment results demonstrate that our best compile-time solution can perform 2.5x-5x faster than original runtime solution, and the CPU-Coprocessor code with it can achieve 1.5x-2.5x speedup over the 16-thread CPU version.

Categories and Subject Descriptors

D.1.3 [**Programming Techniques**]: [Concurrent Programming — Parallel Programming]

Keywords

Coprocessors, Static Analysis, Runtime Analysis, Offloading

1. TECHNICAL DESCRIPTION

Accelerating parallel computation using many-core coprocessors requires specification of code regions that can be profitably offloaded to the coprocessor and executed as independent tasks. These code regions have been specified by the developer using low-level APIs till recently. The software available with Xeon Phi, as well as the emerging *directive-based* models for GPU programming, are providing much higher-level APIs for using accelerators. However, even with such high-level APIs, there are many challenging issues. Particularly, orchestrating data transfers for multi-level pointers using `in`/`out` or equivalent clauses is cumbersome and error-prone.

With the goal of further improving productivity of HPC programmers while also maintaining performance, we focus on easing data transfer related efforts, considering both compile-time and

ICS'14, June 10–13, 2014, Muenchen, Germany

ACM 978-1-4503-2642-1/14/06.

http://dx.doi.org/10.1145/2597652.2600114

runtime solutions. While such data transfers for static arrays can be handled by ICC compiler[1] today, and solutions proposed previously by the literature [2, 1] can handle dynamically allocated one-dimensional arrays, the open problem is handling dynamically allocated multi-dimensional arrays or other structures with multi-level pointers.

It turns out that the problem is quite complex, particularly because the choice of the mechanism used for automatically inserting data transfer clauses impacts memory layouts and access functions (subscripts) on the coprocessor. Because of the nature of the accelerators and complex interactions between the resulting source-code and the native compiler on the accelerator, the performance can be impacted in multiple ways. Overall, our work considers four metrics: 1) Minimization of redundant data transfers, 2) Utilization of Direct Memory Accesses (DMA), 3) Minimization of memory allocation overheads on the accelerator (or even the host), and 4) Preservation of aggressive memory-related compiler optimizations (e.g., vectorization and prefetching) by proper memory layout and accesses for the accelerator.

Our work describes an automated framework that uses both compile time and runtime solutions to address this problem. This system includes a simple but effective compile-time solution, where we linearize the heap without having to modify the memory accesses (subscripts), by using a *pointer reset* approach. This method scores well on all of our metrics and maintains code readability.

For the cases where our compile-time approach cannot apply, we also explore runtime solutions. The background is that a system like Xeon Phi also has shared memory implementations available between the main processor and accelerator. We also investigate and optimize the performance of the runtime memory management approach, by providing certain improvements to the existing coherence protocol. The best compile-time solution consistently performs better than the optimized runtime scheme, but is not as generally applicable. In order to combine performance with generality, we describe a mechanism for integrating the two disjoint approaches using a simple source-to-source transformation.

We have implemented our compile-time solution as a source-to-source transformation using the Apricot framework and evaluated it within the context of application execution on Xeon Phi coprocessor.

2. REFERENCES

[1] S. Lee and R. Eigenmann. OpenMPC: Extended OpenMP Programming and Tuning for GPUs. In *SC*, 2010.

[2] N. Ravi, Y. Yang, T. Bao, and S. Chakradhar. Apricot: an Optimizing Compiler and Productivity Tool for x86-Compatible Many-Core Coprocessors. In *ICS*, pages 47–58, 2012.

---

[1]Intel C++ Compiler. http://www.intel.com/Compilers.

Parallelizing and Optimizing Sparse Tensor Computations

Muthu Manikandan
Baskaran
Reservoir Labs Inc.
baskaran@reservoir.com

Benoit Meister
Reservoir Labs Inc.
meister@reservoir.com

Richard Lethin
Reservoir Labs Inc.
lethin@reservoir.com

ABSTRACT

Irregular computations over large-scale sparse data are prevalent in critical data applications and they have significant room for improvement on modern computer systems from the aspects of parallelism and data locality. We introduce new techniques to efficiently map large irregular computations with multi-dimensional sparse arrays (or *sparse tensors*) onto modern multi-core systems with non-uniform memory access (NUMA) behavior. We implement a static-cum-dynamic task scheduling scheme with low overhead for effective parallelization of sparse computations. We introduce locality-aware optimizations to the task scheduling mechanism that are driven by the sparse input data pattern. We evaluate our techniques on key sparse tensor decomposition methods that are widely used in areas such as data mining, graph analysis, and elsewhere. We achieve around 4-5x improvement in performance over existing parallel approaches and observe "scalable" parallel performance on modern multi-core systems with up to 32 processor cores.

OUR APPROACH

Improving the parallel performance of sparse tensor computations is a non-trivial challenge due to the following reasons: 1) the amount of parallelism is dependent on the non-zero pattern of the input sparse tensor data that is known only at runtime, 2) tensor computations have "mode-specific operations" - operations that access data with respect to the orientation of a mode or dimension of the multi-dimensional data - that make optimizations specific to a mode ineffective. The techniques that we developed to address the challenges in optimizing sparse tensor computations center around the following aspects: 1) identifying and extracting more concurrency, 2) reducing barrier synchronizations or thread waits, 3) improving data locality, 4) improving load balance among processors, and 5) reducing parallelization overheads such as the task scheduling overhead.

Our approach works as follows. The computations are performed in a fine-grained parallel manner and dynamically assigned to processors such that the non-zeros are distributed in to partitions that result in no synchronization as far as possible. This dynamic scheduling of blocks of computations (or tasks) to processors and partitioning of the workload is done by a light-weight runtime layer. When there are multiple iterations of a computation block and if the computation block is to be distributed across processors and if the non-zero structure of the sparse tensor (or the data access pattern of the sparse tensor) does not change within the block, the first iteration of the block is peeled and executed it with a dynamic task scheduling scheme. The runtime layer logs "state" information about the processor workload (such as which portions of the computation block (or tasks) get executed on which processor). In the subsequent iterations, the logged information about the processor workload is used to schedule tasks across processors, thereby avoiding the need for dynamic scheduling to balance load at runtime, and execute the computation block with low scheduling overhead. This static-cum-dynamic (or hybrid) task scheduling approach greatly reduces the task scheduling overhead and also guarantees an improved load balance across processors.

The light-weight runtime layer during the dynamic scheduling phase migrates tasks across processors to improve load balancing. However to improve data locality, task migration is done by respecting the NUMA topology of the system. Tasks are migrated from 'overloaded' processors to topologically closer 'underloaded' processors to facilitate data sharing between NUMA neighbors.

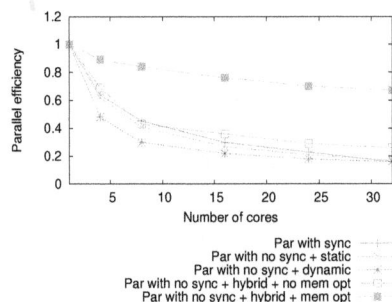

Figure 1: Parallel efficiency on CP method

We evaluate our techniques on an important sparse tensor computation method, namely, the CANDECOMP/PARAFAC (CP) tensor decomposition, using a $63891 \times 63891 \times 1591$ sparse tensor with 737934 non-zeros (derived from a real Facebook dataset) on a quad socket 8-core Intel x86 system. Figure 1 shows improved parallel efficiency and scalability with increasing number of cores (for up to 32 cores) with our techniques.

ICS'14, June 10–13 2014, Munich, Germany.
ACM 978-1-4503-2642-1/14/06.
http://dx.doi.org/10.1145/2597652.2600115.

Revealing Applications' Access Pattern in Collective I/O for Cache Management

Yin Lu, Yong Chen
Computer Science
Texas Tech University
yin.lu@ttu.edu,
yong.chen@ttu.edu

Rob Latham
Mathematics and Computer
Science Division
Argonne National Laboratory
robl@mcs.anl.gov

Yu Zhuang
Computer Science
Texas Tech University
yu.zhuang@ttu.edu

ABSTRACT

Collective I/O is a critical I/O strategy on high-performance parallel computing systems that enables programmers to reveal parallel processes' I/O accesses collectively and makes possible for the parallel I/O middleware to carry out I/O requests in a highly efficient manner. Collective I/O has been proven as a core parallel I/O optimization technique. However, due to the collective nature of collective I/O, the access pattern of each individual process can be lost after I/O requests are aggregated at the parallel I/O middleware layer. In this study, we analyze this issue in detail. We show that such lost access pattern can have a negative impact on underlying caching algorithms' view of locality and can result in many unnecessary cache misses in low level buffer caches and additional disk accesses. To address this issue, we propose to reveal unseen access patterns - performing collective I/O but more importantly retaining applications' access patterns to underlying cache management. With such an idea, we have prototyped a new collective I/O aware cache management methodology. The evaluations with various cache management algorithms have confirmed clear advantages over the existing collective I/O strategy that throws away applications' original access pattern.

Categories and Subject Descriptors

B.4.3 [**Input/Output and Data communications**]: Parallel I/O; D.4.3 [**File Systems Management**]: Access methods

General Terms

Algorithms, Design, Performance

Keywords

Parallel I/O, collective I/O, high performance computing

1. INTRODUCTION

Scientific applications, simulations, and visualizations running on high-performance computing clusters produce and

ICS '14 June 10 - 13 2014, Muenchen, Germany
Copyright 2014 ACM 978-1-4503-2642-1/14/06 ...$15.00.
http://dx.doi.org/10.1145/2597652.2597686

consume growing massive amounts of data. For example, The EarthScience project hosted on Intrepid system accesses a total of 3.5 PiB of data volumes within two months [3]. Similarly, remarkable data volumes moved by accurate climate modeling expect to reach hundreds of exabytes by 2020 [8]. Such massive data sets require extreme amounts of I/O to store and retrieve results for later use and analysis. The disk access latencies of these data-intensive applications have resulted in I/O becoming a significant performance bottleneck.

Many efforts have been taken to tackle the I/O bottleneck issue from different angles. From the system architecture point of view, buffer caches are widely used in high performance storage systems to alleviate disk access latencies for data-intensive applications. Large-scale high performance computing platforms typically are hierarchically organized and can employ buffer caches in multiple layers. Such architectures can significantly enhance the scalability and availability of the systems and reduce I/O operation costs. Clearly, how to take advantage of such buffer cache hierarchy in high performance computing platforms for data-intensive scientific applications is critical from the performance point of view.

From the software perspective, a large-scale data-intensive application may use several layers of software for I/O optimizations. For example, I/O middleware such as an MPI-IO implementation organizes and coordinates I/O within applications using their access patterns. Collective I/O [18] is one of the most important I/O access optimizations in MPI-IO. MPI collective I/O layer in Figure 1a illustrates how a group of read operations can benefit from a collective routine. Four processes P_0, P_1, P_2 and P_3 from application layer request four data blocks at four times respectively. Collective I/O aggregates and services requests from all processes together instead of making several read calls separately. As shown in Figure 1a, the implementation of collective I/O aggregates requests from all those processes and exchanges their access offsets at time t_4. After analyzing the access requests of different processes, collective I/O filters overlapping requests, combines the interleaved noncontiguous requests, and carries out a large contiguous data access.

However, from this example we can observe that, with collective I/O the detailed access patterns available at the application level are changed when the aggregated I/O request reaches the low level buffer cache. How many times a block

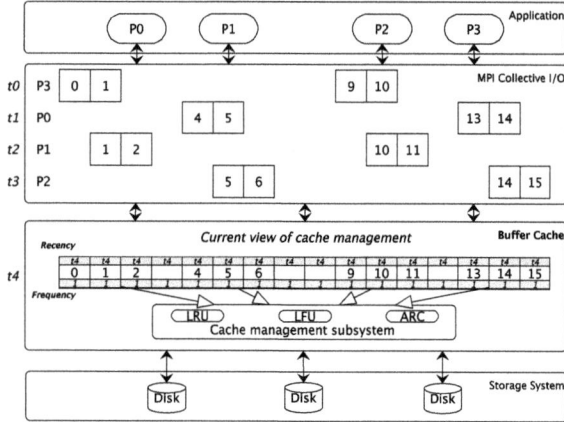

(a) Collective I/O and current cache managment

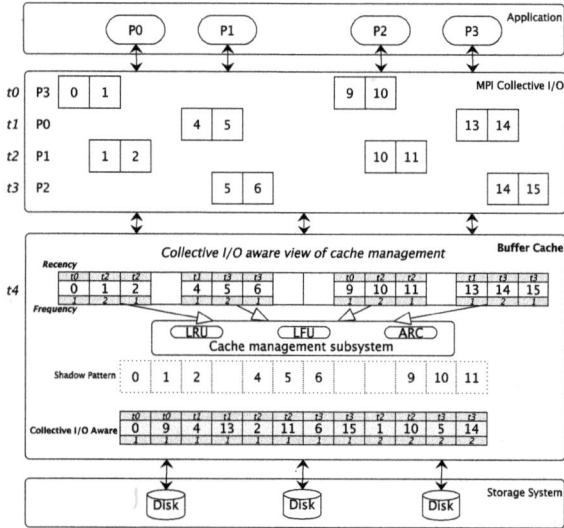

(b) New cache managment

Figure 1: Collective I/O Hides Applications' Original Access Pattern (Recency and Frequency of Requested Blocks) Away

the original pattern of access stream and has the better potential to exploit it. The buffer cache layer in Figure 1a versus the buffer cache layer in Figure 1b demonstrate the comparison of two cache layouts with the same application data accesses. One layout is the effect of the hidden access pattern stemming from current collective I/O. Another cache layout is optimized with our proposed CIO-aware approach. With the proposed strategy, the data elements in buffer cache are organized based on the actual pattern from application level (please note the difference of both recency and frequency between Figure 1a and Figure 1b) and stored in consecutive locations, which helps minimize the number of data blocks occupied in buffer cache and makes the cache management much more efficient than the existing strategy.

The primary contributions of the study are as follows:

- We investigate the impact of collective I/O on the low level buffer cache management and analyze the potential limitation and improvement.

- We propose a CIO-aware cache management scheme which integrates enhanced collective I/O module with pattern detection threads to improve the performance of underlying buffer cache without dedicating extra resources.

- Compared to current scheme, the beauty of the CIO-aware cache management is that, collective I/O is still performed, but more importantly the original true access patterns are revealed to low level buffer caches.

- We implemented CIO-aware cache management scheme within ROMIO [17], the most popular implementation of the MPI-IO middleware. Both pattern detection and cache management are transparent to the users and collective I/O interfaces remain unchanged. Furthermore, CIO-aware cache management is implemented in the file-system-independent layer of ROMIO, allowing it to be easily ported.

- We evaluated CIO-aware buffer cache management with three widely-used parallel I/O benchmarks. Our results show that CIO-aware buffer cache can significantly reduce the total run time and improve the applications' overall performance. Through our experiments, we also found that CIO-aware buffer cache management can help I/O middleware to reduce the actual I/O bandwidth usage, by reducing the data movement between compute and storage nodes.

The rest of this paper is organized as follows. Section II briefly discusses collective I/O and middleware caching as the related work of this study. The design and implementation of collective I/O aware cache management strategy are presented in Section III, and the evaluation methodology and experimental results with analysis are given in Section IV. We conclude this study in Section V.

2. RELATED WORK

Extensive studies have focused on improving the I/O performance of high performance computing systems. We briefly review closely related work with this study along three lines:

is requested and the original temporal information are all thrown away and not known to the low level buffer cache after being aggregated by collective I/O. Therefore data blocks could reside in low level buffer caches undiscerningly for a long period of time before they become cold enough to be replaced by a local replacement algorithm. Furthermore, collective I/O can potentially bring to low level cache more data elements than it needs. For instance, in Figure 1a, at t_4 four blocks in the combined large data chunk are extra data not truly required by processes. These extra data blocks increases the pressure on the low level buffer caches. The effective cache capacity is reduced, which in turn affects application performance. Without a proper coordination between I/O middleware and the low level buffer cache, the *shadow pattern* caused by collective I/O can lead to the buffer cache seriously under-utilized.

To address these limitations, in this paper we propose a collective I/O aware (CIO-aware in short) buffer cache management scheme, in which the buffer cache is exposed with parallel I/O and collective I/O, cache management at storage and file systems level, and cache management at middleware and library level.

2.1 Parallel I/O and Collective I/O

There have been significant amount of research efforts in optimizing parallel I/O performance, such as collective I/O [4, 11, 18], data sieving, server-direct I/O, disk-directed I/O, lightweight I/O [15], partitioned collective I/O [21], layout-aware collective I/O [4], ADIOS library [12], and resonant I/O [22]. These strategies collect and aggregate small requests into larger ones at the I/O client/middleware/server level. Abbasi et. al. recently proposed a DataStager framework with data staging services that move output data to dedicated staging or I/O nodes prior to storage, which has been proven effective in reducing the I/O overheads and interferences on compute nodes [1]. Zheng et. al. proposed a preparatory data analytics (PreDatA) approach to preparing and characterizing scientific data when generated (e.g. data reorganization and metadata annotation) to speedup subsequent data access [23]. These approaches have shown considerable performance improvement with dedicated output staging services and preparatory analysis. Advanced I/O libraries, such as Hierarchical Data Format (HDF), Parallel netCDF (PnetCDF) [9], and Adaptable IO System (ADIOS) [12], provide high-level abstractions, map the abstractions onto I/O in one way or another, and complement parallel programming models in managing data access activities.

2.2 Cache Management at Storage and File Systems Level

Numerous prior work focus on improving the behavior of storage (or second-level) cache management because the behavior of the second-level cache is often hard to characterize, making cache management schemes inadequate. Particularly, Zhou et al. investigated multi-queue, eviction-based, and CLOCK replacement policies [24]. Choi et al. proposed a fine-grained file-level characterization of chunk references in buffer management [5]. Vilayannur et al. introduced selective caching because caching of certain blocks is not always beneficial [19]. Sarhan and Das proposed to use the on-disk buffers for caching intervals between successive streams, while multimedia-on-demand servers improve resource sharing by intelligent request schedulers [16]. Our approach complements these existing caching policies with improved cache locality view via revealing the original access pattern that is hidden by collective I/O.

Recently, several studies looked into cache management for multi-level storage hierarchies. The main motivation for these studies is that the modern networked storage systems have a hierarchy of caches, and special care needs to be taken in order to manage those cache hierarchies efficiently. A key idea is how to reduce negative interference while keeping most valuable blocks in shared cache. Techniques to extract and predict the most valuable blocks include transforming application-level requirement into I/O reservations, correlating program counters with program context, exploiting reference regularities, locality of file chunks of non-uniform strength, and automatic application reference pattern detection. For example, Wong and Wilkes explored the exclusive cache policies against the prevalent inclusive ones [20].

These studies are system-level approaches and are therefore orthogonal to our approach. Our approach is also along this direction but is unique because it specifically addresses hidden pattern and locality issues to low level buffer cache management when collective I/O is heavily used in parallel computing systems.

2.3 Cache Management at Middleware and Library Level

Cooperative caching [6] seeks to improve network file system performance by mutually sharing the contents of client data caches. In cluster environments where high performance, low latency message passing networks are frequently available, accessing remote clients to retrieve cached data may result in improved file system throughput. Cooperative caching offers the most opportunity for performance improvements when the client exhibits a large degree of inter-client sharing. Many projects have explored the use of cooperative caching within the file system as an effective means for improving file system performance. The Center for Ultra-Scale Computing and Information Security at Northwestern University has prototyped several file cache designs [2] with ROMIO [17], an open source implementation of the MPI-IO standard. The basic approach involves partitioning the file into a set of fixed size pages. Pages are then assigned to a single computation node by taking the modulo of the page number. Clients processes access file data by requesting it from the client responsible for the cache page rather by accessing the file system, a cooperative caching approach. In one scheme the file data may only be cached at nodes responsible for the cached page. Another scheme implements directories at the responsible node so that another node may cache the page. All of these schemes require that file data is cached at only one node and that all file accesses occur on page aligned boundaries. Our study leverages these existing work, identifies, and addresses the issue of hidden access pattern to low level cache management due to collective I/O.

3. COLLECTIVE I/O AWARE CACHE MANAGEMENT

Each I/O request from applications represents a caching opportunity for the lower level storage systems. In this section, we introduce the proposed collective I/O aware cache management framework to make applications' access pattern available to low level cache. We also present methods for exploiting this knowledge to improve the overall caching performance.

3.1 CIO-Aware Cache Management Framework

Figure 2 illustrates the high-level view of the proposed CIO-aware cache framework. As shown in the figure, the computations of parallel scientific applications are carried out on compute processes, which generate a number of I/O requests for underlying parallel file system. Each parallel process launches a main thread to perform I/O related operations. The caching helper thread is attached to each main thread for cache management. It delivers the original accesses of each parallel process to the pattern detection module.

A pattern detection module is embedded inside the MPI I/O library. It collects and processes the stream of access requests dispatched from caching helper threads. The current

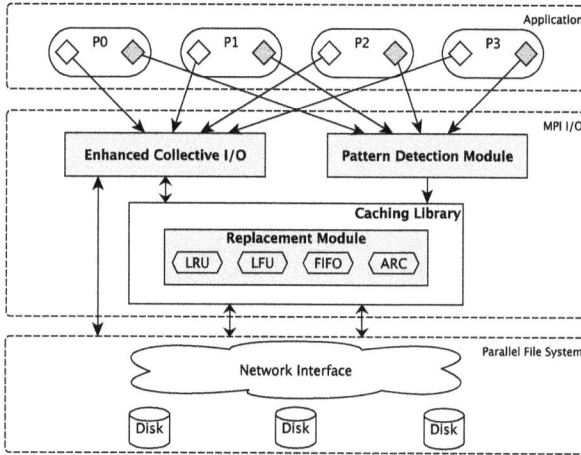

Figure 2: Collective I/O Aware Cache Management

file pointer offsets from caching helper threads are maintained in an implicit file table. The pattern detection module explores the access information from this file table to build pattern views and pass them to the underlying MPI I/O caching library. The pattern detection module also tracks function-call identifiers to synchronize the caching helper thread and the main thread collective I/O calls.

The cache library maintains a global buffer cache among multiple processes. This library is implemented at user space and integrated in the MPI I/O library. It captures the access patterns transferred from the pattern detection module and manages the actual data fetching to the buffer cache. The regular collective I/O is enhanced to take advantages of the cached data residing in the buffer cache. An I/O requesting process must first check the caching status of the requested blocks before exchanging I/O accesses with other processes. If the requested blocks are cached, the requesting process will fetch data from buffer cache directly.

The proposed CIO-aware cache management can work with any cache replacement algorithm. In this study, we focus on four typical replacement algorithms, LRU, LFU, FIFO, and ARC, and study the impact of CIO-aware cache management with any one of these cache replacement algorithms. Such a functionality is implemented in the replacement module.

3.2 MPI I/O Access Pattern Detection

The success of the proposed CIO-aware buffer cache management relies on extracting and utilizing original I/O access information before the collective I/O aggregation. We choose a multi-threading approach to obtain the actual access information of each parallel process. A caching helper thread is constructed in each MPI process when opening the file and destroyed when closing the file. Figure 3 shows several key lines in our prototype to illustrate the thread execution. As shown in Figure 3, the caching helper thread shares certain resources with the main thread, such as process rank, MPI file handles, and file views. While the main thread performs enhanced collective I/O, the caching helper only performs essential computation for data address calculation. A list

of offsets and request sizes are created and maintained in a pattern record corresponding to one process.

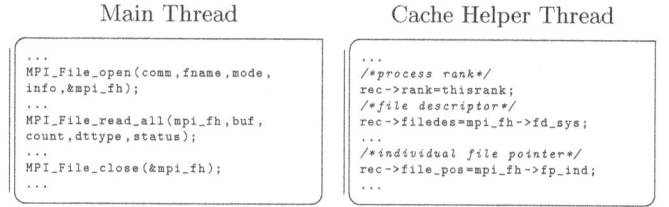

Figure 3: Collective I/O Aware Access Pattern Detection

One caching helper thread only evaluates how a file is accessed by a local process and transfers the records to the pattern detection module. The pattern detection module receives local patterns from all processes involved in collective I/O operations. It analyzes these local patterns and combines them into a global pattern. The pattern detection module considers the following four factors when producing the global pattern: I/O operation type, spatial locality, temporal pattern, and iterative behavior.

The I/O operation type is classified as read, write, or read-/write. The spatial locality can be contiguous, noncontiguous, and the combinations of contiguous and noncontiguous patterns. When the application conducts one collective I/O operation, each process may access several noncontiguous portions of a file while the requests of multiple processes are often overlapped. These gaps and overlaps can help the caching library identify the potential candidate data blocks to be placed into buffer caches. Capturing temporal patterns is also helpful for organizing the cache blocks. If at one point a particular data block is requested by one process, it is likely that the same block will be requested again in the near future. The replacement module in our proposed caching library manage the cache blocks by using the temporal information obtained from the previous I/O accesses. Scientific parallel programs using MPI I/O usually issue data requests with a few loops. This I/O access pattern can be described as iterative behavior. When repetitive I/O access patterns are captured, identified data blocks can be effectively kept longer in the cache. The cached data can be completely used before evicting them to make room for the new blocks.

Taking the factors mentioned above into account, the global pattern stores information of the file descriptor, process id, I/O operation, time stamp, dimension, starting offset, request sizes and number of repetitions. Consider, as an example, a global pattern value with parameters {[3],READ, 0.023184, 1, [(2622716, 510080), (1573632, 510080)], 64} indicates a one dimensional read access pattern. At time 0.023184, the third MPI process accesses a region whose starting offsets are 2622716 and 1573632 respectively. The request size is 510080 bytes for both accesses. This one dimensional pattern repeats 64 times. Using the pattern value and data block sizes, caching library can identify the set of data blocks captured in the buffer cache.

184

3.3 MPI IO Caching Library

MPI-IO based data cache can leverage other MPI library components to take advantage of the collective nature of parallel I/O. Incorporating the caching into the MPI library also increases the implementation portability. MPI-IO based caching can easily interface with different underlying file systems. Several research projects have been working on MPI-IO caching libraries. Liao et al. developed a collective caching library implemented at the MPI-IO level[10, 14]. Collective caching maintains a global buffer cache among multiple processes in the client side. We use this library as the starting point for our study. Each client contributes part of its memory to construct the global cache pool. The cached data is transfered among clients through the high-speed interconnect network. Metadata of cached blocks is maintained to locate data quickly. A simplified cache-coherency protocol is used to maintain consistency among cache copies in the cache pool. At most a single copy of file data is allowed to be cached among all MPI processes. Since the read/write mix varies considerably by application domain and read workloads are as prevalent as writes on leadership platforms [3], in this study we customize the collective caching prototype implementation by enabling read caching only. In addition, we utilize a replacement module in conjunction with pattern detection results to direct caching policy. The details will be discussed in the next subsection.

3.4 CIO-Aware Cache Management

The replacement module in the MPI-IO caching library manages the cache by applying specific replacement policies that best utilize the cache under that access pattern. By taking full benefits of original access patterns delivered from the pattern detection module and used for making the block replacement decisions, caching performance can be enhanced. There has been an extensive research on designing cache replacement algorithms, e.g. LRU [7], LFU, FIFO and ARC [13], etc. In this subsection, we illustrate how cache replacement policies are extended to take advantage of original access pattern from MPI-IO processes.

3.4.1 CIO-Aware LRU

We extend the Least Recently Used (LRU) cache replacement policy and exploit original access temporal locality filtered by collective I/O to manage the LRU list and to decide whether or not to cache accessed blocks.

The new replacement policy of *CIO-aware LRU* first extracts the values of starting offset and request size from each global pattern value. The request is divided into blocks of size equal to the buffer cache block size. We check whether each block is already in the buffer cache or not. If the block is cached, the block is directly copied from buffer cache to user's buffer by using *memcpy()* function call. The exact location where the buffer cache should be copied to is decided by the index of the requested block in user's buffer. Meanwhile, the last access time of this block is updated with its original temporal information and this block is moved to the most-recently-used position. For blocks not placed in the cache buffer, collective reads are first performed directly from the underlying file system. Then these blocks are fetched into the buffer frame held by LRU victims. The general design of CIO-aware LRU is summarized in Algorithm 1.

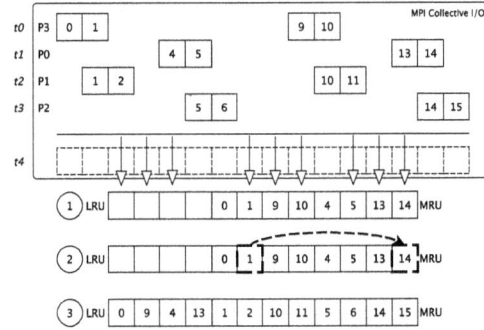

Figure 4: LRU with Collective I/O Awareness

Figure 4 demonstrates how data blocks are arranged by LRU by exploiting their original access temporal locality filtered by collective I/O. We assume the buffer cache is clean at the beginning with twelve frames/slots. Blocks 0, 1, 9 and 10 are referenced by P_3 at t_0 and blocks 4, 5, 13 and 14 are referenced by P_0 at t_1 respectively. Each data block is copied from the data file on the file system into a buffer in the cache. The LRU list holds all these blocks as shown in the first status. The second status demonstrates block 1 referenced by P_1 at t_2 is moved to the most recently used (MRU) position of the LRU list. Other buffers age toward the LRU position of the LRU list. The third status shows the cache content after all data blocks required through one collective I/O have been organized by LRU with their actual timestamps. By leveraging the virtue of the original access pattern, buffer cache avoid copying extra data blocks which are not requested by processes.

Algorithm 1: CIO-Aware LRU

> **input** : A sequence of global pattern values S_v from pattern detection module
> **output**: The contents of buffer cache
>
> **foreach** *global pattern value $g_v \in S_v$* **do**
>   split data requests with g_v into blocks B_s ;
>   uncatched data blocks set $U_s \leftarrow \emptyset$;
>   **foreach** *block $b_i \in B_s$* **do**
>   **if** *$b_i \in$ buffer cache* **then**   // cache hit
>   hits++;
>   // copy data b_i to user using memcpy()
>   user specified buffer $\leftarrow b_i$ in buffer cache;
>   // update b_i last access time
> $Last(b_i) \leftarrow b_i$ time stamp;
>   **else**   // cache miss
>   // perform I/O from disk
>   user specified buffer $\leftarrow b_i$ in file system ;
>   // evicting the LRU block
>   min $\leftarrow$ current time;
>   **foreach** *block $b_j \in$ buffer cache* **do**
>   **if** *$Last(b_j) < min$* **then**
>   victim $\leftarrow b_j$;
>   min $\leftarrow Last(b_j)$;
>   **if** *victim == dirty* **then**
>   flush the victim to the disk;
>   fetch b_i into the buffer frame held by victim;
> $Last(b_i) \leftarrow b_i$ time stamp;

To interact with the replacement module and benefit from caching, the current collective I/O implementation is modified to be able to access the buffer cache for requested data.

When I/O requests are issued, the replacement module extracts the global pattern values from the pattern detection module. The requests are divided into blocks of size equal to the buffer cache block size. The enhanced collective I/O module first checks whether each block is already in the buffer cache or not. If the block is cached, the block is directly copied from buffer cache to user's buffer by using the *memcpy()* function call as discussed earlier. The general design of cooperation mechanism between enhanced collective I/O and CIO-aware LRU module follows Algorithm 1.

3.4.2 CIO-Aware LFU

A potential problem with LRU is that it may quickly replace some data blocks that do not provide hits for a short period of time, although they are beneficial in the long run. In addition, LRU might also fail when the access pattern is such that all requested data blocks can not fit into the buffer cache and the data blocks are requested in a round robin fashion. What will happen in case of LRU is that data blocks will constantly enter and leave the cache, with no client request ever hitting the cache. Under the same condition however, the Least Frequently Used (LFU) will perform much better, with most of the cached items resulting in a cache hit. In I/O intensive scientific applications, a large amount of overlaps exist among the file regions required by multiple processes. Obviously, the overlapped data are referenced more than other data blocks. Under such a circumstance, we anticipate that LFU can better identify these blocks and they can have higher priorities to stay in cache.

The pseudo code for collective I/O aware LFU is similar to that of Algorithm 1 and thus is not included here. Instead of utilizing temporal information, the algorithm keeps the hit count for each data block in the cache. This is achieved by maintaining two double linked list. One is the access frequency list which is used to link together rectangular hit counters. Each hit counter has a frequency value and connects with a set of circular data blocks that have the same access frequency. All the data blocks with the same access frequency are connected using another doubly linked list.

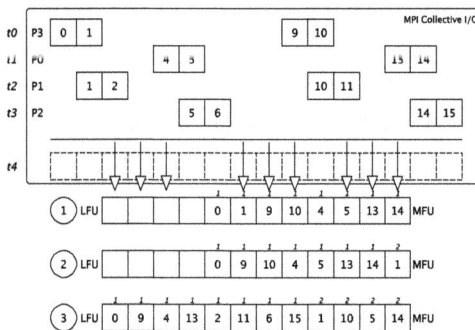

Figure 5: LFU with CIO aware

Figure 5 demonstrates how CIO-aware LFU organizes data blocks using reference frequency hidden by collective I/O. LFU keeps track of the number of times a block is referenced. Status one shows that blocks 0, 1, 9, 10, 4, 5, 13 and 14 are referenced once after t_2. In the second status, block 1 is moved to frequency list with value 2 since it is referenced by P_1 at t_2. The third status illustrates all the data blocks are

arranged with their actual reference frequency at t_3. Without revealing the original access pattern that is hidden away by collective I/O, the cache management will not be able to tell the correct request frequency of blocks. For instance, blocks 1, 5, 10, and 14 are all requested twice, whereas after being aggregated by collective I/O, the requested frequency of these blocks becomes once only to the underlying cache.

3.4.3 CIO-Aware ARC

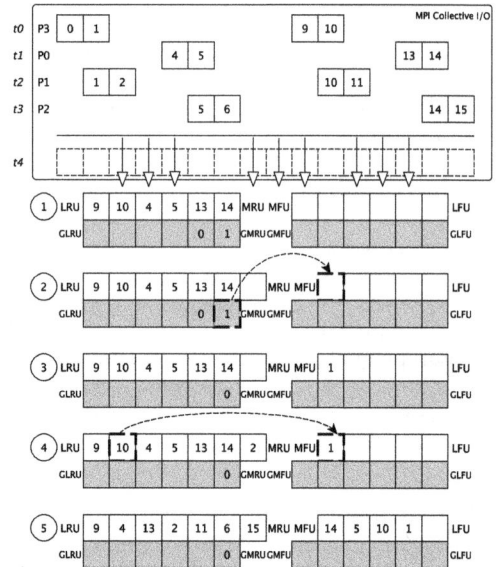

Figure 6: ARC with CIO aware

The standard LFU policy has shortfalls as well. The most significant drawback is that LFU pays no attention to temporal history. Potentially it may accumulate stale pages with high frequency counts that may no longer be useful. Thus LFU does not adapt well to the changing access patterns. Adaptive Replacement Cache (ARC) [13] bridges the gap between LRU and LFU by capturing both recency and frequency. ARC maintains two lists of cache pages, one list for the most recently used pages and another list for the most frequently used pages. In addition, ARC maintains two ghost cache directories that remembers twice as many pages as in the cache memory. Both ghost lists do not cache data, but track the recently evicted pages from the list of most recently used pages and the most frequently used pages respectively. A hit on them affects the behavior of the cache.

The key idea of ARC is to adaptively decide how many top pages from each list to maintain in the cache. Figure 6 shows how CIO-aware ARC performs in response to the same workload we have demonstrated in the previous subsections. GLRU and GLFU represent most recently evicted pages from LRU list and LFU list respectively. When a block is referenced by any processes at first time, it is placed in the recently used list. Status one indicates that blocks 0 and 1 are evicted from the LRU list at t_1 when the LRU list is filled up. These two blocks are put onto the list of recently evicted pages. When block 1 is referenced by P_1 at t_2, this block is on the list of already evicted pages. Such an attempt to read leads to a phantom cache hit. As the block 1 has already

Algorithm 2: CIO-Aware ARC

input : A sequence of global pattern values S_v from pattern detection module; T_1 and T_2 hold pages metadata in the cache; B_1 and B_2 are ghost caches; c is the cache size; p is a tunable parameter

output: The contents of buffer cache

Set $p = 0$ and Set T_1, T_2, B_1 and $B_2 \leftarrow \emptyset$;
foreach *global pattern value* $g_v \in S_v$ **do**
    split data requests with g_v into blocks B_s ;
    foreach *block* $b_i \in B_s$ **do**
        if $b_i \in T_1$ *or* T_2 **then**
            Move b_i to top of T_2;
        else if $b_i \in B_1$ **then**
            $p = \min\left(c, p + \max\left(\frac{|B_2|}{|B_1|}, 1\right)\right)$;
            `replace`(b_i, p);
            Move b_i to top of T_2;
        else if $b_i \in B_2$ **then**
            $p = \max\left(0, p - \max\left(\frac{|B_1|}{|B_2|}, 1\right)\right)$;
        else   // page not in $T_1, T_2, B_1, or\, B_2$
            if $(|T_1| + |B_1|) == CacheSize$ **then**
                if $T_1 < CacheSize$ **then**
                    Remove LRU page in B_1;
                    `replace`(b_i, p);
                else
                    Remove LRU page in T_1;
            else if $(|T_1| + |B_1| + |T_2| + |B_2|) >= CacheSize$ **then**
                if $(|T_1| + |B_1| + |T_2| + |B_2|) >= 2 \times CacheSize$ **then**
                    Remove LRU page in B_2;
                else
                  `replace`(b_i, p);
            Put b_i at the top of T_1;

Replace *(page, p)*
    if $|T_1| \geqslant 1 \wedge (|T_1| \geqslant p \vee (|T_1| == p \wedge page \in B_2))$ **then**
        Move LRU page in T_1 to top of B_1 ;
    else
        Move LRU page in T_2 to top of B_2 ;

---

been evicted from cache, the system has to read it from underlying file system. Since this was a recently evicted page and not a page referenced just the first time, as shown in status two and three, ARC first places this block in the LFU list. This phantom hit also indicates the capacity of LRU list is not enough. In this case the length of LRU list in cache is increased by one. Obviously this reduces the place for LFU list by one. The same mechanism is applied on the other side. If we get a hit on the list of recently evicted pages of LFU list, the available space for frequently used pages will be increased by one. Obviously the list for currently cached recently used pages will be decreased by one. The status five exhibits the cache contents and the adapted lists' size after collective I/O performed. Algorithm 2 demonstrates a high-level description of CIO-aware ARC.

4. EVALUATIONS

In this section, we present the evaluation results of the CIO-aware cache management prototype tested with a variety of benchmarks. We present results that quantitatively demonstrate the benefits of revealing unseen access pattern in collective I/O and confirm the feasibility of our design.

4.1 Methodology

We quantify the extent to which the CIO-aware cache management scheme improves upon the traditional cache management schemes with respect to two key metrics: I/O throughput and buffer cache hit rate. The I/O throughput is expressed as the ratio of the total number of bytes transferred to/from file system to the time required to transfer data. A higher I/O throughput can lead to better performance of the application, i.e. less application execution time. We also choose the cache hit rate metric because it has a direct impact on application execution time. The buffer cache hit rate is defined as the ratio of the total number of buffer cache hits to the total number of I/O accesses made by the application.

The experiments were conducted on a 640-node Linux-based cluster test bed with DataDirect Network storage systems. Each node contains two Intel Xeon 2.8 GHz 6-core processors with 24 GB main memory. All nodes are connected with double-data-rate Infiniband networking that provides full cross-section bandwidth among the parallel nodes. A 600TB Lustre file system and MPICH-3.0.2 library manage the storage system and runtime environment. Files were striped over all I/O servers with the round robin default striping strategy (with 1 MB unit size in the experiments).

In the following experiments, we compare the CIO-aware cache management and the baseline scenario, in which client applications are configured to access the shared file system directly via MPI-IO layer. In addition to the experimental setup described above, we have also built a trace driven buffer cache simulator to measure the cache hit rates. In order to compare the hit rate of our strategy with the hit rate of a traditional system, the trace collector captures the traces of our applications twice while they ran on the cluster. The I/O operation parameters are collected once by using the Profiling MPI interface (PMPI) before the actual collective I/O function is issued and second time in ADIO layer after I/O requests are aggregated.

4.2 MPI-Tile-IO Benchmark

MPI-Tile-IO is a widely used benchmark designed to test the performance of non-contiguous data access. In this application, data I/O access is issued in a single step by using collective I/O. It tests the performance of concurrently accessing a two-dimensional dense data set, simulating the type of workload that exists in visualization and numerical applications. In our experiments, each process renders one tile with 1024×1024 pixels and the size of each element is 8 bytes. Tiles overlap by 128 elements in X axis, 128 elements in Y axis. Because this benchmark closes the file between write and read operations, we slightly modified the benchmark to avoid close/re-open in order to show the effect of collective buffer cache.

Figure 7 compares the total execution time for the implementation with CIO-aware strategy and the native approach which is oblivious of the application access pattern. The experimental results were measured with 8, 16, 32, 64, 128, 256, 512, and 1024 processes on Lustre respectively. The total data are set as 10GB in each I/O phase. The buffer cache size at each client was set as 64MB. We measure the latency for each processes' number by 10-time runs and

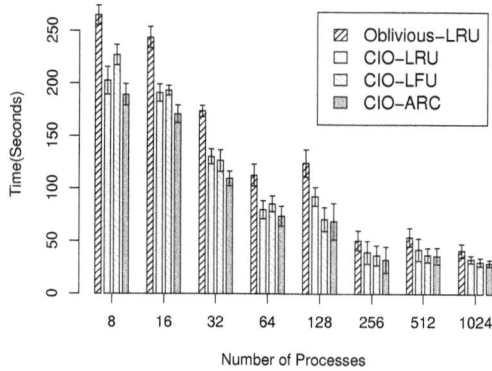

Figure 7: Total execution time comparison of Mpi-Tile-IO, each run with 10 GB data and 64 MB buffer cache per process

plot the figure with the median value. In the Figure 7, the first bar of every column represents the original execution time. The second, third and fourth bar represent the execution time with CIO-aware strategy under LRU, LFU and ARC replacement schemes.

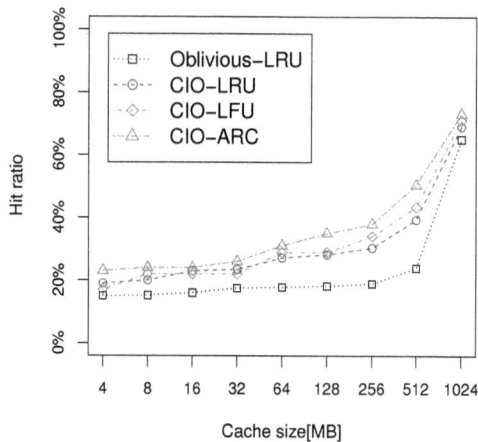

Figure 8: Hit rate comparison of cache replacement schemes for Mpi-Tile-IO, each run with 32 processes

The proposed CIO-aware cache management is on top of existing collective buffer optimization technique and complements the existing approaches. We observe that CIO-aware approach can reduce I/O access latency further when combined with existing collective buffering techniques. Additionally, the improvement increases with the number of processes. The decrease in read execution time was up to 80.6%. Overall, the average execution time decrement was 31.1%, 38.5% and 52.6% in CIO-LRU, CIO-LFU and CIO-ARC schemes respectively. These performance improvements are attributed to two causes: the improvement of buffer cache organizations and the reduction of underlying file system accesses. With CIO-aware buffer cache, subsequent collec-

tive read operations takes better advantage of cache capacity than the native approach. These results also indicate that the choice of a good replacement policy is crucial to CIO-aware scheme. It can be observed that the CIO-aware approach with ARC policy outperforms the LRU and LFU based schemes by 16.4% and 10.7%, respectively.

Figure 8 shows the hit ratios of different cache replacement algorithms. The original collective I/O trace managed by LRU was selected as the baseline. Compared to the original approach, the ARC with CIO-aware strategy provided the best hit rate among all the algorithms. It improved the hit rate by as much as 110.8% with an average of 66.7% improvement over the nine cache sizes. With limited cache size, CIO-aware LRU provides a relatively high hit rate with small cache size. Each block in an LRU cache has a long life before it is discarded, and thus has a high possibility to be referenced again by different clients with high-correlated workloads. The gain becomes smaller as the buffer cache is larger, since a large cache size retains a block for a long enough time, within which it is accessed by most clients.

4.3 IOR benchmark

The Interleaved Or Random (IOR) benchmark measures the performance of parallel I/O through different I/O interfaces, including MPI-IO, POSIX as well as high-level libraries. In this study, we performed interleaved read operations to a file as we varied the number of processes for collective I/O. The tests were carried out with 8MB I/O message size per process.

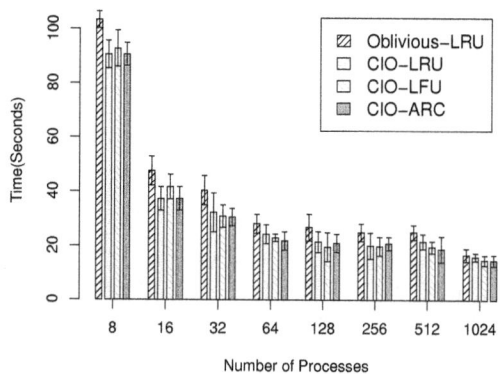

Figure 9: Total execution time comparison of IOR, each run with 10 GB data and 64 MB buffer cache per process

The total execution time results with IOR benchmark are plotted in Figure 9. From Figure 9, clear improvements of CIO-aware cache management over the original strategy can be observed. At 64MB cache size per process with CIO-aware strategy, the execution for CIO-LRU, CIO-LFU and CIO-ARC was decreased by 19%, 22.8% and 24.6%, respectively. Figure 10 shows the hit ratios for IOR benchmark under different cache sizes. Our results with 32 processes and CIO-aware cache showed that the percentage improvements brought by our scheme over the original LRU replacement are 54.4%, 50.8%, 75.5% for CIO-LRU, CIO-LFU and

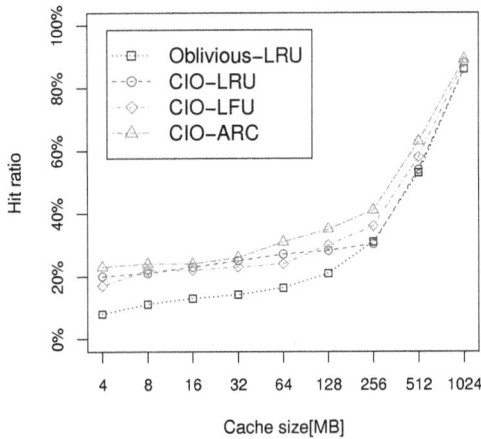

Figure 10: Hit rate comparison of cache replacement schemes for IOR, each run with 32 processes

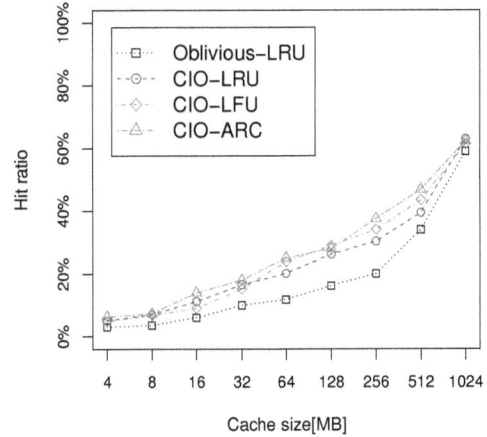

Figure 12: Hit rate comparison of cache replacement schemes for MPI-IO-Test, each run with 32 processes

CIO-ARC, respectively.

Both sets of experiments have verified the proposed collective I/O aware cache management achieved considerable hit rate increments and sustained bandwidth improvements.

4.4 MPI-IO-Test Benchmark

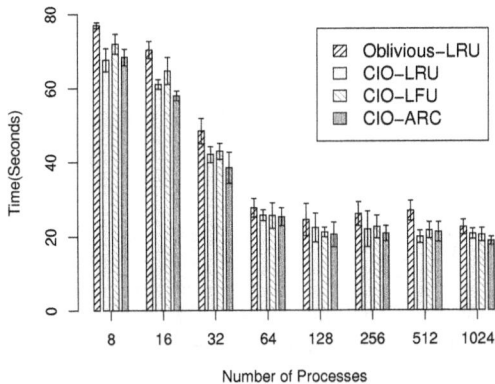

Figure 11: Total execution time comparison of MPI-IO-Test, each run with 10 GB data and 64 MB buffer cache per process

We have carried out various tests with the mpi-io-test benchmark as well. Figure 11 compares the execution time with normal collective I/O and CIO-aware strategy at 64 MB buffer cache per process with a varying number of processes at each run. Compared to the normal collective I/O, the average performance improvements for read is 15.6%, 12.8% and 20.1% for CIO-LRU, CIO-LFU and CIO-ARC. We can observe that the caching improves the performance, but the improvement is not very substantial. One reason is that read caching can perform well if large amount of data reuse exists. If there is no much data reuse, the read caching may not per-

form as well as expected. Figure 12 reports another set of test where we used 32 processes for evaluating the cache hit rate with increasing the buffer cache size. The average hit rate improvement was 58.2%, 59.5%, 83% respectively for CIO-LRU, CIO-LFU and CIO-ARC in this series of tests. Compared with the IOR benchmark, the mpi-io-test cache hit rate increased but at a relatively moderate rate with an increasing cache size.

All these results indicate that the CIO-aware cache management is beneficial to achieve better throughput for collective I/O operations and higher hit rate for the underlying buffer cache.

5. CONCLUSION

Parallel I/O systems have become increasingly critical due to many growingly data-intensive high-performance computing simulations and applications. These data-intensive scientific simulations and applications rely on a highly efficient parallel I/O system to make productive scientific discovery. In current parallel I/O software stack, collective I/O has been widely recognized as a critical I/O strategy that leverages correlations among parallel processes to carry out parallel I/O requests more efficiently. The current collective I/O and parallel I/O software stack, however, are not well integrated and suffer dropping out useful access patterns from applications during the aggregation process of the collective I/O strategy.

In this study, we have thoroughly demonstrated and analyzed this issue. We have shown that the collective I/O filters away many useful I/O access patterns that can be critical to underlying cache management. These thrown-away access patterns can have a negative impact on cache management algorithms on their views of locality, which leads to many unnecessary cache misses in low level buffer caches and additional disk accesses. We have thus proposed a new collective I/O aware cache management methodology that reveals unseen access pattern to underlying caching algorithms. We have prototyped such an idea and the new methodology. We have also carried out evaluations with widely-used cache management algorithms based on recency and frequency of access patterns. The evaluations have confirmed the performance advantage of revealing unseen access patterns in collective I/O. We believe that the issue identified in this study and the new methodology proposed can be helpful and can provide guidance for the community to build an even more efficient parallel I/O system.

6. ACKNOWLEDGMENT

This research is sponsored in part by the National Science Foundation under grant CNS-1162488 and supported by the U.S. Department of Energy, Office of Science, under Contract DE-AC02-06CH11357. The authors thank the High Performance Computing Center (HPCC) at Texas Tech University at Lubbock for providing HPC resources.

7. REFERENCES

[1] H. Abbasi, M. Wolf, and G. e. Eisenhauer. DataStager: Scalable Data Staging Services for Petascale Applications. In *HPDC*, 2009.

[2] S. Byna, Y. Chen, X.-H. Sun, R. Thakur, and W. Gropp. Parallel I/O Prefetching Using MPI File Caching and I/O Signatures. In *Proceedings of the 2008 ACM/IEEE conference on Supercomputing*, 2008.

[3] P. Carns, K. Harms, W. Allcock, C. Bacon, S. Lang, R. Latham, and R. Ross. Understanding and Improving Computational Science Storage Access through Continuous Characterization. In *Mass Storage Systems and Technologies (MSST), 2011 IEEE 27th Symposium on*, 2011.

[4] Y. Chen, X.-H. Sun, R. Thakur, P. Roth, and W. Gropp. LACIO: A New Collective I/O Strategy for Parallel I/O Systems. In *Parallel Distributed Processing Symposium (IPDPS), 2011 IEEE International*, pages 794 –804, 2011.

[5] J. Choi, S. H. Noh, S. L. Min, and Y. Cho. Towards Application/File-level Characterization of Block References: A Case for Fine-Grained Buffer Management, 2000.

[6] M. D. Dahlin, R. Y. Wang, T. E. Anderson, and D. A. Patterson. Cooperative Caching: Using Remote Client Memory to Improve File System Performance. In *Proceedings of the first Symposium on Operating Systems Design and Implmentation*, 1994.

[7] A. Dan and D. Towsley. An Approximate Analysis of the LRU and FIFO Buffer Replacement Schemes. In *Proceedings of the 1990 ACM SIGMETRICS conference on Measurement and modeling of computer systems*, SIGMETRICS '90, 1990.

[8] J. Dongarra, P. H. Beckman, and T. M. etc. The International Exascale Software Project roadmap. *IJHPCA*, 25(1):3–60, 2011.

[9] J. Li, W. keng Liao, A. Choudhary, R. Ross, R. Thakur, R. Latham, A. Siegel, B. Gallagher, and M. Zingale. Parallel netCDF: A high-performance Scientific I/O Interface. In *Proceedings of Supercomputing*, 2003.

[10] W.-K. Liao, A. Ching, K. Coloma, A. Choudhary, and L. Ward. An Implementation and Evaluation of Client-Side File Caching for MPI-IO. In *Parallel and Distributed Processing Symposium, 2007. IPDPS 2007. IEEE International*, 2007.

[11] W.-K. Liao and A. Choudhary. Dynamically Adapting File Domain Partitioning Methods for Collective I/O based on Underlying Parallel File System Locking Protocols. In *Proceedings of the ACM/IEEE Conference on Supercomputing (SC)*, SC'08, 2008.

[12] J. F. Lofstead, S. Klasky, and K. e. Schwan. Flexible IO and Integration for Scientific Codes through the Adaptable IO System (ADIOS). In *Proceedings of the 6th international workshop on Challenges of large applications in distributed environments*, 2008.

[13] N. Megiddo and D. Modha. ARC: A Self-Tuning, Low Overhead Replacement Cache. In *Proceedings of the 2003 Conference on File and Storage Technologies (FAST)*, pages 115–130, 2003.

[14] A. Nisar, W.-k. Liao, and A. Choudhary. Scaling Parallel I/O Performance through I/O Delegate and Caching System. In *Proceedings of the 2008 ACM/IEEE conference on Supercomputing*, SC '08, pages 9:1–9:12, 2008.

[15] R. Oldfield, L. Ward, R. Riesen, A. B. Maccabe, P. Widener, and T. Kordenbrock. Lightweight I/O for Scientific Applications. In *CLUSTER*, 2006.

[16] N. J. Sarhan and C. R. Das. Caching and Scheduling in NAD-Based Multimedia Servers. *IEEE Trans. Parallel Distrib. Syst.*, 15(10):921–933, Oct. 2004.

[17] R. Thakur, W. Gropp, and E. Lusk. *Users Guide for ROMIO: A High-Performance, Portable MPI-IO Implementation*. Mathematics and Computer Science Division, Argonne National Laboratory, Oct. 1997.

[18] R. Thakur, W. Gropp, and E. Lusk. Data Sieving and Collective I/O in ROMIO. In *Proceedings of the The 7th Symposium on the Frontiers of Massively Parallel Computation*, FRONTIERS '99, 1999.

[19] M. Vilayannur, A. Sivasubramaniam, M. Kandemir, R. Thakur, and R. Ross. Selective Caching for Parallel File Systems on Clusters. *Special Issue on Parallel I/O in Computational Grids and Cluster Computing Systems*, Jan 2006.

[20] T. M. Wong and J. Wilkes. My Cache or Yours? Making Storage More Exclusive. In *Proceedings of the General Track of the Annual Conference on USENIX Annual Technical Conference*, 2002.

[21] W. Yu and J. Vetter. ParColl: Partitioned Collective I/O on the Cray XT. In *Proceedings of the 2008 37th International Conference on Parallel Processing*, ICPP '08, 2008.

[22] X. Zhang, S. Jiang, and K. Davis. Making Resonance a Common Case: A high-performance Implementation of Collective I/O on Parallel File Systems. In *Proceedings of the 2009 IEEE International Symposium on Parallel&Distributed Processing*, 2009.

[23] F. Zheng, H. Abbasi, C. Docan, J. F. Lofstead, Q. Liu, S. Klasky, M. Parashar, N. Podhorszki, K. Schwan, and M. Wolf. PreDatA - Preparatory data Analytics on Peta-scale Machines. In *IPDPS'10*, pages 1–12, 2010.

[24] Y. Zhou, J. F. Philbin, and K. Li. The Multi-Queue Replacement Algorithm for Second Level Buffer Caches. In *Proceedings of the 2001 USENIX Annual Technical Conference*, pages 91–104, 2001.

Supporting Storage Configuration for I/O Intensive Workflows

Lauro Beltrão Costa, Samer Al-Kiswany, Hao Yang, Matei Ripeanu
NetSysLab, Electrical and Computer Engineering Department
University of British Columbia, Vancouver, BC, Canada
{lauroc,samera,haoy,matei}@ece.ubc.ca

ABSTRACT

System provisioning, resource allocation, and system configuration decisions for I/O-intensive workflow applications are complex even for expert users. Users face choices at multiple levels: allocating resources to individual sub-systems (e.g., the application layer, the storage layer) and configuring each of these optimally (e.g., replication level, chunk size, caching policies in case of storage) all having a large impact on overall application performance. This paper presents our progress on addressing the problem of supporting these provisioning, allocation and configuration decisions for workflow applications. To enable selecting a good choice in a reasonable time, we propose an approach that accelerates the exploration of the configuration space based on a low-cost performance predictor that estimates total execution time of a workflow application in a given setup. Our evaluation shows that: (i) the predictor is effective in identifying the desired system configuration, (ii) it can scale to model a workflow application run on an entire cluster, while (iii) using over 2000x less resources (machines x time) than running the actual application.

Categories and Subject Descriptors

D.4 [**Operating systems**]: [Storage management]; D.4.8 [**Performance**]: Modeling and Prediction

Keywords

performance prediction; distributed storage systems

1. INTRODUCTION

Assembling workflow applications by putting together standalone binaries has become a popular approach to support large-scale science [9, 21, 28]. The processes spawned from these binaries communicate via temporary files stored on a shared storage system. In this setup, the workflow runtime engines are basically schedulers that build and manage a task-dependency graph based on the tasks' input/output files (e.g., SWIFT [27]).

To avoid accessing the platform's backend storage system (e.g., NFS or GPFS or Amazon S3), recent proposals [4, 28] advocate using some of the nodes allocated to the application to deploy a *intermediate storage system*. That is, aggregating (some of) the resources of an application allocation to provide a shared temporary in-memory storage system dedicated to (and co-deployed with) the application.

This approach offers a number of advantages: higher performance - as applications benefit from a wider I/O channel obtained by striping data across several nodes; higher efficiency – as it improves resource utilization; incremental scalability – as it is possible to increase system capacity in small increments. This scenario also opens the opportunity for optimizing the intermediate storage system for the target workflow application: a storage system used by a single workflow, and co-deployed on the application allocation, can be configured specifically for the I/O patterns generated by the workflow (e.g., specify chunk-size to optimize data-transfers, configure striping and replication to eliminate hot spots, use a data placement policy to maximize data access locality) [25].

These benefits, however, come at a price: configuring the intermediate storage system becomes increasingly complex for multiple reasons. First, the optimization techniques commonly used in distributed environments expose trade-offs that rarely exist in centralized solutions [22, 23]. Second, each application may obtain peak performance at a different configuration point [3, 4, 22, 23]. Third, depending on the context, there are multiple metrics of interest to optimize [11, 22, 25]: time-to-solution, throughput, energy, or, increasingly common in cloud computing environments, the cost of resources.

The Problem. In this scenario, the role of the application administrator/user is non-trivial: if the user wants to extract maximum performance, in addition to being in charge with running the workflow application, the user has to configure the deployment and the intermediate-storage system to achieve high performance (e.g., in terms of application turnaround time, storage footprint, energy consumption, or financial cost). This involves allocating resources and configuring the storage system (e.g., chunk size, stripe width, data placement policy, and replication level). Thus, the decision space revolves around: *provisioning the allocation* - total number of nodes, deciding on node type(s) (or node specification) for cloud environments; *allocation partitioning* – splitting or not these nodes between the application and the intermediate storage system; and *storage system configuration parameters* – choosing the values for several configuration parameters, e.g., choosing chunk size, replication level, cache/prefetching and data placement policies for the intermediate storage system. Consequently, provisioning the system entails searching a complex multidimensional configuration space to determine the user's ideal cost/performance balance point (see examples in §3).

In this complex space, generally the user's goal is to optimize a multi-objective problem, in at least two dimensions: maximize performance (e.g., reduce application execution time) while minimizing cost (e.g., reduce the total CPU hours or dollar amount spent). More concretely the user is often interested in answering specific questions: *What is the configuration that can achieve the lowest total cost? How should I partition the allocation among application and storage nodes to achieve the highest performance? Which is the allocation that has lowest cost per unit of performance?*

Manually fine-tuning the storage system configuration parameters and allocation decisions is hard, and time-consuming due to the time to consider the potentially large configuration space, and non-linear interaction among the possible decisions.

Our long-term goal is to design a configuration exploration framework able to explore the multidimensional configuration space to find the provisioning and the storage system configuration that optimizes a user-specific metric [14]. To reach this goal, we design a prediction mechanism - the focus of this paper - that is able to predict the application performance given a certain resources and storage system configuration.

This paper presents our progress to date on designing and harnessing a performance prediction mechanism for an intermediate object-based storage system in the context of workflow applications. Given a storage system configuration, an application I/O profile, and a characterization of the deployment platform based on a simple system identification process (e.g., storage nodes service time, network characteristics), the mechanism predicts the application turnaround. This approach can support *autotuning*: a software tool that relies on the proposed mechanism can enable efficiently configuring the storage system [14, 22, 23], through exploring the configuration space without actually running the application.

The contributions of this paper lie over multiple axes. It:

- Synthesizes the key requirements for a prediction mechanism (§2.1).

- Describes a prediction mechanism that relies on a uniform queue-based model for distributed, object-based storage systems (§2.3). More important, it proposes a system identification procedure to seed the model that is simple, lightweight, effective, and does not require storage system or kernel changes to collect monitoring information (§2.4).

- Evaluates the prediction mechanism for workflow applications and synthetic benchmarks in the context of making configuration choices for different scenarios (§3). The evaluation shows that the predictor is lightweight (up to 2000× less resources (machines × time) than running the actual applications) and effective (identify the configuration that achieves the best performance in the experiments).

- Finally, this paper discusses our experience and lessons learnt (§5) from using the prediction mechanism as a performance testing and debugging tool for distributed storage system development.

2. THE DESIGN OF A PERFORMANCE ESTIMATION MECHANISM

Making accurate performance predictions for distributed systems is a challenge. Since in most cases purely analytical models cannot provide adequate accuracy, simulation is the commonly adopted solution. At the one end of the design spectrum, current practice (e.g., NS2 simulator [2]) suggests that while simulating a system at low granularity (e.g., packet-level simulation in NS2) can provide high accuracy, the complexity of the model, the complexity of the seeding process, and the number of events generated make accurately simulating large-scale systems infeasible, and reduces the generality of the model. Further, the improvement in accuracy may not add much value. At the other end, coarse grained simulations (e.g., PeerSim [20]) scale at the cost of lower accuracy.

Two key observations enable us to reduce simulation complexity and increase its scalability: First, as the goal is to support configuration choice for a specific workload, achieving perfect accuracy is less critical as long as the configuration decisiodummy.psns are good. Second, we take advantage of workload characteristics generated by workflow applications: relatively large files, and specific data access patterns. These observations enable us to reduce the simulation complexity by not simulating in detail some of the control paths that do not significantly impact accuracy (e.g., the chunk transfer time is dominated by the time to send the data, not accounting the time of the acknowledgments and all metadata messages will not tangibly impact accuracy).

Our solution uses a queue-based storage system model for the system components' operations and their interactions. The model requires three inputs from the user: the storage system configuration, a workload description, and the performance characteristics of storage system components (i.e., system identification §2.4). The simulator instantiates the storage system model with the specific component characteristics and configuration, and simulates the application run as described by the workload description.

This section discusses the requirements for a practical performance prediction mechanism (§2.1) and presents the key aspects of the object-based storage system architecture modeled (§2.2). Then, it focuses on the proposed solution: it presents the model (§2.3), its implementation (§2.5), the system identification process to seed the model (§2.4), and an overview of the workload description (§2.6).

2.1 Solution Requirements

A practical performance prediction mechanism should meet the following, partially conflicting, requirements that bind the solution space:

- **Accuracy.** The mechanism should provide *adequate accuracy*. Although higher accuracy is always desirable, in the face of practical limitations to achieve perfect accuracy, there are decreasing incremental gains for improved accuracy. For example, to support configuration decisions, a predictor only needs to correctly estimate relative performance or trends resulting from changing a configuration parameter.

- **Scalability and Response Time.** The predictor should enable quick exploration of the configuration space. The mechanism should offer performance predictions quickly and scale with: (i) the system size; and (ii) the I/O intensity of I/O workflow applications.

- **Usability and Generality.** The predictor should not impose a burdensome effort to be used. Specifically, the bootstrapping/seeding process should be simple and it should not require storage system redesign (or a particular initial design) to collect performance measurements. Additionally, using the predictor should not require in-depth knowledge of storage system protocols and architecture.

2.2 Object-based Storage System Design

We focus on a widely-adopted object-based storage system architecture (e.g., UrsaMinor [3], PVFS [15], and MosaStore [4]). This architecture includes three main components: a centralized metadata manager, storage nodes, and a client-side system access interface (SAI). The manager maintains the stored files' metadata and system state. To speed up data storage and retrieval, the architecture employs striping: files are split into chunks stored across several storage nodes. Client SAIs implement data access protocols.

Data placement. The default data placement generally adopted is round-robin: when a new file is created on a stripe of n nodes the file's chunks are placed in a round-robin fashion across these nodes. Additionally, and key for workflows, application driven data placement policies that optimize for a specific application access patterns have seen increasing adoption [25,30]. For instance, the following data placement policies are used to optimize for the workflow applications' data access patterns: local, co-locate and broadcast (detailed in §3).

Replication. Data replication is often used to improve reliability or access performance. However, while a higher replication level reduces contention on the node storing a popular file, it increases the file write time and the storage space consumption.

We explore the accuracy of the prediction mechanism assuming that the chunk size, stripe width, replication level, and data placement policy are configurable as suggested in [3, 4, 25]. Our approach can be extended to support other configuration parameters.

2.3 System Model

All participating machines are modeled similarly, regardless of their specific role (Figure 1): each machine hosts a network component and can host one or more system components (each modeled as a service with its own queue).

A system component and its queue represent a specific functionality: The *manager* component is responsible for storing files' and storage nodes' metadata. The *storage* component is responsible for storing and replicating data chunks. Finally, the *client* component receives the read and write operations from the application, implements, at the high-level the storage system protocol by sending control or data requests to other services, and once a storage operation finished it communicates again with the application. Each of these components is modeled as service that takes requests from its queue (fed by the network service or by the application for the client service) and sends responses back through the network service.

The network component and its in- and out- queues model the network-related activity of a host. Key here is to model network-related contention while avoiding modeling the de-

tails of the transport protocol (e.g., dealing with packet loss, connection establishment and teardown details). The requests in the out-queue of a network component are broken in smaller pieces that represent network frames and sent to the in-queue of the destination host. Once the network service processes all the frames of a given request in the in-queue, it assembles the request and places it in the queue of the destination service.

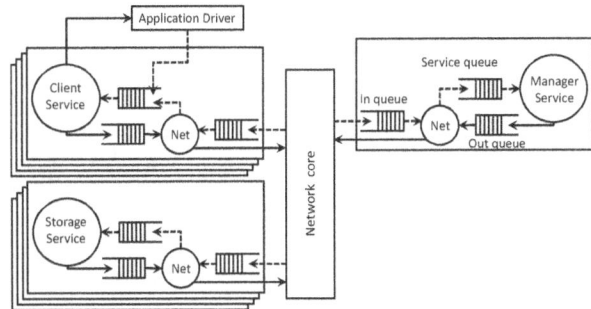

Figure 1: Queue-based model of a distributed storage system. Each component (manager, client component, and storage component) has a single system service that processes requests from its queue. Additionally, each host has a network component with an in- and out- queue. The network core connects and routes the messages between the different components in the system and can model network latency and contention at the aggregate network fabric level. Solid lines show the flow going out from a storage system component while dashed lines show the in-flow path.

The system components can be collocated on the same host (e.g., the client and storage components on the same host). Requests between these collocated services also go through the network, but have a faster service time than remote requests - representing a loopback data transfer (§2.4).

Space limitations prevent us from presenting the full details of the model. A technical report [12] presents more details on the prediction mechanism. As a rule, we accurately model the data paths of the storage system at chunk-level granularity, and the control paths at a coarser granularity: modeling only one control message to initiate a specific storage function while an implementation may have multiple rounds of control messages.

2.4 System Identification

To instantiate the storage system model, one needs to specify the number of storage and client components in the system, and the service times for the network (μ^{net}) and the system components (storage - μ^{sm}, manager - μ^{ma}, and client - μ^{cli}).

Compared to past work (e.g., [23]), our approach focuses on making this *process simple, and not intrusive as no changes are required to the storage system or kernel modules*. The system identification process is automated with a script as follows. First, to measure the service time per chunk/request T^{net}), a script runs a network throughput measurement utility tool (e.g., iperf), to measure the throughput of both: remote and local (loopback) data transfers. Second, this script measures the time to read/write a number of files to identify client and storage service time per data chunk. To this end, the system identification script deploys one client, one storage node and the manager on different machines, and writes/reads a number of files. For each file read/write the benchmark records the total operation time. The script computes the average read/write time T^{tot}. The number of files read/written is set to achieve 95% confidence intervals with $\pm 5\%$ error.

The operation total time (T^{tot}) includes the client side processing time (T^{cli}), the storage node processing time (T^{sm}), the total time related to the manager operations (T^{man}) , and the network transfer time (T^{net}). The network service time for the network (μ^{net}) is based on a simple analytical model based on network throughput and proportional to the amount of data to be transferred in a packet.

To isolate just $T^{cli} + T^{man}$, the script runs a set of reads and writes of 0-size. This forces a request to go through the manager, but it does not touch the storage module. Since decomposing T^{cli} and T^{man} is not possible without probes in the storage system code, we opted to associate the $T^{cli} = 0$ and associate the whole cost of 0-size operations to the manager. While iperf can estimate T^{net}, and the script can infer $T^{cli} + T^{man}$, and therefore $T^{sm} = T^{tot} - T^{net} - T^{man}$. To obtain the service time per chunk, the times are normalized by chunk size. Therefore, $\mu^{sm} = \frac{T^{sm}}{chunkSize}$.

2.5 Model Implementation: The Simulator

We have implemented the above model as a discrete-event simulator in Java. The simulator receives as inputs: a summarized description of the application workload (§2.6), the system configuration (currently, it supports replication level, stripe-width, and data-placement per file; and chunk size system-wide), the deployment parameters (number of storage nodes and clients, whether they are collocated on the same hosts), and a performance characterization of system components: service times for network, client, storage, and manager (§2.4).

Once the simulator instantiates the storage system, it starts the application driver that processes the application workload. The driver reads the description of the application workload, creates the corresponding events (e.g., read from file x at offset y, z bytes) and places them in the client service queue. File-specific configuration [3, 25] is described as part of the operations in the workload description.

As in a real system, the manager component maintains the metadata of the system (i.e., implements data placement policies, and keeps track of file to chunk mapping and chunk placement). To make the process clearer, consider the following example for a file write operation. First, the client contacts the manager asking for free space, the manager replies specifying a set of storage services with free chunks. Then, the client requests each storage service to store chunks in a round-robin fashion. After processing a request to store a chunk, a storage service replies to the client acknowledging the operation success. After sending all the chunks, the client sends to the manager the chunk-map. Once the manager acknowledges, the client returns success to the application driver. In total the write operation generates two requests to the manager and one request per chunk to the storage nodes.

The manager implements a number of data placement policies. The default policy selects, for a write operation, a "stripe-width" of storage services. To model per-file optimizations, the client can overwrite system-wide configurations by requesting the manager to use a specific data place-ment policy. For example, the client may require that a file is stored locally, that is, on a storage service that is located on the same host. In this case, the manager attempts to allocate space on that specific storage service for that write operation. The file-specific data placement policy is part of the workload description.

2.6 Workload Description

The predictor takes as input a description of the workload. This description contains two pieces of information: per client I/O operations trace (i.e., open, read, write, close calls with timestamp, operation type, size, offset, and client id), and files' dependency graph (capturing workflow execution plan) for scheduling and data placement purposes. The client traces are obtained by running and logging the application operations. The execution plan can be provided by the workflow scheduler (e.g., Swift [27]), by an expert user or extracted from log files. Currently, we use the workflow execution plan from PyFlow scheduler and client traces from MosaStore storage logs, which required no further modification for this work. We have developed a FUSE wrapper to log the storage operations, if the storage system does not provide the needed information. The predictor preprocess the logs to infer the operations' elapsed times and interarrival times based on timestamps, aggregate some operations, and create the events to be simulated.

3. EVALUATION

This section aims to evaluate the mechanism's prediction accuracy and, more important, to demonstrate through a set of experiments the mechanism's ability to support correctly identifying quasi-optimal configuration for a specific application. To this end, we use a set of synthetic benchmarks and real applications. The synthetic benchmarks are designed to mimic the access patterns [25] of workflow applications.

To understand how the prediction mechanisms can be used in a real set-up, we use two real workflow applications: BLAST [5] and Montage [16]. The goal is to evaluate the mechanism's ability to predict time-to-solution to support decisions on the storage configuration and allocation.

Storage system. We use an open source distributed object based storage system [4]. We choose to experiment with RAMDisks as they are frequently used to support workflow applications as intermediate storage: it offers higher performance and are the only option in most supercomputers that do not have spinning disks (e.g., IBM BG/P machines).

Testbeds. We use two testbeds. The first testbed (TB20) is our lab cluster with 20 machines. Each machine has Intel Xeon E5345 4-core, 2.33-GHz CPU, 4GB RAM, and 1Gbps NIC. The second testbed (TB100), used for larger scale experiments, includes 100 nodes on Grid5000 'Nancy' cluster [10]. Each machine has Intel Xeon X3440 4-core, 2.53-GHz CPU, 16GB RAM, 1Gbps NIC, and 320GB SATA II.

In all the experiments, one node runs the metadata manager and the workflow coordination scripts, while the other nodes run the storage nodes, the client SAI, and the application processes. The networks is shared with applications running on different machines. The simulator is seeded according to the procedure described in §2.4.

3.1 Synthetic Benchmarks: Workflow Patterns

This section evaluates the accuracy of the prediction mechanism in capturing the system behavior with multiple clients, multiple applications, and different data-placement policies designed to support workflow applications [25]. We use synthetic benchmarks that mimic common data access patterns of workflow applications: pipeline, reduce, and broadcast (Figure 2). These are the most popular patterns uncovered by studying over 20 scientific workflow applications by Wozniak et al. [28], Shibata et al. [21], and Bharathi et al. [9]).

The *synthetic benchmarks are designed to explore the limitations of the predictor* as they are composed exclusively of I/O operations, which generates high network and disk contention in the system.

Summary of results. The predictor has good accuracy: our approach leads to prediction errors of 5% on average, lower than 8% in 80% of the studied scenarios, and within 14% in the worst case. More important, the mechanism correctly differentiates between the different configurations and can support choosing the best configuration for each evaluated scenario.

Experimental setup. We use the storage system setup as described above on the TB20 testbed. We use the *DSS* label for experiments where we use the (Default Storage System) configuration: client and storage modules run on all machines, client stripes data over all 19 machines, and no optimizations are enabled for any data-access pattern. We use the *WASS* label (Workflow Aware Storage System) when the system configuration is optimized for a specific access pattern (including data placement, stripe width or replication) [25]. All WASS experiments assume data location aware scheduling: for a given compute task, if the input file chunks exist on a single storage node, the task is scheduled on that node to increase access locality.

The goal of showing results for two different configurations choices is two-fold: (i) demonstrate the accuracy of the predictions for two different scenarios, and (ii), most important, show that the predictions correctly indicate which configuration is the best. To understand the impact of the data size, for each benchmark, we use three workloads labeled as *medium* (data sizes are indicated in Figure 2), the *small* (10x smaller than medium), and where possible, a 10x larger, *large* workload. We omit results for a *small* workload, since it exhibits a similar performance between different configurations and the predictions are inside the confidence interval.

For actual performance, the figures show the average turnaround time and standard deviation (in error bars) for 15 trials (which was enough to guarantee a 95% confidence level).

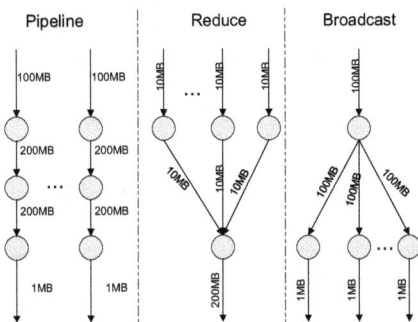

Figure 2: Pipeline, Reduce, and Broadcast benchmarks. Nodes represent workflow stages and arrows represent data transfers through files. The file sizes represent the *medium* workload. The part of the flow that is repeated, ran over 19 machines in this evaluation.

Pipeline benchmark. A set of compute tasks are chained in a sequence such that the output of one task is the input of the next task in the chain (Figure 2). A pipeline-optimized storage system will store the intermediate pipeline files on the storage node co-located with the application. Later, the workflow scheduler places the task that consumes the file on the same node, increasing data access locality. Here, 19 application pipelines run in parallel and go through three processing stages that read and write files from/to the intermediate storage. (The large workload produces too much data to fit in the in-memory intermediate storage system in the TB20 testbed.)

Evaluation of the results. For the optimized configuration (WASS) the predictor has almost perfect accuracy (Figure 3). For the default data placement policy (DSS), however, predictions are 9% lower than actual results. For this case, all clients stripe (write) data to all machines in the system; similarly, all machines read from all others. This creates, complex interactions among all components in the system leading to contention and chunk transfer retries due to connection initiation timeouts caused by network congestion which, we believe, are the main source of prediction inaccuracies.

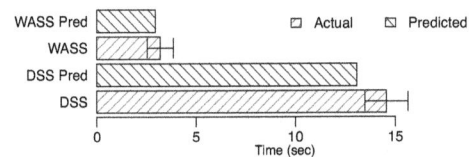

Figure 3: Actual and predicted average execution time for the pipeline benchmark and medium workload.

Reduce benchmark. A single compute task uses input files produced by multiple tasks. In the benchmark, 19 processes run in parallel on different nodes, consume an input file, and produce an intermediate file. In the next stage of the workflow, a single process reads all intermediate files and produces the final output file. A possible data placement optimization is the use of collocation - placing input files on one node and expose their location, which will later be used by the scheduler to run the reduce task on that machine. For WASS configuration, this collocation optimization is enabled for the files used in the reduce stage, for the remaining files the locality optimization is enabled.

Evaluation of the results. Similar to the pipeline benchmark, predictions for the reduce benchmark are close to the actual performance. In fact, they are within 9% of the actual average for medium workload, and 13% of the actual performance for large (Figure 4). More important, they capture the relative improvements the pattern-specific data placement policies bring. We note that Figure 4(b) captures the behavior of a heterogeneous scenario: to accommodate the amount of data produced, we used a faster machine with a larger RAMDisk to run the reduce stage. With proper seeding, the predictor captures the system performance with accuracy similar to a homogeneous system.

When the collocation and locality optimizations are not enabled, the challenge of capturing exactly the system behavior is similar to the pipeline case: capture the complex interactions among all machines in the system. When the specific data placement is enabled though, the challenge is different: there is a high contention created by having several clients writing to the same storage machine (the one that

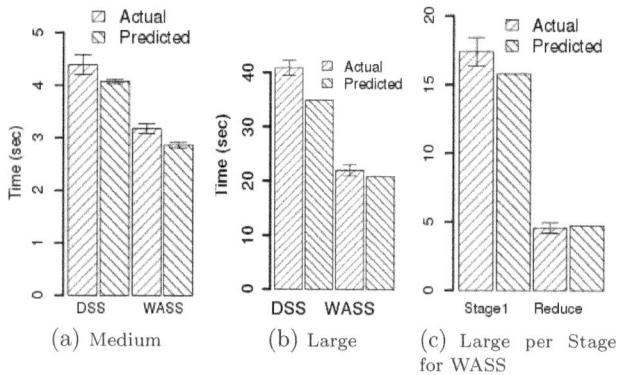

(a) Medium   (b) Large   (c) Large per Stage for WASS

Figure 4: Actual and predicted average execution time for the reduce benchmark for the medium, large workloads, and per stage for large workload.

performs the reduce phase). Figure 4(c) shows the results per-stage for the two stages of the large workload separately to show how the predictor captures these cases.

Broadcast benchmark. A single task produces a file that is consumed by multiple tasks. In this benchmark, 19 processes running in parallel on different machines consume a file that is created in earlier stage by one task. A possible optimization for this pattern is to create replicas of the file that will be consumed by several different tasks.

Evaluation of the results. The results show for broadcast pattern with medium workload with the WASS system have similar performance of aproximately 3 seconds when configured with 1, 2, or 4 replicas (the large workload shows a similar trend) [12]. For this benchmark all predictions match the actual results: predictions are inside the interval of mean of actual ± standard deviation, just 1-3% difference from the mean.

This experiment highlights an interesting case for the predictor. According to the structure of the pattern and the results reported in [25], creating replicas will improve the performance of the broadcast pattern. The results, however, show that creating replicas does not really help here. This happens because data striping already avoids the contention of a single node holding the file. So, although creating replicas reduces the number of accesses to a given machine (since chunks are read in sequence), this gain is not paid off by the overhead of creating a replica. More important, this is another situation where the *predictor captures the impact of different configurations, showing, in this case that they are equivalent and the user can stick with one replica and save storage space.*

3.2 The pipeline benchmark at scale

This section expands the analysis of the synthetic benchmarks to answer the following questions: *"How accurate is the predictor estimates for a different platform?"*, and *"How does the predictor capture the behavior of larger scale systems?"* To answer these question, we ran the pipeline benchmark at scale on our Grid 5000 testbed, TB100. We chose this benchmark because it is the one with the biggest gap between predicted and actual, and it is the most I/O intensive benchmark which stresses the network and the metadata manager, a component well-known for being a potential bottleneck for this type of cluster-based storage system.

We executed this benchmark for a weak scaling set-up using three different scales (25, 50, and 100 nodes), the medium workload, and the two configurations (DSS and WASS). The stripe width is set to 4, reflecting a typical value in distributed storage setup [4, 15].

Figure 5 shows the results. The predictor produces estimates that differ 15% of the actual time on average, are within 22% of the actual results for all cases, and are close to the interval delimited by the standard deviation. Different from the TB20 results, most of the scenarios on TB100 show cases where the predictor underestimate the time, instead of overestimating. We believe it happens because the faster machines of TB100 offer higher parallelism.

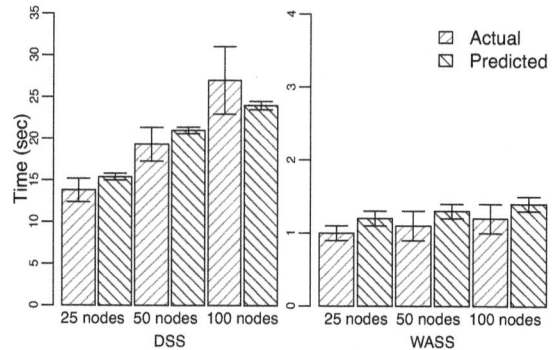

Figure 5: Actual and predicted average execution time for the pipeline benchmark medium workload on TB100.

3.3 Supporting decisions for a real application

Section 3.1 evaluated predictor's ability to accurately estimate the turnaround time of synthetic benchmarks and the impact of different data placement optimizations. This section targets more complex scenarios where the user has to deal with a real application, allocation decisions, as well as the choice of the storage system configuration. Further, *the previous section evaluated prediction accuracy when the application and storage system are co-deployed on the same nodes, this section evaluates accuracy when they are deployed on separate nodes.*

This section demonstrates the predictor's ability to properly guide the user or a search algorithm to the desired configuration focusing on two provisioning scenarios:

- Scenario I assumes that the user has full access to a fixed-size cluster, a common set-up in several university research labs. *Problem: How should the system be partitioned between the application and the intermediate storage and what will be the intermediate storage system configuration for best overall performance?*

- Scenario II explores the provisioning problem with cost constraints (e.g., in HPC centers with limited user budget or cloud environments). *Problem: For a fixed workload; what is the cost/turnaround time trade-off space among the deployment options?*

Workload. We explore these two scenarios with a real workflow application: BLAST [5] a DNA search tool for finding similarities between DNA sequences. In the BLAST workflow, each node receives a set of DNA queries as input (a file for each node with 200 search queries) and all nodes search the same DNA database file stored on intermediate storage (total size of 1.67 GB). Each machine produces one output file, and the files are combined at the end of the application execution. The input files are transferred to the intermediate storage system prior to application execution.

Deployment scenario. Among the 20 machines of the testbed TB20; one node coordinates BLAST tasks' execution and runs the storage system manager. The remaining nodes can either execute tasks from the workload or act as storage nodes.

Experimental methodology. The plots report the average of at least 20 runs, leading to 95% confidence intervals for all experiments. Since standard deviation is low (less than 5%), we omit it in plots to reduce clutter.

3.3.1 Scenario I: Configuring a Fixed-size Cluster

We explore the following question: Given a fixed size cluster, *how should the nodes be partitioned between the application and the intermediate storage, and what is the intermediate storage system configuration to yield highest application performance?*

Figure 6 shows the application execution time for different partitioning and storage system configurations. For this application *chunk size* is the configuration parameter that has the highest impact on performance, thus, to limit the number of possible configurations in the figure, we focus on it only. (We note that the predictor correctly captures the lack of impact for other parameters). Additionally, this scenario covers a configuration parameter not evaluated in §3.1.

Figure 6 highlights several important points: First, the performance difference between the different configurations is significant: up to 10x difference between the best and the worst configuration even for the same chunk size. Second, the results show that the system achieves the fastest processing time with a partitioning of 14 application nodes and 5 storage nodes, and chunk size of 256KB (4x smaller than the default size) a non-obvious configuration beforehand. Third, the experiment shows that the predictor accurately captures the system performance under different partitioning strategies, and storage system configurations. Actually, the overall error of the predictions are small (always within the standard deviation), and smaller than obtained for synthetic benchmarks since there is less stress on the storage system. Finally, the most important point is that the predictor can correctly lead the user or a search algorithm to the desired configuration.

3.3.2 Scenario II: Provisioning in an Elastic and Metered Environment

This scenario assumes an environment where users are charged (proportional to the cumulative CPU-hours used) and have a more complex tradeoff between cost and time-to-solution to make, for example, they aim for the best application turnaround within a certain dollar budget. We aim to inform the user's provisioning decisions by revealing the details of this trade-off. Specifically, this scenario helps the user to answer the following question: *What is the allocation size, and how should it be partitioned and configured to best fit the constraints and optimization criterion?*

Figure 7 shows, on different Y-axes, the application execution time and allocation cost (measured as number of nodes x allocation time) for different cluster sizes, different partitioning, and different chunk size. Similar to Scenario I, Figure 7 shows that the predictor captures the system performance with reasonable accuracy.

Figure 7 also shows that the an allocation of 11 nodes,

with partitioning of 8 application, 2 storage nodes, and chunk size of 256KB offers the lowest cost. However, this figure points out an interesting case for the analysis of cost vs. time-to-solution: The user can analyze the plot to verify that an option with an allocation of 20 nodes actually offers almost 2x higher performance at a marginal 2% higher cost.

3.4 Increasing workflow complexity: Montage

This section aims to answer the following question: *"Can the predictor support user decisions for more complex applications than the one presented in §3.3"*. To answer this question, we focus on evaluating how accurate the estimates are for Montage [16], a complex astronomy workflow composed of 10 different stages (Figure 8) with varying characteristics.

To verify that the predictor can support user's decision, we have executed Montage for different deployments sizes on TB20. For this application, we use clients collocated with storage nodes, verifying yet another configuration parameter. We omit chunk size variations since it does not impact actual Montage (also well captured by the predictor).

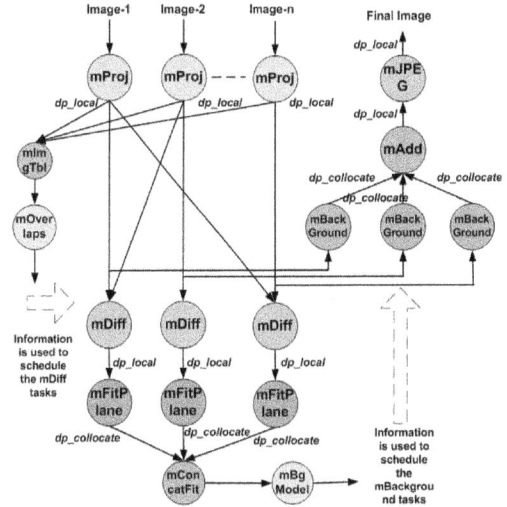

Figure 8: Montage workflow.

Workflow characteristics. The I/O communication intensity between workflow stages is highly variable (presented in Table 1 for the workload we use). Overall the workflow generates over 650 files with sizes from 1KB to over 100MB and about 3GB of data are read/written from storage.

Stage	Data	#Files	File Size
stageIn	109MB	57	1.7MB-2.1MB
mProject	438MB	113	3.3MB-4.2MB
mImgTbl	17KB	1	
mOverlaps	17KB	1	
mDiff	148MB	285	100KB - 3MB
mFitPlane	576KB	142	4KB
mConcatFit	16KB	1	
mBgModel	2KB	1	
mBackground	438MB	113	3.3MB - 4.2MB
mAdd	330MB	2	165MB
mJPEG	4.7MB	1	
stageOut	170MB	2	4.7MB-165MB

Table 1: Characteristics of Montage workflow stages

Evaluation of the Results. Figure 9 shows the execution time, actual and predicted, for Montage on different cluster sizes. The average summarizes 20 trials. The standard deviation is approximately 3% and omitted to reduce

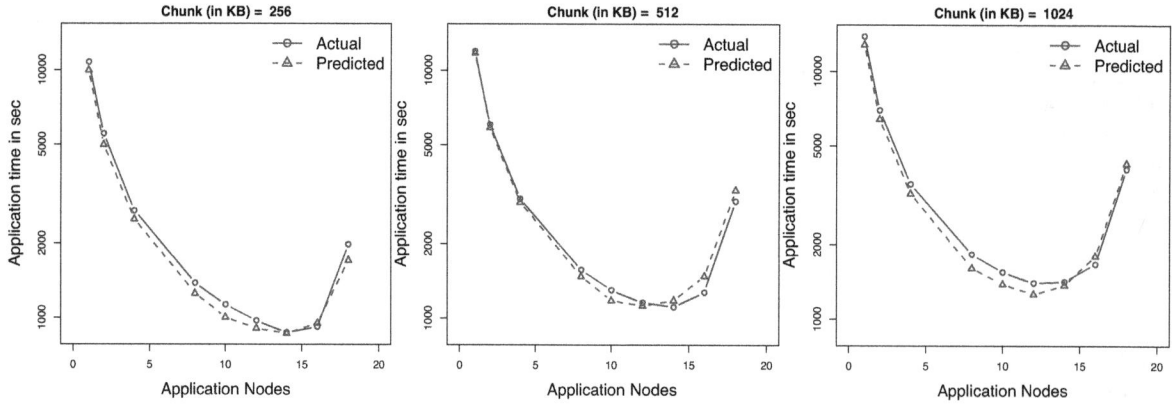

Figure 6: Application runtime (log-scale) for a fixed-size cluster of 20 nodes. X-axis represents number of nodes allocated for the application/storage. Each plot presents results for a different configuration of chunk size.

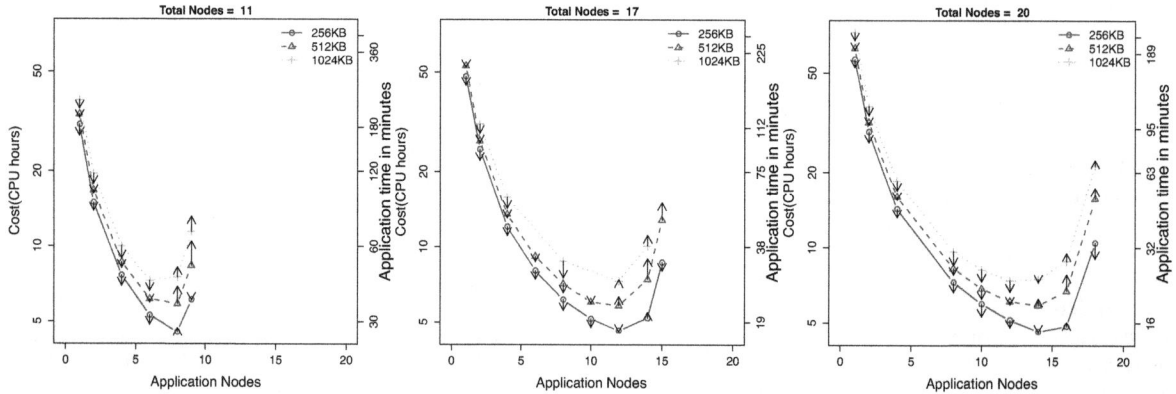

Figure 7: Allocation cost (CPU-hours, log-scale, left Y axis) and application time (right Y axis, log-scale, different scale among plots) for fixed size clusters and different chunk sizes. X-axis represents number of nodes allocated to the application/storage. Lines and arrows present the actual and the predicted cost/performance, respectively.

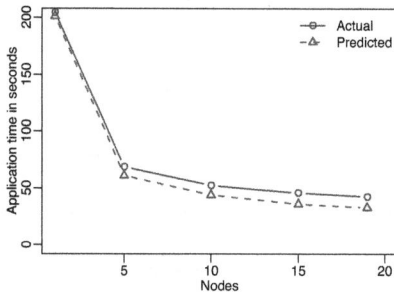

Figure 9: Montage time to solution for fixed size deployments between 1 and 19 nodes - an extra node runs the storage manager on TB20.

clutter. Figure 9 shows that, overall, the predictor captures well the application performance. The increased workflow complexity is a challenge: the predictor is not as accurate as for the BLAST application presented earlier (here the average prediction error is 9%, the smallest is than 1%, and the maximum prediction error is 15%). However, the overall accuracy is "good-enough" to support the provisioning decisions, and the difference is barely visible in the plot.

4. RELATED WORK

This section describes previous work on different approaches to predict storage system performance and tune its configuration parameters.

Model based analysis. A number of projects use model-based approach to estimate the storage system performance with a given configuration or workload. Ergastulum [7] targets centralized storage solution based on one enclosure to recommend an initial system configuration, and Hippodrome [6] relies on Ergastulum to improve the configuration based on online monitoring of the workload. By considering a distributed system, our solution handles more complex interaction among the system components and more configuration options.

Simulation based systems. IMPIOUS (Imprecisely Modeling Parallel I/O is Usually Successful) [19] is a trace-driven simulator that uses an abstract storage system models designed to capture the key mechanism of parallel file systems. The simulator is oversimplified to be able to simulate thousands of client and storage nodes. Consequently the simulator is not accurate, producing performance estimates that under- or over- estimates the performance by up to 60%. PFSsim is a trace-driven simulator designed specifically for evaluating I/O scheduling algorithms in parallel file systems. PFSsim simulates the storage system at low component level, simulating the network using OMNeT++ [26] and disks using DiskSim [1]. Liu et al. [17,18] build a simulation framework for simulating the storage system of supercomputing machines. The framework simulates all hardware components including compute ad IO nodes, storage subsystem, and the supercomputing interconnect. Similar to this work, Thereska et al. [23] proposed a predictor mechanism for a distributed storage system with a detailed model. To provide such information, they propose Stardust [24] a detailed monitoring information system that required changes to the storage system and kernel modules to add monitoring points. This approach enabled their predictor to achieve prediction within 18% of the actual predictions depending on the workload. Our approach has achieved similar accuracy on our target workloads, however with a lightweight approach to seed the model, not requiring changes to the system design or kernel modules.

Unlike these efforts, our approaches targets simulating a generic distributed storage system architecture in a cluster infrastructure (not special supercomputer machines) without simulating particular storage system operations. Our approach avoids detailed low-level simulation (e.g., disk or packet level simulation), without significantly compromising accuracy, enabling our framework to efficiently simulate large-scale deployments.

An important difference to past work on storage systems simulation is our focus on a whole workflow application and the potential interaction among the workflow's phases instead of the average performance for a batch [6,7] of operations, and of predicting performance of the system from the perspective of one client [23] at a time. Additionally, our work targets the partitioning problem of splitting the nodes among application and intermediate storage.

Monitoring based tuning. Behzad et al. [8] present an auto tuning framework for HDF5 IO library. The proposed solution injects optimization parameters into parallel HDF5 I/O calls. Further, the framework monitors the I/O performance, and explores the tuning parameter space using a genetic algorithm. Zhang et al. [29] propose an approach to determine the storage bottleneck for workflow applications using a set of benchmarks and target workflow application runs.

The approach we propose enables a richer exploration of the system at a lower cost since the predictor is able to estimate performance of a scenario that adds or reduces resources and change the configuration without requiring new runs of the application for new generations of the genetic algorithm. Additionally, we target simulating generic POSIX-based storage system not a specific I/O library.

5. SUMMARY AND DISCUSSION

Summary. This paper makes the case for a prediction mechanism to support automating provisioning choices for workflow applications. We focus on predicting the performance of workflow applications when running on top of an intermediate object-based storage system. We propose a solution based on a queue-based model with a number of attractive properties: a generic and uniform system model; supported by a simple system identification process that does not require specialized probes or system changes to perform the initial benchmarking; with a low runtime to obtain predictions; and, finally, with adequate accuracy for the cases we study.

This paper focuses on predicting the application time-to-solution (turnaround time) of the applications and benchmarks, but we note that the model and approach presented apply to other optimization metrics (e.g., cost, amount of data transferred).

We intend to expand this work in multiple directions: (i) explore a richer space of configuration parameters, (ii)

evaluate the system using additional benchmarks and applications, (iii) enable different optimization criteria [22] including energy [11], and (iv) explore different optimization solvers to search the configuration space.

The discussion below aims to clarify our understanding of the limitations of our work and the lessons we have learned.

What are the main sources of inaccuracies? Currently, there are sources of inaccuracies at multiple levels: First, the model does not capture all the details of the storage system (e.g., support services like garbage collection or storage node heartbeats; the control paths are simplified to match what we believe generic object-based storage would do - while we know that a FUSE-based implementation would need more complex control paths; we model all control messages as having the same size) and the environment (e.g., contention at the network fabric level or scheduling). Second, we constrain and simplify system identification even further at the cost of additional accuracy loss. Third, we do not model the infrastructure in detail (e.g., we do not model the network protocols or the spinning disks). Finally, so far the application driver uses an idealized image of the workflow application (e.g., all pipelines are launched in the simulation exactly at the same time while in the actual experiments coordination overheads make them slightly staggered). We believe the latter one is the main reason of current inaccuracies in the system. In fact, our initial evaluation verified that for Montage the overhead can be up to 5% of the total time.

Can the prediction mechanism support the *development process* of a storage system? Do you have specific experience in this context? One of the lessons we have learned so far is the utility of the mechanism to support the development of the storage system itself. Back of the envelope calculations are a common mechanism to evaluate expected performance bounds for a given system. The predictor takes this a step further and is useful in complex scenarios where back of the envelope estimates are intractable. Not only the developers can use it to evaluate the potential gains of implementing a new complex optimizations or to study the impact of faster network and nodes, but to obtain a performance baseline to detect performance anomalies.

More concretely, we have encountered a number of situations where the predicted and actual performance differed significantly. In some cases these highlighted simplifications in the model or in our simulator. But, there were cases that highlighted complex performance-related anomalies in the storage system such as: non-trivial implementation problems (e.g., limited randomness in the data placement decisions that led to an artificial bottleneck, or unreasonable locking overheads). Similarly, the prediction mechanism helped us revisit assumptions about the middleware stack the storage system is implemented over (e.g., significant impact of the TCP connection initiation timeout of 3s in some scenarios). Finally, the predictions highlighted shortcomings of the seeding process or incorrect assumptions about the deployment platform (e.g., we were ignoring platform heterogeneity). A technical report describes this experience [13].

How general is the proposed prediction mechanism? We have designed the predictor to model a generic object-based storage system and all the system identification process to work at the application level only (thus, easily portable across storage systems and deployment platforms). While so far we have evaluated the predictor in depth only for the DSS/WASS storage system we have encouraging preliminary experience with using it to predict the relative application performance on two other storage solutions, Ceph and GlusterFS, for a limited number of scenarios.

Acknowledgements

This research was supported in part by the DoE ASCR XStack program (ER26013) and by the Natural Sciences and Engineering Research Council of Canada.

6. REFERENCES

[1] DiskSim. http://www.pdl.cmu.edu/DiskSim/.
[2] The network simulator NS2.
http://www.isi.edu/nsnam/ns/, 2012.
[3] M. Abd-El-Malek, W. V. C. II, C. Cranor, G. R. Ganger, J. Hendricks, A. J. Klosterman, M. P. Mesnier, M. Prasad, B. Salmon, R. R. Sambasivan, S. Sinnamohideen, J. D. Strunk, E. Thereska, M. Wachs, and J. J. Wylie. Ursa minor: Versatile cluster-based storage. In *Proc. of the Conf. on File and Storage Technologies*, Dec. 2005.
[4] S. Al-Kiswany, A. Gharaibeh, and M. Ripeanu. The case for a versatile storage system. *SIGOPS Oper. Syst. Rev.*, 44:10–14, March 2010.
[5] S. F. Altschul, W. Gish, W. Miller, E. W. Myers, and D. J. Lipman. Basic Local Alignment Search Tool. *J. of Molecular Biology*, 215(3):403–410, Oct. 1990.
[6] E. Anderson, M. Hobbs, K. Keeton, S. Spence, M. Uysal, and A. Veitch. Hippodrome: Running circles around storage administration. In *Proc. of the Conf. on File and Storage Technologies*, pages 175–188, 2002.
[7] E. Anderson, S. Spence, R. Swaminathan, M. Kallahalla, and Q. Wang. Quickly finding near-optimal storage designs. *ACM Trans. Comput. Syst.*, 23(4):337–374, Nov 2005.
[8] B. Behzad, H. V. T. Luu, J. Huchette, S. Byna, Prabhat, R. A. Aydt, Q. Koziol, and M. Snir. Taming Parallel I/O Complexity with Auto-Tuning. In *SC*, 2013.
[9] S. Bharathi, A. Chervenak, E. Deelman, G. Mehta, M.-H. Su, and K. Vahi. Characterization of scientific workflows. In *Workflows in Support of Large-Scale Science, 2008. WORKS 2008. 3rd Workshop on*, pages 1–10, 2008.
[10] F. Cappello, E. Caron, M. Daydé, F. Desprez, Y. Jégou, P. Primet, E. Jeannot, S. Lanteri, J. Leduc, N. Melab, G. Mornet, R. Namyst, B. Quetier, and O. Richard. Grid'5000: a large scale and highly reconfigurable grid experimental testbed. In *Grid Comp.. Proc of the 6th IEEE/ACM Intl. Workshop on*, 2005.
[11] L. B. Costa, S. Al-Kiswany, R. V. Lopes, and M. Ripeanu. Assessing data deduplication trade-offs from an energy and performance perspective. In *2011 Intl. Green Computing Conf. and Workshops*, 2011.
[12] L. B. Costa, A. Barros, S. Al-Kiswany, E. Vairavanathan, and M. Ripeanu. Predicting intermediate storage performance for workflow applications. *CoRR*, abs/1302.4760, 2013.
[13] L. B. Costa, J. Brunet, L. Hattori, and M. Ripeanu. Experience on Applying Performance Prediction during Development: a Distributed Storage System Tale. Technical report, UBC/ECE/NetSysLab, Sep. 13. http://www.ece.ubc.ca/~lauroc/tr/tech2.pdf.
[14] L. B. Costa and M. Ripeanu. Towards Automating the Configuration of a Distributed Storage System. In

[15] I. F. Haddad. Pvfs: A parallel virtual file system for linux clusters. *Linux Journal*, 2000(80es), Nov. 2000.
[16] A. C. Laity, N. Anagnostou, G. B. Berriman, J. C. Good, J. C. Jacob, D. S. Katz, and T. Prince. Montage: An Astronomical Image Mosaic Service for the NVO. In *Astronomical Data Analysis Software and Systems XIV*, volume 347 of *Astronomical Society of the Pacific Conf. Series*, page 34, Dec 2005.
[17] N. Liu, C. Carothers, J. Cope, P. Carns, R. Ross, A. Crume, and C. Maltzahn. Modeling a leadership scale storage system. In *Proc. of the 9th Intl. Conf. on Parallel Processing and Applied Mathematics - Vol. Part I*, PPAM'11, pages 10–19, 2012.
[18] N. Liu, J. Cope, P. Carns, C. Carothers, R. Ross, G. Grider, A. Crume, and C. Maltzahn. On the role of burst buffers in leadership class storage systems. In *Mass Storage Systems and Technologies (MSST), 2012 IEEE 28th Symp. on*, pages 1–11, 2012.
[19] E. Molina-Estolano, C. Maltzahn, J. Bent, and S. Brandt. Building a Parallel File System Simulator. 180(1):012050, 2009.
[20] A. Montresor and M. Jelasity. PeerSim: A scalable P2P simulator. In *Proc. of the 9th Int. Conf. on Peer-to-Peer (P2P'09)*, pages 99–100, Sep 2009.
[21] T. Shibata, S. Choi, and K. Taura. File-access patterns of data-intensive workflow applications and their implications to distributed filesystems. In *Proc. of the 19th ACM Intl. Symp. on High Perf. Distributed Computing*, HPDC '10, pages 746–755, 2010.
[22] J. D. Strunk, E. Thereska, C. Faloutsos, and G. R. Ganger. Using utility to provision storage systems. In *6th USENIX Conf. on File and Storage Technologies, FAST*, pages 313–328, 2008.
[23] E. Thereska, M. Abd-El-Malek, J. J. Wylie, D. Narayanan, and G. R. Ganger. Informed data distribution selection in a self-predicting storage system. In *Proc. of the 3rd Intl. Conf. on Autonomic Computing*, pages 187–198, 2006.
[24] E. Thereska, B. Salmon, J. D. Strunk, M. Wachs, M. Abd-El-Malek, J. López, and G. R. Ganger. Stardust: tracking activity in a distributed storage system. In *SIGMETRICS/Perf.*, pages 3–14, 2006.
[25] E. Vairavanathan, S. Al-Kiswany, L. B. Costa, Z. Zhang, D. S. Katz, M. Wilde, and M. Ripeanu. A workflow-aware storage system: An opportunity study. In *Cluster Computing and the Grid, IEEE Intl. Symp. on*, pages 326–334, 2012.
[26] A. Varga. Using the OMNeT++ Discrete Event Simulation System in Education. *Education, IEEE Trans. on*, 42(4), 1999.
[27] M. Wilde, M. Hategan, J. M. Wozniak, B. Clifford, D. S. Katz, and I. T. Foster. Swift: A language for distributed parallel scripting. *Parallel Computing*, 37(9):633–652, 2011.
[28] J. M. Wozniak and M. Wilde. Case studies in storage access by loosely coupled petascale applications. In *Proc. of the 4th Workshop on Petascale Data Storage*, PDSW '09, pages 16–20, 2009.
[29] Z. Zhang, D. S. Katz, M. Wilde, J. M. Wozniak, and I. Foster. MTC Envelope: Defining the Capability of Large Scale Computers in the Context of Parallel Scripting Applications. In *Proc. of the 22Nd Intl. Symp. on High Perf. Parallel and Distributed Computing*, HPDC '13, pages 37–48, 2013.
[30] Z. Zhang, D. S. Katz, J. M. Wozniak, A. Espinosa, and I. Foster. Design and analysis of data management in scalable parallel scripting. In *Proc. of the Intl. Conf. on High Performance Computing, Networking, Storage and Analysis*, SC '12, pages 85:1–85:11, 2012.

11th ACM/IEEE Intl. Conf. on Grid Computing - Grid 2010, Oct. 2010.

Understanding the Impact of Threshold Voltage on MLC Flash Memory Performance and Reliability

Wei Wang
Computational Science
Research Center
San Diego State University
wang@rohan.sdsu.edu

Tao Xie
Computer Science
Department
San Diego State University
txie@mail.sdsu.edu

Deng Zhou
Computational Science
Research Center
San Diego State University
zhoud@rohan.sdsu.edu

ABSTRACT

MLC (multi-level cell) NAND flash memory based solid state drives (SSDs) have been increasingly used in supercomputing centers because of their merits in cost, performance, and energy-efficiency. However, as each cell starts to store two or more bits, a threshold voltage range employed to represent a state has to be continuously shrunk, and a narrowed threshold voltage range causes more bit errors. An ad-hoc solution to this problem is to apply an enhanced ECC (error correction code) scheme. Still, a comprehensive understanding of the impact of threshold voltage on MLC flash performance and reliability is an open question. In this paper, we first empirically measure the correlations between threshold voltage and program/erase (P/E) performance as well as reliability. After analyzing experimental results, we make several interesting observations: 1) a memory cell programmed to a lower threshold voltage has a faster programming speed (up to 31%) as well as a fewer number of bit errors; 2) the programming time of an MSB page is about 2 to 3 times shorter than that of an LSB page; 3) erase performance is highly correlated to threshold voltage. These new findings provide system implications for the development of a better SSD. Further, to demonstrate how these findings can be leveraged to enhance MLC flash, we propose an approach called threshold voltage reduction (TVR), which increases programming speed and longevity by 50% and 7.1%, respectively. Finally, we conduct a study on TVR-powered SSDs. Simulation results show that overall mean response time can be reduced by up to 35%.

Categories and Subject Descriptors

B.3.3 [**Memory Structure**]: Performance Analysis and Design Aids; C.4 [**Performance of Systems**]: Design studies; D.4.2 [**Operating Systems**]: Storage Management

Keywords

MLC flash; threshold voltage; P/E performance; reliability; solid state disk

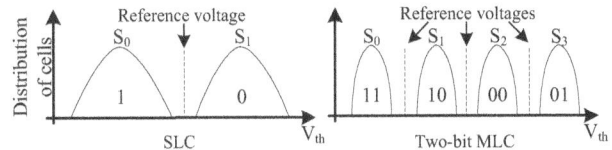

Figure 1: Threshold voltage levels in SLC and MLC flash.

1. INTRODUCTION

SLC (single-level cell) flash memory has been the main choice for SSDs in data centers due to its high performance and endurance [13, 22]. Recently, less-expensive MLC has started to enter into the storage market of data centers thanks to the advanced controller technology that can provide a larger ECC capability to compensate MLC's shorter life span and higher error correction overhead [12, 13, 18]. However, as manufacturers are aggressively pushing flash memory into smaller geometries and each memory cell has to store more bits [10], the improved controller and processing technology might not be able to keep pace with the shrinking NAND lithography [12], which makes the future of MLC flash SSD in data centers unclear. One reason is that the rate of increasing bit errors exceeds the capacity of enhanced ECC schemes [10, 12]. When a memory cell is pushed to store more bits, it is prone to more bit errors due to a much narrowed threshold voltage range [10].

Threshold voltages are used to represent different states in flash memory [3]. As illustrated in Figure 1, an SLC flash cell has two threshold voltage states (i.e., S_0, S_1), which indicate data '1' and '0', respectively. A 2-bit MLC flash cell provides four states (i.e., '11', '10', '00', '01') defined by four threshold voltage ranges (see Figure 1). Each of them is roughly half of that of an SLC flash cell. A programming operation is to charge a memory cell to a particular threshold voltage, whereas an erase operation is a reversal procedure [3]. If a cell's threshold voltage shifts across the reference voltage, the stored data will be misinterpreted, and thus, a bit error occurs [3, 21]. Obviously, MLC trends to generate more bit errors as a narrowed threshold voltage range could not tolerate even a slight threshold voltage shift. Between two adjacent threshold voltage ranges, a wide margin is reserved to combat retention errors. It is because a memory cell loses charge over time, which causes a left shift of threshold voltage [21]. As a threshold voltage range is continuously shrunk, its negative impact on endurance and program/erase (P/E) performance becomes more noticeable

[7, 28]. For example, while a typical SLC flash can tolerate ~100k P/E cycles with a 200 μs programming delay, a 2-bit MLC can only survive ~10k P/E cycles with a 600~900 μs delay [9]. Apparently, threshold voltage greatly influences MLC's performance, endurance and reliability.

Unfortunately, little investigation on the impact of threshold voltage on P/E performance and reliability of flash memory has been reported in the literature. To understand the role of threshold voltage in flash memory's performance and reliability, in this paper we empirically study the correlations between threshold voltage and MLC flash memory[1] P/E performance as well as reliability. All experiments are conducted on a hardware platform including an FPGA evaluation board [27] and a flash daughter board [6], which can issue chip-level commands to raw flash chips without ECC. To the best of our knowledge, this is the first work that empirically evaluates the impact of threshold voltage on MLC flash memory performance and reliability. Our experimental results demonstrate that the level of threshold voltage significantly impacts MLC flash performance and reliability. Since there exists a one-one correspondence between a threshold voltage and a particular state or data [3] (see Figure 1), we can indirectly adjust a memory cell's threshold voltage by programming it to different data. Our new findings, in turn, provide SSD designers with insights to developing a better SSD.

Our new findings and key contributions include:

- *Reliability and Endurance*

  Flash memory reliability in terms of number of bit errors is highly correlated with threshold voltage. A memory cell that is programmed to a higher threshold voltage is likely to generate more bit errors. Further, a memory cell programmed in a high threshold voltage ages faster as the number of bit errors increases more rapidly. Based on the experimental results, a reliability model is derived to explore the relationship between threshold voltage and a cell's reliability in terms of bit error number. These observations provide a new venue for further reliability enhancement of MLC flash.

- *P/E Performance*

  Programming a page to a lower threshold voltage is much faster than programming a page to a higher threshold voltage. For example, in a 2-bit MLC flash the speed of programming a memory cell to state S_0 (i.e., cell programmed as '11') is 15.5%, 23%, and 31% faster than that of programming it to state S_1, S_2, and S_3, respectively. Furthermore, irrelevant to its threshold voltage, a memory cell's programming speed always increases when its number of P/E cycles enlarges. On average, a memory cell's programming speed could improve 11.4% at the end of its lifetime. Besides, the time to program an MSB (most significant bit) page is around 2 to 3 times shorter than that of programming an LSB (least significant bit) page. In addition, under different threshold voltages, the erasing speed of a cell slightly changes. For instance, while erasing a block programmed as '11' costs 3.3 ms, erasing a block programmed as '01' only takes 3.1 ms.

---

[1] in this study we only investigate 2-bit MLC flash, which is currently the dominant type of MLC flash.

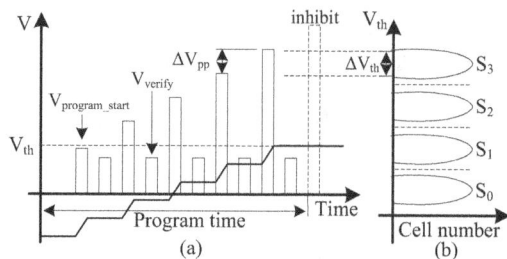

Figure 2: (a) An illustrative example of ISPP; the increased bars show the programming voltage, and the stair-step line shows the change of threshold voltage during the whole ISPP process; (b) distribution of cells in four levels for MLC flash.

- *Threshold Voltage Reduction*

  Inspired by our findings, we propose a new approach called threshold voltage reduction (TVR) that can trade an over-provisioned retention time for an increased write speed and longevity. Its basic idea is to shrink the margin between two neighbor states by reducing their threshold voltages. It can increase write speed by up to 50% while prolonging flash memory lifetime by 7.1%. A simulation study on TVR-powered SSDs shows that overall mean response time can be reduced by up to 35%. TVR serves as a case study to show how the system implications provided by our new findings can be applied to enhance MLC flash SSDs.

The remainder of the paper is organized as follows. Section 2 analyzes threshold voltage in related flash models. An empirical threshold voltage reliability model derived from experimental results is introduced in Section 3. Section 4 investigates the correlations between threshold voltage and P/E performance. The TVR technique is presented in Section 5. Section 6 briefly summarizes the related work. The paper is concluded in Section 7.

2. BACKGROUND AND MODEL ANALYSIS

2.1 ISPP Model

The basic storage unit in flash memory is a floating gate transistor, which is also called as memory cell [3]. An array of memory cells can form one or several pages depending on the number of bits that a cell can store. Typically, 64 or 128 pages are grouped as one block. While page is the smallest granularity for read and program operation, erase operation can only be performed on a block level. Because of the variation of characteristics of memory cells, the threshold voltage on each cell under the same programmed state is not uniform among cells, which results in a bell-shape threshold voltage distribution.

An incremental step pulse programming (ISPP) with a bit-by-bit verifying method [3, 25], therefore, is used to control the precision of final threshold voltage (see Figure 2). ISPP gradually increases the programming voltage from the starting voltage to the maximum voltage step by step. Between two consecutive steps, a bit-by-bit verifying operation is performed [21]. Within this process, the cells whose threshold voltages already reach their state voltage levels will be inhibited to program in next step. The step length between two adjacent steps, ΔV_{pp}, is the most important parameter for programming performance and threshold voltage distribution. First of all, the width of threshold voltage ΔV_{th} is in direct proportion to ΔV_{pp} [3]. The smaller a step length is, the more precise threshold voltage is. Also, ΔV_{pp} is proportional to programming speed [14, 23] for programming time can be shortened if ΔV_{pp} is increased. However, the programming performance improvement is at the cost of an increased raw bit error rate (RBER) [23]. From the study of Jung $et\ al.$ [14], we can approximately model the threshold voltage programmed by ISPP as:

$$V_{th} = V_{start} + \beta \Delta V_{pp} N_s \ . \qquad (1)$$

N_s represents the number of steps that a programming process needs. V_{start} is the initial voltage level of a programmed cell and β is a material related coefficient. Clearly, programming speed can be improved by reducing the number of programming steps N_s [17, 23]. Alternatively, we may also reduce the value of V_{th} while keeping ΔV_{pp} unchanged to obtain a smaller N_s based on equation (1).

2.2 Threshold Voltage Distribution Model

The threshold voltages of cells that are programmed to the same state are not identical. Therefore, a probability density function is used to describe the threshold voltage distribution of threshold voltage for each state. Even though there are asymmetries in a threshold voltage distribution, it still can be approximated by a sum of Gaussian distributions [16, 20]. Thus, the model of M-bit cell threshold voltage distribution is given by:

$$f(x) = \sum_{s=0}^{2^M-1} P(S_s) \frac{1}{\sqrt{2\pi}\delta_s} \exp\{\frac{-(x-\mu_s)^2}{2\delta_s^2}\} \ . \qquad (2)$$

$P(S_s)$ is the probability of state S_s. μ_s and δ_s are the associated mean and variance in the Gaussian probability density function. Ideally, $P(S_s)$ for every state is approximately equal to $\frac{1}{2^M}$ as there are a large amount of memory cells in one flash chip.

Figure 2b illustrates the threshold voltage distribution of a 2-bit flash memory. Without losing generality, 2-bit MLC flash is used as an example in the remainder of this paper. A threshold voltage distribution for more-than-2-bit cell flash memory can be readily derived from the 2-bit cell case. While S_0 is the erase state that represents data '11', S_1, S_2, and S_3 are the other three program states, which represent '10', '00', and '01', respectively. This mapping method is known as Gray-mapping [26]. Two bits data in one cell are separated into an LSB page and an MSB page in the LSB/MSB programming scheme [7], which is widely adopted in current MLC flash memories. A margin with approximately equal width of ΔV_{th} is implemented between two adjacent states in modern flash memory. The wide margin is designed to provide a reliability mechanism for flash memory to combat the voltage drift due to memory cell defects and long retention time [3]. However, the retention problem is almost negligible when the lifetime of data is much shorter than the JEDEC standard[17, 24].

2.3 Cell-to-Cell Interference

Cell-to-cell interference, a major noise also referred to as floating gate coupling, can significantly widen the threshold voltage distribution curve for each state [8]. It degrades the overall reliability of flash memory. The reason behind is that the threshold voltage of a cell is largely affected by its surrounding cells' threshold voltages. To minimize its impact, the page programming order is restricted to an ascending order in a block [15]. In the worst case, a cell is affected by its five neighbor cells [8]. For simplicity, the floating gate coupling influence caused by the upper right cell and upper left cell is ignored because their coupling effect is relatively small compared with other direct neighbors [8]. The change of threshold voltage due to its neighbors' interference can be modeled as [8]:

$$\Delta V_{th}^{(p,q)} = \gamma_{fg1}\Delta V_{th}^{(p,q+1)} + \gamma_{fg2}(\Delta V_{th}^{(p-1,q)} + \Delta V_{th}^{(p+1,q)}) \ . \qquad (3)$$

p and q denote the pth bitline and the qth wordline in a memory block. γ_{fg1} and γ_{fg2} are the floating gate coupling ratios in a bitline and in a wordline, respectively. The values of the two coupling ratios are determined by the materials and structure [8]. In the worst scenario, the ΔV_{th} between two cells is equal to the difference between V_{th} of state S_0 and V_{th} of state S_3. We can simply calculate the voltage change by:

$$\Delta V_{th}^{(p,q)} = (\gamma_{fg1} + 2\gamma_{fg2})\Delta V_{th}^{max} \ . \qquad (4)$$

Cho $et\ al.$ discovered that the worst floating gate coupling effect is even larger than the incremental step voltage ΔV_{pp} [8]. Intuitively, without increasing the complexity of manufacturing and degrading the programming performance, we can directly reduce ΔV_{th}^{max} to tighten the threshold voltage distribution curve. For example, in case that $\gamma_{fg1} = 0.02$, $\gamma_{fg2} = 0.006$, and $\Delta V_{th}^{max} = 5.4$ [8], a $2V$ reduction of ΔV_{th}^{max} can decrease the floating gate coupling effect by 37% based on equation (4).

2.4 Read Disturb

Whenever a flash memory cell is read, a voltage V_{pass} is applied to all deselected wordlines in that block [21]. V_{pass} must be higher than the highest threshold voltage so that the deselected cells on the same wordline can serve as transfer gates, which let the read current from the cell being read to be measured [21]. The V_{pass} unintentionally injects electrons into the floating gate through either stress-induced leakage current (SILC) or tunnel oxide traps filling [21]. Consequently, it introduces bit errors if the increased V_{th} caused by injected electrons exceeds the value of read reference voltage. Mielke $et\ al.$ found that mistakenly reading state S_0 as state S_1 is the dominant read disturb error [21]. The reason behind this is that the gap between V_{pass} and V_{th} of state S_0 is the most significant, which causes the highest field stress in the tunnel oxide under read bias. The leakage current, I, generated by field stress grows exponentially with the voltage across the tunnel oxide [2]:

$$I = I_0 \cdot e^{b_0 v_{ox}} \ . \qquad (5)$$

I_0 and b_0 are two constants, and v_{ox} is the voltage applied on the tunnel oxide. Although read disturb is negligible compared with write error [21], a reduced V_{pass} determined by the highest V_{th} could eventually decrease RBER caused by read disturb.

3. IMPACT ON RELIABILITY

Several studies [7, 21, 28] characterized flash error patterns and trends to understand the correlation between flash memory reliability and P/E cycles on page level. However, since one memory cell is being pushed to store more bits, two or more pages are logically divided from one physical memory cell page. Existing page level reliability investigations [7, 21, 28] cannot reveal the relationship between the threshold voltage of an individual flash memory cell and its reliability. In this section, we empirically evaluate the reliability of flash memory cells under various threshold voltages on a hardware platform [6, 27].

3.1 Testing Methodology

The number of bit errors per page is currently used as an indicator of flash memory reliability [3]. When the number of bit errors per page exceeds the ECC capability, the original data on that page can no longer be recovered, which results in a bad block problem [3]. Because of MLC flash memory mapping scheme, a threshold voltage change (e.g., state S_0 to state S_1) on a cell can result in two consequences. Either an error occurs in both associated LSB page and MSB page or an error happens only in one associated page (i.e., either an LSB page or an MSB page) [7, 28]. The mapping scheme also leads to a phenomenon that the LSB pages generally have a higher RBER than that of MSB pages [28]. We think that the number of cell errors is more suitable than the number of bit errors per page for measuring MLC flash reliability because the influence from logical layer mapping scheme can be avoided. In our experiments, the bit errors are collected and counted in a cell level. Any bit flip in a 2-bit cell, no matter which page it belongs to, is recorded as a cell error.

Figure 3 illustrates the program/erase scheme that is used to collect cell errors in our experiments. In this scheme, P/E procedures are performed on selected blocks cycle-by-cycle. In each P/E cycle, the entire block is first erased. Next, data are programmed into each page within the block. Once all the pages have been programmed, data are immediately read back and then are compared with their original values. Finally, the number of bit flips is recorded for future analysis. The error collecting procedure is repeated for thousands of cycles until the flash memory comes to the end of its lifetime. Since current flash memory does not provide a hardware mechanism for users to dynamically adjust its threshold voltage, programming different data patterns to indirectly change threshold voltage becomes the only feasible solution. This is because MLC flash employs distinct threshold voltages to represent different data patterns [26]. In other words, programming different data patterns (i.e., '11', '10', '00', or '10') onto a cell results in distinct threshold voltages. An MSB page and its associated LSB page are grouped as a cell page. Several scattered cell pages within one block are selected in a way that cell-to-cell interference among them can be ignored. During each P/E cycle, different cell pages are programmed with different data patterns. Within each cell page, however, all cells are programmed with the same data pattern, which represents a particular threshold voltage (i.e., V_{th0}, V_{th1}, V_{th2}, or V_{th3}). In this way, different cell pages are programmed to different threshold voltages in every P/E cycle. After N cycles, the accumulated threshold voltage for each page is NV_{th0}, NV_{th1}, NV_{th2}, and NV_{th3}, respectively.

The program/erase testing scheme explained above eliminates the cell-to-cell interference within one cell page because the same content is programmed across the entire

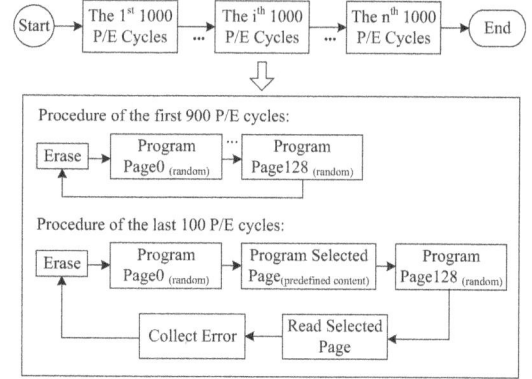

Figure 3: Flash memory error collecting scheme.

Table 1: An example of selected pages.

Page No.	Wordline	Page Type	Program Pattern
10	4	MSB page	1
16	4	LSB page	1
26	8	MSB page	1
32	8	LSB page	0
42	12	MSB page	0
48	12	LSB page	0
58	16	MSB page	0
64	16	LSB page	1

page. In order to mimic a practical flash memory usage pattern, the cell-to-cell interference effect needs to be taken into consideration. Therefore, in our testing scheme, the available P/E cycles of a flash memory are divided into multiple segments, with each consisting of 1,000 P/E cycles. During the first 900 P/E cycles of each segment, the same content is repeatedly programmed into each cell of a selected cell page to simply increase the accumulated threshold voltage without counting the cell errors. Periodically programming the same content to a particular cell page makes the discrepancies of accumulated threshold voltage among cell pages more obvious. Next, in the last 100 P/E cycles a batch of pseudo-random data are programmed and cell errors are collected after immediate reading back so that the testing scheme can simulate a real application environment, whereas the impact of different threshold voltages can still be measured. Figure 3 shows an illustrative example of this procedure. An example of selected pages are shown in Table 1. Page 10 and 16 belong to the same cell page that resides on wordline 4. While page 10 is an MSB page, page 16 is an LSB page. This cell page will be programmed by content '11', which can be performed by programming '1' to page 10 at first, and then writing one-page '1' data to page 16. Page 26 and 32 form a cell page and will be programmed as '10'. Cell page that contains page 42 and 48 will be programmed as '00'. The cell page on wordline 16 will be written as '01'.

A hardware platform, which consists of a Xilinx XUPV5-Lx110t evaluation board [27] and a Ming II flash daughter board [6], is built so that commands can be issued directly to raw flash chips without ECC. The flash memory used in our experiments is 2-bit MLC NAND flash, which is specified to

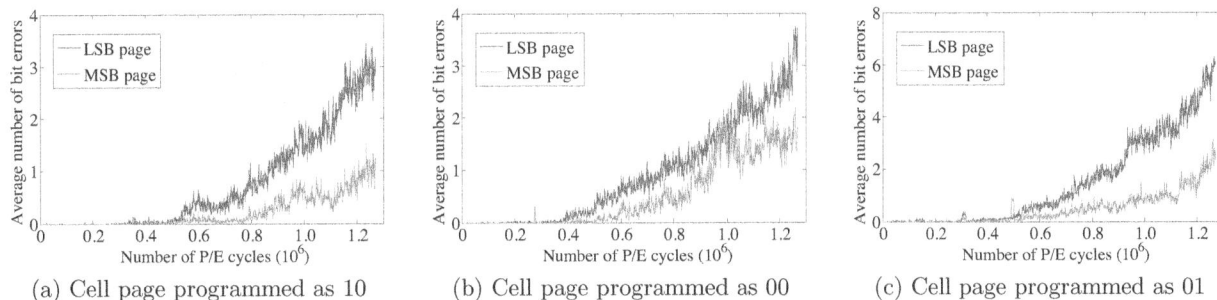

(a) Cell page programmed as 10   (b) Cell page programmed as 00   (c) Cell page programmed as 01

Figure 4: Programming errors in LSB and MSB page within one cell page.

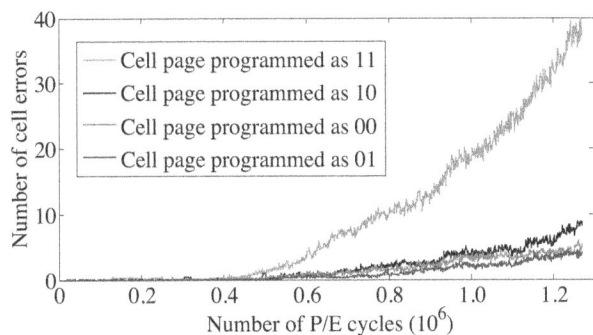

Figure 5: Average number of cell errors versus P/E cycles.

survive 10,000 P/E cycles under 10 year data retention time by using a minimum of 4-bit ECC per 528 bytes of data and a bad-block replacement algorithm [19]. All experiments are conducted in a controlled laboratory environment with a room temperature. The error data are collected from a limited number of blocks on a few flash chips from a particular manufacturer.

3.2 Experimental Results

Figure 5 shows the number of cell errors during the entire flash memory's lifetime. The cell errors are collected in the last 100 P/E cycles within each 1,000 P/E segment. All the lines are serrated because the number of cell errors between two consecutive P/E cycle segments fluctuates significantly. Clearly, the cell errors increase as the number of P/E cycles becomes larger. Further, pages programmed to different threshold voltages generate different number of cell errors. The number of cell errors in each cell page grows exponentially when the number of P/E cycles enlarges.

The cell page programmed as '11' exhibits the most unreliable characteristic as it has much more errors than that of the other three pages. In addition, the number of cell errors on this cell page grows much faster than the other three cell pages as the number of P/E cycles increases. In fact, errors in this cell page are erase errors, whereas the other three cell pages have programming errors. Since '11' represents the erase state, no programming process is carried out when '11' is written to a memory cell. This result suggests that a flash memory cell is more likely to be unreliable if either it is continuously erased without any data programmed or it is always programmed as '11' during a long period of time. The reason behind this is that a negative voltage is applied

on the floating-gate during an erase operation, which causes damage to the tunnel oxide [20]. A programming process, on the other hand, can neutralize and mitigate such damage because of a positive voltage applied on that gate. Therefore, memory cells without programming processes cannot alleviate the erase damage, and thus, generate much more errors compared with the cells on which erase and program operation are alternately performed.

Experimental results obtained from the other three cell pages are consistent with real applications. Figure 5 illustrates that among those three cell pages the cell page programmed as '01' has the largest number of cell errors. On the contrary, the cell page programmed as '10' is more reliable because of the smallest number of cell errors. The number of cell errors from the cell page programmed as '00' lies between that of the '01' cell page and the '10' cell page. According to the mapping method used, it is clear that the cell page always programmed to the lowest threshold voltage (i.e., '10') is more reliable than the cell pages often programmed to a higher threshold voltage (i.e., '00' and '01'). A detailed mathematical analysis will be provided to establish a model, which defines the relationship between threshold voltage and flash memory reliability.

In a 2-bit MLC flash memory, one cell page contains two logical pages referred to as MSB page and LSB page, respectively. Figure 4 shows the bit errors in an MSB page and an LSB page. From the figure, we can see that LSB pages generally have a larger number of bit errors than that of MSB pages under all programming cases. This is due to the fact that the assignment of 2-bit data to threshold voltages within a cell makes an LSB page more susceptible to error than an MSB page [28, 16]. Therefore, the conclusion that LSB pages are more prone to errors than MSB pages holds under various threshold voltages. The errors of '11' cell page are erase errors, while the errors in the other three pages are programming errors. Therefore, the error data of '11' is not illustrated here.

System implications: Continuously programming '11' to a cell page or erasing a block without any data programmed should be avoided, otherwise the reliability of the certain cell page degrades rapidly. Besides, writing data patterns that are represented by a lower threshold voltage could prolong flash's lifetime.

3.3 Model Establishment

In this section, we build an empirical threshold voltage reliability model for MLC flash memory. Cell pages programmed as '11' do not reflect real application situations

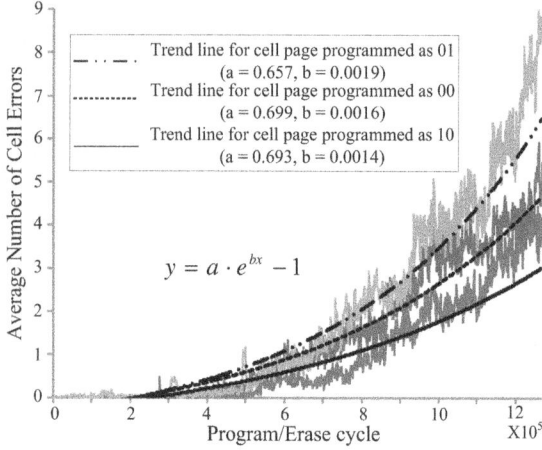

Figure 6: Fitting to exponential trends.

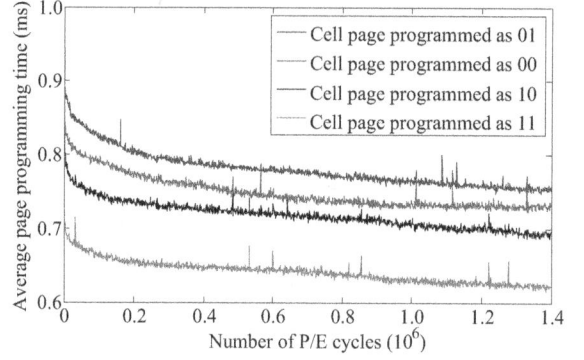

Figure 7: Average page programming performance.

because they only generate erase errors. Thus, we only consider the data collected from the other three cell pages.

Figure 6 clearly demonstrates that the cell errors increase exponentially as the P/E cycle becomes larger. We adopt the exponential law model to describe reliability behavior of the three cell pages in Figure 6 (nonlinear least squares fitting method). Two new parameters a and b are defined in this model. We determine them through parameter fitting. It is clear that each cell page has its own value of a and b as shown in Figure 6. This model, however, only gives us the relationship between the number of cell errors (i.e., reliability) and the P/E cycles for a cell page. It is obvious that threshold voltages of cell pages vary because they are programmed to distinct data patterns. Hence, we can then apply the parameter fitting method again for the three cell pages to obtain the relationship between a threshold voltage and a combination of a and b.

Using the mean distribution voltage values listed in Figure 11a, we can approximate the threshold voltage for the three cell pages. Applying the parameter fitting we get the two equations (6) and (7) to describe the relationship between threshold voltage and parameters a and b.

$$a = -5E^{-4}ln(V_{th}) + 0.0019 \ , \tag{6}$$

$$b = 0.036ln(V_{th}) + 0.6616 \ . \tag{7}$$

We substitute a and b in the exponential law model and get an empirical reliability model with respect to threshold voltage V_{th} shown as below:

$$Err = (-5E^{-4}ln(V_{th}) + 0.0019)e^{(0.036ln(V_{th})+0.6616)N} - 1 \ , \tag{8}$$

where V_{th} is the threshold voltage of flash memory cells. N is the number of P/E cycles, and Err is the number of cell errors. The value of cell errors is the indicator of flash reliability. Equation (8) can be generalized as:

$$Err = (\alpha_1 ln(V_{th}) + \beta_1)e^{(\alpha_2 ln(V_{th})+\beta_2)N} - 1 \ . \tag{9}$$

The parameters $\alpha_1, \beta_1, \alpha_2,$ and β_2 are determined by the characteristics of a flash memory. The empirical reliability model presented by equation (9) discloses the relationship between threshold voltage and flash reliability.

The empirical threshold voltage reliability model in its current format has one limitation. The error data is col-

lected by reading the programmed data back immediately. Therefore, the time-dependent behavior of RBER is not considered in our model. However, Belgal et al. discovered that in the first few weeks of flash retention period almost no retention error is detected [2]. A study on a wide range of real-world traces found that 49-99% of writes require less than 1-week retention time [17]. Therefore, time-dependent characteristics can be safely ignored by the model for workloads that require short retention time.

4. IMPACT ON P/E PERFORMANCE

The P/E performance of MLC flash under different threshold voltages are examined in this section. Similar to the testing methodology used in Section 3, a P/E procedure is performed on flash cycle-by-cycle until flash reaches the end of its lifetime. In each P/E cycle, all cell pages in a block are programmed one-by-one to a particular threshold voltage and then the entire block is erased. By measuring the programming and erase time we can evaluate the P/E performance under a particular threshold voltage.

4.1 Page Programming

Page programming time under different threshold voltages is shown in Figure 7. It is obtained by averaging the programming time of all pages within a block whose memory cells are programmed to a particular threshold voltage. Two interesting observations are made. Firstly, pages programmed to a lower threshold voltage have a better programming performance. For example, programming a page to state S_0 (i.e., cell page programmed as '11') typically costs 672 μs, whereas pages programmed to state S_3 need roughly 880 μs. On average, the speed of programming a page to state S_0 is 15.5%, 23%, and 31% faster than that of programming a page to state S_1, S_2, and S_3, respectively. Secondly, under all threshold voltage situations the programming time decreases as the number of P/E cycles increases. The rationale behind it is that as the tunnel oxide of a memory cell wears out (i.e., the number of P/E cycles increases) electrons are more easily to be injected into a cell's floating gate [20]. Further, the programming time decreases rapidly in the early lifetime of MLC flash. In the range of 1 to 2×10^5 P/E cycles, programming time reduces 10.3% on average. In the rest of flash memory's lifetime, programming time only decreases 4.8%.

Figure 8 illustrates the programming performance of different page types. Figure 8a shows average programming

(a) MSB page programming time

(b) LSB page programming time

(c) Page programming time in a block

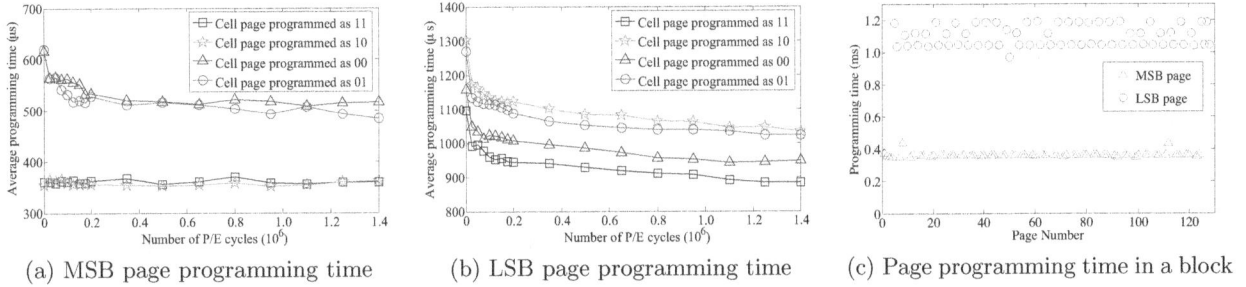

Figure 8: Programming time of LSB and MSB page in a block.

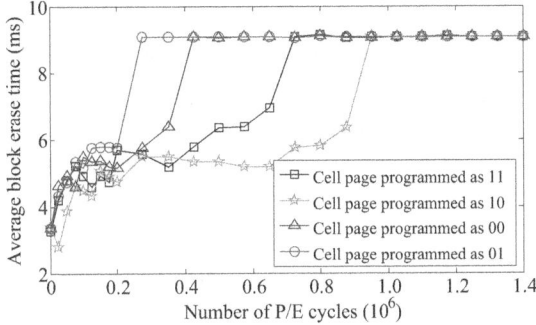

Figure 9: Average block erase time.

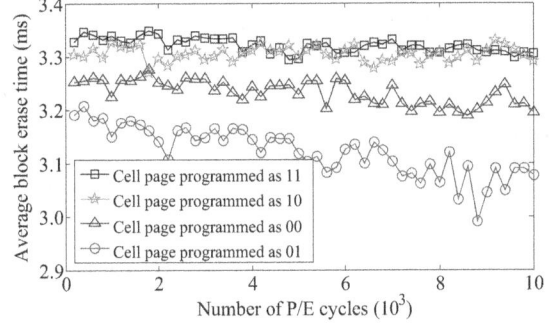

Figure 10: Average block erase time in small P/E cycles.

time of MSB pages versus P/E cycles and Figure 8b gives that of LSB pages. It is clear that programming speed of an MSB page is much faster than that of an LSB page. For example, MSB pages programmed as '11' (i.e., the lowest threshold voltage) only take around 380 μs for a programming operation. Writing the same content onto an LSB page, surprisingly, needs around 1,100 μs. Besides, programming time of MSB pages that are programmed as '00' and '01' (i.e., state S_2 and S_3) is 1.42 times longer than that of MSB pages programmed as '11' and '10' (i.e., state S_1 and S_1) on average. The programming time of LSB pages, on the contrary, does not show the same trend as that of MSB pages does. LSB pages programmed as '11' have the lowest programming time (on average 919 μs), whereas programming an LSB page to '10' state takes the longest programming time (1,082 μs). Figure 8c illustrates the programming speed of each page within a block, which is consistently programmed as '11' when the number of P/E cycles equals to 2,000. It is obvious that the programming time of each page varies. While MSB pages have almost the same programming time, the programming time of LSB pages varies substantially. Further, the programming time of MSB pages is much shorter than that of LSB pages.

4.2 Block Erase

Figure 9 shows the block erase time under different threshold voltages in a flash memory's entire lifetime. It is clear that the erase time increases and varies largely as the number of P/E cycles enlarges. The erase time in all threshold voltage situations increases to 9 ms when flash comes to the end of its lifetime. When the number of P/E cycles is greater than 2×10^5, the erase time of differently programmed blocks exhibits noticeable differences. for in-

stance, the erase time of blocks programmed as '01' rapidly goes to 9 ms, whereas erase time of blocks programmed as '10' increases much slower. The reason why erase time in all situations finally becomes 9 ms is uncertain.

Figure 10 illustrates the erase time in flash's early lifetime (P/E cycles $< 1 \times 10^4$). Blocks programmed to a higher threshold voltage have a better erase performance. On average, blocks programmed as '01' have the fastest erase speed, which is 3.1 ms. Blocks programmed as '11' on average need 3.3 ms to finish an erase operation.

System implications: 1) programming content that is represented by a lower threshold voltage can have a higher P/E performance; 2) judiciously rearranging the programming order could improve SSD's overall performance as the programming speeds on an MSB page and an LSB page are noticeably different; 3) intentionally choosing blocks that have a faster erase speed can reduce garbage collection cost.

5. TVR: A CASE STUDY

This section demonstrates an example of how to apply the system implications provided by our new findings on SSD design. We first present the TVR approach based on an approximate V_{th} distribution [23]. Next, a method of calculating the amount of reduced V_{th} is illustrated. Finally, after quantitatively analyzing programming speed improvements caused by TVR, a simulation study on its impact on SSDs is briefly presented.

5.1 Threshold Voltage Reduction

A standard 2-bit MLC threshold voltage distribution model [16] is illustrated in Figure 11a. Three margins ($D_0, D_1,$ and D_2) between every two adjacent states are configured to increase reliability so that after a long period of time data can still

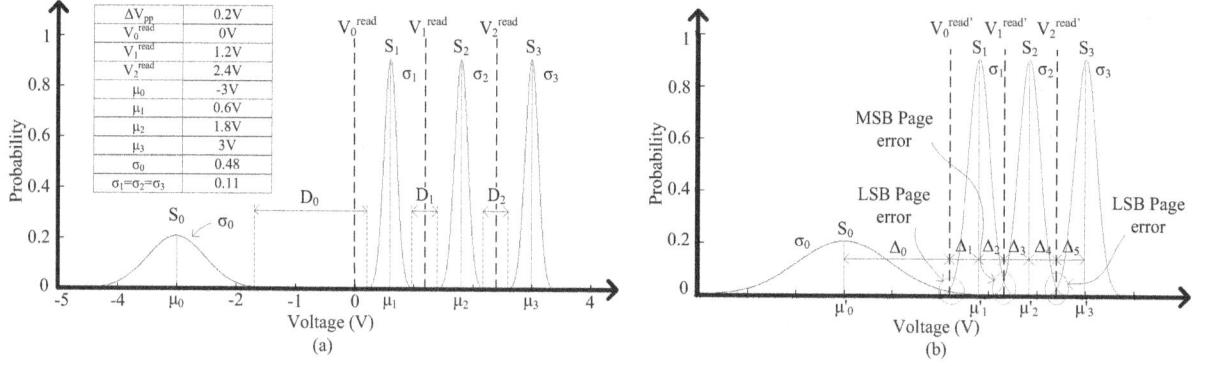

Figure 11: 2-bit MLC flash memory threshold voltage distribution; (a) the threshold voltage distribution simulation result of the flash memory with standard threshold voltage levels; the value of parameters used in the simulation is shown in the table; (b) an example of a retention free threshold voltage distribution; μ_0', δ_0, δ_1, δ_2, and δ_3 are the same as the value in (a).

be read correctly with changed threshold voltage distributions. A recent investigation [17] on a wide range of real-world workloads, however, discoveries that data retention capability offered by the worst-case oriented design is always under-utilized, especially in the early lifetime of a flash memory when data retention problem even does not exist. For example, it finds that 49-99% of writes require less than 1-week retention time [17]. In typical data center workloads like proxy and MapReduce, most data are overwritten frequently, which suggests a short data retention in only days or even hours [17]. Therefore, in a retention relaxation situation such as flash memory used to store log data, the width of those margins can be largely reduced without affecting reliability. Based on the observation of over-provisioned data retention time from [17] and our new findings, we propose the TVR approach. It improves programming performance and reliability by reducing threshold voltages of all states. As a result, margins between two adjacent states can be shrunk. The amounts of reduced threshold voltages lie in a range between zero to a standard margin width. An extreme scenario of TVR is to shrink the width of all the three margins to zero (see Figure 11b), which is called a retention free case. In the remainder of this section, we use the retention free case to quantitatively analyze the maximum improvement in performance and reliability for TVR-powered flash.

In our analysis, the tails of a Gaussian distribution curve are used to calculate RBER because raw bit errors only occur in the overlap area between the tails of two neighbor threshold voltage distribution curves [16]. The two Gaussian tails are asymmetric because V_{th} is more prone to enlarge in a programming process, while retention time diminishing the value of V_{th} [21]. However, since the retention free case does not consider retention errors, the retention free threshold voltage distribution simply takes the two Gaussian tails as symmetric, which is also suggested by [16, 23].

Similar to the simplification used in [23], we set the variances of the three non-erased states as the same ($\delta_1 = \delta_2 = \delta_3$). According to [4], parameters like μ_s, δ_s, V_s^{read}, and ΔV_{pp} are set as the values shown in Figure 11a. Based on the simulation using the defined parameters, it is clear that the erase state S_0 has a flattened bell-shape while the three non-erased states S_1, S_2, and S_3 are much taller and tighter due to the small value of step length in a programming process. Three read reference voltages (i.e., V_0^{read}, V_1^{read}, and V_2^{read})

are set for read operation. V_1^{read} is used to identify the content in an MSB page. If a cell's threshold voltage is higher than V_1^{read}, it is read as '0'. Otherwise, it is read as '1'. For an LSB page, two voltage comparisons are performed. If a cell's threshold voltage lies between V_0^{read} and V_2^{read}, it is taken as '0'. Otherwise, the content is identified as '1'. Based on this strategy, the bit errors in an MSB page always happen in an area around V_1^{read} while bit errors in an LSB page come from the areas around V_0^{read} and V_2^{read}.

5.2 Quantitative Analysis of TVR

Figure 11b illustrates a threshold voltage distribution after applying TVR. When TVR is applied, RBER increases because the voltages of cells at the tail of the distribution will be misread when they pass the read reference voltage. The probability that the voltages of cells cross the read reference voltage can be calculated by the tail probability function [16, 29]. This value is the same as RBER. However, the calculation methods for MSB pages and LSB pages are different for their reading/programming schemes are distinct [16].

Since the number of errors caused by misinterpreting a state as a non-immediate-neighbor state is very small [7, 16], only the errors generated by state changes in two adjacent states are considered in our computation. For an MSB page, misreading errors are around $V_1^{read'}$. RBER is computed by the equation below:

$$\text{RBER}_{\text{MSBpage}} = \frac{1}{4}Q_1\left(\frac{|\Delta_2|}{\delta_1}\right) + \frac{1}{4}Q_2\left(\frac{|\Delta_3|}{\delta_2}\right). \quad (10)$$

For an LSB page, however, misreading errors are around $V_0^{read'}$ and $V_2^{read'}$. Therefore, the calculation of RBER is revised as:

$$\begin{aligned}
\text{RBER}_{\text{LSBpage}} = &\frac{1}{4}Q_0\left(\frac{|\Delta_0|}{\delta_0}\right) + \frac{1}{4}Q_1\left(\frac{|\Delta_1|}{\delta_1}\right) \\
&+ \frac{1}{4}Q_2\left(\frac{|\Delta_4|}{\delta_2}\right) + \frac{1}{4}Q_3\left(\frac{|\Delta_5|}{\delta_3}\right).
\end{aligned} \quad (11)$$

Δ_i ($0 \leq i \leq 5$) is the distance from μ_s' to its adjacent read reference voltage $V_s^{read'}$ as shown in the Figure 11b. $Q_s(x)$ ($s = 0, ..., 3$) is the tail probability function of each state. As explained in Section 4.1, the threshold voltage distribution is asymmetric as the errors caused by a state change from a lower voltage state to a higher voltage state (i.e., $Q_0\left(\frac{|\Delta_0|}{\delta_0}\right)$, $Q_1\left(\frac{|\Delta_2|}{\delta_1}\right)$, and $Q_2\left(\frac{|\Delta_4|}{\delta_2}\right)$) are mainly generated by programming processes. Majority errors due to a reverse change (i.e., $Q_1(\frac{|\Delta_1|}{\delta_1})$, $Q_2(\frac{|\Delta_3|}{\delta_2})$, and $Q_3(\frac{|\Delta_5|}{\delta_3})$) are caused by retention time [21]. To simplify the computation, we assume that the errors made by a forward state change (i.e., from a lower voltage state to a higher voltage state) and a backward state change (i.e., from a higher voltage state to a lower voltage state) have the same probability. Hence, we have:

$$Q_1(\frac{|\Delta_2|}{\delta_1}) = Q_2(\frac{|\Delta_3|}{\delta_2}) \,, \tag{12}$$

$$Q_0(\frac{|\Delta_0|}{\delta_0}) = Q_1(\frac{|\Delta_1|}{\delta_1}) = Q_2(\frac{|\Delta_4|}{\delta_2}) = Q_3(\frac{|\Delta_5|}{\delta_3}) \,. \tag{13}$$

The maximum RBER tolerated by flash memory is determined by the adopted ECC capability and the size of redundant area fabricated by manufacturers [3, 21]. For modern flash memory, RBER must be lower than 4.5×10^{-4} if the uncorrectable bit error rate requirement is set to be 10^{-16} [17] . By solving equations (10) and (11) using parameters shown in Figure 11a, we obtain:

$$\Delta_0 \approx 1.40; \; \Delta_1 = \Delta_4 = \Delta_5 \approx 0.36; \; \Delta_2 = \Delta_3 \approx 0.34.$$

Δ_i ($0 \le i \le 5$) gives the distance between mean threshold voltage of each state and its neighbor read reference voltage in the maximum threshold voltage reduction situation. Finally, the reduced threshold voltages can be calculated based on μ_0' and Δ_i ($0 \le i \le 5$). We find that Δ_i ($i = 2, 3$) is smaller than Δ_j ($j = 1, 4, 5$).

5.3 Programming Speed Improvement

Compared with read operation, the programming speed in flash memory is one order of magnitude slower. Thus, the programming speed is a main performance bottleneck for flash memory. Flash memory programming speed depends on the slowest memory cell in an ISPP programming process [25]. Equation (1) gives the relationship between a threshold voltage and the number of programming steps under certain step length ΔV_{pp}. It can be rearranged as:

$$\lceil N_s \rceil = \frac{\Delta V_{th}}{\beta \Delta V_{pp}} \,. \tag{14}$$

$\Delta V_{th} = V_{th} - V_{start}$ and $\lceil N_s \rceil$ stands for the smallest integer bigger than N_s. Parameter β is determined by the ISPP model based on the curve-fitting values shown in [14]. When $\Delta V_{pp} = 0.2V$ (see Figure 11a) the model fits empirical data [14] very well with β equal to 1.14.

According to reading and programming strategy in MLC flash memory, the largest ΔV_{th} in an MSB page is given by $\mu_2 - \mu_0$ (i.e., from state S_0 to S_2), whereas $\mu_1 - \mu_0$ (i.e., from state S_0 to S_1) yields the largest ΔV_{th} in an LSB page. Therefore, before TVR is applied, the programming time for an MSB page is $22 \cdot t_{step}$ according to equation (14), where t_{step} is the time for one ISPP step. For an LSB page, the programming time is approximately equal to $16 \cdot t_{step}$. On average, the programming time can be evaluated by $19 \cdot t_{step}$.

After applying TVR, the largest ΔV_{th} in an MSB page programming process is $\sum_{i=0,1,2,3} \Delta_i = 2.44$. Hence, programming time can be reduced to $11 \cdot t_{step}$. Similarly, in an LSB page, the largest ΔV_{th} is $\sum_{i=0,1} \Delta_i = 1.76$ and programming time is $8 \cdot t_{step}$. The average programming time after applying TVR is $9.5 \cdot t_{step}$. Compared with a non-TVR scenario, programming speed is improved by 50%.

5.4 Reliability Improvement

By using the empirical reliability model established in Section 3, it is easy for us to evaluate the reliability improvement via threshold voltage reduction. If data size written to each cell page is sufficiently large and random, we can assume that the four different threshold voltage states shown in Figure 11 have an equal chance to be written into a cell page. Thus, we can use the mean voltage throughout flash memory's lifetime to get the number of cell errors at a given P/E cycle. Using the results got from Section 5.2, if RBER is lower than 4.5×10^{-4} [17] the maximum number of P/E cycles is 12.469×10^5 according to equation (8). In the TVR approach, however, the maximum number of P/E cycles that a flash memory can reach is 13.35×10^5. Therefore, the TVR can improve the flash memory reliability by 7.1%.

5.5 Impact on SSDs

To understand the impact of TVR on the overall performance of SSDs, we carry an experimental study on TVR-powered SSDs based on a validated simulation environment (i.e., DiskSim 4.0 [5] and the Microsoft SSD module [1]) and six real-world traces including enterprise data center applications (e.g., Financial1, Financial2) as well as file system benchmarks on workstations (e.g., Iozone, Postmark). Simulation results demonstrate that TVR can reduce SSD's overall mean response time including read and write by 11% to 35%. Besides, TVR consistently increases an SSD's overall performance as the number of packages enlarges. Due to space limit, detailed simulation results are not included.

6. RELATED WORK

Several recent studies [11, 17, 29] have discussed about how to tactfully control the threshold voltage to improve the performance and endurance of flash memory and SSD. The threshold voltage distribution will drift as the number of P/E cycles and retention time increase [29]. Hence, the predetermined fixed read reference voltage often results in significant asymmetric errors in flash memory's lifetime. To overcome this problem, Zhou et al. introduced a dynamic reading thresholds scheme, which is applied to single-level cells to reduce raw bit errors caused by voltage drift [29]. Further, Sala et al. extended their dynamic reading thresholds scheme to MLC memories [11]. The enhanced dynamic threshold voltage scheme combined with new ECC can significantly improve the reliability of a flash memory especially when it is aged. In contrast, in this research TVR dynamically changes both read reference voltages and state voltages in an MLC flash to improve the write speed.

The write speed of flash memory is in direct proportion to the number of programming steps in ISPP [25]. By examining such process, Pan et al. first proposed a device-aware design strategy exploiting the under-utilized ECC redundancy to improve flash memory performance [23]. Its basic idea is to reduce the number of programming steps by increasing the step length in ISPP and use the under-utilized ECC redundancy to correct the errors caused by step length increasing. Liu et al., on the other hand, found that the redundant ECC capability and data retention are usually under-utilized after studying a wide range of real-world traces [17]. A retention-aware flash translation layer is proposed to optimize the overall performance of flash SSDs [17]. TVR employs a totally different approach to exploiting flash SSDs' over-provisioned data retention capability to improve performance and reliability. Instead of shrinking step length, TVR reduces threshold voltages to trade the over-provisioned data retention capability for an improved performance and longevity.

7. CONCLUSIONS

Thanks to recent advances in flash controller technology, cost-effective MLC flash SSDs are gradually becoming popular storage devices in data centers [12, 13, 18]. To further decrease its cost, manufacturers are aggressively pushing flash into smaller geometries and to store more bits per cell. As a result, the reliability of MLC flash continuously decreases, which demands an increasing ECC capacity and controller capability [10]. However, the speed of controller technology development might lag behind the increasing error rate [12]. A main reason for the increasing error rate is that threshold voltage ranges have been largely reduced [10, 28]. Since threshold voltage plays a central role in flash reliability and performance, in this paper we investigate the impact of threshold voltage on the performance and reliability of MLC flash memory. We find that the P/E performance and reliability of MLC flash are highly correlated to threshold voltages. Several important observations have been made. Next, a flash reliability model is established based on experimental results to reveal the relationship between the threshold voltage and the number of bit errors. Finally, we conduct a case study (i.e., the TVR approach) on how to apply the insights derived from our new findings on enhancing MLC flash SSDs. TVR can transform over-provisioned flash memory data retention capability into an increased write speed and longevity. A mathematical analysis demonstrates that TVR improves write speed by up to 50% and prolong flash memory's lifetime by 7.1%. A simulation study shows that TVR reduces mean response time by up to 35%.

In future work, we will conduct a comprehensive study on the system implications provided by this research and their interplay on the overall performance and reliability of MLC flash SSDs. For example, MLC flash P/E performance and reliability can be improved by judiciously rearranging page programming order and reassembling page content.

Acknowledgments

We would like to thank Steven Swanson and his Non-volatile Systems Laboratory for their support on the hardware platform. Also, we would like to thank the anonymous reviewers for their constructive comments that improve this paper. This work was supported in part by the U.S. National Science Foundation under grant CNS (CAREER)-0845105.

8. REFERENCES

[1] N. Agrawal, et al. Design tradeoffs for ssd performance. In *USENIX ATC*, pages 57–70, 2008.

[2] H. P. Belgal, et al. A new reliability model for post-cycling charge retention of flash memories. In *Reliability Physics Symposium*, pages 7–20, 2002.

[3] R. Bez, et al. Introduction to flash memory. *Proceedings of the IEEE*, 91(4):489–502, 2003.

[4] J. Brewer and M. Gill. *Nonvolatile Memory Technologies with Emphasis on Flash: A Comprehensive Guide to Understanding and Using Flash Memory Devices*. Wiley-IEEE Press, 2011.

[5] J. S. Bucy, et al. The disksim simulation environment version 4.0 reference manual. *CMU*, 2008.

[6] T. Bunker, M. Wei, and S. J. Swanson. Ming ii: A flexible platform for nand flash-based research. Technical report, UCSD, 2012.

[7] Y. Cai, et al. Error patterns in mlc nand flash memory: Measurement, characterization, and analysis. In *DATE*, pages 521–526, 2012.

[8] T. Cho, et al. A dual-mode nand flash memory: 1-gb multilevel and high-performance 512-mb single-level modes. *Solid-State Circuits, IEEE Journal of*, 2001.

[9] J. Cooke. The inconvenient truths about nand flash memory. *Micron MEMCON*, 7, 2007.

[10] E. Deal. Trends of nand flash memory error correction. *Cyclic Design, June*, 2009.

[11] S. Frederic, G. Ryan, and D. Lara. Dynamic threshold schemes for multi-level nonvolatile memories. Non-volatile Memory Workshop, 2013.

[12] C. George. Will MLC SSD Replace SLC?, 2011.

[13] J. He, et al. Dash: a recipe for a flash-based data intensive supercomputer. In *SC*, pages 1–11, 2010.

[14] T.-S. Jung, et al. A 117-mm^2 3.3-v only 128-mb multilevel nand flash memory for mass storage applications. *Solid-State Circuits, IEEE Journal of*, 31(11):1575–1583, 1996.

[15] T.-S. Jung, et al. A 3.3 V 128 Mb multi-level nand flash memory for mass storage applications. In *42nd IEEE ISSCC*, pages 32–33, 1996.

[16] Y. Kim, et al. Verify level control criteria for multi-level cell flash memories and their applications. *Journal on Advances in Signal Processing*, 2012.

[17] R.-S. Liu, et al. Optimizing nand flash-based ssds via retention relaxation. *In UESNIX FAST*, 2012.

[18] H. Marks. SSDs in the data center: SLC out, MLC in, Dec. 2012.

[19] Micron. MT29F8G08MAAWC datasheet.

[20] N. Mielke, et al. Flash eeprom threshold instabilities due to charge trapping during program/erase cycling. *IEEE TDMR*, 4(3):335–344, 2004.

[21] N. Mielke, et al. Bit error rate in nand flash memories. In *IEEE IRPS*, pages 9–19, 2008.

[22] M. Moshayedi and P. Wilkison. Enterprise ssds. *Queue*, 6(4):32–39, 2008.

[23] Y. Pan, G. Dong, and T. Zhang. Exploiting memory device wear-out dynamics to improve nand flash memory system performance. In *USENIX FAST*, 2011.

[24] J. Standard. Stress-test-driven qualification of integrated circuits. *JEDEC*, pages 1–26, 2010.

[25] K.-D. Suh, et al. A 3.3 v 32 mb nand flash memory with incremental step pulse programming scheme. *Journal of Solid-State Circuits*, 30(11), 1995.

[26] Z. Wang, et al. Reliable mlc nand flash memories based on nonlinear t-error-correcting codes. In *IEEE DSN*, pages 41–50, 2010.

[27] Xilinx. Xilinx university program xupv5-lx110t development system.

[28] E. Yaakobi, et al. Error characterization and coding schemes for flash memories. In *GLOBECOM Workshops*, pages 1856–1860. IEEE, 2010.

[29] H. Zhou, et al. Error-correcting schemes with dynamic thresholds in nonvolatile memories. In *ISIT*, 2011.

DWC: Dynamic Write Consolidation for Phase Change Memory Systems

Fei Xia*† Dejun Jiang* Jin Xiong* Mingyu Chen* Lixin Zhang* Ninghui Sun*

*SKL Computer Architecture, ICT, CAS, Beijing, China
†University of Chinese Academy of Sciences, Beijing, China
{xiafei2011, jiangdejun, xiongjin, cmy, zhanglixin, snh}@ict.ac.cn

ABSTRACT

Phase change memory (PCM) is promising to become an alternative main memory thanks to its better scalability and lower leakage than DRAM. However, the long write latency of PCM puts it at a severe disadvantage against DRAM. In this paper, we propose a Dynamic Write Consolidation (DWC) scheme to improve PCM memory system performance while reducing energy consumption. This paper is motivated by the observation that a large fraction of a cache line being written back to memory is not actually modified. DWC exploits the unnecessary burst writes of unmodified data to consolidate multiple writes targeting the same row into one write. By doing so, DWC enables multiple writes to be send within one. DWC incurs low implementation overhead and shows significant efficiency. The evaluation results show that DWC achieves up to 35.7% performance improvement, and 17.9% on average. The effective write latency are reduced by up to 27.7%, and 16.0% on average. Moreover, DWC reduces the energy consumption by up to 35.3%, and 13.9% on average.

Categories and Subject Descriptors

C.0 [**Computer Systems Organization**]: General—*System architectures*

Keywords

Phase Change Memory; Write consolidation; Performance optimization

1. INTRODUCTION

DRAM has been the choice for the main memory for decades. However, it is becoming difficult for DRAM to keep scaling down to smaller cells [4] due to limitations such as capacitor placement, device leakages and charge sensing. On the other hand, larger DRAMs result in increasing energy consumption which accounts for 20% to 40% of the total server energy [17, 22, 33]. Recently, some emerging non-volatile memories (NVM) have shown great potential to become the promising choices for the main memory [14, 37, 31] due to their better scalability and lower leakage. Phase Change Memory (PCM), which is already commercially available [28], is one of such NVMs.

It is projected by ITRS [4] that the PCM will have similar write energy and write parallelism with DRAM in near future. However, PCM still has a major weakness: long write latency, which raises a challenging issue to its adoption in the main memory [4]. Several approaches have been proposed to reduce the impact of PCM's long write latency on memory system performance. For instance, PreSET[24] and two-stage-write [35] exploits PCM asymmetries of writing bit one and writing bit zero to reduce the time to write the PCM array. These studies have shown that reducing the unexpected impacts of long PCM write latency is critical to improve the system performance.

PCM employs burst accesses to memory chips. The PCM memory controller uses one write command and multiple bursts (called Burst Length, BL) to transfer a cache line data to PCM chips. It has been observed by many that a large fraction of data written to main memory is not actually modified. We also observe from our study that 54% of eight-byte words written back to the memory from the caches are unmodified. In the conventional system, these unmodified data is written to the memory as part of its respective cache lines. We argue that the bursts used to send unmodified data can be saved to send modified data of other write commands.

The silent store scheme [19] reduces unnecessary writes to the memory by not sending unmodified whole cache line, but it cannot handle partially modified cache lines. Lee et al use partial writes to PCM array by tracking dirty data from L1 cache to memory banks at different granularities [14]. Their approach does not reduce the time to transfer cache line data to the memory. To the best of our knowledge, there is no prior work that exploits the unnecessary bursts of unmodified data blocks to process other writes.

In this paper, we propose a new write scheme *Dynamic Write Consolidation (DWC)* to improve PCM main memory performance while reducing energy consumption. The main idea of DWC is to consolidate multiple write commands in BL bursts by utilizing unnecessary burst writes of unmodified data blocks. Figure 1 shows the timing diagram of the conventional write scheme, silent store scheme and DWC. There are three consecutive write commands target-

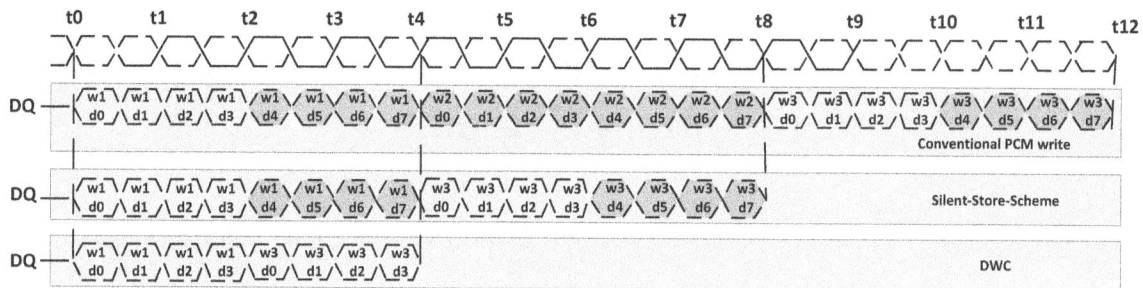

Figure 1: Timing diagram for different PCM writing schemes. The number of modified data blocks of W1, W2, W3 are 4, 0 and 4. The gray hexagon represents transferring an unmodified data block in the burst write mode.

ing the same row. A cache line has eight eight-byte words [1] and BL is eight. The number of modified data blocks of W1 and W3 is 4, and all data blocks of W2 are unmodified. The conventional write scheme completes three writes at time t12 regardless whether whole cache line data or only a few words are modified. Silent store scheme does not write unmodified cache line data, thus W2 is eliminated. It completes writes at time t8. In DWC, unmodified words are not written back to the memory, and thus W2 is also unnecessary. Moreover, W1 and W3 are consolidated to write modified data blocks in BL bursts. Thus DWC completes at time t4. To apply the DWC in real PCM memory systems, we need to address the following three challenges:

1. How to let the memory controller get the modification information of evicted cache line data.

2. How to find write commands that can be consolidated with a write command selected to be issued. Write commands that can be consolidated should satisfy three conditions: i), they access the same row of the same bank; ii), there is no read command between them that accesses the same column; iii), the sum of modified data blocks of these write commands is equal to or less than BL.

3. What modifications of PCM chips should be made to support DWC. Specifically, a PCM chip must be able to handle two or more write commands within one BL burst.

We identify whether a data block is modified or not in the cache hierarchy and propagate the information to the memory controller. Within the memory controller, we propose a two-stage low-overhead searching mechanism to find write commands that can be consolidated. To support DWC, we propose to add a few extra column address buffers and column decoders to a PCM chip. This paper makes the following contributions:

- We propose a new write scheme *DWC* that allows PCM main memory to reduce the impact of its long write latency on the overall system performance. DWC fully utilizes the burst writes of unmodified data and consolidates multiple writes into one write command, which achieves improved performance.

[1] An eight-byte word is also called a data block in this paper.

- We quantitatively evaluate the latency, area and power overheads in implementing DWC with CACTI 6.0 and synthesizing RTL codes. The results show that DWC incurs low implementation overhead.

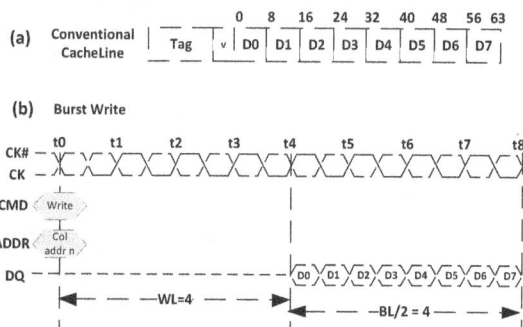

Figure 2: Conventional 64B cache line and burst write process

- We conduct an extensive evaluation to show the effectiveness and efficiency of DWC. The experimental results show that DWC can achieve up to 35.7% performance improvement, and 17.9% on average. DWC can reduce energy consumption by up to 35.3%, and 13.9% on average. We also show the sensitivity of DWC under varying queue depths, page sizes, LLC sizes and replacement policies.

2. BACKGROUND AND MOTIVATION

2.1 Burst reads/writes

PCM is designed to adopt interface specifications similar to DRAM, in which the memory controller sends read and write requests in burst mode. Burst reads prefetch more than one column data and transfer the data through the external data bus to cache line in pipeline. Similarly, one write command triggers burst writes by only sending the command and a starting column address. The memory controller then transfers data of consecutive columns after the starting address. Figure 2 shows an example of burst writes for a 64B cache line. Assuming that the data bus width is 64bit (8B), a cache line can be divided into eight eight-byte words as shown in Figure 2(a). Figure 2(b) shows the burst write process of DDR3. At time t0, the memory controller

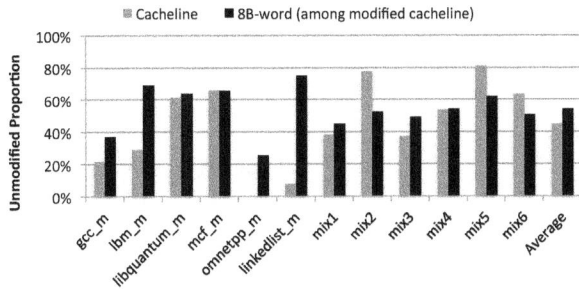

Figure 3: Unmodified data proportions at different granularities

issues a write command and sends column address to address bus. After WL[2] cycles, the memory controller starts to transfer cache line data through data bus in continuous burst mode at time t4. A cache line data needs eight burst writes. The data blocks are transferred at both rising and falling edges of the external bus clock. Therefore, the memory controller completes data transfer at time t8.

2.2 Motivation

The key observation that motivates our work is that a large fraction of a cache line data written back to memory is not actually modified. Figure 3 shows the proportions of unmodified data at 64B (cache line) and 8B (word) granularity. On average 44.8% of data is not modified at cache line granularity, which means that these cache lines do not need to be written back to memory though they are dirty.

Among modified cache line data, there are still 54.1% of words that are not modified on average. The result indicates that more than half of burst writes are wasted to transfer unmodified data within one write command. This motivates us to propose dynamic write consolidation, namely DWC. By avoiding unnecessary burst writes and consolidating multiple writes in BL bursts, DWC can effectively improve PCM memory performance.

3. DYNAMIC WRITE CONSOLIDATION

In this section, we present the design details of DWC. Figure 4 shows the architecture overview of DWC. DWC requires collaboration of cache hierarchy, memory controller, and memory chips. DWC first needs to identify the unmodified data blocks within a cache line. Thus, the cache hierarchy records and propagates the data block modification information of last level cache to memory controller. When memory controller issues a write command, it needs to find other write commands that can be consolidated in the command queue based on the data block modification information. To support DWC, the peripheral circuitry of PCM chips also needs to be modified. Especially, we discuss the implementation overhead of each part.

Although DWC targets to improve performance of PCM memory system, one can also apply it to DRAM memory system. However, it is more critical to reduce the unexpected impact of long write latency of PCM memory for the exploration of next generation memory system using ad-

---

[2]WL represents the time interval between column access command and the start of data occurred in data bus.

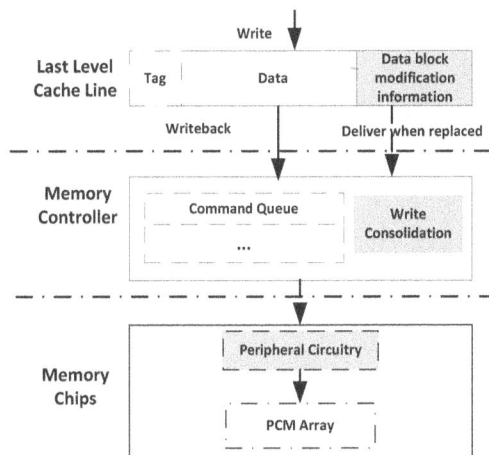

Figure 4: Overview of DWC architecture

vanced features of PCM chips. Thus, we concentrate our attention and discussion on PCM main memory in this paper.

3.1 Cache hierarchy

We first present the modification of cache hierarchy to support DWC. A cache line data can be divided into multiple data blocks. In DWC, only the modified data blocks in cache line are written back to memory. Therefore, DWC needs to distinguish the unmodified data blocks from the modified ones in cache hierarchy. DWC relies on the design choice of employing a *Modified Block Vector (MBV)* to identify the modification information. Similar technique is also proposed in [16]. When data in L2 cache is evicted and written back to LLC, the old data is read from LLC. Then, an added comparator compares the old data with the new one at data bus granularity. The comparison results are stored in MBV, which are then propagated to memory controller when last level cache line data is evicted to main memory.

Overheads. To identify the modification information of data blocks in LLC, one needs to read existing old data from LLC. The read can be implemented using an atomic cache operation called *read-modify-write(RMW)* [18], which is used in ECC-protected caches. The read operation does not incur extra latency overhead because it can be overlapped with tag matching of the write operation [16].

The cache line size is 64B and the data bus width is 64bit in our system. Thus, an 8-bit MBV is needed to store modification information for a 64B cache line. Another 64-bit comparator is required to compare the old data with the new data at each bus transmission. We use CACTI 6.0 [23] to evaluate the total area and power overheads of the modified LLC hierarchy at 32nm technology process. We evaluate the overheads of comparator and MBV by synthesizing RTL codes using 90nm process library and the results are scaled to 32nm. Evaluation results show that our modification in LLC incurs 2.2% area overhead and 2.8% power overhead, compared to the whole LLC architecture [3].

3.2 Memory controller

In the conventional DDRx write scheme, memory controller adopts burst mode to send data of write commands.

---

[3]Detailed cache configuration parameters are shown in Section 4.

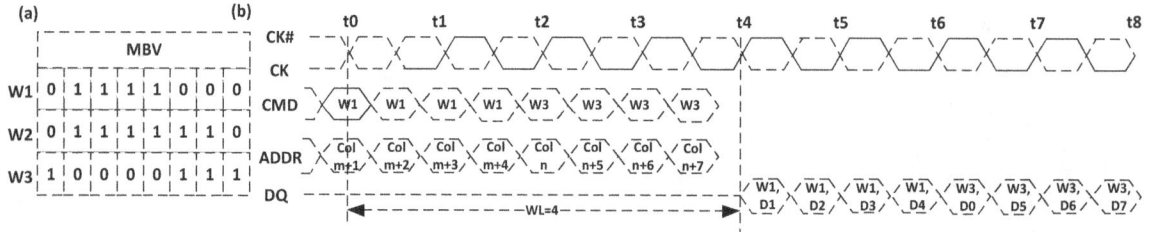

Figure 5: (a). The MBV of W1, W2 and W3 commands. "1" represents that the data block of the cache line is modified and "0" represents not. (b).The timing of DWC that consolidates W3 with W1.

After sending a write command and its starting column address, memory controller uses BL bursts to send the consecutive data blocks starting from the target column address. Each burst sends a data block at the data bus granularity. Unlike the conventional write scheme, DWC identifies the unmodified data blocks and does not write them back to memory. Thus, the bursts used to send unmodified data can be saved to send modified data of other write commands, which is the dynamic write consolidation in our proposed scheme. However, dynamic write consolidation is nontrivial. One cannot consolidate any two write commands arbitrarily. An effective write consolidation requires the following three conditions.

1. The consolidated write commands access the same row of the same bank. Otherwise, the data in row buffer should be first written back to memory array after one write command finishes. In such case, successive write command can not be issued before an ACTIVATE command activates the corresponding row.

2. There is no read command accessing the same column of the same row in front of the write commands to be consolidated in the command queue. It is essential to guarantee the read correctness. Otherwise, the read command gets the data of the consolidated write command, which introduces application errors.

3. The sum of modified data blocks of the consolidated write commands is less than or equal to BL. This guarantees that the modified data blocks can be transferred to memory chip within BL bursts. Thus, the timing of DDRx is preserved as before.

To find write commands that can be consolidated with the issuing write command, the intuitive approach is to search the command queue sequentially and determine whether a write command can be consolidated. This approach searches the queue to the end until BL modified data blocks of writes that can be consolidated are found. This searching approach suffers from large latency overhead, which degrades the system performance unexpectedly.

Instead, DWC employs a two-stage searching with low latency overhead. In the first stage, DWC identifies write commands accessing the same row by comparing their addresses. In the second stage, DWC searches write commands that can be consolidated. For each identified write command in the first stage, DWC adds its modified data blocks with those of the issuing write. In case that the added result is less than or equal to BL, DWC considers the corresponding write command is suitable for consolidation. Then, DWC

chooses the oldest write command among all writes that can be consolidated, and finally consolidates it with the current issuing write. Although it is ideal to consolidate as many writes as possible with current issuing write, it introduces large latency overhead and circuitry complexity which is not desirable in terms of a cost-effective design. We also show the performance speedup achieved by DWC is close to that of the ideal scheme in section 5.

Note that DWC can use the First-Ready-First-Come-First-Served (FR-FCFS) [29] memory scheduling policy to search write commands that access the same row. However, DWC imposes more constraints on the scheduling process and aims to execute possible write consolidations after scheduling.

Double Data Rate Command/Address Bus. In the conventional DDRx memory system, the frequency of command/address bus is lower than that of data bus. Memory controller only needs to send the starting column address in one cycle, while data bursts need four cycles for one write command. However, DWC requires double data rate command/address bus [20, 34] as the modified data blocks may not be in continuous columns. Thus, each column address of modified data blocks must be sent to memory chips at the frequency of data bus.

Figure 5 shows the timing of DWC for consolidating two write commands. Assume write command W3 can be consolidated with the write command W1. Figure 5(a) gives the modification information of W1, W2 and W3. We use the DDR3 protocol, and thus BL is 8. Figure 5(b) shows the timing of the consolidation of W1 and W3. In the first 2 cycles, memory controller sends W1 and its column addresses of modified data blocks. The left 2 cycles are used to process W3 similarly. The data bus transfers the modified data blocks of W1 and W3 using burst writes like before.

Overheads. We set the command queue depth to be 64 for overhead evaluation. We evaluate the area and power overheads of the two-stage searching by implementing it in Verilog HDL and synthesizing the design using Synopsys Design Compiler with the technology library of TSMC at 90nm. The synthesization results show that the searching can be implemented in 2 cycles under 400 MHz, which is much less than the write latency of PCM. We include the latency overhead in our evaluation. The power and area overheads are 0.94 mW and 0.0105 mm^2, respectively.

3.3 Memory chips

Assuming the PCM chip is organized similar to conventional DRAM chip, the column address is in the column address buffer and then sent to the column decoder. The column decoder selects successive multiple columns to store data buffered in the data-in-buffer.

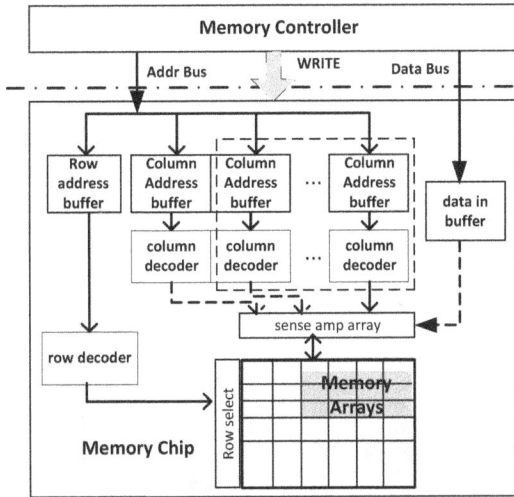

Figure 6: Modification to PCM chip

In order to support DWC, we need to modify the peripheral circuitry of PCM chip. The dashed frame in Figure 6 shows our modification to the simplified memory chip structure. Since DWC requires memory controller to send column address at double data rate, multiple column address buffers are needed to buffer column addresses. Multiple column decoders are also needed to select different columns of row buffer in parallel. The total number of column address buffers is equal to BL, so does column decoders. This is because memory controller sends BL column addresses to memory chip with one write command as Figure 5(b) shows. DWC does not require any modification to row address buffer and row decoder. This is because write consolidation targets the write commands accessing the same row of the same bank. Thus, DWC only needs to add (BL - 1) column address buffers and column decoders per PCM chip.

Overheads. The modification to PCM chip does not incur extra latency overhead, because the added decoders work with the original decoder in parallel. We estimate the area and power overheads of our added column address buffers and column decoders by CACTI 6.0 and synthesizing RTL codes. We use 2Gb DDR3 memory chip in our evaluation. Therefore, 7 column address buffers and 7 column decoders are needed per PCM chip. By using a 32nm technology process, our modification incurs 0.04% area overhead and 0.47% power overhead, compared to an original memory chip.

4. EVALUATION METHODOLOGY

We evaluate DWC using the multiprocessor full-system simulator Gem5 [8] and the cycle accurate memory system simulator DRAMSim2 [30]. We model both the latency and energy consumption of PCM by enhancing the memory module of DRAMSim2.

4.1 System configurations

We simulate an 8-core out-of-order multiprocessors at 2GHz. Table 1 shows the detailed baseline system configurations. The baseline has a 32MB last level cache to filter frequent accesses to PCM. The memory controller schedules read requests of read queue (RDQ) with high priority until write queue (WRQ) is great than 80% full, when write requests

Table 1: Baseline system configurations

Processor	8-cores, Out-of-Order, 2GHz
L1 caches	32KB I-caches, 64KB D-caches, 2-way associative, 64B cache line, 1-cycle latency
L2 caches	512KB, 8-way associative, 64B cache line, 6-cycle latency, write-back
LLC	32MB, 16-way associative, 64B cache line, 30-cycle latency, write-back, LRU replacement policy
Memory controller	64-entry RDQ and WRQ, 64-entry command queues per bank, channel/rank/bank/row/col address mapping, FCFS, read priority scheduling (unless WRQ is great than 80% full)
Main memory	64bit width DDR3-800, 8 x8 2Gb PCM chips, 2 ranks per channel, 8 banks per rank, 32768 rows/bank, 1024 columns/row, tRCD: 55ns, tRP: 150ns, tCL: 12.5ns, tWR: 15ns, Array read: 2.47pJ/bit, Array write: 16.82pJ/bit, Buffer read: 0.93pJ/bit, Buffer write: 1.02pJ/bit

Table 2: Workload characteristics

Workloads	Description	MPKI	R/W ratio
gcc_m	8 copies of gcc	1.92	1.44
lbm_m	8 copies of lbm	23.34	1.41
libquantum_m	8 copies of libquantum	2.17	2.89
mcf_m	8 copies of mcf	17.76	2.92
omnetpp_m	8 copies of omnetpp	1.05	1.12
linkedlist_m	8 copies of linkedlist	15.67	1.08
mix_1	2bzip2-2cactusADM -2lbm-2libquantum	12.13	1.62
mix_2	2bzip-2hmmer -2lbm-2sjeng	11.07	4.48
mix_3	2gcc-2libquantum -2mcf-2omnetpp	5.69	1.78
mix_4	2gcc-2leslied3d -2wrf-2omnetpp	13.08	2.15
mix_5	2astar-2libquantum -2linkedlist-2omnetpp	10.70	5.32
mix_6	2astar-2lbm -2linkedlist-2mcf	13.52	2.72

are issued. The timing and energy parameters of PCM are derived from the widely-used configurations in [14].

4.2 Workloads

We choose a set of workloads from SPEC CPU2006 benchmark [2] and the micro benchmark Linked List [1]. Since multiple workloads usually run on the same physical server simultaneously, we also provide 6 mixed workloads to evaluate the efficiency of DWC to serve such memory access patterns. We execute the applications in the multiprogrammed mode on Gem5. For each workload, we execute 10 millions memory access instructions after warming up last level cache.

Table 2 summarizes the characteristics of these workloads, including the LLC Misses Per-Kilo Instructions (MPKI) and read-to-write ratio (R/W ratio). Note that the number of writes does not include the writes of unmodified cache line data. These workloads have varying MPKIs, ranging from 1.05 to 23.34, which includes both less intensive ones and intensive ones.

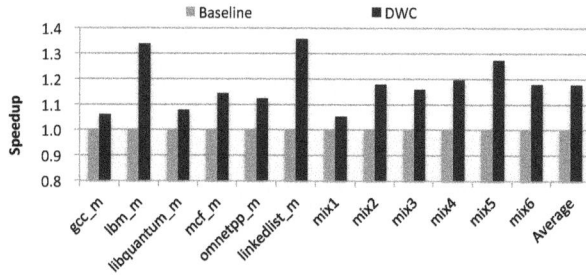

Figure 7: Execution time speedup

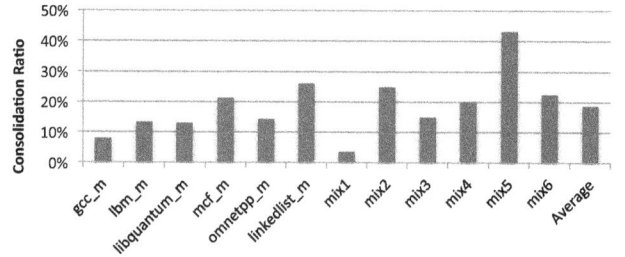

Figure 8: Consolidation ratio

5. EVALUATION RESULTS

In this section, we first evaluate the performance, effective latency and energy consumption of DWC. We use the silent store scheme as the baseline system. Second, we compare DWC with the ideal scheme to evaluate the tradeoff of improvement and overhead. We also compare DWC with FR-FCFS memory scheduling policy. Then, we measure the command/address bus utilization to evaluate the impact of DWC on the parallelism of bank access. Memory system behavior varies under different system configurations, such as queue depth, page size, LLC size and LLC replacement policy. As such, we apply a sensitivity analysis to DWC to show its efficiency against varying configurations at last.

5.1 Performance improvement

We first evaluate the performance improvement of DWC. Figure 7 shows the execution time speedup[4] of DWC against the baseline system. DWC achieves the performance improvement by 17.9% on average. Especially, DWC speeds up the execution time of workload *linkedlist_m* by up to 35.7%. The performance improvement of DWC mainly results from two aspects. First, DWC reduces writes to PCM array and data transfer time by write consolidation. Second, DWC reduces additional reads to row buffer before write. We further record the actually consolidated writes and the total writes for each workload. We calculate the consolidation ratios for all workloads and plot the results in Figure 8. The consolidation ratio of *linkedlist_m* is 26.1%, which results in the high performance improvement.

One factor that affects the performance improvement of DWC is the memory accessing intensity. For instance, *lbm_m* and *libquantum_m* have similar consolidation ratios. However, the memory access of *lbm_m* is more intensive than that of *libquantum_m*, which allows the overall execution time of *lbm_m* to benefit more from write consolidation. On the other hand, the R/W ratio also has significant impact on the performance improvement of DWC. For instance, the consolidation ratio of *mix5* is larger than that of *linkedlist_m*. Nevertheless, the R/W ratio of *linkedlist_m* is 1.08, which is less than 5.32 of *mix5*. The low R/W ratio indicates the existence of more write commands that are possibly consolidated. As a result, DWC achieves larger performance speedup for *linkedlist_m* than that of *mix5*. The consolidation ratios of *gcc_m* and *mix1* are less than 10%, which can explain the little achieved performance speedup.

The major factor that affects the consolidation ratio is the unmodified data proportion. The low unmodified data proportions of *gcc_m* and *mix1* (as shown in Figure 3) result

---

[4]Speedup = $ExecTime_{Baseline}$ / $ExecTime_{DWC}$.

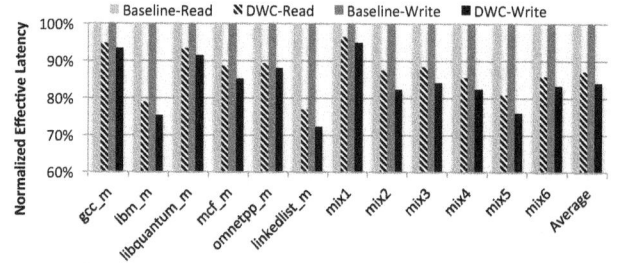

Figure 9: Effective read and write latency

in their low consolidation ratios respectively. We observe that the average unmodified data proportion of *omnetpp_m* is lower than that of *gcc_m*, while the consolidation ratio of *omnetpp_m* is higher than that of *gcc_m*. It is probably due to the nonuniform distribution of unmodified data proportion of writes. We leave the exploration for future work.

5.2 Effective latency reduction

In addition to reducing the application execution time, DWC can also reduce the effective read and write latency. Figure 9 shows the effective latency reduction caused by DWC for all workloads. The results are normalized to the baseline system. DWC can reduce the effective read and write latency by 12.8% and 16.0% on average, separately. DWC reduces the effective read and write latency by up to 23.2% and 27.7% for *linkedlist_m*, respectively. DWC reduces the command queuing time of consolidated writes, which in turn reduces the queuing time of read and unconsolidated write commands. The reduced queuing time in the command queue further reduces the number of stalled requests, and thus the queuing time in the transaction queue. As a result, the effective latency observed by processor is reduced. On the other hand, DWC only requires writing the PCM array once for those consolidated multiple write commands instead of writing once for each write command. This also contributes to the reduction of effective write latency.

5.3 Energy saving

DWC can also reduce memory system energy consumption by consolidating multiple writes together. Since PCM is projected to have similar write energy to DRAM, we do not use differential write scheme. Figure 10 shows the memory energy consumption of DWC normalized to the baseline. DWC saves the energy consumption by up to 35.3% for the workload *libquantum_m*, and 13.9% on average for all workloads. Since DWC avoids unnecessary writes to PCM by not sending unmodified data, DWC can effectively reduce

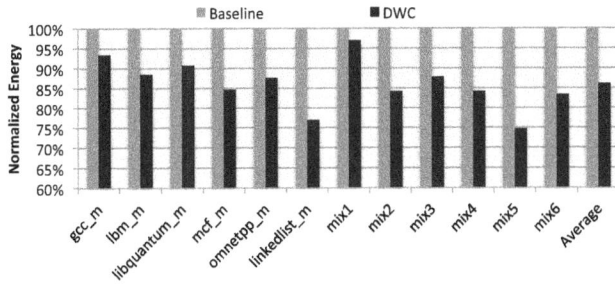

Figure 10: Energy saving

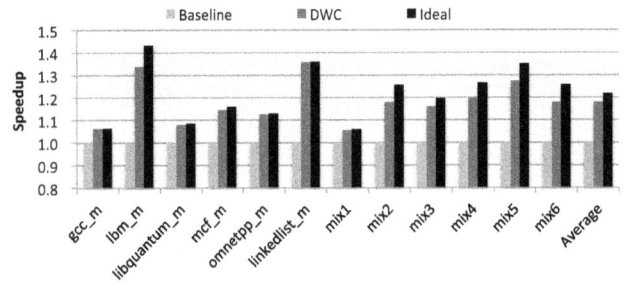

Figure 11: Comparing speedup between DWC and Ideal

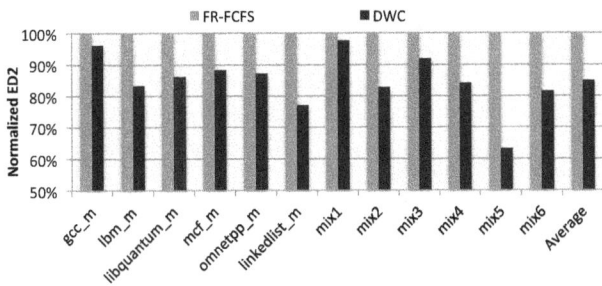

Figure 12: Comparison of ED2 between DWC and FR-FCFS

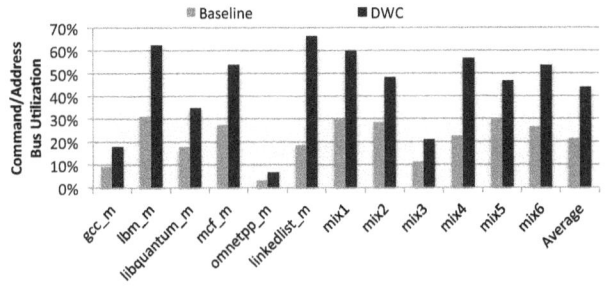

Figure 13: Comparison of the command/address utilization between the conventional memory system and DWC

the write energy consumption of PCM. On the other hand, DWC consolidates multiple writes and writes data into PCM array once together. To serve consolidated writes, PCM only needs to read the addressed data into the row buffer once. This avoids multiple reads in the conventional memory write scheme to serve multiple writes.

5.4 Comparison to the Ideal

So far, we show that DWC can effectively reduce the application execution time, effective latency, and energy consumption. To balance the tradeoff between the performance improvement and the implementation overhead, DWC stops searching the command queue once finding the oldest write that can be consolidated. However, the ideal scheme is to consolidate as many writes as possible in BL bursts. We also implement the ideal scheme in our simulator and compare it with DWC. Figure 11 shows the performance speedup of DWC and Ideal normalized to the baseline. Ideal only achieves less than 5% improvement compared to DWC on average. To consolidate as many writes as possible, the ideal scheme needs to search the command queue to the end at most case and determines whether any write can be consolidated. This process incurs large searching overhead which limits the improvement and requires complex circuitry implementation. Thus, we argue that DWC is much more practical than the ideal scheme with a reasonable tradeoff between the performance improvement and the implementation overhead.

5.5 Comparison to FR-FCFS

DWC can be implemented based on FR-FCFS memory scheduling policy. Thus, we also compare DWC with FR-

FCFS. Figure 12 shows the energy delay squared product (ED2) of DWC normalized to FR-FCFS for all workloads. Compared to FR-FCFS, DWC can reduce ED2 by 15.1% on average. For workload *mix5*, DWC can even achieve an ED2 reduction as much as 36.8%. Unlike FR-FCFS, DWC consolidates multiple writes targeting the same row in addition to reordering them together. DWC fully exploits the burst writes of unmodified data for sending consolidated writes instead. Thus, DWC reduces the average transfer time of write command compared to FR-FCFS. To avoid the bank access starvation, FR-FCFS allows scheduling at most 4 commands before switching to schedule other bank accesses. However, DWC consolidates multiple writes into one write command at every FR-FCFS scheduling, which in turn allows more commands to be scheduled before starting to schedule other bank accesses. This also enables DWC to perform better than FR-FCFS in terms of energy and delay.

5.6 Command/address bus utilization

In conventional DDRx memory systems, the command/address bus can be immediately used to transfer ACTIVATE command of other banks after a write command. However, the command/address bus in DWC is used to send additional column addresses after a write command in successive BL/2 cycles. Other commands can not be transferred during this period. Thus, we finally evaluate the impact of DWC on the parallelism of bank access. We measure the command/address bus utilizations of DWC and the conventional memory system.

As shown in Figure 13, the conventional average command/address bus utilization is only 21.3%, and thus is able to send more commands/addresses without affecting

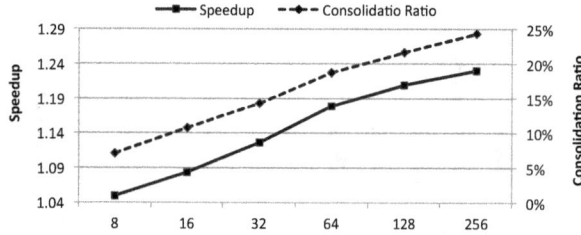

Figure 14: Impact of queue depth

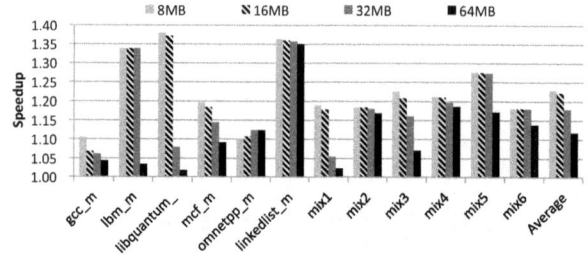

Figure 15: Impact of PCM page size

the bank parallelism. Even one applies DWC to the memory system, the average command/address bus utilization increases to 44.0%, which means that the bus still exists idle. Therefore, DWC can improve application performance without degrading the bank parallelism.

5.7 Sensitivity analysis

The behavior of a memory system usually varies under different configurations. In order to evaluate the impacts of different system configurations on the efficiency of DWC, we conduct a sensitivity analysis to DWC in this section. We include the following two performance-critical factors: queue depth and page size. On the other hand, LLC size and LLC replacement policy affect the memory accessing of PCM main memory. Therefore, we evaluate the impact of LLC size and LLC replacement policy on the efficiency of DWC at last.

5.7.1 Impact of queue depth

Figure 14 shows the average execution time speedup of all workloads when command queue depth varies from 8 to 256. The solid line shows the speedup of execution time, and the dashed line shows the speedup of consolidation ratio. As the command queue depth increases, so does the speedup. This is because a deeper command queue provides more spaces for more writes. Correspondingly, the possibility of finding writes that can be consolidated increases.

However, the speedup does not increase linearly with the increase of command queue depth. The performance improvement is significant when the queue depth increases from 8 to 64. The speedup slows down when the queue depth increases beyond 64. It is because the latency overhead to find consolidated write commands increases significantly when the queue depth is larger than 64. This in turn eliminates the speedup benefit caused by DWC. More importantly, large queue suffers from large area and energy overheads. Therefore, DWC use a 64-entry command queue.

5.7.2 Impact of page size

Scalability is one important advantage of PCM compared to DRAM. Therefore, we can expect that the capacity of PCM chip will increase with the development of material and manufacturing technology. The increased capacity in turn affects the row and column organization of PCM chips. We evaluate the efficiency of DWC as the page size of PCM chip increases. Figure 15 shows the average speedup of all workloads when the PCM page size increases from 2KB to 32KB. We measure both the speedup of execution time and the speedup of consolidation ratio. The speedups increase

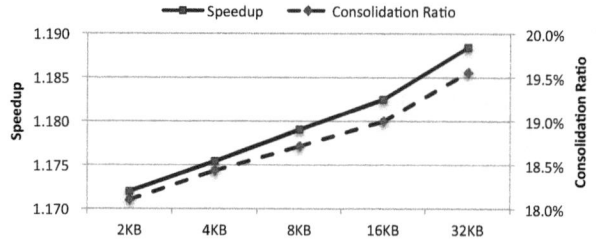

Figure 16: Impact of LLC size

almost linearly with the increasing page size. This is because a larger page results in higher possibility that multiple writes access the same row. Thus, we consider that DWC is a desirable write scheme for future PCM main memory that comprises large PCM pages.

5.7.3 Impact of LLC size

In this section, we evaluate the impact of LLC size on the efficiency of DWC. Figure 16 shows the execution time speedup when the LLC size varies from 8MB to 64MB. The associativity keeps constant at 16-way. The speedup decreases as the LLC size increases for some workloads, such as gcc_m, libquantum_m, and mix3. This is because larger LLC size results in less evictions to PCM and less unmodified blocks of evicted cache line. We can also see that varying LLC size almost does not affect the speedup for some workloads, such as linkedlist_m and mix2. An exception is that the speedup increases as the LLC size increases for workload omnetpp_m. This is because many evicted cache lines are clean when the LLC is small. Therefore, the R/W ratio is high which results in low speedup. The evaluation shows that DWC achieves 11.8% speedup than the baseline when the LLC size is 64MB. Thus, DWC is still efficient with large LLC size.

5.7.4 Impact of LLC replacement policy

So far, we show the efficiency of DWC using the common LRU replacement policy of LLC. Recently, a few works propose optimized LLC replacement policies to reduce writes to PCM memory, such as CLP-N [11]. Therefore, we evaluate the impact of LLC replacement policy on the efficiency of DWC in this section. CLP-N selects the oldest clean cache line among the N least recently used cache lines. If such clean cache line is not found, the LRU cache line is evicted. Among different configurations of N, we set N to be 7 that

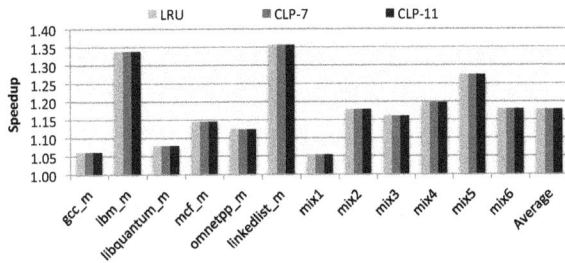

Figure 17: Impact of LLC replacement policy

performs best reported in [11] and 11 that further expends the selection range.

Figure 17 shows the execution time speedups of different LLC replacement policy with 32MB LLC. The speedups of all workloads are almost the same among the LRU, CLP-7 and CLP-11 replacement policy. This is because all cache lines of a cache set in LLC are dirty at most time. The opportunity is low to find other clean cache lines when the LRU cache line is dirty. Thus, the CLP-N replacement policy almost does not affect the efficiency of DWC.

6. RELATED WORK

6.1 PCM main memory

The long write latency of PCM is a major concern when one adopts PCM in main memory. A few research works exploit PCM's asymmetric latency of writing bit one (SET) and writing bit zero (RESET) to improve PCM performance. By proactively setting all the bits in a given memory line immediately after a cache line gets dirty, PreSET [24] allows actual writes taking less time to reduce write latency. Similarly, two-stage-write [35] distinguishes writing bit zero and writing bit one by dividing a write into two stages. In the writing zero stage, all zeros are written at an accelerated speed. In writing one stage, all ones are written with increased parallelism without violating power constraint. Thus, two-stage-write can effectively reduce write latency to PCM array. Since PCM requires multiple writes to flush a row buffer back to the array, partial writes [14] only writes the modified data in row buffer to PCM array to reduce write latency. Flip-N-Write [10] guarantees that each flush includes at most half row buffer to be written by flipping data to reduce write latency. Similarly, DWC can reduce the average write latency to memory array. Moreover, instead of optimizing write latency from row buffer to PCM array, DWC mainly reduces the queuing time and transfer time. To reduce the unexpected impact of long write latency on read requests, write cancellation and write pausing [26] are proposed to serve read requests preemptively. The on-going write operation is cancelled or paused when a newly-arriving read request accesses the same bank. Similarly, DWC can also reduce read latency by reducing queueing time of read commands from write consolidation. A few research efforts focus on write latency optimization for MLC PCM. MLC PCM employs iterative write scheme [7], and thus incurs longer write latency. Morphable memory system [25], Mercury [13], and write truncation [12] are proposed to reduce the write latency of MLC PCM. These

techniques can be complementary to DWC when DWC is applied to MLC PCM-based main memory.

Another related topic is to hide the long write latency of PCM. Hybrid memory system consisting of DRAM and PCM is proposed to reduce writes to PCM by placing the frequent writes in DRAM[14, 15, 27]. OptiPCM [21] takes advantage of photonic links to connect large number of PCM chips, and thus improves bandwidth and performance of PCM memory. However, this paper mainly focuses on consolidation techniques for PCM main memory.

6.2 Memory access scheduling

Memory scheduling policies, such as FR-FCFS [29] and burst scheduling [32], are related to our work closely. FR-FCFS prioritizes memory commands that access the same row. With burst scheduling, memory accesses to the same row of the same bank are clustered into bursts to maximize bus utilization. Read requests are allowed to preempt ongoing writes for reduced read latency. There are two differences between DWC and these techniques. First, FR-FCFS and burst scheduling do not identify unmodified cache line data, while DWC identifies these data and does not send the unmodified data. Moreover, DWC exploits the saved time to send consolidated writes. Second, DWC consolidates multiple writes into one write after reordering these write commands. Unlike DWC, FR-FCFS and burst scheduling do not perform any consolidation.

6.3 Memory access granularity

The access granularity is the product of burst length and the data width of a channel, which is usually equal to the size of a cache line. There are a few works that improve memory system performance by changing the memory access granularity. To be compatible with DDR2, DDR3 supports BC4 (Burst Chop 4) mode [3], in which only half of a cache line data are transferred in four bursts and the other half data are masked. Fine-grained access (FG) of read and write requests is proposed by utilizing the idea of sub-ranked memory, such as Convey's S/G DIMM [9], HP's MC-DIMM [5, 6], and Mini-Rank [36]. FG is based on the observation that only a fraction of data transferred between cache line and memory is actually used. FG utilizes the rest bandwidth to serve other requests in parallel. BC4, FG, and DWC all change the number of data blocks transferred in one command. However, DWC differs from them in two aspects. First, both BC4 and FG do not identify whether the cache line data is modified or not when they are written back to memory. In contrast, DWC only writes the modified data. Second, both BC4 and FG change the memory access granularity of one command, while DWC preserves the memory access granularity by actually consolidating multiple writes in BL bursts.

7. CONCLUSION

With the recent development of emerging non-volatile memories, PCM is promising to become an alternative main memory. However, its long write latency raises a challenging issue for the adoption of PCM in main memory. In this paper, we propose dynamic write consolidation, namely DWC, to improve PCM memory system performance while reducing its energy consumption. DWC identifies unmodified data blocks in cache line and avoids sending these data. By exploiting the burst writes of the unmodified data, DWC consolidates multiple writes into one write command. By doing so, DWC can process multiple writes within BL bursts, which effectively reduces queuing time for both read and write requests. Moreover, DWC reduces the average data transfer time as well as the average write latency from the row buffer to memory array. We conduct an extensive evaluation on DWC to show its efficiency. Furthermore, we show the efficiency of DWC under varying memory system configurations, such as queue depth, page size, LLC size, and LLC replacement policy. On the other hand, although DWC requires changes to cache hierarchy, memory controller, and memory chips, we show that DWC incurs low implementation overhead in terms of area and power.

8. ACKNOWLEDGMENTS

We are grateful to the anonymous reviewers for their valuable comments. This work is supported in part by National Basic Research Program of China under grant No.2011CB302502, National Science Foundation of China under grants No.61379042, 61221062, and 61202063, Huawei Research Program YB2013090048, and the Strategic Priority Research Program of the Chinese Academy of Sciences under grant no. XDA06010401.

9. REFERENCES

[1] Linked list traversal micro-benchmark. http://www.cs.illinois.edu/homes/zilles/llubenchmark.html.

[2] Standard performance evaluation corporation. SPEC CPU 2006. http://www.spec.org/cpu2006/.

[3] DDR3 SDRAM Standard JESD79-3F, 2010. http://www.jedec.org/standards-documents/docs/jesd-79-3d.

[4] PIDS, ITRS, 2012. http://www.itrs.net/Links/2012ITRS/Home2012.htm.

[5] J. H. Ahn, N. P. Jouppi, C. Kozyrakis, J. Leverich, and R. S. Schreiber. Future scaling of processor-memory interfaces. In SC, 2009.

[6] J.-H. Ahn, J. Leverich, R. Schreiber, and N. Jouppi. Multicore DIMM: an energy efficient memory module with independently controlled DRAMs. Computer Architecture Letters, 2009.

[7] F. Bedeschi, R. Fackenthal, C. Resta, E. M. Donze, M. Jagasivamani, E. C. Buda, F. Pellizzer, D. W. Chow, A. Cabrini, G. Calvi, et al. A bipolar-selected phase change memory featuring multi-level cell storage. IEEE Journal of Solid-State Circuits, 2009.

[8] N. Binkert, B. Beckmann, G. Black, S. K. Reinhardt, A. Saidi, A. Basu, J. Hestness, D. R. Hower, T. Krishna, S. Sardashti, R. Sen, K. Sewell, M. Shoaib, N. Vaish, M. D. Hill, and D. A. Wood. The gem5 simulator. SIGARCH Comput. Archit. News, 2011.

[9] T. Brewer. Instruction set innovations for the Convey HC-1 computer. IEEE Micro, 2010.

[10] S. Cho and H. Lee. Flip-N-Write: a simple deterministic technique to improve PRAM write performance, energy and endurance. In MICRO, 2009.

[11] A. Ferreira, M. Zhou, S. Bock, B. Childers, R. Melhem, and D. Mosse. Increasing pcm main memory lifetime. In DATE, 2010.

[12] L. Jiang, B. Zhao, Y. Zhang, J. Yang, and B. Childers. Improving write operations in MLC phase change memory. In HPCA, 2012.

[13] M. Joshi, W. Zhang, and T. Li. Mercury: A fast and energy-efficient multi-level cell based phase change memory system. In HPCA, 2011.

[14] B. C. Lee, E. Ipek, O. Mutlu, and D. Burger. Architecting phase change memory as a scalable DRAM alternative. In ISCA, 2009.

[15] H. G. Lee, S. Baek, C. Nicopoulos, and J. Kim. An energy- and performance-aware DRAM cache architecture for hybrid DRAM/PCM main memory systems. In ICCD, 2011.

[16] Y. Lee, S. Kim, S. Hong, and J. Lee. Skinflint DRAM system: Minimizing DRAM chip writes for low power. In HPCA, 2013.

[17] C. Lefurgy, K. Rajamani, F. Rawson, W. Felter, M. Kistler, and T. W. Keller. Energy management for commercial servers. Computer, 2003.

[18] K. Lepak and M. Lipasti. Silent stores for free. In MICRO, 2000.

[19] K. M. Lepak and M. H. Lipasti. On the value locality of store instructions. In ISCA, 2000.

[20] S. Li, D. H. Yoon, K. Chen, J. Zhao, J. H. Ahn, J. B. Brockman, Y. Xie, and N. P. Jouppi. MAGE: adaptive granularity and ECC for resilient and power efficient memory systems. In SC, 2012.

[21] Z. Li, R. Zhou, and T. Li. Exploring high-performance and energy proportional interface for phase change memory systems. In HPCA, 2013.

[22] K. Lim, P. Ranganathan, J. Chang, C. Patel, T. Mudge, and S. Reinhardt. Understanding and designing new server architectures for emerging warehouse-computing environments. In ISCA, 2008.

[23] N. Muralimanohar, R. Balasubramonian, and N. P. Jouppi. CACTI 6.0: A tool to model large caches. Technical Report HPL-2009-85, HP Laboratories, 2009.

[24] M. K. Qureshi, M. M. Franceschini, A. Jagmohan, and L. A. Lastras. PreSET: Improving performance of phase change memories by exploiting asymmetry in write times. In ISCA, 2012.

[25] M. K. Qureshi, M. M. Franceschini, L. A. Lastras-Montaño, and J. P. Karidis. Morphable memory system: a robust architecture for exploiting multi-level phase change memories. In ISCA, 2010.

[26] M. K. Qureshi, M. M. Franceschini, and L. A. Lastras-Montano. Improving read performance of phase change memories via write cancellation and write pausing. In HPCA, 2010.

[27] L. E. Ramos, E. Gorbatov, and R. Bianchini. Page placement in hybrid memory systems. In ICS, 2011.

[28] J. Rice. Micron announces availability of phase change memory for mobile devices, 2012. http://investors.micron.com/releasedetail.cfm?ReleaseID=692563.

[29] S. Rixner, W. J. Dally, U. J. Kapasi, P. Mattson, and J. D. Owens. Memory access scheduling. In ISCA, 2000.

[30] P. Rosenfeld, E. Cooper-Balis, and B. Jacob. DRAMSim2: A cycle accurate memory system simulator. Computer Architecture Letters, 2011.

[31] S. Sardashti and D. A. Wood. Unifi: Leveraging non-volatile memories for a unified fault tolerance and idle power management technique. In ICS, 2012.

[32] J. Shao and B. Davis. A burst scheduling access reordering mechanism. In HPCA, 2007.

[33] A. N. Udipi, N. Muralimanohar, N. Chatterjee, R. Balasubramonian, A. Davis, and N. P. Jouppi. Rethinking DRAM design and organization for energy-constrained multi-cores. In ISCA, 2010.

[34] D. H. Yoon, M. K. Jeong, and M. Erez. Adaptive granularity memory systems: a tradeoff between storage efficiency and throughput. In ISCA, 2011.

[35] J. Yue and Y. Zhu. Accelerating write by exploiting PCM asymmetries. In HPCA, 2013.

[36] H. Zheng, J. Lin, Z. Zhang, E. Gorbatov, H. David, and Z. Zhu. Mini-rank: Adaptive DRAM architecture for improving memory power efficiency. In MICRO, 2008.

[37] P. Zhou, B. Zhao, J. Yang, and Y. Zhang. A durable and energy efficient main memory using phase change memory technology. In ISCA, 2009.

Palm: Easing the Burden of Analytical Performance Modeling

Nathan R. Tallent and Adolfy Hoisie
Pacific Northwest National Laboratory
{tallent,Adolfy.Hoisie}@pnnl.gov

ABSTRACT

Analytical (predictive) application performance models are critical for diagnosing performance-limiting resources, optimizing systems, and designing machines. Creating models, however, is difficult because they must be both accurate and concise. To ease the burden of performance modeling, we developed Palm (Performance and Architecture Lab Modeling tool), a modeling tool that combines top-down (human-provided) semantic insight with bottom-up static and dynamic analysis. First, Palm provides a source code modeling annotation language for abstracting or expressing complexity. Second, Palm generates hierarchical models according to well-defined rules. Since a model's hierarchy is defined by static and dynamic source code structure, there is a link between a program's organization and its model. By coordinating models and source code, Palm's models are 'first-class' and reproducible. Third, Palm incorporates measurements to focus attention, represent constant behavior, and validate models. We discuss generating models for three different applications.

Categories and Subject Descriptors

C.4 [**Performance of Systems**]: Modeling techniques; I.6.5 [**Simulation and Modeling**]: Model Development—*Modeling methodologies*

Keywords

application modeling; model development; annotation languages; Palm

1. INTRODUCTION

Application performance modeling is an important methodology for diagnosing performance-limiting resources, optimizing application and system performance, and designing machines [7]. There are several ways to model a parallel application, ranging from discrete-event simulations to queuing models. One of the most important classes of application models is the *analytical model*, a quantitative and accurate mapping of an application's characteristics onto system resources with the goal of explaining and predicting the execution time. Unlike a simulation, an analytical model does not divide an application's execution into discrete events. Unlike a queuing model, which takes a system-level view, an analytical model parameterizes an application's constituent parts.

Creating analytical performance models is a complex task that requires the expertise of a performance analyst. A performance model of a parallel program is a model of the execution's critical path. Sometimes, it is challenging to identify the critical path. Furthermore, it is often desirable to capture observed performance using as few parameters as possible. Because of these challenges, application developers whose expertise is elsewhere frequently forgo the insight that an analytical model could provide.

To ease the burden of creating analytical application models, we developed the Palm modeling tool (Performance and Architecture Lab Modeling tool). Palm combines top-down (human-provided) modeling insight with bottom-up static and dynamic analysis of parallel executions. Combining such top-down and bottom-up information corresponds to two of the most important strategies for rapidly developing models: (a) using an analytical function to either abstract or detail components of the critical path; and (b) using performance measurements to focus attention, represent constant behavior, and validate models.

The most important precursor to our work is Alam and Vetter's Modeling Assertions (MA) [4,5]. One way of viewing Palm's contribution is by considering the *form* of a model. Consider an application where Palm's model $\mathcal{M}$ is:

$$\mathcal{M} = \mathcal{T}_1 + \mathcal{M}_{\text{solve}}(2)$$
$$\mathcal{M}_{\text{solve}}(v) = \begin{cases} n\left(\phi(p, \mathcal{T}_{\text{stage}}) + \mathcal{M}_{\text{solve}}(1)\right) & v = 2 \\ \dots & v = 1 \end{cases} \quad (1)$$
$$\phi(p, t) = (p - 1)t$$

Here, $\mathcal{T}_1$ models the time for setup and $\mathcal{M}_{\text{solve}}$ models the pipelined solver. The solver iterates n times. The function ϕ models pipeline fill, where p is the number of pipeline stages and t is the time for a pipeline stage. In contrast, MA's representation of the same model is:

$$t_1 + n\left((p - 1)t_{\text{stage}}\right) + \dots) \quad (2)$$

where t_1 and t_{stage} are provided by the modeler. At first glance, Palm's model utilizes functional abstraction and in-

ICS'14, June 10–13 2014, Munich, Germany.
Copyright 2014 ACM 978-1-4503-2642-1/14/06 ...$15.00.
http://dx.doi.org/10.1145/2597652.2597683.

tegrates performance measurements with models. To enable a tool to generate models in this form, we make several contributions to modeling state-of-the-art.

First, to express high-level modeling insight, Palm provides a modeling annotation language for application source code (§3). Palm's modeling annotations are similar to OpenMP [20] directives in that they have a formal syntax and semantics; they are dissimilar in that Palm's annotations do not affect but (analytically) describe an application's execution. Source code annotations are interesting for several reasons. Annotations provides a mechanism to move from descriptive measurements to predictive (analytical) insight for a block of code. Further, annotations elevate models to first-class citizenship by coordinating modeling insight with source code. The sans serif subscripts in Eq. 1 are annotation names, formally linking source code blocks with model terms. Thus, the blocks of code annotated solve and stage are represented by M_{solve} and T_{stage}, respectively. The practical benefits of citizenship are significant because the inertia of applications is frequently larger than the inertia of an individual machine. Most applications change relatively slowly; they are the product of years of labor whose cumulative costs dwarf the cost of a machine. When an application does change, one can adapt the corresponding model by modifying only the annotations that relate to the change. Finally, annotations facilitate model reproducibility. That is, given annotated source code and a representative execution profile, Palm will generate the same model. For all these reasons, we believe that the effort invested in modeling annotations will pay dividends.

Second, Palm's models automatically integrate measurements (§4). Eq. 1 shows examples of both named (T_{stage}) and anonymous (T_1) measurements, which correspond to annotated and unannotated portions of the execution, respectively. To collect accurate and detailed measurements, Palm uses static analysis to minimize the dynamic impact of annotation instances within Palm's runtime system. One can envision using additional static analysis to supplement annotations or to draw implications from them.

Third, Palm formally links models and measurements. Because measurements are a type of model, Eq. 1 uses the same font for measurements (T) and models (M). Palm's annotation language provides a forward-reference mechanism so that (to-be-generated) models can be used as values in a modeling expression. As a result, a modeler can use T_{stage} — represented only by an annotation — as a well-defined value to pass to the function ϕ (Eq. 1).

Finally, Palm formally links functions and models (§6). Functions unify Palm's modeling annotations and synthesized models: not only can Palm's models use arbitrary functions (ϕ), but a model (M) is a special kind of function. Because models *use* functions (ϕ in Eq. 1), Palm's three annotations are more expressive than the several MA assertions, whose expressions use *variables*. Modelers can build libraries of modeling functions and model with respect to an arbitrarily simple or complex virtual machine. Because models *are* functions, Palm's models are hierarchical, i.e., compositions of other models (functions). Hierarchy is important for understanding and debugging larger models. Palm uses functions to generate models that correspond to the static and dynamic structure of annotations (§5). Furthermore, because measurements are a kind of model, it is possible to define models recursively (M_{solve}).

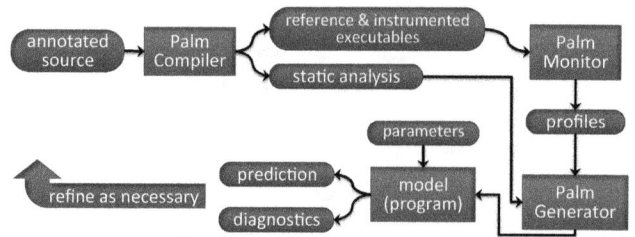

Figure 1: Workflow of the Palm modeling tool.

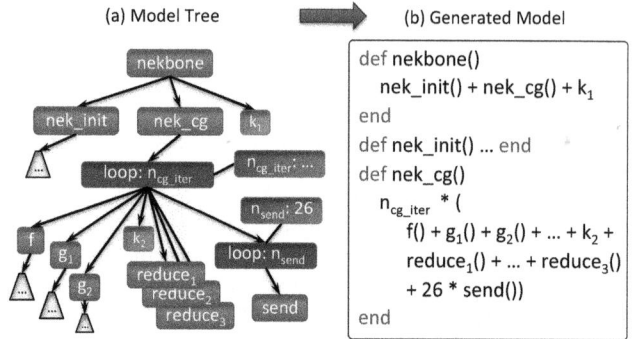

Figure 2: Palm's Generator uses (a) a Model Tree, to synthesize (b) a model (a program).

We describe (§7) modeling Nekbone [11] (weak scaling), GTC [17] (weak scaling), and Sweep3D [1] (weak and strong scaling), three very different applications. For Nekbone and GTC, it is sufficient to use relatively simple annotations. More sophisticated annotations are required for Sweep3D's critical path. We conclude that Palm automates several tasks that would otherwise be manual and can generate models whose forms *match* manually constructed models.

2. OVERVIEW AND DESIGN PRINCIPLES

Palm is based on the following observations. Assume an interest in modeling resource consumption (i.e., monotonically increasing values such as execution time). An analytical performance model of a parallel program is a model of program statement instances along the execution's critical path. To describe the critical path, one can map each statement instance to the amount of resources (e.g., time) it consumes. To *analytically* describe (model) the critical path, one can parameterize each statement instance to form sub-models, group similar sub-models, and sum the result.

Figure 1 shows Palm's workflow. The input is source code annotated with Palm modeling annotations. The most important annotation names and models an instance of a block of code. Given annotated source code, the Palm Compiler produces executables and the Palm Monitor collects a representative performance profile. The Palm Generator synthesizes a model based on the static and dynamic mapping of annotations to program behavior. Figure 2 shows the Palm Generator synthesizing a model for Nekbone [11] (cf. §7.1). The model (a program) is a hierarchical composition of annotation functions, synthesized functions, statistics for runtime values, and performance measurements.

Palm is designed to *facilitate a divide-and-conquer modeling strategy*. Palm enables divide-and-conquer by representing an execution with a hierarchical data structure called a Model Tree, shown in Figure 2(a). Similar to a loop calling context tree (CCT) [24], a Model Tree represents the static and dynamic structure of Palm's source code annotations. Because the Model Tree contains representative profiling measurements, its structure naturally highlights the most important parts of an application's execution. A blue node in the Figure represents a model for that subtree. A red node represents several instances of a model. The subscripts on nodes g and reduce distinguish between distinct calling contexts. Gray nodes are measurement constants for unannotated computation, derived from profiles. White trapezoids are omitted subtrees.

Figure 2(b) summarizes a generated model. The model is a *program*, expressed here in Ruby. Because a Model Tree is hierarchical, Palm's models are hierarchical: each function in the model corresponds to a blue model node in the Model Tree. The model's nekbone and nek_cg functions show how Model Tree nodes are composed using addition and multiplication.

To obtain a prediction, one executes the generated model with parameters. Palm's models can optionally generate diagnostics. The modeler may then choose to refine the modeling annotations and generate another model. As long as measurements either (a) account for a small percentage of the execution or (b) remain constant with respect to model predictions, there is no need to invest more human effort to model the corresponding source code. Once the model is satisfactory, one can perform 'what ifs' by changing parameters or redefining (the generated) model functions.

Palm has been designed to *make the simple easy and the difficult possible*. That is, it provides convenience within a framework that is fully generic. For generality, we designed Palm's annotation language and models around functions. One can use functional abstraction to make models as simple or as sophisticated as desired. For convenience, Palm's annotations assist modeling the critical path. For instance, Palm can capture input values to reduce degrees of freedom and constrain irregularity. In Figure 2(a), the Model Tree's brown nodes are runtime values. As shown by node n_{send}, one can specify a statistic (e.g., average or maximum) to represent varying program values over different instances within *and* across an execution's threads.

3. MODELING LANGUAGE

A Palm user controls the modeling process through the source code annotations summarized in Figure 3(a). The purpose of the annotations is not to affect but to analytically describe the execution of a region of source code. Figure 3(b–c) shows an example of annotated source code for Sweep3D [1], a neutron transport benchmark with pipeline parallelism. There are two basic modeling annotations, def and model, that are sufficient for representing any analytical model. We discuss them in reverse order.

The purpose of the model annotation is to model source code execution. The model annotation names or classifies (*class*) an arbitrary code block and associates with it an optional modeling expression (*expression*); cf. Figure 3(a). The modeling expression models the resource consumption of one instance of that code block. Currently our models focus on time, but one could specify other metrics using the optional *metric* specifier. Figure 3(b), line 11, shows an example of modeling an instance of Sweep3D's solver. It is

often useful to group models into the same class. Figure 3(c) lines 5 and 8 group two distinct communication operations into the same (pipeline) wait class. model annotations have static scope and may be statically nested. If a modeling expression is omitted, the Palm Generator automatically synthesizes one from the dynamic model instances invoked by statements within the annotation's scope.

The def annotation defines a modeling variable or function that may be used by any other annotation. A modeling *variable* typically names important model parameters or captures useful program constants such as per-rank problem size for weak-scaling. Figure 3(b) lines 1–3 define several modeling variables. A modeling *function* enables arbitrary abstraction. Modeling functions are often used to define an abstract machine, such as an interconnect model that predicts message transfer time given message size and distance. Functions can also represent previously validated models for application kernels. Figure 3(b) lines 4–9 define functions that represent the Sweep3D model of Kerbyson et al. [13,15]; our model uses two of those functions (lines 8–9). If convenient, one may place common modeling functions in a modeling library rather than source code. Unlike, model annotations, a def annotation does not introduce scope.

A third annotation, the loop annotation, is used to conveniently represent multiple instances of a model. That is, the loop annotation factors a common loop-trip-count expression from several model annotations. Thus, the loop annotation expression models the number of loop-body instances, not the loop body itself. This annotation's *class* assigns a (possibly non-unique) name to the expression. The loop annotation's static scoping rules are identical to those of the model annotation. Figure 3(c) shows nested model and loop annotations modeling Sweep3D's computational pipeline with wait, grind (compute), and post stages.

Annotations interact with three distinct namespaces, the def-namespace, model-namespace, and the program's namespace. The def-namespace contains the (statically unique) names created by def annotations. This namespace is globally scoped; and there is no need for forward declarations. (Although one could introduce additional static scoping, we have not found it to be helpful.) The model-namespace holds *instances* of a model annotation, grouped according to *class*. Like the def-namespace, it is globally scoped. Unlike the def-namespace, the model-namespace is populated by the data collected by the Palm Monitor.

Interactions with the def-namespace are straightforward. Any annotation's *expression* may refer to a def *name*. Thus, modeling expressions may refer to any modeling function; and a modeling function may refer to any modeling function.

Any annotation's *expression* may use a *program-value reference* to capture statistics for runtime program values. For example, a modeling variable frequently captures a program constant; a modeling expression may capture average message size; a loop annotation's expression typically captures a loop's trip count. Figure 3(c), line 5, shows an example capturing average message size (underlined). The Palm Generator creates a statistic for each program-value reference. The most common statistics are average and maximum.

Models interact with the model-namespace using the *model-class reference*. Recall that members of the model-namespace are placeholders for models synthesized by the Palm Generator. We would like to reference these synthesized models — e.g., to pass them to a modeling function

```
1  pal def name = expression
2  pal def name(args) = expression
3  pal model [metric] class [= expression]
4  pal endmodel
5  pal loop class = expression
6  pal endloop
```

Special *expression* syntax

program-value reference:
  ${scalar-expr}[{statistic}]
model-class reference:
  @{model-class}[{metric}]

```
1  !$pal def n_px = ${npe_i}
2  !$pal def n_pointx = ${n_pointx_gbl} / n_px
3  !$pal def n_py, n_pointy...
4  ! def sweep3d_mdl(g, p, s) = n_solve * (sweep3d(g, p) + s)
5  ! def sweep3d(g, p) = p_fill(g, p) + n_octant * p_octant(g, p) + p_drain(g, p)
6  ! def p_octant(g, p) = (n_sweep - 1) * p_stage(g, p)
7  ! def p_stage(g, p) = (g + (4 * p))
8  !$pal def p_fill(g, p) = (n_px + n_py - 1) * (g + 2 * p)
9  !$pal def p_drain(g, p) = (2 * n_px + 4 * n_py - 2) * (g + 2 * p)
10 !$pal loop n_solve = ... ! hide actual n_solve loop
11 !$pal model sweep = p_fill(@{grind}, @{post1}) + @{sweep} + \
12            p_drain(@{grind}, @{post1})
13   call sweep(...) ! sweep() is the right column
14 !$pal endmodel
15 !$pal endloop
```

```
1  !$pal loop n_octant = ...
2     DO diag = {ne→sw, se→nw, nw→se, sw→ne}
3  !$pal loop n_sweep = ${n_angles * n_zblock}
4     DO z_blk = 1, n_zblock
5  !$pal model wait = recv(${sz_x}{avg} * fp_sz)
6        call receive(sz_x, ew_neighbor, ...)
7  !$pal endmodel
8  !$pal model wait = recv(${sz_y} * fp_sz)
9        call receive(sz_y, ns_neighbor, ...)
10 !$pal endmodel
11 !$pal model grind = @{grind} * (n_pointx / ${n_ptx}) \
12            * (n_pointy / ${n_pty})
13        ! 200 LoC for block of size n_ptx * n_pty
14 !$pal endmodel
15 !$pal model post1 = send(${sz_x} * fp_sz)
16        call send(sz_x, ew_neighbor, ...)
17 !$pal endmodel
18        call send(sz_y, ns_neighbor, ...) ! hide 'model post'
19     END DO ! z_blk
20 !$pal endloop ! n_sweep
21     END DO ! diag
22 !$pal endloop ! n_octant
```

Figure 3: Palm modeling annotations. (a) The top-left inset summarizes annotation syntax. The (b) left and (c) right code listings summarize the annotations used to generate the Sweep3D [1] model in Figures 4 and 5.

or to build other models from them — but need a mechanism to statically name the model *instances*. A model-class reference solves this problem with what we call *anticipatory dynamic scoping*. Given an annotation with a reference to class c, anticipatory dynamic scoping means that c binds to all instances of c occurring during the execution of that annotation instance. The actual reference then evaluates to the sum of all the synthesized models to which c binds. An example of a model-class reference is shown in the sweep model (Figure 3(b), line 11). As the example indicates, we permit self references (underlined), i.e., defining a model in terms of its own synthesized model. The example's self-reference is critical for succinctly modeling Sweep3D's complex pipeline fill and drain dependency chains (see §7.3). The self reference in the grind model (Figure 3(c), line 11) makes it easy to succinctly model 200 lines of code (see §7.3). This model's expression simply scales a reference measurement.

4. ACCURATE MEASUREMENTS

Given annotated source code, the Palm Compiler generates two executables, a reference and instrumented executable (cf. Figure 1). The Palm Monitor, based on a modified version of HPCTOOLKIT [2, 24], monitors an execution of the reference and instrumented executables on a representative input, resulting in two sets of measurements. The two executables are a means for obtaining both accurate measurements and program-value statistics. To collect accurate measurements, we generate a reference executable designed to perform in the same way as an executable generated from unannotated source code. To collect program-value statistics, we generate an instrumented executable that contains the same object code as the reference executable, but with instrumentation inserted to collect runtime program values.

To collect accurate measurements, it is necessary to minimize the runtime impact of annotation instances. Consider a modeling annotation in a 'hot' code region. If this annotation requires runtime assistance, such as through a

library call, it will likely incur high overhead and distort measurements. To minimize the runtime impact of annotation instances in the reference executable, we use static analysis that eliminates the runtime impact of annotations without program-value references. Palm's model directives form a scope tree that statically partitions an application's source code. The Palm Compiler tags with the appropriate scope each program statement and its corresponding object code. The Palm Monitor uses HPCTOOLKIT's sampling-based techniques to collect call path profiles for the reference executable. The Palm Generator maps the static annotation structure of a source code function to its corresponding instances in the call path profile. Thus, if there is no need to collect program values, annotations incur no overhead and measurement overhead is typically less than 5%.

To collect program-value statistics, the Palm Monitor uses extensions to HPCTOOLKIT to collect (call path) value profiles for the instrumented executable. The instrumented executable contains the same object code as the reference executable, but with instrumentation to collect program values.

Given (a) our emphasis on accurate measurements and (b) the cumbrousness of two executables, it is interesting to ask whether there is a way to collect program values with only one executable. Two observations suggest that our two-binary solution is not appreciably different than potential solutions based on one binary. First, suppose we had one executable with a runtime switch; then, there is there is little difference in using two binaries because it is still necessary to use two different executions. Second, low-overhead measurement techniques based on asynchronous sampling will not work because important program values may not be sampled, especially if they occur in infrequently executed code (such as initialization).

5. GENERATING MODELS

The Palm Generator takes data collected by the Palm Monitor and produces a hierarchical model based on the

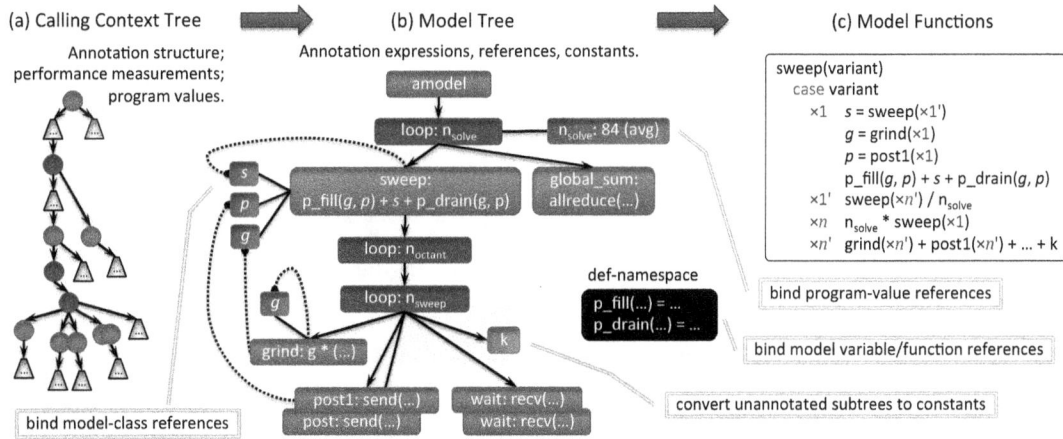

Figure 4: Generating a model. Given (a) a Calling Context Tree, the Palm Generator creates (b) a Model Tree that it uses to generate (c) synthesized modeling functions.

dynamic structure of annotation instances. The Generator first creates a data structure based on a loop calling context tree (CCT) [24]. Figure 4(a) shows a CCT, where interior nodes represent calling or annotation context for program computation. Leaves — hidden by the white trapezoids representing omitted subtrees — represent computation. Blue and red nodes represent model and loop annotations, respectively. This CCT has several important properties designed to facilitate the generation of hierarchical models. Each annotation node (a) is located within its dynamic and static annotation context; (b) is associated with the statement instances it directly invokes; and (c) is associated with its program-value statistics. By viewing the CCT at increasing depths (where the root is depth 0), one views the program execution at finer degrees of resolution. The CCT is relatively compact because program computation with the same context is merged.

Given a CCT, the Generator creates a Model Tree (Figure 4(b)) to represent the final generated model. The basic structure of the Model Tree is the CCT restricted to model and loop annotations. (Compare the blue/red nodes in Figures 4(a)–(b).) This Model Tree represents the Sweep3D annotations from Figure 3. The Model Tree's root node (amodel) represents the entire model. As shown in Figure 4(b), the final Model Tree converts unannotated subtrees to measurement constants, binds def-namespace references to their definitions, binds model-class references, and binds program-value references.

The Generator uses the Model Tree to synthesize modeling functions for each model annotation. The modeling function for sweep is shown in Figure 4(c). Unlike the simplified example in Figure 2(b), sweep's synthesized function has four 'variants.' There are two reasons for the variants.

First, a model node in the Model Tree may represent two distinct modeling expressions. Consider the Model Tree's sweep node. The node has a modeling expression specified by the annotation in Figure 3(b), line 11. But the node simultaneously represents the expression implied by that node's subtree (which itself includes modeling expressions). A modeler may be interested in using either expression.

To navigate expression types and to permit recursive model-class references, Palm orders expressions by 'analyti-

cal content'. For a given model node x, the possible expression types are:

2. annotation expression from x (most analytical)

1. synthesized expression, from x's subtree, with at least one annotation expression

0. synthesized measurement constant from x's subtree

For generating models, Palm uses the two 'most analytical' expressions. Note that expression type 0 is always available (directly or indirectly) as a base case.

Second, there is a tension between (a) Palm's model expressions (that model one instance of a code block) and (b) accurate measurements. Measurement constants can be very important to models. Consider the Model Tree's grind node, which represents the Sweep3D pipeline's compute time. This node's (recursive) annotation expression explicitly requires an accurate measurement (cf. Figure 3(c), line 11). One possible way to compute the constant is to average measurements for each of grind's instances. Unfortunately, many model model instances complete in less than a millisecond. Using current measurement techniques it is difficult to collect accurate per-instance measurements at that level of precision while also collecting context-sensitive measurements. To maintain accuracy, the Palm Monitor collects measurements that aggregate over all (context-sensitive) instances in the execution. The Generator must therefore compose per-instance modeling expressions and multi-instance measurements. To do so, it generates per-instance models that are defined in terms of multi-instance models. For instance sweep variant $\times 1'$ (Figure 4(c)) divides "total cost of sweep" by "number of sweep invocations."

Given a model node in the Model Tree, the Generator synthesizes a modeling function. Each function has up to four variants, as shown in Figure 4(c). Variants $\times 1$ and $\times 1'$ model one instance of the annotation using, respectively, the annotation expression and synthesized expression. Variants $\times n$ and $\times n'$ model multiple (all) instances of the same respective expressions. To improve accuracy, the Generator uses two heuristics. First, to minimize numerical error from floating point division, the Generator prefers the $\times n'$ variant over the $\times 1'$ variant. Second, it distributes loop expressions.

That is, with per-instance and multi-instance variants, it is possible to represent loop nodes in two ways: (a) the product of a loop-instance expression and per-instance loop-body model (factored expression) or (b) a multi-instance loop-body model (distributed expression). The Generator defaults to the latter, which corresponds to preferring multi-instance variants.

The definitions of the $\times 1$ and $\times n$ variants are based on a model node's modeling expression, which models one instance of an annotation. (If the annotation does not have a modeling expression, these variants default to the definitions for the $\times 1'$ and $\times n'$ variants, respectively.) For the $\times 1$ variant, it is necessary to create the modeling expression environment, which binds program-value and model-class references to values. Figure 4(c) shows bindings for sweep's three model-class references (cf. Figure 5, lines 18–19). The bindings for grind and post1 default to the preferred per-instance variant ($\times 1$). The binding for sweep must use the $\times 1'$ variant because it is recursive.

To generate the $\times n$ variant, modeling all instances in a context, we multiply the $\times 1$ variant by the product of all ancestor loop expressions in the Model Tree. Thus, sweep's $\times n$ model expression includes n_{solve} (cf. Figure 5, line 21).

To generate the $\times 1'$ variant, we use the $\times n'$ variant divided by the product of all ancestor loop expressions. Thus, sweep's $\times 1'$ model expression also includes n_{solve} (cf. Figure 5, line 20).

To generate the $\times n'$ variant, we sum the models for that node's *model frontier*. The model frontier for a node x is defined by the set of nodes that represents the first model annotation on each distinct path from x to a leaf. The set is then supplemented with the first non-annotated node on each descendant path such that the model frontier completely 'covers' x's leaves. (That is, each leaf of x's subtree has an ancestor node in the model frontier; and no node in the model frontier is a (strict) ancestor of another node in the model frontier.) The resulting expression is a composition of modeling functions and measurement constants. sweep's model frontier is comprised of three model nodes (grind, post1, wait) and the constant node k (cf. Figure 5, line 22).

6. FUNCTION-ORIENTED MODELS

An analytical model is a program designed for rapid execution. By *rapid execution,* we mean that our models evaluate 'directly' instead of requiring simulators or numerical solvers (cf. POEMS [3]). Any convenient language may be used to represent the model. For example, a scripting language may be convenient for off-line model evaluation. For on-line evaluation (e.g., to inform a run-time decision), object code may be preferable. Because this work focuses on the former case, we generate models in Ruby. We also use Ruby syntax for modeling annotation expressions, but any convenient syntax could be used.

Figure 5 shows an example of a model for Sweep3D [1]. The model was generated from the modeling annotations in Figure 3. The model is represented by a Ruby class, which can be instantiated and evaluated with different parameters (lines 43ff.). Ruby class member functions represent modeling variables (lines 5ff.), modeling functions (lines 9ff.), and synthesized modeling functions (lines 12ff.). (In Figure 5, model variants are represented by Ruby symbols and are therefore prefixed with a colon.)

Generated models have several important properties. First, a model is function-oriented. Each def expression becomes a function or variable definition (where a variable is a function with no arguments); each model and loop expression instance becomes a synthesized function. Thus, the notion of a modeling function unifies Palm's annotations and generated models, enabling model abstraction and reuse. Second, a model is hierarchical because it is an arithmetic expression of modeling functions that themselves are expressions of modeling functions. Third, a model preserves the static naming and nesting structure of annotations. This enables one to name important code blocks (without a modeling expression) and associate model expressions with their corresponding source-code annotations. Fourth, a model contains two types of constants: statistics (for program-value references) and measurements (for portions of the dynamic call structure not represented by annotations).

Each generated model can optionally generate diagnostic reports. We construct a diagnostic report by capturing an expression tree during model evaluation. To build the evaluation expression tree, our models capture values (and operators) from all synthesized model functions. The Contribution Report shows the contribution of each annotation to the overall model prediction. This report makes it easy to identify 'dominant' annotations and to determine whether annotations have appropriate coverage. If unnamed constants contribute significantly to the overall model prediction, then the corresponding source should be annotated.

The Error Report shows the residuals of each annotation's actual prediction with respect to its expected prediction, where *expected* is defined by measurement data. The Error Report is based on the fact that the Generator embeds measurements for each model function in the generated model. The Error report is especially useful for calibrating a model and assessing results of experimentation.

The function-oriented nature of our models makes experimentation easy. Once a model is generated, it easy to inspect the Contribution or Error reports and evaluate the model with different parameters. A common model use case is to evaluate with different machine definitions. Typically, one stores machine definitions in a library so that it is easy to evaluate the model against several different machine instances or even several different machines. Another use case is to experiment with application changes. For changes that do not affect an application's critical path, this experiment involves changing the definition the modeling function that corresponds to the annotated source code.

7. CASE STUDIES

In this section, we describe generating weak or strong models for three very different applications. We generated the models using PNNL's PIC cluster (which pairs dual-Interlagos nodes with an InfiniBand interconnect), Intel's compiler, and MVAPICH2. We used the Palm Monitor to collect representative measurements at 64 cores utilizing 16 cores/node. We present our results in three ways. First, we demonstrate that Palm can elegantly represent validated models, where the most direct evidence is the Sweep3D example of Figures 3 and 5. Second, we describe modeling tasks that Palm automates. Third, we validate our models' predictions through 2048 cores. Since Palm's models match previously validated models, collecting more data would not not have offered additional insight.

```
1  class Model
2    def initialize(exeEnv, paramsGbl = nil) ... end
3    def eval(paramsLcl = nil) ...amodel()... end

4    # model variables; from def annotations
5    def n_px (@n_px) end
6    def n_pointx (@n_pointx_gbl / n_px) end
7    def n_py, n_pointy, n_solve, n_octant, n_sweep, ...

8    # model functions; from def annotations
9    def p_fill(g, p) (n_px + n_py − 1) * (g + 2 * p) end
10   def p_drain(g, p) = (2 * n_px + 4 * n_py − 2) * (g + 2 * p) end

11   # synthesized model functions; from model annotations
12   def amodel(variant = :×n)
13     case variant ...
14     when :×n, :×n′  sweep() + global_sum() + 5.26e5 end
15   end

16   def sweep(variant = :×n)
17     case variant
18     when :×1   g = grind(:×1) ; p = post1(:×1) ; s = sweep(:×1′)
19                p_fill(g, p) + s + p_drain(g, p)
20     when :×1′  sweep(:×n′) / n_solve
21     when :×n   n_solve * sweep(:×1)
22     when :×n′  grind() + post1() + ... + 2.83e5 end
23   end
```

```
24   def grind(variant = :×n)
25     case variant
26     when :×1   g = grind(:×1) ; _n_ptx = 100.0 ; _n_pty = 100.0
27                g * (n_pointx / _n_ptx) * (n_pointy / _n_pty)
28     when :×1′  grind(:×n′) / (n_solve * n_octant * n_sweep)
29     when :×n   (n_solve * n_octant * n_sweep) * grind(:×1)
30     when :×n′  22.5e6 end
31   end

32   def post1(variant = :×n)
33     case variant
34     when :×1   _sz_x = 1500 ; send(_sz_x * 8)
35     when :×1′  post1(:×n′) / (n_solve * n_octant * n_sweep)
36     when :×n   (n_solve * n_octant * n_sweep) * post1(:×1)
37     when :×n′  1.24e6 end
38   end

39   def global_sum(), wait(), ...

40   def send(sz) (@exeEnv.mpiMsgTime(sz)) end
41 end # class Model

42 # Evaluate model
43 require 'pal−machine−pic.rb' # machine library
44 model = Model.new(PAL::ExecutionPIC.new(...))
45 model.eval("@n_px = 32; @n_pointx_gbl = 1600; ...")
```

Figure 5: A model (Ruby program) generated from the annotations in Figure 3.

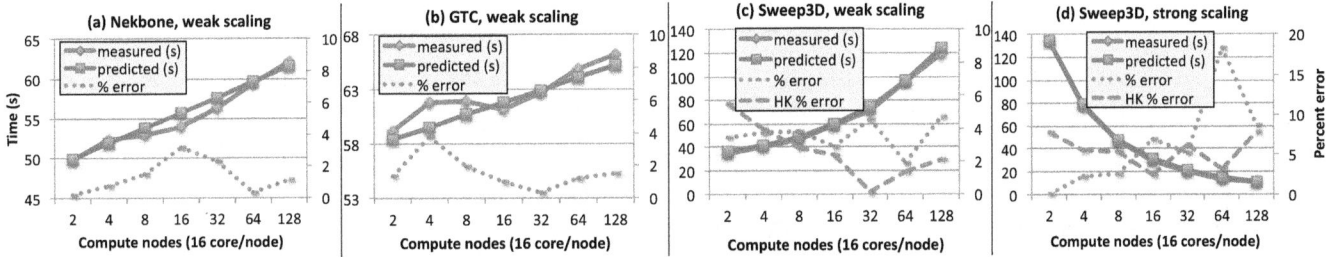

Figure 6: Validation of the models for (a) Nekbone; (b) GTC; and Sweep3D (c) weak and (d) strong scaling.

7.1 Nekbone

Nekbone [11] is a 'proxy application' for Nek5000 [12], an MPI-based scalable computational fluid dynamics solver based on the spectral element method and written in Fortran and C. As an iterative conjugate gradient solver, Nekbone uses a regular 3D decomposition of a 3D domain. On each iteration, a grid element within the domain uses a 'halo exchange' to communicate with all of its neighbors. A manually constructed and validated weak scaling model [14] of one Nekbone iteration has the form

$$t_{\text{local-computation}} + 3t_{\text{allreduce}} + 26t_{\text{send-recv}}$$

where t indicates time, where the middle term represents three synchronous collectives, and where the last term represents the halo exchange for the MPI rank with the most (26) neighbors.

Although Nekbone's weak scaling model is relatively simple, generating that model is not as easy as it might appear. To construct the model above, it is necessary to separate computation from communication. Because Nekbone inherits the modular code structure of Nek5000, the relationship of communication to computation is not apparent within the solver's source code. Second, it is necessary to model the critical path, the MPI rank with the most neighbors with respect to the 3D decomposition. Even if one understands Nekbone's decomposition, the precise implementa-

tion of the halo-exchange is not apparent. It turns out that an application-specific communication descriptor causes the custom communication library to use 26 MPI point-to-point messages. Third, it is necessary to collect accurate measurements for local computation that does not change with scale. Because of Nekbone's modular structure, simple measurement methods face the difficulties of locating the computation/communication boundary and avoiding overhead.

We adopted the following strategy to generate the Nekbone model summarized in Figure 2(b). The strategy is based on the observation that to model weak scaling for a given machine type, one should model (a) communication and (b) any computation that changes with scale. To avoid time-consuming inspection of Nekbone's code layers, we annotated Nekbone's communication library with modeling expressions similar to Figure 3(c), line 5. (One can easily envision inserting such annotations automatically using static analysis and a model template.) Because we do not expect communication contention to be significant, we used a simple LogGP-style [6, 9] communication model. To model the critical path, we used a program-value reference to capture the maximum number of messages generated by the halo-exchange code. For convenience, we used expressionless model annotations to name important parts of the serial computation and model them with named measurement constants. The model's validation results are shown in Figure 6(a).

Although the modeling strategy we adopted was simple, using Palm we were able to generate a weak scaling model whose form (Figure 2) *matches* the manually constructed analytical model given above. This shows that with relatively simple annotations, Palm is able to reduce relatively complex dynamic structure into a succinct analytic expression that captures weak scaling and that matches the human-generated model. Palm automates the laborious tasks of inspecting dynamic structure, capturing semantically meaningful statistics about the application, and collecting constants for local computation. Because of the ease of naming and reducing initialization code to constants, we modeled not just one iteration, but the entire application. Doing so involved an additional loop annotation to capture the number of iterations and an expressionless model annotation to name initialization code.

7.2 GTC

GTC [17] is a scalable 3D general geometry gyrokinetic particle code. As a particle-in-cell code using an unstructured grid, GTC's parallelism is quite different from Nekbone's. However, by adopting the modeling method used for Nekbone, the process of generating a weak-scaling model process was very similar. The resulting model matched a manually constructed and validated analytical model [10]. The model's validation results are shown in Figure 6(b).

7.3 Sweep3D

Sweep3D [1] is a neutron transport benchmark designed for Single Program Multiple Data (SPMD) execution. Sweep3D's deceptively simple code (summarized in Figure 3(c)) implements phased pipeline parallelism on a 2D grid, where receive and send operations correspond to waits and posts, respectively. During one phase, the pipeline's wavefront moves along a diagonal of the 2D processor grid. Figure 7 shows wavefronts moving along

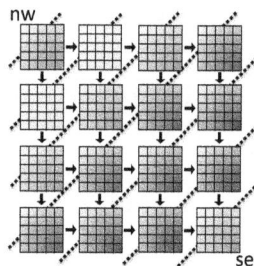

Figure 7: Sweep3D's nw→se wavefront.

the nw→se (northwest→southeast) diagonal. Developing a model of Sweep3D is challenging. During an execution, the pipeline's phase shifts so that the wavefront moves along the four (directed) diagonals of the grid. Depending on the phase shift, there are different amounts of pipeline drain. An accurate model must account for this pipeline drain.

To demonstrate Palm's capabilities, we developed a Sweep3D model that accounts for both weak and strong scaling. The model is shown in Figure 5 and is based on the annotations in Figure 3. The key to the weak-scaling model is joining an analytical description of pipeline fill and drain with a model of the pipeline's steady state. The key to the strong-scaling model is additionally modeling Sweep's grind (compute) loops.

To account for Sweep3D's pipeline, we used insight from a manually constructed Sweep3D model [13,15] to define modeling functions for pipeline fill and drain; they are shown in Figure 3(b), lines 8 and 9. The basic insight is that filling and draining the pipeline requires $O(n\_px + n\_py)$ stages,

where n_px and n_py are the dimensions of the 2D processor core grid; cf. the number of distinct wavefronts in Figure 7. (For a detailed accounting of drain between phase shifts, see Kerbyson et al. [15].) We then modeled an instance of Sweep3D's solver using the three-term expression shown in Figure 3(b), line 11. The respective meanings of the three terms are as follows: one initial pipeline fill, one solver computation, and four pipeline drains (one after each pipeline phase). Notice how model-class references enable one to express sweep's model in a divide-and-conquer fashion. The model-class references capture and name arbitrarily complex helper models. The modeler then treats those models as building blocks for other models.

For a weak scaling model, one may omit an expression for grind (Figure 3(c), line 11), resulting in very simple annotations. To account for strong scaling, it is necessary to model grind's scaling with different input sizes. Palm's annotation language enables us to succinctly model the 200 lines of code that implement grind. The model-class self-reference in the grind model (Figure 3(c), line 11) captures grind's behavior on a given n_ptx × n_pty input. We then simply scale the model relative to that original input.

The generated Sweep3D model is interesting for at least three reasons. First, it is notable that Palm's modeling language succinctly expresses the Sweep3D model. Second, Palm automates the task of collecting measurement constants for the manually constructed model. Third, the generated model incorporates less human insight than the manually generated analytical model. The manually generated model uses four additional modeling functions to model Sweep3D's driver and additional details of the pipeline (Figure 3(b), line 4–7). Palm automatically synthesizes approximations for those four additional modeling functions.

Figures 6(c)–(d) show weak and strong validation results for both our simple and the manually constructed (HK [13,15]) Sweep3D model. Both weak scaling models validate well. The HK strong scaling model is more consistent than our simplified model, but the latter's error rate is still quite good given that the relative importance of computation and pipeline bubbles inverts as the core count increases. It would be possible to make our model more precise by more carefully characterizing the pipeline and by accounting for the scaling of message sizes.

8. RELATED WORK

The closest work to ours is Alam and Vetter's Modeling Assertions (MA) [4,5]. MA's assertions mimic simple def, model, and loop annotations; and MA uses an execution trace to synthesize a modeling expression. Despite these similarities, there are important differences. As previously noted, Eqs. 1 and 2 (§1) summarize those differences. First, whereas MA's models are expressions of variables, Palm's models are expressions of functions. Consequently, Palm's models exploit functional abstraction. Palm's models are also hierarchical, preserving an application's static and dynamic structure. Second, Palm formally links functions, models, and measurements. As a result, much like Eq. 1, Palm can represent Sweep3D using the natural formulation "one pipeline fill, plus one sweep solve, plus four drains." Third, Palm automatically integrates accurate measurements into models. Finally, whereas MA's interface is a library call, Palm formally defines a modeling annotation language. An annotation language permits formal semantics. It eliminates artificial restrictions imposed by library calls (such as representing expressions with strings and limited annotation placement). A language also enables static analysis that minimizes the dynamic impact of annotation instances.

Modeling languages have been used for purposes other than model generation. Systems like Aspen [23], Pace [19], GROPHECY [18] are designed not to *create* but to *represent* and consume models. These systems assume that an application has already been rewritten in their respective modeling language. Therefore, they have nothing that corresponds to the Palm Generator. Of course, it is possible for a model generation tool to emit models in any of these modeling languages.

While our work uses dynamic analysis to assist generating *analytical* models, other tools use dynamic analysis to generate *trace-based* models. The essential difference between a trace-based model and an analytical model is that the latter is predictive whereas the former is (non-analytically) descriptive. For example, Snavely et al. model applications using traces of communication patterns and memory access patterns [22]. Wu et al. [25, 26] automatically generate communication microbenchmarks for SPMD applications. They then generate weak scaling communication models by replaying the communication benchmarks at different scales and fitting a curve through the results. An advantage of these tools is that they do not require source code changes and automate more tasks. A disadvantage is that their models are not analytical. To generate interesting analytical models, we use human insight expressed via annotations.

It is desirable to generate analytical models without requiring source code annotations. To find scalability bugs, Calotoiu et al. automatically generate asymptotic scaling models by fitting performance data to a 'canonical' set of scaling curves [8]. Because the technique focuses on asymptotic behavior, it is not designed to generate the more precise scalability models considered in this paper. Lee et al. use polynomial regression and neural networks to relate input parameters with outputs, ignoring application code [16]. Schindewolf et al. use static analysis to assist model generation [21]. A compiler directs the modeling process by (a) statically estimating dynamic instances of floating point, integer, and memory operations; (b) generating instrumentation to measure these values over several different executions; and (c) generating a model using curve-fitting, in this case quadratic programming. The POEMS [3] project used static and dynamic analysis to generate static and dynamic dependence graphs, respectively. Unfortunately, without manual intervention or human insight, these efforts typically generate useful models only in limited domains.

9. CONCLUSIONS

This paper describes Palm, a tool for generating analytical performance models. Palm combines top-down (human-provided) semantic insight with bottom-up static and dynamic analysis. Given annotated source code, Palm generates a model based on the static and dynamic mapping of annotations to program behavior. The model, which is itself a program, is a hierarchical composition of annotation functions, synthesized functions, statistics for runtime values, and performance measurements.

We describe generating weak scaling models for Nekbone [11], GTC [17], and Sweep3D [1], three very differ-

ent applications. In all cases, we match or closely match manually constructed and validated analytical models. Nekbone's and GTC's models use relatively simple annotations. Sweep3D's model requires more sophisticated annotations because of its complicated critical path. Yet, it is notable that (a) Palm's modeling language elegantly expresses the model and (b) Palm automates several modeling tasks.

We offer the following reflections on our results. First, we have shown that it is possible to model non-trivial critical paths using a combination of program-value statistics, model-class references, and modeling functions.

Second, our work has shown the importance of using modeling functions to unify the seemingly disjoint spaces of modeling annotations and generated models. Functions enable model expressiveness. Functions enable arbitrary abstraction across both spaces. Functions are a means of preserving annotation static and dynamic structure, a key mechanism for model feedback.

Third, pairing accurate and detailed measurements with synthesized modeling functions is a simple but especially effective model generation technique. Collecting accurate measurements automates the generation of modeling constants. Maintaining accurate measurements motivates synthesized modeling functions with multiple variants. Measurements also enable a model's Error Report, a tool for iterative model refinement.

Finally, our work has shown that using a modeling language to coordinate models and source code can be used to generate models that are 'first-class' and reproducible. Given an application, a set of annotations, and a representative execution environment, Palm will generate the same model. We believe this capability presents interesting possibilities for developing, distributing, and validating models.

Recently, we used Palm to generate a model for a benchmark that counts 'triangles' in an undirected graph. The benchmark randomly generates an input graph where edges are distributed according to a power law (a small number of vertices have most of the edges). The benchmark's critical path is dictated by the vertices with the most edges. We used Palm to capture program-value statistics about an important input graph and then converted those statistics to model parameters.

There are several interesting avenues for future work in model generation. We plan to explore energy and data movement models. We also plan to explore ways to use static analysis to assist modeling. Finally, it is important to develop more techniques that assist modeling an application's critical path across different inputs and different machines.

10. ACKNOWLEDGMENTS

We thank Kevin Barker, Darren Kerbyson, Harvey Wasserman, and Scott Pakin for helpful comments. This work was supported by the DOE Office of Science (ASCR), award number 62855 (Beyond the Standard Model). Pacific Northwest National Laboratory is operated by Battelle for the U.S. Department of Energy under contract DE-AC05-76RL01830.

11. REFERENCES

[1] Accelerated Strategic Computing Initiative. The ASCI Sweep3D Benchmark Code (2.2b). http://wwwc3.lanl.gov/pal/software/sweep3d/sweep3d_readme.html, December 1995.

[2] L. Adhianto, S. Banerjee, M. Fagan, M. Krentel, G. Marin, J. Mellor-Crummey, and N. R. Tallent. HPCToolkit: Tools for performance analysis of optimized parallel programs. *Concurr. Comput.: Pract. Exper.*, 22(6):685–701, 2010.

[3] V. S. Adve, R. Bagrodia, J. C. Browne, E. Deelman, A. Dube, E. N. Houstis, J. R. Rice, R. Sakellariou, D. J. Sundaram-Stukel, P. J. Teller, and M. K. Vernon. POEMS: End-to-end performance design of large parallel adaptive computational systems. *IEEE Trans. Softw. Eng.*, 26(11):1027–1048, 2000.

[4] S. Alam and J. Vetter. A framework to develop symbolic performance models of parallel applications. In *Proc. of the 20th IEEE Intl. Parallel and Distributed Processing Symp.*, page 8, 2006.

[5] S. R. Alam and J. S. Vetter. Hierarchical model validation of symbolic performance models of scientific kernels. In W. E. Nagel, W. V. Walter, and W. Lehner, editors, *Proc. of the 12th Intl. Euro-Par Conference*, volume 4128 of *Lecture Notes in Computer Science*, pages 65–77. Springer, 2006.

[6] A. Alexandrov, M. F. Ionescu, K. E. Schauser, and C. Scheiman. LogGP: Incorporating long messages into the LogP model — One step closer towards a realistic model for parallel computation. In *Proc. of the 7th ACM Symp. on Parallel Algorithms and Architectures*, pages 95–105, New York, NY, USA, 1995. ACM.

[7] K. J. Barker, K. Davis, A. Hoisie, D. J. Kerbyson, M. Lang, S. Pakin, and J. C. Sancho. Using performance modeling to design large-scale systems. *Computer*, 42(11):42–49, 2009.

[8] A. Calotoiu, T. Hoefler, M. Poke, and F. Wolf. Using automated performance modeling to find scalability bugs in complex codes. In *Proc. of the 2013 ACM/IEEE Conf. on Supercomputing*, pages 1–12, New York, NY, USA, 2013. ACM.

[9] D. Culler, R. Karp, D. Patterson, A. Sahay, K. E. Schauser, E. Santos, R. Subramonian, and T. von Eicken. LogP: Towards a realistic model of parallel computation. *SIGPLAN Not.*, 28(7):1–12, July 1993.

[10] K. Davis, K. Barker, and D. J. Kerbyson. Performance prediction via modeling: A case study of the ORNL Cray XT4 upgrade. *Parallel Processing Letters*, 19(4):619–640, December 2009.

[11] P. Fischer and K. Heisey. NEKBONE: Nek5000 mini-application, v. 1. https://cesar.mcs.anl.gov/content/software/thermal_hydraulics, April 2013.

[12] P. Fischer, J. Lottes, S. Kerkemeier, A. Obabko, and K. Heisey. Nek5000. http://nek5000.mcs.anl.gov, December 2012.

[13] A. Hoisie, O. Lubeck, and H. Wasserman. Performance and scalability analysis of Teraflop-scale parallel architectures using multidimensional wavefront applications. *Int. J. High Perform. Comput. Appl.*, 14(4):330–346, 2000.

[14] D. J. Kerbyson, D. S. G. Kevin J. Barker, D. Chen, J. R. Brunheroto, K. D. Ryu, G. Chiu, and A. Hoisie. Tracking the performance evolution of Blue Gene systems. In *Proc. of the 2013 Intl. Supercomputing Conference*, 2013.

[15] D. J. Kerbyson, M. Lang, and S. Pakin. Adapting wave-front algorithms to efficiently utilize systems with deep communication hierarchies. *Parallel Computing*, 37(9):550–561, 2011.

[16] B. C. Lee, D. M. Brooks, B. R. de Supinski, M. Schulz, K. Singh, and S. A. McKee. Methods of inference and learning for performance modeling of parallel applications. In *Proc. of the 10th ACM SIGPLAN Symp. on Principles and Practice of Parallel Programming*, pages 249–258, New York, NY, USA, 2007. ACM.

[17] Z. Lin, S. Ethier, and J. Lewandowski. Gyrokinetic Toroidal Code. http://phoenix.ps.uci.edu/GTC/, 2010.

[18] J. Meng, V. Morozov, K. Kumaran, V. Vishwanath, and T. Uram. GROPHECY: GPU performance projection from CPU code skeletons. In *Proc. of the 2011 ACM/IEEE Conf. on Supercomputing*, 2011.

[19] G. R. Nudd, D. J. Kerbyson, E. Papaefstathiou, S. C. Perry, J. S. Harper, and D. V. Wilcox. Pace: A toolset for the performance prediction of parallel and distributed systems. *Int. J. High Perform. Comput. Appl.*, 14(3):228–251, 2000.

[20] OpenMP Architecture Review Board. OpenMP API, v. 4.0. http://www.openmp.org/mp-documents/OpenMP4.0.0.pdf, July 2013.

[21] M. Schindewolf, D. Kramer, and M. Cintra. Compiler-directed performance model construction for parallel programs. In C. Müller-Schloer, W. Karl, and S. Yehia, editors, *Architecture of Computing Systems (ARCS 2010)*, volume 5974 of *Lecture Notes in Computer Science*, pages 187–198. Springer, 2010.

[22] A. Snavely, L. Carrington, N. Wolter, J. Labarta, R. Badia, and A. Purkayastha. A framework for performance modeling and prediction. In *Proc. of the 2002 ACM/IEEE Conf. on Supercomputing*, Los Alamitos, CA, USA, 2002. IEEE Computer Society.

[23] K. L. Spafford and J. S. Vetter. Aspen: A domain specific language for performance modeling. In *Proc. of the 2012 ACM/IEEE Conf. on Supercomputing*, Los Alamitos, CA, USA, 2012. IEEE Computer Society.

[24] N. R. Tallent, L. Adhianto, and J. M. Mellor-Crummey. Scalable identification of load imbalance in parallel executions using call path profiles. In *Proc. of the 2010 ACM/IEEE Conf. on Supercomputing*, Washington, DC, USA, Nov. 2010. IEEE Computer Society.

[25] X. Wu and F. Mueller. ScalaExtrap: Trace-based communication extrapolation for SPMD programs. In *Proc. of the 16th ACM SIGPLAN Symp. on Principles and Practice of Parallel Programming*, pages 113–122, New York, NY, USA, 2011. ACM.

[26] X. Wu, F. Mueller, and S. Pakin. Automatic generation of executable communication specifications from parallel applications. In *Proc. of the 2011 ACM/IEEE Conf. on Supercomputing*, pages 12–21, New York, NY, USA, 2011. ACM.

An End-to-End Analysis of File System Features on Sparse Virtual Disks

Ruijin Zhou
University of Florida
Gainesville, Florida, USA
zhourj@ufl.edu

Sankaran Sivathanu
VMware Inc.
Palo Alto, California, USA
sivathanus@vmware.com

Jinpyo Kim
VMware Inc.
Palo Alto, California, USA
jkim@vmware.com

Bing Tsai
VMware Inc.
Palo Alto, California, USA
bing@vmware.com

Tao Li
University of Florida
Gainesville, Florida, USA
taoli@ece.ufl.edu

ABSTRACT

Software Defined Data Center (SDDC) is now an emerging area drawing considerable attention in enterprise computing. Software-Defined Storage (SDS), as a key element to enable the SDDC concept, is considered one of the most disruptive storage technologies in modern times. SDS introduces a variety of novel features and functionalities thereby changing the traditional view of the storage stack. In VMware's ESXi virtualization platform, several sparse virtual disk formats have been implemented to support critical features for SDS such as virtual machine (VM) snapshots, Fault-Tolerance (FT), thin provisioning and linked clones. Each virtual disk format supports unique features that may incur complex interactions with other layers of the storage stack such as guest file systems and storage devices.

In this paper, we focus on investigating the cross-layer behaviors when applying several key features of modern file systems on sparse virtual disks. Through our experiments, we observe as much as 7x performance degradation for sparse virtual disks if certain file system feature is used improperly. However, we discover that 1) choosing the right set of guest file system features and 2) adopting optimization schemes in virtual disk layer can significantly improve the performance of sparse virtual disks. Based on our observations, we derive valuable insights to assist with the design-decisions made by data-center administrators, file system developers and storage architects.

Categories and Subject Descriptors

C.4 [**Performance of Systems**]: Design studies, Performance attributes; D.4.2 [**Storage Management**]: Storage hierarchies; D.4.3 [**File Systems Management**]: Access methods; D.4.8 [**Performance**]: Measurements

Keywords

Storage Virtualization, File System Design, Sparse Virtual Disk, Cross-layer Analysis

1. INTRODUCTION

The concept of Software Defined Data Center (SDDC) [1] has been recently considered as the future direction of data center evo-lution. As the core technology behind SDDC, virtualization provides numerous advantages such as efficient resource utilization, improved manageability, and a more cost-effective method for provisioning computing, storage, and networking resources. Software Defined Storage (SDS), as a key part of the SDDC concept, targets one of the most critical aspects: storage virtualization. SDS provides several key features to facilitate managing storage resources, including automation with policy-driven virtual storage provisioning [2], and in general, the abstraction of services and capabilities from the underlying physical storage devices.

To support SDS, in VMware's ESXi hypervisor, Virtual Machine File System (VMFS) [3] is closely integrated with the hypervisor kernel. Unlike a general-purpose file system such as ext3, VMFS is a file system solely designed to manage large sized virtual disks for the virtual machines. VMFS supports various virtual disk formats (sparse and non-sparse) offering a greater range of functionalities and flexibilities than the typical nested file system architectures, such as the solutions offered in KVM [4] [5]. Furthermore, unlike the significant performance variance in a nested file system [4], our study has shown predictable performance behaviors for non-sparse virtual disks in VMFS, even when combined with sophisticated features in the guest file system.

However, there are some interesting performance interactions when applying guest file system features on sparse virtual disks. Recently, sparse virtual disk format has become crucial to support efficient provisioning and managing of large number of VMs with the functionalities of VM snapshot, Fault-Tolerance, thin-provisioning and linked clones. As sparse virtual disks rely on Copy-On-Write (COW) feature to track the change of blocks from base disks, it may incur performance penalties by altering the I/O behaviors of workloads. Unfortunately, modern file systems have not been designed to run on sparse virtual disks, which could significantly transform the I/O access patterns. Therefore continuous performance optimizations of sparse virtual disks to consider guest file system's operations become increasingly important to support emerging SDS-oriented use cases such as virtual desktop infrastructure, big data, and cloud storage [6].

This paper studies the performance implications of several key features in modern file systems when enabled on sparse virtual disks in virtualized environments. To the best of our knowledge, this is the first paper to examine thoroughly the combined performance effects of file systems features on sparse virtual disks.

Our main contributions are:
(i) providing a cross-layer performance analysis of different guest file system features on virtualized storage combined with the hypervisor layer and physical devices.

(ii) suggesting design recommendations for both file system developers and storage architects.

Based on our micro benchmark study, we find that some file system features, having certain block allocation scheme and I/O access pattern, favor the COW implementation of sparse virtual disks while others do not. For example, delay allocation can help reduce the performance penalty of sparse virtual disks by as much as 50% while auto online defragmentation can cause 7x performance penalty if not used properly. In our macro benchmark study, we observe that choosing the right set of file system features can improve the performance of sparse virtual disks to be comparable to the non-sparse virtual disks. Take kernel compilation workload for example, choosing ext4 over BtrFS with defragmentation can improve performance of sparse formats by 10~12%. By analyzing the results from the two different virtual disk types, we find that design optimizations in the sparse virtual disk such as I/O coalescing and asynchronous I/O are also crucial for achieving better performance. In our experiments on solid-state drive (SSD), we find that the performance impact by SSD depends on the combination of file system features and virtual disks.

The rest of this paper is organized as follows: Section 2 provides the background on virtual disk formats in ESXi and guest file system features we focus on. Section 3 describes our evaluation methodology. Sections 4 and 5 present our experimental results and key observations. Section 6 discusses related work and Section 7 concludes the paper.

2. UNDERSTANDING VIRTUAL DISK FORMATS AND GUEST FILE SYSTEM FEATURES

2.1. Hypervisor Virtual Disk Formats

In this section, we provide an overview of three virtual machine disk formats (VMDK), which are supported by VMFS and commonly adopted in data centers for enabling SDS.

2.1.1. Thick VMDK

Thick VMDK is the default non-sparse virtual disk format in ESXi. It exists as a file in the VMFS file system. When creating a Thick VMDK, it can be specified as either "lazy-zeroed" or "eager-zeroed". This choice determines whether to write zeroes to all the blocks at the creation of the VMDK file, or to zero each block only before it is actually written to for the first time. VMDK blocks are zeroed before they are written for the following reason. The allocation granularity in VMFS is 1MB, suitable for large VMDK files. However, the guest application is still able to read and write data as small as a single sector, i.e., 512 bytes. Therefore, zeroing a 1MB block prevents the guest from reading residual and invalid data from an allocated 1MB block when only part of this block contains valid data. We use eager-zeroed Thick VMDK as the baseline in this study as it performs very close to a raw physical device.

2.1.2. VMFSsparse

VMFSsparse is a Copy-On-Write (COW) implementation in ESXi used for VM snapshots, incremental backups, etc.. A VMFSsparse virtual disk is always used along with its parent disk because it only stores new contents written to the virtual disk after a snapshot was created. When a snapshot is taken on a VM, VMFS marks the original VMDK (referred to as the parent VMDK) as read-only and creates a new file in the format of VMFSsparse. This file is implemented as a redo-log, which starts off empty and grows as new data written to it (up to the size of its parent VMDK). After the VMFSsparse disk is linked to the VM, all the I/Os will first reach

the VMFSsparse disk. For the write I/Os, the VMFSsparse disk is first checked to see if the block is already allocated, in which case, it gets updated with the new content. If not, new blocks will be allocated and the data will be placed there. For the read I/Os, the VMFSsparse disk is first looked up for the data. If the data is available and up-to-date, the read requests are serviced from here. If the data requested is not completely available, the data is aggregated from both VMFSsparse disk and its parent virtual disk. Figure 1 shows a two-level nested snapshot where a snapshot (VMFSsparse disk) was created from a parent virtual disk and later a second snapshot was created. At any point in the snapshot hierarchy, the lastly created VMFSsparse disk will be linked to the VM. And the read/write IOs will be served as described above. Upon deletion of a snapshot or consolidation of snapshots, the data in the redo-log will be merged with the parent VMDK and the VMFSsparse disk will be deleted. The block size used for VMFSsparse is 512 bytes. This virtual disk format is space-efficient because it maintains snapshots of data and stores only newly written data in a 512-byte (1 sector) granularity. VMFSsparse virtual disk format is therefore used for incremental backups, where snapshots are taken regularly and the data differentials are stored in VMFSsparse.

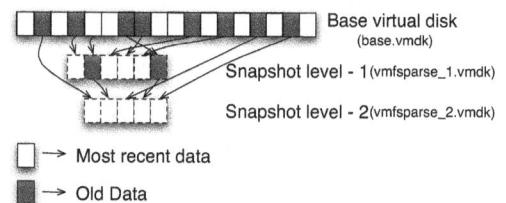

Figure 1. Two level nested snapshot (VMFSsparse)

2.1.3. Space Efficient Sparse (SEsparse)

SEsparse is another variant of COW implementation in ESXi. It is designed for space efficiency and used primarily in linked clones for deploying Virtual Desktop Infrastructure (VDI), where space consolidation can be critical for a large number of virtual desktops. Linked clones enable creation of multiple VMs that can share a single copy of data, while functioning as an independent VM from the user perspective. The implementation of SEsparse is largely similar to VMFSsparse except that the block size in SEsparse is 4KB. Also, SEsparse adopts several optimizations, such as I/O coalescing and asynchronous issue of I/O in the hypervisor storage stack, and zero-block suppression to improve performance. These differences are illustrated in detail in the following sections. Figure 2 shows an example where 'n' VMs share a read-only copy of a single parent *VMDK*, while each of them maintains its own SEsparse disk to hold new writes.

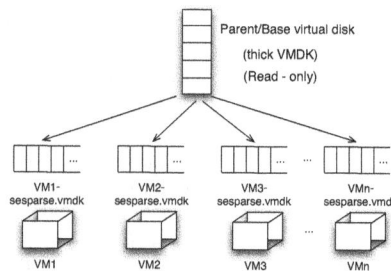

Figure 2. Linked clone VMs share the same parent disk via SEsparse

The most distinct feature of SEsparse is its capability to reclaim storage space that is freed by guest VM's file system and this is illustrated in Figure 3. When a guest file system deletes a block, usually the guest file system metadata is modified, by adding the block to the available free list of blocks. However, the underlying virtual disk layer is not aware that the blocks no longer contain valid data. In the case of VMFSsparse, the space is not reclaimed when a guest file system deletes data. On the contrary, in the case of SEsparse, a daemon running within the guest is invoked to 1) parse through the guest file system, 2) mark the empty blocks, and (3) issue unmap commands to the SEsparse layer. The corresponding bocks are then deleted (called wipe operation) and the freed blocks are compacted to reclaim space (the shrink operation).

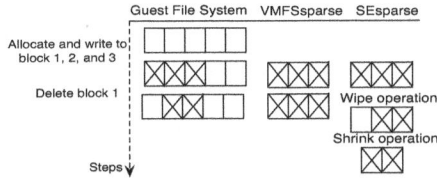

Figure 3. Space reclamation ability of SEsparse

2.2. Guest File System Features

Modern file systems are often equipped with advanced features to enhance performance, security and data consistency. However, these features are mostly designed and optimized for physical servers, where the file system is allowed to interact directly with physical disks. This is not the case in virtualized environments, where the hypervisor manages the physical disks. The combined effects of the guest file system and the hypervisor storage layer can lead to highly complex I/O behaviors. Here we will describe some of the most relevant file system features we studied in this paper:

2.2.1. Copy On Write (COW)

COW [7] is commonly implemented in log-structured file systems such as *BtrFS* [8]. Even on physical servers, COW can alter the eventual randomness in a stream of I/O requests. For example, COW-enabled file systems sequentially allocate new blocks and issue the new write requests to that location. As such, a group of random writes may be written into consecutive locations on disks and complete faster than usual, possibly approaching typical sequential write performance. Consequently, a set of sequential read requests will likely be completed slower and similar to random reads because of the fragmentation caused over time by writes.

The I/O behavior of COW in guest file system can be further complicated in virtualized servers because the implementation of sparse virtual disk is also based on COW. In our experiments in Section 4, the performance gap between sparse and non-sparse virtual disks can be 3x larger in certain situation. To fully understand the combined performance implications, the interactions of guest file systems, virtual disks, and storage devices (e.g. magnetic disks vs. SSD) are studied in this work.

2.2.2. Defragmentation

In COW-enabled file systems like BtrFS, fragmentation is commonly observed when the files are frequently written to and updated. As a result, data blocks that are logically adjacent can easily become physically dispersed. This can disrupt read-ahead mechanisms implemented in various layers of the software stack, which leads to degradation of sequential read performance.

COW-enabled file systems are typically equipped with a daemon process that will rearrange data blocks to reduce fragmentation. This feature is called *auto online defragmentation*, and is usually triggered when a write transaction has been committed. Our experiments show that sequential read performance improves significantly on physical server when auto online defragmentation is enabled.

In a virtualized environment, COW can be enabled in both the guest file system and the hypervisor storage layer. Since the guest file system do not interact with the disk directly, rearranging blocks in the guest may cause unpredictable COW behaviors in the underlying hypervisor, possibly leading to further fragmentation in the physical disks. In our experiments, the performance penalty of sparse virtual disk could be 7x worse. To understand the pros and cons of auto online defragmentation in virtualized environments, we need to examine the block allocation schemes in both the guest file system and the virtual disk layer in ESXi.

2.2.3. Persistent Pre-allocation

The ability to reserve a large disk space upon file creation is crucial for applications such as video streaming services and database servers. In a traditional file system such as Linux's *ext3*, the application itself is responsible for allocating and zeroing out the blocks, which can be quite time consuming. *Persistent pre-allocation* is therefore implemented in the *ext4* file system [9]. Ext4 only updates the meta-data to mark the reserved blocks as uninitialized, and saves the time of zeroing out the blocks. As shown in Figure 4, the pre-allocation time is significantly reduced if persistent pre-allocation is enabled.

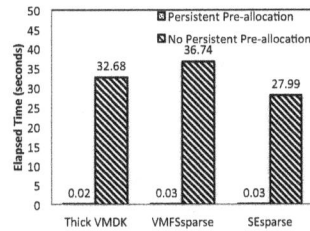

Figure 4. Elapsed time for pre-allocating 1GB space

In a virtualized environment, not only the guest file system but also the hypervisor storage layer can affect the actual block allocations. In ESXi, if the Thick VMDK format is selected, all blocks are allocated and zeroed at initialization. Hence, enabling persistent pre-allocation in the guest has no side effect. With the VMFSsparse format, data blocks are not allocated when the VMDK is created, and the persistent pre-allocation feature will result in file system not actually allocating the blocks in the virtual disk layer. Due to the zero-block suppression optimization in SEsparse, write requests that issue zeros will be returned at virtual disk layer (VMFS) instead of being issued to hard disks. The data blocks are not allocated in SEsparse even after zeroing out the data blocks intentionally. As a result, SEsparse completes the pre-allocation operation 24% faster than VMFSsparse as shown in Figure 4.

Table 1 summarizes all possible block allocation scenarios across different virtual disk formats after the pre-allocation process. Depending on whether the data blocks are allocated, there is significant impact on upcoming file operations such as random write and sequential read. In the worst case, files can be fragmented at virtual disk layer and yield as much as 50x performance penalty.

Table 1. Block allocation scenarios (each entry indicates whether virtual disk blocks are allocated after the file system pre-allocation)

	Persistent Pre-allocation	No Persistent Pre-allocation
Thick VMFS	Allocated	Allocated
VMFSsparse	Not allocated	Allocated
SEsparse	Not allocated	Not allocated

233

2.2.4. Delayed Allocation

In traditional file systems such as ext3, data blocks are allocated immediately on new writes. When multiple writes are issued concurrently to different files, new data blocks belonging to different files are likely to be interleaved with each other during allocation. Over time, fragmentation occurs if the files continue to expand.

Delayed allocation [10] is implemented in ext4 to address the issue discussed above. With this feature, a new block is allocated only when its associated data is flushed out of the file system cache. By doing so, the file system has a better chance to allocate file blocks contiguously on disk, which usually leads to better performance during future reads. However, this situation becomes even more complicated when considering the sparse virtual disk in the hypervisor storage layer. In our study, we find that the type of virtual disk format can have a major impact on the effectiveness of this file system feature.

2.2.5. Tail Packing

When the file size is not a multiple of the file system block size, the last remaining piece of data (called the *tail*), still requires an entire block. A large number of tails can lead to many partially filled blocks, reducing space efficiency. To address this issue, *tail packing* is developed in *ReiserFS* [11] to consolidate the tails into a contiguous location on disk, thereby minimizing the number of partially filled blocks. Even though this method appears to increase fragmentation, the read-ahead feature [12] in file systems is expected to improve sequential-read performance in such situations. Tail packing is known to improve read performance in cases where multiple small files are frequently accessed. In our experiments, we observe around 50% performance improvement for sparse virtual disk if tail packing is used.

3. EVALUATION METHODOLOGY

3.1. Experimental Setup

Our hardware platform is a Dell Power Edge T320 server equipped with a six-core 2.4GHz Xeon processor and 24GB DRAM. This server has one 32GB Intel Solid-State Drive (SSD) and two 500GB 7200RPM magnetic disks (HDDs). We use the latest VMware ESXi 5.5 hypervisor [13]. The virtual machine is configured with four vCPUs and 1GB of memory. We create one 15GB Thick VMDK virtual disk to host the guest operating system (Ubuntu 12.04). For running benchmarks and tests, we create another 20GB virtual disk for the virtual machine. Based on our experiment, we choose to place this second virtual disk on either a hard disk (HDD) or a solid-state disk (SSD).

For VMFSsparse and SEsparse virtual disk types, we use the Thick VMDK format for the base disk format. The base disk is empty at the beginning of each experiment so that all write I/Os will invoke block allocations in the cases of VMFSsparse and SEsparse.

Inside the VM, we format the data volume into three types of file systems, namely, ext4, BtrFS and ReiserFS. We use all the default configuration options in the file systems except for the features under consideration. Using file-system mount options, we turn on or off the COW, auto online defragmentation, delayed allocation and tail-packing features. The persistent pre-allocation feature is enabled in ext4 by default and it is not configurable. Therefore, we simulate the legacy pre-allocation operation in our benchmark instead of using ext4's persistent pre-allocation feature.

To ensure deterministic experimental outcomes, we implement automation scripts to control the key steps in each experiment: 1) creating and formatting the virtual disks, 2) configuring the file

system, 3) running the workloads and 4) detaching and deleting the virtual disk. Furthermore, we run five trials for each experiment and report the average value and standard deviation (as error bars) in the results.

3.2. Benchmarks and Tools

Since existing micro-benchmarks cannot properly exercise some of the more sophisticated file system features, we decide to implement our own tool. In addition to generating basic access patterns such as sequential read, random read, sequential write, and random write. Our tool implements specific functions for file pre-allocation, concurrent writes of multiple files, file aging, etc.

To achieve file-aging effect, we issue write requests to the file for a user-specified x number of times. In a COW-enabled file system, a larger x is expected to cause a higher degree of fragmentation. For pre-allocation function, we leverage the *fallocate()* system call in Linux to reserve disk space if persistent pre-allocation is supported. Otherwise, we manually allocate and write zeroes to the blocks for pre-allocation. For concurrent writes, we use multiple threads to write data into multiple files concurrently with a tunable delay between I/O requests.

We also use a device-level micro-benchmark, *IOmeter* [14] to measure the performance of various virtual disk formats. Sequential write, sequential read, random write, and random read test cases are used. We run IOmeter tests for 5 minutes each and report the average value and standard deviation in the results.

For macro-benchmark experiments, we choose two typical workloads from the *Filebench* suite [15], i.e., *File Server* and *Web Server*. Configurations for the two workloads are shown in Table 2. File Server is a write-dominant workload emulating the I/O behavior of a file server. Each thread only accesses its own set of files and performs a set of operations including create, delete, append, read, write and stat. Web Server is a read-dominant workload with a read/write ratio of 10:1. We use the throughput reported by the benchmark to measure the I/O performance. We use Linux kernel compilation (kernel version 3.8) as a workload that generates substantial I/O (read and write) as well as CPU and memory operations similar to real applications. The performance metric for this workload is the elapsed time from the point of unzipping the source files until the completion of compiling the entire Linux kernel tree.

Table 2. Filebench workload configurations

Workload	Average File Size	Mean Directory Width	Number of Files	I/O Size	Number of Threads	R/W Ratio
File Server	256KB	20	100000	1MB	100	1:2
Web Server	16KB	20	100000	1MB	100	10:1

4. MICRO BENCHMARK RESULTS AND ANALYSIS

In this Section, we first use the block I/O micro benchmark (IOmeter) to study the performance of virtual disk formats. We then use our own file I/O micro benchmark when various guest file system features are studied.

4.1. Performance of Virtual Disk Formats

To better understand the performance of different virtual disk formats, we run IOmeter directly on the raw block devices inside the virtual machine. Besides, we disable all caching effects in the storage stack. IOmeter is configured with 1 outstanding I/O (OIO). The I/O size is varied from 4KB to 64KB. Figure 5 shows the results with 1 OIO and Figure 6 shows the results with multiple OIOs. The following observations are made from our experiments:

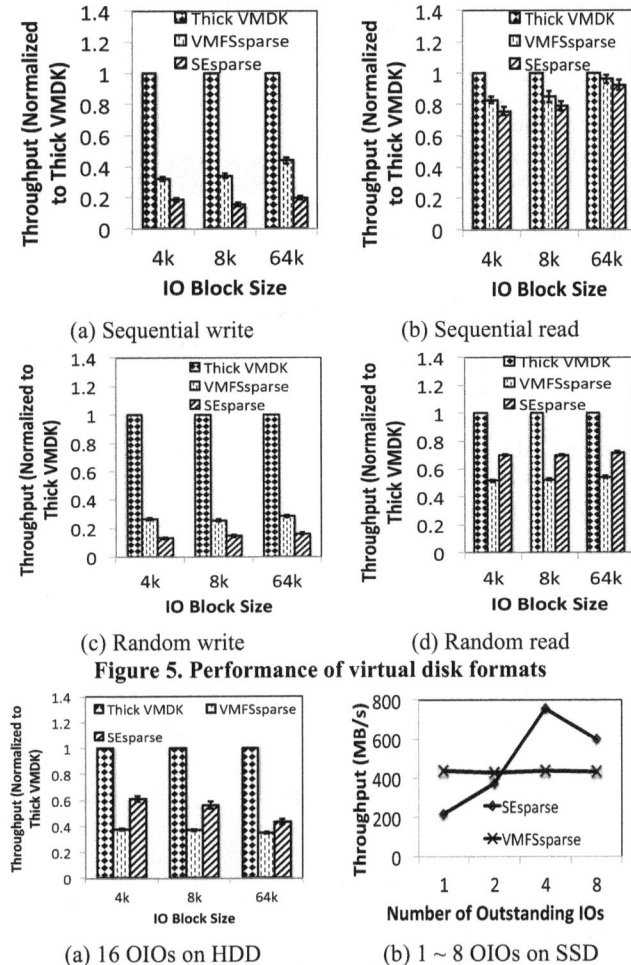

(a) Sequential write   (b) Sequential read

(c) Random write   (d) Random read

Figure 5. Performance of virtual disk formats

(a) 16 OIOs on HDD   (b) 1 ~ 8 OIOs on SSD

Figure 6. Random write throughputs in the case of multiple outstanding IOs (OIOs)

1) Compared to Thick VMDK, VMFSsparse and SEsparse has lower throughput for write operations due to the allocation overhead. As VMFSsparse and SEsparse grow dynamically on writes, new blocks are allocated during writes. This adds overhead in the case of sparse virtual disk format. We therefore observe performance penalty (around 60% and 80% for sequential and random write in Figures 5(a) and 5(c)) in sparse virtual disks when compared to Thick VMDK. For the sequential read case, Figure 5(b) shows that the performance gap is relatively small (about 8% range for 64KB block size) among virtual disk formats. Even though additional on-disk metadata structures need to be traversed for the two sparse formats, parts of metadata can be effectively pre-fetched into memory for sequential reads thereby minimizing the overhead of sparse virtual disk formats for sequential reads.

2) For random I/Os, SEsparse is better optimized compared to VMFSsparse. Random reads and random writes in the sparse formats are expected to perform worse compared to Thick VMDK. This is mainly due to the additional seeks incurred by accessing the on-disk metadata of sparse formats. However, SEsparse implements I/O-coalescing optimization, where multiple small I/Os are combined into larger requests. This reduces the additional round-trip delays in accessing the SEsparse code path for every I/O. As shown in Figure 6(a), in the case of 16 outstanding I/Os the aver-

age throughput of SEsparse is 1.5x higher than that of VMFSsparse for random I/Os.

3) SEsparse scales better than VMFSsparse in handling longer queues for low-latency devices like SSDs. For the results in Figure 6(b), we increase the number of outstanding I/Os in IOmeter from 1 to 8 and measure the throughput of random write workload with SSD device. The throughput of VMFSsparse doesn't scale across increasing number of outstanding I/Os while the throughput of SEsparse scales better. This is because the I/O issuing context is blocked till the I/O request reaches the physical device driver layer due to VMFSsparse's legacy implementation. Whereas for SEsparse, the I/O issue path is made asynchronous right from the upper layer and therefore it performs better in such cases. However, this phenomenon is only visible when the device latency is extremely low as in the case of SSDs. For regular magnetic disks, NAS or SAN-based storage, we expect device latencies to amortize the minor blocking cost in VMFSsparse. Note that when the outstanding I/O count is 1, VMFSsparse achieves higher throughput than SEsparse because the synchronous path in VMFSsparse avoids interrupt-handling delays associated with typical asynchronous implementations.

4.2. Copy on Write Logging

As mentioned in Section 2, COW may alter the sequential and random nature of a stream of requests as it allocates new blocks for every write. To examine the interactions of COW with various virtual disk formats, we create a variety of scenarios in our micro benchmark. We first evaluate the impact of basic operations including sequential rewrite to an existing file, random write to an existing file, and sequential read from a randomly modified file. The normalized elapsed time to complete these operations for a fixed file size is shown in Figures 7, 8, and 9(a). We also tune the degree of fragmentation by varying the number of random writes before the sequential read test is performed. The results are shown in Figure 9(c). Lastly, in Figure 9(b) we show the performance differences in the case of SSD. Note that in Figures 7, 8 and 9, COW refers to the case where copy on write is enabled while NO-COW refers to the case where copy on write is disabled. The following observations are made from our results:

1) With COW enabled in the guest file system, VMFSsparse and SEsparse become less space efficient. When the guest allocates and writes data to new locations as a result of COW, the sparse virtual disks would consider each write as a new write and hence the virtual disk size grows. This has two implications: first, all write operations are subjected to this block allocation overhead till the sparse disk grows to the size of its parent virtual disk. This is evident from the 3x larger performance gap across virtual disk formats in Figure 7, when COW is enabled. Second, the sparse formats become less effective in space savings.

2) COW may lower the performance overhead of VMFSsparse and SEsparse by converting random writes in the guest into sequential writes on physical disks. The performance overhead of VMFSsparse and SEsparse is typically greater in random writes than sequential writes. As shown in Figure 8, the performance gap across virtual disk formats is reduced by 55% when COW is enabled in the guest. Note that the experiment is conducted with a single outstanding IO. As the number of outstanding IOs increases, SEsparse performance further improves as shown in Figures 6(a) and 6(b).

3) Fragmentation in both the guest file system and virtual disk degrades the performance of VMFSsparse. In a fragmented COW-enabled file system, a stream of sequential read requests to a file may become random in the storage layer. In a virtualized environment, fragmentation may also occur in the virtual disk layer. As shown in Figures 5(b) and 5(d), the performance gap across virtual disk formats widens in the case of random reads. Furthermore, a fragmented COW-enabled guest file system amplifies the performance difference (2x larger), as shown in Figure 9(a). The fragmentation does not impact SEsparse as much as VMFSsparse mainly because of the I/O coalescing optimization in SEsparse that keeps the I/Os in queue for some time for the opportunity of combining them into a less random pattern. In Figure 9(c), we show the performance degradation for various degree of fragmentation by tuning the number of blocks randomly modified in the file. As this number grows, the number of file system extents also increases, indicating more fragmentation.

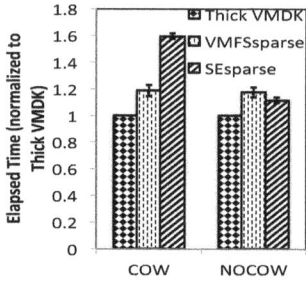

Figure 7. Rewrite to existing file

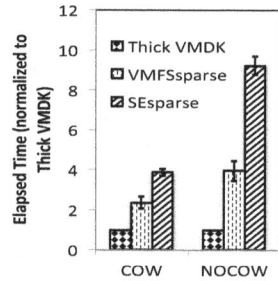

Figure 8. Random write to existing file

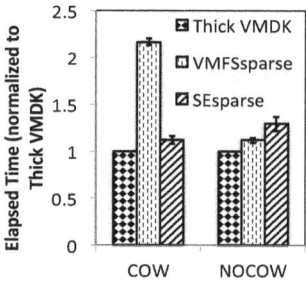

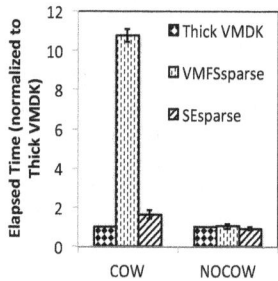

(a) Elapsed time on HDD

(b) Elapsed time on SSD

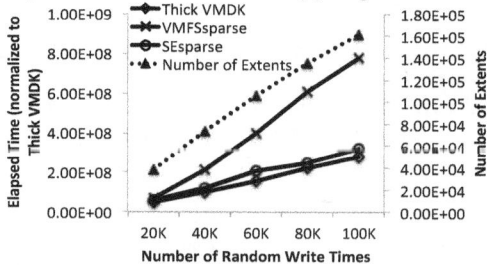

(c) When the fragmentation degree changes

Figure 9. Sequential read from randomly modified file

4) SSD exacerbates the side effect of synchronous I/O implementation in VMFSsparse when COW is used in guest. Even though COW-enabled file systems can fragment data leading to performance degradation in HDDs, this is not a problem in SSDs because SSDs handle random I/Os better than HDDs. Nevertheless, in Figure 9(b) we see that VMFSsparse performs nearly 10x worse than Thick VMDK and SEsparse during a sequential read. This is because, the benchmark does a sequential read of the entire file in 1MB granularity while the file is fragmented in file system layer at 4KB granularity (the block size of random write operations). Therefore, the guest file system issues multiple 4KB I/O requests in order to gather the fragmented 4KB segments of the 1MB data for a single read system call. Since VMFSsparse per-

forms synchronous I/O at virtual disk layer, the overhead of blocking every I/O is significant compared to the low device latency of SSDs. As SEsparse is capable of issuing multiple I/Os asynchronously, it performs close to thick VMDK.

Design Implications: (i) File system developers may consider the underlying virtual disk format before devising default write policies and block allocations. For example, fresh block allocations when modifying an existing data can lead to significant wastage of space for sparse virtual disks. (ii) Synchronous I/O issue path within the storage stack leads to significant performance degradation and worse scalability when adopting low-latency storage devices such as SSDs.

4.3. Auto Online Defragmentation

Auto online defragmentation is a file-system level solution to alleviate fragmentation incurred by COW to improve read performance. However, in a virtualized environment, fragmentation can occur not only in the guest but also in virtual disks. As discussed in Section 2, the defragmentation daemon can only defragment files in the guest level. Here we show the results of performance experiments when auto online defragmentation is enabled. Fragmentation is first generated by randomly modifying a file, and then sequential reads are issued to the fragmented file. The normalized elapsed time for sequentially reading a file of fixed size is shown in Figure 10(a). In addition, we vary the degree of fragmentation by changing the number of random writes in the file as we did in Section 4.2. The elapsed time for sequentially reading an entire file from the HDD is shown in Figure 10(c) and the result from the SSD is shown in Figure 10(d). The key insights derived are:

1) Auto online defragmentation improves thick VMDK performance but not for sparse virtual disk formats. In Thick VMDK, fragmentation only occurs in the guest file system, so auto online defragmentation can effectively re-arrange the data blocks. However, for VMFSsparse and SEsparse, one may observe even worse fragmentation in virtual disks after the defragmentation process completes in the guest. As shown in Figure 10(a), the performance gap between sparse and non-sparse formats is wider (7x for VMFSsparse and 4x for SEsparse) when this feature is enabled in the guest. As indicated in Figures 10(b) and 10(c), the number of extents stays nearly constant regardless of the severity of fragmentation, showing the effectiveness of the defragmentation mechanism in the guest file system. The performance of VMFSsparse is affected more than SEsparse, which confirms that VMFSsparse is more sensitive to fragmentation as we discussed in Section 4.2.

2) Auto online defragmentation helps avoid the side effect of VMFSsparse synchronous I/O for low-latency devices. As described in Section 4.2, due to the limitation of synchronous I/O implementation, VMFSsparse cannot benefit from SSD in the case of sequential read from randomly modified file. With auto online defragmentation, the randomness of data blocks is significantly reduced in the guest after defragmentation. Therefore there is no I/O amplification (single application I/O splitting into multiple smaller I/Os due to defragmentation) at the guest file system layer. A 1MB read request from our benchmark splits into just two 512 KB I/Os (because of limits in the Linux guest operating system) and each of these are issued synchronously to the SSD. As the SSD latency for servicing a 512KB I/O is much larger than the overhead of synchronous I/O issue path and there is only two of those I/Os, we do not see significant performance drop with VMFSsparse as shown in Figure 10(d).

Design Implications: For defragmentation to be useful, the defragmentation daemon should have the physical view of storage devices. Also, new file system features should consider its impact on fragmentation in the virtual disk layer to avoid unpredictable performance.

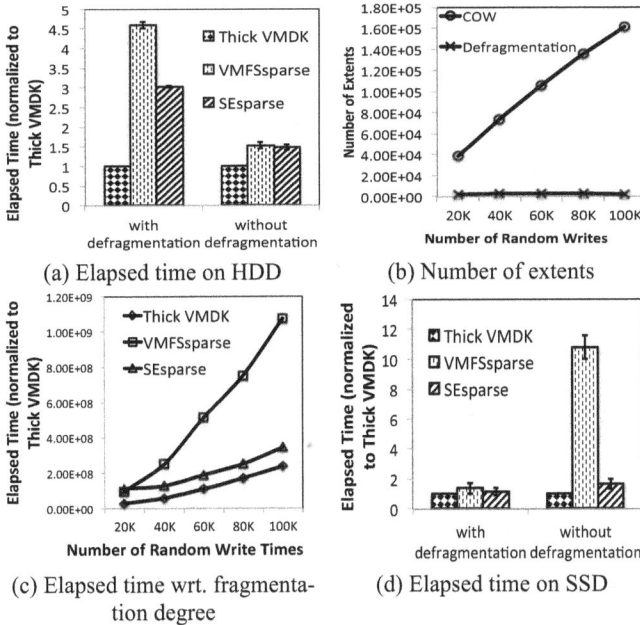

(a) Elapsed time on HDD

(b) Number of extents

(c) Elapsed time wrt. fragmentation degree

(d) Elapsed time on SSD

Figure 10. Sequential read from randomly modified file when auto online defragmentation is used

4.4. Persistent Pre-allocation

With persistent pre-allocation, file systems implement an optimized handler for *fallocate()* system call [16] compared to the generic Linux implementation of the system call handler which manually writes zeroes in order to guarantee the disk space allocation for the file in advance. This impacts the block allocation in virtual disk layer in ways that are shown in Table 1. In this Section, we demonstrate cases that can lead to performance differences due to the block allocation changes in the virtual disk layer caused by persistent pre-allocation. We compare two cases here: (i) "with persistent pre-allocation", where we use the persistent pre-allocation feature to allocate space for the file, and (ii) "without persistent pre-allocation" where we fill the freshly created file by writing zeroes in order to simulate the generic implementation of *fallocate()*. Once the file is pre-allocated, we write data at random offsets and then measure the performance of sequentially reading the file. We do these experiments for both HDD and SSD. The results shown in Figures 11 and 12 represent the normalized elapsed time it takes to complete specific operations. The following are the insights drawn from the experiments:

1) Persistent pre-allocation benefits Thick VMDK. For Thick VMDK, persistent pre-allocation is beneficial because there is no need to write zeros to an already zeroed disk. As the guest file system is able to handle pre-allocation through its metadata without zeroing the file blocks, persistent pre-allocation feature helps in accelerating the time taken for pre-allocation without any side effect on block allocation in the thick virtual disk.

2) The purpose of file pre-allocation is not fulfilled when persistent pre-allocation feature is used with VMFSsparse or SEsparse. With persistent pre-allocation the guest file system just modifies some internal metadata structures to pre-allocate file space. Therefore, in the virtual disk layer, the corresponding blocks are not allocated at this point. Only when data is actually written to

the file, the blocks will be allocated in VMFSsparse and SEsparse. Therefore the purpose of issuing *fallocate()* system call to pre-allocate space for the file is not fulfilled in the case of persistent pre-allocation and sparse virtual disk formats. Figure 11 shows the increased performance degradation (3x larger) in the case of persistent pre-allocation with VMFSsparse and SEsparse due to the additional block allocation overhead during writes even after pre-allocation of the file.

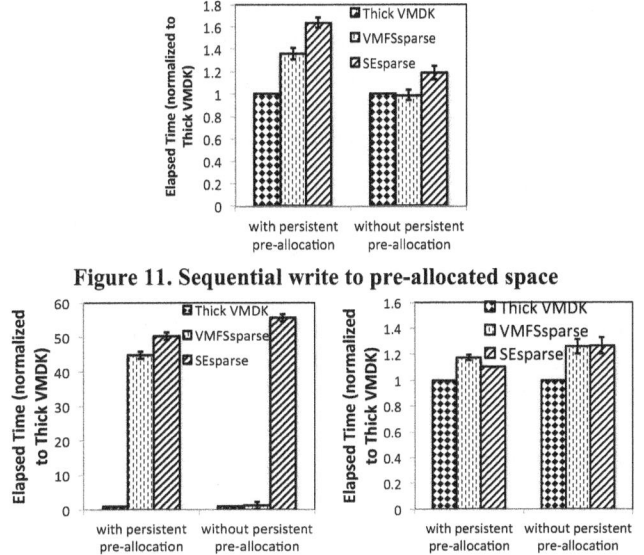

Figure 11. Sequential write to pre-allocated space

(a) Elapsed time on HDD

(b) Elapsed time on SSD

Figure 12. Sequential read of randomly filled file

3) Persistent pre-allocation can cause fragmentation in virtual disk layer and degrade performance for VMFSsparse. With persistent pre-allocation, blocks are not actually pre-allocated in the virtual disk layer. Therefore when an application writes to random offsets in a pre-allocated file, VMFSsparse and SEsparse make the allocations for those random offsets sequentially. This leads to file fragmentation and can lead to poor performance when it is read sequentially. In Figure 12(a), we compare performance of sequential read of the pre-allocated file for the cases with/without persistent pre-allocation. It is clear that with persistent pre-allocation the file fragmentation in the case of VMFSsparse and SEsparse leads to random read performance (~40-50x worse than sequential). Without persistent pre-allocation, VMFSsparse performs nearly as good as Thick VMDK as expected because there is no file fragmentation. However, SEsparse still shows random read performance because SEsparse has the zero block suppression optimization. The block is not actually allocated on disk if zeroes are written to a SEsparse block. Instead, metadata of SEsparse will be changed to track that the specific block contains zeroes. Through this experiment, we found that the zero block suppression optimization has this unintended consequence in the case of file pre-allocation. For SSDs, however, file fragmentation is not an issue as sequential and random reads perform almost similar. This is shown in the Figure 12(b), where there is no significant performance difference for sparse virtual disks.

Design Implications: When changing block allocation policies in file systems it is important to consider different virtual storage implementations to avoid any unintended consequences such as 1) fragmentation at virtual disk layer, and 2) blocks not actually allocated in the lower layers like the virtual disk layer after file system level block allocation.

4.5. Delayed Allocation

Delayed allocation impacts the disk layout of a file especially when there are concurrent writers. Therefore, we implement two write threads in our benchmark. Each of the writers writes to a separate file. Figures 13(a) and 13(b) show the Logic Block Number (LBN) trace when we sequentially read one of the files. The steps in the graphs show the interleaved block allocations for two files written concurrently. Figure 14 shows the time it takes to sequentially read that file with and without delayed allocation. From the experiments, we observe the following:

Larger continuous block allocation yields better performance for VMFSsparse and SEsparse formats. As shown in Figures 13(a) and 13(b), the file is laid out as small number of large continuous blocks when delayed allocation is used and vice versa. As such, this has effect on file fragmentation at the guest file system layer. With VMFSsparse and SEsparse formats, this also leads to extra seeks in accessing on-disk metadata to locate the file blocks resulting in decreased performance. As shown in Figure 14, the performance gap between the virtual disk formats is 2x larger when delayed allocation is disabled. However, in the case of SSD storage, the overhead due to file fragmentation is minimal and therefore the performance gap across virtual disk formats is also less.

Design Implications: It is beneficial in general, to devise file system policies that results in a de-fragmented file during initial placement. Delayed allocation is one such policy that we have verified to improve performance across different virtual disk formats. As discussed in section 4.3, it is more advisable to focus on defragmenting a file during initial placement than to do it at a later stage. There are multiple ways to achieve this goal. For example, cache can be wisely leveraged by applications and file systems to accumulate small blocks into large continuous blocks as in delayed allocation. In addition, file system technologies such as multi block allocation, delayed allocation and extents can be used to lower the chance of small data blocks.

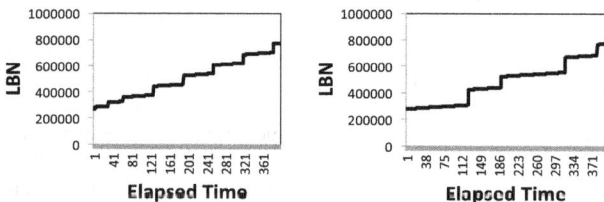

(a) Without delayed allocation   (b) With delayed allocation
Figure 13. Traces for sequential read to one of the files

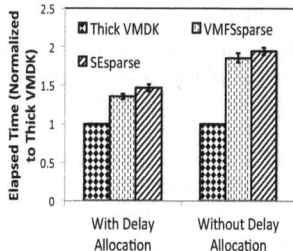

Figure 14. Sequential read to one of the files

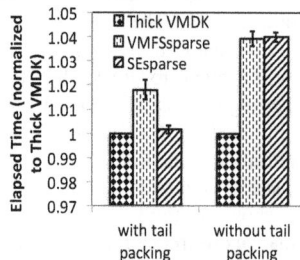

Figure 15. Read 10,000 2KB files

4.6. Tail-packing

As discussed in Section 2, the read efficiency is improved for certain type of accesses by the tail-packing feature. In order to fully exploit the tail-packing effect, we design our experiment to read

10,000 files, each sized 2KB in ReiserFS with a file system block size of 4KB. Figure 15 shows the time taken to read those small files sequentially. We observe the following:

Higher read efficiency leads to lower performance overhead of VMFSsparse and SEsparse formats. With tail packing support, instead of having 2KB invalid data in one data block, the file system use the entire 4KB data block to contain valid data. As a result, the total amount of data that needs to be read is smaller (50% smaller in our experiment). Thus, the number of read requests is less, which leads to less accumulated overhead of accessing VMFSsparse and SEsparse metadata. As can be seen in Figure 15, the performance gap between virtual disk formats is 2x smaller when tail-packing feature is leveraged.

Design Implications: Aggregation of small I/Os into larger I/Os is beneficial in general for sparse virtual disk formats. This is because additional per-I/O overhead of virtual disk formats may manifest into a larger performance gap when large number of small I/Os are used. Techniques such as pre-fetching, I/O coalescing can be leveraged to batch small I/Os.

5. MACRO BENCHMARK RESULTS AND ANALYSIS

In this section, we analyze the behavior of widely used macro-benchmarks and real-world workloads on different virtual disk formats and specific guest file systems that support the features covered in Section 4. The goal of this study is to confirm some of our earlier findings in Section 4 with real-world workloads and to explore if our findings can help in identifying what file system-virtual disk combinations can provide the best performance for certain workloads. We use two workload profiles in *Filebench* macro benchmark, namely *Web Server*, and *File Server*. For the real-world workload, we chose Linux kernel compilation as it has a good mix of reads and writes to leverage most of the file system features we considered.

Here, *BTRFS_NoCOW* refers to BtrFS with COW feature disabled; *BTRFS_Defrag* refers to BtrFS with auto online defragmentation enabled; *EXT4_nodelay* refers to ext4 file system with delayed allocation feature disabled; *ReiserFS_notail* refers to ReiserFS with tail packing feature disabled.

5.1. Read Dominant Workload

We use *Web Server*, which has the read/write ratio of 10:1, as our read dominant workload experiment. Figures 16 and 17 show the throughput of web server workload for the case of HDD and SSD storage. As observed in micro benchmark results, performance difference between virtual disk formats is smaller for SSDs compared to HDDs as the effect of file fragmentation is minimal on SSDs.

For read dominated workloads, the fragmentation and I/O behavior are two most important factors to be considered. Some insights we gathered from micro benchmarks are still valid for the web server workload: (i) disabling COW feature avoids fragmentation, which leads to a better throughput with VMFSsparse and SEsparse. (ii) tail-packing can help achieve higher throughput for read operations. Nevertheless, some observations that were made on micro benchmarks do not apply to the web server workload: (i) auto online defragmentation does not benefit web server workload irrespective of the virtual disk format because its access pattern is mostly random (ii) delayed allocation does not benefit web server workload in the case of VMFSsparse and SEsparse because files are not written in an interleaved manner.

Overall, we find that SEsparse provides better performance compared to VMFSsparse for the web server workload. In summary, file systems that yield less fragmentation and do relatively simpler block allocations achieve lower overhead with sparse virtual disk formats.

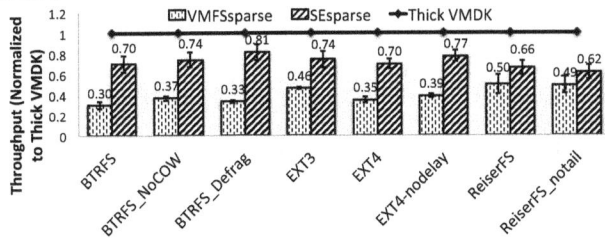

Figure 16. Web server on HDD

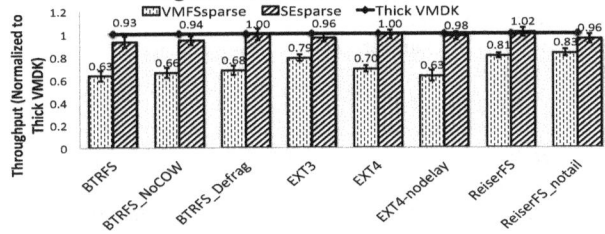

Figure 17. Web server on SSD

5.2. Write Dominant Workload

We use *File Server* workload, which has read/write ratio of 1:2, as our write dominant workload experiment. Figures 18 and 19 show the throughput of file server workload when it runs on HDD and SSD respectively.

For write dominated workloads, the performance depends on two factors: (i) I/O access pattern (random vs. sequential) and (ii) allocation overhead of each write. Figure 18 reveals the following observations: (i) *COW* adds allocation overhead for each write, which leads to less throughput, (ii) auto online defragmentation, which consumes extra disk bandwidth, results in overhead for a write dominant workload, and (iii) Tail packing does not benefit write operations.

As shown in Figure 19, SEsparse achieves better write throughput compared to Thick VMDK in the case of SSDs. This is because the file server workload performs a lot of small writes that may result in a read-modify-write operation in the SSD device, which typically uses a block size of 4KB. As SEsparse does I/O coalescing, these small writes are merged into fewer large writes resulting in significantly better performance with SSDs.

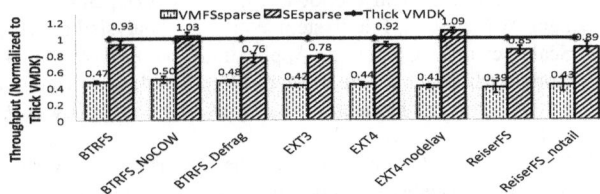

Figure 18. File server on HDD

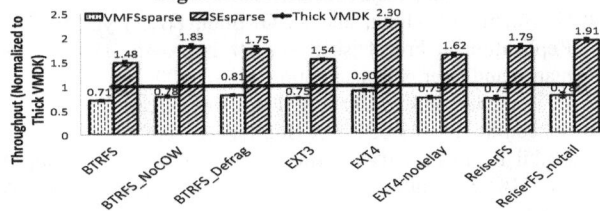

Figure 19. File server on SSD

5.3. Comprehensive Workload

We use kernel compilation as a comprehensive workload for our study. Figures 20 and 21 show the time taken to compile the kernel (normalized to Thick VMDK) on HDD and SSD respectively.

We find that VMFSsparse and SEsparse perform as good as Thick VMDK for the kernel compilation workload and in some cases the sparse formats perform slightly (<10%) better than the thick format. The insights drawn from micro benchmarks can be confirmed here: i) enabling COW feature yields a larger performance gap across virtual disk formats, ii) auto online defragmentation widens the performance gap on HDDs but helps reduce the performance gap on SSDs, iii) delayed allocation helps hide the performance overhead of sparse virtual disk formats. However, due to SSD's high performance, the benefit of delayed allocation is relatively small, and iv) tail packing has minimum impact on kernel compilation.

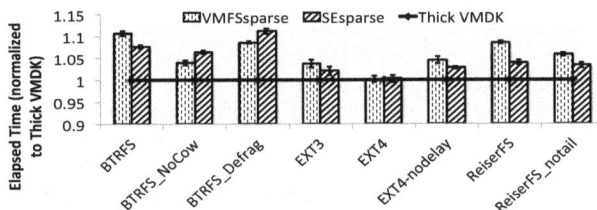

Figure 20. Kernel compilation on HDD

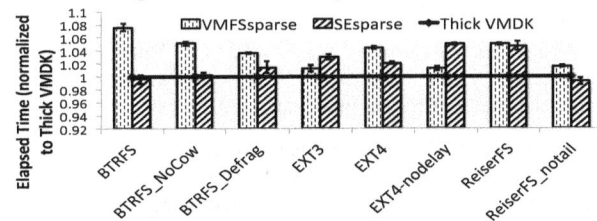

Figure 21. Kernel compilation on SSD

6. RELATED WORK

Many prior works in the field of file and storage systems performance analysis treat each layer in storage stack as separate entities. Prior art that covers performance of storage system layer are as follows: D. Pease et. al. [17] described a distributed storage system design that can perform load balancing according to workload I/O behavior. J. Glider et al. [18] presented a software architecture to control the block management for SAN storage systems. S. Alouf et al. [19] and A. Goyal et al. [20] analyzed storage system performance in different contexts. In the file system layer, J. Douceur et al. [21] studied file system contents on production systems and made observations in terms of common types and sizes of files and their distribution. T. Sato [22] analyzed the performance impact of fragmentation in the file system layer and proposed remedies. In the application layer, there have also been a number of studies on the performance and energy consumption of different file system workloads [23][24][25][26]. While these research contributions are both useful and interesting, they do not focus on cross-layer optimizations and holistic view of the storage stack. However, in the software defined storage era, independently considering individual layers in the storage stack may not be sufficient to fully understand and improve overall I/O performance.

Cross layer analysis and optimization has been adopted in various layers in system stack. K. Miller et al. [27] proposed a memory deduplication scanner that considers the memory pages in both the guest OS and host OS in a virtual environment. In the storage context, K. Duda et al. [28] and H. Huang et al. [29] proposed cross layer design for disk IO scheduler to optimize the performance and energy. Similarly, D. Boutcher et al. [30] and M. Kesavan et al. [31] studied the impact of nested IO schedulers in a virtualized environment. In contrast, we focus primarily on the impact of guest file systems and underlying storage constructs in a virtualized environment.

D. Le et al. [4] analyzed the performance of nested file systems in KVM, where they investigate the interactions between guest and host file systems. They discover significant performance differences when using different combinations of guest and host file systems in a KVM environment. Our study instead focuses on how modern guest file system features interact with sparse virtual disk formats, which lays the foundation for many of the widely used virtualization technologies.

7. CONCLUSION

To implement the concept of Software Defined Storage, VMware ESXi supports two types of sparse virtual disks that lay the foundation for many widely used virtualization features like VM snapshots and linked clones. In this study, we have analyzed the performance impact of guest file system features on these sparse virtual disk formats. Even though sparse virtual disk formats in general has performance penalties compared to thick virtual disk format, we have found that appropriate implementation and tuning of file system features and the sparse virtual disk layer can help sparse virtual disks perform close to thick virtual disk format for certain workloads. SSD would help minimize the performance variance across virtual disk formats due to its better random I/O performance. On the other hand, SSD could exacerbate the performance penalty of certain implementation of sparse virtual disks.

Our study exemplifies the importance of cross-layer performance analysis in virtualized systems. As SDS concept emerges, more storage functionalities will be implemented purely as software. In such cases, a holistic performance analysis and optimization will be even more critical. Based on the observations in our study, we provide suggestions to facilitate future file system designs and virtual disk implementations in the context of SDS.

8. ACKNOWLEDGMENTS

The authors greatly appreciate the anonymous reviewers for their feedback on improving the paper draft. As the project is completed during Ruijin Zhou's internship at VMware Inc., we would also like to thank the Performance Engineering Group at VMware for providing the experimental platform as well as constructive critiques on the work. Especially, we'd like to thank Shilpi Agarwal for her enormous support throughout the whole process. Finally, the authors appreciate the members of The Intelligent Design of Efficient Architectures Laboratory at the University of Florida for helping draft and finalize the paper.

9. REFERENCES

[1] The Software-Defined Data Center, http://www.vmware.com/software-defined-datacenter/index.html.

[2] VMware Virtual SAN Technology http://www.vmware.com/products/virtual-san/.

[3] VMware Virtual Machine File System: Technical Overview and Best Practices, VMware White Paper.

[4] Duy Le, Hai Huang, and Haining Wang, Understanding Performance Implications of Nested File Systems in a Virtualized Environment, FAST, 2012.

[5] Kernel Based Virtual Machine, http://www.linux-kvm.org/page/Main_Page.

[6] Laz Vekiarides, Defining Software Defined Storage, SPDEcon, 2013.

[7] David Hitz, Michael Malcolm, James Lau, and Byron Rakitzis, Copy on Write File System Consistency and Block Usage, US Patent US 6721764 B2.

[8] Howard Powell, ZFS and Btrfs: A Quick Introduction to Modern File Systems, Linux Journal Archive Volume, 2012.

[9] Mingming Cao, et al., Ext4: The Next Generation of Ext2/3 Filesystem, Linux Storage & Filesystem Workshop, 2007.

[10] Adam Sweeney, and Silicon Graphics, Scalability in the XFS File System, USENIX ATC, 1996.

[11] ReiserFS, http://en.wikipedia.org/wiki/ReiserFS.

[12] Ram Pai, Badari Pulavarty, and Mingming Cao, Linux 2.6 Performance Improvement Through Readahead Optimization, Linux Symposium, 2004.

[13] VMware vShpere 5.5, http://www.vmware.com/.

[14] Jerry Sievert. Iometer: The I/O Performance Analysis Tool for Servers. www.intel.com/design/servers/devtools/iometer/index.html.

[15] Richard McDougall, FileBench A Prototype Model Based Workload for File Systems, NAS Conference, 2004.

[16] Alex Depoutovitch, and Andrei Warkentin, File Systems: More Cooperations - Less Integration, Linux Symposium, 2012.

[17] David A. Pease, et al., IBM Storage Tank™ A Distributed Storage System, FAST, 2002.

[18] Joseph S. Glider, et al., The Software Architecture of a SAN Storage Control System, IBM System Journal, 2003.

[19] Sara Alouf, Abdulhalim Dandoush, and Philippe Nain, Performance Analysis of Peer-to-Peer Storage Systems, ITC 2007, LNCS 4516.

[20] Ambuj Goyal, and Tilak Agerwala, Performance Analysis of Future Shared Storage Systems, IBM Journal of Research and Development, 1984.

[21] John R. Douceur, and William J. Bolosky, A Large-Scale Study of File-System Contents, SIGMETRICS 1999.

[22] Takashi Sato, Ext4 Online Defragmentation, Proceedings of the Linux Symposium, 2007.

[23] Priya Sehgal, Vasily Tarasov, and Erez Zadok, Evaluating Performance and Energy in File System Server Workloads, FAST, 2010.

[24] Keith Smith, and Margo Seltzer, File Layout and File System Performance, Harvard Computer Science Technical Report TR-35-94.

[25] Andrew W. Leung, Shankar Pasupathy, Garth Goodson, and Ethan L. Miller, Measurement and Analysis of Large-Scale Network File System Workloads, USENIX ATC, 2008.

[26] Feng Wang, et al., File System Workload Analysis For Large Scale Scientific Computing Applications, IEEE MSST, 2004.

[27] Konrad Miller, et al., XLH: More Effective Memory Deduplication Scanners Through Cross-layer Hints, USENIX ATC, 2013.

[28] Kenneth J. Duda, and David R. Cheriton, Borrowed-Virtual-time (bvt) Scheduling: Supporting Latency-Sensitive Threads in a General-purpose Scheduler. SOSP, 1999.

[29] H. Huang, W. Hung, and K. G. Shin, FS2: Dynamic Data Replication in Free Disk Space for Improving Disk Performance and Energy Consumption, SOSP, 2005.

[30] D. Boutcher, and A. Chandra, Does Virtualization Make Disk Scheduling Passé? USENIX HotStorage, 2009.

[31] Mukil Kesavan, Ada Gavrilovska, and Karsten Schwan, On Disk I/O Scheduling in Virtual Machines. USENIX WIOV, 2010.

Improving Performance by Matching Imbalanced Workloads with Heterogeneous Platforms

Jie Shen
Delft University of Technology
The Netherlands
j.shen@tudelft.nl

Ana Lucia Varbanescu
University of Amsterdam
The Netherlands
a.l.varbanescu@uva.nl

Peng Zou
National University of Defense
Technology, China
zpeng@nudt.edu.cn

Yutong Lu
National University of Defense
Technology, China
ytlu@nudt.edu.cn

Henk Sips
Delft University of Technology
The Netherlands
h.j.sips@tudelft.nl

ABSTRACT

Although GPUs are considered ideal to accelerate massively data-parallel applications, there are still exceptions to this rule. For example, imbalanced applications cannot be efficiently processed by GPUs: despite the massive data parallelism, a varied computational workload per data point remains GPU-unfriendly. To efficiently process imbalanced applications, we exploit the use of heterogeneous platforms (GPUs *and* CPUs) by partitioning the workload to fit the usage patterns of the processors. In this work, we present our flexible and adaptive method that predicts the optimal partitioning. Our method aims to match a quantitative model of the application with the hardware capabilities of the platform, and calculates the optimal match according to a user-given criterion. We evaluate our method in terms of overall performance gain, prediction accuracy, flexibility and adaptivity. Our results, gathered from both synthetic and real-world workloads, show performance gains of up to 60%, accurate predictions for more than 90% of all the 1395 imbalanced workloads we have tested, and confirm that the method adapts correctly to application, dataset, and platform changes (both hardware and software). We conclude that model-based prediction of workload partitioning for heterogeneous platforms is feasible and useful for performance improvement.

Categories and Subject Descriptors

C.4 [**Performance of Systems**]: Modeling techniques; C.1.3 [**Processor Architectures**]: Other Architecture Styles— *heterogeneous (hybrid) systems*

Keywords

Heterogeneous platforms; imbalanced workloads; workload partitioning; GPUs; multi-core CPUs

1. INTRODUCTION

Massively parallel applications are typical workloads for GPUs, under the assumption that the parallelism of the application and the hardware platform match. However, not all massively parallel applications are as regular as needed to fit this profile. For example, *imbalanced applications* (i.e., applications with an imbalanced workload per data point) turn out to be more of a challenge than a fit for GPUs.

Such applications can be found in scientific simulation, numerical method, and graph processing [2,6,19,24,31]. Imagine a scientific simulation using a variable time step as a technique to ensure sufficient accuracy: this approach generates different workloads for different simulation data points. Similarly, many real graphs have power-law degree distributions, where higher-degree nodes require more processing in algorithms like breadth first search (BFS) [9] or finding connected components [23]. These relatively few data points that require more computation drastically limit the GPU utilization and eventually lead to poor performance.

To tackle the issue of imbalanced workloads, we propose an opportunistic exploitation of the native heterogeneity of GPU platforms, i.e., we use the GPU *plus* the host processor (the CPU). Combining the individual strengths of the CPU and the GPU, we aim to achieve improved performance. Related studies [20,21] have shown improved application performance through workload partitioning. This is only possible when the workload is partitioned to best utilize both processors. Moreover, to enable any partitioned execution, the application must be implemented in a portable programming model - like OpenACC [22] or OpenCL [28] - or suitable CPU and GPU implementations must be available.

Optimal workload partitioning is not trivial: hardware capabilities, workload characteristics, and the amount of data that needs transferring must all be taken into account. A trial-and-error search is a possible solution [29], but it is time-consuming (and keeps the target heterogeneous platform occupied to run the search). Understanding or profiling the application and hardware, either analytically (depending on what the application does) [16] or through statistical modeling [7, 14] can also lead to efficient partitioning, but these approaches are too complex, often time-consuming, or less suited for imbalanced workloads.

In this work, we propose *a model-based prediction method for imbalanced workload partitioning*. Our method detects whether partitioning is necessary and, if so, predicts the suitable partitioning point(s) for the heterogeneous platform (CPU+GPU). In this method, we build a *partitioning model*, based on a given fitting criterion (execution time in this paper), that matches a quantitative model of the application (a *workload model*) with the *hardware capabilities* of the given platform. By using the workload model, we quantify the application workload and its characteristics, as well as the data transfer between processors. On the platform side, we estimate hardware capabilities by using a low-cost profiling. This profiling is necessary to cope with the sensitivity of a platform to the application, to the problem size, and to the drivers and compilers. By solving the partitioning model for the given fitting criterion, our method predicts the optimal workload partitioning.

To evaluate our partitioning method, we use synthetic benchmarks (1295 imbalanced workloads), and a real-world application (10 imbalanced workloads), all implemented in OpenCL. We run experiments to evaluate the partitioning impact on performance, and validate the accuracy and adaptiveness of our method. Our results show that partitioning improves application performance by up to 60% compared to the use of a single processor (CPU or GPU). The optimal partitioning point is correctly predicted in more than 90% of the cases, on various platforms and workloads.

To examine the usability of the method, we applied it to a real-world case study [2], showing the systematic recipe that leads to the efficient partitioning. This step-by-step procedure can be repeated for other imbalanced applications.

The main contributions in this work are: (1) we propose a CPU+GPU solution to improve the performance of imbalanced applications; (2) we develop a quantitative workload modeling for imbalanced applications; (3) we design a partitioning model that fits a workload model with a platform's hardware capabilities; (4) we design and implement a prediction method that, by solving the partitioning model for a user-given criterion, predicts the optimal workload partitioning for a given platform; (5) we present a detailed recipe for applying the method to real-life applications.

The rest of the paper is organized as follows. We introduce imbalanced workloads in Section 2. Section 3 then describes the model-based workload partitioning method in detail. The experiment evaluation is given in Section 4, followed by Section 5 with the real-world case study. We discuss related work in Section 6. Finally, in Section 7 we draw conclusion and discuss future work.

2. IMBALANCED WORKLOADS

We define an application having an *imbalanced workload* when it has massive parallelism, but varied workload per data point. A data point is an independent element in the application parallelization space. The *workload* of a data point is a measurable quantity, where the choice of metric depends on the application scenario. For example, scientific simulation can use the number of iterations [2], numerical method can use the number of floating-point operations [19], and graph processing can use the number of child nodes (the degree) [6].

Usually, an application gets an imbalanced workload due to either the algorithm or the dataset. For the algorithm case, for example, in a scientific simulation, the user may be interested in some simulation points, thus making these points run more iterations and perform more computations.

For the dataset case, for example, in graph traversal, because the graph can be quite asymmetric, the nodes with higher degree need more processing than the others. In either case, there are two common features in imbalanced workloads: (1) in the data-point dimension (the parallelization dimension), there is no dependency between two data points; (2) in the workload dimension, the workload of each data point is varied, determined at runtime[1]. By contrast, in a *balanced workload*, each data point has a similar workload known at compile time or even before that. Figure 1 illustrates the difference between imbalanced and balanced workloads.

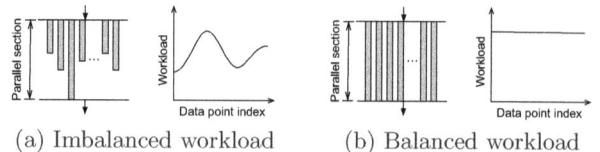

(a) Imbalanced workload   (b) Balanced workload

Figure 1: (a) Imbalanced workload. (b) Balanced workload. Note that the distribution of the workload is in fact discrete per data point. We show it (also for the figures in the rest of the paper) as a continuous distribution to simplify the figure presentation.

For imbalanced workloads, achieving high performance on GPUs is difficult, as the imbalanced part hinders the utilization of the platform. In such situation, using both GPU and CPU with each processor taking a suitable partition will lead to better hardware utilization. Therefore, to improve performance, we propose a new partitioning method that predicts the optimal partitioning for imbalanced workloads.

3. WORKLOAD PARTITIONING

In this section, we present the design and development of our workload partitioning method.

3.1 The Big Picture

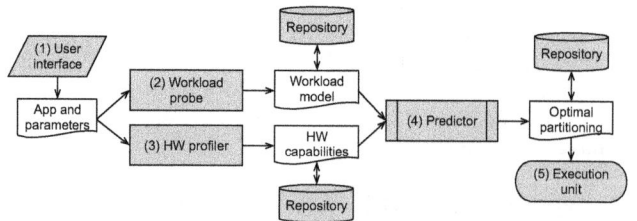

Figure 2: The entire partitioning process.

The entire partitioning process is illustrated in Figure 2. (1) The *user interface* receives a parallel application and its parameters (e.g., problem size), and delivers them to the *workload probe* and the *HW profiler*. (2) The workload probe characterizes the application by its workload features and generates a *workload model*. (3) The HW profiler profiles the processors (CPU and GPU) of the target heterogeneous platform to estimate the *hardware capabilities*. (4) The *predictor* uses the workload model and the hardware capabilities to derive the optimal partitioning. The output generated in (2), (3), and (4) are stored in repositories for reuse,

---

[1]The workload per data point cannot be determined before execution, but the runtime behavior is constant once the algorithm and/or the dataset are fixed.

largely accelerating the partitioning process. (5) Finally, the *execution unit* (the target heterogeneous platform) executes the partitioned workload. The partitioning process can run online, on the same machine as the workload, or offline, on a different machine, which will assist the deployment.

Input applications are parallelized in OpenCL, a unified programming model for heterogeneous platforms [8]. In OpenCL, the host (the CPU) manages data transfers between the host and the devices (the CPU and the GPU), and commands the devices to execute the kernel computation. For the CPU device, as the host and the device share the same physical memory, data transfers can be avoided using zero-copy [10]. For the GPU device, as the host and the device have separate memory spaces, real data copies are performed, and this data-transfer overhead has to be considered into the workload partitioning.

We note that we choose OpenCL for portability, and we assume the same parallel version of the application is used with architecture-specific code specialization [27, 28], thus limiting the effort the users have to put into porting the application to the CPU (while assuming the GPU code is available but underperforms). To enable partitioning, the host code needs to be modified to support OpenCL multi-device initialization, workload distribution, and output gathering. We implement an API to simply the coding. We further note that our partitioning method is *not* dependent on OpenCL. If the users want or have different languages for using this method (e.g., using OpenMP for CPU or CUDA for GPU), it is also possible. In our experience, this does not change the methodology, but only shifts the partitioning one direction or another.

3.2 Workload Modeling

Workload modeling is used to quantify the workload and its characteristics, which is the starting point of workload partitioning and prediction.

Because the workload is imbalanced, we use sorting (i.e., we sort the data points according to their workloads) to reshape the whole workload into a more regular shape. Thus, similar behaving data points will be grouped together, leading to a more intuitive partitioning. Figure 3 shows the workload-reshaping process. A sorted workload can have one of the three basic shapes: a *plateau* shape, a *peak* shape, or a *stair* shape. We note that more apparently complicated workload shapes can be either approximated to one of the basic shapes, or decomposed into the several basic shapes.

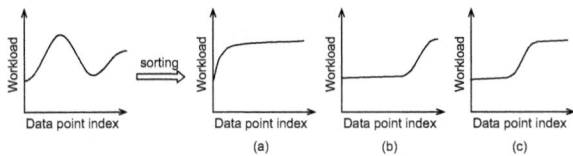

Figure 3: The workload-reshaping process. A workload is sorted into a more regular shape: either (a) plateau shape, (b) peak shape, or (c) stair shape.

From the three basic shapes, an imbalanced workload is best represented by the peak shape. This is because (1) the performance of the plateau-shaped workload is dominated by the plateau part (the flat part), so the imbalanced part will not have much influence on the overall performance; (2) the peak-shaped workload fits the CPU+GPU platforms,

as a GPU with bulk parallel processing is efficient in processing the flat part, and a CPU with better single thread performance is suitable to process the peak part (the part with more irregularity); (3) the stair-shaped workload can be approximated by either a shape with a wider peak (thus covered by the peak shape) or a shape with two dominating plateaus (thus becoming a two-phase balanced workload). For now, we approximate this with a wider peak.

To quantify the characteristics of the peak-shaped workload, we build a workload model (shown in Figure 4), which separates the flat part and the peak part of the workload with an inflection point *ip*. The characteristics of the workload model are: the total problem size, the workload in the flat part (base height), the number of data points in the peak part (peak width), and the maximum workload in the peak part (peak height), noted as n, bh, pw, ph, respectively. From the workload model, we further derive two peak characteristics: s, the slope of the peak ($s = (ph - bh)/pw$), and α, the ratio of pw to n.

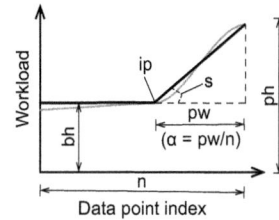

Figure 4: Workload model overview.

Thus, the workload of each data point can be presented by a two-phase linear function:

$$w(i) = \begin{cases} bh & i = 0, ..., n - pw - 1 \\ s \times (i - (n - pw - 1)) + bh & i = n - pw, ..., n - 1 \end{cases}$$

where w is the workload of a data point, and i is the data point index.

In summary, we form a workload model which assumes the imbalanced workload shape is represented by a horizontal line plus a slanted line with an inflection point in between. Its characteristics parameters are n, bh, pw, ph, s, and α.

3.3 Partitioning Method

To achieve our partitioning goal - i.e., the best performance on the platform - is to achieve a perfect execution overlap between the two processors: $T_G + T_D = T_C$. T_G and T_C are the kernel execution time on the GPU and the CPU, respectively. T_D is the data-transfer overhead added on the GPU[2]. This equation is the criterion that defines the optimal partitioning.

We adopt a two-step quantitative approach to model the execution of the workload. In the first step, T_D is removed from the equation, which leads to a partitioning without the influence of data transfers. In the second step, this overhead is added, resulting in a more practical partitioning. By using the two-step modeling, it is possible to evaluate the impact of data transfers on the partitioning. Besides, data-transfer optimizations [12, 13, 17] and integrated CPU+GPU hardware designs (like Intel Sandybridge [11] and AMD APUs [1]) can hide or eliminate this overhead,

---

[2]In this paper, we use the subscript G, C, and D to denote the GPU, the CPU, and the data transfer, respectively.

therefore treating the kernel execution time and the data-transfer time in two phases makes our method applicable to more applications and hardware platforms.

In the first step, we introduce two quantities W and P to evaluate the kernel execution time. W (total workload size) quantifies how much work has to be done in a partition. Due to the workload imbalance, using the problem size (1D) to evaluate W is not sufficient. We define W as a 2D quantity by summing up the workloads of all the data points in a partition. P (processing throughput), measured in amount of workload solved per second, evaluates the hardware capability of a processor, indicating how fast the processor performs the application workload. As a result, the kernel execution time is given by W/P. Substituting W_G, P_G, W_C, and P_C into the first-step target ($T_G = T_C$), we have

$$\frac{W_G}{W_C} = \frac{P_G}{P_C} \qquad (1)$$

Equation 1 implies the workload partitioning into W_G and W_C is affected by the relative hardware capability (P_G/P_C) between the two processors .

In the second step, we further quantify the data-transfer overhead. We use two more quantities O (data-transfer size) and Q (data-transfer bandwidth, measured in bytes per second), and we have $T_D = O/Q$. Q is decided by the bandwidth of the physical connection (e.g., PCIe) that connects the GPU to the CPU. We ignore the latency (smaller than 100 μs in our measurement) for setting up the data transfer, as it has negligible performance impact. Adding the definition of T_D into the second-step target ($T_G + T_D = T_C$) and performing equation transformations, we get

$$\frac{W_G}{W_C} = \frac{P_G}{P_C} \times \frac{1}{1 + (O/W_G) \times (P_G/Q)} \qquad (2)$$

Equation 2 shows the impact of data transfers on the partitioning. Let F be the impact factor ($F = \frac{1}{1+(O/W_G)\times(P_G/Q)}$). As F is smaller than 1, W_G/W_C is decreased to compensate for the data-transfer penalty, resulting in a new partitioning with a part of the GPU workload moved to the CPU. Equation 2 specifies our final partitioning model.

3.4 Predicting the Partitioning

Let β be the fraction of data points assigned to the GPU. Finding the optimal partitioning is equivalent to solving β from Equation 2. There are two types of terms in Equation 2: (1) the partitioning-independent terms (i.e., the β-independent terms), P_G/P_C, P_G/Q; and (2) the partitioning-dependent terms (i.e., the β-dependent terms), W_G/W_C, O/W_G. To solve β from Equation 2, we need to estimate the β-independent terms, and find an expression for the β-dependent terms.

We use profiling to estimate the β-independent terms: the relative hardware capability (P_G/P_C), and the ratio of GPU throughput to data-transfer bandwidth (P_G/Q). As the two ratios depend not only on the processors' hardware characteristics, but further on the application and the problem size that the processors perform, profiling the processors in the (application, problem size) context leads to more realistic estimates. In addition, the use of profiling efficiently addresses the diversity issues of the platforms and the workloads, making the prediction method adaptive to hardware, application, and problem size changes.

Our profiling is based on the *partial execution* of the target workload, i.e., we use a reduced workload to expose the global behavior of the application. As imbalanced applications are usually iterative based, we can limit the workload of every data point to a height vh ($vh_{min} \leq vh \leq bh$)), resulting in a partial workload, noted as V, for profiling (see Figure 5). The choice of vh is a trade-off between profiling accuracy and cost. In general, the use of partial workload makes the profiling much quicker and cheaper than a full profiling. Moreover, profiling results can be reused for multiple workloads with the same problem size but different shapes, thus the profiling becomes a one-time effort, and the overall prediction speed is further accelerated. By executing the V workload on the GPU and the CPU, respectively, we obtain the following estimation:

$$\frac{P_G}{P_C} \approx \frac{W^V/T_G^V}{W^V/T_C^V} = R_{GC}, \quad \frac{P_G}{Q} \approx \frac{W^V/T_G^V}{O^V/T_D^V} = \frac{W^V}{O^V} \times R_{GD} \qquad (3)$$

W^V is calculated according to the definition of W ($W^V = n \times vh$). O^V is obtained from the application, which is the full data-transfer size as we profile the whole problem size. Thus, by measuring the two time ratios T_C^V/T_G^V (noted as R_{GC}), and T_D^V/T_G^V (noted as R_{GD}), we can estimate P_G/P_C and P_G/Q.

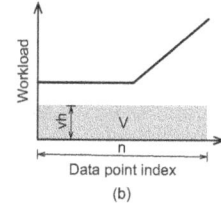

Figure 5: The partial workload V, used in profiling.

Next, we find the expressions for the β-dependent terms: W_G/W_C, O/W_G. We express the three quantities in the terms, W_G, W_C, O, separately. For the data-transfer size (O), depending on the specific application, O can be proportional to the data points assigned to the GPU (thus $O = O^V \times \beta$), or fixed no matter how many data points the GPU gets (thus $O = O^V$). In the latter case, O becomes β independent, reducing the complexity of the problem. For the partition size of the GPU (W_G) and the CPU (W_C), because we define W as the sum of the workloads of all the data points, both of them can be actually expressed by calculating the area (A) of the partition (with the use of the workload model parameters, see Figure 4). Based on the position of the partitioning point, there are two cases of partitioning, and the expressions are accordingly different (see Figure 6). Therefore, we can express W_G and W_C by the known parameters (n, bh, pw, ph, s, and α) captured by the workload model, and the only unknown parameter β.

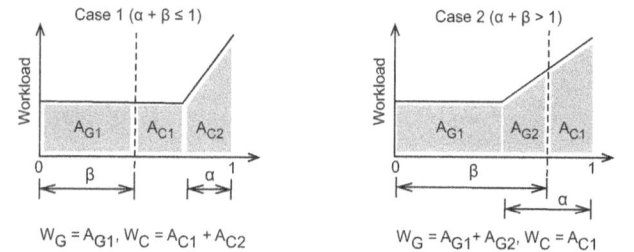

Figure 6: Two cases of partitioning. In Case 1: the partitioning point lies in the flat part. In Case 2, the partitioning point lies in the peak part.

Finally, by substituting the estimates of the β-independent terms and the expressions of the β-dependent terms into Equation 2, we get:

$$\frac{W_G}{W_C} = R_{GC} \times \frac{1}{1 + (\beta \times n \times vh \times R_{GD})/W_G} \quad \text{if } O = O^V \times \beta \quad (4a)$$

$$\frac{W_G}{W_C} = R_{GC} \times \frac{1}{1 + (n \times vh \times R_{GD})/W_G} \quad \text{if } O = O^V \quad (4b)$$

We implement the solver of the two equations into the predictor. Depending on the application's data-transfer type, the predictor chooses to solve Equation 4a or 4b. As it is not possible to determine beforehand whether the partitioning point lies in Case 1 or Case 2, the predictor calculates both cases, and chooses the only one β that falls into the valid range (either $\alpha + \beta \leq 1$ or $\alpha + \beta > 1$). Using the predictor, we obtain the optimal partitioning point in $O(1)$ time.

In summary, enabled by the profiling of the partial workload and the use of the workload model, our prediction method derives the optimal partitioning with fairly low cost, and efficiently tackles platform and workload diversities.

We note that our method can be also applied to workloads where several (adjacent or random) data points are needed to calculate one result (e.g., stencils) by replicating some/all data on both the CPU and the GPU, and multiphase workloads with inter-phase synchronizations by applying our method phase-by-phase.

4. EXPERIMENTAL EVALUATION

In this section, we use synthetic benchmarks to evaluate our partitioning method. We focus on three important aspects: the prediction quality, the partitioning effectiveness, and the adaptiveness of the method. We further apply our method to a real-life application as a case study in Section 5.

4.1 Experimental Setup

Test Workloads: we develop a set of synthetic benchmarks to generate test workloads. These benchmarks are based on iterative vector updates. In each iteration, each data point i performs $A[i] \leftarrow A[i] + B$, where B is computed using 100 floating-point operations, sufficient for timing reliability. The final value of each data point is gathered at the host; thus, the GPU data transfer size is proportional to the partitioning β (we choose to examine the more complex case). To make the workload imbalanced, we vary the number of iterations per data point. The process is controlled at code level by setting the workload model parameters (see Table 1). Varying the values of these parameters, we get a set of benchmarks that generates a set of workloads with different amount of computations and memory operations (present in different workload shapes).

Table 1: The values of each workload model parameter.

n	10^2, 10^3, 10^4, 10^5, 10^6, 10^7, 10^8
α	$(10^{-7}, 10^{-6}, 10^{-5}, 10^{-4}, 10^{-3}, 10^{-2}, 10^{-1}) \times j$, $(j = 1, 2, ..., 9)$, 1.0
pw_{min}	10
bh	500
ph	1000, 200, 3000, 4000, 5000

Table 1 summarizes the values we use: 7 different problem sizes (n), ranging from 10^2 (2KB, within CPU cache) to 10^8 (2GB, around GPU memory size). For each n, we vary the α value to change the peak width (pw). The minimum pw is fixed at 10 to make the peak part have at least 10 data points. The lager n is, the more α values are used,

and the more workloads are generated (e.g., for a problem size of 10^2, the minimum α is 10^{-1}; for a problem size of 10^8, the minimum α is 10^{-7}). The maximum α is set at 1.0 for every n, case in which all the data points form a peak (i.e., there is no flat part in the workload). In the workload dimension, we keep the base height (bh) at 500 and change the peak height (ph) from 1000 to 5000, distinguishing the peak from the flat part at various extents. The slope (s) of the peak part is also varied based on the values of α and ph. Figure 7 illustrates 6 example workload shapes. In total, we generate 1295 different workloads with different shapes (the number of workloads per problem size is shown in Table 3).

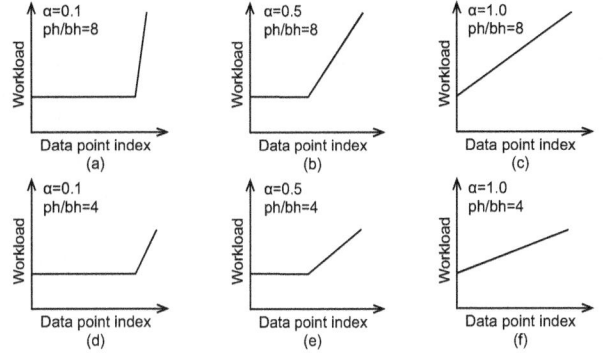

Figure 7: Examples of different workload shapes.

Heterogeneous platforms: we select three heterogeneous platforms for our experiments. The first platform (S1) integrates a dual-socket Intel six-core CPU (E5645, hyper-threading enabled) and an Nvidia Tesla C2050 GPU. The second platform (S2) consists of the same CPU as S1 and an Nvidia Quadro 600 GPU. The third platform (S3) has the same GPU as S1 and a dual-socket Intel quad-core CPU (E5620, hyper-threading enabled). Table 2 summarizes the hardware information. We use OpenCL to parallelize the code. The device-side compiler is Intel OpenCL SDK 2012 and NVIDIA OpenCL SDK 4.2, respectively. The host-side compiler is GCC 4.4.3 with -O3 option.

4.2 Prediction Quality

Our first goal is to validate prediction quality, i.e., to check if the prediction method finds the optimal partitioning. We use the partitioning obtained through auto-tuning as an estimate of the optimal partitioning that meets $T_G + T_D = T_C$. In practice, a threshold δ is applied to control auto-tuning. When $|T_G + T_D - T_C| \leq \delta$, the auto-tuning is stopped and the resulting partitioning is considered as the optimal one.

We measure prediction quality by calculating the execution-time difference D between the predicted partitioning and the optimal partitioning. D shows how the predicted partitioning approximates the optimal partitioning in terms of performance. We use the difference, rather than the relative error, to assess prediction quality. Because the auto-tuning is controlled by a threshold, a certain degree of execution-time variation between the predicted partitioning and the auto-tuned partitioning is acceptable. Thus, we apply the same threshold to D: if $|D| \leq \delta$, we consider that the predicted partitioning is optimal. In this way, we distinguish high-quality predictions from outliers. The threshold δ we use is 1, 1, 2, 3, 5, 15, 60 (ms) for problem sizes from 10^2 to

Table 2: The details of the heterogeneous platforms used in experiments.

Platform	S1		S2		S3	
Device	CPU	GPU	CPU	GPU	CPU	GPU
Processor	2× Intel Xeon E5645	Nvidia Tesla C2050		Nvidia Quadro 600	2× Intel Xeon E5620	
Frequency (GHz)	2.4	1.15		1.28	2.4	
#Cores	24 (HT enabled)	448		96	16 (HT enabled)	
Peak GFLOPS (SP/DP)	460.8/230.4	1030.4/515.2	Same CPU as S1	245.8/122.9	307.2/153.6	Same GPU as S1
Memory Capacity (GB)	24	3		1	24	
Peak Memory Bandwidth (GB/s)	64	144		25.6	51.2	
Connection	Shared memory	PCIe 2.0 ×16		PCIe 2.0 ×16	Shared memory	

10^8, respectively. We choose these values, taking the execution time and the timing measurement error[3] into account.

Table 3: The number of workloads and the hardware profiling results (R_{GC}, R_{GD}), per problem size.

n	10^2	10^3	10^4	10^5	10^6	10^7	10^8
#workloads	50	95	140	185	230	275	320
R_{GC}	0.80	3.76	20.09	30.09	30.47	30.60	30.61
R_{GD}	0.42	0.42	0.36	0.17	0.10	0.09	0.08

The experiment is performed on the S1 platform. To predict β, we measure R_{GC} and R_{GD} (see Equation 3) by profiling the partial workload V. We set $vh = bh$, so we can see the maximum profiling cost. The obtained R_{GC} and R_{GD} are presented in Table 3. Their values are different for different n, proving that profiling in the (application, problem size) context leads to more realistic estimates. The profiling results are reused for all the workloads with the same n, so the profiling cost is amortized (0.9% - 9% of the total execution time of all the workloads). We also find that the choice of vh_{min} is platform dependent. Lowering vh beyond a certain height, the prediction quality will not be acceptable. In this experiment, vh_{min} is empirically set to 100.

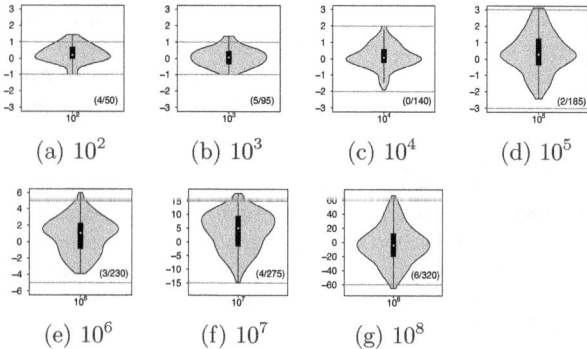

(a) 10^2 (b) 10^3 (c) 10^4 (d) 10^5

(e) 10^6 (f) 10^7 (g) 10^8

Figure 8: The prediction-quality results, in violin plot, per problem size. The vertical (y) axis represents the execution-time difference D. The horizontal lines represent the threshold δ. The violin shape represents the distribution of D values. The numbers between parenthesis show #outliers vs. #total test workloads. (The y-axes of the seven figures have different scales.)

By using the predictor, we obtain β for each workload. By contrast, the auto tuning needs on average 3-8 rounds

of binary search (the execution of the full workload) to get the optimal partitioning. The execution-time difference D per problem size is summarized in Figure 8. We see that the prediction obtains the optimal partitioning in 98.1% of the total tests (1271 out of 1295 tests). For most problem sizes, the distributions of D values are concentrated in the middle of the thresholds, further proving the prediction's high quality. In summary, our method is able to predict the optimal partitioning for imbalanced workloads with very small (0.9% - 9%) profiling cost.

4.3 Partitioning Effectiveness

To evaluate partitioning effectiveness means to understand if workload partitioning on heterogeneous platforms is worth doing, i.e., if our partitioning solution outperforms the homogeneous solution (running the application only on the CPU or the GPU). We use I, the percentage of performance improvement, to evaluate the effectiveness (assuming that partitioning improves performance).

We run the same 1295 workloads on S1. Figure 9(a) shows the performance improvement results. For larger problem sizes (10^6-10^8), the maximum I is smaller than 10%. As the GPU is much capable for the given workloads, and the data-transfer overhead is very small (see Table 3, $R_{GC} > 30$, $R_{GD} \leq 0.1$), the benefit of workload partitioning is limited. Our prediction reflects this by assigning more than 95% of the total data points to the GPU. For the smallest problem size (10^2), most workloads have negative I values (see the 3/4 quartile). Because the CPU has higher capability to process the workloads ($R_{GC} < 1.0$), using the GPU is a waste of resources, and there is no need for partitioning[4]. The median problem sizes (10^3-10^5) benefit the most from partitioning, reaching up to 60% performance improvement. We also notice that the distributions of I values are very scattered in these three problem sizes, and there are also negative I values. This behavior is related to the peak slope s (see Figure 4). When the peak has a small slope, the workload imbalance is less prominent, making the homogeneous solution with no data-transfer overhead a better option. Based on our empirical study, the small-slope upper bound is set to 5. Excluding the small-slope cases for all the problem sizes, we show the new results in Figure 9(b). We see that for the problem sizes of 10^3-10^5, the average I values are increased (above 20%), and the distributions of I values are more concentrated and upward shifted (see the change of the minimums and the quartiles). By contrast, the other problem sizes show no significant changes.

---

[3]The timing measurement error is within the threshold we choose. Each timing test is repeated 50 times. The unstable results in the warm-up phase are discarded, and then the median value in the stable results is selected as the final timing result.

[4]In real life, a problem size of 10^2 is not a usual case for parallelization. We use it to show the "extreme" situation.

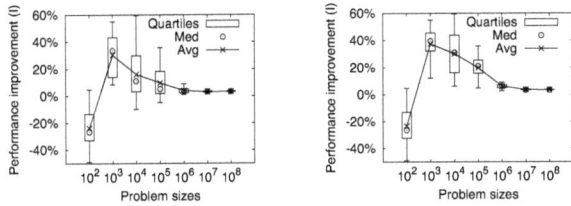

(a) the original results

(b) excluding the small-slope cases

Figure 9: The performance improvement, in box-and-whisker plot, per problem size: (a) the original results, (b) the results after excluding the small-slope cases.

To summarize, partitioning is an effective method for imbalanced workloads, as it leads to better platform utilization than the homogeneous solution. The more imbalanced the workload is, the more performance gain is obtained. There are two cases when using a single processor is better. First, when the dataset has not enough parallelism, using only the CPU (no partitioning) is sufficient. Second, when the GPU has much higher capability to process the workload and the data-transfer overhead is negligible, workload partitioning has limited performance gain. We are able to know this beforehand from prediction ($\beta > 95\%$), and we can use only the GPU for execution.

4.4 Adaptiveness of the method

Another important aspect is the adaptiveness of the method. The above experiments have shown that our method is able to respond to workload and problem size changes. To evaluate its adaptiveness to platform changes, we perform two more experiments.

First, we use the S2 platform that has the same CPU as S1 but a less powerful GPU (both GPUs have the same Fermi architecture). The number of cores, peak GFLOPS, memory capacity, and bandwidth are reduced compared to that in S1. We run the same 1295 workloads on the new platform. As the GPU is changed, we re-profile the GPU, and recalculate R_{GC} and R_{GD} for prediction (the CPU profiling results are reused). We see that the resulting prediction maintains high quality and reacts to the GPU change by shifting the partitioning point one direction or another.

Table 4 summarizes the change of the partitioning point. For smaller problem sizes (10^2-10^3), the new GPU is more efficient in processing their workloads than the old GPU. As a result, the partitioning point is right shifted (the new GPU gets more work), and the performance is improved by 12%. For larger problem sizes (10^4-10^7), the new GPU has much lower capability than the old GPU, thus the partitioning point is largely left shifted (the CPU gets more work), and the performance is decreased by up to 4 times. For the largest problem size (10^8), the calculated GPU partition exceeds the GPU memory. For now, the prediction chooses a smaller partition that fits the memory, but lowers the performance. We aim to solve this limitation in the future by using more complex platforms, i.e., multi-GPUs and integrated CPU+GPU architectures.

Second, we use the S3 platform, where the GPU is the same and the CPU is changed to a lower configuration (dual quad-core, lower peak GFLOPS and memory bandwidth). We repeat the experiment and re-profile only the new CPU. Again the prediction reacts to the CPU change by moving more work onto the GPU. We also find that the performance

difference between S1 and S3 is quite small compared to that between the two CPUs, indicating that the partitioning compensates for the CPU degradation.

Table 4: The change of the partitioning point when using new platforms.

Platform	Problem size	Capability Change	New Partitioning
S2	10^2-10^3	new GPU > old GPU	right shifted
	10^4-10^7	new GPU < old GPU	left shifted
	10^8	new GPU < old GPU	left shifted till it fits the GPU memory
S3	10^2-10^8	new CPU < old CPU	right shifted

To sum up, our partitioning method is able to tackle platform diversity as well. It responds to hardware changes by re-profiling the new hardware and resizing the partitions accordingly.

4.5 The Effect of Compilers

We also investigate how our method responds to compiler performance. As Nvidia and Intel release new versions of their compilers quite often, we make an experiment to test the impact of these changes. We update to Intel SDK 2013 and Nvidia SDK 5.5[5], and re-run the experiment on S1. We find that the Intel compiler improves application performance (on the CPU), while the new Nvidia compiler (the OpenCL part) does not (on the GPU). Our method responds to this change by re-profiling and re-predicting the partitioning point. As a result, the CPU gets more work, and the new partitioning achieves up to 15% performance improvement over the original one.

Thus, we point out that a pure hardware modeling, or a hardware modeling combined with an (application, problem size) modeling, may lead to a sub-optimal partitioning when ignoring the effect of compilers. As updating or altering compilers can affect application performance on the same hardware platform, profiling is essential to achieve the best performing partitioning.

5. A REAL-WORLD CASE STUDY

In this section, we use acoustic ray tracing as an imbalanced application case study, and show how our method is applied to real-world applications.

5.1 The Application

Acoustic ray tracing [2] is developed to calculate, in real time, the propagation of aircraft flyover noise by closely simulating the changes in the ray trajectory as it moves through different media. Figure 10 illustrates the propagation of all the rays launched by the aircraft at different angles.

The ray propagation path is determined by a time-based simulation, where the location and orientation of a ray is calculated in every time step, and saved for later auralization. In the implementation, there are two nested loops: the outer loop traverses all the rays, and the inner loop computes the ray propagation. In the inner loop, the variable time step technique is applied to control the simulation resolution. When a ray meets certain location and orientation conditions, the time step of the ray is dynamically refined to obtain high fidelity (i.e., its propagation is more interesting

---

[5]At the time when we write this paper (January 2014), these are the latest compilers.

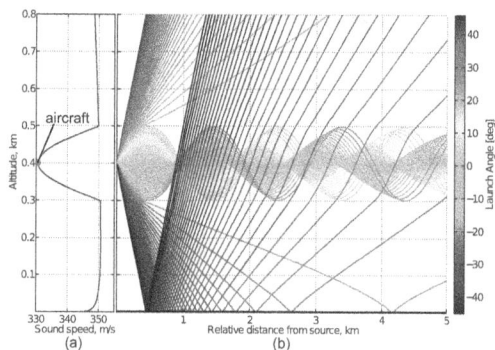

Figure 10: Ray propagation in an *altitue × distance* grid. (a) Sound speed profile. There is headwind (at 0.3-0.5 km altitude) blowing against the aircraft (the red dot at 0.4 km altitude). (b) The propagation profile for all the sound rays emitted by the aircraft.

for the users). It is this use of variable time steps that leads to an imbalanced workload. All the rays are independent from each other and simulated in parallel, but the workload of each ray is dynamically determined at runtime.

By changing the flyover environment (e.g., the headwind speed, the aircraft height), we obtain 10 real imbalanced workloads with different workload shapes. Each workload has 6000 simulated rays (problem size), and the workload of a ray is measured by the number of simulation iterations. Figure 11 shows one such workload.

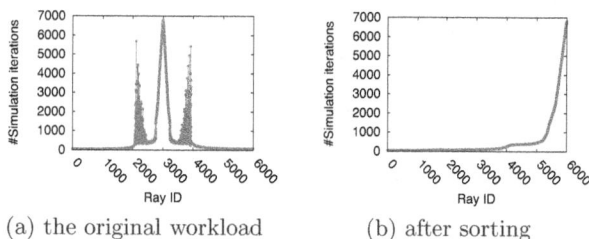

(a) the original workload   (b) after sorting

Figure 11: One workload of acoustic ray tracing: (a) the original workload, (b) the workload after sorting. Each ray is identified by its ray id starting from 0 to 5999, which corresponds to its launching angle ranging from -45 to 45 degree with respect to the horizontal.

5.2 The Partitioning Process

To partition the acoustic ray tracing workload, we need to do three things: model the workload, profile the platform, and perform the prediction.

First, workload modeling extracts the workload model from the original workload. It consists of two steps: workload sorting and workload model approximation. The sorting reshapes the original workload into a peak-shaped workload (Figure 11(b)), making the model approximation easier. Note that a de-sorting is applied at the end of execution to assemble the correct simulation output. The model approximation finds out the inflection point ip between the flat part and the peak part of the sorted workload, and obtains the workload model. It uses a binary search to get the ip that has the largest slope difference Δs (Δs is calculated by connecting ip with the 0-th point and the 5999-th point, and get-

ting the slope difference between the two lines). The three last-searched points are recorded as candidate ip, i.e., we approximate the workload model per ip, predict the partitioning, and choose the best performing one. Figure 12 shows the three workload-model approximations for the workload depicted in Figure 11(b). Next, we profile the platform for this application. The obtained profiling results (R_{GC} and R_{GD}) are used for all the 10 workloads. Finally, the generated workload models and the profiling results are combined in the predictor to get the partitioning.

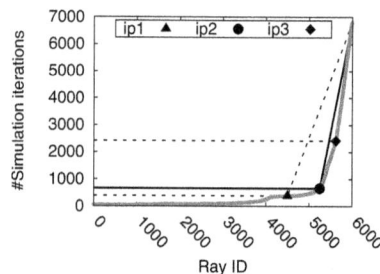

Figure 12: For the workload depicted in Figure 11(b), the three workload-model approximations shown by the straight solid lines and dashed lines. $ip1$, $ip2$, $ip3$ are the three last-searched points. In this example, $ip3$ has the largest Δs, but $ip2$ leads to the closest workload approximation, and thus to the best performing partitioning.

Costs vs. Performance: There is a small cost to model the workload and profile the platform. Depending on the user scenarios, the cost will vary. For example, if the best application performance is the target, we can use total sorting, which potentially guarantees the best performance and takes on average 6% (sorting and de-sorting) of the application execution time. If the performance requirement can be relaxed, a partial sorting [6] or a sampling combined with sorting can be used. This decreases the application performance by 24% (due to a less accurate workload model), but reduces the modeling cost to less than 2% of the application execution time. For workload model approximation, examining three ip candidates leads to three times of runs of application. Choosing only one of them may result in a suboptimal partitioning, but reduces the modeling cost to only the ip searching time (0.2% of application execution time). For profiling the platform, the cost (10% of the application execution time) can be amortized by all the tested workloads, thus the more workloads we run, the less profiling cost we get. The real application scenario is even simpler: different people will hear the same flyover noise simulation, leading to a survey of its annoyance factor. In this scenario, the same flyover environment is set, and the same workload is executed repetitively. Thus, the modeling and the profiling become a one-time effort, as the users can use them just once for prediction, and reuse the prediction by fetching it from the repository.

5.3 The Partitioning Results

We evaluate the prediction quality and the partitioning effectiveness as we have done for synthetic workloads. We perform the experiment on S1 (see Table 2). Figure 13 shows the experimental results (note that because the application has real-time requirement for auralization, the execution time is in ms scale). By comparing the execution time of the predicted partitioning and the best partitioning obtained through auto-tuning [29], we see that, for 9 out of 10 workloads, the execution-time differences are within the threshold ($|D| \leq \delta$, δ is set to 3 ms), with the average D at 1.2 ms. The exception is W3, which actually has a stair-shaped workload. As the workload modeling approximates W3 with a wider peak, this coarse approximation leads to less accurate prediction and degraded performance. We plan to address this issue by refining our workload model to include stair-shaped workloads. By comparing the execution time of the predicted partitioning and the single CPU/GPU solution, we see that the partitioning largely improves application performance, with the average performance improvement I at 51%. The workloads with a larger peak slope get higher performance improvement. Only W4 has limited performance gain. This is mainly because it falls into the small-slope case, in which most of the workload is assigned to the GPU. The predicted partitioning actually indicates this, so we can decide to use only the GPU for W4 without applying and evaluating the partitioning.

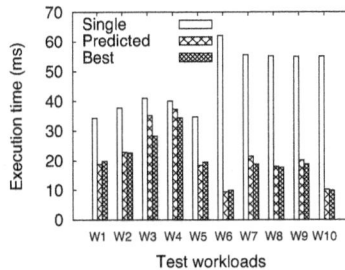

Figure 13: The execution time per real imbalanced workload. W1-W10 denote the 10 workloads. "Single" represents using only the GPU or the CPU (the one with smaller execution time is chosen). "Predicted" represents the predicted partitioning. "Best" represents the best partitioning obtained through auto-tuning.

Summary: In practice, to achieve the best performance for real-world imbalanced applications on heterogeneous platforms, we should apply the following recipe: (1) model the workload, profile the platform, and perform the prediction, (2) decide for partitioning or not based on (1), and if needed, (3) apply the predicted partitioning. The empirical study shows that the decision for partitioning or not is made according to the application problem size and the prediction results. If the application problem size is too small (not enough parallelism), we should use only the CPU. If the prediction decides to run most of the workload on the GPU, we can directly use the GPU, and there is no apparently performance lose.

6. RELATED WORK

Workload partitioning for heterogeneous platforms has been well studied in recent years. Multiple partitioning approaches have been developed aiming to efficiently utilize all the computing resources of the heterogeneous platform.

Merge [15] and the work of Tomov et al. [30] determine the right workload partitioning according to the performance estimate provided by the programmers. These solutions have limited applicability as they largely rely on manual work.

Our previous work [29] has demonstrated the use of auto-tuning for workload partitioning. Because auto-tuning is time-consuming and occupies the target platform unnecessarily, the prediction-based method presented in this paper is a mandatory improvement for our workload partitioning approach.

Grewe et al. [7] adopted a machine learning approach to predict the workload partitioning. They built a predictive model based on static program features extracted from the code. Kofler et al. [14] improved this approach by adding dynamic program features (i.e., problem size related features) into the model. Compared to our approach, both solutions are not adaptive to hardware and software changes. When either changes, a rerun of the whole training phase is needed to rebuild the predictive model, and this training overhead cannot be ignored.

Luk et al. [16] proposed an adaptive approach, Qilin, to map computations to heterogeneous platforms. Qilin uses a large amount of profiling data and curve-fitting to derive the partitioning for the same program with a new input. Our prediction uses a partial workload for profiling, which largely reduces the profiling cost and still generates an accurate prediction. Gharaibeh et al. [5] built a performance model to study the partitioning of graph workloads. They also introduced hardware-capability related metrics to estimate graph processing performance. However, they assumed the metrics are constant independent of actual graph workloads, leading to lower accuracy for some cases. Instead, we use more realistic estimate by measuring the metrics in the (application, problem size) context. Yang et al. [32] predicted application performance on large-scale systems by using relative performance between the target and reference systems. Our partial workload profiling relates to their approach as we both adopt a black-box style performance observation from a very short run of the application. While their prediction is used for large-scale system selection, we focus on workload partitioning over heterogeneous platforms.

On the other hand, studies on dynamic workload scheduling [3, 4, 18, 25, 26] aim to achieve load balancing in heterogeneous systems. Workload scheduling is able to respond to performance variability at runtime, but it may lead to high scheduling and communication overheads depending on the applications, the hardware, and the scheduling algorithms. In our work, we find that workload partitioning is more efficient for accelerating imbalanced workloads on CPU+GPU platforms, as the workload scheduling will generate successive data communication between the CPU and the GPU.

All the above mentioned work only consider the problem-size dimension for partitioning. Our approach takes the workload characteristics into consideration, and generates accurate, efficient partitioning solutions.

7. CONCLUSION

Workload partitioning is essential for efficiently utilizing heterogeneous platforms. In this paper, we propose a model-based partitioning method to match imbalanced workloads with CPU+GPU heterogeneous platforms. Our method predicts the optimal partitioning for imbalanced workloads, leading to the best performance on the platform. Through our experiments on both synthetic workloads and a real-world case study, we show evidence that our method has high prediction quality (above 90% of the total tests get accurate prediction), increases application performance by using both processors (up to 60% performance improvement over a single processor execution), and maintains a very low partitioning cost. We also show that the method is adaptive to application, problem size, hardware, and software changes, obtaining the optimal partitioning for any given (workload, platform) pair.

In the future, we will refine the workload model to include stair-shaped workloads, and extend our method to multi-GPUs and integrated CPU+GPU architectures to solve the memory capacity limitation. We further plan to cover more generic applications (not only imbalanced ones) to make our partitioning method full-fledged.

8. REFERENCES

[1] AMD. APU 101: All about AMD Fusion Accelerated Processing Units. http://developer.amd.com.

[2] M. Arntzen, S. A. Rizzi, H. G. Visser, and D. G. Simons. A framework for simulation of aircraft flyover noise through a non-standard atmosphere. In *the 18th AIAA/CEAS Aeroacoustics Conference*, pages AIAA–2012–2079, 2012.

[3] C. Augonnet, S. Thibault, R. Namyst, and P.-A. Wacrenier. StarPU: a unified platform for task scheduling on heterogeneous multicore architectures. *Concurrency and Computation: Practice and Experience*, 23(2):187–198, 2011.

[4] M. Boyer, K. Skadron, S. Che, and N. Jayasena. Load Balancing in a Changing World: Dealing with Heterogeneity and Performance Variability. In *Computing Frontiers 2013*, pages 21:1–21:10, 2013.

[5] A. Gharaibeh, L. B. Costa, E. Santos-Neto, and M. Ripeanu. A Yoke of Oxen and a Thousand Chickens for Heavy Lifting Graph Processing. In *PACT 2012*, pages 345–354, 2012.

[6] A. Gharaibeh, L. B. Costa, E. Santos-Neto, and M. Ripeanu. On Graphs, GPUs, and Blind Dating: A Workload to Processor Matchmaking Quest. In *IPDPS 2013*, pages 851–862, 2013.

[7] D. Grewe and M. F. P. O'Boyle. A Static Task Partitioning Approach for Heterogeneous Systems Using OpenCL. In *CC 2011*, pages 286–305.

[8] K. Group. The OpenCL Specification v2.0. http://www.khronos.org.

[9] S. Hong, T. Oguntebi, and K. Olukotun. Efficient Parallel Graph Exploration on Multi-Core CPU and GPU. In *PACT 2011*, pages 78–88, 2011.

[10] Intel. Intel SDK for OpenCL Applications - Optimization Guide. http://software.intel.com.

[11] Intel. Sandy Bridge. http://ark.intel.com.

[12] T. B. Jablin, P. Prabhu, J. A. Jablin, N. P. Johnson, S. R. Beard, and D. I. August. Automatic CPU-GPU Communication Management and Optimization. In *PLDI 2011*, pages 142–151, 2011.

[13] J. Kim, H. Kim, J. H. Lee, and J. Lee. Achieving a Single Compute Device Image in OpenCL for Multiple GPUs. In *PPoPP 2011*, pages 277–288, 2011.

[14] K. Kofler, I. Grasso, B. Cosenza, and T. Fahringer. An Automatic Input-Sensitive Approach for Heterogeneous Task Partitioning. In *ICS 2013*, pages 149–160, 2013.

[15] M. D. Linderman, J. D. Collins, H. Wang, and T. H. Y. Meng. Merge: A Programming Model for Heterogeneous Multi-core Systems. In *ASPLOS 2008*, pages 287–296, 2008.

[16] C.-K. Luk, S. Hong, and H. Kim. Qilin: Exploiting Parallelism on Heterogeneous Multiprocessors with Adaptive Mapping. In *MICRO*, pages 45–55, 2009.

[17] D. Lustig and M. Martonosi. Reducing GPU Offload Latency via Fine-Grained CPU-GPU Synchronization. In *HPCA 2013*, pages 354–365.

[18] K. Ma, X. Li, W. Chen, C. Zhang, and X. Wang. GreenGPU: A Holistic Approach to Energy Efficiency in GPU-CPU Heterogeneous Architectures. In *ICPP 2012*, pages 48–57, 2012.

[19] K. K. Matam and K. Kothapalli. Accelerating Sparse Matrix Vector Multiplication in Iterative Methods Using GPU. In *ICPP 2011*, pages 612–621, 2011.

[20] A. F. Murarasu, J. Weidendorfer, and A. Bode. Workload Balancing on Heterogeneous Systems: A Case Study of Sparse Grid Interpolation. In *Euro-Par Workshops*, pages 345–354, 2011.

[21] A. Nere, A. Hashmi, and M. H. Lipasti. Profiling Heterogeneous Multi-GPU Systems to Accelerate Cortically Inspired Learning Algorithms. In *IPDPS 2011*, pages 906–920, 2011.

[22] OpenACC. The OpenACC Application Programming Interface. http://www.openacc-standard.org.

[23] R. A. Pearce, M. Gokhale, and N. M. Amato. Multithreaded Asynchronous Graph Traversal for In-Memory and Semi-External Memory. In *SC 2010*, pages 1–11, 2010.

[24] A. Penders. Accelerating Graph Analysis with Heterogeneous Systems. Master's thesis, TU Delft, 2012.

[25] V. T. Ravi, W. Ma, D. Chiu, and G. Agrawal. Compiler and Runtime Support for Enabling Generalized Reduction Computations on Heterogeneous Parallel Configurations. In *ICS 2010*, pages 137–146, 2010.

[26] T. Scogland, B. Rountree, W. chun Feng, and B. R. de Supinski. Heterogeneous Task Scheduling for Accelerated OpenMP. In *IPDPS 2012*, pages 144–155, 2012.

[27] S. Seo, G. Jo, and J. Lee. Performance characterization of the NAS Parallel Benchmarks in OpenCL. In *IISWC 2011*, pages 137–148, 2011.

[28] J. Shen, J. Fang, H. Sips, and A. L. Varbanescu. An application-centric evaluation of opencl on multi-core cpus. *Parallel Computing*, 39(12):834 – 850, 2013.

[29] J. Shen, A. L. Varbanescu, H. J. Sips, M. Arntzen, and D. G. Simons. Glinda: A Framework for Accelerating Imbalanced Applications on Heterogeneous Platforms. In *Computing Frontiers 2013*, pages 14:1–14:10, 2013.

[30] S. Tomov, J. Dongarra, and M. Baboulin. Towards Dense Linear Algebra for Hybrid GPU Accelerated Manycore Systems. *Parallel Computing*, 36(5-6):232–240, 2010.

[31] R. Vuduc, A. Chandramowlishwaran, J. Choi, M. Guney, and A. Shringarpure. On the Limits of GPU Acceleration. In *HotPar 2010*, pages 13–13, 2010.

[32] L. T. Yang, X. Ma, and F. Mueller. Cross-Platform Performance Prediction of Parallel Applications Using Partial Execution. In *SC 2005*, page 40, 2005.

Long-Term Resource Fairness: Towards Economic Fairness on Pay-as-you-use Computing Systems

Shanjiang Tang, Bu-Sung Lee, Bingsheng He, and Haikun Liu
School of Computer Engineering, Nanyang Technological University
Singapore
{stang5, ebslee, bshe}@ntu.edu.sg, haikunliu@gmail.com

ABSTRACT

Fair resource allocation is a key building block of any shared computing system. However, *MemoryLess Resource Fairness (MLRF)*, widely used in many existing frameworks such as YARN, Mesos and Dryad, is *not* suitable for pay-as-you-use computing. To address this problem, this paper proposes *Long-Term Resource Fairness (LTRF)*, a novel fair resource allocation mechanism. We show that LTRF satisfies several highly desirable properties. First, LTRF incentivizes clients to share resources via group-buying by ensuring that no client is better off in a computing system that she buys and uses individually. Second, LTRF incentivizes clients to submit *non-trivial* workloads and be willing to yield unneeded resources to others. Third, LTRF has a resource-as-you-pay fairness property, which ensures the amount of resources that each client should get according to her monetary cost, despite that her resource demand varies over time. Finally, LTRF is strategy-proof, since it can make sure that a client cannot get more resources by lying about her demand. We have implemented LTRF in YARN by developing *LT-YARN*, a long-term YARN fair scheduler, and shown that it leads to a better resource fairness than other state-of-the-art fair schedulers.

Categories and Subject Descriptors

D.4.1 [**Process Management**]: Scheduling; D.2.8 [**Metrics**]: Process metrics, performance measures; k.6.2 [**Installation Management**]: Pricing and resource allocation

Keywords

Cloud Computing, Long-Term Resource Fairness, MapReduce, YARN

1. INTRODUCTION

Current supercomputers and data centers (e.g., Amazon EC2) typically consist of thousands of servers connected via a high-speed network. At any time, there are tens of thousands of clients concurrently running their high-performance computing applications (e.g., MapReduce [8], MPI, Spark [32]) on the shared computing system (i.e., pay-as-you-use computing system). Clients pay

ICS'14, June 10–13 2014, Munich, Germany.
Copyright 2014 ACM 978-1-4503-2642-1/14/06 ...$15.00.
http://dx.doi.org/10.1145/2597652.2597672.

the money on the basis of their resource usage. To meet different clients' needs, providers generally offer several options of price plans (e.g., on-demand and reservation). When a client has a short-term computation requirement (e.g., several hours), she can choose on-demand price plan that charges compute resources by each time unit (e.g., hour) with fixed price. In contrast, if she has a long-term computation request (e.g., 1 year), choosing reserved price plan can enable her to have a significant discount from the on-demand hourly charge and thereby save the money cost.

Instead of purchasing and utilizing resources individually, recently, there are some researchers and companies (e.g., Tuangru, SalesForce) strongly recommending *group-buying* and *resource sharing*, since *group-buying* can offer resources at significantly reduced prices on the condition that a minimum number of buyers would make the purchase [13] and *resource sharing* can improve the resource utilization. Consider buying the reserved resources for example. With reservation plan, clients need to pay a one-time fee for a long time (e.g., 1 or 3 years). To achieve the full cost savings, customers must commit to have a high utilization. In practice, it is most likely that the resource demand of a customer varies over time, indicating that it's difficult to ensure the resources can be fully utilized all the time.

With group-buying and resource sharing, the above problems can be nicely addressed. First, group buying can get increased discount of reserved resources from sellers, cheaper than buying individually. Second, different clients often have different resource demand at different time. The resource utilization problem can be thereby resolved with resource sharing between clients in a shared system.

Given group-buying resources, the fair resource allocation among clients is a key issue. One of the most popular fair allocation policy is *(weighted) max-min fairness* [11], which maximizes the minimum resource allocation obtained by a user in a shared computing system. It has been widely used in many popular high performance computing frameworks such as Hadoop [4], YARN [2], Mesos [15], Dryad [16] and Choosy [10]. Unfortunately, we observe that the fair polices implemented in these systems are all *memoryless*, i.e., allocating resources fairly at instant time without considering history information. We refer those schedulers as *MemoryLess Resource Fairness (MLRF)*. MLRF is *not* suitable for such pay-as-you-use computing system due to the following reasons.

Trivial Workload Problem. In a pay-as-you-use computing system, we should have a policy to incentivize group members to submit *non-trivial* workloads that they really need (See *Non-Trivial-Workload Incentive* property in Section 3). For *MLRF*, there is an implicit assumption that all users are unselfish and honest towards their requested resource demands, which is however often not true in real world. It can cause trivial workload problem with *MLRF*. Consider two users A and B sharing a system. Let D_A and

D_B be the *true* workload demand for A and B at time t_0, respectively. Assume that D_A is less than its share[1] while D_B is larger than its share. In that case, it is possible that A is selfish and will try to possess all of her share by running some trivial tasks (e.g., running some duplicated tasks of the experimental workloads for double checking) so that her extra unused share will not be preempted by B, causing the inefficiency problem of running non-trivial workloads and also breaking the sharing incentive property (See the definition in Section 3).

Strategy-Proofness Problem. It is important for a shared system to have a policy to ensure that no group member can get any benefits by lying (See *Strategy-proofness* in Section 3). We argue that *MLRF* cannot satisfy this property. Consider a system consisting of three users A, B, and C. Assume A and C are honest whereas B is not. It could happen at a time that both the *true* demands of A and B are less than their own shares while C's *true* demand exceeds its share. In that case, A yields her unused resources to others honestly. But B will provide *false* information about her demand (e.g., far larger than her share) and compete with C for unused resources from A. Lying benefits B, hence violating strategy-proofness. Moreover, it will break the sharing incentive property if all other users also lie.

Resource-as-you-pay Fairness Problem. For group-buying resources, we should ensure that the total resource received by each member is proportional to her monetary cost (See *Resources-as-you-pay Fairness* in Section 3). Due to the varied resource demands (e.g., workflows) for a user at different time, *MLRF* cannot achieve this property. Consider two users A and B. At time t_0, it could happen that the demand D_A is less than its share and hence its extra unused resource will be possessed by B (i.e., lend to B) according to the work conserving property of *MLRF*. Next at time t_1, assume that A's demand D_A becomes larger than its share. With *MLRF*, user A can only use her current share (i.e., cannot get lent resources at t_0 back from B), if D_B is larger than its share, due to *memoryless*. If this scenario often occurs, it will be unfair for A to get the amount of resources that she should have obtained from a long-term view. (See a motivation example in Section 4).

In this paper, we propose *Long-Term Resource Fairness (LTRF)* and show that it can solve the aforementioned problems. LTRF satisfies five good properties including sharing incentive, non-trivial-workload incentive, resource-as-you-pay fairness, strategy-proofness and Pareto Efficiency. *LTRF* provides incentives for users to submit non-trivial workloads and share resources via group-buying by ensuring that no customer is better off in a computing system that she purchases individually. Moreover, *LTRF* can guarantee the amount of resources a user should receive in terms of the monetary cost that she pays, in the case that her resource demand varies over time. In addition, *LTRF* is strategy-proof, as it can make sure that a customer cannot get more resources by lying about her resource demand. Finally, *LTRF* can maximize the system utilization by ensuring that it is impossible for a client to get more resources without decreasing the resource of at least one client.

We have implemented *LTRF* in YARN [2] by developing a long-term fair scheduler *LTYARN*. The experiments show that, 1). LTRF can guarantee SLA via minimizing the sharing loss and bringing much sharing benefit for each client, whereas MLRF cannot; 2). the shared methods using LTRF can get better performance than non-shared one, or at least as fast in the shared system as they do in the non-shared partitioning case. The performance finding is consistent with previous work such as Mesos [15].

This paper is organized as follows. Section 2 reviews the related work. Section 3 gives several payment-oriented resource allocation properties. Section 4 presents LTRF and gives a property analysis, followed by the design and implementation of *LTYARN* in Section 5. Section 6 evaluates the fairness and performance of LT-YARN experimentally. Finally, we conclude and give future work in Section 7.

2. RELATED WORK

We review the existing studies that are closely related to this work from two aspects below:

Fairness Definitions, Policies and Algorithms. Fairness has been studied extensively in HPC and grid computing environment [23, 18, 22, 34, 6]. Sabin et al. [23] consider fair in terms of start time, if no later arriving job delays an earlier arriving job. Jain et al. [18] measured the fairness based on the standard deviation of the turnaround time. Ngubiri et al. [22] compare different fairness definitions on dispersion, start time and queueing time. Zhao et al. [34] and Arabnejad et al. [6] consider fairness for multiple workflows. They define fairness on the basis of *slowdown* that each workflow would experience, where the *slowdown* refers to the difference in the expected execution time between when scheduled together with other workflows and when scheduled alone.

The above fairness definitions are mainly based on the "performance" metrics. In this following, we argue that they are no longer suitable due to the different concerns and meanings of fairness preferred in pay-as-you-use computing systems.

1). The pay-as-you-use computing system is a service-oriented platform with resource guarantee. That is, from service providers' perspective (e.g., Amazon, supercomputer operator), they only need to guarantee the amount of resources allocated to each client over a period of time. That is, the performance metrics for client's applications are not the main concerns for providers. Our proposed LTRF is based on this point in the shared pay-as-you-use computing system. It attempts to make sure that the total amount of resources that each client obtains is larger than or at least the same as that in an non-shared partitioning system, according to her payment.

2). The traditional fair policies and algorithms (e.g., round-robin, proportional resource sharing [29], and weighted fair queueing [9]) on resource allocation in HPC and grid computing are *memoryless*, i.e., instant fairness of a single dimension. In contrast, pay-as-you-use computing system has a monetary cost issue with resources paid by consumed time (e.g., one hour). Its fair policy should have two dimensions, i.e., the size of resources multiplies the execution time that a client consumed. Our LTRF is designed to be a two-dimension fair policy with the historical information considered.

Max-Min Fairness. Max-min fairness is a popular fair policy widely used in many existing systems such as Hadoop [4], YARN [2], Mesos [15], Choosy [10], Quincy [17]. Hadoop [4] partitions resources into map/reduce slots and allocates them fairly across pools and jobs. In contrast, YARN [2] divides resources into containers (i.e., a set of various resources like memory and CPU cores) and tries to guarantee fairness among queues. Mesos [15] enables multiple diverse computing frameworks such as Hadoop and Spark sharing a single system. Choosy [10] extends the max-min fairness by considering placement constraints. Quincy [17] is a fair scheduler for Dryad that achieves the fair scheduling of multiple jobs by formulating it as a min-cost flow problem. Moreover, DRF [11] and its extensions [7, 19, 31, 25] generalize max-min fairness from a single resource type to multiple resource types. However, all of these are indeed *memoryless*, belonging to MLRF. In this paper, we argue that there are three problems in pay-as-

---

[1] By default, we refer to the *current* share at the designated time (e.g., t_0), rather than the *total* share accumulated over time.

you-use computing system regarding MLRF, i.e., trivial workload, strategy-proofness and resource-as-you-pay. In contrast, our proposed LTRF can address all those three problems.

3. PAYMENT-ORIENTED RESOURCE ALLOCATION PROPERTIES

This section presents a set of desirable properties that we believe any payment-oriented resource allocation policy in a shared pay-as-you-use system should meet. Base on these properties, we design our fair allocation policy in the following sections. We have found the following five important properties:

- *Sharing Incentive*: Each client should be better off sharing the resources via group-buying with others, than exclusively buying and using the resources individually. Consider a shared pay-as-you-use computing system with n clients over t period time. Then a client should not be able to get more than $t \cdot \frac{1}{n}$ resources in a system partition consisting of $\frac{1}{n}$ of all resources.

- *Non-Trivial-Workload Incentive*: A client should get benefits by submitting non-trivial workloads and yielding unused resources to others when not needed. Otherwise, she may be selfish and posses all unneeded resources under her share by running some dirty or trivial tasks in a shared computing environment.

- *Resource-as-you-pay Fairness*: The resource that a client gains should be proportional to her payment. This property is important as it is a resource guarantee to clients.

- *Strategy-Proofness*: Clients should not be able to get benefits by lying about their resource demands. This property is compatible with sharing incentive and resource-as-you-pay fairness, since no client can obtain more resources by lying.

- *Pareto Efficiency*: In a shared resource environment, it is impossible for a client to get more resources without decreasing the resource of at least one client. This property can ensure the system resource utilization to be maximized.

4. LONG-TERM RESOURCE FAIRNESS

In this section, we first give a motivation example to show that MemoryLess Resource Fairness (MLRF) is *not* suitable for pay-as-you-use computing system. Then we propose Long-Term Resource Fairness (LTRF), a payment-oriented allocation policy to address the limitations of MLRF and meet the desired properties described in Section 3. Lastly, we introduce our formal fairness definition.

Motivation Example. Consider a shared computing system consisting of 100 resources (e.g., 100GB RAM) and two users A and B with equal share of 50GB each. As illustrated in Table 1, assume that the new requested demands at time t_1, t_2, t_3, t_4 for client A are $20, 40, 80, 60$, and for client B are $100, 60, 50, 50$, respectively. With MLRF, we see in Table 1(a) that, at t_1, the total demand and allocation for A are both 20. It lends 30 unused resources to B and thus 80 allocations for B. The scenario is similar at t_2. Next at t_3 and t_4, the total demand for A becomes 80 and 90, bigger than its share of 50. However, it can only get 50 allocations based on MLRF, being *unfair* for A, since the total allocations for A and B become $160(= 20+40+50+50)$ and $240(= 80+60+50+50)$ at time t_4, respectively. Instead, if we adopt LTRF, as shown in Table 1(b), the total allocations for A and B at t_4 will finally be the same (e.g., 200), being *fair* for A and B.

LTRF Scheduling Algorithm. Algorithm 1 shows pseudo-code for LTRF scheduling. It considers the fairness of total allocated resources consumed by each client, instead of currently allocated

resources. The core idea is based on the '*loan(lending) agreement*' [20] with free interest. That is, a client will yield her unused resources to others as a *lend* manner at a time. When she needs at a later time, she should get the resources back from others that she yielded before (i.e., *return* manner). In our previous two-client example with LTRF in Table 1(b), client A first lends her unused resources of 30 and 10 to client B at time t_1 and t_2, respectively. However, at t_3 and t_4, she has a large demand and then collects all 40 extra resources back from B that she lent before, making *fair* between A and B.

Due to the *lending agreement* of LTRF, in practice, when A yields her unused resources at t_1 and t_2, B might not want to possess extra unused resources from A immediately. In that case, the total allocations for A and B will be $160(= 20+40+50+50)$ and $200(= 50+50+50+50)$ at time t_4, causing the inefficiency problem for the system utilization. To solve this problem, we propose a *discount*-based approach. The idea is that, anybody possessing extra unused resources from others will have a *discount* (e.g., 50%) on resource counting. It will incentivize B to preempt extra unused resources from A, since it is *cheaper* than its own share of resources. For A, it also does not get resource lost, as it can get the same *discount* on the resource counting for the preempted resources from B back later.

Table 1(c) demonstrates this point. It shows the discounted resource allocation for each client over time by discounting the possessed extra unused resource. At time t_1, A yields her 30 unused resources to B and B's discounted resources are $65(= 50+30 \cdot 50\%)$ instead of $80(= 50 + 30)$. Similarly for A at t_3, it preempts 30 resources from B and its discounted resources are $65(= 50 + 30 \cdot 50\%)$. Still, both of them are *fair* at time t_4.

	Client A					Client B				
	Demand		Allocation		Preempt	Demand		Allocation		Preempt
	New	Total	Current	Total		New	Total	Current	Total	
t_1	20	20	20	20	−30	100	100	80	80	+30
t_2	40	40	40	60	−10	60	80	60	140	+10
t_3	80	80	50	110	0	50	70	50	190	0
t_4	60	90	50	**160**	0	50	70	50	**240**	0

(a) Allocation results based on *MLRF*. *Total Demand* refers to the sum of the new demand and accumulated remaining demand in previous time.

	Client A					Client B				
	Demand		Allocation		Preempt	Demand		Allocation		Preempt
	New	Total	Current	Total		New	Total	Current	Total	
t_1	20	20	20	20	−30	100	100	80	80	+30
t_2	40	40	40	60	−10	60	80	60	140	+10
t_3	80	80	80	140	+30	50	70	20	160	−30
t_4	60	60	60	**200**	+10	50	100	40	**200**	−10

(b) Allocation results based on *LTRF*.

	Client A					Client B				
	Demand		Counted Allocation		Preempt	Demand		Counted Allocation		Preempt
	New	Total	Current	Total		New	Total	Current	Total	
t_1	20	20	20	20	−30	100	100	65	65	+30
t_2	40	40	40	60	−10	60	80	55	120	+10
t_3	80	80	65	125	+30	50	70	20	140	−30
t_4	60	60	55	**180**	+10	50	100	40	**180**	−10

(c) Counted allocation results under *discount*-based approach of *LTRF*. There is a discount (e.g., 50%) for the extra unused resources, to incentivize clients to preempt resources actively for system utilization maximization. In this example, although the *counted* allocations for A and B are 180, their real allocations are both 200, which is the same as Table 1(b).

Table 1: A comparison example of *MemoryLess Resource Fairness (MLRF)* and *Long-Term Resource Fairness (LTRF)* in a shared computing system consisting of 100 computing resources for two users A and B.

4.1 Property Analysis for LTRF

THEOREM 1. *LTRF satisfies the sharing incentive property.*

Algorithm 1 LTRF pseudo-code.

1: R: total resources available in the system.
2: $\ddot{R} = (\ddot{R}_1, ..., \ddot{R}_n)$: current allocated resources. $\ddot{R}_i$ denotes the current allocated resources for client i.
3: $U = (u_1, ..., u_n)$: total used resources, initially 0. u_i denotes the total resource consumed by client i.
4: $W = (w_1, ..., w_n)$: weighted share. w_i denotes the weight for client i.

5: **while** there are pending tasks **do**
6:    **Choose** client i with the smallest total weighted resources of u_i/w_i.
7:    $d_i \leftarrow$ the next task resource demand for client i.
8:    **if** $\ddot{R} + d_i \leqslant R$ **then**
9:       $\ddot{R}_i \leftarrow \ddot{R}_i + d_i$. ▷ Update current allocated resources./*Section 5.2.2*/
10:       Update the total resource usage u_i for client i.   ▷ /*Section 5.2.2*/
11:       Allocate resource to client i.   ▷ /*Section 5.2.3*/
12:    **else**   ▷ The system is fully utilized.
13:       **Wait** until there is a released resource r_i from client i.
14:       $\ddot{R}_i \leftarrow \ddot{R}_i - r_i$. ▷ Update current allocated resources/*Section 5.2.2*/

PROOF. Consider a shared pay-as-you-use computing system of R resources group-bought by n clients with equal share (or monetary cost) over t period time. When pursuing individually with the same amount of money, 1). the amount of resources R_1 a client can receive is less than $\frac{R}{n}$, as group-buying has discount over personal buying; 2). Under R_1 resources, she can get at most $t \cdot R_1$ resources, smaller than $t \cdot \frac{R}{n}$. In contrast, with group-buying and fair allocation with LTRF, a client can get at least $t \cdot \frac{R}{n}$ resources. Thus LTRF satisfies sharing incentive property. □

THEOREM 2. *(Non-Trivial-Workload Incentive) Any client who submits non-trivial workloads to the shared pay-as-you-use computing system could get benefits under LTRF.*

PROOF. Recall that LTRF focuses on the fairness over total resources with *lending agreement*. When a client's resource demand is less than its current share, she can *lend* unneeded resources out. Later when she needs more resources in the future, she can get extra amount of resources back from others that she lent before. Reversely, if she submits lots of dirty (or trivial) workloads to the system when her *true* demand is less than her share, she will loose opportunity to get more extra sources, especially when she has lots of important and urgent workloads to compute later. Hence, LTRF meets non-trivial-workload incentive property. □

THEOREM 3. *LTRF achieves resource-as-you-pay fairness in a group-buying shared computing system.*

PROOF. Each client in a *shared* computing system has right to enjoy at least the amount of resources that she pays. One key factor that affects resource-as-you-pay fairness is the varied client's demands at different time (i.e., *unbalanced* workload which can be either less or larger than her current share). LTRF overcomes the unbalanced workload problem by considering the fairness at the level of total allocated resources and following *lending agreement*. It adjusts the current allocation of resources to each client dynamically according to her historical total allocated resources and current demand, ensuring that the total resources a client received are *fair* with each other. Thus, LTRF is resource-as-you-pay fairness. □

THEOREM 4. *LTRF satisfies strategy-proofness property.*

PROOF. Theorem 2 has demonstrated that LTRF satisfies non-trivial-workload incentive property that can make a client be *truly* willing to yield out her unused resources when she does not need. On the other hand, it is possible that an overloaded client lies about her true demands to let her get more allocated resources in preemption with others at a time. Due to *lending agreement* requirement

under LTRF, the consequence of lying is a pre-overconsumption of her resources and she needs to *pay back* at a later time to others. Thus, lying cannot benefit her at all. □

THEOREM 5. *LTRF satisfies pareto efficiency property.*

PROOF. Recall in our LTRF algorithm, we propose a *discount*-based approach to incentivize users to preempt extra unused resources from others. It indicates that the utilization of system is fully maximized whenever there are pending tasks. Therefore, it is impossible for a client to get more resources without decreasing the resources of others. □

Finally, Table 2 summarizes the properties that are satisfied by MLRF and LTRF, respectively. MLRF is *not* suitable for pay-as-you-use computing system due to its lack of support for three important desired properties, whereas LTRF can achieve all those properties.

Property	Allocation Policy	
	MLRF	LTRF
Sharing Incentive	√	√
Non-Trivial Workload Incentive		√
Resource-as-you-pay Fairness		√
Strategy-Proofness		√
Pareto Efficiency	√	√

Table 2: List of properties for MLRF and LTRF.

4.2 Fairness Definition

Due to the varied resource demands and resource preemption in the shared environment, the total resources a client obtained are undermined. Generally, every client wants to get more resources or at least the same amount of resources in a shared computing system than exclusively using the system. We call it *fair* for a client (i.e., sharing benefit) when that can be achieved. In contrast, it is also possible for the total resources a client received are less than that without sharing, which we call *unfair* (i.e., sharing loss). To ensure resource-as-you-pay fairness and the maximization of sharing incentive property in the shared system, it is important to minimize *sharing loss* firstly and then maximize *sharing benefit*.

Without mention, we refer to the *total* resources as *accumulated* resources below. Let $g_i(t)$ be the currently allocated resources for the ith client at time t. Let $f_i(t)$ denote the *accumulated* resources for the ith client at time t. Thus,

$$f_i(t) = \int_0^t g_i(t)\, dt. \tag{1}$$

Let $d_i(t)$ and $S_i(t)$ denote the current demand and current resource share for the ith client at time t, respectively. Given the total resource capacity R of the system and the shared weight w_i for the ith client, there is

$$S_i(t) = R \cdot w_i / \sum_{k=1}^{n} w_k. \tag{2}$$

The fairness degree $\rho_i(t)$ for the ith client at time t is defined as follows:

$$\rho_i(t) = \frac{\int_0^t g_i(t)\, dt}{\int_0^t \min\{d_i(t), S_i(t)\}}. \tag{3}$$

$\rho_i(t) \geqslant 1$ implies the absolute resource fairness for the ith client at time t. In contrast, $\rho_i(t) < 1$ indicates *unfair*. For a client i in a non-shared partition of the system, it always holds $\rho_i(t) = 1$, since it has $g_i(t) = \min\{d_i(t), S_i(t)\}$ at any time t. To measure how much better or worse for sharing with a fair policy than without sharing (i.e., $\rho_i(t) - 1$), we propose two concepts *sharing benefit degree* and *sharing loss degree*. Let $\Psi(t)$ be *sharing benefit degree*, as a sum of all $(\rho_i(t) - 1)$ subject to $\rho_i(t) \geqslant 1$, i.e.,

$$\Psi(t) = \sum_{i=1}^{n} \max\{\rho_i(t) - 1, 0\}. \tag{4}$$

and let $\Omega(t)$ denote *sharing loss degree*, as a sum of all $(\rho_i(t) - 1)$ subject to $\rho_i(t) < 1$, i.e.,

$$\Omega(t) = \sum_{i=1}^{n} \min\{\rho_i(t) - 1, 0\}. \tag{5}$$

We can use this two metrics to compare the quality for different fair policies. Thereby, it always holds that $\Psi(t) \geqslant 0 \geqslant \Omega(t)$. Moreover, in a non-shared partition of the computing system, it always holds $\Psi(t) = \Omega(t) = 0$, indicating that there are neither sharing benefit nor sharing loss. In contrast, in a shared pay-as-you-use computing system, either of them could be nonzero. For a good fair policy, it should be able to maximize $\Omega(t)$ first (e.g., $\Omega(t) \to 0$) and next try to maximize $\Psi(t)$.

5. LTYARN: A LONG-TERM YARN FAIR SCHEDULER

YARN is an emerging resource management and job processing system, and has been viewed as a distributed operating system. As a case study, we implement LTRF on YARN. We propose a long-term YARN fair scheduler called *LTYARN*, by generalizing the default instant max-min fairness.

5.1 Long-Term Max-Min Fairness

We present our long-term max-min fairness model for LTYARN.

5.1.1 Challenges and Approaches

Our long-term max-min fairness policy is based on the *accumulated* resources. When estimating the *accumulated* resources for a task, we need to know the capacity and demand of its requested resources and the execution time that it takes. However, there are several challenges for *online* applications (i.e., refers to applications that arrive over time) on that as follows,

1. the execution time of tasks for each application are often different and unknown in advance.

2. the arriving time for each application can be arbitrary and unknown in advance.

3. the computing resources (e.g., CPU powers) can be heterogeneous in a heterogeneous cluster, and the resource demand (e.g., memory size) for each task can be different.

To deal with the above mentioned challenging issues, we provide several methods below,

Time Quantum-based Approach. It is an approximation approach to deal with the first challenging problem. It gives a concept of *assumed execution time*, initialized with a time quantum, to represent the prior unknown *real* execution time. The assumed execution time is adjusted dynamically to make it close to the real execution time.

The details of our approach are that, we first initialize the *assumed execution time* to be zero for any *pending* task. When a task starts running, we give a time quantum threshold for its *assumed execution time*. For each running task, when its running time exceeds the *assumed execution time*, the *assumed execution time* is updated to the running time. In contrast, for any finished task, its *assumed execution time* is updated to its running time, no matter it is larger or smaller than the time threshold.

Wall Clock-based Approach. It concerns with the second challenging problem of 'online' arriving. Different applications may arrive at different time. It would be no longer suitable to use the accumulated *consumed* resources as a measure to control the fair share. The explanation is that, from the system's (e.g., global-level) perspective, in order to improve its resource utilization, it often follows the idiom that *'the early bird gets the worm'* (we call it *Early Bird Privilege* next) to incentivize users to submit their applications as early as possible. To achieve that, one solution is to give a penalty for the late arriving application, by only starting to consider (or memorize) the fair share of resources from its arriving time. Moreover, our fairness model is on the basis of max-min fairness algorithm [21]. Technically, to implement it, there is a need to top-up a resource cost, named as *Pseudo Accumulated Resources (PAR)*, such that the fair scheduler will not favor the late arriving application. Thus, in contrast to *offline* application whose accumulated resources can be directly set to its accumulated *consumed* resources as expressed by Formula (1) implicitly, the accumulated resources for each *online* application should include both its *PAR* and accumulated consumed resources. That is, for the online application, the definition in Formula (1) should be modified as,

$$f_i(t) = \int_0^t g_i(t)\,dt + \phi_i(t). \tag{6}$$

where $\phi_i(t)$ denotes the *PAR watched* at time t by the application i. Moreover, by taking into account the *discount*-based approach for extra unused resources proposed by Algorithm 1 of LTRF in Section 4, we have the currently *discounted* allocated resource $g_i'(t)$ as follows:

$$g_i'(t) = \min\{g_i(t), S_i(t)\} + \max\{g_i(t) - S_i(t), 0\} \cdot \eta. \tag{7}$$

where $\eta(0 \leqslant \eta \leqslant 1)$ denotes the discount rate. Hence, the definition of Formula (6) should be further modified as,

$$f_i(t) = \int_0^t g_i'(t)\,dt + \phi_i(t). \tag{8}$$

We call this method *Wall Clock-based Approach*, where the *Wall Clock* refers to a time period before the arriving of an application, as illustrated in Figure 1 (a).

Weighted Resource based Approach. It targets at the third challenge. We assign a *weight* to each heterogeneous resource in terms of its computing capacity. For example, the CPU resource can be weighted based on its clock frequency. Thereby, for the ith application,

$$g_i(t) = \sum_{j \in \tau_i(t)} \theta_{i,j} \cdot \delta_{i,j} \cdot \alpha_{i,j}(t). \tag{9}$$

where $\tau_i(t)$ denotes the set of tasks from the ith application that are allocated with resources at the time t. $\theta_{i,j}$ and $\delta_{i,j}$ denote the resource demand (e.g., the size of vcore or memory) and weight for the jth task of the ith application, respectively. $\alpha_{i,j}(t)$ represents the *assumed execution time* for the jth task of the ith application at time t. It is our future work to extend the definition to other hardware resources like GPUs [14].

5.1.2 Long-Term Max-Min Fairness Model

This subsection proposes long-term max-min fairness model for LTYARN. YARN is a hierarchical tree structure of multi-level fairness: applications at the bottom and queues at the higher level. We apply the same mechanism for different levels. The following design considers the bottom-level (i.e., application-level).

Let $\Lambda = \{\Lambda_1, \Lambda_2, \Lambda_3, ...\}$ denote the set of submitted applications, and $\tilde{\Lambda}$ be the set of its active applications (the 'active' means there are pending or running tasks available). Let a_i be the arriving time for the application Λ_i. According to the *Early Bird Privilege* and max-min fairness policy, the *PAR* $\phi_i(t)$ for the active application Λ_i should be,

(a) Fully Long-Term Max-Min Fairness Model (F-LTMM)

(b) Semi-Long-Term Max-Min Fairness Model (S-LTMM)

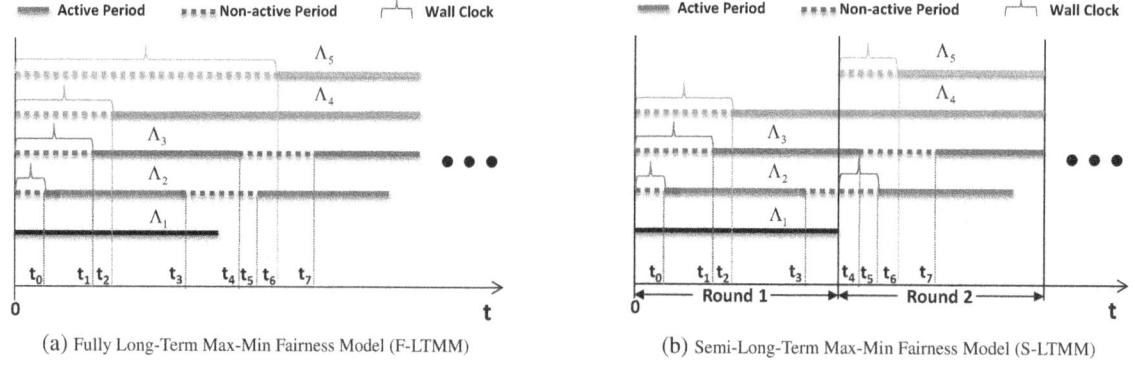

Figure 1: The long-term max-min fairness models for *LTYARN*. For an application, *Active Period* refers to the time interval when it has pending/running tasks available. Otherwise, it belongs to *Non-active Period*. *Wall Clock* refers to a time period before the arriving of an application with respect to the starting time of the current round.

$$\phi_i(t) = \begin{cases} \max_{\Lambda_k \in \tilde{\Lambda}} \{f_k(t) | a_k < a_i\} = \\ \max_{\Lambda_k \in \tilde{\Lambda}} \{\int_0^t g'_k(t)\,dt + \phi_k(t) | a_k < a_i\}, & (a_i > \min_{\Lambda_k \in \tilde{\Lambda}}\{a_k\}). \\ 0, & \text{others.} \end{cases}$$
(10)

Let $n_i^p(t)$ denote the number of pending (i.e., runnable) tasks for the application Λ_i at time t. Let ω_i be the shared weight for the ith application. Based on the weighted max-min fairness strategy and Formula (6), (9), (10), the application Λ_i to be chosen at time t for fair resource allocation should satisfy the following condition,

$$\frac{f_i(t)}{\omega_i} = \min_{\Lambda_k \in \tilde{\Lambda}} \left\{ \frac{f_k(t)}{\omega_k} | n_i^p(t) > 0 \right\}.$$
(11)

We name this fairness model *Fully Long-Term Max-Min Fairness Model (F-LTMM)*, as illustrated in Figure 1(a), considering that it is *recording* the consumed resources all the way since YARN system starts working.

In practice, we may not want the system to be fully long-term. Instead, the definition can be applied to a period of time (e.g., 24 hours). It motives us further to propose a time window-based long-term fairness model below.

Semi-Long-Term Max-Min Fairness Model (S-LTMM). The key idea is that, instead of fully memorizing resources all the time since the system starts working, we can divide system working time into a set of time windows (by default, we call the *time window* as *round*). Within the round (i.e., *Intra-Round Phase*), we adopt the fully long-term fairness model. When the system moves to the next round (i.e., *Inter-Round Phase*), it ignores all jobs' history information from the previous round and starts memorizing from the beginning. It is a hybrid of fully long-term fairness model at intra-round phase and memoryless fairness model at inter-round phase.

Figure 1(b) illustrates the model. Let L denote the time length of a computation round, and t^s be the start time of the current computation round. Then we can compute t^s with the following formula,

$$t^s = \begin{cases} t^s + \lfloor \frac{t - t^s}{L} \rfloor \cdot L, & (t > 0). \\ 0, & (t = 0). \end{cases}$$
(12)

Moreover, all of the *F-LTMM*-related elements, including *Wall Clock*, *PAR* and accumulated consumed resources for each application, should be updated and counted from t^s instead. Then Formula (6) should be updated to be,

$$f_i(t) = \int_{t^s}^t g'_i(t)\,dt + \phi_i(t).$$
(13)

Unlike *F-LTMM* whose *Wall Clock* is just equal to the application's arriving time, the *Wall Clock* in *S-LTMM* is round-based, referring to a non-active period of an application since t^s, e.g., Λ_2

in Figure 1(b). We define *Round Arriving Time* $\breve{a}_i$ for Λ_i to be the starting time point at which the application becomes active since t^s, e.g., t_5 for Λ_2 at Round 2 in Figure 1(b). It can be computed based on the following formula,

$$\breve{a}_i = \begin{cases} a_i, & (t^s \leqslant a_i). \\ t^s, & (\exists j \in \tau_i(t), t_{i,j}^s \leqslant t^s < t_{i,j}^c). \\ \min_{j \in \tau_i(t)} \{t_{i,j}^s | t_{i,j}^s > t^s\}, & \text{others.} \end{cases}$$
(14)

Let $t_{i,j}^s$, $t_{i,j}^c$ denote the start time and finished time for the jth task of the application Λ_i, respectively. Particularly, for the finished tasks of each application in *S-LTMM*, only the jth task satisfying $t_{i,j}^c > t^s$ will count. According to the time quantum-based approach, we then have,

$$\alpha_{i,j}(t) = \begin{cases} t_{i,j}^c - \max\{t^s, t_{i,j}^s\}, & (t^s < t_{i,j}^c \leqslant t). \\ \max\{Q, t - \max\{t^s, t_{i,j}^s\}\}, & (t < t_{i,j}^c \leqslant t^s + L). \\ 0, & \text{others.} \end{cases}$$
(15)

where Q denotes the time quantum. And accordingly, Formula (10) should be updated to

$$\phi_i(t) = \begin{cases} \max_{\Lambda_k \in \tilde{\Lambda}} \{\int_{t^s}^t g'_k(t)\,dt + \phi_k(t) | \breve{a}_k < \breve{a}_i\}, & (\breve{a}_i > \min_{\Lambda_k \in \tilde{\Lambda}}\{\breve{a}_k\}). \\ 0, & \text{others.} \end{cases}$$
(16)

Finally, by combining Formula (12), (15), (9), (16), (13), similar to *F-LTMM*, we can obtain *S-LTMM* by allocating resources to the application Λ_i subject to Formula (9) stringently at time t.

5.2 Design and Implementation of LTYARN

In YARN, the resources are organized into multiple queues with hierarchical tree structure. Each queue can represent an organization and the resources are shared among them. Figure 3 shows an example of three-level structure. There is a root node called *Root Queue*. It distributes the resources of the whole system to the intermediate nodes called *Parent Queues*. Each parent queue further re-distributes resources into its sub-queues (parent queues or leaf queues) recursively until to the bottom nodes called *Leaf Queues*. Finally, users' submitted applications within the same leaf queue share the resources.

Figure 2 gives an overview on the design and implementation of LTYARN. It consists of three key components: *Quantum Updater (QU)*, *Resource Controller (RC)*, and *Resource Allocator (RA)*. QU is responsible for updating the time quantum for each queue dynamically. RC manages the allocated resources for each application/queue and computes the accumulated resources periodically. RA performs the resource allocation based on the accumulated resources of each application/queue. In the following, we present some implementation details about each component.

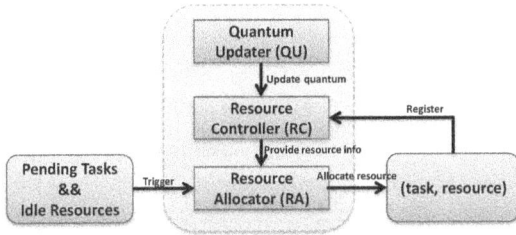

Figure 2: Overview of LTYARN.

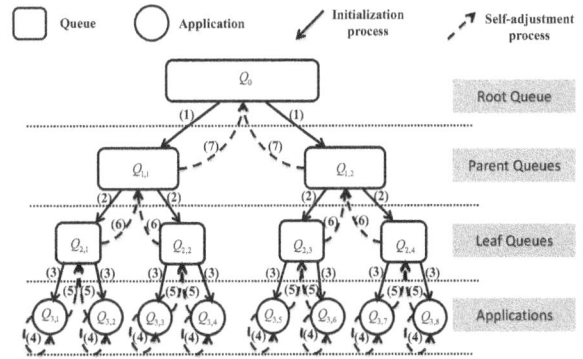

Figure 3: The adaptive task quantum policy for YARN. The *top-to-bottom* data flow is a task time quantum initialization process for new applications. The *bottom-to-top* data flow is a quantum self-adjustment process for existing applications/queues.

5.2.1 Quantum Updater (QU)

For LTYARN, the suitable value of the time quantum Q is very important for *fairness convergency*, which refers to the convergency of unfair applications for their long-term resources at a time point and after that they share the resources fairly with each other. To achieve fast convergency, we need to make Q as close to the real execution time of tasks as possible. Ideally, we need to adapt Q to different applications/tasks and also varied types of applications in different queues for YARN in practice, ensuring that each queue owns a suitable Q for its own applications so that they do not interfere with each other.

We propose an adaptive task quantum policy. It is a multi-level self-tunning approach by extending the hierarchical structure of YARN's resource organization, as shown in Figure 3. The top-to-bottom data flow is a quantum value assignment process. It works when a new element (e.g., queue or application) is added. In contrast, the bottom-to-top data flows are a self-tunning procedure, refreshing periodically by a small fixed time interval (e.g, 1 second).

Initially, the system administrator provides a threshold value for root-level quantum Q_0. When a new application is submitted to the system, it will perform the initialization process from the top to bottom. First, it will check whether its parent queue is new one or not (Arrow (1) in Figure 3). If yes, it will assign the root-queue quantum to its parent-queue quantum, e.g., $Q_{1,1} \leftarrow Q_0$. Next, it checks its sub-queues (e.g., leaf-queue) (Arrow (2) in Figure 3). If it is a new one, it will assign its parent-queue quantum to its sub-queue quantum, e.g., $Q_{2,1} \leftarrow Q_{1,1}$. Lastly, it initializes its application quantum with its leaf-queue quantum, e.g., $Q_{3,1} \leftarrow Q_{2,1}$ (Arrow (3) in Figure 3).

QU checks the system periodically for new completed tasks. When a task finished, the self-adjustment process performs from the bottom to top. First, it will update the time quantum for applications with the average task completion time (Arrow (4) in Figure 3). Next, it updates its leaf-queue quantum with its average application quantum (Arrow (5) in Figure 3). Similarly, it updates its parent-queue quantum using the average value of its leaf-queue quantum (Arrow (6) in Figure 3). Finally, the root-queue quantum is updated with the average value of parent-queue quantum (Arrow (7) in Figure 3).

5.2.2 Resource Controller (RC)

Resource Controller (RC) is the main component of LTYARN. Its principle responsibility is to manage and update the accumulated resources for each queue, needed by RA, on the basis of the model S-LTMM. It tracks the allocated resource (e.g., container in YARN) and the execution time for each task. Based on this information, it performs the resource updating periodically (e.g., 1 second). In the updating procedure, it first updates the starting time of the current round based on Formula (12) and the round arriving time for each application based on Formula (14). Next, based on time quantum-based approach, it estimates the assumed execution time for each running/completed task with the updated quantum

value from QU, according to Formula (15). The currently allocated resource for each task can then be estimated with Formula (7). After that, it estimates the Pseduo Accumulated Resources (PAR) for each application based on Formula (16). Finally, it updates the accumulated resource for each application/queue based on Formula (13).

5.2.3 Resource Allocator (RA)

Resource Allocator (RA) is responsible for resource allocation at each queue of different levels, as shown in Figure 3. It is triggered whenever there are pending tasks or idle resources. RA can now support FIFO, memoryless max-min fairness and long-term max-min fairness for each queue. Users can choose either of them accordingly. For long-term max-min fairness, it performs fair resource allocation for each application/queue with the provided resource information from RC, based on Formula (11). We provide two important configuration arguments for each queue, e.g., time quantum Q and round length L in the default configuration file, to meet different requirements for different queues. Moreover, we also support minimum (maximum) resource share for queues under long-term max-min fairness.

In practice, it is better for its root queue to use the long-term max-min fairness, viewing each of its sub-queues as a client or an organization to it. We need to guarantee the resource-as-you-pay fairness for them. For each parent-queue representing an organization, we should also adopt the long-term max-min fairness if its subqueues (i.e., members of the organization) require resource-as-you-pay fairness. In contrast, when a queue belongs to a client, there might be no need to ensure resource-as-you-pay fairness for its sub-queues. In that case, we can choose either memoryless max-min fairness, long-term max-min fairness or FIFO.

6. EVALUATION

We ran our experiments in a cluster consisting of 10 compute nodes, each with two Intel X5675 CPUs (6 CPU cores per CPU with 3.07 GHz), 24GB DDR3 memory and 56GB hard disks. The latest version of YARN-2.2.0 is chosen in our experiment, used with a two-level hierarchy. The first level denotes the root queue (containing 1 master node, and 9 slave nodes). For each slave node, we configure its total memory resources with 24GB. The second level denotes the applications (i.e., workloads).

6.1 Macro-benchmarks

We ran a macro-benchmark consisting of four different workloads. Thus, four different queues are configured in YARN/LTYARN,

Bin	Job Type	# Maps	# Reduces	# Jobs
1	rankings selection	1	NA	38
2	grep search	2	NA	18
3	uservisits aggregation	10	2	14
4	rankings selection	50	NA	10
5	uservisits aggregation	100	10	6
6	rankings selection	200	NA	6
7	grep search	400	NA	4
8	rankings-uservisits join	400	30	2
9	grep search	800	60	2

Table 3: Job types and sizes for each bin in our synthetic Facebook workloads.

namely, *Facebook*, *Purdue*, *Spark*, *HIVE/TPC-H*, corresponding to the following workloads, respectively. 1). A MapReduce instance with a mix of small and large jobs based on the workload at Facebook. 2). A MapReduce instance running a set of large-sized batch jobs generated with Purdue MapReduce Benchmarks Suite [1]. 3). Hive [24] running a series of TPC-H queries. 4). Spark [32] running a series of machine learning applications.

Synthetic Facebook Workload. We synthesize our Facebook workload based on the distribution of jobs sizes and inter-arrival time at Facebook in Oct. 2009 provided by Zaharia et. al. [33]. The workload consists of 100 jobs. We categorize them into 9 bins of job types and sizes, as listed in Table 3. It is a mix of large number of small-sized jobs (1 ∼ 15 tasks) and small number of large-sized jobs (e.g., 800 tasks[2]). The job submission time is derived from one of SWIM's Facebook workload traces (e.g., FB-2009_samples_24_times_1hr_1.tsv) [12]. The jobs are from Hive benchmark [5], containing four types of applications, i.e., rankings selection, grep search (selection), uservisits aggregation and rankings-uservisits join.

Purdue Workload. We select five benchmarks (e.g., Word-Count, TeraSort, Grep, InvertedIndex, HistogramMovices) randomly from Purdue MapReduce Benchmarks Suite [1]. We use 40G wikipedia data [26] for WordCount, InvertedIndex and Grep, 40G generated data for TeraSort and HistogramMovices with their provided tools. To emulate a series of regular job submissions in a data warehouse, we submit these five jobs sequentially at a fixed interval of 3 mins to the system.

Hive / TPC-H. To emulate continuous analytic query, such as analysis of users' behavior logs, we ran TPC-H benchmark queries on Hive [3]. 40GB data are generated with provided data tools. Four representative queries Q1, Q9, Q12, and Q17 are chosen, each of which we create five instances. We launch one query after the previous one finished in a round robin fashion.

Spark. Latest version of Spark has supported its job to run on the YARN system. We consider two CPU-intensive machine learning algorithms, namely, kmeans and alternating least squares (ALS) with provided example benchmarks. We ran 10 instances of each algorithm, which are launched by a script that waits 2 minutes after each job completed to submit the next.

6.2 LTRF Resource Allocation Flow

To understand the dynamic history-based resource allocation mechanism of LTRF under LTYARN, we sample the resource demands, currently allocated resources and accumulated resources for four workloads over a short period of 0 ∼ 260 seconds, as illustrated in Figure 4. Figure 4(a) and 4(b) show the normalized results of the current resource demand and currently allocated resources for each workload with respect to its current share. Figure 4(c) presents the

---

[2]We reduce the size of the largest jobs in [33] to have the workload fit our cluster size.

normalized accumulated resources for four workloads with respect to the system capacity.

Figure 4(a) shows that workloads have different resource demands over time. At the beginning, Purdue, Spark and Hive / TPC-H have an overloaded demand period (e.g., Purdue: 24 − 131, Spark: 28 − 118, HIVE / TPC-H: 28 − 146). Figure 4(b) shows the allocation details for each workload over time. During the common overloaded period of 28 − 118, the curves for Purdue, Spark and Hive / TPC-H are fluctuated, indicating that LTRF is dynamically adjusting the amount of resource allocation to each workload, instead of simply assigning each workload the same amount of resources like MLRF. Through dynamic adjusting, the accumulated resources for the three workloads are balanced (i.e., the curves are close to each other) during the period 80 − 118, as shown in Figure 4(c). However, for Facebook workload, its overloaded period occurs from 204 − 260. During this period, the Purdue workload is also overloaded, as shown in Figure 4(a). To achieve the accumulated resource fairness, LTRF allocated a large amount of resource to it (e.g., 3.85/4.0 = 96.25% at point 222) shown in Figure 4(b), to make it catch up with others. As in the accumulated resource results in Figure 4(c) that, during 204 − 260, there is a significant increment for Facebook workload, whereas other workloads increase slightly.

6.3 Macrobenchmark Fairness Results

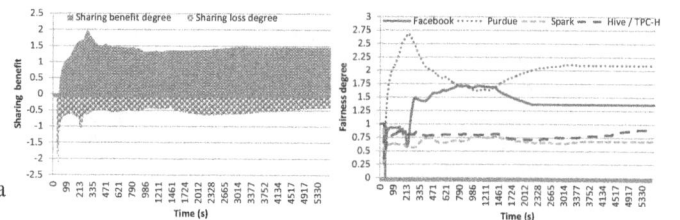

(a) Sharing benefit/loss degree with MLRF based on Formula (4) and (5).

(b) Detailed fairness degree for four queues with MLRF based on Formula (3).

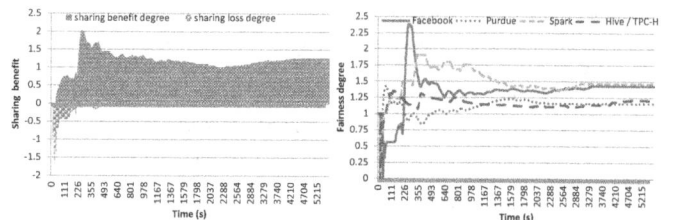

(c) Sharing benefit/loss degree with LTRF based on Formula (4) and (5).

(d) Detailed fairness degree for four queues with LTRF based on Formula (3).

Figure 5: Comparison of fairness results over time for workloads under MLRF and LTRF in YARN. All results are relative to the static partition scenario (i.e., non-shared case) whose fairness degree is always one and sharing benefit/loss is zero. (a) and (c) show the overall benefit/loss relative to the non-sharing scenario. (b) and (d) present the detailed fairness degree for each queue: 1). A queue gets sharing benefit when its fairness degree is larger than one; 2). Otherwise, it arises sharing loss problem when a queue's fairness degree is below one.

In Section 4.2, we have shown that a good sharing policy should be able to first minimize the sharing loss, and then maximize the sharing benefit as much as possible (i.e., Sharing incentive). We make a comparison between MLRF and LTRF for four workloads over time in Figure 5. All results are relative to the static partition case (without sharing) with fairness degree of one and sharing benefit/loss degrees of zero. Figures 5(a) and 5(c) present the sharing benefit/loss degrees based on Formulas (4) and (5), respectively, for

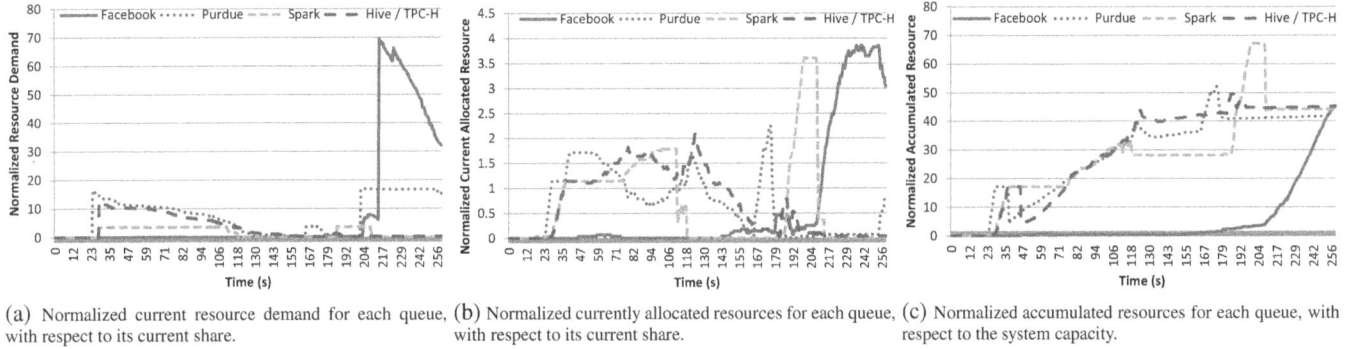

(a) Normalized current resource demand for each queue, with respect to its current share.

(b) Normalized currently allocated resources for each queue, with respect to its current share.

(c) Normalized accumulated resources for each queue, with respect to the system capacity.

Figure 4: Overview of detailed fairness resource allocation flow for LTRF.

MLRF and LTRF. Figures 5(b) and 5(d) show the detailed fairness degree for each queue (workload) over time. We have the following observations:

First, the sharing policies of both MLRF and LTRF can bring sharing benefits for queues (workloads). For example, both Facebook and Purdue workloads, illustrated in Figure 5(b) and 5(d) obtain benefits under the shared scenario. This is due to the sharing incentive property, i.e., each queue has an opportunity to consume more resources than her share at a time, better off running at most all of her shared partition in a non-shared partition system.

Second, LTRF has a much better result than MLRF. Specifically, Figure 5(a) indicates that the sharing loss problem for MLRF is constantly available until all the workloads complete (e.g., ≈ -0.5 on average), contributed primarily by Spark and TPC-H workloads given by Figure 5(b). In contrast, there is no more sharing loss problem after 650 seconds for LTRF, i.e., all workloads get sharing benefits after that. The major reason is that MLRF does not consider historical resource allocation. Due to the varied demands for each workload over time, it easily occurs two extreme cases: 1). some workloads get much more resources over time (e.g., Facebook and Purdue workloads in Figure 5(b)); 2). some workloads obtain much less resources that without sharing over time (e.g., Spark and TPC-H workloads in Figure 5(b)). In contrast, LTRF is a history-based fairness resource allocation policy. It can dynamically adjust the allocation of resources to each queue in terms of their historical consumption and *lending agreement* so that each queue can obtain a much closer amount of total resources over time.

Finally, regarding the sharing loss problem at the early stage (e.g., 0 ~ 650 seconds) of LTRF in Figure 5(c), it is mainly due to the unavoidable waiting allocation problem at the starting stage, i.e., a first coming and running workload possess all resources and leads late arriving workloads need to wait for a while until some tasks complete and release resources. The problem exists in both MLRF and LTRF. Still, LTRF can smooth this problem until it disappears over time via *lending agreement*, while MLRF cannot.

6.4 Macrobenchmark Performance Results

Figure 6 presents the performance results (i.e., speedup) for four workloads under Static Partitioning, MLRF and LTRF, respectively. All results are normalized with respect to Static Partitioning (i.e., non-shared executions). We see that, 1). the shared cases (i.e., MLRF and LTRF) can possibly achieve better performance than or at least the same as the non-shared case. For example, for Facebook and Purdue workloads, both MLRF and LTRF have much better performance results (e.g., 14% ~ 19% improvement for MLRF, and 10% ~ 23% for LTRF) than exclusively using a static partitioning system. The finding is consistent with previous works such as Mesos [15]. The performance gain is mainly due to the resource

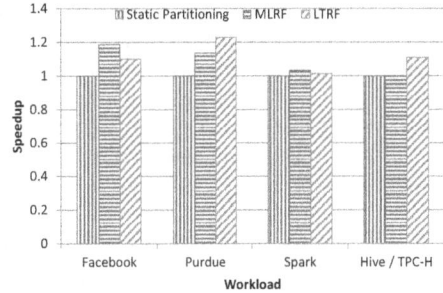

Figure 6: The normalized performance results (e.g., speedup)for Static Partitioning, MLRF and LTRF, with respect to Static Partitioning.

preemption of unused resources from other queues in a shared system. The statement can also be validated in Figure 5(b) and 5(d) in Section 6.3. The fairness degrees for both Facebook and Purdue workloads are above one (i.e., get sharing benefit) during the most of time. 2). There is no conclusive result regarding which one is absolutely better than the other between MLRF and LTRF. For example, MLRF is better than LTRF for Facebook by about 7% and Spark by about 2%. However, LTRF outperforms MLRF for Purdue workload by about 8% and TPC-H by about 10%.

6.5 Adaptive Task Quantum Policy Evaluation

To demonstrate the importance and effectiveness of adaptive task quantum policy for YARN, we study the effects of accumulated resource results over time under the fixed time quantum and the adaptive task quantum mechanism proposed in Section 5.2.1.

We consider a scenario where the configured task quantum (e.g., 600s) is much larger than the real task execution time of workloads. Figure 7 shows the compared accumulated results for LTRF over time within one hour, which are normalized with respect to system capacity. We have the following observations:

First, Figure 7(a) illustrates that the accumulated resource under the fixed task time quantum policy fluctuates significantly over time, making it unable to be an indicator for resource-as-you-pay fairness. This is due to the computation method for assumed execution time in the time quantum-based approach: 1). the assumed execution time for the completed task is equal to its real execution time; 2). for the running task, we compute its assumed execution time using the maximum value of the configured time quantum and its real execution time. Take Facebook workload as an example. Its average task execution time is about 11s. At time 1439s, there are 107 running tasks, whose assumed execution time is 600, and its normalized accumulated resource is 1019. However, at time 1450s (i.e., after 11s), there are 31 running tasks, indicating that at least 76 tasks completed during this period and a significant drop occurs for its normalized accumulated resource (e.g., 630).

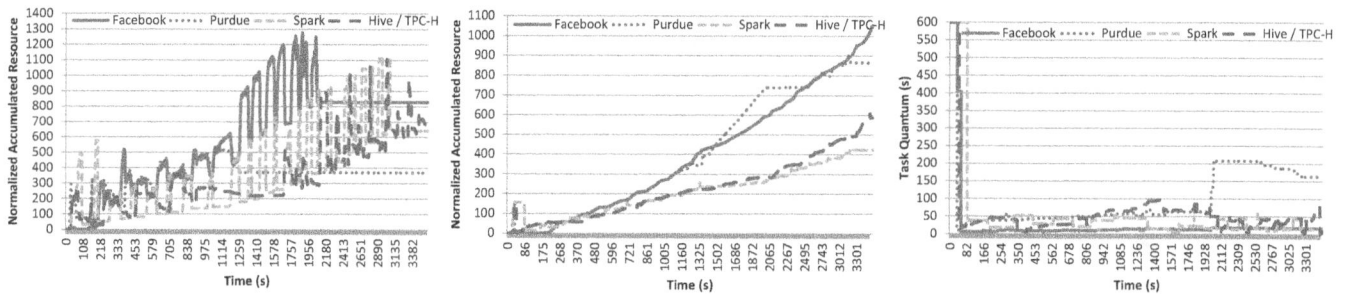

(a) Normalized accumulated resources under the fixed task time quantum of 600s, with respect to the system capacity.

(b) Normalized accumulated resources with adaptive task quantum mechanism, with respect to the system capacity.

(c) Adaptive task quantum, initially 600s.

Figure 7: The adaptive task quantum results for LTRF in one hour.

In contrast, with adaptive task quantum policy, as shown in Figure 7(b), the curves of accumulated resource become much smoother, making it good as an indicator for resource-as-you-pay fairness. Figure 7(c) shows the adaptive task quantum results over time for four workloads. We see that each workload has varied task quantum and our policy can adjust them dynamically for all the workloads, validating the effectiveness of our adaptive approach.

7. CONCLUSION AND FUTURE WORK

Pay-as-you-use computing systems have been become emerging in data centers and supercomputers. Resource fairness is an important consideration for such shared environments. However, this paper finds that, the classical *memoryless* resource fairness policies, widely used in many existing popular frameworks and schedulers, including Hadoop, YARN, Mesos, Choosy, Quincy, DHFS [27], MROrder [28], are *not* suitable in pay-as-you-use computing system due to three serious problems, i.e., trivial workload problem, strategy-proofness problem and resource-as-you-pay problem. To address these problems, we propose LTRF and demonstrate that it is *suitable* for pay-as-you-use computing system. Besides, we also propose five payment-oriented properties as metrics to measure the quality for any fair policy in a pay-as-you-use computing system. We developed *LTYARN*, a long-term max-min fair scheduler for the latest version of YARN and our experiments demonstrate the effectiveness of our approaches. As future work, we plan to extend our fairness definition to different price schemes [30] and multiple resource types (such as DRF [11]).

The implementation of LTYARN can be found in http://sourceforge.net/projects/ltyarn/.

8. ACKNOWLEDGMENT

We thank the anonymous reviewers for their constructive comments. Bingsheng He was partly supported by a startup Grant of Nanyang Technological University, Singapore.

9. REFERENCES

[1] F. Ahmad, S. Y. Lee, M. Thottethodi, T. N. Vijaykumar. *PUMA: Purdue MapReduce Benchmarks Suite*. ECE Technical Reports, 2012.
[2] Apache. *YARN*. https://hadoop.apache.org/docs/current2/index.html
[3] Apache. *TPC-H Benchmark on Hive*. https://issues.apache.org/jira/browse/HIVE-600.
[4] Apache. *Hadoop*. http://hadoop.apache.org.
[5] Apache. *Hive performance benchmarks*. https://issues.apache.org/jira/browse/HIVE-396.
[6] H. Arabnejad, J. Barbosa. *Fairness Resource Sharing for Dynamic Workflow Scheduling on Heterogeneous Systems*, ISPA, pp. 633-639, 2012.
[7] A. Bhattacharya, D. Culler, E. Friedman, A. Ghodsi, S. Shenker, I. Stoica. *Hierarchical Scheduling for Diverse Datacenter Workloads*. SOCC'14, 2014.
[8] J. Dean and S. Ghemawat. *MapReduce: Simplified Data Processing on Large Clusters*. OSDI'04, 2004.

[9] A. Demers, S. Keshav, S. Shenker. *Analysis and Simulation of a Fair Queuing Algorithm*. In SIGCOMM'89, pp. 1-12, 1989.
[10] A. Ghodsi, M. Zaharia, S. Shenker and I. Stoica. *Choosy: Max-Min Fair Sharing for Datacenter Jobs with Constraints*, EuroSys 2013, April 2013.
[11] A. Ghodsi, M. Zaharia, B. Hindman, A. Konwinski, S. Schenker,I. Stoica. *Dominant Resource Fairness: Fair Allocation of Multiple Resource Types*. In NSDI'11, pp. 24-37, 2011.
[12] GitHub. *Facebook workload traces*. https://github.com/SWIMProjectUCB/SWIM/wiki/Workloads-repository.
[13] Group Buying. http://en.wikipedia.org/wiki/Group_buying.
[14] B.S. He, W.B. Fang, Q. Luo, N.K. Govindaraju, T.Y. Wang. *Mars: A MapReduce Framework on Graphics Processors*, In PACT'08, pp.260-269, 2008.
[15] B. Hindman, A. Konwinski, M. Zaharia, A. Ghodsi, A.D. Joseph, R. Katz, S. Shenker and I. Stoica, *Mesos: A Platform for Fine-Grained Resource Sharing in the Data Center*, NSDI 2011, March 2011.
[16] M. Isard, M. Budiu, Y. Yu, A. Birell, D. Fetterly. *Dryad: Distributed Data-Parallel Programs from Sequential Building Blocks*. Eurosys'07, pp.59-72, 2007.
[17] M. Isard, V. Prabhakaran, J. Currey, U. Wieder, K. Talwar, A. Goldberg. *Quincy: Fair Scheduling for Distributed Computing Clusters*, In SOSP'09, pp 261-276, 2009.
[18] R. Jain, D. M. Chiu, and W. Hawe. *A quantitative measure of fairness and discrimination for resource allocation in shared computer system*. Technical Report EC-TR-301, 1984.
[19] I. Kash, A. D. Procaccia, N. Shah. *No agent left behind: dynamic fair division of multiple resources*. In AAMAS'13, PP. 351-358, 2013.
[20] Loan agreement. http://en.wikipedia.org/wiki/Loan_agreement.
[21] Max-Min Fairness (Wikipedia). http://en.wikipedia.org/wiki/Max-min_fairness.
[22] J. Ngubiri, M. V. Vliet. *A Metric of Fairness for Parallel Job Schedulers*. Journal of Concurrency and Computation: Practice & Experience. Vol 21, PP. 1525-1546, 2009.
[23] G. Sabin, G. Kochhar, P. Sadayappan. *Job Fairness in Non-Preemptive Job Scheduling*. ICPP, pp. 186-194, 2004.
[24] A. Thusoo, J. S. Sarma, N. Jain, Z. Shao, P. Chakka, N. Zhang, S. Antony, H. Liu. *Hive- A Petabyte Scale Data Warehouse Using Hadoop*. ICDE, pp. 996-1005, 2010.
[25] D. C. Parkes, A. D. Procaccia, N. Shah. *Beyond Dominant Resource Fairness: Extensions, Limitations, and Indivisibilities*. In ACM Conference on Electronic Commerce, pp. 808-825, 2012.
[26] PUMA Datasets. http://web.ics.purdue.edu/ĩahmad/benchmarks/datasets .htm.
[27] S.J. Tang, B.S. Lee, B.S. He. *Dynamic slot allocation technique for MapReduce clusters*, In CLUSTER'13, pp. 1-8, 2013.
[28] S.J. Tang, B.S. Lee, B.S. He. *MROrder: Flexible Job Ordering Optimization for Online MapReduce Workloads*, In Euro-Par'13, pp. 291-304, 2013.
[29] C.A. Waldspurger, W. E. Weihl. *Lottery Scheduling: Flexible Proportional-Share Resource Management*. In OSDI'94, 1994.
[30] H. Wang, Q. Jing, R. Chen, B. He, Z. Qian, L. Zhou. *Distributed systems meet economics: pricing in the cloud*, In HotCloud'10, pp.1-6, 2010.
[31] W. Wang, B. C. Li, B. Liang. *Dominant Resource Fairness in Cloud Computing Systems with Heterogeneous Servers*. INFOCOM'14, 2014.
[32] M. Zaharia, M. Chowdhury, M. J. Franklin, S. Shenker, I. Stoica. *Spark: Cluster Computing with Working Sets*. HotCloud'10, pp. 10-16. 2010.
[33] M. Zaharia, D. Borthakur, J. Sarma, K. Elmeleegy,S. Schenker, I. Stoica, *Delay scheduling: A simple technique for achieving locality and fairness in cluster scheduling*. In Proceedings of EuroSys, pp. 265-278, 2010.
[34] H. N. Zhao, R. Sakellariou. *Scheduling multiple DAGs onto heterogeneous systems*. IPDPS, pp. 159-172, 2006.

The Future of Supercomputing

Marc Snir

Argonne National Laboratory

9700 South Cass Avenue, Argonne, Illinois 60439

snir@mcs.anl.gov

1 630-252-8808

Abstract

For over two decades, supercomputing evolved in a relatively straightforward manner: Supercomputers were assembled out of commodity microprocessors and leveraged their exponential increase in performance, due to Moore's Law. This simple model has been under stress since clock speed stopped growing a decade ago: Increased performance has required a commensurate increase in the number of concurrent threads. The evolution of device technology is likely to be even less favorable in the coming decade: The growth in CMOS performance is nearing its end, and no alternative technology is ready to replace CMOS. The continued shrinking of device size requires increasingly expensive technologies, and may not lead to improvements in cost/performance ratio; at which point, it ceases to make sense for commodity technology. These obstacles need not imply stagnation in supercomputer performance. In the long run, new computing models will come to the rescue. In the short run, more exotic, non-commodity device technologies can provide two or more orders of magnitude improvements in performance. Finally, better hardware and software architectures can significantly increase the efficiency of scientific computing platforms. While continued progress is possible, it will require a significant international research effort and major investments in future large-scale "computational instruments".

Categories and Subject Descriptors

C.5.1 [Large and Medium ("Mainframe") Computers]: Super (very large) computers

Keywords

Exascale; High-Performance Computing

1. CONTENTS

Supercomputing underwent a major technology revolution twenty years ago, as vector machines built of bipolar circuits were replaced by clusters of microprocessors built out of MOS circuits. The changed occurred because bipolar ECL technology was consuming too much power, and possible replacement materials, such as gallium arsenide, were not ready for prime time. It was an example of a "good enough" technology replacing a better one (at that time) [3]. Early clusters were less performing and much harder to program than leading vector supercomputers. On the other hand, they leveraged a cheaper technology with a large and growing market that had a clear evolution path (Moore's Law).

We are now facing a similar inflection point, since current CMOS technology is reaching the end of its roadmap, hampered by its high power consumption, while replacement materials are not ready for prime time. There is, however, a huge difference: No "good enough", broadly used technology is waiting in the wings to replace CMOS. Continued increase in supercomputer performance may require not only different technological approaches, but also a very different ecosystem.

The presentation will cover the following subjects:

- Technological obstacles to continued performance improvements of CMOS
- Possible alternatives technologies
- Economic obstacles to the continuation of "Moore's Law"
- Do we need continued increases in supercomputing performance?
- Technical approaches to continued performance increase "beyond Moore"
- The need for new policies and a new ecosystem

References relevant to this presentation are listed below.

Acknowledgement

This work was supported by the U.S. Department of Energy, Office of Science, Advanced Scientific Computing Research, under Contract DE-AC02-06CH11357.

REFERENCES

[1] Borkar, S. Designing Reliable Systems from Unreliable Components: the Challenges of Transistor Variability and Degradation. *IEEE Micro*, 25(6), 10--16, 2005.

[2] Cavin, R., Lugli, P. and Zhirnov, V. Science and Engineering beyond Moore's Law. *Proceedings of the IEEE*, 100,1720—1749, 2012.

ICS'14, June 10–13, 2014, Munich, Germany.

ACM 978-1-4503-2642-1/14/06.

http://dx.doi.org/10.1145/2597652.2616585

[3] Christensen, C., *The Innovator's Dilemma: When New Technologies Cause Great Firms to Fail*. Harvard Business Review Press, 2013.

[4] Colwell, R. The Chip Design Game at the End of Moore's Law. *Hot Chips*, Aug. 2013

[5] Courtland, R. The Status of Moore's Law: It's Complicated. *IEEE Spectrum,* Oct 2013. http://spectrum.ieee.org/semiconductors/devices/the-status-of-moores-law-its-complicated

[6] Fuller, S. and Millett, L. (eds.), *The Future of Computing Performance: Game Over or Next Level?* National Academies Press, 2010.

[7] Heck, S., Kaza, S. and Pinner, D. *Creating value in the semiconductor industry*. McKinsey&Company, San Francisco, 2011.

[8] ITRS, *International Technology Roadmap for Semiconductors, 2013 Edition: Executive Summary.* http://public.itrs.net/Links/2013ITRS/2013Chapters/2013ExecutiveSummary.pdf

[9] Kogge P. and Resnick D. *Yearly Update: Exascale Projections for 2013*. Technical Report SAND2013-9229, Sandia National Laboratories, 2013. Snir, M., Gropp, W. and Kogge, P., *Exascale Research: Preparing for the Post---Moore Era*. Technical Report, UIUC, 2011.http://hdl.handle.net/2142/25468

[10] Tiwari, S. and Theis, N. Recommendations from the NSF Workshop on Interdisciplinary Challenges beyond the Scaling Limits of Moore's Law, Aug. 2010. http://www.nnin.org/sites/default/files/files/NSF_Wksp_August_2010/NSF_BeyondMoore_Report_final.pdf

Short Bio

Marc Snir is Director of the Mathematics and Computer Science Division at the Argonne National Laboratory and Michael Faiman and Saburo Muroga Professor in the Department of Computer Science at the University of Illinois at Urbana-Champaign. He currently pursues research in parallel computing.

He was head of the Computer Science Department from 2001 to 2007. Until 2001 he was a senior manager at the IBM T. J. Watson Research Center where he led the Scalable Parallel Systems research group that was responsible for major contributions to the IBM SP scalable parallel system and to the IBM Blue Gene system.

Marc Snir received a Ph.D. in Mathematics from the Hebrew University of Jerusalem in 1979, worked at NYU on the NYU Ultracomputer project in 1980-1982, and was at the Hebrew University of Jerusalem in 1982-1986, before joining IBM. Marc Snir was a major contributor to the design of the Message Passing Interface. He has published numerous papers and given many presentations on computational complexity, parallel algorithms, parallel architectures, interconnection networks, parallel languages and libraries and parallel programming environments.

Marc is Argonne Distinguished Fellow, AAAS Fellow, ACM Fellow and IEEE Fellow. He has Erdos number 2 and is a mathematical descendant of Jacques Salomon Hadamard. He recently won the IEEE Awrd for Excellence in Scalable Computing.

Acceleration of Derivative Calculations with Application to Radial Basis Function – Finite-Differences on the Intel MIC Architecture

Gordon Erlebacher
Department of Scientific Computing
Florida State University
gordon.erlebach@gmail.com

Natasha Flyer
Computational and Information Systems
Laboratory
UCAR
flyer@ucar.edu

Erik Saule
Department of Computer Science
University of North Carolina at Charlotte
esaule@uncc.edu

Evan Bollig
Minnesota Supercomputer Institute
University of Minnesota
bollig@gmail.com

ABSTRACT

In this paper, we develop an efficient scheme for the calculation of derivatives within the context of Radial Basis Function Finite-Difference (RBF-FD). RBF methods express functions as a linear combination of spherically symmetric basis functions on an arbitrary set of nodes. The Finite-Difference component expresses this combination over a local set of nodes neighboring the point where the derivative is sought. The derivative at all points takes the form of a sparse matrix/vector multiplication (SpMV).

In this paper, we consider the case of local stencils with a fixed number of nodes at each point and encode the sparse matrix in ELLPACK format. We increase the number of operations relative to memory bandwidth by interleaving the calculation of four derivatives of four different functions, or 16 different derivatives. We demonstrate a novel implementation on the Intel MIC architecture, taking into account its advanced swizzling and channel interchange features. We present benchmarks on a real data set that show an almost sevenfold increase in speed compared to efficient implementations of a single derivative, reaching a performance of almost 140 Gflop/s in single precision. We explain the results through consideration of operation count versus memory bandwidth.

Categories and Subject Descriptors

F.2 [**Analysis of Algorithms and Problem Complexity**]: Numerical Algorithms and Problems

Keywords

MIC; SIMD; SpMV; Sparse Matrix; Radial Basis Function

ICS'14, June 10–13 2014, Munich, Germany.
Copyright 2014 ACM 978-1-4503-2642-1/14/06 ...$15.00.
http://dx.doi.org/10.1145/2597652.2597656.

1. INTRODUCTION

The multiplication of a sparse matrix by a dense vector (SpMV) is an important kernel in many applied fields such as fluid dynamics [3], recommendation systems [4] and graph drawing [12]). Naturally, improving the performance of SpMV has captured the interest of many researchers; including the development of various implementations for CPUs [5, 28] and GPUs [2, 13, 26, 15]. The main challenge to obtain good performance for matrix vector multiplication in general, and sparse matrix vector multiplication in particular, is the low ratio of floating point operations to memory bandwidth. When the matrix is not dense, the problem is exacerbated due to non-uniform access patterns.

Common improvement techniques such as bandwidth reduction (matrix reordering [9]), register blocking, partitioning to fit in cache or TLB [18, 22, 23], unrolling [17] have impacts that are very dependent on the matrix and overall do not lead to dramatic improvement. (The state-of-the-art techniques in OSKI [27] provide some useful yet limited improvements). Register blocking [23] does not work well to many of the matrices in general use (although it can be applied with virtually no overhead thanks to compressed representations [6].) Indeed, there are about 8 bytes of the matrix to transfer from memory per nonzero in single precision; each nonzero requires two floating point operations leading to a flop-to-byte ratio of at most $\frac{1}{4}$. This limits the obtained performance to at most a quarter of the bandwidth of the architecture, wasting a lot of potentially useful cycles. The commonly used techniques are mostly designed to reach that bound rather than overcome it.

Fortunately that fate is not inevitable. One solution would be to schedule a more instruction-intensive kernel simultaneously with the execution of SpMV, relying on some hardware threading capabilities, such as HyperThreading, to reduce the cycle wastage. However, most of the applications that use SpMV do not typically have an instruction-intensive kernel to run simultaneously.

Another solution, pursued in this paper, is to compute multiple SpMVs using matrices with identical spasity patterns, but with different matrix elements. Obviously not all the applications have such a property. However, important classes of applications such as graph recommendation [14], and the computation of derivatives for solving systems of PDEs using Radial Basis Function-generated Finite Differences (RBF-FD) [10] fall into the category of applications that require multiple SpMVs simultaneously. RBF-FD is a meshless method, which easily handles irregular geometries and local refinement with algorithmic complexity independent of dimensionality, and which can produce high-order derivative approximations. These methods are rapidly gaining ground in science and engineering modeling communities [1, 7, 11, 10, 21]. As a result, it is of interest to develop an efficient implementation on novel computer platforms for the calculation of derivatives within the context of RBF-FD; derivative calculations that account for the bulk of computer resources when running a numerical simulation implemented with RBF-FD. Typical equations solved by RBF-FD depend on multiple derivatives of multiple functions. Rather than compute each derivative individually, this paper investigates how to compute all derivatives simultaneously in an interleaved fashion. Specifically, we calculate four different derivatives (corresponding to four different sparse matrices with identical sparsity pattern) of four different functions (a common scenario in 3D fluid dynamics modeling) for a total of 16 derivatives.

To perform our analysis, we focus our attention on the improvement that can be achieved on the Intel Xeon Phi processor. It follows the Many Integrated Core (MIC) architecture, which has a significant memory bandwidth and peak flop throughput thanks to its 512-bit large SIMD registers. The Xeon Phi processor has been shown to be promising for sparse linear algebra compared to more classical CPU or GPU architectures [19, 16, 8].

In Section 2, we introduce and further motivate the RBF-FD method, giving an example of how calculating the derivatives for a common system of PDEs in fluid dynamics can be expressed as sixteen multiplications of four vectors by four sparse matrices with identical sparsity patterns.

Section 3 presents an estimation of the instruction intensity of various forms of the computations. We show that a sevenfold improvement can be expected when computing the sixteen multiplications simultaneously to reach a total of about 210 Gflop/s. This performance represents approximately 10% of the available flop/s of a Xeon Phi coprocessor. Provided the computation is mostly irregular, it is necessary to have an implementation that organizes the data in such a way it can perform a fully efficient Fused Multiply-Add every 10 cycles. We describe in Section 4 the details of the MIC architecture and how to use specialized load, store, swizzle and permutation instructions to efficiently bring the data from memory into the vector registers to be processed. Section 5 presents results on memory access and computational speed and their relation to choices made in the SpMV kernels. It also provides the actual performance of the various kernels on multiple classes of matrices, some generated for purpose of analysis, and some extracted from an application of RBF-FD. A performance of 135 Gflop/s in single precision is achieved using RBF-FD differentiation matrices, which is 3.75 times better than the theoretical peak performance of an SpMV operation. Concluding remarks and perspectives are provided in Section 6.

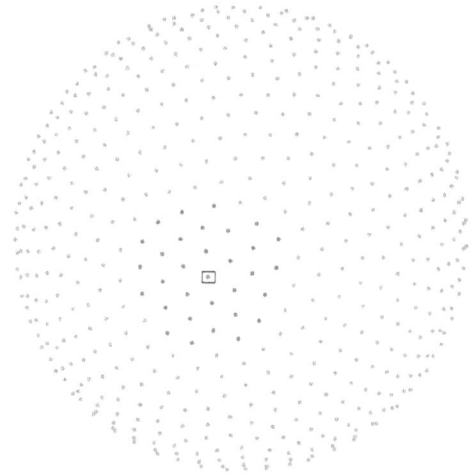

Figure 1: An example of an RBF-FD stencil of size $n = 32$ on a sphere of $N = 1024$ nodes to approximate any derivative operator at the point in the square. In nonsparse format, the DM is 1024×1024 with 32 nonzero entries per row.

2. INTRODUCTION AND MOTIVATION FOR RBF-FD

RBFs approximate a function $f(\mathbf{x}) \in \mathbb{R}^d$ sampled at N distinct node locations by linearly combining translates of a single radially symmetric function, e.g. $\phi(r) = e^{-\varepsilon^2 r^2}$, where $r = \|\mathbf{x} - \mathbf{x}_i\|$ denotes the Euclidean distance between where the function $f(\mathbf{x})$ is evaluated, $\mathbf{x}$, and where the RBF, ϕ, is centered $\mathbf{x}_i$. The parameter ε controls the shape of the RBF. Note that the argument of an RBF is simply a scalar distance, r, independent of any coordinate system or dimension. As a result, nodes can be scattered as desired across complex physical domains with the implementation of the method being independent of dimensionality. Thus, no mesh generation is needed and algorithmic complexity does not increase with dimension.

To obtain a RBF derivative approximation at a node location that will result in a sparse differentiation matrix (DM), the RBF-FD method has been developed over the last decade [24, 25, 20, 29]. RBF-FD is conceptually similar to standard finite differences (FD). However, the differentiation weights for approximating a derivative at a given node (forming one row of the RBF-FD derivative matrix (DM)) enforce that the linear combination of function values at the $n << N$ nearest node locations (a stencil) be exact for RBFs centered at each of the n nodes rather than polynomials. The result is a sparse matrix with only n entries in each of its N rows, resulting in a total of nN nonzero entries. An example stencil is shown in Figure 1.

Due to the above attributes and its simplicity of implementation, the RBF-FD is gaining popularity in modeling systems of PDEs in a variety of fields in fluid dynamics (e.g., geosciences, combustion, aerodynamics [1, 7, 11, 10, 21]). For example, the full shallow water equations in a 3D Cartesian coordinate system for a rotating fluid are as follows:

$$\frac{\partial u}{\partial t} = -\left(u\frac{\partial u}{\partial x} + v\frac{\partial u}{\partial y} + w\frac{\partial u}{\partial z} + f(yw - zv) + g\frac{\partial h}{\partial x} \right)$$

$$\frac{\partial v}{\partial t} = -\left(u\frac{\partial v}{\partial x} + v\frac{\partial v}{\partial y} + w\frac{\partial v}{\partial z} + f(zu - xw) + g\frac{\partial h}{\partial x} \right)$$

$$\frac{\partial w}{\partial t} = -\left(u\frac{\partial w}{\partial x} + v\frac{\partial w}{\partial y} + w\frac{\partial w}{\partial z} + f(xv - yu) + g\frac{\partial h}{\partial x} \right)$$

$$\frac{\partial h}{\partial t} = -\left(\frac{\partial(uh)}{\partial x} + \frac{\partial(vh)}{\partial y} + h\frac{\partial(wh)}{\partial z} \right),$$

where f is the Coriolis force, $\{u, v, w\}$ are the components of the velocity vector in the respective $\{x, y, z\}$ directions, and h is the geopotential height (analogous to pressure). Thus, we have four variables $\{u, v, w, h\}$ and three DMs, D_x, D_y, D_z representing $\partial_x, \partial_y, \partial_z$, respectively. Moreover, in order to stably time step the equations with an explicit time-stepping scheme, most numerical methods (including RBF-FD) require a fourth operator, hyperviscosity, to be added to each equation. Hyperviscosity takes the form of $\triangle^p$ ($\triangle$ denotes the Laplacian operator), where $p \geq 3$, which is approximated by the matrix D_{hyp}. Therefore, in order to solve this system of PDEs, the application of 4 DM to 4 unknowns, i.e. 16 SpMV is required at every time step. Due to the fact that RBFs are independent of a coordinate system, taking into account only distances to nearest neighbors, the DMs have the following properties:

- For a given n, regardless of the operator approximated, e.g., ∂_x, or the Laplacian, RBF-FD DMs will have the same number of nonzeros per row.

- For a given n and N, regardless of the operator approximated, the DMs will have the same sparsity pattern. Examples of an RBF-FD DM can be seen in Figures 8d-e.

Multiple variables transform a SpMV into a SpMM (Sparse Matrix/dense Matrix multiplication), which improves register utilization and decreases cache misses by vectorizing over the multiple source vectors. Furthermore, due to the properties just mentioned, multiple derivatives of a single function can be calculated rather than computing a single derivative of multiple functions. Using the PDE system above as an example, the block structure of the SpMM for computing all derivatives needed is

$$\begin{pmatrix} \underline{u}_x & \underline{v}_x & \underline{w}_x & \underline{h}_x \\ \underline{u}_y & \underline{v}_y & \underline{w}_y & \underline{h}_y \\ \underline{u}_z & \underline{v}_z & \underline{w}_z & \underline{h}_z \\ \underline{u}_{hyp} & \underline{v}_{hyp} & \underline{w}_{hyp} & \underline{h}_{hyp} \end{pmatrix} = \begin{pmatrix} D_x \\ D_y \\ D_z \\ D_{hyp} \end{pmatrix} \times (\underline{u}\ \underline{v}\ \underline{w}\ \underline{h}) \quad (1)$$

where $\{\underline{u}, \underline{v}, \underline{w}, \underline{h}\}$ are the functions values at all nodes of the corresponding variables with the left hand side being the resulting derivative approximations. The increased memory bandwidth due to an increase in the number of derivative matrices is offset by improved cache utilization, leading to an overall performance benefit. In practice however, the number of vectors whose derivatives are required is limited, capping the performance of the matrix/vector multiplication. Similarly, the number of different derivatives in a particular computation is finite. It is for this reason that we seek to combine the benefits of multiple vectors and multiple matrices simultaneously. We limit this initial study to four vectors and four matrices, which is a common number found in fluid dynamic calculations. Equation 1 is of the form $Y = AX$, where Y encodes the x, y, z discrete derivatives (and hyperviscosity operator) of u, v, w, h, X encodes

the variables (u, v, w, h) and A represents the 16 discrete differentiation operators.

We also note that the DMs are time-independent. They are computed once at the beginning of the simulation and used repeatedly to update the solution in time (for each iteration of the simulation). Thus, the cost to calculate the derivatives, although high (on the order of 1000 SpMVs), is amortized by the very long numerical simulations. The startup cost is eliminated when performing parameter studies on a given node distribution. Furthermore, the computation of the derivative matrices are done serially, but are trivially parallelizable.

3. MODELING THE POTENTIAL IMPROVEMENTS

We saw in the previous section that one can express the RBF problem as a multiplication of four matrices by four vectors. We present here an estimation of the variation on the flop intensity of the computation and its impact on the expected performance of the application. Relevant notation are given in Figure 2.

b_i	number of bytes per index
b_x	number of bytes per value
n_z	number of nonzeros per row of A
n_r	number of column/rows of A
n_c	total number of nonzeros
n_v	number of $\mathbf{x}$ vectors
n_m	number of matrices
s_M	size of the n_m matrices in bytes
s_x	size of the n_v $\mathbf{x}$ vectors in bytes
s_y	size of the $n_v n_m$ $\mathbf{y}$ vectors in bytes
cl	size of a cache line in bytes
b_{wT}	number of bytes written to memory
b_{rT}	minimum number of bytes read from memory
b_T	minimum number of bytes transferred
B_{rT}	maximum number of bytes read from memory
B_T	maximum number of bytes transferred
O	number of floating point operations
I_b	maximum computational intensity
I_w	minimum computational intensity

Figure 2: Notation relative to the application problem (upper section) and to the benchmarks (lower section.)

Each vector in the problem is of dimension n_r and each entry takes b_x bytes. There are n_v $\mathbf{x}$ vectors and $n_v n_m$ $\mathbf{y}$ vectors, which lead to the size of the $\mathbf{x}$ and $\mathbf{y}$ vectors:

$$s_x = n_v b_x n_r, \quad s_y = n_v n_m b_x n_r$$

The matrix is composed of n_r rows and columns with n_z nonzeros per row leading to a total of

$$n_c = n_r n_z$$

nonzero entries in the matrix. Each of these nonzero entries has one index of size b_i and n_m values of size b_x. The matrices have a total size of

$$s_M = n_c(b_i + b_x n_m) = n_r n_z(b_i + b_x n_m)$$

If we assume an algorithm where the rows are processed one after the other, the amount of memory written is precisely the size of the $\mathbf{y}$ vector. (This assumption removes the possibility of blocking or cache partitioning techniques.)

$$b_{wT} = s_y = n_v n_m b_x n_r$$

(a) Best case.

nb vectors \ nb matrices	1	2	4	6	8	10	12	16
16	2.67	3.56	4.27	4.57	4.74	4.85	4.92	5.02
12	2.18	2.91	3.49	3.74	3.88	3.97	4.03	4.11
10	1.90	2.54	3.05	3.27	3.39	3.46	3.52	3.59
8	1.60	2.13	2.56	2.74	2.84	2.91	2.95	3.01
6	1.26	1.68	2.02	2.17	2.25	2.30	2.33	2.38
4	0.89	1.19	1.42	1.52	1.58	1.62	1.64	1.67
2	0.47	0.63	0.75	0.81	0.84	0.86	0.87	0.89
1	0.24	0.32	0.39	0.42	0.43	0.44	0.45	0.46

(b) Worst case.

nb vectors \ nb matrices	1	2	4	6	8	10	12	16
16	0.43	0.80	1.39	1.85	2.21	2.50	2.74	3.12
12	0.33	0.61	1.07	1.43	1.71	1.95	2.15	2.46
10	0.27	0.51	0.90	1.21	1.45	1.66	1.83	2.11
8	0.22	0.41	0.73	0.98	1.19	1.36	1.50	1.73
6	0.16	0.31	0.55	0.75	0.91	1.04	1.15	1.33
4	0.11	0.21	0.37	0.51	0.62	0.71	0.79	0.91
2	0.06	0.10	0.19	0.26	0.31	0.36	0.40	0.47
1	0.03	0.05	0.09	0.13	0.16	0.18	0.20	0.24

(c) Worst case (No cacheline effects)

nb vectors \ nb matrices	1	2	4	6	8	10	12	16
16	0.43	0.80	1.39	1.85	2.21	2.50	2.74	3.12
12	0.42	0.76	1.30	1.69	2.00	2.24	2.44	2.74
10	0.41	0.73	1.23	1.59	1.86	2.07	2.24	2.50
8	0.39	0.70	1.14	1.45	1.68	1.86	2.00	2.21
6	0.37	0.64	1.02	1.27	1.45	1.59	1.69	1.85
4	0.33	0.55	0.84	1.02	1.14	1.23	1.30	1.39
2	0.25	0.39	0.55	0.64	0.70	0.73	0.76	0.80
1	0.16	0.25	0.33	0.37	0.39	0.41	0.42	0.43

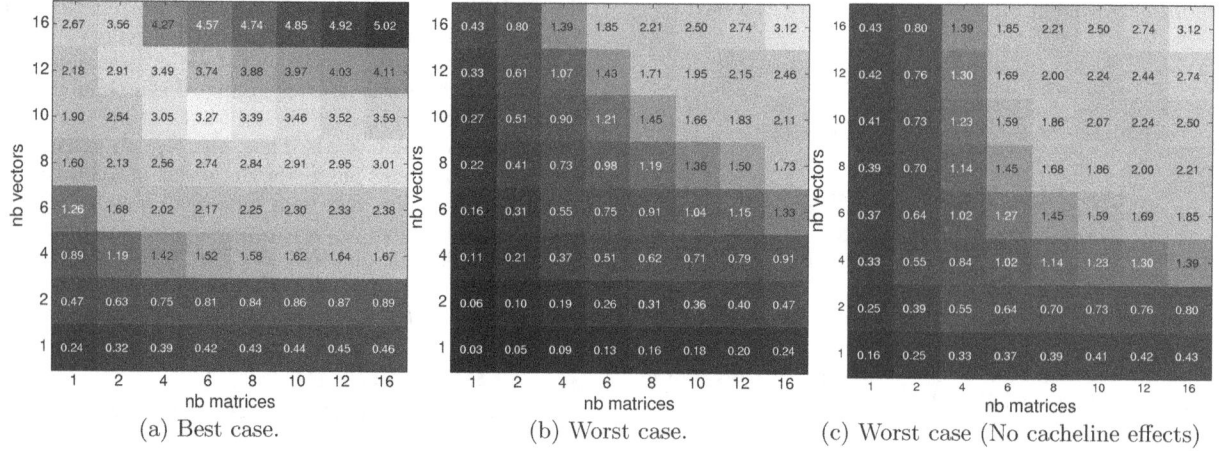

Figure 3: Ratio of flops to bytes in single precision: 3(a) **best case**; 3(b) **worst case when** $cl = 64$; **and** 3(c) **worst case neglecting that the memory transfers are with a granularity of one cache line (equivalent to** $cl = 1$**)**

The amount of data read from memory depends highly on both the algorithm's execution path, and on how the matrix is structured. But in the best case both the matrix A and the source vector $\mathbf{x}$ are read once from the main memory. (We assume that all the elements of $\mathbf{x}$ are involved in the SpMV.) Thus,

$$b_{rT} = s_M + s_x = n_r n_z (b_i + b_x n_m) + n_v b_x n_r$$

$$b_T = b_{rT} + b_{wT} = n_r n_z (b_i + b_x n_m) + n_v b_x n_r (1 + n_m)$$

Notice that there is no reason for a piece of the matrix to be read multiple times. But assuming that each element of the $\mathbf{x}$ vector is read a single time is a strong assumption. If using a single core, it assumes that either the cache of the architecture can store the full $\mathbf{x}$ vector or that the matrix is sufficiently well structured to cause no cache trashing. If using multiple cores, this assumes that no element of the $\mathbf{x}$ vectors will be used by multiple cores. [19] showed that there is very little cache trashing in practice; however having elements of the vectors used by multiple cores can have a significant impact on the performance (growing with n_v).

On the other hand, in the worst case, every time the $\mathbf{x}$ vector is accessed, the value needs to be transferred from memory again. So in total, there are as many transfers as the number of nonzeros in the matrix. Note however that most architectures cannot read memory a single byte at a time. Instead, a minimum number of bytes, equal to the size of a cacheline cl, are transferred at once. When there are multiple vectors, each nonzero element uses n_v consecutive entries. In the worst case, the number of bytes read and transferred is

$$B_{rT} = s_M + n_c cl \left\lceil \frac{n_v b_x}{cl} \right\rceil$$

$$B_T = n_v n_m b_x n_r + n_r n_z \left(b_i + b_x n_m + cl \left\lceil \frac{n_v b_x}{cl} \right\rceil \right)$$

In SpMV, each nonzero of the matrix requires two floating point operations: one for performing the multiplication and one for accumulating the result row-wise. Here we are dealing with $n_v n_m$ simultaneous SpMVs and the number of floating point operations is

$$O = 2 n_v n_m n_c = 2 n_v n_m n_z n_r$$

The computation intensity is the amount of floating point operations performed per byte transferred. In the worst case and in the best case, we have

$$I_b = \frac{O}{b_T} = \frac{2 n_v n_m}{(b_i + b_x n_m) + n_v n_m b_x n_z^{-1} + n_v b_x n_z^{-1}}$$

$$I_w = \frac{O}{B_T} = \frac{2 n_v n_m}{(b_i + b_x n_m) + n_v n_m b_x n_z^{-1} + cl \left\lceil \frac{n_v b_x}{cl} \right\rceil}$$

Figure 3 presents the flop to byte ratios for single precision computation in the best and the worst case on a classical cache-based architecture ($cl = 64$) and assuming $cl = 1$. We can easily see the potential improvement in the computational intensity when the number of matrices or vectors increases. There is a significant difference between the best and the worst case: there is a eightfold difference in the one matrix – one vector ($n_m = n_v = 1$) case but that gap closes with the increase in the number of vectors and matrices to a fourfold difference in the four matrices and four vectors ($n_m = n_v = 4$) case and 1.6 fold in the $n_m = n_v = 16$ case. The ratios computed with $cl = 1$ are mostly similar to the one with $cl = 64$ when the number of vectors is large. But the differences are important when the number of vectors is low: this highlights that accessing the memory with a granularity of one cache line is a main problem faced when performing a standard SpMV computation.

Figure 4 shows how these ratios translate into actual performance. This figure provides projected best and worst Gflop/s achievable assuming the computation is memory-bound and the architecture reaches 150 GB/s. Notice that [19] showed a higher peak bandwidth, but we will show in Section 5 why 150 GB/s is a better estimate of what one might achieve in these kernels. In single precision, the worse that one could achieve by using four vectors and four matrices is much higher than the best achievable using a classical SpMV computation. The best performance reachable is 210 Gflop/s: almost six times higher than the peak of the classical SpMV case.

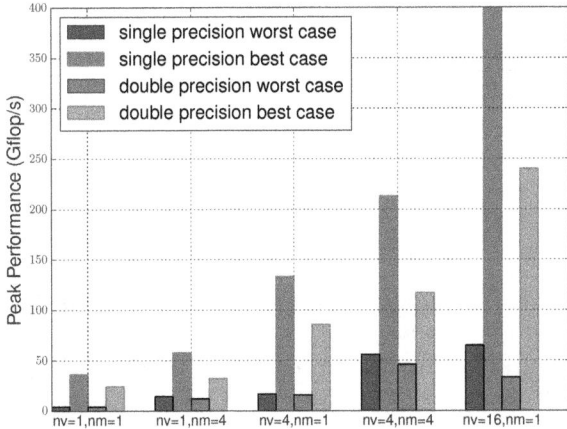

Figure 4: Estimation of the maximum achievable performance using a device with a bandwidth from memory to computational units of 150 GB/s when varying the number of vectors and matrices.

4. EFFICIENT IMPLEMENTATION ON THE INTEL XEON PHI PROCESSOR

4.1 Intel Xeon Phi

In this work, we use an Intel Xeon Phi 5110P coprocessor. This card has 8 memory controllers that can each execute 5 billion transactions per second. Each has two 32-bit channels, achieving a total bandwidth of 320 GB/s aggregated across all the memory controllers. There are 60 cores clocked at 1.05 GHz. Their memory interfaces are 32-bit wide with two channels and the total bandwidth is 8.4 GB/s per core. Thus, the cores should be able to consume 504 GB/s at most. However, the bandwidth between the cores and the memory controllers is limited by the ring network that connects the cores and the memory controller. Its precise bandwidth is believed to be between 200 GB/s and 250 GB/s.

Each core in the architecture has a 32 kB L1 data cache, a 32 kB L1 instruction cache, and a 512 kB L2 cache. The architecture of a core is based on the traditional Pentium architecture, which has been extended to 64-bit with hyperthreading. A core can hold four hardware contexts at any given time (240 threads in total). At each clock cycle, instructions from a single thread are executed. Due to some hardware constraints, two hardware contexts must be used to reach the peak instruction throughput in that architecture. Similar to the Pentium architecture, a core has two different concurrent instruction pipelines that allow the execution of two instructions per cycle. However, only one vector or floating point instruction can be executed per cycle.

Most of the performance of the architecture comes from the vector processing unit. Each core has 32 512-bit SIMD registers that can be used for double or single precision, that is, either as a vector of eight 64-bit values or as a vector of 16 32-bit values, respectively. The vector processing unit can perform arithmetic (addition and multiplication) instructions making it possible to reach 16 single precision (or 8 double precision) operations per cycle. The unit also supports Fused Multiply-Add (FMA) operations, which are typically counted as two operations when benchmarking.

Therefore, the peak performance of the 5110P card is one Tflop/s in double precision and two Tflop/s in single precision. If FMA cannot be used, only half of these rates can be achieved.

4.2 Bringing the data into the vector register

As explained in Section 3, we expect to achieve a performance of about 210 Gflop/s in single precision in the best case. We will focus on the single precision case with four vectors and four matrices. Similar techniques apply for other combinations. This target performance represents 10% of the peak performance of the architecture, which cannot be reached without an efficient vectorization. Indeed, to reach such a performance, a Fused Multiply-Add instruction on fully loaded registers must be executed at most every 10 cycles.

In term of memory layout, we adopt a format similar to the ELLPACK format to store the matrix since the number of nonzeros per row is constant throughout the matrix. The matrix is given in two arrays. The first array is `col_id` that describes the sparsity structure of the matrix. Each row of `col_id` consists of n_z entries that label the column index of each nonzero in A. The other array is `data` that gives the values of the nonzeros in the four matrices. The values of the matrices are interleaved by groups of four so that the value $A^l_{col\_id[k]}$ of the kth nonzero of the lth matrix is at index $\lfloor \frac{k-1}{4} \rfloor * 4 * n_m + (l-1) * 4 + (k-1)\%4$. (In other words, the first four entries are from A^1 and the next four are from A^2.) The vectors $\mathbf{x}$ are interleaved so that $\mathbf{x}^l_i$ and $\mathbf{x}^{l+1}_i$ are consecutive in memory. The vector $\mathbf{y}$ is similarly grouped in sets of 16, which correspond to four derivatives applied to four functions, at a single point.

We discuss how the implementation of the v4m4 kernel works using vector instructions. The code is given for reference in Figure 5 along with a graphical depiction of the content of the registers. (We will show in Section 5 that an implementation that relies on compiler vectorization does not lead to desirable performance, which confirms the results of [19].) The registers in the MIC architecture are 512 bits wide and can store 16 floats or integers. (In comparison to OpenCL or CUDA, one can think of these registers as a warp.) The end goal is to load and format the nonzero values $A^1_h, A^2_h, A^3_h, A^4_h$ and the vector entries $x^1_m, x^2_m, x^3_m, x^4_m$ into two vector registers and apply Fused Multiply-Add on them, which is depicted in the `accu` line of Figure 5. Bringing the data into the vector register as shown in the figure is the difficult component of our proposed algorithm, which we proceed to explain further. A thread will perform the multiplications one row at a time, and parallelism is achieved by giving blocks of rows to each thread using an OpenMP construct.

The core of the technique is to load the maximum amount of data into large the registers and format the data for processing within these registers, minimizing the amount of interaction with memory. The Intel MIC is more for these operations than classical CPUs because it features larger vector registers and more elaborate vector reorganization instructions, such as swizzling, permutations and broadcasts. (The AVX instruction sets on classical CPUs are more primitive in that aspect.) A vector of 512 bits is composed of four lanes (sometimes called channels) of 128 bits, which are made of four segments of 32 bits. A swizzling operation allows the reorder of the elements within each lane (see

```
const __m512i offsets = _mm512_set4_epi32(3,2,1,0);
const __m512i four = _mm512_set4_epi32(4,4,4,4);
int int_mask = 0x1111;
__mmask16 mask = _mm512_int2mask(int_mask);

#pragma omp parallel for
for (int r=0; r < nb_rows; r++) {
__m512 accu = _mm512_setzero_ps();

 for (int n=0; n < nz; n+=4) {
   float* a = &dom.col_id[0]+n+nz*r;
   __m512i vect_i = _mm512_setzero_ps();
   vect_i = _mm512_mask_loadunpacklo_ps(vect_i, mask, a);
   vect_i = _mm512_mask_loadunpackhi_ps(vect_i, mask, a);
   vect_i = _mm512_swizzle_ps(vect_i, _MM_SWIZ_REG_AAAA);
   vect_i = _mm512_fmadd_epi32(vect_i, four, offsets);

   all_vect = _mm512_i32gather_ps(vect_i, dom.vec_vt, scale);

   mat_ent = _mm512_load_ps(dom.data + nb_mat*(n + r*nz));

   //perform first tensor multiplication with AAAA pattern
   vect = permute(all_vect, _MM_PERM_AAAA);
   mat = _mm512_swizzle_ps(mat_ent, _MM_SWIZ_REG_AAAA);
   accu = _mm512_fmadd_ps(vect, mat, accu);

   //three more times with BBBB, CCCC, and DDDD patterns
 }
 _mm512_storenrngo_ps(dom.result_vt+nb_mat*nb_vec*r, accu);
```

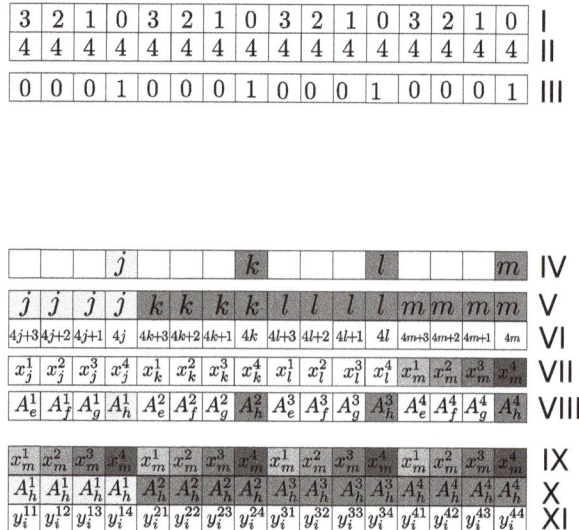

(a) Source code   (b) Content of the vector registers.

Figure 5: Code snippet of the multiplication of 4 vectors with 4 matrices. When a line changes the content of a vector register its new content is shown on the right. The effects of swizzling and permutations are highlighted using a color code.

how `mat` is extracted from `mat_ent` in Figure 5 line VIII to X). On the other hand, a permutation reorders entire lanes, without changing their contents (see for instance how `vect` is generated from `all_vect` in Figure 5 line VII to IX). Both permutation and swizzling support common reordering and broadcast. In the code, the "permute" function needs to use the `_mm512_permute4f128_epi32` instruction which is only defined on integers and therefore in place typecasts are necessary to convert a vector to and from integer type. (Note that we prefer swizzling to permutation if possible because we believe it is cheaper. Many instructions have swizzling capability, while permutation is its own instruction.)

Every operation that loads data from memory into a register transfers 512 bits, or 16 floats at a time. A single nonzero in the matrix will cause 16 operations to be performed, but it only uses four floats from the matrix and four floats from the `x` vector. So we would like to execute a single instruction to load the data for four nonzeros in the matrix, and another instruction to load the data for four nonzeros from the vectors. (The number of nonzeros on a row in our application is always a multiple of four; if it weren't, we would add some explicit zeros in the data structure for padding.)

The values from the nonzero elements in the matrix are the simplest to load. One can load the 16 floating point values for four nonzeros of the matrix at once. The four floats coming from each matrix are naturally grouped within each lane of the SIMD register. One can use a swizzle operation to broadcast the four elements of a single matrix to fill the whole register. (The broadcast of $A_h^1, A_h^2, A_h^3, A_h^4$ is shown in Figure 5.)

Loading the entries from the `x` vector is more involved. First, the column pointers of four different nonzeros are loaded into a vector register and the values are distributed

one per lane of the vector register using an **unpack** operation in line IV[1] (The column pointers are named j, k, l, m in Figure 5.) They are replicated so that each value fills a single vector lane using a swizzle operation (in line V). Then each value is multiplied by four (because $n_v = 4$) and the offset vector $(3, 2, 1, 0)$ is added to each lane to obtain the correct index of the elements of the `x` vector within each lane using a Fused Multiply-Add operation in line VI. A **gather** operation is then performed in line VII to bring the 16 entries of the `x` vector into the SIMD register. At this point we have a register where each lane is the four vector entries for a nonzero element. Using a broadcast permutation, one can replicate an entry of the four vectors across each lane. (The broadcast of $x_m^1, x_m^2, x_m^3, x_m^4$ is shown in Figure 5 in line IX.)

Now that $A_h^1, A_h^2, A_h^3, A_h^4$ and $x_m^1, x_m^2, x_m^3, x_m^4$ are properly laid out in the vectors, a partial value for y_i can be computed in line XI. Once all the nonzeros of the row have been processed, the exact y_i value can be sent to memory using a the "No Read No Global Order" hint to optimize write traffic on the memory bus.

The model of Section 3 establishes that the memory transfer caps the computation at 210 GFlop/s, which is 10% of the peak single precision of the architecture. To reach this value, the cores need to execute one "useful" Fused Multiply-Add operation every ten cycles. The inner loop of the kernel spends 7 vector instructions to layout the data and then 3 per tensor product for a total of 12 vector instructions. Most of these instruction have a one cycle throughput cost except the gather operations which might need to perform up to

---

[1]Notice that there are two calls to **unpack** for the LSB and MSB. Both are mandatory even if one is known to be nilpotent according to the documentation of the hardware.

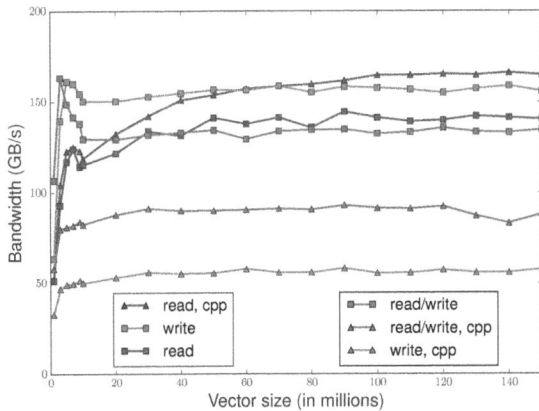

Figure 6: Bandwidth performance under idealized conditions. Entries with "cpp" (triangles) denote cases where vectorization is compiler generated.

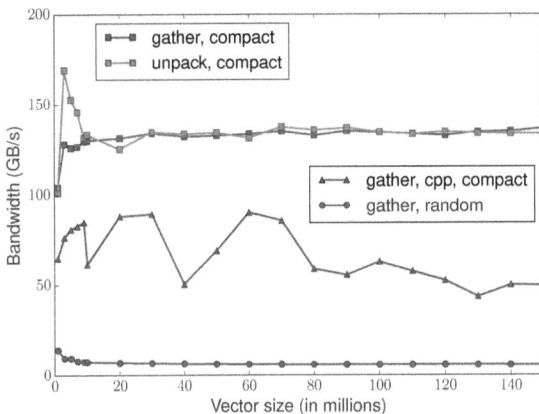

Figure 7: Performance of gather and unpack operations.

16 memory accesses. There are also some scalar operations but there are few of them and are executed on a different pipeline than the vector operations. Overall, the inner loop can emit the 4 Fused Multiply-Add in less than 40 cycles.

5. EXPERIMENTAL VALIDATION

In this section, we describe a series of numerical experiments to confirm the performance predictions of Section 3. To better understand our results, we first perform some bandwidth measurements, followed by the actual SpMV computations. All the codes are compiled with the Intel C Compiler version 13 and -O3 optimization. The codes use the IMCI instructions exposed by the compiler through intrinsics.

5.1 Bandwidth

Figure 6 shows a benchmark that computes the bandwidth achieved when reading and/or writing large arrays on the MIC card. The read benchmark performs a simple sum of the array. The write benchmark sets all the elements of the array to zero, while the read/write benchmarks copies the array into another one. We also investigate the

difference between a straight C++ implementation (compiled with -O3 with proper tagging to inform the compiler of memory alignments) and an implementation with explicit use of the vector registers.

The `read_cpp` implementation reaches a performance of 168 GB/s which is better than the `read` implementation which only achieves 145 GB/s. This is explained by the compiler adding loop unrolling and software prefetching in the assembly code in the `read_cpp` case, which is not added in the `read` case. On the other hand, the `write` case reaches a performance of 158 GB/s while the `write_cpp` implementation never exceeds 58 GB/s. This difference is the result of `_mm512_store_nrngo_ps`, an instruction, which bypasses the "Read For Ownership" protocol and allows the writes to be performed in any order. The compiler can not use this instruction on its own because this would break the memory convention useful for some parallel algorithms. The `read-/write` benchmark performs at 140 GB/s while the `read-/write_cpp` benchmark performs at about 90 GB/s.

Note that SpMV kernels are not likely to use only simple read and simple writes. We also benchmark the performance we can achieve using `gather` and `unpack` operations and we present the results in Figure 7. The `unpack` instruction can reach a performance of 140 GB/s. (There is no easy way to implement the equivalent of the `unpack` operation without using explicit registers.) The performance of the `gather` operations depends in which order the array is read. If the indices are ordered (`compact`) then a performance of 140 GB/s is reached. If the indices are completely randomized, the performance drops below 5 GB/s. We can see that implementing the indirection mechanism without vector instructions lowers the performance significantly. (In the `compact` case, it never surpasses 100 GB/s and is close to 50 GB/s most of the time.)

To summarize, using vector instructions appears necessary in order to reach the highest bandwidth on the MIC architecture. For the instructions used in a typical SpMV computation, one can expect a bandwidth between 140 GB/s to 160 GB/s. That is why we use in our estimations a best achievable bandwidth of 150 GB/s despite the fact that a code carefully crafted to maximize bandwidth can reach higher values [19].

5.2 Instances

The different matrices used to perform our experiments and analysis are presented in Figure 8. The **Supercompact** matrices (Figure 8(a)) have been generated to only have nonzero elements in the first 32 columns of the matrix. As a result, only 32 values of x are read from memory, and the expense associated with cache misses is removed from consideration. The cost associated with A remains. The **Compact** matrices (Figure 8(b)) are generated to have 32 nonzeros per row centered around the diagonal and it represents the ideal case for many applications that rely on sparse matrix vector multiplication. The nonzero elements of the **Random** matrices (Figure 8(c)) see their nonzero elements randomly (uniformly) distributed in the matrix; they represent the worst case scenario for a cache-based architecture where the cache reutilisation is the lowest from one row to the next. The other type of matrix is used in derivative stencils in 3D RBF-FD calculations (Figure 8(d) shows a 32-point stencil of a 3D 8^3 grid).

We also apply a Reverse Cuthill-Mckee reordering to all the matrices. This ordering technique aims to reduce the distance between the nonzeros and the diagonal, hopefully increasing the cache hit ratio. The reordered version of the matrix can be seen in Figure 8(e).

5.3 Computations

We now investigate the actual performance that we can obtain when multiplying four vectors by four matrices in single precision. Figure 9 presents results for different types of matrices and also shows the minimum and maximum performance predicted in Section 3. Figure 9(a) gives the results for the `supercompact` and `random` matrices that represent both the best and the worst case for such a practical computation. The `supercompact` case peaks at 208 Gflop/s which is very close to the predicted peak performance of 213 Gflop/s. Conversely the performance of the `random` case decreases to 56 Gflop/s which is close to the lowest predicted performance of 55 Gflop/s. One can see that RCM ordering helps the `random` case but the impact decreases when the size of the matrix increases.

Figure 9(b) gives the results on the `compact` case, which represents the best realistic matrix one could find with very structured grids and a `RBF` derivative matrix extracted from a real 3D application. In the `compact` case, the performance can be as high as 195 Gflop/s, which is within 15% of the predicted peak performance. The performance of the `RBF` case varies between 100 and 140 Gflop/s. Most of the time, the RCM ordering provides an improvement which can be as high as 30 Gflop/s.

We finally investigate the central questions of this paper. Do we gain actual performance by transforming classical SpMV computation into the multiplication of four vectors by four matrices for the computation of the derivative of RBFs? Does using manual vectorization improve actual application performance? Figure 10 compares the performance achieved by a classical SpMV and by the multiplication of four vectors by four matrices using either standard C++ code and our optimized implementation. The classical SpMV computation reaches 14 Gflop/s. The standard C++ implementation reaches a performance of 38 Gflop/s while our optimized implementation almost reaches 140 Gflop/s. Notice that RCM ordering has no impact in the standard C++ implementation while it provides a significant improvement in our manually vectorized version. Thus, the C++ implementation is likely instruction-bound while our manually vectorized implementation is most likely memory-bound.

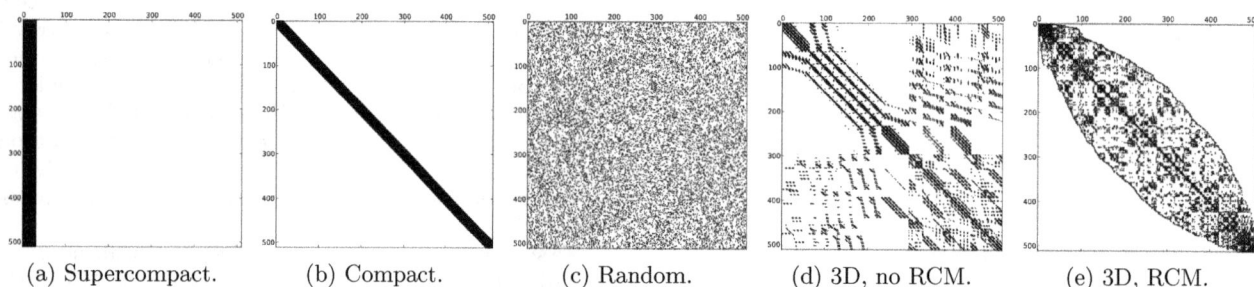

(a) Supercompact.   (b) Compact.   (c) Random.   (d) 3D, no RCM.   (e) 3D, RCM.

Figure 8: Different sparsity distributions. In all cases, there are 512 rows and 32 nonzeros per row. The last two matrices corresponds to a derivative stencil in 3D RBF-FD calculations (with and without RCM ordering).

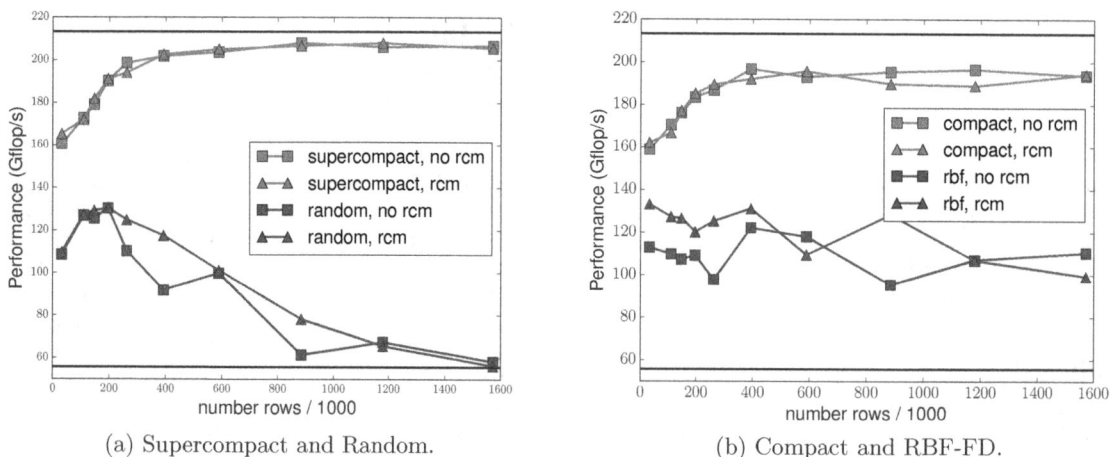

(a) Supercompact and Random.   (b) Compact and RBF-FD.

Figure 9: Performance of the manually vectorized code. The two horizontal lines depict the worst and the best predicted performances.

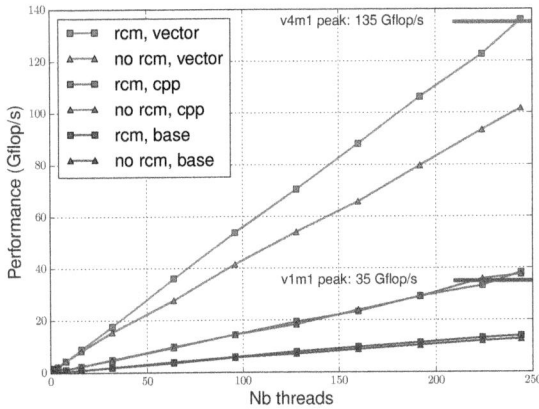

Figure 10: Performance of $y = Ax$ for a RBF derivative stencil of a 96^3 3D grid. Classical "one-matrix one-vector" SpMV ($n_m = n_v = 1$ given in blue) has low performance. The manually vectorized code (red) is 3.5 times faster than the compiler generated one (green). RCM ordering (squares) only improves the performance for our manually vectorized code. We also show peak theoretical performance for v1m1 and v4m1 on the MIC. Not shown is the peak theoretical performance of 210 Gflops for v4m4.

The main idea of this paper, computing 16 derivatives at a time, can be applied on different architectures such as multiprocessor multicore or GPU. To illustrate this fact, we conducted similar experiments on Cascade at the Minnesota Supercomputing Institute using two Intel Xeon E5 2670 nodes (8 cores, 2 threads and 20 Mbytes of L2 cache per core, with hyperthreading disabled.) The cores support the AVX instruction set. Both the compiler-generated code and the code written with the help of the AVX instruction set reach a read bandwidth of 85 GB/s. Using cache lines of 512 bits, we find a best/worst speeds of 2.4/20 Gflops/s and 32/120 Gflops/s, respectively for the 1vec/1mat and 4vec/4mat cases. Our implementation on Cascade reaches 45 Gflops for the 4/4 case, or 45/120=37% of peak theoretical performance on this particular processor setup. For reference, we achieve 140/210=66% of peak theoretical performance on the MIC. Note that peak performance is not that of the processor, but of the best possible algorithm on the processor. The gain in the 4/4 case with respect to 4x 1/1 case is 4x on the MIC and 2.5x on the front end, respectively.

6. CONCLUSION

In the previous sections, we have explored the practical implementation on an Intel Xeon Phi card of multiple derivative operators acting on multiple vectors within the context of RBF-FD. Each derivative has an associated sparse matrix with a fixed number of nonzeros on each row. While computing a single derivative of multiple functions is rather common, we accelerate the algorithm further by considering multiple matrices, with identical sparsity patterns, acting on multiple vectors. We specialize our study to four matrices and four derivatives, with 16 outputs, computed as a sum of outer products.

Our implementation makes use of the IMCI MIC instruction set and includes a number of swizzling and channel swapping operations, for an extremely efficient tensor product implementation. On a 96^3 3D grid, it reaches a performance of 140 Gflop/s which is 2.7 times faster than the best possible performance achievable for a single vector and a single derivative and more than 7 times faster than a best case practical 1/1 implementation.

In future work, we will examine the effect of larger stencil sizes and double precision. The presented performance does not reach the predicted peak and we believe that common techniques from SpMV such as cache partitioning can be successfully applied. We will also integrate the techniques presented in this paper within a fluid simulation using RBF-FD. We will also look into developing a similar technique on the Kepler family of GPUs, which offers swizzling and channeling operations.

Acknowledgment

Erlebacher was supported under NSF grant DMS-#0934331 (FSU), and the use of the MIC at FSU and at LCSE/U. Minnesota (provided by Prof. D. Yuen). NCAR is sponsored by NSF. Flyer acknowledges support of NSF grant DMS-0934317.

7. REFERENCES

[1] V. Bayona and M. Kindelan. Propagation of premixed laminar flames in 3D narrow open ducts using Rbf-generated finite differences. *Combustion Theory and Modelling*, 17:789–803, 2013.

[2] N. Bell and M. Garland. Efficient sparse matrix-vector multiplication on CUDA. NVIDIA Technical Report NVR-2008-004, NVIDIA Corporation, December 2008.

[3] J. Bolz, I. Farmer, E. Grinspun, and P. Schröder. Sparse matrix solvers on the gpu: conjugate gradients and multigrid. *ACM Trans. Graph.*, 22(3):917–924, 2003.

[4] S. Brin and L. Page. The anatomy of a large-scale hypertextual web search engine. In *Proc. of WWW*, 1998.

[5] A. Buluç, J. Fineman, M. Frigo, J. Gilbert, and C. Leiserson. Parallel sparse matrix-vector and matrix-transpose-vector multiplication using compressed sparse blocks. In *Proc. SPAA '09*, pages 233–244, 2009.

[6] A. Buluç, S. Williams, L. Oliker, and J. Demmel. Reduced-bandwidth multithreaded algorithms for sparse matrix-vector multiplication. In *Proc. IPDPS*, 2011.

[7] P. P. Chinchapatnam, K. Djidjeli, P. B. Nair, and M. Tan. A compact RBF-FD based meshless method for the incompressible Navier-Stokes equations. *J. Eng. Maritime Env.*, 223:275–290, 2009.

[8] T. Cramer, D. Schmidl, M. Klemm, and D. an Mey. Openmp programming on intel xeon phi coprocessors: An early performance comparison. In *Proc. of MARC*, November 2012.

[9] E. Cuthill and J. McKee. Reducing the bandwidth of sparse symmetric matrices. In *Proc. ACM national conference*, pages 157–172, 1969.

[10] N. Flyer, E. Lehto, S. Blaise, G. B. Wright, and A. St-Cyr. A guide to RBF-generated finite differences

for nonlinear transport: Shallow water simulations on a sphere. *J. Comput. Phys*, 231:4078–4095, 2012.

[11] B. Fornberg and E. Lehto. Stabilization of RBF-generated finite difference methods for convective PDEs. *J. Comput. Phys.*, 230:2270–2285, 2011.

[12] Y. Koren. Drawing graphs by eigenvectors: Theory and practice. *Computers and Mathematics with Applications*, 49:1867–1888, 2005.

[13] M. Kreutzer, G. Hager, G. Wellein, H. Fehske, A. Basermann, and A. Bishop. Sparse matrix-vector multiplication on gpgpu clusters: A new storage format and a scalable implementation. In *IPDPS Workshops*, pages 1696–1702, 2012.

[14] O. Küçüktunç, K. Kaya, E. Saule, and Ü. Çatalyürek. Fast recommendation on bibliographic networks with sparse-matrix ordering and partitioning. *Social Network Analysis and Mining*, 2013.

[15] M.K. Kumar. Accelerating sparse matrix kernels on graphics processing units. 2012.

[16] X. Liu, M. Smelyanskiy, E. Chow, and P. Dubey. Efficient sparse matrix-vector multiplication on x86-based many-core processors. In *Proc. of ICS*, 2013.

[17] J. Mellor-Crummey and J. Garvin. Optimizing sparse matrix-vector product computations using unroll and jam. *Int. J. High Perform. Comput. Appl.*, 18(2), May 2004.

[18] R. Nishtala, R. Vuduc, J. Demmel, and K. Yelick. When cache blocking of sparse matrix vector multiply works and why. *Appl. Algebra Eng., Commun. Comput.*, 18(3):297–311, May 2007.

[19] E. Saule, K. Kaya, and Ü. Çatalyürek. Performance evaluation of sparse matrix multiplication kernels on intel xeon phi. Technical Report arXiv1302.1078, 2013.

[20] C. Shu, H. Ding, and K. S. Yeo. Local radial basis function-based differential quadrature method and its application to solve two-dimensional incompressible Navier-Stokes equations. *Comput. Meth. Appl. Mech. Engrg.*, 192:941–954, 2003.

[21] D. Stevens, H. Power, M. Lees, and H. Morvan. The use of PDE centers in the local RBF hermitean method for 3D convective-diffusion problems. *J. Comput. Phys.*, 228:4606–4624, 2009.

[22] O. Temam and W. Jalby. Characterizing the behavior of sparse algorithms on caches. In *Proc. of SuperComputing*, pages 578–587, 1992.

[23] S. Toledo. Improving memory-system performance of sparse matrix-vector multiplication. In *PPSC*. SIAM, 1997.

[24] A. I. Tolstykh. On using RBF-based differencing formulas for unstructured and mixed structured-unstructured grid calculations. *Proc. of IMACS World Congress*, 228:4606–4624, 2000.

[25] A. I. Tolstykh and D. A. Shirobokov. On using radial basis functions in a "finite difference mode" with applications to elasticity problems. *Comput. Mech.*, 33:68–79, 2003.

[26] F. Vazquez, José-Jesús Fernández, and Ester M. Garzón. A new approach for sparse matrix vector product on nvidia gpus. *Concurrency and Computation: Practice and Experience*, 23(8):815–826, 2011.

[27] R. Vuduc, J. Demmel, and K. Yelic. OSKI: A library of automatically tuned sparse matrix kernels. In *Proc. SciDAC 2005, J. of Physics: Conference Series*, 2005.

[28] S. Williams, L. Oliker, R. Vuduc, J. Shalf, K. Yelick, and J. Demmel. Optimization of sparse matrix-vector multiplication on emerging multicore platforms. In *Proc. SC '07*, pages 38:1–38:12, 2007.

[29] G. B. Wright and B. Fornberg. Scattered node compact finite difference-type formulas generated from radial basis functions. *J. Comput. Phys.*, 212:99–123, 2006.

An Efficient Two-Dimensional Blocking Strategy for Sparse Matrix-Vector Multiplication on GPUs

Arash Ashari, Naser Sedaghati, John Eisenlohr, and P. Sadayappan
Department of Computer Science and Engineering
The Ohio State University
Columbus, OH 43210
{ashari,sedaghat,eisenloh,saday@cse.ohio-state.edu}

ABSTRACT

Sparse matrix-vector multiplication (SpMV) is one of the key operations in linear algebra. Overcoming thread divergence, load imbalance and non-coalesced and indirect memory access due to sparsity and irregularity are challenges to optimizing SpMV on GPUs.

In this paper we present a new blocked row-column (BRC) storage format with a novel two-dimensional blocking mechanism that effectively addresses the challenges: it reduces thread divergence by reordering and grouping rows of the input matrix with nearly equal number of non-zero elements onto the same execution units (i.e., warps). BRC improves load balance by partitioning rows into blocks with a constant number of non-zeros such that different warps perform the same amount of work. We also present an efficient auto-tuning technique to optimize BRC performance by judicious selection of block size based on sparsity characteristics of the matrix. A CUDA implementation of BRC outperforms NVIDIA CUSP and cuSPARSE libraries and other state-of-the-art SpMV formats on a range of unstructured sparse matrices from multiple application domains. The BRC format has been integrated with PETSc, enabling its use in PETSc's solvers.

Categories and Subject Descriptors

D.1.3 [**Software**]: Programming Techniques—*Parallel Programming*; G.1.0 [**Mathematics of Computing**]: Numerical Analysis—*Parallel Algorithms*

Keywords

BRC; CUDA; GPU; SpMV

ICS'14, June 10–13 2014, Munich, Germany.
Copyright is held by the owner/author(s). Publication rights licensed to ACM.
ACM 978-1-4503-2642-1/14/06 ...$15.00.
http://dx.doi.org/10.1145/2597652.2597678 .

1. INTRODUCTION

In the last decade, there has been a growing trend in the use of many-core throughput-oriented architectures in scientific computing. In particular, with the emergence of programmer-friendly APIs such as OpenCL [12] and CUDA [6, 14], scientists from a broad range of disciplines have started leveraging the computation throughput of GPUs. Sparse Matrix-Vector multiplication (SpMV) is one of the computational operations that have received much attention since it is a core kernel used in many algorithms such as iterative methods for solving large-scale linear systems. Recently, the high performance conjugate gradient (HPCG) benchmark, in which SpMV is one of the main kernels, was announced as a new benchmark for ranking high performance computing Systems [9].

GPUs are very well suited for dense matrix computations, but several challenges are faced in achieving high performance for sparse matrix computations. In the case of SpMV ($y = y + Ax$), sparsity and irregularity of the matrix A cause a) irregular and non-coalesced accesses to both matrix A and vector x, b) load imbalance among threads and warps, and c) thread divergence at the warp level. cuSPARSE [8] and CUSP [4, 7] are two widely-used CUDA libraries that support different sparse matrix formats, e.g. Diagonal (DIA), ELLPACK (ELL), Compressed Sparse Row (CSR), Coordinate (COO), and also hybrid (HYB) which combines ELL and COO. As the best-performing format, HYB splits the matrix into two parts: a compressed part that contains typical number of non-zeros per row well-suited to ELL, and a sparser part with the remaining non-zeros, suited to COO format. However HYB suffers from performing redundant computations (inherent in the ELL part) and also redundant data transfer (due to the padded elements). Several studies, [3, 5, 23], proposed enhanced formats that work better than HYB for certain types of matrices. All these methods achieve coalesced accesses for the matrix A, but lack the generality of HYB and so cannot outperform HYB in general. The main shortcoming of existing methods is the lack of an adaptive format that can tune itself for different matrix structures and achieve consistently superior performance across matrices from various application domains.

In this paper we propose a new adaptive format that addresses intra-warp thread divergence, redundant computation and redundant data transfer introduced by the ELL format. We also address synchronization overhead caused by the reduction/atomic operations in COO. The proposed format, blocked row-column (BRC), is a hybrid sparse matrix representation with the property that in an SpMV operation each warp is assigned the same number of rows (a block of 32 rows) and all the rows have equal non-zero elements less than or equal to a tile size. By using a dense structured blocked format, BRC alleviates thread divergence and redundant computation while achieving a load balanced execution. We also propose an auto-tuning framework for the model parameter – width of block along matrix column. It achieves 96% of the performance obtained from exhaustive search in a bounded domain of this parameter.

On an NVIDIA Kepler GPU, the CUDA implementation of auto-tuned BRC is up to 4.8× and 4.3× (and average 2.7× and 2.5×) faster than the HYB in single and double precision, respectively. BRC also achieves a maximal speedup of 3.6× and 2.2× (and average 2× and 1.7×) over the CSR (the most commonly used format) for single and double precision, respectively. Integrating BRC into PETSc [1, 2] shows that using BRC as the SpMV kernel reduces the total runtime by 16% and 70% for *ILU(0)* and *Polynomial* preconditioners, respectively and when compared to the PETSc AIJ-CUSP format which uses NVIDIA CUSP [7] for SpMV.

The rest of the paper is organized as follows: Section 2 reviews the existing SpMV formats. In Section 3, we describe the BRC format. Section 4 describes evaluation methodology and Section 5 presents the results. Section 6 describes integration of BRC with PETSc. Related work is discussed in Section 7. We conclude in Section 8.

2. BACKGROUND

In this paper, we target the SpMV problem in the form $y = y + Ax$ where y and x are one-dimensional vectors and A is a two-dimensional sparse matrix. Due to sparsity of the matrix, there are many computations and memory usage that can be ignored (e.g. zero elements) in order to save memory and computational resources. To do so, many formats/optimizations have been proposed. Bell and Garland [4] and Vuduc [21] have reviewed some of the existing formats. In this section, we briefly review those that are related to our proposal and against which we have compared our results.

In order to illustrate different formats, we use an example sparse matrix A with 10 non-zero elements (namely, A to J) distributed unevenly across 4 rows and 6 columns (thus leaving total number of 14 zero elements):

$$A = \begin{bmatrix} 0 & A & 0 & B & 0 & 0 \\ 0 & 0 & C & 0 & D & 0 \\ E & F & G & 0 & H & I \\ 0 & 0 & 0 & J & 0 & 0 \end{bmatrix} \quad (1)$$

2.1 Coordinate (COO) Format

COO is a very simple format in which the sparse matrix A is transformed into three dense vectors: *data* that contains only the non-zero data values, *column index* that contains the column index of the elements corresponding to data vector, and *row index* that contains the row index of the elements corresponding to data vector

Figure 1-a shows matrix A in COO format. The SpMV kernel that receives matrix in COO format assigns every non-zero element to a separate GPU thread. As a result, atomic operation is used to collect contributions of different threads (mapped to the same row) and to finalize the reduced results in vector y [4]. One major drawback to COO format is the use of atomic operations especially when un-

even distribution of non-zero elements per row causes some rows to be denser than others. Such a distribution has a drastic impact on performance because of unbalanced executions across threads. Even though improvement attempts such as segmented reduction [4, 20] have been proposed to decrease this overhead, it is still not completely invariant to the distribution of the non-zero elements per row [4].

2.2 Compressed Sparse ROW (CSR) Format

CSR works at the granularity of threads per row(s). This format is similar to COO with the difference that CSR does not need to keep the row indices. Instead, it keeps only the row offsets, as shown by Figure 1-a. In this format, non-zero elements of row i and corresponding column indices are located respectively in the data and column index vectors at index $r : RowOffset[i] \leq r < RowOffst[i+1]$. This way, we save both memory space and load, because for all elements in each row, we keep only the start and end offset of that row.

2.3 ELLPACK (ELL) Format

ELLPACK (ELL) [17] is another format that works at the granularity of thread per row but with the expense of redundant memory usage, data transfer and computation power. In this format, first the non-zero elements of the matrix in each row are compressed, then each row is padded (with extra "0" elements) such that all the rows have the same size as the row with largest number of non-zero elements. Along with the padded data matrix, there is a column matrix that holds the corresponding column index of non-zero elements. Figure 1-b shows the ELL format of our example matrix. While ELL format achieves high performance on dense matrices or on matrices with nearly equal numbers of non-zero elements per row, it suffers from redundant memory usage due to padded rows, redundant computation and data transfer for other matrices (i.e. with variant number of non-zero elements per row).

2.4 HYB Format

Hybrid COO-ELL [4] is a hybrid of COO and ELL in which the ELL part is a complete $row \times k$ matrix. If a row has less than k non-zero elements, it is padded with 0s. And if a row has more than k non-zeros, then the remaining elements are packed into a COO format. k is the maximum value, such that, there is at least $R = max(4096, \frac{M}{3})$ rows with k or more non-zero elements (M is the total number of non-zero elements of the matrix). For a given $k = 2$, Figure 1-c shows the corresponding HYB format of the example matrix A.

2.5 Jagged Diagonal Storage (JDS) Format

JDS [18, 19] is designed to eliminate the redundant memory usage, data transfer and computation of the ELL format. In JDS, rows are rearranged in decreasing order of number of non-zero elements. In this format, Matrix A is represented by the following components (Figure 1-d): *data* that contains non-zero values of the matrix A, ordered by number of non-zeros in each row; *perm*, a vector whose elements indicate the original place of each permuted row; *column begin* that contains the beginning index of each column in the new format; *column index* that holds the column index of non-zero elements, corresponding to vector data; and *non-zeros* that holds the number of non-zeros of each row. This format

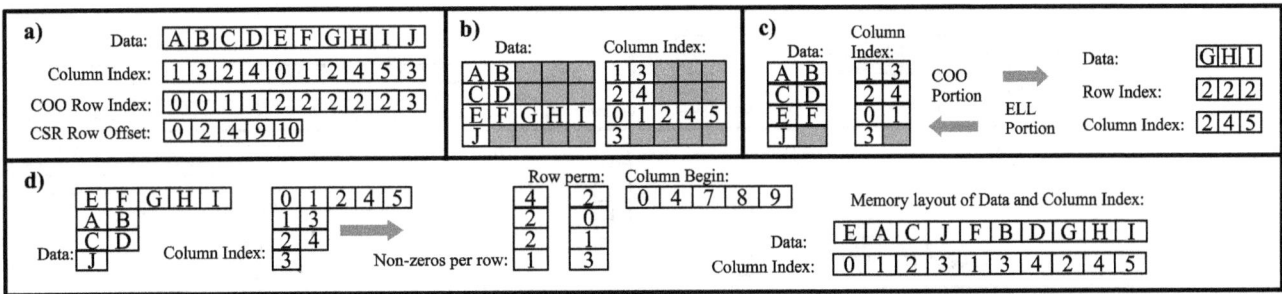

Figure 1: Sparse matrix A transformed into different formats: a) COO/CSR, b) ELL, c) HYB, and d) JDS.

works well when the number of non-zero elements of consecutive rows (in the ordered version) that are packed into a warp/block are the same. However, it suffers from thread divergence when rows with different numbers of non-zero elements are assigned to the same warp/block.

Note that in ELL and JDS (and the ELL portion of HYB), data is stored in column-major order so that SpMV has coalesced accesses. This layout is shown explicitly in Figure 1-d. Moreover, the cost of transforming Matrix A into a customized format is assumed to be amortized and thus can be ignored because is paid once, before launching a large-scale iterative algorithm such as conjugate gradient solver [11].

3. THE BRC FORMAT

ELL format only works well for matrices with equal numbers of non-zeros per row; otherwise, it suffers from redundant computation (for padded rows). Moreover, for matrices with large numbers of non-zeros (e.g. *WEB, LP* in Table 1), size of the GPU device memory becomes a serious issue for ELL [22, 4]. Also, padding overhead becomes worse when performing double-precision computation. COO performs a minimum number of computations, but because of the fine-grained element-to-thread mapping it must perform (usually expensive) atomic (write) operations. The contention due to the increasing number of atomic writes (as the number of non-zeros per row increases) causes COO to fail for large matrices. Although segmented reduction [20] can decrease this overhead in very large matrices, it still suffers high computation due to reduction process. JDS assigns one row to each thread and thus, its performance is dependent on the matrix structure and distribution of elements. This is because branch divergence will not be improved when different (sorted) rows, mapped to threads in the same warp, work on different numbers of elements. Moreover, JDS doesn't promise load-balanced execution when different warps work on rows with different numbers of non-zeros.

To address these problems, we propose the BRC (blocked row-column) format with a novel two-dimensional blocking (i.e. grouping) mechanism in which row-blocking of the matrix A is done to reduce thread divergence and column-blocking to improve load-balance.

3.1 Blocked Row

We first propose row-blocking in which the row permutation (based on the number of non-zeros in each row) of JDS is combined with ELL padding mechanism. However, unlike ELL, we do not pad the entire matrix. Instead, after permuting the rows, we group them into blocks of consecutive rows. Then, in each block we adaptively pad rows based on the number of non-zeros in the first row of that block. Note that, since rows are sorted, first row of each block will have the maximum number of non zeros in that block. This way, we decrease the amount of memory usage, redundant computation and data transfer. In addition, by assigning one warp to each block, we remove in-warp thread divergence.

Figure 2-a shows the example matrix A in blocked-row format. In this figure, the array labeled "Data" contains the actual non-zeros and padded elements; "Column Index" contains the corresponding column indices; "Non-zeros per block" holds the number of non-zeros in each row of the block; "Block begin" holds the beginning address of each block; and "Row perm" keeps the original row of the permuted rows. $B1$, the number of rows in a block that maps to a warp (more description later in this section), is the only parameter used for row-blocking. When SpMV is executed for a matrix in blocked-row format, each block is processed by one warp and each warp may process multiple blocks in order to hide data transfer latency and to have load-balanced execution for all SMs. To avoid extra accesses to vector x in global memory, we use the same column index of the previous rows in the block for the zero-padded rows (those elements will be cached when executing global loads from preceding threads in the same thread block).

3.2 Blocked Row-Column (BRC)

In sparse matrices with unstructured rows, *Blocked-row* format produces blocks in which first row may have a much larger number of non-zeros than the last row. In addition to redundant computation, data transfer and memory usage, this also causes warp-level load imbalance that may not be addressed even by assigning multiple blocks to each warp. Furthermore, blocks that pack longer rows will become a performance bottleneck. To solve this problem, we propose to add another reformatting step after row-blocking in which the matrix A is blocked again along the column dimension (V-Blocks in Figure 2-b). This format is called *blocked row-column* (BRC).

In BRC, we group neighboring rows into smaller blocks such that the maximum number of non-zeros is controlled by a parameter (i.e. $B2$). To do so, we scan the sparse matrix from the first row (rows are already ordered) and create each block by grouping $B1$ rows and packing maximum of $B2$ non-zeros of each row. By scanning the matrix row-wise and then column-wise (*H-Block* and *V-Block* in Figure 2, respectively), each block will have a size of $B1 \times T$ where:

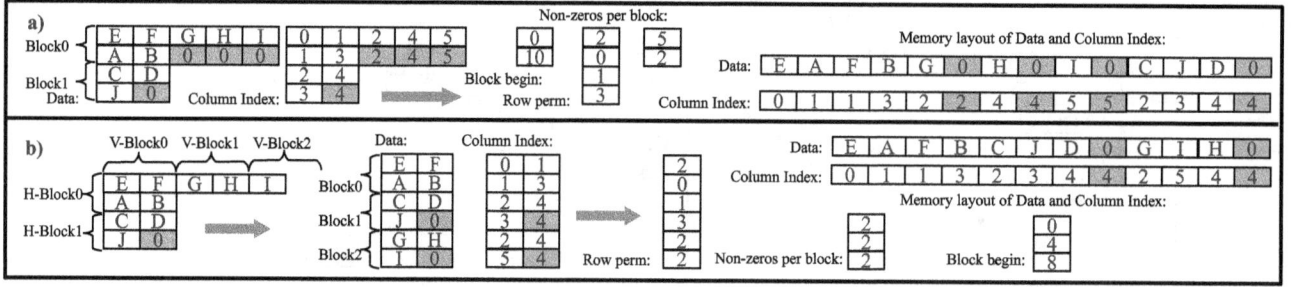

Figure 2: The proposed BRC format: a) blocked-row, b) blocked row-column.

$$T = min(B2, max_{i \in block}(\text{non-zeros of row i})) \qquad (2)$$

Such a blocking scheme is completely adaptive and accounts for the matrix characteristics (e.g. sparsity) as well.

Figure 2-b shows the example matrix A transformed into BRC format. After constructing each block, we decrease the number of non-zeros of the rows by T (if one row has been packed n times into the block, we decrease its non-zeros by $n \times T$). When building a block, if there are not enough rows with non-zeros to be filled up, we use rows from the next vertical block. For example, when scanning rows in V-Block1, we only have one row to use for building Block2. Therefore, the remaining rows of Block2 are filled by rows from V-Block2. And if the last block is not full, we pad it with zeros. As in row-blocking, we use the column index of the previous row in the same block for the padded elements. Moreover, as in all previous formats, we put the data and column index into a column-based one-dimensional array. Figure 2-b also shows the final memory layout of BRC. Unlike blocked-row where each row is processed by only one thread, BRC may require a row to be processed by multiple threads. Therefore, we use atomic write ($atomicAdd()$) to update vector y.

```
__global__ void brc_spmv (
  float* y, float* data, float* x, int* nnz_per_block,
  int* column_index, int* block_offset, int* row_perm,
  int num_blocks, int rep, int B1) {

  int tid = blockIdx.x*blockDim.x+threadIdx.x;
  int cb = tid / B1; // current block
  int b_row = tid % B1;
  for (i=0; i< rep; i++){
    float tmp = 0.0;
    for (j=0; j < nnz_per_block[cb]; j++){
      int index = block_offset[cb]+j*B1+b_row;
      tmp += data[index]*x[column_index[index]];
    }
    atomicAdd(row_perm[tid], tmp);
    tid += gridDim.x * blockDim.x;
    cb += gridDim.x * blockDim.x / B1;
  }
}
```

Figure 3: An example kernel in BRC format

Algorithm 1 demonstrates transformation of a matrix from CSR to BRC. We also present an example CUDA kernel in BRC format in Figure 3 in which rep corresponds to the coarsening factor (described later in this section). In this kernel, each iteration of the i (i.e. coarsening) loop takes care of a padded block of size $B1 \times T$. In the j loop, each

thread takes care of one row in the block and performs T corresponding computations where $T = nnz\_per\_block[cb]$.

3.3 Model Parameters

The first parameter needs to be set for BRC is $B1$ (block height). Since each thread computes one row in a block, $B1$ is important for the following two reasons.

1. Consecutive threads will access consecutive elements in memory (respect memory coalescing)

2. Having row segments with the same number of non-zeros (including padded zeros) means threads in the same warp will perform same amount of computation, and thus control divergence will be removed.

For example, in order to have coalesced DRAM accesses, and for a given burst size of 64 bytes, we set $B1$ to be multiple of 16, for single-precision computation. However, if there is only one warp per thread block, $B1$ has to be chosen as the warp size (e.g. 32 in our experiments). For all the experiments in this paper, we have set $B1$ to be 32. The reason is, for cases with uneven distribution of non-zeros of the rows in one block (e.g. difference between max and min is high), larger $B1$ introduces redundant memory accesses and also computations. Therefore, when standard deviation in the number of non-zeros is small, $B1$ can be chosen to be as big as the thread block size.

The second parameter to be set is $B2$ (block width). If the matrix is row-wise sparse (i.e. averages a small number of non-zero elements per row), it is better to have a smaller block along columns to avoid redundant computation and load imbalance. When the matrix is denser, $B2$ can be bigger in order to avoid the extra cost of atomic data writes. This sizing depends on the matrix sparsity and especially to the mean number of non-zeros per row, standard deviation of non-zeros and size of the matrix (i.e. number of rows and columns). To respect this characteristic, we set $B2$ using the following heuristic:

$$B2 = min(C \times round(\mu + \sigma), MaxNZ) \qquad (3)$$

in which C is a constant, μ is the mean number of non-zeros per row, σ is the standard deviation and $MaxNZ$ is the maximum non-zeros per row. Depending on σ, we choose $B2$ to be close to the μ value. Note that having a small σ means that we have a matrix in which most of the rows have the same number of non-zeros and that number is close to μ. If σ is large, then we choose $B2$ to be larger as well. However, note that we do not necessarily pad all the blocks with $B2$ elements along the row dimension. Our method is

Algorithm 1: BRC Format Transformation

---

input : CSR matrix: $data$, $column\_index$, row_offset
output: BRC matrix: $data$, $column\_index$, row_perm, nnz_per_block, $block\_offset$, num_blocks

begin

  Extract μ, σ and vector nnz_per_row from row_offset;
  Let $Qrows$ be a queue contains list of rows (sorted based on nnz_per_row) with its permutation;
  $num\_block = 0$; $block\_offset[0] = 0$;
  $B1 = 32$; $rep = 1$; $B2 =$ "Equation 3";
  if $\sigma > \mu$ **then**
    $\lfloor$ $rep = MaxOfCoalescing$

  while $Qrows \neq \emptyset$ **do**
    Extract a block of size $B1$ ($current\_block$) as follows and add it to the list of blocks;
    begin
      $current\_block = \emptyset$;
      for $i = 1 : B1$ **do**
        $r\_ptr = Qrows.front$;
        $r\_nnz = r\_ptr.NNZ$;
        add row r_ptr with $min(r\_nnz, B2)$ to $current\_block$;
        add original row_index to row_perm;
        delete $Qrows.front$;
        if $r\_nnz - B2 > 0$ **then**
          $r\_ptr.NNZ = r\_ptr.NNZ - B2$;
          insert r_ptr back to $Qrows$;

        if $Qrows = \emptyset$ **then**
          break;

    store $current\_block{\rightarrow}data$ into $BRC{\rightarrow}data$ (in column order);
    set $BRC{\rightarrow}column\_index$ accordingly;
    set $nnz\_per\_block[num\_block]$ as the max non_zero in rows of $current\_block$;
    pad the smaller rows in $current\_block$ with zeros and column as previous row accordingly;
    add dummy rows if necessary (i.e. loop exited with $i < B1$);
    $num\_block + +$;
    $block\_offset[num\_block] = block\_offset[num\_block - 1] + B1 * nnz\_per\_block[num\_block - 1]$;

---

adaptive and each block chooses its block width based on the value T defined by the Equation 2. That means blocks at the top of the row-order may have a much bigger size than blocks at the bottom due to bigger block width. Meanwhile, Equation 3 respects the load balance among the threads, because $\mu + \sigma$ presents a measure of where the density of the number of non-zeros in each row is focused. Therefore, when we transform the matrix into BRC, in each vertical-block scan of the matrix, threads in each block and also neighboring blocks get almost equal amount of work. If a block has a lower load compared to others, it means that block has all the remaining non-zero elements of some rows which have been scanned completely. In the result section, we show that Equation 3 is experimentally accepted.

Such a $B2$ value is theoretically acceptable unless it is so large that performing SpMV on each row becomes a bottleneck (i.e. when there are rows with large number of non-zeros close to $B2$). In those cases, our solution is to break down the $B2$ further. To do so, we apply the following refinement to our $B2$ selection: we choose its value as the minimum among what has been calculated in Equation 3 and a predefined maximum $B2$ size. Such a maximum can be chosen depending on the device characteristic, computation type and latency of the computation and data transfer. In our case, we have used a maximum of 200 by a simple search. We also apply a final refinement to our parameter selection to deal with the load imbalance issue. In particular, when $\mu < \sigma$, there are big blocks at the top rows and small blocks around the bottom rows, resulting in load imbalance on the warps. To handle this case, we apply a level of thread coarsening and assign each thread more than one row to work on.

4. EVALUATION METHODOLOGY

In order to evaluate the effectiveness of the BRC format, we selected a diverse set of sparse matrices that have been used in previous studies [22, 4]. These matrices are in Matrix Market Coordinate Format [15]. Table 1 shows the $B2$ value chosen for each matrix along with other characteristics of each matrix: min, max, mean (μ) and standard deviation (σ) of the number of non-zeros per row. Our auto-tuning model sets $B2$ such that it falls into the range of min and max, is close to μ and covers a broad range of non-zeros. Since our method is adaptive at the warp level, the padding cost is negligible. As Table 1 shows, if σ is small, then $B2$ is equal to μ. If μ is too large, $B2$ is chosen to be a number small enough such that each thread processes a limited number of elements and does not become a computation bottleneck. The thread block size was set to 128, so that there are enough warps to mask the latency of data transfer in each block.

We report performance in terms of computation rate (as number of floating point operations per second in GFLOPs). Each SpMV experiment was repeated 50 times and the average (arithmetic mean) is reported. We exclude the time spent transferring data between host and device and other one-time SpMV data transformation overhead that is performed on the CPU side (for compatibility reasons). However, we later also report performance in a real use scenario with PETSc, including all data conversion and transfer overheads, where it is shown that these overheads are negligible.

The experiments are run on two different generations of NVIDIA GPUs, $GTX580$ (Fermi) and $GTXTitan$ (Kepler), each hosted by an Intel Core i7 CPU. Details of the GPUs peak are listed in the Table 2. We used NVIDIA compiler ($nvcc$) version 5.5, with all the general optimizationsenabled

Matrix	Abbrv.	Rows	Columns	Total NZ	Mean NZ (μ)	SD NZ (σ)	Min NZ	Max NZ	B2	HYB-k
FEM/Cantilever	CAN	62,451	62,451	4,007,383	64	14	1	78	78	75
FEM/Spheres	SPH	83,334	83,334	6,010,480	72	19	1	81	91	81
FEM/Accelerator	ACC	121,192	121,192	2,624,331	22	14	8	81	36	23
Dense	DEN	2,000	2,000	4,000,000	2000	0	2000	2000	200	0
Economics	ECO	206,500	206,500	1,273,389	6	4	1	44	10	7
Epidemiology	EPI	525,825	525,825	2,100,225	4	0	2	4	4	4
Protein	PRO	36,417	36,417	4,344,765	119	32	18	204	151	138
Wind Tunnel	WIN	217,918	217,918	11,634,424	53	5	2	180	58	54
QCD	QCD	49,152	49,152	1,916,928	39	0	39	39	39	39
LP	LP	4,284	1,092,610	11,279,748	2633	4209	1	56181	200	23
FEM/Harbor	HAR	46,835	46,835	2,374,001	51	28	4	145	79	55
Circuit	CIR	170,998	170,998	958,936	6	4	1	353	10	5
FEM/Ship	SHI	140,874	140,874	7,813,404	55	11	24	102	66	54
Webbase	WEB	1,000,005	1,000,005	3,105,536	3	25	1	4700	28	2

Table 1: Set of matrices used in our experiments (NZ: non-zero, SD: standard deviation (σ), B2: width of vertical blocks, HYB-k: number of columns in ELL portion of the HYB format).

GPU Model	GTX 580	GTX Titan
Architecture	Fermi (GF110)	Kepler (K20X)
Compute capability	2.0	3.5
Multiprocessors, cores per MP	16 , 32	14 , 192
Warp size	32	32
Max threads per block/MP	1024/1536	1024/2048
Shared memory (KB) per block	48	48
L2 cache (KB)	768	1536
Total global memory (MB)	1535	6143
Peak off-chip BW (GB/s)	192	288
Peak SP TFLOPS (FMA)	1.5	4.5

Table 2: GPUs hosted the experiments.

BRC vs.	Fermi		Kepler	
	SP	DP	SP	DP
CSR	1.71 ×	1.19 ×	1.96 ×	1.64 ×
HYB	1.67 ×	1.45 ×	2.68 ×	2.47 ×
JDS	1.64 ×	1.30 ×	4.91 ×	3.54 ×
RG12 [16]	1.19 ×	1.08 ×	2.30 ×	1.69 ×

Table 3: Average BRC speedup.

using -O3. The input vector x was placed in texture memory to improve the accesses when locally cached in SM. As the baseline, we use the best performance among the HYB and CSR formats (from cuSPARSE [8] and CUSP [7] libraries), JDS format [18], and also improved CSR recently developed by Reguly and Giles [16]. We also compared BRC against a state-of-the-art format recently developed for the Intel Xeon Phi many-core system [13].

5. EXPERIMENTAL RESULTS

In the first experiment, we compared BRC with CSR, HYB, JDS and the enhanced CSR approach recently developed by Reguly and Giles [16]. For BRC, $B1$ was set to 32, and $B2$ set according to Equation 3. Figure 4 shows the performance obtained (in GFLOPs) with the different SpMV formats, for single and double precision computation, on the Kepler GPU. BRC outperforms all other SpMV formats, except for one case (matrix EPI) where HYB is slightly better. *EPI* is a very sparse matrix with rows that mostly have 4 non-zero elements, with a few rows with some 2 or 3 non-zeros. With the HYB format, this matrix with $\mu = 4$ and $\sigma \simeq 0$ is represented entirely using the ELL format (no COO part), which is the best match for such a sparse matrix. This avoids the penalty of reading row permutations and uncoalesced memory write that BRC requires due to the

row reordering. Figure 5 shows performance on the Fermi GPU. Here again the BRC format is generally superior, except for a few cases (ECO, EPI, CIR, and WEB). These are the cases where the average number of non-zero elements per row is very small ($max = 6$) and thus there is not much to do due to the low bandwidth utilization of the GPU global memory. In the case of LP matrix, we are limited by the overhead of the atomic add operation. This can be improved by reduction. Later in this section, we report on additional experiments that shed light on the performance with these matrices. Table 3 summarizes the average speedup of BRC over other SpMV formats, for single (SP) and double (DP) precision computation on the two GPUS.

To test the effectiveness of the model for selecting the $B2$ parameter, we first compare performance of BRC by choosing different values for $B2$, either from the range of $[min, max]$ number of non-zeros in each matrix, or from Equation 3. Figure 6 shows this result for double precision on the Kepler GPU. In this case, there is no thread coarsening. As the figure shows, increasing $B2$ improves the performance until it reaches the range of "$\mu + \sigma$". After that point, higher values of $B2$ either have negligible impact (i.e. small fluctuations) or hurt the performance. Also, except for three cases (CIR, ECO, LP), the value of $B2$ chosen by BRC gives the best performance. In the case of LP, BRC thread coarsening improves performance when $B2$ is chosen by Equation 3, while it does not improve performance when $B2 = \{1k, 2k, 4k\}$. And in the case of CIR and ECO, the difference is very small.

We also performed an exhaustive search in a bounded domain of model parameters of size 24. The model had an efficiency of 96% compared to the result of this bounded search. This search is similar to the optimal method proposed by Reguly and Giles [16]. The results suggest that using such a search would help find the optimal model parameters in a few runs. Such a parameter search can be used when the number of iterations of SpMV is large in comparison with the search size. Figure 7 compares BRC to the optimal performance achieved by the enhanced CSR [16]. It can be observed that BRC outperforms [16] on all the test matrices. This was also true for other matrices tested by Reguly and Giles [16], which are not included in Figure 7.

Furthermore, we compared BRC against the EBS scheme of Liu et al. [13] (state-of-the-art many-core CPU solution to SpMV). Figure 8 shows performance of BRC and KNC-adaptive (referred in the figure as *LSCD13*) on the set of

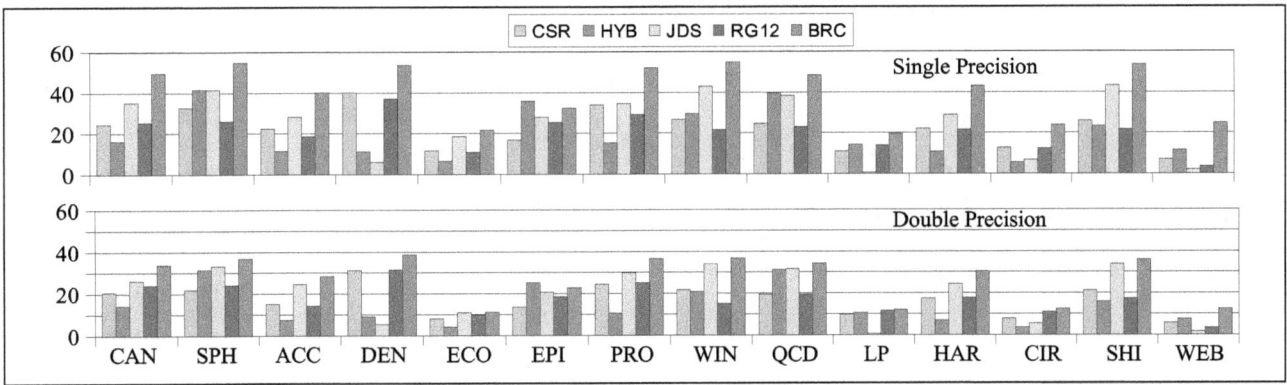

Figure 4: BRC performance (GFLOPs) on Kepler vs. other formats (*RG12* refers to Reguly and Giles [16]).

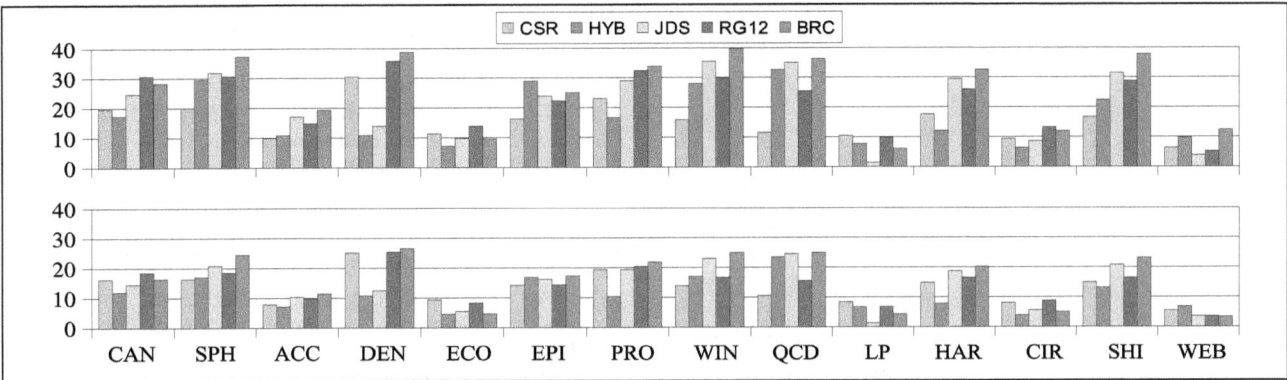

Figure 5: BRC performance (GFLOPs) on Fermi vs. other formats (*RG12* refers to Reguly and Giles [16]).

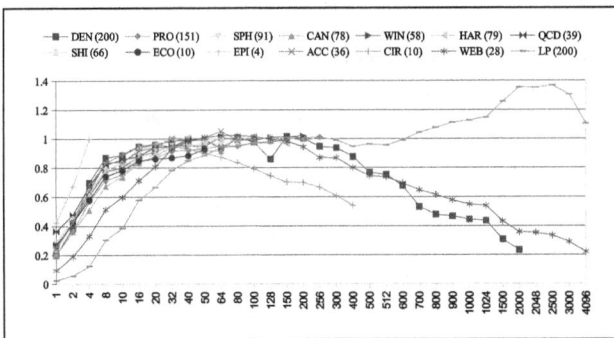

Figure 6: Change in BRC performance for different values of B2 (X-axis), compared to the baseline BRC (i.e. B2 from Equation 3, shown in the legend).

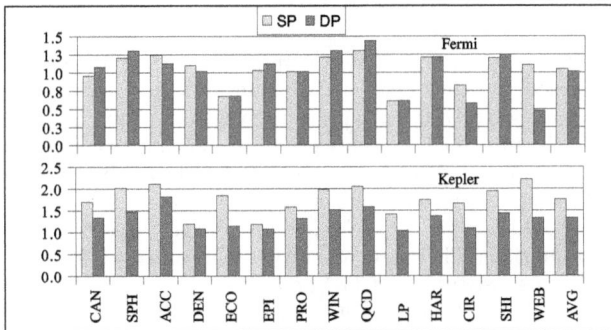

Figure 7: Auto-tuned BRC speedup vs RG12 [16].

matrices that have been tested in [13]. *LSCD13* data in this figure are extracted from *Figure 9* in [13]. As shown by the figure, BRC is 1.27× faster than EBS. However, EBS performs better on matrix *circuits5M*, a large sparse matrix with average of 11 non-zeros in 5*M* rows that are mostly located around the diagonal. In this case, EBS leverages locality of vector *x* in each column partition. EBS is also a bit faster on matrices *rail4284* and *spal-004*, which are matrices with much smaller number of rows in comparison with columns, and large μ and σ. We next describe how

a hybrid of ELL and BRC can perform better with such matrices.

In another experiment, we studied replacing either of the COO or ELL parts of the HYB format by BRC. The last column in Table 1 shows the column size of the ELL part, chosen by HYB. Furthermore, Table 4 provides more information on how HYB partitions the matrix into COO and ELL parts. In this table, the first column shows the fraction of non-zeros that fall into the COO portion (CNZ). The second column shows the fraction of the total time taken by COO computation (CTR). The third and fourth columns show the time of COO and ELL in *ms*, respectively (CTA and ETA). As Table 4 shows, in the case of matrices which

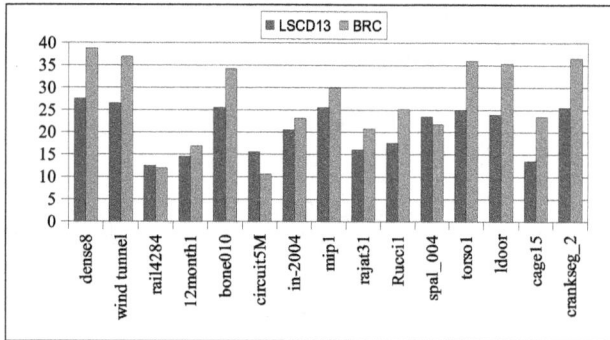

Figure 8: GFLOPs for BRC vs Liu et al. [13].

Matrix	CNZ(%)	CTR(%)	CTA(ms)	ETA(ms)
CAN	0.323	38.189	0.181	0.293
SPH	0	0	0	0.413
ACC	17.248	52.727	0.254	0.228
DEN	100	100	0.672	0
ECO	18.879	69.635	0.268	0.117
EPI	0	0	0	0.149
PRO	4.026	41.016	0.220	0.316
WIN	0.561	23.602	0.2	0.647
QCD	0	0	0	0.121
LP	99.147	98.640	2.782	0.038
HAR	18.673	61.616	0.247	0.154
CIR	21.775	74.862	0.238	0.080
SHI	6.850	38.363	0.270	0.433
WEB	35.788	75.702	0.508	0.163

Table 4: Timing analysis for the CUSP HYB

are less regular, COO takes care of a high percentage of non-zeros and thus takes most of the total time. However, in cases where ELL can finish up computation for most of the non-zeros, the COO part plays a significant role as well. For example, in *Cantilever* matrix, COO has only 0.3% of the non-zeros but takes 38% of the total time. In *Wind Tunnel*, COO has 0.56% of the non-zeros while it takes 23.6% of the total time. Therefore, it is very important to use formats that can substitute the COO portion.

We individually substituted both ELL and COO portion of the HYB format with BRC and then compared the performance with COO and ELL. Figure 9 shows the result of applying BRC on the COO and ELL portions separately. It also shows the performance of the original COO and ELL in HYB. For the COO portion, it may be seen that BRC always outperforms COO. This implies that BRC can always be substituted for COO in the HYB format for improved performance. However, this observation does not hold for the ELL portion. In the matrices *ECO, EPI, LP*, and *WEB*, ELL works better than BRC. These are matrices that either have zero standard deviation of non-zeros like *EPI*, or have very high standard deviation (in comparison with mean) of non-zeros and a big portion of them can be separated and put into ELL format. This observation suggests that in the cases where HYB outperforms BRC, a hybrid of BRC and ELL is likely to perform even better. This could be done via empirical auto-tuning for cases where the same matrix is used multiple times.

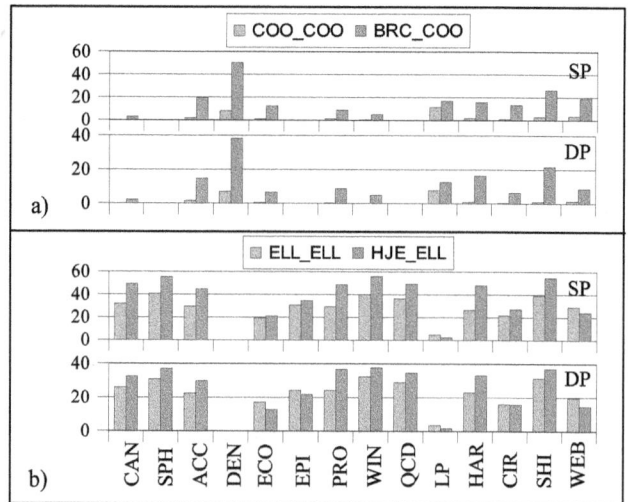

Figure 9: Performance in GFLOPs for a) COO portion of HYB solved using COO (COO_COO) or BRC (BRC_COO) and b) ELL portion of HYB solved using ELL (ELL_ELL) or BRC (BRC_ELL)

6. INTEGRATION OF BRC IN PETSC

In order to facilitate the practical use of the developments reported in this paper, we have incorporated it into the widely used PETSc framework [1, 2]. PETSc has an object-oriented architecture and supports many implementations of the abstract Matrix type. One of these implementations is called the AIJ matrix type and is PETSc's version of the CSR matrix format for sparse matrices. We have implemented the BRC matrix format in PETSc by deriving it from the AIJ type. Our BRC type inherits all functionality implemented in AIJ except the creation and sparse matrix vector multiply functions. The creation routine creates the BRC format version of the sparse matrix and stores the data on the GPU while the sparse matrix vector multiply function uses the BRC format of the matrix. When, for example, an ILU preconditioner is needed for a BRC matrix, the L and U factors are created just as they are for the AIJ superclass and are stored in the same format. The AIJ code is used for the forward and backward substitution steps when using the ILU preconditioner in an iterative solver. However, sparse matrix vector multiplications are performed on the GPU using the BRC format.

To test this implementation we ran one of the PETSc example simulations which must solve systems of non-linear equations. For each iteration of this non-linear solve a system of linear equations must be solved using an iterative method with the user's choice of preconditioner. We ran the simulation using the BRC matrix type and a couple of different preconditioners. During the simulation we measured the elapsed time spent in the routines MatMult, which performs the sparse matrix vector multiplication, and the routine PCApply, which applies the preconditioner. These are called during each step of the iterative solver which was chosen to be GMRES. The time spent in these routines is tabulated in Table 5. We compare the results of running the simulation with three different matrix types – AIJ, CUSP and BRC. The CUSP matrix type is also derived from the AIJ type but stores the matrix data on the GPU in the CSR

Platform	Precon	Format	Iter 1	Iter 2	Conv 1	Conv 2	SpMV1	SpMV 2	PC 1	PC 2	Total
Fermi	ILU(0)	AIJ	657	770	—	—	3.048	3.571	3.756	4.400	26.864
		CUSP	657	770	—	—	1.068	1.248	5.383	6.290	17.345
		BRC	657	770	0.044	0.044	0.412	0.483	4.376	5.117	13.891
	Polynomial	AIJ	299	345	—	—	1.435	1.602	37.680	43.461	91.269
		CUSP	299	345	—	—	0.500	0.558	10.359	11.957	25.783
		BRC	299	345	0.045	0.043	0.194	0.217	4.454	5.137	11.994
Kepler	ILU(0)	AIJ	657	770	—	—	3.113	3.649	3.667	4.298	27.600
		CUSP	657	770	—	—	1.218	1.427	4.453	5.201	15.143
		BRC	657	770	0.040	0.039	0.248	0.290	4.201	4.914	12.683
	Polynomial	AIJ	299	345	—	—	1.467	1.638	38.534	44.446	94.639
		CUSP	299	345	—	—	0.494	0.551	10.078	11.634	24.831
		BRC	299	345	0.040	0.039	0.110	0.123	2.657	3.065	7.540

Table 5: Performance (sec) of PETSc ex19 on two GPU platforms

format and a GPU implementation of sparse-matrix multiplication using NVIDIA's CUSP library. The CUSP matrix type also uses the AIJ format for its ILU preconditioner but overrides the sparse matrix vector multiplication function. For both the CUSP and BRC types, the time spent in SpMV includes the time to transfer the vector values from main memory to GPU memory before the multiplication and to transfer the resulting vector back to main memory. The AIJ implementation of SpMV is done on the CPU.

Table 5 shows the time for running this PETSc example with 2 different preconditioners for 3 matrix formats on two different machines, one with a Fermi GPU and one with a Kepler GPU. The columns labeled *Iter 1* and *Iter 2* show the number of GMRES iterations required for each of the two linear solves. *Conv 1* and *Conv 2* show the time to convert the Jacobian matrix to BRC format while the *SpMV* and *PC* columns show the time in sparse matrix vector multiplication and application of the preconditioner, respectively. As can be seen, for ILU the time to apply the PC is roughly the same for all three matrix types but for the polynomial preconditioner the two GPU formats are better, with BRC being superior. This is because the application of the polynomial preconditioner is based on matrix vector multiplication. The time reported in the *SpMV* columns shows the benefit of the BRC format. The time spent in conversion to the BRC format is more than made up for by the speedup of SpMV.

7. RELATED WORK

There is an extensive amount of work in the literature on customizing sparse matrix formats and optimizing SpMV on different platforms. Vuduc [21] has studied SpMV on single-core CPUs and presented an automated system for generating efficient implementations of SpMV on these platforms. Williams et al. [22] moves toward multi-core platforms with the implementation of parallel SpMV kernels. With the emergence of heterogeneous computing and many-core systems, SpMV kernels have been studied and optimized for GPUs as well. Bell and Garland have implemented sparse matrix formats in CUDA [4, 7, 8]. They have also proposed HYB (hybrid of ELL and COO), which is generally the fastest format for a broad class of unstructured matrices.

Baskaran and Bordawekar [3] have optimized Compressed Sparse Row (CSR) so that it performs about the same (modestly faster with more memory cost) as CSR-Vector [4] (in which each warp takes care of a row with segmented re-

duction). However in general, it does not reach the same performance as CUSP-HYB [4] on unstructured matrices.

Choi et al. [5] also combine the idea of blocking, CSR and ELLPACK (ELL), and present BCSR and BELLPACK. These formats of SpMV outperform HYB in matrices with dense block substructure but on average their auto-tuned version is still behind HYB for general unstructured and sparse matrices. Although we have not compared our method with theirs on the same machine with the same set of matrices, our average speed up over HYB is higher than the max they have reported with exhaustive search on their model.

Yang et al. [23] present a fast SpMV for matrices that present large graphs with power-low characteristics. They combine ideas from Transposed Jagged Diagonal Storage (TJDS) [10] with COO and tiling. They first order columns of the matrix based on non-zero elements in each column and then they tile the columns and work on each tile separately. They do a row ordering on each tile separately and assign the same amount of work to each warp in this order. The last step is a COO-like process that has the overhead of atomic memory write/reduction. It differs from our algorithm in that our format does not need column-based ordering and our method guarantees blocks to have same number of non-zero elements (rarely with the help of padding). Furthermore, our method is general and not limited to very big matrices with power-law characteristics.

Liu et al. [13] propose ELLPACK Sparse Block (ESB) for the Intel Xeon Phi Co-processor, code-named Knights Corner (KNC), that partitions the matrix coarsely by rows and columns into large sparse blocks and applies ELL on those blocks. They first partition the matrix column-wise, sort each column partition separately and block it row-wise. Then each block is saved in ELL format. Their result shows that on average ESB outperforms cuSPARSE on NVIDIA Tesla K20X. However, it still suffers from redundant computation, overhead of separate sorting per column partition, overhead of memory space and load of row permutation per column partition. Furthermore, on the same device, BRC shows superior performance in comparison with ESB. Figure 8 shows performance of BRC on the same set of matrices has been used in [13].

Reguly and Giles [16] present an auto-tuning algorithm on top of CSR format in which they choose the size of a thread group that works on a given row depending on the available resources on the device and matrix specification. This method also selects the number of rows for a thread to work on. It improves on CSR performance but all rows are treated similarly, and thus this approach lacks a complete load balance on threads and warps for matrices with diverse sparsity of rows. We have compared BRC against [16] and our result shows that BRC outperforms it.

8. CONCLUSION AND FUTURE WORK

In this paper, we have presented BRC, a 2D row-column blocked sparse matrix format for GPUs. BRC outperforms NVIDIA CUSP and cuSPARSE libraries, JDS and other formats. The key feature of the BRC format is its adaptivity to the matrix characteristic. This format performs fewer redundant memory accesses and computations than the ELL format, while it eliminates warp-level thread divergence. Our auto-tuning parameter selection sets the blocking parameters so that we have a balanced work distribution among all the warps.

We also studied the COO and ELL portions of HYB separately and showed that BRC can improve the COO part that is the bottleneck of the HYB format. A hybrid format of ELL and BRC works better than either pure BRC or pure HYB in matrices with $0 < \sigma \leq \frac{2}{3}\mu$. In future work, ELL and BRC can be combined to make a more effective hybrid format. In this format, ELL would represent the dense portion of the matrix, while BRC handles the rest. However, parameter tuning needs to be studied further. For example, in the case of banded matrices with few non-zeros per row, but the same number across all rows (e.g. the QCD and Epidemiology matrices), we can have a value k such that ELL covers all the matrix. In other cases, most of the load goes to the BRC part.

In our auto-tuning model, we fixed the size of vertical blocks based on the matrix characteristics. However, scanning the rows, we know that after building the first vertical block, the remaining rows are mostly among the top-ordered rows. As we scan these blocks (from left to the right), we move toward the top part of the row order. Therefore, one can increase the $B2$ size after scanning each block in order to decrease the number of blocks. Another similar idea for further investigation is to choose $B2$ depending on the row order.

9. ACKNOWLEDGMENTS

We thank the anonymous reviewers for their suggestions that helped improve the quality of this paper. We also thank Reguly and Giles [16] for providing us with the source code of their implementation.

10. REFERENCES

[1] S. Balay, J. Brown, , K. Buschelman, V. Eijkhout, W. D. Gropp, D. Kaushik, M. G. Knepley, L. C. McInnes, B. F. Smith, and H. Zhang. PETSc users manual. Technical Report ANL-95/11 - Revision 3.4, Argonne National Laboratory, 2013.

[2] S. Balay, J. Brown, K. Buschelman, W. D. Gropp, D. Kaushik, M. G. Knepley, L. C. McInnes, B. F. Smith, and H. Zhang. PETSc Web page, 2013. http://www.mcs.anl.gov/petsc.

[3] M. M. Baskaran and R. Bordawekar. Optimizing sparse matrix-vector multiplication on gpus. In *Technical report, IBM Research Report RC24704 (W0812-047)*, 2008.

[4] N. Bell and M. Garland. Implementing sparse matrix-vector multiplication on throughput-oriented processors. In *Conference on High Performance Computing Networking, Storage and Analysis*, 2009.

[5] J. W. Choi, A. Singh, and R. W. Vuduc. Model-driven autotuning of sparse matrix-vector multiply on GPUs. In *ACM SIGPLAN Symp. Principles and Practice of Parallel Programming (PPoPP)*, January 2010.

[6] CUDA. A parallel computing platform and programming model invented by nvidia. https://developer.nvidia.com/cuda-home-new.html.

[7] CUSP. The nvidia library of generic parallel algorithms for sparse linear algebra and graph computations on cuda architecture gpus. https://developer.nvidia.com/cusp.

[8] cuSPARSE. The nvidia cuda sparse matrix library. https://developer.nvidia.com/cusparse.

[9] J. Dongarra and M. A. Heroux. Toward a new metric for ranking high performance computing systems. *UTK EECS Tech Report and Sandia National Labs Report SAND2013-4744*, June 2013.

[10] A. Ekambaram and E. Montagne. An alternative compressed storage format for sparse matrices. In *ISCIS*, pages 196–203, 2003.

[11] R. Helfenstein and J. Koko. Parallel preconditioned conjugate gradient algorithm on gpu. *Journal of Computational and Applied Mathematics*, 236(15):3584–3590, 2012.

[12] Khronos OpenCL Working Group. *The OpenCL Specification, version 1.0.29*, 8 December 2008.

[13] X. Liu, M. Smelyanskiy, E. Chow, and P. Dubey. Efficient sparse matrix-vector multiplication on x86-based many-core processors. *International Conference on Supercomputing*, pages 273–282, 2013.

[14] J. Nickolls, I. Buck, M. Garland, and K. Skadron. Scalable parallel programming with cuda. *ACM Queue*, 6(2):40–53, 2008.

[15] N. I. of Standards and Technology. The matrix market format.

[16] I. Reguly and M. Giles. Efficient sparse matrix-vector multiplication on cache-based gpus. In *Innovative Parallel Computing (InPar)*, pages 1–12, 2012.

[17] D. M. Y. Roger G. Grimes, David Ronald Kincaid. *ITPACK 2.0: User's Guide*. 1980.

[18] Y. Saad. Krylov subspace methods on supercomputers. *SIAM J. SCI. STAT. COMPUT*, 10:1200–1232, 1989.

[19] Y. Saad. Sparskit: a basic tool kit for sparse matrix computations - version 2. 1994.

[20] S. Sengupta, M. Harris, Y. Zhang, and J. D. Owens. Scan primitives for gpu computing. In *Graphics Hardware*, pages 97–106, 2007.

[21] R. W. Vuduc. *Automatic performance tuning of sparse matrix kernels*. PhD thesis, University of California, January 2004.

[22] S. Williams, L. Oliker, R. W. Vuduc, J. Shalf, K. A. Yelick, and J. Demmel. Optimization of sparse matrix-vector multiplication on emerging multicore platforms. *Parallel Computing*, 35(3):178–194, 2009.

[23] X. Yang, S. Parthasarathy, and P. Sadayappan. Fast sparse matrix-vector multiplication on gpus: implications for graph mining. *Proc. VLDB Endow.*, 4(4):231–242, 2011.

A Programming System for Xeon Phis with Runtime SIMD Parallelization

Xin Huo, Bin Ren, and Gagan Agrawal
Department of Computer Science and Engineering
The Ohio State University
Columbus, OH 43210
huox@cse.ohio-state.edu, ren@cse.ohio-state.edu, agrawal@cse.ohio-state.edu

ABSTRACT

The Intel Xeon Phi offers a promising solution to coprocessing, since it is based on the popular x86 instruction set. However, to fully utilize its potential, applications must be vectorized to leverage the wide SIMD lanes, in addition to effective large-scale shared memory parallelism. Compared to the SIMT execution model on GPGPUs with CUDA or OpenCL, SIMD parallelism with a SSE-like instruction set imposes many restrictions, and has generally not benefitted applications involving branches, irregular accesses, or even reductions in the past. In this paper, we consider the problem of accelerating applications involving different communication patterns on Xeon Phis, with an emphasis on effectively using available SIMD parallelism. We offer an API for both shared memory and SIMD parallelization, and demonstrate its implementation. We use implementations of overloaded functions as a mechanism for providing SIMD code, which is assisted by runtime data reordering and our methods to effectively manage control flow. Our extensive evaluation with 6 popular applications shows large gains over the SIMD parallelization achieved by the production (ICC) compiler, and we even outperform OpenMP for MIMD parallelism.

Categories and Subject Descriptors

D.1.3 [**Programming Techniques**]: Concurrent Programming—*Parallel programming*; C.1.2 [**Processor Architectures**]: Multiple Data Stream Architectures (Multiprocessors)—*Single-instruction-stream, multiple-data-stream processors (SIMD)*

Keywords

Xeon Phi; SIMD; API; Communication Patterns

1. INTRODUCTION

Over the last 6-7 years, high-end computing systems have changed significantly with respect to the *intra-node* architectures, with popularity of coprocessors. Over the last 3 years, as many as three of the five fastest supercomputers (at any time, based on the bi-annual top 500 list) in the world involved coprocessors on each node, as they offered excellent performance-price and performance-power ratios.

A recent development along the same lines has been the emergence of Xeon Phi chips, based on the Intel MIC architecture. Xeon Phi is a promising system, because it allows x86 compatible software to be used. Thus, users could potentially continue to use their MPI and/or OpenMP applications, and not have to program in (and

ICS'14, June 10–13 2014, Munich, Germany.
Copyright 2014 ACM 978-1-4503-2642-1/14/06 ...$15.00.
http://dx.doi.org/10.1145/2597652.2597682.

learn a) new language like OpenCL or CUDA for the use of accelerators. At the same time, there are many similarities between GPUs and Xeon Phis. Both of these systems have a small amount of memory per thread/core, and moreover, both of them extensively employ a form of SIMD parallelism. NVIDIA GPUs have relied on SIMT (Single Thread Multiple Threads) model. Xeon Phi is built on top of the long-existing Intel SSE (Streaming SIMD Instructions), and particularly, supports IMCI (Initial Many Core Instructions) instruction set for use of SIMD. The SIMD width has been extended to 512 bits (16 floats), potentially offering large benefits for applications.

Use of SSE-like instruction sets has always been a hard problem, and it turns out that such parallelism has not been consistently used for applications outside dense matrix or imaging kernels. Moreover, there are significant programming differences between CUDA and SSE-like instruction sets, since they target SIMT and SIMD models, respectively. Specifically, while coalesced memory accesses are important for performance in SIMT programming, parallelism is still available, whereas programmers need to explicitly create aligned and contiguous accesses in the case of SSE or IMCI. Similarly, while branches are automatically managed in SIMT, with masks internally implemented, programmers or compilers must identify instructions executed by all threads with SSE/IMCI.

Effectively exploiting the power of a coprocessor like Xeon Phi requires that we exploit both MIMD and SIMD parallelism. While the former can be done through Pthreads or OpenMP, it is much harder to extract SIMD performance. This is because the restrictions on the model make hand-parallelization very hard. At the same time, productions compilers are unable to exploit SIMD parallelism for many of the cases.

This paper focuses on the problem of application development on any system that supports both shared memory parallelism and SSE-like SIMD parallelism, with a specific emphasis on the Intel Xeon Phi system. We describe an API and a runtime system that helps extract both shared memory and SIMD parallelism. One of the key ideas in our approach is to exploit the information about underlying communication patterns, to both partition and schedule the computation for MIMD parallelism, and reorganize the data for achieving better SIMD parallelism. While our approach is general, we currently focus on stencil computations, generalized reductions, and irregular reductions.

In the context of SIMD parallelization, though there is large volume of existing work on compiler-based code generation [7, 20, 9, 14], our work is driven by three observations. First, advanced features, like *scatter* and *gather* operations and *masks* need to be exploited for supporting different types of applications with the IMCI instruction sets. Second, increasing width requires that new approaches be exploited, for example considering aggressive inter-iteration parallelism for irregular reductions, unlike the existing work on this topic [14]. Finally, we observe that some of the advances in research prototype compilers have not made it to production-level compilers (as evidenced by our experiments with ICC compiler), and alternative approaches to simplifying SIMD code generation may be needed. Overall, with our approach, it is possible to use SIMD lanes for code involving irregular accesses, reductions, and control flow, unlike the previous work in this area.

Our work is significant in multiple ways: 1) We provide an *end-to-end* application development system for the Xeon Phi architecture, or more broadly, any system with both shared memory and SIMD parallelism, 2) Our work can be viewed as providing a CUDA or OpenCL-like programming API for SSE-like instructions, where the responsibility for determining contiguous vs. non-contiguous accesses or managing conditionals is the responsibility of the underlying library, 3) we offer potential intermediate language which may be generated by a compiler (for example, systems similar to the ones that generate CUDA code), and subsequently, runtime transformations and libraries be used for SIMD parallelization. Compared to the existing code generation approaches, we can simplify SIMD compilation process and make it more portable.

We have extensively evaluated our framework using six applications, which involve generalized reductions, stencil computations, and irregular reductions. Our evaluations shows: 1) on larger of the two datasets used for each application, the SIMD parallelization speedup from our system ranges from 1.6 to 7.8 (average of 2.8) whereas the corresponding gain from production compiler (ICC) is between 0.95 and 3.5 (average of 1.5), 2) as compared to hand-written IMCI code, the overheads of our framework is negligible, 3) by combining MIMD and SIMD parallelism on Xeon Phi, we achieve a speedup between 33 and 580 over single thread execution, outperforming Pthreads with ICC based vectorization by an average of 1.9x, and 4) we outperform parallelism with OpenMP at both MIMD and SIMD levels, even though we offer a comparable programming API.

2. PARALLELIZATION AND PERFORMANCE ISSUES IN INTEL XEON PHI

2.1 Intel Xeon Phi Architecture

The x86-compatible Intel Xeon Phi coprocessor, which is a latest commercial release of the Intel Many Integrated Core (MIC) architecture, has already been incorporated in 9 of the top 100 supercomputers at the time of writing this paper [1]. MIC is designed to leverage existing x86 experience and benefit from traditional multi-core parallelization programming models, libraries, and tools.

In the available MIC systems, there are 60 or 61 x86 cores organized with shared memory. These cores are low frequency in-order ones, and each supports as many as 4 hardware threads. Additionally, there are 32 512-bit vector registers on each core for SIMD operations. The main memory sizes vary from 8 GB to 16 GB, and the memory is shared by all cores. The L1 cache is 32 KB, entirely local to each core, whereas each core has a coherent L2 cache, 512 KB, where cache for different cores are interconnected in a ring.

Our work focuses on three important features of Intel MIC architecture, which need to be exploited for obtaining high performance:
Wide SIMD Registers and Vector Processing Units (VPU): VPU has been treated as the most significant feature of Xeon Phi by many previous studies [16, 27, 21, 6]. The reason is that the Intel Xeon Phi coprocessor has doubled the SIMD lane width compared to Intel Xeon processor, i.e., 256-bit to 512-bit, which means that it is possible to process 16 (8) identical floating point (double precision) operations at the same time. In addition, we have a new 512-bit SIMD instruction set called Intel Initial Many Core Instructions (Intel IMCI), which has built-in *gather* and *scatter* operations that allow irregular memory accesses, a hardware supported *mask* data type, and *write-mask* operations that allow operating on some specific elements within the same SIMD register. Even though all of these new instructions could potentially be simulated by the programers in the SIMD Streaming Extension (SSE) model, explicit new instructions allow easier implementation of more irregular parallelism. Note that SIMD instructions can be generated by the ICC compiler through the *auto-vectorization* option, or the programmers could use IMCI instruction set directly. The former needs low programming effort, though current compilation systems have several limitations and do not always obtain high performance. In comparison, the latter op-

tion can achieve the best performance, however, is tedious and error prone, and creates non-portable code.
Large Number of Concurrent Threads: Each Xeon Phi core allows up to 4 hyper-threads, in another word, we can have as many as 240/244 hardware threads sharing the same memory on Xeon Phi. This provides us with massive Multiple Instruction Multiple Data (MIMD) parallelism with shared memory, which has not been common in the past.
Coherent Distributed L2 Cache: Intel Xeon Phi architecture uses coherent L2 Cache with ring interconnection. When a L2 cache miss occurs for a specific core, an address request is sent to the ring. If the address is found in another core's L2 cache, the corresponding data is forwarded back along the ring. In worst case, the entire process may take hundreds of clock cycles. Thus, Xeon Phi reduces the number of L2 cache misses, but even an L2 cache hit can be very expensive. Thus, data locality is crucial for the overall performance.

2.2 Our Approach

Our approach for providing a solution for application development on Xeon Phi systems, including SIMD parallelization, is based on the observation that most applications follow a small number of *patterns* or *dwarfs* (e.g. as summarized by Collela and also described in Berkeley landscape on parallel computing [3]). By exploiting knowledge of individual patterns, needed data transformations and partitioning approaches can be used. Indeed, many previous efforts on SIMD (and SIMT) parallelization have focused specifically on particular patterns, like stencil computations [5, 9, 8] or irregular reductions [11, 14, 29].

We focus on a more general framework for specifying the computations, but where underlying patterns are explicitly known and exploited. Though the idea can be applied to a variety of patterns, we focus on stencil computations, generalized reductions, and irregular reductions in this paper. Among these, stencil computations and generalized reductions are well understood. As a background for our presentation, we show an example of an irregular reduction here.

```
Real    X(num_nodes), Y(num_edges) ;      {* data arrays *}
Integer IA(num_edges,2) ;                  {* indirection array *}

for(i = 0; i < num_edges; i++) {
    X(IA(i,1)) = X(IA(i,1)) + Y(i) ;
    X(IA(i,2)) = X(IA(i,2)) - Y(i) ;
}
```

Figure 1: A simple loop involving indirection

A typical irregular reduction is shown in Figure 1. In iteration i of the loop, the code makes two indirect references to the array X using $IA(i,1)$ and $IA(i,2)$. Codes from many important scientific and engineering domains contain loops with such indirection array sections. When a problem is modeled using an unstructured grid, a list of edges (with the nodes they connect) is explicitly stored. A computation that iterates over all edges in the grid and updates the attributes associated with the two end-points of the edge will have structure similar to the code in Figure 1. However, such codes can arise in other contexts - for instance, molecular dynamics contains similar loops, as the nodes represent molecules, and the edges denote the interaction between a pair of molecules.

2.3 Challenges and Opportunities

There are two levels of parallelism one can seek on the Xeon Phi: MIMD parallelism supported by large number of hyper-threads, and SIMD parallelism provided by the wide VPU. There are challenges associated with each of them, as well as opportunities to exploit information from specific communication patterns. The issues for applications with different types of patterns are summarized in Table 1.

2.3.1 MIMD Parallelization Issues

A Xeon Phi can be viewed as a SMP machine, in which all the cores not only share the same memory address, but also a coherent

Com Pattern	MIMD Challenge	SIMD Challenge
Generalized Reduction	job partition	unaligned/non-unit-stride access control flow dependency data dependency/conflicts
Stencil Computation	job partition	unaligned memory access control flow dependency
Irregular Reduction	job partition load balance	unaligned/random memory access control flow dependency data dependency/conflicts

Table 1: Parallelization Challenges of Different Communication Patterns

cache space. Thus, the traditional MIMD parallelization methods, like OpenMP, can also be applied with the support of the Intel compiler. Yet, there are many opportunities for exploiting information about specific communication patterns.

Particularly, applications with different communication patterns usually have different requirements on task partitioning and scheduling. For stencil computation and generalized reductions, static scheduling could provide better performance, since it can achieve load balance with a small scheduling overhead. For irregular reductions, a technique like the *reduction space partitioning* [11] can be used to avoid conflicts between the threads. Moreover, dynamic, fine-grained, scheduling could achieve better performance over static scheduling by achieving better load balance.

Communication pattern specific information can also help in other ways. Data reorganization is one of the optimizations to support vectorization, but data reordering can also provide better cache locality for irregular reductions. These optimizations are normally not performed by a more general framework, such as an OpenMP implementation.

2.3.2 SIMD Parallelization Issues

In SIMD execution, one memory access operation can load (store) multiple data elements simultaneously from (to) the memory. However, there are strict restrictions on how and when such operations can be applied.

Unaligned/Non-unit Stride Accesses: For using SIMD parallelism, the start of the read or write memory address has to be 64 bytes aligned on Xeon Phi. But, it is difficult to satisfy this requirement for almost any kind of application. For instance, stencil computation usually needs to access one node's neighbors in different directions. In a one dimension matrix, if the address of matrix[i] is aligned by 64 bytes, addresses of its neighbors, matrix[i-1] and matrix[i+1], will not be aligned. Similar problems will also arise for a matrix with more dimensions. In addition, different SIMD lanes can only access continuous memory address. Thus, accesses of elements from an array of structures or data accessed through indirection arrays cannot exploit SIMD parallelism directly.

Control Flow Dependencies: At any time, all the SIMD lanes have to execute the same instructions on different data elements. However, in the different branches of an *if-else* clause, different lanes may execute different instructions, which is not supported by SIMD. This kind of control flow arises very commonly in generalized reduction and irregular reductions.

Data Dependencies and Conflicts: When different SIMD lanes try to write to the same location, the behavior is undefined, as there is no locking operation. In the case of both generalized reductions and irregular reductions, such write conflicts arise. Thus, how to solve the data dependencies and conflicts for SIMD effectively and efficiently is another challenge.

3. API FOR APPLICATION DEVELOPMENT ON XEON PHI

Our parallelization framework provides a set of user API. Next, we introduce our MIMD and SIMD API, and then show how to use it in a variety of sample kernels.

User Interface API (class Task)	
API	**Descriptions**
struct Configuration	Configuration of the Task size, offset, and accessing stride.
enum Patterns	Declare the communication pattern(Generalized Reduction, Stencil, and Irregular Reduction).
tuple</*Parameter Lists*/>Parameters	Define the input parameters for a specific application.
void Kernel(vector<int> &index)	The kernel function provides the computing logic for a single data, given by the index vector.
MIMD Parallel Framework API (class MIMD_Framework)	
API	**Descriptions**
void run(Task &task)	The run function has the capability of register the user defined task to MIMD framework, invoking runtime optimizations, task partitioning, and scheduling on MIC architecture.
void join()	It will block, until the execution on MIC is finished.

Table 2: User Interface and MIMD Parallel Framework API

3.1 Shared Memory (MIMD) API

MIMD parallelization API is shown in Table 2. The first four parameters correspond to a *Task class*, which has four attributes, *Configuration*, *Pattern*, *Parameters*, and the *Kernel* function. The *Configuration* comprises three vector type variables, representing the size, offset, and stride of the computation space across different dimensions. *Pattern* is used to indicate which communication pattern the given task belongs to. Based on the pattern information, MIMD parallelization framework applies different partitioning methods, and this information is used by the SIMD parallel framework as well. In addition, users need to define the *Parameters* types, which includes the input and output parameters for a specific application. The most important part in the user interface is the *Kernel* function, which gives the smallest computation logic on one data element. It has only one input parameter representing the index of the target data element. Moreover, users need to guarantee that the kernel function is independent between different input indices. The independency can be achieved by either replicating the shared writing data or using locks while updating.

The last two API are related to the execution and optimization of the applications. The *run* function receives a user defined *task*, with a specification of the four set of parameters, and automatically invokes runtime optimizations, including partitioning and scheduling methods, for parallel execution on the Xeon Phi. The strategies employed in partitioning, scheduling, and optimizations are based on the parameters from the user interface. We will elaborate it in detail in Section 4. After these preprocessing, run function will launch a group of threads, each of which executes the kernel function with different input indices. The *run* function is a non-blocking function, which will return immediately after launching a job. Next, the users can call the *join* function to wait, until the execution of the *task* finishes.

Overall, our MIMD API provides a way to port applications to the Xeon Phi architecture with a very small efforts on part of the users. After giving a *task* definition, users can call *run(Task)* directly to execute the target applications.

3.2 SIMD API

The main idea of our SIMD API is to express collections of data elements on which parallel operations can be applied. The actual layout and scheduling of the operations is left up to the runtime system.

Before introducing the API for operations, we first introduce the definition of the new data types. We introduce three data types in SIMD API, which are shown in Table 3. *Scalar Type* is the basic data type, which only contain one data element - the implication is that if this variable is involved in a SIMD operation, it will be shared

Data Type	Name	Description
Scalar Type	int, float, double, ...	Data is shared by all the SIMD lanes. All the basic data types or temporary variables are belonged to shared type.
Vector Type	vint, vfloat, vdouble, ...	It includes multiple data scaling to all the SIMD lanes.
Mask Type	mask	It helps handling control flow in vectorization

Table 3: The data types defined in SIMD API

vint v1, v2; int s; mask m;
op represents the supported mathematic or logic operations;

API	Examples
Assignment API	
Support assignment between vector types, and scalar type to vector type.	v1 = v2; v1 = s; v1 op= v2; v1 op= s;
Mathematic API	
Support most mathematic operations, including +, -, *, /, %, between vector types and scalar types.	v1 = v2 op v1; v1 = v2 op s;
Logic API	
Support most logic operations, including ==, !=, <, >, <=, >=, between vector types and scalar types. Return type is mask type.	m = v1 op v2; m = v1 op s;
Load/Store API	
void load(void *src);	v1.load(addr);
void store(void *dst);	v1.store(addr);
void load(void *src, const vint &index, int scale)	v1.load(addr,index,scale);
void store(void *dst, const vint &index, int scale)	v1.store(addr,index,scale);
Generalized Reduction API	
template<class ReducComp = reducAdd > void reduction(int *update, int scale, int offset, vint *index, type value, [mask m])	reduction(update, scale, offset, index, v1);
Mask API	
mask()	v1.mask()
Mask_State Object	
Members	Descriptions
mask m	mask type variable
type old_val	the default value for unset vector lanes
set_mask(const mask &m, type &old_val);	set mask and default value
void clear_mask();	clear default value and set all vector lanes to active

Table 4: SIMD API

by all the SIMD lanes. In contrast, *Vector Type*, which is represented as *vint or vfloat*, includes an array of data elements. Thus, if we declare one array as *Vector Type*, each time SIMD lanes will access a group of contiguous data elements. However, when SIMD lanes access a *Scalar Type*, the same data element will be automatically duplicated for all the lanes. This automatic duplication is supported by the implicit conversion from *Scalar Type* to *Vector Type* in our implementation.

The last data type is the *Mask Type*. Because SIMD vectorization does not support control flow, we require use of a mask variable to express what computations are applied on which elements. The mask type is implemented as a bit set, in which each bit represents one vector lane. Two values, 1 and 0, represent set and unset, respectively.

The supported operations on different data types are shown in Table 4. The main idea is to *overload* most operators on vector types, or even operations involving one vector type and a scalar type. Thus, the difference between the serial codes and the vectorized codes by using our API is quite small, as we will show through several examples. As shown in Table 4, for assignments and mathematical operations, users can use the same operator in serial codes for vector types and a combination of vector and scalar types. The overloaded oper-

ator implementation will automatically perform vectorization on the input parameters. For logic operations, the difference from the traditional logic operators is with respect to the return type. Because there is no support for control flow in SIMD, in the logic operation API, the return type is the mask type, which is then used to express the conditional clause that will be applied for a particular element.

Moving onto the rest of the API, there are two types of load and store functions, which are for reading and writing contiguous and non-contiguous addresses, respectively. A load (store) with a single source or destination parameter provide the function of read and write between the vector type and a contiguous memory address space. On the other hand, a function with the extra *index* and *scale* parameters helps exploit *gather* and *scatter* operations in the IMCI instruction set for non-contiguous memory accessing. For the applications, which data reorganization can be applied, such as generalized reductions and stencil computations, there is no need for non-contiguous load and store API. However, for irregular applications, in which data reorganization cannot eliminate indirect memory accessing, non-contiguous load and store API can provide an alternative way.

One specific feature is a reduction function. As we had stated before, multiple SIMD lanes cannot update the same element, and as a result, implementation of a reduction function using SIMD instructions is more complex. The specific reduction function is given as a parameter in the template. Our runtime system ensures that SIMD lanes are correctly used for such computation.

The goal of the mask function is the conversion of a unmask vector type to the mask vector type. After this conversion, all the operations on this collection start using the *mask_state object* to determine which elements an operation is applied to. Function *set_mask* is used to setup the mask for current *mask_state object* on one thread, which is then used till it is cleared or updated.

3.3 Sample Kernels

We now illustrate the API using functions involving different communication patterns. We establish how code using our API is similar to sequential code, and much simpler than a hand-written vectorized code.

3.3.1 Stencil Application

Listing 1: Sobel: Stencil Computation with serial codes

```
void kernel(int i, int j){
    float Dx = 0.0, Dy = 0.0;
    for(int p = -1; p <= 1; p++){
        for(int q = -1; q <= 1; q++){
            Dx += weight_H[p+1][q+1]*b[i+p][j+q];
            Dy += weight_V[p+1][q+1]*b[i+p][j+q];
        }
    }
    float z = sqrt(Dx*Dx + Dy*Dy);
    a[i][j] = z;
}
```

Listing 2: Sobel: Stencil Computation with SIMD API

```
void kernel(int i, int j){
    vfloat Dx = 0.0, Dy = 0.0;
    //Compute the weight for a node in a 3x3 area
    for(int p = -1; p <= 1; p++){
        for(int q = -1; q <= 1; q++){
            Dx += weight_H[p+1][q+1]*b[X(i,p,q)][Y(j,p,q)];
            Dy += weight_V[p+1][q+1]*b[X(i,p,q)][Y(j,p,q)];
        }
    }
    vfloat z = sqrt(Dx*Dx + Dy*Dy);
    z.store(&a[i][j]);
}
```

Listing 3: Sobel: Stencil Computation with manual vectorization

```
void kernel(int i, int j){
    __m512 Dx = _mm_set1_ps(0.0), Dy = _mm_set1_ps(0.0);
    //Compute the weight for a node in a 3x3 area
    for(int p = -1; p <=1; ++p){
        for(int q = -1; q <=1; ++q){
            __m512 *tmp = (__m512*)&b[i+q][j+p*vec_width];
            __m512 tmpx = _mm512_mul_ps(*tmp,weight_H[p+1][q+1]);
            Dx = _mm512_add_ps(Dx, tmpx);
            __m512 tmpy = _mm512_mul_ps(*tmp,weight_V[p+1][q+1]);
            Dy = _mm512_add_ps(Dy, tmpy);
        }
    }
    __m512 sqDX = _mm512_mul_ps(Dx, Dx);
    __m512 sqDy = _mm512_mul_ps(Dy, Dy);
    __m512 ret = _mm512_add_ps(sqDx, sqDy);
    ret = _mm512_sqrt_ps(ret);
    _mm512_store_ps(&a[i][j], ret);
}
```

In Listing 1, 2, and 3, we take a simple stencil computation, the sobel filter, and compare serial, vectorized using our API, and manually vectorized versions.

Comparing between Listing 1 and 2, the vectorized codes in our API are almost as same as the serial version, except new vector types (*vfloat*) are introduced to replace the original scalar types (*float*). Another difference is that the assignment from vector type to scalar type is achieved through the *store* API, because it needs to involve multiple data copies from the vector variable to the target memory locations. Also, to facilitate a possible data reorganization at runtime, a function *Dim(idx, offset1, offset2, ...)* is provided to calculate the transformed index in each dimension by applying offsets on different dimensions. For example, in Listing 2, $X(i, p, q)$ calculates the transformed index in the X-dimension when applying p and q offsets on the original X and Y dimensions, respectively.

To summarize, our API provide a convenient way to achieve vectorization with very little modification on the serial code. It is also clear that the manual vectorization codes, shown in Listing 3, introduces more new Intel IMCI API, and is much more complicated compared to serial and our SIMD API versions, as about 40% extra lines are added.

3.3.2 Generalized Reduction

Listing 4: Kmeans: Generalized Reduction with SIMD API

```
void kernel(vfloat *data, int i){
    vfloat min = FLT_MAX;
    vint min_index = 0;
    for(int j = 0; j < k; ++j){
        //step 1 (Computation): compute the distance
        vfloat dis = 0.0;
        for(int m = 0; m < 3; ++m){
            dis += (data[i+m*n]-cluster[j*3+m]) *
                   (data[i+m*n]-cluster[j*3+m]);
        }
        dis = sqrt(dis);
        //step 2 (Control flow): update index
        mask m = dis < min;
        set_mask(m, min);
        min.mask() = dis.mask();
        set_mask(m, min_index);
        min_index.mask() = j;
    }
    //step 3 (Reduction): reduction
    reduction(update, 5, min_index, 0, data[i]);
    reduction(update, 5, min_index, 1, data[i+n]);
    reduction(update, 5, min_index, 2, data[i+n*2]);
    reduction(update, 5, min_index, 3, 1.0);
    reduction(update, 5, min_index, 4, min);
}
```

In Listing 4, we show the main function of Kmeans, a simple data mining kernel, with vectorization by using our API. The procedures of Kmeans can be divided into three steps: 1) compute the distance between one node and the candidate clusters, 2) update index to the cluster with the minimum distance, 3) do reduction on the cluster found in the step 2. Thus, the step 1 is only simple arithmetic operations, whereas steps 2 and 3 involve control flow and generalized reduction, respectively.

In the step 1, similar to the stencil computation, the only modification is the data types of corresponding variables are changed from

scalar type to the vector type. As a result, the computation is automatically vectorized by loading values from the *data* array to all vector lanes, and computing the distance between the data in each lane and the clusters. The step 2 introduces a branch, specifically, if the distance is smaller than the current minimum distance (min), we update the min and min_index, otherwise, min and min_index are not changed. Using our mask API, we represent this computation as *if-else* branch, in which the *else* branch just assigns its own value to itself. As we can see in step 2 of the Listing 4, a mask variable m is returned by the logic computation. Then, m and the default value for *else* branch are set by *set_mask* function. Next, the *mask()* function will do the conversion from unmask vector type to the mask vector type. In the step 3, reduction is performed on the array *update* with the add operation. It is not safe to perform the reduction using the general arithmetic and assignment operations, due to the potential written conflict between different vector lane. Thus, we use the API for reduction. Here, *add* operation, which is the default reduce operation for reduction function, is used to reduce values to the array *update*.

To summarize, in our API, the code with arithmetic operations is almost as same as the original (serial) code. The reduction in our API is provided through a function interface, which allows us to vectorize these codes, whereas most compile-time solutions fail to do this. The most complicated part of our API is handling of control flow, where branches are replaced by mask operations. However, we note that existing vectorizing compilers do not handle control flow at all (as we will show through experimental results), and manual vectorization in presence of control flow is very complicated (please see an example in Figure 4).

4. RUNTIME SCHEDULING FRAMEWORK

We now describe the implementation of the framework, and particularly, how runtime scheduling that is applied for both MIMD and SIMD parallelization.

4.1 MIMD Parallelization

Though MIMD parallelization is performed by a number of existing frameworks, our focus is on providing automatic or guided task partitioning and scheduling for three different communication patters (generalized reduction, stencil computation and irregular reduction) on the Xeon Phi. In each of these patterns, the computation is an iteration over a set of *indices*, where the following two steps are applied on each index: Step 1 - Loading the index of the targeted data and other auxiliary data for computation, and Step 2 - Executing the computation logic, including both computation and writing results, for the target data. In MIMD parallelization, each thread will load a different index in the Step 1, and execute Step 2 simultaneously and independently, except for handling possible race conditions on the output elements. Our API allows the user to provide a *task* function, which is the serial code for computations associated with a single target data element, which is used for Step 2.

Our runtime system has two major components, task partitioning and runtime scheduling, to parallelize the target applications on the Xeon Phi. Task partitioning can potentially be applied on the *computation space* or the *reduction space*. Computation space refers to the space of the computation loop. For example, the num_edges loop in Figure 1 is belonged to *computation space*. Reduction space refers to the space in which a reduction is executed. The X array in Figure 1 is an example of reduction space for this loop. For generalized reductions and stencil computations, it is straightforward to perform task partitioning on the computation space. Particularly, the task partitioning component can just divide the computation loop into a number of blocks with an equal size, and pass these blocks to the dynamic scheduling component to execute.

However, for irregular reduction applications, there is a tradeoff between computation space partitioning and reduction space partitioning [11]. Briefly, computation space can introduce significant overhead on locking operations when different threads trying to update the results on the same reduction index, whereas, reduction space partitioning can completely avoid competition between threads by assigning different reduction space to different threads. Thus, all threads can execute independently by updating non-overlapping parts of the reduction space. Thus, in our framework, different task partitioning strategies will be launched based on the types of the applications, provided by the users.

In the runtime scheduling component, we include three scheduling methods. The first is the static scheduling, in which all the tasks from task partitioning module will be equally distributed to the all the available threads. The static method introduces the smallest scheduling overhead, and for stencil computations, this scheduling method achieves better performance, because it can still achieve good load balance. However, for generalized reductions and irregular reductions, the workload in each task partition may be different. Especially, for an irregular reduction, after reduction space partitioning, the workload in each partition may be quite different, and depends on the number of edges associated with each node in the reduction space. Thus, a dynamic scheduling method based on factoring is provided in our framework, which assigns large number of tasks to the threads at first, and reduces the number of assigned tasks as execution progresses. The third and the final scheduling method is the *user-defined* method, where a user can define the number of tasks in each partition.

4.2 SIMD Parallelization Support

Our SIMD parallelization support has three components: implementation of overloaded functions which supports SIMD execution, runtime data reorganization, and handling of control flow.

4.2.1 SIMD Parallelization Through Implementation of Overloaded Functions

```
int func(vfloat *a, vfloat *b, vfloat *c){
    for(int i = 0; i < n; ++i)
        c[i] = a[i] + b[i];
}
(a) An vectorized function by using overloaded functions
int func(float *a, float *b, float *c){
    for(int i = 0; i < n; i+=16){
        __mm512 *s_a = (__mm512*)a[i];
        __mm512 *s_b = (__mm512*)b[i];
        __mm512 *s_c = (__mm512*)c[i];
        *s_c = _mm512_add_ps(*s_a, *s_b);
    }
}
(b) The expansion of the overloaded functions in (a)
```

Figure 2: An example of vectorization in overloaded functions

Our primary method for auto vectorization is based on the implementation of the overloaded functions we had listed in Table 4. The basic idea is as follows - overloaded functions are used inside definition of a *task*, which applies computation to a particular point. Since these computations can be applied in parallel, an overloaded function's implementation uses SIMD instructions to achieve parallel execution.

An example is shown in Figure 2. The initial function performs an add operation between arrays *a* and *b*, and writes the results to the array *c*. The sub-figure (a) shows the code with our API, which is the sequential code, except for *vector-type* declarations. SIMD parallelization is now automatically applied based on the overloaded add operator on the vector types. Sub-figure (b) shows the expansion of the overloaded function. First, it applies a translation between the scalar type and the vector types on the arrays involved. Then, a SIMD add function is called on the translated arrays to perform 16 add and write operations in the SIMD manner. Next, the index is moved to the start of the next 16 operands.

Overall, unlike hand-code SIMD parallelization, our framework uses numerous overloaded functions to provide a convenient way to achieve the same performance. There is no need for application developers to consider address translation, different vectorization instructions for different operand types, operations, and architectures,

Assume SIMD Width = 4

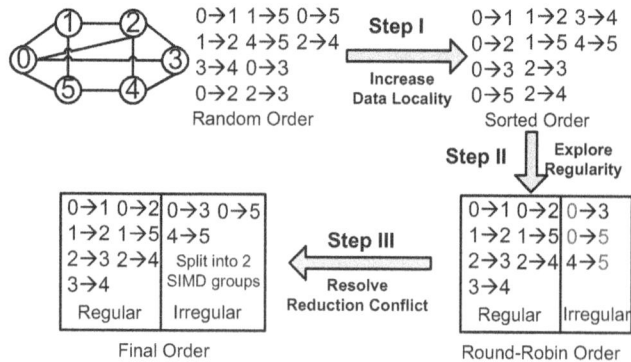

Figure 3: Irregular Reduction Edges Reorder

and the position of the next computing index. However, in practice, there are many complications in the application of overloaded functions, particularly, when data elements are not contiguous, and/or when branches are involved. We discuss these issues in the rest of this section.

4.2.2 Data Reorganization

SIMD operations on Xeon Phis (or any SSE-like instruction set) can only be applied if there are continuous and aligned memory access. Many applications have non-unit stride and unaligned or even random memory accesses. Such kind of accesses impede compiler vectorization. In our framework, we exploit the knowledge about underlying communication patterns to reorganize the data and facilitate SIMD parallelization.

Generalized Reductions: For generalization reductions, data array is usually given as an *Array of Structures* (AoS). For instance, in Kmeans, the input point array comprises x, y, and z dimensional information (for three dimensional-points). During vectorization, the Vector Processing Unit (VPU) will apply the same operation for 16 elements, which means that the VPU needs to access 16 continuous values from each dimension. However, with AoS storage, values corresponding to one particular attribute are non-contiguous. Moreover, if the x dimension data is stored aligned, y and z dimension, data is likely to be unaligned. Therefore, both non-continuous and unaligned memory accesses can either prevent vectorization or impact vectorization performance negatively by the compiler or programing having to introduce extra gather and scatter operations.

Our system applies the standard AoS to SoA *Structure of Array* transformation. In the SoA format, instead storing each member of the structure continuously, all values for a particular member are grouped together. Thus, accesses to the same member will be continuous. Moreover, aligned accesses can be ensured by adding padding at the end of each member array. Because AoS can be viewed as a matrix, in which columns represent different members of the structure, our framework employs a parallel matrix transpose to apply the transformation efficiently.

Stencil Computations: Unaligned memory accesses is the major problem for vectorization on stencil computations. When computing the value for a target point, we need to access all its neighbors. Thus, in the original format, it is impossible to ensure that the target point and its neighbors are both aligned. In the literature [8], a non-linear data layout transformation has been proposed to make the target point and its neighbors aligned at the same time, achieved by *dimension lifting* and a *matrix transposition*. In our framework, we invoke this data reorganization to be able to achieve aligned memory accesses.

Irregular Reductions: In an irregular reduction kernel, indirect data references can cause very random memory accesses. If we want to vectorize these operations, a large number of *gather* and *scatter* operations must be invoked. There are many existing efforts trying to solve or alleviate this problem from different perspectives. Kim and

Han [14] design an algorithm to replace unnecessary gather and scatter operations by scalar operations. Wu *et al.* [28] try to resolve a very similar problem, coalesced memory access, within the context of the GPU architecture. Focusing on inter-iteration parallelism on an irregular reduction for a SSE-like instruction set, we address this problem by a novel computation (edges data) reordering method, which we describe below.

Our method is explained with the help of an example shown in Figure 3. First, the motivation for our method is as follows. The gather and scatter operations incur a very long latency when the data locality is poor, because each gather and scatter operation works at the unit of the entire cache line. For example, when the required data is split across multiple cache lines, we need multiple gather operations to load them. So, the first objective of the our data reorganization method is to reorder the edge data, and increase data locality. To achieve this objective, based on the partitioning algorithm that is used for task partitioning at the MIMD level, we further reorder the *edge* data according to their first nodes (Step I in Figure 3). As a result, at least for one of the end-points of the edge, data is likely to be in the same cache line.

The second objective is to replace *gather* and *scatter* operations by normal SIMD *load* and *store* operations to the extent possible. To achieve this objective, we partition the edges into *regular partitions* and *irregular partitions*, as explained below. First, we further reorder the *edges* data (Step II in Figure 3), so that the edges are ordered in a round-robin manner according to their first nodes, and we have a consecutive set of first node for the set of edges that will be processed in one SIMD step (a *regular partition*). Now, clearly, given a set of edges, we cannot ensure that we can simply reorganize them as a set of regular partitions. A set of edges that will be processed in one SIMD step but whose first nodes do not form a consecutive set is an *irregular partition*. Thus, we will likely have a set of regular partitions and irregular partitions. After this, we can further apply AoS to SoA to duplicate all the first nodes of edges in the regular partition. In such case, we can apply normal SIMD *load* and *store* operations for the first nodes of edges in the regular partition, and only apply *gather* and *scatter* operations for the remaining nodes.

The third objective is to resolve write conflicts within the same SIMD register for the second nodes of edges in a regular partition and for all the nodes in an irregular partition. Note that this issue arises for generalized reductions as well. The problem is that unless we are careful, different SIMD lanes may update the same element of the SIMD register, causing a race condition. A larger SIMD width increases this possibility, and moreover, indirect accesses can make it hard to avoid such situations. In order to resolve this problem, we have two options: a) serialized reduction; and b) further data/computation reorder. For serialized reduction, we provides a way to automatically serialize all the reduction operations to eliminate the possible conflicts. Alternatively, we can further reorder the elements into blocks according to the SIMD width, even introducing *bubble* elements. For irregular reductions, we can further reorder the edges (computation order) as shown in Step III of Figure 3, by which, we can make sure there is no write conflict within the same SIMD register.

4.2.3 Resolving Control Flow

Control flow (presence of branches) has been a severe impediment to SIMD parallelization, from the time of the initial version of SSE released decades ago. Without hardware support, in SSE and AVX, one has to *simulate* the *mask* operations, which is cumbersome. We show an example in Figure 4, where sub-figure(b) shows hand-written SIMD parallelization, where a set of tasks are applying the code in sub-figure (a). It is easy to see that a statement with simple control flow leads to very complex and the size of the code is increased dramatically.

Our framework helps manage this complexity, building on top of the *mask* data type and *mask* operations in latest Xeon Phi (and the IMCI instruction set). As shown in Figure 4 (c), logic operations between the vector variables can return a mask type variable, and we can use the mask variable as part of the *mask* arithmetic operations

```
if(a < b) a += b;
else a -= b;
(a) An example of control follow

__mm128i mask1 = _mm_cmplt_epi32(a, b);
__mm128i mask0 = _mm_andnot_si128(mask1,
    _mm_set1_epi32(0xffffffff));
__mm128i res = _mm_and_si128(_mm_add_epi32(a, b), mask1);
__mm128i oldval = _mm_and_si128(a, mask0);
a = _mm_or_si128(res, oldval);
res = _mm_and_si128(_mm_sub_epi32(a, b), mask0);
oldval = _mm_and_si128(a, mask1);
a = _mm_or_si128(res, oldval);
(b) The vectorization code of control follow in (a)

__mmask16 mask1 = _mm512_cmplt_epi32(a, b);
__mmask16 mask0 = _mm512_cmpge_epi32(a, b);
a = _mm512_mask_add_epi32(a, mask1, a, b);
a = _mm512_mask_sub_epi32(a, mask0, a, b);
(c) The vectorization code of control follow with mask type in (a)
```

Figure 4: An example of control follow (a) without vectorization (b) with vectorization (c) with vectorization and mask type

to get results from different branches. Thus, compared to the code in sub-figure (b), control flow can be handled in a more concise fashion. However, users are still required to be familiar with the new intrinsics, which is still complicated and error prone. This is addressed in our framework.

Initially, we further elaborate on the available *Mask_State Object*, shown in Table 4. There are two members, a mask type m, and a scalar or vector type *old_val*. *old_val* is the default value assigned to the *unset* or *inactive* SIMD lanes. The idea is that the inactive SIMD lanes still need to execute the instruction, but they simply produce *old_val*. So, as one can see from Figure 4 (c), we set a as the *old_val*. Thus, when executing $a+ = b$, for the lanes in which a is greater than or equal to b, the *old_val* or a, will be assigned to itself in the end. Similar operations occur when executing $a- = b$.

The API we support is simpler, and was summarized towards the end of Tables 3 and 4. The key thing to note is that interface of the operations that involve a mask is same as the operations that do not involve any mask. Each thread owns a local mask_state object for its entire life. The mask_state object is declared as a global and static variable for each thread. Each mask_state object includes the information about the *mask* and *old_val* for current control flow. After users set a mask_state object by the *set_mask* function (example shown in Listing 4), it is effective, until a new *mask* is set, or the current mask is cleared (using the *clear_mask* function). Each thread's mask information is used to provide two implementations of each overloaded operation: *unmask* (default) and with *mask*. If a mask is set, versions with mask are invoked, and use the thread's local mask_state object as a parameter. Listing 4 includes an example of how to translate unmask vector type to mask vector type.

5. EVALUATION

In this section, we evaluate our framework using various applications that involve the communication patterns we have focused on. The objectives of our experiments were: 1) Comparing the performance of applications developed using framework, over hand-written parallel versions (using Pthreads), and evaluating the SIMD parallelization in our framework, over the ICC compiler generated SIMD code, 2) Quantifying the overheads of our runtime framework, by comparing performance against the hand-written SIMD code for SIMD parallelization, 3) Comparing the performance of MIMD parallelization from our framework against OpenMP, another high-level framework, and further evaluating the SIMD parallelization by our framework against what is achieved by ICC compiler with OpenMP directives. All experiments were conducted on a Xeon Phi SE10P card, which has 61 cores each running at 1.1 GHz, with four hyper-threads per core, along with a 32 MB L2 cache and 8 GB GDDR5 memory. The compiler that we used is Intel ICC compiler 13.1.0. All benchmarks are compiled with the *-O3* optimization. Compiler vectorization is turned on and off by *-vec* and *-no-vec* options, respectively. *#pragma vector always* was always used with OpenMP. We also attempted SIMD pragmas, such as *#pragma ivdep* and *#pragma simd*, as well as the SIMD Pragmas introduced by OpenMP 4.0. However, none of them could handle irregular and some generalized reductions, due to data dependencies, complicated deferences, and the need for outer loop vectorization for our target class of applications. All experiments are conducted in the *Native Model* with the *-mmic* option.

5.1 Benchmarks

Six benchmarks are selected from various benchmark suites, two each involving generalized reductions, stencil computations, and irregular reductions. **Kmeans** [12] is a very popular data clustering kernel - in each iteration, it processes each point in the dataset, determines the closest center to this point, and computes how this center's location should be updated. Our experiments used two different values of the parameter K, the number of clusters, $K = 10$ and $K = 100$. **Naive Bayes Classifier (NBC)** [25] is a simple classification algorithm based on observed probabilities. We used two datasets, 50 MB and 200 MB. **Sobel** is a stencil computation. For 2D Sobel, two 3×3 *weight templates* are used to compute the weight on the target point. Two matrices, with the size of 8192×8192 and 16384×16384, respectively, were used. **Heat3D** [2] simulates heat transmission in a 3D space, involving a 7-point stencil. The small and large datasets used in the experiments are $512 \times 256 \times 256$ and $512 \times 512 \times 512$, respectively. **Molecular Dynamics (MD)** is an irregular reduction kernel used to study the structural, equilibrium, and dynamic properties of molecules. The simulation iterates over all the edges, and updates the attributes associate with the two end nodes. The small dataset used in the experiments has 16K nodes and 2M edges, while the large one has 256K nodes and 32M edges. **Euler** is another irregular reduction kernel based on Computational Fluid Dynamics (CFD) that takes description of the connectivity of a mesh and calculates quantities like velocities ate each mesh point. The small dataset used in our experiments has 182K nodes and 1.13M edges, while the large one has 1.4M nodes and 8.9M edges.

5.2 Speedups from Our Framework

Our first set of experiments focused on comparing the SIMD parallelization with our framework against compiler generated GDDR5 code (auto-vectorization), and hand-written SIMD code. Compiler SIMD parallelization was applied on Pthreads code, so as to also allow shared memory parallelization. Pthreads-based shared memory parallel versions used similar style (and thus obtain similar performance) as the shared memory parallelization supported by our framework, though the programmer effort is much smaller with our framework. In Figure 5, we compared the best performance between the pthread versions with and without compiler vectorization, and the vectorization versions with hand-coding and our API, for *small* and *large* datasets described earlier. The performance, shown in Figure 5, is the one with the number of threads that leads to the best performance (which maybe different across versions). The numbers reported are relative speedups, with baseline of Pthreads version without vectorization.

For generalized reductions, both Kmeans and NBC show similar trends. The SIMD-API version achieves better performance compared to the Pthread versions with or without compiler generated SIMD code. Moreover, the runtime overhead introduced by SIMD-API is very small compared to the hand-written SIMD versions. In Kmeans, compiler vectorization can only be applied in the innermost loop, which is the loop calculating the distance between one node and all the cluster centers. The performance is sensitive to the amount of computation in this loop, which depends upon the number of clusters, K. Thus, with $K = 10$, `pthread-vec` version is even slower than the `pthread-novec` version. With $K = 100$, `pthread-vec` gains 3.5x speedup compared to `pthread-novec`.

However, with `SIMD-API`, the vectorization is applied on the outermost loop, which is the loop iterating over all input points. In addition, with data reorganization and effective management of branches, we can further improve the performance. Thus, `SIMD-API` gains 2.5 and 7.8 times speedups with $K = 10$ and $K = 100$. Another optimization applicable to Kmeans is the reordering of reduction. When K is smaller than the number of vector lanes, it is impossible to eliminate the write-conflicts, but this optimization is effective with a large K.

Now, considering NBC, large number of branches causes significant overhead on vectorization. So, the available production compiler failed to vectorize the kernel function in NBC, i.e, the difference between `pthread-novec` and `pthread-vec` is negligible. However, with the help of the mask operations introduced in our framework, `SIMD-API` still gains 1.5 and 1.6 times speedups on small and large datasets, respectively.

For stencil computations, one of the major problems for vectorization is unaligned memory accesses. In our framework, we overcome this limitation by reorganizing the datasets. However, the ICC compiler also has the capability to do the automatic vectorization. In Heat3D, we can see that `pthread-vec` achieves the best performance, which is very close to `SIMD-API` and `SIMD-Manual`. But for Sobel, compiler vectorization fails due to the extra inner loop that applies weights on the neighbors of the target node. Thus, the performance of `pthread-vec` is very similar to that of `pthread-novec`, whereas `SIMD-API` can still achieve more than 2x speedup, because vectorization is not limited to the inner loop.

For irregular reductions, the production compiler cannot vectorize a loop with indirection-based memory access at all. In our framework, we use data reordering together with a reduction in the use of gather and scatter operations to vectorize such kind of loops, which turns out to be effective when the datasets are large. We achieve 1.5 and 2.5 times speedup over the pthread versions for Euler and MD, respectively. For small datasets, the performance of the best `SIMD-API` version is comparable to the pthread versions. However, the best configuration with `SIMD-API` involves fewer threads (60 instead of 244). In other words, for the smaller datasets, enough parallelism is not available to exploit both MIMD and SIMD features. Comparing to the best `SIMD-manual` versions, `SIMD-API` incurs neglectable overheads.

5.3 Overall Scalability

In Figure 6, we compare the scalability of `pthread-novec`, `pthread-vec`, `SIMD-API`, and `SIMD-Manual` with an increasing number of threads. Execution with a single thread and no vectorization on Xeon Phi is used as the baseline, and thus, we are evaluating the combined benefits of shared memory parallelization (61 cores), hardware multi-threading (4 threads per core) and SIMD units. The performance scales well for all the versions. `SIMD-API` outperforms both `pthread-vec` and `pthread-novec` in most cases, consistent with what we reported earlier. `SIMD-API` achieves better relative performance when the number of threads is small. For instance, when the number of threads is one, `SIMD-API` is 20 times better than the `Pthreads-novec` version. With small datasets, as the number of threads increases, the vectorization advantage with `SIMD-API` becomes restricted due to limited amount of overall work. The overall speedups obtained range between 580 and 33, depending upon the application. Thus, we can see that our framework is effective in allowing users to exploit the Xeon Phi chip. As an aside, benefits of hardware multi-threading (more than 1 thread per core) seem limited, except for Kmeans (speedup from 2 threads per core, but slowdown from 4 threads per core) and the irregular applications (where latency is masked by hardware multi-threading). In the future, we will examine this issue further and develop a module for automatically choosing the number of threads for a given application.

5.4 Comparison with OpenMP

Our last set of experiments had two distinct goals. First, we wanted to examine how SIMD parallelization with our framework compares

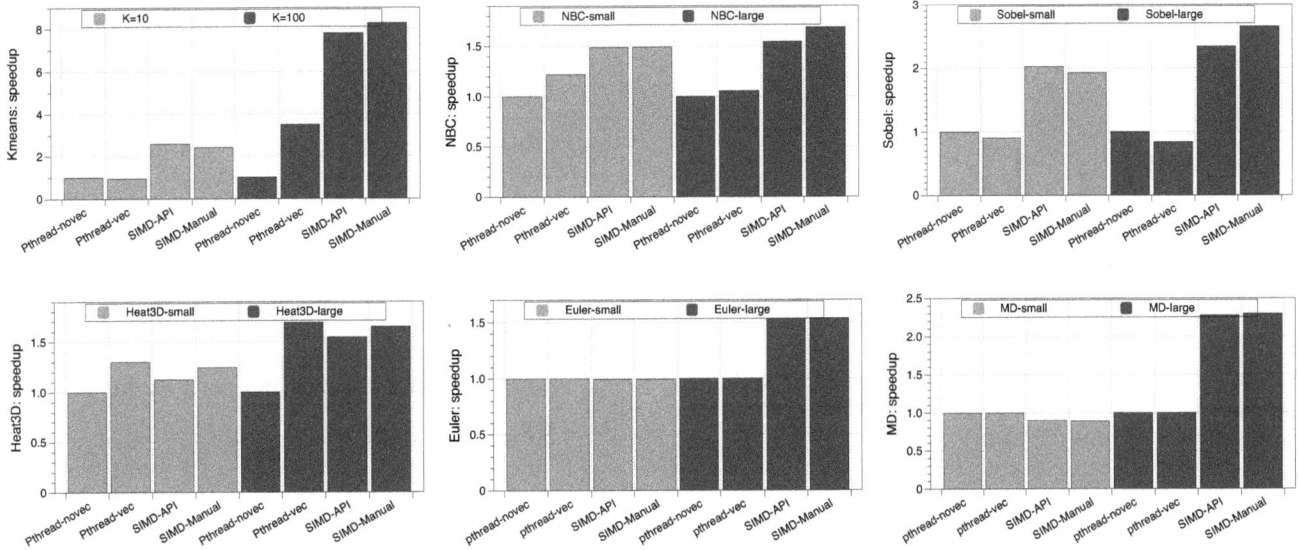

Figure 5: Speedup of Pthread without SIMD (`Pthread-novec`), Pthread with auto-SIMD (`Pthread-vec`), MIC SIMD with our framework (`SIMD-API`), and hand-written SIMD (`SIMD-manual`): Kmeans, NBC, Sobel, Heat3D, Euler, and MD with `small` and `large` datasets each

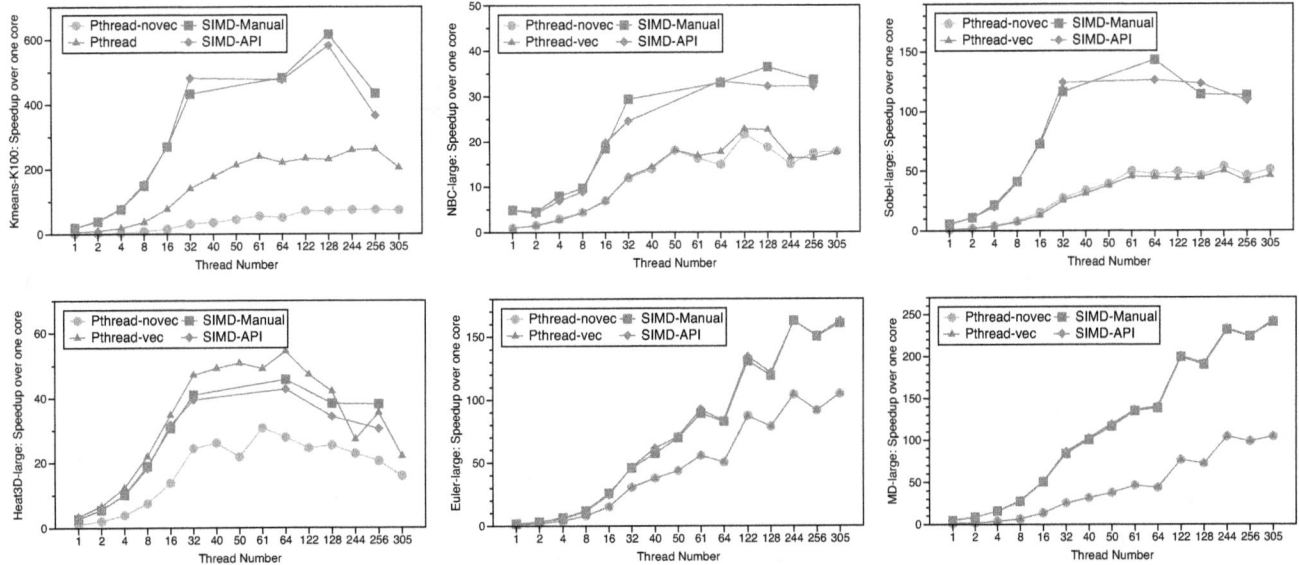

Figure 6: Scalability with Increasing Number of Threads: Pthread without vectorization (`Pthread-novec`), Pthread with auto-vectorization (`Pthread-vec`), SIMD with API (`SIMD-API`), and hand-written SIMD (`SIMD-manual`) with Kmeans, NBC, Sobel, Heat3D, Euler, and MD (large datasets) - Relative Speedups Over 1 Thread Execution on Xeon Phi with no Vectorization

against SIMD parallelization performed by the ICC compiler with OpenMP directives. Second, because both OpenMP and the MIMD API in our framework provide a high-level model for developing shared memory applications, we wanted to examine if our framework offers any performance advantages, possibly because it exploits the knowledge of the underlying communication patterns.

In Figure 7, we compared our MIMD parallel framework with and without SIMD parallelization to the OpenMP MIMD parallelization with and without the compiler vectorization. Comparing `MIMD+SIMD` to `OpenMP-vec`, more than 3 times speedup is achieved in Kmeans and NBC, due to the better SIMD parallelization and efficient MIMD parallelism. For Heat3D, OpenMP with compiler vectorization can provide good performance, but our parallel framework still outperforms the OpenMP version, due to the more efficient MIMD parallelism. Sobel, where SIMD parallelization is not achieved by the

compiler, our framework gains significant speedups compared to the OpenMP version.

Now, focusing just on MIMD parallelization, our parallel framework still obtains better performance compared to OpenMP. The benefits of our framework are modest for Kmeans and stencil computations, but more significant for NBC and the two irregular applications. Overall, combining both MIMD and SIMD parallelization, our framework is better for all six applications, has relative speedup of 2.5 or better for five of the six applications, and for the two irregular reductions, it has an improvement by a factor of 4 and 7, respectively. As discussed throughout the paper, these advantages come from a number of factors, e.g., our framework can vectorize an irregular kernel with indirection-based memory accesses, while OpenMP compiler cannot, and pattern-aware MIMD partitioning and scheduling can avoid locking overheads.

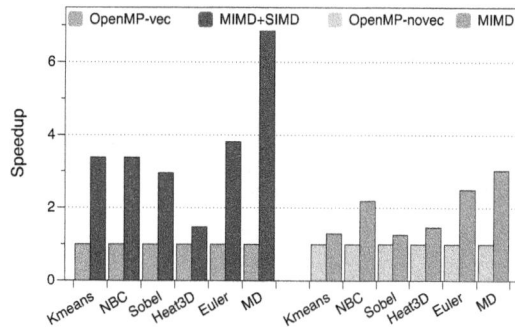

Figure 7: Benefits of MIMD+SIMD Execution in our Framework (Comparison with `OpenMP-vec` - left) and MIMD-only execution (Comparison with `OpenMP-novec` - right)

6. RELATED WORK

Intel SSE has been a part of the x86 since 1999, and there have been many efforts to automatically accelerate various applications using these instructions. For vectorizing stencils, memory alignment is a key problem, which was addressed by Eichenberger *et al.* [7] and Nuzman *et al.* [20] with data reorganization methods. More Recently, Henretty *et al.* [9] propose a system that involved improving data locality and utilizing short-vector SIMD optimizations, and Kong *et al.* [15] designed a Polyhedral compiler to perform loop transformation, optimization and vectorization for imperfectly nested loops.

Vectorizing irregular applications on SSE has also gained considerable interest in recent years. Kim and Han [14] propose a compiler method to generate efficient SIMD code for irregular kernels containing indirection based memory accesses. However, their work is on Cell SPU, with much shorter SIMD unit compared to the Xeon Phi and their method primarily focuses on intra-iteration vectorization. We focus on aggressive inter-iteration parallelism, consistent with presence of wide SIMD lanes. Tian *et al.* [26] provided an extension to the current directive vectorization methods to support function call. ISPC [22] provides a compiler based solution supporting function calls, SOA data structure, and control flow. The focus of our work is different, as we are providing a template based runtime solution for auto-vectorization. It utilizes the knowledge of patterns to automatically conduct data reorganization for different patterns. Moreover, it can also help resolving data dependencies in runtime, which is difficult to be handled for compiler solutions. Ren *et al.* [23] design a *virtual machine* together with domain-specific *bytecodes* method for pointer data traversals. There are also efforts on hand-optimizing irregular applications on SSE and other vector units [24, 13].

Some of the GPU compilation efforts have a similar favor, because SIMT is closely related to SIMD. This includes work on parallelizing stencil applications on GPUs [5, 18, 19, 10, 4]. For irregular applications on GPU, the coalesced memory access problem has also been addressed [28, 29]. However, because of the differences in the architectures (e.g. lack of atomic stores), our data reorganization methods are different. Overall, as compared to the existing work on SIMD compilation, the key distinctive aspects of our work are: 1) handling branches in a general way, 2) exploiting features in the IMCI instruction set, 3) using knowledge of communication patterns for runtime data reorganization, and 4) use of an overloaded function approach, which is unlike all previous efforts on SIMD parallelization, and can simplify the compiler code generation in the future.

There are also many efforts to parallelize various applications on Xeon Phi, which includes the work of Liu *et al.* [16] on Sparse Matrix-Vector Multiplication, Pennycook *et al.* [21] on parallelizing a Molecular Dynamic application, and Lu *et al.* [17] on optimizing the MapReduce framework. We have, to the best of our knowledge,

offered the first general and end-to-end system for exploiting both MIMD and SIMD parallelism on the Xeon Phis.

7. CONCLUSIONS

This paper has presented and evaluated a framework for parallelization on the Xeon Phi coprocessors. Two distinct aspects of our work are 1) use of the knowledge of underlying patterns to perform job partitioning and scheduling in MIMD setting and data reorganization for SIMD parallelization, and 2) a very different approach for SIMD code execution, based on the implementation of overloaded functions, with runtime management of masks. Overall, we perform SIMD parallelization in presence of control flow, irregular accesses, and reductions, unlike previous work with SSE-like instruction sets. Moreover, our work can also be seen as providing a CUDA-like language (and its implementation) for using SSE-like instruction sets.

8. REFERENCES

[1] http://www.top500.org/lists/2013/11/.
[2] http://dournac.org/info/parallel_heat3d.
[3] K. Asanovic, R. Bodik, B. C. Catanzaro, J. J. Gebis, P. Husbands, K. Keutzer, D. A. Patterson, W. L. Plishker, J. Shalf, S. W. Williams, et al. The landscape of parallel computing research: A view from berkeley. Technical Report EECS-2006-183, EECS Department, University of California, Berkeley, 2006.
[4] L. Chen, X. Huo, and G. Agrawal. Scheduling methods for accelerating applications on architectures with heterogeneous cores. In *HCW13*, 2013.
[5] K. Datta, M. Murphy, V. Volkov, S. Williams, J. Carter, L. Oliker, D. A. Patterson, J. Shalf, and K. A. Yelick. Stencil computation optimization and auto-tuning on state-of-the-art multicore architectures. In *SC*, page 4. IEEE/ACM, 2008.
[6] J. Dokulil, E. Bajrovic, S. Benkner, S. Pllana, M. Sandrieser, and B. Bachmayer. Efficient hybrid execution of c++ applications using intel xeon phi coprocessor. *CoRR*, abs/1211.5530, 2012.
[7] A. E. Eichenberger, P. Wu, and K. O'Brien. Vectorization for simd architectures with alignment constraints. In *PLDI*, pages 82–93. ACM, 2004.
[8] T. Henretty, K. Stock, L.-N. Pouchet, F. Franchetti, J. Ramanujam, and P. Sadayappan. Data layout transformation for stencil computations on short-vector simd architectures. In *CC'11/ETAPS'11*, pages 225–245, Berlin, Heidelberg, 2011. Springer-Verlag.
[9] T. Henretty, R. Veras, F. Franchetti, L.-N. Pouchet, J. Ramanujam, and P. Sadayappan. A stencil compiler for short-vector simd architectures. In *ICS*, pages 13–24, 2013.
[10] J. Holewinski, L.-N. Pouchet, and P. Sadayappan. High-performance code generation for stencil computations on gpu architectures. In *Proceedings of the international conference on Supercomputing*, pages 311–320. ACM, 2012.
[11] X. Huo, V. Ravi, W. Ma, and G. Agrawal. An execution strategy and optimized runtime support for parallelizing irregular reductions on modern gpus. In *Proceedings of the international conference on Supercomputing*, pages 2–11. ACM, 2011.
[12] A. K. Jain and R. C. Dubes. *Algorithms for Clustering Data*. Prentice-Hall, Inc., Upper Saddle River, NJ, USA, 1988.
[13] C. Kim, J. Chhugani, N. Satish, E. Sedlar, A. Nguyen, T. Kaldewey, V. Lee, S. Brandt, and P. Dubey. FAST: Fast Architecture Sensitive Tree Search on Modern CPUs and GPUs. In *Proceedings of the International Conference on Management of Data*. ACM, 2010.
[14] S. Kim and H. Han. Efficient simd code generation for irregular kernels. *ACM SIGPLAN Notices*, 47(8):55–64, 2012.
[15] M. Kong, R. Veras, K. Stock, F. Franchetti, L.-N. Pouchet, and P. Sadayappan. When polyhedral transformations meet simd code generation. In *Proceedings of the 34th ACM SIGPLAN conference on Programming language design and implementation*, pages 127–138. ACM, 2013.
[16] X. Liu, M. Smelyanskiy, E. Chow, and P. Dubey. Efficient sparse matrix-vector multiplication on x86-based many-core processors. In *Proceedings of the 27th international ACM conference on supercomputing*, pages 273–282. ACM, 2013.
[17] M. Lu, L. Zhang, H. P. Huynh, Z. Ong, Y. Liang, B. He, R. S. M. Goh, and R. Huynh. Optimizing the mapreduce framework on intel xeon phi coprocessor. *CoRR*, abs/1309.0215, 2013.
[18] J. Meng and K. Skadron. A performance study for iterative stencil loops on gpus with ghost zone optimizations. *International Journal of Parallel Programming*, 39(1):115–142, 2011.
[19] A. D. Nguyen, N. Satish, J. Chhugani, C. Kim, and P. Dubey. 3.5-d blocking optimization for stencil computations on modern cpus and gpus. In *SC*, pages 1–13. IEEE, 2010.
[20] D. Nuzman, I. Rosen, and A. Zaks. Auto-vectorization of interleaved data for simd. In *PLDI*, pages 132–143. ACM, 2006.
[21] S. Pennycook, C. Hughes, M. Smelyanskiy, and S. Jarvis. Exploring simd for molecular dynamics, using intel xeon processors and intel xeon phi coprocessors. In *IPDPS*, 2013.
[22] M. Pharr and W. R. Mark. ispc: A spmd compiler for high-performance cpu programming. In *Innovative Parallel Computing (InPar), 2012*, pages 1–13. IEEE, 2012.
[23] B. Ren, G. Agrawal, J. R. Larus, T. Mytkowicz, T. Poutanen, and W. Schulte. Simd parallelization of applications that traverse irregular data structures. In *Code Generation and Optimization (CGO), 2013 IEEE/ACM International Symposium on*, pages 1–10. IEEE, 2013.
[24] J. Sewall, J. Chhugani, C. Kim, N. Satish, and P. Dubey. PALM: Parallel Architecture-Friendly Latch-Free Modifications to B+ Trees on Many-Core Processors. *PVLDB*, 4(11):795–806, 2011.
[25] P.-N. Tan, M. Steinbach, and V. Kumar. *Introduction to Data Mining, (First Edition)*. Addison-Wesley Longman Publishing Co., Inc., Boston, MA, USA, 2005.
[26] X. Tian, H. Saito, M. Girkar, S. Preis, S. Kozhukhov, A. G. Cherkasov, C. Nelson, N. Panchenko, and R. Geva. Compiling c/c++ simd extensions for function and loop vectorizaion on multicore-simd processors. In *IPDPS Workshops*, pages 2349–2358. IEEE Computer Society, 2012.
[27] S. Williams, D. D. Kalamkar, A. Singh, A. M. Deshpande, B. Van Straalen, M. Smelyanskiy, A. Almgren, P. Dubey, J. Shalf, and L. Oliker. Optimization of geometric multigrid for emerging multi- and manycore processors. SC '12, 2012.
[28] B. Wu, Z. Zhao, E. Z. Zhang, Y. Jiang, and X. Shen. Complexity analysis and algorithm design for reorganizing data to minimize non-coalesced memory accesses on gpu. In *Proceedings of the SIGPLAN symposium on Principles and practice of parallel programming*, 2013.
[29] E. Z. Zhang, Y. Jiang, Z. Guo, K. Tian, and X. Shen. On-the-fly elimination of dynamic irregularities for gpu computing. In *ASPLOS*, pages 369–380, 2011.

Unified On-chip Memory Allocation for SIMT Architecture

Ari B. Hayes and Eddy Z. Zhang
Department of Computer Science
Rutgers University
Piscataway, NJ 08554
{arihayes, eddy.zhengzhang} @cs.rutgers.edu

ABSTRACT

The popularity of general purpose Graphic Processing Unit (GPU) is largely attributed to the tremendous concurrency enabled by its underlying architecture – single instruction multiple thread (SIMT) architecture. It keeps the context of a significant number of threads in registers to enable fast "context switches" when the processor is stalled due to execution dependence, memory requests and etc. The SIMT architecture has a large register file evenly partitioned among all concurrent threads. Per-thread register usage determines the number of concurrent threads, which strongly affects the whole program performance. Existing register allocation techniques, extensively studied in the past several decades, are oblivious to the register contention due to the concurrent execution of many threads. They are prone to making optimization decisions that benefit single thread but degrade the whole application performance.

Is it possible for compilers to make register allocation decisions that can maximize the whole GPU application performance? We tackle this important question from two different aspects in this paper. We first propose an unified on-chip memory allocation framework that uses scratch-pad memory to help: (1) alleviate single-thread register pressure; (2) increase whole application throughput. Secondly, we propose a characterization model for the SIMT execution model in order to achieve a desired on-chip memory partition given the register pressure of a program. Overall, we discovered that it is possible to automatically determine an on-chip memory resource allocation that maximizes concurrency while ensuring good single-thread performance at compile-time. We evaluated our techniques on a representative set of GPU benchmarks with non-trivial register pressure. We are able to achieve up to 1.70 times speedup over the baseline of the traditional register allocation scheme that maximizes single thread performance.

Permission to make digital or hard copies of all or part of this work for personal or classroom use is granted without fee provided that copies are not made or distributed for profit or commercial advantage and that copies bear this notice and the full citation on the first page. Copyrights for components of this work owned by others than ACM must be honored. Abstracting with credit is permitted. To copy otherwise, or republish, to post on servers or to redistribute to lists, requires prior specific permission and/or a fee. Request permissions from permissions@acm.org.
ICS'14, June 10–13 2014, Munich, Germany.
Copyright 2014 ACM 978-1-4503-2642-1/14/06 ...$15.00.
http://dx.doi.org/10.1145/2597652.2597685.

Categories and Subject Descriptors

D.3.4 [**Programming Languages**]: Processors—*code generation, compilers, optimization*; D.1.3 [**Programming Techniques**]: Concurrent Programming—*parallel programming*

General Terms

Performance, Management

Keywords

GPU; Register Allocation; Shared Memory Allocation; Compiler Optimization; Concurrency

1. INTRODUCTION

Existing compilation techniques for on-chip memory resource allocation, including register allocation, mainly target single-thread performance. In the past several decades, efficient techniques have been studied and widely adopted in mainstream compilers. In the context of single instruction multiple threads (SIMT) architecture for general purpose Graphic Processing Unit (GPU), the whole program performance not only depends on single thread performance, but also the interaction between the group of threads that run concurrently – mainly the process to hide each other's latency caused by execution dependence, data request, synchronization and other reasons. The number of concurrent threads depends on the physical on-chip memory constraint as well as the per-thread on-chip memory demand from a given program. The latter mainly depends on compile-time decision. The traditional register allocation technique for CPU program tends to gives the maximal number of physical registers to a single thread according to its register pressure.

The goal of traditional register allocation technique is to minimize the number of register spills and maximize single thread performance. However, this strategy does not necessarily work well for programs running on SIMT architecture. Allocating registers according to a single thread's register pressure may lead to resource contention among concurrently executing threads and lead to sub-optimal performance. We show this phenomenon using the results of a case study over a set of important GPU applications in physics simulation, numerical analysis, and image processing [6] [20]. We control per-thread register count at compile-time and we compile one program into different versions over a range of register usage from 20 or 32[1]to the maximal register de-

---

[1]We choose 20 for Fermi and 32 for Kepler because this leads to the maximal number of concurrent threads. Having

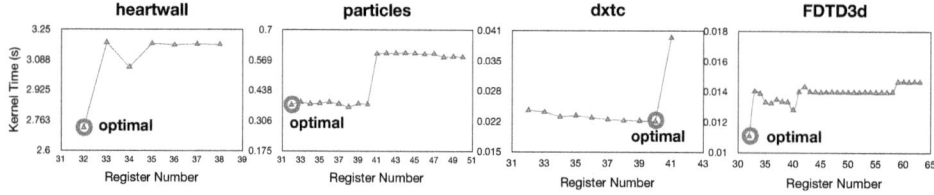

Figure 1: Performance of compiled programs with various per-thread register usage. The *x-axis* represents the per-thread register usage for every compiled version. The *y-axis* shows the running time in seconds. We used an NVIDIA Kepler [21] GTX680. The range of register count is from 32 to the maximal register demand.

mand. We show the results of four benchmarks *heartwall*, *particles*, *dxtc* and *FDTD3d* in Fig. 1. As can be seen in Fig. 1, using as many registers as needed to avoid spilling does not necessarily yield optimal performance. Furthermore, using the smallest number of registers per-thread does not necessarily yield best performance either. For instance, the *dxtc* benchmark's best per-thread register count is 40, which is too high to allow maximal occupancy, yet lower than the register demand.

A fundamental question arises: what is the best per-thread register usage for a given program on a given GPU architecture? An intuitive approach is to try all possible register count, compile the program and profile performance over different runs. However, exhaustive search is prohibitive when the range of possible register counts is large. It can be up to 255 for current GPUs[21]. Furthermore, depending on the input parameters, the number of profiling runs needed for a fully representative input set can be exponential.

To have a good answer to this fundamental question, we need to understand the implications of compile-time on-chip memory allocation decision on the efficiency of concurrent execution. Per-thread register usage, as well as other on-chip memory usage, is tightly correlated with the concurrency level a program can achieve. Using fewer registers per thread may lead to high concurrency, but more local memory loads and stores due to register spills. The local memory resides in DRAM, which has large access latency. How can we minimize per-thread register usage while maintaining good single-thread performance? And how can we strike a balance between the benefits brought by high concurrency and the overhead brought by extra off-chip memory operations?

In this paper, we study the implications of concurrent execution on many-core GPUs and exploit these implications to develop efficient compile-time on-chip memory allocation strategies. We address the above challenges from two main aspects. We first propose a unified on-chip memory allocation framework that not only uses registers but also on-chip scratch-pad memory, to store thread context. The scratch-pad memory acts as a buffering layer between registers and off-chip memory, alleviates single-thread register pressure, and increases the concurrency level. We develop a novel inter-procedure scratch-pad memory allocation scheme that maximizes reuse across procedure boundaries, and implement a prototype on-chip memory allocator. To ensure

compatibility, we only use scratch-pad memory not already allocated by the user. Secondly, we characterize the relationship between the program performance and the concurrency level. Our characterization predicts the desired concurrency level for a given program, and guides the selection of per-thread register count and scratch-pad memory usage.

There is a large body of research work on register allocation for CPUs and embedded processors [4] [5] [23] [12] [22] [3] [7]. They have shown promising results for single-thread applications. Some studies investigated scratch-pad memory allocation techniques on embedded architectures [9] [17] [26], but not on GPUs equipped with a bulk synchronous parallel (BSP) execution model. Gebhart and others [11] proposed techniques to dynamically partition on-chip memory into cache, scratch-pad and register memory according to application's register/scratch-pad memory demand with architecture support. However, it does not address the problems of how to reduce and how to determine register pressure for a given program. Overall, there is a lack of exploration in the implications of compile-time on-chip memory allocation on the concurrent execution efficiency of GPU applications.

In this paper, we propose efficient on-chip memory allocation techniques to enable maximal utilization of many-core GPU processors. We summarize our contributions as follows:

- **On-Chip Memory Allocation** We build an unified on-chip memory allocation framework for GPU applications. We offload register pressure to scratch-pad memory when necessary and we determine the corresponding per-thread register and scratch-pad memory usage for maximal concurrency level. Under this framework, we develop a novel inter-procedure on-chip memory allocation strategy, which maximizes the reuse of on-chip memory across procedure boundaries.

- **Concurrency-oriented Program Analysis** We reveal that severe resource contention can be caused by static memory resource allocation for GPU programs. For the first time, we address the problem of mapping GPU program features to its achievable concurrency and its desirable concurrency level. We propose efficient characterization model to determine if increased concurrency level will always yield better whole program performance. Our model is a pure static model and yet it is effective.

- **Implemented Allocator for Real GPU Systems** We reverse engineered the NVIDIA hardware ISA and

---

a smaller per-thread register count does not improve concurrency; it only degrades single thread performance, leading to worse performance overall.

294

implemented our prototype on-chip memory allocator for programs that run on real GPUs. Our approach can be readily deployed and does not require any architecture level extension.

The rest of the paper is outlined as follows: Section 2 reviews background on GPU programming model. Section 3 details our unified on-chip memory allocation framework. Section 4 describes program characterization and concurrency selection techniques. Section 5 and Section 6 respectively analyzes experiment results and presents related work.

2. BACKGROUND

Although the GPU as a whole acts as a single instruction multiple thread (SIMT) processor, with different threads following different execution paths, it has small groups of threads execute in lockstep, in the manner of a single instruction multiple data (SIMD) processor. Such a SIMD-like processor is called a Streaming Multi-Processor (SM) in NVIDIA terminology. We use NVIDIA terminology to describe GPU architecture throughout this paper. A group of threads that run in lockstep on one SM is called a thread warp. A thread warp is the minimal scheduling unit on every SM. When one thread warp yields an SM, if there is another ready thread warp, it will be scheduled to run. Otherwise the SM processor remains idle until one thread warp is ready. Typically there is a much larger number of active warps than the total number of SMs. All of their states are saved in registers. When one thread warp is swapped out of the processor, its states remain in registers. When one thread warp is switched in to run, it does not need to load its states from off-chip memory into registers unless per-thread register allocation is not enough to hold its state. Therefore it is different from a traditional CPU "context switch". A set of warps form a block, whose threads share access to the same partition of scratch-pad memory. A set of blocks forms a grid, which is launched by the same function. A function that runs on GPU is called a *kernel function* .

There are two types of memory on a GPU card – on-chip memory and off-chip memory. On-chip memory includes registers, scratch-pad memory, and caches. Registers are the fastest on-chip memory storage. Every SM has a large register file and it is divided evenly among co-running threads. Since every thread executes the same *kernel function*, it uses the same number of registers. At one time, only a limited number of threads can run simultaneously due to hardware constraints on the size of register and scratch-pad memory. We refer to these threads as *active* threads. A *kernel function* typically launches a significant number of threads which are further partitioned into multiple batches of *active* threads. A batch does not yield the SMs until all threads within it complete execution. Only thread warps within the same batch can co-run and help hide each other's instruction latency. Every GPU architecture with different computing capabilities also specifies the maximal hardware allowed *active* threads per SM (*active* is used in NVIDIA terminology, however we denote these threads as concurrent threads throughout this paper). In NVIDIA terminology, the ratio between the actual number of active threads and the hardware limit is defined as *occupancy*, which is a number between 0 and 1.

Another important type of on-chip memory is scratch-pad memory. It is referred to as *shared memory* in CUDA. For the rest of the paper, we use *shared memory* to refer to GPU scratch-pad memory. The shared memory can be managed explicitly by software. It is fast, with a latency of several cycles, comparable to the L1 cache. Shared memory is also equally partitioned among different threads.

Off-chip memory includes *global memory* and *local memory*, which might be a hundred times slower than registers. *Local memory* is used to store local variables for every procedure, and is manageable during compile-time. If a register is spilled to off-chip memory, it resides in local memory. *Global memory* can be explicitly managed by programmers. Other types of off-chip memory include *constant* memory, *texture* memory and etc. They are used for special purposes, such as read-only memory storage or multi-dimensional data locality.

3. UNIFIED ON-CHIP MEMORY ALLOCATION

3.1 Framework Overview

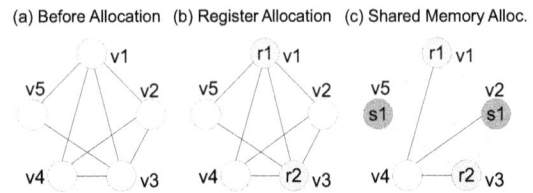

Figure 2: Unified On-Chip Memory Allocation

In this Section, we describe our transformation framework that uses shared memory to store local variables and to alleviate register pressure, which ultimately leads to better GPU concurrency and whole program performance. This framework uses shared memory to store live variables that cannot fit in registers, as if we are spilling registers into shared memory. We perform register allocation first and select the variables that can stay in registers. For the rest of the variables, we perform shared memory allocation and choose a subset of them to be stored in shared memory.

The target of the unified on-chip memory allocation is to store as many local variables into a fixed number of registers and shared memory slots as possible. We treat both registers and shared memory as one type of memory – the on-chip memory. Then we perform on-chip memory allocation as if we are performing register allocation for traditional CPU programs. We illustrate this idea in Fig. 2. Assume we have two registers, one shared memory slot, and one local memory slot. In Fig. 2 (a), we show the interference graph of five local variables $v1, v2, v3, v4, v5$. Two variables interfere with each other if they are both live at one or more instructions. It implies the two variables cannot be assigned to the same register or shared memory slot. If two variables interfere, there is an edge between the nodes representing them. In Fig. 2 (b), we show the result after register allocation. Variables $v1$ and $v2$ are assigned to registers $r1$ and $r2$ respectively. Now we have three variables that are not assigned and we have one shared memory slot. In Fig. 2 (c), we assign variables $v2$ and $v5$ to shared memory slot $s1$. By this step, we have completed assigning as many variables as we can to registers and shared memory. We then let the last variable *v4* stay in local memory. The minimal number of variables to be stored in local memory is 1 in this case.

Register allocation techniques have been extensively studied in the past three decades [4] [5] [23] [12] [22] [3] [7]. However, they mainly focus on single procedure register allocation. A few of them [15] [8] have studied reuse of registers across procedures but mainly focus on minimizing register pressure penalty at procedure calls. Typically, the content of most of the registers in the caller procedure are saved in local memory at procedure calls so that the registers can be reused in the callee procedure. Previous work [15] [8] avoid saving all the registers when procedure calls happen by determining if the registers will be used or not in the callee procedure. We leverage the register allocation algorithms for single procedure on-chip memory allocation and we develop an algorithm that maximizes reuse of on-chip memory across procedure boundaries. We describe this approach in Section 3.2.

In summary, with a given number of registers and shared memory, our unified on-chip memory allocation framework performs both register allocation and shared memory allocation. To separate the coupling effects from other phases of compilation, we build a experiment platform that takes binary as input. As in the binary file, the other phases like instruction scheduling have already completed, and we can simply replace the live variable accesses as shared memory access or off-chip memory accesses and add corresponding instructions. Therefore, the only effect we are testing is the placement of live variables. We use the binary generated by *nvcc* with a fixed register count. Then we analyze the other variables that are spilled into local memory and transform them correspondingly given a fixed number of shared memory slots. The NVIDIA GPU hardware instruction set architecture (ISA) and application binary interface (ABI) is proprietary. We reverse engineered part of the ISA and ABI for CUDA computing capability 3.0 with information from the open source project *asfermi* [13] on CUDA computing capability 2.0. We are able to decode the instructions, parse the assembly code and perform data flow analysis. In the following section, we elaborate inter-procedure shared memory allocation.

3.2 Shared Memory Allocation

3.2.1 *Inter-procedure Shared Memory Reuse*

We start describing our technique on enhancing inter-procedure reuse of shared memory with an example. Note that CUDA does not allow objects with virtual functions to be parameters, and every CUDA kernel we have seen has a call graph which can be determined statically.

We first show that there are opportunities to reuse shared memory slots across procedure calls. In Fig. 3, we show the stack status of a call sequence that involves three procedures: *proc_A, proc_B, proc_C* . *proc_A* calls *proc_B*. *proc_B* calls *proc_C*. Assume the stack memory space for every procedure can hold exactly four different variables. This means at any instruction in this procedure, at most four variables can be live at the same time. The variables that are live when *proc_A* calls *proc_B* are stored in locations *La1*, *La3*. In *proc_B*, when *proc_C* is called, variables are saved in locations *Lb2* and *Lb3*. In Fig. 3, we first show what the call stack looks like with traditional CPU procedure local memory management – labeled as *traditional*. The cells with dark

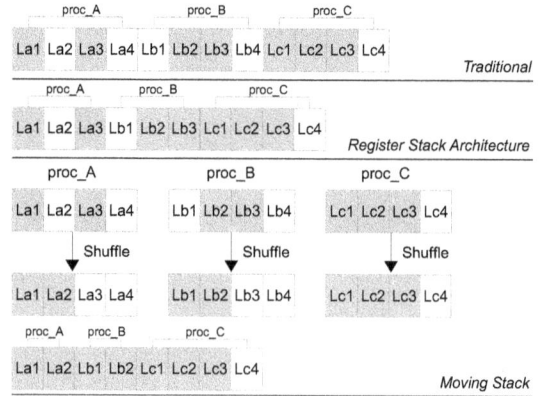

Figure 3: Reuse shared memory across procedure boundaries

background represent that the variable in the corresponding location is live when another procedure is called. With the traditional approach, we can see that the local memory space of different procedures in the call sequence is stacked. Therefore, for these three procedures, the size of the local memory space needed in the call context is 12 slots, assuming one slot can hold one variable. Even if some variables are not live when a procedure is called, the memory stack is incremented from its original maximal stack depth. This is because the size of local memory for a CPU procedure is trivial compared to the size of the off-chip memory.

In the second approach described in Fig. 3, we show a CPU architecture that utilizes a register stack when an architecture has relatively large register space to hold callee-saved registers across multiple procedures [7]. This is only made possible with special architecture support [7]. This architecture utilizes the available register region at the end of the register stack when a procedure is called. In the subfigure marked as *Register Stack Architecture* in Fig. 3, *proc_B* can reuse the last available slot in *proc_A*'s stack, and its stack pointer starts from the end of *La3*. Similarly, *proc_C* can reuse the last slot in the stack for *proc_B*. In this case, we use 10 slots in the stack. This approach is related to inter-procedure register usage, but it can be applied to shared memory allocation across procedure boundaries. It saves 2 slots compared to the approach denoted as *Traditional* in Fig. 3. However, there are still slots that are not used when *proc_B* and *proc_C* are called.

In the third approach described in Fig. 3, we show our approach – *Moving Stack* approach, which minimizes unused stack space when there are nested procedure calls. Our resource allocator emits instructions to be inserted in the original binary, which shuffles variables in the stack so that the used variables will be stored in consecutive memory space. Then we emit code to shift the stack pointer before the callee procedure is invoked. For instance, in Fig. 3 *Moving Stack* section, when *proc_B* is called, the variable in *La3* is shuffled to the second slot. Then we let *proc_B* use the space from *La3*. Similarly, when *proc_B* calls *proc_C*, we move the variable in *Lb3* to *Lb1*. Therefore *proc_C* can use the third slot in *proc_B*'s stack space, which is the 6th slot in the overall runtime stack space. In this case, we use 8 slots in total and no local memory slot is wasted. Compared to the original case that uses 12 slots, we save more than 30% stack space.

3.2.2 Inter-procedure Shared Memory Assignment

In the last section, we presented an approach to maximize the reusability of shared memory slots across procedures. If we have a large amount of shared memory to hold all local variables, then we can directly start assigning shared memory slots to individual variables. However, the shared memory is a scarce resource, as its size is the same or even smaller than the register file size. Therefore, we need to select a subset of local variables to reside in shared memory. Meanwhile, we need to determine how many shared memory slots every procedure gets assigned. Then we can perform shared memory assignment on a per-procedure basis.

In this Section, we describe our approach to map selected local memory variables to shared memory variables. We define *Live-on-exit* to be set of variables live at the exit of an instruction. *Max-live* is defined as the maximum number of simultaneously live variables at the exit of an instruction. *Max-live* of a procedure that does not call any other procedure is easy to acquire. We can traverse all instructions in the procedure and pick the largest *Live-on-exit* set. For procedures that call other procedure calls, we propose a recursive approach built on the following idea. We obtain the number of live variables for an instruction that calls another procedure P_{callee} as the sum of its local $|Live\text{-}on\text{-}exit|$ and $Max\text{-}live(P_{callee})$. If the *Max-live* of the callee procedure is unknown, we recurse into the callee procedure to find its *Max-live*.

Assume we have N_{smem} available shared memory slots. If *Max-live* of the main GPU kernel function is greater than N_{smem}, we need to prune at least $Max\text{-}live$ - N_{smem} variables from the *Live-on-exit* sets and let these variables reside in local memory. Our heuristic approach ranks different variables based on a pre-defined priority function. We prune low priority variables until the updated *Max-live* is less than or equal to N_{smem}. This approach is simple, yet effective.

We rank local variables from different procedures and give them a global ranking. We first define a *composition instruction*. It is a list of 2-tuples used to specify a call sequence. If the instruction $inst_2$ at $func_0$ calls $func_1$, and instruction $inst_3$ at $func_1$ calls $func_2$, and the specific executing instruction in $func_2$ is $inst_0$, then the resulting composition is { ($func_0$, $inst_2$), ($func_1$, $inst_3$), ($func_2$, $inst_0$) }. The call context information exposed in a composition instruction helps keep track of caller instructions so that we can obtain the *Live-on-exit* set easily from a union of live variables at all relevant instructions in this calling context. Then we can compare these variables from different procedures as if they are from the same procedure.

Our inter-procedure variable pruning algorithm takes the following steps:

- **Step 1:** We find the set of all composition instructions whose *Live-on-exit* > N_{smem}. We call it the *Over-smem-limit* set.

- **Step 2:** For all live variables in the union of *live-on-exit var* sets of composition instructions in the *Over-smem-limit* set, we compute their priority values based on the priority function. We use the priority function of variable frequency in the union live variable set.

- **Step 3:** We eliminate one variable from the above set with lowest priority value and check whether *Max-live* is less than or equal to N_{smem} after this variable is

eliminated from all *Live-on-exit* sets. If it is, then we go to Step 4. Otherwise we go back to **Step 3**.

- **Step 4:** We have successfully pruned all the necessary variables. We return the set of variables that are candidates to be placed in shared memory.

Individual Shared Memory Slot Assignment.

The eliminated variables are the ones that stay in local memory and the rest are mapped to shared memory. With this information, we can compute up-to-date *Max-live* for every procedure again. This is used as the maximal number of shared memory slots assigned to every procedure. Then we perform shared memory slot assignment in a way similar to register allocation. We use a heuristic graph coloring approach that starts with the node of highest degree in the interference graph. We assign this node a shared memory slot that does not conflict with any of its neighbors that are already assigned. If there are multiple choices, then we choose the shared memory slot that was previously assigned to some other variable. We process every node. If a variable cannot be assigned to any shared memory slot without conflicting with its neighbors, we map it to local memory. If the interference graph has a chordal property, then we will not have any spills [22]. In most cases, we don't need to spill any shared-memory mapped variable into local memory.

4. GPU PROGRAM OCCUPANCY CHARACTERIZATION

Our transformation framework in Section 3 tackles the problem of minimizing local memory spills given a fixed amount of registers and shared memory. What would be the best amount of registers and shared memory to allocate for every running thread in any given GPU program? Given a typically much larger number of registers than on CPUs, usually in the scale of tens of thousands, we have many possible combinations of register count and shared memory consumption per thread. In this large search space, exhaustive search is prohibitive. In this section, we address the problem of finding best per-thread register and shared memory usage.

The number of registers and the amount of shared memory used per-thread determine the number of concurrent threads on every streaming processor. The number of concurrent threads can be estimated using the formula [2] below:

$$Active.Thread$$
$$= min(\frac{Total.Reg.Num}{PerThread.Reg.Num}, \frac{Total.Smem}{PerThread.Smem}).$$

Essentially, the specific questions on per-thread register and shared-memory usage all boil down to one fundamental question: what would be the most desirable concurrency level for any GPU program on a specific GPU architecture? If we know the best concurrency level, we can estimate per-thread register and shared memory usage by solving the above equation. The optimal concurrency level has

---

[2]The total number of threads is also bound by the register bank alignment and the thread block sizes for CUDA programs. This formula illustrates the idea that per-thread register/shared-memory usage dominates the number of concurrent threads. We use the GPU occupancy calculator [19] to get the accurate number of active threads based on all other factors in our experiments.

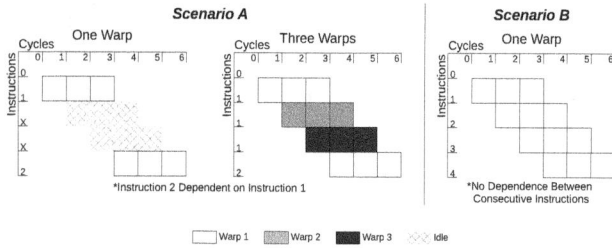

Figure 4: Concurrency Level Sensitivity

the capability of overlapping different types of operations and minimizing computing unit idleness. The number of different operations and how much they can be overlapped depends on the characteristics of a program. The problem of desired concurrency level is thus closely related to the problem of GPU program characterization in a many-thread cooperation/contention context. We describe our characterization approach first and concurrency level determination algorithm secondly.

4.1 Model Many-thread Running Process

We can start from the minimal concurrency level indicated by the maximal register/shared-memory request in the program, keep increasing the concurrency level by spilling live variables into shared memory and/or local memory, and keep increasing concurrency level until the point that the overhead of extra local memory spilling cannot be offset by the benefit brought by increased program concurrency. However, increasing concurrency level does not alway help; in fact it helps for most programs except one special case.

This exception is the case which we define as *computation intensive* case; it is when single thread instruction level parallelism (ILP) is inherently good in the program so that the latency is well hidden when a thread is running by itself. We illustrate it with an example in Fig. 4 *Scenario B*. In Fig. 4, assume every instruction takes three cycles, and the processor is able to dispatch one instruction in every cycle. The *x-axis* represents the cycle number. The *y-axis* represents the instruction number. In *Scenario B*, instruction 2 does not directly depend on instruction 1, and it can be dispatched immediately at the beginning of the second cycle. It is similar for instructions 2, 3, and 4. We only need one thread per-core in *Scenario B* to fully utilize the computation pipeline (one thread warp for one SM). In this cases, an increased concurrency level does not help improve performance, and they are not concurrency-bound cases. Next we show a concurrency-bound case in which increased concurrency helps improve performance. In Fig. 4 *Scenario A*, assume we have dependences between instruction 2 and instruction 1. Instruction 2 can't start until instruction 1 finishes. If we have only one warp, we cannot dispatch instruction 2 until the beginning of the fourth cycle in the *One Warp* case of *Scenario A*. The processor pipeline is thus not fully utilized. However, if we have three warps, in the *Three Warps* case in *Scenario A* of Fig. 4, at the beginning of the second cycle, we can schedule warp 2 to run instruction 1, and at the beginning of the third cycle, we can schedule warp 3 to run instruction 1. Therefore the processor pipeline is fully utilized. Overall, in *Scenario A*, we need three warps to fully utilize the computing units. Increasing the number of concurrent thread warps from one to three helps improve

performance. These cases belong to the concurrency-bound category.

In summary, we want to optimize concurrency-bound programs with multi-level on-chip memory resource allocation strategies. We use a heuristic metric to distinguish between programs that can benefit from increased concurrency and the ones that do not necessarily benefit from increased concurrency. The metric is the average dispatch interval between every two adjacent instructions in the same thread specified statically in the GPU binary code. The average dispatch interval reflects the ratio between the idle cycles and the busy cycles in the pipeline. As illustrated in Fig. 4 *scenario A* and *scenario B*, the dispatch intervals are 3 and 1 respectively. The minimal number of warps to fully utilize the processor pipeline happens to be 3 and 1 for these two cases respectively. The average dispatch interval [3] can also be used as an initial estimate of the number of active warps for every SM. We elaborate our algorithm for concurrency selection in next section.

4.2 Concurrency Level Search

The main idea of our concurrency level search algorithm is to make the benefits of increased concurrency outweigh the overhead of local memory spilling. With limited registers and shared memory, increasing the concurrency level may force live variables to be spilled into slow local memory. How many local memory spills can be allowed depends on the concurrency level we select. We start from an initially estimated number of active threads as the product of average dispatch interval and the number of cores per SM (every SM is the same so we discuss how to find concurrency level for every SM). Based on the initial estimate, we derive the number of registers and the amount of shared memory for every thread. We then perform shared memory allocation with the initial per-thread register number and shared memory amount. Then we check the number of local memory spills to see if we should decrease or increase the concurrency level. In this algorithm, we use a heuristic criteria to check whether a given concurrency level is good enough; we keep increasing concurrency level above the initial concurrency level if the criteria is met, or keep decreasing concurrency level below the initial concurrency level until the criteria is met. We set the criteria in a way that the local memory spilling overhead can be overlapped with the arithmetic and other non off-chip memory instructions. We use $COMPUTE\_inst_{trsf}$ to denote the number of instructions that are not off-chip memory instructions after transformation and we use MEM_inst_{trsf} to denote the number of off-chip memory instructions after transformation. We refer to this criteria as Computation Interleaving predicate – CI_pred and we describe it as follows:

$$CI_{pred} : \frac{COMPUTE\_inst_{trsf} * AD\_int}{MEM\_inst_{trsf}} > MAX\_cmratio$$

(1)

---

[3] NVIDIA kepler GPU architecture uses a static instruction scheduling approach instead of architecture based instruction scheduling. Dispatch interval is encoded in the instructions if we compile with nvcc for computing capability of 3.0 and above. We reverse-engineered the ISA and parsed instructions to get the dispatch interval for every two adjacent instructions.

```
┌─ Find Desired concurrency Level ──────────────────┐
│ 1: if ( Program is concurrency Bound) {           │
│ 2:    ActTnum = AD_interval * SM_cores;           │
│ 3:    (Reg,Smem) = getRegSmem(ActTnum);           │
│ 4:    transformProg(Reg,Smem);                    │
│ 5:    get(CL_pred);                               │
│ 6:    if (CI_pred) TraverseUp=TRUE;               │
│ 7:    else TraverseUp = FALSE;                    │
│ 8:    ActTnum_cur = ActTnum;                      │
│ 9:    if ( TraverseUp ) {                         │
│10:       while(ActTnum_cur < MaxThrd) {           │
│11:          get(CI_pred);                         │
│12:          if ( CI_pred )                        │
│13:             ActThrd_opt = ActTnum_cur;         │
│14:       ActTnum_cur += BlkSize; }                │
│15:    else if(ActTnum ≥ SmemFitTnum) {            │
│16:       while(ActTnum_cur > ActTnum_org) {       │
│17:          get(CI_pred);                         │
│18:          if (CI_pred ) {                       │
│19:             ActThrd_opt = ActTnum_cur;         │
│20:             break; }                           │
│21:          ActTnum_cur − = BlkSize; }            │
│22: else                                           │
│23:    ActThrd_opt = ActTnum_org;                  │
│24: return ActThrd_opt;                            │
└───────────────────────────────────────────────────┘
```

Figure 5: Concurrency Level Search

AD_int denotes the average instruction dispatch interval. We obtain this by decoding NVIDIA Kepler's binary ISA. $MAX\_cmratio$ is correlated with the number of cycles for an off-chip memory instruction; it is the number of computation instructions with a specific dispatch interval that are needed to hide the latency of one off-chip memory instruction. Its value varies from architecture to architecture. We obtain this parameter value by measuring the cycles of computation and off-chip memory instructions for a specific architecture. If the condition in Inequality 1 is satisfied, we consider this concurrency level to be beneficial. In our concurrency level search algorithm, if the initially estimated concurrency level is beneficial, we keep increasing it step by step (and we use thread block size as the step since it is the minimal unit to run on a SM). We choose the largest concurrency level which is beneficial. Otherwise, we keep decreasing the concurrency level step by step until we find the first concurrency level that is beneficial.

We illustrate the major components of our concurrency level search algorithm in Fig. 5. Note that when the algorithm traverses down, it stops when it hits a threshold $SmemFitTnum$. This is the number of concurrent threads which results in no spills into the off-chip memory, which means the live variables can completely fit into registers and shared memory. The variable $ActTnum$, denotes the number of active threads per SM, and the variable $ActThrd\_opt$ denotes the final number of active threads per SM we selected.

5. EVALUATION

In this section, we present our experiment results. We perform experiments on two different machine configurations.

One is NVIDIA Kepler GTX680. It has 8 streaming multi-processors (SM), with 192 cores on each of them and 1536 cores in total. It has CUDA computing capability 3.0. Every streaming multi-processor is equipped with 65536 registers and 48KB shared memory. The maximum number of concurrent threads that can run simultaneously on each streaming multi-processor is 2048. The second machine is configured with NVIDIA Fermi card - Tesla C2075. It has 448 cores in total, with 32 cores on each SM. It has CUDA computing capability 2.0. There are 32768 registers and 48KB shared memory per SM. The maximal number of concurrent threads that can run simultaneously is 1536. Notice that these two configurations impose different constraints on single-thread register count and single-thread shared memory with respect to maximal concurrency supported by hardware. We denote the Kepler card as *Kepler* and the Fermi card as *Fermi*.

We measured computation and off-chip memory instructions latencies with the *clock()* function. Normal algebra instructions like addition and subtraction take 9 cycles and an off-chip memory instruction takes between 300 and 400 cycles. Since reads and writes happen in parallel, we set the average of off-chip memory latency to be between 150-200. Therefore, we choose the larger one 200 and set the parameter $MAX\_cmratio$ in Section 4.2 to be 200. This parameter is used in our automatic occupancy level selection algorithm, and our experiments support this value as being effective.

To process a benchmark, we first extract the assembly code for the kernel function using NVIDIA binary listing tool *cuobjdump*. We decoded necessary parts of the binary instruction set for NVIDIA Kepler architecture, including scheduling instructions omitted by *cuobjdump*, based on *asfermi* [13]. Our binary analysis and modification pass is implemented with the *libelf* library. We implemented our parser with *flex and bison*.Our shared memory allocator then performs program analysis, determines the best occupancy level, and transforms the code. We use one fixed register as a shared-memory stack pointer. If necessary, we use a second fixed register to shuffle shared-memory slots for *Moving Stack* algorithm. Note that this process is done quickly, and takes less than a second on most benchmarks.

We evaluate our methods with seven benchmarks selected from the Rodinia benchmark suite 2.2 [6] and CUDA SDK 5.0. We choose them because they have non-trivial register demand. Note that a lot of benchmarks from Rodinia [6] and CUDA Computing SDK have a low register demand of below 20, which happens to enable maximal hardware supported concurrency for previous and current NVIDIA GPU architectures. Decreasing register pressure for these benchmarks will not help improve concurrency or improve single-thread performance. Our algorithm will choose not to transform these programs, thus we do not include them in discussion. We describe the list of benchmarks used for this paper in Table 1. *RegDemand* is the number of registers needed per-thread if no spilling to on-chip or off-chip memory happens. It is the default choice by nvcc and traditional CPU register allocation approach. *UserSmem* is the bytes of shared memory preallocated by the user per thread. Note that we only use the remaining shared memory left after users' preallocation, and we do not affect the existing concurrency when distributing the available shared memory among concurrent threads. *InstChange* is the increase in size to the transformed kernel function at the auto occupancy.

Benchmark	AppDomain	RegDemand		UserSmem		InstChange		CacheMissRate(%)	
		Fermi	Kepler	Fermi	Kepler	Fermi	Kepler	Fermi	Kepler
cfd [6]	Simulation	61	63	0.00	0.00	1.00	1.12	90.49/90.49	0.00/83.68
dxtc [20]	Imaging	43	49	10.00	12.00	1.03	1.00	32.81/54.39	0.00/0.00
FDTD3d [20]	Numerical Ana.	57	48	7.50	10.00	1.05	1.10	0.00/0.00	0.00/0.00
hotspot [6]	Simulation	36	39	12.00	12.00	1.03	1.03	0.00/48.26	0.00/43.09
imageDenoising [20]	Imaging	63	63	4.00	4.00	1.29	1.06	0.00/72.99	0.00/37.05
particles [20]	Simulation	50	52	0.00	0.00	1.09	1.12	0.00/44.44	0.00/43.41
recursiveGaussian [20]	Imaging	41	42	0.00	0.00	1.00	1.07	0.00/83.69	72.77/90.09

Table 1: Benchmark Description. AppDomain is the benchmark's application. RegDemand is the number of registers the compiler tries to use. UserSmem is the amount of user-allocated shared memory per thread. InstChange is the increase to the instruction count in the auto occupancy. CacheMissRate is the cache miss rate in the auto occupancy; the numerator is with use of shared memory after transformation, and the denominator is with purely global spills before transformation.

CacheMissRate lists cache miss rates for the auto occupancy before and after transformation.

We present both the results of automatically selected occupancy level through our approach, and the exhaustive search through all possible occupancy levels. When an occupancy level is selected, per-thread register and shared-memory limits are determined by the NVIDIA GPU occupancy calculator [19].

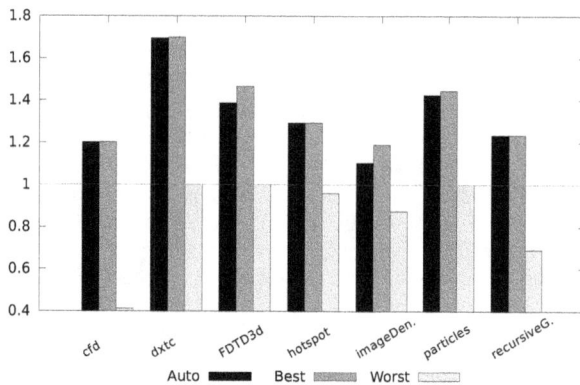

Figure 6: Kepler Performance Results. The Auto bar shows speedup with automatically selected occupancy. The Best bar shows highest speedup among all occupancies by exhaustive search. The Worse bar shows worst speedup among all occupancies. For our baseline, we used the runtime when compiling each benchmark with default settings.

We first present the overall performance results for Kepler in Fig. 6. Each group of bars along the x-axis represents a benchmark. The y-axis represents a particular kernel's speedup compared to its baseline. For our baselines, we compiled each benchmark using nvcc with the default settings, including no register limits. The first bar *Auto* represents the speedup at the concurrency level selected by our concurrency selector. The second bar *Best* represents the best speedup among all possible concurrency levels. The third bar *Worst* represents the speedup in the worst case among all different concurrency levels. The results demonstrate that the automatically transformed program is typically faster than the original, and in most cases is close to the best speedup (from an exhaustive search through concurrency levels). *FDTD3d* and *imageDenoising* fail to reach their best speedup due to our conservative algorithm, which

avoids the highest occupancies in this case due to the number of static memory operations. In our future work, we plan to incorporate dynamic analysis in order to allow more optimal selections. Overall, although no dynamic analysis is performed, we still have good performance improvement for these benchmarks. This demonstrates the importance of static on-chip memory resource allocation.

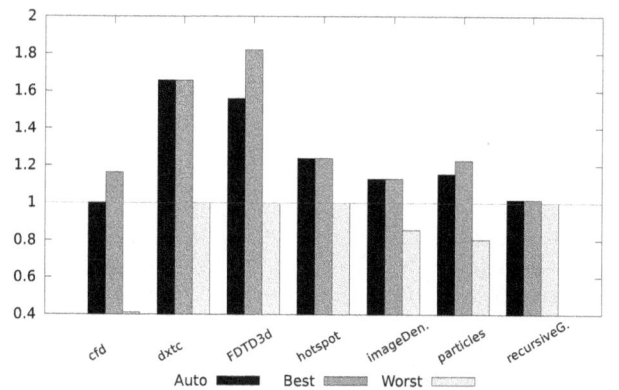

Figure 7: Fermi Performance Results. The Auto bar shows speedup with automatically selected occupancy. The Best bar shows highest speedup among all occupancies by exhaustive search. The Worse bar shows worst speedup among all occupancies. For our baseline, we used the runtime when compiling each benchmark with default settings.

Next we present the results for the Fermi GPU in Fig. 7. For our baseline, we compiled the benchmark using nvcc with the default settings, including no register limits except where necessary for the benchmark to run (due to hardware limitations). The bars and axes have the same meaning as in Fig. 6. Only the *cfd* benchmark here is not improved; this is because *cfd* has an unusually large number of memory instructions, even at the lowest occupancy, and so our conservative algorithm chooses not to increase the occupancy at all. Due to the many memory instructions, increasing the occupancy has less effect than in most benchmarks, regardless. The *particles* and especially the *FDTD3d* benchmarks also have auto speedups below their bestdue to the conservative algorithm choosing a lower occupancy than is optimal in these cases. The *recursiveGaussian* benchmark sees much less improvement than on Kepler. This has to do with the differing limitations of the hardware. On Kepler, a kernel can use up to 63 registers regardless of its block size, but on Fermi, programs with higher block size have a lower register limit, due to the smaller register file. Having a high block size, *recursiveGaussian* must be compiled with less registers to run at all, increasing the initial occupancy, and therefore lessening the extent to which it can be improved.

6. RELATED WORK

Many studies in the past few years have been proposed on register spilling between physical registers and off-chip global memory. A fundamental model is the graph coloring model [4]. In [2], the authors propose an integer linear program modeling of register allocation for CISC machines. In [27] and [14], the authors particularly tackled the problem of register spilling due to software pipelining in loops. Most of these previous studies are for sequential programs, instead of massively parallel architecture. In [1], the authors studied the register allocation schemes for vector machines. However, a vector processor is different from the SIMT processor on modern GPUs. Sampaio and others [24] proposed a divergence aware spilling strategy to save memory, but did not consider concurrency.

The previous studies on GPU also investigate the implication of interaction between concurrent threads on latency minimization. The authors of [25] point out that the ability for memory latency hiding among different vector thread groups is critical. The authors present a model for GPU programs that predicts the performance by calculating *memory warp parallelism (MWP)* and *computation warp parallelism (CWP)*. While this work focused on modeling of concurrent execution, it did not discuss how to achieve the desired concurrency level. Other relevant GPU work includes topics such as GPU exception handling [18], where register states need to be restored for resuming execution after exception, and energy saving [10], where the location of registers is critical to energy consumption because the distance between the registers and processors determines the amount of energy consumed during data movement, and hardware register space saving [29],which combines SRAM and DRAM to store more bits into the die area. In [28], a means of optimizing shared memory is explored in order to prevent user-allocated shared memory from reducing occupancy, whereas our approach makes use of non user-allocated shared memory to lessen the cost of improving occupancy. In [16], an integer programming technique is used to allocate scalars and arrays in shared memory, in order to optimize the code at a higher level than we consider. Most of the aforementioned studies on GPU architecture extensions are implemented and evaluated in hardware simulators.

7. CONCLUSION

In this paper, we propose a unified on-chip memory resource allocation framework for GPU programs. Our on-chip memory resource framework predicts near-optimal partition of on-chip memory resources and adapts GPU program to the best concurrency level according to program characteristics without any online or off-line profiling.

Acknowledgements

We thank Dmitry Mikushin for his insights on decoding NVIDIA Kepler hardware instruction set architecture. We thank the anonymous reviewers for their invaluable comments. This material is based upon the work supported by Rutgers University Research Council Grant and the Department of Education GAANN fellowship. Any opinions, findings, and conclusions or recommendations expressed in this material are those of the authors and do not necessarily reflect the views of our sponsors.

8. REFERENCES

[1] R. Allen and K. Kennedy, "Vector register allocation," *Computers, IEEE Transactions on*, vol. 41, no. 10, pp. 1290 –1317, oct 1992.

[2] A. W. Appel and L. George, "Optimal spilling for cisc machines with few registers," in *Proceedings of the ACM SIGPLAN 2001 conference on Programming language design and implementation*, ser. PLDI '01. New York, NY, USA: ACM, 2001, pp. 243–253. [Online]. Available: http://doi.acm.org/10.1145/378795.378854

[3] I. D. Baev, "Techniques for region-based register allocation," in *Proceedings of the 7th annual IEEE/ACM International Symposium on Code Generation and Optimization*, ser. CGO '09. Washington, DC, USA: IEEE Computer Society, 2009, pp. 147–156. [Online]. Available: http://dx.doi.org/10.1109/CGO.2009.31

[4] G. J. Chaitin, "Register allocation & spilling via graph coloring," in *Proceedings of the 1982 SIGPLAN symposium on Compiler construction*, ser. SIGPLAN '82. New York, NY, USA: ACM, 1982, pp. 98–105. [Online]. Available: http://doi.acm.org/10.1145/800230.806984

[5] G. J. Chaitin, M. A. Auslander, A. K. Chandra, J. Cocke, M. E. Hopkins, and P. W. Markstein, "Register allocation via coloring," in *Computer Languages*, vol. 6, no. 1, 1981, pp. 47–57.

[6] S. Che, M. Boyer, J. Meng, D. Tarjan, J. W. Sheaffer, S.-H. Lee, and K. Skadron, "Rodinia: A benchmark suite for heterogeneous computing," in *Proceedings of the 2009 IEEE International Symposium on Workload Characterization (IISWC)*, ser. IISWC '09. Washington, DC, USA: IEEE Computer Society, 2009, pp. 44–54. [Online]. Available: http://dx.doi.org/10.1109/IISWC.2009.5306797

[7] Y. Choi and H. Han, "Optimal register reassignment for register stack overflow minimization," *ACM Trans. Archit. Code Optim.*, vol. 3, no. 1, pp. 90–114, Mar. 2006. [Online]. Available: http://doi.acm.org/10.1145/1132462.1132467

[8] F. C. Chow, "Minimizing register usage penalty at procedure calls," in *Proceedings of the ACM SIGPLAN 1988 conference on Programming Language design and Implementation*, ser. PLDI '88. New York, NY, USA: ACM, 1988, pp. 85–94. [Online]. Available: http://doi.acm.org/10.1145/53990.53999

[9] A. Dominguez, N. Nguyen, and R. K. Barua, "Recursive function data allocation to scratch-pad memory," in *Proceedings of the 2007 international conference on Compilers, architecture, and synthesis for embedded systems*, ser. CASES '07. New York, NY, USA: ACM, 2007, pp. 65–74. [Online]. Available: http://doi.acm.org/10.1145/1289881.1289897

[10] M. Gebhart, D. R. Johnson, D. Tarjan, S. W. Keckler, W. J. Dally, E. Lindholm, and K. Skadron, "A hierarchical thread scheduler and register file for energy-efficient throughput processors," *ACM Trans. Comput. Syst.*, vol. 30, no. 2, pp. 8:1–8:38, Apr. 2012. [Online]. Available: http://doi.acm.org/10.1145/2166879.2166882

[11] M. Gebhart, S. W. Keckler, B. Khailany, R. Krashinsky, and W. J. Dally, "Unifying primary cache, scratch, and register file memories in a throughput processor," in *Proceedings of the 2012 45th Annual IEEE/ACM International Symposium on Microarchitecture*, ser. MICRO '12. Washington, DC, USA: IEEE Computer Society, 2012, pp. 96–106. [Online]. Available: http://dx.doi.org/10.1109/MICRO.2012.18

[12] S. Hack, D. Grund, and G. Goos, "Register allocation for programs in ssa-form," in *In Compiler Construction 2006, volume 3923 of LNCS*. Springer Verlag, 2006.

[13] Y. Hou, J. Lai, and D. Mikushin, "asfermi: An assembler for the nvidia fermi instruction set." [Online]. Available: http://code.google.com/p/asfermi/

[14] J. Llosa, M. Valero, E. Ayguadé, and A. González, "Hypernode reduction modulo scheduling," in *Proceedings of the 28th annual international symposium on Microarchitecture*, ser. MICRO 28. Los Alamitos, CA, USA: IEEE Computer Society Press, 1995, pp. 350–360. [Online]. Available: http://dl.acm.org/citation.cfm?id=225160.225211

[15] G.-Y. Lueh and T. Gross, "Call-cost directed register allocation," in *Proceedings of the ACM SIGPLAN 1997 conference on Programming language design and implementation*, ser. PLDI '97. New York, NY, USA: ACM, 1997, pp. 296–307. [Online]. Available: http://doi.acm.org/10.1145/258915.258942

[16] W. Ma and G. Agrawal, "An integer programming framework for optimizing shared memory use on gpus," in *High Performance Computing (HiPC), 2010 International Conference on*. IEEE, Dec 2010, pp. 1–10. [Online]. Available: http://dx.doi.org/10.1109/HIPC.2010.5713187

[17] R. McIlroy, P. Dickman, and J. Sventek, "Efficient dynamic heap allocation of scratch-pad memory," in *Proceedings of the 7th international symposium on Memory management*, ser. ISMM '08. New York, NY, USA: ACM, 2008, pp. 31–40. [Online]. Available: http://doi.acm.org/10.1145/1375634.1375640

[18] J. Menon, M. De Kruijf, and K. Sankaralingam, "igpu: exception support and speculative execution on gpus," in *Proceedings of the 39th International Symposium on Computer Architecture*, ser. ISCA '12. Piscataway, NJ, USA: IEEE Press, 2012, pp. 72–83. [Online]. Available: http://dl.acm.org/citation.cfm?id=2337159.2337168

[19] NVIDIA, "Cuda occupancy calculator." [Online]. Available: http://developer.download.nvidia.com/compute/cuda/CUDA_Occupancy_calculator.xls

[20] Nvidia, "Gpu computing sdk." [Online]. Available: https://developer.nvidia.com/gpu-computing-sdk

[21] NVIDIA, "Nvidia's next generation cuda compute architecture: Kepler gk110." [Online]. Available: http://www.nvidia.com/content/PDF/kepler/NVIDIA-Kepler-GK110-Architecture-Whitepaper.pdf

[22] J. Palsberg, "Register allocation via coloring of chordal graphs," in *Proceedings of the thirteenth Australasian symposium on Theory of computing - Volume 65*, ser. CATS '07. Darlinghurst, Australia, Australia: Australian Computer Society, Inc., 2007, pp. 3–3. [Online]. Available: http://dl.acm.org/citation.cfm?id=1273694.1273695

[23] M. Poletto and V. Sarkar, "Linear scan register allocation," *ACM Trans. Program. Lang. Syst.*, vol. 21, no. 5, pp. 895–913, Sep. 1999. [Online]. Available: http://doi.acm.org/10.1145/330249.330250

[24] D. N. Sampaio, E. Gedeon, F. M. Q. a. Pereira, and S. Collange, "Spill code placement for simd machines," in *Proceedings of the 16th Brazilian conference on Programming Languages*, ser. SBLP'12. Berlin, Heidelberg: Springer-Verlag, 2012, pp. 12–26. [Online]. Available: http://dx.doi.org/10.1007/978-3-642-33182-4_3

[25] J. Sim, A. Dasgupta, H. Kim, and R. Vuduc, "A performance analysis framework for identifying potential benefits in gpgpu applications," in *Proceedings of the 17th ACM SIGPLAN symposium on Principles and Practice of Parallel Programming*, ser. PPoPP '12. New York, NY, USA: ACM, 2012, pp. 11–22. [Online]. Available: http://doi.acm.org/10.1145/2145816.2145819

[26] S. Udayakumaran, A. Dominguez, and R. Barua, "Dynamic allocation for scratch-pad memory using compile-time decisions," *ACM Trans. Embed. Comput. Syst.*, vol. 5, no. 2, pp. 472–511, May 2006. [Online]. Available: http://doi.acm.org/10.1145/1151074.1151085

[27] J. Wang, A. Krall, M. A. Ertl, and C. Eisenbeis, "Software pipelining with register allocation and spilling," in *Proceedings of the 27th annual international symposium on Microarchitecture*, ser. MICRO 27. New York, NY, USA: ACM, 1994, pp. 95–99. [Online]. Available: http://doi.acm.org/10.1145/192724.192734

[28] Y. Yang, P. Xiang, M. Mantor, N. Rubin, and H. Zhou, "Shared memory multiplexing: A novel way to improve gpgpu throughput," in *Proceedings of the 21st International Conference on Parallel Architectures and Compilation Techniques*, ser. PACT '12. New York, NY, USA: ACM, 2012, pp. 283–292. [Online]. Available: http://doi.acm.org/10.1145/2370816.2370858

[29] W.-k. S. Yu, R. Huang, S. Q. Xu, S.-E. Wang, E. Kan, and G. E. Suh, "Sram-dram hybrid memory with applications to efficient register files in fine-grained multi-threading," in *Proceedings of the 38th annual international symposium on Computer architecture*, ser. ISCA '11. New York, NY, USA: ACM, 2011, pp. 247–258. [Online]. Available: http://doi.acm.org/10.1145/2000064.2000094

Galaxy: A High-Performance Energy-Efficient Multi-Chip Architecture Using Photonic Interconnects

Yigit Demir[†], Yan Pan[*], Seukwoo Song[‡], Nikos Hardavellas[†], John Kim[‡], and Gokhan Memik[†]

[†]Northwestern University
Dept. of Electrical Eng. and Computer Science
Evanston, IL, USA
yigit@u.northwestern.edu
{nikos, g-memik}@northwestern.edu

[*]Globalfoundries Inc.
Malta, NY, USA
panyan@gmail.com

[‡]KAIST
Dept. of Computer Science
Daejeon, Korea
jjk12@kaist.edu
sukwoo24@gmail.com

ABSTRACT

The scalability trends of modern semiconductor technology lead to increasingly dense multicore chips. Unfortunately, physical limitations in area, power, off-chip bandwidth, and yield constrain single-chip designs to a relatively small number of cores, beyond which scaling becomes impractical. Multi-chip designs overcome these constraints, and can reach scales impossible to realize with conventional single-chip architectures. However, to deliver commensurate performance, multi-chip architectures require a cross-chip interconnect with bandwidth, latency, and energy consumption well beyond the reach of electrical signaling.

We propose Galaxy, an architecture that enables the construction of a many-core "virtual chip" by connecting multiple smaller chiplets through optical fibers. The low optical loss of fibers allows the flexible placement of chiplets, and offers simpler packaging, power, and heat requirements. At the same time, the low latency and high bandwidth density of optical signaling maintain the tight coupling of cores, allowing the virtual chip to match the performance of a single chip that is not subject to area, power, and bandwidth limitations. Our results indicate that Galaxy attains speedup of 2.2x over the best single-chip alternatives with electrical or photonic interconnects (3.4x maximum), and 2.6x smaller energy-delay product (6.8x maximum). We show that Galaxy scales to 4K cores and attains 2.5x speedup at 6x lower laser power compared to a Macrochip with silicon waveguides.

Categories and Subject Descriptions

C.1.2 [**Computer Systems Organization**]: Multiprocessors—*Interconnection architectures;* B.4.3 [**Hardware**]: Interconnections—*Topology;* C.1.4 [**Computer Systems Organization**]: Parallel architectures

Keywords

Interconnection Networks; Nanophotonics; Energy Efficiency

1. INTRODUCTION

The physical limitations in area, yield, off-chip bandwidth, and power, limit the scalability of single-chip designs. Area and yield

considerations push for small die sizes, and the latest ITRS [8] models reflect the competitive requirements for affordability by targeting flat chip-size trends for both cost-performance and high-performance processors (140-260 mm^2). At the same time, while transistor counts grow exponentially, voltage scaling has slowed. This has lead to a dramatic increase in power density with decreasing feature size [11], creating chips that require a power budget beyond what is practical today to operate and leading to "dark silicon" [7,9,17]. In addition, the limited pin count and low efficiency of off-chip communication severely limit the off-chip bandwidth [23], and hamper the scalability and performance of future multicores, even for highly-parallel workloads [9].

Physical constraints limit single chip designs to either a relatively small number of cores, beyond which scaling becomes impractical, or to designs that trade single-core performance for high aggregate instruction throughput, which can only be achieved if all cores are simultaneously employed by the executing workload. For example, a single core in Intel i7-3960X has a peak theoretical performance of 187 *GFLOPS*, but only 6 such cores fit in the chip's area and power budget. In contrast, Intel Phi 5110P features 60 cores, but at only 17 *GFLOPS* per core, and NVIDIA GTX-680 features 1536 CUDA cores but at a paltry 2 *GFLOPS* each.

Aggregating together several discrete smaller dies instead of having a large one (*disintegration*) overcomes the area and yield limitations, as only few dies need to be replaced if they are faulty [3,5]. The total silicon area of the aggregate chip can even scale beyond reticle size limits, allowing the aggregate "virtual" chip to reach scales impossible to realize with a monolithic design (*macrochip integration*). At the same time, a monolithic design forces the use of a technology that is only the best average for all circuit applications that share the die (e.g., cores may strive for a small and fast 16nm process, while an analog component may be more economic to stay at an old 90nm technology node). Disintegration allows each application to optimize its technology independently, reaching a better global optimum design point. However, disintegration and macrochip integration may come at the cost of increased power density, if the dies reside within the same package, or the high energy and latency cost of communication across discrete chips. High power density would force the chips to run at a lower power budget to stay within the thermal envelope, hampering scalability and degrading performance. High-latency high-energy cross-chip communication would render large-scale macrochips impractical. An ideal design would **(a)** mitigate the area and yield constraints, **(b)** achieve a low power profile, and **(c)** provide high-bandwidth, low-latency and low-energy communication across the discrete dies, while **(d)** maintain high scalability. Known alternatives can break free of some physical limitations and satisfy some of these requirements, but not all.

3D-die stacking can ease the area and yield limitations by vertically connecting several smaller dies in a package with through-silicon-vias (TSVs). However, 3D-die stacking incurs significant challenges in power delivery and heat removal, and is best employed when the additional dies implement low-power applications (e.g., DRAM). Thus, 3D integration fails to provide low power density and high scalability (requirements b, d).

Silicon interposers (i.e., 2.5D integration) allow chips to connect laterally within the same package through "bridge" silicon chips, thus exploiting the high density of die-to-package and on-chip wires. However, interposers enable only small-size arrays of chips that can fit in a single package. Scalability is further limited by the low speed of on-chip wires in distances over 10 mm [13,14], and the cooling limitations of a single package. Thus, while silicon interposers run cooler than a 3D-integrated design, they still fail to provide low power density and high scalability (requirements b, d).

Electrical links suffer from severely constrained bandwidth, due to limitations in the density of chip I/O and package routes, which dramatically constrain the number of links that can be routed across discrete chips. A 580 mm^2 die can have 25600 pins to the package substrate at a pitch of 150 μm, but the substrate-to-board pitch is 0.8 mm, which allows only 3844 pins to the board from a 5 cm x 5 cm package [8]. This forces the use of over-clocked and high-power serial links across chips. Unfortunately, electrical links driven by a high-speed serializer/deserializer circuit (*SerDes*) [22] on an FR-4 board incur significant energy consumption or long delays (typically 20 pJ/bit, and at best 2.5 pJ/bit and 2.5 ns latency over 4 inches of electrical strip [22]) as the designers have to trade energy for performance. Thus, SerDes links enable only a small array of chips, and fail to satisfy requirements c and d. To avoid confusion with on-chip wires, in this paper we use "*SerDes*" to refer to conventional electrical links across chips.

With the introduction of nanophotonics, systems can break free of all these limitations. The low latency and high bandwidth density of optical signaling can facilitate efficient off-chip communication and bring physically distant chips effectively close together. This makes it possible to build a physically-large but logically-dense many-core "virtual chip" by optically connecting several chiplets together [3,13,19], each with its own separate package and cooling.

To integrate chiplets into a larger system, NSiP [5] uses silicon-nitride waveguides across chiplets within a package, and the Oracle Macrochip [13] uses silicon waveguides etched on a wafer. While these proposals mitigate the area, yield, and memory bandwidth limitations of conventional designs, they do not address the power constraints. Thereby, designs utilizing waveguides are confined to a small physical space (e.g., a wafer [13] or a package [5]). This increases the thermal density to the point where liquid cooling is required to avoid thermal runaways [13,14], or confines the aggregate "virtual chip" to power limitations not much different from a monolithic design [5]. In addition, the optical loss of silicon waveguides (typically 0.05-0.3 dB/cm [14,4]) makes routing long cross-chiplet optical channels impractical. Macrochip integration may require links over 45 cm [14], for which waveguides impose a 5 ns latency and 2.25 dB loss. Ultra-low-loss waveguides can be manufactured, but their high area occupancy may result in exceedingly narrow chiplet-to-chiplet links (e.g., 2-bit links for an 8x8 chiplet array [13,14]) which in turn impose significant serialization that degrades performance. Thus, to design a large "virtual chip" using waveguides, one has to suffer high optical loss which multiplies the power requirements, or narrow paths which impose serialization, hurt performance, and in turn increase overall energy consumption.

In contrast, Galaxy is designed to push back the power limits, in addition to overcoming the area, yield, and bandwidth constraints, while allowing highly-scalable designs. Optical fibers have tremendously low optical loss (0.2 dB/Km), so very long channels can be drawn at very low power. Galaxy capitalizes on this and uses fibers for cross-chiplet communication. Its design also guarantees that each optical path employs only a small number of couplers, keeping the total optical loss and the corresponding laser power low. These two design choices allow spreading discrete chiplets far apart in space to minimize heat transfer and lower the power density of the virtual chip, which in turn enables each chiplet to operate at higher frequency than power-limited designs. At the same time, the propagation speed of light in fibers (0.676 c) is considerably higher than in silicon waveguides (0.286 c), allowing for low-latency long-distance communication. Compared to SerDes lines, fibers transmit at 33x lower energy per bit [2]. Thus, fibers provide high bandwidth at low power, and enable highly-scalable designs.

Previous research [13] dismissed the use of optical fibers for cross-chiplet communication under the assumption that chips connect to fibers at a relatively large 250 μm core pitch, not the 20 μm pitch of optical proximity couplers that silicon waveguides use. Hence, the chip-to-chip bandwidth over fibers would not improve much over area solder balls connected to package routes. Galaxy overcomes this limitation by exploiting a recently-demonstrated technology that couples an array of fibers into an array of waveguides at 20 μm pitch at the edge of the chip [15]. Our results indicate that fibers provide sufficient bandwidth for communication to chiplets and to memory, allowing for much wider data paths than low-loss but slow silicon waveguides, and boost both the performance and the energy efficiency of the multi-chip system by several times.

In summary, optical fibers are faster, impose lower optical loss, and require lower energy than available alternatives for chiplet communication. They are also flexible and allow for arbitrary placement of chiplets (e.g., across boards within a rack) without additional coupling. Thus, fibers are especially suitable for long, inter-chiplet optical channels, as they are easy to route, and can go off the plane or off the board. Galaxy utilizes optical fibers for cross-chiplet communication and offers simple packaging, power, and heat requirements, yet provides the performance advantages of a tightly-coupled system. While prior works have touched upon some of these issues in the context of multi-chip architectures [2, 3, 5, 13, 14, 19], to the best of our knowledge, this is the first work that quantifies the impact of disintegration and multi-chip integration on power constraints, and analyzes the performance, power, energy, and thermal behavior of multi-chip design alternatives.

It is important to note that Galaxy is just one design that supports processor disintegration and macrochip integration. Other topologies and designs are possible. Our goal is not to perform a full design-space sweep and advocate Galaxy as the optimal solution. Rather, we aim to demonstrate that processor disintegration can match the performance of designs that are not limited by power and off-chip bandwidth, effectively breaking free from the limitations of today's monolithic chips, and at the same time support large-scale macrochip integration. Specifically, our contributions are:

1. We quantify the impact of power and bandwidth constraints in monolithic single-chip designs, and the limitations of electrical links and SOI waveguides when used for chip communication.

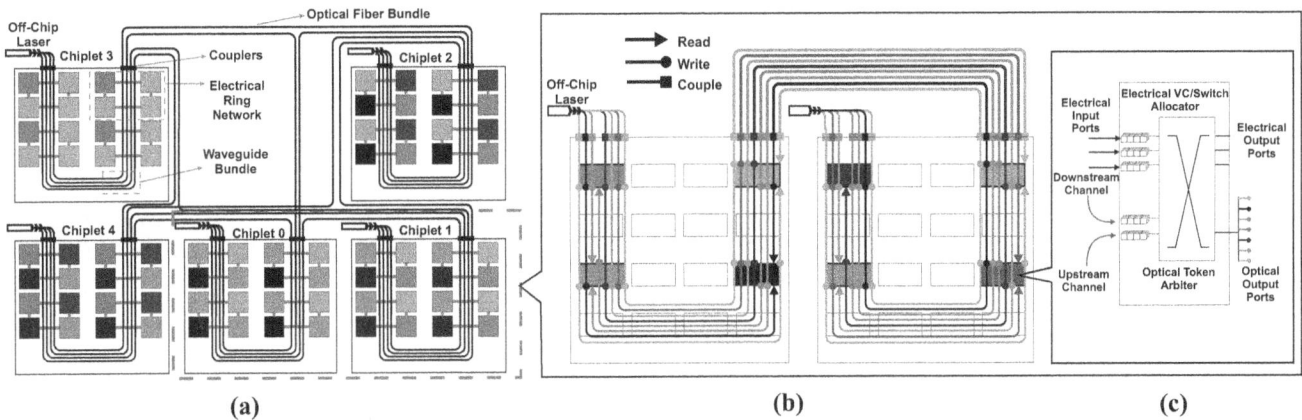

FIGURE 1. (a) Galaxy layout of an example 5-chiplet design, (b) MWSR optical crossbar, and (c) router architecture.

2. We propose Galaxy, an architecture that allows both processor disintegration and macrochip integration. Galaxy builds a many-core "virtual chip" by connecting multiple smaller chiplets through optical fibers.

3. We evaluate the performance, power, energy, and thermal profile of Galaxy, and compare it against single-chip designs (*processor disintegration*) and multi-chip designs (*macrochip integration*). Galaxy is up to 3.4x faster (1.8-2.2x on average) over single-chip alternatives with electrical, photonic, or hybrid interconnects, achieves up to 6.8x smaller energy-delay product (2.6x on average), and scales to 4K cores while being 2.5x faster at 6x lower laser power than a waveguide-based design.

2. THE GALAXY ARCHITECTURE

Galaxy builds a physically-large but logically-dense many-core "virtual chip" by optically connecting many discrete chiplets together. Galaxy aims for high performance while providing high energy efficiency and high scalability. Galaxy builds a point-to-point chip-to-chip network, which outperforms other switched networks in terms of performance and energy efficiency [13]. The chip-to-chip photonic interconnect extends across chiplets by coupling light to SOI waveguides from optical fibers at the edge of the chip [15]. Within a chiplet, Galaxy utilizes electrical signaling for nearest-neighbor communication, and silicon waveguides for long-distance communication. Long-distance on-chip communication has been shown to be more energy efficient with photonics than electrical signaling [21]. Furthermore, we will show that a seamless extension of on-chip optical signaling to chip-to-chip links allows Galaxy to connect an array of distributed chips at a performance comparable to on-chip interconnects [21,28] (Figure 5).

2.1 Network Topology

Galaxy employs a hybrid electrical/photonic interconnect. It extends Firefly [21] to support cross-chiplet communication at low power by minimizing coupler crossings and the number of sharers of each optical path. Figure 1(a) depicts an example 5-chiplet Galaxy design. The colored squares within each chiplet represent routers. The routers within a chiplet are divided into local clusters. Each cluster contains exactly one router per remote chiplet. In our example, there are 4 clusters per chiplet, with 4 routers per cluster. A local cluster in Chiplet 3 consists of neighboring red, orange, blue, and green routers (red outline in Chiplet 3, Figure 1(a)). Each cluster supports a number of cores based on a concentration factor. The cores and routers in a cluster are electrically connected. In our example, we use concentration 1 and an electrical ring within the

cluster (other topologies are possible). A source-destination pair within the same cluster uses only electrical links.

Clusters communicate with each other through optical crossbars. Every optical crossbar is represented by coloring routers with the same color. For example, the pink routers in Chiplet 0 and the pink routers in Chiplet 1 belong to the same optical crossbar. Each optical crossbar extends across only two chiplets. This minimizes coupler crossings and optical loss: every optical path is short, and has at most 3 couplers (including the laser coupling). This way, Galaxy forms a fully connected point-to-point network between chiplets. Also, every crossbar extends across all clusters of the two chiplets it connects. In Figure 1(a), the crossbar between Chiplet 0 and Chiplet 1 consists of the pink routers in Chiplets 0 and 1, the U-shaped waveguides that connect these routers within each chiplet, and the fibers that connect the two chiplets. Figure 1(b) shows a close-up of that crossbar, where the pink routers have been re-colored to assist the detailed explanation of the crossbar later in the section.,

Routing a packet from Chiplet 0 to Chiplet 1 is carried by traversing the corresponding optical crossbar. This is done in 3 steps: (1) Route electrically within the source cluster in Chiplet 0 to a pink router; (2) Take the optical link and arrive at the pink router of the destination cluster in Chiplet 1; (3) Route electrically within the destination cluster to the destination core. Communication between any two clusters is performed similarly. Source-destination cluster pairs within the same chiplet use only the silicon waveguides in that chiplet. If the clusters are at different chiplets, the packet will traverse the waveguides within the source chiplet, the fiber connecting the two chiplets, and the waveguides in the destination chiplet. A packet that traverses an optical link will directly reach a router within the cluster of the destination core, and every packet traverses the optical link only once.

In general, if each chiplet has X clusters, each with Y routers, and a concentration of c, the proposed Galaxy architecture can connect $(Y+1)$ chiplets, using radix-$(2X)$ optical crossbars, supporting a total of $c*Y*X*(Y+1)$ cores. The example in Figure 1 is a case with $X=Y=4$, $c=1$, for a total of 80 cores. It is important to note that it is easy to extend Galaxy to support an arbitrary number of chiplets by having optical routers belong to multiple optical crossbars. However, for ease of explanation, we refrain from this design choice.

Firefly [21] uses Single Writer Multiple Reader (SWMR) optical crossbars, which use global broadcast channels to reserve the data channel, and requires an optical credit stream to control buffer space, thereby increasing power consumption. Galaxy adopts a modified Firefly topology with Multiple Writer Single Reader

(MWSR) optical crossbars which only require a token stream to manage arbitration and buffer space. In MWSR crossbars, each router "listens" on a dedicated channel and sends flits on the listening channels of all the other routers in the crossbar. Figure 1(b) illustrates the MWSR crossbar that extends over chiplets 0 and 1, with 8 senders and 8 receivers. The participating routers were shown in pink color in Figure 1(a), but they are shown with a distinct color here to ease explanation. Every router receives data from its own channel, which is shown with the same color as the receiver router, and writes 7 other channels which are the listening channels of the other routers in the crossbar. Galaxy adopts a 1-pass optical token stream with FairQuota [20] to guarantee that only a single router transmits on a channel at any moment, avoid starvation and packet loss due to buffer overflow, and provide QoS.

Because the optical links are traversed at most once, two Virtual Channels (VCs) are sufficient for the optical channels. The buffers of each optical VC are arbitrated using a separate optical VC token stream. To keep the balance of tokens, the tokens perform a double traversal. The receiver router of a channel first sends the VC tokens in the direction opposite to the data channel (back-traversal), all the way to the origin of the laser injection point, skipping all the senders on the way. Then, the VC token goes through O/E and E/O conversion, and is re-modulated onto a VC token stream in the same direction as the data channel (forward-traversal).

Figure 1(c) shows a hybrid electrical/optical router in Galaxy. Routers store the flits received from the electrical or optical networks in electrical buffers, after an optical to electrical (O/E) conversion if needed. Two electrical input and output ports route packets on the electrical local cluster ring. The third electrical input and output port is used for data injection. Each router has a pair of dedicated optical receiving channels, the upstream and downstream channels. The dark blue and green routers in Figure 1(b) send messages to the purple router through its upstream channel, while the rest send messages to the purple router through its downstream channel. Thus, 2 extra ports are added on the input side of the router to receive packets from the dedicated optical receiving channels from both directions. On the output side, 7 additional output ports switch outgoing packets to different optical channels.

2.2 Inter-Chiplet Connection

Galaxy targets large-scale macrochip integration (e.g., 60+ chiplets) which require fast and energy-efficient long-distance links. Thus, Galaxy connects chiplets via optical fibers, rather than SerDes links [22], or silicon waveguides (0.05 dB/cm [14]). SerDes provide at best 2.5 pJ/bit and 2.5 ns latency over 4 inches of electrical strip [22], thus fibers offer lower latency, and two orders of magnitude lower energy/bit and energy-delay-product across the entire range of possible chiplet-to-chiplet distances (Figure 2). Similarly, fibers are almost 2x faster than SOI waveguides, and achieve between 2-10x lower energy/bit and energy-delay-product

TABLE 1. Nanophotonic Parameters

	per Unit	Total
Splitters	0.2 dB	0.2 dB
Waveguide Loss	0.3 dB/cm	1.5 dB
Fiber Loss	0.2 dB/Km	~0 dB
Nonlinearity	1 dB	1 dB
Coupler Loss	3.8 dB	7.6 dB
Modulator Insertion	0.5 dB	0.5 dB
Ring Through	0.01 dB	1.28 dB
Filter Drop	1.5 dB	1.5 dB
Photodetector	0.1 dB	0.1 dB
Total Loss		**13.68 dB**
Detector Sensitivity	**-20 dBm**	
Modulation/Demodulation	**150 fJ/bit**	
Laser Power per Wavelength		**0.233 mW**
Total Laser Power		**1.195 W**

(Figure 2), mainly due to the high relative optical loss and refractive index of typical silicon waveguides. Fibers are especially suitable for long, inter-chiplet channels, allowing Galaxy to have a thermal-aware design while maintaining high performance and energy efficiency. Figure 2 corroborates prior research [14].

Fibers connect to chiplets through a coupler that tapers an array of fibers at 250 μm pitch down to 20 μm pitch channels, and couples them into an array of SOI waveguides at the edge of the chip [15]. The measured coupling loss is 3.8 dB, including tapering the channels, the refraction index change from fibers to the waveguides, and misalignment [15]. Misalignment within 0.7 μm, 0.4 μm, and 0.7 μm in the lateral, vertical, and optical axes produces losses under 1 dB [15]. The performance of the tapered coupler is comparable to that of an optical proximity coupler (3.5 dB coupler loss, plus 0.5 dB per 1 μm misalignment in the y-axis, plus less than 1 dB loss due to misalignment of 2.5 μm in the x- and z-axis [31]).

2.3 Nanophotonic Parameters and Power

On-chip lasers dissipate a lot of power and heat the chip, thus Galaxy adopts off-chip WDM-compatible lasers. The laser is brought on chip via fibers connected to tapered couplers [15], and a splitter distributes it to on-chip waveguides [4]. Tapered couplers also connect the on-chip waveguides to the off-chip optical fibers. Galaxy uses the modulators, demodulators, drop filters, splitters, and photodetectors introduced in [1]. Optical links run at 10 GHz and are implemented similar to [1]. Table 1 details the optical parameters.

The example configuration of the 5-chiplet Galaxy we evaluate in Section 4.2 consists of 10 radix-8 MWSR crossbars that transfer 64-bit flits. We assume a modest 16-way DWDM, thus Galaxy uses

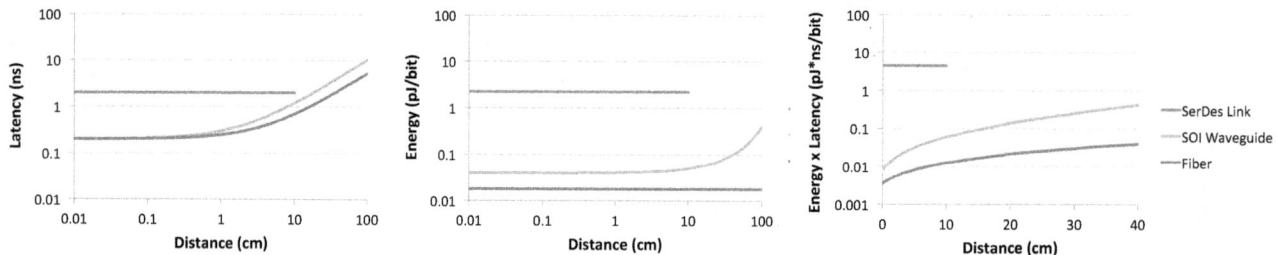

FIGURE 2. Latency, Energy / bit, and Energy x Delay product for SerDes links, SOI waveguides, and fibers.

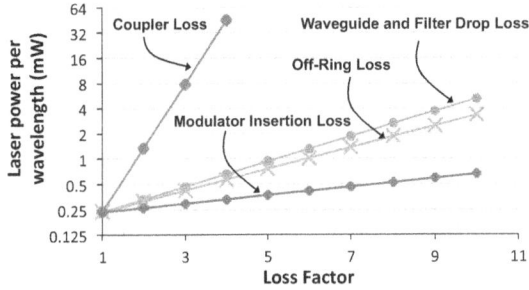

FIGURE 3. Laser power sensitivity to optical parameters.

a total of 320 fibers (128 fibers attached to each chiplet) and 40960 ring resonators (8192 per chiplet covering ~0.9 mm^2). Because every optical channel requires a 1-token-pass arbitration mechanism, a total of 20 additional fibers and 3840 rings are used for arbitration. Another 80 rings and 10 fibers are used for forward clock distribution [14].

To calculate the total ring heating power we extend the method by Nitta *et al.* [18] by incorporating the heat generated by the cores. The cores heat up the photonic layer, and the ring heaters provide the remaining heat necessary to bring the photonic layer within the ring tuning range. As current injection may cause a thermal runaway [18], we only consider trimming by heating. Section 3.1 details the model. We also include the trimming power required for process variations [12]. While Galaxy may benefit from trimming power saving methods [18], they are out of the scope of this paper.

Figure 3 demonstrates the sensitivity of Galaxy's laser power to a change in the loss of each nanophotonic parameter. The laser power is most sensitive to the coupler loss, but relatively insensitive to the other parameters, indicating that our results will likely hold under a wide range of nanophotonic device technologies.

When evaluating laser power consumption, existing literature typically omits inefficiencies in the generation and delivery of the laser [1,13,14,21,28]. By analogy, and to ease comparisons with prior work, we did not include the generation and delivery cost in the laser power calculations in Table 1 and the remainder of this paper. For completeness, however, we report here the laser power including all these overheads. The additional coupling loss increases the laser power to 2.9*W*. Given 10% efficiency for the WDM-compatible laser [32], the wall-socket laser power is 29*W*.

3. EXPERIMENTAL METHODOLOGY

We evaluate the performance of Galaxy for processor disintegration by modeling an example 5-chiplet 80-core Galaxy on a full-system cycle-accurate simulator based on Flexus 4.0 [10,29] integrated with Booksim 2.0 [6] and DRAMSim 2.0 [24]. Table 2 details the architectural modeling parameters. We target a 16 *nm* technology, and have updated our tool chain accordingly based on ITRS projections [8]. We follow the SimFlex sampling methodology [29] with 95% confidence intervals. The simulated system executes a selection of SPLASH and scientific workloads.

We compare Galaxy against three single-chip multicores, all of which implement the architecture described in Table 2. The first multicore uses an all-electrical 2D-Concentrated Mesh on-chip interconnect with express links [6] and concentration of 4 (**CMesh-Exp**). Concentrated mesh is often chosen for on-chip networks as it maps well to a 2D-VLSI planar layout with low complexity. We evaluated a regular 2D-Mesh and a 2D-Concentrated Mesh without express links, and found that CMeshExp outperforms the other

TABLE 2. Architectural Parameters.

Multicore Size	80-cores, 580 mm^2
Processing Cores	ULTRASPARC III ISA, max 5 *GHz*, OoO, 4-wide dispatch/retirement, 96-entry ROB
L1 Cache	split I/D, 64 *KB* 2-way, 2-cycle load-to-use, 2 ports, 64-byte blocks, 32 MSHRs, 16-entry victim cache
L2 Cache	shared, 512 *KB* per core, 16-way, 64-byte blocks, 14-cycle hit, 32 MSHRs, 16-entry victim cache
Memory Controllers	One per 4 cores, or 4 MCs per chip. 1 channel/MC Round-robin page interleaving
Main Memory	DDR3, 80 *GB*, 8 *KB* pages, 20 *ns* access latency Interfaces: (a) Conventional pins, (b) Optically-connected memory (OCM) [1], (c) 3D-stacked [13]
Networks	CMesh, Corona, Firefly, Galaxy, Oracle Macrochip

designs on all metrics (performance, power, and energy). Thus, we only show results for CMeshExp. We model routers with 8 input and output ports and a 3-cycle routing delay. Routers are connected through 166-bit bi-directional links with a 1-cycle link delay.

The second multicore uses an all-optical MWSR crossbar (**Corona** [28]), implemented with 80 MWSR optical busses (256-bit data channels). We model global switch arbitration using an optical token ring. A token for each node, which represents the right to modulate on the node's wavelength, continuously passes around all nodes on a dedicated arbitration waveguide. A node grabs and absorbs a token to transmit a packet, and then releases the token to allow other nodes to obtain it. We estimate 16 *cm* long waveguides for the Corona chip, resulting in 8 cycles token round-trip time.

The third multicore implements a hybrid interconnect where clusters of electrically-connected cores are connected through an SWMR optical crossbar entirely on chip (**Firefly** [21], 256-bit flits, 8 *cm* waveguide, and 1-cycle reservation and electrical-link delay).

We model **Galaxy** with 1-cycle latency for processing an optical token request [20]. Each Galaxy router can initiate a maximum of 8 token requests per cycle, but can utilize at most 2 acquired tokens [20]. Galaxy uses 1-pass token stream arbitration for combined VC and channel arbitration. We estimate that the round-trip time of a token is also 8 cycles (8 *cm* SOI waveguide plus 16 *cm* optical fiber travel time). The input buffers are implemented as a DAMQ [27], with packets queued separately based on their destination. A data packet contains 512 bits, divided into eight 64-bit flits.

3.1 Power and Temperature Modeling

All systems we model employ Dynamic Voltage and Frequency Scaling (DVFS) to lower the voltage and frequency of a chip or chiplet when it reaches the limits of safe operational temperature (without loss of generality, we assume 90°C). Figure 4 shows the flow diagram of our simulation tool chain. We collect runtime statistics from full-system simulations, and use them to calculate the power consumption of compute cores, caches, and memory controllers using McPAT [16], and the power consumption of the electrical and optical networks using DSENT [26] and the analytical model by Joshi *et al.* [12] respectively. Based on these estimates, we calculate the temperature of the chip and chiplet assemblies using HotSpot 5.0 [25] and FloTherm [30], a computational fluid dynamics tool that models the heat transfer between chiplets through air flow and convection. The estimated temperature is then

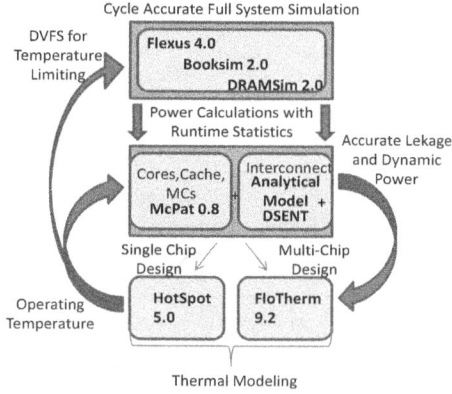

FIGURE 4. Simulation flow chart.

TABLE 3. Galaxy scalability.

# of Cores	Multi-Chip Architecture		Bandwidth per Chip (TB/s)	Laser Power (W)	Serialization Overhead (cycles)	Link Latency (cycles)
320		Fibers	10	4.0	1	2
		Waveguides	5	4.9	2	10
		SerDes links	0.320	3.9	32	12
1088	Galaxy	Fibers	20	27.0	2	10
		Waveguides	5	26.0	8	20
		SerDes links	0.640	26.8	64	12
4160		Fibers	40	47.6	4	10
		Waveguides	10	44.9	16	20
		SerDes links	0.320	47.9	512	12
4096	Oracle MacroChip		0.630	~40.0	64	20

used to refine the leakage power estimate, and we iteratively calculate the power and temperature profiles until the system reaches a stable state. We use the stable-state power and temperature estimates to adjust DVFS, and repeat the process until we identify a DVFS setting for which the chip stays just below 90^oC, or operates at the maximum 5 GHz.

To calculate the total ring heating power for Galaxy, Corona, and Firefly, we extend the method by Nitta *et al.* [18] by additionally accounting for the heating of the photonic die by the operation of the cores. We model the thermal characteristics of a 3D-stacked architecture where the photonic die sits underneath the logic die using the 3D-chip extension of HotSpot [25]. For each target architecture (Corona, Firefly, and Galaxy) we measure the maximum temperature of the logic die during the execution of each one of the workloads. Then, we tune the micro-rings to the maximum of all the observed temperatures that the logic layer reaches across all benchmarks executing on the target architecture, plus a small margin. When a workload executes, we calculate the ring heating power required to maintain the entire photonic die at the micro-ring trimming temperature during the entire execution. We also include the trimming power required to overcome process variations [12].

3.2 Modeling Memory and Physical Constrains

To demonstrate the ability of disintegrated architectures to break free of power and bandwidth limitations, we evaluate Galaxy against all possible single-chip multicore combinations: power-constrained, off-chip bandwidth-constrained, fully constrained (i.e., both power- and bandwidth-constrained), and unconstrained.

We evaluate power-constrained multicores by employing DVFS to keep the chips within 90^oC. To evaluate multicores that are not subject to power constraints, we allow the chips to run at the maximum speed allowed by the design (5 GHz), by disregarding power and thermal limits. We evaluate bandwidth-constrained single-chip multicores by assuming a conventional DDR3 memory, and limit the total memory bandwidth by utilizing ITRS [8] pin projections for a 5 cm x 5 cm package, assuming 1/3 of the pins are used for power, 1/3 are used for I/O, and the remaining 1/3 are used for memory. The memory pins are distributed equally among four memory controllers (MCs). To evaluate designs that are not limited by memory bandwidth, we increase the number of pins well beyond ITRS projections and commensurately increase the number of MCs, until more pins or more MCs no longer increase performance. For our workloads, we reach this point when 5x more pins are distributed across 20 MCs. Fully constrained designs operate within the power, memory bandwidth, and thermal limits. Fully

unconstrained designs operate beyond the power, thermal, and bandwidth limits and cannot realistically be built; however, they provide the highest performance that a particular architecture can achieve, limited only by the maximum speed allowed by the design (5 GHz). While we compare Galaxy to both constrained and unconstrained single-chip multicores, Galaxy is always modeled to conform to realistic power, bandwidth, and temperature limits.

Emerging memory technologies (e.g., optically-connected memory (OCM) [1] or 3D-memory [13]) are not pin-limited, and can remove the memory bandwidth bottleneck for all multicore designs. Thus, we separately evaluate the performance of Galaxy against single-chip multicores with OCM and 3D-memory, where each multicore employs 20 MCs. We model a 10 ns access latency for OCM [1] and 2 ns for 3D-memory [13].

3.3 Modeling Large-Scale Multi-Chip Designs

Galaxy can scale up to 1088 cores with 17 chiplets (64 cores each with concentration 4), and 4160 cores with 65 chiplets. As the number of chiplets grows, the number of point-to-point links and their length increase. In order to keep the network power and component count within reasonable levels, off-chip bandwidth increases slower than the number of point-to-point links. As a result, the datapath width drops for large designs, forcing senders to send messages by sending many smaller flits serially (serialization overhead). Furthermore, messages take longer to travel the longer links. Galaxy does not suffer from high serialization or link delays and remains scalable, because it uses optical fibers, which provide high performance with energy efficiency (Section 2.2). We evaluate Galaxy for macrochip integration by comparing it against (a) **Galaxy with SOI** waveguides and optical proximity (OPC) couplers [31], (b) **Galaxy with SerDes** links, and (c) the **Oracle Macrochip** [13]. For fairness, we adjust the datapath width of Galaxy alternatives so they fit into similar power envelopes, and then we calculate the latency overhead. The Oracle Macrochip model closely follows [13,14,31]. Table 3 details the bandwidth, power

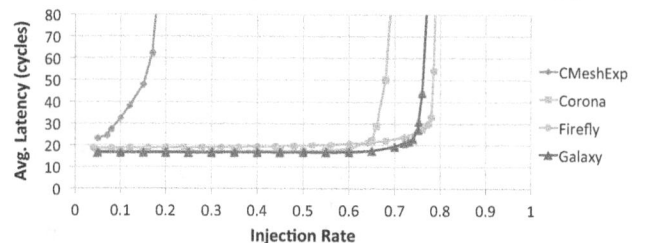

FIGURE 5. Load latency for uniform random traffic.

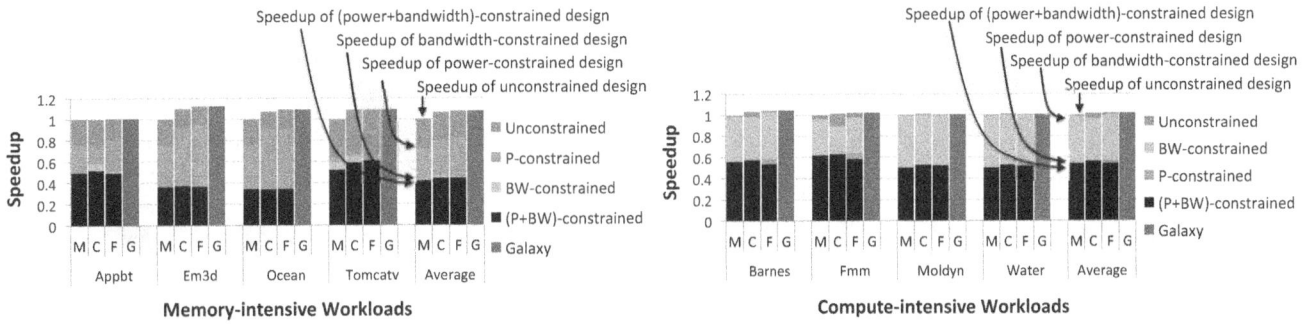

FIGURE 6. Speedup of constrained and unconstrained architectures: CMeshExp (M), Corona (C), Firefly (F), and Galaxy (G).

consumption, serialization delay, and link delay for all designs. To keep the simulations tractable, we estimate the performance of the scaled-out designs by imposing the latency overheads of each scaled-out system from Table 3 to an 80-core 5-chiplet model. The SerDes delay is optimistically kept constant for all sizes. As we impose the scaling overheads onto same-size designs in all cases (80 cores, 5 chiplets), the higher core count of Galaxy compared to the Oracle Macrochip does not affect the results.

4. EXPERIMENTAL RESULTS

4.1 Network Performance

Figure 5 analyzes the load-latency of CMeshExp, Corona, Firefly, and Galaxy. CMeshExp saturates quickly, which is indicative of its relatively low bandwidth. Corona saturates at a little less than 0.7 injection rate, while Firefly reaches an injection rate of almost 0.8 before saturating. Galaxy trails Firefly closely, and falls only slightly short in performance. This is expected because Galaxy is similar to a 2-level Firefly that creates a single datapath between two clusters, while packets in Firefly can take several alternate routes and utilize more of the available bandwidth. Nonetheless, the results indicate that Galaxy is a competitive interconnect.

4.2 Processor Disintegration

Figure 6 shows the speedup achieved by unconstrained single-chip designs (top of blue bar) with CMeshExp, Corona, and Firefly interconnects for memory-intensive and compute-intensive workloads. Submitting the multicores that run compute-intensive workloads (Figure 6 right) to realistic bandwidth constraints results in lower performance, but the loss is relatively small (top of green bar). Submitting them to power constraints, however, results in significant performance drop (top of orange bar). These multicores employ DVFS to stay below 90^oC, which slows down the compute-intensive workloads the most, as they have high core utilization which in turn dissipates more power. For example, Corona runs barnes at only 2.25 GHz from a nominal frequency of 5 GHz, and Firefly exhibits a similar slowdown. In comparison, Galaxy never exceeds 70^oC, and thus it can run at the full 5 GHz and out-

perform all single-chip alternatives by 1.8x on average. Multicores running memory-intensive workloads also show degraded performance when power-constrained (Figure 6 left, top of orange bar), indicating that power limitations are always an important factor. However, they incur the highest performance loss mainly when limited in off-chip bandwidth (top of green bar), while the slow-down due to DVFS is secondary. For example, CMeshExp runs em3d at 4.25 GHz, but Galaxy still demonstrates 3x speedup. Because of this dual slowdown, Galaxy achieves the maximum speedup over fully-constrained single-chip multicores (their performance is indicated by the top of the black bar) on memory-intensive workloads (2.3x on average, and up to 3.5x for ocean). More importantly, Galaxy manages to match or exceed the performance of designs that are entirely unconstrained. This demonstrates the ability of processor disintegration to break free of the power and bandwidth walls of conventional monolithic designs. All the designs we evaluate in the remainder of this paper are subject to power and off-chip bandwidth constraints, where the bandwidth limitations depend on the assumed memory technology.

Optically-connected memory (OCM) [1] overcomes the bandwidth limitations and decreases the memory latency. Corona with OCM outperforms Corona with conventional DDR3 by 3-4x on memory intensive workloads (Figure 7). Firefly and CMeshExp show similar trends. Galaxy, however, still outperforms all alternatives by 1.8x on average, as it runs at the full 5 GHz while DVFS limits the single-chip designs (e.g., Corona with OCM runs em3d at only 3.25 GHz). 3D-stacked memory has a similar effect on Galaxy, while Corona, Firefly, and CMeshExp do not get faster as they are still power limited. Overall, Galaxy outperforms alternative designs by up to 2.95x (2x on average). We conclude that Galaxy can leverage the emerging memory technologies to the fullest, while single-chip multicores are limited by the single-chip power envelope and fail to utilize fully the new memory technologies.

Figure 8 shows the breakdown of the normalized energy-delay product (EDP) and the average energy per instruction of CMeshExp, Corona, Firefly, and Galaxy with conventional memory. The

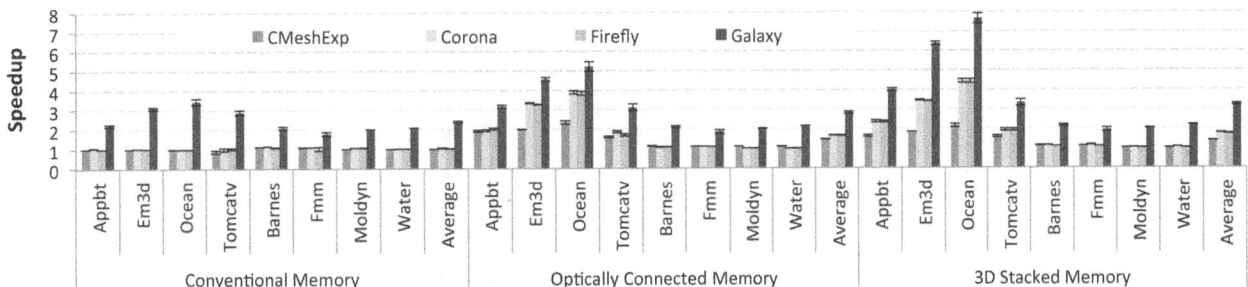

FIGURE 7. Speedup of power-constrained designs with various memory technologies (normalized to CMeshExp with DDR3).

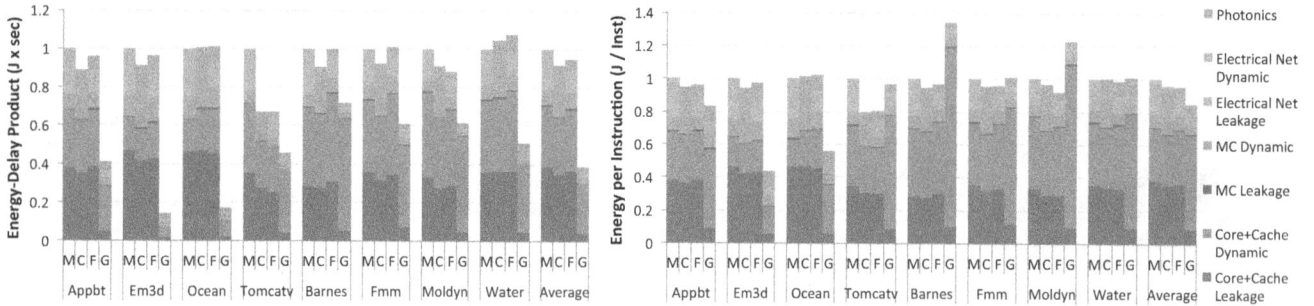

FIGURE 8. (a) Energy x Delay, and (b) Average energy / instruction for CMeshExp (M), Corona (C), Firefly (F), and Galaxy (G).

dynamic energy consumption of cores and caches for Galaxy is higher as it achieves 2.3x speedup on average over single-chip designs. This effect is more pronounced for compute-intensive workloads (barnes, moldyn). However, the chiplets in Galaxy run at only 70^oC and dissipate $55W$ each, compared to 90^oC and $130W$ for CMeshExp-, Corona-, and Firefly-based chips. As a result, Galaxy lowers leakage to just over 10% of energy, while single-chip designs waste 36-40% of their energy on leakage. Overall, single-chip designs consume 1.12-1.2x more energy per instruction than Galaxy (Figure 8(b)). Galaxy reaches its highest energy efficiency increase on memory-bound workloads (2-2.3x), as it achieves over 3x speedup and the chiplets dissipate less power waiting for memory. Galaxy attains up to 6.8x lower EDP than single-chip multi-cores (2.8x on average; Figure 8(a)).

Because Galaxy chiplets run cooler when running memory intensive workloads, the energy consumption of the photonics (including laser power, modulation/demodulation, and ring heating) is higher, as the ring heaters dissipate more power to keep the photonics layer at the trimming temperature. The ring heaters work less with compute intensive workloads, because cores dissipate more power and heat the photonic die.

4.3 Macrochip Integration and Scalability

Galaxy can scale up to 1088 cores with 17 chiplets, and 4160 cores with 65 chiplets (Section 3.3). We evaluate the scalability of Galaxy by comparing it against (a) Galaxy with SOI waveguides and OPC couplers [31], (b) Galaxy with SerDes links, and (c) the Oracle Macrochip [13] (Section 3.3). Table 3 details the power, bandwidth, and latency characteristics of the scaled out designs. Figure 9 compares the performance of these alternatives. The power-hungry SerDes links cannot provide enough bandwidth within the power envelope, resulting in high serialization delay that increasingly hurts performance as the system scales up. Similarly, SOI waveguides fall short because they require higher laser power than fibers, and at the same time light propagates 2.3x slower in waveguides. As a result, fibers increasingly outperform SOI wave-

guides as the system scales up. The performance gap is higher for memory-intensive workloads which stress the interconnect more. A 65-chiplet Galaxy with fibers outperforms Galaxy with SOI waveguides by up to 1.44x (1.24x on average), and Galaxy with SerDes by up to 9.53x (4.58x on average). The Oracle Macrochip [13,14] uses SOI waveguides and OPCs [31] to create point-to-point photonic links across chips. Galaxy outperforms the Oracle Macrochip by 2.5x on average (Figure 9) because the Macrochip implements a 2-bit-wide data channel with SOI waveguides, which impose high serialization and link delay.

We evaluate the sensitivity of laser power to the coupler loss for the Oracle Macrochip and Galaxy (Figure 10), because the coupler loss is the biggest contributor to the laser power consumption (Figure 3). We present laser power consumption of the Oracle Macrochip with measured coupler losses for passive-aligned and active-aligned OPCs [31], as well as under very aggressive OPC loss predictions of 1.2 dB [13,14]. For Galaxy, we present the laser power consumption under SION and SU8 tapered couplers using loss measurements of existing prototypes [15]. From one chiplet to another, laser has to pass through 3 couplers in Macrochip (vs. 2 for Galaxy), so the higher slope of the graph indicates higher sensitivity to coupler loss. The Macrochip with actively-aligned OPCs requires 6x more laser power than Galaxy. Even if the predicted OPC loss is achieved, Galaxy with existing couplers would still require less laser power.

4.4 Thermal Evaluation

To effectively push back the power wall while still employing conventional forced air cooling solutions and cheap packaging appropriate for high-volume markets, a disintegrated design requires the chiplets to be physically far enough from each other to minimize heat transfer. Our thermal modeling using computational fluid dynamics tools [30] and HotSpot [25] indicates that a Galaxy architecture with active heatsinks on each chiplet allows the chiplets to operate at 66.2^oC, sufficiently cool for most applications. In fact, even cheaper cooling solutions seem adequate. Figure 11(a)

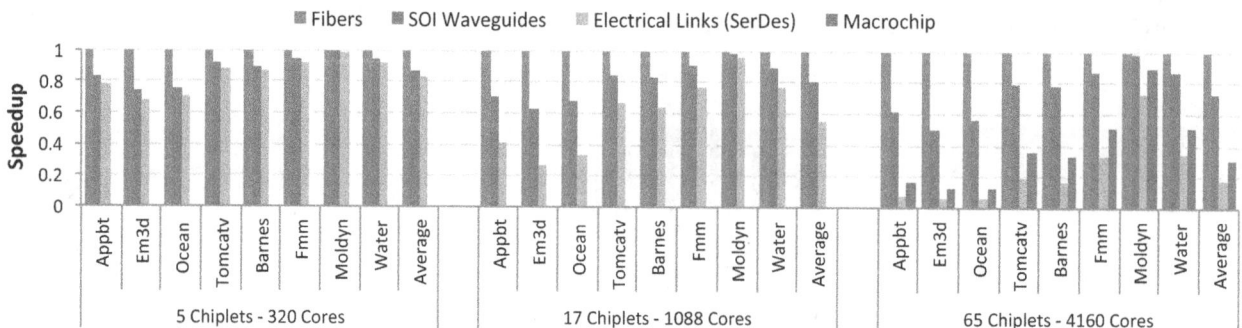

FIGURE 9. Comparison of Galaxy with different chiplet-to-chiplet interconnect technologies, and the Oracle Macrochip.

310

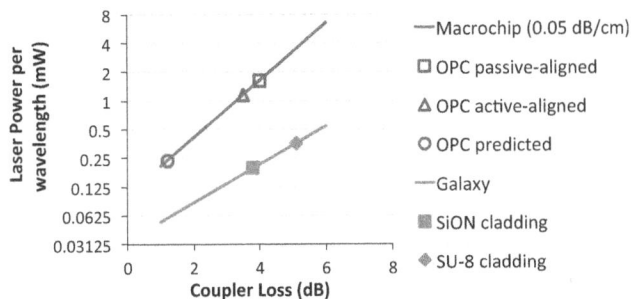

FIGURE 10. Laser power sensitivity to coupler loss.

shows a 5-chiplet Galaxy design which uses passive heatsinks spaced 8 *cm* apart, with a global fan blowing air horizontally in 45°C ambient temperature in a box shell. The fanless (passive) heatsinks cool chiplets to 88.2°C, and deliver low packaging and cooling costs, and increased lifetime. Thus, even very simple and cheap cooling solutions (fanless heatsinks and a global fan) suffice for an 80-core design disintegrated to 5 chiplets with Galaxy.

Optical fibers allow Galaxy to spread chiplets far apart for better cooling, while SOI waveguides and SerDes confine them to limited physical space (e.g. a wafer [13]). We compare the thermal behavior of a Macrochip-like dense design to an equal-size Galaxy by modeling a 9-chiplet design. Both designs use the same heatsinks and dissipate 50W per chiplet. Based on the Macrochip architecture [13,14], we estimate that the heatsinks will almost touch each other resulting in the layout shown at Figure 11(b). We observe that the sites that are further away from the fan reach 249°C, and hence require a special cooling solution. A thermal-aware placement of 9 Galaxy chiplets on a 2D-plane (Figure 11(c)) achieves a maximum temperature of 110°C, which is a full 139°C lower than Macrochip. Furthermore, using optical fibers for cross-chiplet communication allows Galaxy to utilize multiple boards, in which case Galaxy can bring a 9-chiplet design down to a cool 87°C (Figure 11(d)). This freedom of placement gives a significant advantage to Galaxy compared to silicon-waveguide-based designs, and allows it to spread the volume enough to cool even large-scale designs.

5. LIMITATIONS AND CHALLENGES
5.1 Coupler and Fiber Density Considerations
The use of fibers for chiplet-to-chiplet communication in Galaxy brings two new challenges: coupling the fibers on chip, and attaching enough fibers to achieve the highest performance or lowest EDP, depending on the optimization target. Galaxy requires enough length along the periphery of a chiplet to attach the fibers. Even the simulated 116 *mm²* chiplets provide over 43 *mm* in total length along the edge of a chip, allowing up to 172 fibers at a conservative 250 *μm* pitch. The disintegrated design we evaluated assumes 128 fibers per chiplet with 16 DWDM on 64-bit-wide datapaths. Figure 12 indicates that a higher fiber density provides only marginal performance benefits at significantly higher laser power (e.g., 512 fibers provide 3% more speedup at 4x more power), while fewer fibers reduce performance without significant power savings (e.g., 16 fibers are 15.5% slower and save only 1W). This indicates that the power and performance are the real limiting factors, not the fiber density provided by the coupler.

5.2 Yield and Financial Considerations
Galaxy relies on the manufacturing of a photonic die, the 3D integration of the photonic and the logic dies at each chiplet, the man-

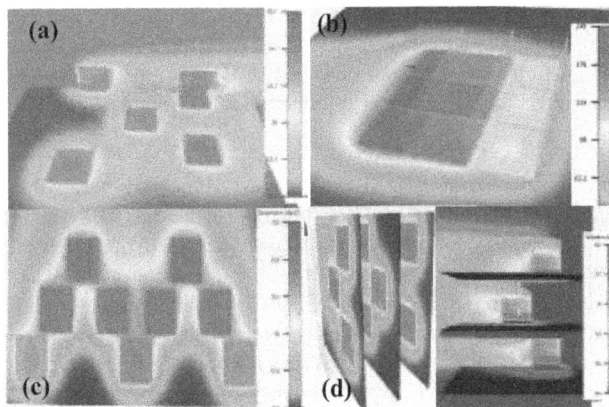

FIGURE 11. Thermal effects of chiplet placement.

ufacturing of tapered couplers and fibers, and their assembly. The absence of yield and manufacturing data for nanophotonic systems does not allow us to make quantitative arguments, but we note that fibers have been manufactured at high volumes and have become relatively cheap. To assist in calculating the additional cost of nanophotonics, Section 2.3 provides component counts for the nanophotonic devices. Processor disintegration allows Galaxy to recover the cost overhead of nanophotonic devices by breaking a monolithic chip into multiple smaller chiplets, increasing yield and lowering non-recurring and marginal costs by a significant factor, as only the defective chiplets need to be replaced rather than an entire large chip ([5]). This is especially important for low and medium volume markets. Furthermore, by allowing for the arbitrary placement of chiplets, Galaxy offers the system architect the flexibility to utilize any point in the trade-off between compute density and cooling, from forced air to liquid cooling and beyond. Fibers allow the chiplets to spread in 3D-space and occupy multiple boards, balancing compute density with board power requirements and cooling, while still performing like a large monolithic tightly-coupled chip (Section 4.4). Even though photonic integration adds to the cost, Galaxy's higher yield, scalability, performance, and energy efficiency may overcome the extra cost and result in competitive and possibly even lower cost of ownership.

6. RELATED WORK
Several on-chip interconnect networks exploiting optical signaling have been proposed [12, 21, 28]. Beamer *et al.* [3] proposed to achieve higher hardware parallelism while using smaller dies with high production yield. Batten *et al.* [1] proposes to connect a many-core processor to the DRAM memory using monolithic silicon. Koka *et al.* [13] discuss the design and implementation of a silicon-photonic network for a large multi-die "macrochip" system. In con-

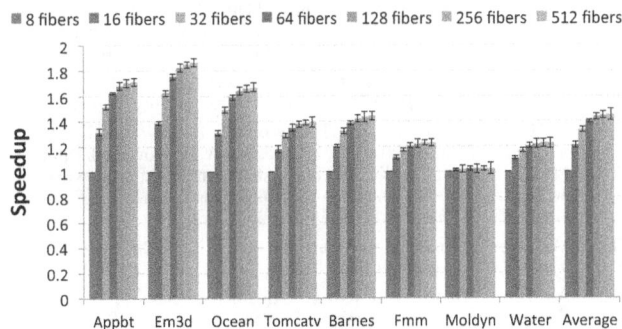

FIGURE 12. Sensitivity to fiber density per chiplet.

trast to these architectures, Galaxy leverages optical fibers to create a high-bandwidth, scalable, low-latency photonic interconnect that can support both processor disintegration and multi-chip integration, and at the same time enable cheap cooling solutions.

7. CONCLUSIONS

In this paper we propose Galaxy, a multi-chip architecture which builds a many-core "virtual chip" by connecting multiple smaller chiplets through optical fibers. Galaxy is designed to push back the power constraints, in addition to overcoming the area and bandwidth limitations, while providing high scalability. We demonstrate that Galaxy achieves 1.8-3.4x average speedup over competing single-chip designs, and achieves 2.6x lower energy-delay product (6.8x maximum). The careful design of optical paths in Galaxy minimizes coupler crossings, and allows it to scale beyond 4K cores, showing significant promise as the foundation of practical large-scale virtual chips. We show that a scaled-out 4K-core Galaxy attains significant speedup and energy efficiency advantages over similar designs such as the Oracle Macrochip, as it achieves at least 2.5x speedup with 6x more power-efficient optical links.

8. ACKNOWLEDGEMENTS

This work was partially supported by National Science Foundation awards CCF-1218768, CCF-0747201, and CCF-0916746, an ISEN booster award, and the June and Donald Brewer Chair in EECS at Northwestern University. John Kim was supported by the IT R&D program of MSIP/KEIT [10041313, UX-oriented Mobile SW Platform] and by the NRF grant funded by the Korea government (MSIP) (NRF-2013R1A2A2A01069132).

9. REFERENCES

[1] C. Batten, A. Joshi, J. Orcutt, A. Khilo, B. Moss, C. W. Holzwarth, M. A. Popovic, H. Li, H. I. Smith, J. L. Hoyt, F. X. Kartner, R. J. Ram, V. Stojanovic, and K. Asanovic. Building many-core processor-to-DRAM networks with monolithic CMOS silicon photonics. *IEEE Micro*, 29(4):8- 21, 2009.

[2] S. Beamer. *Designing Multisocket Systems with Silicon Photonics.* Ph.D. thesis, University of California at Berkeley, 2009.

[3] S. Beamer, K. Asanovic, C. Batten, A. Joshi, and V. Stojanovic. Designing multi-socket systems using silicon photonics. In *International Conference on Supercomputing (ICS)*, pages 521- 522, 2009.

[4] J. Cardenas, C. Poitras, J. Robinson, K. Preston, L. Chen, and M. Lipson. Low loss etchless silicon photonic waveguides. *Optics Express*, 17(6):4752- 4757, 2009.

[5] M. Cianchetti, N. Sherwood-Droz, and C. Batten. Implementing system-in-package with nanophotonic interconnect. *Workshop on the Interaction between Nanophotonic Devices and Systems*, 2010.

[6] W. J. Dally and B. Towles. *Principles and practices of interconnection networks.* Morgan Kaufmann Publishing Inc., 2004.

[7] H. Esmaeilzadeh, E. Blem, R. St. Amant, K. Sankaralingam, and D. Burger. Dark silicon and the end of multicore scaling. In *38th Annual International Symposium on Computer Architecture*, 2011.

[8] European, Japan, Korean, Taiwan, and United States Semiconductor Industry Associations. The international technology roadmap for semiconductors (ITRS). http://www.itrs.net/, 2012 Edition.

[9] N. Hardavellas, M. Ferdman, B. Falsafi, and A. Ailamaki. Toward dark silicon in servers. *IEEE Micro*, 31(4):6- 15, July-August 2011.

[10] N. Hardavellas, S. Somogyi, T. F. Wenisch, R. E. Wunderlich, S. Chen, J. Kim, B. Falsafi, J. C. Hoe, and A. G. Nowatzyk. SimFlex: a fast, accurate, flexible full-system simulation framework for performance evaluation of server architecture. *SIGMETRICS Performance Evaluation Review*, 31(4):31- 35, April 2004.

[11] M. Horowitz. Scaling, power and the future of CMOS. In *20th International Conference on VLSI Design*, page 23, January 2007.

[12] A. Joshi, C. Batten, Y.-J. Kwon, S. Beamer, I. Shamim, K. Asanovic, and V. Stojanovic. Silicon-photonic CLOS networks for global on-chip communication. In *IEEE International Symposium on Networks-on-Chip*, pages 124- 133, 2009.

[13] P. Koka, M. McCracken, H. Schwetman, X. Zheng, R. Ho, and A. Krishnamoorthy. Silicon-photonic network architectures for scalable, power-efficient multi-chip systems. In *37th Annual International Symposium on Computer Architecture*, pages 117- 128, 2010.

[14] A. Krishnamoorthy, R. Ho, X. Zheng, H. Schwetman, J. Lexau, P. Koka, G. Li, I. Shubin, and J. Cunningham. Computer systems based on silicon photonic interconnects. *Proceedings of the IEEE*, 97(7):1337 - 1361, July 2009.

[15] B. Lee, F. Doany, S. Assefa, W. Green, M. Yang, C. Schow, C. Jahnes, S. Zhang, J. Singer, V. Kopp, J. Kash, and Y. Vlasov. 20μm-pitch eight-channel monolithic fiber array coupling 160 Gb/s/channel to silicon nanophotonic chip. In *Conference on Optical Fiber Communications and National Fiber Optic Engineers Conference (OFC/NFOEC)*, pages 1 - 3, March 2010.

[16] S. Li, J. H. Ahn, R. D. Strong, J. B. Brockman, D. M. Tullsen, and N. P. Jouppi. McPAT: an integrated power, area, and timing modeling framework for multicore and manycore architectures. In *42nd Annual International Symposium on Microarchitecture*, 2009.

[17] R. Merritt. ARM CTO: Power surge could create dark silicon. http://www.eetimes.com/electronics-news/4085396/ARM-CTO-power-surge-could-create-dark-silicon-, October 2009.

[18] C. Nitta, M. Farrens, and V. Akella. Addressing system-level trimming issues in on-chip nanophotonic networks. In *17th International Symposium on High Performance Computer Architecture*, 2011.

[19] Y. Pan, Y. Demir, N. Hardavellas, J. Kim, and G. Memik. Exploring benefits and designs of optically connected disintegrated processor architecture. *Workshop on the Interaction between Nanophotonic Devices and Systems (in conjunction. with MICRO-43)*, 2010.

[20] Y. Pan, J. Kim, and G. Memik. FeatherWeight: low-cost optical arbitration with QoS support. In *44th IEEE/ACM Annual International Symposium on Microarchitecture*, pages 105- 116, 2011.

[21] Y. Pan, P. Kumar, J. Kim, G. Memik, Y. Zhang, and A. Choudhary. Firefly: Illuminating future network-on-chip with nanophotonics. In *36th International Symposium on Computer Architecture*, 2009.

[22] J. Poulton, R. Palmer, A. Fuller, T. Greer, J. Eyles, W. Dally, and M. Horowitz. A 14-mW 6.25-Gb/s transceiver in 90-nm CMOS. *IEEE Journal of Solid-State Circuits*, 42(12):2745- 2757, 2007.

[23] B. M. Rogers, A. Krishna, G. B. Bell, K. Vu, X. Jiang, and Y. Solihin. Scaling the bandwidth wall: challenges in and avenues for CMP scaling. In *36th Annual International Symposium on Computer Architecture*, pages 371- 382, 2009.

[24] P. Rosenfeld, E. Cooper-Balis, and B. Jacob. DRAMSIM 2: A cycle accurate memory system simulator. *Computer Architecture Letters*, 10(1):16- 19, 2011.

[25] K. Skadron, M. R. Stan, W. Huang, S. Velusamy, K. Sankaranarayanan, and D. Tarjan. Temperature-aware microarchitecture. In *30th Annual International Symposium on Computer Architecture*, pages 2- 13, 2003.

[26] C. Sun, C.-H. O. Chen, G. Kurian, L. Wei, J. Miller, A. Agarwal, L.-S. Peh, and V. Stojanovic. DSENT- a tool connecting emerging photonics with electronics for opto-electronic networks-on-chip modeling. In *6th International Symposium on Networks-on-Chip*, 2012.

[27] Y. Tamir and G. Frazier. Dynamically-allocated multi-queue buffers for VLSI communication switches. *IEEE Transactions on Computers*, pages 725- 737, 1992.

[28] D. Vantrease, R. Schreiber, M. Monchiero, M. McLaren, N. P. Jouppi, M. Fiorentino, A. Davis, N. Binkert, R. G. Beausoleil, and J. H. Ahn. Corona: system implications of emerging nanophotonic technology. In *35th Annual International Symposium on Computer Architecture*, pages 153- 164, 2008.

[29] T. F. Wenisch, R. E. Wunderlich, M. Ferdman, A. Ailamaki, B. Falsafi, and J. C. Hoe. SimFlex: statistical sampling of computer system simulation. *IEEE Micro*, 26(4):18- 31, July-August 2006.

[30] M. Yang. A comparison of using icepak and flotherm in electronic cooling. In *7th Intersociety Conference on Thermal and Thermomechanical Phenomena in Electronic Systems (ITHERM)*, Vol 1, 2000.

[31] X. Zheng, J. E. Cunningham, I. Shubin, J. Simons, M. Asghari, D. Feng, H. Lei, D. Zheng, H. Liang, C. chih Kung, J. Luff, T. Sze, D. Cohen, and A. V. Krishnamoorthy. Optical proximity communication using reflective mirrors. *Optics Express*, 16(19), Sept. 2008.

[32] A. Zilkie, B. Bijlani, P. Seddighian, D. C. Lee, W. Qian, J. Fong, R. Shafiiha, D. Feng, B. Luff, X. Zheng, J. Cunningham, A. V. Krishnamoorthy, and M. Asghari. High-efficiency hybrid III-V/Si external cavity DBR laser for 3μm SOI waveguides. In *9th IEEE International Conference on Group IV Photonics (GFP)*, 2012.

A Performance Perspective on Energy Efficient HPC Links

Karthikeyan P. Saravanan
karthikeyan.palavedu@bsc.es

Paul M. Carpenter
paul.carpenter@bsc.es

Alex Ramirez
alex.ramirez@bsc.es

Barcelona Supercomputing Center (BSC)/ Universitat Politècnica de Catalunya (UPC)

ABSTRACT

Energy costs are an increasing part of the total cost of owner-ship of HPC systems. As HPC systems become increasingly energy proportional in an effort to reduce energy costs, in-terconnect links stand out for their inefficiency. Commodity interconnect links remain "always-on", consuming full power even when no data is being transmitted. Although various techniques have been proposed towards energy-proportional interconnects, they are often too conservative or are not fo-cused toward HPC. Aggressive techniques for interconnect energy savings are often not applied to HPC, in particular, because they may incur excessive performance overheads. Any energy-saving technique will only be adopted in HPC if there is no significant impact on performance, which is still the primary design objective.

This paper explores interconnect energy proportionality from a performance perspective. We characterize HPC ap-plications over on/off links and propose PerfBound, a tech-nique that reduces link energy, subject to a bound on the ap-plication's performance degradation. We also propose Perf-BoundRatio, which maintains the same performance bound across an entire hierarchical network. Finally, we propose PerfBoundPredict, which improves energy savings using an idle time prediction mechanism. Even when predictions are inaccurate, the performance degradation is still bounded. The techniques require no changes to the application and add no communication between nodes and/or switches. We evaluate our techniques using HPC traces from production supercomputers. Our results show that, configured with a 1% performance bound, 13 out of 15 applications are in-side the bound, and average link energy savings are 60% for PerfBound and 68% for PerfBoundPredict.

Categories and Subject Descriptors

C.5 [**Computer System Implementation**]: *Super (very large) computers*

Keywords

Performance overhead bounding; Energy Efficient Ethernet; Energy proportional interconnects; Idle time prediction

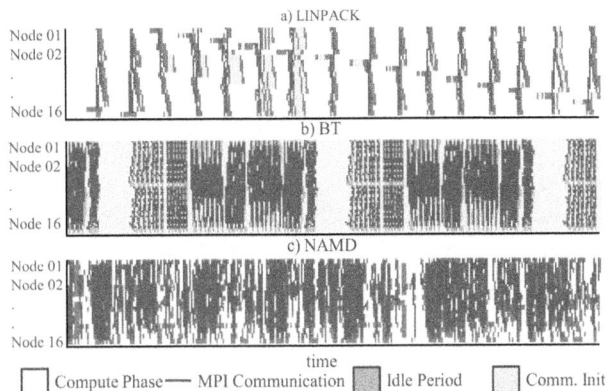

Figure 1: **Communication behavior in HPC applica-tions - LINPACK[1], BT[2] and NAMD[3]**

1. INTRODUCTION

Over the past decade, the field of HPC has become in-creasingly concerned by power consumption and energy ef-ficiency. This is especially true in the design of future exa-scale systems, which will only be practicable through a dra-matic improvement in energy efficiency [4]. Successive tech-nological advances in micro-architecture and process tech-nology have not only sustained tremendous performance scal-ing, but have also considerably increased performance per watt. With energy optimized processors and memory, at-tention is moving towards the interconnect.

Interconnects contribute a significant portion of the sys-tem's energy consumption. D. Abts et al. [5] recently showed that a typical interconnect consumes 12% of the total sys-tem power at full load, and more when the application does not fully utilize the CPU and memory. Improved energy proportionality in the compute elements naturally increases the proportion of energy consumed by the interconnect. The main reason for a lack of energy proportionality is that in-terconnect links, which consume up to 65% of the total in-terconnect power, are essentially "always-on", continually transmitting signals, even when idle, in order to maintain alignment and synchronization [6, 7, 8].

HPC applications require a high-performance intercon-nect, to support their peak communications demand, but the average utilization of the network is low. Moreover, much of the interconnect's idle time is contributed by relatively long idle periods [9, 10]. Figure 1 shows the communication behavior of LINPACK [1], BT [2], and NAMD [3]. Fourteen of the fifteen applications examined in this work exhibited regular patterns similar to Figures 1(a) and 1(b). These ap-plications have short intensive communication bursts, sepa-rated by long computation phases, during which the interconnect is idle. The final application, NAMD, shown in Figure 1(c), appears irregular, but it still exhibited low network utilization and considerable interconnect energy savings.

Several proposals attempt to exploit the above-mentioned opportunities to save energy [5, 11, 12, 13, 14]. These proposals are built upon one of the following underlying mechanisms. Firstly, *on/off links* are powered down during idle periods. An important example is IEEE 802.3az Energy Efficient Ethernet (EEE) [8, 15], approved in 2010, which is primarily designed to save network power consumption in homes, offices and data centres. Alternatively, *bandwidth tunable links* adapt the network bandwidth to the communication requirements, reducing the frequency or the number of channels when demand is low, and therefore also reducing the power consumption. An important example is InfiniBand, which implements variable bandwidth as well as a variable number of active $1\times$ links. Effective use of on/off links is especially important, given that it is the mechanism implemented in Energy Efficient Ethernet, and together, 1Gb and 10Gb Ethernet account for 43% of the systems in the November 2013 TOP500 list.

In both cases, changing power state incurs a delay; for example, EEE on a 10Gbps link requires $3\mu s$ to sleep and $4\mu s$ to wake. Also, the physical layer specification provides the underlying mechanisms, but the decisions as to when to enter and leave power-saving states are left to the vendor. These decisions are critical, especially in HPC, for which, although energy-efficiency is increasingly important, the primary design objective is still performance. Any proposed energy-saving technique will only be adopted if there is no significant reduction in performance.

This paper introduces *PerfBound*, a link energy saving technique for on/off links that reacts to performance overheads. The only parameter is a limit on the performance degradation, which was set to 1% in the evaluation. PerfBound is self-contained, in that the application is not modified and decisions are taken using local state, without any additional communication between nodes and/or switches.

In a multi-hop network, each link in the route may implement power-saving techniques, each of which may incur latency, multiplying the performance overheads. We therefore propose *PerfBoundRatio*, which maintains the same application performance target, across the whole hierarchical on/off network, by automatically adjusting to the application's communication locality. As for PerfBound, the application is not modified, decisions are taken using local state only, and there are no application-dependent parameters.

Finally, we propose *PerfBoundPredict*, which adds an idle time prediction mechanism, based on techniques used in CPU branch predictors. PerfBoundPredict exploits the fact that HPC application communication patterns are typically repetitive, and, when the idle period is predicted to be long, it enables the link to enter sleep mode without first waiting for the timer to elapse, which would otherwise incur unnecessary energy consumption. It also allows the link to be turned back on in time for the next message, avoiding the wake overhead. The interaction with PerfBound or PerfBoundRatio ensures that, even though prediction may be incorrect, the total performance degradation is still controlled.

In summary, in order for HPC to adapt energy proportional interconnects, it's crucial that performance overheads caused by the same are controlled. In this regard, the key novelty behind our work is that we examine and propose on/off link management mechanisms that account for performance degradation. To be specific, the novel contributions of this paper are as follows:

1. A detailed analysis of the communication behavior in HPC applications provides insights on the correct management of on/off links. We identify that, for the application to remain within a given performance overhead bound, a certain number of messages, per unit time, can be allowed to incur wakeup delays. We show how the energy savings depend on making the right choice of messages to delay.

2. We use the above insights to propose PerfBound, a technique that saves energy, subject to a bound on the performance degradation. PerfBound monitors the number of wake-up delays and it adjusts the internal parameters to become more or less aggressive, optimizing energy savings subject to the performance overhead bound. We also propose PerfBoundRatio, which respects the same bound on the total overhead in a hierarchical network.

3. Finally, we propose a prediction mechanism for predicting link idle period durations. Knowing the duration of the next idle period allows the link to be turned off immediately, when doing so is appropriate, and it allows the link to be turned back on in time for the next message, avoiding overheads. Prediction is disabled when idle periods are unpredictable. In addition, prediction is always controlled by PerfBound, and disabled when mis-prediction could breach the performance bound.

The rest of this paper is organized as follows. Section 2 discusses background and prior work. In Section 3, we investigate the causes of performance degradation and, based on insights gathered, make a case for performance bounding in interconnects. We propose our mechanisms and discuss their technical details. Finally in Sections 4 and 5, we discuss the evaluation of our proposed techniques and conclude.

2. BACKGROUND AND RELATED WORK

As discussed in the introduction, interconnect energy proportionality can be supported in two main ways: either through on/off links; e.g. Energy Efficient Ethernet, or through varying the bandwidth; e.g. InfiniBand. This paper focuses on on/off links, for two main reasons. Firstly, bandwidth tunable links at low power mode are still "always-on" at their lowest bandwidth. Recent work [5] found that in the lowest energy state, bandwidth tunable links consume 40% of their maximum power consumption. In contrast, when an on/off link is switched off, it typically consumes about 10% of peak power. Secondly, on/off links are used in Energy Efficient Ethernet, as described below. Although this paper does not discuss bandwidth tunable links any further, the contributions, specifically idle time characterization and prediction, can also be applied to bandwidth tunable links.

Energy Efficient Ethernet (EEE): In 2010, the IEEE 802.3az Energy Efficient Ethernet Task Force published its standard for Ethernet energy efficiency [8, 15]. Since Internet infrastructure is primarily built using Ethernet, the mandate of the task force was to reduce the significant contribution of these network devices to the national power budget [8, 11]. After considering various proposals, including adaptively changing the link rate, the task force adopted the proposal known as Low Power Idle (LPI) [8, 15].

Low Power Idle (LPI) proposes modifications to existing Ethernet standards that allow the link to switch between "sleep" and "wake" modes on demand, to save energy. At low power mode, the link is still periodically refreshed and awaits frames, hence is not completely off. Arrival of a frame triggers the signaling of a wake up transition to turn on the link. Frame transmission starts when both the transceiver and receiver PHY are both active. At the subsequent hop, arriving frames are buffered while a subsequent link is signalled for wake-up. LPI was considered straightforward to implement, since it freezes the state of the transceiver when the link enters sleep and it restores the state when it wakes [15]. Switches that support EEE, targeting data centers, are already commercially available.

The Ethernet family of interconnects is used in the largest share of systems in TOP500; specifically, 43% of the systems in the Nov. 2013 list use 1Gb/10Gb Ethernet. The growing popularity of Ethernet in HPC, coupled with the need for energy proportionality, makes a strong case for performance-aware techniques for EEE. We believe that the insights presented in this paper could help vendors in designing EEE technology for HPC and the standardization effort in the upcoming EEE for 40/100Gb links (IEEE P802.3bm). To this end, as discussed in the methodology section, the figures presented in this paper use timing information from the EEE specification.

2.1 Related Work

Jian Li, et al., [11] discuss on/off networks that use snoop messages that arrive at the NICs as an indication of an impending message. In nodes that have snoop-based coherence, snooping messages would arrive at the link before an impending message, which could be used to trigger the link on, before the actual arrival of the message. They also propose the use of an always-on control network that sends control signals through the routing path of a message to wake up subsequent links. They further propose software enhancements which would have programmers annotate the code signalling an impending message. Similarly, Soteriou, et al., [16] show that on/off networks incur a large performance penalty and hence, they propose software mechanisms such as parallelizing compilers for network power savings.

Gupta, et al., in their work [17], show opportunistic sleeping of links is possible, but their technique increases mean latency. Vassos, et al., [18] discusses a design space analysis for on/off based links. They propose using multiple routing paths available in torus like networks to shut down parts of the network during periods of low load. They evaluate their proposal with message arrivals following a Poisson process. Similarly, Alonso, et al., [19] propose shutting down redundant links (sub-trees) in their fat-tree system to save energy. These proposals do not discuss the performance impact of bursty communications that are typical of HPC. Similarly Ethernet evaluation reports [7, 8] also use synthetic benchmarks to evaluate on/off networks. Relevant work on Energy Efficient Ethernet [7, 8, 15, 20, 21, 22, 23] provide detailed evaluations on EEE for its potential for desktop and IT based systems; however, do not target HPC workloads. Totoni, et al., [24] show that not all links of a network executing an HPC application are utilized hence propose runtime techniques to find links in the network that are never utilized, to turn them off. However, their work does not adaptively turn on/off links.

D. Abts et al., [5] proposed energy proportional interconnects based on reducing the link rates of aggregated links. In their approach, during periods of inactivity, link rates are reduced to a lower link bandwidth to save energy. Work by Kim, et al., [14] evaluate energy proportional networks and compare links based on dynamic voltage scaling and on/off links. They show that dynamic voltage scaling in links causes a significant increase in latency and show that on/off based techniques perform comparatively better. Our previous work [10], presents a case for Energy Efficient Ethernet. We show that increase in latencies due to wake-up could be harmful to certain HPC applications. Furthermore, having the link on for a static period of time after link becomes idle, reduces performance overheads. However, the previous work is a static approach and cannot handle all applications. The difference between this work and the above proposals is that, it targets adaptive link energy savings accounting for application performance degradation.

Yoshi, et al., [25], propose ATPT - a prediction mechanism to find message sizes with src-dest pairs. They show that src-dest pairs could be used to improve prediction accuracy. When the size of the next message size is known, they tune the network frequency to the requirements of the next message size. Their work however does not predict idle link periods which are required for on/off based networks.

3. ENERGY EFFICIENT LINKS FOR HPC – A PERFORMANCE PERSPECTIVE

This section presents our performance-centric approach to energy efficiency in on/off based HPC interconnects.

3.1 Methodology

We used an extension of the Dimemas cluster simulator, which has been found to be accurate to within 10% and validated against production supercomputers, including Blue Gene/L, P, Q, and three generations of MareNostrum [26, 27, 28]. We modified the network model to support a hierarchical network, with on/off links controlled by our proposed techniques. The simulation infrastructure is driven by traces, which record CPU intervals and MPI events, independent of the network configuration, measured from a real execution on MareNostrum. The CPU intervals are scaled by relative CPU performance. MPI events imply dependencies, which ensure correctness. Link energy consumption is modelled as 100% when "on" or during transition between on/off states, and 10% when "off". All energy figures are normalised to percentage of original energy-to-solution.

The simulator is configured to model a cluster with a three-level hierarchical network. Applications are executed on 64, 128 or 256 nodes, grouped into 8, 16, or 32 nodes per rack, respectively, forming eight racks in total. Nodes are connected to the top-of-the-rack switch, which is in-turn connected to a two-level, four-node 2-ary fat tree. The network is statically routed, cut-through flow-control with fully duplex links. Each node is a two-socket high-end CPU with 225GFlops (based on TOP500 machines with two Intel Xeon sockets). The switch latency is configured at 320ns for the first hop and 80ns for subsequent hops. Edge links are configured at 20Gb/s, while the higher two levels are 40Gb/s and 100Gb/s respectively. The two directions of the full-duplex links can be turned on and off separately. We use the wake-up and sleep times of $4\mu s$ and $3\mu s$ for Energy Efficient Ethernet [8, 15].

We used fifteen HPC applications. The original traces were large, on the order of hundreds of gigabytes, so simulation was done for a few iterations of the outer loop, as shown in Figure 1. Traces obtained for ALYA[29], LINPACK[1], BT [2], CG[2], FT[2] and MG[2] where executed on 256 nodes, QUANTUM[30], WRF[31] MILC[32], GROMACS[33] and GADGET[34] on 128 nodes, and NAMD[3], PEPC[35], SP and LU[2] on 64 nodes.

3.2 Motivation

Although the EEE standard defines mechanisms for entering and leaving the sleep mode (low power idle), it does not define how to decide when to do so. A naive, and aggressive, technique is to always turn the link off as soon as it becomes idle and to turn it back on only on demand. There is, however, a fundamental trade-off between energy savings and performance overhead: aggressive techniques, such as the above save more energy but may introduce too much network latency, whereas conservative techniques incur a low performance overhead but they achieve little energy savings.

One difficulty in HPC is that different applications react differently to increases in latency. Figure 2 shows a sensitivity analysis of application performance to wake-up latency, assuming the naive management technique. The x-axis is the wake-up latency (which for EEE is about $4\mu s$/link). Applications that are least sensitive, including Quantum[30] and BT[2], can potentially tolerate an aggressive energy saving technique, since the naive approach incurs only about 2% performance overhead. In contrast, GROMACS[33] and NAMD[3] have unacceptable performance degradation, with their execution time roughly doubled, so they require a rather conservative energy saving scheme.

There are two questions related to the management of on/off links: when to turn the link off, and when to turn it back on. An ideal solution, which obtains maximum energy savings, is to turn the link off immediately after each message and to turn it back on at the correct time in anticipation of the next message (if the idle period is shorter than the sum of the sleep and wake times, then the link is, of course, not switched off). This scheme, however, requires an accurate and precise prediction of the arrival time of the next message. If the prediction is wrong, then, either the link is woken up too late, incurring a performance overhead, or too soon, wasting potential energy savings.

A simple mechanism that can work well is to turn the link off only after a specific duration of idle time, which we call the **LinkOFF threshold**, and to turn it back on when the next message arrives. The naive approach described above corresponds to LinkOFF=0. Our previous study [10] found that this mechanism can work well in HPC. Since different applications have different sensitivities to increases in latencies, the optimal value of LinkOFF depends on the application. This paper proposes PerfBound, which determines the correct LinkOFF threshold to obtain maximum energy savings subject to a performance bound. It also proposes PerfBoundRatio, which extends the scheme to cover hierarchical on/off networks.

Using the LinkOFF timer works well for both short idle periods, for which the link correctly remains on throughout, and long idle periods, for which its disadvantages are negligible: the energy consumption before the timer elapses is small, and so is the performance overhead of waking on demand. It works less well if there are a large number of idle periods of intermediate duration. We therefore propose PerfBoundPredict, which adds an idle time predictor. Since HPC application communication patterns are often

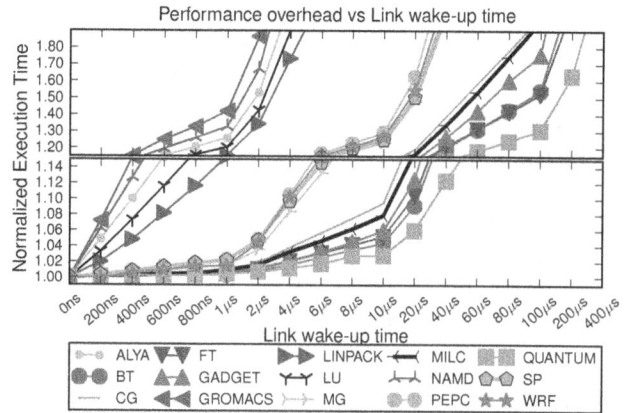

Figure 2: **Application performance overhead as a function of wake-up delay.**

repetitive, the idle time predictor is often able to provide an accurate prediction of the length of the idle period. If the idle period is predicted to be large enough, the link is switched off immediately and switched back on in time to avoid the wake overhead on the following message. This method avoids the energy consumption otherwise incurred before the LinkOFF threshold has elapsed, and it allows the link to be switched off inside much shorter idle periods, since the associated wake up latency is usually avoided. An important disadvantage of prediction is the potential performance impact of mis-prediction. Interaction with the performance bounding mechanism of PerfBound ensures that even when the prediction is not possible or is incorrect, the total performance degradation is still controlled.

Our first key insight, in the development of PerfBound, is that, since every time the link is switched off, one message will later be delayed by the wake-up time, the performance overhead is approximately proportional to the number of times the link is switched off. This is an approximation, since the method cannot track chains of dependencies among nodes. Tracking dependency chains requires either that the user or compiler annotates the application, or that additional messages are sent by the run-time system and monitored by the switches. Either approach adds complexity, with the result that such a proposal would be unlikely to be adopted in practice. We believe, on balance, that our approach gives the right compromise, especially since the results, described in Section 4, show that this approximation is generally sound. In summary, the performance overhead bound translates to a fixed number of messages, per unit time, that can be delayed. The following heuristics ensure that this number of delayed messages is not exceeded, and that the right choice of messages to delay is made, to get the maximum energy savings.

3.3 Understanding the overhead of link wake up and idle time predictability

In order to make overhead-aware decisions for link energy savings, it is important to first understand how wakeup latencies translate to performance overheads. In Figure 2, we showed that different applications have different sensitivities to wake-up latencies. To look at this question in more detail, we examine the application overheads by applying the wake-up delays selectively. From this point in this paper, we refer to "message inter-arrival periods" as **idle link events**.[1]

---

[1]In this paper, we term any duration during which no data is transmitted over a link as an *idle link event*

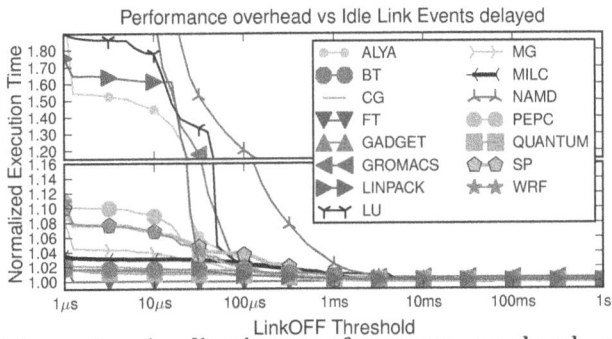

Figure 3: **Application performance overhead as LinkOFF threshold is varied - normalised to execution over an always-on network.**

Figure 3 shows a sensitivity analysis plot relating the LinkOFF threshold, on the x-axis, to application performance. As mentioned previously, the LinkOFF threshold controls the time for which the link must be idle, but kept on, before it is turned off. At low values of the LinkOFF threshold, the links turn off after many short idle periods, which translates to high performance overheads, due to the latency of frequently turning back on when required. As the LinkOFF threshold is increased, the performance overhead drops, eventually approaching zero. This is because, as the threshold is increased, the number of idle link events that exceed the threshold decreases towards zero. If an acceptable level of performance overhead for the application is 5%, for example, then Figure 3 can be used to determine an application-dependent static value for the LinkOFF threshold. For application LU, for instance, we can see that an appropriate value of the LinkOFF threshold would be 80μs. In this case, the link remains on for the first 80μs in each idle period, saving power on all idle link events that are longer than this, but maintaining performance overhead inside the specified bound of 5%.

The application behavior can be understood in greater detail, from the perspective of idle link events, by looking at the heatmaps in Figure 4. All sub-figures show the length of the current idle link event on the x-axis and the length of the next idle link event on the y-axis, for LINPACK[1], BT[2] and NAMD[3] according to the title. Figures 4(a), 4(c) and 4(e) are colored according to the *number of events*, whereas Figures 4(b), 4(d) and 4(f) are colored according to the total idle time contributed by those events. That is, if in Figure 4(a) there are 100 events in position (2ms, 2ms), then their total idle time would be 200ms. The idle link event heatmap gives a sense of the most common idle durations, which is helpful for prediction, and the total idle time helps understand how the idle time translates to energy savings. The results in these figures are averages across all edge links in the network.

Both applications LINPACK and BT are typical examples of HPC applications and shown, the difference between Figures 4(a) and 4(c) is in the clustering of idle link events. In the case of LINPACK, in Figure 4(a), the events are clustered at around 10μs, while the events in BT are clustered at around 1ms. Another key difference between these applications is clearly seen in Figures 4(b) and 4(d): the majority of the idle link events of LINPACK are of 10μs, but most of its total idle time comes from events that are longer than 10ms, even though there are few of them. A similar behavior can be seen in BT, where a small number of events longer than 10ms also contribute to a significant amount of total

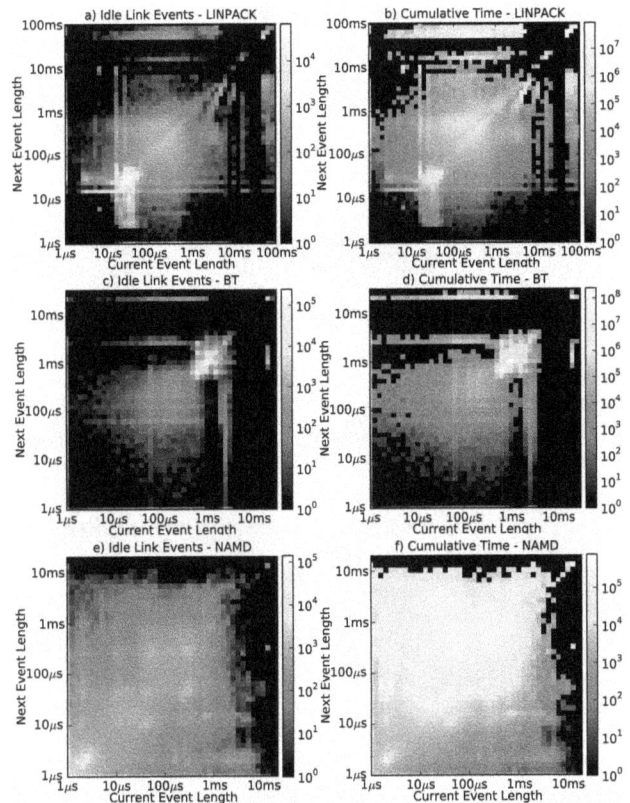

Figure 4: **Idle Link Event distributions of LINPACK(a,b), BT(c,d), NAMD(e,f) - (a),(c),(e) Heat map of the idle link event duration; (b),(d),(f) Heat map of total idle time (Number events × duration)**

idle time. The main difference for BT is that its most common idle link event duration also contributes significantly to the total idle time. Further, as mentioned in the introduction, NAMD is an outlier in our set of applications. In Figures 4(e) and 4(f), it is clear that the application is irregular. In the context of predictability, for any current idle link event of 4(e) there are no event clusters that have an especially high probability. In other words, in the case of NAMD, given knowledge of the current event's length, the next event could have any length. As shown in Figures 4(a) and 4(c), in contrast, LINPACK and BT show reasonable predictability. In the case of LINPACK, for any event of size between 10μs and 100μs, there exists a high probability that the next event is the same size; similarly in the case of BT, for events of between 1ms and 10ms.

Comparing Figures 3 and 4, we can explain the observed performance overheads. Firstly, note from Figure 3, that the performance overhead of LINPACK remains at about 60% until the LinkOFF threshold is increased to 10μs, where it drops to about 2% between 10μs and 100μs. Comparing that to Figure 4(a), the performance overhead has clearly dropped as the LinkOFF threshold crossed the cluster between 10μs and 100μs. In other words, if the link remains on for about 100μs, none of the events in the cluster in Figure 4(a) would incur performance overheads. Similarly, in the case of BT, comparing Figures 3 and 4(c), we can see that the performance overhead of BT, starting from 2%, drops to near zero at about 1ms; this correlates to the clustering found at 1ms in Figure 4(c). Finally, in the case of NAMD, since there are no clusters and the distribution of events is uniform, we find a gradual decrease in performance over-head, as LinkOFF is increased, falling below 1% above a threshold of 2ms, which correlates with Figure 4(e). Note that the clustering observed in Figures 4(a) and 4(c) are due to repetitive patterns in these applications (as seen in Figure 1), which are not seen in irregular application NAMD. Furthermore, BT has low performance overhead, even at low values of the LinkOFF threshold, because, first, at low threshold values in Figure 4(c), no events exist to incur performance delays. Since, for BT, the number of events that exist between $1\mu s$ and 1ms is low, the reduction in the performance overhead is gradual. Secondly, for large events, the ratio of event size to delay incurred is very low. To illustrate, when a delay of $1\mu s$ is applied to an event of 1ms, the added delay corresponds to 0.1%. For LINPACK, most events are clustered at $10\mu s$, so if a $1\mu s$ delay is added to them, each delay adds 10% of the idle time, translating to large performance overheads.

3.4 PerfBound: Bounding performance over-heads in on/off HPC links

The application analysis in Section 3.3 provides several key insights. First, the application overhead is roughly proportional to the number of delayed idle link events. Secondly, the application overhead can be adjusted using the LinkOFF threshold. Thirdly, the best LinkOFF threshold depends on the application, so the algorithm itself must be dynamic, adaptive and application independent. Finally, from an energy standpoint, it is best to delay the events of longest duration. Based on the above, we propose Perf-Bound and PerfBoundRatio. The only parameter to the algorithms is a limit on performance degradation, which we set to 1% in the evaluation. For the purpose of the exposition, we assume that the limit is 1%, but it should be clear how to make the bound into a parameter. The approach is to first determine how many idle link events can be delayed per unit time before the overhead reaches 1%, and then to ensure that the right number of events are delayed and that they are the longest ones. The latter is done by dynamically adjusting the LinkOFF threshold.

3.4.1 Calculating the #events that can be delayed:

We first analyse the case where there is a single hop between two nodes. Since the overhead is assumed to come only from delayed wakeup events, the maximum number of them that can be tolerated, within a 1% bound, in a period of length X is simply $0.01X / T_w$, where T_w is the wakeup delay and 0.01 corresponds to the 1% bound. As X increases, the total number of events that can be delayed also increases, in proportion. This is the value used by **Perf-Bound**, when configured with a local performance bound of 1%. The next section will describe how the LinkOFF threshold is adjusted to delay the correct number of events.

In a multi-hop network, each link in the route may implement PerfBound, multiplying the resulting performance overhead. A three-level network has a maximum hop count of six, so a single message may incur cumulative wakeup delays on three upward links and three downward links. Using the above equation directly leads to a total overhead of up to 6%. The simplest solution is to divide the global 1% performance bound equally among the links, so that each link uses PerfBound with a local performance bound of 0.166%.

This is, however, unnecessarily conservative. An application that mainly communicates at Level 0 (say), would

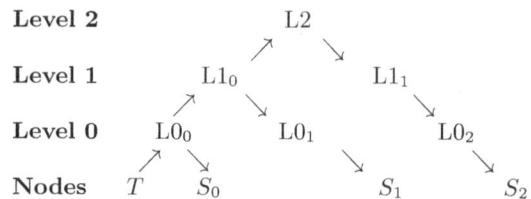

Figure 5: **Example network topology**

Link	Total messages	Messages/level			Proportion to level		
		L0	L1	L2	L0	L1	L2
T to $L0_0$	1000	500	400	100	0.5	0.4	0.1
$L0_0$ to S_0	500	500	0	0	1.0	0	0
$L0_0$ to $L1_0$	500	0	400	100	0	0.8	0.2
$L1_0$ to $L0_1$	400	0	400	0	0	1.0	0
$L0_1$ to S_1	400	0	400	0	0	1.0	0
$L1_0$ to $L2$	100	0	0	100	0	0	1.0
$L2$ to $L1_1$	100	0	0	100	0	0	1.0
$L1_1$ to $L0_2$	100	0	0	100	0	0	1.0
$L0_2$ to S_2	100	0	0	100	0	0	1.0

Table 1: **PerfBoundRatio: Example calculation of local state, when 50%, 40% and 10% of messages reach levels 0, 1 and 2, respectively.**

rarely incur overheads at the upper levels, meaning that the overhead is actually being constrained to 0.33%. Although a lower overhead is better, all else being equal, the configured 1% performance bound would probably have led to greater energy savings. Our solution for multi-hop networks is **PerfBoundRatio**, which is configured with a global performance bound. It adapts dynamically to the locality of the application's communication pattern, using only the information that is available locally at the switch. In order to use PerfBound, each switch must be given enough information about the network topology to be able to calculate the level of the highest switch in the route between any pair of source and destination IP addresses. This may require specific configuration, but for an HPC system, such configuration is tolerable.

We explain PerfBoundRatio using the example three-level network in Figure 5. The switches are labeled with the level and a unique number; e.g. $L1_1$ is one of the switches in level 1 and nodes are labeled T and S_0 to S_2. Let us assume, node T transmits 1000 messages in total, to S_0, S_1 and S_2, in proportion 50%, 40% and 10%, respectively. In a real application, all nodes will transmit, with different distributions to various nodes, but the total counts are simply the sums of the various contributions, and the algorithm still works. It can be best understood by looking at a simple case.

Each link has four counters, one that counts the total number of messages over the link, and three messages/level counters, each corresponding to a level in the network. The messages/level counter for level n counts the number of messages seen whose highest level in the network is exactly n. This information is summarized, for all links, in Table 1. This table also shows the proportion of messages that go to each level, found by dividing by the total number of messages. For example, the link between $L0_0$ and $L1_0$ sees all messages from T that go to either S_1 or S_2. There are 500 such messages, of which 400 go to S_1, reaching level 1, and 100 go to S_2, reaching level 2. The ratios of messages that reach levels 0, 1 and 2, respectively, are 0, 0.8 and 0.2.

The key idea is to divide the global performance bound according to the behavior of the communication traffic. Of the 500 messages that are seen over the link between $L0_0$ and

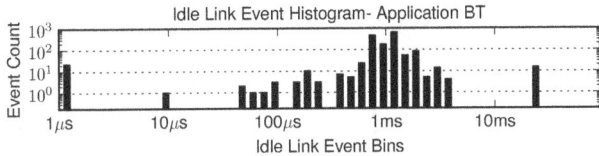

Figure 6: **Snapshot of an Idle Link Event Histogram**

$L1_0$, 80% of the messages that reach network level 1, have four hops on their route, whereas the 20% of messages that reach network level 2, have six hops. The local performance bound is therefore given by $0.8 \times \frac{0.01}{4} + 0.2 \times \frac{0.01}{6}$. In this equation, the weighing factors of 0.8 and 0.2 are given by the message statistics, 0.01 is the global performance bound, and the denominators are the numbers of hops on the routes.

In general, for a particular link, let $LC0$ be the total number of messages that reach maximum level 0, $LC1$ be the total number that reach maximum level 1, and $LC2$ the total number that reach level 2. Let $LC = LC0 + LC1 + LC2$ be the local total message counter. Then the local performance bound (as shown in Table 1) for that link is given by

$$l = \frac{LC0}{LC} \cdot \frac{0.01}{2} + \frac{LC1}{LC} \cdot \frac{0.01}{4} + \frac{LC2}{LC} \cdot \frac{0.01}{6}$$

3.4.2 Calculating the LinkOFF threshold:

After calculating the total number of events that can be delayed, per unit time, the final step is to determine the LinkOFF threshold. As described in Section 3.2, the LinkOFF threshold is the duration of time that the link must remain idle before it is switched off.

The LinkOFF threshold is determined from a histogram of idle link events. In detail, at the end of every idle link event, one new data point is available. This data point is the length of the previous idle link event. As shown in Figure 6, the bin corresponding to this length is determined and its histogram value is incremented. The histogram therefore keeps track of the distribution of link idle interval lengths, and its total mass increases over time. The LinkOFF threshold is found by searching from the right-hand side of the histogram; i.e. from the longest idle intervals, until the correct total number of messages has been found. That is, if the histogram has been collected for total time X, then the previous section gives the number of messages to delay as $N = lX / T_w$, where l is the local performance bound. The threshold is given by the midpoint of the smallest bin that has a total of at most N messages in all bins to its right.

The amount of work per message is constant and rather small, since it is only necessary to update the histogram and search for the correct value of LinkOFF. In our experiments, the LinkOFF threshold value is updated after every idle link event, but clearly it can be updated less frequently if desired. Alternatively, the algorithm can easily be optimized to take advantage of the fact that the correct value of LinkOFF seldom moves by more than one bin at a time.

Figure 7 shows three important characteristics of the algorithm. The x-axis is time, or more accurately a sequence number for the idle link event, and the y-axis is the value of the LinkOFF threshold, measured for a particular, but arbitrary, edge link (other edge links had similar behavior). Firstly, the correct value of the LinkOFF threshold differs dramatically between benchmarks—notice the logarithmic scale on the y-axis. Secondly, most applications rapidly converge to a stable value of the LinkOFF threshold, within just 200 events. This stable value can be compared with the point in Figure 3 where the overhead drops below 1%.

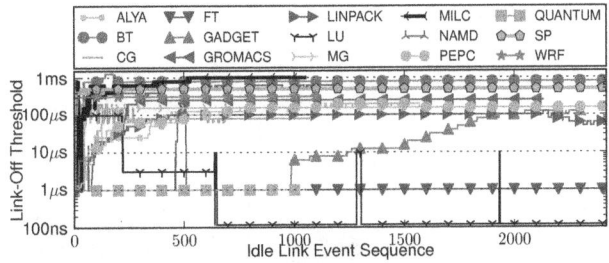

Figure 7: **LinkOFF threshold convergence over time**

Thirdly, for some benchmarks, most clearly LU, LinkOFF threshold is seen to adapt to varying application phases.

Although we discuss our mechanisms per *unit-time*, structures are refreshed in *idle link events*, e.g. every 20,000 idle link events, irrespective of the elapsed time or application. In Figure 7, we show that, for all applications, the algorithm converges within 200 events, which is only 1% of 20,000, hence a negligible fraction. When a new application begins, only the first refresh cycle has events from the old application. In the worst case, at $4\mu s$ and 6 hops/message incurred on all 20,000 events in the first refresh cycle, the overhead is $\leq 480ms$, which is negligible compared with typical application execution times.

3.5 PerfBoundPredict: Prediction over Perf-Bound for On/Off networks

It is clear, both from the above analysis and from the traces in Figure 1, that HPC applications exhibit repetitive behavior. This repetitive behavior translates to periodic and predictable idle link events. We use this insight to propose an idle period predictor that detects repetitive idle link events in order to turn off the link immediately as opposed to waiting for the LinkOFF threshold to expire.

This section describes **PerfBoundPredict**, an idle period predictor, whose performance overhead is controlled by PerfBound. Whenever the length of the upcoming idle period cannot be predicted with high confidence, the algorithm defaults to PerfBound. In addition, whenever the predictor mis-predicts, the performance overhead of one additional wakeup delay is compensated for: either by throttling prediction or by adjusting the LinkOFF threshold.

We borrow from ATPT [25], by predicting based on source-destination pairs. ATPT predicts the total amount of data transferred, whereas PerfBoundPredict is concerned with idle link durations. One challenge in predicting the lengths of idle periods is that there is always some noise; i.e., no two idle link events have *exactly* the same duration. This is handled by effectively quantizing the idle link events; that is, more accurately, by considering two idle link events to be the same if they differ by less than ±20%. We propose this tolerance based on experiments that showed a steep reduction in the number of unique idle link events up to ±20%. This means that the wakeup time must be up to 20% before the predicted event, since that prediction could correspond to a value as small as that. Finally, we ignore all events that are smaller than twice the time required for link wake-up and sleep, since there are many such events but they do not provide significant benefits for energy savings.

Figure 8 shows how classifying idle link events by the src-dest pair for the preceding message helps to identify repetitive behavior. Figure 8(a) plots the event duration on the y-axis for all idle link events, arranged along the x-axis. The data is for a fixed but arbitrary edge link, for application BT;

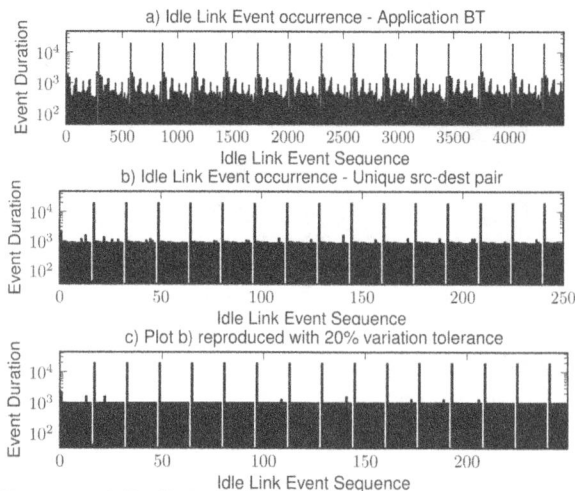

Figure 8: **Idle link events sequence of occurrence**

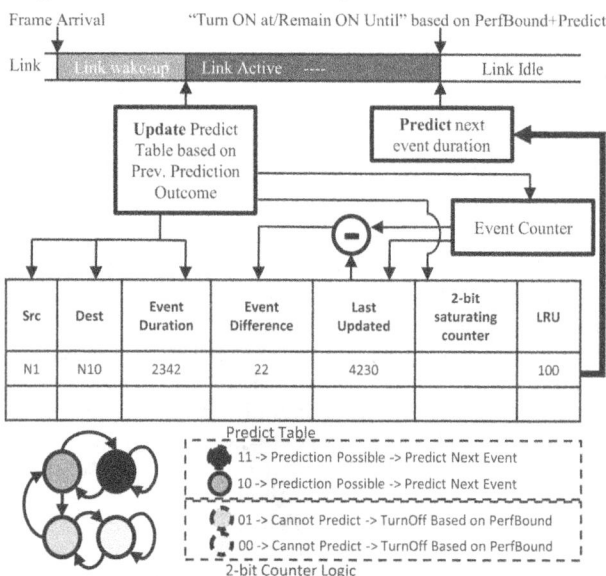

Figure 9: **Block diagram of PerfBoundPredict**

other edge links have similar behavior. Two things are apparent in Figure 8(a). First, large events occur periodically, but smaller events are more sporadic. Figure 8(b) shows only those idle link events that follow a message on a specific src-dest pair. Note that not all src-dest pairs attach to large idle events. Most of the other src-dest pairs we examined had no large idle events at all. In fact, we chose the src-dest pair that contains all of the large events visible in Figure 8(a). In Figure 8(b), all large events are separated from the preceding one by exactly the same number of idle link events. In Figure 8(c), we account for variation in the idle event durations by applying ± 20% variation tolerance.

Figure 9, shows a block diagram of the proposed prediction mechanism. The predictor has two functions, **update** state and **predict** state. As shown in the figure, update state is invoked whenever a link is woken up. During update state, all fields in the predict table are updated with the previous idle link event. Predict state is invoked whenever the link becomes idle. The predict table is accessed, based on the recent src-dest, to make an idle time prediction. When prediction is not possible, algorithm defaults to remain on until LinkOFF threshold.

The predict table contains many entries, each of which

contains the following: src-dest, the previous idle link *Event Duration*, a 2-bit counter for prediction confidence and a *Least Recently Used* (LRU) value. It also contains the *Event Difference* and *Last Updated* values. An *Event Counter* tracks the total number of idle link events that has progressed. The *Last Updated* value is updated, as described below, to contain a previous value of the *Event Counter*. The *Event Difference* is the period between successive similar idle link events.

The update stage, after the link is woken up, updates predict table with the duration of the previous idle link event and the src-dest addresses of the previous message. The predict table is indexed using the src-dest and idle link event duration, to find any already existing entries. If such a src-dest exists, and its event duration falls within ± 20% of the original entry, then an *Event Difference* is calculated as the difference between the current *Event Counter* value and the *Last Updated* value in the entry. If this *Event Difference* matches the entry in the predict table, then a repetitive pattern is found, and the 2-bit counter is incremented. If it does not match, then the 2-bit counter is decremented. In either case, the *Last Updated* field is updated to equal the current *Event Counter*. If, on decrementing, the 2-bit counter reaches zero, then the new *Event Difference* replaces the old one. In any case, the LRU is refreshed, moving the entry to the top of the table. Finally, if there is no matching event, a new one is added, overwriting the entry with the oldest LRU value.

Prediction is done, whenever the link becomes idle based on the src-dest pair of the recent message. First, the src-dest pair is used to obtain a list of all matching entries in the predict table. Each entry in the predict table is checked in turn, starting from the most recent, by first calculating the *Current Event Difference* as the difference between *Event counter+1*, which corresponds to the event counter after this idle period, and the *Last Updated Value* in the entry. If the *Current Event Difference* matches the *Event Difference* in the table, then the entry is a tentative match. In this case, the 2-bit counter is checked for confidence. If it indicates a reliable prediction, then the link is immediately turned off, and scheduled to turn back on after a time given by the *Event Duration* minus 20%. If no tentative match is found whose 2-bit counter indicates a reliable prediction, then the algorithm defaults to PerfBound or PerfBoundRatio, by remaining on for a time given by LinkOFF threshold.

4. RESULTS

Figure 10 shows the normalized application execution time, for each application referenced in the previous section, relative to the same system with an always-on interconnect. Figure 11 is similar, but for *link energy* savings, separately for each level of the network, where level 0 is connected to the nodes and level 2 is the highest. The energy saving mechanisms are identified as follows: Toff turns off each link as soon as it becomes idle. T50us is an arbitrary static LinkOFF threshold which has the link on for 50us before turning off. Since worst-case static LinkOFF threshold and PerfBound are described only for a single hop, results for the 3-level hierarchical network are given for three variants - allocating the 1% performance overhead equally among two, four or six hops. For example Ton4hop is static LinkOFF threshold tolerating a 0.25% overhead per hop; since the wake-up latency is $T_w = 4\mu s$, this bound is enforced whenever the LinkOFF threshold is at least $T_w/0.0025$. In con-

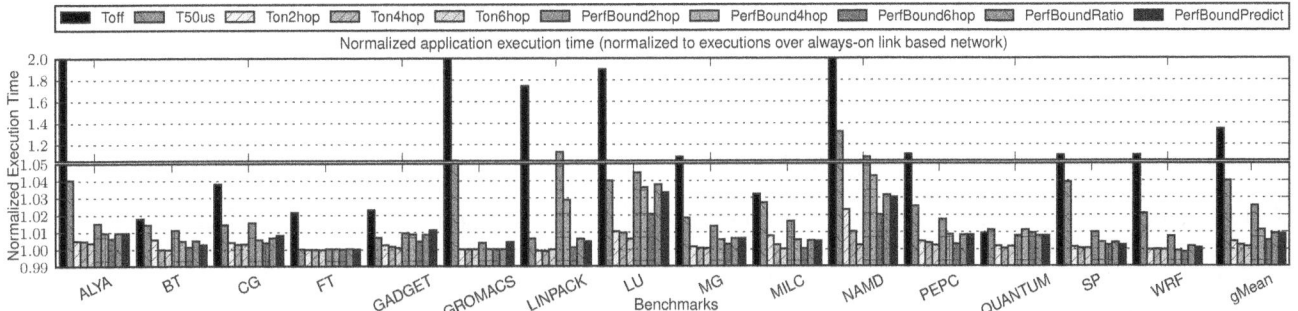

Figure 10: **Application incurred performance overheads over techniques proposed**

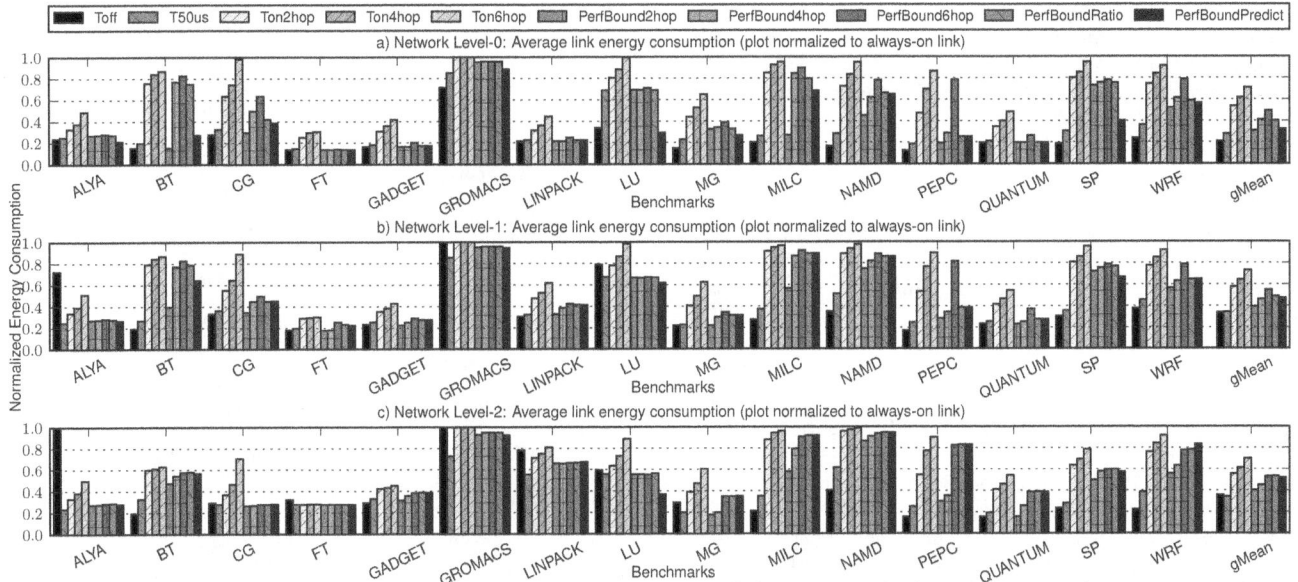

Figure 11: **Average energy consumption of links over techniques proposed**

sequence, Ton2hop has greater energy savings, but, since it allocates 0.5% potential overhead to each hop, total overhead may reach 3%, while Ton6hop is conservative. PerfBound(2,4,6)hop are similar, but they use PerfBound instead of static LinkOFF threshold. Finally, PerfBoundRatio and PerfBoundPredict are the proposed algorithms. Since they naturally support hierarchical networks, the typical number of hops does not need estimating. The results include the full execution time, including warm-up periods for training the predictor and PerfBound mechanisms.

On average, as shown in Figure 10, proposed mechanisms PerfBoundRatio and PerfBoundPredict both remain within the assigned performance degradation bound of 1%. In comparison to Toff, our mechanisms (on average) reduce possible performance degradation from about 40% to assigned 1%. PerfBound2hop, expectedly exceeds assigned PerfBound to about 2.5% while PerfBound6hop is well within 1% at about 0.5%. As mentioned above it is clear from the results that PerfBound2hop and PerfBound4hop are too optimistic while PerfBound6hop is too conservative and PerfBoundRatio performs better at maintaining the assigned PerfBound. Static LinkOFF threshold values Ton(2,4,6)hop and T50us have performance degradation of 0.5% and 4% respectively.

With respect to energy, as shown in Figure 11, on average, Toff and T50us gives the highest link energy savings, followed by PerfBoundPredict and PerfBoundRatio. Note that the difference in energy savings between our proposed PerfBoundRatio or PerfBoundPredict and the naive Toff technique is less than 20%, while on average PerfBound

reduces performance degradation by about 40%. On average, PerfBoundPredict produces 8.5% higher energy savings compared to PerfBoundRatio and overall, PerfBoundPredict saves link energy by 68.5% compared to an always-on network followed by PerfBoundRatio which saves 60% in network Level-1. Similarly, at higher levels 2 and 3, PerfBoundPredict saves 55% and 49% and PerfBoundRatio saves 51% and 48% respectively. Note that higher levels of the network tend to have higher traffic, reducing possible opportunity for energy savings. Prediction technique works best in the lower levels (which contain the highest proportion of links in the network) and less well at the higher levels which are subject to more noise. Note that the lower prediction accuracy has not contributed to higher performance degradation. PerfBound(2,4,6)hop have lower/higher energy savings respective their performance degradation.

Four of the bars in the figures are for static values of the LinkOFF threshold. The 50us static LinkOFF threshold (T50us) achieves good link energy savings, but the worst-case performance degradation of 30% is unacceptable. In comparison, the worst-case overhead for PerfBoundRatio is 4% and for PerfBoundPredict 3.5%. On the other hand, Ton(2,4,6)hop have <=1% overhead, but their energy consumption is more than twice that of PerfBoundRatio and PerfBoundPredict, at 77% rather than 37%. We also performed a sweep to find the best static LinkOFF threshold. We found that a value of 500us or larger is needed to reduce the worst-case overhead, for our benchmarks, to 4%. At this point the average energy consumption increases to 49% of the original, compared with 40% for PerfBoundRatio and 35% for PerfBoundPredict. Moreover, to be confident that the worst case overhead in production is reasonable, a prudent system designer should choose an even larger LinkOFF threshold, similar to the values used by Ton(2,4,6)hop. As previously described, this would lead to link energy consumption roughly double that of PerfBoundRatio/Predict.

In Figures 10 and 11 it is clear that some applications, more than others, benefit from predictability. Application LINPACK, for example, has no benefit from prediction. This lack of benefit is because PerfBoundRatio works very well for LINPACK leaving little scope for improvement. PerfBoundPredict saves energy by switching off the link immediately without having to wait for LinkOFF threshold timer to expire. Hence consequently if LinkOFF timer is small, relative benefit from PerfBoundPredict mechanism is low. LINPACK, as explained in Section 3.3 and as seen in Figures 4(a) and 4(b), contains few events that contribute to majority of the idle time while most events are small and fit into a rather small LinkOFF Threshold value.

Contrary to the above, BT appears to benefit by about 60% from prediction. Unlike LINPACK, BT contains a large number of events that are large and contribute significantly to idle time of the application (Figure 4). Since LinkOFF threshold for BT is large, turning off the link immediately results in larger power savings. Interestingly, in Figure 11, we find that PerfBound2hop performs better than PerfBoundPredict. The reason for this can be seen in Figure 10, since, unlike other mechanisms, PerfBound2hop exceeds the PerfBound value of 1% by a small amount. This small amount is essentially the difference between a LinkOFF threshold larger than or smaller than that of the large cluster of events observed in Figure 4(c). When LinkOFF threshold is larger, as in PerfBoundRatio, 1% PerfBound is maintained, however lesser energy is saved, when smaller, 1% PerfBound is not maintained, as in PerfBound2hop, however higher link energy is saved. Similar behavior can be observed at a smaller scale in applications CG and MILC.

The two outliers whose overhead are not bounded are NAMD and LU, due to dependencies in their messages i.e., messages in these applications are not transmitted until the reception of dependent messages. Further, as shown in Figure 1(c), NAMD does not have patterns to exploit for energy savings. Note that in both cases, performance overhead is still less than 4% with link energy savings up to 70%.

5. CONCLUSIONS

Interconnect inefficiency is a growing problem in HPC. While HPC applications have potential for link energy savings, techniques can only be employed if performance degradation is controlled. In this paper, we presented three techniques towards the above in the context of on/off links - PerfBound, PerfBoundRatio and PerfBoundPredict. We showed that significant energy savings can be obtained while performance overhead is bounded. Our techniques do not require modifications to the application/compilers nor does it introduce extra traffic into the network. The key novelty of our work is the analysis of link energy from a *performance perspective* - linking application performance degradation with link energy savings. Furthermore, we presented detailed analysis and insights on HPC application behavior with respect to link idle periods. We believe that our techniques and analysis could be useful in the upcoming standardization of Energy Efficient Ethernet for 40/100Gb links.

6. ACKNOWLEDGMENTS

This research was supported by the Ministry of Economy and Competitiveness of Spain under the contract TIN2012-34557, HiPEAC-3 Network of Excellence (ICT-287759), European Union's 7th Framework Programme [FP7/2007-2013] under project Mont-Blanc (288777), Generalitat de Catalunya (FI-AGAUR 2012 FI B 00644) and finally Severo Ochoa Program (SEV-2011-00067) of the Spanish Government.

References

[1] D. Teresa et al. High performance linpack benchmark: a fault tolerant implementation without checkpointing. In *International Supercomputing Conference (SC)*, 2011.
[2] NAS Parallel Benchmarks.
[3] R. K. Brunner et al. Scalable Molecular Dynamics for Large Biomolecular Systems. In *Supercomputing Conference*, 2000.
[4] DARPA. Ubiquitous High Performance Computing (UHPC) Broad Agency Announcement (BAA). 2010.
[5] D Abts et al. Energy Proportional Datacenter Networks. In *International Symposium on Computer Architecture*, 2010.
[6] Ripduman Sohan et al. Characterizing 10 Gbps network interface energy consumption. In *LCN*, 2010.
[7] Reviriego P. et al. Performance evaluation of energy efficient ethernet. *Comm. Letters.*, 13(9):697–699, September 2009.
[8] Christensen Ken et al. IEEE 802.3az: the road to energy efficient ethernet. *Comm. Mag.*, 48(11):50–56, nov 2010.
[9] S Conner et al. Link shutdown opportunities during collective communications in 3-D torus nets. In *IPDPS 2007*.
[10] K P Saravanan et al. Power/Performance Evaluation of Energy Efficient Ethernet (EEE) for High Performance Computing. In *IEEE ISPASS*, 2013.
[11] Li Jian et al. Power shifting in Thrifty Interconnection Network. In *High Performance Computer Architecture*, 2011.
[12] Li Shang et al. Dynamic voltage scaling with links for power optimization of interconnection networks. *HPCA*, 2003.
[13] V Soteriou et al. Dynamic power management for power optimization of interconnection networks using on/off links. In *High Performance Interconnects*, pages 15–20. IEEE, 2003.
[14] Eun Jung Kim et al. Energy optimization techniques in cluster interconnects. In *ISLPED*, 2003.
[15] Active/Idle Toggling with Low Power Idle, IEEE 802.3az.
[16] Vassos Soteriou et al. Software-directed power-aware interconnection networks. *TACO*, 2007.
[17] Maruti Gupta et al. Dynamic ethernet link shutdown for energy conservation on ethernet links. In *ICC'07*.
[18] Soteriou et al. Design-space exploration of power-aware on/off interconnection networks. In *ICCD*, 2004.
[19] Alonso Marina et al. Dynamic power saving in fat-tree interconnection networks using on/off links. IPDPS, 2006.
[20] Chamara Gunaratne et al. Ethernet adaptive link rate (alr): Analysis of a buffer threshold policy. In *GLOBECOM*, 2006.
[21] Baoke Zhang et al. Real-time performance analysis of Adaptive Link Rate. In *Local Computer Networks (LCN)*, 2008.
[22] Blanquicet Francisco et al. An Initial Performance Evaluation of Rapid PHY Selection (RPS) for Energy Efficient Ethernet. Local Computer Networks (LCN), 2007.
[23] Koibuchi M. et al. An on/off link activation method for low-power ethernet in PC clusters. IPDPS, 2009.
[24] Totoni et al. Toward Runtime Power Management of Exascale Networks by On/Off Control of Links. In *IPDPS-W'13*.
[25] YS-C Huang et al. Application-driven end-to-end traffic predictions for low power NoC design. In *VLSI Systems*, 2013.
[26] Rosa M. Badia et al. Dimemas: Predicting MPI applications behaviour in Grid environments. GGF8 Workshop, 2003.
[27] Sergi Girona et al. Validation of dimemas communication model for mpi collective operations. In *EuroPVM/MPI'00*.
[28] J. Gonzalez et al. Simulating whole supercomputer applications. In *IEEE MICRO*, 2011.
[29] Alya Red:Computational Biomechanics for Supercomputers.
[30] QUANTUM ESPRESSO: a modular and open-source software project for quantum simulations of materials.
[31] Michalakes et al. The Weather Reseach and Forecast Model: Software Architecture and Performance. In *ECMWF*, 2004.
[32] MIMD lattice computation collaboration.
[33] Hess et al. GROMACS 4: Algorithms for highly efficient, load-balanced, and scalable molecular simulation. *Journal of chemical theory and computation*, 2008.
[34] The cosmological simulation code gadget-2.
[35] PEPC: Pretty Efficient Parallel Coulomb-solve, Interner Bericht Zentralinstitut fur Angewandte Mathematik.

Verifying Micro-Architecture Simulators using Event Traces

Hui Meen Nyew   Nilufer Onder   Soner Onder   Zhenlin Wang

Department of Computer Science
Michigan Technological University
Houghton, MI 49931
{hnyew,nilufer,soner,zlwang}@mtu.edu

ABSTRACT

Contemporary micro-architecture research inherently relies on cycle-accurate simulators to test new ideas. Typical simulator implementations involve tens of thousands of lines of high-level code. Although general software engineering verification and validation techniques can be applied, the mere complexity of simulators makes using formal techniques difficult and calls for domain-specific knowledge to be a part of the verification process. This domain-specific information includes modeling the pipeline stages and the timing behavior of instructions with respect to these stages.

We present an approach to simulator verification that uses domain-specific information to effectively capture a potential mismatch between the assumed architecture model and its simulator. We first discuss how a simulator-generated event trace can be fed into an automatically generated verification program from a first-order logic specification to verify that the simulator obeys the invariants. We then show techniques that extract simulator behavior from traces and present the results to the user in the form of graphs and rules. While the former seeks an assurance of implementation correctness by checking that the model invariants hold, the latter attempts to derive an extended model of the implementation and hence enables a deeper understanding of what was implemented.

Our techniques are applicable to any micro-architecture simulator. We present the application of our techniques to hand-written simulators as well as to those generated from an architecture specification language.

Categories and Subject Descriptors

C.0 [**Computer Systems Organization**]: Modeling of computer architecture; C.1 [**Processor Architecture**]:

General Terms

Verification

Keywords

Architecture simulation, verification, first order logic

ICS'14, June 10–13 2014, Munich, Germany.
Copyright 2014 ACM 978-1-4503-2642-1/14/06 ...$15.00.
http://dx.doi.org/10.1145/2597652.2597680 .

1. INTRODUCTION

State of the art micro-architecture research inherently relies on cycle-accurate simulators to develop and test new ideas. Cycle-accurate simulators need to correctly model the processor behavior in sufficient detail so that accurate information about how a given program will execute under the new design can be quantitatively estimated. Cycle-accurate simulators are rather complex pieces of software as their implementation typically takes tens of thousands of lines of high-level program code, such as C. Cycle-accurate simulators also serve a crucial role in actual processor development and their use is essential to finalize the micro-architecture design. Currently, hand-coded cycle-accurate simulators such as SimpleScalar [3, 16], RSIM [13], M5 [2], GEM5 [1] as well as those generated from domain-specific architecture description languages are used widely both by the industry and academia. Examples of architecture description languages include Mimola, nML, Lisa, Expression, ASIP Meister, TIE, Madl, ADL++, GNR, among others [11].

While generation from an architecture description language can facilitate the application of formal validation techniques, using an architecture description language in itself will not prevent model representation errors. Furthermore, hand-coded simulators are still widely used as companies rely on their developed code base to improve the future versions of existing processors. As a result, verification of simulators is still a difficult task and remains an area dominated by ad-hoc techniques, except for simpler embedded processors where a formal specification language can be used to describe the architectural details. Our motivation therefore is to develop techniques which can identify model representation errors and do so in a simulator independent manner.

Our techniques rely on event traces generated from an execution of the target simulator by using the trace in two complementary processes. Figure 1 shows the general framework. First, we develop a first-order logic based language, which we call *First-Order Logic Constraint Specification Language* (FOLCSL). Using the language, the invariants of the model under consideration are specified. Examples of such invariants include that every fetched instruction must be decoded, no more than two load instructions can simultaneously access the cache, or, the execution step of an integer type instruction takes a single cycle. We then automatically synthesize a verification program from the first-order logic program as shown in Figure 1(a). This verification program reads the event trace generated by running the simulator using a particular benchmark (Figure 1(b) and (c)) and signals whether all invariants are respected. In this approach, if the constraint specification is complete and the verification program returns no errors, it can be stated that the simulator has faithfully followed the model for the set of benchmark programs tested. Unfortunately, the domain of invariants is large and even domain experts may omit the necessary

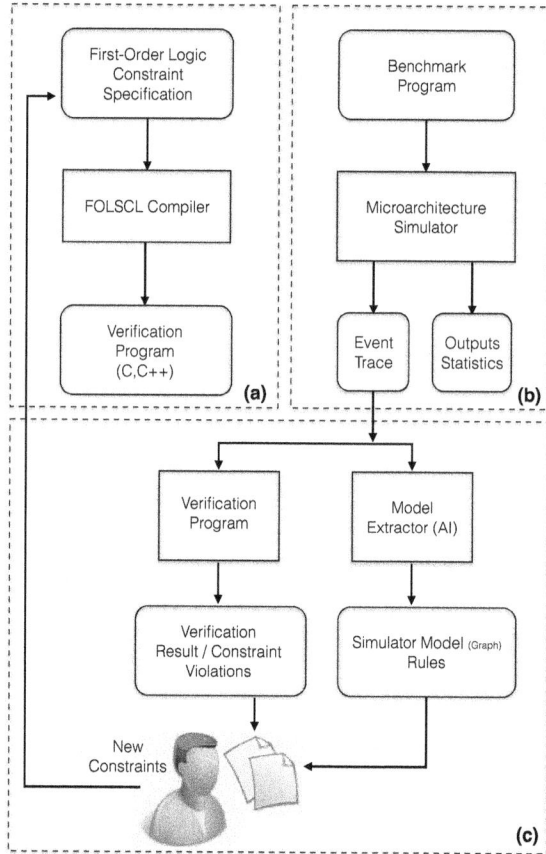

Figure 1: Simulator verification using event traces.

ing, decoding, and executing an instruction are all considered to be events which affect a single instruction. In contrast, events such as a branch misprediction initiated rollback in a superscalar processor simulator is considered to be *global* as it affects every instruction in the processor. One of our contributions is to show that such traces contain sufficient information to verify that the simulator faithfully implements its execution model when these traces are processed with the appropriate algorithms. Although the data sets are very large and these algorithms have bad asymptotic complexity, by applying advanced filtering and windowing techniques, we are able to keep the running times within reasonable limits.

In the remainder of the paper, first, in Section 2, we describe our first-order logic based constraint specification language and its use in the verification process. This section starts by formally describing the properties of the trace.

2. FOLCSL CONSTRAINT LANGUAGE

FOLCSL is designed to specify the invariants which must hold during the execution of the simulator. The language allows constraint specification using first-order logic. The constraints are specified by referencing a particular event and associating it with other events. Expressions refer to the names used in a given trace, therefore, we first formally describe the expected form of trace data.

A trace T is a sequence of *events* $T = \xi^1 \cdots \xi^l$, represented as n-tuples: $\xi^i = < e_1^i, \cdots, e_n^i >$ where, e_j^i refers to the jth attribute of the ith event. Each e_j^i is an integer. For example, $\xi^i = < a^i, c^i, s^i, t^i >$ is an event generated by a processor simulator where a^i is the address of an instruction, c^i is the instance number of the instruction (each instruction can execute multiple times), s^i is the pipeline stage, and t^i is the cycle time at which the ith event has been observed. It can be read as follows: At time t^i, the c^i-th instance of the instruction with address a^i is in state s^i. A sample trace line generated by the simulator is:

```
0xaabbccdd, 2, ID, 1000
```

The above trace line states that the second instance of the instruction fetched from address 0xaabbccdd is at instruction decode stage (ID) and at machine cycle 1000. FOLCSL does not require the declaration of text attributes such as ID above. Text attributes have no domain specific meaning attached to them by the language and they are treated just like any other constant.

A *constraint* C is a quantified statement that includes arithmetic and Boolean expressions and contains domain facts specified by the user. For example, the following constraint specifies that each instruction that goes through the instruction fetch (IF) stage should go through the instruction decode (ID) stage unless a rollback (RB) that flushes the pipeline occurs.

$$\forall z \in T \; \exists y \in T, \; (s^z = IF) \Rightarrow (a^y = a^z) \wedge (c^y = c^z)$$
$$\wedge \, ((s^y = ID) \vee (s^y = RB)) \qquad (C.1)$$

Verbally, the above expression specifies that for every event z that has the s attribute equal to instruction fetch (IF) and the instance attribute c, the verifier needs to find another event y with the same address and instance attribute values such that the stage attribute of event y is equal to instruction decode (ID), or it needs to find another matching event whose stage attribute is rollback (RB).

FOLCSL constraints consists of fully quantified variables, arithmetic expressions and Boolean expressions. The language has the simple grammar shown in Figure 2. Note that a *Terminal* in the language is an integer or an event attribute and an *Identifier* is a variable name or a function. In our current implementation func-

constraints to catch all the errors in the simulator. We therefore developed a second approach complementing the first.

In our second approach, we process the event trace using several artificial intelligence algorithms, and attempt to derive the simulated model from the event trace. This model, presented in the form of temporal graphs and rules, can be inspected by the human user to gain a deeper understanding of what the simulator actually implements. Using the derived model, further invariant constraints can be formulated and added to the initial set of constraints, in essence complementing the former approach. These two processes are used iteratively by repeating the process with different benchmark programs as shown in Figure 1, each time improving the set of constraints.

The strength of the outlined approach lies in its power to verify the implementation by both performing a check of the invariants as well as visually describing what the simulator implements. Furthermore, this is done in a very practical and general manner. Event traces can be easily generated from any type of simulator by inserting output statements, i.e., instruments, at specific points in the simulator. Most existing simulators already provide mechanisms to generate an event trace. For example, SimpleScalar can produce an event trace by simply setting an option. It also is easy to generate an event trace in automatically synthesized simulators by augmenting appropriate points in the description. We consider every type of activity within the simulator to be an *event*, and broadly classify events into two main groups, namely, those events which affect a single instruction and those which globally affect the processor's operation and hence all the instructions. For example, fetch-

```
   constraint → quantification, statement;
    statement → ¬statement
             → statement ∧ statement
             → statement ∨ statement
             → statement ⇔ statement
             → statement ⇒ statement
             → expression relation expression
             → (statement)
             → identifier
   expression → expression + expression
             → expression − expression
             → expression * expression
             → expression / expression
             → (expression)
             → terminal
             → identifier
     relation → > | ≥ | < | ≤ | = | ≠
quantification → ∀ | ∃
```

Figure 2: FOLCSL Grammar.

tions are restricted to built-in functions only, and they are implicitly declared.

2.1 Instrumentation

Trace data is generated by inserting instrumentation statements into the simulator. Each instrumentation statement outputs an event in comma-separated value (CSV) format. For example, *printf("%lld,%lld,%d,%lld", addr, instance, state, cycles)* outputs an event with 4 attributes. SimpleScalar simulator's *-ptrace* option outputs similar data although it is not in CSV format [3, 16]. We translate it to CSV using a postprocessing program instead of modifying the simulator.

Instrumentation statements must be injected into proper locations in the simulation code. Global events which affect a subset of instructions require attaching the event to individual instructions. For example, a rollback is a global event in a processor pipeline but it affects a subset of instructions, namely, all uncommitted instructions that are still in the pipeline. In order to properly handle these types of events, we attach the rollback state to all affected instructions whenever a rollback occurs.

2.2 Stream Processing and Sliding Windows

FOLCSL and the associated trace description treat an instruction as an object which moves through different stages at some time point. The language allows the user to command the full power of first-order logic in specifying the invariants which need to hold. A direct consequence of this flexibility is the enormous size of the trace data which needs to be processed. As an invariant can reference arbitrary events, it may be necessary to compare all events to each other. Given that the number of dynamic instructions for a benchmark program are in the order of billions and each instruction will have multiple events, an uncompressed full trace of a single benchmark program takes many terabytes of storage space. Therefore, instead of storing the trace and processing it afterwards, we process the data as a stream. In our approach, whenever all the *required events* are available they are immediately processed and all the *expired events* are discarded. As a result, a minimum amount

of data is kept in memory during the verification process. In order to reduce the processing time, we employ *sliding windows*.

2.2.1 Sliding Window

The sliding window approach views the trace as a chronologically ordered stream of events. Let ξ^i be our pivot event. We can buffer all events from time $t^i - t_b$ to time $t^i + t_f$ to form a sliding window [9] that pivots at time t^i. If we assume that an instruction's maximum time to live (ttl) in the pipeline is t_{ttl}, then a given constraint can be verified by just checking events in the sliding window that pivots at time t^z with $t_b = t_f = t_{ttl}$. Note that, in the event of a context switch or a roll-back, the ttl values are reset, so the window is always bounded. The *required events* are all those events which reside in the sliding window and the *expired events* are all events such that their occurrence time is less than $t^z - t_b$. Figure 3 depicts the sliding window for constraint C.1, where t^z is the pivot.

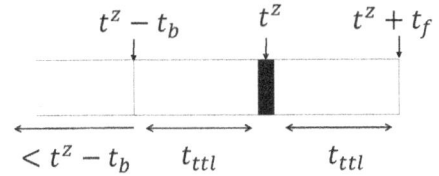

Figure 3: Sliding window.

The sliding window data structure provides three advantages. First, it requires minimal amount of storage space. Second, the verification process can begin even before the full trace is generated, allowing traces with an unknown length to be processed, such as a data stream from a network. Finally, for each pivot event, only the events residing in the sliding window need to be considered instead of all the events in the full trace. This significantly speeds up the verification process and processing very large traces becomes feasible.

2.2.2 Checker

Within a sliding window, all permutations of events are verified against the constraints. A more efficient way would be to view the verification process as an assignment of values to event variables, similar to constraint satisfaction problems (CSP). Using that view, existing CSP algorithms can be used. Our main checker algorithm is a backtracking search algorithm which uses depth-first search by assigning values to each variable and backtracking when a given assertion fails. To further reduce processing time, we prune the search space by evaluating critical expressions of a constraint before all variables get assigned a value. In constraint C.2 shown below, if the evaluation of expression $s^z = IF$ is true and $a^y = a^z$ is false, we know that the constraint is guaranteed to be false regardless of the value x. As a result, we can immediately backtrack and assign another value for y.

$$\forall z \in T \ \forall y \in T \ \exists x \in T,$$
$$(s^z = IF) \Rightarrow (a^y = a^z) \wedge (t^x > t^y) \qquad \text{(C.2)}$$

More efficient CSP heuristics such as propagation, variable ordering and intelligent backtracking [14] can also be applied into the checker.

2.3 Constraint Examples

While the domain of constraints is fairly large, several classes of constraints are particularly interesting to look at as they are necessary to catch some of the most common modeling errors. A common error in simulator development is the violation of resource constraints. For example, if an architecture provides only two memory ports, at no time we should have more than two memory operations performing an access. While such an error would immediately get caught in a real hardware implementation as the hardware would not run, a simulator may continue to execute and yield incorrect results. In this section, we give examples targeting several common modeling errors which occur while modeling the resources involved, the temporal behavior of instructions and modeling competing instructions such as arbitration. In order to easily specify such constraints, FOLCSL includes several built-in functions. One of these functions is *car* which computes the cardinality of a set. The following example specifies a constraint that indicates at most two instructions can simultaneously access the memory ports. Note how sets are utilized to enforce resource based invariants.

$$\forall q \in T, car(set(\forall z \in T, (s^z = MEMPORT)$$
$$\wedge (t^z = t^q))) \leq 2 \qquad \text{(C.3)}$$

Similar to resource constraints, temporal constraints can be violated without a visible indication that such a violation has occurred. Temporal constraint violations include omission of a simulation step (i.e., a corresponding hardware stage), as well as when a particular instruction does not respect the latency of a particular pipeline stage. Such violations are very difficult to catch using ad-hoc techniques, particularly when these violations occur only for a small subset of the executed instructions. The following example encodes the requirement that an instruction that leaves the instruction fetch stage (IF) must either enter the instruction decode (ID) stage or the rollback (RB) stage and in doing so, it should take at least a cycle, but no more than K cycles, where K is a constant:

$$\forall z \in T \; \exists y \in T, \; (s^z = IF) \Rightarrow (a^y = a^z) \wedge (c^y = c^z)$$
$$\wedge (t^y - t^z > 0) \wedge (t^y - t^z \leq K)$$
$$\wedge ((s^y = ID) \vee (s^y = RB)) \qquad \text{(C.4)}$$

When multiple instructions compete for a particular resource a subset of those instructions are granted access. This process, which is typically carried out by an arbiter at the hardware level, is particularly difficult to verify as the combination of the set of instructions must be taken into account while writing the FOLCSL statements. In the following example, we specify through constraint C.5 that $LOAD$ instructions are given priority to move from EX to WB stage.

$$\forall z \in T \; \forall y \in T, \; \exists x \in T \; \exists w \in T$$
$$(s^z = EX) \wedge (h^z = LOAD)$$
$$\wedge (s^y = EX) \wedge (h^y \neq LOAD) \wedge (t^y = t^z) \Rightarrow$$
$$(a^x = a^z) \wedge (c^x = c^z) \wedge (a^w = a^y) \wedge (c^w = c^y)$$
$$\wedge [((s^x = WB) \wedge (s^w = WB) \wedge (t^x \leq t^w))$$
$$\vee (s^x = RB) \vee (s^w = RB)] \qquad \text{(C.5)}$$

As it can be seen through our examples, FOLCSL provides a convenient and easy to use way of specifying the invariants which must hold during the execution of the simulator. The challenge is to produce a sound and complete set of constraints for a given simulator implementation so that the correctness of the simulator can be trusted with high confidence. We have developed a large number of constraints targeting these common errors in modeling and tested two simulators, one automatically synthesized from an Architecture Description Language (ADL) [12] specification and the other for SimpleScalar out-of-order simulator [16]. Both of these

simulators model sophisticated superscalar processor architectures. We found that both simulators respect the timing and resource constraints they are believed to model. During this process, several "errors" we found turned out to be incomplete constraint specifications. Because this is an iterative process, each run yielded better constraint specifications which provided improved coverage. As both of these simulators are mature and have been verified multiple times using different means of verification in the past, the lack of errors is expected.

The fundamental value of our technique is the assurance it provides when these simulators are modified to model an architectural variation of the original design. The verifier's presence will provide confidence that after the modification the resulting simulator remains a trustworthy model of the architecture under consideration.

We tested various hand-written constraints in ADL and SimpleScalar simulators. The constraints that we tested include:

1. For each instruction type, the stages that must be visited are indeed visited.

2. All stage latencies such as integer operations, divide and multiply latencies, cache access latencies, as well as floating point calculation latencies are respected.

3. Global events, such as rollback are properly included.

4. Resource constraints, such as the number and type of available memory ports are respected.

5. The width of each stage, such as the number of instructions fetched, decoded, and retired match the architecture description.

While the invariant verification provides an assurance and a "yes" or "no" answer to simulator correctness, micro-architecture research can benefit immensely from better understanding the implemented model's behavior under various execution scenarios. We therefore extend the utilization of trace data to model extraction. Extracted models provide the user with the ability to develop further constraints and better understand the implications of newly developed techniques. This is the topic of the next section.

3. DERIVING TEMPORAL MODELS FROM THE TRACE

Cycle-accurate simulators typically model the flow of instructions from one pipeline stage to the next, and it is this timing that eventually provides estimates about how many cycles it would take to execute the given program under the modeled architecture. Depending on the modeled architecture, the number of stages and the latency through each stage will be different. In addition, a range of events will affect the flow of instructions through the stages. We directly derive the pipeline structure, stages simulated, how instructions flow from one stage to the next as well as various events taking place from the event trace and represent them on a temporal graph where the nodes of the graph represents the *state* (as opposed to the stage) an instruction is in. This graphical representation is called an SFTAG (State Flow Temporal Analysis Graph) and used to display the paths instructions follow through the pipeline as well as conditions and events under which such flow occurs.

An SFTAG is a labeled, directed graph $< N, E >$, where N represents the set of nodes and E represents the set of edges. Each node includes one or more state titles representing the stage(s) an instruction is in, and the associated conditions. For example, a node titled "IF" means that the instruction is in the "Instruction Fetch" stage. Having multiple titles shows that the instruction is either in many stages, or additional events took place simultaneously while the instruction is in that stage. For example, a node titled "II & $W4O$" means that the instruction is in the "Instruction Issue" stage and is waiting for its operands to be ready. Similarly, in the simulated architecture if two sub-operations are performed in the same clock cycle and the trace contains a separate event data for each sub-operation, they will be combined into a *state* which represents both. For example, if the modeled architecture performs execution (EX) and register-file write (WB) in the same cycle, the corresponding state will be $EX\&WB$.

In a graph, an edge is a quadruple $< n_s, I, r, n_d >$, where, n_s represents the source node, I is an interval representing the time taken for the transition, r represents the ratio of instructions performing the state transition, and n_d represents the destination node. The titles for n_s and n_d come from the set $SS \cup \{\text{Start}\} \cup \{\text{End}\}$, where SS is the set of states shown in the trace file, Start is the special start state showing the entrance of the instructions to the pipeline, and End is the special end state showing the exit of the instructions from the pipeline. An interval I is shown as a [lower bound, upper bound] pair. For example, the three edges emanating from the node titled "II" in Figure 5 show that 2% of the instructions end at the II stage, 63% of the instructions transition from II to EX&WB taking between 1 to 2 cycles, and 35% of the instructions transition to the EX stage taking between 1 to 2 cycles. Note that the instructions that end at the II stage end due to a rollback.

Algorithm 1 Analyze object transition.

Input: Trace T consisting of event triplets $id, state(s), time(t)$, Max. Samples $maxsamples$, Probability $prob$, Window forward time t_f, Window backward time t_b

Output: Graph g
1: $g \leftarrow \emptyset$
2: $BINS \leftarrow \emptyset$
3: $\xi \leftarrow$ first event
4: **while** $length(BINS) < maxsamples$ **do**
5:     **if** $random() < prob$ AND $\xi^{id} \notin BINS$ **then**
6:         $w \leftarrow window(T, \xi, t_f, t_b)$
7:         $bin \leftarrow group(w, o, \xi^{id})$
8:         $bin \leftarrow sort(bin, t)$
9:         $bin \leftarrow cse(bin, s, t)$
10:        $bin \leftarrow cpe(bin, s, t)$
11:        $g \leftarrow merge(g, bin, s)$
12:        $BINS(\xi^o) \leftarrow bin$
13:     **end if**
14:     $\xi \leftarrow$ next event
15: **end while**
16: **return**

We use Algorithm 1 to create an SFTAG from a trace. A trace used to generate an SFTAG contains three attributes, namely, id, state, and time. The id of an instruction consists of its address and instance. In Figure 4(a) we show a trace segment with three instructions. The algorithm uses a sliding window as explained in Section 2.2 setting the window size such that all events related to a particular instruction are within the window. The process starts by grouping instructions into bins based on their unique address and instance (*group* on line 7). Each bin is sorted with respect to time (*sort* on line 8) and duplicate state names are combined (*combine serial events (cse)* on line 9) into one as shown in Figure 4(b). For example, in the original trace, Instruction 1 is in "Instruction Issue"

(II) state at cycles 3 and 4 before transitioning to "Execute" (EX) and "Write Back" (WB) states at cycle 5. The bin contains events $< 1, II, 3 >$, $< 1, EX, 5 >$ and $< 1, WB, 5 >$ to reflect this flow.

We generate a temporary flow graph for each bin as shown in Figure 4(c). In this example, Instruction 1 is in "Execute" and "Write-back" stages at the same time (cycle 5). Therefore, a new state representing parallel states EX and WB is created (*combine parallel events (cpe)* on line 10). Instruction 2 enters the IF state at cycle 1 and the ID state at cycle 5. Therefore, the link from IF to ID is labeled as 4, the time it takes to move from the IF state to the ID state.

Finally, the temporary flow graphs are combined into a single SFTAG as shown in Figure 4(d) and line 11 of the algorithm. For each transition in the SFTAG, the minimum and maximum cycles needed for the transition are computed and presented next to the edge in $[min, max]$ format. For example, the transition times from IF to ID are $\{1, 4, 1\}$, hence the label in the SFTAG is $[1, 4]$. The decimal value on each edge is the ratio of the instructions that move to the destination state among the instructions in the source state. For example, in Figure 4(d), node II has 2 outgoing edges, one to $EX\&WB$ state and one to EX state. Both edges have the ratio of .50 which means that 50% of instructions in II move to $EX\&WB$ and the remaining 50% move to EX.

4. CASE STUDIES

In this section we present three case studies we conducted using empirical data. The data traces were obtained from FAST ADL [12] and SimpleScalar out of order [16] simulators. We manually instrumented various events in FAST ADL simulator. Instrumented events included major pipeline stages, various stall events and various global events. For SimpleScalar, we used its built-in trace generation and manually added extra events such as memory port access. The first of these studies shows how our technique can extract both the pipeline structure and the temporal behavior of the simulated model. We also illustrate how a human interpreter can write new constraints in FOLCSL by examining the temporal graphs. In the second case study, we compare the temporal graphs obtained for two variants of SimpleScalar. The first simulator faithfully implements a Rambus DRAM model while the second models the original SimpleScalar simple DRAM model. Through the generated histograms we conclude the observed behavior matches to expected behavior for these two models. Finally, we present an analysis of a bus arbiter implementation which makes use of the same algorithms which were used for pipeline temporal models but transposes the data so that instead of modeling instruction flow through the states, *flow of states through instructions* is performed. This transposition exposes resource arbitration by combining all those instructions which are simultaneously in the same stage. This is a powerful concept which can also be used to identify the forwarding requirements of a given architecture by allowing instructions to get their data as if full-forwarding is implemented, obtaining the trace data, analyzing it and implementing a realistic forwarding implementation back in the simulator. We believe each of these case studies are representative of common, time-consuming analysis efforts spent by the micro-architecture community.

4.1 Pipeline Temporal Information

When the simulator event traces are fed through the algorithms discussed in the previous section, two graphs shown in Figure 5 and Figure 6 result. These temporal graphs are obtained directly from trace data, without human intervention.

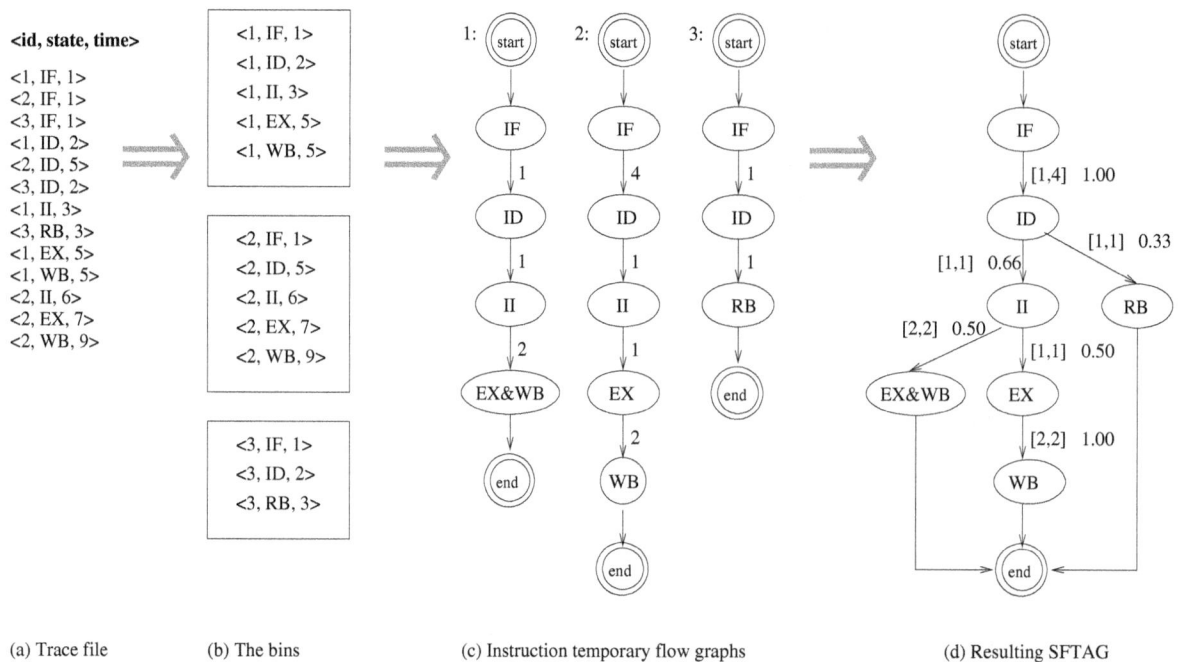

<id, state, time>	<1, IF, 1>	1:	2:	3:	

(a) Trace file (b) The bins (c) Instruction temporary flow graphs (d) Resulting SFTAG

Figure 4: Generating a State Flow Temporal Analysis Graph (SFTAG).

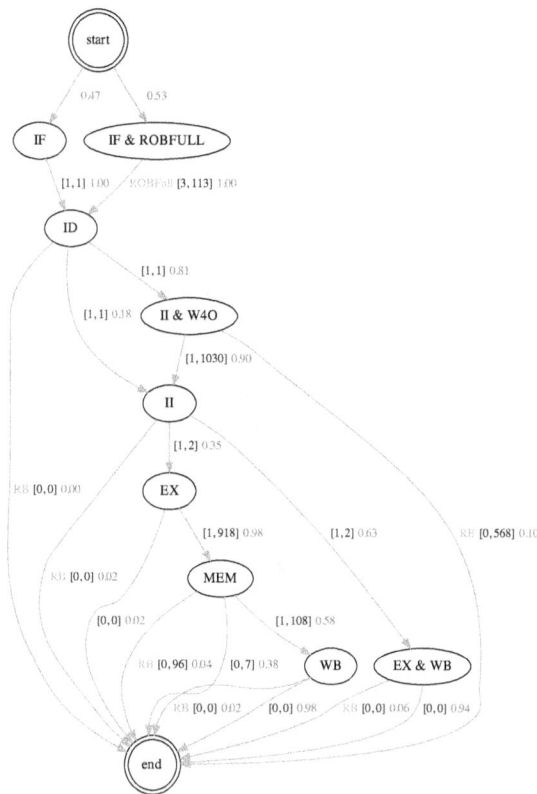

Figure 5: FAST pipeline temporal representation.

Figure 5 can be read as follows: Every instruction starts at IF state or $IF\&ROBFull$ state. The $IF\&ROBFull$ state means that the instruction in IF state and at the same time reorder buffer (ROB) is full. 47% of them will start at IF and the rest will begin with $IF\&ROBFull$ state. Instructions from both states then move to ID. Instructions which move from ID have a transition time of 1 cycle and instructions which originate from $ID\&ROBFull$ have minimum transition time of 3 and maximum transition time of 113. In other words, a full ROB takes minimum 3 cycles and maximum 113 cycles to make itself available again. From ID, instructions can move to II (instruction issue), $II\&W4O$ (instruction issue and waiting for operands) or RB (terminate due to rollback) state. The rest of the graph can be read in a similar fashion.

Figure 6 is similar to Figure 5 except that it represents SimpleScalar out of order architecture. One major difference depicted in both graphs is an instruction's starting state. In FAST, all instructions start at IF but in SimpleScalar an instruction can either start at IF or DA. Looking at the code revealed that SimpleScalar architecture splits *load* or *store* instructions into two instructions in dispatch stage. The trace treats these instructions as generic instructions and since their starting state is in DA (dispatch) and they never visit IF, they appear as if they fork out from the DA state. Alternatively, one can tag those instructions as special instructions and represent them differently but we preferred not to distinguish them. Our approach is to not modify the simulator at all with the exception of adding the necessary instrumentation code and thus keeping the modifications at a minimum. Nevertheless, this is a clear example of how our approach can provide information about what the simulator actually implements. Whether the simulator performed any instruction splitting and if so at which stage were not known to us at the beginning of the case study. This is an example of how the perception of the user and what is actually implemented may differ, which our approach has successfully identified.

Besides showing the user the pipeline temporal information, the graph can also serve as a guide to construct pipeline constraints such as C.4. For example, consider the outgoing edges from ID in

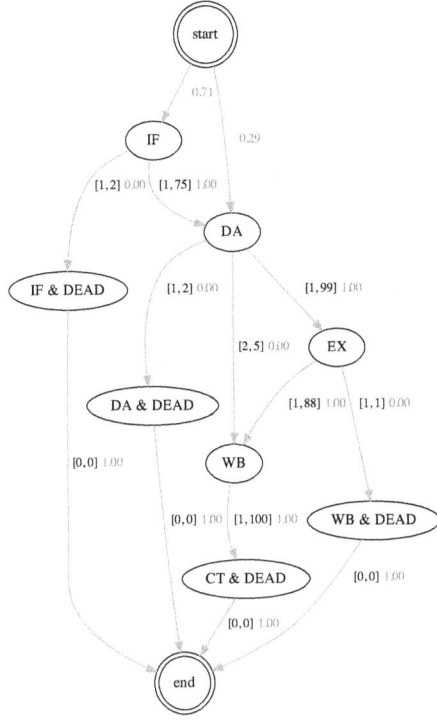

Figure 6: SimpleScalar pipeline temporal representation.

Figure 5. We observe that every instruction that is in ID transitions to one of II state, RB state, or $W4O$ state. This can be encoded in a straight-forward manner as :

$$\forall z \in T \; \exists y \in T \exists x \in T,$$
$$(s^z = ID) \Rightarrow (a^y = a^z) \wedge (c^y = c^z)$$
$$\wedge \Big[(s^y = II)$$
$$\vee \, [(s^y = II) \wedge ((s^x = W4O)$$
$$\wedge (a^x = a^z) \wedge (c^x = c^z))]$$
$$\vee \, (s^y = RB) \Big] \qquad (C.6)$$

Similarly, temporal information can be added as follows:

$$\forall z \in T \; \exists y \in T \exists x \in T,$$
$$(s^z = ID) \Rightarrow (a^y = a^z) \wedge (c^y = c^z)$$
$$\wedge \Big[(s^y = II) \wedge (t^y - t^z = 1)$$
$$\vee \, [(s^y = II) \wedge (s^x = W4O)$$
$$\wedge (a^x = a^z) \wedge (c^x = c^z)$$
$$\wedge (t^y - t^z = 1) \wedge (t^x - t^z = 1)]$$
$$\vee \, (s^y = RB) \wedge (t^y - t^z = 0) \Big] \qquad (C.7)$$

Figures 5 and 6 represent all the possible transitions for instructions. If the behavior of specific types of instructions is of interest, filtering the event trace for an instruction type exposes the specific path taken by the selected instruction type.

4.2 DRAM

One common use of architectural simulators is to verify and test new architectural designs. SFTAGs can help the designer to reason about the behavior of the new design both in its correctness and efficiency. We take SimpleScalar as an example to show how the main memory architecture can affect the processor pipeline.

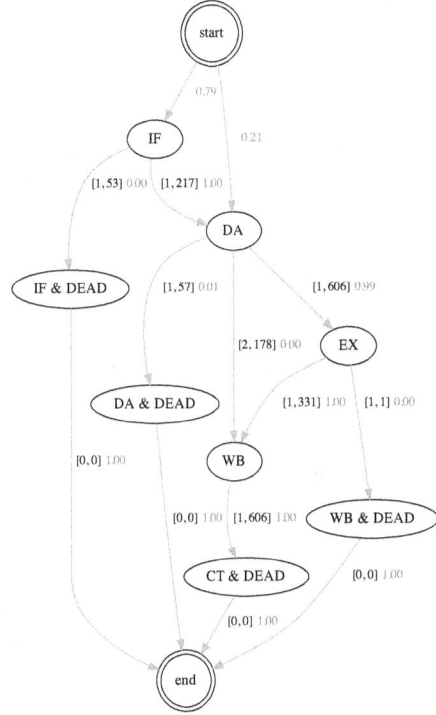

Figure 7: SimpleScalar/Rambus pipeline temporal representation.

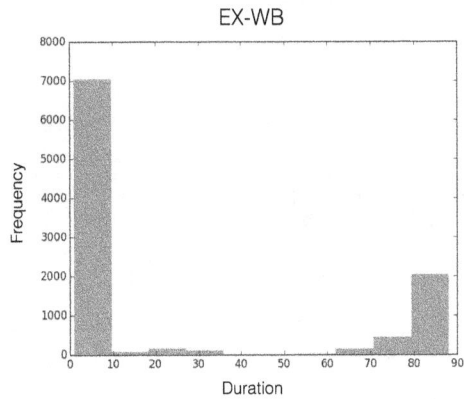

Figure 8: SimpleScalar EX to WB distribution.

Figure 6 shows the SFTAG for a default superscalar machine with a simple DRAM model as used in SimpleScalar 3.0. The SF-TAG shown in Figure 7 is from an extension to SimpleScalar where Rambus DRAM is modeled. The two simulators are configured the same, otherwise. We configured SimpleScalar 3.0 with a memory latency of 72 to 88 cycles. Both simulators execute 171.swim from

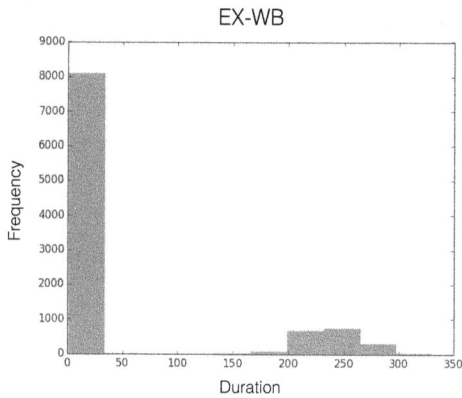

Figure 9: SimpleScalar/Rambus EX to WB distribution.

SPEC CPU2000. The Rambus DRAM can yield a latency of 200 to 300 cycles depending on the memory access pattern. As can be observed from the SFTAGs the increased DRAM latency causes longer transition times between instruction fetch (IF) and dispatch (DA), execute (EX) and write-back (WB), and WB and commit (CT).

We can further generate a histogram for a transition edge of interest in an SFTAG to show the distribution of transition times. The distribution is helpful for us to gain more insight into the simulated architecture and infer its behavior. Figure 8 and Figure 9 show the histograms of the transition from EX to WB for the original SimpleScalar 3.0 and its Rambus extension, respectively. Figure 8 demonstrates that a large number of load instructions indeed cause L2 misses and need to access the main memory. The range of the latencies follows the memory configuration and thus verifies the correctness of memory system simulation. The Rambus DRAM (RDRAM) is much more complicated. Figure 9 suggests that an access to the RDRAM can cause a latency of 200 to 300 cycles. This range fits our configuration of Rambus and thus increases our confidence in the correctness of the implementation.

4.3 Bus Arbiter

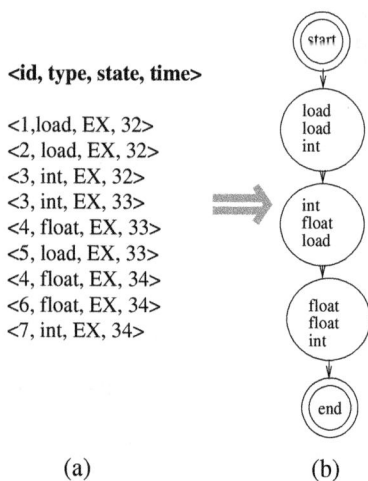

(a)   (b)

Figure 10: Finding the temporal information about the instructions leaving the EX stage.

We use the concept of state flow graph to find patterns of priority in a simulation. The case study we performed was to look at how instructions are prioritized by a bus arbiter. To achieve this, we first filter all the events where the instructions are in the "Execute" (EX) stage as shown in Figure 10(a). Next, we combine parallel events into single nodes (Figure 10(b)). We convert the graph into a tabular representation showing which type of instructions leave the EX stage as shown in the table below. In the table, the columns LOAD, STORE, INT and FLOAT indicate the number of that class of instructions which are simultaneously present at the EX stage, and columns E-LOAD, E-STORE, etc., indicate how many instructions of the given class leave the stage. We feed this table into the CN2 algorithm [4, 5] and find the rules regarding which instructions leave the execute stage. CN2 is a learning algorithm for rule induction. It takes a set of examples and induces rules in the form of IF-THEN statements. The algorithm uses information entropy as the search heuristic during the rule induction process, similar to decision tree induction algorithms.

LOAD	STORE	INT	FLOAT	E-LOAD	E-STORE	E-INT	E-FLOAT
2	0	1	0	2	0	0	0
1	0	1	1	1	0	1	0

This algorithm yields a set of rules which relate the given combination to the observed outcome. The simulated architecture permits up to 4 instructions at EX, and only 2 instructions exit EX at any given time. Below is a list of the rules generated by CN2.

1. **if** LOAD=1, STORE=1 **then** E-LOAD=1, E-STORE=1
   This rule reads as follows: if there is one LOAD and one STORE in EX stage then during the next transition, the LOAD and STORE will exit EX stage having priority over others.

2. **if** LOAD=0, STORE=0, INT=0, FLOAT=0 **then** E-LOAD=0, E-STORE=0, E-INT=0, E-FLOAT=0
   This rule is trivial. If EX stage contains no instructions then nothing will exit the stage.

3. **if** LOAD=2, STORE=0 **then** E-LOAD=2
   This rule states that if EX stage contains two loads, and no stores, they will leave (irrespective of presence of other types of instructions).

4. **if** STORE=1, INT=3 **then** E-STORE=1, E-INT=1
   STORE has precedence over INT instructions. STORE is given priority, remaining slots are filled by the rest.

5. **if** STORE=1, FLOAT=3 **then** E-STORE=1, E-FLOAT=1
   STORE has precedence over FLOAT instructions (same as above).

6. **if** STORE=2, LOAD=0 **then** E-STORE=2
   This rule states that if EX stage contains two stores, and no loads, they will leave (irrespective of presence of other types of instructions).

The above rules clearly match the implemented arbiter which gives precedence to memory instructions over others. Note that the technique can be used to learn additional information about the inner-workings of a given simulator. If the process yields unintended rules, this may point to significant problems in faithfully implementing the desired model.

Just like a simulator implementation may incorrectly implement an arbiter, it may inadvertently embody an "arbiter" when there is none. This problem originates from trying to map the simulation of an inherently parallel implementation onto a sequential representation, a well studied problem by Vachharajani et al. [19]. For example, the polling order of the simulator may always give preference to a particular stage, in essence simulating an architecture which embodies an arbiter that always favors that stage. A concrete example is the utilization of ports. A hardware implementation may grant a particular port on a random basis. If the simulator polls a particular stage first, it always will get priority over others, different from the real implementation. In other words, observing a rule which should not be present is equally important as not observing a rule which should be present.

5. PERFORMANCE

Through the careful selection and implementation of our algorithms, we can process very large traces with reasonable running times. In this section, we give an evaluation of SFTAG generation performance for a large set of SPEC CPU2000 benchmarks. All experiments were performed on a machine which has a Quad Core Intel Core i7 processor running at 3.4 GHZ. The machine has 256 KB L2, 8 MB L3 cache and 24 GB of memory. The operating system is OS X 10.9.2 (13C64) with the kernel version Darwin 13.1.0.

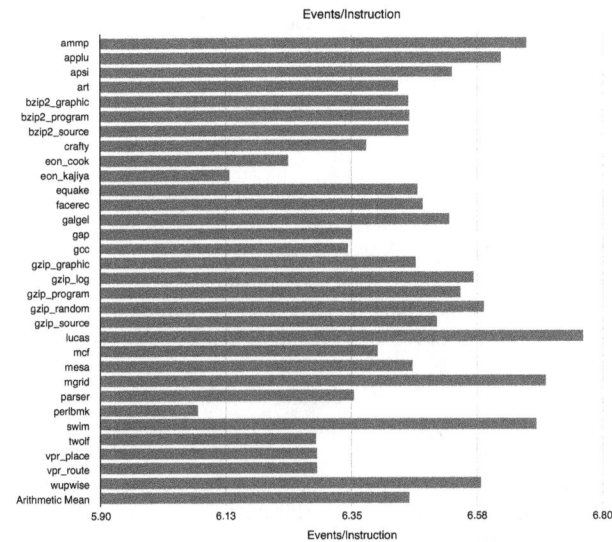

Figure 11: Events per instruction for benchmark programs.

Our algorithm's performance is directly correlated with the number of events that need to be processed. Figure 11 illustrates that the number of events per instruction is variable among different benchmarks, with a mean value of 6.5 events/instruction. SFTAG generation algorithm can process close to a million instructions per second, shown in Figure 12. This rate is close to the performance of an annotated simulator. Hence, on a dual-core system, it is possible to generate SFTAGs in parallel with the simulation as the data becomes available and hence add no extra time on top of the simulation time.

6. RELATED WORK

Mauer et al. [10] give a taxonomy of simulators and classify them into *Integrated*, *Functional-First*, *Timing-Directed* and *Timing-First*. ADL generated simulators used in this study are all *integrated* simulators whereas SimpleScalar simulators can be considered *Functional-First*. Mauer et al. develop the *Timing-First* simulator development approach which relies on a functional simu-

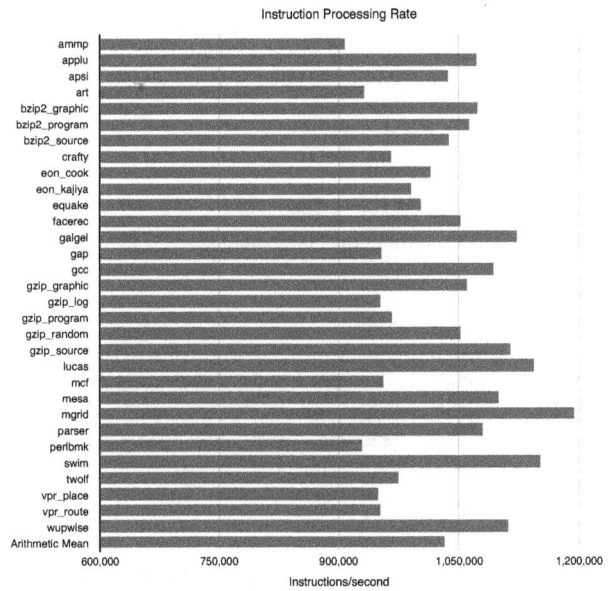

Figure 12: SFTAG processed instructions per second.

lator to verify the functional correctness of the timing simulator. A similar approach is taken by Tomić et al. [18] where dynamic run-time testing is used through a validated emulator. In both approaches, the correctness of the timing simulator needs to be established through manual techniques. Therefore, both techniques can benefit from the approaches presented in this paper. Similarly, one may choose to employ functional validation by relying on an already verified functional simulator and use our techniques to detect timing errors only. Such an approach would have the benefit of specifically concentrating on timing issues and hence reducing the amount of first-order logic invariants that need to be specified.

The FOLCSL framework we developed is a general run-time verification technique, which is applied to the micro-architecture domain. Sargent [15] lists four approaches to decide model validity, namely, model verification, validation, accreditation and credibility [15]. He also discusses two paradigms in the verification and validation process. Various validation techniques such animation, historical data validation and extreme condition tests also mentioned. Sokolsky, et. al. [17] give an overview of runtime verification research, pointing out that there are four important directions. The first is the checking algorithm which includes the property specification language. The second is the generation of traces (instrumentation), i.e., how observations are made and recorded. Third is management of the overhead on system performance imposed by run-time checking. The last direction is feedback and run-time enforcement which address the question of what to do when a violation is discovered. Xiang, et. al. [21] apply various verification and validation in their agent-based simulation model. Agent-based modeling (ABM) is a method used to simulate multiple agents with some type of autonomous behavior. In their conclusion they mention that the suitability of a verification method might depend on the modeling technique used in the simulation.

The Temporal Rover [6] used temporal logic to describe assertions. The assertion statements are written as source code (C, C++, Verilog, VHDL) comments. The assertions are embedded into the original source code via the Temporal Rover parser. IODINE [8] automatically extracts low-level dynamic invariants such as state machine protocols, request-acknowledge pairs and mutual exclusion. GoldMine [20] uses static analysis on RTL design and a decision tree based supervised learning algorithm on simulation traces to generate assertions. Mandouh and Wassal [7] propose a framework that utilizes frequent and sequential pattern mining and known templates to extract RTL design properties.

7. CONCLUSION AND FUTURE WORK

We presented a micro-architecture simulator verification framework which relies on analytical and visual discovery of patterns, as well as invariant checking.

We believe a considerable amount of time is spent in the micro-architecture research community to develop simulators for new techniques and making sure that they faithfully implement the desired models. Our developed framework is a step forward to increase the confidence of researchers in their results. While simulator validation (as opposed to verification) has been carried out for some of the most widely used simulators, such validation is no guarantee that a modified version of the same simulator will correctly simulate the desired model.

Our goal therefore is to develop complete FOLCSL programs for most commonly used simulators which can be used by the researchers together with a given simulator as they are modified. If the new modifications should not change the invariant behavior of the simulator, the FOLCSL specifications can be used as is, or modified accordingly. It is important to note that a limitation of our approach is its reliance on traces generated by a given set of benchmarks. As a result, modeling errors will only be caught if they are exercised by the set of benchmark programs used. While this will not affect the correctness of reported outcomes for the studied benchmark set, uncovered modeling errors may affect future studies when new benchmarks are added. Utilization of a large set of benchmarks upfront may improve the chances that modeling errors will be caught as early as possible.

Our future work involves automatic and semi-automatic derivation of invariant rules from event traces, in addition to the visual and analytical techniques we have outlined. We plan to use additional artificial intelligence techniques to extract further information from event streams. Our intention is to make the developed software available to the micro-architecture research community to contribute towards building simulation frameworks which can be trusted, even after extensive modifications.

8. REFERENCES

[1] N. Binkert, B. Beckmann, G. Black, S. K. Reinhardt, A. Saidi, A. Basu, J. Hestness, D. R. Hower, T. Krishna, S. Sardashti, R. Sen, K. Sewell, M. Shoaib, N. Vaish, M. D. Hill, and D. A. Wood. The Gem5 simulator. *SIGARCH Comput. Archit. News*, 39(2):1–7, Aug. 2011.

[2] N. L. Binkert, R. G. Dreslinski, L. R. Hsu, K. T. Lim, A. G. Saidi, and S. K. Reinhardt. The M5 simulator: Modeling networked systems. *IEEE Micro*, 26:52–60, 2006.

[3] D. Burger and T. M. Austin. The SimpleScalar tool set, version 2.0. *SIGARCH Computer Architecture News*, 25(3):13–25, June 1997.

[4] P. Clark and T. Niblett. The CN2 induction algorithm. *Machine Learning*, 3(4):261–283, March 1989.

[5] J. Demšar, T. Curk, and A. Erjavec. Orange: Data mining toolbox in Python. *Journal of Machine Learning Research*, 14:2349–2353, 2013.

[6] D. Drusinsky. The temporal rover and the ATG rover. In *Proceedings of the 7th International SPIN Workshop on*

SPIN Model Checking and Software Verification, pages 323–330, London, UK, 2000. Springer-Verlag.

[7] E. El Mandouh and A. Wassal. Automatic generation of hardware design properties from simulation traces. In *Circuits and Systems (ISCAS), 2012 IEEE International Symposium on*, pages 2317–2320, 2012.

[8] S. Hangal, S. Narayanan, N. Chandra, and S. Chakravorty. IODINE: A tool to automatically infer dynamic invariants for hardware designs. In *Proceedings of the 42nd Annual Design Automation Conference*, DAC '05, pages 775–778, New York, NY, USA, 2005. ACM.

[9] H. Mannila, H. Toivonen, and A. Inkeri Verkamo. Discovery of frequent episodes in event sequences. *Data Mining and Knowledge Discovery*, 1(3):259–289, Jan. 1997.

[10] C. J. Mauer, M. D. Hill, and D. A. Wood. Full-system timing-first simulation. *SIGMETRICS Perform. Eval. Rev.*, 30(1):108–116, June 2002.

[11] P. Mishra and N. Dutt. *Processor Description Languages*. Morgan Kaufmann, San Francisco, CA, USA, 2008.

[12] S. Önder and R. Gupta. Automatic generation of microarchitecture simulators. In *Proceedings of the 1998 International Conference on Computer Languages*, ICCL '98, pages 80–, Washington, DC, USA, 1998. IEEE Computer Society.

[13] V. S. Pai, P. Ranganathan, and S. V. Adve. RSIM reference manual (version 1.0). Technical Report 9705, Rice University, Dept. of Electrical and Computer Engineering, Aug. 1997.

[14] S. Russell and P. Norvig. *Artificial Intelligence: A Modern Approach*. Prentice Hall Press, Upper Saddle River, NJ, USA, 3rd edition, 2009.

[15] R. G. Sargent. Verification and validation of simulation models. In *Proceedings of the Winter Simulation Conference*, WSC '11, pages 183–198. Winter Simulation Conference, 2011.

[16] SimpleScalar LLC. SimpleScalar toolset. http://www.simplescalar.com. Accessed: 2014-01-01.

[17] O. Sokolsky, K. Havelund, and I. Lee. Introduction to the special section on runtime verification. *International Journal on Software Tools for Technology Transfer*, 14(3):243–247, 2012.

[18] S. Tomic, A. Cristal, O. Unsal, and M. Valero. Rapid development of error-free architectural simulators using dynamic runtime testing. In *Computer Architecture and High Performance Computing (SBAC-PAD), 2011 23rd International Symposium on*, pages 80–87, Oct 2011.

[19] M. Vachharajani, N. Vachharajani, D. A. Penry, J. A. Blome, and D. I. August. The Liberty simulation environment, version 1.0. *Performance Evaluation Review: Special Issue on Tools for Architecture Research*, 31:2004, 2004.

[20] S. Vasudevan, D. Sheridan, S. Patel, D. Tcheng, B. Tuohy, and D. Johnson. Goldmine: Automatic assertion generation using data mining and static analysis. In *Proceedings of the Conference on Design, Automation and Test in Europe*, DATE '10, pages 626–629, 3001 Leuven, Belgium, 2010. European Design and Automation Association.

[21] X. Xiang, R. Kennedy, G. Madey, and S. Cabaniss. Verification and validation of agent-based scientific simulation models. In *Proceedings of the 2005 Agent-Directed Simulation Symposium*, volume 37, pages 47–55, 2005.

Scaling Up Matrix Computations on Shared-Memory Manycore Systems with 1000 CPU Cores *

Fengguang Song
Department of Computer Science
Indiana University-Purdue University
Indianapolis
fgsong@cs.iupui.edu

Jack Dongarra
University of Tennessee at Knoxville
Oak Ridge National Laboratory
University of Manchester
dongarra@eecs.utk.edu

ABSTRACT

While the growing number of cores per chip allows researchers to solve larger scientific and engineering problems, the parallel efficiency of the deployed parallel software starts to decrease. This unscalability problem happens to both vendor-provided and open-source software and wastes CPU cycles and energy. By expecting CPUs with hundreds of cores to be imminent, we have designed a new framework to perform matrix computations for massively many cores. Our performance analysis on manycore systems shows that the unscalability bottleneck is related to Non-Uniform Memory Access (NUMA): memory bus contention and remote memory access latency. To overcome the bottleneck, we have designed NUMA-aware tile algorithms with the help of a dynamic scheduling runtime system to minimize NUMA memory accesses. The main idea is to identify the data that is, either read a number of times or written once by a thread resident on a remote NUMA node, then utilize the runtime system to conduct data caching and movement between different NUMA nodes. Based on the experiments with QR factorizations, we demonstrate that our framework is able to achieve great scalability on a 48-core AMD Opteron system (e.g., parallel efficiency drops only 3% from one core to 48 cores). We also deploy our framework to an extreme-scale shared-memory SGI machine which has 1024 CPU cores and runs a single Linux operating system image. Our framework continues to scale well, and can outperform the vendor-optimized Intel MKL library by up to 750%.

Categories and Subject Descriptors

D.1.3 [**Programming Techniques**]: Concurrent Programming—*Parallel programming*; C.1.2 [**Processor Architectures**]: Multiple Data Stream Architectures (Multiprocessors)—*Parallel processors*

---

*This research was supported by an allocation of advanced computing resources at the National Institute for Computational Sciences and the National Science Foundation.

1. INTRODUCTION

The number of cores per chip keeps increasing due to the requirements to increase performance, to reduce energy consumption and heat dissipation, and to lower operating cost. Today, more and more multicore compute nodes are deployed in high performance computer systems. However, the biggest bottleneck for the high performance systems, is to design software to utilize the increasing number of cores effectively.

The problem is that with an increasing number of cores, the efficiency of parallel software degrades gradually. Since matrix problems are fundamental to many scientific computing applications, we tested and benchmarked the performance of matrix factorizations on a shared-memory machine with 48 cores. Figure 1 shows the performance of Intel MKL [1], TBLAS [18], and PLASMA [3]. As shown in the figure, from one core to 48 cores, the efficiency (i.e., performance per core) of all three libraries decreases constantly.

At first glance, one would think it is the hardware or the operating system that imposes a limit to the parallel software. Indeed, this is true for I/O intensive applications due to limitations in I/O devices and critical sections in device drivers [6, 10, 21], but this argument is rarely true for computation-intensive applications. Computation-intensive applications typically perform in-memory computations and can minimize the overhead of system calls. By our intuitions, their performance should be scalable. However, it is not, as shown in Figure 1. Our paper studies why this unscalability problem can happen and how to solve the problem.

To solve the unscalability problem, we first want to find out what and where the bottlenecks are. We take QR factorization as an example and use PAPI [2] to collect a set of hardware performance counter data. By comparing experiments on a small number of cores to experiments on a large number of cores, we find the main causes for the performance degradation, which are "FPU idle cycles" and "Any stall cycles". However, there are many sources that can contribute to the causes. This leads us to conduct another set of experiments to identify the real reason. The reason we eventually find out is not a big surprise, but confirms one of our speculations. It is the increasing number of remote memory accesses that are incurred by the hierarchical NUMA (Non-Uniform Memory Access) architecture which is commonly found on modern manycore systems.

After finding the reason, we start to seek a solution to the problem. The main idea is as follows. First, at algorithm level, we extend the tile algorithms proposed by Dongarra et al. [8,9] to design new NUMA-aware algorithms. Instead of

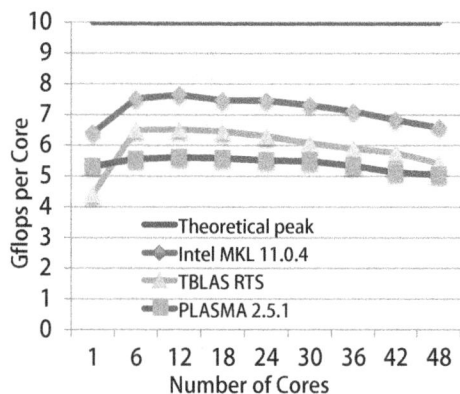

Figure 1: QR factorization on a 48-core AMD Opteron machine. With more cores, the *per-core performance keeps dropping*. Input sizes n = 1000 × NumberCores. One core does not reach the max performance because it is given a small input and has a relatively larger scheduling overhead.

allocating a global matrix and allowing any thread to access any matrix element, we restrict each thread to a fixed subset of the matrix. Since each thread has its own subset of data, a thread can view its own data as *local* and others as *remote*. The NUMA-aware algorithms take into account the number of accesses to remote data. For instance, if a thread needs to access remote data many times, it copies the remote data to its local NUMA node before accessing it. Second, we design a novel dynamic scheduling runtime system to support systems with a large number of CPU cores. The new runtime system follows a push-based data-flow programming model. It also uses work stealing to attain better load balancing. Third, we use a 2-D block cyclic distribution method [13] to map a matrix to different threads. Fourth, each thread owns a memory pool that is allocated from its local NUMA node and uses this memory to store its mapped subset of matrix.

Our experiment with QR factorizations demonstrates great scalability of the new approach. On a Linux machine with 48 cores, our performance per core drops only 3% from one core to 48 cores. This is an improvement of 16% over the previous work. We also test it on an extreme-scale shared-memory system with 1024 CPU cores. The system runs a single Linux operating system image. Based on the experimental results, we can deliver a maximum performance of 3.4 TFlops. It is 750% faster than the Intel MKL library, 75% faster than the Intel MKL ScaLAPACK library, and 42% faster than the PLASMA library [3] developed by the University of Tennessee.

To our best knowledge, this paper makes the following contributions:

1. Performance analysis of the unscalability issue in mathematical software for manycore systems, as well as an approach to solving the issue.

2. An extended matrix computation algorithm with NUMA awareness.

3. An extremely scalable runtime system with new mechanisms to effectively reduce NUMA memory accesses.

4. A novel framework that runs efficiently on manycore systems. It is the first time to demonstrate great scalability on shared-memory massively manycore systems with 1000 CPU cores.

The rest of the paper is organized as follows. Next section conducts performance analysis and identifies the reasons of the unscalability issue. Section 3 introduces our extended NUMA-aware QR factorization algorithm. Sections 4 and 5 describe the implementation of our framework. Section 6 provides the experimental results. Section 7 presents the related work. Finally Section 8 summarizes our work.

2. PERFORMANCE ANALYSIS

We measured the performance of an existing dynamic scheduling runtime system called TBLAS [18] to compute matrix operations. TBLAS was previously tested on quad-core and eight-core compute nodes, but has not been tested on compute nodes with more than sixteen CPU cores.

To measure TBLAS's performance on modern manycore systems, we did experiments with QR factorizations on a shared-memory 48-core machine. The 48-core machine has four 2.5 GHz AMD Opteron chips, each of which has twelve CPU cores. It also runs the CentOS 5.9 operating system and has 256 GB memory partitioned into eight NUMA nodes. Figure 1 displays performance of the QR factorization implemented with TBLAS. Each experiment takes as input a matrix of size $n = 1000 \times NumberCores$. On six cores, TBLAS reaches the highest performance of 6.5 GFlops/core. Then its performance keeps dropping. On 48 cores, its performance becomes as slow as 5.1 GFlops/core (i.e., a 20% loss).

However, we know that QR factorization has a time complexity of $O(\frac{4}{3}n^3)$ and is CPU-bound. With an increased input size, we had expected to see great scalability as previously shown on clusters with thousands of cores [18], because its ratio of communication to computation becomes less and less as the input size increases. Hence, Figure 1 exposes an unexpected unscalable problem. Our immediate task is to investigate what has caused this unscalability problem. Is it due to hardware or software or due to both?

2.1 Performance Analysis Using Hardware Performance Counters

We manually instrumented our matrix factorization program using the PAPI library [2]. Then we compared the differences between one experiment with a small number of cores and another experiment with 48 cores. Since this is a multi-threaded program, we collected performance data of hardware performance counters for each thread. Based on our performance data, each thread spent an equal amount of time on computation. This implies that there is no load imbalance among threads.

Table 1 shows the performance-counter data we collected on 12 and 48 cores, respectively. From the table, we can see that the 48-core experiment keeps the same low cache-miss rate and branch miss-prediction rate, as well as the same low rate of cycles without instructions. By contrast, the TLB miss rate increases a little bit from 7.8% to 8.7%. Moreover, the rate of FPU idle cycles increases by 31% from 3.9% to 5.1%. The rate of any-stall cycles (due to any resources) increases by almost 75%.

Table 1: Data of hardware performance counters collected from a 12-core experiment and a 48-core experiment, respectively.

	On 12 Cores	On 48 Cores
Performance per Core	6.4 GFlops	5.1 GFLops
L1 Data Cache Miss Rate	.5%	.5%
L2 Data Cache Miss Rate	2.98%	2.87%
TLB Miss Rate	7.8%	**8.7%**
Branch Miss-Prediction Rate	1.6%	1.5%
Cycles w/o Inst.	.5%	.6%
FPU Idle Cycles	3.9%	**5.1%**
Any-Stall Cycles	20.6%	**35.9%**

2.2 Reasons for Increased Any-Stall Cycles

We expect there are three possible reasons that can result in lots of stall cycles (due to any resources). They are: (1) thread synchronization, (2) remote memory access latency, and (3) memory bus or memory controller contention.

Thread synchronization can happen during the scheduling of tasks by the TBLAS runtime system. For instance, a thread is waiting to enter a critical section (e.g., a ready task queue) to pick up a task. When a synchronization occurs, the thread cannot do any computation but waiting. Therefore, the synchronization overhead is a part of the thread's non-computation time (i.e., total execution time - computation time). However, as shown in Table 2, the non-computation time of our program is less than 1%. Therefore, we can omit thread synchronization as a possible reason.

Table 2: Analysis of synchronization overhead.

	Total Time (s)	Computation Time (s)
12 Cores	30	29.9
48 Cores	74.8	74

The second possible reason is remote memory accesses. We conduct a different experiment to test the effect of remote memory accesses. In the experiment, the TBLAS program allocates memory only from the NUMA memory nodes from 4 to 7, that is, the second half of the eight NUMA memory nodes as shown in Figure 2. This is enforced by using the Linux command `numactl`. Then, we compare two configurations (see Figure 2): (a) running twelve threads on CPU cores from 0 to 11 located on NUMA nodes 0 and 1, and (b) running twelve threads on CPU cores from 36 to 47 located on NUMA nodes 6 and 7. In the first configuration, TBLAS attains a total performance of 57 GFlops. In the second configuration, it attains a total performance of 63 GFLOPS. Note that the matrix input is stored in NUMA nodes from 4 to 7. The performance difference shows that accessing remote memory does decrease performance. Note that we use Linux command `taskset` to pin each thread to a specific core.

The third possible reason is memory contention that may come from a memory bus or a memory controller. Here we do not differentiate the controller contention from the bus contention, but consider the memory controller an end

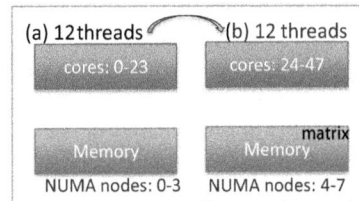

Figure 2: Effect of remote NUMA memory access latency. `matrix` is always allocated on NUMA nodes from 4 to 7. Then we run twelve threads in two different locations: (a) on NUMA nodes 0 and 1 (i.e., far from data), and (b) on NUMA nodes 6 and 7 (i.e., close to data).

point of its attached memory bus. In our third experiment, we run "numactl -i all" to place memory to all the eight NUMA nodes using the round-robin policy. As shown in Figure 3, there are two configurations: (a) we create twelve threads and pin them on cores from 0 to 11, (b) we create twelve thread and each thread runs on one core out of every four cores. In both configurations, each thread must access all the eight NUMA nodes due to the interleaved memory placement. Since the second configuration provides more memory bandwidth to each thread (i.e., lesser contention) than the first configuration, it achieves a total performance of 76.2 GFlops. By contrast, the first configuration only achieves a total performance of 66.3 GFlops. The difference shows that memory contention also has a significant impact on performance. One way to reduce memory contention is to maximize data locality and minimize cross-chip memory access traffic.

The above three experiments together with the performance differences they have made, provide an insight into the unscalability problem and motivate us to perform NUMA memory optimizations. We target at minimizing remote memory accesses since it is able to not only reduce the latency to access remote memories, but also alleviate the pressure on memory buses.

3. THE TILE ALGORITHM

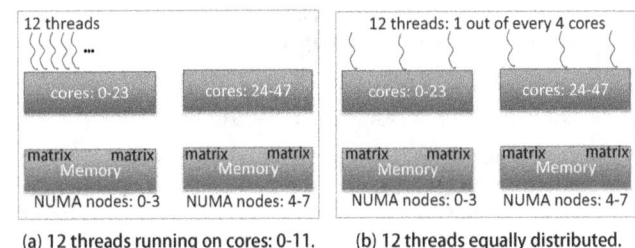

(a) 12 threads running on cores: 0-11.   (b) 12 threads equally distributed.

Figure 3: Effect of memory bus contention. `matrix` is allocated to all eight NUMA nodes using the roundrobin policy. We start twelve threads using two configurations, respectively. (a) 12 threads are located on 12 contiguous cores from 0 to 11. (b) 12 threads, each of which runs on one core out of every four cores.

To achieve the best performance, we must redesign new algorithms that can take advantage of both architecture and the application-level knowledges. We first briefly introduce the existing tile QR factorization algorithm. Then we analyze the algorithm's data-flow and data-reuse patterns. Finally we introduce our extension to make the algorithm NUMA aware.

3.1 Background

The tile QR factorization algorithm [8,9] uses an updating-based scheme that operates on matrices stored in a tile data layout. A tile is a block of submatrix and is stored in memory contiguously. Given a matrix A consisting of $n_b \times n_b$ tiles, matrix A can be expressed as follows:

$$A = \begin{pmatrix} A_{1,1} & A_{1,2} & \dots & A_{1,n_b} \\ A_{2,1} & A_{2,2} & \dots & A_{2,n_b} \\ \vdots & \vdots & \ddots & \vdots \\ A_{n_b,1} & A_{n_b,2} & \dots & A_{n_b,n_b} \end{pmatrix},$$

where $A_{i,j}$ is a square tile of size $b \times b$.

At the beginning, the algorithm computes the QR factorization for tile $A_{1,1}$ only. The factorization output of $A_{1,1}$ is then used to update the set of tiles on $A_{1,1}$'s right hand side in an embarrassingly parallel way (i.e., $\{A_{1,2}, \dots, A_{1,n_b}\}$). As soon as the update on any tile $A_{1,j}$ is finished, the update on tile $A_{2,j}$ can read the modified $A_{1,j}$ and start. In other words, whenever a tile-update in the i-th row completes, its below tile in the $(i+1)$-th row can start if $A_{i+1,1}$ also completes. After updating the tiles in the bottom n_b-th row, tile QR factorization applies the same steps to the trailing submatrix $A_{2:n_b,2:n_b}$ recursively.

3.2 Algorithm Analysis

Figure 4 shows the data-flow graph for solving a matrix of 4×4 tiles using the tile QR factorization algorithm. In the figure, each node denotes a computational task. A task is represented by a function name and an index [i, j]. A task with index [i, j] indicates that the output of the task is tile A[i, j]. An edge from node x to node y indicates that the output of node x will be an input to node y. For instance, SSRFB [2, 4] refers to a task that reads the output of tasks LARFB [1, 4] and TSQRT [2, 1], then modifies its own output of A[2, 4].

There are totally four functions (aka "kernels") in the tile QR factorization algorithm: GEQRT, TSQRT, LARFB, and SS-RFB. For completeness of this paper, we describe them briefly here:

- GEQRT: R[k,k], V[k,k], T[k,k] ← GEQRT(A[k,k]).

  It computes the QR factorization for a tile A[k,k] located on matrix A's main diagonal, and generates three outputs: an upper triangular tile R[k,k], a unit lower triangular tile V[k,k] containing the Householder reflectors, and an upper triangular tile T[k,k] for storing the accumulated transformations.

- TSQRT: R[k,k], V[i,k], T[i,k] ← TSQRT(R[k,k], A[i,k]).

  It updates the tiles located under tile A[k,k]. After GEQRT is called, TSQRT stacks tile R[k,k] on top of tile A[i,k] and computes an updated factorization.

- LARFB: R[k,j] ← LARFB(V[k,k], T[k,k], A[k,j]).

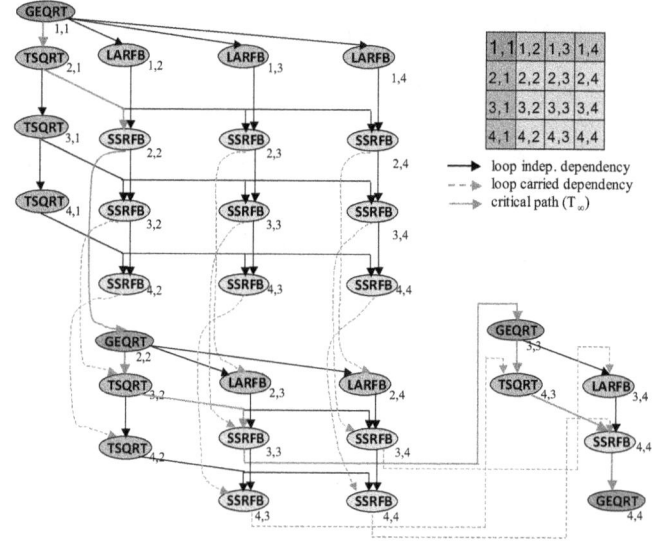

Figure 4: Data flow graph of the tile QR factorization algorithm to solve a matrix of 4×4 tiles.

It updates the tiles located on the right hand side of A[k,k]. LARFB applies GEQRT's output to tile A[k,j] and computes the R factor R[k,j].

- SSRFB: R[k,j], A[i,j] ← SSRFB(V[i,k], T[i,k], R[k,j], A[i,j]).

  It updates the tiles located in the trailing submtrix of $A_{k+1:n_b,k+1:n_b}$. It applies TSQRT's output to a stacked R[k,j] and A[i,j], and updates them correspondingly.

It is important to note that Figure 4 provides not only the information of data dependency, but also the information of data reuse. The previous TBLAS runtime system and many other runtime systems only use the data dependency information to ensure correct computational results.

Data reuse is the other important information to be utilized. It indicates how many times a tile will be used by the other tasks. For instance, in Figure 4, suppose tasks of SSRFB [2,2], [2,3], [2,4] are computed by the same thread running on a NUMA node p, and task TSQRT [2,1] is computed by another thread running on a different NUMA node q. Then due to cache misses, the former thread has to read the remote tile A[2,1] three times. Note that on NUMA systems, the latency to access a remote NUMA node can be much higher than that to access a local NUMA node (e.g., twice higher on our 48-core AMD machine). Therefore, we modify the tile algorithm and the TBLAS runtime system to utilize the data-reuse information to optimize NUMA memory accesses.

3.3 A NUMA-Aware Extension

This subsection describes our extended algorithm to solve QR factorizations by minimizing remote NUMA memory accesses.

We assume that the input to the algorithm is a matrix A with $nb \times nb$ blocks. Given a number of n threads, the $nb \times nb$ blocks are mapped to the n threads using a static dis-

---

Algorithm 1 Extended_NUMA_Tile_QR Algorithm

Thread_init(int tid /*thread id*/, double A[nb][nb])
double* A_{tid}[nb][nb]
for i ← 0 **to** nb-1 **do**
  for j ← 0 **to** nb-1 **do**
    /*Each tile[i,j] is mapped to a thread*/
    if get_assigned_thread(i, j) = tid **then**
      A_{tid}[i][j] ← malloc(tile_size)
      A_{tid}[i][j] ← A[i][j];
    end if
  end for
end for

Thread_entry_point(int tid)
for k ← 0 **to** nb-1 **do**
  if get_assigned_thread(k, k) = tid **then**
    R_{tid}[k,k], V_{tid}[k,k], T_{tid}[k,k] ← geqrt(A_{tid}[k,k])
    [memcpy V_{tid}[k,k], T_{tid}[k,k] to V_{tid_x}[k,k], T_{tid_x}[k,k]
    in threads tid_x, where thread tid_x is waiting for
    V_{tid}/T_{tid}[k,k]]
  end if
  thread_barrier
  for j ← k+1 **to** nb-1 /*along k-th row*/ **do**
    if get_assigned_thread(k, j) = tid **then**
      A_{tid}[k,j] ← larfb(V[k,k], T[k,k], A[k,j])
      [memcpy A_{tid}[k,j] to $A_{tid'}$[k,j], where thread tid' is
      waiting for A_{tid}[k,j]]
    end if
  end for
  thread_barrier
  for i ← k+1 **to** nb-1 **do**
    if get_assigned_thread(i, k) = tid **then**
      R[k,k], V[i,k], T[i,k] ← tsqrt(R[k,k], A[i,k])
      [memcpy V_{tid}[i,k], T_{tid}[i,k] to V_{tid_x}[i,k], T_{tid_x}[i,k]
      in threads tid_x, where thread tid_x is waiting for
      V_{tid}/T_{tid}[i,k]]
    end if
    for j ← k+1 **to** nb-1 **do**
      if get_assigned_thread(i, j) = tid **then**
        A_{tid}[k,j], A_{tid}[i,j]←ssrfb(V_{tid}[i,k], T_{tid}[i,k],
        A_{tid}[k,j], A_{tid}[i,j])
        [memcpy A_{tid}[k,j] to $A_{tid'}$[k,j], where thread tid'
        is waiting for A_{tid}[k,j]]
      end if
    end for
    thread_barrier
  end for
end for

---

tribution method. The static distribution method is defined by the means of an application-specific mapping function `get_assigned_thread(i,j)` which calculates the mapped thread ID of a matrix block [i, j].

Each thread has a thread ID tid. It uses its local NUMA memory to store its assigned subset of the input matrix A denoted by A_{tid}, and intermediate matrix results denoted by V_{tid} and T_{tid}. Those thread-private matrices of A_{tid}, V_{tid}, and T_{tid} are implemented as $nb \times nb$ NULL pointers. Their memories are dynamically allocated when needed.

Algorithm 1 shows the multithreaded version of NUMA-aware tile QR factorization. Before starting computation, each thread tid calls **Thread_init** to copy input to its private A_{tid}, from either a global matrix or a file in parallel. Next, each thread computes QR factorization in parallel as follows: 1) factor block A[k,k] on the main diagonal by calling `geqrt` if A[k,k] is assigned to itself; 2) factor all blocks on the k-th row by calling `larfb`; 3) factor the remaining ma-

trix blocks from A[k+1,k] to A[nb-1,nb-1] by calling `tsqrt` and `ssrfb` in parallel. Note that the algorithm copies certain tasks' output to a set of remote threads explicitly. The set of threads that are waiting for the specific output can be determined by the data flow analysis of the algorithm as shown in Figure 4.

The purpose of `thread_barrier` is only to show a correct working version of the parallel algorithm. We acknowledge that a direct translation of the algorithm may not be the fastest implementation due to the barriers. In our own implementation using a runtime system, however, there is no barrier at all. We use a dynamic data-availability-driven scheduling scheme in the runtime system to trigger new tasks whenever their inputs become available and are able to avoid global synchronizations. As shown in Figure 4, a runtime system can execute any task as long as its inputs are ready. A ready task can be scheduled to start even though some tasks prior to it are blocked. This approach essentially uses the same idea as the out-of-order instruction execution in superscalar processors.

4. OVERVIEW OF OUR FRAMEWORK

To support manycore NUMA systems efficiently, we design a framework that integrates application, runtime system, and architecture together. The framework consists of a static distribution method, an architecture-aware runtime system, and a user program. The user program is used to create (or "eject") new tasks which will be scheduled dynamically by the runtime system.

Our framework adopts a data-centric computing model. It co-allocates both data and tasks to different threads using a static distribution method. A matrix block A[i, j] is first assigned to a thread. Next, the task whose output is block A[i, j] will be assigned to the same thread as the block A[i, j]. On shared-memory systems, the static distribution will not prevent a thread from accessing any data. However, by using the static distribution, we are able to allocate all of a thread's data from its local NUMA memory and minimize remote memory accesses.

A user program is executed by the runtime system. Whenever reading a computational function, the runtime system creates a task and puts it to a queue immediately without doing any computation (i.e., "eject" a task or a job). A created task contains all the information needed for a thread to execute such as function name, locations of input and output. There are two types of task pool: waiting-task pool and ready-task pool. When a new task is created, it first enters the waiting-task pool. After all of its inputs are ready, it becomes a ready task and moves to a ready task pool.

The entire framework follows a data-flow programming model. It drives the user-program execution by data availability. After finishing a task and generating a new output, a compute thread goes to the waiting-task pool to search for the tasks whose input is the same as that output. If a waiting task has the same input as the newly generated output, its input state changes from unready to ready. When all the input states change to ready, the waiting task becomes a ready task and will be later picked up by a compute thread. Note that each compute thread is independent from every other compute thread (i.e., there is no fork-join).

In order to minimize remote NUMA memory accesses, our runtime system copies an output to the waiting threads' local memory nodes. The memory copy operation happens before the input state changes (from unready to ready) so that the local copy of the output can be used by the waiting thread.

In general, each compute thread executes the following steps in a while loop: (1) picks up a ready task, (2) computes the task, (3) searches for tasks that are waiting for the new output, and (4) triggers new ready tasks. Whenever a task is finished, the runtime system will use the newly available output data to trigger a set of new tasks.

5. THE IMPLEMENTATION

Our work builds upon the previous TBLAS runtime system to support scalable matrix computations on shared-memory manycore systems.

5.1 TBLAS

The TBLAS runtime system was originally designed to support matrix computations on distributed multicore cluster systems [18]. Although TBLAS has demonstrated good scalability on clusters, it has been applied only to compute nodes with a maximum number of 12 CPU cores. The structure of TBLAS is very simple. It has one task window and a global ready task queue shared by all the compute threads. The task window is of fixed size and stores all the waiting task (i.e., tasks created but not finished). The ready queue stores all the ready tasks whose input are available to read. The runtime system includes two types of thread: task-generation thread and compute thread. Each CPU core has a compute thread, but the entire runtime system has a single task-generation thread. The task-generation thread executes the user program and create new tasks to fill in the task window. Whenever becoming idle, a compute thread picks up a ready task from the global ready task queue. After finishing the task, the compute thread searches for the finished task's children and triggers new tasks.

5.2 Extensions

To achieve scalability on a shared-memory system with hundreds or even thousands of cores and a complex NUMA memory hierarchy, we have extended the previous TBLAS runtime system in the following aspects. Suppose a shared-memory system has n CPU cores and m NUMA memory nodes, our runtime system will launch n compute threads on n different cores.

- **Static data and tasks partitioning**. A matrix with $n_b \times n_b$ tiles will be partitioned among different threads using a 2-D cyclic distribution method [13]. Assume that n threads are mapped to a 2-D grid of r rows and c columns, where $n = r \times c$. Given a tile A[i, j] that is located at the i-th row and j-th column of matrix A, tile A[i, j] will be assigned to thread[i mod r, j mod c]. This distribution method is called 2-D cyclic distribution. All the matrix tiles assigned to thread i will be stored to thread i's local NUMA memory node. Also, a task whose output is tile A[i, j] will be assigned to the same thread as A[i, j]. This way a thread can always perform write operations to its local NUMA memory.

- **Per-thread ready queue**. As shown in Figure 5, instead of using a global ready task queue, each thread has its own ready task queue. A thread's ready task

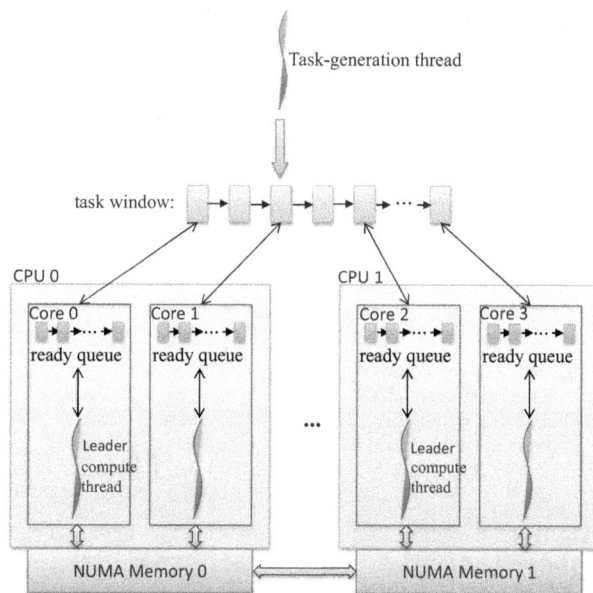

Figure 5: Architecture of the new TBLAS runtime system designed for NUMA many cores. For simplicity, the figure only displays two dual-core CPUs and two NUMA nodes. The actual runtime system can support many cores and many NUMA nodes.

queue only stores the tasks that are assigned to it based on the 2-D cyclic distribution. If a task modifies a tile that is assigned to thread i, the task is added to thread i's ready task queue accordingly. Using a per-thread ready queue not only reduces thread contention but also increases data locality.

- **Thread-private memory allocator**. Each thread allocates memory from its private memory pool to store its assigned submatrix and intermediate results. Before a thread starts, it has pre-allocated a slab of memory for its memory pool. When the thread starts, the first thing it does is to touch all the pages associated with the memory pool. This way all physical memory frames will reside in the thread's local NUMA memory node.

- **Work stealing**. Since each thread is assigned a fixed subset of tasks based on the 2-D cyclic distribution method, it results in a suboptimal performance due to load imbalance. To obtain better load balancing, our runtime system allows each thread to do work stealing when a thread has been idle for a certain amount of time. Note that a thread just steals tasks, but not the tasks' input or output data even if the data are in a remote NUMA node. We have implemented two work stealing policies: 1) locality-based work stealing, where a thread first tries to steal tasks from its neighbors that are on the same NUMA node, then steals from other threads located on remote NUMA nodes; 2) system-wise random work stealing, where a thread steals tasks from any other thread randomly.

- **Inter-NUMA-node memory copy**. If a matrix block owned by thread x is accessed multiple times by a remote thread y, the runtime system calls `memcpy` to copy the block to thread y's local buffer. After `memcpy` is complete, thread y can access the block from its local buffer directly.

Although the output block of a task is stored to a buffer in the destination, it will not stay in the destination forever since our runtime system keeps track of a reference counter for each block. After the consumers read (or consume) the block for a certain number of times, the block will be freed to the runtime system's free-memory pool and can be reused for future memory copies. Therefore, this NUMA optimization method has good scalability in terms of memory usage.

In our current implementation, the algorithm specifies which block should be copied to remote NUMA nodes. Note that given any matrix block, the runtime system knows to which thread the block is assigned by the predefined static 2-D cyclic distribution method.

- **NUMA-group leader thread**. We use leader threads to further reduce the cost of memory copies. Figure 5 illustrates that each NUMA node has a group of compute threads (one thread per core). The thread that runs on the first core of the NUMA node is defined as the "leader thread" of the group. The leader thread has a larger memory pool than its group members. When a data block is needed by multiple threads that reside on a remote NUMA node, the runtime system copies the data block to that NUMA node's leader thread only once. After the block is copied to the remote leader thread, member threads on the remote NUMA node can read data from their leader correspondingly. Note that all accesses from the member threads to their leader are local memory accesses, which saves a lot of remote memory accesses.

We use the above enhancements to attain better locality, load balancing, scalability, reduced synchronizations, and NUMA optimization. In addition, without the support of the runtime system, it will be much more difficult for programmers to manage and copy memory around manually to optimize NUMA memory accesses.

6. EXPERIMENTAL RESULTS

This section presents experimental results with QR factorizations on two *shared-memory* multicore systems: a system with 48 CPU cores, and a system with 1024 CPU cores.

6.1 Evaluation on a 48-core System

The 48-core system is the same one as we used for the performance analysis in Section 2. It has four 12-core AMD Opteron CPUs. Each CPU chip consists of two packages each of which has a dedicated NUMA memory node. Hence the system has eight NUMA memory nodes.

In the following experiments, we choose the appropriate NUMA memory placements to obtain the best performance. For instance, in the single CPU experiment, we use the Linux command "numactl -m node" to allocate memory to the CPU's local NUMA node. And in the largest 48-core experiment, we used "numactl -i all" to interleave allocation to all the NUMA nodes. Note that the performance will become much worse if numactl is not used.

6.1.1 Initial Optimizations

The previous TBLAS runtime system does not have good scalability. Figure 6 shows that the previous TBLAS on a single CPU (i.e. 6 cores) attains a performance of 6.5 GFlops/core. With an increasing number of cores, its performance starts to decrease gradually. Eventually on 48 cores, it drops to 5.4 GFlops/core (i.e., 17% loss). Note that the input matrix is of size $N = 1000 \times$ NumberCores.

The first optimization we apply is to divide a global ready-task queue into multiple queues so that each thread has a private ready task queue. This optimization can reduce thread contention to enter the global queue. We use the 2-D cyclic distribution method to distribute tasks to different threads statically as described in Section 5.2. As shown in Figure 6, adding the 2-D cyclic distribution makes the program scale better (i.e., a more constant GFlops/core). However, on a small number of cores, the previous TBLAS is faster than our extended 2-D cyclic version. This is because the dynamic scheduling method of the previous TBLAS has a better load balancing than the static distribution method. Furthermore, the thread contention overhead is low when only six threads are used.

The second optimization is to use work stealing (WS) to improve load balancing. Figure 6 shows that adding work stealing improves the static 2D cyclic extension by another 6%. When the number of cores is greater than 24, the `2D cyclic + WS` extension starts to outperform the previous TBLAS system.

However, from 24 cores to 48 cores, `2D cyclic + WS` still drops gradually. This shows that load balancing across different cores and using block-based data layout are not sufficient. Based on the insight provided by our performance analysis (Section 2), we start to perform NUMA memory optimizations.

6.1.2 Adding NUMA Optimizations

In order to minimize remote memory accesses, we not only distribute *tasks* to different threads statically, but also distribute *data* to different threads statically. The location of a task and the location of the task's output are always the same. This feature is enforced by the 2-D cyclic distribution method.

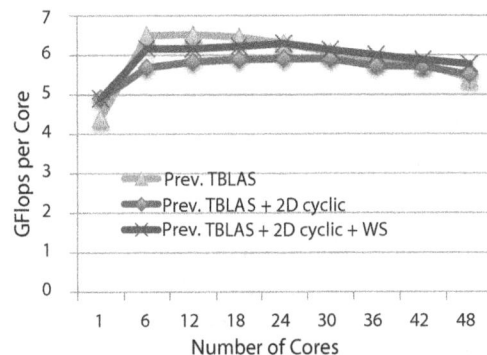

Figure 6: Our initial attempt to add 2-D cyclic distribution and work stealing to the previous TBLAS runtime system. The modified versions have a better scalability but are slower when using a small number of cores.

We have implemented the NUMA-aware QR factorization using our new TBLAS runtime system. The NUMA-aware algorithm decides which matrix block should be copied to remote NUMA memory nodes. Then the runtime system will take care of all the remaining work. For instance, the runtime system first determines which threads are waiting for the block, then pushes the block to the consumer threads' local memory buffers, finally it notifies the consumer threads of the data availability. The major NUMA optimizations added to the TBLAS runtime system are: 1) static partitioning and co-allocation of data and tasks, 2) automatic inter-NUMA memory copy, 3) NUMA-group leaders, 4) thread-private and group-private memory allocators, and 5) locality-aware work stealing. Please refer to Section 5.2 for details.

Figure 7 shows the performance of our new TBLAS that has added the NUMA optimizations. Without work stealing, the new TBLAS runtime system already shows great scalability. For instance, on 18 cores, it attains a maximum performance of 6.3 GFlops/core. On all the 48 cores, it attains 6.1 GFlops/core (i.e., 3% less than the maximum). By enabling work stealing, we are able to further improve the performance slightly (up to 4%). The figure also displays the performance of PLASMA 2.5.1 as a reference. To get the best performance of PLASMA, we have run its experiments with numactl, chosen the static scheduler, and tried various tile sizes. The performance difference between the previous TBLAS and PLASMA is due to the load-balance difference between dynamic scheduling and static scheduling.

It is worthwhile to point out that the new TBLAS with work stealing can perform as well as the previous TBLAS that runs on a single local memory node (i.e., no remote memory accesses). In addition, it is 16% faster than the previous TBLAS when using 48 cores.

6.2 Evaluation on a Massively Manycore System with 1024 Cores

The largest shared-memory manycore system we have access is an SGI UV1000 system [17]. It has 1024 CPU cores (Intel Xeon X7550 2.0GHz), and runs a single operating system image of Red Hat Enterprise Linux 6. It has 4 Terabytes of global shared memory distributed across 64 blades. Each blade consists of two 8-core CPUs and two NUMA memory nodes. All the blades are connected by a NUMAlink 5 interconnection.

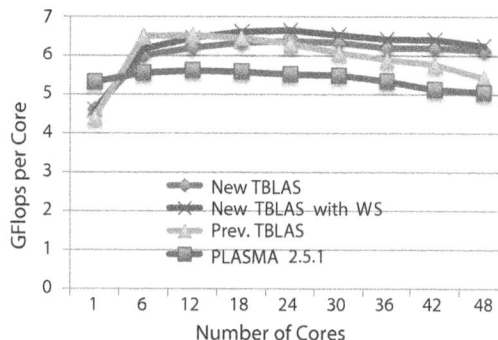

Figure 7: Performance of the new TBLAS runtime system with NUMA optimizations on a 48-core AMD Opteron system.

We run experiments on the SGI UV1000 system using one core to 960 cores. The input matrix size $N = 2000 \times \sqrt{number\_cores}$. As shown in Figure 8, we compare five different programs. To make a fair comparison, we have tuned each program to obtain its best performance. We describe the five programs as follows:

- `Intel MKL (LAPACK) QR`. We use Intel MKL 10.3.6 to compute QR factorizations using its LAPACK routine. It creates one process with a number of threads to perform computations. We run the Linux command "numactl –interleave=memory-nodes" to execute the program.

- `PLASMA QR`. PLASMA is a parallel multithreading library for multicore systems. We test various tile sizes and choose the size that provides the best performance. We also use PLASMA's static scheduler and "numactl –interleave=memory-nodes" to run the experiments.

- `New TBLAS`. Because the new TBLAS runtime system itself manages memory allocation and memory copy to optimize NUMA accesses, we use "numactl –localalloc" to allocate memory on the local NUMA memory node. We tune its tile size to achieve the best performance.

- `Intel MKL (ScaLAPACK) QR`. Intel MKL provides two sets of computational routines: *shared-memory* LAPACK routines, and *distributed-memory* MPI-based ScaLAPACK routines. Since the memory on the SGI UV1000 system is distributed to various blades, another interesting experiment is to test the ScaLAPACK routine which uses the MPI message passing model.

  We tune three optimization parameters for the ScaLAPACK QR factorization: i) selection of one-process-per-node or one-process-per-core, ii) ScaLAPACK block size NB, iii) process grid $P \times Q$, where the total number of processes is equal to $P \times Q$. To attain the highest performance, we choose one-process-per-core, NB=100, and the $P^* \times Q^*$ with the best performance.

- `Intel MKL ScaLAPACK PDGEMM`. PDGEMM is a parallel *matrix multiplication* subroutine in ScaLAPACK. The reason we compare QR factorizations to PDGEMM is that matrix multiplication has a higher computation-to-communication ratio, a higher degree of parallelism, and faster kernel implementations than the QR factorization. Therefore, we can use PDGEMM as an upper bound for QR factorizations. In fact, matrix multiplication can serve as an upper bound for most matrix computations although it may not be a tight upper bound.

Figure 8 (a) shows that our new TBLAS is able to keep up with the speed of PDGEMM, and scales efficiently from one core to 960 cores. Although the SGI UV1000 system has 1024 cores, we were not able to reserve all of them due to long job waiting time and hardware issues. The new TBLAS program delivers 1.05 TFlops, 2.0 TFlops, and 2.9 TFlops on 256, 512, and 784 cores, respectively. On 960 cores, it can deliver 3.4 TFlops. Note that the speedup of PDGEMM slows down a little bit from 784 to 960 cores. We think it might hit some hardware limitation because parallel matrix multiplication typically has a perfect weak-scalability.

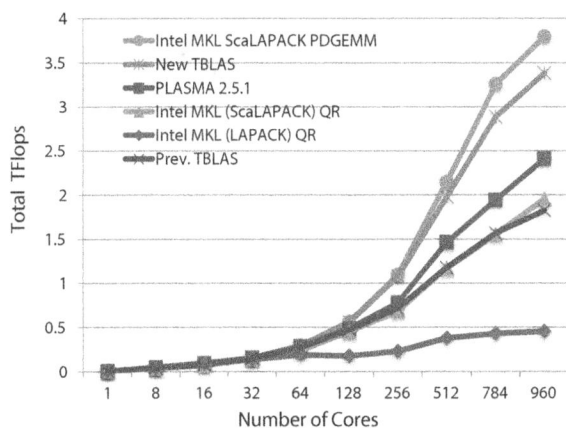

(a) Overall performance.

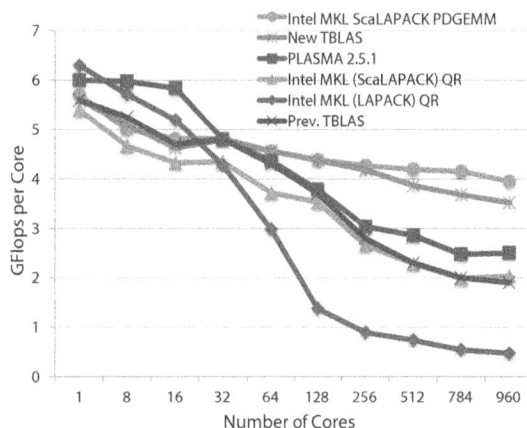

(b) Performance per core.

Figure 8: Comparison of the new TBLAS QR implementation with Intel MKL LAPACK, Intel MKL ScaLA-PACK, PLASMA, previous TBLAS, and parallel matrix multiplications (i.e., PDGEMM) on a shared memory 1024-core SGI UV1000 system.

PLASMA is the second best library, which can deliver 2.4 TFlops using 960 cores. As shown in Figure 8 (b), when the number of cores is less than or equal to 16 (i.e., within one blade), new TBLAS is slower than PLASMA because we disabled work stealing for better performance on large numbers of cores. On the other hand, the Intel MKL 10.3.6 library achieves 0.45 TFlops by using the MKL LAPACK routine, and 1.95 TFlops by using the MKL ScaLAPACK routine, respectively. Figure 8 shows that by taking into account NUMA optimizations, our new TBLAS can outperform its counterpart of Intel MKL LAPACK by 750%, and the ScaLAPACK library by 75%.

7. RELATED WORK

There are a few mathematical libraries that can provide high performance on multicore architectures. Intel MKL, AMD ACML, and IBM ESSL are vendor-provided libraries. They support linear algebra computations as one fundamental area. All the linear algebra subroutines have implemented the standard LAPACK interface [4]. PLASMA is an open source linear algebra library developed at the University of Tennessee [3]. It is a reimplementation of LA-PACK and aims at delivering high performance on multicore architectures. Similar to PLASMA, our work also uses the tile algorithms but extends the algorithms with NUMA optimizations. ScaLAPACK is a high performance linear algebra library for distributed memory machines [5]. ScaLAPACK uses a message passing programming model. Different from ScaLAPACK, our work focuses on how to design scalable software using a shared-memory programming model.

While the existing libraries can utilize all CPU cores, their efficiency (e.g., GFlops per core) keeps dropping when the number of cores increases. This paper targets at this unscalability problem and proposes an approach to improving it. We compare our framework with the most widely used Intel MKL and the latest PLASMA library and demonstrate better scalability.

NUMA-related issues on multicore systems have been studied by many researchers in the high performance computing community. McCurdy and Vetter introduced a tool called *Memphis*, which uses instruction-based sampling to pinpoint

NUMA problems in benchmarks and applications [16]. Tao et al. designed a low-level hardware monitoring infrastructure to identify remote NUMA memory inefficiencies and used the information to specify proper data layout to optimize applications [20]. Li et al. used shared memory to implement NUMA-aware intra-node MPI collectives and have achieved twice speedup over traditional MPI implementations [14]. Tang et al. proposed a two-phase methodology to investigate the impact of NUMA on Google's large workloads and designed load-test to optimize NUMA performance [19]. Frasca et al. improved both CPU performance and energy consumption significantly for large sparse-graph applications by using graph reorganization and dynamic task scheduling to optimize NUMA performance [12].

NUMA issues have also been studied by many researchers in the operating system community. Majo and Gross investigated the NUMA-memory contention problem and developed a model to characterize the sharing of local and remote memory bandwidth [15]. Fedorova et al. designed a contention-aware algorithm *Carrefour* to manage memory traffic congestion in the Linux OS [11]. An extension of the GNU OpenMP, *ForestGOMP* [7], allows developers to provide hints to the runtime system to schedule thread and memory migrations. These system related researches mainly studied how and when to migrate thread and memory with a minimal cost. Differently, we take advantage of the domain-specific knowledge (i.e., matrix computations) and use a combination of 2-D cyclic distribution and work stealing to keep load balancing and minimize thread and memory movement.

8. CONCLUSION AND FUTURE WORK

Despite the increase in the number of cores per chip, parallel software has not been able to take the full advantage of all the cores and to scale efficiently on shared-memory manycore systems. We analyzed the performance of existing software and proposed a new framework that consists of an extended NUMA-aware algorithm and a new runtime system. The framework builds upon a static 2-D cyclic distribution such that tasks are co-located with their accessed data. If a data block is referenced by remote threads multiple times, the runtime system copies the data from a local memory node to a remote memory node. The runtime system uses a data-availability-driven (i.e., data-flow) scheduling method and knows where data are located and which tasks are waiting for the data. This way it is feasible to push data to consumers automatically. The experimental results on a 48-core system and a 1024-core system demonstrate that our approach is effective, and is much more scalable than the existing numerical libraries (e.g., up to 750% faster than Intel MKL on 960 cores).

While our approach is used to solve QR factorization as an example, it can be applied directly to solve other different matrix factorizations, systems of linear equations, and eigenvalue problems. We envision that the same methodology and principles can also be extended to support other types of scientific applications such as computational fluid dynamics, sparse matrix problems, and quantum chemistry. Our future work is to apply the framework to solve other matrix problems, and then extend it to support computational fluid dynamics applications and sparse matrix problems on distributed-memory manycore systems at extreme scale.

9. REFERENCES

[1] Intel Math Kernel Library (MKL). http://software.intel.com/en-us/intel-mkl. Accessed: January, 2014.

[2] PAPI project. http://icl.cs.utk.edu/papi. Accessed: January, 2014.

[3] PLASMA project. http://icl.cs.utk.edu/plasma. Accessed: January, 2014.

[4] E. Anderson. *LAPACK Users' Guide*, volume 9. SIAM, 1999.

[5] L. S. Blackford. *ScaLAPACK User's Guide*, volume 4. SIAM, 1997.

[6] S. Boyd-Wickizer, A. T. Clements, Y. Mao, A. Pesterev, M. F. Kaashoek, R. Morris, and N. Zeldovich. An analysis of Linux scalability to many cores. In *Proceedings of the 9th USENIX Conference on Operating Systems Design and Implementation (OSDI'10)*, pages 1–8. USENIX, 2010.

[7] F. Broquedis, N. Furmento, B. Goglin, R. Namyst, and P.-A. Wacrenier. Dynamic task and data placement over NUMA architectures: an OpenMP runtime perspective. In *Evolving OpenMP in an Age of Extreme Parallelism*, pages 79–92. Springer, 2009.

[8] A. Buttari, J. Langou, J. Kurzak, and J. Dongarra. Parallel tiled QR factorization for multicore architectures. *Concurr. Comput. : Pract. Exper.*, 20(13):1573–1590, 2008.

[9] A. Buttari, J. Langou, J. Kurzak, and J. Dongarra. A class of parallel tiled linear algebra algorithms for multicore architectures. *Parallel Comput.*, 35(1):38–53, 2009.

[10] B. Cantrill and J. Bonwick. Real-world concurrency. *ACM Queue*, 6(5):16–25, 2008.

[11] M. Dashti, A. Fedorova, J. Funston, F. Gaud, R. Lachaize, B. Lepers, V. Quéma, and M. Roth. Traffic management: A holistic approach to memory placement on NUMA systems. In *18th international conference on architectural support for programming languages and operating systems*. ACM, 2013.

[12] M. Frasca, K. Madduri, and P. Raghavan. NUMA-aware graph mining techniques for performance and energy efficiency. In *Proceedings of the International Conference on High Performance Computing, Networking, Storage and Analysis*, SC '12, pages 95:1–95:11. IEEE, 2012.

[13] B. A. Hendrickson and D. E. Womble. The torus-wrap mapping for dense matrix calculations on massively parallel computers. *SIAM J. Sci. Comput.*, 15(5):1201–1226, Sept. 1994.

[14] S. Li, T. Hoefler, and M. Snir. NUMA-aware shared-memory collective communication for MPI. In *Proceedings of the 22Nd International Symposium on High-performance Parallel and Distributed Computing*, HPDC '13, pages 85–96. ACM, 2013.

[15] Z. Majo and T. R. Gross. Memory system performance in a NUMA multicore multiprocessor. In *Proceedings of the 4th Annual International Conference on Systems and Storage*. ACM, 2011.

[16] C. McCurdy and J. Vetter. Memphis: Finding and fixing NUMA-related performance problems on multi-core platforms. In *2010 IEEE International Symposium on Performance Analysis of Systems and Software (ISPASS)*, pages 87–96. IEEE, 2010.

[17] SGI. *Technical Advances in the SGI UV Architecture (white paper)*. 2012.

[18] F. Song, A. YarKhan, and J. Dongarra. Dynamic task scheduling for linear algebra algorithms on distributed-memory multicore systems. In *Proceedings of the Conference on High Performance Computing Networking, Storage and Analysis (SC'09)*, pages 19:1–19:11. ACM, 2009.

[19] L. Tang, J. Mars, X. Zhang, R. Hagmann, R. Hundt, and E. Tune. Optimizing Google's warehouse scale computers: The NUMA experience. In *Nineteenth International Symposium on High-Performance Computer Architecture*. IEEE, 2013.

[20] J. Tao, W. Karl, and M. Schulz. Memory access behavior analysis of NUMA-based shared memory programs. *Sci. Program.*, 10(1):45–53, Jan. 2002.

[21] D. Waddington, J. Colmenares, J. Kuang, and F. Song. KV-Cache: A scalable high-performance web-object cache for manycore. In *Proceedings of the 6th ACM/IEEE International Conference on Utility and Cloud Computings*, UCC 2013. ACM, 2013.

Collective Memory Transfers for Multi-Core Chips

George Michelogiannakis, Alexander Williams, Samuel Williams, John Shalf
Lawrence Berkeley National Laboratory, 1 Cyclotron Road, Berkeley, CA 94720
mihelog@lbl.gov, awilliams@lbl.gov, swwilliams@lbl.gov, jshalf@lbl.gov

ABSTRACT

Future performance improvements for microprocessors have shifted from clock frequency scaling towards increases in on-chip parallelism. Performance improvements for a wide variety of parallel applications require domain decomposition of data arrays from a contiguous arrangement in memory to a tiled layout for on-chip L1 caches and scratchpads. However, DRAM performance suffers under the non-streaming access patterns generated by many independent cores. In this paper, we propose collective memory scheduling (CMS) that uses simple software and inexpensive hardware to identify collective transfers and guarantee that loads and stores arrive in memory address order to the memory controller. CMS actively takes charge of collective transfers and pushes or pulls data to or from the on-chip processors according to memory address order. CMS reduces application execution time by up to 55% (20% average) compared to a state-of-the-art architecture where each processor reads and writes its data independently. CMS also reduces DRAM read power by 2.2× and write power by 50%.

1. INTRODUCTION

In recent years, the primary constraint for microprocessors has shifted from chip area to power consumption, leading to the stall in clock frequencies and the move towards massive parallelism [38, 5]. Emerging data intensive applications for these multicore platforms are projected to have enormous demands on memory bandwidth. However, DRAM bandwidth is not projected to scale proportionally to meet these future demands [43, 41, 33, 10, 17, 2, 30]. Memory bandwidth is already critical in numerous applications such as media applications, which have already been reported to require up to 300GB/s of memory bandwidth to utilize just 48 processors [31]. In addition, processing demands force the Xbox 360 to have 22.4GB/s of GDDR3 bandwidth to satisfy just three processors [43]. The situation will only become worse in the future because computational throughput is projected to improve much faster than memory bandwidth [33]. In fact, projections state that chip pins increase by 10% every year whereas processors double every 18 months [33]. In addition, while memory density nearly doubles every two years, the improvement in cycle time has been hundreds of times less, leading to tens to hundreds of processor cycles per memory access [41]. Energy is also a major

ICS'14, June 10–13 2014, Munich, Germany.
ACM 978-1-4503-2642-1/14/06 ...$15.00.
http://dx.doi.org/10.1145/2597652.2597654.

concern because given that today's DDR3 technology consumes about 70pJ per bit, a system with only 0.2 bytes per FLOP memory bandwidth requires over 160mW of DRAM power [38]. This problem is already crucial in datacenters, where 25%–40% of total power is attributed to DRAM [42]. Maximizing DRAM performance and energy efficiency is critical, especially for future systems where DRAM's contribution will likely be proportionally larger than today [5].

Numerous crucial applications depend on parallel speedups achieved through bulk-synchronous single program multiple data (SPMD) execution where all compute elements are employed in tandem to speed up a single kernel. In fact, data-parallel applications have been cited as the biggest drivers for multi-core, and applications in future multi-cores are expected to follow data-parallelism even for consumer and mobile applications [7]. Bulk-synchronous kernels typically rely on domain decomposition to expose data parallelism. However, copying data from a contiguous representation in DRAM to the domain-decomposed (tiled) layout in on-chip caches poses significant challenges to modern memories. That is because current chip multiprocessors (CMPs) presume each core operates independently, even for SPMD execution. The result is that the memory is presented with uncoordinated and stochastic requests that exhibit poor locality, which degrades performance and power [42, 45, 32, 31]. Even though a plethora of memory controllers have been proposed, they are typically passive elements which do not control how requests arrive to them. Therefore, their degree of freedom is limited to the entries in their finite-size transaction queues [32, 18, 40, 29, 11].

In this paper, we demonstrate a combined software and hardware approach for coordinating DRAM and on-chip data movement for data-parallel applications named collective memory scheduling (CMS). CMS uses the software layer to identify collective transfer opportunities and collect the data layout information. It then uses that information in the hardware to read and write data arrays in the DRAM in strict memory address order. On the on-chip network side, CMS pushes or pulls data to or from processors according to how the data array should be distributed to the on-chip L1 caches or local stores. Memory access and data distribution are handled by a CMS hardware engine co-located with each memory controller, instead of individual processor prefetch or direct memory access (DMA) engines. Essentially, the CMS engine acts as a memory access accelerator and is inexpensive enough to include even in general-purpose systems. CMS shifts the pattern of data movement from concurrent actors (threads or processes in shared mem-

This work was supported by the Director, Office of Science, of the U.S. Department of Energy under Contract No. DE-AC02-05CH11231.

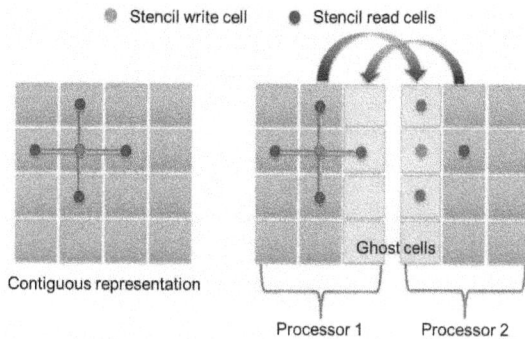

Figure 1: Tiling of a dense array onto a processor grid. Each tile is assigned to a processor. Tiles may include read-only data that replicate neighboring data (shared data). Such an example created by a 2D 5-point stencil is shown.

```
Array = hta(name,
        {[1,3,5], // Tile boundaries before
                  //  rows 1 (start), 3 and 5
         [1,3,5]},// Likewise for columns
         [3,3]);  // Map to a 3x3 processor array
```

Figure 2: Example HTA declaration code.

ory) each requesting data from memory directly and independently, to collaborating actors accessing memory as a group by performing collective operations. CMS guarantees in-order memory access even with row- and column-major mappings which are more productive for programmers but normally produce unfavorable memory access patterns [14]. CMS also performs bandwidth filtering in algorithms where processors share data by reading such data just once from memory and then distributing it to all recipients. This can drastically reduce memory reads in data parallel numerical kernels such as matrix multiplication, stencils and FFTs where working sets are highly overlapping.

To make access to CMS easy for programmers, we augment the hierarchically tiled array (HTA) programming abstraction [15] to efficiently and compactly express collective transfers and pass on the required information to the CMS hardware engine. This way, CMS simplifies the application programming interface (API) since the same *collective* function call is performed by all processors, with no need to calculate individual DMA address ranges [36]. Although we use the HTA library to demonstrate the programming interface for CMS, the concept could easily be exploited by numerous other compiler-based programming systems, such as OpenMP and OpenACC.

We use algorithm kernels from the TORCH and PARSEC collections to demonstrate the effectiveness of CMS across a wide variety of applications [3, 19]. CMS supports arbitrary mappings of data to processors and data array dimensions, but we focus on data-parallel applications with regular tiled layouts such as dense and sparse 2D data arrays because of their broad coverage of typical use cases in consumer electronics and scientific/engineering applications [26, 28, 10, 17], and their projected criticality in future multi-cores [7].

By re-establishing a streaming access pattern, CMS reduces the completion time for a collective read and write operation by 39% for dense 2D data arrays, and 60% for sparse 2D data arrays. Consequently, CMS reduces application execution time by up to 55% (20% average), compared to independent DMA or prefetch operations in each processor. CMS also reduces DRAM read power by 2.2× and DRAM write power by 50%. In addition, CMS eliminates

network congestion by replacing many independent read and write requests which saturate the network with a handful of control packets. CMS achieves this with a simple hardware engine and with no need for costly and deep transaction queues, which modern memory controllers use to partially recover a streaming access pattern [44, 45, 18, 32, 29].

2. BACKGROUND

2.1 Domain Decomposition

Domain decomposition is commonly used to expose parallelism for SPMD algorithms that operate on data much larger that the available on-chip storage. Figure 1 illustrates decomposition of a dense 2D data array into tiles. Tiles are typically sized to fit L1 caches or local storage in each processor [26]. Therefore, processors typically load their next tile, compute on the tile with minimal communication, and then write it back to memory. There is typically minimal data reuse across tiles assigned to the same processor. Accessing tiles in memory is done with local independent hardware prefetch [21] or cache fill streams for a cache-coherent CMP, a list of outstanding load-store requests for a massively multithreaded architecture like a graphical processor unit (GPU), or via a sequence of DMA requests for a local store architecture like STI Cell [36]. Other algorithms consist of sparse data arrays, where some tiles contain a large number of or exclusively zeroes. Applications with dense process grids leave processors with tiles containing only zeroes idle, whereas applications with sparse process grids do not reserve more processors than non-zero tiles. Data-parallel algorithms constitute critical applications in such diverse areas as image processing, seismic imaging, machine learning, electromagnetics, fluid dynamics, climate modeling, and others [26, 28, 10, 17].

2.2 Memory Access Streams and Efficiency

In current architectures and even in SPMD execution, processors access memory independently causing requests to arrive in nearly random order to memory [45, 42]. Random access patterns make prefetching difficult and degrade DRAM performance and power [44, 32, 42] because they cannot take advantage of pre-activated rows and therefore cause more row activations compared to sequential access patterns [42]. As a result, in many workloads an open row is used only once or twice before being closed due to a conflict [42]. Depending on the access pattern, only 14%–97% of peak memory bandwidth can actually be utilized [31].

Overfetch penalizes both latency and power because opening a new row requires charging bit lines, amplification by sense amplifiers, and then writing bits back to the cells. This further aggravates the memory bandwidth bottleneck in modern architectures, causing a wide variety of applications to be constrained by memory bandwidth [10, 43, 41]. Uncoordinated memory requests can also result in redundant memory accesses, because data shared between processors is fetched independently by each processor using transactions potentially separated by long time intervals. Finally, multiple independent requests congest the network waiting for vacancies in the memory controller's queue.

2.3 Hierarchical Tiled Arrays Representation

HTAs are a polyhedral representation language that compactly expresses tiled data arrays [15]. The declaration of

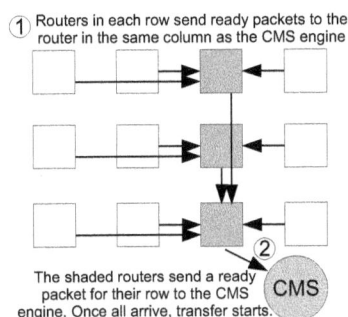

Figure 3: Initiating a synchronous read CMS operation.

HTAs includes how the data array is tiled and how tiles map (are distributed) to processors. The example of Figure 2 divides a 6×6 array into 2×2 tiles and maps those tiles to a 3×3 array of processors, as shown in Figure 8.

3. COLLECTIVE MEMORY TRANSFERS

This Section describes collective read and write operations, different data array layouts, the CMS hardware engine, and finally the programming interface to CMS.

3.1 Collective Read Operations

In read operations, the CMS engine reads memory sequentially and distributes data to the appropriate processors according to the data array's mapping to the processors. Essentially, the CMS engine takes charge of the collective operation and *pushes* data to the processors. Data that is shared between processors, such as ghost zones in stencil computations in the example of Figure 1, is read only once from memory and then distributed to all recipients with multicast or duplicate unicast packets.

The CMS engine initiates the transfer when all processors make the collective read function call for the same data array. This inserts an implicit barrier which can replace existing barrier calls, which are typical in computation loops of data-parallel computations [17]. To coordinate operation start, we employ a simple hierarchical communication pattern, shown in Figure 3. For cases where inserting a barrier would be inefficient, we also implement non-barrier reads where the transfer initiates when only the first processor is ready. This requires non-ready processors to store the next iteration's tile in addition to the current iteration's tile (the tile under computation), and possibly the previous iteration's tile which may be still in the process of being written back to memory. We do not allow processors to be further out of synchronization, to reduce local storage requirements.

3.2 Collective Write Operations

To easily guarantee memory access order, CMS write operations are performed as reads from the standpoint of the CMS engine. In other words, the CMS engine *pulls* data from the processors and writes it to memory. When the processor that holds the first tile line of the data array in memory address order (e.g., processor 1 in the top left of Figure 8) is ready to write its tile, it sends a write ready packet to the CMS engine. The CMS engine then sends read requests to retrieve the whole data array in memory address order. In the mapping of Figure 8, the first read request for elements $(1,1)$ and $(2,1)$ is served by processor 1, $(3,1)$ and $(4,1)$ by processor 2, $(5,1)$ and $(6,1)$ by proces-

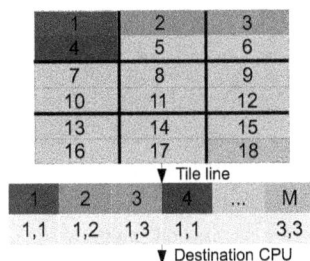

Figure 4: An example data layout array and the resulting mapping of tile lines to a 3×3 processor array.

sor 3, $(1,2)$ and $(2,2)$ by processor 1, and so on. Processors may delay their response until they produce the data.

In order to cover the communication delay and keep the memory constantly busy, there need to be more than one outstanding read requests in flight. Because the network guarantees no ordering, the CMS engine uses a small reorder buffer to enqueue read replies and write data to memory in address order. The size of the reorder buffer represents a tradeoff between eliminating memory idle cycles versus cost and network load. In our 8×8 2D mesh and using dense 2D data arrays, the minimum size which guarantees that the CMS engine constantly has data to write to the memory is six transactions for arrays of 512×512 elements, four transactions for 1024×1024, and three for 2048×2048 arrays.

3.3 Data Array Layout

CMS supports regular and flexible mappings of multi-dimensional data arrays in memory to processors. Regular mappings are for tiled arrays and map each tile to a processor according to a function or a mapping matrix. For example, the dense 2D data array of Figure 8 follows the function $F(x) = x$ because tile i maps to processor i. Regular mappings can also express sparse data arrays. For instance, in the same 3 × 3 processor array, a 3×3 mapping matrix with tile ID 1 in position $(1,1)$ (indicating that processor $(1,1)$ is assigned tile 1), 2 in position $(2,2)$ and 3 in position $(3,3)$ defines a sparse data array with tiles only in the diagonal. By knowing how the data array is mapped to memory addresses (such as row-major), the CMS engine calculates the address ranges of each tile. Regular mappings also have a parameter to define the shared data in each tile. In Figure 8, this parameter has a value of one.

Flexible mappings support any layout of memory addresses to processors. To enable this, the CMS engine maintains a small dedicated data layout array recording which processor owns each data. An example array is shown in Figure 4. To reduce its size, this array is indexed at a granularity defined by the largest contiguous address range that belongs to a single processor. With row- or column-major mapping and tiles, that is a tile line. The CMS engine may also include an identical additional data layout array to record processors that share each tile line.

The size of the data layout and sharer arrays depends on the size of the data array and the indexing granularity. To support a 2048×2048 2D data array in a 64-processor system with 256B tile lines, the data layout array is 20KB, which is less than 0.1% of the cache size in the Intel Xeon Phi, and similarly a very small fraction of other on-chip caches or local storage. Data arrays with finer indexing granularities may need more storage. This can be mitigated by mapping the data array to memory addresses such as to increase the

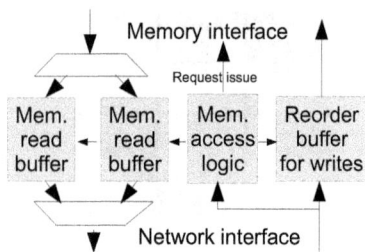

Figure 5: CMS engine outline.

indexing granularity. Instead of adding dedicated storage, the CMS engine can also use part of the L3 cache local to the memory controller the CMS engine is co-located with. If space in the data layout array does not suffice, part of the collective transfer is performed without CMS.

The data layout array is populated by the CMS engine after observing the memory access pattern created when each processor fetches its first tile without coordination. We rely on processors to explicitly mark what read requests are for shared data (data in another processor's tile). The CMS engine also discovers the data layout array indexing granularity during that time by observing the size of read requests. After the initial learning period, all subsequent read and write transfers are performed collectively until the application initiates a new learning period, indicating that it is now accessing a data array with a different layout.

We choose to have the CMS engine discover the layouts of data arrays instead of transferring the data layout information from the processors to the CMS engine in the request packets due to the on-chip data movement that would create. The performance impact from performing the first transfer without coordination is negligible due to the large number of computation iterations typical in data-parallel applications. For most applications, one owner and one reader (sharer) processors suffice. However, if there are more readers than sharer data arrays, the additional readers do not participate in the collective transfers for their read-only (shared) data.

Ready (request) packets contain the starting address of the data array and information about how it maps to processors. For data arrays with regular mappings, ready packets contain the mapping function or matrix as previously discussed, which can easily be contained in a few flits. For flexible mapping arrays, ready packets need only contain an indication of whether a new learning period should initiate.

3.4 Collective Memory Scheduling Engine

We implement the CMS engine atop a typical DMA engine. As illustrated in Figure 5, the CMS engine has a memory interface side and an on-chip network interface side. Read or write requests arrive from the network interface side. At the memory interface side, the CMS engine either sends read requests as fast as the memory controller allows, or it sends write requests whenever it has valid data to write. Once the collective transfer is complete, the CMS engine returns to idle, waiting to accept a new operation.

The memory access logic stores the collective transfer information. In regular mapping mode, the CMS engine stores that information from the collective request packet. Otherwise, the CMS engine uses the logic outlined in Figure 6.

The allowed number of pending memory transactions depends on the size of the CMS engine's buffers. Read operations use two small buffers ("mem. read buffers") for the outstanding DRAM read requests and to permit duplicating

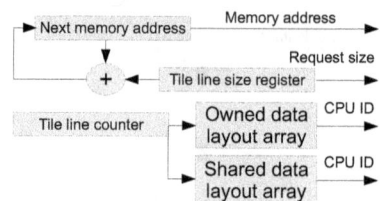

Figure 6: An outline of the memory access logic for data arrays with flexible mapping. Since accessing a tile line in the DRAM requires many cycles, these circuits are pipelined to avoid extending the CMS engine critical path.

Array = hta(name, {[1,3,5], [1,3,5]}, [3,3],
 F(x) = x, // Mapping function
 1); // Tiles share one cell from their edges

Figure 7: An example declaration for a regular mapping. Each tile shares cells adjacent to their boundaries (therefore two rows and two columns in total).

shared data packets. No new DRAM read requests may be issued until one of the two buffers is free. The reorder buffer for write operations tags requests to tiles for their tile lines and uses that tag to write the returned data into the correct location in the reorder buffer such that memory address order is preserved. The CMS engine can also include a small queue to store pending collective transfer requests, but only one is active at a time.

We co-locate a CMS engine with each memory controller in order to reduce communication distance. The CMS engine can be integrated into the memory controller instead of remaining a separate entity. In memory controllers with multiple channels, we can extend the CMS engine to perform different parts of the collective transfer in different channels. Alternatively, we can use one CMS engine per channel to perform multiple concurrent collective transfers. With multiple memory controllers, a large collective transfer is divided into smaller ones, each of which is assigned to a CMS engine. Therefore, a chip-wide operation will activate all CMS engines, each performing a portion of the operation.

Because the CMS engine guarantees memory address order, the memory controller need not be more complex than a FIFO scheduler with just enough transaction queue entries for memory pipelining. Moreover, since the CMS engine performs the entire operation instead of individual-processor DMA engines or prefetch units, these is opportunity to simplify memory controllers and local processor DMA engines or prefetch units. Doing so would outweigh the additional complexity of the CMS engine compared to a typical DMA engine because of the complexity of modern memory controllers with large transaction queues and complex scheduling policies [32, 18, 40, 29, 11]. Even without these cost reductions, as we show in Section 4.2.4, CMS engines are inexpensive enough to be included in general-purpose systems at a minimal cost increase. When there are no collective transfer opportunities, CMS engines remain inactive and can power down, similar to any other accelerator.

3.5 Programming Interface

CMS uses the software to identify transfers as collective, transfer the necessary data layout information to the CMS hardware engine, and make the collective transfer capabilities easily accessible to the programmer. Although a variety of APIs and libraries can take advantage of this kind of collective memory operations (such as OpenMP and OpenACC), we choose the HTA syntax [15] as an interface to

346

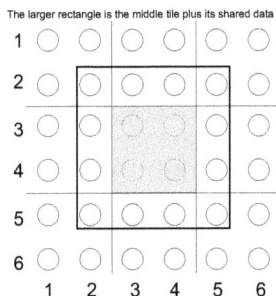

Figure 8: The mapping from our example declaration. Only the shared zones for the shaded (middle) tile are shown. Vertical and horizontal lines are tile boundaries.

Loading a HTA with a CMS read

```
HTA_instance = CMS_read (HTA_instance);
```

Loading the same HTA with DMA operations for each line of data

```
Array[row1] = DMA (Starting_address_row1,
                   Ending_address_row1);
            .
            .
Array[rowN] = DMA (Starting_address_rowN,
                   Ending_address_rowN);
```

Figure 9: Without CMS, the programmer needs to calculate starting and ending addresses for each tile line in a local-store architecture, including shared data.

formally express tiled data arrays. For regular mappings, CMS adds a parameter to HTAs to define the regular mapping, and another parameter for the number of cells shared between neighboring processors to accommodate computations such as stencils, as discussed in Section 3.3. Figure 7 shows an example. The resulting mapping is illustrated in Figure 8. HTAs have been extended to offer an alternative and more complex but also more powerful syntax to declare shared zones of arbitrary shapes and sizes [15], which we can also use for CMS. For flexible mappings, the library can abstractly determine if a new learning period is required, and thus no added parameters are necessary. Flexible mappings that cannot be expressed with HTAs require library modifications or alternative polyhedral representations.

We provide access to CMS functionality using a library that exposes an API similar to DMA function calls [36]. This leaves the programming style intact and simply requires the programmer to use CMS function calls instead of DMA function calls. A CMS read or write function call requires only the HTA instance as parameters. Since the HTA instance contains all tiling, layout, and addressing information, the library abstractly constructs request packets with the information required by the CMS engine. Therefore, all processors that wish to read or write the same HTA *make the exact same function call.*

The CMS API is considerably simpler than DMA operations in local-store architectures such as STI Cell [36]. In the common case that a processor's tile consists of non-contiguous memory addresses [16, 30], a potentially large number of DMA calls is required, which in turn require deep transaction queues in each DMA engine [22]. As an example, to transfer a tile in a 64-core system from a regularly-mapped 2048×2048 data array without architectural support for strided memory access, each processor requires 256 separate DMA transfers. That is because each processor's tile contains 256 rows each of which are disjoint in memory address order with row- or column-major mappings, which

are typically used. The equivalent CMS operation requires only one function call, as shown in Figure 9.

Although our example programming interface is limited to local-store architectures with an explicit API, this is not a requirement. Conventional directives-based approaches such as OpenACC, and Polyhedral representations alternative to HTAs can also use CMS hardware [23, 4]. Alternatively, compilers or run-time systems can analyze memory access patterns and data structure layouts to identify collective transfers. Finally, collective transfers can be performed even using basic language constructs, but this requires the programmer to directly communicate with the CMS engine.

4. EVALUATION

4.1 Methodology

We use DRAMSim2 [34] to model DRAM performance in response to the access patterns generated by our test-cases. We then input these resulting DRAM performance and power models to a heavily-modified version of the Booksim network simulator that includes processors and local stores. This architecture is representative of future many-core chips with local stores, which we use as a proof of concept and later discuss the applicability of CMS to other platforms. All our simulations use dense process grids (all processors participate regardless of the amount of data assigned to them). Initially we simulate writes and barrier read operations of 2D dense and sparse regularly mapped data arrays with no shared data. Variables (cells) in data arrays are 8-byte double precision.

We then present application results for the following important applications: Fluidanimate and streamcluster from the PARSEC benchmark suite [3], seismic wave propagation simulation (RTM) [26], the SOBEL filter used extensively for image processing (SOBEL) [12], LU factorization of a dense matrix (LU), sparse matrix multiply (SpMV), and conjugate gradient (CG) from the TORCH benchmark suite [19], and the Laplacian stencil from [20]. All applications use a regular mapping of tiles to processors, therefore there is no data layout array in the CMS engine. Such regular mapped data arrays comprise the building blocks of applications ranging from image processing in consumer devices to the largest scale high performance computing (HPC) applications such as climate modeling and fluid simulations. SpMV and CG use sparse matrices with approximately 25% non-zeroes, predominantly located in tiles on the diagonal. Similar to past work, only non-zero values are stored in and transferred to and from main memory [6]. LU and streamcluster use dense tiled data arrays, while fluidanimate, RTM, SOBEL and Laplacian use dense tiled data arrays with stencils and therefore use shared data.

For our application results, we model a CMP with an 8×8 array of Intel Xeon Phi co-processors, which are simple in-order x86-based processors and representative of the simple cores projected for future many-core chips [5]. For each application, we calculate the processing time per array variable as well as the shared data size, and simulate ten iterations of each application's execution loop (more iterations produce comparable results). Because thread migration is detrimental to data-parallel applications, we use a static mapping of threads to processors. We assume enough local storage for triple buffering for all tile sizes, which prevents performance degradation due to redundant DRAM or higher-level cache accesses as tile size increases. In general-purpose systems, the software can perform cache blocking to resize tiles to fit available local storage. We use the typically-used row-major mapping of data arrays to memory (column-major produces comparable results) [16, 30, 14].

Our memory subsystem consists of memory channels with independent controllers, which matches the configuration of many contemporary server processor designs [2, 33]. We place four memory controllers at the corners of our CMP, and a CMS engine co-located with each memory controller. We use static address-based mapping to map tile lines (memory addresses) to memory controllers. Therefore, each processor requests each tile line from the appropriate memory controller and CMS engine.

A 2D mesh on-chip network is used with dimension-order routing (DOR) and four-stage input-buffered routers [9]. Input buffers have 4 virtual channels (VCs), with eight flit slots statically assigned to each. Two VCs are used for request packets, and two VCs for replies. The datapath is 128 bits wide. Data-transferring packets carry one line of a processor's tile, plus one head flit.

For the memory, we simulate a 16MB DDR3 1600MHz memory module from Micron with a 64-bit data path and two ranks with 8 banks each. There is a single memory controller for the two ranks. The most significant bits of the address determine the channel, then the row, column, bank, and finally rank. The memory controller has 32-slot transaction and DRAM command reorder queues, and first ready first come first served (FRFCFS) scheduling [32, 45]. Our FRFCFS scheduler uses an open-row policy which respects row buffer locality by prioritizing transactions to open DRAM rows. This essentially performs limited transaction reordering by address, similar to other modern schedulers [32, 18, 29, 11]. We compare CMS against FRFCFS because FRFCFS maximizes memory throughput compared to a variety of other controllers [40, 32]. FRFCFS does not necessarily minimize application execution time because maximizing memory throughput may be unfair to threads [29]. However, we do not model and therefore hold these adversary effects against FRFCFS. Therefore, our FRFCFS represents an optimized state-of-the-art memory controller. We use 1600MHz for all processors and the network.

4.2 Results

4.2.1 Memory Throughput Degradation

First, we quantify the performance of DRAM in response to an uncoordinated access pattern that results from a SPMD algorithm running on a conventional many-core memory subsystem. In this case, our FRFCFS memory controller tries to maximize performance by reconstructing a linear access pattern and respecting row buffer locality using transaction reordering. However, even a sophisticated controller's reordering capability is inherently limited by the depth of its transaction queue since memory controllers do not control the order requests arrive into their queue. In contrast, CMS guarantees in-order memory access without complex reordering schemes or deep queues.

To set up this experiment, we use DRAMsim2 [34] to simulate a synthetic 16MB in-order trace of loads to represent the coordinated memory accesses created by CMS, and an out-of-order trace to simulate the uncoordinated case where loads or stores are presented to the memory controller in random order. A single load accesses a 64-Byte word, causing an eight-cycle burst due to the 64-bit memory controller datapath. The uncoordinated requests are randomly-ordered in sizes of 128 bytes representing one tile line. These traces therefore *accurately represent* the unpredictable memory access stream that would arrive to a memory controller in the baseline case where processors send requests for each tile line without coordination. Experiments with access traces larger than 16MB produce comparable results.

Our results show that for the uncoordinated access pattern (baseline with FRFCFS), DRAM throughput drops by 25% for loads and 41% for stores. Also, median latency increases by 23% for loads and 64% for stores, maximum latency increases by 2× in both cases, and power increases by 2.2× for loads and 50% for stores. Compared to the DRAM peak bandwidth, reads achieve 80% and writes 75% with CMS compared to 60% and 44% respectively for the uncoordinated case. Even streaming unit-stride traces cannot achieve 100% throughput due to refresh operations.

The uncoordinated case exhibits higher power consumption due to an increase in activate and precharge power (5.2× for loads and 3.4× for stores), caused by a 96% row buffer miss rate in the uncoordinated case compared to 3% with CMS. Past work has found similar results, and not even the best-performing memory transaction scheduler can bridge the gap between random and in-order accesses [32, 42, 44, 41]. For example, the row buffer hit rate drops from 60% for a single processor to 35% in a baseline 16-processor CMP, in a variety of benchmarks [42]. Also, in a 16-core CMP, a row fetched into the row buffer is typically used only once or twice before being closed due to a conflict [42].

4.2.2 Operation Completion Time

With the above DRAM results, we then perform collective (coordinated) and uncoordinated transfers of data arrays. The results are shown in Figure 10 (left). Compared to the uncoordinated case, CMS reduces completion time by an average of 39% for both reads and writes for dense data arrays, and 60% for sparse data arrays. These gains are predominantly due to the lower throughput the DRAM provides with random (uncoordinated) memory access patterns. The slightly lower performance gains for CMS writes for 128×128 and smaller data arrays are due to the propagation delay between processors generating request (ready) packets and accessing memory for the first time, which is 22 cycles for barrier reads and 40 for writes by average in our system. This is easily amortized by the duration of a transfer. Larger transfers make these delays negligible.

Larger data arrays increase the tile line size which favors spatial locality in the uncoordinated case. However, larger tile lines also create more severe contention and degrade on-chip network performance because of the long packets. Furthermore, in the uncoordinated case, sparse data arrays create intense hotspots because the majority of the data are destined to the few processors that are assigned the tiles along the diagonal. This provides the performance advantage for sparse arrays compared to dense arrays and illustrates that CMS load balances the network better because it accesses tile lines in processors in an interleaved manner. Otherwise, hotspots can be created depending on the order requests arrive to the memory controller.

We then repeat the experiments, but we add a uniform random (UR) background traffic pattern with a 10% flit in-

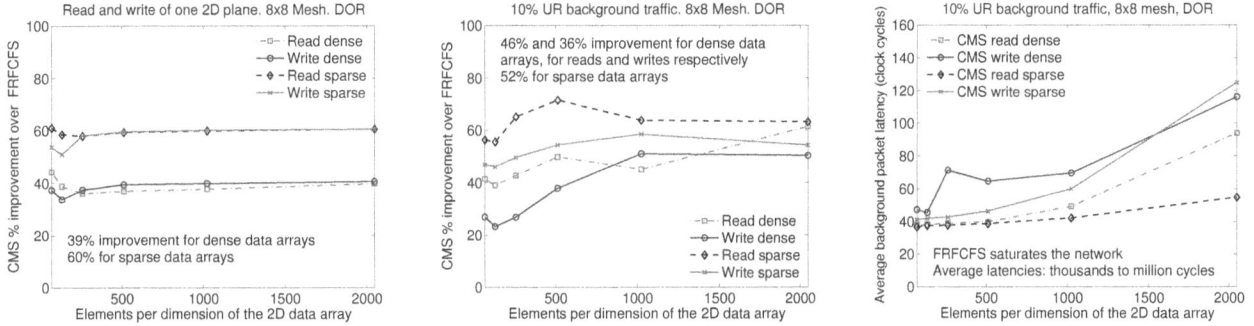

Figure 10: CMS transfer completion time improvement over FRFCFS (uncoordinated) and the impact on background traffic.

jection rate. A 10% injection rate provides non-negligible traffic, but not enough to saturate the network by itself. This traffic is composed of read and write requests and replies similar to DMA traffic, and represents innocent bystander traffic. As shown in Figure 10 (center), the reduction in execution time for CMS in the mesh is 46% for reads and 36% for writes for dense data arrays, and 52% for sparse arrays for both reads and writes. The reduction in speedup for collective writes compared to collective reads for dense arrays illustrates the increased traffic of collective writes compared to reads. While background traffic degrades performance for CMS, it is more adversary to the uncoordinated case (FRFCFS) because that creates hundreds or thousands of request packets that traverse the network most of which are queued in the network for a long time because they cannot be absorbed by the memory controller, thus contenting with the background traffic. Figure 10 (right) illustrates the impact to the background traffic.

Repeating these experiments in a 144-processor system yields comparable results. Finally, having only one or two memory controllers instead of four slightly favors CMS because the baseline case produces more severe network hotspots and stresses the memory more.

4.2.3 Impact on Application Execution Time

We show application results in Figure 11. The gains depend on the ratio of the time spent computing for each tile versus completing a read and then a write operation. This is the application's byte per FLOP ratio. CMS provides a minimal (0%–2%) reduction in execution time for the compute-bound applications in our system (RTM, LU and CG), but CMS still reduces DRAM power. In contrast, memory bandwidth-bound applications directly benefit from CMS in execution time. The geometric mean of the execution time reduction for all applications is 8.5% due to the compute-bound applications in our collection, the average is 20%, and the maximum is 55%.

Figure 11 (right) presents execution time as a function of the bytes per FLOP ratio, in order to estimate execution time for other architectures and applications. Dense data array applications take advantage of CMS beyond 0.6 bytes per FLOP, while applications with sparse arrays similar to our applications benefit beyond 0.5 bytes per FLOP.

Sparse data array applications have their compute time dictated by the tiles with the most non-zeroes, which in our applications are predominantly the tiles on the diagonal. Because even tiles on the diagonal contain zeroes, compute time per tile decreases. This decreases compute time which increases the pressure to memory, therefore allowing

Table 1: RTL synthesis results.

	DMA	CMS
ASIC		
Combinational area (μm^2)	743	16231
Non-combinational area (μm^2)	419	61313
Minimum cycle time (ns)	0.6	0.75
FPGA		
LUTs for logic	245	856
Minimum cycle time (ns)	4.4	5.1

CMS to provide larger execution time benefits. Applications with fewer non-zeroes than our 25% would further benefit CMS for the same reason, assuming they are still memory-bandwidth bound. Dense data array applications are perfectly load-balanced. In addition, we ignore scheduling or other effects which can delay individual processors, because such effects are potentially adversarial to any parallel application. Moreover, our stencil-based applications have the additional benefit of eliminating redundant memory reads in read CMS operations, since shared data is read only once and submitted to the owner and reader processors, instead of each processor retrieving its shared data separately. For example, with a 256×256 dense data array and 5-point stencils, there are 12% fewer memory reads with CMS.

4.2.4 CMS Implementation and Synthesis

We implement a CMS engine and a typical DMA engine in RTL and synthesize them using Synopsys Design Compiler and a 40nm general-purpose technology library. We synthesize the same designs using the Xilinx FPGA design flow for a Virtex-5 FPGA. The CMS and DMA engines are configured for the DDR3 Micron modules with 64 bit datapaths used in our evaluations. For the CMS engine, the two read buffers are 16×128 bits each. The reorder buffer for write operations is sized to hold eight transactions of 16×128 bits each, for a total of 2KB. Eight transactions are enough to keep the memory busy in the write operations of our evaluations, as discussed in Section 3.2. In the ASIC flow, the reorder buffer as well as the small read buffer in the CMS engine are implemented using flip-flop (FF) arrays. The CMS engine does not include a data layout array because the size as well as whether the data layout array is included in a L3 cache are architecture-dependent. Table 1 shows the results.

As shown, cycle time for the CMS engine increases by 25% in the ASIC flow and 16% in the FPGA flow. This is due to the extra complexity of the CMS engine, the write reorder buffer, and the two read buffers. Also due to the buffers, the CMS engine occupies more area. However, to make the CMS engine operate at the same clock frequency as the DMA engine, we can simply pipeline the CMS engine

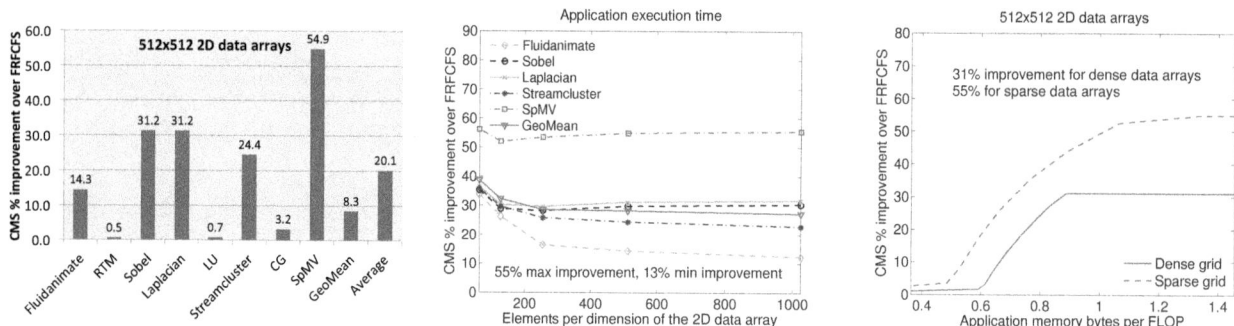

Figure 11: Application execution time improvement of CMS compared to FRFCFS (uncoordinated).

by adding one more stage. The one extra cycle delay is negligible compared to the duration of a collective transfer. The data layout array and handling logic, shown in Figure 6, may further increase area. However, they will not increase cycle time because array access and the handling logic can be heavily pipelined since one memory access covers multiple CMS engine cycles due to the DRAM's burst length.

CMS can simplify other system components in systems that predominantly perform collective transfers. That is because CMS requires only a simple FIFO memory scheduler with just enough transaction queue entries for memory pipelining. Compared to modern memory controllers, this is a significant reduction in cycle time because modern controllers typically hold a few tens of transactions [32] and perform an associative comparison of all requests in their transaction queue every cycle (therefore requiring comparators for every queue entry). They then issue a transaction from any position in the queue based on multi-level priority and other complex schemes [45, 32]. CMS also does not use DMA or prefetch engines in *each* processor allowing for simpler designs. Even without these cost reductions, CMS engines are inexpensive enough to be included in general purpose systems (a CMS engine is required per memory controller instead of per processor). When those systems do not perform collective transfers, CMS engines remain inactive, similar to any other accelerator.

5. DISCUSSION

CMS is targeted at bulk-synchronous SPMD execution models that transfer data arrays to and from memory, and is not intended to address irregular multi-processing workloads. We believe that the kinds of algorithms that are the largest drivers for improved computational performance and multi-core are in fact SPMD kernels such as data-parallel kernels that are seen in image processing, face recognition, machine learning, fluid dynamics, linear algebra, kinetics simulation, and numerous other applications in platforms from HPC to embedded architectures [26, 28, 10, 17]. Many future applications in multi-cores are expected to follow data-parallelism even for consumer and mobile applications [7]

The programming interface to CMS operates in the virtual address space but the CMS hardware engine uses physical addresses. This, however, does not require modifications to existing virtual to physical memory address translation mechanisms such as the TLB in each processor. Even though data placed contiguously in the virtual address space may not be contiguous in the physical address space, CMS guarantees that whether the DRAM page (row) accessed next is

the next contiguous page in the physical address space or not will not affect performance and power so long as every line within that page is used (to the extent made possible by the application) after that page is open. Even if the TLB relocates the page, it will not affect the CMS engine's ability to make maximal use of the data within that open page.

Idle processors can be programmed to mimic the functionality of the CMS engine to avoid dedicated CMS engines. However, this makes some processors unavailable to the application, performs collective transfer at a much higher energy cost, and requires processors with an unrealistically high number of outstanding memory requests to cover the bandwidth–delay product to memory.

Highly threaded SMs within GPUs are similarly challenged by data-parallel applications and the desire to coalesce independent thread accesses into a limited number of accesses to memory [1]. CMS can be used to replace or augment the existing functionality within an SM when data is loaded either into shared memory or the register files. CMS can also be used to view the union of transfers performed by the active set of SMs as a collective and move data to and from their respective load stores. GPUs have programming constructs capable of expressing collective transfers, such as HTAs which have been implemented for OpenCL [47].

In applications that allow a subset of processors to make progress faster than others, CMS would force the fast processors to stall due to the implicit barriers. This typically does not degrade execution time because application performance is commonly dictated by the slowest processors, as is the case with our sparse data array application benchmarks. However, barrier calls are already typical in data-parallel applications that are the focus of CMS [17].

While in local-store architectures such as STI Cell [36] we choose to identify collective transfers by using a software API that replaces DMA function calls, typical cache-coherent CMPs can use hardware prefetch units. In such systems, individual prefetch units in each processor can transmit their predictions to the CMS engine, which can identify collective prefetching opportunities. This would require modifications to the cache coherency protocol to allow L1 caches to receive data they did not request and to identify data to write back to the memory before it is evicted. Prefetch decisions can also be performed by the CMS engine by observing the memory access stream, without prefetch engines at each processor. Alternatively, compilers can also recognize collective transfer opportunities abstractly from the programmer and transfer the same data layout information that the programmer provides through HTAs in our current implementation to the CMS hardware engine.

6. RELATED WORK

Past work has researched collective data transfer techniques in very different contexts. In wide-area TCP/IP networks, coordinating the nodes to send their data to a common destination with a common transfer schedule that avoids conflicts substantially reduces network congestion [8]. Alternative techniques for wide-area networks focus on heterogeneity and use of shared resources by transferring different chunks of the same file from replicas [24]. Collective data transfers have also been applied to server disk-directed I/O, because the access bandwidth for magnetic hard disk drives significantly improves with sequential accesses [37].

Vector machines such as the Cray-1 [35] overcome the inefficiencies of DRAM *overfetch* and access granularity by using massive bank-switching to offer word-granularity accesses. However, vector core designs and memory controllers are costly due to their limited market and sizable engineering costs [13]. VIRAM can also exploit data-level parallelism to overcome the wiring costs of massive bank-switching [25], but the memory capacities offered by the various processor-in-memory approaches are impractically small for the commercial market. Moreover, variations of DMA engines [22] still perform transfers between only two components, thus creating out of order access streams to memory.

The Impulse memory controller reorganizes the memory address stream so that non-contiguous address patterns appear contiguously in the cache hierarchy [46]. However, with Impulse the data arrays remain scattered in the DRAM, thereby leading to inefficient DRAM performance. Moreover, even though data-to-memory address layouts alternative to row- or column-major can produce a more favorable memory access stream for some applications without CMS [16, 30, 14], complex layouts are counter-productive for programming. Such data layout transformations still cannot outperform CMS because CMS guarantees in-order memory access. CMS also makes communication-avoiding optimizations unnecessary, which removes the need for extra local storage or redundant computation which is typical from such optimizations [17, 10].

Sophisticated memory schedulers use complex scheduling policies and can be thread-aware [32, 18, 40, 29, 11]. Many schedulers also perform limited reordering by attempting to exploit row buffer locality and bank parallelism among other metrics [29]. Still, even a memory controller with an ideal policy is inherently incapable of fully reconstructing the memory access stream. That is because controllers are *passive* elements which do not control the order requests arrive to them and decide which one to serve next only from within their transaction queues. In contrast, CMS guarantees in-order memory access by actively controlling the transfer and *pushing* or *pulling* data to and from processor local stores or L1 caches. CMS has similar goals with "memory access scheduling" proposed for stream processors, but memory access scheduling is merely an algorithm that applies to the memory controller, and thus is inherently limited by the size of the memory controller's transaction queue [31]. As we explain in Section 4.1, we compare against FRFCFS with an open-row policy because FRFCFS maximizes throughput compared to many other controllers.

Past work has simplified memory controllers by using the on-chip routers to reorder requests [45]. However, because decisions are made with local knowledge and processors still issue requests independently, this scheme performs slightly lower than a FRFCFS scheduler. Alternative work uses admission control to inject only requests for open DRAM rows [27]. However, this uses a centralized scheme and thus faces limited scalability, and also risks idling memory due to propagation delay. Frequently-accessed data can be placed in the same row to favor open row DRAM policies [41]. Modifications to DRAM internals have also been proposed to reduce the negative power effects of random-order sequences, by avoiding to activate all the bitlines in a row before the exact read request is known [42].

While local and last-level cache (LLC) caches can reduce DRAM accesses during the computation phase of a loop, data is still retrieved from main memory when loading new and storing old data arrays. CMS focuses on fetching new and storing old data, and not on cache interference across tiles during computation. In the wide variety of memory bandwidth-bound applications discussed in this paper, retrieving new and storing old data suffice to saturate memory bandwidth. LLCs may potentially assist in reducing redundant memory reads, which however is not the dominant factor for CMS. LLCs can also partially reconstruct address order for writes with a write back policy, especially with mechanisms such as the virtual write cache which relies on the memory controller having idle cycles to fetch data from the LLC in address order [39]. However, in memory-bandwidth bound applications memory controllers are hardly idle. Also, streaming (write-through) writes are preferable to write back policies in data-parallel computations to prevent polluting higher-level caches because the results of a computation loop are not reused in the next iteration [10, 17].

Prefetching is currently the defacto solution for latency hiding on modern CPU architectures. However, prefetching typically focuses on reducing latency and offers little benefit in systems that are bound by memory bandwidth. In general there are two forms — cache prefetchers (move data from cache to processors) and DRAM prefetchers (move data from DRAM to the LLC). The performance of cache prefetchers often suffers on bulk synchronous applications that cache block dense arrays because the contiguous address stream length is often short. As such, prefetcher latency is not amortized and significant overfetch can occur (a processor inappropriately prefetches data from the next cache block), stressing memory bandwidth. Cache prefetchers also typically perform predictions independently at each processor and thus create out-of-order access patterns [21]. In addition, the performance of a DRAM prefetcher can be particularly sensitive to the number of active threads, how separated their address streams are, and the number of streams the prefetcher can track. Finally, prefetching lacks knowledge from the applications and is thus prone to errors where the wrong data is fetched instead of the data the processor actually requires. This is detrimental to both the memory because it served erroneous requests, but also to the processor. CMS addresses the challenges of both cache and DRAM prefetchers by distilling the core collective memory access pattern and avoiding mispredictions.

7. CONCLUSION

To make optimal use of the limited memory bandwidth of current and future systems, we present CMS that provides a shared responsibility mechanism between the software and an inexpensive hardware engine to coordinate parallel data accesses in a CMP such that data arrays are read from or written to the DRAM in strict memory address order and distributed to or collected from processors. CMS is essentially a memory access accelerator that is inexpensive to include even in general-purpose systems. CMS actively takes control of collective data transfers by *pushing* or *pulling* data to or from on-chip L1 caches or local stores. CMS maximizes memory throughput beyond that possible even by the most aggressive transaction schedulers in modern memory controllers, reduces memory power and latency, simplifies the API to manage bulk-synchronous DMA operations, and alleviates network congestion. CMS reduces application time by up to 55% (20% average), memory read power by up to $2.2\times$, and memory write power by up to 50%.

8. REFERENCES

[1] A. Abdelfattah *et al.*, "Optimizing memory-bound numerical kernels on GPU hardware accelerators," ser. VECPAR, Kobe, Japan, 2012.

[2] D. Abts *et al.*, "Achieving predictable performance through better memory controller placement in many-core CMPs," ser. ISCA, 2009.

[3] C. Bienia, "Benchmarking modern multiprocessors," Ph.D. dissertation, Princeton University, January 2011.

[4] U. Bondhugula *et al.*, "A practical automatic polyhedral parallelizer and locality optimizer," ser. PLDI, 2008.

[5] S. Borkar and A. A. Chien, "The future of microprocessors," *Communications of the ACM*, vol. 54, no. 5, 2011.

[6] A. Buluc *et al.*, "Reduced-bandwidth multithreaded algorithms for sparse matrix-vector multiplication," ser. IPDPS, 2011.

[7] Y.-K. Chen *et al.*, "Convergence of recognition, mining, and synthesis workloads and its implications," *Proceedings of the IEEE*, vol. 96, no. 5, pp. 790–807, 2008.

[8] W. C. Cheng *et al.*, "A coordinated data collection approach: design, evaluation, and comparison," *IEEE Journal on Selected Areas in Communications*, vol. 22, no. 10, 2006.

[9] W. J. Dally and B. Towles, *Principles and Practices of Interconnection Networks*. Morgan Kaufmann Publishers Inc., 2003.

[10] K. Datta *et al.*, "Stencil computation optimization and auto-tuning on state-of-the-art multicore architectures," ser. SC, 2008.

[11] E. Ebrahimi *et al.*, "Parallel application memory scheduling," ser. MICRO, 2011.

[12] W. Gao *et al.*, "An improved sobel edge detection," ser. ICCSIT, vol. 5, 2010.

[13] J. Gebis *et al.*, "Improving memory subsystem performance using ViVA: Virtual Vector Architecture," ser. ARCS. Berlin, Heidelberg: Springer-Verlag, 2009.

[14] C. Gou, G. Kuzmanov, and G. N. Gaydadjiev, "SAMS multi-layout memory: Providing multiple views of data to boost SIMD performance," ser. ICS, 2010.

[15] J. Guo *et al.*, "Writing productive stencil codes with overlapped tiling," *Journal on Concurrency and Computation: Practice and Experience*, vol. 21, no. 1, 2009.

[16] T. Henretty *et al.*, "Data layout transformation for stencil computations on short-vector SIMD architectures," ser. CC/ETAPS, 2011.

[17] J. Holewinski, L.-N. Pouchet, and P. Sadayappan, "High-performance code generation for stencil computations on GPU architectures," ser. ICS, 2012.

[18] Y. Ishii, M. Inaba, and K. Hiraki, "Unified memory optimizing architecture: memory subsystem control with a unified predictor," ser. ICS, 2012.

[19] A. Kaiser *et al.*, "TORCH computational reference kernels: A testbed for computer science research," Tech. Rep. UCB/EECS-2010-144, Dec 2010.

[20] S. Kamil *et al.*, "An auto-tuning framework for parallel multicore stencil computations," ser. IPDPS, 2010.

[21] M. Kandemir, Y. Zhang, and O. Ozturk, "Adaptive prefetching for shared cache based chip multiprocessors," ser. DATE '09, 2009.

[22] H. Kavianipour and C. Bohm, "High performance FPGA-based scatter/gather DMA interface for PCIe," ser. NSS/MIC '12, 2012.

[23] K. Keahey, P. Fasel, and S. Mniszewski, "PAWS: collective interactions and data transfers," ser. HPDC, 2001.

[24] G. Khanna *et al.*, "A dynamic scheduling approach for coordinated wide-area data transfers using GridFTP," ser. IPDPS, 2008.

[25] C. Kozyrakis and D. Patterson, "Scalable, vector processors for embedded systems," *IEEE Micro*, vol. 23, no. 6, 2003.

[26] J. Krueger *et al.*, "Hardware/software co-design for energy-efficient seismic modeling," ser. SC, 2011.

[27] D. Lee, S. Yoo, and K. Choi, "Entry control in network-on-chip for memory power reduction," ser. ISLPED, 2008.

[28] M. Mohiyuddin *et al.*, "A design methodology for domain-optimized power-efficient supercomputing," ser. SC, 2009.

[29] O. Mutlu and T. Moscibroda, "Parallelism-aware batch scheduling: Enhancing both performance and fairness of shared dram systems," ser. ISCA, 2008.

[30] L. Peng *et al.*, "High-order stencil computations on multicore clusters," ser. IPDPS, 2009.

[31] S. Rixner, "A bandwidth-efficient architecture for a streaming media processor," Ph.D. dissertation, Massachusetts Institute of Technology, 2001.

[32] S. Rixner *et al.*, "Memory access scheduling," ser. ISCA, 2000.

[33] B. M. Rogers *et al.*, "Scaling the bandwidth wall: challenges in and avenues for CMP scaling," ser. ISCA, 2009.

[34] P. Rosenfeld, E. Cooper-Balis, and B. Jacob, "DRAMSim2: A cycle accurate memory system simulator," *IEEE Computer Architecture Letters*, vol. 10, no. 1, 2011.

[35] R. M. Russell, "The CRAY-1 computer system," *Communications of the ACM*, vol. 21, no. 1, 1978.

[36] S. Schneider, J.-S. Yeom, and D. S. Nikolopoulos, "Programming multiprocessors with explicitly managed memory hierarchies," *IEEE Computer*, vol. 42, no. 12, 2009.

[37] K. Seamons *et al.*, "Server-directed collective I/O in Panda," ser. SC, 1995.

[38] J. Shalf, S. S. Dosanjh, and J. Morrison, "Exascale computing technology challenges," ser. VECPAR, 2010.

[39] J. Stuecheli *et al.*, "The virtual write queue: Coordinating DRAM and last-level cache policies," ser. ISCA, 2010.

[40] L. Subramanian *et al.*, "MISE: Providing performance predictability and improving fairness in shared main memory systems," ser. HPCA, 2013.

[41] K. Sudan *et al.*, "Micro-pages: increasing DRAM efficiency with locality-aware data placement," ser. ASPLOS, 2010.

[42] A. N. Udipi *et al.*, "Rethinking DRAM design and organization for energy-constrained multi-cores," ser. ISCA, 2010.

[43] A. Vega *et al.*, "Breaking the bandwidth wall in chip multiprocessors," ser. SAMOS, 2011.

[44] D. T. Wang, "Memory DRAM memory systems: performance analysis and a high performance, power-constrained DRAM scheduling algorithm," Ph.D. dissertation, University of Maryland, 2005.

[45] G. L. Yuan, A. Bakhoda, and T. M. Aamodt, "Complexity effective memory access scheduling for many-core accelerator architectures," ser. MICRO, 2009.

[46] L. Zhang *et al.*, "The impulse memory controller," *IEEE Transactions on Computers*, vol. 50, no. 11, 2001.

[47] X. Zhou *et al.*, "Hierarchical overlapped tiling," ser. CGO, 2012.

Scalable Analysis of Multicore Data Reuse and Sharing

Miquel Pericàs[*]
Tokyo Institute of Technology
2-12-1 Ookayama, Meguro-ku
Tokyo, Japan
pericas.m.aa@m.titech.ac.jp

Kenjiro Taura
The University of Tokyo
7-3-1 Hongo, Bunkyo-ku
Tokyo, Japan
tau@eidos.ic.i.u-tokyo.ac.jp

Satoshi Matsuoka
Tokyo Institute of Technology
2-12-1 Ookayama, Meguro-ku
Tokyo, Japan
matsu@is.titech.ac.jp

ABSTRACT

The performance and energy efficiency of multicore systems are increasingly dominated by the costs of communication. As hardware parallelism grows, developers require more powerful tools to assess the data reuse and sharing properties of their algorithms. The reuse distance is an effective metric to study the temporal locality of programs and model private and shared caches. But the application of this method is challenging. First, generating memory traces is very expensive in storage and very intrusive on execution, possibly distorting the parallel schedule. And second, the algorithm is computationally very expensive, limiting the length, memory size and parallelism of analyzable programs.

This paper introduces a novel *coarse-grained* reuse distance method, called *Kernel Reuse Distance* (KRD), which addresses these challenges. KRD enables a quick assessment of data locality by studying the reuse characteristics of the kernels' inputs and outputs. We analyze the performance of the initial prototype implementation and show two use cases comparing different parallel implementations. On a 24-core system, analyzing a trace from a matrix multiplication representing 24 threads, 1.37 terabytes of streamed data and 800 million distinct accesses, the parallel KRD implementation is able to compute the coherence-aware kernel reuse distance histogram for one socket (six cores) in 11.1 seconds.

Categories and Subject Descriptors

D.2.5 [**Software Engineering**]: Testing and Debugging—*Tracing*; D.2.8 [**Software Engineering**]: Metrics—*performance measures*; D.3.4 [**Programming Languages**]: Processors—*Run-time environments*

Keywords

Reuse distance; instrumentation; data reuse and sharing; multithreaded runtime systems

---

[*]Current Address: Chalmers University of Technology, SE-412 96, Gothenburg, Sweden. mpericas@acm.org

ICS'14, June 10–13 2014, Munich, Germany.
Copyright 2014 ACM 978-1-4503-2642-1/14/06 $15.00.
http://dx.doi.org/10.1145/2597652.2597674.

1. INTRODUCTION

Technology forecasts for semiconductor technology indicate that the number of cores per die will continue to increase in the coming years[1]. Overcoming the limitations imposed by power density and interconnect wire delays will become a major requirement to achieve efficient computation. Applications will need to balance parallelism in the control flow and locality in the data access. This means that applications will need to be increasingly *data-aware*, novel concurrent algorithms that reduce communication will need to be devised, and better tools to understand data communication properties will need to be developed.

A powerful metric to analyze data reuse and sharing is the *reuse distance* [15]. The reuse distance method is based on the stack distance algorithm, which measures the number of distinct addresses accessed by a program between two consecutive accesses to the same element. The metric can be used to model and optimize hit rates for highly associative caches. In the context of multithreaded systems the Concurrent Reuse Distance (CRD) and the Private Reuse Distance (PRD) [9] are used. These metrics model private and shared caches, and account for the effects of cache coherence.

The reuse distance is an effective metric, but it has some important limitations. First, generating memory traces is expensive in storage and intrusive on execution, causing a non-uniform increase in execution cycles. It can seriously distort the parallel schedules generated by runtime systems, particularly when threads do not perform identical work. Second, the original stack distance algorithm [15] is computationally very complex. While algorithms based on binary search trees [4] and holes [1] have effectively reduced the complexity, they are still limited by memory and time. As a result the length and parallelism of applications that can be analyzed is limited. This is particularly problematic for HPC codes, which feature long execution times, large working sets and high parallelism.

To address these issues we propose a novel method based on coarse-grained analysis. Instead of working at the individual load-store level, we propose a method that operates at the granularity of *compute kernels*. This paper describes the method, called Kernel Reuse Distance (KRD), and discusses its serial implementation and a general approximate parallel implementation that scales to much larger problems. The KRD method achieves very low instrumentation overhead, reduces trace sizes, and enables quick computation of data reuse distances for shared caches. This paper builds

---

[1]http://public.itrs.net/

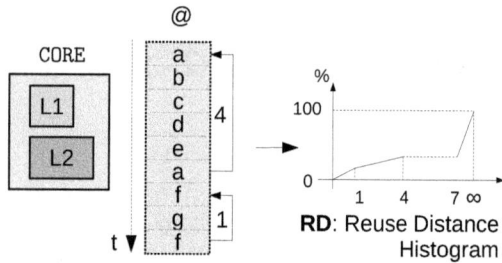

Figure 1: Single-threaded Reuse Distance

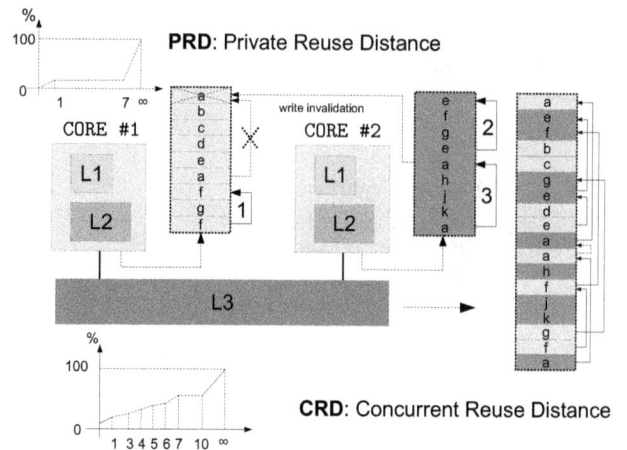

Figure 2: Concurrent and Private Reuse Distance

on recent work on multithreaded locality analysis [23] and makes the following contributions:

- We propose a fast coarse-grained reuse distance method that is cache coherence-aware and can assess reuse quality and detect sharing conflicts across caches.

- We propose a general parallel algorithm to compute approximate reuse distance histograms.

- We apply the KRD method to evaluate the data locality of different implementation options, including choice of programming model and runtime schedulers.

- We explore the limits of KRD when analyzing large multicore executions.

This paper is organized as follows: Section 2 provides background on the reuse distance method. Shortcomings of traditional methods are analyzed in Section 3. In Section 4 we introduce the Kernel Reuse Distance method and evaluate its serial and parallel implementation. Section 5 describes two use cases which showcase the usefulness of the KRD method. The scalability of the method is studied in Section 6. Section 7 summarizes our conclusions.

2. MULTICORE REUSE DISTANCE

The efficient execution of a parallel application requires to (1) maximize exploitation of parallelism and (2) to optimize the sharing and reuse of data access. Analyzing the parallelism of task-parallel applications can be performed via sampling [11, 26] or tracing [3, 10, 27]. Sampling tools can also detect hotspots related to memory accesses [12, 16] but provide little information on the overall data locality.

The stack distance algorithm [15] models the behavior of a fully associative cache with least recently used (LRU) replacement policy. The algorithm processes a trace of memory addresses (or cache lines) and builds a stack of unique elements. The search depth of a matching address is the reuse distance between two identical accesses. Elements accessed for the first time have infinite distance. Figure 1 depicts a trace of memory references generated by a single core and its reuse distance histogram. The trace has of only two reuses: a and f, with stack distances of 4 and 1, respectively, out of 7 total unique addresses.

The stack-based implementation of the reuse distance method is called the *naive* algorithm. For a trace of N elements with M distinct references the computational complexity is $O(NM)$. Since real address traces contain billions of references and millions of distinct accesses, this algorithm is

not practical. Improved algorithms that use a combination of hash tables and self-balancing binary search trees (BST) [1, 4] reduce the overall complexity to $O(NlogM)$.

With the advent of multicores, the reuse distance metric has been extended to model the private and shared caches of these chips [6, 9, 25]. Two new metrics are used: the Concurrent Reuse Distance (CRD) and the Private Reuse Distance (PRD) [9]. The PRD is is the stack distance observed by a private cache plus any cache coherence events that modify it, such as a MESI read-for-ownership (RFO) invalidations. The CRD, defined for a set of threads sharing a cache, is the reuse distance resulting from the interleaving of all memory references of the set, including external cache coherence activity such as inter-socket invalidations. Figure 2 describes these two metrics by extending the example shown in Figure 1 to two cores. It also shows the effect of an invalidating write by core #2 to the element a present in core #1's stack. Since concurrent and private traces include invalidation activity, they are larger than their single-threaded counterparts, further limiting the scale of reuse analysis.

To overcome the algorithm's complexity and process larger traces, several parallelization strategies have been proposed. Niu et al. [18] propose to partition the trace into chunks and compute the reuse distance in parallel. Local misses are sent to the previous chunk iteratively to resolve if they are global misses. Schuff et al. [24] accelerate the calculation of the reuse distance by using an approximate method based on parallel sampling of a subset of addresses. Their method is online, with each thread computing its own reuse distance.

Calculating the reuse distance consists in two steps: collecting memory traces and computing the reuse distance histogram. Most research has focused on the second of these parts, which is by far the most time consuming. Tracing is much faster and can generally be accomplished with overhead below 10× using dynamic instrumentation tools such as PIN [13] or Valgrind [17]. The execution slowdown produced by these instrumentors is not uniform and depends on the particular instruction mix. For the case of parallel applications, it is necessary to ensure that the dynamically instrumented execution still behaves as the native execution. Jiang et al. suggest that symmetric threading cases can be reliably instrumented to obtain realistic reuse distances [9]. In the following section we study the effects of dynamic instrumentation on task-parallel and dataflow codes.

3. EFFECTS OF INSTRUMENTATION

To analyze the effects of instrumenting parallel applications we take a set of applications with different parallelization and data sharing characteristics and run them natively and using PIN [13]. We then analyze if the PIN-based execution has the same properties as the native execution.

3.1 Test Environment

We use two test systems throughout this work. The main system (`westmere`) is a quad-socket machine featuring 4 Intel Xeon E7-4807 chips. Each die contains six *Westmere* cores running at 1.87 GHz and sharing 18 MB of last level cache. The second platform (`magnycours`) is a 4-socket AMD MagnyCours system. Each MagnyCours chip contains 12 *Greyhound+* cores clocked at 2.1 GHz and distributed in two groups of six cores sharing 6 MB of last level cache. The benchmark set consists of the following codes:

Task-parallel Matrix Multiplication (`matmul`): `matmul` is a highly regular code which performs a symmetric divide-and-conquer decomposition. At each step the input/output matrices ($A \times B = C$) are subdivided until the sum of the submatrix sizes (in bytes) falls below a threshold called the *leaf_size*. `sgemm` kernels are only executed at the leaves of the task graph. The default matrix size is 4096×4096 single precision elements.

Task-parallel FMM (`exafmm`): `exafmm` is a task-parallel implementation of the Fast Multipole Method [28]. The parallelization strategy is also divide-and-conquer. The domain decomposition is not symmetric but still very regular. The task graph is irregular, depending on the octree that holds the data. The default input is 1 million particles organized in a plummer distribution. The number of particles per leaf box (q) is 32. We focus on the tree traversal phase which contains the two main kernels: M2L (multipole-to-local) and P2P (particle-to-particle).

Task-parallel Integer Sort (`cilksort`): The `cilksort` benchmark is based on the cilksort code distributed with the Cilk-5.4.6 source distribution. The task graph is regular and symmetric. `cilksort` recursively bisects the input space until a threshold is reached, after which a quicksort is performed to sort a contiguous chunk of data. A merge phase follows which splits the inputs based the median value of each leaf chunk and merges the buffers in parallel. `cilksort` is a data-intensive code that features an irregular reuse pattern, in which kernels read data that partially overlaps with data written by kernels deeper in the task graph. The default input is a set of 100 million random integers.

Dataflow FMM (`kifmm-df`): `kifmm-df` is a dataflow implementation of the KIFMM algorithm [2] featuring kernels that trigger based on data dependencies. We focus on the two dominant kernels: the `pointwise multiplication` and the `direct computation`. The input consists of one million particles organized in an elliptic distribution. We run `kifmm-df` on the `magnycours` system in order to reproduce the infrastructure of the source reference [2].

3.2 Analysis of executions

To compare the native and instrumented executions we first run the benchmarks natively on all cores, and then re-

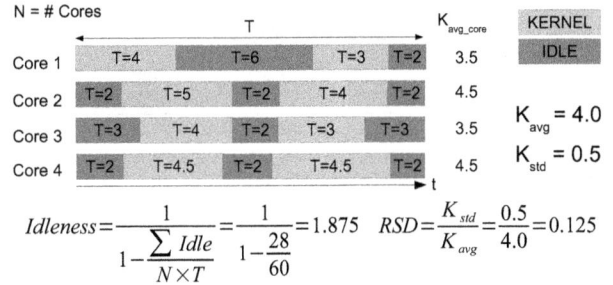

$$Idleness = \frac{1}{1 - \frac{\sum Idle}{N \times T}} = \frac{1}{1 - \frac{28}{60}} = 1.875 \qquad RSD = \frac{K_{std}}{K_{avg}} = \frac{0.5}{4.0} = 0.125$$

Figure 3: Work idleness and relative standard deviation of kernel executions

execute the code using PIN. For the PIN-based executions we specify the `memtrace.so` plug-in, which instruments the code to generate memory traces and could eventually be extended for reuse distance computation. We silently discard the output traces to eliminate storage overheads.

For every execution we collect the execution time, the *work idleness* and the relative standard deviation (RSD) of the average kernel times observed by the different threads. The *work idleness* is the ratio of the execution cycles to the kernel cycles. It quantifies both runtime overheads and load imbalance. The RSD is the ratio of the standard deviation of average kernel times across cores (K_{std}) to the average kernel time (K_{avg}). An RSD is computed for every kernel function. These concepts are explained graphically in Figure 3. The results for the four applications are summarized in Table 1.

Distortions in the PIN-based executions are highlighted in boldface. Several runs were conducted to verify that the measurements are reproducible. All benchmarks suffered from distortions. The worst case happened with `kifmm-df`, where the RSD of both kernel times increased from 15-30% to about 100%. `matmul` and `exafmm` also saw an increase in the work idleness, indicating that PIN caused distortion to the work stealer. These results suggest that for task-parallel and dataflow applications, traces generated using instruction-level instrumentation are not reliable. This motivates the search for a lightweight tracing alternative.

4. THE KERNEL REUSE DISTANCE METHOD

Tracing at the level of load/store instructions is too expensive. Execution time increases, application features are distorted, and storage requirements for offline memory trace analysis become very large. However, not all data recorded in a memory trace is equivalent. For instance, variables local to procedures or loop indexes have very small footprints that have little impact on caching performance, particularly in HPC applications. Yet their temporal locality can be very high, and they may consume considerable storage space in a memory trace.

Cache performance, particularly for large last level caches, is mainly concerned with working set sizes. It is intuitively possible to assess a coarse-grained reuse distance performance by summarizing trace segments into their working sets. Such summaries lose the information on near reuses, but they can accurately represent distant reuses. The accuracy of this method will depend on the size of each trace segment and its corresponding working set. We propose to

Code (Kernels)	matmul (sgemm)		exafmm (M2L/P2P)		cilksort (mergesort/quicksort)		kifmm-df (pointwise/direct)	
Execution Mode	Native	PIN	Native	PIN	Native	PIN	Native	PIN
Execution Time	0.994 sec	4.73 sec	0.787 sec	1.849 sec	1.165 sec	2.492 sec	4.258 sec	26.05 sec
Work Idleness	10.3%	**22.2%**	72.03%	69.45%	6.86%	**19.49%**	56.96%	57.7%
RSD	0%	0%	0.87%/6.47%	**3.75%/19.27%**	5%/0.91%	**5%/19.5%**	29.5%/13.12%	**92.8%/117.1%**

Table 1: Impact of dynamic instrumentation. The kernel names are specified in parenthesis and correspond to the order listed in the RSD column. Distortions to the execution are highlighted in boldface.

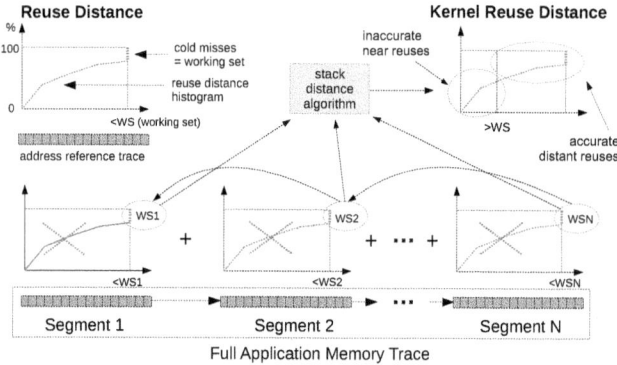

Figure 4: Construction of the Kernel Reuse Distance from a set of segments.

apply this method at the level of kernel executions. Figure 4 describes the relationship between our proposed *Kernel Reuse Distance* (KRD) and the traditional reuse distance. We further simplify trace generation by collecting only persistent data and discarding automatic variables.

This allows to greatly simplify trace collection and to reduce trace size. As Figure 4 shows, to generate KRD histograms we only need the kernel working sets. KRD traces are thus collections of working sets recorded at kernel granularity. A trace entry holds a data block descriptor and a timestamp. The data block descriptor is a application-specific entity that needs to be defined for each case. In this work we define two generic descriptors:

- **Vector**: The *vector* descriptor describes contiguous data in memory. Recording such data requires only two fields: the starting address and the size in bytes.

- **Sparse**: While *vector* is fully general to describe any data block in multiple entries, it can become very inefficient for irregular data structures. Many applications have the property that working sets accessed by different kernels either overlap completely, or not at all. This allows to describe these working sets with an identifier and a size in bytes. We use the starting address as the identifier for the *sparse* descriptor.

The instrumentation to generate these traces can be inserted manually or automatically by an instrumentor (for example, by instrumenting depend clauses in OpenMP 4.0 [21] programs). A program generates first a RAW (reads-and-writes) trace that extends the data descriptor and timestamp with a Read/Write identifier and a thread ID.

The RAW traces are then used to generate concurrent and private traces for multithreaded executions. To generate a

concurrent trace several RAW traces corresponding to a set of threads sharing a cache are first merged into one *merged* RAW trace, sorted by the timestamps. Writes from other traces not sharing the same cache are then integrated as invalidations. The resulting *coherence-aware* trace is called RWI (read-write-invalidate) trace.

Next the reuse distance histograms are computed from the RWI traces. Any existing stack distance algorithm [1,15,20] can be used to process the trace. Upon a reuse or a miss, the histogram increment is weighted by the total number of bytes (or cache lines) of the data block. One issue when using the *vector* interpretation are partially overlapping data blocks. In this case the algorithm needs to record the reuse distance only for the matching data and continues to search further in the stack until all data has been either matched or determined to be a miss. Upon such partial hits, the stack elements need to be readjusted in size and possibly split into multiple elements.

Invalidations are handled by searching for matching elements in the stack and *invalidating* them. The invalidated elements are themselves kept in the stack [25], keeping the distance of stack elements unmodified. When a load/store matches an invalidated element, a miss is accounted for and the invalidation status of the element is removed. Some approaches [25] treat invalidated elements as *holes* that can be filled, in order to more closely model caches. We leave invalidated elements in the stack. This allows to track the origin of all misses, an important property for parallel programs.

This method will yield a reuse histogram for each group of threads sharing a cache along with a count of invalidation misses. A summary can be optionally generated by adding all histograms. Figure 5 shows a diagram with all the steps involved in the KRD method.

4.1 Prototype Implementation

We have developed a prototype implementation of the KRD method targeting Linux-based x86-64 environments. All our codes are written in C and compiled using gcc/g++ version 4.7.

Collection of RAW traces: RAW traces are generated by instrumenting kernels with calls to a tracing library. The parameters are an identifier (address), memory size in bytes, and a read/write flag. The trace data is stored in a large per-thread memory chunk that is allocated at initialization via mmap(). In addition to this data, each element also contains a 64-bit timestamp collected via the x86 timestamp counter (TSC). On each kernel, the calling thread identifies itself via the RDTSCP instruction or sched_getcpu() system call to index the thread-private trace buffer. Traces are written to disk at program termination. For the four applications described in Section 3 the size of the encoded data blocks ranges from 48 bytes (exaFMM's M2L kernel) to 30520

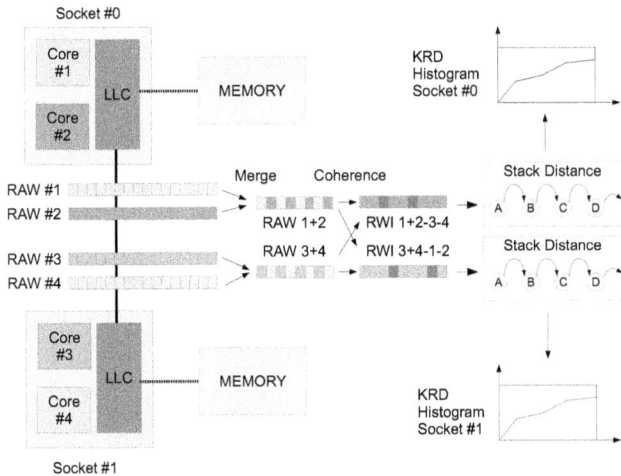

Figure 5: Steps involved in the generation of coherent KRD socket histograms

CPU Core	Westmere	Sandy Bridge	MagnyCours	Interlagos
Frequency	1.87GHz	3.1GHz	2.1GHz	2.1GHz
Sequential	34.50 ns	18.45 ns	73.2 ns	57.11 ns
Random	74.72 ns	47.52 ns	133.9 ns	121.6 ns

Table 2: Overheads for tracing a single element.

We next evaluate the impact of generating KRD traces on a real code in sequential and parallel executions. We use the matmul code and instrument the sgemm kernel with its inputs (A and B) and output (C). Every kernel invocation generates three trace elements corresponding to these sub-matrices. We test different kernel sizes by specifying a range of values for the *leaf_size* parameter. Two experiments are performed: a serial run and a parallel run with 24 cores, both on westmere. Table 3 shows the resulting execution times for several thresholds. The reported sgemm time is the average execution time measured during the non-instrumented (native) run. Sizes are somewhat larger during instrumented runs, but the difference is always below 5%.

The worst case overhead is 12% for a kernel size around 500 ns. No distortions to the *work idleness* and kernels RSD were observed. Considering ~10% as an acceptable overhead, the implementation allows to generate about 6 trace elements per microsecond serially or about 144 trace elements per microsecond on 24 cores. The fact that the overhead is exactly the same at 1 core and 24 cores also indicates that the tracing infrastructure scales well. Among our test applications, the largest overhead was observed with exafmm, which reached about 5% overhead.

4.2 Prototype Performance

Next we analyze the performance of our KRD implementation. We generate and process traces from single threaded runs of the benchmarks introduced in Section 3. Input parameters are set such that the total amount of data streamed through the kernels is around 20-30 GB. Table 4 summarizes the results. *References* is the total number of traced kernel loads/stores while *Elems* (N_K) is the length of the trace (number of data blocks). *Speed-down* is the *KRD time* normalized to the benchmark *Exec Time*. *Depth* (M_K) is the average depth of the stack search. Finally, *References* is the total number of distinct memory references (working set). Each reference is normalized to a 4-byte load or store. The prototype implementation, being based on the naive algorithm, has a complexity of $O(N_K M_K)$. The K subscript indicates that it is the KRD version of the parameter. We identify the parameters N and M to show the reduction in trace and stack size enabled by the KRD method.

There is a huge variation in the performance of the KRD computation, leading to very different speed-downs compared to native execution. These variations are due to different computational complexities, which depend on the number of elements (*Elems*), and the data access pattern of the application (*Depth*). Some KRD executions are actually faster than the native execution (matmul and kifmm-df). cilksort exhibits by far the worst behavior. The partially overlapping mergesort() kernels require the *vector* data interpretation and preclude the Bloom filter. cilksort also has a very distant reuse pattern and large amount of cold misses. Altogether this results in a very deep average search (M_K). Considering such cases, and with applications be-

bytes (cilksort's mergesort). The size of each trace entry (descriptor, timestamp, R/W, thread id) is 32 bytes.

Merging of Traces: Merging of multiple traces and generation of coherent traces is sorted by the TSC timestamps. Synchronization of all clocks is required. All modern x86-64 processors support the invariant TSC feature [7], which keeps all cores on a chip synchronized. Synchronization of cores across sockets is achieved by systems simultaneously sending the RESET signal to all sockets. Although clocks can get out of sync afterward, we confirmed that all the sockets in our test systems were synchronized.

Computation of stack distances: The kernel-based method reduces considerably the number trace elements (N) and the number of distinct elements (M). This allows the prototype to implement the simple *naive* algorithm, despite its $O(NM)$ complexity. An implementation based on self-balancing BSTs is also possible, and should be considered if the requirement arises.

Processing traces with many first time accesses and many non-matching invalidations can be expensive as such references perform long and unnecessary searches on the stack. The impact of these elements can be reduced by adding a Bloom filter that tracks addresses present on the stack. Filtered references can be directly accounted as misses, while filtered invalidations can be ignored. We implemented a Bloom filter with 2^{28} entries using a simple address-modulo hash. The Bloom filter is currently implemented only for the *sparse* data representation. For the *vector* data representation it is more complex to associate an element with a hash entry due to the chance of partially overlapping elements.

Table 2 shows the latency of inserting an element into the memory buffer on four recent processor cores. The measurements show the average time of inserting an element in a tight loop, both sequentially and randomly over 100,000 elements (to avoid prefetching benefits). The table shows that storing a single trace element has always a penalty below 150 ns, and below 75 ns when storing the elements sequentially, as is done in practice.

	Serial	2000	4000	8000	16000	32000	64000	128000
Serial	Leaf Size (A+B+C)	2000	4000	8000	16000	32000	64000	128000
	sgemm time (ns)	486.1	1524	2605	10002	19797	78308	150642
	Native (s)	5.647	3.597	2.937	2.683	2.631	2.579	2.478
	Instrumented (s)	6.311	3.803	3.001	2.693	2.639	2.582	2.477
Parallel	Leaf Size (A+B+C)	2000	4000	8000	16000	32000	64000	128000
	sgemm time (ns)	518.8	1612.3	2731	10785	20472	80222	154171
	Native (s)	0.4302	0.2349	0.2068	0.1511	0.1467	0.1388	0.1315
	Instrumented (s)	0.4782	0.2577	0.2144	0.1528	0.148	0.1419	0.1363

Table 3: KRD overheads for serial and parallel execution on 24 cores (four sockets)

	Parameters	References (N)	Elems (N_K)	Exec Time	KRD time	Speed-down	Depth (M_K)	References (M)
matmul	4096 x 4096 matrices	5.3×10^9	3.15×10^6	21.36 s	5.535 s	0.26x	292.452	50.3×10^6
exafmm	Plummer, $1 * 10^6$ part.	4.6×10^9	61.60×10^6	41.8 s	538.5 s	12.9x	569.158	32.6×10^6
cilksort	100 million integers	6.5×10^9	1.64×10^6	19.84 s	1474 s	74.3x	34252.3	400×10^6
kifmm-df	Uniform, $200 * 10^3$ part.	7.85×10^9	2.77×10^6	13.09 s	12.85 s	0.98x	532.987	43.4×10^6

Table 4: KRD Time and statistics for the benchmark set.

coming larger, we propose a parallel implementation of KRD to further increase the scale of analyzable applications.

4.3 pKRD: parallel Kernel Reuse Distance

The parallel algorithm is based on the observation that reuses interesting for caching happen within a bounded distance. The difference between very far reuses (e.g. > 1 GB) and misses is in practice of little importance. The parallelization strategy uses a chunking plus stack warm-up approach. Each process independently computes the stack distance for a different chunk of the trace. This provides parallelism, but results in an abnormally high number of cold misses, since each process' stack is initially empty. To improve accuracy, the algorithm processes a preceding trace segment (called *warm-up*) before the regular KRD computation. The warm-up phase is similar to the regular phase except that it does not count hits or misses. The parallelism and accuracy are controlled by two parameters: the *partition size* and the *stack warm-up*. The *partition size* sets the length of each chunk, thus determining the parallelism and accuracy degradation. The *stack warm-up* specifies the length of the warm-up phase, thus improving accuracy. We specify both parameters in terms of processed bytes, not number of elements, to make them application independent. Figure 6 explains the parallelization strategy diagrammatically. We refer to the sequential and exact implementation as *sKRD*, while the parallel and approximate version is called *pKRD*.

The pKRD parallelization scheme is conceptually similar to that of PARDA [18]. Both are based on a chunking strategy, but they differ in their approach to detect interchunk reuses. PARDA connects all neighboring processes with MPI. Local misses are sent to the preceding MPI process for inspection until a reuse is found. The whole trace thus needs to be processed in parallel. Our scheme is more redundant than PARDA for high accuracy cases, but it is more flexible in terms of parallelization. For example, pKRD allows to process a trace in small batches. As will be shown later, this *overpartitioning* approach can yield higher performance than processing a full trace in a single batch.

We now analyze the performance and accuracy of the pKRD method on the same set of traces generated in Section 4.2. Table 5 shows the pKRD execution time and speed-up compared to the benchmark execution time for several

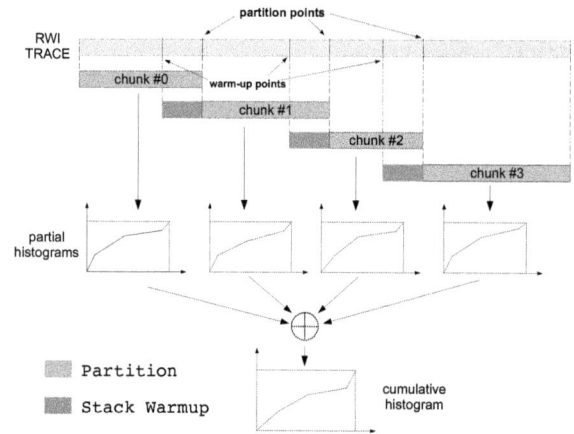

Figure 6: KRD parallelization strategy

partition sizes and a stack warm-up of 144 MB. The pKRD runs were performed on the same 24-core `westmere` system. Figures 7 and 8 show how the accuracy of the method evolves with several partition and stack warm-up sizes for each benchmark. We study two values related to accuracy: *LLC Error* is the percentage error between the pKRD histogram and the sKRD histogram at a reuse distance of 16 MB, which is a common size for today's last level caches. *Cold Error* is the relative increase in the number of cold misses (first time accesses) detected by the pKRD method compared to sKRD.

The table shows the performance achieved on a set of parallel implementations pKRD-P, where P is the number of trace partitions. All pKRD-48 and pKRD-96 runs are faster than the benchmark executions. For most cases, the best performance is obtained at a parallelism degree of 48 partitions, which corresponds to the total hyperthreading capacity of the 24 westmere cores. For the case of `cilksort`, going to 96 partitions continues to improve the performance. The speed-up at 96 partitions is over 300 times, considerably larger than the number of threads (48). In pKRD each parallel computation starts with an empty stack. This considerably improves the average search depth M_K and enables

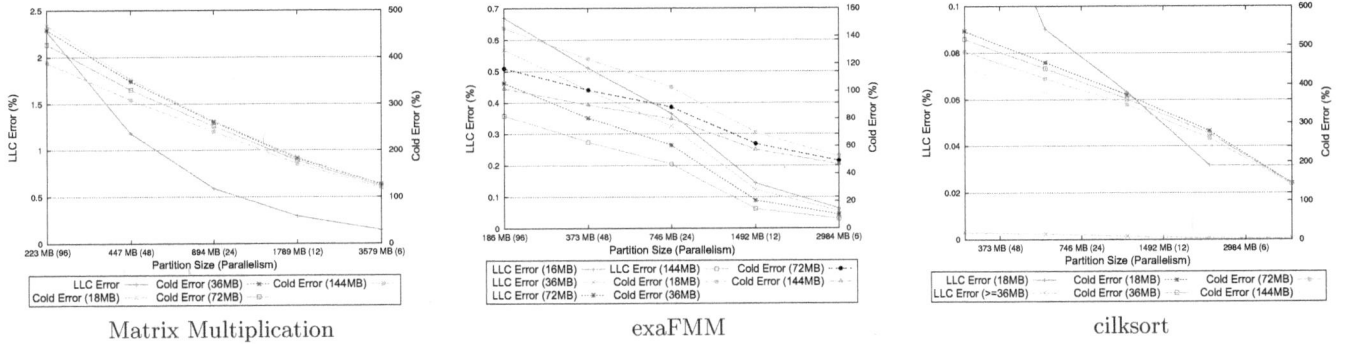

| Matrix Multiplication | exaFMM | cilksort |

Figure 7: LLC Error and Cold Error for the task parallel benchmarks

#Partition	sKRD	pKRD-6	pKRD-12	pKRD-24	pKRD-48	pKRD-96
matmul	5.535	2.620 (2.11x)	1.464 (3.78x)	0.956 (5.78x)	0.827 (6.69x)	1.327 (4.17x)
exaFMM	538.5	103.0 (5.228x)	56.02 (9.6126x)	28.50 (18.89x)	18.67 (28.843x)	24.02 (22.41x)
cilksort	1474	313.3 (4.70x)	81.69 (18.04x)	20.79 (70.89x)	8.588 (171.7x)	4.452 (331.1x)
kifmm-df	12.85	1.382 (9.29x)	0.701 (18.3x)	0.708 (18.15x)	1.005 (12.8x)	2.078 (6.18x)

Table 5: pKRD execution times (s) and speed-up compared to sKRD

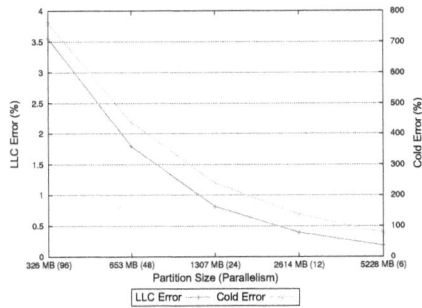

Figure 8: LLC Error and Cold Miss Error for the kifmm-df code

such super-linear speed-ups. In the case of pKRD-96, the average stack search (M_K) of cilksort is only 236 elements, two orders of magnitude smaller than the 34252 elements reported for sKRD (see Table 4). These numbers show that overpartitioning can be interesting even when the number of cores is limited. For the other benchmarks the speed-ups of overpartitioning are more limited. These benchmarks make use of the *sparse* data interpretation and the Bloom filter which already reduces the average search depth and enables good performance even with sKRD.

The parallelization strategy comes at the cost of accuracy. For three of the four benchmarks (all except exafmm), the warm-up size had little effect on the LLC error, which depended exclusively on the partition size. The LLC error can be determined with a fairly small amount of data, so adding a warm-up segment does not have a big influence. Only matmul and kifmm-df experienced an LLC error larger than 1%, which can be reduced by increasing the partition size. The LLC error for exafmm and cilksort was below 1% for all evaluated sizes. The error is particularly small for

cilksort when the warm-up is larger than 36 MB (below 0.005%).

The downside of the pKRD method is the large error observed in cold misses. Even for the largest evaluated sizes of partitions and stack warm-up the error tends to stay above 100%. The number of cold misses is equivalent to the total number of distinct addresses. Only a global analysis of the trace can provide this number. However, for practical purposes the number of cold misses is less critical since locality and caching are optimized at much closer reuse distances.

4.4 Correlation with Cache Misses

To estimate last level cache miss hit rates, two conditions have to be met: 1) the kernels inputs and outputs have to account for the vast majority of distinct addresses, and 2) the working set of each kernel has to be considerably smaller than the size of the last level cache.

We analyze the correlation of KRD and last level cache misses by measuring the number of misses experienced by the serial matmul code and comparing it with the number of distant accesses reported by KRD as we increase the size of the input matrices. The default leaf size of 30 KB is used, yielding submatrix sizes of 4 KB and a 8KB, which is three orders of magnitude smaller than the size of the last level cache. Table 6 shows the values obtained in this experiment. Cold Misses and Over 16MB are the sKRD values for the number of cold accesses and for reuses beyond 16 MB. We use 16 MB since it is the power of 2 most close to the size of the last level cache (18 MB). The number of last level cache misses (LLC_MISSES) is obtained using PAPI [22] and specifying the LAST_LEVEL_CACHE_MISSES counter from the Intel Architectural PerfMon [7]. The table shows clearly how, as the ratio of matrix data to local variables increases, the amount of last level cache misses becomes proportional to the amount of far accesses predicted by the KRD algorithm at size 16 MB. The final value of the fraction Over_16MB/LLC_MISSES means that for every actual LLC miss, sKRD predicts ~13.4 distant accesses. Since the

Matrix Size	256x256	512x512	1024x1024	2048x2048	4096x4096	8192x8192
Exec Time (s)	0.005092	0.03539	0.283	2.261	18.08	145.6
Cold Misses	196.6×10^3 (15%)	786.4×10^3 (7.5%)	3.145×10^6 (3.75%)	12.58×10^6 (1.875%)	50.33×10^6 (0.9375%)	201.3×10^6 (0.46875%)
Over 16MB	196.6×10^3 (15%)	786.4×10^3 (7.5%)	3.145×10^6 (3.75%)	20.971×10^6 (3.125%)	167.8×10^6 (3.125%)	1.342×10^9 (3.125%)
LLC_MISSES	84	98	29822	1.563×10^6	12.30×10^6	100.3×10^6
O16MB/LLC	2340.6	8024.8	105.48	13.416	13.642	13.386

Table 6: Kernel Reuse Distance and Last Level Cache misses measured for `matmul` with several matrix sizes

cache line size is 64 bytes and the elements are single precision (4 bytes), this value is reasonable.

5. CASE STUDIES

This section describes the application of the KRD method to study different implementations of parallel applications.

5.1 Worksharing vs. Dataflow

A common question in dataflow programming models is the impact of dataflow scheduling on the data locality. We compare two implementations of `kifmm` using the dataflow and worksharing (OpenMP) models [2,5]. We run the configurations on `magnycours` and generate coherence-aware KRD histograms for the first NUMA node. The input consists of 4 million particles distributed in an elliptical distribution.

The execution times of the dataflow and OpenMP versions are 16.9 and 13.2 seconds, respectively. The KRD computation indicates that the worksharing execution experiences almost no misses due to invalidations. Since the OpenMP version processes octree data level by level in a producer-consumer relationship, the code never writes to a memory location reused later by a different socket. The dataflow version, on the other hand, experienced about 110 million misses due to invalidations on one NUMA node. This corresponds to 39% of all misses. Figure 5.1 shows the KRD histograms for both executions. Overall the dataflow version has worse temporal locality, particularly close to the cache size (6 MB). While dataflow reduced synchronization overheads, its bad locality caused the work time to inflate, causing reduction in the performance of the dataflow execution. On the other hand, the dataflow implementation had better reuse at short distances. This is an effect of producer-consumer relationships, which are triggered quickly by dataflow scheduling.

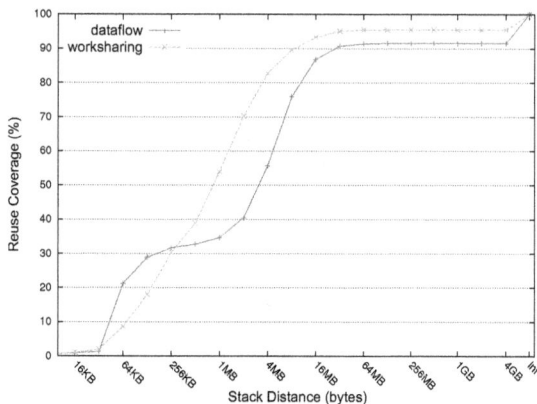

Figure 9: Stack distances of the dataflow and worksharing kifmm code

	matmul	exafmm	cilksort
MassiveThreads	6.09 (**12.5%**)	10.4 (**41.9%**)	179 (**33.9%**)
TBB	88.6 (**63.9%**)	36.1 (**67.1%**)	222 (**38.5%**)
Qthread	3.22 (**8.0%**)	5.43 (**33.0%**)	118 (**25.0%**)

Table 7: Invalidation misses in millions ($\times 10^6$) and percentage of total

5.2 Data Sharing in Task-parallel Runtimes

A common trend in parallel programming is the reliance on runtime systems to handle the mapping of tasks to cores. The schedule and resource mapping determines how data is shared and reused, thus influencing memory subsystem performance. The KRD metric can be used to analyze the data reuse and sharing patterns in such scenarios. We use KRD to evaluate 24-core executions of the three task-parallel benchmarks (`matmul`, `exafmm` and `cilksort`) using three runtimes: MassiveThreads (svn, Jan. 2014) [14], TBB (v41_20130116oss) [8] and Qthread (v1.9) [30]. MassiveThreads and TBB are tasking runtimes based on random work stealing. Qthread includes scheduling policies designed to minimize inter-socket data sharing [19]. We configure Qthread with one *shepherd* per socket and one *worker* per core. The KRD plots for the default inputs described in Section 3 are shown in Figure 10. The figures also show the average kernel times. The total number of misses due to invalidations is reported in Table 7.

The results provide evidence that, for divide-and-conquer applications such as these benchmark codes, performing work stealing at the socket level (Qthread) instead of the core level (MassiveThreads, TBB) can result in better data partitioning and thus less cold misses. In addition, the parallel-depth-first scheduling that Qthread approximates [19], increases the number of near reuses in `matmul` and `cilksort`. This example shows how KRD can be used to evaluate the data locality across different runtimes. Note that final performance also depends on other factors, such as runtime overheads, parallelism and spatial locality [23, 26, 29]. The kernel times shown in Figure 10 are highly correlated to the reuse distance, but they also depend on these other factors.

6. SCALABILITY

To understand the scalability and limitations of KRD we perform parallel experiments on large input sets. We use the `westmere` machine and the MassiveThreads runtime.

Matrix Multiplication: We first stress KRD by running a parallel matrix multiplication with input matrices of size 16384×16384 elements, which translates into 1 GB per matrix (3 GB total). On `westmere` the run completes in 62 seconds, after executing 67 million kernels and streaming a total of 1.37 terabytes of submatrix data. Each core generates a trace of 270 MB. A fully merged trace thus requires 24×270 MB = 6.5 GB of storage space. At this scale, the time for reading and storing the trace to disk becomes non-

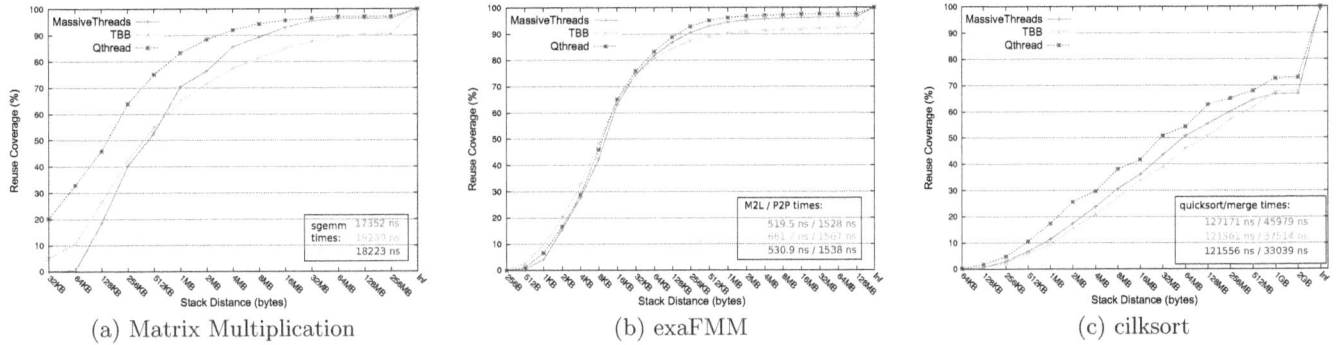

| (a) Matrix Multiplication | (b) exaFMM | (c) cilksort |

Figure 10: KRD plots and kernel times for different runtimes observed on one socket

negligible. The size of the coherent RWI trace for one socket is 3.2 GB, representing about 350 GB of references. We generated KRD plots for both the fully merged trace and for a single socket. We used pKRD with 48 partitions.

Computing the fully merged trace took 555 seconds, about $9\times$ slower than the benchmark run. The average search depth (M_K) was 55 elements for the pKRD-48 run. Generation of the single-socket KRD histogram was much faster and took only 11.1 seconds, about $6\times$ faster than the native execution. For this run almost no misses due to invalidations were detected by the KRD algorithm.

The complexity of generating KRD histograms is considerably simplified because the presence of submatrices on the stack can be quickly determined by the Bloom filter. To understand the effects of the filter, we reran the computation deactivating the Bloom filter. This resulted in an execution of 1402 seconds, $126\times$ slower than the filtered execution.

Integer Sort: The `cilksort` code is a more demanding test case which features a more complex access pattern including partial matches which disable the Bloom filter. For this experiment we ran `cilksort` on the 24 cores of `westmere` with an input consisting of 5 billion (5×10^9) integers (40 GB of data). The execution time was 77.5 seconds, during which 49.68×10^6 kernels were executed. Each socket processed about 416 GB of data (1.66 TB in total).

We generated a coherent trace for a single socket. Again we partition the RWI trace into 48 pieces and ran a warmup of 280 MB. With these parameters the computation of the KRD histogram for one socket took about four hours. Although each partition contains just 8.67 GB of data, the trace also contains 13 GB of invalidations which increase N_K and cannot be filtered. This increases the depth of the average stack search (M_K) which becomes quite large in `cilksort`: 6618.1 elements on average over the 48 partitions. To reduce N_K and M_K we test the overpartitioning property of pKRD introduced in Section 4.3. As we saw, by reducing the size of partitions we can improve performance at the cost of some accuracy. A second experiment was performed partitioning the trace into 512 chunks, with every chunk processing about 800MB of data plus about 1.2 GB of invalidations. The execution was done in in batches of 24 and 48 cores with the computation time taking 3648 and 2506 seconds, respectively. Out of a total of 116.1×10^9 memory references only 1.06×10^6 misses due to invalidations were detected. As with matrix multiplication, a larger input size decreased the overall impact of invalidations. Divide-and-

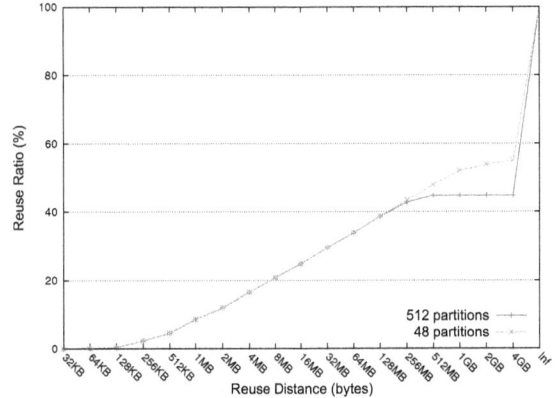

Figure 11: Coherent stack distances for one socket corresponding to `cilksort` sorting 5 billion integers on 24 cores

conquer parallelization schemes, like those of `matmul` and `cilksort`, tend to perform good privatization of data, thus explaining this phenomenon.

Figure 6 shows the KRD plot for the per-socket reuse distance obtained with both partition numbers (48 and 512). The plot shows that the estimate of reuses around 16 MB is basically identical for both cases, but notable divergence happens at distances equal or larger than 512 MB. This is expected, since the accuracy is related to the sum of the stack warm-up and chunk size. For the case of 512 partitions the segment size is 280MB + 800MB. Under these conditions the reuse distance cannot be accurate at distances close or larger than 1 GB. In fact, divergence starts becoming notable already at a reuse distance of 512 MB.

7. CONCLUSIONS

Understanding data reuse and sharing in multicore scenarios is critical to designing scalable and energy efficient applications. To enable quick assessment of reuse and sharing, we propose a coarse-grained approach to the reuse distance method operating at the kernel level. In this paper we described the method and a prototype implementation, and have shown how the technique can be used to compare implementation choices for parallel applications. The scheme is very lightweight and efficient, and can generate reuse plots for parallel runs considerably larger than current approaches. At scale, both computation and I/O slowly become a bottleneck for which new techniques will be needed.

Acknowledgments

This work has been supported by a JSPS postdoctoral fellowship (P-12044). We thank the anonymous reviewers for their valuable feedback.

8. REFERENCES

[1] G. Almasi, C. Cascaval, and D. A. Padua. Calculating Stack Distances Efficiently. In *ACM SIGPLAN Workshop on Memory System Performance*, June 2002.

[2] A. Amer, N. Maruyama, M. Pericàs, K. Taura, R. Yokota, and S. Matsuoka. Fork-Join and Data-Driven Execution Models on Multi-core Architectures: Case Study of the FMM. In *Proceedings of ISC'13*, June 2013.

[3] Barcelona Supercomputing Center. *Extrae User Guide Manual*, May 2013.

[4] B. Bennett and V. J. Kruskal. LRU Stack Processing. *IBM Journal for Research and Development*, pages 353–357, July 1975.

[5] A. Chandramowlishwaran, S. Williams, L. Oliker, I. Lashuk, G. Biros, and R. Vuduc. Optimizing and Tuning the Fast Multipole Method for State-of-the-Art Multicore Architectures. In *Proceedings of IPDPS'10*, May 2010.

[6] C. Ding and T. Chilimbi. A Composable Model for Analyzing Locality of Multi-threaded Programs. Technical Report MSR-TR-2009-107, Microsoft Research, Aug. 2009.

[7] Intel Corporation. Intel 64 and IA-32 Architectures Software Developer's Manual. Volume 3B. http://www.intel.com/content/www/us/en/processors/architectures-software-developer-manuals.html.

[8] Intel Corporation. Intel Threading Building Blocks. https://www.threadingbuildingblocks.org/.

[9] Y. Jiang, E. Z. Zhang, K. Tian, and X. Shen. Is Reuse Distance Applicable to Data Locality Analysis on Chip Multiprocessors? In *Proceedings of the 19th Joint European Conference on Theory and Practice of Software, International Conference on Compiler Construction*, pages 264–282, 2010.

[10] A. Knüpfer, H. Brunst, J. Doleschal, M. Jurenz, M. Lieber, H. Mickler, M. S. Müller, and W. E. Nagel. *The Vampir Performance Analysis Tool-Set*, pages 139–155. Springer Berlin Heidelberg, 2008.

[11] Linux perf-tools Team. perf: Linux profiling with performance counters. https://perf.wiki.kernel.org/index.php/Main_Page.

[12] X. Liu and J. Mellor-Crummey. Pinpointing Data Locality Problems Using Data-centric Analysis. In *Proceedings of CGO'11*, Apr. 2011.

[13] C.-K. Luk, R. Cohn, R. Muth, H. Patil, A. Klauser, G. Lowney, S. Wallace, V. J. Reddi, and K. Hazelwood. Pin: building customized program analysis tools with dynamic instrumentation. In *Proceedings of the 2005 ACM SIGPLAN conference on Programming language design and implementation*, pages 190–200, 2005.

[14] MassiveThreads Team. MassiveThreads: a Lightweight Thread Library for High Productivity Languages. http://code.google.com/p/massivethreads/.

[15] R. L. Mattson, J. Gecsei, D. R. Slutz, and I. L. Traiger. Evaluation techniques for storage hierarchies. *IBM Systems Journal*, 9(2):78–117, 1970.

[16] C. McCurdy and J. Vetter. Memphis : Finding and Fixing NUMA-related Performance Problems on Multi-core Platforms. In *Proceedings of ISPASS 2010*, Mar. 2010.

[17] N. Nethercote and J. Seward. Valgrind: A Framework for Heavyweight Dynamic Binary Instrumentation. In *Proceedings of ACM SIGPLAN 2007 Conference on Programming Language Design and Implementation (PLDI 2007)*, June 2007.

[18] Q. Niu, J. Dinan, Q. Lu, and P. Sadayappan. PARDA: A Fast Parallel Reuse Distance Analysis Algorithm. In *Proceedings of IPDPS'12*, pages 1284–1294, May 2012.

[19] S. L. Olivier, A. K. Porterfield, K. B. Wheeler, and J. F. Prins. Scheduling Task Parallelism on Multi-Socket Multicore Systems. In *Proceedings of ROSS'11*, pages 49–56, 2011.

[20] F. Olken. Efficient Methods for Calculating the Success Function of Fixed Space Replacement Policies. Technical report, Lawrence Berkeley Laboratory, 1981.

[21] OpenMP Architecture Review Board. OpenMP. http://openmp.org/wp/.

[22] PAPI Team. Performance application programming interface. http://icl.cs.utk.edu/papi/.

[23] M. Pericàs, A. Amer, K. Taura, and S. Matsuoka. Analysis of Data Reuse in Task-Parallel Runtimes. In *Workshop on Performance, Modeling, Benchmarking and Simulation (PMBS'13)*, Nov. 2013.

[24] D. L. Schuff, M. Kulkarni, and V. S. Pai. Accelerating Multicore Reuse Distance Analysis with Sampling and Parallelization. In *Proceedings of PACT'10*, pages 53–64, Sept. 2010.

[25] D. L. Schuff, B. S. Parsons, and V. S. Pai. Multicore-Aware Reuse Distance Analysis. In *Parallel & Distributed Processing, Workshops and Phd Forum (IPDPSW), 2010 IEEE International Symposium on*, May 2010.

[26] N. R. Tallent and J. M. Mellor-Crummey. Effective Performance Measurement and Analysis of Multithreaded Applications. In *Proceedings of PPoPP'09*, Feb. 2009.

[27] TAU Team. TAU: Tuning and Analysis Utilities. http://www.cs.uoregon.edu/research/tau/home.php.

[28] K. Taura, R. Yokota, and N. Maruyama. A Task Parallelism Meets Fast Multipole Methods. In *Proceedings of the SCALA'12 workshop*, Nov. 2012.

[29] J. Weinberg, M. O. McCracken, E. Strohmaier, and A. Snavely. Quantifying Locality In The Memory Access Patterns of HPC Applications. In *Proceedings of the 2005 ACM/IEEE conference on Supercomputing*, Nov. 2005.

[30] K. Wheeler, R. Murphy, and D. Thain. Qthreads: An API for Programming with Millions of Lightweight Threads. In *Proceedings of MTAAP '08*, 2008.

Author Index

www.ingramcontent.com/pod-product-compliance
Lightning Source LLC
Chambersburg PA
CBHW080712220326
41598CB00033B/5398